McDougal Littell

THE LANGUAGE OF
LITERATURE

McDougal Littell

THE LANGUAGE OF
LITERATURE

Arthur N. Applebee

Andrea B. Bermúdez

Sheridan Blau

Rebekah Caplan

Franchelle Dorn

Peter Elbow

Susan Hynds

Judith A. Langer

James Marshall

McDougal Littell
A HOUGHTON MIFFLIN COMPANY

Evanston, Illinois ▪ Boston ▪ Dallas

Acknowledgments

Unit One

  Putnam Publishing Group: "Two Kinds" from *The Joy Luck Club* by Amy Tan; Copyright © 1989 by Amy Tan. By permission of G. P. Putnam's Sons, a division of Putnam Publishing Group.

  Rosemary Catacalos: "La Casa," from *Again for the First Time* by Rosemary Catacalos; Copyright © 1984. By permission of the author.

  University of Hawaii Press: "Cranes" by Hwang Sunwŏn, from *Flowers of Fire: Twentieth-Century Korean Stories*, edited and translated by Peter H. Lee; Copyright © 1974, 1986 by the University of Hawaii Press. By permission of the University of Hawaii Press.

  New Directions Publishing Corp. and Watkins/Loomis Agency, Inc.: "Winter Night," from *Fifty Stories* by Kay Boyle; Copyright © 1980 by Kay Boyle. Reprinted by permission of New Directions Publishing Corp. and the estate of Kay Boyle.

  Simon & Schuster, Inc.: Excerpt from *Kaffir Boy* by Mark Mathabane; Copyright © 1986 by Mark Mathabane. Reprinted by permission of Simon & Schuster.

Continued on page 1122

Cover Art

  Background photo: Bali, Indonesia, Copyright © Ian Lloyd / Black Star. **Painting:** *Forbidden Fruit,* Simon Ng. Reprinted with the permission of Simon & Schuster Books for Young Readers, an imprint of Simon & Schuster Children's Publishing Division. From *Tales from Gold Mountain: Stories of the Chinese in the New World,* a Groundwood Book / Douglas & McIntyre. Text Copyright © by Paul Yee, illustrations Copyright © 1989 by Simon Ng. **Statue:** Ere alaafin Shangó [Shangó, Oyo-Ilé warrior-king] (early 19th century), Oyo-Shangó artist. Collection of the Nigerian Museum, Lagos. Photo by Robert Farris Thompson, 1962. **Book:** Photo by Alan Shortall. **Coins and frame:** Photos by Sharon Hoogstraten.

ISBN 0-395-73705-2

Copyright © 1997 by McDougal Littell Inc. All rights reserved.
Printed in the United States of America.

2 3 4 5 6 7 8 9 – RRD – 02 01 00 99 98 97 96

Senior Consultants

The senior consultants guided the conceptual development for *The Language of Literature* series. They participated actively in shaping prototype materials for major components, and they reviewed completed prototypes and/or completed units to ensure consistency with current research and the philosophy of the series.

Arthur N. Applebee Professor of Education, State University of New York at Albany; Director, Center for the Learning and Teaching of Literature; Senior Fellow, Center for Writing and Literacy

Andrea B. Bermúdez Professor of Studies in Language and Culture; Director, Research Center for Language and Culture; Chair, Foundations and Professional Studies, University of Houston-Clear Lake

Sheridan Blau Senior Lecturer in English and Education and former Director of Composition, University of California at Santa Barbara; Director, South Coast Writing Project; Director, Literature Institute for Teachers; Vice President, National Council of Teachers of English

Rebekah Caplan Coordinator, English Language Arts K-12, Oakland Unified School District, Oakland, California; Teacher-Consultant, Bay Area Writing Project, University of California at Berkeley; served on the California State English Assessment Development Team for Language Arts

Franchelle Dorn Professor of Drama, Howard University, Washington, D.C.; Adjunct Professor, Graduate School of Opera, University of Maryland, College Park, Maryland; Co-founder of The Shakespeare Acting Conservatory, Washington, D.C.

Peter Elbow Professor of English, University of Massachusetts at Amherst; Fellow, Bard Center for Writing and Thinking

Susan Hynds Professor and Director of English Education, Syracuse University, Syracuse, New York

Judith A. Langer Professor of Education, State University of New York at Albany; Co-director, Center for the Learning and Teaching of Literature; Senior Fellow, Center for Writing and Literacy

James Marshall Professor of English and English Education, University of Iowa, Iowa City

Contributing Consultants

Tommy Boley Associate Professor of English, University of Texas at El Paso

Jeffrey N. Golub Assistant Professor of English Education, University of South Florida, Tampa

William L. McBride Reading and Curriculum Specialist; former middle and high school English instructor

Multicultural Advisory Board

The multicultural advisors reviewed literature selections for appropriate content and made suggestions for teaching lessons in a multicultural classroom.

Dr. Joyce M. Bell, Chairperson, English Department, Townview Magnet Center, Dallas, Texas

Dr. Eugenia W. Collier, author; lecturer; Chairperson, Department of English and Language Arts; teacher of Creative Writing and American Literature, Morgan State University, Maryland

Kathleen S. Fowler, President, Palm Beach County Council of Teachers of English, Boca Raton Middle School, Boca Raton, Florida

Noreen M. Rodriguez, Trainer for Hillsborough County School District's Staff Development Division, independent consultant, Gaither High School, Tampa, Florida

Michelle Dixon Thompson, Seabreeze High School, Daytona Beach, Florida

Teacher Review Panels

The following educators provided ongoing review during the development of the tables of contents, lesson design, and key components of the program.

FLORIDA
Judi Briant, English Department Chairperson, Armwood High School, Hillsborough County School District

Beth Johnson, Polk County English Supervisor, Polk County School District

Sharon Johnston, Learning Resource Specialist, Evans High School, Orange County School District

Continued on page 1131

Manuscript Reviewers

The following educators reviewed prototype lessons and tables of contents during the development of *The Language of Literature* program.

Carol Alves, English Department Chairperson, Apopka High School, Apopka, Florida

Jacqueline Anderson, James A. Foshay Learning Center, Los Angeles, California

Kathleen M. Anderson-Knight, United Township High School, East Moline, Illinois

Anita Arnold, Thomas Jefferson High School, San Antonio, Texas

Cassandra L. Asberry, Justin F. Kimball High School, Dallas, Texas

Don Baker, English Department Chairperson, Peoria High School, Peoria, Illinois

Continued on page 1133

vi

Student Board

The student board members read and evaluated selections to assess their appeal for tenth-grade students.

Jayme Charak, Niles North High School, Skokie, Illinois

Amy Dobelstein, Shades Valley Resource Learning Center, Birmingham, Alabama

Quoleshna Z. Elbert, Lincoln College Preparatory Academy, Kansas City, Missouri

Katrina Gorski, Loudon County High School, Leesburg, Virginia

Geoffrey L. Harvey, Phineas Banning High School, Wilmington, California

Katherine McGuire, Lyons Township High School, Western Springs, Illinois

Emily Myers, Union High School, Grand Rapids, Michigan

Ronnie G. Pigao, Phineas Banning High School, Wilmington, California

Josh Raub, Lakeview High School, Lakeville, Minnesota

Kevin Schatzman, Miami Killian Sr. High School, Miami, Florida

Stephanie Stone, John Marshall High School, San Antonio, Texas

Cynthia Villicana, Phineas Banning High School, Wilmington, California

Adriana M. Zuñiga, San Marcos High School, San Marcos, Texas

THE LANGUAGE OF LITERATURE
Overview

Student Anthology
Learning the Language of Literature

Literature Connections

Each book in the Literature Connections series combines a novel or play with related readings— poems, stories, plays, essays, articles—that provide new perspectives on the theme or subject matter of the longer work. For example, Nathaniel Hawthorne's *The Scarlet Letter* is combined with the following readings, which focus on modern applications and humorous retellings of the novel and on such topics as the Puritans, scapegoating, sin, and temptation.

John Dunton	**Muddy Brains**
Richard Armour	*from* **The Classics Reclassified**
Kate Chopin	**A Respectable Woman**
Emily Dickinson	**For Each Ecstatic Instant**
Emily Dickinson	**Mine Enemy Is Growing Old**
Bible	**Psalm 32**
Shirley Jackson	**The Lottery**
Toni Locy	**Concerns Raised on "Scarlet Letter" for Drunk Drivers**

The Adventures of Huckleberry Finn*
Mark Twain

. . . And the Earth Did Not Devour Him
Tomás Rivera

Animal Farm
George Orwell

The Crucible
Arthur Miller

Ethan Frome
Edith Wharton

Fallen Angels
Walter Dean Myers

The Friends
Rosa Guy

Hamlet
William Shakespeare

Jane Eyre*
Charlotte Brontë

Julius Caesar
William Shakespeare

Macbeth
William Shakespeare

A Midsummer Night's Dream
William Shakespeare

My Ántonia
Willa Cather

Nervous Conditions
Tsitsi Dangarembga

Picture Bride
Yoshiko Uchida

A Place Where the Sea Remembers
Sandra Benítez

Pygmalion
Bernard Shaw

A Raisin in the Sun
Lorraine Hansberry

The Scarlet Letter
Nathaniel Hawthorne

A Tale of Two Cities*
Charles Dickens

Things Fall Apart
Chinua Achebe

To Kill a Mockingbird: The Screenplay
Horton Foote

The Tragedy of Romeo and Juliet*
William Shakespeare

The Underdogs
Mariano Azuela

West with the Night
Beryl Markham

When Rain Clouds Gather
Bessie Head

*McDougal Littell offers a Spanish version.

Part 2 The Power of Heritage

Part 1 Challenging the System

Part 2 Prisoners of Circumstance

xiii

Part 2 Mysteries of the Heart

REFLECTING ON THEME What Do You Think? 428

Mark Twain ▪ United States	**The Californian's Tale**	FICTION	430
Su Dong Po ▪ China	**To a Traveler** / INSIGHT	POETRY	438
N. Scott Momaday ▪ United States	**Simile**	POETRY	441
Pablo Neruda ▪ Chile	**Tonight I Can Write . . . /** **Puedo Escribir Los Versos . . .**	POETRY	441
Aleksandr Pushkin ▪ Russia	**To . . .**	POETRY	448
Rachel de Queiroz ▪ Brazil	**Metonymy, or The Husband's Revenge**	FICTION	452
Bernard Malamud ▪ United States	**The First Seven Years**	FICTION	460
Anton Chekhov ▪ Russia	**The Bear**	DRAMA	473
Anonymous ▪ China	**The Lady Who Was a Beggar**	FOLK TALE	488

ON YOUR OWN / ASSESSMENT OPTION

WRITING FROM EXPERIENCE   **Informative Exposition**

Guided Assignment: Write a Compare-and-Contrast Essay 500
Prewriting: Exploring Information
Drafting: Getting Your Ideas Down
Revising and Publishing: Finishing Your Essay
SKILLBUILDERS: Using Library Resources, Using Parallel
Structure, Avoiding Double Comparisons

UNIT REVIEW: REFLECT & ASSESS 508

xv

Part 1 Unexpected Realizations

Part 2 What Matters Most

REFLECTING ON THEME   What Do You Think?. 592

WRITING FROM EXPERIENCE   Informative Exposition

Guided Assignment: Write a Cause-and-Effect Essay 658
Prewriting: Answering Questions
Drafting: Making Connections
Revising and Publishing: Clarifying Connections
SKILLBUILDERS: Avoiding Logical Fallacies, Creating Coherence in Paragraphs, Avoiding Sentence Fragments

UNIT REVIEW: REFLECT & ASSESS 666

Part 2 Cultural Crossroads

The Making of Heroes

Electronic Library

The Electronic Library is a CD-ROM that contains additional fiction, nonfiction, poetry, and drama for each unit in *The Language of Literature*.

List of Titles, Grade 10 Electronic Library

Unit 1

Pat Mora	**The Border**
Tacitus	**The Burning of Rome**
Lu Xün	**My Old Home**
Léon Damas	**Hiccups**
Anatole France	**Putois**
Tru Vu	**Who Am I?**
Czeslaw Milosz	**My Faithful Mother Tongue**
Minfong Ho	**The Winter Hibiscus**

Unit 2

Italo Calvino	**Santa's Children**
Henrik Ibsen	**A Doll's House**
Bertolt Brecht	**To Posterity**
Mikhail Zoshchenko	**Bees and People**
Franz Kafka	**A Hunger Artist**
Miguel Hernández	**War**

Unit 3

Karel Čapek	**The Stamp Collection**
Tu Fu	**The Return**
Alfonsina Storni	**One More Time**
Petrarch	**The Spring Returns**
Sappho	**Leaving Crete**
Ovid	**The Story of Pyramus and Thisbe**
Isak Dinesen	**The Ring**
Luigi Pirandello	**War**
Gabriela Mistral	**Intimate**

Note: A complete list of literature available for all grade levels accompanies each CD-ROM.

MᴄDᴏᴜɢᴀʟ Lɪᴛᴛᴇʟʟ

ELECTRONIC LIBRARY

A COMPENDIUM OF OVER 200 LITERARY SELECTIONS ON CD ROM

Selections by Genre, Writing Workshops

LEARNING THE LANGUAGE OF
LITERATURE

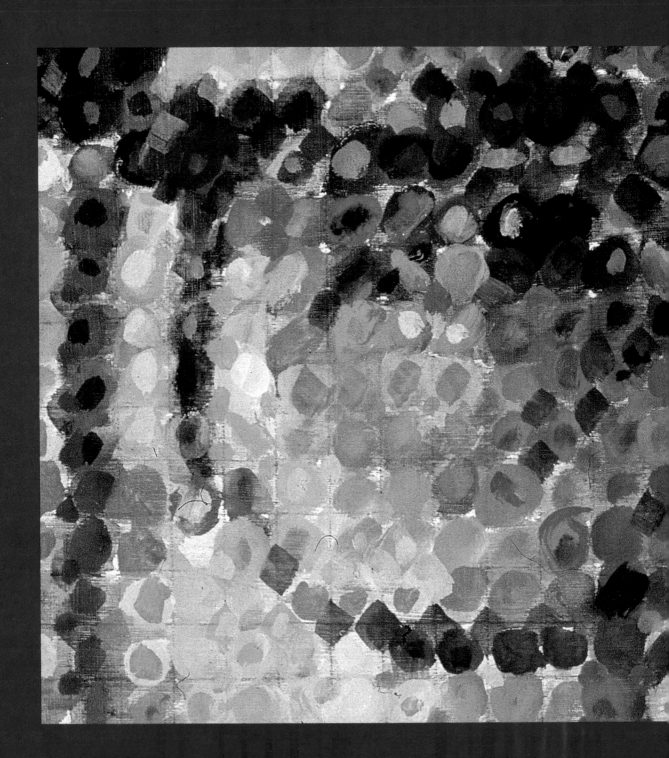

Do You See What I See?

This painting is radiant with striking colors, shapes, and brush strokes. Why do you think the artist composed the painting in this way? The answer lies in the subject matter of the painting. Can you guess what it is?

LOOK AGAIN

In small groups, try to make sense of the painting. Here are some ideas about how to proceed.

1. Have group members take turns holding the book and looking carefully at the image.

2. Try holding the image very close to your face and then moving it farther and farther away.

3. Guess the subject of the painting, and jot down your guess on a small piece of paper.

4. Share guesses as a group. Can the group agree on an answer?

5. When your group is satisfied, compare your answer with the answers arrived at by other groups.

6. If other groups came up with different answers than your group did, describe to them how you got your answer.

7. Can your class agree on what the painting portrays?

CONNECT TO LITERATURE

Just as this painting mixes different colors and shapes to create an image, literature pieces together bits of reality and imagination to create experiences in readers' minds. Once you figure out how the parts work together to create a whole, you can fully enjoy the experience of reading. For a look at what you might encounter, turn the page.

What Can Literature Reveal?

Literature can be an eye-opening experience, as you are sure to discover in this book. Hundreds of destinations and stunning sights await you. What do you think literature might reveal?

WORLDS OF WONDER

Literature can show you the way to Africa, the Americas, Europe, India, China, Japan— the whole world! You can even zoom backward or forward in time. As you journey through the **literature selections** in this book, you'll encounter history and heroes, truth and change, love, and much more. To see how a story can reflect society, take a look through Yukio Mishima's "The Pearl" on page 284.

CLOSE-UPS OF YOU

Literature can give you insights into yourself. Most of the selections begin with a **Previewing** page that taps into your knowledge of a subject and gives you background information as well. On page 51, for example, you'll explore qualities both good and evil before reading a story by Leo Tolstoy. The **Responding** pages after a selection give you opportunities to build on what you have learned from the literature. For a glimpse at some of those opportunities, see the activities on page 62.

HIDDEN LINKS

The people and cultures you read about may seem worlds away, but eventually you'll begin to notice certain links between yourself and the world. When you're ready to share your many discoveries with others, the **Writing About Literature** workshops can show you how. For example, the workshop on page 420 invites you to respond to Shakespeare and other poets. For opportunities to connect unit themes to real life, turn to the **Writing from Experience** workshops. Unit 3, for example, explores how family life varies among cultures. Then in the workshop on page 500, you'll compare two or more cultures.

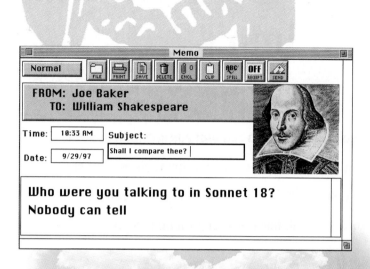

NEW PERSPECTIVES

Sometimes it seems that life is a little too pressing. Literature lets you step back and take stock of your experiences. In the **Reading the World** features, you will see how strategies that help you clarify your understanding of literature can also help you make sense of the world around you. For an exercise in observation, see page 426.

Chuck Close, Self Portrait, 1986 (Detail shown on page 1)

How Do You Bring It into Focus?

You're beginning to see that you can look at literature from a variety of perspectives. Now it is time to learn techniques that can help you get clearer pictures and develop your own unique views.

Portfolio

MULTIPLE PATHWAYS

How do you learn best? Do you prefer to work alone or with the help of a friend? In this book, you are presented with a variety of learning opportunities that allow you to chart the course to your own success, whether your strengths lie mainly in written, oral, dramatic, or artistic activities. In addition, you will collaborate with classmates to share ideas, improve your writing, and make connections to other subject areas. You may even use technological tools such as the Laserlinks and the Writing Coach software program to further personalize your learning.

PORTFOLIO

Many artists, photographers, designers, and writers keep samples of their work in a portfolio to show to others. Like them, you will be collecting your work—writing samples, records of activities, artwork—in a portfolio throughout the year. You probably won't want to put all your work in your portfolio, just carefully chosen pieces. Discuss with your teacher portfolio plans for this year. Suggestions for how to use your portfolio occur throughout this book.

Reading Log

Notebook

"The Interlopers" by Saki

What does "interloper" m...
can I understand the sto...
even know what the titl...
An interloper meddles in ...
of others, often for selfi...

* Look up the word "

Ideas for a paper based on "The Interlopers" by Saki

I didn't think I'd like this story because typically I'm not interested in hunting stories, but when I discovered that the story was about a feud, I became interested.

Now that I've read the entire story, I feel inspired to write about an unfortunate aspect of my life. For five years, my cousin and I have been at each other's throats.

he was in the kitchen learning to cook or in the living room
learning to embroider. She often says she wants me to be
strong and independent. I think she feels strongly about this
because she wasn't raised that way herself.

Sometimes, however, she forgets that she wants me to
independent. Sometimes she complains that I care more
about my friends and activities than I do about her. She'd
say that American girls have too much freedom and that in
Argentina a daughter would stay home and keep her mother
company.

It is true that I haven't stayed home much on the weekends this year. I'm a sophomore now, and there are parties
and dances to go to. My friends expect me to come, and I
want to be with them. Sometimes I change my plans when
Mom complains, but this Friday, I wasn't going to let her
grumbling upset me. I was a flag girl in the band and had to
perform at half-time.

"Sorry, Mom," I answered. "You know there's a football
game tonight. I have to be there in a half hour. "

NOTEBOOK

Choose any type of notebook, and dedicate it to
your study of literature. Divide the notebook into
three sections. Use the first section to jot down
ideas, describe personal experiences, take notes,
and express your thoughts before, while, and after
you read a selection. Also include any charts, diagrams, and drawings that help you connect your
reading to your life. The second section will be for
your reading log, described below. Use the third
section as a writer's notebook to record ideas and
inspirations that may prove useful in your writing.

READING LOG

Your reading log is for a special kind of response
to literature—the comments you make as you
read a selection. The reading strategies detailed
at the right will help you think through what you
read. In your reading log experiment with recording your own comments as you read. Specific
opportunities to use your reading log appear
throughout this book.

Strategies for Reading

To get the most out of literature, you must think
about what you read. The strategies below
describe the kinds of thinking that active readers
do as they read. When you study these strategies,
you will see that you, too, can put them to use.

QUESTION

Question what's happening while you read.
Searching for reasons behind events and characters' feelings can help you feel more involved in
what you're reading. Note confusing words or
statements. Don't worry if you don't understand
everything; further reading will probably make
things clear.

CONNECT

Connect personally with what you're reading.
Think of similarities between the descriptions in
the selection and what you have personally experienced, heard about, or read about.

PREDICT

Try to figure out what will happen next and how
the selection might end. Then read on to see if
you made good guesses.

CLARIFY

Stop occasionally to review what you understand
so far. But get ready to have your understanding
change and develop as you read on. Also, watch
for answers to questions you had earlier.

EVALUATE

Form opinions while you're reading and after
you've finished. Develop your own mental images
of characters and your own ideas about events.

**Now turn the page to see how two student
readers put these strategies to work.**

Alongside "The Interlopers" are the spoken comments made by two tenth-grade students, Robert Wingader and Thanh-Thuy Nguyen (tän tōō ē wǐn), while they were reading the story. Their comments provide a glimpse into the minds of readers actively engaged in the process of reading. You'll notice that in the course of reading, Robert and Thuy (tōō ē) quite naturally used the Strategies for Reading that were introduced on page 5. You'll also note that these readers responded differently to the story—no two readers think the same way.

To benefit most from this model of active reading, read the story first, jotting down your own responses in your reading log. Then read Robert's and Thuy's comments and compare their processes of reading with your own.

THE INTERLOPERS

Saki

Robert: *I've heard of the Carpathians, but I don't know where they are.*
CONNECTING / QUESTIONING

Thuy: *At first I thought he was hunting, but now I think it's like a game to him. He's hunting another man.*
CLARIFYING

Robert: *Why is the land so jealously guarded?*
QUESTIONING

In a forest of mixed growth somewhere on the eastern spurs of the Carpathians, a man stood one winter night watching and listening, as though he waited for some beast of the woods to come within the range of his vision, and, later, of his rifle. But the game for whose presence he kept so keen an outlook was none that figured in the sportman's calendar as lawful and proper for the chase; Ulrich von Gradwitz patrolled the dark forest in quest of a human enemy.

The forest lands of Gradwitz were of wide extent and well stocked with game; the narrow strip of precipitous woodland that lay on its outskirt was not remarkable for the game it harbored or the shooting it afforded, but it was the most jealously guarded of all its owner's territorial possessions. A famous lawsuit, in the days of his grandfather, had wrested it from the illegal possession of a neighboring family of petty landowners; the dispossessed party had never acquiesced in the judgment of the Courts, and a long series of poaching affrays and similar scandals had embittered the relationships between the families for three generations. The neighbor feud had grown into a personal one since Ulrich had come to be head of his family; if there was a man in the world whom he detested and wished ill to it was Georg Znaeym, the inheritor of the quarrel and the tireless game-snatcher and raider of the disputed border-forest. The feud might, perhaps, have died down or been compromised if the personal ill-will of the two men had not stood in the way; as boys they had thirsted for one another's blood, as men each prayed that misfortune might fall on the other, and this wind-scourged winter night Ulrich had banded together his foresters to watch the dark forest, not in quest of four-footed quarry, but to keep a lookout for the prowling thieves whom he suspected of being afoot from across the land boundary. The roebuck, which usually kept in the sheltered hollows during a storm wind, were running like driven things tonight, and there was movement and unrest among the creatures that were wont to sleep through the dark hours. Assuredly there was a disturbing element in the forest, and Ulrich could guess the quarter from whence it came.

He strayed away by himself from the watchers whom he had placed in ambush on the crest of the hill, and wandered far down the steep slopes amid the wild tangle of undergrowth, peering through the tree trunks and listening through the whistling and skirling of the wind and the restless beating of the branches for sight or sound of the marauders. If only on this wild night, in this dark, lone spot, he might come across Georg Znaeym, man to man, with none to witness—that was the wish that was uppermost in his thoughts. And as he stepped around the trunk of a huge beech, he came face to face with the man he sought.

The two enemies stood glaring at one another for a long silent moment.

Each had a rifle in his hand, each had hate in his heart and murder uppermost in his mind. The chance had come to give full play to the passions of a lifetime. But a man who has been brought up under the code of a restraining civilization cannot easily nerve himself to shoot down his neighbor in cold blood and without word spoken, except for an offense against his hearth and honor. And before the moment of hesitation had given way to action a deed of Nature's own violence overwhelmed them both. A fierce shriek of the storm had been answered by a splitting crash over their heads, and ere they could leap aside a mass of falling beech tree had thundered down on them. Ulrich von Gradwitz found himself stretched on the ground, one arm numb beneath him and the other held almost as helplessly in a tight tangle of forked branches, while both legs were pinned beneath the fallen mass. His heavy shooting

Thuy: I picture Ulrich and Georg as having rocky childhoods. These two guys hated each other and were very competitive.
EVALUATING

Thuy: Ulrich is hunting not for animals but for people who are trespassing. That's the game for him.
CLARIFYING

Thuy: He's got vengeance in his eyes; he wants to murder Georg. He's bloodthirsty!
CLARIFYING

Robert: It's ironic that Ulrich found Georg just as he had hoped. Seems unrealistic. I'm reminded that so many wars are just about land. Murder seems too harsh a penalty for a land dispute.
EVALUATING / CONNECTING

Thuy: I'm beginning to think I know where the story is going. I think they'll be caught and then both might die. Or, they might not hate each other in the end and have to work together to save their lives.
PREDICTING

boots had saved his feet from being crushed to pieces, but if his fractures were not as serious as they might have been, at least it was evident that he could not move from his present position till someone came to release him. The descending twigs had slashed the skin of his face, and he had to wink away some drops of blood from his eyelashes before he could take in a general view of the disaster. At his side, so near that under ordinary circumstances he could almost have touched him, lay Georg Znaeym, alive and struggling, but obviously as helplessly pinioned down as himself. All around them lay a thick-strewn wreckage of splintered branches and broken twigs.

Relief at being alive and exasperation at his captive plight brought a strange medley of pious thank offerings and sharp curses to Ulrich's lips. Georg, who was nearly blinded with the blood which trickled across his eyes, stopped his struggling for a moment to listen, and then gave a short, snarling laugh.

"So you're not killed, as you ought to be, but you're caught, anyway," he cried; "caught fast. Ho, what a jest, Ulrich von Gradwitz snared in his stolen forest. There's real justice for you!"

And he laughed again, mockingly and savagely.

"I'm caught in my own forest land," retorted Ulrich. "When my men come to release us, you will wish, perhaps, that you were in a better plight than caught poaching on a neighbor's land, shame on you."

Georg was silent for a moment; then he answered quietly.

"Are you sure that your men will find much to release? I have men, too, in the forest tonight, close behind me, and they will be here first and do the releasing. When they drag me out from under these damned branches, it won't need much clumsiness on their part to roll this mass of trunk right over on the top of you. Your men will find you dead under a fallen beech tree. For form's sake I shall send my condolences to your family."

"It is a useful hint," said Ulrich fiercely. "My men had orders to follow in ten minutes' time, seven of which must have gone by already, and when they get me out—I will remember the hint. Only as you will have met your death poaching on my lands, I don't think I can decently send any message of condolence to your family."

"Good," snarled Georg, "good. We fight this quarrel out to the death, you and I and our foresters, with no cursed interlopers to come between us. Death and damnation to you, Ulrich von Gradwitz."

"The same to you, Georg Znaeym, forest thief, game snatcher."

Both men spoke with the bitterness of possible defeat before them, for each knew that it might be long before his men would seek him out or find him; it was a bare matter of chance which party would arrive first on the scene.

Both had now given up the useless struggle to free themselves from the mass of wood that held them down; Ulrich limited his endeavors to an effort to bring his one partially free arm near enough to his outer coat pocket to draw out his wine flask. Even when he had accomplished that operation, it was long before he could manage the unscrewing of the stopper or get any of the liquid down his throat. But what a heaven-sent draft it seemed! It was an open winter, and little snow had fallen as yet, hence the captives suffered less from the cold than might have been the case at that season of the year; nevertheless, the wine was warming and reviving to the wounded man, and he looked across with something like a throb of pity to where his enemy lay, just keeping the groans of pain and weariness from crossing his lips.

"Could you reach this flask if I threw it over to you?" asked Ulrich suddenly; "there is good wine in it, and one may as well be as comfortable as one can. Let us drink, even if tonight one of us dies."

"No, I can scarcely see anything; there is so much blood caked around my eyes," said Georg, "and in any case I don't drink wine with an enemy."

Ulrich was silent for a few minutes and lay listening to the weary screeching of the wind. An idea was slowly forming and growing in his brain, an idea that gained strength every time that he looked across at the man who was fighting so grimly against pain and exhaustion. In the pain and languor that Ulrich himself was feeling the old fierce hatred seemed to be dying down.

"Neighbor," he said presently, "do as you please if your men come first. It was a fair compact. But as for me, I've changed my mind. If my men are the first to come, you shall be the first to be helped, as though you were my guest. We have quarreled like devils all our lives over this stupid strip of forest, where the trees can't even stand upright in a breath of wind. Lying here tonight, thinking, I've come to think we've been rather fools; there are better things in life than getting the better of a boundary dispute. Neighbor, if you will help me to bury the old quarrel I—I will ask you to be my friend."

Georg Znaeym was silent for so long that Ulrich thought, perhaps, he had fainted with the pain of his injuries. Then he spoke slowly and in jerks.

Robert: It's a good thing that Ulrich finally saw past the feud.
EVALUATING

Thuy: When Ulrich drinks the wine he feels warm and some relief from his suffering. It's the first time he feels pity toward his enemy.
CLARIFYING

Thuy: Ulrich does have some human characteristics; I don't hate him as much as I used to.
EVALUATING

Robert: It's pitiful that Georg wouldn't accept Ulrich's offer. It's hard to believe that he's that uneasy about drinking wine with his enemy.
EVALUATING

Thuy: Ulrich calls Georg "neighbor," which contradicts "enemy." He's almost like a friend now.
CLARIFYING

Thuy: Now I know why they hate each other and have been quarreling all this time—it's because of the forest. They see now that they have been fools in the past because of this.
CLARIFYING / EVALUATING

Thuy: *The whole village knows about the feud. It would be a big surprise if they came back to the village as friends.*
CLARIFYING / PREDICTING

Robert: *All feuds should be settled like this; gangs, for instance, could make peace and avoid futile battles.*
EVALUATING / CONNECTING

Robert: *I wonder how Georg's and Ulrich's men will react to the ending of the feud.*
QUESTIONING

Thuy: *At first, each man wanted his own people to come first so the other would be killed, but now, each wants to be first to save the other's life. They both want to be first to show their friendship.*
CLARIFYING

Robert: *They're finally working together to save themselves.*
CLARIFYING

Robert: *I wonder whose men these are.*
QUESTIONING

"How the whole region would stare and gabble if we rode into the market square together. No one living can remember seeing a Znaeym and a von Gradwitz talking to one another in friendship. And what peace there would be among the forester folk if we ended our feud tonight. And if we choose to make peace among our people, there is none other to interfere, no interlopers from outside. . . . You would come and keep the Sylvester night beneath my roof, and I would come and feast on some high day at your castle. . . . I would never fire a shot on your land, save when you invited me as a guest; and you should come and shoot with me down in the marshes where the wildfowl are. In all the countryside there are none that could hinder if we willed to make peace. I never thought to have wanted to do other than hate you all my life, but I think I have changed my mind about things too, this last half-hour. And you offered me your wine flask. . . . Ulrich von Gradwitz, I will be your friend."

For a space both men were silent, turning over in their minds the wonderful changes that this dramatic reconciliation would bring about. In the cold, gloomy forest, with the wind tearing in fitful gusts through the naked branches and whistling around the tree trunks, they lay and waited for the help that would now bring release and succor to both parties. And each prayed a private prayer that his men might be the first to arrive, so that he might be the first to show honorable attention to the enemy that had become a friend.

Presently, as the wind dropped for a moment, Ulrich broke silence.

"Let's shout for help," he said; "in this lull our voices may carry a little way."

"They won't carry far through the trees and undergrowth," said Georg, "but we can try. Together, then."

The two raised their voices in a prolonged hunting call.

"Together again," said Ulrich a few minutes later, after listening in vain for an answer halloo.

"I heard something that time, I think" said Ulrich.

"I heard nothing but the pestilential wind," said Georg hoarsely.

There was silence again for some minutes, and then Ulrich gave a joyful cry.

"I can see figures coming through the wood. They are following in the way I came down the hillside."

Both men raised their voices in as loud a shout as they could muster.

Border Patrol (1951), Andrew Wyeth. Private collection.

"They hear us! They've stopped. Now they see us. They're running down the hill towards us," cried Ulrich.

"How many of them are there?" asked Georg.

"I can't see distinctly," said Ulrich; "nine or ten."

"Then they are yours," said Georg; "I had only seven out with me."

"They are making all the speed they can, brave lads," said Ulrich gladly.

"Are they your men?" asked Georg. "Are they your men?"

"No," said Ulrich with a laugh, the idiotic chattering laugh of a man unstrung with hideous fear.

"Who are they?" asked Georg quickly, straining his eyes to see what the other would gladly not have seen.

"*Wolves.*" ❖

Thuy: Why "hideous fear"? If men are coming, it doesn't matter who they are.
QUESTIONING

Thuy: Now I see. Now they're going to die together. I like the ending.
CLARIFYING / EVALUATING

Imprints of the Past

One's past is what one is.

Oscar Wilde
*Irish-born poet, playwright,
and novelist
1854–1900*

LASTING IMPRESSIONS

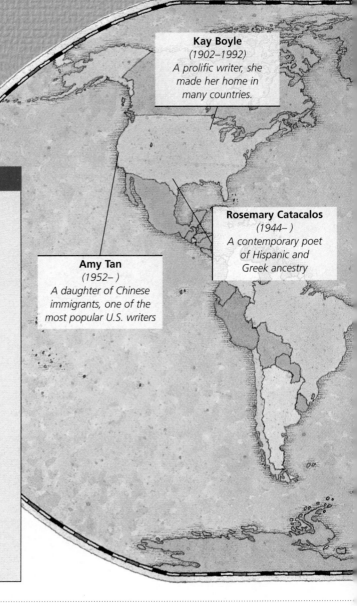

Kay Boyle
(1902–1992)
A prolific writer, she made her home in many countries.

Rosemary Catacalos
(1944–)
A contemporary poet of Hispanic and Greek ancestry

Amy Tan
(1952–)
A daughter of Chinese immigrants, one of the most popular U.S. writers

REFLECTING ON THEME

Why do some people stand out in your memory, even when you haven't seen them for many years? Why do recollections of some distant events linger so long? For each of us, impressions of certain people or events loom large in our memory, lasting perhaps even a lifetime. In this part of Unit One, you will explore how the past has imprinted the lives of characters both real and fictional. You will also tap into your own memories of people who made a lasting impression on you.

What Do You Think? Interview a classmate about a person or an event that made a lasting impression on his or her life. Record the results of your interview in your notebook, and then have the same classmate interview you. Share with the rest of the class what both of you learned from the interviews. In discussion, consider why some impressions have such a lasting impact on people.

Amy Tan	**Two Kinds** *Why won't the daughter live her mother's dreams?*	18
Rosemary Catacalos	**La Casa** / INSIGHT *The old house is still the same,* *but something has changed.*	30
Hwang Sunwŏn	**Cranes** *Two friends now on opposite sides in war*	33
Kay Boyle	**Winter Night** *A mysterious woman shares her past.*	40

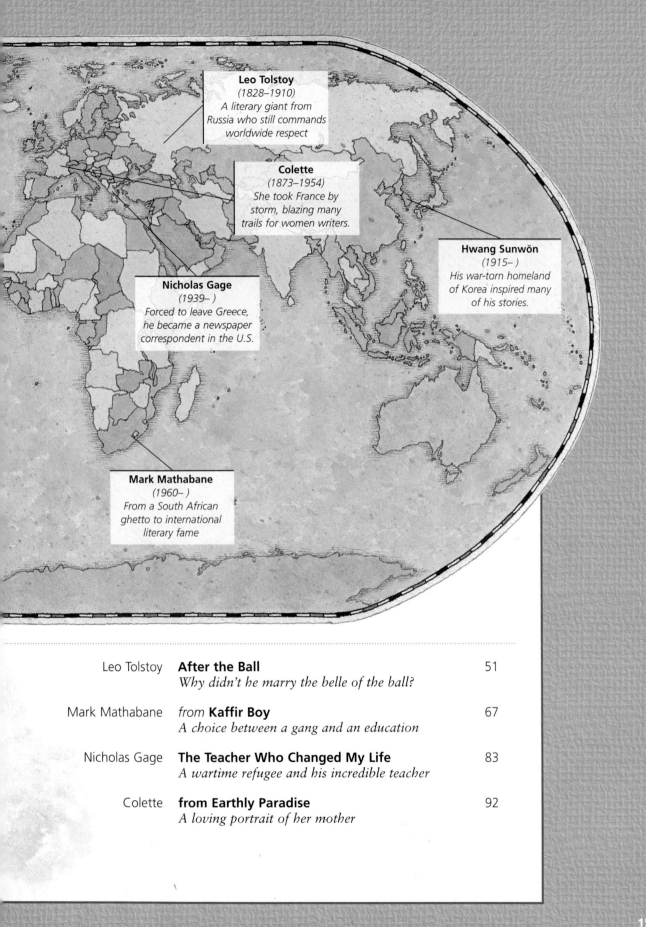

Leo Tolstoy
(1828–1910)
A literary giant from Russia who still commands worldwide respect

Colette
(1873–1954)
She took France by storm, blazing many trails for women writers.

Hwang Sunwŏn
(1915–)
His war-torn homeland of Korea inspired many of his stories.

Nicholas Gage
(1939–)
Forced to leave Greece, he became a newspaper correspondent in the U.S.

Mark Mathabane
(1960–)
From a South African ghetto to international literary fame

FOCUS ON FICTION

The origins of the word *fiction* can be traced to the Latin verb *fingere* (fĭng'gĕ-rĕ), which had two meanings: "to make up or invent" and "to make by shaping." Both meanings are relevant to fiction. A work of **fiction** is a narrative that springs from the imagination of a writer, though it may be based on actual events and real people. The writer shapes his or her narrative to capture the reader's interest and to achieve desired effects.

The two major types of fiction are **novels** and **short stories.** A novel is a fictional prose narrative of considerable length, usually taking several days or even weeks to read. Typically, a novel has a complex plot that unfolds though the actions, speech, and thoughts of the characters. A short story, on the other hand, is a brief work of fiction that can be read at one sitting. Generally, it develops one primary conflict and produces a single effect. Despite these differences in length and complexity, short stories and novels share the elements of **character, setting, plot,** and **theme.**

CHARACTER Characters are the individuals who take part in the action of a story. The events of the story center on the most important characters—the **main characters.** Less prominent characters are known as **minor characters.** Whereas some characters are two-dimensional, with only one or two dominant traits, a fully developed character possesses many traits, mirroring the psychological complexity of a real person. In longer works of fiction, main characters often undergo change as the plot unfolds. Such characters are called **dynamic characters,** as opposed to **static characters,** who remain the same.

SETTING The events of a story occur in a particular time and place, or setting. The setting is

very important in some stories but no more than a backdrop in others. A story can be set in a realistic or an imaginary place, and its events can occur in the past, the present, or the future.

PLOT The word *plot* refers to the chain of related events that take place in a story. The plot is the writer's blueprint for what happens, when it happens, and to whom it happens. Usually, the events of a plot progress because of a **conflict,** or struggle between opposing forces.

Although there are many types of plots, most include the following stages:

Exposition The exposition lays the groundwork for the plot and provides the reader with essential background information. Characters are introduced, the setting is described, and the plot begins to unfold. Although the exposition generally appears at the opening of a story, it may also occur later in the narrative.

Rising Action As the story progresses, **complications** usually arise, causing difficulties for the main characters and making the conflict more difficult to resolve. As the characters struggle to find solutions to the conflict, suspense builds.

Climax The climax is the turning point of the action, the moment when interest and intensity reach their peak. The climax of a story usually involves an important event, decision, or discovery that affects the final outcome.

Falling Action The falling action consists of the events that occur after the climax. Often, the conflict is resolved, and the intensity of the action subsides. Sometimes this phase of the plot is called the **denouement** (dā´nōō-mäɴ´), from a French word that means "untying." In the denouement, the tangles of the plot are untied and mysteries are solved.

THEME A theme is an important idea or message conveyed by a work of fiction. It is a perception about life or human nature that the writer shares with the reader. Some pieces of fiction are intended only for entertainment and, as such, have no underlying themes. Most serious writing, however, comments on life or the human condition. Themes are seldom stated directly; often they can be uncovered only by means of careful reading and thought.

The following suggestions will help you unlock the theme or themes of a work:

- Review what happened to the main character. Did he or she change during the story? What did he or she learn about life?

- Skim the selection for key phrases and sentences—statements that move beyond the action of the story to say something important about life or people.

- Think about the title of the selection. Does it have a special meaning that could lead you to discover a major theme?

STRATEGIES FOR READING FICTION

- **Preview** Before you begin a work of fiction, look ahead to see what the title, the art, or other noticeable features tell you about the story.

- **Visualize and Connect** As you read the exposition, picture in your mind the characters and setting described. Look for specific adjectives that can help you imagine how the opening scene might look. Try connecting what you read with people, places, and situations that you know from personal experience.

- **Observe and Question** Be an active reader by making observations and asking questions about the story. Note whether the narrator is a character within the story or is watching the action from outside. Ask yourself what the central problem, or conflict, seems to be. Ask why the characters behave as they do.

- **Predict** Once you begin to understand the problems the characters face, predict what will happen

next. Think about what the characters might do or say in their situation. Try to imagine what the climax of the story might be.

- **Clarify** As you read, you will notice that the reasons for certain characters' actions become clear. As they do, your impressions of these characters may change. Continue to clarify, or refine, your understanding of the story. Reread relevant sections of the selection to help you understand fully what has happened or why it has happened.

- **Evaluate** Don't forget to make judgments about what you read. Draw your own conclusions about the characters and their actions, just as you would about people you know in real life.

- **Reflect** When you finish reading, take a few minutes to think about your impressions. How do you feel about the story's events and main characters? What did you enjoy about the story?

PREVIEWING

FICTION

Two Kinds
Amy Tan United States

PERSONAL CONNECTION

Think of a time when someone in authority had high expectations of you—expectations that you were not sure you could meet. Perhaps a parent expected straight A's, a bandleader gave you a difficult solo, or a coach put you in a game at a critical moment. Share your experience with your classmates.

CULTURAL CONNECTION

During the 1930s and 1940s, China was invaded by Japan and racked by political upheavals that led to a bitter civil war. Some Chinese citizens escaped these dangers by emigrating to the United States. To many Chinese immigrants, life in the United States was so different from life in war-torn China that anything seemed possible, especially for their children. The children were expected to pursue the American dream of material success, but without sacrificing the traditional Chinese values of obedience and respect for one's elders. "Two Kinds" is narrated by a young woman who, like Amy Tan herself, is the daughter of Chinese immigrants.

WRITING CONNECTION

Why do you think many parents have high expectations of their children? To help you sort out your thoughts on this issue, create a chart similar to the one shown here. Then write a brief explanation of why parents sometimes have high expectations. As you read this story, keep in mind your thoughts on this subject.

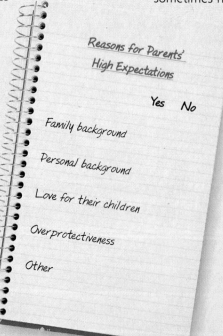

Reasons for Parents' High Expectations

	Yes	No
Family background		
Personal background		
Love for their children		
Overprotectiveness		
Other		

LASERLINKS
• CULTURAL CONNECTION

TWO KINDS

AMY TAN

My mother believed you could be anything you wanted to be in America. You could open a restaurant. You could work for the government and get good retirement. You could buy a house with almost no money down. You could become rich. You could become instantly famous.

Detail of *Laundryman's Daughter* (1988), Tomie Arai.

"Of course you can be prodigy, too," my mother told me when I was nine. "You can be best anything. What does Auntie Lindo know? Her daughter, she is only best tricky."

America was where all my mother's hopes lay. She had come here in 1949 after losing everything in China: her mother and father, her family home, her first husband, and two daughters, twin baby girls. But she never looked back with regret. There were so many ways for things to get better.

We didn't immediately pick the right kind of prodigy. At first my mother thought I could be a Chinese Shirley Temple.[1] We'd watch Shirley's old movies on TV as though they were training films. My mother would poke my arm and say, *"Ni kan"*—You watch. And I would see Shirley tapping her feet, or singing a sailor song, or pursing her lips into a very round O while saying, "Oh my goodness."

"Ni kan," said my mother as Shirley's eyes flooded with tears. "You already know how. Don't need talent for crying!"

Soon after my mother got this idea about Shirley Temple, she took me to a beauty training school in the Mission district[2] and put me in the hands of a student who could barely hold the scissors without shaking. Instead of getting big fat curls, I emerged with an uneven mass of crinkly black fuzz. My mother dragged me off to the bathroom and tried to wet down my hair.

"You look like Negro Chinese," she lamented, as if I had done this on purpose.

The instructor of the beauty training school had to lop off these soggy clumps to make my hair even again. "Peter Pan is very popular these days," the instructor assured my mother. I now had hair the length of a boy's, with straight-across bangs that hung at a slant two inches above my eyebrows. I liked the haircut, and it made me actually look forward to my future fame.

In fact, in the beginning, I was just as excited as my mother, maybe even more so. I pictured this prodigy part of me as many different images, trying each one on for size. I was a dainty ballerina girl standing by the curtains, waiting to hear the right music that would send me floating on my tiptoes. I was like the Christ child lifted out of the straw manger, crying with holy indignity. I was Cinderella stepping from her pumpkin carriage with sparkly cartoon music filling the air.

In all of my imaginings, I was filled with a sense that I would soon become *perfect.* My mother and father would adore me. I would be beyond reproach. I would never feel the need to sulk for anything.

But sometimes the prodigy in me became impatient. "If you don't hurry up and get me out of here, I'm disappearing for good," it warned. "And then you'll always be nothing."

Every night after dinner, my mother and I would sit at the Formica[3] kitchen table. She would present new tests, taking her examples from stories of amazing children she had read in *Ripley's Believe It or Not,* or *Good Housekeeping, Reader's Digest,* and a dozen other magazines she kept in a pile in our bathroom. My mother got these magazines from people whose houses she cleaned. And since she cleaned many houses each week, we had a great assortment. She would look through them all,

---

1. **Shirley Temple:** a popular child movie star of the 1930s.
2. **Mission district:** a residential neighborhood in San Francisco.
3. **Formica** (fôr-mī′kə): a heat-resistant plastic used on tops of kitchen counters, tables, and the like.

searching for stories about remarkable children.

The first night she brought out a story about a three-year-old boy who knew the capitals of all the states and even most of the European countries. A teacher was quoted as saying the little boy could also pronounce the names of the foreign cities correctly.

"What's the capital of Finland?" my mother asked me, looking at the magazine story.

All I knew was the capital of California, because Sacramento was the name of the street we lived on in Chinatown. "Nairobi!"[4] I guessed, saying the most foreign word I could think of. She checked to see if that was possibly one way to pronounce "Helsinki" before showing me the answer.

The tests got harder—multiplying numbers in my head, finding the queen of hearts in a deck of cards, trying to stand on my head without using my hands, predicting the daily temperatures in Los Angeles, New York, and London.

One night I had to look at a page from the Bible for three minutes and then report everything I could remember. "Now Jehoshaphat[5] had riches and honor in abundance and . . . that's all I remember, Ma," I said.

And after seeing my mother's disappointed face once again, something inside of me began to die. I hated the tests, the raised hopes and failed expectations. Before going to bed that night, I looked in the mirror above the bathroom sink and when I saw only my face staring back—and that it would always be this ordinary face—I began to cry. Such a sad, ugly girl! I made high-pitched noises like a crazed animal, trying to scratch out the face in the mirror.

And then I saw what seemed to be the prodigy side of me—because I had never seen that face before. I looked at my reflection, blinking so I could see more clearly. The girl staring back at me was angry, powerful. This girl and I were the same. I had new thoughts, willful thoughts, or rather thoughts filled with lots of won'ts. I won't let her change me, I promised myself. I won't be what I'm not.

So now on nights when my mother presented her tests, I performed listlessly, my head propped on one arm. I pretended to be bored. And I was. I got so bored I started counting the bellows of the foghorns out on the bay while my mother drilled me in other areas. The sound was comforting and reminded me of the cow jumping over the moon. And the next day, I played a game with myself, seeing if my mother would give up on me before eight bellows. After a while I usually counted only one, maybe two bellows at most. At last she was beginning to give up hope.

Two or three months had gone by without any mention of my being a prodigy again. And then one day my mother was watching *The Ed Sullivan Show*[6] on TV. The TV was old and the sound kept shorting out. Every time my mother got halfway up from the sofa to adjust the set, the sound would go back on and Ed would be talking. As soon as she sat down, Ed would go silent again. She got up, the TV broke into loud

> **I won't let her change me, I promised myself. I won't be what I'm not.**

---

4. **Nairobi** (nī-rō′bē): the capital of the African nation of Kenya.

5. **Jehoshaphat** (jə-hŏsh′ə-făt′): a king of Judah in the ninth century B.C.

6. ***The Ed Sullivan Show***: a popular weekly variety show on television from 1948 to 1971.

Laundryman's Daughter (1988), Tomie Arai. Silkscreen print, 22″ × 30″ unframed, printed in an edition of 35 by Avocet Editions.

piano music. She sat down. Silence. Up and down, back and forth, quiet and loud. It was like a stiff, embraceless dance between her and the TV set. Finally she stood by the set with her hand on the sound dial.

She seemed entranced by the music, a little frenzied piano piece with this mesmerizing quality, sort of quick passages and then teasing lilting ones before it returned to the quick playful parts.

"*Ni kan,*" my mother said, calling me over with hurried hand gestures, "Look here."

I could see why my mother was fascinated by the music. It was being pounded out by a little Chinese girl, about nine years old, with a Peter Pan haircut. The girl had the sauciness of a Shirley Temple. She was proudly modest like a proper Chinese child. And she also did this fancy sweep of a curtsy, so that the fluffy skirt of her white dress cascaded slowly to the floor like the petals of a large carnation.

In spite of these warning signs, I wasn't worried. Our family had no piano and we couldn't afford to buy one, let alone <u>reams</u> of sheet music and piano lessons. So I could be generous in my comments when my mother bad-mouthed the little girl on TV.

"Play note right, but doesn't sound good! No singing sound," complained my mother.

"What are you picking on her for?" I said carelessly. "She's pretty good. Maybe she's not the best, but she's trying hard." I knew almost immediately I would be sorry I said that.

"Just like you," she said. "Not the best. Because you not trying." She gave a little huff as she let go of the sound dial and sat down on the sofa.

The little Chinese girl sat down also to play an encore of "Anitra's Dance" by Grieg.[7] I remember the song, because later on I had to learn how to play it.

Three days after watching *The Ed Sullivan Show,* my mother told me what my schedule would be for piano lessons and piano practice. She had talked to Mr. Chong, who lived on the first floor of our apartment building. Mr. Chong was a retired piano teacher and my mother had traded housecleaning services for weekly lessons and a piano for me to practice on every day, two hours a day, from four until six.

When my mother told me this, I felt as though I had been sent to hell. I whined and then kicked my foot a little when I couldn't stand it anymore.

"Why don't you like me the way I am? I'm *not* a genius! I can't play the piano. And even if I could, I wouldn't go on TV if you paid me a million dollars!" I cried.

My mother slapped me. "Who ask you be genius?" she shouted. "Only ask you be your best. For you sake. You think I want you be genius? Hnnh! What for! Who ask you!"

"So ungrateful," I heard her mutter in Chinese. "If she had as much talent as she has temper, she would be famous now."

Mr. Chong, whom I secretly nicknamed Old Chong, was very strange, always tapping his fingers to the silent music of an invisible orchestra. He looked ancient in my eyes. He had lost most of the hair on top of his head and he wore thick glasses and had eyes that always looked tired and sleepy. But he must have been younger than I thought, since he lived with his mother and was not yet married.

I met Old Lady Chong once and that was enough. She had this peculiar smell like a baby that had done something in its pants. And her fingers felt like a dead person's, like an old peach I once found in the back of the refrigerator; the

---

7. **Grieg** (grēg): the Norwegian composer Edvard Grieg (1843–1907).

skin just slid off the meat when I picked it up.

I soon found out why Old Chong had retired from teaching piano. He was deaf. "Like Beethoven!"[8] he shouted to me. "We're both listening only in our head!" And he would start to conduct his frantic silent sonatas.

Our lessons went like this. He would open the book and point to different things, explaining their purpose: "Key! Treble! Bass! No sharps or flats! So this is C major! Listen now and play after me!"

And then he would play the C scale a few times, a simple chord, and then, as if inspired by an old, unreachable itch, he gradually added more notes and running trills and a pounding bass until the music was really something quite grand.

I would play after him, the simple scale, the simple chord, and then I just played some nonsense that sounded like a cat running up and down on top of garbage cans. Old Chong smiled and applauded and then said, "Very good! But now you must learn to keep time!"

So that's how I discovered that Old Chong's eyes were too slow to keep up with the wrong notes I was playing. He went through the motions in half-time. To help me keep rhythm, he stood behind me, pushing down on my right shoulder for every beat. He balanced pennies on top of my wrists so I would keep them still as I slowly played scales and arpeggios.[9] He had me curve my hand around an apple and keep that shape when playing chords. He marched stiffly to show me how to make each finger dance up and down, staccato[10] like an obedient little soldier.

He taught me all these things, and that was how I also learned I could be lazy and get away with mistakes, lots of mistakes. If I hit the wrong notes because I hadn't practiced enough, I never corrected myself. I just kept playing in rhythm. And Old Chong kept conducting his own private reverie.

So maybe I never really gave myself a fair chance. I did pick up the basics pretty quickly, and I might have become a good pianist at that young age. But I was so determined not to try, not to be anybody different, that I learned to play only the most ear-splitting preludes,[11] the most discordant hymns.

Over the next year, I practiced like this, dutifully in my own way. And then one day I heard my mother and her friend Lindo Jong both talking in a loud, bragging tone of voice so others could hear. It was after church, and I was leaning against the brick wall wearing a dress with stiff white petticoats. Auntie Lindo's daughter, Waverly, who was about my age, was standing farther down the wall about five feet away. We had grown up together and shared all the closeness of two sisters squabbling over crayons and dolls. In

I also learned I could be lazy and get away with mistakes, lots of mistakes.

8. **Beethoven** (bā′tō′vən): the German composer Ludwig van Beethoven (1770–1827), who began losing his hearing in 1801 and was deaf by 1819.

9. **arpeggios** (är-pĕj′ē-ōz′): chords in which the notes are played separately in quick sequence rather than at the same time.

10. **staccato** (stə-kä′tō): producing distinct, abrupt breaks between successive tones.

11. **preludes** (prĕl′yo͞odz′): short piano compositions, each usually based on a single musical theme.

WORDS TO KNOW

reverie (rĕv′ə-rē) *n.* a daydream
discordant (dĭ-skôr′dnt) *adj.* having a disagreeable or clashing sound; not in harmony

24

other words, for the most part, we hated each other. I thought she was snotty. Waverly Jong had gained a certain amount of fame as "Chinatown's Littlest Chinese Chess Champion."

"She bring home too many trophy," lamented Auntie Lindo that Sunday. "All day she play chess. All day I have no time do nothing but dust off her winnings." She threw a scolding look at Waverly, who pretended not to see her.

"You lucky you don't have this problem," said Auntie Lindo with a sigh to my mother.

And my mother squared her shoulders and bragged: "Our problem worser than yours. If we ask Jing-mei[12] wash dish, she hear nothing but music. It's like you can't stop this natural talent."

And right then, I was determined to put a stop to her foolish pride.

A few weeks later, Old Chong and my mother conspired to have me play in a talent show which would be held in the church hall. By then, my parents had saved up enough to buy me a secondhand piano, a black Wurlitzer spinet[13] with a scarred bench. It was the showpiece of our living room.

For the talent show, I was to play a piece called "Pleading Child" from Schumann's[14] *Scenes from Childhood*. It was a simple, moody piece that sounded more difficult than it was. I was supposed to memorize the whole thing, playing the repeat parts twice to make the piece sound longer. But I dawdled over it, playing a few bars and then cheating, looking up to see what notes followed. I never really listened to what I was playing. I daydreamed about being somewhere else, about being someone else.

The part I liked to practice best was the fancy curtsy: right foot out, touch the rose on the carpet with a pointed foot, sweep to the

side, left leg bends, look up and smile.

My parents invited all the couples from the Joy Luck Club to witness my debut.[15] Auntie Lindo and Uncle Tin were there. Waverly and her two older brothers had also come. The first two rows were filled with children both younger and older than I was. The littlest ones got to go first. They recited simple nursery rhymes, squawked out tunes on miniature violins, twirled Hula-Hoops,[16] pranced in pink ballet tutus,[17] and when they bowed or curtsied, the audience would sigh in unison, "Awww," and then clap enthusiastically.

When my turn came, I was very confident. I remember my childish excitement. It was as if I knew, without a doubt, that the prodigy side of me really did exist. I had no fear whatsoever, no nervousness. I remember thinking to myself, This is it! This is it! I looked out over the audience, at my mother's blank face, my father's yawn, Auntie Lindo's stiff-lipped smile, Waverly's sulky expression. I had on a white dress layered with sheets of lace, and a pink bow in my Peter Pan haircut. As I sat down I envisioned people jumping to their feet and Ed Sullivan rushing up to introduce me to everyone on TV.

And I started to play. It was so beautiful. I was so caught up in how lovely I looked that at first I didn't worry how I would sound. So it was a surprise to me when I hit the first wrong note and I realized something didn't sound

---

12. **Jing-mei** (jǐng′mā′).

13. **spinet** (spǐn′ǐt): a small upright piano.

14. **Schumann's** (shoo′mänz′): of Robert Schumann (1810–1856), a German composer famous for his piano works.

15. **debut** (dā-byoo′): first public performance.

16. **Hula-Hoops:** plastic hoops that are whirled around the body by means of hip movements similar to those of the hula, a Hawaiian dance.

17. **tutus** (too′tooz): short layered skirts worn by ballerinas.

WORDS TO KNOW **lament** (lə-měnt′) *v.* to express grief or deep regret

25

quite right. And then I hit another and another followed that. A chill started at the top of my head and began to trickle down. Yet I couldn't stop playing, as though my hands were bewitched. I kept thinking my fingers would adjust themselves back, like a train switching to the right track. I played this strange jumble through two repeats, the sour notes staying with me all the way to the end.

When I stood up, I discovered my legs were shaking. Maybe I had just been nervous and the audience, like Old Chong, had seen me go through the right motions and had not heard anything wrong at all. I swept my right foot out, went down on my knee, looked up and smiled. The room was quiet, except for Old Chong, who was beaming and shouting, "Bravo! Bravo! Well done!" But then I saw my mother's face, her stricken face. The audience clapped weakly, and as I walked back to my chair, with my whole face quivering as I tried not to cry, I heard a little boy whisper loudly to his mother, "That was awful," and the mother whispered back, "Well, she certainly tried."

And now I realized how many people were in the audience, the whole world it seemed. I was aware of eyes burning into my back. I felt the shame of my mother and father as they sat stiffly throughout the rest of the show.

We could have escaped during intermission. Pride and some strange sense of honor must have anchored my parents to their chairs. And so we watched it all: the eighteen-year-old boy with a fake mustache who did a magic show and juggled flaming hoops while riding a unicycle. The breasted girl with white makeup who sang from *Madama Butterfly*[18] and got honorable mention. And the eleven-year-old boy who won first prize playing a tricky violin song that sounded like a busy bee.

After the show, the Hsus,[19] the Jongs, and the St. Clairs from the Joy Luck Club came up to my mother and father.

"Lots of talented kids," Auntie Lindo said vaguely, smiling broadly.

"That was somethin' else," said my father, and I wondered if he was referring to me in a humorous way, or whether he even remembered what I had done.

Waverly looked at me and shrugged her shoulders. "You aren't a genius like me," she said matter-of-factly. And if I hadn't felt so bad, I would have pulled her braids and punched her stomach.

But my mother's expression was what devastated me: a quiet, blank look that said she had lost everything. I felt the same way, and it seemed as if everybody were now coming up, like gawkers at the scene of an accident, to see what parts were actually missing. When we got on the bus to go home, my father was humming the busy-bee tune and my mother was silent. I kept thinking she wanted to wait until we got home before shouting at me. But when my father unlocked the door to our apartment, my mother walked in and then went to the back, into the bedroom. No accusations. No blame. And in a way, I felt disappointed. I had been waiting for her to start shouting, so I could shout back and cry and blame her for all my misery.

I assumed my talent-show fiasco meant I never had to play the piano again. But two days later, after school, my mother came out of the kitchen and saw me watching TV.

"Four clock," she reminded me as if it were any other day. I was stunned, as though she were asking me to go through the talent-show

---

18. *Madama* (mä-dä′mä) *Butterfly*: a famous opera by the Italian composer Giacomo Puccini.

19. **Hsus** (shüz).

WORDS TO KNOW	**devastate** (dĕv′ə-stāt′) *v.* to destroy or overwhelm **fiasco** (fē-ăs′kō) *n.* a complete failure

26

The Stairway (1970), Will Barnet. Photo courtesy of Terry Dintenfass Gallery, New York.
© 1995 Will Barnet/Licensed by VAGA, New York, NY.

torture again. I wedged myself more tightly in front of the TV.

"Turn off TV," she called from the kitchen five minutes later.

I didn't budge. And then I decided. I didn't have to do what my mother said anymore. I wasn't her slave. This wasn't China. I had listened to her before and look what happened. She was the stupid one.

She came out from the kitchen and stood in the arched entryway of the living room. "Four clock," she said once again, louder.

"I'm not going to play anymore," I said nonchalantly. "Why should I? I'm not a genius."

She walked over and stood in front of the TV. I saw her chest was heaving up and down in an angry way.

"No!" I said, and I now felt stronger, as if my true self had finally emerged. So this was what had been inside me all along.

"No! I won't!" I screamed.

She yanked me by the arm, pulled me off the

floor, snapped off the TV. She was frighteningly strong, half pulling, half carrying me toward the piano as I kicked the throw rugs under my feet. She lifted me up and onto the hard bench. I was sobbing by now, looking at her bitterly. Her chest was heaving even more and her mouth was open, smiling crazily as if she were pleased I was crying.

"You want me to be someone that I'm not!" I sobbed. "I'll never be the kind of daughter you want me to be!"

"Only two kinds of daughters," she shouted in Chinese. "Those who are obedient and those who follow their own mind! Only one kind of daughter can live in this house. Obedient daughter!"

"Then I wish I wasn't your daughter. I wish you weren't my mother," I shouted. As I said these things I got scared. It felt like worms and toads and slimy things crawling out of my chest, but it also felt good, as if this awful side of me had surfaced, at last.

"Too late change this," said my mother shrilly.

And I could sense her anger rising to its breaking point. I wanted to see it spill over. And that's when I remembered the babies she had lost in China, the ones we never talked about. "Then I wish I'd never been born!" I shouted. "I wish I were dead! Like them."

It was as if I had said the magic words. Alakazam!—and her face went blank, her mouth closed, her arms went slack, and she backed out of the room, stunned, as if she were blowing away like a small brown leaf, thin, brittle, lifeless.

"Only two kinds of daughters," she shouted in Chinese. "Those who are obedient and those who follow their own mind!"

It was not the only disappointment my mother felt in me. In the years that followed, I failed her so many times, each time asserting my own will, my right to fall short of expectations. I didn't get straight A's. I didn't become class president. I didn't get into Stanford. I dropped out of college.

For unlike my mother, I did not believe I could be anything I wanted to be. I could only be me.

And for all those years, we never talked about the disaster at the recital or my terrible accusations afterward at the piano bench. All that remained unchecked, like a betrayal that was now unspeakable. So I never found a way to ask her why she had hoped for something so large that failure was inevitable.

And even worse, I never asked her what frightened me the most: Why had she given up hope?

For after our struggle at the piano, she never mentioned my playing again. The lessons stopped. The lid to the piano was closed, shutting out the dust, my misery, and her dreams.

So she surprised me. A few years ago, she offered to give me the piano, for my thirtieth birthday. I had not played in all those years. I saw the offer as a sign of forgiveness, a tremendous burden removed.

"Are you sure?" I asked shyly. "I mean, won't you and Dad miss it?"

"No, this your piano," she said firmly. "Always your piano. You only one can play."

28

"Well, I probably can't play anymore," I said. "It's been years."

"You pick up fast," said my mother, as if she knew this was certain. "You have natural talent. You could been genius if you want to."

"No I couldn't."

"You just not trying," said my mother. And she was neither angry nor sad. She said it as if to announce a fact that could never be disproved. "Take it," she said.

But I didn't at first. It was enough that she had offered it to me. And after that, every time I saw it in my parents' living room, standing in front of the bay windows, it made me feel proud, as if it were a shiny trophy I had won back.

Last week I sent a tuner over to my parents' apartment and had the piano reconditioned, for purely sentimental reasons. My mother had died a few months before and I had been getting things in order for my father, a little bit at a time. I put the jewelry in special silk pouches. The sweaters she had knitted in yellow, pink, bright orange—all the colors I hated—I put those in mothproof boxes. I found some old Chinese silk dresses, the kind with little slits up the sides. I rubbed the old silk against my skin, then wrapped them in tissue and decided to take them home with me.

After I had the piano tuned, I opened the lid and touched the keys. It sounded even richer than I remembered. Really, it was a very good piano. Inside the bench were the same exercise notes with handwritten scales, the same second-hand music books with their covers held together with yellow tape.

I opened up the Schumann book to the dark little piece I had played at the recital. It was on the left-hand side of the page, "Pleading Child." It looked more difficult than I remembered. I played a few bars, surprised at how easily the notes came back to me.

And for the first time, or so it seemed, I noticed the piece on the right-hand side. It was called "Perfectly Contented." I tried to play this one as well. It had a lighter melody but the same flowing rhythm and turned out to be quite easy. "Pleading Child" was shorter but slower; "Perfectly Contented" was longer, but faster. And after I played them both a few times, I realized they were two halves of the same song. ❖

LA CASA[1]

Rosemary Catacalos

Comadre Rafaelita (1934), Emil J. Bisttram. Courtesy of The Anschutz Collection, Denver. Photo courtesy of James O. Milmoe.

The house by the *acequia*,[2]
its front porch dark and
cool with begonias,
an old house, always there,
5   always of the same adobe,[3]
always full of the same lessons.
We would like to stop.
We know we belonged there once.
Our mothers are inside.
10   All the mothers are inside,
lighting candles, swaying
back and forth on their knees,
begging The Virgin's forgiveness
for having reeled us out
15   on such very weak string.
They are afraid for us.
They know we will not stop.
We will only wave as we pass by.
They will go on praying
20   that we might be simple again.

1. **La Casa** (lä kä′sä) *Spanish:* "The House."
2. *acequia* (ä-sĕ′kyä) *Spanish:* an irrigation ditch or canal.
3. **adobe** (ə-dō′bē): a building material consisting of mud or clay mixed with straw and dried in the sun.

RESPONDING
OPTIONS

FROM PERSONAL RESPONSE TO CRITICAL ANALYSIS

REFLECT   **1.** In your notebook, describe your impressions of the two main characters.

RETHINK   **2.** What might the narrator mean by saying that "Pleading Child" and "Perfectly Contented" are "two halves of the same song"?

Consider
- her behavior as a young girl
- why she takes up playing the piano again
- what the names of the pieces reveal about her relationship with her mother

3. Why do you think the narrator's feelings about being a prodigy change during the story?

Consider
- her daydreams at the beginning of the story
- her response to her mother's expectations
- her opinions about herself

4. Why do you think the mother had such unrealistic expectations for her daughter? Use evidence from the story to support your ideas. You might also review the explanation you wrote for the Writing Connection on page 18.

RELATE   **5.** How does the mother-child relationship presented in the Insight poem "La Casa" compare with the mother-child relationship depicted in "Two Kinds"?

6. In this story, the mother's high expectations have a negative effect on the narrator. When can high expectations have a positive effect? Explain, drawing on your experience.

LITERARY CONCEPTS

The events of a story almost always involve one or more **conflicts,** or struggles between opposing forces. A conflict may be **external,** pitting a character against an outside force—such as another character, a physical obstacle, or an aspect of nature or society—or it may be **internal,** occurring within a character. What are the external and internal conflicts in "Two Kinds"?

ANOTHER PATHWAY

Cooperative Learning

In a small group, make two lists, one of the mother's complaints about her daughter and one of the daughter's complaints. Use story details to complete each list. With the other members of your group, decide which complaints are justified and how they might be effectively resolved. Explain your findings to the class.

QUICKWRITES

1. Write a **diary entry** in which the mother explains her hopes, dreams, and expectations for her daughter, as well as her sense of frustration.

2. Write a **personality profile** of either the mother or the daughter. Describe your subject's distinctive traits.

3. Write a **review** of the talent show for a Chinatown newspaper. Discuss all the performances described in the story.

4. Find out more about Waverly and Auntie Lindo by reading the chapter "Rules of the Game" in Amy Tan's *The Joy Luck Club*. Write an **essay** comparing the mother-daughter relationship in that story with the one in "Two Kinds."

PORTFOLIO Save your writing. You may want to use it later as a springboard to a piece for your portfolio.

ALTERNATIVE ACTIVITIES

1. With a classmate, role-play a **conversation** between the narrator's mother and Auntie Lindo, in which the narrator's mother describes her daughter's talent-show performance.

2. Many of the mother's ideas about the United States come from television and popular magazines. Collect pictures from various magazines and create a **collage** showing the misleading impression of American life that an immigrant might derive from these publications.

THE WRITER'S STYLE

Although Amy Tan's story deals with the serious problem of a parent's unrealistic expectations, **humor** plays an important role in it. Go through the story again and identify places where events or descriptions add a humorous tone to the story. What effect does the humor have on your view of the narrator's problem?

ACROSS THE CURRICULUM

History The 1930s and 1940s were not the only period of time when large numbers of people emigrated from China to the United States. Find out about the influx of Chinese immigrants during the mid-1800s. Present your findings in an oral report to the class.

WORDS TO KNOW

Review the Words to Know at the bottom of the selection pages. On your paper, match each word on the left with a synonym on the right.

1. prodigy	a. mourn
2. indignity	b. disaster
3. reproach	c. genius
4. discordant	d. ruin
5. lament	e. disloyalty
6. ream	f. humiliation
7. reverie	g. condemnation
8. devastate	h. daydream
9. fiasco	i. heap
10. betrayal	j. inharmonious

AMY TAN

Amy Tan, the daughter of Chinese immigrants, was born in Oakland, California. She earned a bachelor's degree in linguistics and English and a master's degree in linguistics at San Jose State University, then went on to become a successful business writer before turning her talents to fiction. "Two Kinds" is part of her popular work *The Joy Luck Club,* a book that weaves together separate stories about four Chinese mothers and their American-born daughters. After its release in 1989,

1952 –

the book spent eight months on the *New York Times* bestseller list; in 1993, it was made into a movie. *The Joy Luck Club* was a finalist for the National Book Award and the National Book Critics Circle Award, and it received the 1990 Bay Area Book Reviewers Award for Fiction. It has been translated into more than 15 languages, including Chinese.

OTHER WORKS "Mother Tongue" in *The Best American Essays 1991, The Kitchen God's Wife*

PREVIEWING

Cranes

Hwang Sunwŏn (hwäng sŏŏn'wən') **Korea**

PERSONAL CONNECTION

Have you ever been in a situation in which your friend became your opponent? Perhaps you were pitted against each other in a competition or found yourselves on opposite sides of an important issue. In your notebook, describe the situation and the feelings that it evoked.

HISTORICAL CONNECTION

This story takes place during the Korean War, a conflict that often pitted friend against friend and even brother against brother. In 1948, shortly after World War II, the nation of Korea, which occupies a peninsula on the eastern shore of Asia, became officially divided. Two separate governments were established: a Communist government in the north and a non-Communist government in the south. In 1950, North Korea invaded South Korea, beginning a civil war in which other nations, including the United States and China, soon became involved. A truce was signed in 1953, but tension between the two Koreas has continued for decades.

Much of the war took place near the 38th parallel of north latitude, the dividing line between the two countries. This area was the scene of hotly contested battles in which thousands died and the control of villages often shifted back and forth between the North Koreans and the South Koreans. One of these villages is the setting of "Cranes."

READING CONNECTION

Making Inferences In a work of fiction, a character's **motives,** or reasons for behaving a certain way, may be implied rather than stated directly. In such a case, the reader must make inferences, based on evidence in the story, about what motivates the character. As you read "Cranes," pay attention to the main character's behavior toward his friend, and try to determine the motives behind that behavior.

LASERLINKS
• *HISTORICAL CONNECTION*   **33**

CRANES

HWANG SUNWŎN

The northern village lay snug beneath the high, bright autumn sky, near the border at the Thirty-eighth Parallel.

White gourds lay one against the other on the dirt floor of an empty farmhouse. Any village elders who passed by extinguished their bamboo pipes first, and the children, too, turned back some distance off. Their faces were marked with fear.

As a whole, the village showed little damage from the war, but it still did not seem like the same village Sŏngsam[1] had known as a boy.

At the foot of a chestnut grove on the hill behind the village he stopped and climbed a chestnut tree. Somewhere far back in his mind he heard the old man with a wen[2] shout, "You bad boy, climbing up my chestnut tree again!"

The old man must have passed away, for he was not among the few village elders Sŏngsam had met. Holding on to the trunk of the tree, Sŏngsam gazed up at the blue sky for a time. Some chestnuts fell to the ground as the dry clusters opened of their own accord.

A young man stood, his hands bound, before a farmhouse that had been converted into a Public Peace Police office. He seemed to be a stranger, so Sŏngsam went up for a closer look. He was stunned: this young man was none other than his boyhood playmate, Tŏkchae.[3]

Sŏngsam asked the police officer who had come with him from Ch'ŏnt'ae[4] for an explanation. The prisoner was the vice-chairman of the Farmers' Communist League and had just been flushed[5] out of hiding in his own house, Sŏngsam learned.

Sŏngsam sat down on the dirt floor and lit a cigaret.

---

1. **Sŏngsam** (sŏng′säm′).
2. **wen:** a harmless skin tumor.
3. **Tŏkchae** (tŏk′jä′).
4. **Ch'ŏnt'ae** (chŏn′tă′).
5. **flushed:** driven from hiding.

Tŏkchae was to be escorted to Ch'ŏngdan[6] by one of the peace police.

After a time, Sŏngsam lit a new cigaret from the first and stood up.

"I'll take him with me."

Tŏkchae averted his face and refused to look at Sŏngsam. The two left the village.

Sŏngsam went on smoking, but the tobacco had no flavor. He just kept drawing the smoke in and blowing it out. Then suddenly he thought that Tŏkchae, too, must want a puff. He thought of the days when they had shared dried gourd leaves behind sheltering walls, hidden from the adults' view. But today, how could he offer a cigaret to a fellow like this?

Once, when they were small, he went with Tŏkchae to steal some chestnuts from the old man with the wen. It was Sŏngsam's turn to climb the tree. Suddenly the old man began shouting. Sŏngsam slipped and fell to the ground. He got chestnut burrs all over his bottom, but he kept on running. Only when the two had reached a safe place where the old man could not overtake them did Sŏngsam turn his bottom to Tŏkchae. The burrs hurt so much as they were plucked out that Sŏngsam could not keep tears from welling up in his eyes. Tŏkchae produced a fistful of chestnuts from his pocket and thrust them into Sŏngsam's . . . Sŏngsam threw away the cigaret he had just lit, and then made up his mind not to light another while he was escorting Tŏkchae.

They reached the pass at the hill where he and Tŏkchae had cut fodder[7] for the cows until Sŏngsam had to move to a spot near Ch'ŏnt'ae, south of the Thirty-eighth Parallel, two years before the liberation.

Sŏngsam felt a sudden surge of anger in spite of himself and shouted, "So how many have you killed?"

For the first time, Tŏkchae cast a quick glance at him and then looked away.

"You! How many have you killed?" he asked again.

Tŏkchae looked at him again and glared. The glare grew intense, and his mouth twitched.

"So you managed to kill quite a few, eh?" Sŏngsam felt his mind becoming clear of itself, as if some obstruction had been removed. "If you were vice-chairman of the Communist League, why didn't you run? You must have been lying low with a secret mission."

Tŏkchae did not reply.

"Speak up. What was your mission?"

Tŏkchae kept walking. Tŏkchae was hiding something, Sŏngsam thought. He wanted to take a good look at him, but Tŏkchae kept his face averted.

Fingering the revolver at his side, Sŏngsam went on: "There's no need to make excuses. You're going to be shot anyway. Why don't you tell the truth here and now?"

"I'm not going to make any excuses. They made me vice-chairman of the League because I was a hardworking farmer and one of the poorest. If that's a capital offense,[8] so be it. I'm still what I used to be—the only thing I'm good at is tilling the soil." After a short pause, he added, "My old man is bedridden at home. He's been ill almost half a year." Tŏkchae's father was a widower, a poor, hardworking farmer who lived only for his son. Seven years before his back had given out, and he had contracted a skin disease.

"Are you married?"

"Yes," Tŏkchae replied after a time.

"To whom?"

"Shorty."

"To Shorty?" How interesting! A woman so small and plump that she knew the earth's

---

6. **Ch'ŏngdan** (chəng'dän').

7. **fodder:** coarsely chopped hay or straw used as food for farm animals.

8. **capital offense:** a crime calling for the death penalty.

vastness, but not the sky's height. Such a cold fish! He and Tŏkchae had teased her and made her cry. And Tŏkchae had married her!

"How many kids?"

"The first is arriving this fall, she says."

Sŏngsam had difficulty swallowing a laugh that he was about to let burst forth in spite of himself. Although he had asked how many children Tŏkchae had, he could not help wanting to break out laughing at the thought of the wife sitting there with her huge stomach, one span around. But he realized that this was no time for joking.

"Anyway, it's strange you didn't run away."

"I tried to escape. They said that once the South invaded, not a man would be spared. So all of us between seventeen and forty were taken to the North. I thought of evacuating, even if I had to carry my father on my back. But Father said no. How could we farmers leave the land behind when the crops were ready for harvesting? He grew old on that farm depending on me as the prop and the mainstay of the family. I wanted to be with him in his last moments so I could close his eyes with my own hand. Besides, where can farmers like us go, when all we know how to do is live on the land?"

Sŏngsam had had to flee the previous June. At night he had broken the news privately to his father. But his father had said the same thing: Where could a farmer go, leaving all the chores behind? So Sŏngsam had left alone. Roaming about the strange streets and villages in the South, Sŏngsam had been haunted by thoughts of his old parents and the young children, who had been left with all the chores. Fortunately, his family had been safe then, as it was now.

They had crossed over a hill. This time Sŏngsam walked with his face averted. The autumn sun was hot on his forehead. This was an ideal day for the harvest, he thought.

When they reached the foot of the hill, Sŏngsam gradually came to a halt. In the middle of a field he espied a group of cranes that resembled men in white, all bent over. This had been the demilitarized zone[9] along the Thirty-eighth Parallel. The cranes were still living here, as before, though the people were all gone.

Once, when Sŏngsam and Tŏkchae were about twelve, they had set a trap here, unbeknown to the adults, and caught a crane, a Tanjŏng crane.[10] They had tied the crane up, even binding its wings, and paid it daily visits, patting its neck and riding on its back. Then one day they overheard the neighbors whispering: someone had come from Seoul[11] with a permit from the governor-general's office to catch cranes as some kind of specimens. Then and there the two boys had dashed off to the field. That they would be found out and punished had no longer mattered; all they cared about was the fate of their crane. Without a moment's delay, still out of breath from running, they untied the crane's feet and wings, but the bird could hardly walk. It must have been weak from having been bound.

The two held the crane up. Then, suddenly, they heard a gunshot. The crane fluttered its wings once or twice and then sank back to the ground.

The boys thought their crane had been shot. But the next moment, as another crane from a nearby bush fluttered its wings, the boys' crane stretched its long neck, gave out a whoop, and disappeared into the sky. For a long while the two boys could not tear their eyes away from the blue sky up into which their crane had soared.

"Hey, why don't we stop here for a crane hunt?" Sŏngsam said suddenly.

---

9. **demilitarized zone:** an area—generally one separating two hostile nations or armies—from which military forces are prohibited.

10. **Tanjŏng** (tän'jəng') **crane:** a type of crane found in Asia.

11. **Seoul** (sōl): the capital and largest city of South Korea.

Yi Dynasty rank badge (about 1600–1700). Colored silk and gold paper, thread on figured silk, Victoria & Albert Museum, London / Art Resource, New York.

Tŏkchae was dumbfounded.

"I'll make a trap with this rope; you flush a crane over here."

Sŏngsam had untied Tŏkchae's hands and was already crawling through the weeds.

Tŏkchae's face whitened. "You're sure to be shot anyway"—these words flashed through his mind. Any instant a bullet would come flying from Sŏngsam's direction, Tŏkchae thought.

Some paces away, Sŏngsam quickly turned toward him.

"Hey, how come you're standing there like a dummy? Go flush a crane!"

Only then did Tŏkchae understand. He began crawling through the weeds.

A pair of Tanjŏng cranes soared high into the clear blue autumn sky, flapping their huge wings. ❖

Translated by Peter H. Lee

RESPONDING
OPTIONS

FROM PERSONAL RESPONSE TO CRITICAL ANALYSIS

REFLECT

1. What went through your mind at the end of the story? Describe your reaction in your notebook.

RETHINK

2. What is Sŏngsam's motivation for letting Tŏkchae go free?
   Consider
   - what Sŏngsam says will happen to Tŏkchae
   - what Sŏngsam learns about Tŏkchae during their walk
   - Sŏngsam's memories of their childhood friendship

3. Do you think Sŏngsam makes the right decision at the end? Give reasons for your answer.

4. What do you think is the significance of the cranes in the story?
   Consider
   - the cranes still living in the demilitarized zone
   - the crane that the boys caught and then freed
   - the last sentence of the story

5. What conclusions can you reach about the author's views on war and friendship?

RELATE

6. Think of situations when loyalty to friends comes into conflict with duty. In such cases, which do you think should take priority—loyalty or duty? Share your thoughts.

ANOTHER PATHWAY

Cooperative Learning

With a small group of classmates, create a time line to show the different phases of the relationship between Sŏngsam and his childhood friend. List major events in the relationship and describe the changes in Sŏngsam's attitude toward Tŏkchae.

QUICKWRITES

1. Create a **comparison chart** showing the similarities and differences between the lives of Sŏngsam and Tŏkchae. Remember to review the observations that you made about the characters' motives while you were reading.

2. Assume the identity of Sŏngsam and write a **letter** to Tŏkchae's father, in which you explain what has happened to his son.

3. Imagine that Sŏngsam chose duty over friendship in the end. Create an **alternative ending;** rewrite the last few paragraphs of the story, changing Sŏngsam's and Tŏkchae's thoughts and actions and the final image of the cranes.

   📁 *PORTFOLIO Save your writing. You may want to use it later as a springboard to a piece for your portfolio.*

LITERARY CONCEPTS

Plot refers to the actions and events presented in a literary work. The plot of a work is often influenced by the work's **setting,** the time and place in which the events unfold. With a partner, make a list of details from "Cranes" that establish the story's setting. Then compare your list with those made by other students. Discuss how the setting influences the plot of the story.

ALTERNATIVE ACTIVITIES

1. Role-play a **dramatic scene** in which Sŏngsam explains Tŏkchae's escape to a superior.

2. Photocopy pictures of Korean and other Asian art depicting cranes, and use the pictures to create an **art exhibit.** In a brief presentation, discuss the feelings that the artwork evokes and compare these feelings to those evoked by the cranes in the story.

ACROSS THE CURRICULUM

History Find out more about the events that led to the outbreak of the Korean War. Present your findings in a pictorial essay.

HWANG SUNWŎN

1915 –

For Korea's Hwang Sunwŏn, becoming a published writer in his native tongue was no easy matter. For the first three decades of Hwang's life, Korea was ruled by Japan. The Japanese tried to stamp out Korean nationalism by setting up Japanese-language schools, arresting Korean scholars, and at one point even forcing Koreans to adopt Japanese names. Hwang had to travel to Japan to receive his higher education. However, his years at Waseda University proved stimulating, and he returned to his homeland to publish his first story collection in 1940.

Two years later, his career plans were temporarily blocked when, at the height of World War II, the Japanese banned all Korean-language publications.

After the Japanese departed at the war's end, Hwang and his family still faced hardships in the Communist-dominated north where they lived. Luckily, they were able to flee to the south, but invasion by the North Korean forces at the start of the Korean War soon made them refugees once again. Only after the signing of the truce in 1953 was Hwang able to return full-time to his writing.

Over the years, Hwang has produced 7 novels and over 100 short stories, which have won him several prestigious awards in his homeland. "Cranes," written in 1953, was the title story of a 1956 collection.
OTHER WORKS *Trees on the Cliff, The Book of Masks, Shadows of a Sound*

PREVIEWING

FICTION

Winter Night

Kay Boyle United States

PERSONAL CONNECTION

Throughout history, war has had a profound effect on the lives of people—both soldiers and civilians. In the story "Cranes," for example, war tests a relationship between old friends. With a group of classmates, create a list of other ways in which war can impact human lives. As you make your list, be sure to consider both the physical and the emotional effects that war can have.

HISTORICAL CONNECTION

After the German dictator Adolf Hitler took power in 1933, he ordered the construction of concentration camps for the imprisonment of minority groups and people who opposed his Nazi party. Over time, more than 20 such camps were built, not only in Germany but also in Poland and other German-occupied countries in Europe. During World War II many of the camps became extermination centers where prisoners were murdered in gas chambers. Most of the 6 million Jews who were killed during the war perished in these concentration camps; Hitler's forces were also responsible for the deaths of more than 5 million others.

Although people living in the United States during World War II did not experience the physical presence of the war, its impact was still felt across the country. The main character in this story is a little girl living in New York whose once-secure life has been changed by the eruption of the war. Her father has left to serve in the armed forces. Her mother works in an office and frequently goes out in the evenings, leaving her with "sitting parents," or baby sitters. On the winter night when the story takes place, the girl's sitting parent is a mysterious woman whose life has also been affected by the war. This woman tells her a story she does not fully understand. You, however, will be able to see meanings that the little girl cannot.

READING CONNECTION

Identifying Mood Mood is the feeling, or atmosphere, that a writer creates for the reader. Descriptive words, setting, dialogue, and figurative language contribute to the mood of a work, as do the sound and rhythm of the language. As you read "Winter Night," think about the story's mood. Does it change as the story progresses? What does the mood reveal about the effects of war?

Winter Night

Kay Boyle

There is a time of apprehension that begins with the beginning of darkness and to which only the speech of love can lend security. It is there, in abeyance, at the end of every day, not urgent enough to be given the name of fear but rather of concern for how the hours are to be reprieved from fear, and those who have forgotten how it was when they were children can remember nothing of this. It may begin around five o'clock on a winter afternoon, when the light outside is dying in the windows. At that hour, the New York apartment in which Felicia lived was filled with shadows, and the little girl would wait alone in the living room, looking out at the winter-stripped trees which stood black in the Park against the isolated ovals of unclean snow. Now it was January, and the day had been a cold one; the water of the artificial lake was frozen fast, but because of the cold and the coming darkness, the skaters had ceased to move across its surface. The street that lay between the Park and the apartment house was wide, and the two-way streams of cars and buses, some with their headlamps already shining, advanced and halted, halted and poured swiftly on, to the tempo of the traffic signals' altering lights. The time of apprehension had set in, and Felicia, who was seven, stood at the window in the evening and waited before she asked the questions. When the signals below changed from red to green again, or when the double-decker bus turned the corner below, she would ask it. The words of it were already there, tentative in her mouth, when the answer came from the far end of the hall.

"Your mother," said the voice among the sound of kitchen things, "she telephoned up before you came in from school. She won't be back in time for supper. I was to tell you a sitter was coming in from the sitting parents' place."

Felicia turned back from the window into the obscurity of the living room, and she looked toward the open door and into the hall beyond it, where the light from the kitchen fell in a clear, yellow angle across the wall and onto the strip of carpet. Her hands were cold, and she put them in her jacket pockets as she walked carefully across the living-room rug and stopped at the edge of light.

"Will she be home late?" she said.

For a moment there was the sound of water running in the kitchen, a long way away, and then the sound of the water ceased, and the high, Southern voice went on, "She'll come home when she gets ready to come home. That's all I have to say. If she wants to spend two dollars and fifty cents and ten cents carfare on top of that three or four nights out of the week for a sitting parent to come in here and sit, it's her own business. It certainly ain't nothing to do with you or me. She makes her money, just like the rest of us does. She works all day down there in the office, or whatever it is, just like the rest of us works, and she's entitled to spend her money like she wants to spend it. There's no law in the world against buying your own freedom. Your mother and me, we're just buying our own freedom, that's all we're doing. And we're not doing nobody no harm."

The voice from the kitchen had no name. It was as variable as the faces and figures of the women who came and sat in the evenings.

"Do you know who she's having supper with?" said Felicia from the edge of dark. There was one more step to take and then she would be standing in the light that fell on the strip of carpet, but she did not take the step.

"Do I know who she's having supper with?" the voice cried out in what might have been derision, and there was the sound of dishes striking the metal ribs of the drainboard by the sink. "Maybe it's Mr. Van Johnson[1] or Mr. Frank Sinatra,[2] or maybe it's just the Duke of Wincers[3] for the evening. All I know is you're having soft-boiled egg and spinach and applesauce for supper, and you're going to have it quick now because the time is getting away."

The voice from the kitchen had no name. It was as variable as the faces and figures of the women who came and sat in the evenings. Month by month the voice in the kitchen altered to another voice, and the sitting parents were no more than lonely aunts of an evening or two, who sometimes returned and sometimes did not to this apartment in which they had sat

before. Nobody stayed anywhere very long any more, Felicia's mother told her. It was part of the time in which you lived, and part of the life of the city, but when the fathers came back, all this would be miraculously changed. Perhaps you would live in a house again, a small one, with fir trees on either side of the short brick walk, and Father would drive up every night from the station just after darkness set in. When Felicia thought of this, she stepped quickly into the clear angle of light, and she left the dark of the living room behind her and ran softly down the hall.

The drop-leaf table stood in the kitchen between the refrigerator and the sink, and Felicia sat down at the place that was set. The voice at the sink was speaking still, and while Felicia ate it did not cease to speak until the bell of the front door rang abruptly. The girl walked around the table and went down the hall, wiping her dark palms in her apron, and, from the drop-leaf table, Felicia watched her step from the angle of light into darkness and open the door.

"You put in an early appearance," the girl said, and the woman who had rung the bell came into the hall. The door closed behind her, and the girl showed her into the living room and lit the lamp on the bookcase, and the shadows were suddenly bleached away. But when the girl turned, the woman turned from the living room, too, and followed her, humbly and in silence, to the threshold of the kitchen. "Sometimes they keep me standing around

---

1. **Van Johnson:** an American film actor popular in the 1940s.
2. **Frank Sinatra:** a famous American singer and movie star.
3. **Duke of Wincers:** a mispronunciation of "Duke of Windsor," the title given King Edward VIII of Great Britain after he gave up the throne to marry the woman he loved in 1937.

WORDS TO KNOW   **derision** (dĭ-rĭzh′ən): *n.* contempt or ridicule

42

waiting after it's time for me to be getting on home, the sitting parents do," the girl said, and she picked up the last two dishes from the table and put them in the sink. The woman who stood in the doorway was small, and when she undid the white silk scarf from around her head, Felicia saw that her hair was black. She wore it parted in the middle, and it had not been cut but was drawn back loosely into a knot behind her head. She had very clean white gloves on, and her face was pale, and there was a look of sorrow in her soft black eyes. "Sometimes I have to stand out there in the hall with my hat and coat on, waiting for the sitting parents to turn up," the girl said, and as she turned on the water in the sink, the contempt she had for them hung on the kitchen air. "But you're ahead of time," she said, and she held the dishes, first one and then the other, under the flow of steaming water.

The woman in the doorway wore a neat black coat, not a new-looking coat, and it had no fur on it, but it had a smooth velvet collar and velvet lapels. She did not move or smile, and she gave no sign that she had heard the girl speaking above the sound of water at the sink. She simply stood looking at Felicia, who sat at the table with the milk in her glass not finished yet. "Are you the child?" she said at last, and her voice was low and the pronunciation of the words a little strange.

"Yes, this here's Felicia," the girl said, and the dark hands dried the dishes and put them away. "You drink up your milk quick, now, Felicia, so's I can rinse your glass."

"I will wash the glass," said the woman. "I would like to wash the glass for her," and Felicia sat looking across the table at the face in the doorway that was filled with such unspoken grief. "I will wash the glass for her and clean off the table," the woman was saying quietly. "When the child is finished, she will show me where her night things are."

"The others, they wouldn't do anything like that," the girl said, and she hung the dishcloth over the rack. "They wouldn't put their hand to housework, the sitting parents. That's where they got the name for them," she said.

Whenever the front door closed behind the girl in the evening, it would usually be that the sitting parent who was there would take up a book of fairy stories and read aloud for a while to Felicia, or else would settle herself in the big chair in the living room and begin to tell the words of a story in drowsiness to her, while Felicia took off her clothes in the bedroom, and folded them, and put her pajamas on, and brushed her teeth, and did her hair. But this time that was not the way it happened. Instead, the woman sat down on the other chair at the kitchen table, and she began at once to speak, not of good fairies or bad, or of animals endowed with human speech, but to speak quietly, in spite of the eagerness behind her words, of a thing that seemed of singular importance to her.

"It is strange that I should have been sent here tonight," she said, her eyes moving slowly from feature to feature of Felicia's face, "for you look like a child that I knew once, and this is the anniversary of that child."

"Did she have hair like mine?" Felicia asked quickly, and she did not keep her eyes fixed on the unfinished glass of milk in shyness any more.

"Yes, she did. She had hair like yours," said the woman, and her glance paused for a moment on the locks which fell straight and thick on the shoulders of Felicia's dress. It may have been that she thought to stretch out her hand and touch the ends of Felicia's hair, for her fingers stirred as they lay clasped together on the table, and then they relapsed into passivity again. "But it is not the hair alone, it is the delicacy of your face, too, and your eyes the same, filled with the same spring-lilac color," the woman said, pronouncing the words carefully. "She had little coats of golden fur on her arms and legs," she said, "and when we were closed up there, the lot of us in the cold, I used to make her laugh when I told her that the fur that was so pretty, like a little fawn's skin on her arms, would always help to keep her warm."

> *"It was not a school, but still there were a lot of children there. It was a camp—that was the name the place had."*

"And did it keep her warm?" asked Felicia, and she gave a little jerk of laughter as she looked down at her own legs hanging under the table, with the bare calves thin and covered with a down of hair.

"It did not keep her warm enough," the woman said, and now the mask of grief had come back upon her face. "So we used to take everything we could spare from ourselves, and we would sew them into cloaks and other kinds of garments for her and for the other children."

"Was it a school?" said Felicia when the woman's voice had ceased to speak.

"No," said the woman softly, "it was not a school, but still there were a lot of children there. It was a camp—that was the name the place had; it was a camp. It was a place where they put people until they could decide what was to be done with them." She sat with her hands clasped, silent a moment, looking at Felicia. "That little dress you have on," she said, not saying the words to anybody, scarcely saying them aloud. "Oh, she would have liked that little dress, the little buttons shaped like hearts, and the white collar—"

"I have four school dresses," Felicia said.

"I'll show them to you. How many dresses did she have?"

"Well, there, you see, there in the camp," said the woman, "she did not have any dresses except the little skirt and the pullover. That was all she had. She had brought just a handkerchief of her belongings with her, like everybody else— just enough for three days away from home was what they told us, so she did not have enough to last the winter. But she had her ballet slippers," the woman said, and her clasped fingers did not move. "She had brought them because she thought during her three days away from home she would have the time to practice her ballet."

"I've been to the ballet," Felicia said suddenly, and she said it so eagerly that she stuttered a little as the words came out of her mouth. She slipped quickly down from the chair and went around the table to where the woman sat. Then she took one of the woman's hands away from the other that held it fast, and she pulled her toward the door. "Come into the living room and I'll do a pirouette[4] for you," she said, and then she stopped speaking, her eyes halted on the woman's face. "Did she—did the little girl— could she do a pirouette very well?" she said.

"Yes, she could. At first she could," said the woman, and Felicia felt uneasy now at the sound of sorrow in her words. "But after that she was hungry. She was hungry all winter," she said in a low voice. "We were all hungry, but the children were the hungriest. Even now," she said, and her voice went suddenly savage, "when I see milk like that, clean, fresh milk standing in a glass, I want to cry out loud, I want to beat my hands on the table, because it did not have to be!" She had drawn her fingers abruptly away from Felicia now, and Felicia stood before her, cast off, forlorn, alone again in the time of apprehension. "That was three years ago," the

---

4. **pirouette** (pĭr′o͞o-ĕt′): in ballet, a full turn of the body on the point of the toe or the ball of the foot.

Elizabeth in a Red Chair (1961), Fairfield Porter. Oil on canvas, 44¾″ × 39¾″, Collection of the Heckscher Museum, Huntington, New York, gift of the family of Fairfield Porter (1982.3).

woman was saying, and one hand was lifted, as if in weariness, to shade her face. "It was somewhere else, it was in another country," she said, and behind her hand her eyes were turned upon the substance of a world in which Felicia had played no part.

"Did—did the little girl cry when she was hungry?" Felicia asked, and the woman shook her head.

"Sometimes she cried," she said, "but not very much. She was very quiet. One night, when she heard the other children crying, she said to me, 'You know, they are not crying because they want something to eat. They are crying because their mothers have gone away.'"

"Did the mothers have to go out to supper?" Felicia asked, and she watched the woman's face for the answer.

"No," said the woman. She stood up from her chair, and now that she put her hand on the little girl's shoulder, Felicia was taken into the sphere of love and intimacy again. "Shall we go into the other room, and you will do your pirouette for me?" the woman said, and they went from the kitchen and down the strip of carpet on which the clear light fell. In the front room, they paused, hand in hand, in the glow of the shaded lamp, and the woman looked about her, at the books, the low tables with the magazines and ashtrays on them, the vase of roses on the piano, looking with dark, scarcely seeing eyes at these things that had no reality at all. It was only when she saw the little white clock on the mantelpiece that she gave any sign, and then she said quickly, "What time does your mother put you to bed?"

Felicia waited a moment, and in the interval of waiting, the woman lifted one hand and, as if in reverence, touched Felicia's hair.

"What time did the little girl you knew in the other place go to bed?" Felicia asked.

"Ah, God, I do not know, I do not remember," the woman said.

"Was she your little girl?" said Felicia softly, stubbornly.

"No," said the woman. "She was not mine. At least, at first she was not mine. She had a mother, a real mother, but the mother had to go away."

> *"They are not crying because they want something to eat. They are crying because their mothers have gone away."*

"Did she come back late?" asked Felicia.

"No, ah, no, she could not come back, she never came back," the woman said, and now she turned, her arm around Felicia's shoulders, and she sat down in the low, soft chair. "Why am I saying all this to you, why am I doing it?" she cried out in grief, and she held Felicia close against her. "I had thought to speak of the anniversary to you, and that was all, and now I am saying these other things to you. Three years ago today, exactly, the little girl became my little girl because her mother went away. That is all there is to it. There is nothing more."

Felicia waited another moment, held close against the woman, and listening to the swift, strong heartbeats in the woman's breast.

"But the mother," she said then, in the small, persistent voice, "did she take a taxi when she went?"

"This is the way it used to happen," said the woman, speaking in hopelessness and bitterness in the softly lighted room. "Every week they used to come into the place where we were and they would read a list of names out. Sometimes it would be the names of children they would read out, and then a little later they would have to go away. And sometimes it would be the grown people's names, the names of the mothers or big sisters, or other women's names. The men were not with us. The fathers were somewhere else, in another place."

"Yes," Felicia said. "I know."

"We had been there only a little while, maybe ten days or maybe not so long," the woman went on, holding Felicia against her still, "when they read the name of the little girl's mother out, and that afternoon they took her away."

"What did the little girl do?" Felicia said.

"She wanted to think up the best way of getting out, so that she could go find her mother," said the woman, "but she could not think of anything good enough until the third or fourth day. And then she tied her ballet slippers up in the handkerchief again, and she went up to the guard standing at the door." The woman's voice was gentle, controlled now. "She asked the guard please to open the door so that she could go out. 'This is Thursday,' she said, 'and every Tuesday and Thursday I have my ballet lessons. If I miss a ballet lesson, they do not count the money off, so my mother would be just paying for nothing, and she cannot afford to pay for nothing. I missed my ballet lesson on Tuesday,' she said to the guard, 'and I must not miss it again today.'"

Felicia lifted her head from the woman's shoulder, and she shook her hair back and looked in question and wonder at the woman's face.

"And did the man let her go?" she said.

"No, he did not. He could not do that," said the woman. "He was a soldier and he had to do what he was told. So every evening after her mother went, I used to brush the little girl's hair for her," the woman went on saying. "And while I brushed it, I used to tell her the stories of the ballets. Sometimes I would begin with *Narcissus*,"[5] the woman said, and she parted Felicia's locks with her fingers, "so if you will go and get your brush now, I will tell it while I brush your hair."

"Oh, yes," said Felicia, and she made two

whirls as she went quickly to her bedroom. On the way back, she stopped and held onto the piano with the fingers of one hand while she went up on her toes. "Did you see me? Did you see me standing on my toes?" she called to the woman, and the woman sat smiling in love and contentment at her.

"Yes, wonderful, really wonderful," she said. "I am sure I have never seen anyone do it so well." Felicia came spinning toward her, whirling in pirouette after pirouette, and she flung herself down in the chair close to her, with her thin bones pressed against the woman's soft, wide hip. The woman took the silver-backed, monogrammed brush and the tortoise-shell comb in her hands, and now she began to brush Felicia's hair. "We did not have any soap at all and not very much water to wash in, so I never could fix her as nicely and prettily as I wanted to," she said, and the brush stroked regularly, carefully down, caressing the shape of Felicia's head.

"If there wasn't very much water, then how did she do her teeth?" Felicia said.

"She did not do her teeth," said the woman, and she drew the comb through Felicia's hair. "There were not any toothbrushes or toothpaste, or anything like that."

Felicia waited a moment, constructing the unfamiliar scene of it in silence, and then she asked the tentative question.

"Do I have to do my teeth tonight?" she said.

"No," said the woman, and she was thinking of something else, "you do not have to do your teeth."

"If I am your little girl tonight, can I pretend there isn't enough water to wash?" said Felicia.

"Yes," said the woman, "you can pretend that if you like. You do not have to wash," she said, and the comb passed lightly through Felicia's hair.

---

5. *Narcissus* (när-sĭs′əs): a ballet based on the myth of Narcissus, a handsome youth who pined away for love of his own reflection in a pool of water.

"Will you tell me the story of the ballet?" said Felicia, and the rhythm of the brushing was like the soft, slow rocking of sleep.

"Yes," said the woman. "In the first one, the place is a forest glade with little, pale birches growing in it, and they have green veils over their faces and green veils drifting from their fingers, because it is the springtime. There is the music of a flute," said the woman's voice softly, softly, "and creatures of the wood are dancing—"

"But the mother," Felicia said, as suddenly as if she had been awaked from sleep. "What did the little girl's mother say when she didn't do her teeth and didn't wash at night?"

"The mother was not there, you remember," said the woman, and the brush moved steadily in her hand. "But she did send one little letter back. Sometimes the people who went away were able to do that. The mother wrote it in a train, standing up in a car that had no seats," she said, and she might have been telling the story of the ballet still, for her voice was gentle and the brush did not falter on Felicia's hair. "There were perhaps a great many other people standing up in the train with her, perhaps all trying to write their little letters on the bits of paper they had managed to hide on them, or that they had found in forgotten corners as they travelled. When they had written their letters, then they must try to slip them out through the boards of the car in which they journeyed, standing up," said the woman, "and these letters fell down on the tracks under the train, or they were blown into the fields or onto the country roads, and if it was a kind person who picked them up, he would seal them in envelopes and send them to where they were addressed to go. So a letter came back like this from the little girl's mother," the woman said, and the brush followed the comb, the comb the

brush, in steady pursuit through Felicia's hair. "It said goodbye to the little girl, and it said please to take care of her. It said, 'Whoever reads this letter in the camp, please take good care of my little girl for me, and please have her tonsils looked at by a doctor if this is possible to do.'"

"And then," said Felicia softly, persistently, "what happened to the little girl?"

"I do not know. I cannot say," the woman said. But now the brush and comb had ceased to move, and in the silence Felicia turned her thin, small body on the chair, and she and the woman suddenly put their arms around each other. "They must all be asleep now, all of them," the woman said, and in the silence that fell on them again, they held each other closer. "They must be quietly asleep somewhere and not crying all night because they are hungry and because they are cold. For three years I have been saying 'They must all be asleep, and the cold and the hunger and the seasons or night or day or nothing matters to them.'"

It was after midnight when Felicia's mother put her key in the lock of the front door, and pushed it open, and stepped into the hallway. She walked quickly to the living room, and just across the threshold she slipped the three blue-fox skins from her shoulders and dropped them, with her little velvet bag, upon the chair. The room was quiet, so quiet that she could hear the sound of breathing in it, and no one spoke to her in greeting as she crossed toward the bedroom door. And then, as startling as a slap across her delicately tinted face, she saw the woman lying sleeping on the divan, and Felicia, in her school dress still, asleep within the woman's arms. ❖

RESPONDING
OPTIONS

FROM PERSONAL RESPONSE TO CRITICAL ANALYSIS

REFLECT

1. In your notebook, jot down some words and phrases that express the mood of this story. Then, jot down anything you have questions about.

RETHINK

2. How would you describe Felicia's life?
Consider
- Felicia's "time of apprehension" at the beginning of the story
- the description of the apartment in which she lives
- how the war has affected her life
- her curiosity about the little girl in the sitting parent's story

3. What kind of person is the sitting parent?
Consider
- the way she treats Felicia
- how she has been affected by the war
- her relationship with the little girl in the camp

4. How do you account for the immediate bond that forms between Felicia and the sitting parent? Use details from the story to support your response.

5. Imagine both Felicia and the sitting parent ten years after their encounter. What impact, if any, might the war still have on each of them?

RELATE

6. What lessons can others learn from the experiences of survivors of war?

LITERARY CONCEPTS

Characters are the people (and occasionally animals or fantasy creatures) who participate in the action of literary works. A character may be considered either main or minor, depending on the extent of the character's development and on his or her importance in a work. Like "Winter Night," a piece of literature may include a story within a story, complete with main and minor characters of its own. Make a list of the main and minor characters in "Winter Night," and tell what they add to the story.

ANOTHER PATHWAY

Cooperative Learning

Work with a small group to create a chart that compares and contrasts Felicia and the girl in the camp. If you have a graphics program on your computer, use it to help you construct the chart.

QUICKWRITES

1. Write a **continuation** of the story, starting where Kay Boyle left off. Try to maintain the mood of the selection and to include dialogue and descriptive images characteristic of Boyle's style.

2. Imagine that you are Felicia, as an adult, writing her autobiography. Write a **chapter** titled "The Mysterious Sitter," in which she focuses on her encounter with the sitting parent.

3. Write an **editorial** explaining what you think are the universal needs of children, no matter what their life circumstances. Use examples and quotations from the story to support your views.

📁 *PORTFOLIO Save your writing. You may want to use it later as a spring-board to a piece for your portfolio.*

ALTERNATIVE ACTIVITIES

1. Get together with classmates and prepare a **dramatic reading** of "Winter Night." Three people can read the dialogue; a fourth can be the narrator. As a group, decide which paragraphs the narrator needs to read and which parts of the narration can be communicated through the actions of the characters.

2. Make a charcoal or pencil **sketch** of a scene from "Winter Night." Try to use light and dark images the way Kay Boyle does in her writing.

ACROSS THE CURRICULUM

History Study oral histories of Holocaust survivors—either in print or on film—to see if their memories are similar to the ones shared by the sitting parent in "Winter Night." Present your findings to the class.

WORDS TO KNOW

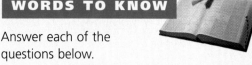

Answer each of the questions below.

1. Is a performer in a school play more likely to feel **apprehension** before going on stage or after the play is over?

2. If debate on an issue is in **abeyance,** is the issue debated now or later?

3. If a queen **reprieves** a prisoner, will the prisoner be executed immediately?

4. Is a person in **obscurity** more likely to be standing in a dense forest or in an open field?

5. Who is a more likely object of **derision**—a wise counselor or an annoying fool?

THE WRITER'S STYLE

Throughout "Winter Night," Kay Boyle uses images of light and dark to add meaning and to establish mood. Look for these images as you carefully review the story, keeping a list of the examples you find. Then get together with classmates and discuss how these images affect your reading of the story.

KAY BOYLE

Kay Boyle began writing stories when she was a young child, making books for family members as birthday and Christmas presents. She went on to become a prolific writer of short stories, as well as novels, poetry, and essays. Among the many honors and literary awards she received in her lifetime were two Guggenheim fellowships and two O. Henry awards for best short story of the year.

1902–1992

Boyle was born in St. Paul, Minnesota, but she spent her early childhood and much of her adulthood in Europe. She was living in France with her husband and children when the country was invaded by Nazi Germany in 1940, and she was unable to move back to the United States until the summer of 1941. Several of her novels concern this period of the war in France. Boyle returned to Europe after the war; she lived in France and West Germany from 1946 to 1953 while serving as a foreign correspondent for *The New Yorker* magazine. Later, she taught at several colleges and universities in the United States.

The human need for love is an underlying theme in much of Boyle's writing, but her work also focuses on moral responsibility and social justice. In an interview with the *Los Angeles Times*, Boyle once said, "The older I grow, the more I feel that all writers should be more committed to their times and write of their times and of the issues of their times."

OTHER WORKS *The White Horses of Vienna and Other Stories, The Smoking Mountain: Stories of Post-War Germany, Fifty Stories, Life Being the Best and Other Stories*

PREVIEWING

FICTION

After the Ball
Leo Tolstoy Russia

PERSONAL CONNECTION

In your notebook, list the qualities and behaviors that you associate with a good person, and then list those that you associate with an evil person. Now think of several famous people you have heard of, and try to classify each as good or evil. Can you always tell whether a person is good or evil?

HISTORICAL CONNECTION

Leo Tolstoy was an important Russian writer, reformer, and moral thinker of the 19th century. For much of his life he was preoccupied with questions of good and evil, the meaning of life, and the structure of society. The major events in "After the Ball" take place in the 1840s. The characters belong to the polite society of the time, where lavish dances, or balls, were major social events.

READING CONNECTION

Evaluating Characters As you read this story, use a chart like the one below to keep track of the personal qualities and behaviors of the main characters. Decide whether you think each quality or behavior is good or evil, and record it in the appropriate section of the chart.

A court ball at the Winter Palace, St. Petersburg, Russia, 1888. Culver Pictures.

Qualities and Behaviors		
Character	**Good**	**Evil**
Ivan Vassilievich		
Varenka		
Varenka's father, the colonel		

LASERLINKS
• *VISUAL VOCABULARY*

51

The Reception (about 1883–1885), James Tissot. Oil on canvas, 56″ × 40″, Albright-Knox Art Gallery, Buffalo, New York, gift of William M. Chase, 1909.

After the Ball

Leo Tolstoy

"You say a man can't tell good from evil, that everything depends on circumstances, that circumstances determine everything. While I think everything depends on chance. I speak from my own experience."

These were the much-respected Ivan Vassilievich's[1] introductory words following a discussion we had had about the necessity of changing living conditions before people could improve themselves. Strictly speaking, no one had said it was impossible to tell good from evil, but Ivan Vassilievich had a way of answering the thoughts a discussion provoked in his own mind, and then recounting episodes of his own life related to these thoughts. He was often so transported by his story, particularly since he told stories earnestly and honestly, that he completely forgot his reason for telling it. That is what happened this time, too.

"I speak from my own experience. My whole life took one direction instead of another, not because of circumstances, but something completely different."

---

1. **Ivan Vassilievich** (ĭ-vän′ və-syĭl′yə-vĭch′).

"What was it then?" we asked.

"Well, that's a long story. To make you understand, I'd have to explain it at length."

"Well, tell us."

Ivan Vassilievich became thoughtful, nodded his head.

"Yes," he said. "My whole life was changed by one night, or rather by one morning."

"But what happened?"

"It happened that I was greatly in love. I had been in love many times, but this was my greatest love. It's past: she has married daughters by now. It was B——, yes, Varenka B—— (Ivan Vassilievich mentioned her surname). At the age of fifteen, she was already a remarkable beauty. As a young girl of eighteen, she was enchanting: tall, well-formed, graceful, majestic—most of all, majestic. She carried herself unusually erect as though she were unable to do otherwise, tipping her head slightly back. Despite her slenderness, even boniness, this posture gave her, with her beauty and her height, a sort of queenly aspect which would have frightened people away from her had it not been for her tenderness, the merry smile on her lips, her enchanting, sparkling eyes, and her whole sweet young self."

"How well Ivan Vassilievich describes her!"

"No matter how much I described her, I could never make you realize what she was like. But that's beside the point; what I wanted to tell about happened in the forties. I was then a student in a provincial university. Whether it was good or bad I don't know, but at that time we had no clubs or theories in our universities; and we were simply young men, living as young men do: studying and being merry. I was a very

"At the age of fifteen, she was already a remarkable beauty. As a young girl of eighteen, she was enchanting: tall, well formed, graceful, majestic—most of all, majestic."

gay and venturesome boy, and rich as well. I had a fast trotter and used to take sleigh rides in the hills with the ladies (skates were not yet in fashion) and carouse with my comrades (at that time we drank nothing but champagne; if we had no money, we didn't drink, but we never drank vodka as we do now). Parties and balls were my greatest pleasures. I was a good dancer and not ugly."

"No need to be modest," interrupted one of the ladies. "After all, we've seen your daguerreotype.[2] You weren't just not ugly; you were handsome."

"Handsome or not, that's beside the point. The point is that at the time of my greatest love for her, I was at a ball given the last day of Shrovetide[3] by the provincial governor, an affable old man, rich, a generous host, and a nobleman. His wife received equally graciously in a puce velvet dress with her diamond coronet on her head, and her bare, old, plump, white shoulders and throat like the portrait of Elizabeth Petrovna.[4] The ball was marvelous: an excellent ballroom, singers, and musicians—the serfs of a music-loving landowner who were then famous, a magnificent buffet, and a sea of champagne. Although I loved champagne, I did not drink because I was drunk with love without wine, but

---

2. **daguerreotype** (də-gâr′ə-tīp′): an early type of photograph.

3. **the last day of Shrovetide:** Mardi Gras, a day of festivity preceding the fasting and penance of the Christian season of Lent.

4. **Elizabeth Petrovna** (pə-trôv′nə): empress of Russia from 1741 to 1762.

WORDS TO KNOW

majestic (mə-jĕs′tĭk) *adj.* showing lofty dignity or nobility; stately

54

I danced until exhausted; I danced quadrilles[5] and waltzes and polkas; everything I could, of course, with Varenka. She wore a white dress, a pink sash, and white kid gloves just short of her thin, sharp elbows, and white satin slippers. The detestable Engineer Anisimov[6] beat me to the mazurkas[7]—to this day I haven't forgiven him for that. He had invited her just as she arrived, while I had had to go to the hairdresser's and to fetch a pair of gloves, and was late. So it happened that I danced the mazurka not with her, but with a German girl I had courted a bit before. But I'm afraid I was not very polite to her; I didn't talk to her, didn't look at her; I saw only the tall, well-formed figure in the white dress with the pink sash, her radiant, pink-cheeked, dimpled face and her gentle, kind eyes. I was not alone; everyone looked at her and loved her; men and women loved her, in spite of the fact that she eclipsed them all. It was impossible not to love her.

According to the rules, so to speak, I was not her partner for the mazurkas; but in reality, I danced with her almost all the time. In cotillions,[8] she would cross the whole ballroom straight to me without embarrassment, and I would jump up without waiting for her invitation, and she would thank me for my perspicacity with a smile. When she failed to guess what character trait I had chosen to represent, she would give her hand to someone other than me with a shrug of her thin shoulders and would smile at me as a sign of regret and consolation. When the mazurka featured a waltz, I would waltz with her for a long time, and she, often out of breath, would smile and say 'Encore'[9] to me. And I would waltz again, feeling completely bodiless."

"Come, how could you feel bodiless! I should think you would feel quite the opposite when you took her by the waist; not only your own body, but hers," said one of the guests.

Ivan Vassilievich suddenly blushed and almost shouted in his anger:

"Yes, that's like you, indeed, today's youth. You see nothing but bodies. In our day it wasn't like that. The more I loved her, the more ethereal she became for me. Now you can see feet, ankles, and still more; you denude the women you love; for me, as Alphonse Karr said—now there was a good writer—the object of my love always wore clothes of bronze. We not only did not denude them but tried to cover up their nakedness, like the good son of Noah. But you wouldn't understand . . . "

"Don't listen to him. What happened next?" said one of us.

"Yes. So I danced some more with her not noticing how time was passing. The musicians had already reached a sort of desperate stage of tiredness, you know, as often happens at the end of a ball; they kept repeating the same mazurka; the papas and mamas had already gotten up from the card tables in the salons and were waiting for supper; the lackeys[10] ran back and forth more and more frequently. It was after two. I had to make use of the last remaining minutes. I chose her once more, and we went across the ballroom for the hundredth time.

"'Then, after supper, the quadrille is mine?' I asked her, escorting her back to her place.

---

5. **quadrilles** (kwŏ-drĭlz′): dances performed by groups of four couples.

6. **Anisimov** (ə-nyĭs′ĭ-môv′).

7. **mazurkas** (mə-zûr′kəz): lively Polish dances similar to the polka.

8. **cotillions** (kō-tĭl′yənz): ballroom dances for couples.

9. *encore* (äN-kôr′) *French*: again; once more.

10. **lackeys**: servants.

55

"'Of course; if they don't take me home,' she said, smiling.

"'I won't give you up,' I said.

"'Give me back my fan, anyway,' she said.

"'It's hard to give it back,' I said, handing back her unassuming, white fan.

"'Then I'll give you something so you won't be sad,' she said and tore off a feather from the fan to give me.

"I took the feather and could only express all my enthusiasm and gratitude with a look. I was not only merry and content, I was happy, blessed; I was pure; I was not I, but a kind of unearthly being, knowing no evil and capable only of good. I hid the feather in my glove and stood there, powerless to leave her.

"'Look, Papa is asking someone to dance,' she said to me, pointing out the tall, dignified figure of her father, a colonel with silver epaulettes,[11] standing at the entrance with the hostess and other ladies.

"'Varenka, come here,' we heard the deep voice of the hostess with her diamond coronet and Elizabethan shoulders say.

"Varenka went to the entrance, and I followed her.

"'Come, *ma chère,*[12] your father will dance with you. Please, now, Piotr Vladislavich.' The hostess turned toward the colonel.

"Varenka's father was a very handsome, imposing, and well-preserved old man. His face was rosy with curled, white mustaches *à la* Nikolai I[13] joining his equally white sideburns with their curls combed forward at the temples. His eyes and lips wore the same gentle, joyous smile as his daughter's. He had a handsome build: long, well-formed legs, strong shoulders,

> "The entire ballroom followed the couple's every movement. As for me, I was not just admiring, but was watching them with intense emotion."

and a military chest bearing large, unornate decorations. He was a military commander in the tradition of Nikolai I.

"When we reached the entrance, the colonel was protesting, saying he had forgotten how to dance, but just the same, smiling, bending his left hand behind him, he unbuckled his sword, handed it to an obliging young man, and pulling his chamois[14] glove on his right hand—'Must observe the rules,' he said, smiling—he took his daughter's hand and stood in the third row, waiting for the beat.

"At the beginning of the mazurka theme, he nimbly tapped one leg, bent the other, and his tall, robust figure moved around the ballroom, now quietly and smoothly, now noisily and energetically, clicking his feet together. The graceful figure of Varenka swam around him, from time to time imperceptibly shortening or lengthening the steps of her tiny, white satin shoes. The entire ballroom followed the couple's every movement. As for me, I was not just admiring, but was watching them with intense emotion. I was particularly impressed by his boots, drawn tight with straps—fine, calf boots, but unfashionable, ancient ones with square toes and no heels. They were obviously designed as battle boots. 'So his beloved daughter can be well dressed and go out, he wears

---

11. **epaulettes** (ĕp'ə-lĕts'): ornamental fringed shoulder pads on a military uniform.

12. *ma chère* (mä shĕr) *French:* my dear.

13. *à la* **Nikolai** (nyĭk-ə-lī') **I:** in the style of Nicholas I, czar of Russia from 1825 to 1855.

14. **chamois** (shăm'ē): a soft leather made from the skin of an antelope.

56

Self-Portrait (about 1865), James Tissot. The Fine Arts Museums of San Francisco, Mildred Anna Williams Collection (1961.16).

primitive shoes instead of buying fashionable new ones,' I thought, and those square toes on his boots particularly affected me. It was evident that he had once danced beautifully, but now he was heavy, and his legs were not sufficiently limber for all the elegant, rapid steps he tried to execute. But he completed two turns of the room skillfully, just the same. Everyone burst into loud applause when, quickly spreading his legs apart then joining them together again, he dropped, although somewhat heavily, on one knee, while she, smiling and straightening her skirt, which he had ruffled, turned smoothly around him. Raising himself with some effort, he tenderly and gently placed his hands on his daughter's ears and, kissing her on the forehead, led her back to me on the assumption that I had the next dance. I said that I was not her partner.

"'Well, it doesn't matter; go with her now,' he said, smiling kindly and replacing his sword.

"It was as though a huge stream had been poured into a bottle which was only one drop short of full—that was how my love for Varenka released all the hidden capacities for love in my heart. I embraced the whole world with my love then. I loved the hostess in her coronet with her Elizabethan bust, and her husband, and her guests, and her lackeys, and even the sulking Engineer Anisimov. Toward her father, with his clumsy boots and his gentle smile so like hers, I felt an intense, tender emotion.

"The mazurka came to an end, and the hostess asked the guests to come to supper, but Colonel B. declined, saying he had to get up early the following day, and he bid the hosts good-by. I was afraid he would take her away, but she stayed with her mother.

"After supper I danced the promised quadrille with her, and although it seemed to me I was already infinitely happy, my happiness kept growing and growing. We never spoke of love. I never even asked either her or myself

whether she loved me. It was sufficient for me that I loved her. The only thing I feared was that something might spoil my happiness.

*W*hen I reached home, undressed and thought of sleep, I realized that sleeping was out of the question. In my hand lay the feather from her fan and the glove she had given me when she got into her carriage, and I had helped seat first her mother, then her. I looked at these things and without closing my eyes saw her before me when, choosing between two partners, she guessed the character trait I was representing; I could hear her sweet voice as she said: 'It's pride. Right?'—and gladly gave me her hand. I saw her, as she sipped a glass of champagne at supper and looked up at me with her tender eyes. But I saw her most clearly as she danced with her father, glided smoothly around him, and glanced with pride and joy at the admiring spectators. And I unconsciously included them both in the same gentle, tender emotion.

"At that time, my late brother and I lived alone. My brother did not like society at all and did not go to balls; he was preparing himself for his baccalaureate[15] at that time and led a particularly regulated life. He was asleep. I looked at his head buried in his pillow and half-covered with a flannel blanket, and I felt an affectionate pity for him; pity because he did not know or share my happiness. Our servant, Petrusha, met me with a candle and wanted to help me undress, but I let him go. The sight of his sleepy face and disheveled hair seemed very touching to me. Trying to make no noise, I went to my own room on tiptoe and sat down on the bed. No, I was too happy; I could not sleep. Then I began to feel too hot in the heated rooms, and, still dressed, I went quietly out to

---

15. **baccalaureate** (băk′ə-lôr′ē-ĭt): bachelor's degree.

the entry, put on my over-coat, opened the outer door and went into the street.

"I had left the ball at five o'clock, then gone home and sat there a bit; two hours had gone by, and when I went out it was already light. It was typical Shrovetide weather: fog, water-soaked snow melting on the roads, and water dripping from all the roofs. The B———s then lived at the edge of town, next to a big field with a promenade[16] at one end and a girl's school at the other. I went through our deserted side street and came out onto a big road, where I began to encounter people on foot and others carting firewood on sleds, whose runners scraped the pavement. The horses, rhythmically swinging their wet heads under the glistening shaft bows, and the drivers covered with sacking, splashing in huge boots near their wagons, and the houses looking very tall in the fog—all seemed particularly dear and meaningful to me.

"When I came to the field where her house stood, I saw at the end of it, in the direction of the promenade, something large and black, and I heard the sounds of a fife and drum coming from there. All this time I had continued humming and hearing the theme of the mazurka intermittently. But this was a different, cruel, evil music.

"'What can it be?' I thought, and crossing the middle of the field over a slippery path, I walked in the direction of the sound. After covering a hundred paces, I began to discern a number of black forms through the fog. Soldiers, obviously. 'It must be a drill,' I thought, and along with a blacksmith in his greasy coat and apron, carrying something and walking in front of me, I went closer. Soldiers in dark uniforms were drawn up in two ranks facing each other, standing motionless, holding

"I looked in that direction and between the ranks caught sight of something dreadful moving toward me."

their rifles at their sides. Behind them stood the drummer and the fifer, repeating the same unpleasant, shrill melody without stopping.

"'What are they doing?' I asked the blacksmith, who had stopped next to me.

"'They're whipping a Tartar[17] for running off,' the blacksmith said angrily, glancing at the farthest end of the ranks.

"I looked in that direction and between the ranks caught sight of something dreadful moving toward me. It was a man stripped to the waist, tied to the rifles of two soldiers, who led him. Next to him walked a tall officer in an overcoat and forage cap whose face seemed familiar to me. Resisting with his whole body, his feet splashing in the melting snow, the victim was lurching toward me under the blows falling on him from both sides; now he keeled over backward—and the sergeants who were dragging him by their rifles shoved him forward; then he fell forward—and the sergeants, preventing him from falling, pulled him back. And never leaving the victim's side, halting and advancing with a firm tread, was the tall officer. It was her father, with his rosy face and white mustache and sideburns.

"At each blow, the victim, as if surprised, turned his pain-distorted face to the side from which it fell and, disclosing his white teeth, repeated the same words over and over. It was only when he was very close that I heard these words clearly. He sobbed rather than said: 'Brothers, have mercy. Brothers, have mercy.' But his brothers did not have mercy, and when the procession was even with me, I saw how the soldier standing opposite me stepped forward

16. **promenade:** a public walkway.

17. **Tartar:** a member of a Turkic people of southern Russia.

The Monument to Peter I on Senate Square in Petersburg (1870), Vasilii Ivanovich Surikov. The State Russian Museum, St. Petersburg, Russia.

decisively and, swinging his stick through the air with a swish, brought it down hard on the Tartar's back. The Tartar pulled forward, but the sergeants held him back, and an identical blow fell on him from the other side, and then again from this side, and again from the other side. The colonel walked on, looking now at the victim, now at his own feet, drawing in his breath, blowing out his cheeks, and letting the air out slowly through his puckered mouth. When the procession had passed the spot where I stood, I caught a glimpse of the victim's back between the ranks. It was striped, wet, red; unrecognizable to the point that I could not believe it was the body of a man.

"'Oh, God,' murmured the blacksmith beside me.

"The procession was moving on, and the blows continued to fall from both sides just as before on the stumbling, shrinking man, and the drum beat as before, and the fife played, and, as before, the tall, dignified figure of the colonel moved with a firm tread next to the victim. Suddenly the colonel stopped and approached one of the soldiers abruptly.

"'I'll trounce you,' I heard his irate voice say. 'Will you beat now? Will you?'

"And I saw him pummel the frightened, under-

WORDS TO KNOW

irate (ī-rāt') *adj.* extremely angry; enraged
pummel (pŭm'əl) *v.* to hit repeatedly; beat

sized, frail soldier with his strong, chamois-gloved hand for not having brought his stick down hard enough on the Tartar's red back.

"'Form fresh gauntlets!'[18] he cried and, glancing around, caught sight of me. He pretended he did not know me; he frowned threateningly and maliciously, hurriedly turned around. All the way home I kept hearing first the roll of the drum beating and the whistle of the fife, and then the self-assured, irate voice of the colonel shouting: 'Will you beat now? Will you?' And in my heart there was an almost physical anguish approaching nausea, so strong that I stopped several times, and I felt as though I were about to vomit all the horror with which the spectacle had filled me. I don't remember how I got home and into bed. But as soon as I started to fall asleep, I heard and saw everything again and jumped up.

"'Obviously, he knows something I don't know,' I thought in reference to the colonel. 'If I knew what he knows, I would understand what I saw, and it would not disturb me.' But no matter how much I thought about it, I couldn't figure out what it was the colonel knew, and I went to sleep only toward evening, and then only after visiting a friend and drinking with him until I was completely drunk.

"I suppose you think that I decided then that what I had seen was an evil thing? Not at all. 'If this was done with such conviction and recognized as necessary by all, then it must be that they knew something that I didn't know,' I thought, and I tried to find out what. But no matter how I tried, I could not find out. And not having found out, I could not go into military service, as I had previously wanted to, and not only did I not go into service, but I never served anywhere and, as you see, was never fit for anything."

"Come, we know how you were never fit for anything," said one of us. "But tell us: how many people are really fit for anything, if you're not?"

"Come, that's complete nonsense," Ivan Vassilievich said with sincere chagrin.

"But what about love?" we asked.

"Love? From that day, love went into a decline. When, as frequently happened, she became thoughtful, although still smiling, I would immediately remember the colonel on the field; it became somehow awkward and unpleasant for me, and I began seeing her less frequently. And so love came to nothing. That's how these things happen, and that's what changes and determines a man's whole life. And you say . . . ," and thus he finished. ❖

Translated by Arthur Mendel and
Barbara Makanowitzky

---

18. **gauntlets** (gônt′lĭts): two parallel lines of people who deliver punishment by striking with clubs or other weapons a person forced to run between them.

61

RESPONDING
OPTIONS

FROM PERSONAL RESPONSE TO CRITICAL ANALYSIS

REFLECT

1. What images and ideas from the story linger in your mind? Record them in your notebook and share them with a partner.

RETHINK

2. Why do you think the colonel's actions lead to a change in Ivan Vassilievich's feelings for Varenka?

3. Ivan reveals that when the colonel caught sight of him the morning after the ball, "he pretended he did not know me; he frowned threateningly and maliciously, hurriedly turned around." Why do you think Tolstoy includes this detail in his story?

4. Do you think Ivan is better off because of what he saw after the ball?
   Consider
   • how his friends describe him
   • how the course of his life was changed
   • how he views his life

5. Ivan tells his story to illustrate that everything depends on "chance" rather than "circumstances." Do you think he succeeds? Explain your answer.

6. Compare the chart you made for the Reading Connection on page 51 with those of your classmates, giving reasons for your assessment of each character as good or evil.

RELATE

7. In American society, corporal (bodily) punishment is less common than it once was, but it still exists. Drawing on your own ideas and observations and on the depiction of corporal punishment in "After the Ball," comment on whether you think its use is ever justified.

ANOTHER PATHWAY

Cooperative Learning

Work with a small group to adapt the plot of "After the Ball" to a contemporary American setting. For example, you might have the events take place at a high school prom, or you might have Varenka's father be a police officer. Perform your adaptation as an improvisation for the class.

QUICKWRITES

1. Imagine that you are a gossip columnist for a Russian newspaper. Write a **newspaper column** about the ball. Include descriptions of Varenka, her father, and Ivan, as well as details about romance in the making.

2. Write a **dramatic scene** in which the colonel explains to his daughter the beating of the Tartar.

3. Varenka may know nothing of the event that turns Ivan's love away from her. Create a **letter** that Varenka writes to an advice column, explaining her situation and feelings. Also provide a reply.

4. With a partner, devise an alternative to the gauntlet as a means of punishing deserters. Write a **proposal** to the czar in which you explain your idea.

📁 *PORTFOLIO Save your writing. You may want to use it later as a springboard to a piece for your portfolio.*

LITERARY CONCEPTS

A **flashback** is an account of a conversation, an episode, or an event that happened before the beginning of a story. Often a flashback interrupts the chronological flow of a story to give information that can help readers to understand a character's present situation. "After the Ball" is a story told almost entirely in flashback. The events that happened to Ivan as a young man help readers to understand why he now believes that chance is more important than circumstances in determining the course of a person's life.

With four or five classmates, re-create the chronology of events in this story. Then have one person retell the story in strict chronological order, without the use of a flashback. As a whole group, compare the retelling with the original. What does Tolstoy gain or lose by using a flashback?

CRITIC'S CORNER

The Russian critic Leo Shestov said: "In his youth Tolstoy described life as a fascinating ball; and later, when he was old, it was like the running of the gauntlet." How does this comment apply to "After the Ball" (which, by the way, was written when Tolstoy was in his 70s)?

ART CONNECTION

How does the portrait on page 57 compare to your own mental image of the young Ivan?

ALTERNATIVE ACTIVITIES

1. Put together a series of **musical recordings** that represent the different parts of the story. For example, you might choose a waltz or mazurka to represent the ball; a darker, more serious piece of music might represent Ivan's witnessing the beating. Share your recordings with the class.

2. Create a **costume sketch** of the clothing of one or more of the characters. Use details from the story as well as books about the fashions of 19th-century Russian society for ideas.

Russian gown

ACROSS THE CURRICULUM

History Find out more about Tolstoy's philosophy of nonviolent resistance and its effects on such 20th-century reformers as Martin Luther King, Jr., and Mohandas K. Gandhi. Present your findings in the form of a magazine article.

Detail of *Self-Portrait* (about 1865), James Tissot. The Fine Arts Museums of San Francisco, Mildred Anna Williams Collection (1961.16).

WORDS TO KNOW

EXERCISE A Determine the relationship between each pair of capitalized words below. On your paper, write the letter of the choice that shows the most similar relationship.

1. QUEEN : MAJESTIC :: (a) comedy : tragic (b) sky : dark (c) recreation : sports (d) monster : gruesome (e) education : elementary

2. CHAGRIN : EMBARRASSMENT :: (a) ability : musical (b) expense : tax (c) misery : joy (d) sleep : death (e) worry : anxiety

3. BOXERS : PUMMEL :: (a) teachers : punish (b) lawyers : win (c) detectives : investigate (d) scholars : cheat (e) collectors : lose

4. HEAVEN : ETHEREAL :: (a) grass : dried (b) water : muddy (c) baseball : athletic (d) desert : arid (e) soup : cold

5. PERSPICACITY : SHARP :: (a) intelligence : clever (b) fool : wise (c) courage : stupid (d) shyness : sociable (e) sense : visual

EXERCISE B Using your understanding of the boldfaced word, write on your paper the letter of the word or phrase that best completes each sentence below.

1. Tolstoy talked **maliciously** about his wife Sonya because he (a) admired her, (b) fought bitterly with her, (c) enjoyed her wit.

2. She became **irate** when he (a) showed her kindness, (b) wanted to give away their wealth, (c) managed their estate wisely.

3. The pilgrims to Tolstoy's estate found him **imposing** because of his (a) reputation, (b) forgetfulness, (c) unruly hair.

4. Sonya thought the visitors were **detestable** because they (a) lacked refinement, (b) enjoyed her company, (c) earned her respect.

5. In old age, Tolstoy was **unassuming** about his earlier works; he judged them (a) boldly original, (b) perfect, (c) flawed.

LEO TOLSTOY

1828–1910

When the 82-year-old Tolstoy died at a small railroad station just days after running away from his wife and family, the event became front-page news around the world. Nothing about Tolstoy's life, or death, was small.

Born into a wealthy, aristocratic family, Tolstoy was orphaned by the age of nine and, along with his three brothers, was raised by aunts. As a young man dissatisfied with his life, he volunteered in the Russian army. Tolstoy led an unsettled life, with periodic bouts of excess. His experience as a soldier in the Crimean War (a war between Russia and British, French, and Turkish troops) provided material for *Sevastopol Sketches* (1855), a collection of stories that won him literary fame. The next 25 years saw the publication of his two greatest novels, *War and Peace* (1869) and *Anna Karenina* (1877).

At the height of his creativity, Tolstoy underwent a spiritual crisis that led him to reexamine his life and works. In the last 30 years of his life, he became a kind of prophet, preaching his own gospel for the world's salvation. Though Tolstoy continued literary work, he now believed that literature must teach moral truths. He wrote many books and essays about his beliefs, which included love for humanity, rejection of private property, and suspicion of all forms of government.

Tolstoy's efforts to free himself from the burdens of property led to bitter quarrels with his wife, Sonya, the mother of his 13 children. He eventually decided to leave her, fleeing in the company of his youngest daughter and his doctor. He became ill on a train journey and died days later.

OTHER WORKS *The Death of Ivan Ilych and Other Stories, Master and Man and Other Stories, Essays and Letters, Childhood*

LASERLINKS
• AUTHOR BACKGROUND

FOCUS ON NONFICTION

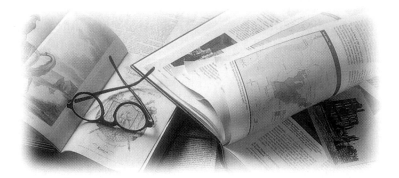

Nonfiction is prose writing about real people, places, and events. Unlike fiction, nonfiction is largely concerned with factual information, although the writer shapes the information according to his or her purpose and viewpoint. Nonfiction includes an amazingly diverse range of writing; newspaper articles, cookbooks, letters, movie reviews, editorials, speeches, true-life adventure stories—all are considered nonfiction. Some of the major types of nonfiction that are represented in this book are described below.

AUTOBIOGRAPHY An **autobiography** is a writer's account of his or her own life and is almost always told in the first person—that is, with the writer using the pronoun *I* to refer to himself or herself. In an autobiography, the writer focuses on the most significant events and people in his or her life. In this book, the selections by Mark Mathabane, Le Ly Hayslip, and Yevgeny Yevtushenko are drawn from their autobiographies.

An autobiography is usually book length because it covers a long span of years. Shorter types of autobiographical narratives include **journals, diaries,** and **letters,** which often originate as private writing. Some types of autobiographical writing, such as the **autobiographical essay,** focus on single persons or events in the authors' lives—for example, Nicholas Gage's "The Teacher Who Changed My Life" and Santha Rama Rau's "By Any Other Name." Other types—such as *Night* by Elie Wiesel and

Farewell to Manzanar by Jeanne Wakatsuki Houston and her husband, James—focus on important periods in the authors' lives.

BIOGRAPHY A **biography** is an account of a person's life, written by another person. The writer of a biography, or biographer, often researches his or her subject in order to present accurate information. A biographer may also draw upon personal knowledge of his or her subject. For example, Coretta Scott King's *My Life with Martin Luther King, Jr.* (from which "Montgomery Boycott" is drawn) is based on the author's intimate knowledge of her subject. Although biographies are usually book length, there are also shorter forms of biographical writing, such as the excerpt from Colette's *Earthly Paradise,* which is a biographical sketch of the writer's mother, and Doris Herold Lund's "Gift from a Son Who Died," which focuses on the life of Lund's son.

ESSAY An **essay** is a brief composition on a single subject, usually presenting the personal views of the writer. Because essays can be put to so many different uses, they are difficult to classify. An essay may seek to persuade, as does E. M. Forster's "Tolerance." An essay may offer a reflection on an episode in the writer's life, in the manner of E. B. White's "Once More to the Lake." Other essays, such as Roger Rosenblatt's "The Man in the Water" and Brent Staples's "Black Men and Public Space," are reflections on current events or social problems. Of course, there are many types of essays other than those included in this book, ranging from political and historical analysis to humorous commentary.

Other forms of nonfiction represented in this book are the **true-life adventure** (the excerpt from Yossi Ghinsberg's *Back from Tuichi*) and the **speech** (Elie Wiesel's Nobel Prize acceptance speech).

Keep in mind that many works of nonfiction fit into more than one category. For example, Nicholas Gage's "The Teacher Who Changed My Life" is an autobiographical essay. It has the brevity and single focus of an essay; at the same time, it is autobiographical.

STRATEGIES FOR READING NONFICTION

When reading narrative types of nonfiction—-such as autobiographies, biographies, true-life adventures, and some essays—you can apply the same strategies that you use in reading fiction. When reading informative types of nonfiction, you can apply the strategies described below.

- **Preview.** For clues to what a nonfiction selection is about, look first at the title and at any headings, pictures, graphs, charts, and other noticeable features. If you are looking for specific information, previewing will help you decide whether a particular piece addresses your needs.

- **Think about what you already know.** Once you know the topic of a selection, take a moment to think about what you might already know about that topic. Activating your prior knowledge helps you understand what you read.

- **Set purposes.** As you begin to read, focus your thinking by setting purposes to guide your reading. Ask yourself what information you want or expect to find.

- **Identify the method of organization.** Writers of informative nonfiction organize their works according to their purpose for writing. In a selection meant to inform or persuade, the writer may organize the material around main ideas. In a selection meant to explain a process or a subject, the writer may use a step-by-step organization or a chronological presentation of facts. Some nonfiction, especially in history and science textbooks, includes headings that state the topics of individual sections.

- **Separate facts from opinions.** It is important to weigh and evaluate the facts that a writer presents. **Facts** are statements that can be proved. **Opinions** are unprovable statements that express a writer's beliefs. Sometimes, however, a writer presents an opinion as if it were a fact. Be sure to recognize which statements are facts and which are opinions.

- **Consider the writer's tone.** The attitude a writer takes toward a subject is called his or her tone. A writer's tone may, for example, be critical, amused, cynical, or nostalgic. To identify a writer's tone, look closely at the writer's choice of words and the kinds of statements he or she makes.

- **Summarize.** When you have finished reading a selection, take a few moments to summarize or restate the main points. Reread anything that is still unclear. If the selection has headings, use them as guidelines for your review of the text. For longer works, you may wish to summarize at the end of each chapter and take notes in the form of an outline. Summarizing shows you what you have learned and what you might still want to find out.

PREVIEWING

NONFICTION

from Kaffir Boy

Mark Mathabane (mä′tä-bä′nə) **South Africa / United States**

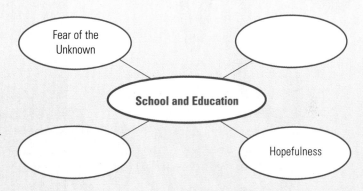

PERSONAL CONNECTION

Think back to your earliest memories of school. What was your attitude toward school and education then? Use a word web like the one shown to explore your early attitude.

HISTORICAL CONNECTION

For black South Africans who lived under apartheid (ə-pärt′hīt′), education was difficult to attain. Apartheid laws—in effect from 1948 to 1991—prescribed a rigid separation of races. Black South Africans were forced to reside in overcrowded, disease-ridden areas, such as Alexandra—a township just outside Johannesburg (jō-hăn′ĭs-bûrg)—where Mark Mathabane and his family lived. Apartheid laws also severely limited blacks' job opportunities and forced black children to attend separate, inferior schools.

In his autobiography *Kaffir Boy,* Mathabane describes what it was like to grow up under these conditions. The word *Kaffir* (kăf′ər), an insulting term that many white South Africans applied to blacks, reflects the racism he experienced.

READING CONNECTION

Using a Reading Log The reading strategies introduced on page 5 showed the kinds of connections active readers make when they read. To help you practice some of those strategies, questions have been inserted periodically throughout *Kaffir Boy*. Record your responses to each of the questions in your reading log. Also record other thoughts and feelings that come to you. After you have finished reading, discuss some of your responses with your classmates.

from Kaffir Boy

Mark Mathabane

When my mother began dropping hints that I would soon be going to school, I vowed never to go because school was a waste of time. She laughed and said, "We'll see. You don't know what you're talking about." My philosophy on school was that of a gang of ten-, eleven- and twelve-year-olds whom I so revered that their every word seemed that of an oracle.

A boy peeks around a wall in a South African village. South Light / Gamma Liaison Network.

These boys had long left their homes and were now living in various neighborhood junkyards, making it on their own. They slept in abandoned cars, smoked glue and benzene,[1] ate pilchards[2] and brown bread, sneaked into the white world to caddy and, if unsuccessful, came back to the township to steal beer and soda bottles from shebeens,[3] or goods from the Indian traders on First Avenue. Their life-style was exciting, adventurous and full of surprises; and I was attracted to it. My mother told me that they were no-gooders, that they would amount to nothing, that I should not associate with them, but I paid no heed. What does she know? I used to tell myself. One thing she did not know was that the gang's way of life had captivated me wholly, particularly their philosophy on school: they hated it and considered an education a waste of time.

They, like myself, had grown up in an environment where the value of an education was never

---

1. **benzene:** a clear, poisonous liquid derived from petroleum, used in cleaning and as a motor fuel.
2. **pilchards** (pĭl'chərdz): sardines.
3. **shebeens** (shə-bēnz'): unlicensed taverns.

emphasized, where the first thing a child learned was not how to read and write and spell, but how to fight and steal and rebel; where the money to send children to school was grossly lacking, for survival was first priority. I kept my membership in the gang, knowing that for as long as I was under its influence, I would never go to school.

One day my mother woke me up at four in the morning.

"Are they here? I didn't hear any noises," I asked in the usual way.

"No," my mother said. "I want you to get into that washtub over there."

"What!" I balked, upon hearing the word *washtub*. I feared taking baths like one feared the plague. Throughout seven years of hectic living the number of baths I had taken could be counted on one hand with several fingers missing. I simply had no natural inclination for water; cleanliness was a trait I still had to acquire. Besides, we had only one bathtub in the house, and it constantly sprung a leak.

PREDICT

What do the mother's actions seem to be leading to?

"I said get into that tub!" My mother shook a finger in my face.

Reluctantly, I obeyed, yet wondered why all of a sudden I had to take a bath. My mother, armed with a scrobbrush and a piece of Lifebuoy soap, purged me of years and years of grime till I ached and bled. As I howled, feeling pain shoot through my limbs as the thistles of the brush encountered stubborn calluses, there was a loud knock at the door.

Instantly my mother leaped away from the tub and headed, on tiptoe, toward the bedroom. Fear seized me as I, too, thought of the police. I sat frozen in the bathtub, not knowing what to do.

"Open up, Mujaji[4] [my mother's maiden name]," Granny's voice came shrilling through

the door. "It's me."

My mother heaved a sigh of relief; her tense limbs relaxed. She turned and headed to the kitchen door, unlatched it, and in came Granny and Aunt Bushy.

"You scared me half to death," my mother said to Granny. "I had forgotten all about your coming."

What's going on? What's Granny doing at our house this ungodly hour of the morning?

"Are you ready?" Granny asked my mother.

"Yes—just about," my mother said, beckoning me to get out of the washtub.

She handed me a piece of cloth to dry myself. As I dried myself, questions raced through my mind: What's going on? What's Granny doing at our house this ungodly hour of the morning? And why did she ask my mother, "Are you ready?" While I stood debating, my mother went into the bedroom and came out with a stained white shirt and a pair of faded black shorts.

"Here," she said, handing me the togs, "put these on."

"Why?" I asked.

"Put them on I said!"

I put the shirt on; it was grossly loose fitting. It reached all the way down to my ankles. Then I saw the reason why: it was my father's shirt!

"But this is Papa's shirt," I complained. "It don't fit me."

"Put it on," my mother insisted. "I'll make it fit."

"The pants don't fit me either," I said. "Whose are they anyway?"

4. **Mujaji** (mōō-jä′jē).

"Put them on," my mother said. "I'll make them fit."

Moments later I had the garments on; I looked ridiculous. My mother started working on the pants and shirt to make them fit. She folded the shirt in so many intricate ways and stashed it inside the pants, they too having been folded several times at the waist. She then choked the pants at the waist with a piece of sisal rope to hold them up. She then lavishly smeared my face, arms and legs with a mixture of pig's fat and vaseline. "This will insulate you from the cold," she said. My skin gleamed like the morning star, and I felt as hot as the center of the sun, and I smelled God knows like what. After embalming me, she headed to the bedroom.

"Where are we going, Gran'ma?" I said, hoping that she would tell me what my mother refused to tell me. I still had no idea I was about to be taken to school.

"Didn't your mother tell you?" Granny said with a smile. "You're going to start school."

"What!" I gasped, leaping from the chair where I was sitting as if it were made of hot lead. "I am not going to school!" I blurted out and raced toward the kitchen door.

My mother had just reappeared from the bedroom, and guessing what I was up to, she yelled, "Someone get the door!"

Aunt Bushy immediately barred the door. I turned and headed for the window. As I leaped for the windowsill, my mother lunged at me and brought me down. I tussled, "Let go of me! I don't want to go to school! Let me go!" but my mother held fast onto me.

"It's no use now," she said, grinning triumphantly as she pinned me down. Turning her head in Granny's direction, she shouted, "Granny! Get a rope quickly!"

Granny grabbed a piece of rope nearby and came to my mother's aid. I bit and clawed every hand that grabbed me, and howled protestations against going to school; however, I was no match for the two determined matriarchs.[5] In a jiffy they had me bound, hands and feet.

"What's the matter with him?" Granny, bewildered, asked my mother. "Why did he suddenly turn into an imp when I told him you're taking him to school?"

"You shouldn't have told him that he's being taken to school," my mother said. "He doesn't want to go there. That's why I requested you come today, to help me take him there. Those boys in the streets have been a bad influence on him."

As the two matriarchs hauled me through the door, they told Aunt Bushy not to go to school but stay behind and mind the house and the children.

The sun was beginning to rise from beyond the veld[6] when Granny and my mother dragged me to school. The streets were beginning to fill with their everyday traffic: old men and women, wizened, bent and ragged, were beginning their rambling; workless men and women were beginning to assemble in their usual coteries[7] and head for shebeens in the backyards where they discussed how they escaped the morning pass raids[8] and contemplated the conditions of life amidst intense beer drinking and vacant, uneasy laughter; young boys and girls, some as young as myself, were beginning their aimless wanderings along the narrow, dusty streets in search of food, carrying bawling infants piggyback.

As we went along some of the streets, boys and girls who shared the same fears about school as I were making their feelings known

---

5. **matriarchs** (mā′trē-ärks′): female rulers of families, clans, or tribes.

6. **veld** (vĕlt): in South Africa, an area of grassland.

7. **coteries** (kō′tə-rēz): close circles of friends, usually with common interests.

8. **pass raids:** police raids regularly conducted under apartheid to check that black South Africans had the papers authorizing them to be in particular areas.

Children play among the roughly built shacks, or shanties, in Khayelitsha, South Africa, a settlement near Cape Town. Copyright © Louise Gubb / JB Pictures Ltd.

in a variety of ways. They were howling their protests and trying to escape. A few managed to break loose and make a mad dash for freedom, only to be recaptured in no time, admonished or whipped, or both, and ordered to march again.

As we made a turn into Sixteenth Avenue, the street leading to the tribal school I was being taken to, a short, chubby black woman came along from the opposite direction. She had a scuttle[9] overflowing with coal on her *doek*-covered (cloth-covered) head. An infant, bawling deafeningly, was loosely swathed with a piece of sheepskin onto her back. Following closely behind the woman, and picking up pieces of coal as they fell from the scuttle and placing

them in a small plastic bag, was a half-naked, potbellied and thumb-sucking boy of about four. The woman stopped abreast. For some reason we stopped too.

"I wish I had done the same to my oldest son," the strange woman said in a regretful voice, gazing at me. I was confounded by her stopping and offering her <u>unsolicited</u> opinion.

"I wish I had done that to my oldest son," she repeated and suddenly burst into tears; amidst sobs, she continued, "before . . . the street claimed him . . . and . . . turned him into a *tsotsi*."[10]

---

9. **scuttle:** a metal pail for carrying coal.
10. *tsotsi* (tsŏt′sē): a street hoodlum armed with a knife or some other weapon.

WORDS TO KNOW

unsolicited (ŭn′sə-lĭs′ĭ-tĭd) *adj.* not requested

72

Granny and my mother offered consolatory remarks to the strange woman.

"But it's too late now," the strange woman continued, tears now streaming freely down her puffy cheeks. She made no attempt to dry them. "It's too late now," she said for the second time, "he's beyond any help. I can't help him even if I wanted to. *Uswile*[11] [He is dead]."

"How did he die?" my mother asked in a sympathetic voice.

"He shunned school and, instead, grew up to live by the knife. And the same knife he lived by ended his life. That's why whenever I see a boy child refuse to go to school, I stop and tell the story of my dear little *mbitsini*[12] [heartbreak]."

Having said that, the strange woman left as mysteriously as she had arrived.

"Did you hear what that woman said!" my mother screamed into my ears. "Do you want the same to happen to you?"

I dropped my eyes. I was confused.

"Poor woman," Granny said ruefully. "She must have truly loved her son."

Finally, we reached the school, and I was ushered into the principal's office, a tiny cubicle facing a row of privies[13] and a patch of yellowed grass.

"So this is the rascal we'd been talking about," the principal, a tall, wiry man, foppishly[14] dressed in a black pinstriped suit, said to my mother as we entered. His <u>austere</u>, shiny face, <u>inscrutable</u> and imposing, reminded me of my father. He was sitting behind a brown table upon which stood piles of dust and cobweb-covered books and papers. In one upper pocket of his jacket was arrayed a variety of pens and pencils; in the other nestled a lily-white handkerchief whose presence was more decorative than <u>utilitarian</u>. Alongside him stood a disproportionately portly black woman, fashionably dressed in a black skirt and a white blouse. She had but one pen, and this she held in her hand. The room was hot and stuffy and buzzing with flies.

"Yes, Principal," my mother answered, "this is he."

"He's just like the rest of them . . . Once they get out into the streets, they become wild."

"I see he's living up to his notoriety," remarked the principal, noticing that I had been bound. "Did he give you too much trouble?"

"Trouble, Principal," my mother sighed. "He was like an imp."

"He's just like the rest of them, Principal," Granny sighed. "Once they get out into the streets, they become wild. They take to the many vices of the streets like an infant takes to its mother's milk. They begin to think that there's no other life but the one shown them by the *tsotsis*. They come to hate school and forget about the future."

"Well," the principal said. "We'll soon remedy all that. Untie him."

"He'll run away," my mother cried.

---

11. *Uswile* (o͞o-swē'lä).
12. *mbitsini* (əm-bĭt-sē'nē).
13. **privies** (prĭv'ēz): outhouses.
14. **foppishly:** with great attention to niceties of clothing; in the manner of a fop, a vain man who pays too much attention to his clothes.

"I don't think he's that foolish to attempt that with all of us here."

"He *is* that foolish, Principal," my mother said as she and Granny began untying me. "He's tried it before. Getting him here was an ordeal in itself."

The principal rose from his seat, took two steps to the door and closed it. As the door swung closed, I spotted a row of canes of different lengths and thicknesses hanging behind it. The principal, seeing me staring at the canes, grinned and said, in a manner suggesting that he had wanted me to see them, "As long as you behave, I won't have to use any of those on you."

Use those canes on me? I gasped. I stared at my mother—she smiled; at Granny—she smiled too. That made me abandon any <u>inkling</u> of escaping.

"So they finally gave you the birth certificate and the papers," the principal addressed my mother as he returned to his chair.

"Yes, Principal," my mother said, "they finally did. But what a battle it was. It took me nearly a year to get all them papers together."

EVALUATE

What conclusions can you draw about the mother's attitude toward education?

She took out of her handbag a neatly wrapped package and handed it to the principal. "They've been running us around for so long that there were times when I thought he would never attend school, Principal," she said.

"That's pretty much standard procedure, Mrs. Mathabane," the principal said, unwrapping the package. "But you now have the papers, and that's what's important.

"As long as we have the papers," he continued, minutely perusing the contents of the package, "we won't be breaking the law in admitting your son to this school, for we'll be in full compliance with the requirements set by the authorities in Pretoria."[15]

"Sometimes I don't understand the laws from Pitori,"[16] Granny said. "They did the same to me with my Piet[17] and Bushy. Why, Principal, should our children not be allowed to learn because of some piece of paper?"

"The piece of paper you're referring to, Mrs. Mabaso [Granny's maiden name]," the principal said to Granny, "is as important to our children as a pass is to us adults. We all hate passes; therefore, it's only natural we should hate the regulations our children are subjected to. But as we have to live with passes, so our children have to live with the regulations, Mrs. Mabaso. I hope you understand; that is the law of the country. We would have admitted your grandson a long time ago, as you well know, had it not been for the papers. I hope you understand."

"I understand, Principal," Granny said, "but I don't understand," she added <u>paradoxically</u>.

One of the papers caught the principal's eye, and he turned to my mother and asked, "Is your husband a Shangaan,[18] Mrs. Mathabane?"

"No, he's not, Principal," my mother said. "Is there anything wrong? He's Venda,[19] and I'm Shangaan."

The principal reflected for a moment or so and then said, concernedly, "No, there's nothing seriously wrong. Nothing that we can't take care of. You see, Mrs. Mathabane, technically,

---

15. **Pretoria** (prĭ-tôr'ē-ə): a city north of Johannesburg that serves as the administrative capital of South Africa.

16. **Pitori** (pĭ-tôr'ē): a mispronunciation of "Pretoria."

17. **Piet** (pēt).

18. **Shangaan** (shäng-gän'): a member of an ethnic group of northeastern South Africa.

19. **Venda** (věn'də): a member of another ethnic group of northeastern South Africa.

WORDS TO KNOW **inkling** (ĭng'klĭng) *n.* a vague idea or notion
paradoxically (păr'ə-dŏk'sĭ-klē) *adv.* in a seemingly contradictory way

74

the fact that your child's father is a Venda makes him ineligible to attend this tribal school because it is only for children whose parents are of the Shangaan tribe. May I ask what language the children speak at home?"

"Both languages," my mother said worriedly, "Venda and Shangaan. Is there anything wrong?"

The principal coughed, clearing his throat, then said, "I mean which language do they speak more?"

"It depends, Principal," my mother said, swallowing hard. "When their father is around, he wants them to speak only Venda. And when he's not, they speak Shangaan. And when they are out at play, they speak Zulu and Sisotho."[20]

"Well," the principal said, heaving a sigh of relief. "In that case, I think an exception can be made. The reason for such an exception is that there's currently no school for Vendas in Alexandra. And should the authorities come asking why we took in your son, we can tell them that. Anyway, your child is half-half."

Everyone broke into a nervous laugh, except me. I was bewildered by the whole thing. I looked at my mother, and she seemed greatly relieved as she watched the principal register me; a broad smile broke across her face. It was as if some enormously heavy burden had finally been lifted from her shoulders and her conscience.

"Bring him back two weeks from today," the principal said as he saw us to the door. "There're so many children registering today that classes won't begin until two weeks hence. Also, the school needs repair and cleaning up after the holidays. If he refuses to come, simply notify us, and we'll send a couple of big boys to come fetch him, and he'll be very sorry if it ever comes to that."

As we left the principal's office and headed home, my mind was still against going to school. I was thinking of running away from home and joining my friends in the junkyard.

I didn't want to go to school for three reasons: I was reluctant to surrender my freedom and independence over to what I heard every school-going child call "tyrannous discipline." I had heard many bad things about life in tribal school—from daily beatings by teachers and mistresses who worked you like a mule to long school hours—and the sight of those canes in the principal's office gave ample credence to rumors that school was nothing but a torture chamber. And there was my allegiance to the gang.

But the thought of the strange woman's lamentations over her dead son presented a somewhat strong case for going to school: I didn't want to end up dead in the streets. A more compelling argument for going to school, however, was the vivid recollection of all that humiliation and pain my mother had gone through to get me the papers and the birth certificate so I could enroll in school. What should I do? I was torn between two worlds.

But later that evening something happened to force me to go to school.

I was returning home from playing soccer when a neighbor accosted me by the gate and told me that there had been a bloody fight at my home.

"Your mother and father have been at it again," the neighbor, a woman, said.

"And your mother left."

I was stunned.

"Was she hurt badly?"

"A little bit," the woman said. "But she'll be all right. We took her to your grandma's place."

I became hot with anger.

---

20. **Zulu** (zōō'lōō) **and Sisotho** (sĭ-sō'tō): languages spoken by two peoples of eastern South Africa.

WORDS TO KNOW

credence (krēd'ns) *n.* belief or believability
accost (ə-kôst') *v.* to approach and speak to, especially in a pushy way

"Is anyone in the house?" I stammered, trying to control my rage.

"Yes, your father is. But I don't think you should go near the house. He's raving mad. He's armed with a meat cleaver. He's chased out your brother and sisters, also. And some of the neighbors who tried to intervene he's threatened to carve them to pieces. I have never seen him this mad before."

I brushed aside the woman's warnings and went. Shattered windows convinced me that there had indeed been a skirmish of some sort. Several pieces of broken bricks, evidently broken after being thrown at the door, were lying about the door. I tried opening the door; it was locked from the inside. I knocked. No one answered. I knocked again. Still no one answered, until, as I turned to leave:

"Who's out there?" my father's voice came growling from inside.

"It's me, Johannes,"[21] I said.

"Go away, . . . !" he bellowed. "I don't want you or that . . . mother of yours setting foot in this house. Go away before I come out there and kill you!"

"Let me in!" I cried. "Dammit, let me in! I want my things!"

"What things? Go away, you black swine!"

I went to the broken window and screamed obscenities at my father, daring him to come out, hoping that if he as much as ever stuck his black face out, I would pelt him with the half-a-loaf brick in my hand. He didn't come out. He continued launching a tirade of obscenities at my mother and her mother. . . . He was drunk, but I wondered where he had gotten the money to buy beer because it was still the middle of the week and he was dead broke. He had lost his entire wage for the past week in dice and had had to borrow bus fare.

"I'll kill you someday for all you're doing to my mother," I threatened him, overwhelmed with rage. Several nosey neighbors were begin-

Most children in South Africa dress in Western-style clothing.

ning to congregate by open windows and doors. Not wanting to make a spectacle of myself, which was something many of our neighbors seemed to always expect from our family, I backtracked away from the door and vanished into the dark street. I ran, without stopping, all the way to the other end of the township where Granny lived. There I found my mother, her face swollen and bruised and her eyes puffed up to the point where she could scarcely see.

"What happened, Mama?" I asked, fighting to hold back the tears at the sight of her disfigured face.

21. **Johannes** (yō-hän′əs): the author's original name, which he later changed to Mark.

"Nothing, child, nothing," she mumbled, almost apologetically, between swollen lips. "Your papa simply lost his temper, that's all."

"But why did he beat you up like this, Mama?" Tears came down my face. "He's never beaten you like this before."

My mother appeared reluctant to answer me. She looked searchingly at Granny, who was pounding millet with pestle and mortar and mixing it with sorghum and nuts for an African delicacy. Granny said, "Tell him, child, tell him. He's got a right to know. Anyway, he's the cause of it all."

"Your father and I fought because I took you to school this morning," my mother began. "He had told me not to, and when I told him that I had, he became very upset. He was drunk. We started arguing, and one thing led to another."

"Why doesn't he want me to go to school?"

"He says he doesn't have money to waste paying for you to get what he calls a useless white man's education," my mother replied. "But I told him that if he won't pay for your schooling, I would try and look for a job and pay, but he didn't want to hear that, also. 'There are better things for you to work for,' he said. 'Besides, I don't want you to work. How would I look to other men if you, a woman I owned, were to start working?' When I asked him why shouldn't I take you to school, seeing that you were now of age, he replied that he doesn't believe in schools. I told him that school would keep you off the streets and out of trouble, but still he was belligerent."

CLARIFY

Why do you think the father has such a negative attitude toward education?

"Is that why he beat you up?"

"Yes, he said I disobeyed his orders."

"He's right, child," Granny interjected. "He paid *lobola* [bride price] for you. And your father ate it all up before he left me."

To which my mother replied, "But I desper-ately want to leave this beast of a man. But with his *lobola* gone I can't do it. That worthless thing you call your husband shouldn't have sold Jackson's scrawny cattle and left you penniless."

"Don't talk like that about your father, child," Granny said. "Despite all, he's still your father, you know. Anyway, he asked for *lobola* only because he had to get back what he spent raising you. And you know it would have been taboo for him to let you or any of your sisters go without asking for *lobola.*"

"You and Papa seemed to forget that my sisters and I have minds of our own," my mother said. "We didn't need you to tell us whom to marry, and why, and how. If it hadn't been for your interference, I could have married that schoolteacher."

Granny did not reply; she knew well not to. When it came to the act of "selling" women as marriage partners, my mother was vehemently opposed to it. Not only was she opposed to this one aspect of tribal culture, but to others as well, particularly those involving relations between men and women and the upbringing of children. But my mother's sharply differing opinion was an exception rather than the rule among tribal women. Most times, many tribal women questioned her sanity in daring to question well-established mores.[22] But my mother did not seem to care; she would always scoff at her opponents and call them fools in letting their husbands enslave them completely.

Though I disliked school, largely because I knew nothing about what actually went on there, and the little I knew had painted a dreadful picture, the fact that a father would not want his son to go to school, especially a father who didn't go to school, seemed hard to understand.

"Why do you want me to go to school, Mama?" I asked, hoping that she might, some-

---

22. **mores** (môr′āz′): traditional customs of a social group.

how, clear up some of the confusion that was building in my mind.

"I want you to have a future, child," my mother said. "And, contrary to what your father says, school is the only means to a future. I don't want you growing up to be like your father."

The latter statement hit me like a bolt of lightning. It just about shattered every defense mechanism and every <u>pretext</u> I had against going to school.

"Your father didn't go to school," she continued, dabbing her puffed eyes to reduce the swelling with a piece of cloth dipped in warm water; "that's why he's doing some of the bad things he's doing. Things like drinking, gambling and neglecting his family. He didn't learn how to read and write; therefore, he can't find a decent job. Lack of any education has narrowly focused his life. He sees nothing beyond himself. He still thinks in the old, tribal way and still believes that things should be as they were back in the old days when he was growing up as a tribal boy in Louis Trichardt.[23] Though he's my husband, and your father, he doesn't see any of that."

"Why didn't he go to school, Mama?"

"He refused to go to school because his father led him to believe that an education was a tool through which white people were going to take things away from him, like they did black people in the old days. And that a white man's education was worthless insofar as black people were concerned because it prepared them for jobs they can't have. But I know it isn't totally so, child, because times have changed somewhat. Though our lot isn't any better today, an education will get you a decent job. If you can read or write, you'll be better off than those of us who can't. Take my situation: I can't find a job because I don't have papers, and I can't get papers because white people mainly want to register people who can read and write. But I want things to be different for you, child. For you and your brother and sisters. I want you to go to school, because I believe that an education is the key you need to open up a new world and a new life for yourself, a world and life different from that of

"I want you to go to school, because I believe that an education is the key you need to open up a new world . . ."

either your father's or mine. It is the only key that can do that, and only those who seek it earnestly and perseveringly will get anywhere in the white man's world. Education will open doors where none seem to exist. It'll make people talk to you, listen to you and help you; people who otherwise wouldn't bother. It will make you soar, like a bird lifting up into the endless blue sky, and leave poverty, hunger and suffering behind. It'll teach you to learn to embrace what's good and shun what's bad and evil. Above all, it'll make you a somebody in this world. It'll make you grow up to be a good and proud person. That's why I want you to go to school, child, so that education can do all that, and more, for you."

A long, awkward silence followed, during which I reflected upon the significance of my

---

23. **Louis Trichardt** (loo′ĭs trĭch′ərt): a town in northern South Africa.

WORDS TO KNOW   **pretext** (prē′tĕkst′) *n.* a pretended reason; excuse

mother's lengthy speech. I looked at my mother; she looked at me.

Finally, I asked, "How come you know so much about school, Mama? You didn't go to school, did you?"

"No, child," my mother replied. "Just like your father, I never went to school." For the second time that evening, a mere statement of fact had a thunderous impact on me. All the confusion I had about school seemed to leave my mind, like darkness giving way to light. And what had previously been a dark, yawning void in my mind was suddenly transformed into a beacon of light that began to grow larger and larger, until it had swallowed up, blotted out, all the blackness. That beacon of light seemed to reveal things and facts, which, though they must have always existed in me, I hadn't been aware of up until now.

"But unlike your father," my mother went on, "I've always wanted to go to school but couldn't because my father, under the sway of tribal traditions, thought it unnecessary to educate females. That's why I so much want you to go, child, for if you do, I know that someday I too would come to go, old as I would be then. Promise me, therefore, that no matter what, you'll go back to school. And I, in turn, promise that I'll do everything in my power to keep you there."

With tears streaming down my cheeks and falling upon my mother's bosom, I promised her that I would go to school "forever." That night, at seven and a half years of my life, the battle lines in the family were drawn. My mother on the one side, illiterate but determined to have me drink, for better or for worse, from the well of knowledge. On the other side, my father, he too illiterate, yet determined to have me drink from the well of ignorance. Scarcely aware of the magnitude of the decision I was making or, rather, the decision which was being emotionally thrust upon me, I chose to fight on my mother's side, and thus my destiny was forever altered. ❖

RESPONDING
OPTIONS

FROM PERSONAL RESPONSE TO CRITICAL ANALYSIS

REFLECT

1. What incident in the selection stands out most vividly in your mind? Why?

RETHINK

2. What do you think is Mrs. Mathabane's greatest challenge in getting her son an education?

   Consider
   - the regulations that discourage black education
   - her husband's attitude toward education
   - tribal traditions about a woman's status
   - the influence of the gang on her son

3. What is your opinion of Mathabane's father? Support your opinion with details from the selection.

4. Why do you think the mother and the grandmother have such different opinions about a woman's role in marriage?

RELATE

5. What do you think is the most important message that Mathabane conveys in this selection?

   Consider
   - how apartheid affects the lives of blacks
   - the effect of tribal marriage traditions on women's lives
   - the doors that may or may not be opened by education

6. For Mathabane, the prediction "Education will open doors where none seem to exist" came true. Do you think this statement is generally true in our society? Why or why not?

ANOTHER PATHWAY

Cooperative Learning

With a few classmates, adapt a scene from the selection as a radio play. Your adaptation should consist mainly of dialogue, with some sound effects and perhaps a narrator's remarks. Try to capture the personalities of the characters.

QUICKWRITES

1. Imagine that you are young Mark Mathabane and that a gang member confronts you about your decision to attend school. Using dialogue in the selection as a model, write a **dialogue** in which you defend your decision to the gang member.

2. Write a script for a **public-service announcement** on South African television, in which the adult Mark Mathabane advises young South African blacks to go to school.

3. Write a **eulogy,** or memorial speech, that the woman on Sixteenth Avenue might have delivered at her son's funeral. Use details from her conversation with the Mathabanes for ideas about what she might say.

📁 *PORTFOLIO Save your writing. You may want to use it later as a springboard to a piece for your portfolio.*

LITERARY CONCEPTS

Dialogue is conversation between two or more characters. The use of dialogue in writing brings characters to life and gives the reader insights into the characters' personality traits. For example, consider the dialogue between the strange woman and Mathabane's mother. This conversation between a mother who has lost her son and a mother fighting to keep hers dramatizes the regret and sorrow of the one and the sympathy and determination of the other. With a partner, examine another passage of dialogue in the selection. What does the dialogue reveal about the characters who participate in it? Share your ideas with your classmates.

LITERARY LINKS

Compare and contrast Mark Mathabane's childhood rebelliousness with that of the narrator of "Two Kinds."

ALTERNATIVE ACTIVITIES

1. Design a **poster** in which art or photos are used to encourage students from Mark Mathabane's township to stay in school.

2. Create a **drawing** that illustrates two different ways of viewing school. One way should be that of Mathabane's mother; the other should be the gang's.

CRITIC'S CORNER

One newspaper review praised *Kaffir Boy* as an autobiography "told with relentless honesty." What details in the selection support this evaluation? Do you agree that "relentless honesty" is praiseworthy in an autobiography? Explain your opinion.

ACROSS THE CURRICULUM

History Find out more about apartheid. How did this system originate? What were its effects on people's lives? What brought an end to apartheid? Present your findings in a research paper.

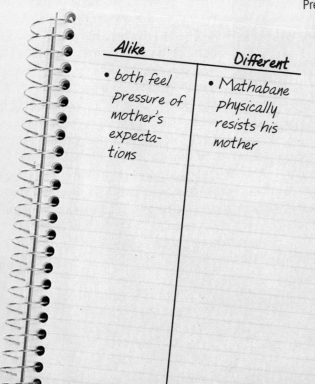

Alike	Different
• both feel pressure of mother's expectations	• Mathabane physically resists his mother

WORDS TO KNOW

EXERCISE A On your paper write the word that best completes each sentence below.

1. Apartheid laws set up separate black schools on the (pretext, credence) that such schools would preserve tribal traditions.

2. The schools for blacks were underfunded and had (austere, unsolicited) budgets.

3. The dream of educating her son had (accosted, captivated) Mrs. Mathabane for years.

4. (Paradoxically, Unsolicited), Mark's father limited his own future by refusing to cooperate with the white-controlled schools.

5. Books and documents seem (utilitarian, inscrutable) to those who cannot read.

6. When Mark entered school, he had no (inkling, pretext) of the fame that he would eventually achieve.

EXERCISE B Find an object or a picture of an object that can be described with one of the four adjectives among the Words to Know.

MARK MATHABANE

Inspired by his mother's sacrifices, young Mark Mathabane became a top student at his school and began learning English—his fifth language—when he was about ten. To help with his family's meager finances, he also started doing odd jobs at the home of the white family for whom his grandmother worked. From that family, who did not believe in apartheid, Mathabane received copies of classic novels like *Treasure Island* and *David Copperfield;* he also received an old tennis racket. His interest in tennis skyrocketed when, a year later, the African-American tennis star Arthur Ashe—an outspoken critic of apartheid—was allowed to play in South Africa for the first time.

In 1977 Mathabane met another American tennis champion, Stan Smith, who helped him win a tennis

1960–

scholarship to an American college. Once there, however, Mathabane realized that his tennis skills would never be of Smith's and Ashe's caliber. He began to devote most of his attention to his studies and, during his junior year, started writing his autobiography. Published in 1986, *Kaffir Boy* quickly became an international bestseller. Nevertheless, it was banned in South Africa until the political situation there began to change in the early 1990s.

Mathabane hopes that the story of his life will inspire "other boys and girls into believing that you can still grow up to be as much of an individual as you have the capacity to be."

OTHER WORKS *Kaffir Boy in America, Love in Black and White*

PREVIEWING

The Teacher Who Changed My Life
Nicholas Gage Greece / United States

PERSONAL CONNECTION

Think of the various people who have influenced the course of your life. When you look back, 10 or 20 years from now, which of these people do you think will have made a lasting impression on you? In your notebook, jot down your thoughts about one of these people.

BIOGRAPHICAL CONNECTION

Nicholas Gage was born in 1939 in Lia, a mountain village in northwestern Greece. Nicholas lived his early years with his mother, Eleni, and four older sisters. His father, Christos, had left his impoverished village to find work in the United States, eventually settling in Worcester, Massachusetts. Before World War II began, his father had been able to return home for extended visits, but the war and the German occupation of Greece made such travel impossible.

After World War II, Eleni and her five children found themselves caught in Greece's bitter civil war between the Communists and the royalists, those who supported rule by the king. In 1947 the Communists took control of Lia, blocking all exit opportunities. In the spring of 1948, the Communists began retreating into nearby Albania, taking the village children with them. Eleni made secret arrangements for the family to flee, but her plan was only partially successful. Though Nicholas and three sisters escaped, one daughter and the mother were left behind. Eventually, Nicholas and his three sisters were able to join their father in the United States.

READING CONNECTION

Understanding Cause and Effect
As you read this selection, focus on the changes in the author's life that were brought about by his teacher's influence. Use a diagram like the one below to record the effects of her influence.

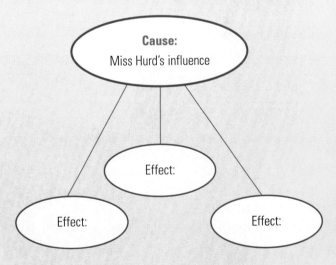

Cause:
Miss Hurd's influence

Effect:

Effect:

Effect:

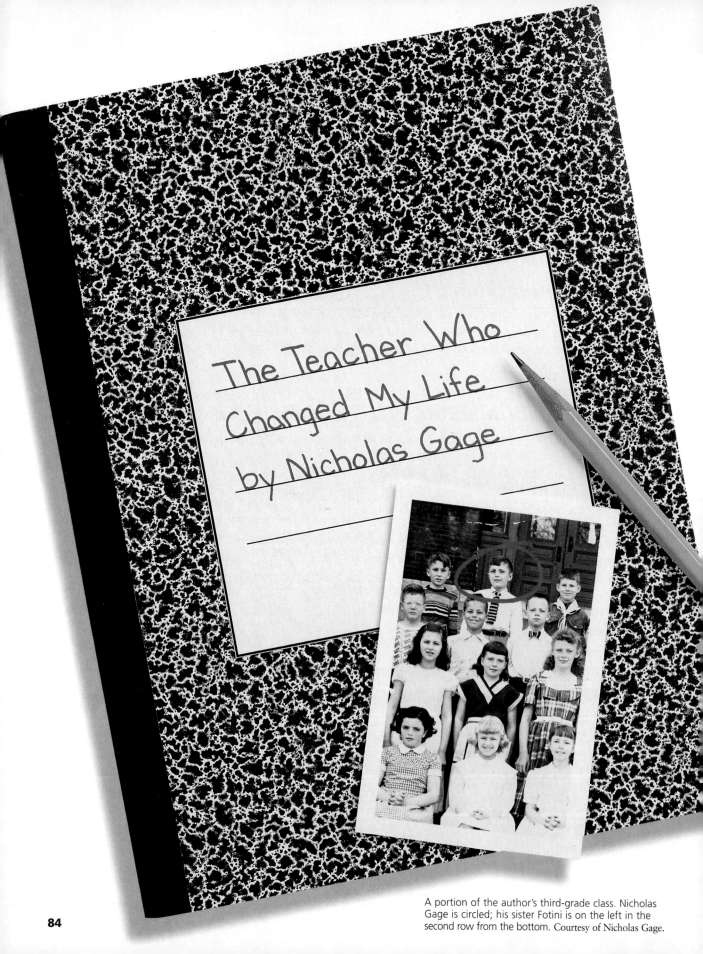

The Teacher Who Changed My Life

by Nicholas Gage

A portion of the author's third-grade class. Nicholas Gage is circled; his sister Fotini is on the left in the second row from the bottom. Courtesy of Nicholas Gage.

The person who set the course of my life in the new land I entered as a young war refugee—who, in fact, nearly dragged me onto the path that would bring all the blessings I've received in America—was a salty-tongued, no-nonsense schoolteacher named Marjorie Hurd. When I entered her classroom in 1953, I had been to six schools in five years, starting in the Greek village where I was born in 1939.

When I stepped off a ship in New York Harbor on a gray March day in 1949, I was an undersized 9-year-old in short pants who had lost his mother and was coming to live with the father he didn't know. My mother, Eleni Gatzoyiannis,[1] had been imprisoned, tortured and shot by Communist guerrillas for sending me and three of my four sisters to freedom. She died so that her children could go to their father in the United States.

The portly, bald, well-dressed man who met me and my sisters seemed a foreign, <u>authoritarian</u> figure. I secretly resented him for not getting the whole family out of Greece early enough to save my mother. Ultimately, I would grow to love him and appreciate how he dealt with becoming a single parent at the age of 56, but at first our relationship was prickly, full of hostility.

As Father drove us to our new home—a tenement in Worcester, Mass.—and pointed out the huge brick building that would be our first school in America, I clutched my Greek notebooks from the refugee camp, hoping that my few years of schooling would impress my teachers in this cold, crowded country. They didn't. When my father led me and my 11-year-old sister to Greendale Elementary School, the grim-faced Yankee principal put the two of us in a class for the mentally retarded. There was no facility in those days for non-English-speaking children.

By the time I met Marjorie Hurd four years later, I had learned English, been placed in a normal, graded class and had even been chosen for the college preparatory track in the Worcester public school system. I was 13 years old when our father moved us yet again, and I entered Chandler Junior High shortly after the beginning of seventh grade. I found myself surrounded by richer, smarter and better-dressed classmates, who looked askance at my strange clothes and heavy accent. Shortly after I arrived, we were told to select a hobby to pursue during "club hour" on Fridays. The idea of hobbies and clubs made no sense to my immigrant ears, but I decided to follow the prettiest girl in my class—the blue-eyed daughter of the local Lutheran minister. She led me through the door marked "Newspaper Club" and into the presence of Miss Hurd, the newspaper adviser and English teacher who would become my <u>mentor</u> and my <u>muse</u>.

A <u>formidable</u>, solidly built woman with salt-and-pepper hair, a steely eye and a flat Boston accent, Miss Hurd had no patience with layabouts. "What are all you goof-offs doing here?" she bellowed at the would-be journalists. "This is the Newspaper Club! We're going to put out a *newspaper*. So if there's anybody in this room who doesn't like work, I suggest you go across to the Glee Club now, because you're going to work your tails off here!"

I was soon under Miss Hurd's spell. She did indeed teach us to put out a newspaper, skills I

---

1. Eleni Gatzoyiannis (ĕ-lĕ′nē gät′zô-yän′ĭs).

Passport photo of Nicholas Gage and three of his sisters.
Courtesy of Nicholas Gage.

honed during my next 25 years as a journalist. Soon I asked the principal to transfer me to her English class as well. There, she drilled us on grammar until I finally began to understand the logic and structure of the English language. She assigned stories for us to read and discuss; not tales of heroes, like the Greek myths I knew, but stories of underdogs—poor people, even immigrants, who seemed ordinary until a crisis drove them to do something extraordinary. She also introduced us to the literary wealth of Greece—giving me a new perspective on my war-ravaged, impoverished homeland. I began to be proud of my origins.

One day, after discussing how writers should write about what they know, she assigned us to compose an essay from our own experience. Fixing me with a stern look, she added, "Nick, I want you to write about what happened to your family in Greece." I had been trying to put those painful memories behind me and left the assignment until the last moment. Then, on a warm spring afternoon, I sat in my room with a yellow pad and pencil and stared out the window at the buds on the trees. I wrote that the coming of spring always reminded me of the last time I said goodbye to my mother on a green and gold day in 1948.

I kept writing, one line after another, telling how the Communist guerrillas occupied our village, took our home and food, how my mother started planning our escape when she learned that the children were to be sent to re-education camps[2] behind the Iron Curtain[3] and

---

2. **re-education camps:** camps where people were forced to go to be indoctrinated with Communist ideas and beliefs.

3. **behind the Iron Curtain:** on the Communist side of the imaginary divide between the democracies of Western Europe and the Communist dictatorships of Eastern Europe; in this case, the camps were in Albania.

WORDS
TO
KNOW

hone (hōn) v. to sharpen

86

how, at the last moment, she couldn't escape with us because the guerrillas sent her with a group of women to thresh wheat in a distant village. She promised she would try to get away on her own, she told me to be brave and hung a silver cross around my neck, and then she kissed me. I watched the line of women being led down into the ravine and up the other side, until they disappeared around the bend—my mother a tiny brown figure at the end who stopped for an instant to raise her hand in one last farewell.

I wrote about our nighttime escape down the mountain, across the minefields and into the lines of the Nationalist soldiers, who sent us to a refugee camp. It was there that we learned of our mother's execution. I felt very lucky to have come to America, I concluded, but every year, the coming of spring made me feel sad because it reminded me of the last time I saw my mother.

For the first time I began to understand the power of the written word. A secret ambition took root in me.

I handed in the essay, hoping never to see it again, but Miss Hurd had it published in the school paper. This <u>mortified</u> me at first, until I saw that my classmates reacted with sympathy and <u>tact</u> to my family's story. Without telling me, Miss Hurd also submitted the essay to a contest sponsored by the Freedoms Foundation at Valley Forge, Pa., and it won a medal. The Worcester paper wrote about the award and quoted my essay at length. My father, by then a "five-and-dime-store chef," as the paper described him, was ecstatic with pride, and the Worcester Greek community celebrated the honor to one of its own.

For the first time I began to understand the power of the written word. A secret ambition took root in me. One day, I vowed, I would go back to Greece, find out the details of my mother's death and write about her life, so her grandchildren would know of her courage. Perhaps I would even track down the men who killed her and write of their crimes. Fulfilling that ambition would take me 30 years.

Meanwhile, I followed the literary path that Miss Hurd had so forcefully set me on. After junior high, I became the editor of my school paper at Classical High School and got a part-time job at the Worcester *Telegram and Gazette.* Although my father could only give me $50 and encouragement toward a college education, I managed to finance four years at Boston University with scholarships and part-time jobs in journalism. During my last year of college, an article I wrote about a friend who had died in the Philippines—the first person to lose his life working for the Peace Corps—led to my winning the Hearst Award for College Journalism. And the plaque was given to me in the White House by President John F. Kennedy.

For a refugee who had never seen a motorized vehicle or indoor plumbing until he was 9, this was an unimaginable honor. When the Worcester paper ran a picture of me standing next to President Kennedy, my father rushed out to buy a new suit in order to be properly dressed to receive the congratulations of the Worcester Greeks. He clipped out the photograph, had it laminated in plastic and carried it in his breast pocket for the rest of his life to show everyone he met. I found the much-worn photo in his pocket on the day he died 20 years later.

WORDS TO KNOW
mortify (môr′tə-fī′) *v.* to cause to feel shame or humiliation
tact (tăkt) *n.* the sensitivity to say and do what is appropriate when dealing with other people

In our isolated Greek village, my mother had bribed a cousin to teach her to read, for girls were not supposed to attend school beyond a certain age. She had always dreamed of her children receiving an education. She couldn't be there when I graduated from Boston University, but the person who came with my father and shared our joy was my former teacher, Marjorie Hurd. We celebrated not only my bachelor's degree but also the scholarships that paid my way to Columbia's Graduate School of Journalism. There, I met the woman who would eventually become my wife. At our wedding and at the baptisms of our three children, Marjorie Hurd was always there, dancing alongside the Greeks.

She would alternately bully and charm each one with her own special brand of tough love until the spark caught fire.

By then, she was Mrs. Rabidou, for she had married a widower when she was in her early 40s. That didn't distract her from her vocation of introducing young minds to English literature, however. She taught for a total of 41 years and continually would make a "project" of some balky student in whom she spied a spark of potential. Often these were students from the most troubled homes, yet she would alternately bully and charm each one with her own special brand of tough love until the spark caught fire. She retired in 1981 at the age of 62 but still avidly follows the lives and careers of former students while overseeing her adult stepchildren and driving her husband on camping trips to New Hampshire.

Miss Hurd was one of the first to call me on Dec. 10, 1987, when President Reagan, in his television address after the summit meeting with Gorbachev,[4] told the nation that Eleni Gatzoyiannis's dying cry, "My children!" had helped inspire him to seek an arms agreement "for all the children of the world."

"I can't imagine a better monument for your mother," Miss Hurd said with an uncharacteristic catch in her voice.

Although a bad hip makes it impossible for her to join in the Greek dancing, Marjorie Hurd Rabidou is still an honored and enthusiastic guest at all our family celebrations, including my 50th birthday picnic last summer, where the shish kebab was cooked on spits, clarinets and *bouzoukis*[5] wailed, and costumed dancers led the guests in a serpentine line around our Colonial farmhouse, only 20 minutes from my first home in Worcester.

My sisters and I felt an aching <u>void</u> because my father was not there to lead the line, balancing a glass of wine on his head while he danced, the way he did at every celebration during his 92 years. But Miss Hurd was there, surveying the scene with quiet satisfaction. Although my parents are gone, her presence was a consolation, because I owe her so much.

This is truly the land of opportunity, and I would have enjoyed its bounty even if I hadn't walked into Miss Hurd's classroom in 1953. But she was the one who directed my grief and pain into writing, and if it weren't for her, I wouldn't have become an investigative reporter and foreign correspondent, recorded the story of my mother's life and death in *Eleni* and now my father's story in *A Place for Us,* which is

---

4. **summit meeting with Gorbachev** (gôr′bə-chôf′): a high-level meeting between U.S. president Ronald Reagan and Mikhail Gorbachev, the last premier of the Soviet Union.

5. *bouzoukis* (boo-zoo′kēz): traditional Greek stringed instruments resembling mandolins.

WORDS
TO   **void** *n.* a feeling of loss; emptiness
KNOW

88

Pictured at left, Marjorie Hurd Rabidou and Nicholas Gage. Copyright © Eddie Adams / SYGMA. At right, Nicholas Gage and his family at the harbor in Piraeus, Greece, ready to set out for the United States. Courtesy of Nicholas Gage.

also a testament to the country that took us in. She was the catalyst that sent me into journalism and indirectly caused all the good things that came after. But Miss Hurd would probably deny this emphatically.

A few years ago, I answered the telephone and heard my former teacher's voice telling me, in that won't-take-no-for-an-answer tone of hers, that she had decided I was to write and deliver the eulogy at her funeral. I agreed (she didn't leave me any choice), but that's one assignment I never want to do. I hope, Miss Hurd, that you'll accept this remembrance instead. ❖

89

RESPONDING
OPTIONS

FROM PERSONAL RESPONSE TO CRITICAL ANALYSIS

REFLECT

1. What words and phrases sum up your response to this selection? Write them in your notebook.

RETHINK

2. Review the cause-and-effect diagram that you made about Miss Hurd's influence on the author. What do you think were the most important effects that she had on his life?

   Consider
   - the hardships of Nicholas Gage's childhood
   - Miss Hurd's essay assignment
   - their friendship

3. Gage says that Miss Hurd would probably deny that she "was the catalyst that sent [him] into journalism and indirectly caused all the good things that came after." Why do you think he says this?

   Consider
   - what you learned about her personality and teaching style
   - how she might view his tribute to her influence

RELATE

4. Would you want Miss Hurd for your teacher? Give reasons for your answer.

5. In your opinion, what personal qualities helped Nicholas Gage to succeed in his adopted homeland? Do you think these same qualities would prove helpful to immigrants today?

ANOTHER PATHWAY

Cooperative Learning

Work with a small group to list the characteristics you think are necessary in a good teacher. Then evaluate Miss Hurd in terms of those characteristics, citing evidence from the selection to support your evaluation. Share your findings with the rest of the class.

QUICKWRITES

1. Write an **essay** about someone who has made a lasting impression on your life. You may want to use what you jotted down for the Personal Connection on page 83 as a starting point.

2. Describe either Nicholas Gage or Miss Hurd in a **character sketch.** Include details from the selection.

   PORTFOLIO Save your writing. You may want to use it later as a springboard to a piece for your portfolio.

LITERARY CONCEPTS

An **essay** is a brief nonfiction work, usually offering an opinion on a subject. Its main purpose may be to express ideas and feelings, to analyze, to inform, to entertain, or to persuade. Work with a partner to identify Gage's purpose for writing. Make a list of the statements in his essay that helped you to identify that purpose.

Purposes of Essays

- to express ideas and feelings
- to analyze
- to entertain
- to inform
- to persuade

ALTERNATIVE ACTIVITIES

1. Create a **photo essay** about someone who has influenced your life. Include captions that explain what the photographs depict.

2. Read *Eleni*, Nicholas Gage's 1983 book about his mother, or view the 1985 movie adaptation of it on videocassette. Then summarize the book or film in an **oral report** to classmates.

3. Imagine that you are the author's father. Perform a **dramatic monologue** in which you tell the story of your son's life and explain your feelings about him.

LITERARY LINKS

Compare and contrast Miss Hurd with Mark Mathabane's mother in *Kaffir Boy*. What similarities and differences do you see in the women's personalities, their values, and their effects on the lives of others?

WORDS TO KNOW

On your own paper match each word on the left with the word on the right that is most nearly *opposite* in meaning. Use each word only once.

1. authoritarian	a. fullness
2. mentor	b. opponent
3. muse	c. flatter
4. formidable	d. weakly
5. hone	e. awkwardness
6. mortify	f. lenient
7. tact	g. result
8. void	h. unimpressive
9. catalyst	i. pupil
10. emphatically	j. dull

NICHOLAS GAGE

1939–

Miss Hurd's influence helped launch Nicholas Gage (originally Nikola Gatzoyiannis) on a remarkable career as an investigative reporter. For the *Boston Herald Traveler* he exposed shocking conditions at a school for the mentally retarded; for the *Wall Street Journal* he reported on organized crime in both the United States and Great Britain. In 1970 Gage was recruited by the *New York Times*. While there, he wrote news stories on a number of controversial issues, including drug trafficking and government corruption in Latin America and an attempt to sell New York's Metropolitan Museum of Art a fake vase for a million dollars. During this time he also wrote two novels, as well as nonfiction about his native Greece.

In 1980 Gage retired from journalism to devote all his time to researching a book about his mother. His investigations led him to the man responsible for his mother's death, whom he considered killing. In the end, however, he refused to exact vengeance, realizing that to do so would be to "become like him, purging myself as he did of all humanity or compassion."

OTHER WORKS *Eleni, Hellas: A Portrait of Greece, A Place for Us*

THE TEACHER WHO CHANGED MY LIFE **91**

from Earthly Paradise

Colette ❦ France

The French writer Colette lovingly remembers her mother, Sido (sē-dō'), in these three excerpts from a collection of her autobiographical writings. The first excerpt, beginning "I could live in Paris . . . ," describes Colette's memories of her childhood with Sido, when they lived together in a French country village. The second excerpt, beginning "The time came . . . ," presents Sido many years later, when she was an old woman living alone. The third excerpt, beginning "Sir, You ask me . . . ," is a reflection on a letter that Sido wrote to Colette's second husband and captures Sido's remarkable spirit.

"I could live in Paris . . ."

"I could live in Paris only if I had a beautiful garden," she would confess to me. "And even then! I can't imagine a Parisian garden where I could pick those big bearded oats I sew on a bit of cardboard for you because they make such sensitive barometers." I chide myself for having lost the very last of those rustic barometers made of oat grains whose two awns,[1] as long as a shrimp's feelers, crucified on a card, would turn to the left or the right according to whether it was going to be fine or wet.

No one could equal Sido, either, at separating and counting the talc-like skins of onions. "One—two—three coats; three coats on the onions!" And letting her spectacles or her lorgnette[2] fall on her lap, she would add pensively: "That means a hard winter. I must have the pump wrapped in straw. Besides, the tortoise has dug

itself in already, and the squirrels round about Guillemette[3] have stolen quantities of walnuts and cobnuts for their stores. Squirrels always know everything."

If the newspapers foretold a thaw, my mother would shrug her shoulders and laugh scornfully. "A thaw? Those Paris meteorologists can't teach me anything about that! Look at the cat's paws!" Feeling chilly, the cat had indeed folded her paws out of sight beneath her, and shut her eyes tight. "When there's only going to be a short spell of cold," went on Sido, "the cat rolls herself into a turban with her nose against the

---

1. **awns:** slender bristles on the ears of certain grasses.
2. **lorgnette** (lôrn-yĕt'): a pair of eyeglasses attached to a handle.
3. **Guillemette** (gē-mĕt').

Old House and Garden, East Hampton, Long Island (1898), Frederick Childe Hassam. Oil on canvas, 24 1/16″ × 20″, Henry Art Gallery, University of Washington, Seattle, Horace C. Henry Collection (26.70).

root of her tail. But when it's going to be really bitter, she tucks in the pads of her front paws and rolls them up like a muff."

All the year round she kept racks full of plants in pots standing on green-painted wooden steps. There were rare geraniums, dwarf rose bushes, spiraeas with misty white and pink plumes, a few "succulents," hairy and squat as crabs, and murderous cacti. Two warm walls formed an angle which kept the harsh winds from her trial ground, which consisted of some red earthenware bowls in which I could see nothing but loose, dormant earth.

"Don't touch!"

"But nothing's coming up!"

"And what do you know about it? Is it for you to decide? Read what's written on the labels stuck in the pots! These are seeds of blue lupin; that's a narcissus bulb from Holland; those are seeds of winter cherry; that's a cutting of hibiscus—no, of course it isn't a dead twig!— and those are some seeds of sweet peas whose flowers have ears like little hares. And that . . . and that . . ."

"Yes, and that?"

My mother pushed her hat back, nibbled the chain of her lorgnette, and put the problem frankly to me:

"I'm really very worried. I can't remember whether it was a family of crocus bulbs I planted there, or the chrysalis of an emperor moth."

"We've only got to scratch to find out."

A swift hand stopped mine. Why did no one ever model or paint or carve that hand of Sido's, tanned and wrinkled early by household tasks, gardening, cold water, and the sun, with its long, finely tapering fingers and its beautiful, convex,[4] oval nails?

"Not on your life! If it's the chrysalis, it'll die as soon as the air touches it, and if it's the crocus, the light will shrivel its little white shoot and we'll have to begin all over again. Are you taking in what I say? You won't touch it?"

"No, Mother."

As she spoke, her face, alight with faith and an all-embracing curiosity, was hidden by another, older face, resigned and gentle. She knew that I should not be able to resist, any more than she could, the desire to know, and that like herself I should ferret in the earth of that flowerpot until it had given up its secret. I never thought of our resemblance, but she knew I was her own daughter and that, child though I was, I was already seeking for that sense of shock, the quickened heartbeat, and the sudden stoppage of the breath—symptoms of the private ecstasy of the treasure seeker. A treasure is not merely something hidden under the earth or the rocks or the sea. The vision of gold and gems is but a blurred mirage. To me the important thing is to lay bare and bring to light something that no human eye before mine has gazed upon.

She knew then that I was going to scratch on the sly in her trial ground until I came upon the upward-climbing claw of the cotyledon, the sturdy sprout urged out of its sheath by the spring. I thwarted the blind purpose of the bilious-looking, black-brown chrysalis, and hurled it from its temporary death into a final nothingness.

"You don't understand . . . you can't understand. You're nothing but a little eight-year-old murderess—or is it ten? You just can't understand something that wants to live." That was the only punishment I got for my misdeeds; but that was hard enough for me to bear.

Sido loathed flowers to be sacrificed. Although her one idea was to give, I have seen her refuse a request for flowers to adorn a hearse or a grave. She would harden her heart, frown, and answer "No" with a vindictive[5] look.

"But it's for poor Monsieur Enfert,[6] who died

---

4. **convex:** having a surface that curves outward.

5. **vindictive** (vĭn-dĭk′tĭv): spiteful; vengeful.

6. **Monsieur Enfert** (mə-syœ′ än-fĕr′).

last night! Poor Madame Enfert's so pathetic, she says if she could see her husband depart covered with flowers, it would console her! And you've got such lovely moss roses, Madame Colette."

"My moss roses on a corpse! What an outrage!"

It was an involuntary cry, but even after she had pulled herself together she still said: "No. My roses have not been condemned to die at the same time as Monsieur Enfert."

But she gladly sacrificed a very beautiful flower to a very small child, a child not yet able to speak, like the little boy whom a neighbor to the east proudly brought into the garden one day, to show him off to her. My mother found fault with the infant's swaddling clothes, for being too tight, untied his three-piece bonnet and his unnecessary woolen shawl, and then gazed to her heart's content on his bronze ringlets, his cheeks, and the enormous, stern black eyes of a ten months' old baby boy, really so much more beautiful than any other boy of ten months! She gave him a *cuisse-de-nymphe-émue*[7] rose, and he accepted it with delight, put it in his mouth, and sucked it; then he kneaded it with his powerful little hands and tore off the petals, as curved and carmine[8] as his own lips.

"Stop it, you naughty boy!" cried his young mother.

But mine, with looks and words, applauded his massacre of the rose, and in my jealousy I said nothing.

She also regularly refused to lend double geraniums, pelargoniums, lobelias, dwarf rose bushes and spiraea for the wayside altars on Corpus Christi day, for although she was baptized and married in church, she always held aloof from Catholic trivialities and pageantries. But she gave me permission, when I was between eleven and twelve, to attend catechism classes and to join in the hymns at the evening service.

On the first of May, with my comrades of the catechism class, I laid lilac, camomile, and roses before the altar of the Virgin, and returned full of pride to show my "blessed posy." My mother laughed her irreverent laugh and, looking at my bunch of flowers, which was bringing the May bugs into the sitting room right under the lamp, she said: "Do you suppose it wasn't already blessed before?"

I do not know where she got her aloofness from any form of worship. I ought to have tried to find out. My biographers, who get little information from me, sometimes depict her as a simple farmer's wife and sometimes make her out to be a "whimsical bohemian."[9] One of them, to my astonishment, goes so far as to accuse her of having written short literary works for young persons!

In reality, this Frenchwoman spent her childhood in the Yonne,[10] her adolescence among painters, journalists, and musicians in Belgium, where her two elder brothers had settled, and

---

7. *cuisse-de-nymphe-émue* (kwēs′də-nănf′ā-mü′): the French name of a variety of rose.

8. **carmine** (kär′mĭn): red or purplish-red.

9. **bohemian** (bō-hē′mē-ən): an artistic person who lives in a free, unconventional way.

10. **Yonne** (yän): a rural region in central France, named for the Yonne River.

then returned to the Yonne, where she married twice. But whence, or from whom, she got her sensitive understanding of country matters and her discriminating appreciation of the provinces, I am unable to say. I sing her praises as best I may, and celebrate the native lucidity[11] which, in her, dimmed and often extinguished the lesser lights painfully lit through the contact of what she called "the common run of mankind."

I once saw her hang up a scarecrow in a cherry tree to frighten the blackbirds, because our kindly neighbor of the west, who always had a cold and was shaken with bouts of sneezing, never failed to disguise his cherry trees as old tramps and crown his currant bushes with battered opera hats. A few days later I found my mother beneath the tree, motionless with excitement, her head turned toward the heavens in which she would allow human religions no place.

"Sssh! Look!"

A blackbird, with a green and violet sheen on his dark plumage, was pecking at the cherries, drinking their juice and lacerating their rosy pulp.

"How beautiful he is!" whispered my mother. "Do you see how he uses his claw? And the movements of his head and that arrogance of his? See how he twists his beak to dig out the stone! And you notice that he only goes for the ripest ones."

"But, mother, the scarecrow!"

"Sssh! The scarecrow doesn't worry him!"

"But, mother, the cherries!"

My mother brought the glance of her rain-colored eyes back to earth: "The cherries? Yes, of course, the cherries."

In those eyes there flickered a sort of wild gaiety, a contempt for the whole world, a lighthearted disdain which cheerfully spurned me along with everything else. It was only momentary, and it was not the first time I had seen it. Now that I know her better, I can interpret those sudden gleams in her face. They were, I feel, kindled by an urge to escape from everyone and everything, to soar to some high place where only her own writ ran.[12] If I am mistaken, leave me to my delusion.

But there, under the cherry tree, she returned to earth once more among us, weighed down with anxieties, and love, and a husband and children who clung to her. Faced with the common round of life, she became good and comforting and humble again.

"Yes, of course, the cherries . . . you must have cherries too."

The blackbird, gorged, had flown off, and the scarecrow waggled his empty opera hat in the breeze. . . .

The time came . . .

The time came when all her strength left her. She was amazed beyond measure and would not believe it. Whenever I arrived from Paris to see her, as soon as we were alone in the afternoon in her little house, she had always some sin to confess to me. On one occasion she turned up the hem of her dress, rolled her stocking down over her shin, and displayed a

---

11. **lucidity** (loo-sĭd′ĭ-tē): a state of being clear-headed or rational.

12. **writ ran:** law was enforced.

96

purple bruise, the skin nearly broken.

"Just look at that!"

"What on earth have you done to yourself this time, Mother?"

She opened wide eyes, full of innocence and embarrassment.

"You wouldn't believe it, but I fell downstairs!"

"How do you mean—'fell'?"

"Just what I said. I fell, for no reason. I was going downstairs and I fell. I can't understand it."

"Were you going down too quickly?"

"Too quickly? What do you call too quickly? I was going down quickly. Have I time to go downstairs majestically like the Sun King? And if that were all . . . But look at this!"

On her pretty arm, still so young above the faded hand, was a scald forming a large blister.

"Oh goodness! Whatever's that!"

"My footwarmer."

"The old copper footwarmer? The one that holds five quarts?"

"That's the one. Can I trust anything, when that footwarmer has known me for forty years? I can't imagine what possessed it, it was boiling fast, I went to take it off the fire, and crack, something gave in my wrist. I was lucky to get nothing worse than the blister. But what a thing to happen! After that I let the cupboard alone. . . ."

She broke off, blushing furiously.

"What cupboard?" I demanded severely.

My mother fenced, tossing her head as though I were trying to put her on a lead.

"Oh, nothing! No cupboard at all!"

"Mother! I shall get cross!"

"Since I've said, 'I let the cupboard alone,' can't you do the same for my sake? The cupboard hasn't moved from its place, has it? So, shut up about it!"

The cupboard was a massive object of old walnut, almost as broad as it was high, with no carving save the circular hole made by a Prussian bullet that had entered by the right-hand door and passed out through the back panel.

"Do you want it moved from the landing, Mother?"

An expression like that of a young she-cat, false and glittery, appeared on her wrinkled face.

"I? No, it seems to me all right there—let it stay where it is!"

All the same, my doctor brother and I agreed that we must be on the watch. He saw my mother every day, since she had followed him and lived in the same village, and he looked after her with a passionate devotion which he hid. She fought against all her ills with amazing elasticity, forgot them, baffled them, inflicted on them signal if temporary defeats, recovered, during entire days, her vanished strength; and the sound of her battles, whenever I spent a few days with her, could be heard all over the house till I was irresistibly reminded of a terrier tackling a rat.

At five o'clock in the morning I would be awakened by the clank of a full bucket being set down in the kitchen sink immediately opposite my room.

"What are you doing with that bucket, Mother? Couldn't you wait until Josephine arrives?"

And out I hurried. But the fire was already blazing, fed with dry wood. The milk was boiling on the blue-tiled charcoal stove. Nearby, a bar of chocolate was melting in a little water for my breakfast, and, seated squarely in her cane armchair, my mother was grinding the fragrant coffee which she roasted herself. The morning hours were always kind to her. She wore their rosy colors in her cheeks. Flushed with a brief return to health, she would gaze at the rising sun, while the church bell rang for early Mass, and rejoice at having tasted, while we still slept, so many forbidden fruits.

The forbidden fruits were the overheavy bucket drawn up from the well, the firewood split with a billhook on an oaken block, the spade, the mattock, and above all the double steps propped against the gable window of the woodhouse. There were the climbing vine whose shoots she trained up to the gable windows of the attic, the flowery spikes of the too-tall lilacs, the dizzy cat that had to be rescued from the ridge of the roof. All the accomplices of her old existence as a plump and sturdy little woman, all the minor rustic divinities who once obeyed her and made her so proud of doing without servants, now assumed the appearance and position of adversaries. But they reckoned without that love of combat which my mother was to keep till the end of her life. At seventy-one, dawn still found her undaunted, if not always undamaged. Burnt by the fire, cut with the pruning knife, soaked by melting snow or spilled water, she had always managed to enjoy her best moments of independence before the earliest risers had opened their shutters. She was able to tell us of the cats' awakening, of what was going on in the nests, of news gleaned, together with the morning's milk and the warm loaf, from the milkmaid and the baker's girl, the record in fact of the birth of a new day.

It was not until one morning when I found the kitchen unwarmed, and the blue enamel saucepan hanging on the wall, that I felt my mother's end to be near. Her illness knew many respites, during which the fire flared up again on the hearth, and the smell of fresh bread and melting chocolate stole under the door together with the cat's impatient paw. These respites were periods of unexpected alarms. My mother and the big walnut cupboard were discovered together in a heap at the foot of the stairs, she having determined to transport it in secret from the upper landing to the ground floor. Whereupon my elder brother insisted that my mother should keep still and that an old servant should sleep in the little house. But how could an old servant prevail against a vital energy so youthful and mischievous that it contrived to tempt and lead astray a body already half fettered by death? My brother, returning before sunrise from attending a distant patient, one day caught my mother red-handed in the most wanton of crimes. Dressed in her nightgown, but wearing heavy gardening sabots, her little gray septuagenarian's plait of hair turning up like a scorpion's tail on the nape of her neck, one foot firmly planted on the crosspiece of the beech trestle, her back bent in the attitude of the expert jobber, my mother, rejuvenated by an indescribable expression of guilty enjoyment, in defiance of all her promises and of the freezing morning dew, was sawing logs in her own yard.

"Sir, You ask me . . ."

"Sir,

"You ask me to come and spend a week with you, which means I would be near my daughter, whom I adore. You who live with her know how rarely I see her, how much her presence delights me, and I'm touched that you should ask me to come and see her. All the same I'm not going to accept your kind invitation, for the time being at any rate. The reason is that my pink cactus is probably going to flower. It's a very rare plant I've been given, and I'm told that in our climate it flowers only once every four years. Now, I am already a very old woman, and if I went away when my pink cactus is about to flower, I am certain I shouldn't see it flower again.

"So I beg you, sir, to accept my sincere thanks and my regrets, together with my kind regards."

This note, signed *"Sidonie Colette, née Landoy,"* was written by my mother to one of my husbands, the second. A year later she died, at the age of seventy-seven.

Whenever I feel myself inferior to everything about me, threatened by my own mediocrity, frightened by the discovery that a muscle is losing its strength, a desire its power, or a pain the keen edge of its bite, I can still hold up my head and say to myself: "I am the daughter of the woman who wrote that letter—that letter and so many more that I have kept. This one tells me in ten lines that at the age of seventy-six she was planning journeys and undertaking them, but that waiting for the possible bursting into bloom of a tropical flower held everything up and silenced even her heart, made for love. I am the daughter of a woman who, in a mean, close-fisted, confined little place, opened her village home to stray cats, tramps, and pregnant servant girls. I am the daughter of a woman who many a time, when she was in despair at not having enough money for others, ran through the wind-whipped snow to cry from door to door, at the houses of the rich, that a child had just been born in a poverty-stricken home to parents whose feeble, empty hands had no swaddling clothes for it. Let me not forget that I am the daughter of a woman who bent her head, trembling, between the blades of a cactus, her wrinkled face full of ecstasy over the promise of a flower, a woman who herself never ceased to flower, untiringly, during three quarters of a century." ❖

*Translated by Enid McCleod
and Una Vincenzo Troubridge*

COLETTE

Sidonie-Gabrielle Colette (sē-dô-nē′ gä-brē-ĕl′ kô-lĕt′), known simply as Colette, was a major French writer. Her novels, short stories, and autobiographical writings are marked by a fine attention to sensory detail and a sensitivity to the complexities of human desire.

Colette's first husband, Henri Gauthier-Villars (äɴ-rē′ gō-tyā′vē-lär′), was a hack writer who discovered Colette's talent and encouraged her to publish her "Claudine" novels under his pen name, Willy, in the years 1900–1903. These novels tell about the escapades of a young, mischievous woman as she learns about life and love.

After a divorce in 1906, Colette pursued an independent career for several years both as a writer and as a music-hall performer. She wrote about this period of her life in *The Vagabond* (1910) and *Recaptured*

1873–1954

(1913). She produced her finest work in the 1920s, including *Chéri* (1920) and *The Last of Chéri* (1926). Of *Chéri*, the story of an older woman's devotion to a younger man, Colette said, "For the first time in my life, I felt morally certain of having written a novel for which I needed neither blush nor doubt. . . . I know where my best work as a writer is to be found."

By then a legendary figure, Colette spent her final years confined to her Paris apartment, crippled by arthritis and surrounded by her beloved cats. When she died in 1954, she had produced an impressive variety of works and had received a number of distinguished literary honors. Her funeral was the first state funeral ever given to a woman in France. **OTHER WORKS** *Creatures Great and Small, Journey for Myself: Selfish Memories, Gigi, Sido*

DISCUSSING A PORTRAYAL

What does the conversation between Felicia and the woman in "Winter Night" tell you about their past? How does dialogue show character in "Two Kinds"? On the following pages, you will see and hear how dialogue gives you a better understanding of events and characters. You will also

- study how writers use dialogue
- write your response to the portrayal of a group or event
- think about how media shapes your impressions

The Writer's Style: Creating Dialogue Writers use the words of a character to show what the character is like, to show what is going on, and to add interest.

Read the Literature

Notice how writers use dialogue in these excerpts.

Literature Models

Dialogue Reveals Background Information
What background information does this dialogue provide?

"They read the name of the little girl's mother out, and that afternoon they took her away."

"What did the little girl do?" Felicia said.

"She wanted to think up the best way of getting out, so that she could go find her mother," said the woman, "but she could not think of anything good enough until the third or fourth day. And then she tied her ballet slippers up in the handkerchief again, and she went up to the guard standing at the door."

Kay Boyle, from "Winter Night"

Dialogue Reveals Conflict
What does this dialogue reveal about the relationship between these characters?

"You want me to be someone I'm not!" I sobbed. "I'll never be the kind of daughter you want me to be!"

"Only two kinds of daughters," she shouted in Chinese. "Those who are obedient and those who follow their own mind! Only one kind of daughter can live in this house. Obedient daughter!"

"Then I wish I wasn't your daughter. I wish you weren't my mother," I shouted.

Amy Tan, from "Two Kinds"

Connect to Life

You read dialogue in books, magazines, and newspapers, and you listen to dialogue whenever people talk to one another on TV or in movies. Of course, you engage in dialogue each time you talk to someone. Read the dialogue between the cartoon characters below.

Cartoon

CALVIN AND HOBBES © 1986 Watterson. Dist. by UNIVERSAL PRESS SYNDICATE. Reprinted with permission. All rights reserved.

Dialogue Reveals Character
What does this dialogue reveal about the differences between these two characters?

Try Your Hand: Writing Dialogue

1. **Say It in Dialogue** Revise the following paragraph to include dialogue that reveals character:

   Jake and I are best friends, but we disagree about everything. Our personalities, at times, are exact opposites. The argument over the way he treats Randy really shows how differently we view our world!

2. **Present Events** Choose one of the following topics and write a dialogue that provides important information:

   • two old friends recall a practical joke they once played
   • a newcomer learns why nobody goes near the old house

3. **Write Your Own Dialogue** Write a dialogue between you and someone you'd like to have a conversation with.

Personal Response

Well-written dialogue and description can help create a strong image of a particular event, group, or individual. The image created by the writer may or may not match an image or idea you already have in your head. Personally responding to a portrayal helps you sort out these ideas or images.

GUIDED ASSIGNMENT

Write a Personal Response The following pages will help you write a personal response to the portrayal of an event, a group, or an individual in a selection from this unit.

Student's Prewriting List

The Portrayal of the Holocaust

Notes and my reactions

Felicia reminds the woman of a little girl at the concentration camp. Story reminds me of movies and books I have read about the Holocaust
—reminds me to value my personal freedom
—need for hope in the world
—universal idea of love

Examples and Quotes

"We were all hungry, but the children were the hungriest."
"That afternoon they took her away."
"They must be quietly asleep somewhere and not crying all night because they are hungry and because they are cold."
—the first quote in the story about love

1 Prewrite and Explore

Think about the selections in this unit. Did one of the authors portray an event, a group, or a person in a way that seemed to match your ideas?

EXAMINING THE SELECTION

As you review each of the selections, jot down your responses to the portrayal of a group or event. Reflect on these questions:

- What did I think about this group or an event before I read the selection?
- What was my initial reaction to the author's portrayal?
- Do I agree with the author's ideas? Why or why not?
- How does the portrayal make me feel?
- How does the dialogue contribute to my reaction?

GATHERING INFORMATION

Your personal response should include an explanation of your own impression of what is portrayed, as well as details and examples from the selection to explain the reasons for your feelings, opinions, and insights. You can use a simple list like the one at the left to help you gather examples. This sample shows one student's reaction to the portrayal of the Holocaust in "Winter Night."

② Write and Analyze a Discovery Draft

Begin drafting by writing freely about ideas on your prewriting list. Remember that you'll eventually want to organize your draft to help your reader understand your response.

The discovery draft below includes the student's analysis on yellow notes.

Student's Discovery Draft

What other specific descriptions of the event can I include?

This story was about the Holocaust. I felt sorry for the woman and angry at injustice. Felicia's mother acting selfishly angered me too. I can't forget the mother standing on the train scratching a note on a piece of paper, hoping that it would reach the hands of someone who cares.

I feel sadness, but I feel hopeful too. The woman is a strong individual and a loving person. She sees beyond injustice and loss. In this story, the Holocaust is portrayed as a horrifying, senseless event. It's also portrayed as a stern lesson in love. I agree with both of these ideas.

Which ideas should I expand? I want to use this idea in my conclusion.

③ Draft and Share

Now you are ready to write a rough draft with an introduction that gives your readers enough information about the work. Your draft should also contain an explanation of why you feel as you do and a conclusion that sums up your overall reaction. The SkillBuilder on using elaboration will help you to include support. Consider the following questions:

- Does my response clearly explain my feelings?
- Have I included enough specific examples and quotations?

When you are finished, invite a peer to read your rough draft.

 PEER RESPONSE

- Do I explore my reactions to the selection in depth? How?
- Which quotes and details clearly support my response?

4 Revise and Edit

Check the Standards for Evaluation below as you revise your draft. Look back at your prewriting list to make sure you supported your response. Reread your draft. Does it reflect your thoughts and feelings about the points that are most important to you?

Student's Final Draft

Response to the Portrayal of the Holocaust in "Winter Night"

"There is a time of apprehension that begins with the beginning of darkness and to which only the speech of love can lend security." This opening sentence of "Winter Night" by Kay Boyle sets the tone for me. It makes me feel as if the darkness is the Holocaust and only love can begin to help heal. The story of the Holocaust is told through the dialogue of a sad woman and an innocent little girl. Even though she has survived a terrible experience, the woman speaks of love. The content of this conversation fascinates me and makes me angry too.

Notice how the student uses a quotation from the story to provide an interesting introduction.

How does the student use personal knowledge and experience to support ideas?

As the woman puts her arms around Felicia and gives her love, I feel hope and am reminded of a book. This book, by a hopeful survivor of the Holocaust, is about the power of love in the face of injustice. The woman speaks of this injustice when she says, "I want to beat my hands on the table, because it did not have to be!" I agree with the sad woman, but I also believe in the security that love can provide.

Standards for Evaluation

A personal response
- identifies the author and title of the story and introduces an overall response in the first paragraph
- provides readers with enough information about the story for them to understand the response
- clearly supports your ideas with quotations or other details

Grammar in Context

Pronouns and Their Antecedents In any writing you do, including responding to literature, all pronouns should have clear antecedents—words naming the persons or things to which the pronouns refer.

As the woman puts her arms around Felicia and gives her love, I feel hope and am reminded of a book. This book, by a hopeful survivor of the Holocaust, is about the power of love in the face of injustice. *The woman* ~~She~~ speaks of this injustice when she says, "I want to beat my hands on the table, because it did not have to be!" I agree with *the sad woman* ~~her~~, but I also believe in the security that love can lend.

If you use *she, he, it,* or other pronouns without clear antecedents, you'll confuse your readers. Look at the third sentence in the model. Three antecedents—*the woman*, *Felicia*, and *a hopeful survivor*—are possible for the word *she*. Before the edit, the reference was not clear.

Try Your Hand: Pronouns and Antecedents

On a separate sheet of paper, revise the following paragraph so that each pronoun has a clear antecedent:

The little girl was thrilled that the sad woman was listening to her. She twirled around and around, pretending to be a ballerina. Then she nestled in her lap and listened to her tell a story about the past. The story was about a little girl who liked the ballet, just like her. She continued to talk about her mother and the strange cold camp where she could not brush her teeth. Finally, she yawned and snuggled closer to her. Her dreams were filled with a little girl practicing her ballet.

GRAMMAR FROM WRITING

Achieving Pronoun-Antecedent Agreement

A pronoun must agree with its antecedent in number, gender, and person. Some examples follow:

Some indefinite antecedents such as *all, some, any,* and *none* may require either a singular or a plural pronoun, depending on the meaning of the sentence.

Singular Antecedent	Pronoun
anybody, no one, somebody, everyone	his or her

Plural Antecedent	Pronoun
both, few, many, several	our, your, their

APPLYING WHAT YOU'VE LEARNED
On a separate sheet of paper, correct the sentences below.

1. Everyone brought their belongings to the camp.
2. None of them had his winter clothes.
3. Few of the people remained with his or her family.

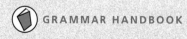

GRAMMAR HANDBOOK

For more information on pronoun–antecedent agreement, see page 1071 of the Grammar Handbook.

SETTLE FOR SECOND

WE LOVE

shop-till-you-drop sweepstakes

'TEEN

JULY 1995

what to say to **him?**

(we'll tell you!)

10 ways to fuller, shinier hair

practically free fashion

best buys under $30

QUIZ could you be chasing boys away?

babewatch! films &

GUYS MOUTH OFF About

106

READING THE WORLD

PORTRAYAL OF A GROUP

You've explored how writers create a particular image of a group or event. In our everyday world, advertisers, TV directors, and other media professionals are busy doing the same thing. How do these images affect your attitudes and beliefs? Take a closer look at how women are portrayed in the world around you.

View As you look at the image, jot down your thoughts. Do you know many people who look like this? What other information appears on this cover?

Interpret How would you summarize the portrayal of women in this image? How do the headlines contribute to the overall impression?

Discuss In a group, discuss various responses to the image. What key ideas influence the reactions that your classmates have? You might list them on a separate sheet or in your notebook. Now use the SkillBuilder on evaluating images to reinforce your understanding.

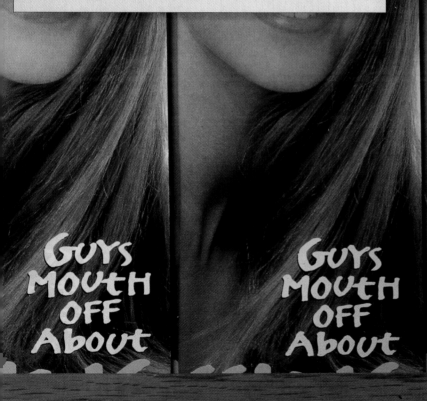

SkillBuilder

 CRITICAL THINKING

Evaluating Images

"Consider the source!" You've probably heard this warning before. Each time you view or read advertisements, magazines, newspapers, and television, you should consider why that source has chosen to portray a group or an event in a specific way. What image is being conveyed?

Why does the editor of a magazine choose to portray a group in a certain light? Who will be receiving the message a magazine conveys? What does that fact tell you about the message?

The next time you notice that a group or an event is portrayed by the media in a certain way, decide for yourself whether you agree with that portrayal.

APPLYING WHAT YOU'VE LEARNED
Use the image on this page as a starting point. Create a list of phrases that describe women as they are portrayed in the media.

In a group, evaluate other portrayals in the media such as

- the portrayal of traditional families
- the portrayal of the elderly
- the portrayal of teenagers

THE POWER OF HERITAGE

REFLECTING ON THEME

How would you define heritage? Would you describe it in terms of ethnic or racial background? Is it shaped by family, religious, or cultural traditions? In this part of Unit One, you will read about characters and real people who come to important realizations about their heritage and its power. You will also be asked to explore your own heritage.

What Do You Think? Create a pie graph showing the different aspects of your own heritage. Use separate labels, such as "Family," "Religion," "Social Groups," and "Ethnic Background" to identify each piece of your heritage pie. The sizes of the pieces should reflect the relative importance of each aspect of your heritage. The largest piece should represent the most important aspect; the smallest should represent the least important.

Tom Whitecloud
(1912–1972)
A Native American writer, doctor, and public servant

Robert Hayden
(1913–1980)
An African-American scholar and teacher— and celebrated poet

Teresa Paloma Acosta
(1949–)
Her Mexican heritage has inspired her poetry.

Langston Hughes
(1902–1967)
His poetry about African Americans has inspired generations.

Alice Walker
(1944–)
A daughter of poor farmers, now a major African-American voice in contemporary literature

Alice Walker	**Everyday Use** *Which daughter will inherit Grandma's quilts?*	110
Teresa Paloma Acosta	**My Mother Pieced Quilts** / INSIGHT *The fabric of memory*	120
Tom Whitecloud	**Blue Winds Dancing** *A long journey home*	124
D. H. Lawrence	**Piano** *The music stirs his memory.*	135
Robert Hayden	**Those Winter Sundays** *Remembering a father's sacrifice*	135

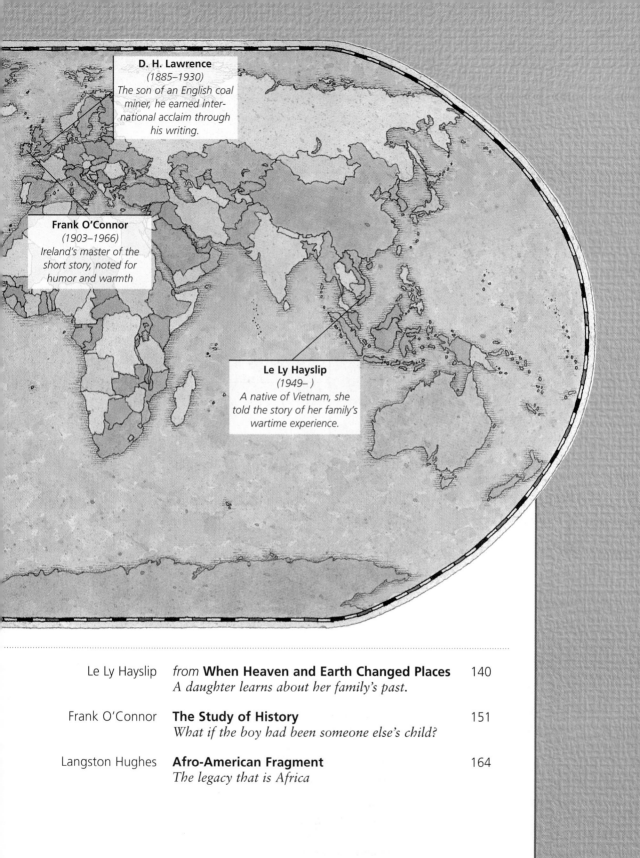

D. H. Lawrence
*(1885–1930)
The son of an English coal miner, he earned international acclaim through his writing.*

Frank O'Connor
*(1903–1966)
Ireland's master of the short story, noted for humor and warmth*

Le Ly Hayslip
*(1949–)
A native of Vietnam, she told the story of her family's wartime experience.*

<table>
<tr><td>Le Ly Hayslip</td><td>from **When Heaven and Earth Changed Places**
A daughter learns about her family's past.</td><td>140</td></tr>
<tr><td>Frank O'Connor</td><td>**The Study of History**
What if the boy had been someone else's child?</td><td>151</td></tr>
<tr><td>Langston Hughes</td><td>**Afro-American Fragment**
The legacy that is Africa</td><td>164</td></tr>
</table>

PREVIEWING

FICTION

Everyday Use
Alice Walker United States

PERSONAL CONNECTION

What aspects of your family's heritage are especially important to you? In your notebook, make a chart similar to the one shown. Under each heading in the chart, record one or more examples drawn from your heritage. For example, under "Language" you might write expressions that you have heard your parents or grandparents use. Then share your heritage chart with a small group of classmates. Be sure to save your work for use after you read the selection.

Heritage	
Family Treasures	Traditional Foods
Holidays	Language

HISTORICAL CONNECTION

This story is set in the rural South of the 1960s, a time when many African Americans sought to learn more about their heritage. The "black pride" movement, which grew out of the civil rights campaigns of that era, called upon African Americans to appreciate their African roots and to affirm all aspects of their cultural identity. The advocates of black pride were often young and rebellious; they were impatient with their elders, who they believed were too fearful of offending or displeasing whites. The movement helped to spur interest in black history, literature, art, and fashion.

As an expression of black pride, young people sometimes adopted African names and styles of dress. Others even changed their religious affiliations and practices. During this time, the Black Muslims gained national prominence. This group combined aspects of the Islamic religion (based on the teachings of Mohammed) with political activism. The Black Muslims encouraged blacks to separate from whites and to achieve economic independence.

READING CONNECTION

Drawing Conclusions In reading "Everyday Use," you will be using clues, facts, or other evidence to draw important conclusions about three women. As you read, jot down in your notebook what you conclude about each of the three women and her sense of heritage.

Using Your Reading Log Use your reading log to record your responses to the questions inserted at various points in this selection.

LASERLINKS
• HISTORICAL CONNECTION

110

Everyday Use

Alice Walker

Working Woman (1947),
Elizabeth Catlett. Oil on canvas,
courtesy of the Barnett-Aden Collection,
Museum of African American Art, Tampa, Florida.

I will wait for her in the yard that Maggie and I made so clean and wavy yesterday afternoon. A yard like this is more comfortable than most people know. It is not just a yard. It is like an extended living room.

When the hard clay is swept clean as a floor and the fine sand around the edges lined with tiny, irregular grooves, anyone can come and sit and look up into the elm tree and wait for the breezes that never come inside the house.

Maggie will be nervous until after her sister goes: she will stand hopelessly in corners, homely and ashamed of the burn scars down her arms and legs, eying her sister with a mixture of envy and awe. She thinks her sister has held life always in the palm of one hand, that "no" is a word the world never learned to say to her.

You've no doubt seen those TV shows where the child who has "made it" is confronted, as a surprise, by her own mother and father, tottering in weakly from backstage. (A pleasant surprise, of course: What would they do if parent and child came on the show only to curse out and insult each other?) On TV mother and child embrace and smile into each other's faces. Sometimes the mother and father weep, the child wraps them in her arms and leans across the table to tell how she would not have made it without their help. I have seen these programs. Sometimes I dream a dream in which Dee and I are suddenly brought together on a TV program of this sort. Out of a dark and soft-seated limousine I am ushered into a bright room filled with many people. There I meet a smiling, gray, sporty man like Johnny Carson who shakes my hand and tells me what a fine girl I have. Then we are on the stage and Dee is embracing me with tears in her eyes. She pins on my dress a large orchid, even though she has told me once that she thinks orchids are tacky flowers.

EVALUATE

What impression have you formed of Dee so far?

In real life I am a large, big-boned woman with rough, man-working hands. In the winter I wear flannel nightgowns to bed and overalls during the day. I can kill and clean a hog as mercilessly as a man. My fat keeps me hot in zero weather. I can work outside all day, breaking ice to get water for washing; I can eat pork liver cooked over the open fire minutes after it comes steaming from the hog. One winter I knocked a bull calf straight in the brain between the eyes with a sledge hammer and had the meat hung up to chill before nightfall. But of course all this does not show on television. I am the way my daughter would want me to be: a hundred pounds lighter, my skin like an uncooked barley pancake. My hair glistens in the hot bright lights. Johnny Carson has much to do to keep up with my quick and witty tongue.

But that is a mistake. I know even before I wake up. Who ever knew a Johnson with a quick tongue? Who can even imagine me look-ing a strange white man in the eye? It seems to me I have talked to them always with one foot raised in flight, with my head turned in which-ever way is farthest from them. Dee, though. She would always look anyone in the eye. Hesitation was no part of her nature.

How do I look, Mama?" Maggie says, showing just enough of her thin body enveloped in pink skirt and red blouse for me to know she's there, almost hidden by the door.

"Come out into the yard," I say.

Have you ever seen a lame animal, perhaps a dog run over by some careless person rich enough to own a car, <u>sidle</u> up to someone who is ignorant enough to be kind to him? That is the way my Maggie walks. She has been like this, chin on chest, eyes on ground, feet in shuffle, ever since the fire that burned the other house to the ground.

Dee is lighter than Maggie, with nicer hair and a fuller figure. She's a woman now, though sometimes I forget. How long ago was it that the other house burned? Ten, twelve years? Sometimes I can still hear the flames and feel Maggie's arms sticking to me, her hair smoking and her dress falling off her in little black papery flakes. Her eyes seemed stretched open, blazed open by the flames reflected in them. And Dee. I see her standing off under the sweet gum tree she used to dig gum out of; a look of concentration on her face as she watched the last dingy gray board of the house fall in toward the red-hot brick chimney. Why don't you do a dance around the ashes? I'd wanted to ask her. She had hated the house that much.

I used to think she hated Maggie, too. But that was before we raised the money, the church and me, to send her to Augusta[1] to school. She used to read to us without pity; forcing words, lies, other folks' habits, whole lives upon us two, sitting trapped and ignorant underneath her voice. She washed us in a river of make-believe, burned us with a lot of knowledge we didn't necessarily need to know. Pressed us to her with the serious way she read, to shove us away at just the moment, like dimwits, we seemed about to understand.

Dee wanted nice things. A yellow organdy dress to wear to her graduation from high school; black pumps to match a green suit she'd made from an old suit somebody gave me. She was determined to stare down any disaster in her efforts. Her eyelids would not flicker for minutes at a time. Often I fought off the temptation to shake her. At sixteen she had a style of her own: and knew what style was.

I never had an education myself. After second grade the school was closed down. Don't ask me why: in 1927 colored asked fewer questions than they do now. Sometimes Maggie reads to me. She stumbles along good-naturedly but can't see well. She knows she is not bright. Like good looks and money, quickness passed her by. She will marry John Thomas (who has mossy teeth in an earnest face) and then I'll be free to sit here and I guess just sing church songs to myself. Although I never was a good singer. Never could carry a tune. I was always better at a man's job. I used to love to milk till I was hooked in the side in '49. Cows are soothing and slow and don't bother you, unless you try to milk them the wrong way.

I have <u>deliberately</u> turned my back on the house. It is three rooms, just like the one that burned, except the roof is tin; they don't make shingle roofs any more. There are no real windows, just some holes cut in the sides, like the portholes in a ship, but not round and not square, with rawhide holding the shutters up on the outside. This house is in a pasture, too, like the other one. No doubt when

> **EVALUATE**
>
> What conclusions have you drawn so far about the narrator and Maggie?

---

1. **Augusta:** a city in Georgia.

113

Nia: Purpose (1991), Varnette Honeywood. Monoprint, collection of Karen Kennedy.
Copyright © Varnette P. Honeywood, 1991.

Dee sees it she will want to tear it down. She wrote me once that no matter where we "choose" to live, she will manage to come see us. But she will never bring her friends. Maggie and I thought about this and Maggie asked me, "Mama, when did Dee ever *have* any friends?"

She had a few. Furtive boys in pink shirts hanging about on wash-day after school. Nervous girls who never laughed. Impressed with her they worshiped the well-turned phrase, the cute shape, the scalding humor that erupted like bubbles in lye. She read to them.

When she was courting Jimmy T she didn't have much time to pay to us, but turned all her faultfinding power on him. He *flew* to marry a cheap city girl from a family of ignorant flashy people. She hardly had time to recompose herself.

When she comes I will meet—but there they are!

Maggie attempts to make a dash for the house, in her shuffling way, but I stay her with my hand. "Come back here," I say. And she stops and tries to dig a well in the sand with her toe.

It is hard to see them clearly through the strong sun. But even the first glimpse of leg out of the car tells me it is Dee. Her feet were always neat-looking, as if God himself had shaped them with a certain style. From the other side of the car comes a short, stocky man. Hair is all over his head a foot long and hanging from his chin like a kinky mule tail. I hear Maggie suck in her breath. "Uhnnnh," is what it sounds like. Like when you see the wriggling end of a snake just in front of your foot on the road. "Uhnnnh."

Dee next. A dress down to the ground, in this hot weather. A dress so loud it hurts my eyes. There are yellows and oranges enough to throw back the light of the sun. I feel my whole face warming from the heat waves it throws out. Ear-rings gold, too, and hanging down to her shoulders. Bracelets dang-ling and making noises when she moves her arm up to shake the folds of the dress out of her armpits. The dress is loose and flows, and as she walks closer, I like it. I hear Maggie go "Uhnnnh" again. It is her sister's hair. It stands straight up like the wool on a sheep. It is black as night and around the edges are two long pigtails that rope about like small lizards disappearing behind her ears.

"Wa-su-zo-Tean-o!" she says, coming on in that gliding way the dress makes her move. The short stocky fellow with the hair to his navel is all grinning and he follows up with "Asalamalakim,[2] my mother and sister!" He moves to hug Maggie but she falls back, right up against the back of my chair. I feel her trembling there and when I look up I see the perspiration falling off her chin.

"Don't get up," says Dee. Since I am stout it takes something of a push. You can see me trying to move a second or two before I make it. She turns, showing white heels through her sandals, and goes back to the car. Out she peeks next with a Polaroid. She stoops down quickly and lines up picture after picture of me sitting

> HER FEET WERE
> ALWAYS NEAT–LOOKING,
> AS IF GOD HIMSELF HAD
> SHAPED THEM

---

2. **Wa-su-zo-Tean-o!** (wä-sōō′zō-tē′nō) . . . **Asalamalakim!** (ə-săl′ə-mə-lăk′əm): greetings used by members of the Black Muslims.

there in front of the house with Maggie cowering behind me. She never takes a shot without making sure the house is included. When a cow comes nibbling around the edge of the yard she snaps it and me and Maggie *and* the house. Then she puts the Polaroid in the back seat of the car, and comes up and kisses me on the forehead.

Meanwhile Asalamalakim is going through motions with Maggie's hand. Maggie's hand is as limp as a fish, and probably as cold, despite the sweat, and she keeps trying to pull it back. It looks like Asalamalakim wants to shake hands but wants to do it fancy. Or maybe he don't know how people shake hands. Anyhow, he soon gives up on Maggie.

"Well," I say. "Dee."

"No, Mama," she says. "Not 'Dee,' Wangero Leewanika Kemanjo!"[3]

"What happened to 'Dee'?" I wanted to know.

"She's dead," Wangero said. "I couldn't bear it any longer, being named after the people who oppress me."

"You know as well as me you was named after your aunt Dicie," I said. Dicie is my sister. She named Dee. We called her "Big Dee" after Dee was born.

"But who was *she* named after?" asked Wangero.

"I guess after Grandma Dee," I said.

"And who was she named after?" asked Wangero.

"Her mother," I said, and saw Wangero was getting tired. "That's about as far back as I can trace it," I said. Though, in fact, I probably could have carried it back beyond the Civil War through the branches.

"Well," said Asalamalakim, "there you are."

"Uhnnnh," I heard Maggie say.

"There I was not," I said, "before 'Dicie' cropped up in our family, so why should I try to trace it that far back?"

He just stood there grinning, looking down on me like somebody inspecting a Model A[4] car. Every once in a while he and Wangero sent eye signals over my head.

"How do you pronounce this name?" I asked.

"You don't have to call me by it if you don't want to," said Wangero.

"Why shouldn't I?" I asked. "If that's what you want us to call you, we'll call you."

"I know it might sound awkward at first," said Wangero.

"I'll get used to it," I said. "Ream it out again."

Well, soon we got the name out of the way. Asalamalakim had a name twice as long and three times as hard. After I tripped over it two or three times he told me to just call him Hakim-a-barber.[5] I wanted to ask him was he a barber, but I didn't really think he was, so I didn't ask.

"You must belong to those beef-cattle peoples down the road," I said. They said "Asalamalakim" when they met you, too, but they didn't shake hands. Always too busy: feeding the cattle, fixing the fences, putting up salt-lick shelters, throwing down hay. When the white folks poisoned some of the herd the men

***

"I COULDN'T BEAR IT ANY LONGER, BEING NAMED AFTER THE PEOPLE WHO OPPRESS ME."

***

3. **Wangero Leewanika Kemanjo** (wän-gär′ō lē-wä-nē′kə kĕ-män′jō).

4. **Model A:** an automobile manufactured by Ford from 1927 to 1931.

5. **Hakim-a-barber** (hä-kē′mə-bär′bər).

stayed up all night with rifles in their hands. I walked a mile and a half just to see the sight.

Hakim-a-barber said, "I accept some of their doctrines, but farming and raising cattle is not my style." (They didn't tell me, and I didn't ask, whether Wangero (Dee) had really gone and married him.)

We sat down to eat and right away he said he didn't eat collards and pork was unclean. Wangero, though, went on through the chitlins and corn bread, the greens and everything else. She talked a blue streak over the sweet potatoes. Everything delighted her. Even the fact that we still used the benches her daddy made for the table when we couldn't afford to buy chairs.

"Oh, Mama!" she cried. Then turned to Hakim-a-barber. "I never knew how lovely these benches are. You can feel the rump prints," she said, running her hands underneath her and along the bench. Then she gave a sigh and her hand closed over Grandma Dee's butter dish. "That's it!" she said. "I knew there was something I wanted to ask you if I could have." She jumped up from the table and went over in the corner where the churn stood, the milk in it clabber[6] by now. She looked at the churn and looked at it.

"This churn top is what I need," she said. "Didn't Uncle Buddy whittle it out of a tree you all used to have?"

"Yes," I said.

"Uh huh," she said happily. "And I want the dasher,[7] too."

"Uncle Buddy whittle that, too?" asked the barber.

Dee (Wangero) looked up at me.

"Aunt Dee's first husband whittled the dash," said Maggie so low you almost couldn't hear her. "His name was Henry, but they called him Stash."

"Maggie's brain is like an elephant's," Wangero said, laughing. "I can use the churn top as a centerpiece for the alcove table," she said, sliding a plate over the churn, "and I'll think of something artistic to do with the dasher."

When she finished wrapping the dasher the handle stuck out. I took it for a moment in my hands. You didn't even have to look close to see where hands pushing the dasher up and down to make butter had left a kind of sink in the wood. In fact, there were a lot of small sinks; you could see where thumbs and fingers had sunk into the wood. It was beautiful light yellow wood, from a tree that grew in the yard where Big Dee and Stash had lived.

After dinner Dee (Wangero) went to the trunk at the foot of my bed and started rifling through it. Maggie hung back in the kitchen over the dishpan. Out came Wangero with two quilts. They had been pieced by Grandma Dee and then Big Dee and me had hung them on the quilt frames on the front porch and quilted them. One was in the Lone Star pattern. The other was Walk Around the Mountain. In both of them were scraps of dresses Grandma Dee had worn fifty and more years ago. Bits and pieces of Grandpa Jarrell's Paisley shirts. And one teeny faded blue piece, about the size of a penny matchbox, that was from Great Grandpa Ezra's uniform that he wore in the Civil War.

---

6. **clabber:** curdled milk.

7. **dasher:** the plunger of a churn, a device formerly used to stir cream or milk to produce butter.

WORDS TO KNOW **doctrine** (dŏk′trĭn) *n.* a principle or rule taught by a religious, political, or philosophic group

117

"Mama," Wangero said sweet as a bird. "Can I have these old quilts?"

I heard something fall in the kitchen, and a minute later the kitchen door slammed.

"Why don't you take one or two of the others?" I asked. "These old things was just done by me and Big Dee from some tops your grandma pieced before she died."

"No," said Wangero. "I don't want those. They are stitched around the borders by machine."

"That'll make them last better," I said.

"That's not the point," said Wangero. "These are all pieces of dresses Grandma used to wear. She did all this stitching by hand. Imagine!" She held the quilts securely in her arms, stroking them.

"Some of the pieces, like those lavender ones, come from old clothes her mother handed down to her," I said, moving up to touch the quilts. Dee (Wangero) moved back just enough so that I couldn't reach the quilts. They already belonged to her.

"Imagine!" she breathed again, clutching them closely to her bosom.

"The truth is," I said, "I promised to give them quilts to Maggie, for when she marries John Thomas."

She gasped like a bee had stung her.

"Maggie can't appreciate these quilts!" she said. "She'd probably be backward enough to put them to everyday use."

"I reckon she would," I said. "God knows I been saving 'em for long enough with nobody using 'em. I hope she will!" I didn't want to bring up how I had offered Dee (Wangero) a quilt when she went away to college. Then she had told me they were old-fashioned, out of style.

"But they're *priceless!*" she was saying now, furiously; for she has a temper. "Maggie would put them on the bed and in five years they'd be in rags. Less than that!"

"She can always make some more," I said. "Maggie knows how to quilt."

Dee (Wangero) looked at me with hatred. "You just will not understand. The point is *these* quilts, these quilts!"

"Well," I said, stumped. "What would *you* do with them?"

"Hang them," she said. As if that was the only thing you *could* do with quilts.

Maggie by now was standing in the door. I could almost hear the sound her feet made as they scraped over each other.

"She can have them, Mama," she said, like somebody used to never winning anything, or having anything reserved for her. "I can 'member Grandma Dee without the quilts."

I looked at her hard. She had filled her bottom lip with checkerberry snuff and it gave her face a kind of dopey, hangdog look. It was Grandma Dee and Big Dee who taught her how to quilt herself. She stood there with her scarred hands hidden in the folds of her skirt. She looked at her sister with something like fear but she wasn't mad at her. This was Maggie's portion. This was the way she knew God to work.

When I looked at her like that something hit me in the top of my head and ran down to the soles of my feet. Just like when I'm in church and the spirit of God touches me and I get happy and shout. I did something I never had done before: hugged Maggie to me, then dragged her on into the room, snatched the quilts out of Miss Wangero's hands and dumped them into Maggie's lap. Maggie just sat there on my bed with her mouth open.

"Take one or two of the others," I said to Dee.

But she turned without a word and went out to Hakim-a-barber.

"You just don't understand," she said, as Maggie and I came out to the car.

"What don't I understand?" I wanted to know.

"Your heritage," she said. And then she turned to Maggie, kissed her, and said, "You ought to try to make something of yourself, too, Maggie. It's really a new day for us. But from the way you and Mama still live you'd never know it."

She put on some sunglasses that hid every-

QUESTION

What does Dee mean when she says that her mother doesn't understand her heritage?

thing above the tip of her nose and her chin. Maggie smiled; maybe at the sunglasses. But a real smile, not scared. After we watched the car dust settle I asked Maggie to bring me a dip of snuff. And then the two of us sat there just enjoying, until it was time to go in the house and go to bed. ❖

My Mother Pieced Quilts

Teresa Paloma Acosta

they were just meant as covers
in winters
as weapons
against pounding january winds

5 but it was just that every morning I awoke to
these
october ripened canvases
passed my hand across their cloth faces
and began to wonder how you pieced
all these together

10 these strips of gentle communion cotton and
flannel nightgowns
wedding organdies
dime store velvets

how you shaped patterns square and oblong
and round
positioned
15 balanced
then cemented them
with your thread
a steel needle
a thimble

20 how the thread darted in and out
galloping along the frayed edges, tucking
them in
as you did us at night
oh how you stretched and turned and rearranged
your michigan spring faded curtain pieces
25 my father's santa fe work shirt[1]
the summer denims, the tweeds of fall
in the evening you sat at your canvas
—our cracked linoleum floor the drawing
board
me lounging on your arm
30 and you staking out the plan
whether to put the lilac purple of easter
against the red plaid of winter-going-

into-spring
whether to mix a yellow with blue and white
and paint the
corpus christi[2] noon when my father held
your hand
35 whether to shape a five-point star from the
somber black silk you wore to grandmother's
funeral

you were the river current
carrying the roaring notes
forming them into pictures of a little boy
reclining
40 a swallow flying
you were the caravan master at the reins
driving your threaded needle artillery across
the mosaic cloth bridges
delivering yourself in separate testimonies.

oh mother you plunged me sobbing and
laughing
45 into our past
into the river crossing at five
into the spinach fields
into the plainview[3] cotton rows
into tuberculosis wards
50 into braids and muslin dresses
sewn hard and taut to withstand the
thrashings of twenty-five years

stretched out they lay
armed/ready/shouting/celebrating

knotted with love
55 the quilts sing on

---

1. **santa fe work shirt:** work shirt bearing the insignia of the Santa Fe Railroad.
2. **corpus christi:** of Corpus Christi, a port city in southern Texas.
3. **plainview:** of Plainview, a city in northwestern Texas.

RESPONDING
OPTIONS

FROM PERSONAL RESPONSE TO CRITICAL ANALYSIS

REFLECT

1. How did you react to the characters in this story? Briefly describe your reactions in your notebook.

RETHINK

2. Which character in this story do you like best, and which do you like least? Review the notes you jotted down about the three women characters.

3. Do you agree with the narrator's decision to give the quilts to Maggie rather than to Dee? Explain your answer.

4. Who do you think better appreciates her heritage, Dee or Maggie?
   Consider
   - why Dee takes photographs of her family and their house
   - which sister knows more about the family's history
   - Dee's African clothing, name, hairstyle, and greeting
   - why Dee now wants the churn and the quilts
   - Maggie's own ability to quilt

5. In your opinion, what is Alice Walker's ultimate judgment of Dee? In supporting your opinion, cite examples of what Walker might admire in Dee and what she might dislike about Dee.

RELATE

6. Which of the characters in "Everyday Use" do you think would most appreciate the quilts described in the Insight poem "My Mother Pieced Quilts"?

7. In recent years, many people have come to take an interest in their heritage—both family traditions and cultural past. What do you think accounts for this interest?

ANOTHER PATHWAY

Cooperative Learning

Imagine a scenario in which the narrator and Dee are reunited on a television show after a long separation. With three of your classmates, decide who should play the parts of the narrator, Dee, Maggie, and the television host, then role-play the scenario.

QUICKWRITES

1. Review Walker's vivid and imaginative descriptions of her characters. Then write a **description** of the physical appearance of someone in your family.

2. Maggie and Dee are obviously very different. Draft an **essay** describing how you are different from one of your brothers, sisters, or best friends.

3. If you were going to direct a film based on this short story, what actors would you choose to play the narrator, Maggie, Dee, and "Hakim-a-barber"? Write a **memo** to the producer of the film, explaining your choices.

4. Write a **sequel** showing what might happen at a Johnson family reunion held ten years after the events of this story.

📁 *PORTFOLIO Save your writing. You may want to use it later as a springboard to a piece for your portfolio.*

LITERARY CONCEPTS

Figurative language is language that communicates ideas other than the literal meanings of the words. Although what is said is not literally true, it stimulates vivid pictures or concepts in the mind of the reader. An example in this selection is the passage in which Dee's pigtails are said to "rope about like small lizards disappearing behind her ears." Look through the story for three other examples of figurative language, and compare your findings with those of another student.

LITERARY LINKS

Compare and contrast the parent-child relationships portrayed in this story with those portrayed in Amy Tan's "Two Kinds."

CRITIC'S CORNER

A critic has written that Walker's poetry "reveals a sensitive African-American intellectual coming to terms with disparate strands of her own existence." How might this statement be applied to her writing of this story?

ALTERNATIVE ACTIVITIES

1. Design a **story quilt** that depicts important characters, objects, and events in "Everyday Use." Be sure to use colors that help convey the mood of the story.

2. Create a **collage, mobile,** or **sculpture,** using objects that you associate with your family. For example, you might include photographs, pieces of cloth, toys, household objects, recipe cards, invitations, and graduation programs. Drawings or magazine photographs of these objects can also be included. You might find it useful to refer to the heritage chart you created for the Personal Connection on page 110.

ACROSS THE CURRICULUM

History With a partner, research the sharecropping system of the rural South. Find out how sharecropping developed as an economic system and how it operated in the 20th century. Then review the story to find details that suggest the Johnson family's participation in this system. Present your findings in an oral report.

Economics Research the activities of the Black Muslim movement in the 1960s and 1970s. Find out about their ideas for encouraging the economic independence of African Americans. Where possible, describe economic enterprises that were established by the Black Muslims. Present your findings in a written report.

ART CONNECTION

Look again at the painting *Working Woman* on page 111. What qualities of this painting are also present in "Everyday Use"?

Detail of *Working Woman* (1947), Elizabeth Catlett. Oil on canvas, courtesy of the Barnett-Aden Collection, Museum of African American Art, Tampa, Florida.

WORDS TO KNOW

Review the Words to Know at the bottom of the selection pages. Then, on your paper, write the word that best completes each sentence.

1. The presence of Dee seemed to _____ Maggie, making it difficult for her to feel comfortable.

2. Dee _____ dressed in clothing that expressed her African heritage.

3. Maggie's _____ expression showed her lack of self-confidence.

4. Maggie would often _____ up to her mother for protection and comfort.

5. The narrator of the story believes in the _____ of hard work and simple living.

ALICE WALKER

In the poems, short stories, and novels of the Pulitzer Prize–winning writer Alice Walker, African-American women struggle to survive in the face of poverty, alienation, racism, and sexism. These issues are quite familiar to Walker, who, like Dee and Maggie in "Everyday Use," was a daughter of poor Georgia sharecroppers.

Although neither of her parents made it past the fifth grade and she was nearly blinded by a shot from her brother's BB gun when she was eight, Walker was determined to succeed in

1944–

school. She started school early and graduated at the top of her high school class. After college, she worked for the civil rights movement in Mississippi, traveled, and taught at a number of universities. Today, she is considered an important voice in American literature.

OTHER WORKS *Revolutionary Petunias and Other Poems, In Love and Trouble: Stories of Black Women, The Color Purple, In Search of Our Mothers' Gardens, Horses Make a Landscape Look More Beautiful*

PREVIEWING

Blue Winds Dancing
Tom Whitecloud United States

PERSONAL CONNECTION

When and where do you feel most comfortable or accepted? Who or what makes you feel as if you really belong? Discuss with classmates the different people, places, and situations that give you a sense of belonging.

CULTURAL CONNECTION

Tom Whitecloud's sense of belonging came from a place called home, a Chippewa (chĭp'ə-wô') village in Wisconsin where he spent much of his youth. The Chippewa, also called Ojibwa (ō-jĭb'wā'), are a Native American people of the Great Lakes region. They traditionally lived in small villages on the edge of the area's vast forests, where birch trees provided bark used for shelters, canoes, arts and crafts, and the sacred scrolls on which Chippewa medicine men scratched symbols recording important events and rituals. Chippewa customs have also been preserved orally; even today, some Chippewa gather at the local medicine lodge, celebrating their traditions and perpetuating their culture in song, dance, and storytelling.

In "Blue Winds Dancing," Tom Whitecloud reflects on his heritage as he makes a Christmastime journey home from college in California. His journey took place during the Great Depression of the 1930s, when travelers too poor to pay train fare often hid themselves on freight trains to get a free ride.

WRITING CONNECTION

What comes to mind when you hear the word *outsider?* What does a person who is an outsider look like? Why might a person feel like an outsider? In your notebook, write a paragraph or two about someone who is an outsider, and tell what the person might do to satisfy his or her need for a sense of belonging. Keep these issues in mind as you read about Tom Whitecloud's journey.

Chippewa settlement in Wisconsin (about 1939).
Courtesy of Milwaukee (Wisconsin) Public Museum.

LASERLINKS
• *HISTORICAL CONNECTION*

Blue Winds Dancing

Tom Whitecloud

There is a moon out tonight. Moon and stars and clouds tipped with moonlight. And there is a fall wind blowing in my heart. Ever since this evening, when against a fading sky I saw geese wedge southward. They were going home. . . . Now I try to study, but against the pages I see them again, driving southward. Going home.

Across the valley there are heavy mountains holding up the night sky, and beyond the mountains there is home. Home, and peace, and the beat of drums, and blue winds dancing over snow fields. The Indian lodge will fill with my people, and our gods will come and sit among them. I should be there then. I should be at home.

But home is beyond the mountains, and I am here. Here where fall hides in the valleys, and winter never comes down from the mountains. Here where all the trees grow in rows; the palms stand stiffly by the roadsides, and in the groves the orange trees line in military rows and endlessly bear fruit. Beautiful, yes; there is always beauty in order, in rows of growing things! But it is the beauty of captivity. A pine fighting for existence on a windy knoll[1] is much more beautiful.

In my Wisconsin, the leaves change before the snows come. In the air there is the smell of wild rice and venison cooking; and when the winds come whispering through the forests, they carry the smell of rotting leaves. In the evenings, the loon calls, lonely; and birds sing their last songs before leaving. Bears dig roots and eat late fall berries, fattening for their long winter sleep. Later, when the first snows fall, one awakens in the morning to find the world white and beautiful and clean. Then one can look back over his trail and see the tracks following. In the woods there are tracks of deer and snowshoe rabbits, and long streaks where partridges slide to alight. Chipmunks make tiny footprints on the limbs; and one can hear squirrels busy in hollow trees, sorting acorns. Soft lake waves wash the shores, and sunsets burst each evening over the lakes and make them look as if they were afire.

That land which is my home! Beautiful, calm—where there is no hurry to get anywhere, no driving to keep up in a race that knows no ending and no goal. No classes where men talk and talk and then stop now and then to hear their own words come back to them from the students. No constant peering into the maelstrom of one's mind; no worries about grades and honors; no hysterical preparing for life until that life is half over; no anxiety about one's place in the thing they call Society.

I hear again the ring of axes in deep woods, the crunch of snow beneath my feet. I feel again

---

1. **knoll** (nōl): a small, rounded hill.

WORDS TO KNOW

maelstrom (mãl'strəm) *n.* a violent turbulence; whirlpool

125

the smooth velvet of ghost-birch bark. I hear the rhythm of the drums. . . . I am tired. I am weary of trying to keep up this bluff of being civilized. Being civilized means trying to do everything you don't want to, never doing anything you want to. It means dancing to the strings of custom and tradition; it means living in houses and never knowing or caring who is next door. These civilized white men want us to be like them—always dissatisfied—getting a hill and wanting a mountain.

Then again, maybe I am not tired. Maybe I'm licked. Maybe I am just not smart enough to grasp these things that go to make up civilization. Maybe I am just too lazy to think hard enough to keep up.

Still, I know my people have many things that civilization has taken from the whites. They know how to give; how to tear one's piece of meat in two and share it with one's brother. They know how to sing—how to make each man his own songs and sing them; for their music they do not have to listen to other men singing over a radio. They know how to make things with their hands, how to shape beads into designs and make a thing of beauty from a piece of birch bark.

But we are inferior. It is terrible to have to feel inferior; to have to read reports of intelligence tests and learn that one's race is behind. It is terrible to sit in classes and hear men tell you that your people worship sticks of wood—that your gods are all false, that the Manitou[2] forgot your people and did not write them a book.

I am tired. I want to walk again among the ghost-birches. I want to see the leaves turn in autumn, the smoke rise from the lodgehouses, and to feel the blue winds. I want to hear the drums; I want to hear the drums and feel the blue whispering winds.

There is a train wailing into the night. The trains go across the mountains. It would be easy to catch a freight. They will say he has gone back to the blanket;[3] I don't care. The dance at Christmas. . . .

A bunch of bums warming at a tiny fire talk politics and women and joke about the Relief and the WPA[4] and smoke cigarettes. These men in caps and overcoats and dirty overalls living on the outskirts of civilization are free, but they pay the price of being free in civilization. They are outcasts. I remember a sociology professor lecturing on adjustment to society; hobos and prostitutes and criminals are individuals who never adjusted, he said. He could learn a lot if he came and listened to a bunch of bums talk. He would learn that work and a woman and a place to hang his hat are all the ordinary man wants. These are all he wants, but other men are not content to let him want only these. He must be taught to want radios and automobiles and a new suit every spring. Progress would stop if he did not want these things. I listen to hear if there is any talk of communism or socialism in the hobo jungles. There is none. At best there is a sort of disgusted philosophy about life. They seem to think there should be a better distribution of wealth, or more work, or something. But they are not <u>rabid</u> about it. The radicals live in the cities.

I find a fellow headed for Albuquerque and talk road-talk with him. "It is hard to ride fruit cars. Bums break in. Better to wait for a cattle

---

2. **Manitou** (măn′ĭ-tōo′): in the traditional religious beliefs of the Chippewa and many other Native Americans, the deity or spiritual force that permeates the world and is possessed to some degree by every being.

3. **gone back to the blanket:** returned to the Native American tribal way of life.

4. **the Relief and the WPA:** public assistance and the Works Progress Administration—programs set up by the federal government during the Great Depression of the 1930s to combat unemployment and poverty.

WORDS TO KNOW

rabid (răb′ĭd) *adj.* extremely enthusiastic; fanatical

Descending Stars, Zoltan Szabo. 9″ × 10½″.

car going back to the Middle West and ride that." We catch the next eastbound and walk the tops until we find a cattle car. Inside, we crouch near the forward wall, huddle, and try to sleep. I feel peaceful and content at last. I am going home. The cattle car rocks. I sleep.

Morning and the desert. Noon and the Salton Sea, lying more lifeless than a <u>mirage</u> under a somber sun in a pale sky. Skeleton mountains rearing on the skyline, thrusting out of the desert floor, all rock and shadow and edges. Desert. Good country for an Indian reservation. . . .

Yuma[5] and the muddy Colorado. Night again, and I wait shivering for the dawn.

Phoenix. Pima[6] country. Mountains that look like cardboard sets on a forgotten stage. Tucson. Papago[7] country. Giant cacti that look like <u>petrified</u> hitchhikers along the highways. Apache[8] country. At El Paso my road-buddy decides to

---

5. **Yuma** (yōō′mə): a city in southwestern Arizona.

6. **Pima** (pē′mə): a Native American people of south central Arizona.

7. **Papago** (păp′ə-gō′): a Native American people of southern Arizona and northwestern Mexico.

8. **Apache** (ə-păch′ē): a Native American people of southeastern Arizona, southwestern New Mexico, and nearby areas.

WORDS TO KNOW **mirage** (mĭ-räzh′) *n.* an optical illusion producing the appearance of water where none exists
petrified (pĕt′rə-fīd′) *adj.* having been turned to stone **petrify** *v.*

127

go on to Houston. I leave him and head north to the mesa[9] country. Las Cruces and the terrible Organ Mountains, jagged peaks that instill fear and wondering. Albuquerque. Pueblos along the Rio Grande. On the boardwalk there are some Indian women in colored sashes selling bits of pottery. The stone age offering its art to the twentieth century. They hold up a piece and fix the tourist with black eyes until, embarrassed, he buys or turns away. I feel suddenly angry that my people should have to do such things for a living. . . .

So many things seem to be clear now that I am away from school and do not have to worry about some man's opinion of my ideas.

Santa Fe trains are fast, and they keep them pretty clean of bums. I decide to hurry and ride passenger coal tenders.[10] Hide in the dark, judge the speed of the train as it leaves, and then dash out and catch it. I hug the cold steel wall of the tender and think of the roaring fire in the engine ahead and of the passengers back in the dining car reading their papers over hot coffee. Beneath me there is a blur of rails. Death would come quick if my hands should freeze and I fall. Up over the Sangre De Cristo range, around cliffs and through canyons to Denver. Bitter cold here, and I must watch out for Denver Bob. He is a railroad bull[11] who has thrown bums from fast freights. I miss him. It is too cold, I suppose. On north to the Sioux[12] country.

Small towns lit for the coming Christmas. On the streets of one I see a beam-shouldered young farmer gazing into a window filled with shining

silver toasters. He is tall and wears a blue shirt buttoned, with no tie. His young wife by his side looks at him hopefully. He wants decorations for his place to hang his hat to please his woman. . . .

Northward again. Minnesota, and great white fields of snow; frozen lakes, and dawn running into dusk without noon. Long forests wearing white. Bitter cold, and one night the northern lights. I am nearing home.

I reach Woodruff[13] at midnight. Suddenly I am afraid, now that I am but twenty miles from home. Afraid of what my father will say, afraid of being looked on as a stranger by my own people. I sit by a fire and think about myself and all other young Indians. We just don't seem to fit in anywhere—certainly not among the whites and not among the older people. I think again about the learned sociology professor and his professing. So many things seem to be clear now that I am away from school and do not have to worry about some man's opinion of my ideas. It is easy to think while looking at dancing flames.

Morning. I spend the day cleaning up and buying some presents for my family with what is left of my money. Nothing much, but a gift is a gift, if a man buys it with his last quarter. I wait until evening, then start up the track toward home.

Christmas Eve comes in on a north wind. Snow clouds hang over the pines, and the night

---

9. **mesa** (mā′sə): a broad, flat-topped hill with clifflike sides, common in the southwestern United States.

10. **ride passenger coal tenders:** illegally hitch rides on the railroad cars that carry coal as fuel for the passenger trains' steam locomotives.

11. **railroad bull:** a guard employed by a railway to eject nonpaying passengers.

12. **Sioux** (sōō): a group of Native American peoples of northern Nebraska, North and South Dakota, and nearby areas.

13. **Woodruff:** a town in northern Wisconsin.

comes early. Walking along the railroad bed, I feel the calm peace of snowbound forests on either side of me. I take my time; I am back in a world where time does not mean so much now. I am alone; alone but not nearly so lonely as I was back on the campus at school. Those are never lonely who love the snow and the pines; never lonely when the pines are wearing white shawls and snow crunches coldly underfoot. In the woods I know there are the tracks of deer and rabbit; I know that if I leave the rails and go into the woods, I shall find them. I walk along feeling glad because my legs are light and my feet seem to know that they are home. A deer comes out of the woods just ahead of me and stands silhouetted on the rails. The North, I feel, has welcomed me home. I watch him and am glad that I do not wish for a gun. He goes into the woods quietly, leaving only the design of his tracks in the snow. I walk on. Now and then I pass a field, white under the night sky, with houses at the far end. Smoke comes from the chimneys of the houses, and I try to tell what sort of wood each is burning by the smoke; some burn pine, others aspen, others tamarack. There is one from which comes black coal smoke that rises lazily and drifts out over the tops of the trees. I like to watch houses and try to imagine what might be happening in them.

Just as a light snow begins to fall, I cross the reservation boundary; somehow it seems as though I have stepped into another world. Deep woods in a white-and-black winter night. A faint trail leading to the village.

The railroad on which I stand comes from a city sprawled by a lake—a city with a million people who walk around without seeing one another; a city sucking the life from all the country around; a city with stores and police and intellectuals and criminals and movies and apartment houses; a city with its politics and libraries and zoos.

Laughing, I go into the woods. As I cross a frozen lake, I begin to hear the drums. Soft in the night the drums beat. It is like the pulse beat of the world. The white line of the lake ends at a black forest, and above the trees the blue winds are dancing.

I come to the outlying houses of the village. Simple box houses, etched black in the night. From one or two windows soft lamplight falls on the snow. Christmas here, too, but it does not mean much; not much in the way of parties and presents. Joe Sky will get drunk. Alex Bodidash will buy his children red mittens and a new sled. Alex is a Carlisle man[14] and tries to keep his home up to white standards. White standards. Funny that my people should be ever falling farther behind. The more they try to imitate whites, the more tragic the result. Yet they want us to be imitation white men. About all we imitate well are their vices.

The village is not a sight to instill pride, yet I am not ashamed; one can never be ashamed of his own people when he knows they have dreams as beautiful as white snow on a tall pine.

Father and my brother and sister are seated around the table as I walk in. Father stares at me for a moment, then I am in his arms, crying on his shoulder. I give them the presents I have brought, and my throat tightens as I watch my sister save carefully bits of red string from the packages. I hide my feelings by wrestling with my brother when he strikes my shoulder in token of affection. Father looks at me, and I know he

---

14. **Carlisle** (kär-līl′) **man:** a graduate of the Carlisle Indian School in Pennsylvania, which stressed assimilation into white society.

has many questions, but he seems to know why I have come. He tells me to go on alone to the lodge, and he will follow.

I walk along the trail to the lodge, watching the northern lights forming in the heavens. White waving ribbons that seem to pulsate with the rhythm of the drums. Clean snow creaks beneath my feet, and a soft wind sighs through the trees, singing to me. Everything seems to say, "Be happy! You are home now—you are free. You are among friends—we are your friends; we, the trees, and the snow, and the lights." I follow the trail to the lodge. My feet are light, my heart seems to sing to the music, and I hold my head high. Across white snow fields blue winds are dancing.

Before the lodge door I stop, afraid. I wonder if my people will remember me. I wonder—"Am I Indian, or am I white?" I stand before the door a long time. I hear the ice groan on the lake and remember the story of the old woman who is under the ice, trying to get out, so she can punish some runaway lovers. I think to myself, "If I am white, I will not believe that story; if I am Indian, I will know that there is an old woman under the ice." I listen for a while, and I know that there is an old woman under the ice. I look again at the lights and go in.

Inside the lodge there are many Indians. Some sit on benches around the walls, others dance in the center of the floor around a drum. Nobody seems to notice me. It seems as though I were among a people I have never seen before. Heavy women with long black hair. Women with children on their knees—small children that watch with intent black eyes the movements of the dancers, whose small faces are solemn and serene. The faces of the old people are serene,

too, and their eyes are merry and bright. I look at the old men. Straight, dressed in dark trousers and beaded velvet vests, wearing soft moccasins. Dark, lined faces intent on the music. I wonder if I am at all like them. They dance on, lifting their feet to the rhythm of the drums, swaying lightly, looking upward. I look at their eyes and am startled at the rapt attention to the rhythm of the music.

The dance stops. The men walk back to the walls and talk in low tones or with their hands. There is little conversation, yet everyone seems to be sharing some secret. A woman looks at a small boy wandering away, and he comes back to her.

Strange, I think, and then remember. These people are not sharing words—they are sharing a mood. Everyone is happy. I am so used to white people that it seems strange so many people could be together without someone talking. These Indians are happy because they are together, and because the night is beautiful outside, and the music is beautiful. I try hard to forget school and white people, and be one of these—my people. I try to forget everything but the night, and it is a part of me; that I am one with my people and we are all a part of something universal. I watch eyes and see now that the old people are speaking to me. They nod slightly, imperceptibly, and their eyes laugh into mine. I look around the room. All the eyes are friendly; they all laugh. No one questions my being here. The drums begin to beat again, and I catch the invitation in the eyes of the old men. My feet begin to lift to the rhythm, and I look out beyond the walls into the night and see the lights. I am happy. It is beautiful. I am home. ❖

WORDS TO KNOW

pulsate (pŭl'sāt') *v.* to expand and contract rhythmically; beat
serene (sə-rēn') *adj.* calm; undisturbed
rapt (răpt) *adj.* deeply absorbed; engrossed
imperceptibly (ĭm'pər-sĕp'tə-blē) *adv.* so slightly or gradually as to be barely noticeable

RESPONDING
O P T I O N S

FROM PERSONAL RESPONSE TO CRITICAL ANALYSIS

REFLECT

1. What went through your mind as you finished this essay? Respond in your notebook, and then share your thoughts with a partner.

RETHINK

2. Why do you think Whitecloud called this essay "Blue Winds Dancing"?

3. Reread the third paragraph. Do you agree with Whitecloud's definition of beauty in the natural world? Explain your answer.

4. How would you describe the author's attitude toward "Society"?
   Consider
   - what he says about his school and his teachers
   - what "being civilized" means to him
   - how he says his people are treated by whites
   - his opinions about the people in the hobo jungles

RELATE

5. This essay was written more than half a century ago. Do you think people today still experience conflicts between their own cultural heritages and mainstream American society? Are there strong pressures to assimilate or to act like other people in order to fit in? Give reasons for your opinions.

ANOTHER PATHWAY
Cooperative Learning
Imagine that while Tom Whitecloud is home for Christmas, he talks to his family about whether he should return to college in California. Working with a small group of classmates, write and perform a skit that realistically captures the scene.

LITERARY CONCEPTS

Description is writing that helps a reader to picture scenes, events, and characters. Effective description enables a reader to see, hear, smell, taste, or feel the subject that is described. Notice the effect of Whitecloud's descriptive language: "Clean snow creaks beneath my feet, and a soft wind sighs through the trees, singing to me." Rewrite two of the following sentences, adding descriptive details so that the style resembles Tom Whitecloud's.
- The train went through the town.
- Those mountaintops are covered with snow.
- I could tell that leaves were burning.

QUICKWRITES

1. Imagine that 30 years after graduating from college, Tom Whitecloud returns to campus to give a commencement speech. Write the **speech** Whitecloud might give to the graduating class, focusing on the meaning and importance of cultural heritage.

2. Whitecloud mentions a story about "the old woman who is under the ice." Supplying details from your imagination, create a **legend** about the old woman that could be included in a book of folklore.

PORTFOLIO Save your writing. You may want to use it later as a springboard to a piece for your portfolio.

ALTERNATIVE ACTIVITIES

1. Trace a **map** of the United States and label all the bodies of water, mountain ranges, cities, and states mentioned in the essay. Then draw a line on the map to indicate the route Tom Whitecloud may have taken on his journey.

2. Create a **landscape painting** of one of the scenes described in "Blue Winds Dancing." Try to capture the mood of the scene.

CRITIC'S CORNER

When asked to comment on this story, student reviewer Amy Dobelstein remarked: "The imagery made you feel you were with the narrator, walking through snow, smelling pine, etc." Do you agree? Explain your answer.

THE WRITER'S STYLE

Analyze the relationship between the setting and the mood of "Blue Winds Dancing."

WORDS TO KNOW

Review the Words to Know at the bottom of the selection pages. Then choose the word that could be substituted for the italicized word or phrase in each sentence below.

1. The author found it difficult to adjust to the *hectic swirl* of life in college.
2. He longed for his *peaceful* Chippewa home.
3. He criticized society, but he was not *fanatical* about his opinions.
4. When the hoboes told their stories, he was a *completely attentive* audience.
5. The hoboes displayed many *wicked habits,* yet he enjoyed their straightforward talk.
6. As the train shook from side to side, the sound of the wheels on the tracks seemed to *beat a rhythm* in the passenger's ears.
7. Staring out the window at the desert sands, he saw a *false vision of water.*
8. A mountain was *outlined* against the morning sky.
9. A deer stood *like stone* in the middle of the road.
10. The old woman smiled *so slightly that it was difficult to observe.*

TOM WHITECLOUD

Born in New York City, Tom Whitecloud (1912–1972) spent part of his youth on the Lac du Flambeau (läk' də flăm'bō) Chippewa reservation in Wisconsin, where his father's family had its roots. As a young man, Whitecloud worked at various jobs—from boxer to farm hand—before deciding to pursue a career in medicine. He studied at the University of New Mexico and at the University of Redlands in California, where he earned his undergraduate degree, and went on to study medicine at Tulane University in New Orleans. Dr. Whitecloud devoted himself to improving the health of Native Americans, and he helped found the American Association of Indian Physicians.

Because writing was not his primary career, most of Whitecloud's essays, poems, and stories remained unpublished during his lifetime. An exception is "Blue Winds Dancing," which appeared as a prize-winning essay in *Scribner's Magazine* in 1938, when Whitecloud was a senior in college.

OTHER WORKS "An Indian Prayer," in *Return of the Indian Spirit* (ed. Vinson Brown); *"Thief,"* in *American Indian Prose and Poetry* (ed. Gloria Levitas et al.)

FOCUS ON POETRY

Of the four major genres, poetry may be the most difficult to define because of its wide-ranging variety. Yet most people can recognize poetry immediately by the arrangement of lines on the page. In poetry, the physical aspects of language—the look and sound of it—are inseparable from meaning. Like a sculptor, a poet pays close attention to all the aspects of the materials (that is, words) used in his or her creation. The word *poet* comes from the Greek *poietes,* meaning "one who makes or fashions." Indeed, writing poetry involves the careful crafting of words.

The language of poetry is more compressed than that of prose and often more musical, designed to stir the imagination and the emotions. Samuel Taylor Coleridge, a famous British poet, once described poetry as "the best words in the best order." To the French poet Paul Valéry, "prose was walking, poetry dancing."

FORM At its simplest, the form of a poem is the physical arrangement of words on the page, including the length and placement of the lines and the grouping of lines into stanzas. The term *form* can also refer to other types of patterning in a poem, including rhythm and other sound patterns.

SOUND Because poetry depends so much upon sound, it should be read aloud. Here are some techniques that poets use to create sound effects:

Alliteration is a repetition of initial consonant sounds.

So long lives this, and this gives life to thee.
(Shakespeare)

Assonance is a repetition of a vowel sound within nonrhyming words.

from labor in the weekday weather made /
banked fires blaze . . . (Robert Hayden)

Consonance is a repetition of consonant sounds within and at the ends of words.

I call out for you against the jutted stars
(Amy Lowell)

Onomatopoeia is the use of words—like *creak, whir,* and *clunk*—whose pronunciations suggest their meanings.

. . . the tinkling piano our guide
(D. H. Lawrence)

Rhyme is a repetition of the sound of the stressed vowels and all succeeding sounds in two or more words. Note the two rhymes in the following example:

I recollect that wondrous meeting,
That instant I encountered you,

When like an apparition <u>fleeting</u>
Like beauty's spirit, past you <u>flew</u>.
(Aleksandr Pushkin)

Repetition is the repeating of a sound, word, phrase, line, or unit for the purpose of emphasis.
<u>So</u> long,
<u>So</u> far away
Is Africa. (Langston Hughes)

Rhythm is a pattern or flow of sound created by the arrangement of stressed and unstressed syllables in a line of poetry. Some poems contain a regular pattern, or **meter,** of stressed and unstressed syllables. In the following example, stressed syllables are marked with a ′ and unstressed or lightly stressed syllables are marked with a ˘.

Nŏr yét ă flóatĭng spár tŏ mén thăt sínk
Ănd rise ănd sínk ănd rise ănd sínk ăgáin
(Edna St. Vincent Millay)

Other poems do not have strict meters, making use of rhythm in less formal ways.

IMAGERY Poets choose words that help readers see, hear, feel, taste, and smell the things being described. This kind of description is called imagery. Note the senses being appealed to.

There will come soft rains and the smell of the
  ground,
And swallows circling with their shimmering
  sound;
And frogs in the pools singing at night,
And wild plum-trees in tremulous white . . .
(Sara Teasdale)

FIGURATIVE LANGUAGE Figurative language is language that communicates ideas beyond the ordinary, literal meanings of the words.

Similes are comparisons of two dissimilar things by means of the word *like* or *as*. N. Scott Momaday uses a simile to draw a comparison between people in a damaged relationship and deer: ". . . now we are as the deer / who walk in single file."

Metaphors are direct comparisons of unlike things, as when the main character in Lucille Clifton's "Miss Rosie" is described as a "wet brown bag of a woman."

Personification is the giving of human qualities to an object, animal, or idea. In Dahlia Ravikovitch's "Pride," human physical attributes are given to rocks in the phrases "they lie on their backs."

STRATEGIES FOR READING POETRY

- **Read a poem at least three times.** First, read through it quickly to get a general idea of the meaning. Then read it slowly and carefully, stopping to look up any unfamiliar words. Finally, read the poem aloud.

- **Pay close attention to the poem's title,** which often supplies key information.

- **Identify the speaker.** Often, a poet creates a speaker with a distinctive identity. The speaker in Gwendolyn Brooks's "Kitchenette Building" is a poor resident of substandard housing.

- **Visualize the setting and situation.** Use details and your imagination to help you envision the

poem's setting. Where and when does it take place? Are there people portrayed? If so, who are they?

- **Reflect upon parts that puzzle or confuse you.** Because poetry is so concentrated in form, its meanings are often not immediately clear. When you encounter something that doesn't make sense, reread that portion of the poem. Try to figure it out within the context of the whole poem.

- **Determine the theme.** What important ideas about life or human nature does the poem convey? If the poem is humorous, is there a deeper meaning beneath the humor?

PREVIEWING

Piano
D. H. Lawrence England

Those Winter Sundays
Robert Hayden United States

PERSONAL CONNECTION

Recall a routine household activity from your childhood that now evokes strong feelings in you. Perhaps your mother read to you at night, your father patiently helped you with homework, or your grandmother baked a weekly pie. In your notebook, create a simple chart, like the one shown here, to record sensations that you associate with that memory. Fill in all applicable boxes.

Sense	Sensation Associated with Memory
Sight	
Hearing	
Touch	
Smell	
Taste	

BIOGRAPHICAL CONNECTION

The two poems that you are about to read draw upon the poets' memories of their own childhood. D. H. Lawrence, the son of a coal miner and his cultured wife, grew up in the late 19th century near Nottingham, England. Robert Hayden, born in 1913, was raised by poor, hard-working foster parents in Detroit, Michigan. Each poet, coincidentally, examines a parent's legacy by recalling activities of long-ago winter Sundays.

READING CONNECTION

Visualizing Images As you read these two poems, develop your own mental pictures of the characters and scenes that are described. Pay close attention to the details that convey memories in the poems.

Piano

D. H. Lawrence

Softly, in the dusk, a woman is singing to me;
Taking me back down the vista of years, till I see
A child sitting under the piano, in the boom of the
    tingling strings
And pressing the small, poised feet of a mother who
    smiles as she sings.

5 In spite of myself, the insidious mastery of song
Betrays me back, till the heart of me weeps to belong
To the old Sunday evenings at home, with winter outside
And hymns in the cozy parlour, the tinkling piano
    our guide.

So now it is vain for the singer to burst into clamour
10 With the great black piano appassionato. The glamour
Of childish days is upon me, my manhood is cast
Down in the flood of remembrance, I weep like a child
    for the past.

2 vista (vĭs′tə): a passage affording a distant view.

5 insidious (ĭn-sĭd′ē-əs): working subtly and gradually; treacherous.

9 vain: useless.

10 appassionato (ə-pä′sē-ə-nä′tō): an Italian word meaning "with deep emotion," used as a musical direction.

FROM PERSONAL RESPONSE TO CRITICAL ANALYSIS

REFLECT   **1.** When you finished this poem, what picture lingered in your mind? In your notebook, draw a quick sketch of that mental image or describe it in words.

RETHINK   **2.** Why does the speaker "weep like a child for the past"?
Consider
- what he means by "the glamour of childish days"
- what he values about "the old Sunday evenings at home"

3. Why does the speaker say that "now it is vain for the singer to burst into clamour"?
Consider
- why the woman might be singing to him
- the difference between his situations now and in the past

Sunday Morning Breakfast (1943), Horace Pippin. Private collection, courtesy of Galerie St. Etienne, New York.

Those Winter Sundays

Robert Hayden

Sundays too my father got up early
and put his clothes on in the blueblack cold,
then with cracked hands that ached
from labor in the weekday weather made
5 banked fires blaze. No one ever thanked him.

I'd wake and hear the cold splintering, breaking.
When the rooms were warm, he'd call,
and slowly I would rise and dress,
fearing the chronic angers of that house,

10 Speaking indifferently to him,
who had driven out the cold
and polished my good shoes as well.
What did I know, what did I know
of love's austere and lonely offices?

9 chronic (krŏn'ĭk): lasting or recurring for a long time.

14 austere (ô-stîr'): stern; severe; **offices:** duties; ceremonies.

RESPONDING
OPTIONS

FROM PERSONAL RESPONSE TO CRITICAL ANALYSIS

REFLECT

1. In your notebook, jot down three words or phrases that explain the sensations you experienced while reading "Those Winter Sundays."

RETHINK

2. What is your opinion of the speaker? **Consider**
   - the speaker's observations in lines 5 and 10
   - the question that ends the poem
   - the possible reason that the speaker recalls this memory

3. What lessons might be learned from this poem? Explain your answer.

RELATE

4. Compare and contrast the speakers' attitudes toward their childhood in "Piano" and "Those Winter Sundays."

5. In what way does each of these two poems relate to the theme of this part of Unit One, "The Power of Heritage"?

6. What feelings or memories from your own life did these poems awaken?

ANOTHER PATHWAY

Working with a small group of classmates, prepare a choral reading of one of these poems. Discuss what emotions should be communicated, where pauses should fall, and which words or phrases should be given emphasis. Then practice your reading aloud, perfecting your timing and enunciation. Perform your reading for the class.

LITERARY CONCEPTS

Imagery involves the use of words and phrases to create sensory experiences for readers. Each such experience, or **image,** appeals to one or more of the five senses: sight, hearing, taste, smell, and touch. For example, "A child sitting under the piano" appeals to the sense of sight, "the boom of the tingling strings" appeals to the senses of hearing and touch, and "pressing the small, poised feet" appeals to the senses of sight and touch. List three more images from "Piano" and three images from "Those Winter Sundays," naming the sense or senses to which each appeals. Then decide which poem, in your opinion, uses sensory images more effectively.

QUICKWRITES

1. Use the chart you created for the Personal Connection on page 135 as the starting point for a **poem** about your childhood memory. Include vivid imagery that appeals to different senses.

2. Write a **eulogy** that the speaker of "Piano" might deliver for his mother or one that the speaker of "Those Winter Sundays" might deliver for his father.

📁 *PORTFOLIO Save your writing. You may want to use it later as a springboard to a piece for your portfolio.*

ALTERNATIVE ACTIVITIES

1. For an audience of your classmates, play live or recorded **music** that you think captures the mood of one of these poems.

2. Begin a **dictionary** of sensory images. Under the headings "Sight," "Hearing," "Touch," "Taste," and "Smell," record words and phrases from your reading, including those encountered in "Piano" and "Those Winter Sundays." Refer to the dictionary when completing future writing assignments.

LITERARY LINKS

Compare the speaker in "Piano" with the narrator of "Two Kinds." How does each feel about his or her experience with music?

D. H. LAWRENCE

1885–1930

David Herbert Lawrence grew up in poverty in the coal-mining district of Nottinghamshire, England. His father was a hardworking, hard-drinking coal miner; his mother, to whom he was deeply attached, was a former schoolteacher who instilled in her son a love of learning and culture. A sickly but intellectually gifted child, Lawrence attended school on scholarships and after graduation became a schoolteacher himself, writing fiction and poetry in his spare time.

Lawrence's first poems were published when a girlfriend submitted them to a magazine whose editor was impressed with Lawrence's efforts. With the editor's help, Lawrence was able to publish his first novel, *The White Peacock,* in 1911. He went on to produce a string of critically acclaimed novels, many of which focus on male-female relationships with a frankness that shocked the public of his day.

Lawrence has for decades been recognized as a first-rate poet. "Piano," a famous example of his poetic craftsmanship, was written in 1918, seven years after his mother died.

OTHER WORKS *Sons and Lovers, The Complete Short Stories of D. H. Lawrence, The Complete Poems of D. H. Lawrence*

ROBERT HAYDEN

1913–1980

Robert Hayden grew up in Detroit, Michigan, where he was raised by foster parents who made great sacrifices to insure his education. Their efforts were also encouraged by Hayden's natural mother, who occasionally sent him books to read. Hayden began writing poems in elementary school, although for years he doubted that he could make a career of it. In 1938 he was employed by the Federal Writers' Project to research African-American history and folklore. Soon afterward, he began working part-time for an African-American weekly paper whose editor helped him publish his first book of poetry, *Heart-Shape in the Dust* (1940).

In 1941, Hayden enrolled in graduate school at the University of Michigan, where one of his most inspiring professors was the British poet W. H. Auden. Eventually becoming a professor himself, Hayden taught for over 20 years at Fisk University in Nashville, Tennessee. As his reputation as a scholar grew, so did his fame as a poet. "Those Winter Sundays," one of his best-known shorter poems, was first collected in the volume *A Ballad of Remembrance,* published in 1962.

OTHER WORKS *Angle of Ascent: New and Selected Poems, Collected Prose, Robert Hayden: Collected Poems*

PREVIEWING

from When Heaven and Earth Changed Places
Le Ly Hayslip (lā′ lē′ hā′slĭp) **Vietnam / United States**

PERSONAL CONNECTION

With another student, create a list of words and phrases that come to mind when you hear the word *Vietnam.* Compare your list with those of other classmates.

The author's parents.
Courtesy of Le Ly Hayslip.

BIOGRAPHICAL CONNECTION

Vietnam has had a long history of war. For centuries, the Vietnamese fought against Chinese domination. In the late 1800s, the French invaded Vietnam and began to rule it as a colony. After World War II, the Vietnamese—led by Ho Chi Minh (hō′ chē′ mĭn′) and his Communist organization, the Vietminh (vē-ĕt′mĭn′)—fought a long war of independence against the French (1946–1954). Following France's defeat, the country was divided into Communist North Vietnam and the non-Communist Republic of South Vietnam.

Another war broke out in South Vietnam in 1955, when the Vietcong—Communist rebels backed by North Vietnam—began to fight against the republican forces, who were supported by the United States. The Vietcong sought to unite both parts of the country under Communist leadership, whereas the republican forces wanted to keep out the Communists and preserve their capitalistic way of life. During this time, the writer of this selection was growing up in the village of Ky La (kē′ lä′) in central Vietnam. In this excerpt from her autobiography, she shares childhood memories of her father and reveals the war's impact on her family.

READING CONNECTION

Evaluating As you read about the writer's recollections of Vietnam, identify the statements that seem to you to be most important. After your reading, reevaluate your choices. List your final choices on a sheet of paper or in your notebook.

LASERLINKS
• *HISTORICAL CONNECTION*

from **When Heaven and Earth Changed Places**

Le Ly Hayslip

After my brother Bon went North, I began to pay more attention to my father.

He was built solidly—big boned—for a Vietnamese man, which meant he probably had well-fed, noble ancestors. People said he had the body of a natural-born warrior.

He was a year younger and an inch shorter than my mother, but just as good-looking. His face was round, like a Khmer or Thai,[1] and his complexion was brown as soy from working all his life in the sun. He was very easygoing about everything and seldom in a hurry. Seldom, too, did he say no to a request—from his children or his neighbors. Although he took everything in stride, he was a hard and diligent worker. Even on holidays, he was always mending things or tending to our house and animals. He would not wait to be asked for help if he saw someone in trouble. Similarly, he always said what he thought, although he knew, like most honest men, when to keep silent. Because of his honesty, his empathy, and his openness to people, he understood life deeply. Perhaps that is why he was so easygoing. Only a half-trained mechanic thinks everything needs fixing.

He loved to smoke cigars and grew a little tobacco in our yard. My mother always wanted him to sell it, but there was hardly ever enough to take to market. I think for her it was the principle of the thing: smoking cigars was like burning money. Naturally, she had a song for such gentle vices—her own habit of chewing betel[2] nuts included:

Get rid of your tobacco,
And you will get a water buffalo.
Give away your betel,
And you will get more paddy land.[3]

Despite her own good advice, she never abstained from chewing betel, nor my father from smoking cigars. They were rare luxuries that life and the war allowed them.

My father also liked rice wine, which we made, and enjoyed an occasional beer, which he purchased when there was nothing else we needed. After he'd had a few sips, he would tell jokes

and happy stories, and the village kids would flock around. Because I was his youngest daughter, I was entitled to listen from his knee—the place of honor. Sometimes he would sing funny songs about whoever threatened the village, and we would feel better. For example, when the French or Moroccan[4] soldiers were near, he would sing:

There are many kinds of vegetables;
Why do you like spinach?
There are many kinds of wealth;
Why do you use Minh money?
There are many kinds of people;
Why do you love terrorists?

We laughed because these were all the things the French told us about the Viet Minh fighters whom we favored in the war. Years later, when the Viet Cong were near, he would sing:

There are many kinds of vegetables;
Why do you like spinach?
There are many kinds of money;
Why do you use Yankee dollars?
There are many kinds of people;
Why do you disobey your ancestors?

This was funny because the words were taken from the speeches the North Vietnamese cadres[5] delivered to shame us for helping the Republic. He used to have a song for when the Viet Minh were near too, which asked in the same way,

---

1. **Khmer** (kmâr) **or Thai** (tī): a member of the Khmer people of Cambodia or the Thai people of Thailand.
2. **betel** (bēt′l) **nuts:** seeds of the betel palm, chewed as a mild stimulant.
3. **paddy land:** fields for growing rice.
4. **Moroccan** (mə-rŏk′ən): from the North African nation of Morocco, then a French colony.
5. **cadres** (kăd′rēz): tightly knit groups of revolutionaries.

"Why do you use francs?"[6] and "Why do you love French traitors?" Because he sang these songs with a comical voice, my mother never appreciated them. She couldn't see the absurdity of our situation as clearly as we children. To her, war and real life were different. To us, they were all the same.

Even as a parent, my father was more <u>lenient</u> than our mother, and we sometimes ran to him for help when she was angry. Most of the time it didn't work, and he would lovingly rub our heads as we were dragged off to be spanked. The village saying went: "A naughty child learns more from a whipping stick than a sweet stick." We children were never quite sure about that but agreed the whipping stick was an eloquent teacher. When he absolutely had to punish us himself, he didn't waste time. Wordlessly, he would find a long, <u>supple</u> bamboo stick and let us have it behind our thighs. It stung, but he could have whipped us harder. I think seeing the pain in his face hurt more than receiving his halfhearted blows. Because of that, we seldom did anything to merit a father's spanking—the highest penalty in our family. Violence in any form offended him. For this reason, I think, he grew old before his time.

One of the few times my father ever touched my mother in a way not consistent with love was during one of the yearly floods, when people came to our village for safety from the lower ground. We sheltered many in our house, which was nothing more than a two-room hut with woven mats for a floor. I came home one day in winter rain to see refugees and Republican soldiers milling around outside. They did not know I lived there, so I had to elbow my way inside. It was nearly suppertime, and I knew my mother would be fixing as much food as we could spare.

In the part of the house we used as our kitchen, I discovered my mother crying. She and my father had gotten into an argument outside a few minutes before. He had assured the refugees he would find something to eat for everyone, and she insisted there would not be enough for her children if everyone was fed. He repeated his order to her, this time loud enough for all to hear. Naturally, he thought this would end the argument. She persisted in contradicting him, so he had slapped her.

> *Even as a parent, my father was more lenient than our mother, and we sometimes ran to him for help when she was angry.*

This show of male power—we called it *do danh vo*[7]—was usual behavior for Vietnamese husbands but unusual for my father. My mother could be as strict as she wished with his children, and he would seldom interfere. Now, I discovered there were limits even to his great patience. I saw the glowing red mark on her cheek and asked if she was crying because it hurt. She said no. She said she was crying because her action had caused my father to lose face in front of strangers. She promised that if I ever did what she had done to a husband, I would have both cheeks glowing: one from his blow and one from hers.

Once, when I was the only child at home, my

---

6. **francs:** French money.
7. *do danh vo* (dô zän′yə vô).

WORDS TO KNOW

lenient (lē′nē-ənt) *adj.* tolerant or merciful in disposition
supple (sŭp′əl) *adj.* easily bent; pliant

143

Images for this selection are from the movie *Heaven and Earth*, directed by Oliver Stone.
Copyright © Warner Bros./Regency Enterprises/Le Studio Canal.

mother went to Danang[8] to visit Uncle Nhu, and my father had to take care of me. I woke up from my nap in the empty house and cried for my mother. My father came in from the yard and reassured me, but I was still cranky and continued crying. Finally, he gave me a rice cookie to shut me up. Needless to say, this was a tactic my mother never used.

The next afternoon I woke up, and although I was not feeling cranky, I thought a rice cookie might be nice. I cried a fake cry, and my father came running in.

"What's this?" he asked, making a worried face. "Little Bay Ly[9] doesn't want a cookie?"

I was confused again.

"Look under your pillow," he said with a smile.

I twisted around and saw that, while I was sleeping, he had placed a rice cookie under my pillow. We both laughed, and he picked me up like a sack of rice and carried me outside while I gobbled the cookie.

In the yard, he plunked me down under a tree and told me some stories. After that, he got some scraps of wood and showed me how to make things: a doorstop for my mother and a toy duck for me. This was unheard of—a father doing these things with a child that was not a son! Where my mother would instruct me on cooking and cleaning and tell stories about brides, my father showed me the mystery of hammers and explained the customs of our people.

His knowledge of the Vietnamese went back to the Chinese Wars in ancient times. I learned how one of my distant ancestors, a woman named Phung Thi Chinh,[10] led Vietnamese fighters against the Han.[11] In one battle, even though she was pregnant and surrounded by Chinese, she delivered the baby, tied it to her back, and cut her way to safety wielding a sword in each hand. I was amazed at this warrior's bravery and impressed that I was

her descendant. Even more, I was amazed and impressed by my father's pride in her accomplishments (she was, after all, a humble female), and his belief that I was worthy of her example. *"Con phai theo got chan co ta"*[12] (Follow in her footsteps), he said. Only later would I learn what he truly meant.

Never again did I cry after my nap. Phung Thi women were too strong for that. Besides, I was my father's daughter, and we had many things to do together.

On the eve of my mother's return, my father cooked a feast of roast duck. When we sat down to eat it, I felt guilty, and my feelings showed on my face. He asked why I acted so sad.

"You've killed one of mother's ducks," I said. "One of the fat kind she sells at the market. She says the money buys gold which she saves for her daughters' weddings. Without gold for a dowry—*con o gia*[13]—I will be an old maid!"

My father looked suitably concerned, then brightened and said, "Well, Bay Ly, if you can't get married, you will just have to live at home forever with me!"

I clapped my hands at the happy prospect.

My father cut into the rich, juicy bird and said, "Even so, we won't tell your mother about the duck, okay?"

I giggled and swore myself to secrecy.

The next day, I took some water out to him in the fields. My mother was due home any time, and I used every opportunity to step outside and watch for her. My father stopped working, drank gratefully, then took my hand and led me to the top of a nearby hill. It had a

---

8. **Danang** (də-năng′): a seaport in central Vietnam.

9. **Bay Ly** (bī′ lē′): the author's childhood nickname, indicating that she was the sixth child of her parents.

10. **Phung Thi Chinh** (pŏŏng′ tē′ jĭn′yə).

11. **Han:** the principal ethnic group of China.

12. *Con phai theo got chan co ta* (kôn pī tĕ-ô′ gô jän kô tä).

13. *con o gia* (kôn ŭ jē-ä′).

good view of the village and the land beyond it, almost to the ocean. I thought he was going to show me my mother coming back, but he had something else in mind.

He said, "Bay Ly, you see all this here? This is the Vietnam we have been talking about. You understand that a country is more than a lot of dirt, rivers, and forests, don't you?"

I said, "Yes, I understand." After all, we had learned in school that one's country is as sacred as a father's grave.

"Good. You know, some of these lands are battlefields where your brothers and cousins are fighting. They may never come back. Even your sisters have all left home in search of a better life. You are the only one left in my house. If the enemy comes back, you must be both a daughter and a son. I told you how the Chinese used to rule our land. People in this village had to risk their lives diving in the ocean just to find pearls for the Chinese emperor's gown. They had to risk tigers and snakes in the jungle just to find herbs for his table. Their payment for this hardship was a bowl of rice and another day of life. That is why Le Loi, Gia Long,[14] the Trung sisters, and Phung Thi Chinh fought so hard to expel the Chinese. When the French came, it was the same old story. Your mother and I were taken to Danang to build a runway for their airplanes. We labored from sunup to sundown and well after dark. If we stopped to rest or have a smoke, a Moroccan would come up and whip our behinds. Our reward was a bowl of rice and another day of life. Freedom is never a gift, Bay Ly. It must be won and won again. Do you understand?"

I said that I did.

"Good." He moved his finger from the patchwork of brown dikes, silver water, and rippling stalks to our house at the edge of the village. "This land here belongs to me. Do you know how I got it?"

I thought a moment, trying to remember my mother's stories, then said honestly, "I can't remember."

He squeezed me lovingly. "I got it from your mother."

"What? That can't be true!" I said. Everyone in the family knew my mother was poor and my father's family was wealthy. Her parents were dead, and she had to work like a slave for her mother-in-law to prove herself worthy. Such women don't have land to give away!

"It's true." My father's smile widened. "When I was a young man, my parents needed someone to look after their lands. They had to be very careful about who they chose as wives for their three sons. In the village, your mother had a reputation as the hardest worker of all. She raised herself and her brothers without parents. At the same time, I noticed a beautiful woman working in the fields. When my mother said she was going to talk to the matchmaker about this hard-working village girl she'd heard about, my heart sank. I was too attracted to this mysterious tall woman I had seen in the rice paddies. You can imagine my surprise when I found out the girl my mother heard about and the woman I admired were the same.

"Well, we were married, and my mother tested your mother severely. She not only had to cook and clean and know everything about children, but she had to be able to manage several farms and know when and how to take the extra produce to the market. Of course, she was testing her other daughters-in-law as well. When my parents died, they divided their several farms among their sons, but you know what? They gave your mother and me the biggest share because they knew we would take care of it best. That's why I say the land came from her, because it did."

I suddenly missed my mother very much and looked down the road to the south, hoping to

---

14. **Le Loi** (lā′ loi′), **Gia Long** (jē-ä′ lông′).

see her. My father noticed my sad expression.

"Hey." He poked me in the ribs. "Are you getting hungry for lunch?"

"No. I want to learn how to take care of the farm. What happens if the soldiers come back? What did you and Mother do when the soldiers came?"

My father squatted on the dusty hilltop and wiped the sweat from his forehead. "The first thing I did was to tell myself that it was my duty to survive—to take care of my family and my farm. That is a tricky job in wartime. It's as hard as being a soldier. The Moroccans were very savage. One day the rumor passed that they were coming to destroy the village. You may remember the night I sent you and your brothers and sisters away with your mother to Danang."

"You didn't go with us!" My voice still held the horror of the night I thought I had lost my father.

"Right! I stayed near the village—right on this hill—to keep an eye on the enemy and on our house. If they really wanted to destroy the village, I would save some of our things so that we could start over. Sure enough, that was their plan.

"The real problem was to keep things safe and avoid being captured. Their patrols were everywhere. Sometimes I went so deep in the forest that I worried about getting lost, but all I had to do was follow the smoke from the burning huts and I could find my way back.

"Once, I was trapped between two patrols that had camped on both sides of a river. I had to wait in the water for two days before one of them moved on. When I got out, my skin was shriveled like an old melon. I was so cold I could hardly move. From the waist down, my body was black with leeches.[15] But it was worth all the pain. When your mother came back, we still had some furniture and tools to cultivate the earth. Many people lost everything. Yes, we were very lucky."

My father put his arms around me. "My

> "The first thing I did was to tell myself that it was my duty to survive—to take care of my family."

brother Huong[16]—your uncle Huong—had three sons and four daughters. Of his four daughters, only one is still alive. Of his three sons, two went north to Hanoi,[17] and one went south to Saigon.[18] Huong's house is very empty. My other brother, your uncle Luc, had only two sons. One went north to Hanoi; the other was killed in the fields. His daughter is deaf and dumb. No wonder he has taken to drink, eh? Who does he have to sing in his house and tend his shrine when he is gone? My sister Lien[19] had three daughters and four sons. Three of the four sons went to Hanoi, and the fourth went to Saigon to find his fortune. The girls all tend their in-laws and mourn slain husbands. Who will care for Lien when she is too feeble to care for herself? Finally, my baby sister Nhien[20] lost her husband to French bombers. Of her two sons, one went to Hanoi, and the other joined the Republic, then defected, then was murdered in his house. Nobody knows which side killed him. It doesn't really matter."

My father drew me out to arm's length and

---

15. **leeches:** bloodsucking worms that live in water.

16. **Huong** (hŏŏ-ông').

17. **Hanoi** (hă-noi'): the capital of North Vietnam from 1954 until 1976; now the capital of the unified country of Vietnam.

18. **Saigon** (sī-gŏn'): the capital of South Vietnam from 1954 until 1976; now called Ho Chi Minh City.

19. **Lien** (lē-ĕn').

20. **Nhien** (nē-ĕn').

looked me squarely in the eye. "Now, Bay Ly, do you understand what your job is?"

I squared my shoulders and put on a soldier's face. "My job is to avenge my family. To protect my farm by killing the enemy. I must become a woman warrior like Phung Thi Chinh!"

My father laughed and pulled me close. "No, little peach blossom. Your job is to stay alive— to keep an eye on things and keep the village safe. To find a husband and have babies and tell the story of what you've seen to your children and anyone else who'll listen. Most of all, it is to live in peace and tend the shrine of our ancestors. Do these things well, Bay Ly, and you will be worth more than any soldier who ever took up a sword." ❖

RESPONDING
OPTIONS

FROM PERSONAL RESPONSE TO CRITICAL ANALYSIS

REFLECT
1. What is your impression of the writer's life during the Vietnam War? Write your thoughts in your notebook.

RETHINK
2. What qualities of the writer's father emerge in this portrayal of him?
   Consider
   - the songs he sang before the soldiers
   - his treatment of the refugees
   - his relationship with his family
   - what he did to save the family's property

3. The writer's father tells his daughter that her job is not to fight but to stay alive and raise a family. What do you think of his advice?

4. If the writer had not been the youngest daughter and the only child left at home, how do you think her relationship with her father might have been different?

5. What have you learned about Vietnam from this selection? Compare your insights with the list you made for the Personal Connection on page 140.

RELATE
6. What lessons have you learned from this selection that can be applied to your own life?

ANOTHER PATHWAY

Cooperative Learning
Working with a small group of classmates, review the lists of important statements you made for the Reading Connection on page 140. Then choose one statement that you think best represents the spirit of the selection. Share your results with the rest of the class, explaining why you chose that statement.

QUICKWRITES

1. Write an **autobiographical essay** in which you describe the impact that a particular event has had on your family.

2. Write a magazine **advice column** on child rearing that Hayslip's father might have written.

3. Create **song lyrics** that convey your own attitude toward war.

4. Do research to find out more about modern Vietnamese culture. Present your information in a **chart** that compares the Vietnamese and American cultures in terms of values, family unity, types of work, economy, and social customs.

📁 *PORTFOLIO Save your writing. You may want to use it later as a springboard to a piece for your portfolio.*

LITERARY CONCEPTS

An **autobiography** is a person's account of his or her own life. Often, a person writing an autobiography—an autobiographer—looks back on his or her past in an effort to understand it better. The autobiographer can then make judgments about people or events of the past in a way that might not have been possible earlier. For example, Hayslip looks back on her father's dread of violence and concludes, "For this reason, I think, he grew old before his time."

Working with a partner, look through the selection to find at least two more instances in which Hayslip makes judgments about events that took place in her girlhood. Share your examples with your classmates.

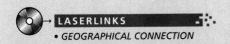

LASERLINKS
• *GEOGRAPHICAL CONNECTION*

ALTERNATIVE ACTIVITIES

1. Conduct a **debate** on whether women can better serve their country by fighting alongside men or by remaining at home to care for their families. Organize the class into two groups, each arguing a different side of the issue.

2. Read the rest of *When Heaven and Earth Changed Places*. With other students, prepare a **skit** that depicts another event in Le Ly Hayslip's life.

ACROSS THE CURRICULUM

History Find out more about the involvement of the United States in the Vietnam War. How did it begin? What did the United States hope to accomplish in Vietnam? What were the effects of our nation's participation in the war? Share the results in an oral report.

WORDS TO KNOW

Write the letter of the word or phrase that best completes each sentence below.

1. You would know that a farmer was **diligent** if he or she (a) took on extra responsibilities, (b) composed humorous songs, (c) enjoyed a good meal.

2. Hayslip's father showed **empathy** when he (a) slapped his wife, (b) hid from soldiers, (c) showed awareness of his daughter's feelings.

3. The author's parents would **abstain** from physical punishment if they (a) no longer spanked their children, (b) spanked their children only for serious offenses, (c) explained their reasoning to their children.

4. If Hayslip's mother were more **lenient,** she would (a) punish her daughter more often, (b) overlook some of her daughter's misdeeds, (c) show more affection for her husband.

5. A bamboo stick is **supple** because it is (a) hard, (b) flexible, (c) long.

LE LY HAYSLIP

1949–

Le Ly Hayslip grew up in a traditional Buddhist family in the rural village of Ky La in central Vietnam. When she was 12, the Vietnam War turned her life into a nightmare of imprisonments, torture, and threats of execution. Her father, who refused to leave the family's home, did not survive the war. Separated from his wife and children, harassed by both the Vietcong and the American forces, and saddened by the destruction of his village, he eventually committed suicide.

Hayslip married an American serviceman and left Vietnam in 1970, settling in California. After the Vietnam War ended, she helped to found the East Meets West Foundation, a nonprofit organization that builds clinics and schools in Vietnam. In 1986, Hayslip returned to Vietnam for a reunion with remaining family members. She realized one of her fondest dreams three years later, when the East Meets West Foundation opened a clinic in her childhood home of Ky La.

Published in 1989, Hayslip's book *When Heaven and Earth Changed Places* is one of the few autobiographical accounts of the Vietnam War from a Vietnamese point of view. It was used as the basis of the film *Heaven and Earth* by the director Oliver Stone.

OTHER WORKS *Child of War, Woman of Peace*

PREVIEWING

FICTION

The Study of History
Frank O'Connor Ireland

The author's parents. Courtesy of Harriet O'Donovan.

PERSONAL CONNECTION

What would your life have been like if your ancestors had made different decisions before you were born? For example, what if your family had decided to settle in a different country? What if your mother had chosen a different mate, so that you had a different father? Imagine a different set of circumstances in your family background. Then freewrite in your notebook for five minutes about who you might be or what your life might be like.

BIOGRAPHICAL CONNECTION

The boy who would come to be known as Frank O'Connor often daydreamed about who he might have been if his family background had been different. Born Michael Francis O'Donovan in 1903, O'Connor grew up in Barrackton, a slum on the outskirts of Cork in southwestern Ireland. He shared a close bond with his mother, and he adopted her maiden name when he decided to write under a pseudonym.

Not only did O'Connor write two autobiographies; he also wrote autobiographical fiction about a boy named Laurence ("Larry") Delaney. Larry appears in a number of O'Connor's short stories, and like the author himself, he is an only child who is sometimes frustrated by the sharp contrasts between the rich and the poor in Cork. Naive and full of insecurities, he is often embarrassed by the commonness of his parents. Larry Delaney is the main character in the story you are about to read.

READING CONNECTION

Analyzing Details As you read "The Study of History," pay attention to the details that O'Connor uses in describing his characters. What do these details tell you about the characters' personalities, attitudes, and family backgrounds?

LASERLINKS
• *HISTORICAL CONNECTION*

THE STUDY OF HISTORY

Frank O'Connor

The discovery of where babies came from filled my life with excitement and interest. Not in the way it's generally supposed to, of course. Oh, no! I never seem to have done anything like a natural child in a standard textbook. I merely discovered the fascination of history.

Up to this, I had lived in a country of my own that had no history, and accepted my parents' marriage as an event ordained from the creation; now, when I considered it in this new, scientific way, I began to see it merely as one of the turning points of history, one of those apparently trivial events that are little more than accidents but have the effect of changing the destiny of humanity. I had not heard of Pascal, but I would have approved his remark about what would have happened if Cleopatra's nose had been a bit longer.[1]

It immediately changed my view of my parents. Up to this, they had been principles, not characters, like a chain of mountains guarding a green horizon. Suddenly a little shaft of light, emerging from behind a cloud, struck them, and the whole mass broke up into peaks, valleys, and foothills; you could even see whitewashed farmhouses and fields where people worked in the evening light, a whole world of interior perspective. Mother's past was the richer subject for study. It was extraordinary the variety of people and settings that woman had had in her background. She had been an orphan, a parlormaid, a companion, a traveler; and had been proposed to by a plasterer's apprentice, a French chef who had taught her to make superb coffee, and a rich and elderly shopkeeper in Sunday's Well.[2] Because I liked to feel myself different, I thought a great deal about the chef and the advantages of being a Frenchman, but the shopkeeper was an even more vivid figure in my imagination because he had married someone else and died soon after—of disappointment, I had no doubt—leaving a large fortune. The fortune was to me what Cleopatra's nose was to Pascal: the ultimate proof that things might have been different.

"How much was Mr. Riordan's fortune, Mummy?" I asked thoughtfully.

"Ah, they said he left eleven thousand,"

Mother replied doubtfully, "but you couldn't believe everything people say."

That was exactly what I could do. I was not prepared to minimize a fortune that I might so easily have inherited.

"And weren't you ever sorry for poor Mr. Riordan?" I asked severely.

"Ah, why would I be sorry, child?" she asked with a shrug. "Sure, what use would money be where there was no liking?"

That, of course, was not what I meant at all. My heart was full of pity for poor Mr. Riordan who had tried to be my father; but, even on the low level at which Mother discussed it, money would have been of great use to me. I was not so fond of Father as to think he was worth eleven thousand pounds, a hard sum to visualize but more than twenty-seven times greater than the largest salary I had ever heard of—that of a Member of Parliament. One of the discoveries I was making at the time was that Mother was not only rather hard-hearted but very impractical as well.

But Father was the real surprise. He was a brooding, worried man who seemed to have no proper appreciation of me and was always wanting me to go out and play or go upstairs and read, but the historical approach changed him like a character in a fairy tale. "Now let's talk about the ladies Daddy nearly married," I would say; and he would stop whatever he was doing

---

1. **Pascal** (păskăl') . . . **longer:** The 17th-century French philosopher and mathematician Blaise Pascal wrote that if Cleopatra's nose had been shorter (not longer, as the narrator says), "the whole face of the world would have been changed." Cleopatra (69–30 B.C.), a queen of Egypt famous for her beauty, affected history through her romances with the Roman leaders Julius Caesar and Mark Antony.

2. **in Sunday's Well:** on Sunday's Well Road, a street in the wealthier part of the city of Cork.

WORDS TO KNOW
ordained (ôr-dānd') *adj.* established by authority or fate **ordain** *v.*
brooding (brōō'dĭng) *adj.* having a moody or depressed disposition **brood** *v.*

153

and give a great guffaw. "Oh, ho, ho!" he would say, slapping his knee and looking slyly at Mother, "you could write a book about them." Even his face changed at such moments. He would look young and extraordinarily mischievous. Mother, on the other hand, would grow black.

"You could," she would say, looking into the fire. "Daisies!"

"'The handsomest man that walks Cork!'" Father would quote with a wink at me. "That's what one of them called me."

"Yes," Mother would say, scowling. "May Cadogan!"

"The very girl!" Father would cry in astonishment. "How did I forget her name? A beautiful girl! 'Pon my word, a most remarkable girl! And still is, I hear."

"She should be," Mother would say in disgust. "With six of them!"

"Oh, now, she'd be the one that could look after them! A fine head that girl had."

"She had. I suppose she ties them to a lamp-post while she goes in to drink and gossip."

That was one of the peculiar things about history. Father and Mother both loved to talk about it but in different ways. She would only talk about it when we were together somewhere, in the Park or down the Glen, and even then it was very hard to make her stick to the facts, because her whole face would light up and she would begin to talk about donkey carriages, or concerts in the kitchen, or oil lamps, and though nowadays I would probably value it for atmosphere, in those days it sometimes drove me mad with impatience. Father, on the other hand, never minded talking about it in front of her, and it made her angry—particularly when he mentioned May Cadogan. He knew this perfectly well, and he would wink at me and make me laugh outright, though I had no idea of why I laughed, and, anyway, my sympathy was all with her.

"But, Daddy," I would say, presuming on his high spirits, "if you liked Miss Cadogan so much, why didn't you marry her?"

At this, to my great delight, he would let on to be filled with doubt and distress. He would put his hands in his trousers pockets and stride to the door leading into the hallway.

"That was a delicate matter," he would say, without looking at me. "You see, I had your poor mother to think of."

"I was a great trouble to you," Mother would say, in a blaze.

"Poor May said it to me herself," he would go on as though he had not heard her, "and the tears pouring down her cheeks. 'Mick,' she said, 'that girl with the brown hair will bring me to an untimely grave.'"

"She could talk of hair!" Mother would hiss. "With her carroty mop!"

"Never did I suffer the way I suffered then, between the two of them," Father would say with deep emotion as he returned to his chair by the window.

"Oh, 'tis a pity about ye!" Mother would cry in an exasperated tone and suddenly get up and go into the front room with her book to escape his teasing. Every word that man said she took literally. Father would give a great guffaw of delight, his hands on his knees and his eyes on the ceiling, and wink at me again. I would laugh with him, of course, and then grow wretched because I hated Mother's sitting alone in the front room. I would go in and find her in her wicker chair by the window in the dusk, the book open on her knee, looking out at the Square. She would always have regained her composure when she spoke to me, but I would have an uncanny feeling of unrest in her and stroke her and talk to her soothingly as if we had changed places and I were the adult and she the child.

Jimmy O'D (about 1925), Robert Henri. Oil on canvas, 24″ × 20″, Collection of the Montclair (New Jersey) Art Museum, museum purchase, Picture Buying Fund (26.1).

But if I was excited by what history meant to them, I was even more excited by what it meant to me. My potentialities were double theirs. Through Mother I might have been a French boy called Laurence Armady or a rich boy from Sunday's Well called Laurence Riordan. Through Father I might, while still remaining a Delaney, have been one of the six children of the mysterious and beautiful Miss Cadogan. I was fascinated by the problem of who I would have been if I hadn't been me, and, even more, by the problem of whether or not I would have known that there was anything wrong with the arrangement. Naturally, I tended to regard Laurence Delaney as the person I was intended to be, and so I could not help wondering whether as Laurence Riordan I would not have been aware of Laurence Delaney as a real gap in my make-up.

I remember that one afternoon after school I walked by myself all the way up to Sunday's Well, which I now regarded as something like a second home. I stood for a while at the garden gate of the house where Mother had been working when she was proposed to by Mr. Riordan, and then went and studied the shop itself. It had clearly seen better days, and the cartons and advertisements in the window were dusty and sagging. It wasn't like one of the big stores in Patrick Street, but at the same time, in size and fittings, it was well above the level of a village shop. I regretted that Mr. Riordan was dead, because I would have liked to see him for myself instead of relying on Mother's impressions, which seemed to me to be biased. Since he had, more or less, died of grief on Mother's account, I conceived of him as a really nice man; lent him the countenance and manner of an old gentleman who always spoke to me when he met me on the road; and felt I could have become really attached to him as a father. I could imagine it all: Mother reading in the parlor while she waited for me to come home up Sunday's Well in a school-cap and blazer, like the boys from the Grammar School,[3] and with an expensive leather satchel instead of the old cloth school bag I carried over my shoulder. I could see myself walking slowly and with a certain distinction, lingering at gateways and looking down at the river; and later I would go out to tea in one of the big houses with long gardens sloping to the water, and maybe row a boat on the river along with a girl in a pink frock. I wondered only whether I would have any awareness of the National School[4] boy with the cloth school bag who jammed his head between the bars of a gate and thought of me. It was a queer, lonesome feeling that all but reduced me to tears.

But the place that had the greatest attraction of all for me was the Douglas Road, where Father's friend Miss Cadogan lived, only now she wasn't Miss Cadogan but Mrs. O'Brien. Naturally, nobody called Mrs. O'Brien could be as attractive to the imagination as a French chef or an elderly shopkeeper with eleven thousand pounds, but she had a physical reality that the other pair lacked. As I went regularly to the library at Parnell Bridge, I frequently found myself wandering up the road in the direction of Douglas and always stopped in front of the long row of houses where she lived. There were high steps up to them, and in the evening the sunlight fell brightly on the house fronts till they looked like a screen. One evening as I watched a gang of boys playing ball in the street outside, curiosity overcame me. I spoke to one of them. Having been always a child of solemn and unnatural politeness, I probably scared the wits out of them.

"I wonder if you could tell me which house Mrs. O'Brien lives in, please?" I asked.

"Hi, Gussie!" he yelled to another boy. "This fellow wants to know where your old one lives."

This was more than I had bargained for. Then a thin, good-looking boy of about my own age detached himself from the group and came up to me with his fists clenched. I was feeling distinctly panicky, but all the same I studied him closely. After all, he was the boy I might have been.

"What do you want to know for?" he asked suspiciously.

Again, this was something I had not anticipated.

"My father was a great friend of your mother," I explained carefully, but, so far as he was concerned, I might as well have been talking a foreign language. It was clear that Gussie O'Brien had no sense of history.

"What's that?" he asked incredulously.

At this point we were interrupted by a woman I had noticed earlier, talking to another over the railing between the two steep gardens. She was small and untidy looking and occasionally rocked

---

3. **Grammar School:** a private school.
4. **National School:** a public school funded by the government.

WORDS TO KNOW

biased (bī′əst) *adj.* marked by an unfair preference; prejudiced
incredulously (ĭn-krĕj′ə-ləs-lē) *adv.* in a manner expressing skepticism or disbelief

the pram[5] in an absent-minded way as though she only remembered it at intervals.

"What is it, Gussie?" she cried, raising herself on tiptoe to see us better.

"I don't really want to disturb your mother, thank you," I said, in something like hysterics, but Gussie anticipated me, actually pointing me out to her in a manner I had been brought up to regard as rude.

"This fellow wants you," he bawled.

"I don't really," I murmured, feeling that now I was in for it. She skipped down the high flight of steps to the gate with a laughing, puzzled air, her eyes in slits and her right hand arranging her hair at the back. It was not carroty as Mother described it, though it had red lights when the sun caught it.

"What is it, little boy?" she asked coaxingly, bending forward.

"I didn't really want anything, thank you," I said in terror. "It was just that my daddy said you lived up here, and, as I was changing my book at the library, I thought I'd come up and inquire. You can see," I added, showing her the book as proof, "that I've only just been to the library."

"But who is your daddy, little boy?" she asked, her gray eyes still in long, laughing slits. "What's your name?"

"My name is Delaney," I said. "Larry Delaney."

"Not *Mike* Delaney's boy?" she exclaimed wonderingly. "Well, for God's sake! Sure, I should have known it from that big head of yours." She passed her hand down the back of my head and laughed. "If you'd only get your hair cut, I wouldn't be long recognizing you. You wouldn't think I'd know the feel of your old fellow's head, would you?" she added roguishly.

"No, Mrs. O'Brien," I replied meekly.

"Why, then indeed I do, and more along with it," she added in the same saucy tone, though the meaning of what she said was not clear to me. "Ah, come in and give us a good look at you! That's my eldest, Gussie, you were talking to," she added, taking my hand. Gussie trailed behind us for a purpose I only recognized later.

"Ma-a-a-a, who's dat fella with you?" yelled a fat little girl who had been playing hopscotch on the pavement.

"That's Larry Delaney," her mother sang over her shoulder. I don't know what it was about that woman but there was something about her high spirits that made her more like a regiment than a woman. You felt that everyone should fall into step behind her. "Mick Delaney's son from Barrackton. I nearly married his old fellow once. Did he ever tell you that, Larry?" she added slyly. She made sudden swift transitions from brilliance to intimacy that I found attractive.

"Yes, Mrs. O'Brien, he did," I replied, trying to sound as roguish as she, and she went off into a delighted laugh, tossing her red head.

"Ah, look at that now! How well the old divil didn't forget me! You can tell him I didn't forget him either. And if I married him, I'd be your mother now. Wouldn't that be a queer old three and fourpence?[6] How would you like me for a mother, Larry?"

"Very much, thank you," I said complacently.

"Ah, go on with you, you would not," she exclaimed, but she was pleased all the same. She struck me as the sort of woman it would be easy enough to please. "Your old fellow always said it: your mother was a *most* superior woman, and you're a *most* superior child. Ah, and I'm not

---

5. **pram:** a baby carriage.

6. **a queer old three and fourpence:** slang expression meaning "an odd thing."

WORDS TO KNOW

saucy (sô'sē) *adj.* disrespectful in a bold or high-spirited way; pert
complacently (kəm-plā'sənt-lē) *adv.* in a contented, unconcerned manner

Spring in St. John's Wood (1933), Dame Laura Knight. Oil on canvas, $51\frac{3}{4}'' \times 45\frac{1}{2}''$, Board of Trustees of the National Museums and Galleries on Merseyside, Walker Art Gallery, Liverpool, Great Britain.

too bad myself either," she added with a laugh and a shrug, wrinkling up her merry little face.

In the kitchen she cut me a slice of bread, smothered it with jam, and gave me a big mug of milk. "Will you have some, Gussie?" she asked in a sharp voice as if she knew only too well what the answer would be. "Aideen," she said to the horrible little girl who had followed us in, "aren't you fat and ugly enough without making a pig of yourself? Murder the Loaf we call her," she added smilingly to me. "You're a polite little boy, Larry, but damn the politeness you'd have if you had to deal with them. Is the book for your mother?"

"Oh, no, Mrs. O'Brien," I replied. "It's my own."

"You mean you can read a big book like that?" she asked incredulously, taking it from my hands and measuring the length of it with a puzzled air.

"Oh, yes, I can."

"I don't believe you," she said mockingly. "Go on and prove it!"

There was nothing I asked better than to prove it. I felt that as a performer I had never got my due, so I stood in the middle of the kitchen, cleared my throat, and began with great feeling to enunciate one of those horribly involved opening paragraphs you found in children's books of the time. "On a fine evening in Spring, as the setting sun was beginning to gild the blue peaks with its lambent[7] rays, a rider, recognizable as a student by certain niceties[8] of attire, was slowly, and perhaps regretfully, making his way . . ." It was the sort of opening sentence I loved.

"I declare to God!" Mrs. O'Brien interrupted in astonishment. "And that fellow there is one age with you, and he can't spell *house*. How well you wouldn't be down at the library, you caubogue,[9] you! . . . That's enough now, Larry,"

she added hastily as I made ready to entertain them further.

"Who wants to read that blooming[10] old stuff?" Gussie said <u>contemptuously</u>.

Later, he took me upstairs to show me his air rifle and model airplanes. Every detail of the room is still clear to me: the view into the back garden with its jungle of wild plants where Gussie had pitched his tent (a bad site for a tent as I patiently explained to him, owing to the danger from wild beasts); the three cots still unmade; the scribbles on the walls; and Mrs. O'Brien's voice from the kitchen telling Aideen to see what was wrong with the baby, who was screaming his head off from the pram outside the front door. Gussie, in particular, fascinated me. He was spoiled, clever, casual; good-looking, with his mother's small clean features; gay and calculating. I saw that when I left and his mother gave me a sixpence.[11] Naturally I refused it politely, but she thrust it into my trousers pocket, and Gussie dragged at her skirt, noisily demanding something for himself.

"If you give him a tanner,[12] you ought to give me a tanner," he yelled.

"I'll tan you," she said laughingly.

"Well, give up a lop[13] anyway," he begged, and she did give him a penny to take his face off her, as she said herself, and after that he followed me down the street and suggested we should go to the shop and buy sweets. I was

---

7. **lambent:** flickering lightly on a surface.

8. **niceties:** fine points or details.

9. **caubogue** (kô-bōg′): simpleton; bumpkin (from the Irish *cábóg*).

10. **blooming:** in Ireland and Britain, a slang word used to add intensity to a statement.

11. **sixpence:** a coin worth six British pennies.

12. **tanner:** another term for a sixpence.

13. **lop:** chunk; piece.

WORDS TO KNOW
contemptuously (kən-tĕmp′chōō-əs-lē) *adv.* in a way that shows one's low opinion of someone or something; scornfully

159

simple-minded, but I wasn't an out-and-out fool, and I knew that if I went to a sweetshop with Gussie, I should end up with no sixpence and very few sweets. So I told him I could not buy sweets without Mother's permission, at which he gave me up altogether as a sissy or worse.

It had been an exhausting afternoon but a very instructive one. In the twilight I went back slowly over the bridges, a little regretful for that fast-moving, colorful household, but with a new appreciation of my own home. When I went in, the lamp was lit over the fireplace and Father was at his tea.

"What kept you, child?" Mother asked with an anxious air, and suddenly I felt slightly guilty, and I played it as I usually did whenever I was at fault—in a loud, demonstrative, grown-up way. I stood in the middle of the kitchen with my cap in my hand and pointed it first at one, then at the other.

"You wouldn't believe who I met!" I said dramatically.

"Wisha,[14] who, child?" Mother asked.

"Miss Cadogan," I said, placing my cap squarely on a chair and turning on them both again. "Miss May Cadogan. Mrs. O'Brien as she is now."

"Mrs. O'Brien?" Father exclaimed, putting down his cup. "But where did you meet Mrs. O'Brien?"

"I said you wouldn't believe it. It was near the library. I was talking to some fellows, and what do you think but one of them was Gussie O'Brien, Mrs. O'Brien's son. And he took me home with him, and his mother gave me bread and jam, and she gave me *this.*" I produced the sixpence with a real flourish.

"Well, I'm blowed!" Father gasped, and first he looked at me, and then he looked at Mother and burst into a loud guffaw.

"And she said to tell you she remembers you too, and that she sent her love."

"Oh, by the jumping bell of Athlone!"[15] Father crowed and clapped his hands on his knees. I could see he believed the story I had told and was delighted with it, and I could see, too, that Mother did not believe it and that she was not in the least delighted. That, of course, was the trouble with Mother. Though she would do anything to help me with an intellectual problem, she never seemed to understand the need for experiment. She never opened her mouth while Father cross-questioned me, shaking his head in wonder and storing it up to tell the men in the factory. What pleased him most was Mrs. O'Brien's remembering the shape of his head, and later, while Mother was out of the kitchen, I caught him looking in the mirror and stroking the back of his head.

But I knew too that for the first time I had managed to produce in Mother the unrest that Father could produce, and I felt wretched and guilty and didn't know why. This was an aspect of history I only studied later.

That night I was really able to indulge my passion. At last I had the material to work with. I saw myself as Gussie O'Brien, standing in the bedroom, looking down at my tent in the garden, and Aideen as my sister, and Mrs. O'Brien as my mother, and, like Pascal, I re-created history. I remembered Mrs. O'Brien's laughter, her scolding, and the way she stroked my head. I knew she was kind—casually kind—and hot-tempered, and recognized that in dealing with her I must somehow be a different sort of person. Being good at reading would never satisfy her. She would almost compel you to be as Gussie

---

14. **wisha:** in Ireland, an introductory interjection meaning "Well!" or "Indeed!"

15. **by the jumping bell of Athlone** (ăth-lōn′): a humorous exclamation. Athlone is a town in central Ireland.

was: flattering, impertinent, and exacting. Though I couldn't have expressed it in those terms, she was the sort of woman who would compel you to flirt with her.

Then, when I had had enough, I deliberately soothed myself as I did whenever I had scared myself by pretending that there was a burglar in the house or a wild animal trying to get in the attic window. I just crossed my hands on my chest, looked up at the window, and said to myself: "It is not like that. I am not Gussie O'Brien. I am Larry Delaney, and my mother is Mary Delaney, and we live in Number 8, Wellington Square. Tomorrow I'll go to school at the Cross, and first there will be prayers, and then arithmetic, and after that composition."

For the first time the charm did not work. I had ceased to be Gussie, all right, but somehow I had not become myself again, not any self that I knew. It was as though my own identity was a sort of sack I had to live in, and I had deliberately worked my way out of it, and now I couldn't

get back again because I had grown too big for it. I practiced every trick I knew to reassure myself. I tried to play a counting game; then I prayed, but even the prayer seemed different, as though it didn't belong to me at all. I was away in the middle of empty space, divorced from mother and home and everything permanent and familiar. Suddenly I found myself sobbing. The door opened, and Mother came in in her nightdress, shivering, her hair over her face.

"You're not sleeping, child," she said in a wan and complaining voice.

I snivelled, and she put her hand on my forehead.

"You're hot," she said. "What ails you?"

I could not tell her of the nightmare in which I was lost. Instead, I took her hand, and gradually the terror retreated, and I became myself again, shrank into my little skin of identity, and left infinity and all its anguish behind.

"Mummy," I said, "I promise I never wanted anyone but you." ❖

RESPONDING
OPTIONS

FROM PERSONAL RESPONSE TO CRITICAL ANALYSIS

REFLECT

1. Did you find this story humorous? serious? both? Describe your impressions.

RETHINK

2. How would you describe young Larry Delaney?
   Consider
   - how he spends his free time
   - his relationship with each of his parents
   - why he fantasizes about a different family background
   - his encounter with Gussie and Mrs. O'Brien

3. Do you think Larry would be happy as Mrs. O'Brien's son? Why or why not?

4. What seems to be the narrator's attitude toward his own childhood? Support your response with details from the story.

5. Frank O'Connor once said that storytelling "doesn't deal with problems; it doesn't have any solutions to offer; it just states the human conditions." What do you think the writer is trying to say about the human condition in this story?

RELATE

6. Which do you feel is more influential in determining what kind of person a child becomes—biological factors (inherited genes) or environmental factors (culture, friendships, economic status, and so forth)? Explain your opinion.

ANOTHER PATHWAY

Plan a film version of "The Study of History" by designing and drawing a storyboard— a series of sketches showing the sets and the positions of the actors in one or more scenes of the story.

QUICKWRITES

1. Write an **autobiographical incident** that, like Larry Delaney's story, deals with a turning point in your life. If you prefer, write from the point of view of the person you might have become if the circumstances of your birth had been different, using as a springboard the freewriting you did for the Personal Connection on page 151.

2. Write several **love letters** that Michael Delaney and May Cadogan might have exchanged. Alternatively, write a love letter in which Mr. Riordan proposes marriage to Larry's mother, then write her "Dear John" response.

📁 *PORTFOLIO Save your writing. You may want to use it later as a springboard to a piece for your portfolio.*

LITERARY CONCEPTS

Characterization consists of the techniques that a writer uses to develop characters. There are four basic methods of characterization: **1.** through physical description; **2.** through a character's speech, thoughts, feelings, and actions; **3.** through the speech, thoughts, feelings, and actions of other characters; and **4.** through the narrator's direct comments about the character's nature. O'Connor uses all four techniques to bring the characters in "The Study of History" to life. Choose one of the characters in the story and find passages that illustrate each different method of characterization.

ACROSS THE CURRICULUM

Science Prepare a diagram of your family tree as far back as you can research it. Try to include information about genetic traits that are passed along from generation to generation, such as eye color and hair color.

Sister-in-law Maria

sister Jenny · Me · brother Rob

Uncle Luis · Dad — Mom

Grandma & Grandpa Lopez

Grandma & Grandpa Ortiz

Family Tree

LITERARY LINKS

Compare and contrast Larry's attitude toward his parents with that of another character in a fiction or nonfiction selection in Unit One.

FRANK O'CONNOR

Frank O'Connor grew up in a troubled, impoverished home, but he found refuge in the imaginary world of literature. He was an avid reader as a young boy and by the time he was 12 had already begun to pursue his life's work as a writer, creating an anthology of his own biographies, poems, and essays on Irish history.

For many years, O'Connor worked as a librarian in Cork and in Dublin, his occupation being one that gave him time to write. Eventually he became one of Ireland's most influential literary figures, producing everything from poetry to novels,

1903–1966

travel books to literary criticism. O'Connor is best known for his intimate and realistic short stories, however. According to James Matthews, O'Connor's biographer, "Only when he had a story banging around in the echo chamber of his mind was Frank O'Connor really alive." His passion for writing is evident not only in his work but also in his writing habits: he was known to revise his stories over and over again, even after they were published.

OTHER WORKS *Domestic Relations, An Only Child, Collected Stories*

Afro-American Fragment
LANGSTON HUGHES UNITED STATES

So long,
So far away
Is Africa.
Not even memories alive
5 Save those that history books create,
Save those that songs
Beat back into the blood—
Beat out of blood with words sad-sung
In strange un-Negro tongue—
10 So long,
So far away
Is Africa.

Subdued and time-lost
Are the drums—and yet
15 Through some vast mist of race
There comes this song
I do not understand,
This song of atavistic[1] land,
Of bitter yearnings lost
20 Without a place—
So long,
So far away
Is Africa's
Dark face.

---

1. **atavistic** (ăt′ə-vĭs′tĭk): showing a recurrence of characteristics possessed by remote ancestors.

Haitian drum (1940s), artist unknown.
Wood and goat skin, 43 × 24 × 24 inches.
Collection of Virgil Young.

LANGSTON HUGHES

Langston Hughes was among the foremost figures in 20th-century African-American literature. Born in Joplin, Missouri, James Langston Hughes was the son of a schoolteacher mother and a shopkeeper father who separated soon after his birth. Until he was 12, he was raised principally by his grandmother. After her death, he lived with his mother and stepfather, eventually settling in Cleveland, Ohio. At the age of 19, Hughes published the poem "The Negro Speaks of Rivers" in a prestigious magazine. During the same year, he moved to New York City, where he briefly attended Columbia University. Hughes next held a series of varied jobs that took him to Africa and Europe as a sailor and to Paris, where he worked as a cook. On returning to the United States, he took a job as a busboy at a Washington, D.C., hotel, where one night he served the famous American poet Vachel Lindsay. Hughes daringly

1902–1967

dropped a few of his poems beside Lindsay's plate; Lindsay was so impressed that he read them aloud at a poetry recital he attended that very night. Soon afterward, Hughes had his poetry published in the African-American journal *Opportunity* and in a now-famous volume, *The Weary Blues* (1926).

Settling in Harlem, the New York City neighborhood that was a mecca for African-American artists in the 1920s, Hughes began a long and influential career marked by achievements in virtually every form of literature—plays, novels, short stories, essays, biographies, and, of course, poetry. He also championed the careers of younger black writers and edited several anthologies of African and African-American literature.

OTHER WORKS *The Big Sea, The Dream Keeper and Other Poems, I Wonder As I Wander, Selected Poems*

WRITING FROM EXPERIENCE

WRITING A FIRSTHAND NARRATIVE

As you have seen in Unit One, "Imprints of the Past," the families and cultures in which people grow up help mold them into the people they become. Having an awareness of your heritage can help you better understand yourself and others.

GUIDED ASSIGNMENT

Write About an Autobiographical Incident Many people have stories about times they suddenly understood the value of their heritage or times they rebelled against their heritage, perhaps in order to grow. Writing about an autobiographical incident can help you recognize and understand the significance of such an experience and share that discovery with others.

1 Analyze What You Read

In a small group, discuss the items on these pages. What information do you get from the table of statistics and its footnote? What ideas about heritage do the cartoon and the novel excerpt show? Make notes of your ideas.

2 Examine Your Heritage

Think of ways you experience your heritage or culture. Remember that you are the product of several cultures—a family culture, an American culture, and perhaps a regional, religious, social, or ethnic culture. Think about any conflicts that you have experienced among these cultures, beliefs, or customs. Then write a paragraph about your culture or heritage.

3 Collect Your Ideas

Look over your notes. List several autobiographical incidents you could write about that would tell something about your culture, heritage, beliefs, customs, or family history.

Statistical Table

U.S. Population by Selected Ancestry Group: 1990

Race*	Number
African-American	23,777,000
American Indian	8,708,000
Asian Indian	570,000
Chinese	1,505,000
Cuban	860,000
Czech	1,296,000
Dutch	6,227,000
English	32,652,000
Filipino	1,451,000
French	10,321,000
French Canadian	2,167,000
German	57,947,000
Greek	1,110,000
Irish	38,736,000
Italian	14,665,000
Japanese	1,005,000
Korean	837,000
Mexican	11,587,000
Norwegian	3,869,000
Polish	9,366,000
Puerto Rican	1,955,000
Russian	2,953,000
Scottish	5,394,000
Slovak	1,883, 000
Spanish	2,024,000
Swedish	4,681,000
Vietnamese	536,000

*The concept of race as used by the U.S. Census Bureau reflects self-identification; it does not denote any scientific classification based on biological stock. Persons who reported one or more ancestry groups may be included in more than one category.

Source: U.S. Bureau of the Census, 1990 Census of Population.

Novel Excerpt

The narrator is starting to feel her Chinese heritage in her blood.

Cartoon

THE FAR SIDE   By GARY LARSON

"This is your side of the family, you realize."

The narrator thought being Chinese meant acting weird.

I felt different about being Argentinean after I spent a week in Argentina.

Family Heirloom

A PAIR OF TICKETS

The minute our train leaves the Hong Kong border and enters Shenzhen, China, I feel different. I can feel the skin on my forehead tingling, my blood rushing through a new course, my bones aching with a familiar old pain. And I think, My mother was right. I am becoming Chinese.

"Cannot be helped," my mother said when I was fifteen and had vigorously denied that I had any Chinese whatsoever below my skin. I was a sophomore at Galileo High in San Francisco, and all my Caucasian friends agreed: I was about as Chinese as they were. But my mother had studied at a famous nursing school in Shanghai, and she said she knew all about genetics. So there was no doubt in her mind, whether I agreed or not: Once you are born Chinese, you cannot help but feel and think Chinese.

"Someday you will see," said my mother. "It is in your blood, waiting to be let go."

And when she said this, I saw myself transforming like a werewolf, a mutant tag of DNA suddenly triggered, replicating itself insidiously into a *syndrome,* a cluster of telltale Chinese behaviors, all those things my mother did to embarrass me—haggling with store owners, pecking her mouth with a toothpick in public, being color-blind to the fact that lemon yellow and pale pink are not good combinations for winter clothes.

But today I realize that I've never really known what it means to be Chinese. I am thirty-six years old. My mother is dead and I am on a train, carrying with me her dreams of coming home. I am going to China.

306

THE JOY LUCK CLUB   AMY TAN

LASERLINKS
• *WRITING SPRINGBOARD*

WRITING COACH

WRITING FROM EXPERIENCE   **167**

Exploring Experiences

A Closer Look Now that you've thought about what makes up your heritage and culture, you're ready to decide on a story to tell about it. The ideas on these pages will help you choose an autobiographical incident and begin writing about it.

1 Brainstorm Further

Take several sheets of paper. On each page, write a word or phrase that has to do with heritage or culture, such as *values* or *traditions*. On each page, complete a web with examples from your experience or family history. Think of autobiographical incidents you could relate about these that would say something about your heritage or culture.

Student's Brainstorming Web

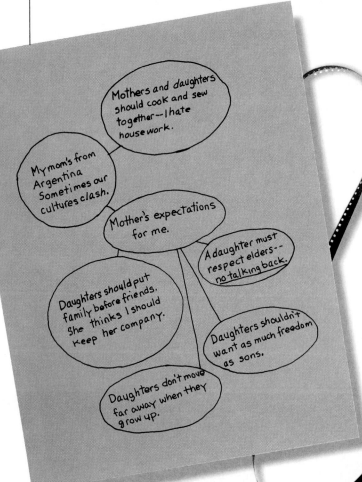

2 Choose Your Topic

You may have several ideas for a story. Asking yourself questions like the following will help you choose one idea.

- Which idea interests me the most?
- Which memory brings up strong emotions?
- Which incident would make the best story?
- Am I comfortable sharing this story?
- Will this story say something significant about my heritage?

③ Talk Over Your Idea

Share your story idea with your classmates.

- Pay attention to your classmates' reactions to your story idea. This will help you know what you need to explain about your heritage or about a family custom if you write this story.
- Listen carefully to your classmates' story ideas. Learning about other people's backgrounds can help you to see your own more clearly.

④ Get the Facts Straight

Do you have the information you need to begin writing?

- If you are telling a story from your past, do you remember everything clearly? List your questions and consult with others who shared the experience.
- If you are telling about a family tradition or holiday celebration, is the history or meaning of the tradition or celebration ⌐ear to you? The SkillBuilder at the right can help you do ⌐me research to find out more about the custom.

⌐nk About Audience and Purpose

⌐ider your audience as you think about what form your ⌐ might take. If you intend to share your story at a school ⌐eighborhood festival celebrating heritage, you may tell it ⌐rently than if you intend to share it with friends. Whatever ⌐audience, remember that if you can make clear why an ⌐ent from your past or a part of your heritage is important ⌐u, your story will hold their interest.

⌐cus on your audience and purpose, jot down the answers ⌐me of these questions:

⌐hat information do your readers need about the ⌐aracters or setting of your story?
⌐hat other background information do they need?
⌐hat dialogue or description will help to tell your story?
⌐hat point do you want to make with your story?

SkillBuilder

RESEARCH SKILLS

Locating Information

If you are telling about your family history or about a tradition or custom, there may be some questions that you want to have answered before you write. You may want to

- talk to an expert on your heritage—someone connected with a church or cultural center, perhaps
- look for information in a library or museum
- interview a grandparent or an older relative or friend

APPLYING WHAT YOU'VE LEARNED
Decide what sources you will use to find answers for a question you have about your heritage. If one of your sources is a family member or expert, contact this person. Be sure to take notes or record interviews electronically.

THINK & PLAN

Reflecting on Your Idea

1. How did you decide what story to tell? How do you think you will share your story?
2. How did sharing your idea with your classmates help you plan your story?
3. Which of the methods you used to gather ideas were particularly helpful? Which will you want to try again?

DRAFTING

Getting Your Ideas Down

The Story Begins Once you have thought about your story, you can begin writing it. Some people dive in and write a story from beginning to end. Others start in the middle of an important scene and fill in the background later. Begin in the way that seems best for getting the significance of your story across to your audience.

❶ Write a Rough Draft

Write your story down as it comes to you. Don't worry yet about how it sounds.

Student's Rough Draft

I guess I want to show how I resented Mom's demands on my time.

It was Friday night and my mother had just asked me to stay home and read romance novels with her.

"Sorry, Mom," I answered. "You know there's a football game tonight. I have to be there in a half hour." I was a flag girl in the band and had to perform at halftime.

Add dialogue to help show Mom's disappointment?

Mom looked hurt. She had often accused me of caring more about my friends and activities than her. In Argentina, ~~where she's from~~, daughters stay home and keep their mothers company.

This year, I hadn't stayed home much on the weekends. I was a sophomore now, and there were parties and dances to go to. My friends expected me to come, and I wanted to be with them.

Check with Mom to see how she remembers this incident.

We ∧Mom and I often read books together, comparing plots in Agatha Christie stories or making fun of bookcovers that showed overly dramatic characters in flowing costumes. We would also have serious talks. Mom said she *grew up in Argentina and* ∧wanted me to be strong and independent because she hadn't been raised that way. Sometimes, however, she said I was "too modern."

❷ Evaluate Your Rough Draft

Asking yourself questions like these may help you decide whether you've told the incident the way you wanted to.

- Does the story make the point I want to make?
- What actions, descriptions, or dialogue could I add to help make my point?
- Do I need to explain any terms or ideas that my readers might not know?
- Do I need to insert a flashback, add background information, or reorganize my story to make it clear?

The example at the left shows the changes one student considered making to her rough draft.

❸ Rework and Share

The guidelines below can help you revise your rough draft and make your story clearer and more interesting to your readers.

LET YOUR STORY FLOW

- Begin your story in a way that makes the significance of the event you describe clear to your readers.
- Use transitions such as *before, next, after, meanwhile,* and *finally* to make the sequence of events clear to your reader.

CREATE VIVID IMAGES

- Use sensory details to describe important characters or settings in your story.
- Add details and dialogue that will help to make the incident real to your readers.
- Use vivid action verbs to tell what characters do.

 PEER RESPONSE

A peer reviewer can help you identify the strengths and weaknesses of your draft. Ask questions like the following:

- What was unclear about my story?
- What more do you need to know about the characters, setting, events, or background of my story?
- Why do you think I chose to tell this incident?

Finishing Your Story

The Final Touch To create a strong impression in your readers' minds, your narrative should be free of distracting errors in spelling, grammar, and punctuation. Follow the steps on these pages to put the finishing touches on your story.

① Revise and Edit

Read your draft aloud slowly. Look for awkward phrasings and places where you can remove unnecessary description, dialogue, or explanation that gets in the way of your story. Look for errors. Underline words, sentences, or sections you want to revise, and write notes or questions to yourself in the margins.

- Use peer comments and the Standards for Evaluation to decide which terms or ideas need more explanation.
- Use the Editing Checklist in the SkillBuilder on the next page to help you use dialogue effectively.
- The model shows how one student revised and edited her draft, using details to develop the setting and characters.

What transitional words keep the sequence of events clear?

Student's Revised Draft

What details help set the scene?

Mom walked through the door of our small apartment at a few minutes after 7 P.M., her old canvas bag in hand. After work she had stopped at the library for a few mysteries and romance novels. It was Mom's Friday-night ritual: curl up on the couch with a juicy book and a cup of coffee. She plopped onto the couch, slipped off her shoes, and rubbed her feet. "Want to do some light reading tonight?" she asked.

I knew I wasn't living up to her expectations, and sometimes I felt guilty about that. Other times I just felt resentful. How could I be the strong, independent American daughter she wanted and the dutiful Argentinean one too?

When I told Mom I wasn't staying home, I thought she'd get mad. Usually, she does. This time, she didn't say anything. She just looked lonely. I thought about how I sometimes missed her too. I remembered how much my friends liked her.

"Mom, why don't you come with me?" I asked her. "In fact, I'd really like it if you would."

Mom liked the idea. She has been coming to all of the home football games ever since.

Poster for heritage festival and a student's note cards

 GRAMMAR FROM WRITING

Using Quotation Marks in Dialogue
Dialogue can make characters seem real or help move a story along. For direct quotations, use quotation marks.

"If we don't leave now," Pam said, "we're going to be late."

Do not use quotation marks with indirect quotations.

Pam said that if we didn't leave immediately we would be late.

GRAMMAR HANDBOOK

For more information on using quotation marks, see page 1096 of the Grammar Handbook.

Editing Checklist Use the following editing tips as you revise:

- Are words spelled correctly?
- Are sentences, including dialogue, punctuated correctly?

② Share Your Work

Are you craving a wider audience? You may want to share your story at a school or neighborhood festival celebrating heritage. Think about photographs and other visual aids that could accompany your story.

PUBLISHING IDEAS

- Your class could collect stories about heritage and publish them in an illustrated booklet.
- Stories could be part of a radio broadcast about heritage.
- Your story could be published in a family newsletter.
- You could save your story in a family memory album.

Standards for Evaluation
A firsthand narrative
• includes details that develop settings, characters, and events
• has dialogue that makes characters seem real
• reveals why the incident was significant

REFLECT & ASSESS

Evaluating the Experience

1. What method of generating writing ideas worked for you?
2. Which of the stories shared in class did you like best? Why?
3. What did you learn about heritage from this assignment?

PORTFOLIO You may want to add your story and your evaluation to your portfolio.

REFLECT & ASSESS

UNIT ONE: IMPRINTS OF THE PAST

How have your own views about the past been affected by the selections in this unit? How have you developed or improved your skills? Explore these questions by completing one or more of the options in each of the following sections.

REFLECTING ON THEME

OPTION 1 **Classifying Imprints of the Past** Draw a horizontal line in the middle of a sheet of paper. On the top half, list characters or real people from this unit who you think have been positively affected by the past. On the bottom half, list characters who you think have been negatively affected. Add yourself or people you know to either category. Then, with a small group compare your lists.

OPTION 2 **Nominating a Guest Speaker** Imagine that your school's administration has asked for suggestions on how to improve the annual Heritage Day assembly. In past years, the speakers at this assembly have been known to cause drowsiness and boredom. Choose from this unit a character or writer who might breathe new life into the event. The person you choose should be not only interesting but also capable of communicating valuable insights about the importance of heritage. Write a nominating speech in which you explain your choice.

OPTION 3 **Role-Playing** This unit begins with a quotation from Oscar Wilde: "One's past is what one is." (See page 12.) How do you think the various characters, real people, and writers in this unit would respond to that quotation? Would they agree with it or disagree with it? Work with a small group of classmates to conduct a role-playing activity, with each member of the group assuming the identity of a character, real person, or writer in the unit. Then share your own views about the quotation.

Self-Assessment: Now that you have considered how your views about the past have been affected by the selections in this unit, make a chart. In the first column, record insights about how the past influences people's lives; in the second, list selections that prompted the insights.

REVIEWING LITERARY CONCEPTS

OPTION 1 **Understanding Conflict** In the selections in this unit, individuals become involved in a variety of external and internal conflicts. In a chart similar to the one shown, name at least six characters or real people in the unit and describe an important

Character or Person/Selection	Type of Conflict	Description of Conflict	Difficulty of Resolving Conflict
Mark Mathabane/ *Kaffir Boy*	External	Mark resists his mother's plans to enroll him in school.	4

conflict that each one faces. Then rate the difficulty of resolving each conflict, from 1 (somewhat difficult) to 5 (extremely difficult). Compare your chart with those of your classmates and discuss the differences.

OPTION 2 **Examining Plot** Review the selections that you have read in this unit. In which does the narrative proceed in chronological order? In which does the narrative not follow a strict chronological sequence? Discuss the advantages and the disadvantages of both types of narration with a small group of classmates, drawing on the selections for examples. Then share your group's conclusions with the rest of the class.

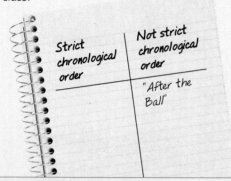

Self-Assessment: *On a sheet of paper, copy the following list of literary terms introduced in this unit. Underline the terms that you feel you understand completely. Put question marks next to any terms that you do not understand fully. You may want to review the terms you marked with question marks.*

conflict	*essay*
plot	*figurative language*
setting	*description*
characters	*imagery*
flashback	*autobiography*
dialogue	*characterization*

PORTFOLIO BUILDING

- **QuickWrites** For some of the QuickWrites activities in this unit, you assumed the identities of characters or real people depicted in selections. Review your writing for those activities, and pick out one or two pieces that you feel are particularly successful in portraying a character's personality or views. In a cover note, explain what makes the piece or pieces that you selected effective. Add the pieces and the note to your portfolio.

- **Writing About Literature** In this unit you responded personally to a writer's portrayal of a group or an event. Write a note to accompany your response. Briefly tell what a personal response is, what the subject of your response was, and whether you feel that the response was successful. Then tell what you learned about the importance of portraying a subject fairly and accurately.

- **Writing from Experience** By now you've written a firsthand narrative about your cultural heritage. How would you describe that writing experience? List two or three things that you discovered about yourself and your cultural heritage from your research and writing. Decide whether to include your note in your portfolio.

- **Personal Choice** Reflect upon all the activities and writing that you have completed for this unit, including any work that you may have done on your own. Also look over the evaluations and responses that you have received from peers. Which of the activities or writing projects proved the most rewarding? Write a note that explains your choice, and add it to your portfolio.

Self-Assessment: *At this point, you may just be beginning your portfolio. Review the pieces that you have chosen for your portfolio. Do they have anything in common? What do they suggest about your strengths and interests as a writer?*

SETTING GOALS

As you worked through the activities in this unit, you probably became more aware of your strengths and weaknesses in reading and writing skills. After reviewing the work that you did for this unit, create a list of skills that you would like to work on in the next unit.

Reflecting on Society

Literature

is one

of a society's

instruments

of self-awareness.

ITALO CALVINO
*Italian novelist and short story writer
1923-1985*

Central America: Children in
Transition (1982), Betty LaDuke.
From Multi-Cultural Celebrations,
the Paintings of Betty LaDuke
1972–1992.

CHALLENGING THE SYSTEM

REFLECTING ON THEME

How do you respond to problems or injustices in society—or in your own immediate surroundings? Do you take action, even if it means going against the crowd? Or do you stand by and watch, perhaps feeling powerless? This part of Unit Two focuses on people who take a stand. You'll encounter a woman who deceives Nazi officers, a young boy who exposes corruption, and others who challenge the system—sometimes with surprising results.

What Do You Think? Skim a daily newspaper or weekly newsmagazine to find articles related to social issues. Based on what you find, jot down a list of those issues that you care about—the ones that touch your heart, raise your temper, or maybe even spur you to action. Then share your list with a partner and discuss how it reflects your values and concerns.

W. P. Kinsella
(1935–)
This Canadian writer turned a baseball diamond into a field of dreams.

Margaret Walker
(1915–)
A prominent African-American poet, a chronicler of her times

Coretta Scott King
(1927–)
A prominent civil rights activist—and widow of Dr. Martin Luther King, Jr.

Armando Valladares
(1937–)
Twenty-two years in a Cuban prison; his poetry is a cry for freedom

Luisa Valenzuela
(1944–)
A native of Argentina, today a major voice in Latin American writing

Josephine Tey	**The Pen of My Aunt** *A Nazi soldier at her door, a stranger's life in her hands*	182
W. P. Kinsella	**The Thrill of the Grass** *What turns these men into conspirators?*	198
Heinrich Böll	**The Balek Scales** *A boy uncovers the truth.*	211
Coretta Scott King	from **Montgomery Boycott** *An episode in civil rights history remembered*	221
Margaret Walker	**Sit-Ins** / INSIGHT *An act of civil disobedience*	229

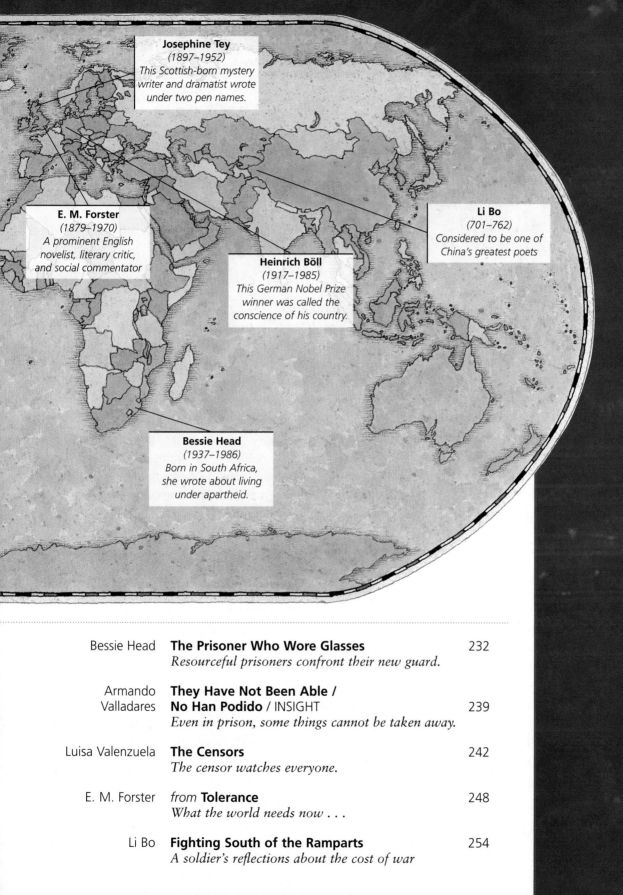

Josephine Tey
(1897–1952)
This Scottish-born mystery writer and dramatist wrote under two pen names.

E. M. Forster
(1879–1970)
A prominent English novelist, literary critic, and social commentator

Heinrich Böll
(1917–1985)
This German Nobel Prize winner was called the conscience of his country.

Li Bo
(701–762)
Considered to be one of China's greatest poets

Bessie Head
(1937–1986)
Born in South Africa, she wrote about living under apartheid.

Bessie Head	**The Prisoner Who Wore Glasses** *Resourceful prisoners confront their new guard.*	232
Armando Valladares	**They Have Not Been Able /** **No Han Podido** / INSIGHT *Even in prison, some things cannot be taken away.*	239
Luisa Valenzuela	**The Censors** *The censor watches everyone.*	242
E. M. Forster	*from* **Tolerance** *What the world needs now . . .*	248
Li Bo	**Fighting South of the Ramparts** *A soldier's reflections about the cost of war*	254

FOCUS ON DRAMA

What comes to mind when you hear the word *drama?* Do you see a troupe of actors on a stage beneath the glaring lights, with an audience in rapt attention? Or perhaps you recall a spellbinding movie. Broadly defined, drama is any story in dialogue that is performed by actors before an audience. A Broadway play, a television comedy, a Hollywood movie—all can be defined as drama.

The origin of the word *drama*, from the Greek word *dran*, meaning "to do" or "to act," reminds us that all dramas portray human actions. Unlike other forms of literature, such as fiction and poetry, a work of drama requires the collaboration of many people in order to come to life. In an important sense, a drama in printed form is an incomplete work of art. It is a skeleton that must be fleshed out by a director, actors, set designers, and others who interpret the work and stage a performance, whether before cameras or a live audience. From ancient times to the present, drama has always been a communal activity.

Most forms of drama share certain elements, described below.

PLOT As in fiction, the plot in drama is a series of interrelated actions. Typically, a drama opens with a problem or conflict, which then intensifies, reaches a peak, and is eventually resolved. The elements of plot—**exposition, rising action, climax, falling action,** and **dénouement**—are described in detail on pages 16–17.

Dramatic plots are often divided into **scenes.** Each scene establishes a different time or place. Long plays, such as Shakespeare's *Julius Caesar*, are divided into **acts,** with each act comprising related scenes.

CHARACTERS Many of the same types of characters that populate fiction can be found in drama. A **round character** (also known as a **dynamic character**), for example, is one that goes through a change or development in the course of the drama, while a **flat character** (or **static character**) is one that remains the same throughout. A **protagonist** is usually the central character, often the one that the audience most closely identifies with. The **antagonist** opposes the protagonist, which results in the central conflict. In Sophocles' *Antigone*, the protagonist is Antigone; she seeks to bury her brother, who has been killed in a civil war. Creon, the **antagonist,** has forbidden burial rites for those who rebelled, which leads to a series of confrontations between him and Antigone.

DIALOGUE Dialogue, or conversation between characters, is the lifeblood of drama. Virtually everything of consequence, from plot details to character revelations, flows from the dialogue. Of course, dialogue plays an important role in fiction and sometimes in poetry, but usually such dialogue is framed by the commentary of a narrator or speaker. In drama, dialogue is seldom filtered through a controlling viewpoint (though some dramas do make use of narrators). As a result, the director, the performers, and the audience have more freedom to form their own interpretations.

In addition to speech between two or more characters, drama may make use of **monologue,** a long speech spoken by a single character to himself or herself or to the audience. Drama may also make use of an **aside,** a short speech delivered to the audience, beyond the hearing of the remaining characters.

STAGE DIRECTIONS In the history of drama, stage directions are relatively new; they did not become common until the 19th century, which explains why Chekhov used them but Sophocles did not. The stage directions in a script serve as a kind of instructional manual for the director, actors, and stage crew as well as the general reader. Often the stage directions are printed in italic type, and they may be enclosed in parentheses or brackets. Directions may describe the **scenery,** or **setting,** the environment created on stage or on film that produces the illusion of a specific time or place. Directions may also describe the **props**—objects, furniture, and the like—that are used during a performance. Stage directions may describe lighting, costumes, music, sound effects, or, in the case of film productions, camera angles and shots. Most important, the stage directions usually provide hints to the performers on how the characters look, move, and speak.

STRATEGIES FOR READING DRAMA

- **Pay close attention to the beginning.** Much important information is revealed at the very beginning of a play. Before you begin reading, review the cast of characters and familiarize yourself with the names. Read the opening stage directions carefully to learn about the characters and the setting. Likewise, go slowly through the opening scene, which usually reveals crucial background information and introduces the main conflict or problem.

- **Search for the conflicts.** As you read, always be on the lookout for any signs of tension, turmoil, or unresolved problems. Watch for both **external conflict,** that is, conflict between characters, and internal conflict, the struggle between opposing tendencies within a single character.

- **Stage the play in your mind.** It is not enough just to read the words; you need to visualize the action. Imagine the feelings behind the dialogue

and the stage directions that accompany the dialogue. Form an image of each major character and try to hear the words as he or she speaks. To read a drama successfully, you need to be a director as well as a reader.

- **Take sides with the characters.** Drama is always more enjoyable if you look for a character you can identify with, one who can engage your interest and sympathies. As you read, decide where the characters stand in relation to your own values and beliefs. Taking sides with the characters will help you to become more involved.

- **Read the play aloud with others.** After you have read a play silently, read it aloud with others. When possible, get together with friends or classmates to stage a "read through," with each person reading a different character's lines. Better yet, stage a production of a scene or of the entire play.

PREVIEWING

The Pen of My Aunt
Josephine Tey Scotland

PERSONAL CONNECTION

Imagine that you live in a country occupied by a foreign military power that uses terror and brutality to maintain control. How do you think you would respond to such a situation? Would you resist? Share your ideas with your classmates.

HISTORICAL CONNECTION

The Pen of My Aunt is set in Nazi-occupied France during World War II. On June 22, 1940, France surrendered to the invading forces of Germany, who occupied first part and then all of the nation. Some French soldiers escaped to England and established the Free French forces, who joined in the Allied fight against the Nazis. In France itself, many people also fought the Nazis, banding together in a resistance movement that practiced a kind of underground warfare. The French resistance conducted raids, bombings, ambushes, and other missions designed to weaken the Nazis. The resistance also organized an escape network for downed Allied pilots and resistance fighters who needed to flee the country. For anyone caught working with the resistance, the usual punishment was execution.

Some French citizens, however, fully cooperated with the forces of the German occupation. These people, who were called collaborators, often helped the Nazi cause, even to the point of betraying their fellow citizens. Aided by collaborators, the Nazis exerted strict control over the everyday lives of French citizens. At all times, people needed to carry identification papers, which helped the police to monitor their activities and travels.

WRITING CONNECTION

In your notebook, list the qualities that you think someone who participates in a resistance movement would need to have. As you read, determine whether the main character, Madame, exhibits those qualities.

LASERLINKS
• *HISTORICAL CONNECTION*

The Pen of My Aunt

Josephine Tey

Characters

Madame **Stranger**
Simone **Corporal**

The scene is a French country house during the Occupation. The lady of the house is seated in her drawing room.[1]

Simone (*approaching*).
Madame! Oh, madame!
Madame, have you—

Madame. Simone.

Simone. Madame, have you seen what—

Madame. Simone!

Simone. But madame—

Madame. Simone, this may be an age of barbarism, but I will have none of it inside the walls of this house.

Simone. But madame, there is a—there is a—

Madame (*silencing her*). Simone. France may be an occupied country, a ruined nation, and a conquered race, but we will keep, if you please, the usages of civilization.

Simone. Yes, madame.

Madame. One thing we still possess, thank God; and that is good manners. The enemy never had it; and it is not something they can take from *us*.

Simone. No, madame.

---

1. **drawing room:** a large, often elegant room where guests are entertained.

183

Madame. Go out of the room again. Open the door—

Simone. Oh, *madame!* I wanted to tell you—

Madame. —open the door, shut it behind you—quietly—take two paces into the room, and say what you came to say. (Simone *goes hastily out, shutting the door. She reappears, shuts the door behind her, takes two paces into the room, and waits.*) Yes, Simone?

Simone. I expect it is too late now; they will be here.

Madame. Who will?

Simone. The soldiers who were coming up the avenue.

Madame. After the last few months I should not have thought that soldiers coming up the avenue was a remarkable fact. It is no doubt a party with a billeting order.[2]

Simone (*crossing to the window*). No, madame, it is two soldiers in one of their little cars, with a civilian between them.

Madame. Which civilian?

Simone. A stranger, madame.

Madame. A stranger? Are the soldiers from the combatant branch?

Simone. No, they are those beasts of administration.[3] Look, they have stopped. They are getting out.

Madame (*at the window*). Yes, it is a stranger. Do you know him, Simone?

Simone. I have never set eyes on him before, madame.

Madame. You would know if he belonged to the district?

Simone. Oh, madame, I know every man between here and St. Estèphe.[4]

Madame (*dryly*). No doubt.

Simone. Oh, merciful God, they are coming up the steps.

Madame. My good Simone, that is what the steps were put there for.

Simone. But they will ring the bell and I shall have to—

Madame. And you will answer it and behave as if you had been trained by a butler and ten upper servants instead of being the charcoal-burner's daughter from over at Les Chênes.[5] (*This is said encouragingly, not in unkindness.*) You will be very calm and correct—

Simone. Calm! Madame! With my inside turning over and over like a wheel at a fair!

Madame. A good servant does not have an inside, merely an exterior. (*comforting*) Be assured, my child. You have your place here; that is more than those creatures on our doorstep have. Let that hearten you—

Simone. Madame! They are not going to ring. They are coming straight in.

Madame (*bitterly*). Yes. They have forgotten long ago what bells are for. (*Door opens.*)

Stranger (*in a bright, confident, casual tone*). Ah, there you are, my dear aunt. I am so glad. Come in, my friend, come in. My dear aunt, this gentleman wants you to identify me.

Madame. Identify you?

Corporal. We found this man wandering in the woods—

Stranger. The corporal found it inexplicable that anyone should wander in a wood.

Corporal. And he had no papers on him—

---

2. **billeting order:** a written order demanding that troops be lodged in a private home or another location.

3. **combatant branch . . . beasts of administration:** The German occupying force included both combat troops fighting the war and officials who administered and controlled the occupied territory.

4. **St. Estèphe** (săṅ′tĕs-tĕf′).

5. **Les Chênes** (lā-shĕn′).

184

Stranger. And I rightly pointed out that if I carry all the papers one is supposed to these days, I am no good to God or man. If I put them in a hip pocket, I can't bend forward; if I put them in a front pocket, I can't bend at all.

Corporal. He said that he was your nephew, madame, but that did not seem to us very likely, so we brought him here.

(*There is the slightest pause; just one moment of silence.*)

Madame. But of course this is my nephew.

Corporal. He is?

Madame. Certainly.

Corporal. He lives here?

Madame (*assenting*). My nephew lives here.

Corporal. So! (*recovering*) My apologies, madame. But you will admit that appearances were against the young gentleman.

Madame. Alas, Corporal, my nephew belongs to a generation who delight in flouting appearances. It is what they call "expressing their personality," I understand.

Corporal (*with contempt*). No doubt, madame.

Madame. Convention is anathema to them, and there is no sin like conformity. Even a collar is an offense against their liberty, and a discipline not to be borne by free necks.

Corporal. Ah yes, madame. A little more discipline among your nephew's generation, and we might not be occupying your country today.

Stranger. You think it was that collar of yours that conquered my country? You flatter yourself, Corporal. The only result of wearing a collar like that is varicose veins in the head.

Madame (*repressive*). Please! My dear boy. Let us not descend to personalities.

Stranger. The matter is not personal, my good aunt, but scientific. Wearing a collar like that retards the flow of fresh blood to the head, with the most disastrous consequences to the grey matter of the brain. The hypothetical grey matter. In fact, I have a theory—

Corporal. Monsieur,[6] your theories do not interest me.

Stranger. No? You do not find speculation interesting?

Corporal. In this world one judges by results.

Stranger (*after a slight pause of reflection*). I see. The collared conqueror sits in the high places, while the collarless conquered lies about in the woods. And who comes best out of that, would you say? Tell me, Corporal, as man to man, do you never have a mad, secret desire to lie unbuttoned in a wood?

Corporal. I have only one desire, monsieur, and that is to see your papers.

Stranger (*taken off guard and filling in time*). My papers?

Madame. But is that necessary, Corporal? I have already told you that—

Corporal. I know that madame is a very good collaborator and in good standing—

Madame. In that case—

Corporal. But when we begin an affair we like to finish it. I have asked to see monsieur's papers, and the matter will not be finished until I have seen them.

Madame. You acknowledge that I am in "good standing," Corporal?

Corporal. So I have heard, madame.

---

6. **monsieur** (mə-syœ′): A French form of address, corresponding to "sir" or "mister."

WORDS TO KNOW

anathema (ə-năth′ə-mə) *n.* something or someone to be shunned or despised; a curse
repressive (rĭ-prĕs′ĭv) *adj.* causing or inclined to put down by force or hold back
speculation (spĕk′yə-lā′shən) *n.* consideration of a subject, especially based on incomplete or unclear evidence; guesswork

185

The Suitor (1893), Edouard Vuillard. Oil on millboard panel, Smith College Museum of Art, Northampton, Massachusetts. Purchased, Drayton Hillyer Fund, 1938.

Madame. Then I must consider it a discourtesy on your part to demand my nephew's credentials.

Corporal. It is no reflection on madame. It is a matter of routine, nothing more.

Stranger (*murmuring*). The great god Routine.

Madame. To ask for his papers was routine; to insist on their production is discourtesy. I shall say so to your commanding officer.

Corporal. Very good, madame. In the meantime, I shall inspect your nephew's papers.

Madame. And what if I—

Stranger (*quietly*). You may as well give it up, my dear. You could as easily turn a steamroller. They have only one idea at a time. If the corporal's heart is set on seeing my papers, he shall see them. (*moving towards the door*) I left them in the pocket of my coat.

Simone (*unexpectedly, from the background*). Not in your *linen* coat?

Stranger (*pausing*). Yes. Why?

Simone (*with apparently growing anxiety*). Your *cream* linen coat? The one you were wearing yesterday?

Stranger. Certainly.

Simone. Merciful Heaven! I sent it to the laundry!

Stranger. To the laundry!

Simone. Yes, monsieur; this morning; in the basket.

Stranger (*in incredulous anger*). You sent my coat, *with my papers in the pocket,* to the laundry!

Simone (*defensive and combatant*). I didn't know monsieur's papers were in the pocket.

Stranger. You didn't know! You didn't know that a packet of documents weighing half a ton were in the pocket. An identity card, a *laisser passer,*[7] a food card, a drink card, an army discharge, a permission to wear civilian clothes, a permission to go farther than ten miles to the east, a permission to go more than ten miles to the west, a permission to—

Simone (*breaking in with spirit*). How was I to know the coat was heavy! I picked it up with the rest of the bundle that was lying on the floor.

Stranger (*snapping her head off*). My coat was on the back of the chair.

Simone. It was on the floor.

Stranger. On the back of the chair!

Simone. It was on the floor with your dirty shirt and your pajamas, and a towel and what not. I put my arms round the whole thing and then—woof! into the basket with them.

Stranger. I tell you that coat was on the back of the chair. It was quite clean and was not going to the laundry for two weeks yet—if then. I hung it there myself, and—

Madame. My dear boy, what does it matter? The damage is done now. In any case, they will find the papers when they unpack the basket, and return them tomorrow.

Stranger. If someone doesn't steal them. There are a lot of people who would like to lay hold of a complete set of papers, believe me.

Madame (*reassuring*). Oh, no. Old Fleureau[8] is the soul of honesty. You have no need to worry about them. They will be back first thing tomorrow, you shall see; and then we shall have much pleasure in sending them to the administration office for the corporal's inspection. Unless, of course, the corporal insists on your personal appearance at the office.

Corporal (*cold and indignant*). I have seen monsieur. All that I want now is to see his papers.

Stranger. You shall see them, Corporal, you shall see them. The whole half-ton of them. You may inspect them at your leisure. Provided,

---

7. *laisser passer* (lĕs′ā pä-sā′) *French:* a travel pass.

8. **Fleureau** (flœ-rō′).

that is, that they come back from the laundry to which this idiot has consigned them.

Madame (*again reassuring*). They will come back, never fear. And you must not blame Simone. She is a good child, and does her best.

Simone (*with an air of belated virtue*). I am not one to pry into pockets.

Madame. Simone, show the corporal out, if you please.

Simone (*natural feeling overcoming her for a moment*). He knows the way out. (*recovering*) Yes, madame.

Madame. And Corporal, try to take your duties a little less literally in future. My countrymen appreciate the spirit rather than the letter.

Corporal. I have my instructions, madame, and I obey them. Good day, madame. Monsieur.

(*He goes, followed by* Simone—*door closes. There is a moment of silence.*)

Stranger. For a good collaborator, that was a remarkably quick adoption.

Madame. Sit down, young man. I will give you something to drink. I expect your knees are none too well.

Stranger. My knees, madame, are pure gelatine. As for my stomach, it seems to have disappeared.

Madame (*offering him the drink she has poured out*). This will recall it, I hope.

Stranger. You are not drinking, madame?

Madame. Thank you, no.

Stranger. Not with strangers. It is certainly no time to drink with strangers. Nevertheless, I drink the health of a collaborator. (*He drinks.*) Tell me, madame, what will happen tomorrow when they find that you have no nephew?

Madame (*surprised*). But of course I have a nephew. I tell lies, my friend; but not *silly* lies. My charming nephew has gone to Bonneval[9] for the day. He finds country life dull.

Stranger. Dull? This—this heaven?

Madame (*dryly*). He likes to talk and here there is no audience. At headquarters in Bonneval he finds the audience sympathetic.

Stranger (*understanding the implication*). Ah.

Madame. He believes in the brotherhood of man—if you can credit it.

Stranger. After the last six months?

Madame. His mother was American, so he has half the Balkans[10] in his blood. To say nothing of Italy, Russia, and the Levant.[11]

Stranger (*half-amused*). I see.

Madame. A silly and worthless creature, but useful.

Stranger. Useful?

Madame. I—borrow his cloak.

Stranger. I see.

Madame. Tonight I shall borrow his identity papers, and tomorrow they will go to the office in St. Estèphe.

Stranger. But—he will have to know.

Madame (*placidly*). Oh, yes, he will know, of course.

Stranger. And how will you persuade such an enthusiastic collaborator to deceive his friends?

Madame. Oh, that is easy. He is my heir.

Stranger (*amused*). Ah.

Madame. He is, also, by the mercy of God, not too unlike you, so that his photograph will not startle the corporal too much tomorrow. Now tell me what you were doing in my wood.

---

9. **Bonneval** (bôn-väl´).

10. **Balkans** (bôl´kɘnz): the Balkan Peninsula of southeastern Europe. Madame is insulting her nephew, suggesting that his collaboration with the Nazis can be blamed on his mixed ancestry.

11. **Levant** (lɘ-vănt´): the countries bordering the eastern Mediterranean Sea, today including Turkey, Syria, Lebanon, Israel, and Egypt.

Stranger. Resting my feet—I am practically walking on my bones. And waiting for tonight.

Madame. Where are you making for? (*as he does not answer immediately*) The coast? (*He nods.*) That is four days away—five if your feet are bad.

Stranger. I know it.

Madame. Have you friends on the way?

Stranger. I have friends at the coast, who will get me a boat. But no one between here and the sea.

Madame (*rising*). I must consult my list of addresses. (*pausing*) What was your service?

Stranger. Army.

Madame. Which regiment?

Stranger. The 79th.

Madame (*after the faintest pause*). And your colonel's name?

Stranger. Delavault[12] was killed in the first week, and Martin[13] took over.

Madame (*going to her desk*). A "good collaborator" cannot be too careful. Now I can consult my notebook. A charming color, is it not? A lovely shade of red.

Stranger. Yes—but what has a red quill pen to do with your notebook?—Ah, you write with it of course—stupid of me.

Madame. Certainly I write with it—but it is also my notebook—look—I only need a hairpin—and then—so—out of my quill pen comes my notebook—a tiny piece of paper—but enough for a list of names.

Stranger. You mean that you keep that list on your desk? (*He sounds disapproving.*)

Madame. Where did you expect me to keep it, young man? In my corset?[14] Did you ever try to get something out of your corset in a hurry? What would you advise as the ideal quality in a hiding place for a list of names?

Stranger. That the thing should be difficult to find, of course.

Madame. Not at all. That it should be easily destroyed in emergency. It is too big for me to swallow—I suspect they do that only in books—and we have no fires to consume it, so I had to think of some other way. I did try to memorize the list, but what I could not be sure of remembering were those that—that had to be scored off. It would be fatal to send someone to an address that—that was no longer available. So I had to keep a written record.

Stranger. And if you neither eat it nor burn it when the moment comes, how do you get rid of it?

Madame. I could, of course, put a match to it, but scraps of freshly-burned paper on a desk take a great deal of explaining. If I ceased to be looked on with approval, my usefulness would end. It is important therefore that there should be no sign of anxiety on my part: no burned paper, no excuses to leave the room, no nods and becks[15] and winks. I just sit here at my desk and go on with my letters. I tilt my nice big inkwell sideways for a moment and dip the pen into the deep ink at the side. The ink flows into the hollow of the quill, and all is blotted out. (*consulting the list*) Let me see. It would be good if you could rest your feet for a day or so.

Stranger (*ruefully*). It would.

Madame. There is a farm just beyond the Marnay[16] crossroads on the way to St. Estèphe— (*She pauses to consider.*)

Stranger. St. Estèphe is the home of the single-minded corporal. I don't want to run into him again.

---

12. **Delavault** (də-lä-vō′).

13. **Martin** (mär-tăɴ′).

14. **corset** (kôr′sĭt): a close-fitting, reinforced undergarment worn to give shape or support to the figure.

15. **becks:** summoning gestures.

16. **Marnay** (mär-nĕ′).

Madame. No, that might be awkward; but that farm of the Cherfils[17] would be ideal. A good hiding place, and food to spare, and fine people—

Stranger. If your nephew is so friendly with the invader, how is it that the corporal doesn't know him by sight?

Madame (*absently*). The unit at St. Estèphe is a noncommissioned one.

Stranger. Does the brotherhood of man exclude sergeants, then?

Madame. Oh, definitely. Brotherhood does not really begin under field rank, I understand.

Stranger. But the corporal may still meet your nephew somewhere.

Madame. That is a risk one must take. It is not a very grave one. They change the personnel every few weeks, to prevent them becoming too <u>acclimatized</u>. And even if he met my nephew, he is unlikely to ask for the papers of so obviously well-to-do a citizen. If you could bear to go *back* a little—

Stranger. Not a step! It would be like—like denying God. I have got so far, against all the odds, and I am not going a yard back. Not even to rest my feet!

Madame. I understand; but it is a pity. It is a long way to the Cherfils farm—two miles east of the Marnay crossroads it is, on a little hill.

Stranger. I'll get there; don't worry. If not tonight then tomorrow night. I am used to sleeping in the open by now.

Madame. I wish we could have you here, but it is too dangerous. We are liable to be billeted on at any moment, without notice. However, we can give you a good meal, and a bath. We have no coal, so it will be one of those flat-tin-saucer baths.[18] And if you want to be very kind to Simone, you might have it somewhere in the kitchen regions and so save her carrying water upstairs.

Stranger. But of course.

Madame. Before the war I had a staff of twelve. Now I have Simone. I dust and Simone sweeps, and between us we keep the dirt at bay. She has no manners but a great heart, the child.

Stranger. The heart of a lion.

Madame. Before I put this back you might memorize these: Forty Avenue Foch,[19] in Crest,[20] the back entrance.

Stranger. Forty Avenue Foch, the back entrance.

Madame. You may find it difficult to get into Crest, by the way. It is a closed area. The pot boy[21] at the Red Lion in Mans.[22]

Stranger. The pot boy.

Madame. Denis[23] the blacksmith at Laloupe.[24] And the next night should take you to the sea and your friends. Are they safely in your mind?

Stranger. Forty Avenue Foch in Crest: the pot boy at the Red Lion in Mans: and Denis the blacksmith at Laloupe. And to be careful getting into Crest.

Madame. Good. Then I can close my notebook— or roll it up, I should say—then—it fits neatly, does it not? Now let us see about some food for you. Perhaps I could find you other clothes. Are these all you—

---

17. **Cherfils** (shĕr-fēs′).

18. **flat-tin-saucer baths:** sponge baths.

19. **Foch** (fôsh).

20. **Crest** (krĕst).

21. **pot boy:** a boy or man who serves customers and does chores at a public inn.

22. **Mans** (mäɴ).

23. **Denis** (də-nē′).

24. **Laloupe** (lä-lōōp′): a town in northwestern France; also spelled *La Loupe.*

WORDS TO KNOW **acclimatized** (ə-klī′mə-tīzd′) *adj.* accustomed to something, especially an area or an environment **acclimatize** *v.*

190

L'Arlésienne: Madame Joseph-Michel Ginoux (Marie Julien, 1848–1911) (1888), Vincent van Gogh. Oil on canvas, 36″ × 29″, The Metropolitan Museum of Art, bequest of Sam A. Lewisohn, 1951 (51.112.3).

(*The* Corporal's *voice is heard mingled in fury with the still more furious tones of* Simone. *She is yelling:* "Nothing of the sort, I tell you, nothing of the sort," *but no words are clearly distinguishable in the angry row.*

The door is flung open, and the Corporal *bursts in dragging a struggling* Simone *by the arm.*)

Simone (*screaming with rage and terror*). Let me go, you foul fiend, you murdering foreigner, let me go. (*She tries to kick him.*)

Corporal (*at the same time*). Stop struggling, you lying deceitful little bit of no-good.

Madame. Will someone explain this extraordinary—

Corporal. This creature—

Madame. Take your hand from my servant's arm, Corporal. She is not going to run away.

Corporal (*reacting to the voice of authority and automatically complying*). Your precious servant was overheard telling the gardener that she had never set eyes on this man.

Simone. I did not! Why should I say anything like that?

Corporal. With my own ears I heard her, my own two ears. Will you kindly explain that to me if you can.

Madame. You speak our language very well, Corporal, but perhaps you are not so quick to understand.

Corporal. I understand perfectly.

Madame. What Simone was saying to the gardener was no doubt what she was announcing to all and sundry at the pitch of her voice this morning.

Corporal (*unbelieving*). And what was that?

Madame. That she *wished* she had never set eyes on my nephew.

Corporal. And why should she say that?

Madame. My nephew, Corporal, has many charms, but tidiness is not one of them. As you may have <u>deduced</u> from the episode of the coat. He is apt to leave his room—

Simone (*on her cue; in a burst of scornful rage*). Cigarette ends, pajamas, towels, bedclothes, books, papers—all over the floor like a *flood.* Every morning I tidy up, and in two hours it is as if a bomb had burst in the room.

Stranger (*testily*). I told you already that I was sor—

Simone (*interrupting*). As if I had nothing else to do in this enormous house but wait on you.

Stranger. Haven't I said that I—

Simone. And when I have climbed all the way up from the kitchen with your shaving water, you let it get cold; but will you shave in cold? Oh, no! I have to bring up another—

Stranger. I didn't ask you to climb the damned stairs, did I?

Simone. And do I get a word of thanks for bringing it? Do I indeed? You say: "*Must* you bring it in that hideous jug; it offends my eyes."

Stranger. So it does offend my eyes!

Madame. Enough, enough! We had enough of that this morning. You see, Corporal?

Corporal. I could have sworn—

Madame. A natural mistake, perhaps. But I think you might have used a little more common sense in the matter. (*coldly*) And a great deal more dignity. I don't like having my servants manhandled.

Corporal. She refused to come.

Simone. Accusing me of things I never said!

Madame. However, now that you are here again you can make yourself useful. My nephew wants to go into Crest the day after tomorrow, and that requires a special pass. Perhaps you would make one out for him.

WORDS TO KNOW

deduce (dĭ-dōōs′) *v.* to reach a conclusion by reasoning; to figure out
testily (tĕs′tĭ-lē) *adv.* in an irritated or impatient manner

Corporal. But I—

Madame. You have a little book of permits in your pocket, haven't you?

Corporal. Yes. I—

Madame. Very well. Better make it valid for two days. He is always changing his mind.

Corporal. But it is not for me to grant a pass.

Madame. You sign them, don't you?

Corporal. Yes, but only when someone tells me to.

Madame. Very well, if it will help you, I tell you to.

Corporal. I mean, permission must be granted before a pass is issued.

Madame. And have you any doubt that a permission will be granted to my nephew?

Corporal. No, of course not, madame.

Madame. Then don't be absurd, Corporal. To be absurd twice in five minutes is too often. You may use my desk—and my own special pen. Isn't it a beautiful quill, Corporal?

Corporal. Thank you, madame, no. *We* Germans have come a long way from the geese.

Madame. Yes?

Corporal. I prefer my fountain pen. It is a more efficient implement. (*He writes.*) For the 15th and the 16th. "Holder of identity card number"—What is the number of your identity, monsieur?

Stranger. I have not the faintest idea.

Corporal. You do not know?

Stranger. No. The only numbers I take an interest in are lottery numbers.

Simone. I know the number of monsieur's card.

Madame (*afraid that she is going to invent one*). I don't think that likely, Simone.

Simone (*aware of what is in her mistress's mind, and reassuring her*). But I really *do* know, madame. It is the year I was born, with two

ones after it. Many a time I have seen it on the outside of the card.

Corporal. It is good that someone knows.

Simone. It is—192411.

Corporal. 192411. (*He fills in the dates.*)

Madame (*as he nears the end*). Are you going back to St. Estèphe now, Corporal?

Corporal. Yes, madame.

Madame. Then perhaps you will give my nephew a lift as far as the Marnay crossroads.

Corporal. It is not permitted to take civilians as passengers.

Stranger. But you took me here as a passenger.

Corporal. That was different.

Madame. You mean that when you thought he was a miscreant you took him in your car, but now that you know he is my nephew you refuse?

Corporal. When I brought him here it was on service business.

Madame (*gently reasonable*). Corporal, I think you owe me something for your general lack of tact this afternoon. Would it be too much to ask you to consider my nephew a miscreant for the next hour while you drive him as far as the Marnay crossroads?

Corporal. But—

Madame. Take him to the crossroads with you and I shall agree to forget your—your lack of efficiency. I am sure you are actually a very efficient person, and likely to be a sergeant any day now. We won't let a blunder or two stand in your way.

Corporal. If I am caught giving a lift to a civilian, I shall *never* be a sergeant.

Madame (*still gentle*). If I report on your conduct this afternoon, tomorrow you will be a private.

Corporal (*after a long pause*). Is monsieur ready to come now?

Stranger. Quite ready.

Corporal. You will need a coat.

Madame. Simone, get monsieur's coat from the cupboard in the hall. And when you have seen him off, come back here.

Simone. Yes, madame. (*Exit* Simone.)

Corporal. Madame.

Madame. Good day to you, Corporal. (*Exit* Corporal.)

Stranger. Your talent for blackmail is remarkable.

Madame. The place has a yellow barn. You had better wait somewhere till evening, when the dogs are chained up.

Stranger. I wish I had an aunt of your <u>caliber</u>. All mine are authorities on crochet.

Madame. I could wish you were my nephew. Good luck, and be careful. Perhaps one day you will come back, and dine with me, and tell me the rest of the tale.

(*The sound of a running engine comes from outside.*)

Stranger. Two years today, perhaps?

Madame. One year today.

Stranger (*softly*). Who knows? (*He lifts her hand to his lips.*) Thank you, and *au revoir.*[25] (*turning at the door*) Being sped on my way by the enemy is a happiness I had not anticipated. I shall never be able to repay you for that. (*He goes out.*) (*off*) Ah, my coat—thank you, Simone.

(*Sound of car driving off. Madame pours out two glasses. As she finishes, Simone comes in, shutting the door correctly behind her and taking two paces into the room.*)

Simone. You wanted me, madame?

Madame. You will drink a glass of wine with me, Simone.

Simone. With you, madame!

Madame. You are a good daughter of France and a good servant to me. We shall drink a toast together.

Simone. Yes, madame.

Madame (*quietly*). To Freedom.

Simone (*repeating*). To Freedom. May I add a bit of my own, madame?

Madame. Certainly.

Simone (*with immense satisfaction*). And a very bad end to that corporal!

Curtain

---

25. *au revoir* (ō´rə-vwär´) *French:* good-bye.

RESPONDING
OPTIONS

FROM **PERSONAL RESPONSE** *TO* **CRITICAL ANALYSIS**

REFLECT

1. As you read the play, what images of the set and characters came to mind? Sketch one of those images in your notebook.

RETHINK

2. What is your opinion of each of the characters in the play? Give your reasoning.

3. Do you think that the way Madame, the Stranger, and Simone succeed in fooling the Corporal is believable?
Consider
- the explanations offered for the Stranger's unkempt appearance, his wandering in the woods, and his missing papers
- the explanation for Simone's comment that she "had never set eyes" on the Stranger
- the improvised roles adopted by Madame, the Stranger, and Simone

4. Does Madame exhibit the qualities that you associate with a resistance fighter, as you described for the Writing Connection? Explain, using examples from the play to support your opinion.

5. In your judgment, what is the theme of the play?
Consider
- the personal qualities exhibited by the French characters
- the contrast between Madame's real nephew and the Stranger
- what the French hope to achieve by their resistance

RELATE

6. Though Madame plays the role of a collaborator, she actually works for the resistance. Under what circumstances, if any, would you consider playing a double role in order to serve a worthy cause?

ANOTHER PATHWAY
Cooperative Learning

Stage a Readers Theater performance of the play. In Readers Theater, performers read their lines from the text, paying close attention to how the lines should be interpreted. They rely on the oral reading alone to convey their characters' thoughts and feelings.

QUICKWRITES

1. Write an additional **scene** for this play, showing, perhaps, the return of the real nephew or the Stranger's return to thank Madame after France is liberated. Include both dialogue and stage directions.

2. Write a **review** of the play, based either on the text or on an imagined performance.

3. Write a **monologue** in which Madame offers her reflections on the war and on the differences between her nephew and the Stranger.

4. Write the **log entry** that the Corporal might have written on the day of the play's events. Think about what he would have deliberately included or omitted.

PORTFOLIO Save your writing. You may want to use it later as a springboard to a piece for your portfolio.

LITERARY CONCEPTS

As you know, **stage directions** are the notes included in a play to help actors and directors put on the play and to help readers picture the action. The stage directions may describe setting, lighting, sound effects, the gestures and movements of the actors, or the way in which dialogue is to be spoken. With a small group of classmates, choose a section of the play, such as the first confrontation with the Corporal, and add more stage directions, focusing on how the performers should act. Rehearse your section, making sure that you follow the stage directions, and then perform it for the rest of the class. When you have finished, discuss whether the additional stage directions enhanced your performance.

CONCEPT REVIEW: Plot On the horizontal axis of a line graph like the one started below, list in sequence the plot events of the play. On the vertical axis, rank the events according to the suspense that they generate. The highest point of your graph should be the event that creates the most suspense.

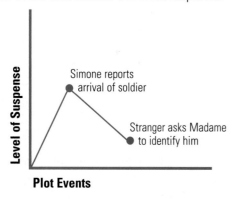

ALTERNATIVE ACTIVITIES

1. Draw a **set design** for a production of this play. Be sure to include the furniture and props mentioned in the dialogue and stage directions.

2. On a detailed map of France, locate some of the place names mentioned in the play. Then create a **map** of the Stranger's likely escape route.

THE WRITER'S STYLE

Besides being suspenseful, this play employs wit and humor. With a partner, examine the section where Madame describes her nephew to the Stranger (page 188), or a section of your choice. In your opinion, what lines would make the audience laugh? How does the use of humor contribute to the development of the characters? Share your observations with your classmates.

ACROSS THE CURRICULUM

World Languages The title *The Pen of My Aunt* is the literal translation of the French expression *la plume de ma tante* (lä-plüm′də-mä-tänt′). Find the French translations of several words or phrases that you think are important in the play, such as *collaborator, civilian, notebook,* and *occupation.* Read aloud the French words to your classmates, and have them guess the meanings.

WORDS TO KNOW

EXERCISE A Write the letter of the word pair that expresses the relationship that is most similar to the relationship of the word pair in capital letters.

1. MISCREANT : WRONGDOING :: (a) hero : cowardice, (b) traitor : treason, (c) collaborator : resistance
2. DICTATORSHIP : REPRESSIVE :: (a) tyranny : democratic, (b) war : peaceful, (c) injury: painful
3. ANATHEMA : BLESSING :: (a) sin : virtue, (b) crime : punishment, (c) preacher : prayer
4. CALIBER : QUALITY :: (a) frankness : sincerity, (b) courage : cowardice, (c) inch : foot
5. PENCIL : IMPLEMENT :: (a) thermometer : heat, (b) hammer : tool, (c) plume : quill
6. EXPLAIN : INEXPLICABLE :: (a) change : variable, (b) rely : reliable, (c) dispute : indisputable

7. SPECULATION : CERTAINTY :: (a) science : experiment, (b) practicality : usefulness, (c) danger : safety
8. ANNOYED : TESTILY :: (a) worried : nervously, (b) insulted : politely, (c) overjoyed : calmly
9. DEDUCE : CONCLUSION :: (a) deceive : truth, (b) judge : objectivity, (c) search : discovery
10. CLIMATE : ACCLIMATIZED :: (a) circle : circular, (b) custom : accustomed, (c) mortality : immortal

EXERCISE B Choose one of the Words to Know to act out in front of a small group of classmates. Feel free to use props if appropriate. See whether the others can guess your word.

JOSEPHINE TEY (GORDON DAVIOT)

1897–1952

Josephine Tey and Gordon Daviot were the two pen names of Elizabeth Mackintosh, a Scottish-born writer who first went to England to study and teach physical education. Literary success came in 1929, with the publication of a novel called *The Man in the Queue*. Thereafter, Mackintosh devoted herself to writing, with literary achievements as divergent as the two pen names she adopted. Writing as Josephine Tey, she produced well-crafted detective novels that won the praise of critics and mystery fans alike. Using the pen name of Gordon Daviot, she created several hit plays for the London stage; the most famous of these, *Richard of Bordeaux* (1933), starred the famous British actor Sir John Gielgud and was successful enough to be brought overseas for a run in New York City.

Many of Tey's mysteries feature Alan Grant, an inspector with Scotland Yard. In *The Daughter of Time* (1951), Grant investigates one of English history's most brutal crimes, the murder of two young princes in the Tower of London, which most historians—and playwright William Shakespeare—lay at the feet of King Richard III. This book has been widely praised as one of the best mysteries of all time.

OTHER WORKS *Leith Sands and Other Short Plays, Miss Pym Disposes, The Singing Sands, Plays by Gordon Daviot*

PREVIEWING

The Thrill of the Grass
W. P. Kinsella Canada

PERSONAL CONNECTION

Baseball is often called America's national pastime. Why do you think so many people have such strong feelings about the game? Discuss your opinions with classmates.

CULTURAL CONNECTION

Like other sports, the game of baseball has changed over the years. A major change occurred in 1965 when the city of Houston built its Astrodome, the first indoor baseball stadium. This stadium featured a nylon, grasslike carpet called AstroTurf® that served as a substitute for natural grass. Over the next few decades, variations of this artificial turf, which is padded and covers an asphalt surface, came to be used in other stadiums. People who support the use of artificial turf note that it holds up well in any weather and requires little maintenance. Critics, however, point out that its hard surface causes injuries and makes the ball bounce in unusual ways. They also regret the loss of natural grass, which they associate with pleasant memories of baseball in years past.

   "The Thrill of the Grass" deals with the issue of artificial turf and the strong feelings that it elicits from fans. The story is set during the baseball strike of 1981, when, for 49 days, major-league players refused to play while they awaited a new contract.

WRITING CONNECTION

In your notebook, write about a time when your strong feelings for a person or an issue motivated you to take drastic action, perhaps to do something that you would never have imagined yourself doing. As you read the story, compare your experience with that of the narrator.

AstroTurf® is a registered trademark of Southwest Recreational Industries, Inc.

LASERLINKS
• CULTURAL CONNECTION

THE THRILL OF THE GRASS

W. P. Kinsella

1981: the summer the baseball players went on strike. The dull weeks drag by, the summer deepens, the strike is nearly a month old. Outside the city the corn rustles and ripens in the sun.

Busch Stadium (1982), Jim Dow. Three-panel panorama from 8″ × 10″ color negatives.

Summer without baseball: a disruption to the psyche.[1] An unexplainable aimlessness engulfs me. I stay later and later each evening in the small office at the rear of my shop. Now, driving home after work, the worst of the rush hour traffic over, it is the time of the evening I would normally be heading for the stadium.

I enjoy arriving an hour early, parking in a far corner of the lot, walking slowly toward the stadium, rays of sun dropping softly over my shoulders like tangerine ropes, my shadow gliding with me, black as an umbrella. I like to watch young families beside their campers, the mothers in shorts, grilling hamburgers, their men drinking beer. I enjoy seeing little boys dressed in the home team uniform, barely toddling, clutching hotdogs in upraised hands.

I am a failed shortstop. As a young man, I saw myself diving to my left, graceful as a toppling tree, fielding high grounders like a cat leaping for butterflies, bracing my right foot and tossing to first, the throw true as if a steel ribbon connected my hand and the first baseman's glove. I dreamed of leading the American League in hitting—being inducted into the Hall of Fame. I batted .217 in my senior year of high school and averaged 1.3 errors per nine innings.

I know the stadium will be deserted; nevertheless I wheel my car down off the freeway, park, and walk across the silent lot, my footsteps rasping and mournful. Strangle-grass and creeping charlie are already inching up through

_____

1. **psyche** (sī′kē): the human spirit or soul.

the gravel, <u>surreptitious</u>, surprised at their own ease. Faded bottle caps, rusted bits of chrome, an occasional paper clip, recede into the earth. I circle a ticket booth, sun-faded, empty, the door closed by an oversized padlock. I walk beside the tall, machinery-green, board fence. A half mile away a few cars hiss along the freeway; overhead a single-engine plane fizzes lazily. The whole place is silent as an empty classroom, like a house suddenly without children.

It is then that I spot the door-shape. I have to check twice to be sure it is there: a door cut in the deep green boards of the fence, more the promise of a door than the real thing, the kind of door, as children, we cut in the sides of card-board boxes with our mother's paring knives. As I move closer, a golden circle of lock, like an acrimonious[2] eye, establishes its certainty.

I stand, my nose so close to the door I can smell the faint odour of paint, the golden eye of a lock inches from my own eyes. My desire to be inside the ballpark is so great that for the first time in my life I commit a criminal act. I have been a locksmith for over forty years. I take the small tools from the pocket of my jacket, and in less time than it would take a speedy runner to circle the bases I am inside the sta-dium. Though the ballpark is open-air, it smells

---

2. **acrimonious** (ăk′rə-mō′nē-əs): harsh; bitter.

WORDS TO KNOW   **surreptitious** (sûr′əp-tĭsh′əs) *adj.* done or made by secretive means; stealthy

201

BASEBALL IS MEANT TO BE PLAYED ON SUMMER EVENINGS AND SUNDAY AFTERNOONS, ON GRASS JUST CUT BY A HORSE-DRAWN MOWER.

of abandonment; the walkways and seating areas are cold as basements. I breathe the odours of rancid popcorn and wilted cardboard.

The maintenance staff were laid off when the strike began. Synthetic grass does not need to be cut or watered. I stare down at the ball diamond, where just to the right of the pitcher's mound, a single weed, perhaps two inches high, stands defiant in the rain-pocked dirt.

The field sits breathless in the orangy glow of the evening sun. I stare at the potato-coloured earth of the infield, that wide, dun[3] arc, surrounded by plastic grass. As I <u>contemplate</u> the prickly turf, which scorches the thighs and buttocks of a sliding player as if he were being seared by hot steel, it stares back in its uniform ugliness. The seams that send routinely hit ground balls veering at tortuous angles, are vivid, grey as scars.

I remember the ballfields of my childhood, the outfields full of soft hummocks[4] and brown-eyed gopher holes.

I stride down from the stands and walk out to the middle of the field. I touch the stubble that is called grass, take off my shoes, but find it is like walking on a row of toothbrushes. It was an evil day when they stripped the sod from this ballpark, cut it into yard-wide swathes,[5] rolled it, memories and all, into great green-and-black cinnamon-roll shapes, trucked it away. Nature temporarily defeated. But Nature is patient.

Over the next few days an idea forms within me, ripening, swelling, pushing everything else into a corner. It is like knowing a new, wonderful joke and not being able to share. I need an accomplice.

I go to see a man I don't know personally, though I have seen his face peering at me from the financial pages of the local newspaper, and the *Wall Street Journal,* and I have been watching his profile at the baseball stadium, two boxes to the right of me, for several years.

He is a fan. Really a fan. When the weather is intemperate, or the game not close, the people around us disappear like flowers closing at sunset, but we are always there until the last pitch. I know he is a man who attends because of the beauty and mystery of the game, a man who can sit during the last of the ninth with the game decided innings ago, and draw joy from watching the first baseman adjust the angle of his glove as the pitcher goes into his windup.

He, like me, is a first-base-side fan. I've always watched baseball from behind first base. The positions fans choose at sporting events are like politics, religion, or philosophy: a view of the world, a way of seeing the universe. They make no sense to anyone, have no basis in anything but stubbornness.

I brought up my daughters to watch baseball from the first-base side. One lives in Japan and sends me box scores from Japanese newspapers, and Japanese baseball magazines with pictures of superstars politely bowing to one another. She has a season ticket in Yokohama;[6] on the first-base side.

---

3. **dun:** brownish gray.
4. **hummocks:** low, rounded hills.
5. **swathes** (swŏths): strips as wide as the blade of a mowing machine.
6. **Yokohama** (yō′kə-ha′mə): a large city in Japan.

WORDS TO KNOW **contemplate** (kŏn′təm-plāt′) *v.* to look at attentively and thoughtfully; to consider carefully

"Tell him a baseball fan is here to see him," is all I will say to his secretary. His office is in a skyscraper, from which he can look out over the city to where the prairie rolls green as mountain water to the limits of the eye. I wait all afternoon in the artificially cool, glassy reception area with its yellow and mauve chairs, chrome and glass coffee tables. Finally, in the late afternoon, my message is passed along.

"I've seen you at the baseball stadium," I say, not introducing myself.

"Yes," he says. "I recognize you. Three rows back, about eight seats to my left. You have a red scorebook and you often bring your daughter . . . "

"Granddaughter. Yes, she goes to sleep in my lap in the late innings, but she knows how to calculate an ERA[7] and she's only in Grade 2."

"One of my greatest regrets," says this tall man, whose moustache and carefully styled hair are polar-bear white, "is that my grandchildren all live over a thousand miles away. You're very lucky. Now, what can I do for you?"

"I have an idea," I say. "One that's been creeping toward me like a first baseman when the bunt sign is on.[8] What do you think about artificial turf?"

"Hmmmf," he snorts, "that's what the strike should be about. Baseball is meant to be played on summer evenings and Sunday afternoons, on grass just cut by a horse-drawn mower," and we smile as our eyes meet.

"I've discovered the ballpark is open, to me anyway," I go on. "There's no one there while the strike is on. The wind blows through the high top of the grandstand, whining until the pigeons in the rafters flutter. It's lonely as a ghost town."

"And what is it you do there, alone with the pigeons?"

"I dream."

"And where do I come in?"

"You've always struck me as a man who dreams. I think we have things in common. I think you might like to come with me. I could show you what I dream, paint you pictures, suggest what might happen . . . "

He studies me carefully for a moment, like a pitcher trying to decide if he can trust the sign his catcher has just given him.

"Tonight?" he says. "Would tonight be too soon?"

"Park in the northwest corner of the lot about 1:00 a.m. There is a door about fifty yards to the right of the main gate. I'll open it when I hear you."

He nods.

I turn and leave.

The night is clear and cotton warm when he arrives. "Oh, my," he says, staring at the stadium turned chrome-blue by a full moon. "Oh, my," he says again, breathing in the faint odours of baseball, the reminder of fans and players not long gone.

"Let's go down to the field," I say. I am carrying a cardboard pizza box, holding it on the upturned palms of my hands, like an offering.

When we reach the field, he first stands on the mound, makes an awkward attempt at a windup, then does a little sprint from first to about half-way to second. "I think I know what you've brought," he says, gesturing toward the box, "but let me see anyway."

I open the box, in which rests a square foot of sod, the grass smooth and pure, cool as a swatch of satin, fragile as baby's hair.

"Ohhh," the man says, reaching out a finger to test the moistness of it. "Oh, I see."

---

7. **ERA:** earned run average for a baseball pitcher; that is, the average number of earned runs—runs scored without the aid of an error—a pitcher allows every nine innings.

8. **when the bunt sign is on:** when the coach has signaled the batter to tap at the pitched ball instead of swinging at it.

We walk across the field, the harsh, prickly turf making the bottoms of my feet tingle, to the left-field corner where, in the angle formed by the foul line and the warning track, I lay down the square foot of sod. "That's beautiful," my friend says, kneeling beside me, placing his hand, fingers spread wide, on the verdant[9] square, leaving a print faint as a veronica.[10]

I take from my belt a sickle-shaped blade, the kind used for cutting carpet. I measure along the edge of the sod, dig the point in and pull carefully toward me. There is a ripping sound, like tearing an old bed sheet. I hold up the square of artificial turf like something freshly killed, while all the time digging the sharp point into the packed earth I have exposed. I replace the sod lovingly, covering the newly bared surface.

"A protest," I say.

"But it could be more," the man replies.

"I hoped you'd say that. It could be. If you'd like to come back . . . "

"Tomorrow night?"

"Tomorrow night would be fine. But there will be an admission charge . . . "

"A square of sod?"

"A square of sod two inches thick . . . "

"Of the same grass?"

"Of the same grass. But there's more."

"I suspected as much."

"You must have a friend . . . "

"Who would join us?"

"Yes."

"I have two. Would that be all right?"

"I trust your judgment."

"My father. He's over eighty," my friend says. "You might have seen him with me once or twice. He lives over fifty miles from here, but if I call him, he'll come. And my friend . . . "

"If they pay their admission, they'll be welcome . . . "

"And *they* may have friends . . . "

"Indeed they may. But what will we do with this?" I say, holding up the sticky-backed square of turf, which smells of glue and fabric.

"We could mail them anonymously to baseball executives, politicians, clergymen."

"Gentle reminders not to tamper with Nature."

We dance toward the exit, rampant with excitement.

"You will come back? You'll bring others?"

"Count on it," says my friend.

They do come, those trusted friends, and friends of friends, each making a live, green deposit. At first, a tiny row of sod squares begins to inch along toward left-centre field. The next night even more people arrive, the following night more again, and the night after there is positively a crowd. Those who come once seem always to return accompanied by friends, occasionally a son or young brother, but mostly men my age or older, for we are the ones who remember the grass.

Night after night the pilgrimage continues. The first night I stand inside the deep green door, listening. I hear a vehicle stop; hear a car door close with a snug thud. I open the door when the sound of soft-soled shoes on gravel tells me it is time. The door swings silent as a snake. We nod curt greetings to each other. Two men pass me, each carrying a grasshopper-legged sprinkler. Later, each sprinkler will sizzle like frying onions as it wheels, a silver sparkler in the moonlight.

During the nights that follow, I stand sentinel-like at the top of the grandstand, watching as my cohorts arrive. Old men walking across a parking lot in a row, in the dark, carrying

---

9. verdant (vŭr′dnt): covered with green growth.

10. **a print faint as a veronica** (və-rŏn′ĭ-kə): a simile referring to the image of Jesus' face supposedly left on the handkerchief offered to him by Saint Veronica for wiping away his blood on the way to the crucifixion.

WORDS TO KNOW

rampant (răm′pənt) *adj.* unchecked; unrestrained; out of control
cohort (kō′hôrt′) *n.* a member of the same group; a companion or an associate

Michael W. Straus (1961), Fairfield Porter. Oil on canvas, 45 3/16″ × 39 1/2″.

IT IS LIKE MY COMPATRIOTS AND I ARE INVOLVED IN A RITUAL FOR TRUE BELIEVERS ONLY.

coiled hoses, looking like the many wheels of a locomotive, old men who have slipped away from their homes, skulked down their sturdy sidewalks, breathing the cool, grassy, after-midnight air. They have left behind their sleeping, grey-haired women, their immaculate bungalows, their manicured lawns. They continue to walk across the parking lot, while occasionally a soft wheeze, a nibbling, breathy sound like an old horse might make, divulges their humanity. They move methodically toward the baseball stadium which hulks against the moon-blue sky like a small mountain. Beneath the tint of starlight, the tall light standards which rise above the fences and grandstand glow purple, necks bent forward, like sunflowers heavy with seed.

My other daughter lives in this city, is married to a fan, but one who watches baseball from behind third base. And like marrying outside the faith, she has been converted to the third-base side. They have their own season tickets, twelve rows up just to the outfield side of third base. I love her, but I don't trust her enough to let her in on my secret.

I could trust my granddaughter, but she is too young. At her age she shouldn't have to face such responsibility. I remember my own daughter, the one who lives in Japan, remember her at nine, all knees, elbows and missing teeth—remember peering in her room, seeing her asleep, a shower of well-thumbed baseball cards scattered over her chest and pillow.

I haven't been able to tell my wife—it is like my compatriots and I are involved in a ritual for true believers only. Maggie, who knew me when I still dreamed of playing professionally myself—Maggie, after over half a lifetime together, comes and sits in my lap in the comfortable easy chair which has adjusted through the years to my thickening shape, just as she has. I love to hold the lightness of her, her tongue exploring my mouth, gently as a baby's finger.

"Where do you go?" she asks sleepily when I crawl into bed at dawn.

I mumble a reply. I know she doesn't sleep well when I'm gone. I can feel her body rhythms change as I slip out of bed after midnight.

"Aren't you too old to be having a change of life," she says, placing her toast-warm hand on my cold thigh.

I am not the only one with this problem.

"I'm developing a reputation," whispers an affable man at the ballpark. "I imagine any number of private investigators following any number of cars across the city. I imagine them creeping about the parking lot, shining pen-lights on licence plates, trying to guess what we're up to. Think of the reports they must prepare. I wonder if our wives are disappointed that we're not out discoing with frizzy-haired teenagers?"

Night after night, virtually no words are spoken. Each man seems to know his assignment. Not all bring sod. Some carry rakes, some hoes, some hoses, which, when joined together, snake across the infield and outfield, dispensing the blessing of water. Others cradle in their arms bags of earth for building up the infield to meet the thick, living sod.

I often remain high in the stadium, looking down on the men moving over the earth, dark as ants, each sodding, cutting, watering, shaping. Occasionally the moon finds a knife blade as it trims the sod or slices away a chunk of artificial turf, and tosses the reflection skyward like a bright ball. My body tingles. There should be symphony music playing. Everyone should be humming "America the Beautiful."

Toward dawn, I watch the men walking away in groups, like small patrols of soldiers, carrying instead of arms, the tools and utensils which breathe life back into the arid ballfield.

Row by row, night by night, we lay the little squares of sod, moist as chocolate cake with green icing. Where did all the sod come from? I picture many men, in many parts of the city, surreptitiously cutting chunks out of their own lawns in the leafy midnight darkness, listening to the uncomprehending protests of their wives the next day—pretending to know nothing of it—pretending to have called the police to investigate.

When the strike is over, I know we will all be here to watch the workouts, to hear the recalcitrant[11] joints crackling like twigs after the forced inactivity. We will sit in our regular seats, scattered like popcorn throughout the stadium, and we'll nod as we pass on the way to the exits, exchange secret smiles, proud as new fathers.

For me, the best part of all will be the surprise. I feel like a magician who has gestured hypnotically and produced an elephant from thin air. I know that I am not alone in my wonder. I know that rockets shoot off in half-a-hundred chests—the excitement of birthday mornings, Christmas eves, and hometown doubleheaders, boils within each of my conspirators. Our secret rites[12] have been performed with love, like delivering a valentine to a sweetheart's door in that blue-steel span of morning just before dawn.

Players and management are meeting around the clock. A settlement is <u>imminent</u>. I have watched the stadium covered square foot by square foot until it looks like green graph paper. I have stood and felt the cool odours of the grass rise up and touch my face. I have studied the lines between each small square, watched those lines fade until they were visible to my eyes alone, then not even to them.

What will the players think, as they straggle into the stadium and find the miracle we have created? The old-timers will raise their heads like ponies, as far away as the parking lot, when the thrill of the grass reaches their nostrils. And, as they dress, they'll recall sprawling in the lush fields of childhood, the grass as cool as a mother's hand on a forehead.

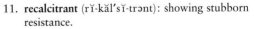

---

11. **recalcitrant** (rĭ-kăl′sĭ-trənt): showing stubborn resistance.

12. **rites:** ceremonies.

WORDS TO KNOW   **imminent** (ĭm′ə-nənt) *adj.* likely to happen soon

Stretching at First (about 1976), John Dobbs. Oil on canvas, 36″ × 40″, collection of Gilbert Kinney, Washington, D.C.

"Goodbye, goodbye," we say at the gate, the smell of water, of sod, of sweat, small perfumes in the air. Our secrets are safe with each other. We go our separate ways.

Alone in the stadium in the last chill darkness before dawn, I drop to my hands and knees in the centre of the outfield. My palms are sodden. Water touches the skin between my spread fingers. I lower my face to the silvered grass, which, wonder of wonders, already has the ephemeral[13] odours of baseball about it. ❖

---

13. **ephemeral** (ĭ-fĕm′ər-əl): short-lived; passing quickly.

RESPONDING OPTIONS

FROM PERSONAL RESPONSE TO CRITICAL ANALYSIS

REFLECT
1. Do you approve of the action taken by the narrator and his friends? Explain your opinion in your notebook.

RETHINK
2. Why do you think the narrator and his friends take such drastic action?

   Consider
   - your discussion for the Personal Connection on page 198 about the feelings associated with baseball
   - how the narrator describes his feelings
   - the memories that the men associate with natural grass
   - what the men might hope to accomplish

3. When the narrator chooses his first accomplice, how does he know this man will share his dream?

4. Do you agree with the story's message about the value of challenging the system? Cite details to support your opinion.

RELATE
5. Do you think what happens in this story could really happen? Explain your position.

6. Do you think that such spectator sports as baseball, basketball, and football play a positive role in the lives of their fans? Explain your opinion.

ANOTHER PATHWAY

Cooperative Learning

Conduct a mock trial of the lawbreakers in this story. Assign the roles of prosecutor, defense attorney, judge, defendants, and witnesses such as police, stadium staff, turf company officials, and the team owner. The rest of the class can serve as the jury.

QUICKWRITES

1. Write a **description,** in either poetry or prose, of a baseball player or another athlete in action. Use vivid similes, as Kinsella does in his story.

2. Write a **television commercial** to promote the game of baseball. Try to convey "the beauty and mystery of the game" that so captivated the narrator and his fellow conspirators.

3. Write a **newspaper article** reporting the discovery of real grass at the ballpark. Include the reactions of players, fans, and others.

   📁 *PORTFOLIO Save your writing. You may want to use it later as a springboard to a piece for your portfolio.*

LITERARY CONCEPTS

A **simile** is a figure of speech, usually containing the word *like* or *as,* that makes a comparison between two unlike things that nevertheless have something in common. In "The Thrill of the Grass," for example, the narrator describes his shadow as being "black as an umbrella."

Divide into teams to find other similes in the story. List the similes on the board, then discuss why Kinsella might have chosen to use so many similes in the story.

ALTERNATIVE ACTIVITIES

1. Conduct a **survey,** asking people whether they think baseball deserves to be known as our national pastime. Tabulate the results of your survey on a bar graph or a circle graph.

2. View the film *Field of Dreams,* based on Kinsella's novel *Shoeless Joe.* Then present an **oral movie review** similar to those provided by television movie critics. In your review, include comparisons with "The Thrill of the Grass."

WORDS TO KNOW

Write the letter of the word that is not similar in meaning to the other words in each numbered set.

1. (a) sneaky, (b) **surreptitious,** (c) candid, (d) secret
2. (a) **contemplate,** (b) ignore, (c) examine, (d) observe
3. (a) restrained, (b) **rampant,** (c) uncontrollable, (d) wild
4. (a) outsider, (b) colleague, (c) **cohort,** (d) companion
5. (a) **skulk,** (b) slink, (c) stoop, (d) prowl
6. (a) spotless, (b) smeared, (c) stainless, (d) **immaculate**
7. (a) tell, (b) reveal, (c) **divulge,** (d) disguise
8. (a) **methodically,** (b) carelessly, (c) systematically, (d) deliberately
9. (a) friendly, (b) distant, (c) **affable,** (d) pleasant
10. (a) probable, (b) **imminent,** (c) delayed, (d) approaching

CRITIC'S CORNER

One reviewer described W. P. Kinsella's novel *Shoeless Joe* as "not so much about baseball as . . . about dreams, magic, life." How might this quote apply to "The Thrill of the Grass"?

ACROSS THE CURRICULUM

Mathematics Conduct a math workshop, showing how math applies to baseball. For example, you might explain the narrator's .217 batting average, a pitcher's ERA, and other statistics. Define the baseball terms so that classmates who are not fans will understand.

W. P. KINSELLA

Success did not come easily to William Patrick Kinsella. Born in Edmonton, Alberta, Canada, Kinsella says that he always thought of himself as a writer, though he wrote more than 50 stories before getting published. He also worked at various odd jobs, such as running his own pizza restaurant, managing a credit agency, and driving a taxicab. Kinsella did not begin college until he was in his 30s.

Kinsella grew up loving the game of baseball, though he was a poor player himself. He penned his first baseball story, a murder mystery called "Diamond

1935–

Doom," when he was in the eighth grade. Kinsella published his first collection of baseball stories, *Shoeless Joe Jackson Comes to Iowa,* in 1980. He expanded the title story into his award-winning novel *Shoeless Joe* (1982), which garnered much attention when it was adapted and produced as the 1989 Hollywood movie *Field of Dreams.*

OTHER WORKS *Dance Me Outside, The Alligator Report, The Iowa Baseball Confederacy, The Further Adventures of Slugger McBatt*

PREVIEWING

FICTION

The Balek Scales
Heinrich Böll (hĭn'rĭk bœl) Germany

PERSONAL CONNECTION

What does the word *justice* mean to you? Explore the meaning of the word and its associations by filling out a diagram like the one shown. Then compare your ideas with those of your classmates.

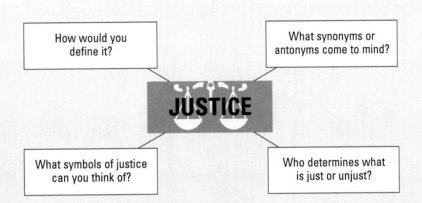

How would you define it?

What synonyms or antonyms come to mind?

JUSTICE

What symbols of justice can you think of?

Who determines what is just or unjust?

HISTORICAL CONNECTION

This story takes place in central Europe around 1900. In that era, much of Europe was characterized by a strict social hierarchy in which a person's social position was largely determined by birth. At the top of the social ladder were such royal figures as kings or emperors, followed by counts and barons and other members of the aristocracy who passed their titles down to their children. Ranking below the aristocracy were wealthy landowners who had no titles but who often hoped to acquire them as a reward for service or influence. At the bottom of the social ladder were the common people, the vast bulk of the population.

In the story you are about to read, the Baleks, a wealthy family, have controlled the lives of the common people for five generations, even to the point of creating laws to control the system of justice. The Baleks live in an elegant chateau (shă-tō'), or country house, and own much of the land in the area. Most of the common people work on Balek land, crushing and drying flax plants used to make fabric.

A European chateau. Copyright © Charlie Waite / Tony Stone Images

READING CONNECTION

Making Predictions Predicting is a useful reading strategy because it helps you to focus your attention and to sharpen your perceptiveness. Based on the title, "The Balek Scales," and on the information provided on this page, what do you predict about the role of justice in this story? As you read, compare your prediction with what actually happens.

Using Your Reading Log Use your reading log to record your responses to the questions inserted throughout the selection. Also jot down other thoughts and feelings that come to you as you read.

LASERLINKS
• *HISTORICAL CONNECTION*

211

The Balek Scales

Heinrich Böll

Where my grandfather came from, most of the people lived by working in the flax sheds. For five generations they had been breathing in the dust which rose from the crushed flax stalks, letting themselves be killed off by slow degrees, a race of long-suffering, cheerful people who ate goat cheese, potatoes, and now and then a rabbit; in the evening they would sit at home spinning and knitting; they sang, drank mint tea and were happy.

During the day they would carry the flax stalks to the antiquated machines, with no protection from the dust and at the mercy of the heat which came pouring out of the drying kilns.[1] Each cottage contained only one bed, standing against the wall like a closet and reserved for the parents, while the children slept all around the room on benches. In the morning the room would be filled with the odor of thin soup; on Sundays there was stew, and on feast days[2] the children's faces would light up with pleasure as they watched the black acorn coffee turning paler and paler from the milk their smiling mother poured into their coffee mugs.

The parents went off early to the flax sheds, the housework was left to the children: they would sweep the room, tidy up, wash the dishes and peel the potatoes, precious pale-yellow fruit whose thin peel had to be produced afterwards to dispel any suspicion of extravagance or carelessness.

As soon as the children were out of school, they had to go off into the woods and, depending on the season, gather mushrooms and herbs: woodruff and thyme, caraway, mint and foxglove, and in summer, when they had brought in the hay from their meager fields, they gathered hayflowers. A kilo[3] of hayflowers was worth one pfennig,[4] and they were sold by the apothecaries[5] in town for twenty pfennigs a kilo to highly strung ladies. The mushrooms were highly prized: they fetched twenty pfennigs a kilo and were sold in the shops in town for one mark twenty.[6] The children would crawl deep into the green darkness of the forest during the autumn when dampness drove the mushrooms out of the soil, and almost every family had its own places where it gathered mushrooms, places which were handed down in whispers from generation to generation.

The woods belonged to the Baleks, as well as the flax sheds, and in my grandfather's village the Baleks had a chateau, and the wife of the head of the family had a little room next to the dairy where mushrooms, herbs and hayflowers were weighed and paid for. There on the table stood the great Balek scales, an old-fashioned, ornate bronze-gilt[7] contraption, which my grandfather's grandparents had already faced when they were children, their grubby hands holding their little baskets of mushrooms, their paper bags of hayflowers, breathlessly watching the number of weights Frau[8] Balek had to throw on the scale before the swinging pointer came to rest exactly over the black line, that thin line of justice which had to be redrawn every year. Then Frau Balek would take the big book covered in brown leather, write down the weight, and pay out the money, pfennigs or ten-pfennig pieces and very, very occasionally, a mark. And when my grandfather was a child, there was a big glass jar of lemon drops standing there, the kind that cost one mark a kilo, and when Frau Balek—whichever one happened to be presiding over the little room—was in a good mood, she would put her hand into this jar and give each

---

1. **kilns** (kĭlnz): ovens, used here to dry the flax.
2. **feast days:** holidays, especially religious holidays honoring saints.
3. **kilo** (kē′lō): short for *kilogram*, a metric measure equal to 1,000 grams, or about 2.2 pounds.
4. **pfennig** (fĕn′ĭg): a coin equal to a hundredth of a deutsche mark, the basic unit of German currency. The word *pfennig* is related to the English *penny*.
5. **apothecaries** (ə-pŏth′ĭ-kĕr′ēz): pharmacists; druggists.
6. **one mark twenty:** one mark and twenty pfennigs.
7. **bronze-gilt:** covered with a thin layer of bronze.
8. **Frau** (frou): a German title indicating a married woman.

WORDS TO KNOW **antiquated** (ăn′tĭ-kwā′tĭd) *adj.* old-fashioned; outmoded
meager (mē′gər) *adj.* lacking quantity, fullness, strength, or fertility; feeble; scanty
preside (prĭ-zīd′) *v.* to hold the chief position of authority or control

213

child a lemon drop, and the children's faces would light up with pleasure, the way they used to when on feast days their mother poured milk into their coffee mugs, milk that made the coffee turn paler and paler until it was as pale as the flaxen pigtails of the little girls.

One of the laws imposed by the Baleks on the village was: no one was permitted to have any scales in the house. The law was so ancient that nobody gave a thought as to when and how it had arisen, and it had to be obeyed, for anyone who broke it was dismissed from the flax sheds, he could not sell his mushrooms or his thyme or his hayflowers, and the power of the Baleks was so far-reaching that no one in the neighboring villages would give him work either or buy his forest herbs. But since the days when my grandfather's parents had gone out as small children to gather mushrooms and sell them in order that they might season the meat of the rich people of Prague[9] or be baked into game pies, it had never occurred to anyone to break this law: flour could be measured in cups, eggs could be counted, what they had spun could be measured by the yard, and besides, the old-fashioned bronze-gilt, ornate Balek scales did not look as if there was anything wrong with them, and five generations had entrusted the swinging black pointer with what they had gone out as eager children to gather from the woods.

True, there were some among those quiet people who <u>flouted</u> the law, poachers bent on making more money in one night than they could earn in a whole month in the flax sheds, but even these people apparently never thought of buying scales or making their own. My grandfather was the first person bold enough to test the justice of the Baleks, the family who lived in the chateau and drove two carriages, who always maintained one boy from the village while he studied theology at the seminary[10] in Prague, the family with whom the priest played taroc[11] every Wednesday, on whom the local reeve,[12] in his carriage emblazoned with the Imperial coat of arms, made an annual New Year's Day call and on whom the Emperor conferred a title on the first day of the year 1900.

My grandfather was hard-working and smart: he crawled further into the woods than the children of his clan had crawled before him, he penetrated as far as the thicket where, according to legend, Bilgan the Giant was supposed to dwell, guarding a treasure. But my grandfather was not afraid of Bilgan: he worked his way deep into the thicket, even when he was quite little, and brought out great quantities of mushrooms; he even found truffles,[13] for which Frau Balek paid thirty

PREDICT

Why do you think the Baleks outlawed the ownership of scales?

---

9. **Prague** (präg): the capital of the present-day Czech (chĕk) Republic, which borders southeastern Germany. At the time of the story, Prague was ruled by German-speaking Austria and was home to many German merchants as well as native Czechs.

10. **studied theology at the seminary:** studied religious philosophy at the school for training members of the clergy.

11. **taroc** (tăr′ɔk): a European card game played with a 78-card pack; also spelled *tarok*.

12. **reeve** (rēv): a local authority, here representing the emperor's government.

13. **truffles** (trŭf′ɔlz): edible fungi that resemble mushrooms but are far rarer and are considered a great delicacy.

WORDS TO KNOW **flout** (flout) *v.* to show contempt for; to scorn

pfennigs a pound. Everything my grandfather took to the Baleks he entered on the back of a torn-off calendar page: every pound of mushrooms, every gram of thyme, and on the right-hand side, in his childish handwriting, he entered the amount he received for each item; he scrawled in every pfennig, from the age of seven to the age of twelve, and by the time he was twelve the year 1900 had arrived, and because the Baleks had been raised to the aristocracy by the Emperor, they gave every family in the village a quarter of a pound of real coffee, the Brazilian kind; there was also free beer and tobacco for the men, and at the chateau there was a great banquet; many carriages stood in the avenue of poplars leading from the entrance gates to the chateau.

But the day before the banquet the coffee was distributed in the little room which had housed the Balek scales for almost a hundred years, and the Balek family was now called Balek von Bilgan because, according to legend, Bilgan the Giant used to have a great castle on the site of the present Balek estate.

My grandfather often used to tell me how he went there after school to fetch the coffee for four families: the Cechs, the Weidlers, the Vohlas[14] and his own, the Brüchers.[15] It was the afternoon of New Year's Eve: there were the front rooms to be decorated, the baking to be done, and the families did not want to spare four boys and have each of them go all the way to the chateau to bring back a quarter of a pound of coffee.

And so my grandfather sat on the narrow wooden bench in the little room while Gertrud the maid counted out the wrapped four-ounce packages of coffee, four of them, and he looked at the scales and saw that the pound weight was still lying on the left-hand scale; Frau Balek von Bilgan was busy with preparations for the banquet. And when Gertrud was about to put her hand into the jar with the lemon drops to give my grandfather one, she discovered it was empty: it was refilled once a year and held one kilo of the kind that cost a mark.

Gertrud laughed and said: "Wait here while I get the new lot," and my grandfather waited with the four four-ounce packages which had been wrapped and sealed in the factory, facing the scales on which someone had left the pound weight, and my grandfather took the four packages of coffee, put them on the empty scale, and his heart thudded as he watched the black finger of justice come to rest on the left of the black line: the scale with the pound weight stayed down, and the pound of coffee remained up in the air; his heart thudded more than if he had been lying behind a bush in the forest waiting for Bilgan the Giant, and he felt in his pocket for the pebbles he always carried with him so he could use his catapult[16] to shoot the sparrows which pecked away at his mother's cabbage plants—he had to put three, four, five pebbles beside the packages of coffee before the scale with the pound weight rose and the pointer at last came to rest over the black line. My grandfather took the coffee from the scale, wrapped the five pebbles in his kerchief,

---

14. **the Cechs** (chĕks), **the Weidlers** (vīd′lərz), **the Vohlas** (vō′läz).

15. **Brüchers** (brü′ĸĦ ərz): The name *Brücher* derives from the German words for "to break" and "to breach."

16. **catapult** (kăt′ə-pŭlt′): here, a slingshot.

and when Gertrud came back with the big kilo bag of lemon drops which had to last for another whole year in order to make the children's faces light up with pleasure, when Gertrud let the lemon drops rattle into the glass jar, the pale little fellow was still standing there, and nothing seemed to have changed. My grandfather only took three of the packages, then Gertrud looked in startled surprise at the white-faced child who threw the lemon drop onto the floor, ground it under his heel, and said: "I want to see Frau Balek."

"Balek von Bilgan, if you please," said Gertrud.

"All right, Frau Balek von Bilgan," but Gertrud only laughed at him, and he walked back to the village in the dark, took the Cechs, the Weidlers and the Vohlas their coffee, and said he had to go and see the priest.

CLARIFY

What has the grand-father discovered?

Instead he went out into the dark night with his five pebbles in his kerchief. He had to walk a long way before he found someone who had scales, who was permitted to have them; no one in the villages of Blaugau and Bernau[17] had any, he knew that, and he went straight through them till, after two hours' walking, he reached the little town of Dielheim[18] where Honig[19] the apothecary lived. From Honig's house came the smell of fresh pancakes, and Honig's breath, when he opened the door to the half-frozen boy, already smelled of punch, there was a moist cigar between his narrow lips, and he clasped the boy's cold hands firmly for a moment, saying: "What's the matter, has your father's lung got worse?"

"No, I haven't come for medicine, I wanted . . ." My grandfather undid his kerchief, took out the five pebbles, held them out to Honig and said: "I wanted to have these weighed." He glanced anxiously into Honig's face, but when Honig said nothing and did not get angry, or even ask

him anything, my grandfather said: "It is the amount that is short of justice," and now, as he went into the warm room, my grandfather realized how wet his feet were. The snow had soaked through his cheap shoes, and in the forest the branches had showered him with snow which was now melting, and he was tired and hungry and suddenly began to cry because he thought of the quantities of mushrooms, the herbs, the flowers, which had been weighed on the scales which were short five pebbles' worth of justice. And when Honig, shaking his head and holding the five pebbles, called his wife, my grandfather thought of the generations of his parents, his grandparents, who had all had to have their mushrooms, their flowers, weighed on the scales, and he was overwhelmed by a great wave of injustice and began to sob louder than ever, and, without waiting to be asked, he sat down on a chair, ignoring the pancakes, the cup of hot coffee which nice plump Frau Honig put in front of him, and did not stop crying till Honig himself came out from the shop at the back and, rattling the pebbles in his hand, said in a low voice to his wife: "Fifty-five grams, exactly."

M y grandfather walked the two hours home through the forest, got a beating at home, said nothing, not a single word, when he was asked about the coffee, spent the whole evening doing sums on the piece of paper on which he had written down everything he had sold to Frau Balek, and when midnight struck, and the cannon could be heard from the chateau, and the whole village rang with shouting and laughter and the noise of rattles, when the family kissed and embraced all

---

17. **Blaugau** (blou′gou′) **and Bernau** (bĕr′nou).
18. **Dielheim** (dēl′hīm′).
19. **Honig** (hô′nĭkH).

Une Battue en Campine [Beating the bushes in Campine] (about 1882–1885), Théodor Verstræte. Oil on canvas, 41¼″ × 71″, collection of Crédit Communal, Brussels, Belgium.

around, he said into the New Year silence: "The Baleks owe me eighteen marks and thirty-two pfennigs." And again he thought of all the children there were in the village, of his brother Fritz who had gathered so many mushrooms, of his sister Ludmilla; he thought of the many hundreds of children who had all gathered mushrooms for the Baleks, and herbs and flowers, and this time he did not cry but told his parents and brothers and sisters of his discovery.

When the Baleks von Bilgan went to High Mass on New Year's Day, their new coat of arms—a giant crouching under a fir tree— already emblazoned in blue and gold on their carriage, they saw the hard, pale faces of the people all staring at them. They had expected garlands in the village, a song in their honor, cheers and hurrahs, but the village was com-

pletely deserted as they drove through it, and in church the pale faces of the people were turned toward them, mute and hostile, and when the priest mounted the pulpit to deliver his New Year's sermon, he sensed the chill in those otherwise quiet and peaceful faces, and he stumbled painfully through his sermon and went back to the altar drenched in sweat. And as the Baleks von Bilgan left the church after Mass, they walked through a lane of mute, pale faces. But young Frau Balek von Bilgan stopped in front of the children's pews, sought out my grandfather's face, pale little Franz Brücher, and asked him, right there in the church: "Why didn't you take the coffee for your mother?" And my grandfather stood up and said: "Because you owe me as much money as five kilos of coffee would cost." And he pulled the five pebbles from his pocket, held them out to the young woman and said: "This much, fifty-five grams, is short in every pound of your justice"; and before the woman could say anything the men and women in the church lifted up their voices and sang: "The justice of this earth, O Lord, hath put Thee to death. . . ."

While the Baleks were at church, Wilhelm Vohla, the poacher, had broken into the little room, stolen the scales and the big fat leather-bound book in which had been entered every kilo of mushrooms, every kilo of hayflowers, everything bought by the Baleks in the village, and all afternoon of that New Year's Day the men of the village sat in my great-grandparents' front room and calculated, calculated one tenth of everything that had been bought—but when they had calculated many thousands of talers[20] and had still not come to an end, the reeve's gendarmes[21] arrived, made their way into my great-grandfather's front room, shooting and stabbing as they came, and removed the scales and the book by force. My grandfather's little sister Ludmilla lost her life, a few men were wounded, and one of the gendarmes was stabbed to death by Wilhelm Vohla the poacher.

Our village was not the only one to rebel: Blaugau and Bernau did too, and for almost a week no work was done in the flax sheds. But a great many gendarmes appeared, and the men and women were threatened with prison, and the Baleks forced the priest to display the scales publicly in the school and demonstrate that the finger of justice swung to and fro accurately. And the men and women went back to the flax sheds—but no one went to the school to watch

the priest: he stood there all alone, helpless and forlorn with his weights, scales, and packages of coffee.

And the children went back to gathering mushrooms, to gathering thyme, flowers and foxglove, but every Sunday, as soon as the Baleks entered the church, the hymn was struck up: "The justice of this earth, O Lord, hath put Thee to death," until the reeve ordered it proclaimed in every village that the singing of this hymn was forbidden.

EVALUATE

Why do you think the Baleks were able to return to business as usual?

My grandfather's parents had to leave the village and the new grave of their little daughter; they became basket weavers but did not stay long anywhere because it pained them to see how everywhere the finger of justice swung falsely. They walked along behind their cart, which crept slowly over the country roads, taking their thin goat with them, and passers-by could sometimes hear a voice from the cart singing: "The justice of this earth, O Lord, hath put Thee to death." And those who wanted to listen could hear the tale of the Baleks von Bilgan, whose justice lacked a tenth part. But there were few who listened. ❖

Translated by Leila Vennewitz

20. **talers** (tä′lərz): silver coins used in central Europe until around the turn of the century.
21. **gendarmes** (zhän′därmz′): police officers.

WORDS TO KNOW   **forlorn** (fər-lôrn′) *adj.* appearing sad or lonely because one has been left alone

218

RESPONDING
OPTIONS

FROM PERSONAL RESPONSE TO CRITICAL ANALYSIS

REFLECT 1. What were your reactions to the final outcome of the villagers' protests? Record your thoughts in your notebook.

RETHINK 2. How would you describe the narrator's grandfather as a boy? Support your answer with details from the story.

3. Consider the thoughts about justice that you explored for the Personal Connection on page 211. In your opinion, what is the worst injustice in the story? Explain your position.

4. How would you explain the main message about justice that is communicated in this story? *Consider*
   - the hymn sung by villagers when the Baleks enter church
   - why it took so long for the inaccuracy of the scales to be discovered
   - what the Balek scales symbolize
   - why the narrator's grandfather and his family found that "the finger of justice swung falsely" everywhere they went

5. How does the prediction you made in the Reading Connection on page 211 compare with what actually happens in the story?

RELATE 6. The Baleks seem to control nearly every aspect of life in the village, from the weighing of mushrooms to the activities of the police and clergy. Do you think wealthy people in the United States today exert a similar kind of power? Explain your reasoning.

LITERARY LINKS

Compare the outcome of challenging the system in this story with the outcomes in *The Pen of My Aunt* and "The Thrill of the Grass."

ANOTHER PATHWAY
Cooperative Learning
Create a pie graph that shows who may be held responsible for injustices in the story. Each segment should represent a different person or group and should be proportional to the degree of responsibility.

QUICKWRITES

1. Imagine that a new priest is assigned to the village and learns about the events related to the scales. Write a **sermon** in which the priest offers his moral judgment of these events.

2. Write a guest **editorial** that the Balek family might have placed in the local paper in which they attempt to win back the favor of the villagers.

3. Write a **journal entry** in which the grandfather, as an adult, reflects upon the lessons about justice that he learned as a result of discovering the scales' false measure.

📁 **PORTFOLIO** *Save your writing. You may want to use it later as a springboard to a piece for your portfolio.*

THE BALEK SCALES **219**

LITERARY CONCEPTS

Tone is the attitude a writer or narrator takes toward a subject. The language and details a writer chooses help to create the tone, which might be playful, serious, bitter, angry, or detached, among other possibilities. To identify the tone of a work, you might find it helpful to read the work aloud, as if giving a dramatic reading. The emotions that you convey in reading should give you hints as to the tone of the work. With a small group of classmates, read aloud the opening and closing paragraphs of "The Balek Scales." Then come up with the words or phrases that describe the tone of these paragraphs. Compare your descriptions with those of other groups.

CRITIC'S CORNER

Editor Ralph Ley described Böll as "the humane and incorruptible conscience of his country." What does this story reveal about Böll's conscience?

WORDS TO KNOW

Review the Words to Know at the bottom of the selection pages. Then, on your paper, match each example below with the appropriate vocabulary word.

1. The machines used for drying the flax were so old that no one could remember when they had first been used.

2. Most of the people had very little to eat; even milk was considered a treat.

3. By refusing the coffee, the grandfather ridiculed the authority of the Baleks.

4. In the next generation, another Frau Balek would be in control of the room with the scales.

5. The grandfather and his family must have felt lonely as they moved from town to town.

HEINRICH BÖLL

1917–1985

Heinrich Böll grew up in Cologne (kə-lōn'), Germany, the descendant of English Catholics who centuries before had fled to the Continent to escape religious persecution. Raised in a tolerant household at a time when many Germans were embracing intolerance, Böll watched in growing horror as the Nazis rose to power. During World War II, he was forced to join the German army; he was wounded four times and was captured and imprisoned by American forces. After the war, he began to publish novels and short stories. His early novels were harshly critical of warfare, which the Nazis had glorified. In *The Train Was on Time* (1949), he traced the despair of a sensitive young German soldier, not unlike himself; in *Adam, Where Art Thou?* (1951), he compared warfare to a contagious and deadly disease.

With time, Böll broadened his themes, though he remained a social critic. The corruption of power, the victimization of the innocent by those in power, and the dehumanizing effects of modern life are often treated in his novels and short stories. Böll also championed the rights of oppressed fellow writers, providing lodgings for Russian author Aleksandr Solzhenitsyn (ăl'ĭk-săn'dər sōl'zhə-nēt'sĭn) when he was forced to leave his then-Communist homeland. Over the years, Böll produced nearly 40 books and was honored with a Nobel Prize. "The Balek Scales," one of his most widely read stories, was first published in German in 1955.

OTHER WORKS *Eighteen Stories, The Stories of Heinrich Böll, What's to Become of the Boy?*

PREVIEWING

NONFICTION

from Montgomery Boycott
Coretta Scott King United States

Rosa Parks being fingerprinted. AP/Wide World Photos.

Dr. Martin Luther King, Jr., leading a protest march. UPI/Bettmann.

PERSONAL CONNECTION

What do you know about the civil rights movement and two of its key participants, Rosa Parks and Martin Luther King, Jr.? Share your knowledge with your classmates in a class discussion.

HISTORICAL CONNECTION

In the 1890s and early decades of the 20th century, many states, especially in the South, passed laws to ensure segregation, the complete separation of the races in public places. These so-called Jim Crow laws—named after a character in an old song— discriminated against African Americans. After World War II, opponents of these laws challenged their legality. In 1954 the Supreme Court, reversing an earlier decision, declared that it was unconstitutional to force whites and blacks to attend separate schools. Soon afterward, African Americans in Montgomery, Alabama, began the bus boycott that is the subject of the following selection.

A pivotal event in the civil rights movement, the Montgomery boycott first brought to national attention the Reverend Martin Luther King, Jr., the writer's husband. King's eye-opening efforts of nonviolent protest helped inspire many others in the struggle for civil rights. In 1960, for example, African-American students in Greensboro, North Carolina, initiated a new protest strategy, the sit-in, when they risked arrest for insisting on being served at a local segregated lunch counter.

READING CONNECTION

Identifying Multiple Effects "Montgomery Boycott" reports a now-famous incident from the civil rights movement in which one woman's refusal to give up her seat on a bus had significant effects. As you read the selection, identify the multiple effects of her decision. Jot them down on a diagram like this one.

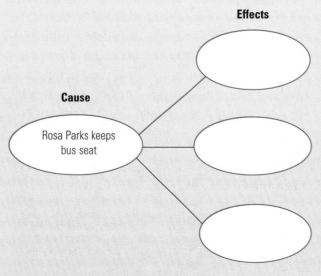

LASERLINKS
• *HISTORICAL CONNECTION*

221

MONTGOMERY BOYCOTT

CORETTA SCOTT KING

Of all the facets of segregation in Montgomery, the most degrading were the rules of the Montgomery City Bus Lines. This northern-owned corporation outdid the South itself. Although seventy percent of its passengers were black, it treated them like cattle—worse than that, for nobody insults a cow. The first seats on all buses were reserved for whites. Even if they were unoccupied and the rear seats crowded, blacks would have to stand at the back in case some whites might get aboard; and if the front seats happened to be occupied and more white people boarded the bus, black people seated in the rear were forced to get up and give them their seats. Furthermore—and I don't think northerners ever realized this—blacks had to pay their fares at the front of the bus, get off, and walk to the rear door to board again. Sometimes the bus would drive off without them after they had paid their fare. This would happen to elderly people or pregnant women, in bad weather or good, and was considered a joke by the drivers. Frequently the white bus drivers abused their passengers, calling them niggers, black cows, or black apes. Imagine what it was like, for example, for a black man to get on a bus with his son and be subjected to such treatment.

There had been one incident in March 1955, when fifteen-year-old Claudette Colvin refused

At one time, signs ordering the segregation of black and white passengers were posted on buses and trains in the South. This photograph was taken the day the Supreme Court banned segregation on public transportation. UPI/Bettmann Newsphotos.

NOTICE
IT IS REQUIRED BY LAW UNDER PENALTY OF FINE OF $5.00 TO $25.00 THAT WHITE AND NEGRO PASSENGERS MUST OCCUPY THE RESPECTIVE SPACE OR SEATS INDICATED BY SIGNS IN THIS VEHICLE
TEXAS PENAL CODE ARTICLE 1659 SEC 4
DALLAS CITY ORDINANCE NO 2904

COLORED →

to give up her seat to a white passenger. The high school girl was handcuffed and carted off to the police station. At that time Martin served on a committee to protest to the city and bus-company officials. The committee was received politely—and nothing was done.

The fuel that finally made that slow-burning fire blaze up was an almost routine incident. On December 1, 1955, Mrs. Rosa Parks, a forty-two-year-old seamstress whom my husband aptly described as "a charming person with a <u>radiant</u> personality," boarded a bus to go home after a long day working and shopping. The bus was crowded, and Mrs. Parks found a seat at the beginning of the black section. At the next stop more whites got on. The driver ordered Mrs. Parks to give her seat to a white man who boarded; this meant that she would have to stand all the way home. Rosa Parks was not in a revolutionary frame of mind. She had not planned to do what she did. Her cup had run over. As she said later, "I was just plain tired, and my feet hurt." So she sat there, refusing to get up. The driver called a policeman, who arrested her and took her to the courthouse. From there Mrs. Parks called E. D. Nixon, who came down and signed a bail bond for her.

Mr. Nixon was a fiery Alabamian. He was a Pullman porter[1] who had been active in A. Philip Randolph's Brotherhood of Sleeping Car Porters, and in civil rights activities. Suddenly he also had had enough; suddenly, it seemed, almost every African American in Montgomery had had enough. It was spontaneous combustion.[2] Phones began ringing all over the black section of the city. The Women's Political Council suggested a one-day boycott of the buses as a protest. E. D. Nixon courageously agreed to organize it.

The first we knew about it was when Mr. Nixon called my husband early in the morning of Friday, December 2. He had already talked to Ralph Abernathy.[3] After describing the incident, Mr. Nixon said, "We have taken this type of thing too long. I feel the time has come to boycott the buses. It's the only way to make the white folks see that we will not take this sort of thing any longer."

Martin agreed with him and offered the Dexter Avenue Church as a meeting place. After much telephoning, a meeting of black ministers and civic leaders was arranged for that evening. Martin said later that as he approached his church Friday evening, he was nervously wondering how many leaders would really turn up. To his delight, Martin found over forty people, representing every segment of African-American life, crowded into the large meeting room at Dexter. There were doctors, lawyers, businessmen, federal-government employees, union leaders, and a great many ministers. The latter were particularly welcome, not only because of their influence, but because it meant that they were beginning to accept Martin's view that "religion deals with both heaven and earth. . . . Any religion that professes to be concerned with the souls of men and is not concerned with the slums that doom them, the economic conditions that strangle them, and the social conditions that cripple them, is dry-as-dust religion." From that very first step, the Christian ministry provided the leadership of our struggle, as Christian ideals were its source.

---

1. **Pullman porter:** a railroad employee who serves people in a Pullman car; that is, a passenger car with seats that can be converted into beds.

2. **spontaneous combustion** (spŏn-tā′nē-əs kəm-bŭs′chən): literally, the situation that occurs when something bursts into flames on its own, without the addition of heat from an outside source.

3. **Ralph Abernathy** (1926–1990): a minister who became a close colleague of Martin Luther King, Jr., and an important civil rights leader.

Martin told me after he got home that the meeting was almost wrecked because questions or suggestions from the floor were cut off. However, after a stormy session, one thing was clear: however much they differed on details, everyone was unanimously for a boycott. It was set for Monday, December 5. Committees were organized; all the ministers present promised to urge their congregations to take part. Several thousand leaflets were printed on the church mimeograph machine, describing the reasons for the boycott and urging all blacks not to ride buses "to work, to town, to school, or anyplace on Monday, December 5." Everyone was asked to come to a mass meeting at the Holt Street Baptist Church on Monday evening for further instructions. The Reverend A. W. Wilson had offered his church because it was larger than Dexter and more convenient, being in the center of the black district.

Saturday was a busy day for Martin and the other members of the committee. They hustled around town talking with other leaders, arranging with the black-owned taxi companies for special bulk fares and with the owners of private automobiles to get the people to and from work. I could do little to help because Yoki[4] was only two weeks old, and my physician, Dr. W. D. Pettus, who was very careful, advised me to stay in for a month. However, I was kept busy answering the telephone, which rang continuously, and coordinating from that central point the many messages and arrangements.

Our greatest concern was how we were going to reach the fifty thousand black people of Montgomery, no matter how hard we worked. The white press, in an outraged exposé, spread the word for us in a way that would have been impossible with only our own resources.

As it happened, a white woman found one of our leaflets, which her black maid had left in the kitchen. The irate woman immediately telephoned the newspapers to let the white community know what the blacks were up to.

Our greatest concern was how we were going to reach the fifty thousand black people of Montgomery.

We laughed a lot about this, and Martin later said that we owed them a great debt.

On Sunday morning, from their pulpits, almost every African-American minister in town urged people to honor the boycott.

Martin came home late Sunday night and began to read the morning paper. The long articles about the proposed boycott accused the NAACP[5] of planting Mrs. Parks on the bus—she had been a volunteer secretary for the Montgomery chapter—and likened the boycott to the tactics of the White Citizens Councils.[6] This upset Martin. That awesome conscience of his began to gnaw at him, and he wondered if he was doing the right thing. Alone in his study, he struggled with the question of whether the boycott method was basically unchristian. Certainly it could be used for unethical ends. But, as he said, "We were using it to give birth to freedom . . . and to urge men to comply with the law of the land. Our concern was not to put

---

4. **Yoki:** nickname of the Kings' daughter Yolanda.

5. **NAACP:** the National Association for the Advancement of Colored People, a prominent civil rights organization.

6. **White Citizens Councils:** groups that formed, first in Mississippi and then throughout the South, to resist the 1954 Supreme Court decision to desegregate the schools.

WORDS
TO
KNOW
exposé (ĕk´spō-zā´) *n.* an account that reveals something negative to the public

225

the bus company out of business, but to put justice in business." He recalled Thoreau's[7] words, "We can no longer lend our cooperation to an evil system," and he thought, "He who accepts evil without protesting against it is really cooperating with it." Later Martin wrote, "From this moment on I conceived of our movement as an act of massive noncooperation. From then on I rarely used the word 'boycott.'"

Serene after his inner struggle, Martin joined me in our sitting room. We wanted to get to bed early, but Yoki began crying and the telephone kept ringing. Between interruptions we sat together talking about the prospects for the success of the protest. We were both filled with doubt. Attempted boycotts had failed in Montgomery and other cities. Because of changing times and tempers, this one seemed to have a better chance, but it was still a slender hope. We finally decided that if the boycott was sixty percent effective we would be doing all right, and we would be satisfied to have made a good start.

A little after midnight we finally went to bed, but at five-thirty the next morning we were up and dressed again. The first bus was due at six o'clock at the bus stop just outside our house. We had coffee and toast in the kitchen; then I went into the living room to watch. Right on time, the bus came, headlights blazing through the December darkness, all lit up inside. I shouted, "Martin! Martin, come quickly!" He ran in and stood beside me, his face lit with excitement. There was not one person on that usually crowded bus!

We stood together waiting for the next bus. It was empty too, and this was the most heavily traveled line in the whole city. Bus after empty bus paused at the stop and moved on. We were so excited we could hardly speak coherently. Finally Martin said, "I'm going to take the car

and see what's happening other places in the city."

He picked up Ralph Abernathy and they cruised together around the city. Martin told me about it when he got home. Everywhere it was the same—a few white people and maybe one or two blacks in otherwise empty buses. Martin and Ralph saw extraordinary sights—the sidewalks crowded with men and women trudging to work; the students of Alabama State College walking or thumbing rides; taxicabs with people clustered in them. Some of our people rode mules; others went in horse-drawn buggies. But most of them were walking, some making a round-trip of as much as twelve miles. Martin later wrote, "As I watched them I knew that there is nothing more majestic than the determined courage of individuals willing to suffer and sacrifice for their freedom and dignity."

Martin rushed off again at nine o'clock that morning to attend the trial of Mrs. Parks. She was convicted of disobeying the city's segregation ordinance and fined ten dollars and costs. Her young attorney, Fred D. Gray, filed an appeal. It was one of the first clear-cut cases of an African American being convicted of disobeying the segregation laws—usually the charge was disorderly conduct or some such thing.

The leaders of the Movement called a meeting for three o'clock in the afternoon to organize the mass meeting to be held that night. Martin was a bit late, and as he entered the hall, people said to him, "Martin, we have elected you to be our president. Will you accept?"

Fear was an invisible presence at the meeting, along with courage and hope. Proposals were voiced to make the organization, which the

---

7. **Thoreau** (thə-rō′): Henry David Thoreau (1817–1862), American writer whose famous essay "Civil Disobedience" helped inspire the ideas of nonviolent resistance used in the civil rights movement.

WORDS TO KNOW   **coherently** (kō-hîr′ənt-lē) *adv.* in a manner that shows clear thinking and makes sense

226

Dr. Martin Luther King, Jr. (*left*), and Coretta Scott King in their early days as civil rights activists. Culver Pictures.

leaders decided to call the Montgomery Improvement Association, or MIA, a sort of secret society, because if no names were mentioned it would be safer for the leaders. E. D. Nixon opposed that idea. "We're acting like little boys," he said. "Somebody's name will be known, and if we're afraid, we might just as well fold up right now. The white folks are eventually going to find out anyway. We'd better decide now if we are going to be fearless men or scared little boys."

That settled that question. It was also decided that the protest would continue until certain demands were met. Ralph Abernathy was made chairman of the committee to draw up the demands.

Martin came home at six o'clock. He said

later that he was nervous about telling me he had accepted the presidency of the protest movement, but he need not have worried, because I sincerely meant what I said when I told him that night: "You know that whatever you do, you have my backing."

Reassured, Martin went to his study. He was to make the main speech at the mass meeting that night. It was now six-thirty and—this was the way it was usually to be—he had only twenty minutes to prepare what he thought might be the most decisive speech of his life. He said afterward that thinking about the responsibility and the reporters and television cameras, he almost panicked. Five minutes wasted and only fifteen minutes left. At that moment he turned to prayer. He asked God "to restore my balance and be with me in a time when I need Your guidance more than ever."

How could he make his speech militant enough to rouse people to action and yet devoid of hate and resentment? He was determined to do both.

Martin and Ralph went together to the meeting. When they got within four blocks of the Holt Street Baptist Church, there was an enormous traffic jam. Five thousand people stood outside the church listening to loudspeakers and singing hymns. Inside it was so crowded, Martin told me, the people had to lift Ralph and him above the crowd and pass them from hand to hand over their heads to the platform. The crowd and the singing inspired Martin, and God answered his prayer. Later Martin said, "That night I understood what the older preachers meant when they said, 'Open your mouth and God will speak for you.'"

First the people sang "Onward, Christian Soldiers" in a tremendous wave of five thousand voices. This was followed by a prayer and a reading of the Scriptures. Martin was introduced. People applauded; television lights beat upon him. Without any notes at all he began to speak. Once again he told the story of Mrs. Parks, and rehearsed some of the wrongs black people were suffering. Then he said,

But there comes a time when people get tired. We are here this evening to say to those who have mistreated us so long, that we are tired. Tired of being segregated and humiliated; tired of being kicked about by the brutal feet of oppression.

The audience cheered wildly, and Martin said,

We have no alternative but to protest. We have been amazingly patient . . . but we

come here tonight to be saved from that patience that makes us patient with anything less than freedom and justice.

Taking up the challenging newspaper comparison with the White Citizens Councils and the Klan,[8] Martin said,

They are protesting for the perpetuation of injustice in the community; we're protesting for the birth of justice . . . their methods lead to violence and lawlessness. But in our protest there will be no cross-burnings, no white person will be taken from his home by a hooded Negro mob and brutally murdered . . . We will be guided by the highest principles of law and order.

Having roused the audience for militant action, Martin now set limits upon it. His study of nonviolence and his love of Christ informed his words. He said,

No one must be intimidated to keep them from riding the buses. Our method must be persuasion, not coercion. We will only say to the people, "Let your conscience be your guide." . . . Our actions must be guided by the deepest principles of the Christian faith. . . . Once again we must hear the words of Jesus, "Love your enemies. Bless them that curse you. Pray for them that despitefully use you." If we fail to do this, our protest will end up as a meaningless drama on the stage of history

---

8. **Klan:** the Ku Klux Klan, a secret society trying to establish white power and authority by unlawful and violent methods directed against African Americans and other minority groups.

WORDS
TO
KNOW

militant (mĭl′ĭ-tənt) *adj.* showing a fighting spirit; aggressive
devoid (dĭ-void′) *adj.* completely lacking; empty
oppression (ə-prĕsh′ən) *n.* unjust or cruel exercise of power or authority
perpetuation (pər-pĕch′oo-ā′shən) *n.* a long-lasting continuation
coercion (kō-ûr′zhən) *n.* the use of power or threats to force someone to do something

and its memory will be shrouded in the ugly garments of shame. . . . We must not become bitter and end up by hating our white brothers. As Booker T. Washington[9] said, "Let no man pull you so low as to make you hate him."

Finally, Martin said,

If you will protest courageously, and yet with dignity and Christian love, future historians will say, "There lived a great people—a black people—who injected new meaning and dignity into the veins of civilization." This is our challenge and our overwhelming responsibility.

As Martin finished speaking, the audience rose cheering in <u>exaltation</u>. And in that speech my husband set the keynote and the tempo of the Movement he was to lead, from Montgomery onward. ❖

---

9. **Booker T. Washington** (1856–1915): African-American educator and writer.

SIT-INS

Margaret Walker

Greensboro, North Carolina, in the Spring of 1960

You were our first brave ones to defy their
   dissonance of hate
With your silence
With your willingness to suffer
Without violence
5 Those first bright young to fling names across pages
Of new southern history
With courage and faith, convictions, and intelligence
The first to blaze a flaming path for justice
And awaken consciences
10 Of these stony ones.

Come, Lord Jesus, Bold Young Galilean[1]
Sit Beside this Counter, Lord, with Me!

---

1. **Galilean** (găl'ə-lē'ən): a term used as a synonym for Jesus, because Galilee was the center of Jesus' ministry.

WORDS
TO
KNOW

exaltation (ĕg'zôl-tā'shən) *n.* the act of glorifying, praising, or honoring

229

RESPONDING
OPTIONS

FROM PERSONAL RESPONSE TO CRITICAL ANALYSIS

REFLECT 1. What feelings did you experience while reading the selection? Describe them in your notebook.

RETHINK 2. Review the cause-and-effect diagram that you completed for the Reading Connection on page 221. What do you think were the most important effects of Rosa Parks's decision not to give up her bus seat?

3. Do you think the phrase "spontaneous combustion" is a good description of the events leading up to the boycott?

Consider
- Rosa Parks's motivation for challenging the system
- how segregation had affected the African-American community

4. What does the selection suggest about the character, goals, and principles of Martin Luther King, Jr.?

5. What is your opinion of Rosa Parks and her accomplishments? Explain your opinion.

RELATE 6. Based on your understanding of "Montgomery Boycott" and the Insight poem "Sit-Ins," what qualities do you think were valued by the early participants in the civil rights movement?

7. Do you think a boycott is an effective and fair means of protest? Use examples to explain your reasoning.

LITERARY CONCEPTS

Author's purpose refers to a writer's main reason for writing. Writers of nonfiction usually write for one or more of the following purposes: to inform, to give an opinion, to entertain, or to persuade. For example, the purpose of a news report is to inform readers about events; the purpose of an editorial may be to persuade readers to do or believe something. What would you identify as Coretta Scott King's main purpose in writing this selection? Cite details to support your response.

ANOTHER PATHWAY

Cooperative Learning

Work together in a small group to write two newspaper editorials on the Montgomery boycott that might have appeared the day after it began. Write one from the perspective of a paper aimed primarily at African-American readers and the second from the perspective of a paper that serves a mostly white readership.

QUICKWRITES

1. Write the diary entry Rosa Parks might have written just after her famous bus ride and arrest. Expand on ideas touched upon in the selection and in your prereading discussion.

2. In describing the boycott, Rosa Parks reported, "Many whites, even white Southerners, told me that even though it may have seemed like the blacks were being freed, they felt more free and at ease themselves." Write an analysis of what you think she meant.

3. Create several protest signs that demonstrators might have carried on the first day of the bus boycott.

📁 *PORTFOLIO Save your writing. You may want to use it later as a springboard to a piece for your portfolio.*

LASERLINKS
• *HISTORICAL CONNECTION*

ALTERNATIVE ACTIVITIES

1. Retell the **story** of the boycott as if you were presenting it to an audience of young children celebrating Martin Luther King Day. If possible, present your story to an audience of children.

2. Find and photocopy news stories and magazine articles that reported the Montgomery boycott when it happened. Use them in a "Moments in History" **bulletin-board display** or **exhibit.**

3. Bring to class and play a recording of a **speech** by Martin Luther King, Jr. Explain when and where he made the speech and why it is significant.

ACROSS THE CURRICULUM

History Research and prepare a time line that identifies and briefly describes events in the civil rights movement. You might begin with the Montgomery boycott or with the 1954 Supreme Court decision in *Brown* v. *Board of Education of Topeka, Kansas.*

LITERARY LINKS

What person, real or fictional, that you have read about in this book do you think is most like Rosa Parks? Explain your answer.

WORDS TO KNOW

Review the Words to Know at the bottom of the selection pages. Then, on a separate sheet, indicate whether the following pairs of words are synonyms or antonyms.

1. degrading—humiliating
2. radiant—dim
3. exposé—tribute
4. oppression—injustice
5. coherently—sensibly
6. militant—meek
7. devoid—full
8. perpetuation—halt
9. coercion—intimidation
10. exaltation—glorification

CORETTA SCOTT KING

As a child in Heiberger, Alabama, Coretta Scott had to walk five miles a day to a one-room schoolhouse while white children rode past her on a school bus. That experience and others made her determined to struggle for racial equality. Recognizing education as the key to winning that struggle, she studied hard and eventually won a scholarship to Antioch College in Ohio, where her sister Edythe had been the first African-American student on campus. After graduation, she moved to Boston to study music and there met Martin Luther King, Jr., then a graduate student at Boston University, whose dreams of fighting for racial equality coincided with her own. The two were married in 1953, two years before the Montgomery boycott.

1927–

Over the years, Coretta Scott King has shown great determination and courage in her fight for civil rights. In 1956 her home was bombed; in 1968 her husband was assassinated in Memphis, Tennessee. Nevertheless, on the day before her husband's funeral, she led a march of striking Memphis garbage collectors, and the next year she published *My Life with Martin Luther King, Jr.,* the book from which "Montgomery Boycott" is taken. Since then, she has remained a tireless champion in the struggle for racial justice, most notably as founder and chief executive officer of the Martin Luther King, Jr., Center for Nonviolent Social Change in Atlanta, Georgia.

OTHER WORKS *The Words of Martin Luther King, Jr.*

PREVIEWING

The Prisoner Who Wore Glasses

Bessie Head **South Africa / Botswana**

PERSONAL CONNECTION

In a class discussion, tell what you think it means to be assertive. Then discuss the possible advantages and disadvantages of acting assertively. Use examples from various social situations—at home, at school, in your community, and so on.

HISTORICAL CONNECTION

From the late 1940s to the early 1990s, black South Africans who tried to be assertive frequently became political prisoners. Some people were imprisoned, for example, simply for speaking out against the government or publicly protesting government policies. South Africa was then ruled by a white minority government whose official policy of apartheid (ə-pärt'hīt') kept the races separate and legally discriminated against the nation's black majority and other people of color. "The Prisoner Who Wore Glasses" is set on a South African prison farm in the years when apartheid was still the law of the land. The two main characters in the story are a black political prisoner and a white prison guard, or warder. The warder is an Afrikaner (ăf'rĭ-kä'nər), a white South African of Dutch descent, who speaks English with a heavy accent.

Riot in Durban, South Africa, 1959. Archive Photos.

WRITING CONNECTION

Do you find it easy to voice your own needs and wants, or are you reluctant to speak up for yourself? In your notebook, rate your own assertiveness on a scale of 0 to 10, like the one to the right, and then explain your reasoning. As you read, notice how assertive the main characters are.

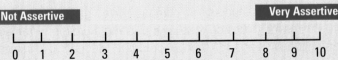

The Prisoner Who Wore Glasses

Bessie Head

Chain Gang (1939–1940), William H. Johnson. National Museum of American Art, Washington, D.C./Art Resource, New York.

Scarcely a breath of wind disturbed the stillness of the day, and the long rows of cabbages were bright green in the sunlight. Large white clouds drifted slowly across the deep blue sky. Now and then they obscured the sun and caused a chill on the backs of the prisoners who had to work all day long in the cabbage field.

233

This trick the clouds were playing with the sun eventually caused one of the prisoners who wore glasses to stop work, straighten up and peer short-sightedly at them. He was a thin little fellow with a hollowed-out chest and comic knobbly knees. He also had a lot of fanciful ideas because he smiled at the clouds.

"Perhaps they want me to send a message to the children," he thought tenderly, noting that the clouds were drifting in the direction of his home some hundred miles away. But before he could frame the message, the warder in charge of his work span[1] shouted:

"Hey, what you tink you're doing, Brille?"[2]

The prisoner swung round, blinking rapidly, yet at the same time sizing up the enemy. He was a new warder, named Jacobus Stephanus Hannetjie.[3] His eyes were the color of the sky but they were frightening. A simple, primitive, brutal soul gazed out of them. The prisoner bent down quickly and a message was quietly passed down the line:

"We're in for trouble this time, comrades."

"Why?" rippled back up the line.

"Because he's not human," the reply rippled down, and yet only the crunching of the spades as they turned over the earth disturbed the stillness.

This particular work span was known as Span One. It was composed of ten men, and they were all political prisoners. They were grouped together for convenience, as it was one of the prison regulations that no black warder should be in charge of a political prisoner lest this prisoner convert him to his views. It never seemed to occur to the authorities that this very reasoning was the strength of Span One and a clue to the strange terror they aroused in the warders. As political prisoners they were unlike the other prisoners in the sense that they felt no guilt nor were they outcasts of society. All guilty men instinctively <u>cower</u>, which was why it was

the kind of prison where men got knocked out cold with a blow at the back of the head from an iron bar. Up until the arrival of Warder Hannetjie, no warder had dared beat any member of Span One and no warder had lasted more than a week with them. The battle was entirely psychological. Span One was assertive and it was beyond the scope of white warders to handle assertive black men. Thus, Span One had got out of control. They were the best thieves and liars in the camp. They lived all day on raw cabbages. They chatted and smoked tobacco. And since they moved, thought and acted as one, they had perfected every technique of group concealment.

Trouble began that very day between Span One and Warder Hannetjie. It was because of the shortsightedness of Brille. That was the nickname he was given in prison and is the Afrikaans[4] word for someone who wears glasses. Brille could never judge the approach of the prison gates, and on several previous occasions he had munched on cabbages and dropped them almost at the feet of the warder, and all previous warders had overlooked this. Not so Warder Hannetjie.

"Who dropped that cabbage?" he thundered.

Brille stepped out of line.

"I did," he said meekly.

"All right," said Hannetjie. "The whole span goes three meals off."

"But I told you I did it," Brille protested.

The blood rushed to Warder Hannetjie's face.

---

1. **work span:** a work group in the prison.
2. **Brille** (brĭl'ə).
3. **Jacobus Stephanus Hannetjie** (yä-kō'büs stä-fän'üs hä'nĕt-yē).
4. **Afrikaans** (ăf'rĭ-kans'): a language closely related to Dutch and spoken by South Africans of Dutch descent.

"Look 'ere," he said. "I don't take orders from a kaffir.[5] I don't know what kind of kaffir you tink you are. Why don't you say Baas.[6] I'm your Baas. Why don't you say Baas, hey?"

Brille blinked his eyes rapidly but by contrast his voice was strangely calm.

"I'm twenty years older than you," he said. It was the first thing that came to mind, but the comrades seemed to think it a huge joke. A titter swept up the line. The next thing Warder Hannetjie whipped out a knobkerrie[7] and gave Brille several blows about the head. What surprised his comrades was the speed with which Brille had removed his glasses or else they would have been smashed to pieces on the ground.

That evening in the cell Brille was very apologetic.

"I'm sorry, comrades," he said. "I've put you into a hell of a mess."

"Never mind, brother," they said. "What happens to one of us, happens to all."

"I'll try to make up for it, comrades," he said. "I'll steal something so that you don't go hungry."

Privately, Brille was very philosophical about his head wounds. It was the first time an act of violence had been perpetrated against him, but he had long been a witness of extreme, almost unbelievable human brutality. He had twelve children and his mind traveled back that evening through the sixteen years of bedlam in which he had lived. It had all happened in a small drab little three-bedroomed house in a small drab little street in the Eastern Cape,[8] and the children kept coming year after year because neither he nor Martha managed the contra-

ceptives the right way and a teacher's salary never allowed moving to a bigger house and he was always taking exams to improve this salary only to have it all eaten up by hungry mouths. Everything was pretty horrible, especially the way the children fought. They'd get hold of each other's heads and give them a good bashing against the wall. Martha gave up somewhere along the line, so they worked out a thing between them. The bashings, biting and blood were to operate in full swing until he came home. He was to be the bogeyman,[9] and when it worked he never failed to have a sense of godhead[10] at the way in which his presence could change savages into fairly reasonable human beings.

Yet somehow it was this chaos and mismanagement at the center of his life that drove him into politics. It was really an ordered beautiful world with just a few basic slogans to learn along with the rights of mankind. At one stage, before things became very bad, there were conferences to attend, all very far away from home.

"Let's face it," he thought ruefully. "I'm only learning right now what it means to be a politician.

> "But I told you I did it,"
> Brille protested.
> The blood rushed to
> Warder Hannetjie's face.

5. **kaffir** (kăf'ər): in South Africa, an insulting term for a black.

6. **Baas** (bäs): Afrikaans for *master*. The word has the same Dutch origins as the English *boss*.

7. **knobkerrie** (nŏb'kĕr´ē): a short club with a knobbed end.

8. **the Eastern Cape:** the eastern part of the Cape Province in southern South Africa.

9. **bogeyman** (bŏŏg´ē-măn´): a terrifying figure of fear, dread, or harassment.

10. **godhead:** divinity; the quality or state of being a god.

WORDS TO KNOW

perpetrate (pûr'pĭ-trāt') *v.* to commit
bedlam (bĕd'ləm) *n.* a place or situation of great noise and confusion
chaos (kā'ŏs') *n.* total disorder
ruefully (rōō'fə-lē) *adv.* with regret

Le nègre Scipion [Black Scipio] (about 1866–1868), Paul Cézanne. Museu de Arte de São Paulo (Brazil) Assis Chateaubriand. Photo by Luiz Hossaka.

All this while I've been running away from Martha and the kids."

And the pain in his head brought a hard lump to his throat. That was what the children did to each other daily and Martha wasn't managing, and if Warder Hannetjie had not interrupted him that morning, he would have sent the following message:

"Be good comrades, my children. Cooperate, then life will run smoothly."

The next day Warder Hannetjie caught this old man with twelve children stealing grapes from the farm shed. They were an enormous quantity of grapes in a ten-gallon tin,[11] and for this misdeed the old man spent a week in the

---

11. **tin:** the British word for a can, used in South Africa and many other former British colonies.

isolation cell. In fact, Span One as a whole was in constant trouble. Warder Hannetjie seemed to have eyes at the back of his head. He uncovered the trick about the cabbages, how they were split in two with the spade and immediately covered with earth and then unearthed again and eaten with split-second timing. He found out how tobacco smoke was beaten into the ground, and he found out how conversations were whispered down the wind.

For about two weeks Span One lived in acute misery. The cabbages, tobacco and conversations had been the pivot of jail life to them. Then one evening they noticed that their good old comrade who wore the glasses was looking rather pleased with himself. He pulled out a four-ounce packet of tobacco by way of explanation, and the comrades fell upon it with great greed. Brille merely smiled. After all, he was the father of many children. But when the last shred had disappeared, it occurred to the comrades that they ought to be puzzled. Someone said:

"I say, brother. We're watched like hawks these days. Where did you get the tobacco?"

"Hannetjie gave it to me," said Brille.

There was a long silence. Into it dropped a quiet bombshell.

"I saw Hannetjie in the shed today," and the failing eyesight blinked rapidly. "I caught him in the act of stealing five bags of fertilizer, and he bribed me to keep my mouth shut."

There was another long silence.

"Prison is an evil life," Brille continued, apparently discussing some irrelevant matter. "It makes a man contemplate all kinds of evil deeds."

He held out his hand and closed it.

"You know, comrades," he said. "I've got Hannetjie. I'll betray him tomorrow."

Everyone began talking at once.

"Forget it, brother. You'll get shot."

Brille laughed.

"I won't," he said. "That is what I mean about evil. I am a father of children, and I saw today that Hannetjie is just a child and stupidly truthful. I'm going to punish him severely because we need a good warder."

The following day, with Brille as witness, Hannetjie confessed to the theft of the fertilizer and was fined a large sum of money. From then on Span One did very much as they pleased while Warder Hannetjie stood by and said nothing. But it was Brille who carried this to extremes. One day, at the close of work Warder Hannetjie said:

"Brille, pick up my jacket and carry it back to the camp."

"But nothing in the regulations says I'm your servant, Hannetjie," Brille replied coolly.

"I've told you not to call me Hannetjie. You must say Baas," but Warder Hannetjie's voice lacked conviction. In turn, Brille squinted up at him.

"I'll tell you something about this Baas business, Hannetjie," he said. "One of these days we are going to run the country. You are going to clean my car. Now, I have a fifteen-year-old son, and I'd die of shame if you had to tell him that I ever called you Baas."

Warder Hannetjie went red in the face and picked up his coat.

On another occasion Brille was seen to be walking about the prison yard, openly smoking tobacco. On being taken before the prison commander he claimed to have received the tobacco from Warder Hannetjie. All throughout the tirade from his chief, Warder Hannetjie failed to defend himself, but his nerve broke completely. He called Brille to one side.

"Brille," he said. "This thing between you and me must end. You may not know it, but I have a wife and children, and you're driving me to suicide."

"Why don't you like your own medicine, Hannetjie?" Brille asked quietly.

"I can give you anything you want," Warder Hannetjie said in desperation.

"It's not only me but the whole of Span One," said Brille cunningly. "The whole of Span One wants something from you."

Warder Hannetjie brightened with relief.

"I tink I can manage if it's tobacco you want," he said.

Brille looked at him, for the first time struck with pity and guilt. He wondered if he had carried the whole business too far. The man was really a child.

"It's not tobacco we want, but you," he said. "We want you on our side. We want a good warder because without a good warder we won't be able to manage the long stretch ahead."

Warder Hannetjie interpreted this request in his own fashion, and his interpretation of what was good and human often left the prisoners of Span One speechless with surprise. He had a way of slipping off his revolver and picking up a spade and digging alongside Span One. He had a way of producing unheard-of luxuries like boiled eggs from his farm nearby and things like cigarettes, and Span One responded nobly and got the reputation of being the best work span in the camp. And it wasn't only taken from their side. They were awfully good at stealing <u>commodities</u> like fertilizer which were needed on the farm of Warder Hannetjie. ❖

> "You may not know it, but I have a wife and children, and you're driving me to suicide."

WORDS TO KNOW

commodity (kə-mŏd'ĭ-tē) *n.* an item—especially a farming or mining product—that can be turned to commercial use or that can provide another advantage

THEY HAVE NOT BEEN ABLE   NO HAN PODIDO

ARMANDO VALLADARES
(är-män′dô bä-yä-dä′rĕs)

They have not been able to take away
the rain's song
not yet
not even in this cell
5 but perhaps they'll do it tomorrow
that's why I want to enjoy it now,
to listen to the drops
drumming against
the boarded windows.
10 And suddenly it comes
through I don't know what crack
through I don't know what opening
that pungent odor
of wet earth
15 and I inhale deeply
filling myself to the brim
because perhaps they will also
prohibit that tomorrow.

*Translated by
Marguerite Guzman Bouvard*

*No han podido quitarme
todavía
en este encierro
el canto de la lluvia
5 pero quizás lo hagan mañana
por eso quiero ahora disfrutarlo
escuchar las gotas
más allá de mis ojos
y los esperos muros
10 golpear con insistencia
las ventanas tapiadas.
Y de pronto me llega
no sé por qué ranura
no sé por qué intersticio
15 ese olor agradable
de la tierra mojada
y la aspiro muy hondo
para llenarme bien
porque quizás también
20 lo prohiban mañana.*

Hombre y su sombra [Man and his shadow] (1971), Rufino Tamayo. Oil on canvas, 50 cm × 40 cm, collection of INBA-Museo de Arte Moderno, Mexico City.

RESPONDING OPTIONS

FROM PERSONAL RESPONSE TO CRITICAL ANALYSIS

REFLECT
1. What are your thoughts and feelings about the relationship between Brille and Hannetjie? Describe your response in your notebook.

RETHINK
2. Why do you think Hannetjie becomes such a "good warder" at the end of the story?

3. How does Brille's relationship with his children compare with his relationship with Hannetjie?

4. In your opinion, what is this story saying about assertiveness and cooperation?
   Consider
   • how the different characters assert themselves
   • the effectiveness of assertive acts in the story
   • how the men cooperate at the end of the story

RELATE
5. Compare Brille's attitude with that of the speaker in the Insight poem "They Have Not Been Able."

6. Consider the hardships endured by Brille and the other prisoners of Span One. What do you think would be the most difficult aspect of life in prison?

ANOTHER PATHWAY

Cooperative Learning

In a small group, identify the incidents involving conflict between Brille and Hannetjie. Then create a chart in which you describe each incident, note the beliefs that motivate Brille and Hannetjie, and explain how the incident reflects the larger conflict between whites and blacks in South Africa.

LITERARY CONCEPTS

Point of view refers to the narrative method used in a literary work. In **first-person point of view,** the narrator is a character in the story who describes the action in his or her own words, referring to himself or herself with first-person pronouns such as *I*, *me*, and *us*. In **third-person point of view,** the narrator is not a character but instead stands outside the action, referring to all characters with third-person pronouns such as *he, she,* and *they.* "The Prisoner Who Wore Glasses" uses third-person point of view. Why do you think Bessie Head chose *not* to have Brille tell the story himself?

CONCEPT REVIEW: Setting The story is set in South Africa at a time when apartheid was still in effect. Why do you think Head set the story in a prison instead of a factory, a slum, or some other place?

QUICKWRITES

1. Assume Brille's identity and write a **letter** to his children. In it, reveal what you have learned as a result of your experience in prison. Include some advice about assertiveness and cooperation.

2. Draft a **personal essay** in which you compare Brille's response to his warder with your likely response to such a situation.

3. If Brille had not caught Hannetjie stealing fertilizer, how might the outcome of the story be different? Write a **plot summary** of the events that might have happened.

📁 *PORTFOLIO Save your writing. You may want to use it later as a springboard to a piece for your portfolio.*

The Censors

Luisa Valenzuela

Poor Juan![1] One day they caught him with his guard down before he could even realize that what he had taken as a stroke of luck was really one of fate's dirty tricks. These things happen the minute you're careless, as one often is. Juancito[2] let happiness—a feeling you can't trust—get the better of him when he received from a confidential source Mariana's new address in Paris and knew that she hadn't forgotten him. Without thinking twice, he sat down at his table and wrote her a letter. *The* letter that now keeps his mind off his job during the day and won't let him sleep at night (what had he scrawled, what had he put on that sheet of paper he sent to Mariana?).

Juan knows there won't be a problem with the letter's contents, that it's irreproachable, harmless. But what about the rest? He knows

that they examine, sniff, feel, and read between the lines of each and every letter, and check its tiniest comma and most accidental stain. He knows that all letters pass from hand to hand and go through all sorts of tests in the huge censorship offices and that, in the end, very few continue on their way. Usually it takes months, even years, if there aren't any snags; all this time the freedom, maybe even the life, of both sender and receiver is in jeopardy. And that's why Juan's so troubled: thinking that something might happen to Mariana because of

---

1. **Juan** (hwän).
2. **Juancito** (hwän-sē′tô): an affectionate nickname for Juan.

WORDS TO KNOW   **irreproachable** (ĭr′ĭ-prō′chə-bəl) *adj.* perfect or blameless in every respect; faultless

his letters. Of all people, Mariana, who must finally feel safe there where she always dreamt she'd live. But he knows that the Censor's Secret Command operates all over the world and cashes in on the discount in air fares; there's nothing to stop them from going as far as that hidden Paris neighborhood, kidnapping Mariana, and returning to their cozy homes, certain of having fulfilled their noble mission.

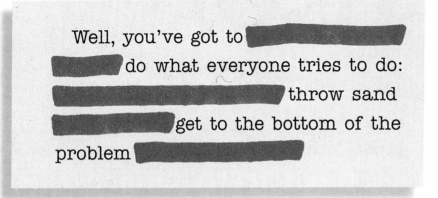

Well, you've got to beat them to the punch, do what everyone tries to do: sabotage the machinery, throw sand in its gears, get to the bottom of the problem so as to stop it.

This was Juan's sound plan when he, like many others, applied for a censor's job—not because he had a calling[3] or needed a job: no, he applied simply to intercept his own letter, a consoling albeit unoriginal idea. He was hired immediately, for each day more and more censors are needed and no one would bother to check on his references.

Ulterior motives[4] couldn't be overlooked by the Censorship Division, but they needn't be too strict with those who applied. They knew how hard it would be for the poor guys to find the letter they wanted and even if they did, what's a letter or two when the new censor would snap up so many others? That's how Juan managed to join the Post Office's Censorship Division, with a certain goal in mind.

The building had a festive air on the outside that contrasted with its inner staidness. Little by little, Juan was absorbed by his job, and he felt at peace since he was doing everything he could to get his letter for Mariana. He didn't even worry when, in his first month, he was sent to Section K where envelopes are very carefully screened for explosives.

It's true that on the third day, a fellow worker had his right hand blown off by a letter, but the division chief claimed it was sheer negligence on the victim's part. Juan and the other employees were allowed to go back to their work, though feeling less secure. After work, one of them tried to organize a strike to demand higher wages for unhealthy work, but Juan didn't join in; after thinking it over, he reported the man to his superiors and thus got promoted.

You don't form a habit by doing something once, he told himself as he left his boss's office. And when he was transferred to Section F, where letters are carefully checked for poison dust, he felt he had climbed a rung in the ladder.

By working hard, he quickly reached Section E, where the job became more interesting, for he could now read and analyze the letters'

---

3. **had a calling:** had an inner urge to go into a particular occupation or career.

4. **ulterior motives:** reasons for doing something that are concealed in order to deceive.

WORDS TO KNOW   **staidness** (stād'nĭs) *n.* a quiet, often strait-laced dignity

244

contents. Here he could even hope to get hold of his letter, which, judging by the time that had elapsed, had gone through the other sections and was probably floating around in this one.

Soon his work became so absorbing that his noble mission blurred in his mind. Day after day he crossed out whole paragraphs in red ink, pitilessly chucking many letters into the censored basket. These were horrible days when he was shocked by the <u>subtle</u> and <u>conniving</u> ways employed by people to pass on <u>subversive</u> messages; his instincts were so sharp that he found behind a simple "the weather's unsettled" or "prices continue to soar" the wavering hand of someone secretly scheming to overthrow the Government.

His zeal brought him swift promotion. We don't know if this made him happy. Very few letters reached him in Section B—only a hand-ful passed the other hurdles—so he read them over and over again, passed them under a mag-nifying glass, searched for microprint with an electronic microscope, and tuned his sense of smell so that he was beat by the time he made it home. He'd barely manage to warm up his soup, eat some fruit, and fall into bed, satisfied with having done his duty. Only his darling mother worried, but she couldn't get him back on the right track. She'd say, though it wasn't always true: Lola called, she's at the bar with the girls, they miss you, they're waiting for you. Or else she'd leave a bottle of red wine on the table. But Juan wouldn't overdo it: any distraction could make him lose his edge, and the perfect censor had to be alert, keen, attentive, and sharp to nab cheats. He had a truly patriotic task, both self-denying and uplifting.

His basket for censored letters became the best fed as well as the most cunning basket in the whole Censorship Division. He was about to congratulate himself for having finally discovered his true mission, when his letter to Mariana reached his hands. Naturally, he censored it without regret. And just as naturally, he couldn't stop them from executing him the following morning, another victim of his devotion to his work. ❖

Translated by David Unger

RESPONDING
OPTIONS

FROM PERSONAL RESPONSE TO CRITICAL ANALYSIS

REFLECT

1. What is your reaction to the ending of the story? Record your reaction in your notebook.

RETHINK

2. What is your opinion of Juan? Support your opinion with examples from the story.

3. *Absurd* means "ridiculously incongruous or unreasonable." What parts of the story would you describe as absurd?

4. How has the story influenced your understanding of censorship? Explain your views.

RELATE

5. Why do you think censorship is more severe in dictatorships than in democracies?

6. Do you think that censorship is necessary in certain circumstances? Use examples to explain your views.

ANOTHER PATHWAY

With a partner, evaluate Juan as a citizen. Create a list of criteria by which to judge him, and then give him a grade for each of the criteria. Share your results with your classmates.

LITERARY CONCEPTS

Irony is a contrast between what is expected and what actually exists or happens. Three types of irony follow:

Situational irony is the contrast between what a character or reader expects and what actually happens. For example, when Juan begins his job, the reader may expect that he will find a way to interfere with the censors. However, Juan becomes an enthusiastic censor himself.

Verbal irony occurs when a character or narrator says one thing and means another. For instance, the narrator tells the reader that Juan "had a truly patriotic task." The narrator really means that Juan's work was harmful.

Dramatic irony refers to the contrast between what a character knows and what the reader or audience knows. For example, Juan believes that the phrase "the weather's unsettled" really means that someone is scheming to overthrow the government. The reader knows, however, that the letter writer was only describing the weather.

With a partner, list three or four other examples of irony in this story. Determine why each example is ironic, and identify the type of irony it represents.

QUICKWRITES

1. Expand the writing you did for the Writing Connection on page 242 into a **dramatic scene** about life in a dictatorship with strict censorship.

2. Write Juan's **letter** to Mariana. Then censor it as you think Juan might have. Explain to the class how you decided to censor it.

3. Create a **list of rules** for the workers in the Post Office's Censorship Division. Include at least five do's and five don'ts.

📁 *PORTFOLIO Save your writing. You may want to use it later as a springboard to a piece for your portfolio.*

ALTERNATIVE ACTIVITIES

1. Create a **poster** that might be used to recruit new employees for the Post Office's Censorship Division.

2. Conduct **interviews** with administrators or teachers to learn if there are any official policies about censorship that apply to the school library, the school newspaper, or the classroom.

ACROSS THE CURRICULUM

History Read the Bill of Rights to find the amendments guaranteeing freedoms that limit the power of government to impose censorship. Then hold a class discussion on how these freedoms affect the everyday lives of citizens.

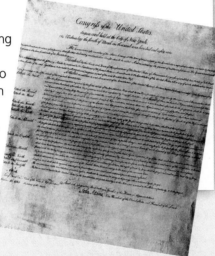

Use your understanding of the boldfaced words below to complete each of the sentences.

1. An **irreproachable** censor would (a) never work, (b) always do his job well, (c) whine about the demands of the job.

2. A **subtle** message in a letter would (a) be easy to understand, (b) reveal the ignorance of the writer, (c) not be immediately obvious.

3. **Conniving** citizens might be expected to (a) try to fool the authorities, (b) follow all the rules, (c) be reluctant to take action of any kind.

4. A government agency characterized by **staidness** would (a) have a festive air, (b) be noted for its efficiency, (c) be a sober place to work.

5. A **subversive** employee might (a) dutifully attend to details, (b) work to topple the government, (c) look for ways to advance his or her career.

LUISA VALENZUELA

1944–

When Luisa Valenzuela was very young, her older sister used to read her horror stories to make her eat. "I would open my mouth in fright and she would stuff it," Valenzuela reports. "I swallowed my fear and my fascination along with the food." Literature continued to play a role in Valenzuela's life. Her mother was a well-known writer, and their home in Buenos Aires, Argentina, was often visited by literary figures. When Valenzuela took an interest in writing, her career moved quickly: at age 17 she published her first short story.

Feeling stifled by Argentina's political situation, the adult Valenzuela lived abroad when she could, working in Paris for the French broadcasting agency, attending the International Writers' Program at the University of Iowa, and becoming a writer-in-residence at Columbia University in New York City. She published her first novel, *Something to Smile About*, in 1966 and her first story collection, *The Heretics*, a year later. Valenzuela once said that she writes to shake people up. Much of her best work communicates her ideas about power, politics, and human relationships.

OTHER WORKS *He Who Searches, The Lizard's Tail, Open Door, Strange Things Happen Here*

PREVIEWING

NONFICTION

from Tolerance
E. M. Forster England

PERSONAL CONNECTION

Complete the statement shown on the right with one word that best represents your thinking about what the world needs. You may pick one of the words in the brackets or another word of your choice. In your notebook, explain your reasons for your choice. Then share your ideas with your classmates.

> In the world today, people need to treat one another with _____ [compassion, respect, love, tolerance, kindness, generosity].

HISTORICAL CONNECTION

As the title of the following essay suggests, Great Britain's E. M. Forster ranked tolerance high among the qualities necessary for the world at large. The essay is one of several that Forster broadcast over the radio during or just after World War II (1939–1945) and later collected in his volume *Two Cheers for Democracy* (1951). In these essays, Forster often explores the means by which citizens of democracies can counter the spread of the kind of thinking that leads to brutal dictatorships—dictatorships like that of Nazi Germany, Britain's foe during the war. With their claims of racial superiority, their attempts to conquer neighboring nations that they labeled as inferior, and their mass murder of ethnic groups that they branded as undesirable, the Nazis were the supreme example of *in*tolerance.

READING CONNECTION

Clarifying Concepts As you read this excerpt from Forster's essay, try to pin down exactly what Forster means by his use of the word *tolerance*. Create a chart like the one below, and record on it brief notes about Forster's intent.

Tolerance
Words and phrases that describe or define tolerance:
Benefits of tolerance:
Why tolerance is needed:

Italian Landscape II: Europa (1944), Ben Shahn.
Copyright © 1995 Estate of Ben Shahn /
Licensed by VAGA, New York.

from
TOLERANCE
E. M. Forster

Surely the only sound foundation for a civilisation is a

sound state of mind. Architects, contractors, international

commissioners, marketing boards, broadcasting corpora-

tions will never, by themselves, build a new world.

They must be inspired by the proper spirit, and there must be the proper spirit in the people for whom they are working. . . .

What though is the proper spirit? . . . There must be a sound state of mind before diplomacy or economics or trade conferences can function. But what state of mind is sound? Here we may differ. Most people, when asked what spiritual quality is needed to rebuild civilisation, will reply "Love." Men must love one another, they say; nations must do likewise, and then the series of cataclysms[1] which is threatening to destroy us will be checked.

Respectfully but firmly, I disagree. Love is a great force in private life; it is indeed the greatest of all things: but love in public affairs does not work. It has been tried again and again: by the Christian civilisations of the Middle Ages, and also by the French Revolution, a secular movement which reasserted the brotherhood of man.[2] And it has always failed. The idea that nations should love one another, or that business concerns or marketing boards should love one another, or that a man in Portugal should love a man in Peru of whom he has never heard—it is absurd, unreal, dangerous. It leads us into perilous and vague sentimentalism.[3] "Love is what is needed," we chant and then sit back, and the world goes on as before. The fact is we can only love what we know personally. And we cannot know much. In public affairs, in the rebuilding of civilisation, something much

> NO ONE HAS EVER WRITTEN AN ODE TO TOLERANCE OR RAISED A STATUE TO HER. YET THIS IS THE QUALITY WHICH WILL BE MOST NEEDED AFTER THE WAR.

less dramatic and emotional is needed, namely, tolerance. Tolerance is a very dull virtue. It is boring. Unlike love, it has always had a bad press. It is negative. It merely means putting up with people, being able to stand things. No one has ever written an ode[4] to tolerance or raised a statue to her. Yet this is the quality which will be most needed after the war. This is the sound state of mind which we are looking for. This is the only force which will enable different races and classes and interests to settle down together to the work of reconstruction.

The world is very full of people—appallingly full; it has never been so full before, and they are all tumbling over each other. Most of these people one doesn't know, and some of them one doesn't like; doesn't like the colour of their skins, say, or the shapes of their noses, or the way they blow them or don't blow them, or the way they talk, or their smell, or their clothes, or their fondness for jazz or their dislike of jazz, and so on. Well, what is one to do? There are two solutions. One of them is the Nazi solution. If you don't like people, kill them, banish them, segregate them, and then strut up and down

---

1. **cataclysms** (kăt′ə-klĭz′əmz): violent upheavals causing great change and destruction.

2. **French Revolution . . . brotherhood of man:** the French Revolution, which lasted from 1789 to 1799, had the motto "Liberty! Equality! Brotherhood!"

3. **sentimentalism** (sĕn′tə-mĕn′tl-ĭz′əm): a tendency toward too much tender, often shallow emotion.

4. **ode** (ōd): a usually formal poem on a serious subject.

WORDS TO KNOW

diplomacy (dĭ-plō′mə-sē) *n.* the art or practice of conducting international relations and discussing and resolving differences among nations
secular (sĕk′yə-lər) *adj.* worldly rather than spiritual; not specifically related to religion
perilous (pĕr′ə-ləs) *adj.* dangerous
appallingly (ə-pô′lĭng-lē) *adv.* in an upsetting manner; shockingly; dreadfully

proclaiming that you are the salt of the earth.[5] The other way is much less thrilling, but it is on the whole the way of the democracies, and I prefer it. If you don't like people, put up with them as well as you can. Don't try to love them: you can't; you'll only strain yourself. But try to tolerate them. On the basis of that tolerance a civilised future may be built. Certainly I can see no other foundation for the postwar world.

For what it will most need is the negative virtues: not being huffy, touchy, irritable, revengeful. I have lost all faith in positive militant ideals; they can so seldom be carried out without thousands of human beings getting maimed or imprisoned. Phrases like "I will purge this nation," "I will clean up this city," terrify and disgust me. They might not have mattered when the world was emptier: they are horrifying now, when one nation is mixed up with another, when one city cannot be organically separated from its neighbours. . . .

I don't then regard tolerance as a great eternally established divine principle, though I might perhaps quote "In my Father's house are many mansions"[6] in support of such a view. It is just a makeshift, suitable for an overcrowded and overheated planet. It carries on when love gives out, and love generally gives out as soon as we move away from our home and our friends and stand among strangers in a queue[7] for potatoes. Tolerance is wanted in the queue; otherwise we think, "Why will people be so slow?"; it is wanted in the tube,[8] or "Why will people be so fat?"; it is wanted at the telephone, or "Why are they so deaf?" or conversely, "Why do they mumble?" It is wanted in the street, in the office, at the factory, and it is wanted above all between classes, races, and nations. It's dull. And yet it entails imagination. For you have all the time to be putting yourself in someone else's place. Which is a desirable spiritual exercise. ❖

---

5. **salt of the earth:** the finest or noblest people. The expression derives from a statement in the New Testament of the Bible (Matthew 5:13).

6. **"In my Father's house are many mansions":** a quotation from the New Testament (John 14:2).

7. **queue** (kyo͞o): a chiefly British expression for a line of people.

8. **tube:** British term for the Underground, or London subway.

RESPONDING OPTIONS

FROM PERSONAL RESPONSE TO CRITICAL ANALYSIS

REFLECT

1. Did you find Forster's arguments convincing? Describe your reaction in your notebook.

RETHINK

2. Do you agree with Forster's view that tolerance is a negative virtue?

   Consider
   - how Forster defines "negative virtue"
   - the chart that you completed for the Reading Connection on page 248
   - his contrast between "negative virtues" and "positive militant ideals"

3. Do you agree with Forster that tolerance is more useful than love as a foundation of civilization?

   Consider
   - why he thinks "love in public affairs does not work"
   - his belief that "we can only love what we know personally"
   - your own views about love and tolerance

4. Why do you think Forster describes tolerance as a "makeshift, suitable for an overcrowded and overheated planet"?

RELATE

5. Do you think that the world is becoming a more tolerant place in which to live? Use examples from current affairs to support your opinion.

ANOTHER PATHWAY

Cooperative Learning

In a small group, review a newspaper or newsmagazine to find an article about a conflict between two groups of people in your community or in the world. Analyze the conflict in light of Forster's essay, then list specific steps that might be taken to promote tolerance between the two groups.

QUICKWRITES

1. Expand your ideas from the Personal Connection on page 248 into an **essay** about a quality that you believe is needed in the world today. Directly state your theme, and support it with details and logical arguments.

2. Write a **critical analysis** in which you explain the meaning of the biblical quotation "In my Father's house are many mansions" and its relevance to Forster's theme.

3. Write a **fable** or **parable** that illustrates Forster's theme about tolerance.

   PORTFOLIO Save your writing. You may want to use it later as a spring-board to a piece for your portfolio.

LITERARY CONCEPTS

Theme is the central idea or message in a work of literature. Theme should not be confused with subject, or what the work is about. Rather, theme is a perception about life or human nature. Sometimes the theme is directly stated within the work; at other times it is implied, and the reader must infer the theme. In one sentence, state what you feel is the theme of the excerpt from "Tolerance." Then compare your statement of the theme with the statements of your classmates. Discuss whether the theme is stated directly or implied.

CONCEPT REVIEW: Tone In your opinion, is the tone of the excerpt formal or informal?

ALTERNATIVE ACTIVITIES

1. Rehearse and deliver Forster's essay as a **speech** to be broadcast on the radio.

2. Design a **poster** for an ad campaign promoting tolerance. If you have access to a computer with graphic applications, you may wish to design the poster electronically.

ACROSS THE CURRICULUM

Media Find out more about the role of radio during World War II, especially how it affected public information and morale. Report your findings in a multimedia presentation that includes original recordings or your own simulations of actual broadcasts.

WRITER'S STYLE

With a partner, review Forster's essay and list all the sentences that have six or fewer words. What effects do you think Forster is trying to achieve by using such brief sentences?

ART CONNECTION

Why do you think the painting on page 249, *Italian Landscape II: Europa,* was chosen to illustrate Forster's essay?

Detail of *Italian Landscape II: Europa* (1944), Ben Shahn. Copyright © 1995 Estate of Ben Shahn/Licensed by VAGA, New York.

WORDS TO KNOW

Match each numbered word with its synonym.

1. makeshift	a. risky
2. maim	b. cleanse
3. proclaiming	c. negotiation
4. secular	d. worldly
5. perilous	e. stand-in
6. conversely	f. disable
7. entail	g. require
8. purge	h. oppositely
9. diplomacy	i. disturbingly
10. appallingly	j. broadcasting

E. M. FORSTER

Edward Morgan Forster, who was born in Coventry, England, spent the early part of his life hating the private boys' school that he attended, where he was subject to the taunts of classmates and the severity of teachers. He felt liberated by his subsequent years of study at Cambridge University, which enabled him to expand his intellectual horizons, make close friends, and dedicate himself to the literary life. Forster began publishing stories soon after graduation and published his first novel in 1905. There followed a number of acclaimed novels; the best known of these—*A Room with a View* (1908), *Howards End* (1910),

1879–1970

and *A Passage to India* (1924)—have recently enjoyed a resurgence of popularity sparked by successful film adaptations.

During the 1920s, Forster achieved prominence as a literary critic, but in the next two decades he turned increasingly to social criticism and virtually gave up writing fiction. Horrified by events in Germany and elsewhere, Forster reacted with lectures and radio broadcasts that stressed the value of goodwill and reason in combating totalitarian thinking.

OTHER WORKS *Abinger Harvest, The Collected Tales of E. M. Forster, Two Cheers for Democracy*

Fighting South of the Ramparts

Li Bo   China

In the past, China was ruled by dynasties, successions of rulers from the same family or line. Under the Han dynasty (206 B.C. to A.D. 220)—one of the most famous in Chinese history—the country more than doubled in size through warfare against such peoples as the Huns in the north, the Vietnamese in the south, and the central Asians and the Tartars in the west.

Li Bo wrote the following poem around the year 751, basing it on an earlier folk song about the border wars during the Han dynasty. To fight those wars, the Han government raised taxes and forced the Chinese peasants to leave their lands and join the army, causing popular unrest. In describing these events from China's past, Li Bo was actually criticizing similar policies of the Tang dynasty, the dynasty in power during his lifetime. In the early 700s, the Tang dynasty extended China's borders even farther than the Han dynasty had done. Once again, however, the warfare was proving expensive, and peasants were being forced from their lands to fight in remote border areas.

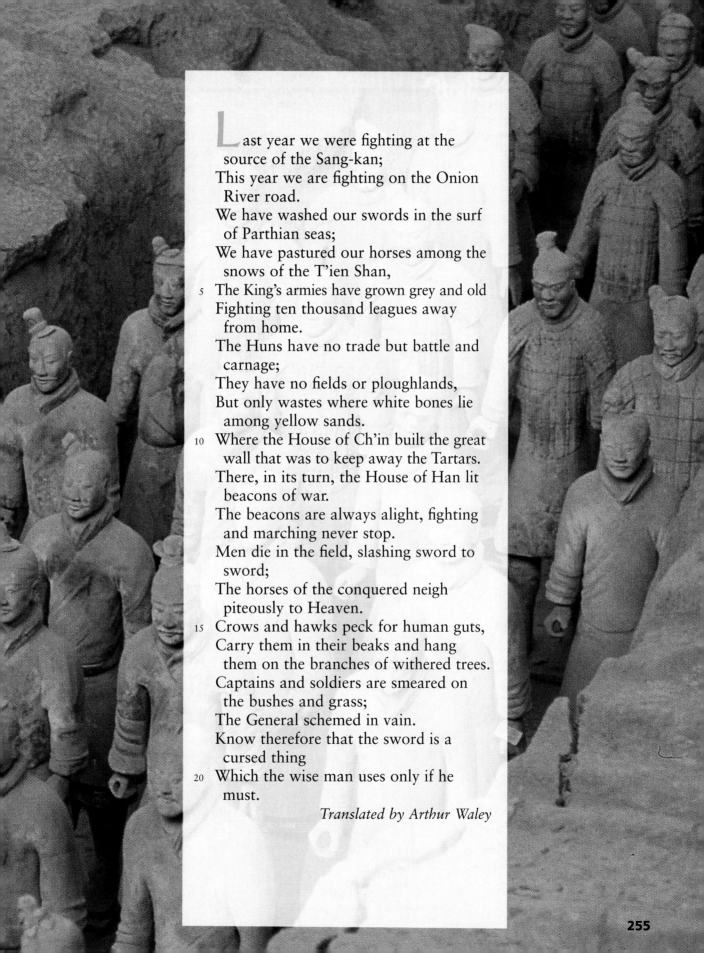

Last year we were fighting at the
source of the Sang-kan;
This year we are fighting on the Onion
River road.
We have washed our swords in the surf
of Parthian seas;
We have pastured our horses among the
snows of the T'ien Shan,
5 The King's armies have grown grey and old
Fighting ten thousand leagues away
from home.
The Huns have no trade but battle and
carnage;
They have no fields or ploughlands,
But only wastes where white bones lie
among yellow sands.
10 Where the House of Ch'in built the great
wall that was to keep away the Tartars.
There, in its turn, the House of Han lit
beacons of war.
The beacons are always alight, fighting
and marching never stop.
Men die in the field, slashing sword to
sword;
The horses of the conquered neigh
piteously to Heaven.
15 Crows and hawks peck for human guts,
Carry them in their beaks and hang
them on the branches of withered trees.
Captains and soldiers are smeared on
the bushes and grass;
The General schemed in vain.
Know therefore that the sword is a
cursed thing
20 Which the wise man uses only if he
must.

Translated by Arthur Waley

255

SETTING THE SCENE

Could you picture the stadium in "The Thrill of the Grass"? Did the description in "House Taken Over" seem to put you in the scene? Understanding setting, in stories and in real life, helps you see how much your own surroundings affect you and others. On the next pages you will

- explore the ways writers organize the details of a setting
- write about the relation of setting to events in a story
- examine how real-world settings affect you

The Writer's Style: Paragraph Coherence When writing a description, writers arrange details in an order that helps readers imagine the subject and understand its impression.

Read the Literature

Note how writers organize the details in the following excerpts.

Literature Models

Order of Impression
Notice how the writer presents details in the order the narrator perceives them.

Strangle-grass and creeping charlie are already inching up through the gravel, surreptitious, surprised at their own ease. Faded bottle caps, rusted bits of chrome, an occasional paper clip, recede into the earth. I circle a ticket booth, sun-faded, empty, the door closed by an oversized padlock. I walk beside the tall, machinery-green, board fence. A half mile away a few cars hiss along the freeway; overhead a single-engine plane fizzes lazily.

W. P. Kinsella, from "The Thrill of the Grass"

Spatial Order
How does presenting the details in order of their physical position help you to picture the setting? Which words help to show relationships among the details?

One entered the house through a vestibule with enameled tiles, and a wrought-iron grated door opened onto the living room. You had to come in through the vestibule and open the gate to go into the living room; the doors to our bedrooms were on either side of this, and opposite it was the corridor leading to the back section; going down the passage, one swung open the oak door beyond which was the other part of the house.

Julio Cortázar, from "House Taken Over"

Connect to Life

Travel books and articles often organize details of a setting by describing the manner in which items are positioned or seen. Sometimes, though, a writer uses both spatial order and order of impression to create a picture in the reader's mind. Using both techniques helps the reader imagine the setting.

Travel Article

Just north of the little town of Wickenburg, Arizona, I turned off U.S. Highway 89 and headed slowly down a narrow country road. At once everything seemed to signal a return to the storybook West. Whiteface cattle ambled across my path, rolling their eyes. Beyond a barbed wire fence a massive Brahman bull grazed. In the next field a handsome, high-strung yearling colt reared, wheeled, and galloped away. A snake at least four feet long wriggled across the road just ahead of my car. I rattled over the cattle guard at the portal to the Kay El Bar Guest Ranch and thought to myself: The rough, tough frontier is alive and well.

Merrill Windsor, from "Welcome to Wickenburg," *National Geographic Traveler*, Winter 1984/85

Combined Order
Which details are presented in spatial order? How does the writer also use order of impression for details?

Try Your Hand: Ordering the Details

1. **Use Spatial Order** Choose one of the following topics, and write a descriptive paragraph using spatial order.

   - your hangout
   - the scene from a rooftop
   - the scene surrounding you at a sporting event

2. **Describe a Place** In a paragraph, describe a place that's special to you. Organize details to emphasize spatial order.

3. **Double Description** Describe your classroom during the last period of the day in two ways—first using order of impression and then spatial order.

SkillBuilder

WRITER'S CRAFT

Using Transition Words and Phrases
To relate details and show connections between ideas, writers use transition words and phrases. The list below shows some words that can be used to present ideas in the order of physical position, or spatial order.

Words and Phrases Used to Show Spatial Relationships

behind	in front of
around	over
here	through
inside	on the right of
beneath	down
there	above

APPLYING WHAT YOU'VE LEARNED
Locate words or phrases showing spatial relationships in the following paragraph:

The men walked through the parking lot in anticipation. Inside the ballpark, they gazed at the spectacle—empty seats above them and cold plastic grass beneath them. After placing squares of sod on top of the packed earth, they looked down from the seats behind home plate and smiled.

 WRITING HANDBOOK

For more information on transition words, see page 1027 of the Writing Handbook. For more information on organizing details, see page 1032 of the Writing Handbook.

Analysis

When writers describe a setting, they are doing more than simply presenting a place. They may use setting to create a mood or as a driving force in a story. You can analyze how a writer uses setting to create a particular impression. Closely analyzing information about setting helps you make connections—in stories and in everyday life.

GUIDED ASSIGNMENT

Analyze a Setting The following pages will help you think about the setting from a selection and analyze how it plays an important role in your impression of the story.

① Prewrite and Explore

Begin thinking about two or three selections in which setting seems to play a key role. Why is the setting significant? Perhaps it creates a mood, affects a character's actions and feelings, provides details, or makes the story convincing.

Student's Prewriting Chart

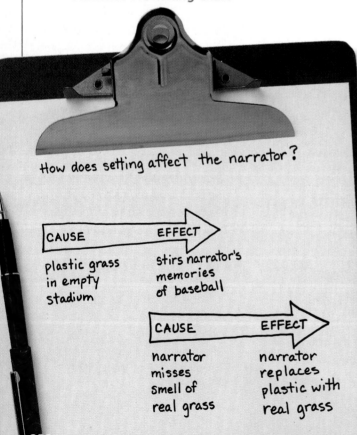

How does setting affect the narrator?

CAUSE → EFFECT
plastic grass in empty stadium → stirs narrator's memories of baseball

CAUSE → EFFECT
narrator misses smell of real grass → narrator replaces plastic with real grass

EXAMINING SETTINGS

The following questions might help you explore why a particular setting seems important to a story.

- Where and when does the story take place?
- How does the setting affect events?
- How does it affect how characters act or feel?
- How would a change in setting affect the story?
- What mood is created by descriptions of the setting?

Decision Point Based on your responses, which setting would you most like to explore?

LOOK FOR CONNECTIONS

Creating a cause-and-effect chart can help you visualize the connections between the setting, mood, events, and characters. Remember that a chart does not need to be all facts. Feel free to include your feelings and reactions.

❷ Write and Analyze a Discovery Draft

With so many possibilities, how can you choose a focus for your writing about setting? Begin freewriting using the topics from your cause-and-effect chart.

Student's Discovery Draft

When I think about the setting in "The Thrill of the Grass," I picture the empty stadium. It's so lonely and artificial—it doesn't even have real grass. That's it! Without the setting, there would be no story. The narrator is deeply affected by its emptiness and lack of green grass. It stirs his emotions.

I think I'll include how he feels before and after he changes the setting.

The setting is the cause for the narrator's action—main point.

The narrator physically changes the setting by removing squares of the plastic grass and adding sod. I see that as the setting changes, his feelings about the stadium and baseball change too. The grass smells like baseball and he feels at home.

Following are some questions that you can ask yourself when you finish your writing.

- What main point about the setting seems to surface?
- Do I want to focus on a specific aspect of the setting or the overall role of the setting in the story?
- What examples from the selection can I use for support?

❸ Draft and Share

Now it's time to write a focused draft. Analysis, on page 1040 of the Writing Handbook, will help you to write an analysis about setting. If you will be discussing how the setting creates a mood, consult the SkillBuilder on creating mood. Trade your paper with a writing partner and ask for a response.

 PEER RESPONSE

- What is my main point about the setting?
- Is there anything in my paper that confuses you or seems beside the point?

4 Revise and Edit

Review your thoughts and the responses of your peers. How have you made your ideas clear? Do you include enough support? Did you use good quotes or comment on the writer's word choice if these support your main point? After you make your final copy, reflect on how your thoughts have changed.

Student's Final Draft

What will this essay be about? What is the student's main point?

The Thrill of the Grass

Sometimes the scent of a certain place or setting can stir a memory or feeling from long ago. In "The Thrill of the Grass" by W. P. Kinsella, scents of a baseball stadium—particularly fresh grass—remind the narrator of days in the outfield as a child and the pure pleasure of a baseball game. However, the lonely stadium in his town, whose outfield is plastic grass, lacks the scent of baseball. The setting itself, a silent stadium, causes the narrator to take action during the summer of a baseball strike.

How do the details and quotations show that setting affects the narrator's actions?

As the narrator and his accomplices change the setting—the outfield—his feelings change too. He used to feel mournful; now he feels full of wonder. The scent of the grass stirs something within him. Alone in the newly sodded setting, he bows in the center of the outfield to pay respect. He says, "I lower my face to the silvered grass, which, wonder of wonders, already has the ephemeral odours of baseball about it."

Standards for Evaluation

The setting analysis
- identifies the selection by author and title and briefly describes it
- clearly describes the point the writer wants to make
- presents an organized analysis of the setting or a specific aspect of it
- offers support for the writer's points by using details and quotations

Grammar in Context

Prepositional Phrases When creating descriptions, writers often use spatial order to organize the details. Prepositional phrases show spatial order, or the physical position of objects or people in a description. As a review, examine the following excerpt from the student's draft and note the prepositional phrases that show spatial relationships.

The narrator parks his car. *at the far end of the lot* As he walks slowly, *across the lot toward the stadium* he dreams about his childhood baseball days. When he arrives, *at the deserted stadium* he stands and contemplates breaking in. *within inches of the door* As he thinks about what lies on the other side, *of the door* he skillfully picks the padlock. *under the latch* He enters and feels rejuvenated.

Prepositional phrases can add richness to a piece of writing. In the example above, the inserted prepositional phrases show how elements in the story are physically related. For more information about prepositional phrases, see page 1064 of the Grammar Handbook.

Try Your Hand: Using Prepositional Phrases

Revise the following paragraph to include prepositional phrases that describe spatial relationships.

> After walking through the door, the narrator saw the ballpark. It felt cold and desolate. The plastic grass shimmered. Seams stood out. Rows of bleachers loomed. The dugouts looked lonely. Even the pressbox wasn't impressive.

GRAMMAR FROM WRITING

Achieving Subject-Verb Agreement with Prepositional Phrases

Making sure your subjects and verbs agree when you use prepositional phrases can be challenging. Try not to mistake a word in a prepositional phrase for the subject of a sentence.

*The **narrator**, with his accomplices, **decides** to plant sod in the outfield.*

(The subject, *narrator*, is singular; *with his accomplices* is a prepositional phrase; therefore, the verb, *decides*, is singular.)

***Scents** of a baseball stadium **remind** the narrator of days in the outfield.*

(The subject, *scents*, is plural; *of a baseball stadium* is a prepositional phrase; the verb, *remind*, is plural.)

APPLYING WHAT YOU'VE LEARNED
Choose the verb that agrees with its subject.

1. The stadium in the shadows (stand/stands) mournfully.
2. The men with their boxes of sod (arrive/arrives) after midnight.

 GRAMMAR HANDBOOK

Consult page 1064 in the Grammar Handbook to review subject-verb agreement with prepositional phrases.

THE IMPACT OF SETTING

Just as setting in literature affects characters and events, so setting in your life affects your reaction to events. How do you respond to the settings in your world?

View Examine the situation shown in this photo. Describe what you see. What is your reaction to the bride and groom in this setting?

Interpret Think about why the setting is important. How might the setting affect your assumptions about the couple?

Discuss In a group, discuss why this image is newsworthy. What is important about this photo? With your group, share ideas on how setting affects your understanding of events. Now use the SkillBuilder on the next page to help you analyze the components of setting.

 → **CRITICAL THINKING**

Analyzing Components of Setting

Have you ever seen a movie or play in which the setting played a starring role? What made it memorable? Setting can create a mood, affect a person's feelings or actions, or even portray symbols.

When you analyze, you take apart, examine, and explain an idea or a subject. Think about how you might use these skills to analyze the importance of settings in your life. How is the backdrop of an urban school meant to affect people's perceptions of a politician's speech on the importance of education for all young people? How might your response change if the same speech were given in front of a video arcade or outside a mansion? Can you think of other examples?

APPLYING WHAT YOU'VE LEARNED
In a small group, discuss the memorable settings of books, television shows, plays, or movies. Talk about real-life settings too. In your discussion, analyze how setting plays an important role. Consider differences in group members' analyses of the settings.

PRISONERS OF CIRCUMSTANCE

Lucille Clifton
(1936–)
Another major voice in African-American poetry

Tim O'Brien
(1946–)
His fiction about the Vietnam War has won him fame.

Jeanne Wakatsuki Houston (1934–) and **James D. Houston** (1933–)
This husband and wife wrote about her experience in a Japanese-American detention camp.

Brent Staples
(1951–)
A leading African-American journalist and author

Gwendolyn Brooks
(1917–)
The first African-American poet to win a Pulitzer Prize

Julio Cortázar
(1914–1984)
A leading Argentinean writer, noted for experimentation

REFLECTING ON THEME

Do you ever feel trapped by society? Do you ever worry that your dreams may be blocked by forces beyond your control? As you will see in this part of Unit Two, individuals can be trapped or imprisoned by many circumstances. War, poverty, prejudice, injustice, pressures to conform—such forces can cast a net around an individual. People respond to such restrictions in different ways. Some manage to fight their way free.

What Do You Think? With several classmates, create a two-column chart. In the left column, list individuals or groups of people who seem to be prisoners of circumstance. In the right column, list the factors—such as poverty, ignorance, and so on—that restrict each individual or group. Present your chart to the rest of the class.

Tim O'Brien	**On the Rainy River** *Will he fight in Vietnam or flee to Canada?*	266
Yukio Mishima	**The Pearl** *A social gathering gets out of hand.*	284
Brent Staples	**Black Men and Public Space** *Put yourself in his place.*	297
Lucille Clifton	**Miss Rosie** *How did she get like this?*	303
Gwendolyn Brooks	**Kitchenette Building** *Can dreams survive?*	303

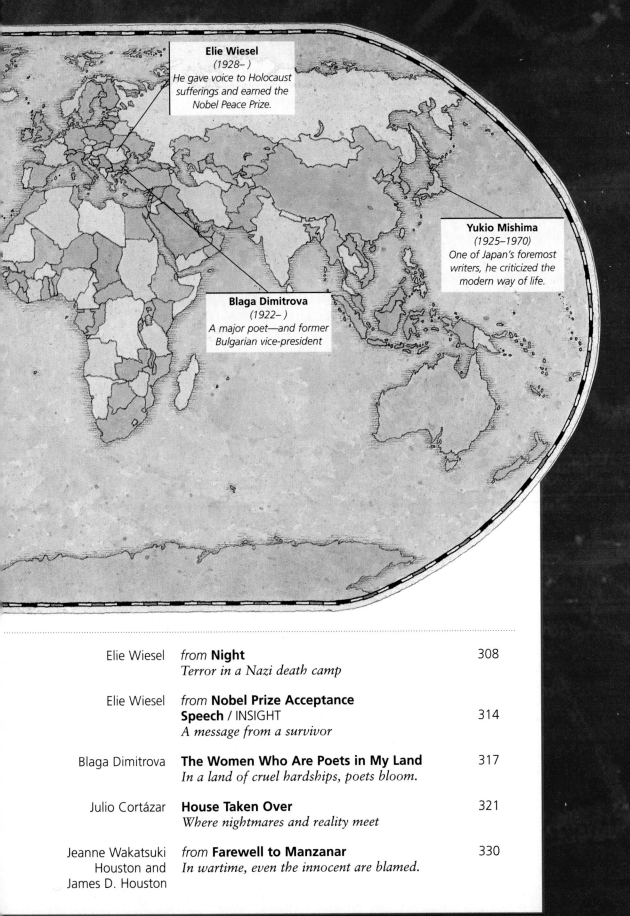

Elie Wiesel
(1928–)
He gave voice to Holocaust sufferings and earned the Nobel Peace Prize.

Yukio Mishima
(1925–1970)
One of Japan's foremost writers, he criticized the modern way of life.

Blaga Dimitrova
(1922–)
A major poet—and former Bulgarian vice-president

PREVIEWING

On the Rainy River
Tim O'Brien United States

PERSONAL CONNECTION

In this story, a young man must decide whether to fight in a war he opposes. Under what conditions would you be willing to fight in a war? Under what conditions would you be unwilling to fight? Respond in your notebook by listing your ideas in a chart like the one to the right.

I would fight if . . .	I would not fight if . . .

HISTORICAL CONNECTION

The Vietnam War (1957–1975), a war between South and North Vietnam, was the longest and one of the most controversial military conflicts in which the United States has been involved. The United States entered the war in 1964 in hopes of preventing the spread of communism throughout Southeast Asia. During the course of the war, nearly 3 million Americans were sent overseas to defend the South Vietnamese government against a takeover by Communist North Vietnam and the Viet Cong, a South Vietnamese Communist rebel force. The last American troops were pulled out of Vietnam in 1973, and two years later the South Vietnamese government surrendered to North Vietnam.

During the war, nearly 2 million men were drafted into the military, first by a system that allowed college students and others to defer their service and later by a lottery that allowed fewer exemptions. Those who were drafted but who opposed the war faced a difficult decision: whether to risk their lives in a foreign war they couldn't justify or risk imprisonment at home by refusing to serve. Some burned their draft cards as a form of protest; others fled the country, most often by crossing the border into Canada.

READING CONNECTION

Drawing Conclusions As you read "On the Rainy River," pay particular attention to the narrator's judgments. Decide whether you agree with his views about war and with his ultimate decision.

Vietnam War protest march in the late 1960s.
Copyright © Peter de Krassel / Photo Researchers, Inc.

LASERLINKS
- *GEOGRAPHICAL CONNECTION*
- *HISTORICAL CONNECTION*

Portrait of Donald Schrader (1962), Fairfield Porter. The Metropolitan Museum of Art, bequest of Arthur M. Bullowa, 1993 (1993.406.12). Copyright © 1995 The Metropolitan Museum of Art.

On the *Rainy River*

Tim O'Brien

This is one story I've never told before. Not to anyone. Not to my parents, not to my brother or sister, not even to my wife. To go into it, I've always thought, would only cause embarrassment for all of us, a sudden need to be elsewhere, which is the natural response to a confession. Even now, I'll admit, the story makes me squirm. For more than twenty years I've had to live with it, feeling the shame, trying to push it away, and so by this act of remembrance, by putting the facts down on paper, I'm hoping to relieve at least some of the pressure on my dreams.

Still, it's a hard story to tell. All of us, I suppose, like to believe that in a moral emergency we will behave like the heroes of our youth, bravely and forthrightly, without thought of personal loss or discredit. Certainly that was my conviction back in the summer of 1968. Tim O'Brien: a secret hero. The Lone Ranger. If the stakes ever became high enough—if the evil were evil enough, if the good were good enough—I would simply tap a secret reservoir of courage that had been accumulating inside me over the years. Courage, I seemed to think, comes to us in finite quantities, like an inheritance, and by being frugal and stashing it away, and letting it earn interest, we steadily increase our moral capital in preparation for that day when the account must be drawn down. It was a comforting theory. It dispensed with all those bothersome little acts of daily courage; it offered hope and grace to the repetitive coward; it justified the past while amortizing the future.

In June of 1968, a month after graduating from Macalester College, I was drafted to fight a war I hated. I was twenty-one years old. Young, yes, and politically naive, but even so the American war in Vietnam seemed to me wrong. Certain blood was being shed for uncertain reasons. I saw no unity of purpose, no consensus on matters of philosophy or history or law. The very facts were shrouded in uncertainty: Was it a civil war? A war of national liberation or simple aggression? Who started it, and when, and why? What really happened to the U.S.S. *Maddox* on that dark night in the Gulf of Tonkin?[1] Was Ho Chi Minh[2] a Communist stooge, or a nationalist savior, or both, or neither? What about the Geneva Accords?[3] What about SEATO[4] and the Cold War?[5] What about dominoes?[6] America was divided on these and a thousand other issues, and the debate had spilled out across the floor of the United States Senate and into the streets,

> I was too *good* for this war. Too smart, too compassionate, too everything.

and smart men in pinstripes could not agree on even the most fundamental matters of public policy. The only certainty that summer was moral confusion. It was my view then, and still is, that you don't make war without knowing why. Knowledge, of course, is always imperfect, but it seemed to me that when a nation goes to war it must have reasonable confidence in the justice and imperative of its cause. You can't fix your mistakes. Once people are dead, you can't make them undead.

In any case those were my convictions, and back in college I had taken a modest stand against the war. Nothing radical, no hothead

---

1. **U.S.S. *Maddox* . . . Gulf of Tonkin:** an alleged attack on the U.S. destroyer *Maddox* in the Gulf of Tonkin, off the coast of North Vietnam, in 1964, which provided a basis for expanding U.S. involvement in the Vietnam conflict.

2. **Ho Chi Minh** (hō′ chē′ mǐn′): a political leader who waged a successful fight against French colonial rule and established a Communist government in North Vietnam.

3. **Geneva Accords:** a 1954 peace agreement providing for the temporary division of Vietnam into North and South Vietnam and calling for national elections.

4. **SEATO:** the Southeast Asia Treaty Organization, an alliance of seven nations, including the United States, formed to halt Communist expansion in Southeast Asia after Communist forces defeated France in Indochina.

5. **Cold War:** a term for the post–World War II struggle for influence between Communist and democratic nations.

6. **dominoes:** refers to the domino theory, which holds that if a nation becomes a Communist state, neighboring nations will also become Communist.

WORDS TO KNOW

consensus (kən-sĕn′səs) *n.* general agreement by a group
imperative (ĭm-pĕr′ə-tĭv) *n.* urgent necessity or duty

stuff, just ringing a few doorbells for Gene McCarthy,[7] composing a few tedious, uninspired editorials for the campus newspaper. Oddly, though, it was almost entirely an intellectual activity. I brought some energy to it, of course, but it was the energy that accompanies almost any abstract endeavor; I felt no personal danger; I felt no sense of an impending crisis in my life. Stupidly, with a kind of smug removal that I can't begin to fathom, I assumed that the problems of killing and dying did not fall within my special province.

The draft notice arrived on June 17, 1968. It was a humid afternoon, I remember, cloudy and very quiet, and I'd just come in from a round of golf. My mother and father were having lunch out in the kitchen. I remember opening up the letter, scanning the first few lines, feeling the blood go thick behind my eyes. I remember a sound in my head. It wasn't thinking, it was just a silent howl. A million things all at once—I was too *good* for this war. Too smart, too compassionate, too everything. It couldn't happen. I was above it. I had the world—Phi Beta Kappa and summa cum laude and president of the student body and a full-ride scholarship for grad studies at Harvard. A mistake, maybe—a foul-up in the paperwork. I was no soldier. I hated Boy Scouts. I hated camping out. I hated dirt and tents and mosquitoes. The sight of blood made me queasy, and I couldn't tolerate authority, and I didn't know a rifle from a slingshot. I was a *liberal:* If they needed fresh bodies, why not draft some back-to-the-stone-age hawk? Or some dumb jingo[8] in his hardhat and Bomb Hanoi button? Or one of LBJ's[9] pretty daughters? Or Westmoreland's[10] whole family—nephews and nieces and baby grandson? There should be a law, I thought. If you support a war, if you think it's worth the price, that's fine, but you have to put your own

life on the line. You have to head for the front and hook up with an infantry unit and help spill the blood. And you have to bring along your wife, or your kids, or your lover. A *law,* I thought.

I remember the rage in my stomach. Later it burned down to a smoldering self-pity, then to numbness. At dinner that night my father asked what my plans were.

"Nothing," I said. "Wait."

spent the summer of 1968 working in an Armour meat-packing plant in my hometown of Worthington, Minnesota. The plant specialized in pork products, and for eight hours a day I stood on a quarter-mile assembly line—more properly, a disassembly line—removing blood clots from the necks of dead pigs. My job title, I believe, was Declotter. After slaughter, the hogs were decapitated, split down the length of the belly, pried open, eviscerated, and strung up by the hind hocks on a high conveyer belt. Then gravity took over. By the time a carcass reached my spot on the line, the fluids had mostly drained out, everything except for thick clots of blood in the neck and upper chest cavity. To remove the stuff, I used a kind of water gun. The machine was heavy, maybe eighty pounds, and was suspended from the ceiling by a heavy rubber cord. There was some bounce to it, an

---

7. **Gene McCarthy:** Eugene McCarthy, U.S. senator from Minnesota and Vietnam War critic who unsuccessfully sought the 1968 Democratic presidential nomination.

8. **jingo** (jĭng′gō): one who aggressively supports his or her country and favors war as a means of settling political disputes.

9. **LBJ:** Lyndon B. Johnson, U.S. president from 1963 to 1969.

10. **Westmoreland's:** referring to William Westmoreland, American general and the senior commander of U.S. forces in Vietnam from 1964 to 1968.

269

elastic up-and-down give, and the trick was to maneuver the gun with your whole body, not lifting with the arms, just letting the rubber cord do the work for you. At one end was a trigger; at the muzzle end was a small nozzle and a steel roller brush. As a carcass passed by, you'd lean forward and swing the gun up against the clots and squeeze the trigger, all in one motion, and the brush would whirl and water would come shooting out and you'd hear a quick splattering sound as the clots dissolved into a fine red mist. It was not pleasant work. Goggles were a necessity, and a rubber apron, but even so it was like standing for eight hours a day under a lukewarm blood-shower. At night I'd go home smelling of pig. I couldn't wash it out. Even after a hot bath, scrubbing hard, the stink was always there—like old bacon, or sausage, a dense greasy pig-stink that soaked deep into my skin and hair. Among other things, I remember, it was tough getting dates that summer. I felt isolated; I spent a lot of time alone. And there was also that draft notice tucked away in my wallet.

In the evenings I'd sometimes borrow my father's car and drive aimlessly around town, feeling sorry for myself, thinking about the war and the pig factory and how my life seemed to be collapsing toward slaughter. I felt paralyzed. All around me the options seemed to be narrowing, as if I were hurtling down a huge black funnel, the whole world squeezing in tight. There was no happy way out. The government had ended most graduate school deferments; the waiting lists for the National Guard and Reserves[11] were impossibly long; my health was solid; I didn't qualify for CO[12] status—no religious grounds, no history as a pacifist.[13] Moreover, I could not claim to be opposed to war as a matter of general principle. There were occasions, I believed, when a nation was justified in using military force to achieve its ends, to stop a Hitler or some comparable evil, and I told myself that in such circumstances I would've willingly marched off to the battle. The problem, though, was that a draft board did not let you choose your war.

Beyond all this, or at the very center, was the raw fact of terror. I did not want to die. Not ever. But certainly not then, not there, not in a wrong war. Driving up Main Street, past the courthouse and the Ben Franklin store, I sometimes felt the fear spreading inside me like weeds. I imagined myself dead. I imagined myself doing things I could not do—charging an enemy position, taking aim at another human being.

At some point in mid-July I began thinking seriously about Canada. The border lay a few hundred miles north, an eight-hour drive. Both my conscience and my instincts were telling me to make a break for it, just take off and run like hell and never stop. In the beginning the idea seemed purely abstract, the word Canada printing itself out in my head; but after a time I could see particular shapes and images, the sorry details of my own future—a hotel room in Winnipeg, a battered old suitcase, my father's eyes as I tried to explain myself over the telephone. I could almost hear his voice, and my mother's. Run, I'd think. Then I'd think, Impossible. Then a second later I'd think, *Run.*

---

11. **National Guard and Reserves:** military reserve units run by each state in the United States. Some men joined these units to avoid service in Vietnam.

12. **CO:** conscientious objector, a person exempted from military service because of strongly held moral or religious beliefs that do not permit participation in war.

13. **pacifist** (păs′ə-fĭst): one who opposes war or other violence as a means of settling disputes.

It was a kind of schizophrenia.[14] A moral split. I couldn't make up my mind. I feared the war, yes, but I also feared exile. I was afraid of walking away from my own life, my friends and my family, my whole history, everything that mattered to me. I feared losing the respect of my parents. I feared the law. I feared ridicule and censure.[15] My hometown was a conservative little spot on the prairie, a place where tradition counted, and it was easy to imagine people sitting around a table at the old Gobbler Café on Main Street, coffee cups poised, the conversation slowly zeroing in on the young O'Brien kid, how the damned sissy had taken off for Canada. At night, when I couldn't sleep, I'd sometimes carry on fierce arguments with those people. I'd be screaming at them, telling them how much I detested their blind, thoughtless, automatic acquiescence to it all, their simple-minded patriotism, their prideful ignorance, their love-it-or-leave-it platitudes, how they were sending me off to fight a war they didn't understand and didn't want to understand. I held them responsible. By God, yes I *did*. All of them—I held them personally and individually responsible—the polyestered Kiwanis boys, the merchants and farmers, the pious churchgoers, the chatty housewives, the PTA and the Lions club and the Veterans of Foreign Wars and the fine upstanding gentry out at the country club. They didn't know Bao Dai[16] from the man in the moon. They didn't know history. They didn't know the first thing about Diem's[17] tyranny, or the nature of Vietnamese nationalism, or the long colonialism of the French—this was all too damned complicated, it required some reading—but no matter, it was a war to stop the Communists, plain and simple, which was how they liked things, and you were treasonous if you had second thoughts about killing or dying for plain and simple reasons.

I was bitter, sure. But it was so much more than that. The emotions went from outrage to terror to bewilderment to guilt to sorrow and then back again to outrage. I felt a sickness inside me. Real disease.

Most of this I've told before, or at least hinted at, but what I have never told is the full truth. How I cracked. How at work one morning, standing on the pig line, I felt something break open in my chest. I don't know what it was. I'll never know. But it was real. I know that much, it was a physical rupture—a cracking-leaking-popping feeling. I remember dropping my water gun. Quickly, almost without thought, I took off my apron and walked out of the plant and drove home. It was midmorning, I remember, and the house was empty. Down in my chest there was still that leaking sensation, something very warm and precious spilling out, and I was covered with blood and hog-stink, and for a long while I just concentrated on holding myself together. I remember taking a hot shower. I remember packing a suitcase and carrying it out to the kitchen, standing very still for a few minutes, looking carefully at the familiar objects all around me. The old chrome toaster, the telephone, the pink and white Formica on the kitchen counters. The room was full of bright sunshine.

SUPPORT OUR BOYS IN VIETNAM

---

14. **schizophrenia** (skĭt′sə-frē′nē-ə): a mental disorder. Here, the narrator refers to a split personality.

15. **censure** (sĕn′shər): an expression of strong disapproval or harsh criticism.

16. **Bao Dai** (bou′dī′): the last emperor of Vietnam (1926–1945) and chief of state from 1949 to 1955.

17. **Diem:** Ngo Dinh Diem (nō′ dĭn′ dē-ĕm′), the first president of South Vietnam, who led his country like a brutal dictator. He was murdered by his own generals in 1963.

WORDS TO KNOW
acquiescence (ăk′wē-ĕs′əns) *n.* passive agreement; agreement without protest
platitude (plăt′ĭ-tood′) *n.* a trite or unoriginal statement, especially one expressed as if it were original or significant; a cliché

Everything sparkled. My house, I thought. My life. I'm not sure how long I stood there, but later I scribbled out a short note to my parents.

What it said exactly, I don't recall now. Something vague. Taking off, will call, love Tim.

I drove north.

It's a blur now, as it was then, and all I remember is a sense of high velocity and the feel of the steering wheel in my hands. I was riding on adrenaline.[18] A giddy feeling, in a way, except there was the dreamy edge of impossibility to it—like running a dead-end maze—no way out—it couldn't come to a happy conclusion and yet I was doing it anyway because it was all I could think to do. It was pure flight, fast and mindless. I had no plan. Just hit the border at high speed and crash through and keep on running. Near dusk I passed through Bemidji, then turned northeast toward International Falls. I spent the night in the car behind a closed-down gas station a half mile from the border. In the morning, after gassing up, I headed straight west along the Rainy River, which separates Minnesota from Canada, and which for me separated one life from another. The land was mostly wilderness. Here and there I passed a motel or bait shop, but otherwise the country unfolded in great sweeps of pine and birch and sumac. Though it was still August, the air already had the smell of October, football season, piles of yellow-red leaves, everything crisp and clean. I remember a huge blue sky. Off to my right was the Rainy River, wide as a lake in places, and beyond the Rainy River was Canada.

For a while I just drove, not aiming at anything, then in the late morning I began looking for a place to lie low for a day or two. I was exhausted, and scared sick, and around noon I pulled into an old fishing resort called the Tip Top Lodge. Actually, it was not a lodge at all,

just eight or nine tiny yellow cabins clustered on a peninsula that jutted northward into the Rainy River. The place was in sorry shape. There was a dangerous wooden dock, an old minnow tank, a flimsy tar paper boathouse along the shore. The main building, which stood in a

> **It was pure flight, fast and mindless. I had no plan. Just hit the border at high speed . . . and keep on running.**

cluster of pines on high ground, seemed to lean heavily to one side, like a cripple, the roof sagging toward Canada. Briefly, I thought about turning around, just giving up, but then I got out of the car and walked up to the front porch.

The man who opened the door that day is the hero of my life. How do I say this without sounding sappy? Blurt it out—the man saved me. He offered exactly what I needed, without questions, without any words at all. He took me in. He was there at the critical time—a silent, watchful presence. Six days later, when it ended, I was unable to find a proper way to thank him, and I never have, and so, if nothing else, this story represents a small gesture of gratitude twenty years overdue.

Even after two decades I can close my eyes and return to that porch at the Tip Top Lodge. I can see the old guy staring at me. Elroy Berdahl: eighty-one years old, skinny and shrunken and mostly bald. He wore a flannel shirt and brown work pants. In one hand, I remember, he carried a green apple, a small paring knife in the other. His eyes had the bluish gray color of a razor

---

18. **adrenaline** (ə-drĕn′ə-lĭn): a hormone that is released into the bloodstream in response to physical or mental stress, such as fear, and that initiates or heightens several physical responses, including an increase in heart rate.

blade, the same polished shine, and as he peered up at me I felt a strange sharpness, almost painful, a cutting sensation, as if his gaze were somehow slicing me open. In part, no doubt, it was my own sense of guilt, but even so I'm absolutely certain that the old man took one look and went right to the heart of things—a kid in trouble. When I asked for a room, Elroy made a little clicking sound with his tongue. He nodded, led me out to one of the cabins, and dropped a key in my hand. I remember smiling at him. I also remember wishing I hadn't. The old man shook his head as if to tell me it wasn't worth the bother.

"Dinner at five-thirty," he said. "You eat fish?"

"Anything," I said.

Elroy grunted and said, "I'll bet."

e spent six days together at the Tip Top Lodge. Just the two of us. Tourist season was over, and there were no boats on the river, and the wilderness seemed to withdraw into a great permanent stillness. Over those six days Elroy Berdahl and I took most of our meals together. In the mornings we sometimes went out on long hikes into the woods, and at night we played Scrabble or listened to records or sat reading in front of his big stone fireplace. At times I felt the awkwardness of an intruder, but Elroy accepted me into his quiet routine without fuss or ceremony. He took my presence for granted, the same way he might've sheltered a stray cat—no wasted sighs or pity—and there was never any talk about it. Just the opposite. What I remember more than anything is the man's willful, almost ferocious silence. In all that time together, all those hours, he never asked the obvious questions: Why was I there?

Why alone? Why so preoccupied? If Elroy was curious about any of this, he was careful never to put it into words.

My hunch, though, is that he already knew. At least the basics. After all, it was 1968, and guys were burning draft cards, and Canada was just a boat ride away. Elroy Berdahl was no hick. His bedroom, I remember, was cluttered with books and newspapers. He killed me at the Scrabble board, barely concentrating, and on those occasions when speech was necessary, he had a way of compressing large thoughts into small, cryptic[19] packets of language. One evening, just at sunset, he pointed up at an owl circling over the violet-lighted forest to the west.

"Hey, O'Brien," he said. "There's Jesus."

The man was sharp—he didn't miss much. Those razor eyes. Now and then he'd catch me staring out at the river, at the far shore, and I could almost hear the tumblers clicking in his head. Maybe I'm wrong, but I doubt it.

One thing for certain, he knew I was in desperate trouble. And he knew I couldn't talk about it. The wrong word—or even the right word—and I would've disappeared. I was wired and jittery. My skin felt too tight. After supper one evening I vomited and went back to my cabin and lay down for a few moments and then vomited again; another time, in the middle of the afternoon, I began sweating and couldn't shut it off. I went through whole days feeling dizzy with sorrow. I couldn't sleep; I couldn't lie still. At night I'd toss around in bed, half awake, half dreaming, imagining how I'd sneak down to the beach and quietly push one of the old man's boats out into the river and start paddling my way toward Canada. There were times when I thought I'd gone off the psychic edge. I

---

19. **cryptic** (krĭp'tĭk): having a hidden or mysterious meaning; mystifying.

WORDS TO KNOW **preoccupied** (prē-ŏk'yə-pīd') *adj.* absorbed in one's thoughts; distracted **preoccupy** *v.*

273

couldn't tell up from down, I was just falling, and late in the night I'd lie there watching weird pictures spin through my head. Getting chased by the Border Patrol—helicopters and searchlights and barking dogs—I'd be crashing through the woods, I'd be down on my hands and knees—people shouting out my name—the law closing in on all sides—my hometown draft board and the FBI and the Royal Canadian Mounted Police. It all seemed crazy and impossible. Twenty-one years old, an ordinary kid with all the ordinary dreams and ambitions, and all I wanted was to live the life I was born to—a mainstream life—I loved baseball and hamburgers and cherry Cokes—and now I was off on the margins of exile, leaving my country forever, and it seemed so impossible and terrible and sad.

I'm not sure how I made it through those six days. Most of it I can't remember. On two or three afternoons, to pass some time, I helped Elroy get the place ready for winter, sweeping down the cabins and hauling in the boats, little chores that kept my body moving. The days were cool and bright. The nights were very dark. One morning the old man showed me how to split and stack firewood, and for several hours we just worked in silence out behind his house. At one point, I remember, Elroy put down his maul[20] and looked at me for a long time, his lips drawn as if framing a difficult question, but then he shook his head and went back to work. The man's self-control was amazing. He never pried. He never put me in a position that required lies or denials. To an extent, I supposed, his reticence was typical of that part of Minnesota, where privacy still held value, and even if I'd been walking around with some horrible deformity— four arms and three heads—I'm sure the old man would've talked about everything except those extra arms and heads. Simple politeness was part

of it. But even more than that, I think, the man understood that words were insufficient. The problem had gone beyond discussion. During that long summer I'd been over and over the various arguments, all the pros and cons, and it was no longer a question that could be decided by an act of pure reason. Intellect had come up against emotion. My conscience told me to run, but some irrational and powerful force was resisting, like a weight pushing me toward the war. What it came down to, stupidly, was a sense of shame. Hot, stupid shame. I did not want people to think badly of me. Not my parents, not my brother and sister, not even the folks down at the Gobbler Café. I was ashamed to be there at the Tip Top Lodge. I was ashamed of my conscience, ashamed to be doing the right thing.

Some of this Elroy must've understood. Not the details, of course, but the plain fact of crisis.

Although the old man never confronted me about it, there was one occasion when he came close to forcing the whole thing out into the open. It was early evening, and we'd just finished supper, and over coffee and dessert I asked him about my bill, how much I owed so far. For a long while the old man squinted down at the tablecloth.

"Well, the basic rate," he said, "is fifty bucks a night. Not counting meals. This makes four nights, right?"

I nodded. I had three hundred and twelve dollars in my wallet.

Elroy kept his eyes on the tablecloth. "Now that's an on-season price. To be fair, I suppose we should knock it down a peg or two." He leaned back in his chair. "What's a reasonable number, you figure?"

"I don't know," I said. "Forty?"

"Forty's good. Forty a night. Then we tack

---

20. **maul** (môl): heavy, long-handled hammer.

274

Sea Air (1987), Douglas Brega. Dry brush on paper, 14″ × 21″, courtesy of the artist.

on food—say another hundred? Two hundred sixty total?"

"I guess."

He raised his eyebrows. "Too much?"

"No, that's fair. It's fine. Tomorrow, though . . . I think I'd better take off tomorrow."

Elroy shrugged and began clearing the table. For a time he fussed with the dishes, whistling to himself as if the subject had been settled. After a second he slapped his hands together.

"You know what we forgot?" he said. "We forgot wages. Those odd jobs you done. What we have to do, we have to figure out what your time's worth. Your last job—how much did you pull in an hour?"

"Not enough," I said.

"A bad one?"

"Yes. Pretty bad."

Slowly then, without intending any long sermon, I told him about my days at the pig plant. It began as a straight recitation of the facts, but before I could stop myself I was talking about the blood clots and the water gun and how the smell had soaked into my skin and how I couldn't wash it away. I went on for a long time. I told him about wild hogs squealing in my dreams, the sounds of butchery, slaughterhouse sounds, and how I'd sometimes wake up with that greasy pig-stink in my throat.

When I was finished, Elroy nodded at me.

"Well, to be honest," he said, "when you first showed up here, I wondered about that. The aroma, I mean. Smelled like you was awful damned fond of pork chops." The old man almost smiled. He made a snuffling sound, then sat down with a pencil and a piece of paper. "So what'd this crud job pay? Ten bucks an hour? Fifteen?"

"Less."

Elroy shook his head. "Let's make it fifteen. You put in twenty-five hours here, easy. That's three hundred seventy-five bucks total wages. We subtract the two hundred sixty for food and lodging. I still owe you a hundred and fifteen."

He took four fifties out of his shirt pocket and laid them on the table.

"Call it even," he said.

"No."

"Pick it up. Get yourself a haircut."

The money lay on the table for the rest of the evening. It was still there when I went back to my cabin. In the morning though, I found an envelope tacked to my door. Inside were the four fifties and a two-word note that said EMERGENCY FUND.

The man knew.

Looking back after twenty years, I sometimes wonder if the events of that summer didn't happen in some other dimension, a place where your life exists before you've lived it, and where it goes afterward. None of it ever seemed real. During my time at the Tip Top Lodge I had the feeling that I'd slipped out of my own skin, hovering a few feet away while some poor yo-yo with my name and face tried to make his way toward a future he didn't understand and didn't want. Even now I can see myself as I was then. It's like watching an old home movie: I'm young and tan and fit. I've got hair—lots of it. I don't smoke or drink. I'm wearing faded blue jeans and a white polo shirt. I can see myself sitting on Elroy Berdahl's dock near dusk one evening, the sky a bright shimmering pink, and I'm finishing up a letter to my parents that tells what I'm about to do and why I'm doing it and how sorry I am that I've never found the courage to talk to them about it. I ask them not to be angry. I try to explain some of my feelings, but there aren't enough words, and so I just say that it's a thing that has to be done. At the end of the letter I talk about the vacations we used to take up in this north country, at a place called Whitefish Lake, and how the scenery here reminds me of those good times. I tell them I'm fine. I tell them I'll write again from Winnipeg or Montreal or wherever I end up.

On my last full day, the sixth day, the old man took me out fishing on the Rainy River. The afternoon was sunny and cold. A stiff breeze came in from the north, and I remember how the little fourteen-foot boat made sharp rocking motions as we pushed off from the dock. The current was fast. All around us, I remember, there was a vastness to the world, an unpeopled rawness, just the trees and the sky and the water reaching out toward nowhere. The air had the brittle scent of October.

For ten or fifteen minutes Elroy held a course upstream, the river choppy and silver-gray, then he turned straight north and put the engine on full throttle. I felt the bow lift beneath me. I remember the wind in my ears, the sound of the old outboard Evinrude. For a time I didn't pay attention to anything, just feeling the cold spray against my face, but then it occurred to me that at some point we must've passed into Canadian waters, across that dotted line between two different worlds, and I remember a sudden tightness in my chest as I looked up and watched the far shore come at me. This wasn't a daydream. It was tangible and real. As we came in toward land, Elroy cut the engine, letting the boat fishtail lightly about twenty yards off shore. The old man didn't look at me or speak. Bending down, he opened up his tackle box and busied himself with a bobber and a piece of wire leader, humming to himself, his eyes down.

It struck me then that he must've planned it. I'll never be certain, of course, but I think he meant to bring me up against the realities, to guide me across the river and to take me to the edge and to stand a kind of vigil as I chose a life for myself.

I remember staring at the old man, then at my hands, then at Canada. The shoreline was dense with brush and timber. I could see tiny red berries on the bushes. I could see a squirrel up in one of the birch trees, a big crow looking at me from a boulder along the river. That close— twenty yards—and I could see the delicate latticework of the leaves, the texture of the soil, the browned needles beneath the pines, the configurations of geology and human history. Twenty yards. I could've done it. I could've jumped and started swimming for my life. Inside me, in my chest, I felt a terrible squeezing pressure. Even now, as I write this, I can still feel that tightness. And I want you to feel it—the wind coming off the river, the waves, the silence, the wooded frontier. You're at the bow of a boat on the Rainy River. You're twenty-one years old, you're scared, and there's a hard squeezing pressure in your chest.

What would you do?

Would you jump? Would you feel pity for yourself? Would you think about the family and your childhood and your dreams and all you're leaving behind? Would it hurt? Would it feel like dying? Would you cry, as I did?

I tried to swallow it back. I tried to smile, except I was crying.

Now, perhaps, you can understand why I've never told this story before. It's not just the embarrassment of tears. That's part of it, no doubt, but what embarrasses me much more, and always will, is the paralysis that took my heart. A moral freeze: I couldn't decide, I couldn't act, I couldn't comport myself with even a pretense of modest human dignity.

All I could do was cry. Quietly, not bawling, just the chest-chokes.

At the rear of the boat Elroy Berdahl pretended

> **I think he meant to bring me up against the realities . . . to stand a kind of vigil as I chose a life for myself.**

not to notice. He held a fishing rod in his hands, his head bowed to hide his eyes. He kept humming a soft, monotonous little tune. Everywhere, it seemed, in the trees and water and sky, a great worldwide sadness came pressing down on me, a crushing sorrow, sorrow like I had never known before. And what was so sad, I realized, was that Canada had become a pitiful fantasy. Silly and hopeless. It was no longer a possibility. Right then, with the shore so close, I understood that I would not do what I should do. I would not swim away from my hometown and my country and my life. I would not be brave. That old image of myself as a hero, as a man of conscience and courage, all that was just a threadbare pipe dream.[21] Bobbing there on the Rainy River, looking back at the Minnesota shore, I felt a sudden swell of helplessness come over me, a drowning sensation, as if I had toppled overboard and was being swept away by the silver waves. Chunks of my own history flashed by. I saw a seven-year-old boy in a white cowboy

---

21. **pipe dream:** daydream or fantasy that will never happen; vain hope.

277

Atascadero Dusk (about 1990), Robert Reynolds. Watercolor, 22″ × 15″. *From Painting Nature's Beautiful Places,* published by North Light Books.

278

hat and a Lone Ranger mask and a pair of holstered six-shooters; I saw a twelve-year-old Little League shortstop pivoting to turn a double play; I saw a sixteen-year-old kid decked out for his first prom, looking spiffy in a white tux and a black bow tie, his hair cut short and flat, his shoes freshly polished. My whole life seemed to spill out into the river, swirling away from me, everything I had ever been or ever wanted to be. I couldn't get my breath; I couldn't stay afloat; I couldn't tell which way to swim. A hallucination, I suppose, but it was as real as anything I would ever feel. I saw my parents calling to me from the far shoreline. I saw my brother and sister, all the townsfolk, the mayor and the entire Chamber of Commerce and all my old teachers and girlfriends and high school buddies. Like some weird sporting event: everybody screaming from the sidelines, rooting me on—a loud stadium roar. Hotdogs and popcorn—stadium smells, stadium heat. A squad of cheerleaders did cart-wheels along the banks of the Rainy River; they had megaphones and pompoms and smooth brown thighs. The crowd swayed left and right. A marching band played fight songs. All my aunts and uncles were there, and Abraham Lincoln and Saint George,[22] and a nine-year-old girl named Linda who had died of a brain tumor back in fifth grade, and several members of the United States Senate, and a blind poet scribbling notes, and LBJ, and Huck Finn, and Abbie Hoffman,[23] and all the dead soldiers back from the grave, and the many thousands who were later to die—villagers with terrible burns, little kids without arms or legs—yes, and the Joint Chiefs of Staff[24] were there, and a couple of popes, and a first lieutenant named Jimmy Cross, and the last surviving veteran of the American Civil War, and Jane Fonda dressed up as Barbarella,[25] and an old man sprawled beside a pigpen, and my grandfather, and Gary Cooper,[26] and a kind-faced woman carrying an umbrella and a copy of Plato's *Republic*,[27] and a million

ferocious citizens waving flags of all shapes and colors—people in hardhats, people in head-bands—they were all whooping and chanting and urging me toward one shore or the other. I saw faces from my distant past and distant future. My wife was there. My unborn daughter waved at me, and my two sons hopped up and down, and a drill sergeant named Blyton sneered and shot up a finger and shook his head. There was a choir in bright purple robes. There was a cabbie from the Bronx. There was a slim young man I would one day kill with a hand grenade along a red clay trail outside the village of My Khe.[28]

The little aluminum boat rocked softly beneath me. There was the wind and the sky.

I tried to will myself overboard.

I gripped the edge of the boat and leaned forward and thought, *Now.*

I did try. It just wasn't possible.

All those eyes on me—the town, the whole universe—and I couldn't risk the embarrassment. It was as if there were an audience to my life, that swirl of faces along the river, and in my head I could hear people screaming at me. Traitor! they yelled. Turncoat! I felt myself

---

22. **Saint George:** Christian martyr (killed about A.D. 303) and patron saint of England who, according to legend, slew a frightening dragon.

23. **Abbie Hoffman:** social organizer and radical anti–Vietnam War activist known for his humor and politically inspired pranks.

24. **Joint Chiefs of Staff:** the principal military advisors of the U.S. president, including the chiefs of the army, navy, and air force and the commandant of the marines.

25. **Jane Fonda dressed up as Barbarella:** anti–Vietnam War activist and actress Jane Fonda (1937–), dressed as Barbarella, the title character she played in a 1968 science fiction film.

26. **Gary Cooper:** American actor famous for playing strong, quiet heroes.

27. **Plato's *Republic:*** a famous work in which the ancient Greek philosopher Plato describes the ideal state or society.

28. **My Khe** (mē′ kē′).

blush. I couldn't tolerate it. I couldn't endure the mockery, or the disgrace, or the patriotic ridicule. Even in my imagination, the shore just twenty yards away, I couldn't make myself be brave. It had nothing to do with morality. Embarrassment, that's all it was.

And right then I submitted.

I would go to the war—I would kill and maybe die—because I was embarrassed not to.

That was the sad thing. And so I sat in the bow of the boat and cried.

It was loud now. Loud, hard crying.

Elroy Berdahl remained quiet. He kept fishing. He worked his line with the tips of his fingers, patiently, squinting out at his red and white bobber on the Rainy River. His eyes were flat and impassive. He didn't speak. He was simply there, like the river and the late-summer sun. And yet by his presence, his mute watchfulness, he made it real. He was the true audience. He was a witness, like God, or like the gods, who look on in absolute silence as we live our lives, as we make our choices or fail to make them.

"Ain't biting," he said.

Then after a time the old man pulled in his line and turned the boat back toward Minnesota.

I don't remember saying goodbye. That last night we had dinner together, and I went to bed early, and in the morning Elroy fixed breakfast for me. When I told him I'd be leaving, the old man nodded as if he already knew. He looked down at the table and smiled.

At some point later in the morning it's possible that we shook hands—I just don't remember—but I do know that by the time I'd finished packing the old man had disappeared. Around noon, when I took my suitcase out to the car, I noticed that his old black pickup truck was no longer parked in front of the house. I went inside and waited for a while, but I felt a bone certainty that he wouldn't be back. In a way, I thought, it was appropriate. I washed up the breakfast dishes, left his two hundred dollars on the kitchen counter, got into the car, and drove south toward home.

The day was cloudy. I passed through towns with familiar names, through the pine forests and down to the prairie, and then to Vietnam, where I was a soldier, and then home again. I survived, but it's not a happy ending. I was a coward. I went to the war. ❖

WORDS TO KNOW **impassive** (ĭm-păs′ĭv) *adj.* revealing no emotion; expressionless

RESPONDING
OPTIONS

FROM PERSONAL RESPONSE TO CRITICAL ANALYSIS

REFLECT

1. In your notebook, write your reaction to the narrator's final decision.

RETHINK

2. The narrator feels he was a coward for fighting in the Vietnam War. Do you share his opinion? Why or why not?

3. What do you think the narrator means when he says that Elroy Berdahl "saved" him?

Consider
- the effect of Elroy's silence
- his offer of money to the narrator
- why he takes the narrator fishing

4. The narrator gives a detailed description of his summer job in a meat-packing plant. Why do you think this description is included?

5. If you had been in the narrator's position, would you have chosen to fight in the war or to flee to Canada? Consider the chart you created for the Personal Connection on page 266.

6. "Prisoners of Circumstance" is the title given to this part of Unit Two. In what sense is the narrator a prisoner of circumstance?

RELATE

7. Should a government be able to compel citizens to fight in wars? Why or why not?

United States Marines in Vietnam, 1965. Copyright © Larry Burrows Collection.

ANOTHER PATHWAY

Cooperative Learning

With your entire class, conduct a point/counterpoint discussion that explores both sides of the narrator's conscience. One side of the class should argue in favor of military service; the other side should argue in favor of fleeing to Canada. Use evidence from the story to support your views.

QUICKWRITES

1. Assume the identity of Elroy in "On the Rainy River" and write a **letter** to a relative, telling about your unusual week with the narrator.

2. Draft a **definition essay** about courage, showing how your personal definition is similar to or different from the narrator's. If you are using a computer, don't forget to use the spelling checker before you print your essay.

3. Imagine that when the narrator feels the impulse to jump from the boat and swim toward Canada, he actually does so. Write an **alternative ending** to the story from this point on.

4. Recall a time when you wrestled with your conscience about the right thing to do. Write a **personal essay** about the experience.

📁 *PORTFOLIO Save your writing. You may want to use it later as a springboard to a piece for your portfolio.*

LITERARY CONCEPTS

Point of view refers to the narrative method, or the kind of narrator, used in a literary work. In the **first-person point of view,** the narrator is a character in the story who tells everything in his or her own words. The first-person point of view can sometimes make a fictional story seem more true to life, particularly when the writer gives the narrator his or her own name, as Tim O'Brien did. How does O'Brien's use of the first-person point of view affect how you feel about the narrator? How does it affect your understanding of Elroy Berdahl?

LITERARY LINKS

In the excerpt from *When Heaven and Earth Changed Places* in Unit One, Le Ly Hayslip's father says, "Freedom is never a gift. . . . It must be won and won again." What do you think freedom means to this Vietnamese father? What do you think it means to the American narrator of "On the Rainy River"? If the two men had met in Vietnam, what might they have said to each other?

ART CONNECTION

What do you think is the connection between the painting *Portrait of Donald Schrader* on page 267 and the first part of the story?

ALTERNATIVE ACTIVITIES

1. Create a **collage** based on the vision the narrator has while he's on the Rainy River (pages 277–279). You may include photos, clippings from newspapers and magazines, and your own drawings of the images that the narrator thinks he sees.

2. Bring in recordings of folk and rock **protest songs** from the Vietnam War era and play them for your class. Discuss how these songs express moral and political objections to the conflict.

ACROSS THE CURRICULUM

History *Cooperative Learning*
Working with a group of classmates, conduct research on the Vietnam War. What was the United States trying to achieve by participating in the conflict? Why did some people support our role in the war, and why did others oppose it? Divide your group in two and hold a debate that might have taken place between hawks and doves in 1968.

Journalism Tape-record or videotape interviews with people who lived through the Vietnam War era. Have them describe their feelings about the war and their experiences with the draft, the fighting itself, and the rallies or protests on the home front. Then write a feature story for the school newspaper.

WORDS TO KNOW

Review the Words to Know at the bottom of the selection pages. Then choose the word that best completes each of the following sentences.

1. Grandma says that long before Dad was drafted, he was so _____ with the Vietnam War that he couldn't focus on his schoolwork and his grades were falling.
2. Dad believed in the _____ of defending one's country, but he didn't understand how the Vietnam War was connected to freedom at home.
3. He found the tangled web of Vietnamese politics difficult to _____.
4. In the United States, there was no _____ about the war; hawks said one thing, and doves said another.
5. My grandfather understood Dad's reluctance to fight in that war; he used to say "War is hell," but that was only a _____.

6. After receiving his draft notice, Dad stayed up all night holding a lonely _____.
7. Since Dad was usually so cheerful and talkative in the morning, his _____ at the breakfast table the next day made my grandfather feel sad.
8. To Grandma he seemed calm, but that was merely _____, for deep down he was troubled.
9. He kept his face _____ so that Grandma could not observe his feelings.
10. When Grandma asked if he would soon be going overseas to fight, he nodded in _____.

TIM O'BRIEN

Though the events depicted in "On the Rainy River" are fictional, many details in the story match the writer's own experiences. Like the narrator, the real Tim O'Brien grew up in Minnesota and was an exceptional student at Macalester College. He also was drafted into the U.S. Army immediately after graduation, and he was later admitted to graduate school at Harvard. An opponent of the Vietnam War,

1946–

O'Brien, like the narrator, debated fleeing the country (his choice of destination was Sweden, not Canada), but ultimately he decided to serve. "I did not want to be a soldier, not even an observer to war," he later wrote. "But neither did I want to upset a peculiar balance between the order I knew, the people I knew, and my own private world."

During the Vietnam War, O'Brien was promoted to the rank of sergeant; he also was wounded in combat and awarded the Purple Heart. His experiences in the army affected him profoundly and have inspired much of his writing. His first book, *If I Die in a Combat Zone, Box Me Up and Ship Me Home* (1973), is a nonfiction memoir of his tour of duty. O'Brien's popular second novel about Vietnam, *Going After Cacciato,* won two O. Henry Memorial Awards and the 1978 National Book Award. "On the Rainy River" appeared in *The Things They Carried* (1990), a collection of interrelated stories about the Vietnam War and its victims. Despite the presence of a narrator named Tim O'Brien, the stories in the collection are fictional. For O'Brien, whether a story is literally true is less important than the truths it conveys. "I want you to feel what I felt," he once explained. "I want you to know why story truth is truer sometimes than happening truth."

OTHER WORKS *Northern Lights, In the Lake of the Woods*

FICTION

The Pearl

Yukio Mishima (yōō′kē-ō mĭ-shē′mä) Japan

PERSONAL CONNECTION

Have you ever been caught in an awkward or embarrassing moment at a party or social event? What did you do? In your notebook, describe a time when you felt you needed to "save face," or keep your standing in the eyes of others.

CULTURAL CONNECTION

Polite behavior is important in Japanese society, as it is in American society, but the customs and the rules of etiquette in the two cultures are often quite different. In Japan it is considered rude to sneeze or blow your nose in public, for example, and you must be careful not to accidentally bump someone with your foot because feet are considered unclean. Japanese society places great value on self-restraint and duty, and the need to maintain dignity in embarrassing or awkward situations often motivates personal behavior. This was particularly true three or four decades ago, when the following story takes place. Set in Tokyo, the capital of Japan, "The Pearl" portrays five friends from middle-class Japanese society who become entangled in an awkward social situation.

Two businessmen in Osaka, Japan.
Copyright © Will and Deni McIntyre / Tony Stone Images.

READING CONNECTION

Understanding Problems and Solutions "The Pearl" takes several twists and turns as each character independently tries to resolve the awkward situation that has affected the entire group. To keep track of the action in the story, copy this problem-and-solution chart into your notebook and fill it out as you read.

Character	Problem(s)	Solution(s)
Mrs. Sasaki		
Mrs. Yamamoto		
Mrs. Matsumura		
Mrs. Azuma		
Mrs. Kasuga		

Using Your Reading Log Use your reading log to record your responses to the questions inserted throughout the selection. Also, jot down other thoughts and feelings that come to you as you read.

The Pearl

Yukio Mishima

December 10 was Mrs. Sasaki's[1] birthday, but since it was Mrs. Sasaki's wish to celebrate the occasion with the minimum of fuss, she had invited to her house for afternoon tea only her closest friends. Assembled were Mesdames Yamamoto, Matsumura, Azuma, and Kasuga[2] —all four being forty-three years of age, exact contemporaries of their hostess.

These ladies were thus members, as it were, of a Keep-Our-Ages-Secret Society and could be trusted implicitly not to divulge to outsiders the number of candles on today's cake. In inviting to her birthday party only guests of this nature, Mrs. Sasaki was showing her customary prudence.

On this occasion Mrs. Sasaki wore a pearl ring. Diamonds at an all-female gathering had not seemed in the best of taste. Furthermore, pearls better matched the color of the dress she was wearing on this particular day.

Shortly after the party had begun, Mrs. Sasaki was moving across for one last inspection of the cake when the pearl in her ring, already a little loose, finally fell from its socket. It seemed a most inauspicious event for this happy occasion, but it would have been no less embarrassing to have everyone aware of the misfortune, so Mrs. Sasaki simply left the pearl close by the rim of the large cake dish and resolved to do something about it later. Around the cake were set out the plates, forks, and paper napkins for herself and the four guests. It now occurred to Mrs. Sasaki that she had no wish to be seen wearing a ring with no stone while cutting this cake, and accordingly she removed the ring from her finger and very deftly,

---

1. **Sasaki** (sä-sä′kē).

2. **Mesdames Yamamoto** (mā-däm′ ya′mə-mō′tō), **Matsumura** (mät′sōō-mōō′rə), **Azuma** (ə-zōō′mä), **and Kasuga** (kə-sōō′gä): *Mesdames* is the plural form of the French title for a married woman, *Madame,* which is equivalent to the English title *Mrs.*

Firescreen (1935), Vanessa Bell. Gouache on board, 104 × 107 cm, The Charleston Trust, East Sussex. Photo by Susanna Price.

without turning around, slipped it into a recess in the wall behind her back.

Amid the general excitement of the exchange of gossip, and Mrs. Sasaki's surprise and pleasure at the thoughtful presents brought by her guests, the matter of the pearl was very quickly forgotten. Before long it was time for the customary ceremony of lighting and extinguishing the candles on the cake. Everyone crowded excitedly about the table, lending a hand in the not untroublesome task of lighting forty-three candles.

Mrs. Sasaki, with her limited lung capacity, could hardly be expected to blow out all that number at one puff, and her appearance of

utter helplessness gave rise to a great deal of hilarious comment.

The procedure followed in serving the cake was that, after the first bold cut, Mrs. Sasaki carved for each guest individually a slice of whatever thickness was requested and transferred this to a small plate, which the guest then carried back with her to her own seat. With everyone stretching out hands at the same time, the crush and confusion around the table was considerable.

On top of the cake was a floral design executed in pink icing and liberally interspersed with small silver balls. These were silver-painted crystals of sugar—a common enough decoration on birthday cakes. In the struggle to secure helpings, moreover, flakes of icing, crumbs of cake, and a number of these silver balls came to be scattered all over the white tablecloth. Some of the guests gathered these stray particles between their fingers and put them on their plates. Others popped them straight into their mouths.

In time all returned to their seats and ate their portions of cake at their leisure, laughing. It was not a homemade cake, having been ordered by Mrs. Sasaki from a certain high-class confectioner's,[3] but the guests were unanimous in praising its excellence.

Mrs. Sasaki was bathed in happiness. But suddenly, with a tinge of anxiety, she recalled the pearl she had abandoned on the table, and, rising from her chair as casually as she could, she moved across to look for it. At the spot where she was sure she had left it, the pearl was no longer to be seen.

Mrs. Sasaki abhorred losing things. At once and without thinking, right in the middle of the party, she became wholly engrossed in her search, and the tension in her manner was so obvious that it attracted everyone's attention.

"Is there something the matter?" someone asked.

"No, not at all, just a moment. . . ."

Mrs. Sasaki's reply was ambiguous, but before she had time to decide to return to her chair, first one, then another, and finally every one of her guests had risen and was turning back the tablecloth or groping about on the floor.

Mrs. Azuma, seeing this commotion, felt that the whole thing was just too deplorable for words. She was incensed at a hostess who could create such an impossible situation over the loss of a solitary pearl.

Mrs. Azuma resolved to offer herself as a sacrifice and to save the day. With a heroic smile she declared: "That's it then! It must have been a pearl I ate just now! A silver ball dropped on the tablecloth when I was given my cake, and I just picked it up and swallowed it without thinking. It *did* seem to stick in my throat a little. Had it been a diamond, now, I would naturally return it—by an operation, if necessary—but as it's a pearl, I must simply beg your forgiveness."

This announcement at once resolved the company's anxieties, and it was felt, above all, that it had saved the hostess from an embarrassing predicament. No one made any attempt to investigate the truth or falsity of Mrs. Azuma's confession. Mrs. Sasaki took one of the remaining silver balls and put it in her mouth.

"Mm," she said. "Certainly tastes like a pearl, this one!"

QUESTION

Why are Mrs. Sasaki and her guests laughing?

Thus, this small incident, too, was cast into the crucible[4] of good-humored teasing, and there—amid general laughter—it melted away.

When the party was over, Mrs. Azuma drove off in her two-seater sportscar, taking with her in the other seat her close friend and neighbor Mrs. Kasuga. Before two minutes had passed, Mrs. Azuma said, "Own up! It was you who swallowed the pearl, wasn't it? I covered up for you and took the blame on myself."

This unceremonious manner of speaking concealed deep affection, but, however friendly the intention may have been, to Mrs. Kasuga a wrongful accusation was a wrongful accusation. She had no recollection whatsoever of having swallowed a pearl in mistake for a sugar ball. She was—as Mrs. Azuma too must surely

---

3. **confectioner's** (kən-fĕk'shə-nərz): a shop or caterer specializing in candies, cakes, and other sweets.

4. **crucible** (krōō'sə-bəl): test or trial.

WORDS TO KNOW **ambiguous** (ăm-bĭg'yōō-əs) *adj.* open to more than one interpretation
incensed (ĭn-sĕnst') *adj.* extremely angered **incense** *v.*

287

know—<u>fastidious</u> in her eating habits, and, if she so much as detected a single hair in her food, whatever she happened to be eating at the time immediately stuck in her gullet.

"Oh, really now!" protested the timid Mrs. Kasuga in a small voice, her eyes studying Mrs. Azuma's face in some puzzlement. "I just couldn't do a thing like that!"

"It's no good pretending. The moment I saw that green look on your face, I knew."

The little disturbance at the party had seemed closed by Mrs. Azuma's frank confession, but even now it had left behind it this strange awkwardness. Mrs. Kasuga, wondering how best to demonstrate her innocence, was at the same time seized by the fantasy that a solitary pearl was lodged somewhere in her intestines. It was unlikely, of course, that she should mistakenly swallow a pearl for a sugar ball, but in all that confusion of talk and laughter, one had to admit that it was at least a possibility. Though she thought back over the events of the party again and again, no moment in which she might have inserted a pearl into her mouth came to mind—but, after all, if it was an unconscious act, one would not expect to remember it.

Mrs. Kasuga blushed deeply as her imagination chanced upon one further aspect of the matter. It had occurred to her that when one accepted a pearl into one's system, it almost certainly—its luster a trifle dimmed, perhaps, by gastric juices[5]—reemerged intact within a day or two.

And with this thought the design of Mrs. Azuma, too, seemed to have become transparently clear. Undoubtedly Mrs. Azuma had viewed this same prospect with embarrassment and shame and had therefore cast her responsibility onto another, making it appear that she had considerately taken the blame to protect a friend.

Meanwhile Mrs. Yamamoto and Mrs. Matsumura, whose homes lay in a similar direction, were returning together in a taxi. Soon after the taxi had started, Mrs. Matsumura opened her handbag to make a few adjustments to her make-up. She remembered that she had done nothing to her face since all that commotion at the party.

As she was removing the powder compact, her attention was caught by a sudden dull gleam as something tumbled to the bottom of the bag. Groping about with the tips of her fingers, Mrs. Matsumura retrieved the object and saw to her amazement that it was a pearl.

Mrs. Matsumura stifled an exclamation of surprise. Recently her relationship with Mrs. Yamamoto had been far from cordial, and she had no wish to share with that lady a discovery with such awkward implications for herself.

Fortunately Mrs. Yamamoto was gazing out of the window and did not appear to have noticed her companion's momentary start of surprise.

Caught off balance by this sudden turn of events, Mrs. Matsumura did not pause to consider how the pearl had found its way into her bag but immediately became a prisoner of her own private brand of school-captain morality. It was unlikely—she thought—that she would do a thing like this, even in a moment of abstraction. But since, by some chance, the object had found its way into her handbag, the proper course was to return it at once. If she failed to do so, it would weigh heavily upon her conscience. The fact that it was a pearl, too—an article you could call neither all that expensive nor yet all

---

5. **gastric juices:** fluids used by the stomach during digestion.

WORDS TO KNOW   **fastidious** (fă-stĭd′ē-əs) *adj.* showing meticulous attention to detail; excessively careful in matters of taste or manners

that cheap—only made her position more ambiguous.

At any rate, she was determined that her companion, Mrs. Yamamoto, should know nothing of this incomprehensible development—especially when the affair had been so nicely rounded off, thanks to the selflessness of Mrs. Azuma. Mrs. Matsumura felt she could remain in the taxi not a moment longer, and on the pretext of remembering a promise to visit a sick relative on her way back, she made the driver set her down at once, in the middle of a quiet residential district.

Mrs. Yamamoto, left alone in the taxi, was a little surprised that her practical joke should have moved Mrs. Matsumura to such abrupt action. Having watched Mrs. Matsumura's reflection in the window just now, she had clearly seen her draw the pearl from her bag.

Mrs. Yamamoto . . . was a little surprised that her practical joke should have moved Mrs. Matsumura to such abrupt action.

At the party Mrs. Yamamoto had been the very first to receive a slice of cake. Adding to her plate a silver ball which had spilled onto the table, she had returned to her seat—again before any of the others—and there had noticed that the silver ball was a pearl. At this discovery she had at once conceived a <u>malicious</u> plan. While all the others were preoccupied with the cake, she had quickly slipped the pearl into the handbag left on the next chair by that insufferable hypocrite Mrs. Matsumura.

Stranded in the middle of a residential district where there was little prospect of a taxi, Mrs.

Matsumura fretfully gave her mind to a number of reflections on her position.

First, no matter how necessary it might be for the relief of her own conscience, it would be a shame indeed, when people had gone to such lengths to settle the affair satisfactorily, to go and stir up things all over again; and it would be even worse if in the process—because of the inexplicable nature of the circumstances—she were to direct unjust suspicions upon herself.

Secondly—notwithstanding these considerations—if she did not make haste to return the pearl now, she would forfeit her opportunity forever. Left till tomorrow (at the thought Mrs. Matsumura blushed), the returned pearl would be an object of rather disgusting speculation and doubt. Concerning this possibility, Mrs. Azuma herself had dropped a hint.

It was at this point that there occurred to Mrs. Matsumura, greatly to her joy, a master scheme which would both salve[6] her conscience and at the same time involve no risk of exposing her character to any unjust suspicion. Quickening her step, she emerged at length onto a comparatively busy thoroughfare, where she hailed a taxi and told the driver to take her quickly to a certain celebrated pearl shop on the Ginza.[7] There she took the pearl from her bag and showed it to the attendant, asking to see a pearl of slightly larger size and clearly superior quality. Having made her purchase, she proceeded once more, by taxi, to Mrs. Sasaki's house.

Mrs. Matsumura's plan was to present this newly purchased pearl to Mrs. Sasaki, saying she had found it in her jacket pocket. Mrs. Sasaki would accept it and later attempt to fit it into the ring. However, being a pearl of a different size, it would not fit into the ring, and Mrs. Sasaki—puzzled—would try to return it to Mrs.

---

6. **salve** (săv): soothe, heal, or ease.

7. **Ginza** (gĭn′zə): an elegant shopping district in Tokyo.

WORDS TO KNOW **malicious** (mə-lĭsh′əs) *adj.* deliberately harmful; spiteful

289

Matsumura, but Mrs. Matsumura would refuse to have it returned. Thereupon Mrs. Sasaki would have no choice but to reflect as follows: The woman has behaved in this way in order to protect someone else. Such being the case, it is perhaps safest simply to accept the pearl and forget the matter. Mrs. Matsumura has doubtless observed one of the three ladies in the act of stealing the pearl. But at least, of my four guests, I can now be sure that Mrs. Matsumura, if no one else, is completely without guilt. Whoever heard of a thief stealing something and then replacing it with a similar article of greater value?

CLARIFY

Why does Mrs. Matsumura purchase a new pearl for Mrs. Sasaki instead of returning the original one that was lost?

By this device Mrs. Matsumura proposed to escape forever the infamy of suspicion and equally—by a small outlay of cash—the pricks of an uneasy conscience.

To return to the other ladies. After reaching home, Mrs. Kasuga continued to feel painfully upset by Mrs. Azuma's cruel teasing. To clear herself of even a ridiculous charge like this—she knew—she must act before tomorrow or it would be too late. That is to say, in order to offer positive proof that she had not eaten the pearl, it was above all necessary for the pearl itself to be somehow produced. And, briefly, if she could show the pearl to Mrs. Azuma immediately, her innocence on the gastronomic count (if not on any other) would be firmly established. But if she waited until tomorrow, even though she managed to produce the pearl, the shameful and hardly mentionable suspicion would inevitably have intervened.

The normally timid Mrs. Kasuga, inspired with the courage of impetuous action, burst from the house to which she had so recently

returned, sped to a pearl shop in the Ginza, and selected and bought a pearl which, to her eye, seemed of roughly the same size as those silver balls on the cake. She then telephoned Mrs. Azuma. On returning home, she explained, she had discovered in the folds of the bow of her sash the pearl which Mrs. Sasaki had lost, but, since she felt too ashamed to return it by herself, she wondered if Mrs. Azuma would be so kind as to go with her, as soon as possible. Inwardly Mrs. Azuma considered the story a little unlikely, but since it was the request of a good friend, she agreed to go.

Mrs. Sasaki accepted the pearl brought to her by Mrs. Matsumura and, puzzled at its failure to fit the ring, fell obligingly into that very train of thought for which Mrs. Matsumura had prayed; but it was a surprise to her when Mrs. Kasuga arrived about an hour later, accompanied by Mrs. Azuma, and returned another pearl.

Mrs. Sasaki hovered perilously on the brink of discussing Mrs. Matsumura's prior visit but checked herself at the last moment and accepted the second pearl as unconcernedly as she could. She felt sure that this one at any rate would fit, and as soon as the two visitors had taken their leave, she hurried to try it in the ring. But it was too small and wobbled loosely in the socket. At this discovery Mrs. Sasaki was not so much surprised as dumbfounded.

On the way back in the car both ladies found it impossible to guess what the other might be thinking, and, though normally relaxed and loquacious[8] in each other's company, they now lapsed into a long silence.

Mrs. Azuma, who believed she could do nothing without her own full knowledge, knew

---

8. **loquacious** (lō-kwā′shəs): very talkative.

WORDS TO KNOW

infamy (ĭn′fə-mē) *n.* evil fame or reputation
impetuous (ĭm-pĕch′ᴐᴐ-əs) *adj.* abrupt or impulsive; spontaneous

290

Illustration by Leslie Wu.

for certain that she had not swallowed the pearl herself. It was simply to save everyone from embarrassment that she had cast shame aside and made that declaration at the party—more particularly, it was to save the situation for her friend, who had been fidgeting about and looking conspicuously guilty. But what was she to think now? Beneath the peculiarity of Mrs. Kasuga's whole attitude, and beneath this elaborate procedure of having herself accompany her as she returned the pearl, she sensed that there lay something much deeper. Could it be that Mrs. Azuma's intuition had touched upon a weakness in her friend's make-up which it was forbidden to touch upon and that by thus driving her friend into a corner she had transformed an unconscious, impulsive kleptomania[9] into a deep mental derangement beyond all cure?

---

9. **kleptomania** (klĕp´tə-mā´nē-ə): obsessive impulse to steal, regardless of economic need.

Mrs. Kasuga, for her part, still retained the suspicion that Mrs. Azuma had genuinely swallowed the pearl and that her confession at the party had been the truth. If that was so, it had been unforgivable of Mrs. Azuma, when everything was smoothly settled, to tease her so cruelly on the way back from the party, shifting the guilt onto herself. As a result, timid creature that she was, she had been panic-stricken and, besides spending good money, had felt obliged to act out that little play—and was it not exceedingly ill-natured of Mrs. Azuma that, even after all this, she still refused to confess it was she who had eaten the pearl? And if Mrs. Azuma's innocence was all pretense, she herself—acting her part so painstakingly—must appear in Mrs. Azuma's eyes as the most ridiculous of third-rate comedians.

PREDICT

Do you think that, by the end of the story, Mrs. Sasaki and the other women will learn the truth about what happened to the pearl?

To return to Mrs. Matsumura. That lady, on her way back from obliging Mrs. Sasaki to accept the pearl, was feeling now more at ease in her mind and had the notion to make a leisurely reinvestigation, detail by detail, of the events of the recent incident. When going to collect her portion of the cake, she had most certainly left her handbag on the chair. Then, while eating the cake, she had made liberal use of the paper napkin—so there could have been no necessity to take a handkerchief from her bag. The more she thought about it, the less she could remember having opened her bag until she touched up her face in the taxi on the way home. How was it, then, that a pearl had rolled into a handbag which was always shut?

She realized now how stupid she had been not to have remarked this simple fact before, instead of flying into a panic at the mere sight of the pearl. Having progressed this far, Mrs.

Matsumura was struck by an amazing thought. Someone must purposely have placed the pearl in her bag in order to incriminate her. And of the four guests at the party the only one who would do such a thing was, without doubt, the detestable Mrs. Yamamoto. Her eyes glinting with rage, Mrs. Matsumura hurried toward the house of Mrs. Yamamoto.

From her first glimpse of Mrs. Matsumura standing in the doorway, Mrs. Yamamoto knew at once what had brought her. She had already prepared her line of defense.

However, Mrs. Matsumura's cross-examination was unexpectedly severe, and from the start it was clear that she would accept no evasions.

"It was you, I know. No one but you could do such a thing," began Mrs. Matsumura, deductively.

"Why choose me? What proof have you? If you can say a thing like that to my face, I suppose you've come with pretty conclusive proof, have you?" Mrs. Yamamoto was at first icily composed.

To this Mrs. Matsumura replied that Mrs. Azuma, having so nobly taken the blame on herself, clearly stood in an incompatible relationship with mean and despicable behavior of this nature; and as for Mrs. Kasuga, she was much too weak-kneed for such dangerous work; and that left only one person—yourself.

Mrs. Yamamoto kept silent, her mouth shut tight like a clamshell. On the table before her gleamed the pearl which Mrs. Matsumura had set there. In the excitement she had not even had time to raise a teaspoon, and the Ceylon tea she had so thoughtfully provided was beginning to get cold.

"I had no idea that you hated me so." As she said this, Mrs. Yamamoto dabbed at the corners of her eyes, but it was plain that Mrs. Matsumura's resolve not to be deceived by tears was as firm as ever.

"Well, then," Mrs. Yamamoto continued,

"I shall say what I had thought I must never say. I shall mention no names, but one of the guests . . . "

"By that, I suppose, you can only mean Mrs. Azuma or Mrs. Kasuga?"

"Please, I beg at least that you allow me to omit the name. As I say, one of the guests had just opened your bag and was dropping something inside when I happened to glance in her direction. You can imagine my amazement! Even if I had felt *able* to warn you, there would have been no chance. My heart just throbbed and throbbed, and on the way back in the taxi—oh, how awful not to be able to speak even then! If we had been good friends, of course, I could have told you quite frankly, but since I knew of your apparent dislike for me . . . "

"I see. You have been very considerate, I'm sure. Which means, doesn't it, that you have now cleverly shifted the blame onto Mrs. Azuma and Mrs. Kasuga?"

"Shifted the blame! Oh, how can I get you to understand my feelings? I only wanted to avoid hurting anyone."

"Quite. But you didn't mind hurting me, did you? You might at least have mentioned this in the taxi."

"And if you had been frank with me when you found the pearl in your bag, I would probably have told you, at that moment, everything I had seen—but no, you chose to leave the taxi at once, without saying a word!"

For the first time, as she listened to this, Mrs. Matsumura was at a loss for a reply.

"Well, then. Can I get you to understand? I wanted no one to be hurt."

Mrs. Matsumura was filled with an even more intense rage.

"If you are going to tell a string of lies like that," she said, "I must ask you to repeat them, tonight if you wish, in my presence, before Mrs. Azuma and Mrs. Kasuga."

At this Mrs. Yamamoto started to weep.

"And thanks to you," she sobbed reprovingly,[10] "all my efforts to avoid hurting anyone will have come to nothing."

It was a new experience for Mrs. Matsumura to see Mrs. Yamamoto crying, and, though she kept reminding herself not to be taken in by tears, she could not altogether dismiss the feeling that perhaps somewhere, since nothing in this affair could be proved, there might be a modicum[11] of truth even in the assertions of Mrs. Yamamoto.

"One of the guests had just opened your bag and was dropping something inside when I happened to glance in her direction."

In the first place—to be a little more objective— if one accepted Mrs. Yamamoto's story as true, then her reluctance to disclose the name of the guilty party, whom she had observed in the very act, argued some refinement of character. And just as one could not say for sure that the gentle and seemingly timid Mrs. Kasuga would never be moved to an act of malice, so even the undoubtedly bad feeling between Mrs. Yamamoto and herself could, by one way of looking at things, be taken as actually lessening the likelihood of Mrs. Yamamoto's guilt. For if she were to do a thing like this, with their relationship as it was, Mrs. Yamamoto would be the first to come under suspicion.

"We have differences in our natures," Mrs. Yamamoto continued tearfully, "and I cannot deny that there are things about yourself which

---

10. **reprovingly** (rĭ-prōo′vĭng-lē): in a manner that finds fault or conveys disappointment.

11. **modicum** (mŏd′ĭ-kəm): a small amount.

I dislike. But, for all that, it is really too bad that you should suspect me of such a petty trick to get the better of you. . . . Still, on thinking it over, to submit quietly to your accusations might well be the course most consistent with what I have felt in this matter all along. In this way I alone shall bear the guilt, and no other will be hurt."

After this pathetic pronouncement Mrs. Yamamoto lowered her face to the table and abandoned herself to uncontrolled weeping.

Watching her, Mrs. Matsumura came, by degrees, to reflect upon the impulsiveness of her own behavior. Detesting Mrs. Yamamoto as she had, there had been times in her castigation[12] of that lady when she had allowed herself to be blinded by emotion.

When Mrs. Yamamoto raised her head again after this prolonged bout of weeping, the look of resolution on her face, somehow remote and pure, was apparent even to her visitor. Mrs. Matsumura, a little frightened, drew herself upright in her chair.

"This thing should never have been. When it is gone, everything will be as before." Speaking in riddles, Mrs. Yamamoto pushed back her disheveled hair and fixed a terrible, yet hauntingly beautiful, gaze upon the top of the table. In an instant she had snatched up the pearl from before her, and, with a gesture of no ordinary resolve, tossed it into her mouth. Raising her cup by the handle, her little finger elegantly extended, she washed the pearl down her throat with one gulp of cold Ceylon tea.

Mrs. Matsumura watched in horrified fascination. The affair was over before she had time to protest. This was the first time in her life she had seen a person swallow a pearl, and there was in Mrs. Yamamoto's manner something of that desperate finality one might expect to see in a person who had just drunk poison.

However, heroic though the action was, it was above all a touching incident, and not only did Mrs. Matsumura find her anger vanished into thin air, but so impressed was she by Mrs. Yamamoto's simplicity and purity that she could only think of that lady as a saint. And now Mrs. Matsumura's eyes too began to fill with tears, and she took Mrs. Yamamoto by the hand.

"Please forgive me, please forgive me," she said. "It was wrong of me."

For a while they wept together, holding each other's hands and vowing to each other that henceforth they would be the firmest of friends.

When Mrs. Sasaki heard rumors that the relationship between Mrs. Yamamoto and Mrs. Matsumura, which had been so strained, had suddenly improved, and that Mrs. Azuma and Mrs. Kasuga, who had been such good friends, had suddenly fallen out, she was at a loss to understand the reasons and contented herself with the reflection that nothing was impossible in this world.

However, being a woman of no strong scruples, Mrs. Sasaki requested a jeweler to refashion her ring and to produce a design into which two new pearls could be set, one large and one small, and this she wore quite openly, without further mishap.

Soon she had completely forgotten the small commotion on her birthday, and when anyone asked her age, she would give the same untruthful answers as ever. ❖

Translated by Geoffrey W. Sargent

---

12. **castigation** (kăsʹtĭ-gāʹshən): the act of punishing or criticizing severely.

WORDS TO KNOW   **scruple** (skrōoʹpəl) *n.* an ethical principle that inhibits action

RESPONDING
OPTIONS

FROM PERSONAL RESPONSE TO CRITICAL ANALYSIS

REFLECT

1. In your notebook, jot down your impressions of the five women and their problems.

RETHINK

2. Who do you think is most responsible for the confusion resulting from the loss of the pearl? Explain your opinion.

3. Why do you think these women behave as they do?

   Consider
   - how the women relate to one another
   - the positions in which the women are placed when the pearl is lost
   - the ways in which they try to save face
   - the mores of their culture

4. Explain whether you think Mrs. Yamamoto's swallowing of the pearl is a good resolution to the situation. What do you think you would have done?

5. If the story had been told by one of the women rather than by a narrator outside the story, how might "The Pearl" have been different?

RELATE

6. Do you think the incidents described in the story could happen in American society today? Why or why not?

ANOTHER PATHWAY

Cooperative Learning

Working in a small group, organize information from "The Pearl" in a time line. For each scene in the story, indicate the location and the events and characters involved. Share your time line with other groups of classmates. Then discuss what you learned about the story by doing this activity.

QUICKWRITES

1. Using a formal, polite tone, write the **dialogue** for a telephone conversation in which two characters in the story explain their behavior and offer apologies.

2. Imagine that you are directing an adaptation of "The Pearl" for the stage. To help your actresses prepare for their roles, write a brief **character sketch** of each of the five women.

3. Write a draft of a **satiric story** based on an awkward situation you've experienced. The writing you did for the Personal Connection on page 284 can help get you started.

📁 *PORTFOLIO Save your writing. You may want to use it later as a springboard to a piece for your portfolio.*

LITERARY CONCEPTS

Satire is a literary technique in which ideas, customs, behaviors, or institutions are ridiculed for the purpose of improving society. Satire may be gently witty, mildly abrasive, or bitterly critical, and it often uses exaggeration to force readers to see something in a more critical light. What aspects of society would you say "The Pearl" is ridiculing? What improvements to society might Mishima be trying to promote?

CONCEPT REVIEW: Tone In a small group, discuss Mishima's tone, or the attitude he takes toward his subject. List phrases or sentences from the story that support your group's opinions. Then, for each quotation, jot down what you think is being satirized.

ALTERNATIVE ACTIVITIES

1. Draw **caricatures** of the women in "The Pearl" using the medium of your choice. To visualize the characters, review the story, looking for descriptive details and mannerisms that help to portray both the action of the story and the emotional state of each woman. Then choose one line from the story as a caption for each drawing.

2. *Cooperative Learning* In a small group, create and rehearse a satirical **skit** that is a sequel to "The Pearl," a skit in which the five women meet again, at another social gathering. Then perform the skit for your classmates.

THE WRITER'S STYLE

Yukio Mishima wrote "The Pearl" in a formal style that the translator has tried to preserve. The phrasing is often elaborate and indirect. For example, in the fourth paragraph, Mishima wrote, "It now occurred to Mrs. Sasaki that she had no wish to be seen" instead of simply "Mrs. Sasaki did not want to be seen." Find three more examples of formal word choice or indirect phrasing. Why do you think Mishima used such a formal style for this particular story?

WORDS TO KNOW

On your paper, indicate whether the words in each numbered pair below are synonyms or antonyms.

1. infamy—notoriety
2. malicious—wicked
3. prudence—foolishness
4. fastidious—sloppy
5. impetuous—cautious
6. inauspicious—promising
7. incensed—infuriated
8. ambiguous—unclear
9. implicitly—unquestioningly
10. scruple—qualm

YUKIO MISHIMA

1925–1970

Born Kimitake Hiraoka (kē'mĭ-tä'kē hĭ'rä-ō'kä) in Tokyo, Japan, Yukio Mishima adopted his pen name in 1941 when he published his first long work, "The Forest in Full Bloom," in a school magazine. Three years later, as his school's star pupil, Mishima received a special graduation prize from the emperor of Japan. Mishima went on to study law at Tokyo University. He worked for several years in the Ministry of Public Finance before devoting himself to writing.

Mishima's first novel, the semiautobiographical *Confessions of a Mask,* became an instant popular and critical success when it was published in 1949. His writing career then flourished, and he became famous for his many novels, short stories, and essays, as well as for his film writing, acting, and directing. Throughout his lifetime, Mishima was devoted to Japanese culture, values, and history, and his fascination with the Japanese past led him to adapt many traditional plays for the modern stage. Shortly before his premature death by *seppuku,* a ritual form of suicide, Mishima wrote, "I came to wish to sacrifice myself for the old, beautiful tradition of Japan, which is disappearing very quickly day by day."

OTHER WORKS *The Sound of Waves, The Temple of the Golden Pavilion, The Sailor Who Fell from Grace with the Sea, Death in Midsummer and Other Stories, Five Modern No Plays*

PREVIEWING

NONFICTION

Black Men and Public Space

Brent Staples **United States**

PERSONAL CONNECTION

Consider the types of people you encounter on the street that make you fearful or uneasy. Why do you think you feel uncomfortable around these people? Are your fears reasonable, or do you think they might be exaggerated? In a group discussion, share your experiences and opinions with your classmates.

Outdoor mall in Manhattan, New York City.
Copyright © Rafael Macia/Photo Researchers, Inc.

CULTURAL CONNECTION

Much of the news we are exposed to on television, on the radio, and in newspapers concerns crime; the number of reported car jackings, drive-by shootings, robberies, assaults, and even murders seems to be ever on the rise. Crime rates increase for a variety of reasons, including population growth, drug use, inadequate education, and lack of economic opportunities, especially for the urban poor. Because crime has become widespread, people are often fearful or suspicious of strangers—particularly those that are different from themselves—even when the strangers mean no harm. In the essay you are about to read, writer Brent Staples shows that while crime itself is a problem, the fear in which people sometimes live creates another set of problems.

WRITING CONNECTION

If you were walking down the street late at night, do you think other people on the street might feel afraid of you? Explore your thoughts in a paragraph or two in your notebook. Then put yourself in Brent Staples's shoes as you read his essay.

Fear of Crime Fuels Debate

CRIME WAVE HITS THE CITY

Crime Rates on the Rise

BLACK MEN AND PUBLIC

Homage to Sterling Brown (1972), Charles White. Collection of Dr. Edmund Gordon, courtesy of the Heritage Gallery, Los Angeles.

S P A C E

BRENT STAPLES

My first victim was a woman—white, well dressed, probably in her early twenties. I came upon her late one evening on a deserted street in Hyde Park, a relatively <u>affluent</u> neighborhood in an otherwise mean, impoverished section of Chicago. As I swung onto the avenue behind her, there seemed to be a discreet, uninflammatory[1] distance between us. Not so. She cast back a worried glance. To her, the youngish black man—a broad six feet two inches with a beard and billowing hair, both hands shoved into the pockets of a bulky military jacket—seemed menacingly close. After a few more quick glimpses, she picked up her pace and was soon running in earnest. Within seconds she disappeared into a cross street.

That was more than a decade ago. I was twenty-two years old, a graduate student newly arrived at the University of Chicago. It was in the echo of that terrified woman's footfalls that I first began to know the <u>unwieldy</u> inheritance I'd

---

1. **uninflammatory** (ŭnˊĭn-flămˊə-tôrˊē): not likely to rouse excitement, anger, or violence.

298

come into—the ability to alter public space in ugly ways. It was clear that she thought herself the quarry[2] of a mugger, a rapist, or worse. Suffering a bout of insomnia, however, I was stalking sleep, not defenseless wayfarers. As a softy who is scarcely able to take a knife to a raw chicken—let alone hold one to a person's throat—I was surprised, embarrassed, and dismayed all at once. Her flight made me feel like an accomplice in tyranny. It also made it clear that I was indistinguishable from the muggers who occasionally seeped into the area from the surrounding ghetto. That first encounter, and those that followed, signified that a vast, unnerving gulf lay between nighttime pedestrians—particularly women—and me. And I soon gathered that being perceived as dangerous is a hazard in itself. I only needed to turn a corner into a dicey[3] situation, or crowd some frightened, armed person in a foyer somewhere, or make an errant move after being pulled over by a policeman. Where fear and weapons meet—and they often do in urban America—there is always the possibility of death.

In that first year, my first away from my hometown, I was to become thoroughly familiar with the language of fear. At dark, shadowy intersections, I could cross in front of a car stopped at a traffic light and elicit the *thunk, thunk, thunk, thunk* of the driver—black, white, male, or female—hammering down the door locks. On less traveled streets after dark, I grew accustomed to but never comfortable with people crossing to the other side of the street rather than pass me. Then there were the standard unpleasantries with policemen, doormen, bouncers, cabdrivers, and others whose business it is to screen out troublesome individuals *before* there is any nastiness.

I moved to New York nearly two years ago, and I have remained an avid night walker. In central Manhattan, the near-constant crowd cover minimizes tense one-on-one street encounters. Elsewhere—in SoHo,[4] for example, where sidewalks are narrow and tightly spaced buildings shut out the sky—things can get very taut indeed.

After dark, on the warrenlike[5] streets of Brooklyn where I live, I often see women who fear the worst from me. They seem to have set their faces on neutral, and with their purse straps strung across their chests bandolier-style, they forge ahead as though bracing themselves against being tackled. I understand, of course, that the danger they perceive is not a hallucination. Women are particularly vulnerable to street violence, and young black males are drastically overrepresented among the perpetrators of that violence. Yet these truths are no solace against the kind of alienation that comes of being ever the suspect, a fearsome entity[6] with whom pedestrians avoid making eye contact.

It is not altogether clear to me how I reached the ripe old age of twenty-two without being conscious of the lethality[7] nighttime pedestrians attributed to me. Perhaps it was because in Chester, Pennsylvania, the small, angry industrial town where I came of age in the 1960s, I was scarcely noticeable against a backdrop of

---

2. **quarry:** prey; object of pursuit.

3. **dicey:** risky; hazardous.

4. **SoHo** (sō'hō'): a neighborhood in Manhattan.

5. **warrenlike** (wôr'ən-līk): like a rabbit warren, the area in which a colony of rabbits lives in burrows; like a maze, a place where one may easily become lost.

6. **entity** (ĕn'tĭ-tē): thing or being.

7. **lethality** (lē-thăl'ĭ-tē): the ability to cause extreme harm or death.

gang warfare, street knifings, and murders. I grew up one of the good boys, had perhaps a half-dozen fistfights. In retrospect, my shyness of combat has clear sources.

As a boy, I saw countless tough guys locked away; I have since buried several, too. They were babies, really—a teenage cousin, a brother of twenty-two, a childhood friend in his mid-twenties—all gone down in episodes of bravado[8] played out in the streets. I came to doubt the virtues of intimidation early on. I chose, perhaps unconsciously, to remain a shadow—timid, but a survivor.

The fearsomeness mistakenly attributed to me in public places often has a perilous flavor. The most frightening of these confusions occurred in the late 1970s and early 1980s, when I worked as a journalist in Chicago. One day, rushing into the office of a magazine I was writing for with a deadline story in hand, I was mistaken for a burglar. The office manager called security and, with an ad hoc posse,[9] pursued me through the labyrinthine[10] halls, nearly to my editor's door. I had no way of proving who I was. I could only move briskly toward the company of someone who knew me.

Another time I was on assignment for a local paper and killing time before an interview. I entered a jewelry store on the city's affluent Near North Side. The proprietor excused herself and returned with an enormous red Doberman pinscher straining at the end of a leash. She stood, the dog extended toward me, silent to my questions, her eyes bulging nearly out of her head. I took a cursory look around, nodded, and bade her good night.

Relatively speaking, however, I never fared as badly as another black male journalist. He went to nearby Waukegan, Illinois, a couple of summers ago to work on a story about a murderer who was born there. Mistaking the reporter for the killer, police officers hauled him from his car at gunpoint and but for his press credentials would probably have tried to book him. Such episodes are not uncommon. Black men trade tales like this all the time.

Over the years, I learned to smother the rage I felt at so often being taken for a criminal. Not to do so would surely have led to madness. I now take precautions to make myself less threatening. I move about with care, particularly late in the evening. I give a wide berth[11] to nervous people on subway platforms during the wee hours, particularly when I have exchanged business clothes for jeans. If I happen to be entering a building behind some people who appear skittish,[12] I may walk by, letting them clear the lobby before I return, so as not to seem to be following them. I have been calm and extremely congenial on those rare occasions when I've been pulled over by the police.

And on late-evening constitutionals[13] I employ what has proved to be an excellent tension-reducing measure: I whistle melodies from Beethoven and Vivaldi and the more popular classical composers. Even steely New Yorkers hunching toward nighttime destinations seem to relax, and occasionally they even join the tune. Virtually everybody seems to sense that a mugger wouldn't be warbling bright, sunny selections from Vivaldi's *Four Seasons*. It is my equivalent to the cowbell that hikers wear when they know they are in bear country. ❖

---

8. **bravado** (brə-vä′dō): pretended courage or defiant confidence when there is really little or none.

9. **ad hoc posse:** a group of people that has been brought together to form a search party.

10. **labyrinthine** (lăb′ə-rĭn′thĭn): like a labyrinth, or maze.

11. **wide berth:** ample space or distance to avoid an unwanted consequence.

12. **skittish:** nervous; jumpy.

13. **constitutionals:** walks taken for one's health.

WORDS
TO
KNOW

retrospect (rĕt′rə-spĕkt′) *n.* a review or examination of things in the past
cursory (kûr′sə-rē) *adj.* performed with haste and little attention to detail
congenial (kən-jēn′yəl) *adj.* agreeable; sociable; sympathetic

RESPONDING OPTIONS

FROM PERSONAL RESPONSE TO CRITICAL ANALYSIS

REFLECT 1. What is your response to this essay? Record your response in your notebook.

RETHINK 2. How would you describe Brent Staples?
Consider
- his description of himself in the first two paragraphs
- what he says about his childhood
- the fact that he takes precautions to make himself "less threatening"

3. What is your opinion of the way people respond to Staples? Be sure to draw on examples from the selection in explaining your point of view.

4. Do you approve of the ways Staples chooses to deal with the fears of others? Explain your opinion.

5. Why do you think Staples concludes his essay with the image of a hiker wearing a bell in bear country?

RELATE 6. Think back to your discussion in the Personal Connection and to what you wrote for the Writing Connection on page 297. Did anything in Staples's essay cause you to reexamine your own feelings and behavior?

ANOTHER PATHWAY

Write a review of "Black Men and Public Space" for a column in a student newspaper. Explain your opinion about the essay and about the problems Staples describes. Be sure to include a summary of the essay in your review.

QUICKWRITES

1. Write a **descriptive paragraph** of Staples from the point of view of the female "victim" presented in the first paragraph of the essay. Then write another paragraph that describes Staples as he sees himself.

2. Write a **dramatic scene** based on one of the incidents in Staples's essay. Include dialogue as well as stage directions describing action.

3. In an **editorial** for your school or local newspaper, explain how people's prejudices or fears have threatened or damaged the dignity of African-American men or some other group.

4. Draft a **personal narrative** describing a time when another person did not perceive the truth about you.

PORTFOLIO Save your writing. You may want to use it later as a springboard to a piece for your portfolio.

LITERARY CONCEPTS

Structure is the way in which a work of literature is put together. In prose, structure is the arrangement of units or parts of a selection. Staples begins his essay "Black Men and Public Space" by describing a woman's perception of him that contrasts with his true identity. Next, he describes the predicament he faces as an African American and elaborates on his experience by providing specific examples. He concludes by explaining how he has adapted his behavior over time. With a partner, discuss how the structure of the essay affected your thoughts and feelings about the author. How did your ideas about him change from the beginning to the end of the selection?

LITERARY LINKS

What do you think Martin Luther King, Jr., Coretta Scott King, or another person featured in "Montgomery Boycott" might have said to Staples about his predicament and about the way he altered his behavior to make himself seem less threatening?

ART CONNECTION

Why do you think the painting on page 298, titled *Homage to Sterling Brown,* was chosen to accompany the essay "Black Men and Public Space"?

Detail of *Homage to Sterling Brown* (1972), Charles White. Collection of Dr. Edmund Gordon, courtesy of Heritage Gallery, Los Angeles.

WORDS TO KNOW

EXERCISE A Write the letter of the word that is most nearly the opposite of the word in bold print.

1. **cursory:** (a) polite, (b) unclear, (c) thorough
2. **unwieldy:** (a) clumsy, (b) manageable, (c) huge
3. **congenial:** (a) ill, (b) unspoken, (c) unfriendly
4. **taut:** (a) relaxed, (b) stern, (c) ignorant
5. **retrospect:** (a) review, (b) test, (c) forecast
6. **affluent:** (a) dry, (b) poor, (c) bilingual
7. **avid:** (a) uninterested, (b) wet, (c) eager
8. **solace:** (a) distress, (b) friendship, (c) dimness
9. **elicit:** (a) allow, (b) stifle, (c) accuse
10. **errant:** (a) roaming, (b) false, (c) truthful

EXERCISE B Working with a partner, write the ten Words to Know on small pieces of paper, fold the pieces, and mix them up. Then take turns choosing a word and drawing a picture to illustrate the word for your partner. To make the game more challenging, set a time limit for drawing and guessing the words.

ACROSS THE CURRICULUM

Psychology Interview a police officer to find out how to avoid becoming a victim of a street crime or how to avoid being perceived as a threat. Share your findings with the class in an oral report.

BRENT STAPLES

The incidents Brent Staples recounts in this essay were incorporated into his 1994 memoir, *Parallel Time: Growing Up in Black and White,* a work that shows how he escaped his difficult home life and impoverished neighborhood in the racially mixed industrial city of Chester, Pennsylvania. Staples came from a family of nine children, and gang violence, drugs, and street crime were prevalent in his community. In fact, Staples's own brother Blake became a drug dealer and

1951–

was shot to death at the age of 22 by a former customer. By the time his younger brother was killed, however, Staples had already graduated from college and earned his doctorate in psychology from the University of Chicago. He then became a journalist, writing for the *Chicago Sun Times* and other publications before joining the staff of the *New York Times* in 1985. He is now on that paper's editorial board, and he writes on politics and culture.

PREVIEWING

POETRY

Miss Rosie
Lucille Clifton United States

Kitchenette Building
Gwendolyn Brooks United States

PERSONAL CONNECTION

Think about a person or a place in your everyday life that means something to you. How would you describe your subject? What essential images would you use if you were to write a poem about that person or place? Brainstorm a list of words or phrases to describe your subject. Remember that sometimes you can define what something is by showing what it is not.

BIOGRAPHICAL CONNECTION

The poems you are about to read were written by two widely read and critically acclaimed African-American poets. Lucille Clifton, author of "Miss Rosie," has been inspired to write by the urban community in which she lives. She also acknowledges that she writes from her experience as a woman, or more particularly, as a black woman. Like Lucille Clifton, Gwendolyn Brooks writes from personal experience and from what she sees and hears in her community. She says, "In my writing I am proud to feature people and their concerns, their troubles as well as their joys." Her poem "Kitchenette Building" is about everyday life in a type of apartment house found in low-income urban areas, in which the small apartments have compact kitchens and the bathrooms are shared by the tenants on a floor.

READING CONNECTION

Making Inferences in Poetry An inference is a logical guess or conclusion based on known facts or evidence. When reading a poem, you can make inferences from ideas that are stated directly as well as from ideas that are presented in figurative language. In the two poems that follow, the literal and figurative details allow you to make inferences about the everyday people and places they describe. In your notebook, make a chart like the one below for each of the two poems and fill it out as you read.

Detail from Poem	Inference
"old man's shoes with the little toe cut out"	She's too poor to buy shoes for herself.

Public housing project in Chicago.
AP/Wide World Photos.

Miss Rosie

Lucille Clifton

When I watch you
wrapped up like garbage
sitting, surrounded by the smell
of too old potato peels
5   or
when I watch you
in your old man's shoes
with the little toe cut out
sitting, waiting for your mind
10   like next week's grocery
I say
when I watch you
you wet brown bag of a woman
who used to be the best looking gal in Georgia
15   used to be called the Georgia Rose
I stand up
through your destruction
I stand up

FROM PERSONAL RESPONSE TO CRITICAL ANALYSIS

REFLECT   1. What person or persons does Miss Rosie remind you of? Discuss your response with a partner.

RETHINK   2. Describe your mental picture of Miss Rosie.

3. How do you think the speaker feels about Miss Rosie?
   Consider
   • why the speaker keeps repeating "when I watch you"
   • the meaning of "I stand up / through your destruction" (lines 16–17)

4. What speculations can you make about the way Miss Rosie used to live and about the way she lives now? Use information from the chart you created for the Reading Connection on page 303.

Kitchenette Building

Gwendolyn Brooks

Shaded Lives (1988), Phoebe Beasley. Collage, 40″ × 30″, collection of Alex Gallery, Washington, D.C.

We are things of dry hours and the
   involuntary plan,
Grayed in, and gray. "Dream" makes a giddy
   sound, not strong
Like "rent," "feeding a wife," "satisfying
   a man."

But could a dream send up through onion fumes
5 Its white and violet, fight with fried potatoes
And yesterday's garbage ripening in the hall,
Flutter, or sing an aria[1] down these rooms

Even if we were willing to let it in,
Had time to warm it, keep it very clean,
10 Anticipate a message, let it begin?

We wonder. But not well! not for a minute!
Since Number Five is out of the bathroom now,
We think of lukewarm water, hope to get in it.

---

1. **aria** (är′ē-ə): a song or melody for a solo voice in an opera.

RESPONDING
OPTIONS

FROM PERSONAL RESPONSE TO CRITICAL ANALYSIS

REFLECT 1. What images from everyday life came to mind as you were reading "Kitchenette Building"? Describe or draw them in your notebook.

RETHINK 2. What words and phrases would you use to describe the kind of life the tenants of the kitchenette building lead?

   Consider
   - what the phrases "dry hours," "involuntary plan," and "grayed in, and gray" might mean (lines 1–2)
   - what lines 4–7 say about the tenants' environment
   - the concerns named in lines 3 and 12–13
   - information from the chart you created for the Reading Connection on page 303

ANOTHER PATHWAY

Cooperative Learning

With a small group of classmates, prepare a dramatic reading of the poems. To do this, you will first need to discuss the meaning of each poem and determine the tone. Present your reading to the entire class.

3. How would you describe the kind of dream this poem is talking about? Use details from the poem to support your response.

4. Does the speaker seem to think a dream can survive in this building?

RELATE 5. Do you think that the characters in "Miss Rosie" and "Kitchenette Building" are prisoners of the same circumstances? What is similar and what is different about their situations?

6. Which poem's imagery do you think has stronger sensory appeal? Why?

LITERARY CONCEPTS

The **speaker** in a poem is the voice that talks to the reader, similar to the narrator in fiction. Through inference the reader can learn many things about the speaker in a poem, insights that in turn enhance the poem's meaning. Who is the speaker in "Miss Rosie"? What do you think is that speaker's relationship to Rosie? Who is the speaker in "Kitchenette Building"? Why do you think the speaker uses the pronoun "we"?

CONCEPT REVIEW: Theme Do the messages about life communicated in these two poems apply to both the rich and the poor? Explain your answer.

QUICKWRITES

1. Adapt each poem into a new **poem** with a different speaker. For example, you might make Miss Rosie the speaker of one poem.

2. Prepare a **report card** for Clifton and Brooks in which you evaluate each poem on the basis of theme, imagery, word choice, and overall effectiveness.

📁 *PORTFOLIO Save your writing. You may want to use it later as a springboard to a piece for your portfolio.*

ALTERNATIVE ACTIVITIES

1. Working with a small group of classmates, select additional poems by Gwendolyn Brooks and Lucille Clifton for **oral reading**. After presenting the poems, try to identify the speaker of each one, and compare the content and style of the new poems with that of "Miss Rosie" and "Kitchenette Building."

2. Paint or sketch two **portraits** of Miss Rosie, one showing her as she is today and another showing her when she was called the Georgia Rose.

CRITIC'S CORNER

According to critic Audrey T. McCluskey, "Lucille Clifton writes with conviction; she always takes a moral and hopeful stance." Based on your reading of "Miss Rosie," do you think this statement is true? Would you say the observation is true of Gwendolyn Brooks? Explain your opinions.

THE WRITER'S STYLE

Lucille Clifton once said. "I am interested in trying to render big ideas in a simple way." To what extent does "Miss Rosie" illustrate Clifton's approach to writing?

LUCILLE CLIFTON

1936–

Lucille Clifton writes frequently about the struggles and triumphs of African-American families living in urban communities, emphasizing "endurance and strength through adversity." Of her youth in Depew, New York, Clifton says, "I grew up a well-loved child in a loving family, and so I have always known that being poor, which we were, had nothing to do with lovingness or familyness or character." She tries to bring this understanding to her writing, particularly to her works for young people. A mother of six, Clifton has published more than 20 books for children, including a popular series about a little boy named Everett Anderson. Among her collections of poetry for adults are *Good Times,* which includes "Miss Rosie," and *Book of Light.* She also coauthored the Emmy Award–winning television program *Free to Be . . . You and Me.* Clifton has received many awards and honors for her writing, including a Pulitzer Prize nomination and National Endowment for the Arts awards. She served as the poet laureate of Maryland from 1979 to 1982.

OTHER WORKS *Good News About the Earth: New Poems; Generations: A Memoir*

GWENDOLYN BROOKS

1917–

A lifelong resident of Chicago, Illinois, Gwendolyn Brooks frequently writes about the lives of the urban poor. As a child she was an avid reader, and she began writing poetry at a very early age. Brooks was encouraged by such well-known poets as James Weldon Johnson and Langston Hughes after sending them samples of her work, and she became a published poet at the age of 13.

In 1950, Brooks became the first African-American author to win a Pulitzer Prize. She was named the poet laureate of Illinois in 1968, and at the age of 68, she became the first African-American woman appointed Poetry Consultant to the Library of Congress. Brooks is a great champion of young writers, visiting schools nationwide and sponsoring literary awards programs in her home state. Through her poetry, Brooks reveals what she calls the "neglected miracles of everyday experience," and she encourages her students to do the same. She offers students this reminder: "Your poem does not need to tell your reader everything. A little mystery is fascinating."

OTHER WORKS *Annie Allen, Maud Martha, Selected Poems, The World of Gwendolyn Brooks, Blacks*

LASERLINKS
• *AUTHOR BACKGROUND*

PREVIEWING

NONFICTION

from Night

Elie Wiesel (el'ē vē-sĕl') **Romania / United States**

PERSONAL CONNECTION

With a small group of classmates, share what you know about the Holocaust, the slaughter of millions of Jews in Europe during World War II. Where did you learn what you know? How did you react when you learned it?

HISTORICAL CONNECTION

In the 1920s and 1930s, Germany was in the throes of a major economic depression; millions were unemployed. When Adolph Hitler became chancellor in 1933, he promised people jobs while providing them with a scapegoat for the nation's problems: the Jews. Hitler's Nazi party began its campaign against the Jews by revoking their citizenship, boycotting their businesses, and banning them from certain professions.

Germany's invasion of Poland in 1939 marked the beginning of World War II. Hitler's goal was to expand his empire across Europe and to eliminate the Jews at the same time. In Germany and from each nation Germany occupied, Jews—as well as gypsies, homosexuals, and intellectuals and artists who opposed Hitler—were transported to the concentration camps. Everyone entering the camps was tattooed with a number on the left forearm, replacing people's names with numbers. Most of the 6 million Jews who were killed during World War II died in concentration camps. They were put to death in gas chambers, were shot by firing squads, or succumbed to starvation, torture, and disease. This selection is from the memoir of a survivor who was only 15 when he was imprisoned.

WRITING CONNECTION

In your notebook, list words and phrases that you think might describe the thoughts and feelings of someone living in a death camp during the Holocaust. As you read, compare your list with Elie Wiesel's thoughts and feelings.

Major Concentration Camps in Europe, World War II

LASERLINKS
• *HISTORICAL CONNECTION*

Survivors of a Nazi concentration camp, 1945. The Bettmann Archive.

FROM
NIGHT

Elie Wiesel

The SS[1] gave us a fine New Year's gift.

We had just come back from work. As soon as we had passed through the door of the camp, we sensed something different in the air. Roll call did not take so long as usual. The evening soup was given out with great speed and swallowed down at once in anguish.

1. SS: an elite military unit of the Nazi party that served as Hitler's personal guard and as a special security force.

I was no longer in the same block as my father. I had been transferred to another unit, the building one, where, twelve hours a day, I had to drag heavy blocks of stone about. The head of my new block was a German Jew, small of <u>stature</u>, with piercing eyes. He told us that evening that no one would be allowed to go out after the evening soup. And soon a terrible word was circulating—selection.

We knew what that meant. An SS man would examine us. Whenever he found a weak one, a *musulman* as we called them, he would write his number down: good for the crematory.

After soup, we gathered together between the beds. The veterans said:

"You're lucky to have been brought here so late. This camp is paradise today, compared with what it was like two years ago. Buna[2] was a real hell then. There was no water, no blankets, less soup and bread. At night we slept almost naked, and it was below thirty degrees. The corpses were collected in hundreds every day. The work was hard. Today, this is a little paradise. The Kapos[3] had orders to kill a certain number of prisoners every day. And every week— selection. A merciless selection. . . . Yes, you're lucky."

"Stop it! Be quiet!" I begged. "You can tell your stories tomorrow or on some other day."

They burst out laughing. They were not veterans for nothing.

"Are you scared? So were we scared. And there was plenty to be scared of in those days."

The old men stayed in their corner, dumb, motionless, haunted. Some were praying.

An hour's delay. In an hour, we should know the verdict—death or a reprieve.

And my father? Suddenly I remembered him. How would he pass the selection? He had aged so much. . . .

The head of our block had never been outside concentration camps since 1933. He had already been through all the slaughterhouses, all the factories of death. At about nine o'clock, he took up his position in our midst:

"Achtung!"[4]

There was instant silence.

"Listen carefully to what I am going to say." (For the first time, I heard his voice quiver.) "In a few moments the selection will begin. You must get completely undressed. Then one by one you go before the SS doctors. I hope you will all succeed in getting through. But you must help your own chances. Before you go into the next room, move about in some way so that you give yourselves a little color. Don't walk slowly, run! Run as if the devil were after you! Don't look at the SS. Run, straight in front of you!"

He broke off for a moment, then added:

"And, the essential thing, don't be afraid!"

Here was a piece of advice we should have liked very much to be able to follow.

I got undressed, leaving my clothes on the bed. There was no danger of anyone stealing them this evening.

Tibi and Yossi, who had changed their unit at the same time as I had, came up to me and said:

"Let's keep together. We shall be stronger."

Yossi was murmuring something between his teeth. He must have been praying. I had never realized that Yossi was a believer. I had even always thought the reverse. Tibi was silent, very pale. All the prisoners in the block stood naked

---

2. **Buna** (boō'nə): a forced-labor camp in Poland, near the Auschwitz concentration camp.

3. **Kapos** (kä'pōz): the prisoners who served as foremen, or heads, of each building or cell block.

4. **Achtung!** (äкн-tŏŏng') *German:* Attention!

WORDS
TO
KNOW   **stature** (stăch'ər) *n.* a person's height

310

between the beds. This must be how one stands at the last judgment.

"They're coming!"

There were three SS officers standing around the <u>notorious</u> Dr. Mengele,[5] who had received us at Birkenau.[6] The head of the block, with an attempt at a smile, asked us:

"Ready?"

Yes, we were ready. So were the SS doctors. Dr. Mengele was holding a list in his hand: our numbers. He made a sign to the head of the block: "We can begin!" As if this were a game!

The first to go by were the "officials" of the block: *Stubenaelteste,*[7] Kapos, foremen, all in perfect physical condition of course! Then came the ordinary prisoners' turn. Dr. Mengele took stock of them from head to foot. Every now and then, he wrote a number down. One single thought filled my mind: not to let my number be taken; not to show my left arm.

There were only Tibi and Yossi in front of me. They passed. I had time to notice that Mengele had not written their numbers down. Someone pushed me. It was my turn. I ran without looking back. My head was spinning: you're too thin, you're too weak, you're too thin, you're good for the furnace. . . . The race seemed <u>interminable</u>. I thought I had been running for years. . . . You're too thin, you're too weak. . . . At last I had arrived exhausted. When I regained my breath, I questioned Yossi and Tibi:

"Was I written down?"

"No," said Yossi. He added, smiling: "In any case, he couldn't have written you down, you were running too fast. . . ."

I began to laugh. I was glad. I would have

liked to kiss him. At that moment, what did the others matter! I hadn't been written down.

Those whose numbers had been noted stood apart, abandoned by the whole world. Some were weeping in silence.

> ## ONE SINGLE THOUGHT FILLED MY MIND: NOT TO LET MY NUMBER BE TAKEN; NOT TO SHOW MY LEFT ARM.

The SS officers went away. The head of the block appeared, his face reflecting the general weariness.

"Everything went off all right. Don't worry. Nothing is going to happen to anyone. To anyone."

Again he tried to smile. A poor, <u>emaciated,</u> dried-up Jew questioned him avidly in a trembling voice:

"But . . . but, *Blockaelteste,*[8] they did write me down!"

The head of the block let his anger break out. What! Did someone refuse to believe him!

"What's the matter now? Am I telling lies then? I tell you once and for all, nothing's going to happen to you! To anyone! You're wallowing

---

5. **Dr. Mengele** (mĕng′ə-lə): Josef Mengele, a German doctor who personally selected nearly half a million prisoners to die in gas chambers at Auschwitz. He also became infamous for his medical experiments on inmates.

6. **Birkenau** (bîr′kə-nou): a large section of the Auschwitz concentration camp.

7. *Stubenaelteste* (shtōō′bən-ĕl′tə-stə): a rank of Kapos; literally "elders of the rooms."

8. *Blockaelteste* (blôk′ĕl′tə-stə): a rank of Kapos; literally "elders of the building."

in your own despair, you fool!"

The bell rang, a signal that the selection had been completed throughout the camp.

With all my might I began to run to Block 36. I met my father on the way. He came up to me:

"Well? So you passed?"

"Yes. And you?"

"Me too."

How we breathed again, now! My father had brought me a present—half a ration of bread obtained in exchange for a piece of rubber, found at the warehouse, which would do to sole a shoe.

The bell. Already we must separate, go to bed. Everything was regulated by the bell. It gave me orders, and I automatically obeyed them. I hated it. Whenever I dreamed of a better world, I could only imagine a universe with no bells.

Several days had elapsed. We no longer thought about the selection. We went to work as usual, loading heavy stones into railway wagons. Rations had become more meager: this was the only change.

We had risen before dawn, as on every day. We had received the black coffee, the ration of bread. We were about to set out for the yard as usual. The head of the block arrived, running.

"Silence for a moment. I have a list of numbers here. I'm going to read them to you. Those whose numbers I call won't be going to work this morning; they'll stay behind in the camp."

And, in a soft voice, he read out about ten numbers. We had understood. These were numbers chosen at the selection. Dr. Mengele had not forgotten.

The head of the block went toward his room. Ten prisoners surrounded him, hanging onto his clothes:

"Save us! You promised . . . ! We want to go to the yard. We're strong enough to work. We're good workers. We can . . . we will . . . ."

He tried to calm them to reassure them about their fate, to explain to them that the fact that they were staying behind in the camp did not mean much, had no tragic significance.

> "THOSE WHOSE NUMBERS I CALL WON'T BE GOING TO WORK THIS MORNING; THEY'LL STAY BEHIND IN THE CAMP."

"After all, I stay here myself every day," he added.

It was a somewhat feeble argument. He realized it, and without another word went and shut himself up in his room.

The bell had just rung.

"Form up!"

It scarcely mattered now that the work was hard. The essential thing was to be as far away as possible from the block, from the crucible of death, from the center of hell.

I saw my father running toward me. I became frightened all of a sudden.

"What's the matter?"

Out of breath, he could hardly open his mouth.

"Me, too . . . me, too . . . ! They told me to stay behind in the camp."

They had written down his number without his being aware of it.

"What will happen?" I asked in anguish.

But it was he who tried to reassure me.

"It isn't certain yet. There's still a chance of escape. They're going to do another selection today . . . a decisive selection."

I was silent.

He felt that his time was short. He spoke quickly. He would have liked to say so many things. His speech grew confused; his voice choked. He knew that I would have to go in a few moments. He would have to stay behind alone, so very alone.

"Look, take this knife," he said to me. "I don't need it any longer. It might be useful to you. And take this spoon as well. Don't sell them. Quickly! Go on. Take what I'm giving you!"

The inheritance.

"Don't talk like that, Father." (I felt that I would break into sobs.) "I don't want you to say that. Keep the spoon and knife. You need them as much as I do. We shall see each other again this evening, after work."

He looked at me with his tired eyes, veiled with despair. He went on:

"I'm asking this of you. . . . Take them. Do as I ask, my son. We have no time. . . . Do as your father asks."

Our Kapo yelled that we should start.

The unit set out toward the camp gate. Left, right! I bit my lips. My father had stayed by the block, leaning against the wall. Then he began to run, to catch up with us. Perhaps he had forgotten something he wanted to say to me. . . . But we were marching too quickly . . . Left, right!

We were already at the gate. They counted us, to the <u>din</u> of military music. We were outside.

The whole day, I wandered about as if sleep-walking. Now and then Tibi and Yossi would throw me a brotherly word. The Kapo, too, tried to reassure me. He had given me easier work today. I felt sick at heart. How well they were treating me! Like an orphan! I thought: even now, my father is still helping me.

I did not know myself what I wanted—for the day to pass quickly or not. I was afraid of finding myself alone that night. How good it would be to die here!

At last we began the return journey. How I longed for orders to run!

The military march. The gate. The camp.

I ran to Block 36.

Were there still miracles on this earth? He was alive. He had escaped the second selection. He had been able to prove that he was still useful. . . . I gave him back his knife and spoon. ❖

WORDS TO KNOW   **din** (dĭn) *n.* a jumble of loud noises

from Nobel Prize Acceptance Speech

Elie Wiesel

It is with a profound sense of humility that I accept the honor you have chosen to bestow upon me. I know: your choice transcends me. This both frightens and pleases me.

It frightens me because I wonder: do I have the right to represent the multitudes who have perished? Do I have the right to accept this great honor on their behalf? I do not. That would be presumptuous. No one may speak for the dead, no one may interpret their mutilated dreams and visions.

It pleases me because I may say that this honor belongs to all the survivors and their children, and through us, to the Jewish people with whose destiny I have always identified.

I remember: it happened yesterday or eternities ago. A young Jewish boy discovered the kingdom of night. I remember his bewilderment, I remember his anguish. It all happened so fast. The ghetto. The deportation. The sealed cattle car. The fiery altar upon which the history of our people and the future of mankind were meant to be sacrificed.

I remember: he asked his father: "Can this be true? This is the 20th century, not the Middle Ages. Who would allow such crimes to be committed? How could the world remain silent?"

And now the boy is turning to me: "Tell me," he asks. "What have you done with my future? What have you done with your life?"

And I tell him that I have tried. That I have tried to keep memory alive, that I have tried to fight those who would forget. Because if we forget, we are guilty, we are accomplices.

And then I explained to him how naive we were, that the world did know and remain silent. And that is why I swore never to be silent whenever and wherever human beings endure suffering and humiliation. We must always take sides. Neutrality helps the oppressor, never the victim. Silence encourages the tormentor, never the tormented.

RESPONDING OPTIONS

FROM PERSONAL RESPONSE TO CRITICAL ANALYSIS

REFLECT

1. Make a sketch, painting, or drawing that depicts your reaction to this selection about the Holocaust.

RETHINK

2. What do you consider the worst circumstance in this portion of Wiesel's concentration camp experiences? Explain.

3. What are your impressions of the people portrayed in this excerpt?

RELATE

4. How would you describe Wiesel's tone?
   Consider
   - his saying that the SS "gave us a fine New Year's gift"
   - his calling the knife and spoon his "inheritance"

5. Why do you think Wiesel called his book *Night*?
   Consider
   - the circumstances he recounts
   - what the word *night* might symbolize
   - Wiesel's remarks on accepting the Nobel Peace Prize, provided in the Insight

6. Do you agree with Wiesel's statement from his Nobel Prize acceptance speech that "neutrality helps the oppressor, never the victim"? Support your opinion.

ANOTHER PATHWAY

Cooperative Learning

What can you glean about life—and death—in a concentration camp on the basis of this short excerpt from *Night*? Get together with a small group of classmates and make a list of generalizations you can draw about people's experiences in the camps. Also list the words and phrases from the selection that have led you to your conclusions.

QUICKWRITES

1. Rewrite the **excerpt** from Wiesel's father's point of view. Try to show what it might have felt like to fear for your life—and that of your son—in these circumstances.

2. Imagine that you are one of the soldiers who helped to liberate a concentration camp at the end of World War II and that the first thing you saw when you arrived was the group of prisoners pictured on page 309. Using the photo and Wiesel's description of his experiences as your inspiration, write an **eyewitness account** of your experience.

3. Make a **list of questions** you would ask Wiesel if you had the chance to talk to him.

📁 *PORTFOLIO Save your writing. You may want to use it later as a springboard to a piece for your portfolio.*

LITERARY CONCEPTS

Style is the way in which a literary work is written. Style refers not to what is said but to how it is said. Elements that contribute to a writer's personal style include word choice; sentence length, structure, and variety; tone; imagery; and use of dialogue. In this selection, for example, Wiesel tends to use simple vocabulary and short sentences along with questions and exclamations. How do you think these elements of style affect Wiesel's tone? What overall impact does this style have on readers? Review the selection again and identify other elements of Wiesel's style.

ALTERNATIVE ACTIVITIES

1. Perform a **dramatic reading** of Wiesel's Nobel Prize acceptance speech. You may read the portion on page 314 or obtain a copy of the complete speech from the *New York Times,* December 11, 1986.

2. Read all of *Night* to find out more about Wiesel's experiences during the Holocaust, as well as what his life was like before being deported and imprisoned. Present a summary in an **oral report.**

ACROSS THE CURRICULUM

Media Obtain and view a video recording of *Schindler's List,* the 1993 film about a man who enabled more than a thousand Jews to escape the Holocaust. Discuss the impact of the film in an oral review.

WORDS TO KNOW

Review the Words to Know at the bottom of the selection pages. Then, on your paper, indicate which of these words could best replace the italicized word or phrase in each sentence below.

1. To those in concentration camps, the war seemed *as if it would never end.*

2. Auschwitz was *famous in a negative way* for torture and mass murder.

3. Those not killed immediately were fed little and soon grew *incredibly skinny.*

4. Backbreaking labor bent once tall prisoners to half their *size.*

5. Daily, the *clashing background sound* of German patriotic music tore at the prisoners' ears.

ELIE WIESEL

1928–

Elie Wiesel was born in the town of Sighet (sē'gĕt), Transylvania, an area of Romania that the Germans made part of Hungary when they overran both nations in 1940, during World War II. Cut off by the war from most communication, the 15,000 Jews of Sighet had no idea where they were going when, in the spring of 1944, the Nazis ordered their deportation and shipped them on a cattle train to Auschwitz in Poland. Wiesel's mother and one of his three sisters were murdered there. In 1945, Wiesel and his father were sent to Buchenwald concentration camp in Germany, but sadly, Wiesel's father died of starvation and dysentery less than three months before the camp was liberated by the Allies.

After the war, Wiesel settled in France. He studied at the Sorbonne and worked as a writer and journalist, but he made a vow to write nothing about his concentration camp experience for ten years. "I didn't want to use the wrong words," he later explained. "I was afraid that words might betray it." Wiesel's 800-page autobiographical account was first written in Yiddish, the language of his childhood, and published in 1956. He condensed the work to just over 100 pages and published it in French as *La Nuit* in 1958. Two years later, the book was published in English as *Night.* Wiesel has written numerous histories, novels, and stories about the Holocaust and its survivors, and he has received scores of literary awards. A U.S. citizen since 1963, Wiesel has worked tirelessly to call attention to human rights violations in countries around the world, including South Africa, Cambodia, Bangladesh, and Bosnia. He was awarded the Nobel Peace Prize in 1986.

OTHER WORKS *Dawn, The Accident, A Beggar in Jerusalem, Legends of Our Time, A Jew Today, The Oath, One Generation After*

PREVIEWING

The Women Who Are Poets in My Land

Blaga Dimitrova (blä′gä dĭ-mē′trə-və) **Bulgaria**

PERSONAL CONNECTION

Do you think that there are equal opportunities in our society for both men and women? Create a chart like the one shown, indicating whether you think there is equal opportunity in each category. Then, in a group discussion, debate these issues.

	Yes	No
Education		
Careers		
Social Customs		

HISTORICAL/CULTURAL CONNECTION

During its long history, Blaga Dimitrova's native country of Bulgaria has experienced many forms of oppression and strife. For centuries, it was ruled by Turkey's Ottoman Empire, and much of its native culture was suppressed. It became a fully independent monarchy in 1908 but was torn by competing political factions until World War II, after which it became a Communist state. In the late 1980s, when communism began to crumble throughout Eastern Europe, Bulgaria moved toward democracy. Despite continued unrest, the nation elected its first non-Communist government in 1991.

During its four decades of communism, Bulgaria moved away from its centuries-old agricultural economy. However, other traditions proved more deep-seated. Though the Communists paid lip service to the idea of equality of the sexes, the traditional dominance of males continued in Bulgarian society. Dimitrova recognized this discrepancy; thus her writing often focuses on the lives and concerns of women.

WRITING CONNECTION

Imagine yourself living in a society in which your choices of career, marriage, and lifestyle were not your own. In your notebook, describe how you would feel about this situation. As you read the following poem, decide whether the world portrayed by the speaker is one in which freedom and equality are valued.

The Women Who Are Poets in My Land

Blaga Dimitrova

Never Ending Work (1990), Lelde Vinters-Ore. Private collection.

When I think of them,
numberless, armorless,
it's not the distant
humming at the cradle that I hear,
5   nor the reaper's[1] harmonies,
unbearable, or any strumming
at the loom—the rug they weave
of many strings—or widows winding
graves into their song.

10 Instead I think of cruel
silences: the girl grown mute
in wedlock, so as not
to talk back; and the bride
sworn in her home to be
15 dumb as a doornail all her life,
nor bother her mother-in-law;
the lonely schoolteachers
in every little town,
pale-lipped, home-bound.

20 And all the beauties taken abroad
and wed for life unto a foreign tongue,
all those who died without
a word—O future in my blood—to lose
in silence what is most your own,
25 before your lover and your world,
before your hearth[2] and self, unsung,
misunderstood—That's why

there are so many poets
among women in my land.
30 The mute whose speech
is suddenly restored
will rend[3] the air
with a moan or a shout—
centuries of silence
35 crying to come out.

*Translated by Niko Boris and
Heather McHugh*

---

1. **reaper:** a person who cuts and gathers grain or another crop.
2. **hearth** (härth): the paved floor of a fireplace, which usually extends into a room; figuratively, one's home or family life.
3. **rend:** split apart in rage; pierce or disturb with sound.

RESPONDING
OPTIONS

FROM PERSONAL RESPONSE TO CRITICAL ANALYSIS

REFLECT
1. Which lines of the poem did you find most memorable, powerful, or surprising? Share your response with your classmates.

RETHINK
2. How would you describe the world portrayed by the speaker of this poem? *Consider*
   - what has caused the "cruel silences" described in stanzas 2 and 3
   - why so many poets inhabit this world
   - how a woman in this world might fill out the chart for the Personal Connection on page 317

3. What do you predict will happen when "speech is suddenly restored" (lines 30–35)? Give reasons for your prediction.

4. Review the description you wrote for the Writing Connection on page 317. Now that you have read the poem, would you change anything about your description?

5. Assuming that the subject matter in this poem remained the same, how do you think this poem would be different if Dimitrova were a man?

RELATE
6. Compare and contrast your own ideas about the institution of marriage with the speaker's ideas as reflected in this poem.

ANOTHER PATHWAY
Cooperative Learning

Working with a few classmates, take turns reading the poem aloud. Remember that the punctuation can guide your reading. Commas, dashes, and colons indicate a brief pause; semicolons and periods signal a complete stop. After each period, stop and discuss what you think the speaker is saying.

QUICKWRITES

1. Use the description you wrote for the Writing Connection as a starting point for a **speech** you deliver to classmates on the importance of a person's determining his or her own direction in life.

2. Write your own **poem** called "The Women Who Are Poets in My Land," but instead of Bulgaria, use your native country as the setting. Try to express what you know about the ways women's lives are affected by your country's social norms and conventions.

3. Imagine that you are one of the "beauties taken abroad and wed for life unto a foreign tongue." Write a **letter** to your sister in Bulgaria. Explain how your life changed.

📁 *PORTFOLIO Save your writing. You may want to use it later as a springboard to a piece for your portfolio.*

LITERARY CONCEPTS

Many poems are organized into **stanzas,** or groups of two or more lines, that can work the same way paragraphs do in prose. This poem, for example, is organized into four stanzas, each of which presents a different, complete idea. Notice that the third stanza is linked to the fourth with the transitional phrase, "That's why." Write down in your own words the main idea of each stanza.

CONCEPT REVIEW: Imagery List five images in the poem. Why do you think so many of the images appeal to the sense of sound?

ALTERNATIVE ACTIVITIES

1. Create a **bulletin-board display** of original drawings and/or art and photo reproductions to illustrate the women described in this poem.

2. Working with a partner, **dramatize** "The Women Who Are Poets in My Land." Use pantomime and facial expressions to depict the images in each stanza. Present your drama to the class.

LITERARY LINKS

Compare the ways in which voices are silenced in Blaga Dimitrova's poem "The Women Who Are Poets in My Land" with the ways they are silenced in Luisa Valenzuela's story "The Censors."

CRITIC'S CORNER

The poet and scholar Alexander Shurbanov once wrote that "words are especially dear to Blaga Dimitrova. . . . [She said,] 'If they should put a ban on my words, how could I quench this thirst of mine?'" What kind of "thirst" do you think Dimitrova is talking about? What evidence can you find in the poem to show how important language is to her?

ACROSS THE CURRICULUM

Music Obtain recordings of Bulgarian folk music, and play the recordings in class. Share information that accompanying printed materials provide about the songs' lyrics or histories.

Folk dancers in Bulgaria. Balkan Holidays-USA.

BLAGA DIMITROVA

Blaga Dimitrova (1922–) is one of the most popular and respected writers in Eastern Europe today. Remarkably, she was able to write and publish despite Bulgaria's long-time repressive Communist regime and its totalitarian control over the arts. She was an outspoken opponent of communism and in 1989 joined the "Club for the Promotion of Glasnost and Perestroika." She stayed at the forefront of the struggle for human rights, women's rights, and democracy and was elected to the Bulgarian parliament in 1991. She became vice president of Bulgaria in January 1992, but she resigned her post 18 months later because she opposed the president's policies and feared her nation was headed toward dictatorship.

Born in northwestern Bulgaria, Dimitrova attended Sofia University in Bulgaria's capital and earned her Ph.D. at Moscow University's A. M. Gorky Institute of World Literature. Later, she worked as an editor for a Sofia publishing house. She has written more than 20 works of poetry, fiction, drama, criticism, and translation; much of her own work has been translated into eight languages. Among her poetry volumes are *Forbidden Sea,* which includes poems about her harrowing experiences as a cancer victim, and *Night Diary*, a collection of poems written between 1989 and 1992, the years of Bulgaria's transition from communism to democracy.

OTHER WORKS *Because the Sea Is Black, Journey to Oneself,* poems in *Poets of Bulgaria* and in *The Devil's Dozen: Thirteen Contemporary Bulgarian Women Poets, The Last Rock Eagle*

PREVIEWING

FICTION

House Taken Over

Julio Cortázar (hōō′lyô kôr-tä′sär) **Argentina**

PERSONAL CONNECTION

Sometimes the images in our dreams fade as soon as we open our eyes; sometimes the images stay with us. Can you remember a dream you had last night? last week? years ago? Try to recall one of your dreams, and think about what real-life details or situations it contained. Did it also contain fantastic events that could never actually occur? In your notebook, jot down what you remember about the dream, and indicate whether the events belong to the world of reality or to the world of fantasy. You might organize them in a diagram like this one.

Event 1

Reality: I'm heading home from school.

Fantasy: Airplanes are lined up in middle of street.

Event 2

Reality: I fall crossing the street.

Fantasy: I try crawling to the curb, but it keeps moving away from me.

Event 3

Reality: A traffic light turns green.

Fantasy: Airplanes rush at me.

BIOGRAPHICAL CONNECTION

Dreams and fantasy play a large role in the writings of Argentine author Julio Cortázar—a role evident in the story you are about to read. Cortázar's taste for fantasy developed in childhood, when he was fond of horror and mystery stories. It was further nurtured by his early association with the great Argentine writer Jorge Luis Borges (hôr′hĕ lōō-ĕs′ bôr′hĕs), whose experimental prose often blurred the borders between fact and fiction.

Cortázar was deeply dissatisfied with life under the dictators who ruled Argentina for decades, and his discomfort with his country's political situation helped inspire some of his darker fantasies. "House Taken Over" first appeared in 1946 in a literary journal that Borges edited. The story takes place in Argentina's capital, Buenos Aires, not far from where Cortázar grew up. It is based on one of the author's recurring nightmares.

READING CONNECTION

Recognizing Fantasy As you read the story, consider its dreamlike qualities. What true-to-life details does it contain? How does it mingle real-life experiences with events that could never happen?

Street scene from the 1940s, Buenos Aires, Argentina. Culver Pictures.

HOUSE TAKEN OVER

JULIO CORTÁZAR

We liked the house because, apart from its being old and spacious (in a day when old houses go down for a profitable auction of their construction materials), it kept the memories of great-grandparents, our paternal grandfather, our parents and the whole of childhood.

Irene and I got used to staying in the house by ourselves, which was crazy; eight people could have lived in that place and not have gotten in each other's way. We rose at seven in the morning and got the cleaning done, and about eleven I left Irene to finish off whatever rooms and went to the kitchen. We lunched at noon precisely; then there was nothing left to do but a few dirty plates. It was pleasant to take lunch and com-mune with the great, hollow, silent house, and it was enough for us just to keep it clean. We ended up thinking, at times, that that was what had kept us from marrying. Irene turned down two suitors for no particular reason, and María Esther went and died on me before we could manage to get engaged. We were easing into our forties with the unvoiced concept that the quiet, simple marriage of sister and brother was the indispensable end to a line established in this house by our grandparents. We would die here someday, obscure and distant cousins would inherit the place, have it torn down, sell the bricks and get rich on the building plot; or more justly and better yet, we would topple it ourselves before it was too late.

Irene never bothered anyone. Once the morning housework was finished, she spent the rest of the day on the sofa in her bedroom, knitting. I couldn't tell you why she knitted so much; I think women knit when they discover that it's a fat excuse to do nothing at all. But Irene was not like that, she always knitted necessities, sweaters for winter, socks for me, handy morning robes and bedjackets for herself. Sometimes she would do a jacket, then unravel it the next moment because there was something that didn't please her; it was pleasant to see a pile of tangled wool in her knitting basket fighting a losing battle for a few hours to retain its shape. Saturdays I went downtown to buy wool; Irene had faith in my good taste, was pleased with the colors and never a skein[1] had to be returned. I took advantage of these trips to make the rounds of the bookstores, uselessly asking if they had anything new in French literature. Nothing worthwhile had arrived in Argentina since 1939.[2]

But it's the house I want to talk about, the house and Irene; I'm not very important. I wonder what Irene would have done without her knitting. One can reread a book, but once a pullover is finished you can't do it over again; it's some kind of disgrace. One day I found that the drawer at the bottom of the chiffonier,[3] replete with mothballs, was filled with shawls: white, green, lilac. Stacked amid a great smell of camphor—it was like a shop; I didn't have the nerve to ask her what she planned to do with them. We didn't have to earn our living, there was plenty coming in from the farms each month, even piling up. But Irene was only interested in the knitting and showed a wonderful dexterity, and for me the hours slipped away watching her, her hands like silver sea urchins, needles flashing, and one or two knitting baskets on the floor, the balls of yarn jumping about. It was lovely.

---

1. skein (skān): a length of yarn or thread wound into a loose coil.
2. 1939: the year in which World War II began. The war prevented most exports from France to South America.
3. chiffonier (shĭf′ə-nîr′): a narrow, high chest of drawers, often with a mirror attached.

How not to remember the layout of that house. The dining room, a living room with tapestries, the library and three large bedrooms in the section most recessed, the one that faced toward Rodríguez Peña.[4] Only a corridor with its massive oak door separated that part from the front wing, where there was a bath, the kitchen, our bedrooms and the hall. One entered the house through a vestibule with enameled tiles, and a wrought-iron grated door opened onto the living room. You had to come in through the vestibule and open the gate to go into the living room; the doors to our bedrooms were on either side of this, and opposite it was the corridor leading to the back section; going down the passage, one swung open the oak door beyond which was the other part of the house; or just before the door, one could turn to the left and go down a narrower passageway which led to the kitchen and the bath. When the door was open, you became aware of the size of the house; when it was closed, you had the impression of an apartment, like the ones they build today, with barely enough room to move around in. Irene and I always lived in this part of the house and hardly ever went beyond the oak door except to do the cleaning. Incredible how much dust collected on the furniture. It may be Buenos Aires is a clean city, but she owes it to her population and nothing else. There's too much dust in the air, the slightest breeze and it's back on the marble console tops and in the diamond patterns of the tooled-leather desk set. It's a lot of work to get it off with a feather duster; the motes[5] rise and hang in the air, and settle again a minute later on the pianos and the furniture.

I'll always have a clear memory of it because it happened so simply and without fuss. Irene was knitting in her bedroom, it was eight at night, and I suddenly decided to put the water up for maté.[6] I went down the corridor as far as the oak door, which was ajar, then turned into the hall toward the kitchen, when I heard something in the library or the dining room. The sound came through muted and indistinct, a chair being knocked over onto the carpet or the muffled buzzing of a conversation. At the same time or a second later, I heard it at the end of the passage which led from those two rooms toward the door. I hurled myself against the door before it was too late and shut it, leaned on it with the weight of my body; luckily, the key was on our side; moreover, I ran the great bolt into place, just to be safe.

I went down to the kitchen, heated the kettle, and when I got back with the tray of maté, I told Irene:

"I had to shut the door to the passage. They've taken over the back part."

She let her knitting fall and looked at me with her tired, serious eyes.

"You're sure?"

I nodded.

"In that case," she said, picking up her needles again, "we'll have to live on this side."

I sipped at the maté very carefully, but she took her time starting her work again. I remember it was a gray vest she was knitting. I liked that vest.

The first few days were painful, since we'd both left so many things in the part that had been taken over. My collection of French literature, for example, was still in the library. Irene had left several folios of stationery and a pair of slippers that she used a lot in the winter. I missed my briar pipe, and Irene, I think, regretted the loss of an ancient bottle of Hesperidin.[7] It happened repeatedly (but only in the first few days) that we would close some drawer or

---

4. **Rodríguez Peña** (rô-drē′gĕz pě′nyä): a wealthy, mostly residential street in central Buenos Aires.

5. **motes:** small particles; specks.

6. **maté** (mä-tě′): a tealike beverage popular in South America.

7. **Hesperidin** (hě-spĕr′ĭ-dĭn): a natural citrus flavoring.

El novio [The groom] (1974), Jacobo Borges. Oil on canvas, 120.5 cm × 120.5 cm, collection of Clara Diament Sujo, New York.

That Which I Should Have Done I Did Not Do
(1931–1941), Ivan Le Lorraine Albright. Oil on canvas,
246.5 cm × 91.5 cm, The Art Institute of Chicago, Mary and
Leigh B. Block Charitable Fund (1955.645). Photo Copyright
© 1994, The Art Institute of Chicago, all rights reserved.

cabinet and look at one another sadly.

"It's not here."

One thing more among the many lost on the other side of the house.

But there were advantages, too. The cleaning was so much simplified that, even when we got up late, nine-thirty for instance, by eleven we were sitting around with our arms folded. Irene got into the habit of coming to the kitchen with me to help get lunch. We thought about it and decided on this: while I prepared the lunch, Irene would cook up dishes that could be eaten cold in the evening. We were happy with the arrangement because it was always such a bother to have to leave our bedrooms in the evening and start to cook. Now we made do with the table in Irene's room and platters of cold supper.

Since it left her more time for knitting, Irene was content. I was a little lost without my books, but so as not to inflict myself on my sister, I set about reordering papa's stamp collection; that killed some time. We amused ourselves sufficiently, each with his or her own thing, almost always getting together in Irene's bedroom, which was more comfortable. Every once in a while, Irene might say:

"Look at this pattern I just figured out, doesn't it look like clover?"

After a bit it was I, pushing a small square of paper in front of her so that she could see the excellence of some stamp or another from Eupen-et-Malmédy.[8] We were fine, and little by little we stopped thinking. You can live without thinking.

(Whenever Irene talked in her sleep, I woke up immediately and stayed awake. I never could get used to this voice from a statue or a parrot, a voice that came out of the dreams, not from a throat. Irene said that in my sleep I flailed about

---

8. **Eupen-et-Malmédy** (ə-pě′nä-mäl-mä′dē): a region in Belgium.

enormously and shook the blankets off. We had the living room between us, but at night you could hear everything in the house. We heard each other breathing, coughing, could even feel each other reaching for the light switch, when, as happened frequently, neither of us could fall asleep.

Aside from our nocturnal rumblings, everything was quiet in the house. During the day there were the household sounds, the metallic click of knitting needles, the rustle of stamp-album pages turning. The oak door was massive; I think I said that. In the kitchen or the bath, which adjoined the part that was taken over, we managed to talk loudly, or Irene sang lullabies. In a kitchen there's always too much noise, the plates and glasses, for there to be interruptions from other sounds. We seldom allowed ourselves silence there, but when we went back to our rooms or to the living room, then the house grew quiet, half-lit, we ended by stepping around more slowly so as not to disturb one another. I think it was because of this that I woke up irremediably[9] and at once when Irene began to talk in her sleep.)

Except for the consequences, it's nearly a matter of repeating the same scene over again. I was thirsty that night, and before we went to sleep, I told Irene that I was going to the kitchen for a glass of water. From the door of the bedroom (she was knitting) I heard the noise in the kitchen; if not the kitchen, then the bath, the passage off at that angle dulled the sound. Irene noticed how brusquely I had paused, and came up beside me without a word. We stood listening to the noises, growing more and more sure

that they were on our side of the oak door, if not the kitchen then the bath, or in the hall itself at the turn, almost next to us.

We didn't wait to look at one another. I took Irene's arm and forced her to run with me to the wrought-iron door, not waiting to look back. You could hear the noises, still muffled but louder, just behind us. I slammed the grating and we stopped in the vestibule. Now there was nothing to be heard.

"They've taken over our section," Irene said. The knitting had reeled off from her hands and the yarn ran back toward the door and disappeared under it. When she saw that the balls of yarn were on the other side, she dropped the knitting without looking at it.

"Did you have time to bring anything?" I asked hopelessly.

"No, nothing."

We had what we had on. I remembered fifteen thousand pesos in the wardrobe in my bedroom. Too late now.

I still had my wristwatch on and saw that it was 11 P.M. I took Irene around the waist (I think she was crying), and that was how we went into the street. Before we left, I felt terrible; I locked the front door up tight and tossed the key down the sewer. It wouldn't do to have some poor devil decide to go in and rob the house, at that hour and with the house taken over. ❖

Translated by Paul Blackburn

---

9. **irremediably** (ĭr′ĭ-mē′dē-ə-blē): in a way that cannot be remedied, corrected, or repaired.

327

RESPONDING OPTIONS

FROM PERSONAL RESPONSE TO CRITICAL ANALYSIS

REFLECT

1. What is your reaction to this story? Record your thoughts in your notebook and share them with classmates.

RETHINK

2. How would you describe the background and social class of the narrator and his sister?

3. What is your opinion of the way the brother and sister react to the discovery that "they" have taken over the back part of the house?

4. The story is intentionally ambiguous, or open to different interpretations. What might the mysterious invaders represent?

5. In what sense might the narrator and his sister be considered prisoners of circumstance? Explain your view.

6. Judging from the details in the story, predict what will happen to the brother and sister after the story's end.

RELATE

7. How do you think the dreams we have at night are related to our daytime experiences? Explain your views in a class discussion.

ANOTHER PATHWAY

In a chart like the one below, differentiate between the situations and details from the story that can be considered realistic and those that can be considered fantastic. If any details about the lives of the two characters can be considered absurd or inconsistent with what is customary—even before the house is "taken over"—list them in the "Fantastic" category.

Realistic	Fantastic

LITERARY CONCEPTS

Julio Cortázar is considered a master of **magical realism,** a style of writing that often includes exaggeration, unusual humor, magical and bizarre events, dreams that come true, and superstitions that prove warranted. Magical realism differs from pure fantasy in that it combines fantastic elements with realistic elements such as recognizable characters, believable dialogue, a true-to-life setting, a matter-of-fact tone, and a plot that sometimes contains historic events. How does "House Taken Over" fit this definition of magical realism? Cite details from the story to support your answer.

CONCEPT REVIEW: Setting Why do you think Cortázar describes the house in such detail? What role does the house play in the lives of the two main characters?

QUICKWRITES

1. Draft an **essay** in which you explain your interpretation of "House Taken Over." Be sure to defend your point of view with details from the story.

2. Write a **story,** in the style of magical realism, based on the dream you described in the Personal Connection on page 321.

📁 *PORTFOLIO Save your writing. You may want to use it later as a springboard to a piece for your portfolio.*

ALTERNATIVE ACTIVITIES

1. Create a **painting** of the "house taken over" or its mysterious invaders. Blend realistic details with fantastic ones.

2. Put together a **recording** of several pieces of music that evoke the same mood of suspense and mystery as this story does.

ART CONNECTION

Examine the painting on page 325 titled *The Groom*. In what way might the term *magical realism* be applied to it?

Detail of *El Novio* [The groom] (1974), Jacobo Borges. Oil on canvas, 120.5 cm x 120.5 cm, collection of Clara Diament Sujo, New York.

WORDS TO KNOW

On a separate sheet of paper, answer each question below.

1. If you answer a question **brusquely,** are you more likely to seem rude or to seem long-winded?

2. If a waiter displays **dexterity,** does he or she serve smoothly or clumsily?

3. Will a person who **communes** with nature be more likely to leave a camping site virtually unchanged or to leave litter behind?

4. If your shelf is **replete** with trophies, have you won or have you lost many tournaments?

5. Is an **obscure** actress famous, or is she known to few people?

CRITIC'S CORNER

In commenting on this story, student Kevin Schatzman said, "The thing I liked best about it was the suspense. It kept me wondering what was going to happen next and made me want to read more." How does this compare with your own experience reading the story?

JULIO CORTÁZAR

1914–1984

Although Julio Cortázar was born in Brussels, Belgium, he was raised by his Argentine parents in a suburb of Buenos Aires from the time he was four years old. Even as a child, Cortázar was an avid reader and writer. He attended the Teachers College of Buenos Aires and then taught literature at both the high school and the university level before working as a translator and publishing his own writing.

Cortázar opposed Argentine dictator Juan Perón (hwän pě-ron'), who rose to power in the 1940s. In 1951, dissatisfied with the Perón regime, Cortázar immigrated to Paris, France, and continued to write. A lifelong jazz fan and trumpet player, he won much attention with his 1959 novella *The Pursuer,* whose hero is modeled after American jazz musician Charlie "Bird" Parker. Cortázar's fame increased with the publication of *Rayuela,* an experimental novel that was translated into English and published as *Hopscotch* in 1966. In that same year, one of his stories was used as the basis for the critically acclaimed film *Blow-Up.* By the end of the 1960s, Cortázar—despite his self-imposed exile in Europe—was internationally acknowledged as one of Latin America's most influential authors. Cortázar was also a "man of conscience," remaining politically active throughout his life.

OTHER WORKS *The Winners, End of the Game and Other Stories, We Love Glenda So Much and Other Tales*

from FAREWELL TO MANZANAR

★ ★

Jeanne Wakatsuki Houston and James D. Houston
United States

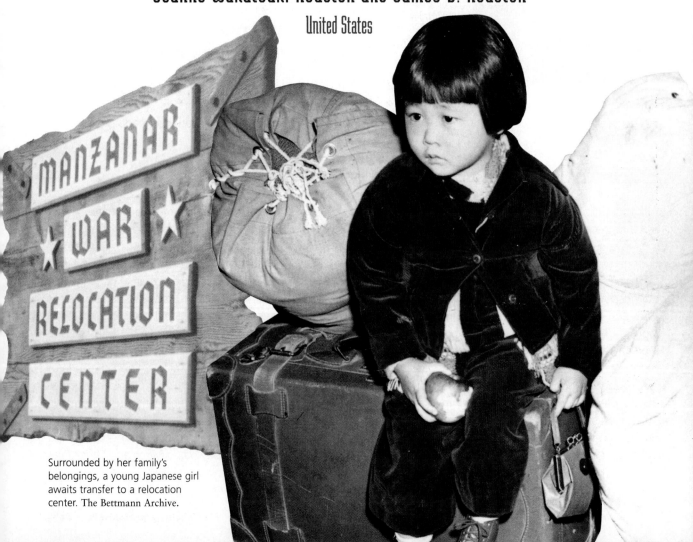

Surrounded by her family's belongings, a young Japanese girl awaits transfer to a relocation center. The Bettmann Archive.

When Japan's attack on Pearl Harbor drew the United States into World War II in December 1941 people on the West Coast began to fear further attacks from those of Japanese descent living in their communities. The fears were racist and completely irrational (most of the Japanese had become U.S. citizens or legal residents and had been living and working on the coast for decades), yet suspicion fueled public policy. In February 1942 President Franklin D. Roosevelt signed an order that cleared the way for the removal of Japanese people from their homes. Virtually the entire Japanese-American population of the West Coast, about 110,000 people, was bused to ten inland "relocation" centers in the Western states and Arkansas, where they were interned, or confined, for the duration of the war. With sometimes only 24 hours' notice, they were forced to abandon their homes, farms, and businesses and to leave behind most of their possessions in what has been called "the most blatant mass violation of civil liberties in American history."

Jeanne Wakatsuki was 7 years old and living in Ocean Park, California, when the United States entered the war. On the night after the Pearl Harbor attack, her father showed his loyalty to his adoptive land by burning the Japanese flag he had brought with him from Japan 35 years before. Nevertheless, he was arrested and sent to a detention camp in North Dakota. The rest of the family moved to a Japanese-American community in Terminal Island, California, but the area was soon declared off-limits to Japanese Americans because of its proximity to the Long Beach Naval Station. The Wakatsukis were forced to relocate to a minority ghetto in Los Angeles, where they are living when the following selection begins. The selection is an excerpt from the memoir that Jeanne Wakatsuki Houston wrote with her husband three decades after the war.

The American Friends Service[1] helped us find a small house in Boyle Heights, another minority ghetto, in downtown Los Angeles, now inhabited briefly by a few hundred Terminal Island refugees. Executive Order 9066 had been signed by President Roosevelt, giving the War Department authority to define military areas in the western states and to exclude from them anyone who might threaten the war effort. There was a lot of talk about internment, or moving inland, or something like that in store for all Japanese Americans. I remember my brothers sitting around the table talking very intently about what we were going to do, how we would keep the family together. They had seen how quickly Papa was removed, and they knew now that he would not be back for quite a while. Just before leaving Terminal Island, Mama had received her first letter, from Bismarck, North Dakota. He had been imprisoned at Fort Lincoln, in an all-male camp for enemy aliens.

---

1. **American Friends Service:** a Quaker charity often aiding political and religious refugees and other displaced persons.

Papa had been the patriarch.[2] He had always decided everything in the family. With him gone, my brothers, like councilors in the absence of a chief, worried about what should be done. The ironic thing is, there wasn't much left to decide. These were mainly days of quiet, desperate waiting for what seemed at the time to be inevitable. There is a phrase the Japanese use in such situations, when something difficult must be endured.

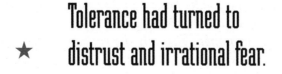

Tolerance had turned to distrust and irrational fear.

You would hear the older heads, the Issei,[3] telling others very quietly, *"Shikata ga nai"* (It cannot be helped). *"Shikata ga nai"* (It must be done).

Mama and Woody went to work packing celery for a Japanese produce dealer. Kiyo and my sister May and I enrolled in the local school, and what sticks in my memory from those few weeks is the teacher—not her looks, her remoteness. In Ocean Park my teacher had been a kind, grandmotherly woman who used to sail with us in Papa's boat from time to time and who wept the day we had to leave. In Boyle Heights the teacher felt cold and distant. I was confused by all the moving and was having trouble with the classwork, but she would never help me out. She would have nothing to do with me.

This was the first time I had felt outright hostility from a Caucasian. Looking back, it is easy enough to explain. Public attitudes toward the Japanese in California were shifting rapidly. In the first few months of the Pacific war, America was on the run. Tolerance had turned to distrust and irrational fear. The hundred-year-old tradition of anti-Orientalism on the west coast soon resurfaced, more vicious than ever. Its result became clear about a month later, when we were told to make our third and final move.

The name Manzanar meant nothing to us when we left Boyle Heights. We didn't know where it was or what it was. We went because the government ordered us to. And, in the case of my older brothers and sisters, we went with a certain amount of relief. They had all heard stories of Japanese homes being attacked, of beatings in the streets of California towns. They were as frightened of the Caucasians as Caucasians were of us. Moving, under what appeared to be government protection, to an area less directly threatened by the war seemed not such a bad idea at all. For some it actually sounded like a fine adventure.

Our pickup point was a Buddhist church in Los Angeles. It was very early, and misty, when we got there with our luggage. Mama had bought heavy coats for all of us. She grew up in eastern Washington and knew that anywhere inland in early April would be cold. I was proud of my new coat, and I remember sitting on a duffel bag trying to be friendly with the Greyhound driver. I smiled at him. He didn't smile back. He was befriending no one. Someone tied a numbered tag to my collar and to the duffel bag (each family was given a number, and that became our official designation until the camps were closed), someone else passed out box lunches for the trip, and we climbed aboard.

I had never been outside Los Angeles County, never traveled more than ten miles from the coast, had never even ridden on a bus. I was full of excitement, the way any kid would be, and wanted to look out the window. But for the first few hours the shades were drawn. Around me other people played cards, read magazines,

---

2. **patriarch** (pā′trē-ärk′): the man who heads his family or clan.

3. **Issei** (ēs′sā′): people born in Japan who immigrate to the United States.

dozed, waiting. I settled back, waiting too, and finally fell asleep. The bus felt very secure to me. Almost half its passengers were immediate relatives. Mama and my older brothers had succeeded in keeping most of us together, on the same bus, headed for the same camp. I didn't realize until much later what a job that was. The strategy had been, first, to have everyone living in the same district when the evacuation began, and then to get all of us included under the same family number, even though names had been changed by marriage. Many families weren't as lucky as ours and suffered months of anguish while trying to arrange transfers from one camp to another.

We rode all day. By the time we reached our destination, the shades were up. It was late afternoon. The first thing I saw was a yellow swirl across a blurred, reddish setting sun. The bus was being pelted by what sounded like splattering rain. It wasn't rain. This was my first look at something I would soon know very well, a billowing flurry of dust and sand churned up by the wind through Owens Valley.[4]

We drove past a barbed-wire fence, through a gate, and into an open space where trunks and sacks and packages had been dumped from the baggage trucks that drove out ahead of us. I could see a few tents set up, the first rows of black barracks, and beyond them, blurred by sand, rows of barracks that seemed to spread for miles across this plain. People were sitting on cartons or milling around, with their backs to the wind, waiting to see which friends or relatives might be on this bus. As we approached, they turned or stood up, and some moved toward us expectantly. But inside the bus no one stirred. No one waved or spoke. They just stared out the windows, ominously silent. I didn't understand this. Hadn't we finally arrived, our whole family intact? I opened a window, leaned out, and yelled happily. "Hey! This whole bus is full of Wakatsukis!"

Outside, the greeters smiled. Inside there was an explosion of laughter, hysterical, tension-breaking laughter that left my brothers choking and whacking each other across the shoulders.

We had pulled up just in time for dinner. The mess halls weren't completed yet. An outdoor chow line snaked around a half-finished building that broke a good part of the wind. They issued us army mess kits, the round metal kind that fold over, and plopped in scoops of canned Vienna sausage, canned string beans, steamed rice that had been cooked too long, and on top of the rice a serving of canned apricots. The Caucasian servers were thinking that the fruit poured over rice would make a good dessert. Among the Japanese, of course, rice is never eaten with sweet foods, only with salty or savory foods. Few of us could eat such a mixture. But at this point no one dared protest. It would have been impolite. I was horrified when I saw the apricot syrup seeping through my little mound of rice. I opened my mouth to complain. My mother jabbed me in the back to keep quiet. We moved on through the line and joined the others squatting in the lee[5] of half-raised walls, dabbing courteously at what was, for almost everyone there, an inedible concoction.

After dinner we were taken to Block 16, a cluster of fifteen barracks that had just been finished a day or so earlier—although finished was hardly the word for it. The shacks were built of one thickness of pine planking covered with tarpaper. They sat on concrete footings, with about two feet of open space between the floorboards and the ground. Gaps showed between the planks, and as the weeks passed

---

4. **Owens Valley:** referring to the valley of the Owens River in south central California west of Death Valley, where Manzanar was built. The once lush and green valley had become dry and deserted in the 1930s after water was diverted to an aquaduct supplying Los Angeles.

5. **lee:** the side sheltered from the wind.

The 550-acre Manzanar internment camp was located 200 miles northeast of Los Angeles at the foot of the Sierra Nevada. When the war ended in 1945, the camp's staff buildings and barracks were quickly disassembled and auctioned off. AP/Wide World Photos.

and the green wood dried out, the gaps widened. Knotholes gaped in the uncovered floor.

Each barracks was divided into six units, sixteen by twenty feet, about the size of a living room, with one bare bulb hanging from the ceiling and an oil stove for heat. We were assigned two of these for the twelve people in our family group; and our official family "number" was enlarged by three digits—16 plus the number of this barracks. We were issued steel army cots, two brown army blankets each, and some mattress covers, which my brothers stuffed with straw.

The first task was to divide up what space we had for sleeping. Bill and Woody contributed a blanket each and partitioned off the first room: one side for Bill and Tomi, one side for Woody and Chizu and their baby girl. Woody also got the stove, for heating formulas.

The people who had it hardest during the first few months were young couples like these, many of whom had married just before the evacuation began, in order not to be separated and sent to different camps. Our two rooms were crowded, but at least it was all in the family. My oldest

night—the parents wanted their boys asleep by 9:00 p.m.—and they continued arguing over matters like that for six months, until my sister and her husband left to harvest sugar beets in Idaho. It was grueling work up there, and wages were pitiful, but when the call came through camp for workers to alleviate the wartime labor shortage, it sounded better than their life at Manzanar. They knew they'd have, if nothing else, a room, perhaps a cabin of their own.

That first night in Block 16, the rest of us squeezed into the second room—Granny; Lillian, age fourteen; Ray, thirteen; May, eleven; Kiyo, ten; Mama; and me. I didn't mind this at all at the time. Being youngest meant I got to sleep with Mama. And before we went to bed I had a great time jumping up and down on the mattress. The boys had stuffed so much straw into hers, we had to flatten it some so we wouldn't slide off. I slept with her every night after that until Papa came back.

We woke early, shivering and coated with dust that had blown up through the knotholes and in through the slits around the doorway. During the night Mama had unpacked all our clothes and heaped them on our beds for warmth. Now our cubicle looked as if a great laundry bag had exploded and then been sprayed with fine dust. A skin of sand covered the floor. I looked over Mama's shoulder at Kiyo, on top of his fat mattress, buried under jeans and overcoats and sweaters. His eyebrows were gray, and he was starting to giggle. He was looking at me, at my gray eyebrows and coated hair, and pretty soon we were both giggling. I looked at Mama's face to see if she thought Kiyo was funny. She lay very still next to me on our mattress, her eyes scanning everything—bare rafters, walls, dusty kids—scanning slowly, and I think the mask of her face would have cracked had not Woody's voice just then come at us through the wall. He was rapping on the

sister and her husband were shoved into one of those sixteen-by-twenty-foot compartments with six people they had never seen before—two other couples, one recently married like themselves, the other with two teenage boys. Partitioning off a room like that wasn't easy. It was bitter cold when we arrived, and the wind did not abate. All they had to use for room dividers were those army blankets, two of which were barely enough to keep one person warm. They argued over whose blanket should be sacrificed and later argued about noise at

planks as if testing to see if they were hollow.

"Hey!" he yelled. "You guys fall into the same flour barrel as us?"

"No," Kiyo yelled back. "Ours is full of Japs."

All of us laughed at this.

"Well, tell 'em it's time to get up," Woody said. "If we're gonna live in this place, we better get to work."

He gave us ten minutes to dress, then he came in carrying a broom, a hammer, and a sack full of tin can lids he had scrounged somewhere. Woody would be our leader for a while now, short, stocky, grinning behind his mustache.

The simple truth is the camp was no more ready for us when we got there than we were ready for it.

He had just turned twenty-four. In later years he would tour the country with Mr. Moto, the Japanese tag-team wrestler, as his sinister assistant Suki— karate chops through the ropes from outside the ring, a chunky leg reaching from under his kimono to trip up Mr. Moto's foe. In the ring Woody's smile looked sly and crafty; he hammed it up. Offstage it was whimsical, as if some joke were bursting to be told.

"Hey, brother Ray, Kiyo," he said. "You see these tin can lids?"

"Yeah, yeah," the boys said drowsily, as if going back to sleep. They were both young versions of Woody.

"You see all them knotholes in the floor and in the walls?"

They looked around. You could see about a dozen.

Woody said, "You get those covered up before breakfast time. Any more sand comes in here through one of them knotholes, you have to eat it off the floor with ketchup."

"What about sand that comes in through the cracks?" Kiyo said.

Woody stood up very straight, which in itself was funny, since he was only about five-foot-six.

"Don't worry about the cracks," he said. "Different kind of sand comes in through the cracks."

He put his hands on his hips and gave Kiyo a sternly comic look, squinting at him through one eye the way Papa would when he was asserting his authority. Woody mimicked Papa's voice: "And I can tell the difference. So be careful."

The boys laughed and went to work nailing down lids. May started sweeping out the sand. I was helping Mama fold the clothes we'd used for cover, when Woody came over and put his arms around her shoulder. He was short; she was even shorter, under five feet.

He said softly, "You okay, Mama?"

She didn't look at him, she just kept folding clothes and said, "Can we get the cracks covered too, Woody?"

Outside the sky was clear, but icy gusts of wind were buffeting our barracks every few minutes, sending fresh dust puffs up through the floorboards. May's broom could barely keep up with it, and our oil heater could scarcely hold its own against the drafts.

"We'll get this whole place as tight as a barrel, Mama. I already met a guy who told me where they pile all the scrap lumber."

"Scrap?"

"That's all they got. I mean, they're still building the camp, you know. Sixteen blocks left to go. After that, they say maybe we'll get some stuff to fix the insides a little bit."

Her eyes blazed then, her voice quietly furious. "Woody, we can't live like this. Animals live like this."

It was hard to get Woody down. He'd keep smiling when everybody else was ready to explode. Grief flickered in his eyes. He blinked it away and hugged her tighter. "We'll make it better, Mama. You watch."

We could hear voices in other cubicles now. Beyond the wall Woody's baby girl started to cry.

"I have to go over to the kitchen," he said, "see if those guys got a pot for heating bottles. That oil stove takes too long—something wrong with the fuel line. I'll find out what they're giving us for breakfast."

"Probably hotcakes with soy sauce," Kiyo said, on his hands and knees between the bunks.

"No." Woody grinned, heading out the door. "Rice. With Log Cabin syrup and melted butter."

I don't remember what we ate that first morning. I know we stood for half an hour in cutting wind waiting to get our food. Then we took it back to the cubicle and ate huddled around the stove. Inside, it was warmer than when we left, because Woody was already making good his promise to Mama, tacking up some ends of lath[6] he'd found, stuffing rolled paper around the door frame.

Trouble was, he had almost nothing to work with. Beyond this temporary weather stripping, there was little else he could do. Months went by, in fact, before our "home" changed much at all from what it was the day we moved in— bare floors, blanket partitions, one bulb in each compartment dangling from a roof beam, and open ceilings overhead so that mischievous boys like Ray and Kiyo could climb up into the rafters and peek into anyone's life.

The simple truth is the camp was no more ready for us when we got there than we were ready for it. We had only the dimmest ideas of what to expect. Most of the families, like us, had moved out from southern California with as much luggage as each person could carry. Some old men left Los Angeles wearing Hawaiian

shirts and Panama hats and stepped off the bus at an altitude of 4000 feet, with nothing available but sagebrush and tarpaper to stop the April winds pouring down off the back side of the Sierras.[7]

The War Department was in charge of all the camps at this point. They began to issue military surplus from the First World War—olive-drab knit caps, earmuffs, peacoats, canvas leggings. Later on, sewing machines were shipped in, and one barracks was turned into a clothing factory. An old seamstress took a peacoat of mine, tore the lining out, opened and flattened the sleeves, added a collar, put arm holes in and handed me back a beautiful cape. By fall, dozens of seamstresses were working full-time transforming thousands of these old army clothes into capes, slacks, and stylish coats. But until that factory got going and packages from friends outside began to fill out our wardrobes, warmth was more important than style. I couldn't help laughing at Mama walking around in army earmuffs and a pair of wide-cuffed, khaki-colored wool trousers several sizes too big for her. Japanese are generally smaller than Caucasians, and almost all these clothes were oversize. They flopped, they dangled, they hung.

It seems comical, looking back; we were a band of Charlie Chaplins[8] marooned in the California desert. But at the time, it was pure chaos. That's the only way to describe it. The evacuation had been so hurriedly planned, the camps so hastily thrown together, nothing was completed when we got there, and almost nothing worked.

I was sick continually, with stomach cramps and diarrhea. At first it was from the shots they

---

6. **lath** (lăth): a thin strip of wood.

7. **Sierras** (sē-ĕr'əz): referring to the Sierra Nevada mountain range in eastern California.

8. **Charlie Chaplins:** referring to actor and director Charlie Chaplin, who portrayed a tramp in baggy clothing in several comedy films of the 1920s and 1930s.

gave us for typhoid, in very heavy doses and in assembly-line fashion: swab, jab, swab, *Move along now,* swab, jab, swab, *Keep it moving.* That knocked all of us younger kids down at once, with fevers and vomiting. Later, it was the food that made us sick, young and old alike. The kitchens were too small and badly ventilated. Food would spoil from being left out too long. That summer, when the heat got fierce, it would spoil faster. The refrigeration kept breaking down. The cooks, in many cases, had never cooked before. Each block had to provide its own volunteers. Some were lucky and had a professional or two in their midst. But the first chef in our block had been a gardener all his life and suddenly found himself preparing three meals a day for 250 people.

"The Manzanar runs" became a condition of life, and you only hoped that when you rushed to the latrine, one would be in working order.

That first morning, on our way to the chow line, Mama and I tried to use the women's latrine in our block. The smell of it spoiled what little appetite we had. Outside, men were working in an open trench, up to their knees in muck—a common sight in the months to come. Inside, the floor was covered with excrement, and all twelve bowls were erupting like a row of tiny volcanoes.

Mama stopped a kimono-wrapped woman stepping past us with her sleeve pushed up against her nose and asked, "What do you do?"

"Try Block Twelve," the woman said, grimacing. "They have just finished repairing the pipes."

It was about two city blocks away. We followed her over there and found a line of women waiting in the wind outside the latrine. We had no choice but to join the line and wait with them.

Inside it was like all the other latrines. Each block was built to the same design just as each of the ten camps, from California to Arkansas, was built to a common master plan. It was an open room, over a concrete slab. The sink was a long metal trough against one wall, with a row of spigots for hot and cold water. Down the center of the room twelve toilet bowls were arranged in six pairs, back to back, with no partitions. My mother was a very modest person, and this was going to be agony for her, sitting down in public, among strangers.

One old woman had already solved the problem for herself by dragging in a large cardboard carton. She set it up around one of the bowls, like a three-sided screen. OXYDOL was printed in large black letters down the front. I remember this well, because that was the soap we were issued for laundry; later on, the smell of it would permeate these rooms. The upended carton was about four feet high. The old woman behind it wasn't much taller. When she stood, only her head showed over the top.

She was about Granny's age. With great effort she was trying to fold the sides of the screen together. Mama happened to be at the head of the line now. As she approached the vacant bowl, she and the old woman bowed to each other from the waist. Mama then moved to help her with the carton, and the old woman said very graciously, in Japanese, "Would you like to use it?"

Happily, gratefully, Mama bowed again and said, *"Arigato"* (Thank you). *"Arigato gozaimas"* (Thank you very much). "I will return it to your barracks."

"Oh, no. It is not necessary. I will be glad to wait."

The old woman unfolded one side of the cardboard, while Mama opened the other; then she bowed again and scurried out the door.

Those big cartons were a common sight in the spring of 1942. Eventually sturdier partitions appeared, one or two at a time. The first were built of scrap lumber. Word would get around that Block such and such had partitions now, and Mama and my older sisters would walk halfway across the camp to use them. Even after every latrine in camp was screened, this quest for privacy continued. Many would wait in line at night. Ironically, because of this, midnight was often the most crowded time of all.

Like so many of the women there, Mama never did get used to the latrines. It was a humiliation she just learned to endure: *shikata ga nai*, this cannot be helped. She would quickly subordinate her own desires to those of the family or the community, because she knew cooperation was the only way to survive. At the same time, she placed a high premium on

personal privacy, respected it in others and insisted upon it for herself. Almost everyone at Manzanar had inherited this pair of traits from the generations before them who had learned to live in a small, crowded country like Japan. Because of the first, they were able to take a desolate stretch of wasteland and gradually make it livable. But the entire situation there, especially in the beginning—the packed sleeping quarters, the communal mess halls, the open toilets—all this was an open insult to that other, private self, a slap in the face you were powerless to challenge. ❖

JEANNE WAKATSUKI HOUSTON AND JAMES D. HOUSTON

The daughter of a Japanese father and a Japanese-American mother, Jeanne Wakatsuki Houston and her mother, brothers, and sisters were among the first to be interned at Manzanar and among the last to be released. In the foreword to her book *Farewell to Manzanar*, Houston says that it took her 25 years to be able to talk about what happened to her and her family in the internment camp. Writing the book, she says, was "a way of coming to terms with the impact these years have had on my entire life." The book, coauthored with her writer husband, James D. Houston, won instant attention and critical praise when it was published in 1973; three years later, the Houstons collaborated on an award-winning screenplay based on the book.

1934–

1933–

The Houstons have spent most of their lives on the West Coast and have written mainly about their home state of California. They met as students at San Jose State University in California and married in 1957. James Houston served in the U.S. Air Force from 1957 to 1960 and went on to become an award-winning writer of novels and short stories as well as nonfiction.

OTHER WORKS by Jeanne Wakatsuki Houston: *Don't Cry, It's Only Thunder* (with Paul G. Hensler); *Beyond Manzanar and Other Views of Asian-American Womanhood*

OTHER WORKS by James D. Houston: *Between Battles; Gig; Californians: Searching for the Golden State*

WRITING TO PERSUADE

In Unit Two, "Reflecting on Society," many challenged unjust systems and brought about change. To right society's wrongs, it is necessary to take a stand, present convincing arguments, and ask for support. In this lesson you will learn techniques that will help you gain the support of others.

GUIDED ASSIGNMENT

Write a Persuasive Essay Did you ever find a situation that made you say, "Someone ought to do something!"? Have you ever thought that the someone could be you? Fight for your cause! Write an essay persuading readers to correct a situation or to support your position on an issue.

❶ Explore Issues

Find an issue you feel strongly about. Your issue may involve a local, a national, or an international problem.

Looking Close to Home Look into local or state issues that affect your family or that affect you personally. Think about school policies you disagree with or support.

Exploring the Media Scan magazine and newspaper articles, letters to the editor, and political cartoons. Television news stories, documentaries, and movies may also present controversial issues. For example, the news articles and statistics on these pages concern children's rights. Note your initial reactions to each item. What issues are involved in each situation?

❷ Look for Bias

As you come across interesting topics, ask yourself:

- Are all sides of the story reported here?
- What is the writer's position? What is left out?
- What would I need to know before I could take a stand on this issue?

In a small group, discuss issues that interest you and your classmates. Note the feelings and opinions of group members on these issues.

Newspaper Article

Fed up with custody shuffle, boy seeks 'divorce' from parents

Gregory K. wants a divorce.

From his parents.

This isn't the movies, where a poor little rich girl . . . pouts precociously as her Hollywood-gorgeous parents bicker about their marriage.

It's the sad life of a real 11-year-old . . . boy, who–according to court records–has been passed from an abusive, alcoholic dad to a neglectful mom, to a foster home, back to Mom, to another foster home, to a boys ranch and finally to another foster family.

Enough already, Gregory pleads in [his lawsuit]. All he has ever wanted is "a place to be," Gregory once tearfully told a social worker, the lawsuit says.

The boy's attorney . . . says the bespectacled 5th grader, who likes to read and is now making A's and B's, wants to stay with his latest foster family–a couple with eight children of their own. They want to adopt Gregory as their ninth.

The biological parents say no.

Patty Shillington,
from *Chicago Tribune*, April 22, 1992

I think this boy was old enough to decide where he wants to live.

Newspaper Article

Don't laws protect adopted children from being "reclaimed" by their biological parents?

The State of America's Children

Living Arrangements of Children, 1970–1990

1970
- 11%
- 1%
- 3%
- 85%

1990
- 22%
- 3%
- 3%
- 72%

■ Both parents
■ Mother only
■ Father only
■ Neither parent

Children who grow up without fathers are five times more likely to drop out of high school
3 million children were reported abused and neglected in 1993—a number triple that of 1980
1 in 4 homeless people in 1994 was a child under the age of 18
9.4 million children were without health insurance in 1993
Suicide is the third-leading cause of death for young people ages 15–27
5,379 children and teens were killed by gunfire in 1992

Sources: Statistical Abstract of the United States, 1992, 1994

Graph & Data
Circle graphs do not show actual numbers. What do they show?

"Baby Michael" to be taken from the only parents he has ever known

"Baby Michael" will be sleeping in an unfamiliar bed tonight. For the four years of his life, since he was three days old, he has been tucked into bed each night by the adoptive parents who have raised him.

After weeks of hostile negotiations between lawyers for the biological father and the adoptive parents of the boy and hours of sessions with both sets of parents and psychiatric experts, the time has arrived for Michael to be turned over to the biological father he has never met.

"This is the most moving experience I have ever had," said the attorney for the biological father, Melvin Nelson. "We are so happy and excited!"

"This is a tragedy for the boy and for my clients," said the attorney for the adoptive parents. "We thought this could never be allowed to happen."

Negotiations over the transfer of Michael began November 22, the day the Wisconsin Supreme Court, for the second time in six months, ordered Michael to Nelson's custody.

Nelson's efforts to obtain custody of Michael began more than three years ago. He was unaware of the boy's birth and adoption because he was out of the country at the time. Michael's mother, Margaret Clinton, gave the child up for adoption and told the father the child had died. Nelson—now married and the father of a second child—sued for custody of Michael as soon as he learned the truth about him.

This really upsets me! What if I were taken from my adoptive parents?

❸ Record Your Reactions

Spend five to ten minutes writing down your ideas about an issue that has aroused your emotions. What do you already know about this issue? What is your initial position on it? Why do you feel this way? Write freely to see where your thoughts lead you. You may decide to explore another topic if your QuickWrite does not lead you in a satisfying direction.

LASERLINKS
• *WRITING SPRINGBOARD*
WRITING COACH

Investigating the Issue

Filling In the Gaps It is not enough to care about an issue and want to do something about it. You must make sure that your feelings are based on good information and that you've examined the issue from other viewpoints. You must identify questions you have about the issue and begin to answer them.

❶ Analyze Your Position

Examine why you feel strongly about your issue. A tree diagram like the one below may help you to do this. A student's stance on the issue is written on the trunk. Arguments that support his position are written as branches, and basic beliefs underlying his position are written as roots.

Decision Point After thinking about why you feel as you do on an issue, you may decide to change your position or to choose another issue.

Student's Tree Diagram

❷ Collect Information

Consider a variety of sources to fill gaps in your knowledge and to find evidence that supports your position.

- Check magazine, newspaper, and on-line indexes for articles on your topic.
- Interview people directly involved in or affected by your issue.
- Scan the phone book for organizations or agencies concerned with your issue.
- Poll your classmates or computer on-line users to get their opinions.
- Use the Multimedia Handbook for help in researching your topic.

If the information you find does not support your initial position on the issue, you may want to modify or even reverse your position.

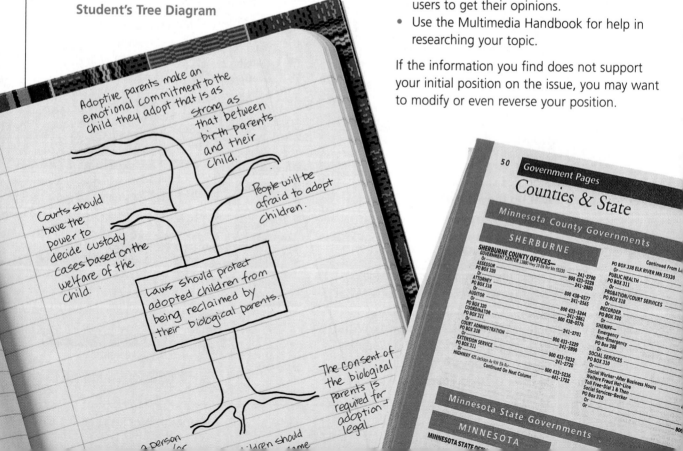

❸ Define Your Audience and Purpose

In a persuasive essay, it is not enough to support your position with valid evidence. To change your readers' minds, you must know who they are. Listing some characteristics of your audience may help you know how you can speak directly to them. Ask yourself the following questions:

- How much does my audience know about the issue?
- What does my audience need to know in order to believe or do what I ask?
- What are some other ways I could publish the arguments in my essay in order to reach my audience? (See Share Your Work, page 347.)

❹ Look Through Others' Eyes

Be aware that there are more viewpoints than yours on your issue. Readers who disagree with your position or who haven't made up their minds will be more likely to consider your arguments if they see that you have considered other points of view. To prepare to defend your position, try any of these activities.

- In a group, brainstorm arguments against your position.
- Do a tree diagram listing arguments and underlying beliefs from another viewpoint.
- With a partner, debate the issue. Ask your partner to argue your position. You should play "devil's advocate" and argue opposing positions in order to understand them better.

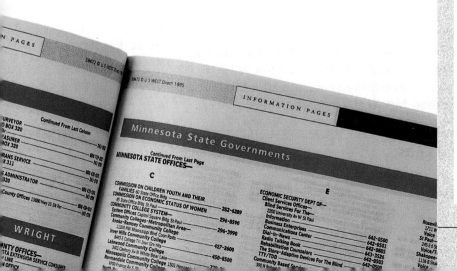

DRAFTING

Getting Your Ideas Down

Building Your Argument By now, you have probably collected a great deal of information. Until you start drafting, however, you may not be sure how you want to use all of it. Let your ideas take shape as you write. Try out different ways of stating your position and of organizing arguments that support it.

1 Write a Discovery Draft

Begin by freewriting. Get down as many arguments and as much important information as you can.

- As you write, think about what's most important. Strengthen some arguments; drop others.
- Include any new ideas you have as you write.
- Keep your goal in mind—to get the support of your audience.
- The Writing Coach can help you at this point.

Student's Discovery Draft

A Case for Adoption

My Discovery Draft

My Comments
My Discovery Draft

Kids' Constitutional Rights Ignored

"This is a travesty of justice," said Governor Smith when he heard the court's decision about "Baby Michael." I agree wholeheartedly with what he said. The child will be torn away forever from his adoptive parents—the only family he has ever known—and placed in the hands of his biological father and the father's wife, people he has never met.

Not only were Michael's rights ignored (the Constitution guarantees ALL people the right to pursue happiness, and Michael was never asked what he wanted) (1st argument), but the judges have placed the four-year-old in the care of people who, in my opinion, do not love him enough to put his interests before their own. (2nd argument)

Michael's adoptive parents made an emotional commitment when they adopted him and every day since then for four years. To take him away is unjust. (3rd argument)

"What about the rights of biological parents?" you might ask. Fathering a child does not mean owning a child. It's true that Michael's biological father sought custody as soon as he learned of the boy's birth. For over three years, the adoptive parents have refused to allow him to see the boy.

Better to begin with explaining my own feelings on adoption?

What is my purpose? Need to say what can be done not just about this case but about larger issue of protecting rights of adopted children and adoptive parents.

This case is more complicated than I thought.

② Review with Your Purpose in Mind

As you read your discovery draft, focus on your ideas. Is your position clear on this issue? Decide whether the arguments and information in your draft support your position and whether they will be clear to your audience and will accomplish your purpose. Think about how you could order your arguments in a way that will convince your readers.

③ Rework and Share

As you write your second draft, the suggestions below may help you.

Hook Them from the Start Ask a question, tell an anecdote, list statistics, or provide a quotation. Make it clear why your audience should care about the issue.

Decide What Comes Next Before giving your arguments, you could give background information or explain the problem. Look over the organizing patterns in the Writing Handbook on page 1042, and choose one that fits your subject.

Order Your Evidence Win the trust of your audience by beginning with statements everyone can agree with. Then progress to more controversial or more emotional arguments.

Call to Action If you want your audience to take specific action, say so clearly and forcefully. Then give them the information they need to take the recommended action.

End on a Powerful Note Restate your original position. It will now carry with it the strength of your evidence and arguments.

 PEER RESPONSE

Before you begin to revise your writing, ask a peer to review your draft and to give you feedback. Questions like the following will help you target your strengths and weaknesses.

- What do you think I'm trying to accomplish?
- What are my strongest arguments?
- Where do you think I need to add more support?

Fine-Tuning Your Essay

Polishing Before Publishing Before presenting your essay, prepare any visuals you'll use when you present your ideas to your audience. Read your draft aloud and listen for places where language could be more precise or powerful. The tips on this page will help you correct and improve your draft.

Student's Final Draft

A Case for Adoption

When I first heard the news that "Baby Michael" would be taken from his adoptive family—the only family he had ever known—and placed in the custody of his biological parents—people he had never met—I was overcome with a familiar feeling of fear. You see, I'm adopted. And for many of my younger years I lived with the haunting dread that something like this could happen to me.

As I watched my nightmare being played out on the six o'clock news, I wondered how one of the highest courts of this land could impose such a horrible sentence upon an innocent boy.

The laws that allowed this must be changed. Courts must protect the rights of adopted children. We must make sure that other children do not suffer Michael's fate.

The institution of adoption itself is endangered. Since 1970, adoptions have decreased by nearly fifty percent, and as more and more cases like Michael's are publicized, the number of children in foster homes grows: 276,000 in 1986; 470,000 now.

What about the rights of biological parents? Just because a person gives birth to or fathers a child does not mean that the person owns that child. The legal system has made some advances from the days of ancient Rome, when a father had the legal right to kill his unwanted children. There are now laws that protect children. "Where we haven't made sufficient progress," says Diane Geraghy, a professor of law at Loyola University and an expert on children's rights, "is in the aggressive implementation of these laws."

① Revise and Edit

Put your draft aside for a day, and then return to it with a fresh, critical eye. Revise your essay to eliminate anything that could detract from your arguments.

- Be sure that you explain the issue and your position in an introduction.
- Check that you have provided support for your arguments and addressed opposing views.
- Use peer comments to identify arguments that are not logical or that need additional support.

Why does the student tell about his own situation?

How does the quotation from an expert help support the student's position and add credibility?

Words are not your only tools of persuasion. How might these visual aids clarify ideas, convey additional information, or intensify interest?

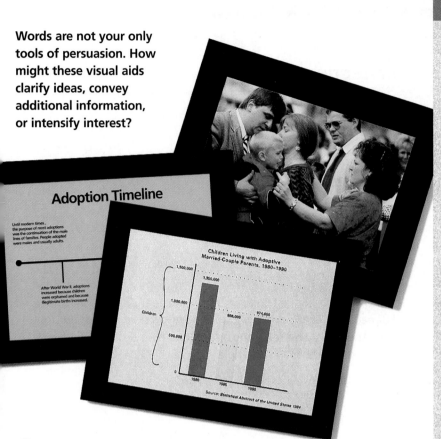

➋ Share Your Work

When you feel strongly about an issue, you want to get your message to as many people as possible. You could publish your essay as an illustrated pamphlet. Charts, photographs, and other illustrations could help to persuade your audience. Also consider these options:

- A letter to the editor of a local newspaper will reach a wide audience.
- Your essay could be an editorial in a school newspaper.
- You could argue your case in a persuasive speech.

Standards for Evaluation

An effective persuasive essay
- sets forth the issue and the writer's position in the introduction
- uses logical arguments that are supported by evidence
- anticipates and answers possible challenges
- uses language effectively and precisely

 GRAMMAR FROM WRITING

Using Pronouns
Use the first- and second-person pronouns *we, us, our, you,* and *your* to make your audience feel more involved and responsive to your arguments. Revise these sentences by adding pronouns.

1. Citizens should not tolerate another tax hike.
2. The school board has made plans to use the money without reporting its plans.

GRAMMAR HANDBOOK

For more information on using pronouns, see page 1069 of the Grammar Handbook.

Editing Checklist Use the following editing tips as you revise.

- Have I checked the spelling of names and accuracy of dates?
- Do the visual aids I'm using accurately represent the information in my essay?

REFLECT & ASSESS

Evaluating the Experience

1. Has this assignment changed your thinking about your issue?
2. How could you have argued your point differently?

PORTFOLIO How well did you argue your position? Put this evaluation in your portfolio along with your published essay.

REFLECT & ASSESS

UNIT TWO: REFLECTING ON SOCIETY

*What insights have you gained into the relationship between
society and individuals as a result of your readings in this unit?
Explore this question by completing one or more of the options
in each of the following sections.*

REFLECTING ON THEME

OPTION 1 **Drawing a Mirror of Society** Consider the different views of society presented in this unit. Choose three selections that made you think about the power of society and its impact on individuals' lives. For each selection, draw a mirror containing words, phrases, and images that suggest your view of the society portrayed in the selection. Then put a check by the mirror that most closely reflects your own views about society.

OPTION 2 **Social-Issues Freewriting** Review the selections you have read, jotting down the problems they address. Circle two or three issues that seem particularly relevant to your life. Then do some freewriting about one or more of those issues. Consider why each issue matters to you and whether your opinions about it have changed as a result of your reading.

OPTION 3 **Charting One's Destiny** Can individuals control their own destinies in society? Working with a partner, decide which of this unit's selections suggest

an affirmative answer to that question and which suggest a negative answer. Then create a two-column chart. In the first column, list examples—drawn both from the selections and from your experience—of individuals who seem to control their own destinies. In the second, list examples of individuals who seem to be controlled by society. On the basis of your perception of your own life, put yourself in one of the two categories.

Self-Assessment: Now that you have had a chance to reflect upon society and its relationship to individuals, create two cluster diagrams. The first should be centered on the topic "My Views of Society"; the second, on the topic "My Place in Society." Put an X next to any entry that represents an insight prompted by a selection in this unit.

REVIEWING LITERARY CONCEPTS

OPTION 1 **Identifying Irony** After reviewing the definition of *irony* on page 246, identify at least four selections in this unit that contain examples of irony. Then fill out a chart similar to the one shown. For each selection, list one or more examples of irony, putting each example in the appropriate column. When finished, pair up with a classmate and compare charts.

Selection	Examples of		
	Situational Irony	Verbal Irony	Dramatic Irony
"The Thrill of the Grass"	Responsible adults break into a stadium and destroy private property—all for the love of a game.		

OPTION 2 **Discussing Point of View** The use of point of view in writing fiction may be compared to the use of a camera in making a movie. A close-up shot brings viewers very close to the subject, offering an intimate view. A wide-angle shot, on the other hand, presents a large scene. Which stories in this unit offer the most intimate view of their subjects? Are those stories told from a first-person or a third-person point of view? Discuss how point of view can affect a reader's sense of closeness to a character.

Self-Assessment: On a sheet of paper, copy the following list of literary terms introduced in this unit. Put a check next to the terms that you believe you could easily define in your own words. Underline the terms that you feel are not easy to define. Then get together with a small group of classmates to discuss the meanings of the terms that seem difficult to define.

stage directions	*first-person point*
simile	*of view*
tone	*satire*
author's purpose	*structure*
third-person point	*speaker*
of view	*style*
irony	*stanza*
theme	*magical realism*

PORTFOLIO BUILDING

- **QuickWrites** In many of the QuickWrites features in this unit, you were asked to write in order to persuade others to adopt or understand a certain view on a social issue. Choose the two of your responses that you think would be most successful at persuading people. Write a cover note supporting your choices, and add the note and the two pieces of writing to your portfolio.

- **Writing About Literature** Earlier, you analyzed a setting presented in one of the selections in this unit. Review your analysis and write a journal entry about it. How easy or difficult was it for you to write the analysis? How successful do you think your analysis is? Why? What did you learn about setting as you wrote your analysis? You may wish to include a copy of your journal entry in your portfolio.

- **Writing from Experience** Review your persuasive essay. As you researched and wrote the essay, what did you discover about your topic? Did your attitude toward your topic change as you worked? If so, how and why do you think it changed? What advice would you give to someone who wants to write persuasively? Jot down your answers to these questions and attach them to your essay.

- **Personal Choice** Look back through all the activities and writing you have completed for this unit, including any work you have done on your own. Which of the activities or writing assignments was the most challenging to work on? Write a note explaining your choice, and add it to your portfolio.

Self-Assessment: Think about the pieces you have just added to your portfolio. How do they compare with the items you added previously? Are your choices beginning to reveal any preferences you may have for certain types of writing or activities?

SETTING GOALS

As you worked through the reading and writing activities in this unit, you probably encountered some people or issues you would like to learn more about. Look back through the unit, making a list of subjects you would like to follow up on in your personal reading.

UNIT THREE

The Lovers (Somali Friends) (1950), Lois Mailou Jones. Casein on canvas, The Evans-Tibbs Collection, Washington, D.C.

In the Name of Love

Great literature,

past or present, is the

expression of great

knowledge of the

human heart.

Edith Hamilton
German-born educator,
writer, and classical scholar
1867-1963

351

THE TIES THAT BIND

Edna St. Vincent Millay
(1892–1950)
One of the most popular American poets of her day

Amy Lowell
(1874–1925)
From an illustrious American family, she dedicated her life to poetry.

Luis Lloréns Torres
(1878–1944)
He came to be known as the poet of Puerto Rico.

Gabriela Mistral
(1889–1957)
Chilean poet, Nobel Prize winner, and diplomat

REFLECTING ON THEME

The writers who created the original Star Trek series for television imagined an entire race of people—the Vulcans—defined by their logic and absence of emotion. For the Vulcans, love's passions posed a threat to reason. In this part of Unit Three, you will read selections that would certainly puzzle the Vulcans. Here, you will encounter a variety of ties created by love.

What Do You Think? Think about a love relationship in your own life. In your notebook, list various feelings that you experience in that relationship. Then create a bar graph that shows the relative frequencies of these feelings. For example, the longest bar might be used to represent contentment, while the shortest bar might be used to represent anger. As you read, compare your experience of love with those described in the selections.

Rosamunde Pilcher	**Lalla** *Which boy will she choose?*	354
Luis Lloréns Torres	**Love Without Love** *What he asks of his love*	370
Amy Lowell	**The Taxi** *Raw emotions with an urban edge*	370
William Shakespeare	**Sonnet 18** *"Shall I compare thee to a summer's day?"*	375
Edna St. Vincent Millay	**Sonnet 30** *All that love is not*	375

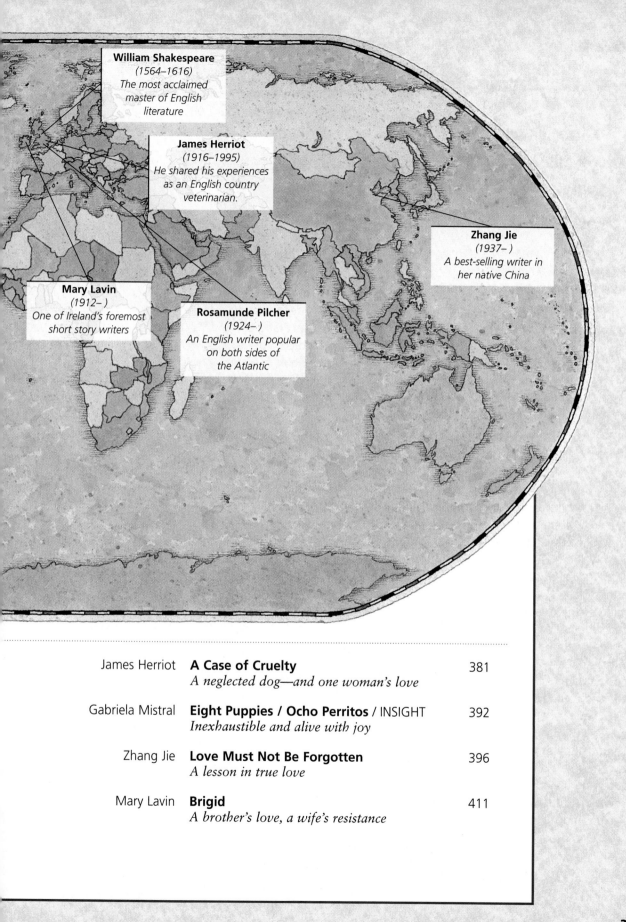

William Shakespeare
(1564–1616)
The most acclaimed master of English literature

James Herriot
(1916–1995)
He shared his experiences as an English country veterinarian.

Zhang Jie
(1937–)
A best-selling writer in her native China

Mary Lavin
(1912–)
One of Ireland's foremost short story writers

Rosamunde Pilcher
(1924–)
An English writer popular on both sides of the Atlantic

PREVIEWING

Lalla
Rosamunde Pilcher England

PERSONAL CONNECTION

When you set a goal for your life or make another important decision, you probably base that decision on your values, the ideals or beliefs that are most important to you. Think about the values that you would consider when setting a goal or making a major decision. In your notebook, list five values that are important to you, then rank them from one to five, with one being the most important.

GEOGRAPHICAL CONNECTION

In the selection you are about to read, Lalla, the main character, makes several life decisions based on her values. One choice she faces is whether to live in the cosmopolitan capital city of London or in a rural village in the county of Cornwall, on the remote southwest coast of England.

Cornwall is popular with tourists and artists for its rugged beauty. The county occupies a long, narrow peninsula that juts into the Atlantic Ocean. The area is mainly rural, with small farming villages scattered through the inland countryside and picturesque fishing towns along the coast. By contrast, London has been one of the world's largest and busiest cities for centuries. The city boasts many famous museums, art galleries, parks, and cathedrals. It also offers a wide variety of job opportunities, fine shops, and exciting night life. In choosing between the excitement of London and the attractions of Cornwall, Lalla discovers what she values most.

READING CONNECTION

Understanding Point of View Point of view refers to the type of narrator used in a story. The short story "Lalla" uses a first-person point of view, in which the narrator is a character in the story who tells everything in his or her own words. This narrator, a young girl named Jane, describes characters and relates events as she sees and understands them. As you read the selection, look for clues to Jane's values in the comments she makes.

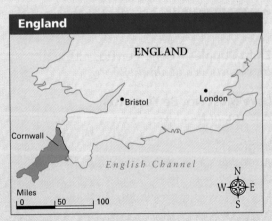

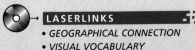

LASERLINKS
- GEOGRAPHICAL CONNECTION
- VISUAL VOCABULARY

Lalla

Rosamunde Pilcher

There was a Before and After. Before was before our father died, when we lived in London, in a tall narrow house with a little garden at the back. When we went on family skiing holidays every winter and attended suitable—and probably very expensive—day schools.

Portrait of Amber (1991), Charles Warren Mundy. Oil on canvas, 8″ × 10″, private collection.

Our father was a big man, outgoing and immensely active. We thought he was immortal, but then most children think that about their father. The worst thing was that Mother thought he was immortal too, and when he died, keeling over on the pavement between the insurance offices where he worked, and the company car into which he was just about to climb, there followed a period of ghastly limbo. Bereft, uncertain, lost, none of us knew what to do next. But after the funeral and a little talk with the family lawyer, Mother quietly pulled herself together and told us.

At first we were horrified. "Leave London? Leave school?" Lalla could not believe it. "But I'm starting 'O' levels[1] next year."

"There are other schools," Mother told her.

"And what about Jane's music lessons?"

"We'll find another teacher."

"I don't mind about leaving school," said Barney. "I don't much like my school anyway."

Mother gave him a smile, but Lalla persisted in her inquisition.[2] "But where are we going to *live?*"

"We're going to Cornwall."

And so it was After. Mother sold the lease of the London house and a removals firm[3] came and packed up all the furniture and we traveled, each silently thoughtful, by car to Cornwall. It was spring, and because Mother had not realized how long the journey would take, it was dark by the time we found the village and, finally, the house. It stood just inside a pair of large gates, backed by tall trees. When we got out of the car, stiff and tired, we could smell the sea and feel the cold wind.

> We were living in the country and there were no boundaries to our new territory.

"There's a light in the window," observed Lalla.

"That'll be Mrs. Bristow," said Mother, and I knew she was making a big effort to keep her voice cheerful. She went up the little path and knocked at the door, and then, perhaps realizing it was ludicrous to be knocking at her own door, opened it. We saw someone coming down the narrow hallway towards us—a fat and bustling lady with grey hair and a hectically flowered pinafore.[4]

"Well, my dear life," she said, "what a journey you must have had. I'm all ready for you. There's a kettle on the hob[5] and a pie in the oven."

The house was tiny compared to the one we had left in London, but we all had rooms to ourselves, as well as an attic for the dolls' house, the books, bricks,[6] model cars and paintboxes we had refused to abandon, and a ramshackle shed alongside the garage where we could keep our bicycles. The garden was even smaller than the London garden, but this didn't matter because now we were living in the country and there were no boundaries to our new territory.

---

1. 'O' levels: in Britain, a series of secondary-school examinations given before students can advance to higher studies.

2. inquisition (ĭn′kwĭ-zĭsh′ən): a lengthy series of questions.

3. removals firm: chiefly British term for a moving company.

4. pinafore (pĭn′ə-fôr): an apron.

5. hob: a warming shelf, especially on the back or side of a fireplace.

6. bricks: chiefly British term for building blocks.

WORDS TO KNOW
bereft (bĭ-rĕft′) *adj.* suffering the death of a loved one; deprived of someone or something important
ludicrous (loo′dĭ-krəs) *adj.* laughably absurd; ridiculous

We explored, finding a wooded lane which led down to a huge inland estuary[7] where it was possible to fish for flounder from the old sea wall.[8] In the other direction, a sandy right-of-way[9] led past the church and over the golf links[10] and the dunes to another beach—a wide and empty shore where the ebb tide[11] took the ocean out half a mile or more.

The Roystons, father, mother and two sons, lived in the big house and were our landlords. We hadn't seen them yet, though Mother had walked, in some trepidation, up the drive to make the acquaintance of Mrs. Royston, and to thank her for letting us have the house. But Mrs. Royston hadn't been in, and poor Mother had had to walk all the way down the drive again with nothing accomplished.

"How old are the Royston boys?" Barney asked Mrs. Bristow.

"I suppose David's thirteen and Paul's about eleven." She looked at us. "I don't know how old you lot are."

"I'm seven," said Barney, "and Jane's twelve and Lalla's fourteen."

"Well," said Mrs. Bristow. "That's nice. Fit in nicely, you would."

"They're far too young for me," said Lalla. "Anyway, I've seen them. I was hanging out the washing for Mother, and they came down the drive and out of the gate on their bicycles. They didn't even look my way."

"Come now," said Mrs. Bristow, "they're probably shy as you are."

"We don't particularly want to know them," said Lalla.

"But . . ." I started and then stopped. I wasn't like Lalla. I wanted to make friends. It would be nice to know the Royston boys. They had a tennis court; I had caught a glimpse of it through the trees. I wouldn't mind being asked to play tennis.

But for Lalla, of course, it was different. Fourteen was a funny age, neither one thing nor the other. And as for the way that Lalla looked! Sometimes I thought that if I didn't love her, and she wasn't my sister, I should hate her for her long, cloudy brown hair, the tilt of her nose, the amazing blue of her eyes, the curve of her pale mouth. During the last six months she seemed to have grown six inches.

I was short and square and my hair was too curly and horribly tangly. The awful bit was, I couldn't remember Lalla ever looking the way I looked, which made it fairly unlikely that I should end up looking like her.

A few days later Mother came back from shopping in the village to say that she had met Mrs. Royston in the grocer's and we had all been asked for tea.

Lalla said, "I don't want to go."

"Why not?" asked Mother.

"They're just little boys. Let Jane and Barney go."

"It's just for tea," pleaded Mother.

She looked so anxious that Lalla gave in. She shrugged and sighed, her face closed in resignation.

We went, and it was a failure. The boys didn't want to meet us any more than Lalla wanted to

---

7. **estuary** (ĕs′chōō-ĕr′ē): the wide part of a river where its currents meet the tides of an ocean or sea.

8. **sea wall:** a wall or embankment built to shelter the coast from storms or erosion.

9. **right-of-way:** a path or road on which the public is allowed to cross private property.

10. **golf links:** a golf course.

11. **ebb tide:** the outgoing tide.

meet them. Lalla was at her coolest, her most remote. I knocked over my teacup, and Barney, who usually chatted to everybody, was silenced by the superiority of his hosts. When tea was over, Lalla stayed with the grown-ups, but Barney and I were sent off with the boys.

"Show Jane and Barney your tree house," Mrs. Royston told them as we trailed out of the door.

They took us out into the garden and showed us the tree house. It was a marvelous piece of construction, strong and roomy. Barney's face was filled with longing. "Who built it?" he asked.

"Our cousin Godfrey. He's eighteen. He can build anything. It's our club, and you're not members."

They whispered together and went off, leaving us standing beneath the forbidden tree house.

When the summer holidays came, Mother appeared to have forgotten about our social debt to the Royston boys, and we were careful not to remind her. So their names were never raised, and we never saw them except at a distance, cycling off to the village or down to the beach. Sometimes on Sunday afternoons they had guests and played tennis on their court. I longed to be included, but Lalla, deep in a book, behaved as though the Roystons didn't exist. Barney had taken up gardening, and, with his usual single-mindedness, was concentrating on digging himself a vegetable patch. He said he was going to sell lettuces,

and Mother said that maybe he was the one who was going to make our fortune.

It was a hot summer, made for swimming. Lalla had grown out of her old swimsuit, so Mother made her a cotton bikini out of scraps. It was pale blue, just right for her tan and her long, pale hair. She looked beautiful in it, and I longed to look just like her. We went to the beach most days and often saw the Royston boys there. But the beach was so vast that there was no necessity for social contact, and we all avoided each other.

Until one Sunday. The tide came in during the afternoon that day, and Mother packed us a picnic so we could set off after lunch. When we got to the beach, Lalla said she was going to swim right away, but Barney and I decided we would wait. We took our spades and went down to where the outgoing tide had left shallow pools in the sand. There we started the construction of a large and complicated harbor. Absorbed in our task, we lost track of time, and never noticed the stranger approaching. Suddenly a long shadow fell across the sparkling water.

I looked up, shading my eyes against the sun. He said "Hello" and squatted down to our level.

"Who are you?" I asked.

"I'm Godfrey Howard, the Roystons' cousin. I'm staying with them."

Illustration by
Robbin Gourley

Barney suddenly found his tongue. "Did you build the tree house?"

"That's right."

"How *did* you do it?"

Godfrey began to tell him. I listened and wondered how any person apparently so nice could have anything to do with those hateful Royston boys. It wasn't that he was particularly good-looking. His hair was mousey, his nose too big and he wore spectacles. He wasn't even very tall. But there was something warm and friendly about his deep voice and his smile.

"Did you go up and look at it?"

Barney went back to his digging. Godfrey looked at me. I said, "They wouldn't let us. They said it was a club. They didn't like us."

"They think you don't like them. They think you come from London and that you're very grand."

This was astonishing. "Grand? *Us?*" I said indignantly. "We never even pretended to be grand." And then I remembered Lalla's coolness, her pale, unsmiling lips. "I mean—Lalla's older—it's different for her." His silence at this was encouraging. "I wanted to make friends," I admitted.

He was sympathetic. "It's difficult sometimes. People are shy." All at once he stopped, and looked over my shoulder. I turned to see what had caught his attention and saw Lalla coming towards us across the sand. Her hair lay like wet silk over her shoulders, and she had knotted her red towel around her hips like a sarong.[12] As she approached, Godfrey stood up. I said, introducing them the way Mother introduced people, "This is Lalla."

"Hello, Lalla," said Godfrey.

"He's the Roystons' cousin," I went on quickly. "He's staying with them."

"Hello," said Lalla.

Godfrey said, "David and Paul are wanting to play cricket. It's not much good playing cricket with just three people and I wondered if you'd come and join us?"

"Lalla won't want to play cricket," I told myself. "She'll snub him and then we'll never be asked again."

But she didn't snub him. She said, uncertainly, "I don't think I'm much good at cricket."

"But you could always try?"

"Yes." She began to smile, "I suppose I could always try."

And so we all finally got together. We played a strange form of beach cricket invented by Godfrey, which involved much lashing out at the ball and hysterical running. When we were too hot to play any longer, we swam. The Roystons had a couple of wooden surfboards, and they let us have turns, riding in on our stomachs on the long, warm breakers of the flood tide.[13] By five o'clock we were ready for tea, and we collected our various baskets and haversacks[14] and sat around in a circle on the sand. Other people's picnics are always much nicer than one's own, so we ate the Royston sandwiches and chocolate biscuits, and they ate Mother's scones with loganberry jam in the middle.

We had a last swim before the tide turned, and then gathered up our belongings and walked slowly home together. Barney and the two Roystons led the way, planning the next day's activities, and I walked with Godfrey and Lalla. But gradually, in the natural manner of events, they fell behind me. Plodding up and over the springy turf of the golf course, I listened to their voices.

12. **sarong:** a skirtlike garment formed by wrapping cloth around the waist.

13. **flood tide:** the incoming tide.

14. **haversacks** (hăv′ər-săks′): supply bags carried over one shoulder, popular with hikers.

First Sail (1993), Charles Warren Mundy. Oil on canvas, 30″ × 40″, private collection.

"Do you like living here?"

"It's different from London."

"That's where you lived before?"

"Yes, but my father died, and we couldn't afford to live there any more."

"I'm sorry, I didn't know. Of course, I envy your living here. I'd rather be at Carwheal than anywhere else in the world."

"Where do you live?"

"In Bristol."

"Are you at school there?"

"I've finished with school. I'm starting college in September. I'm going to be a vet."

"A vet?" Lalla considered this. "I've never met a vet before."

He laughed. "You haven't actually met one yet."

I smiled to myself in satisfaction. They sounded like two grown-ups talking. Perhaps a grown-up friend of her own was all that Lalla had needed. I had a feeling that we had crossed another watershed.[15] After today, things would be different.

---

15. **watershed:** a critical point that marks a division or a change of course; a turning point.

The Roystons were now our friends. Our relieved mothers—for Mrs. Royston, faced with our unrelenting enmity, had been just as concerned and conscience-stricken as Mother—took advantage of the truce, and after that Sunday we were never out of each other's houses. Through the good offices[16] of the Roystons, our social life widened, and Mother found herself driving us all over the county to attend various beach picnics, barbecues, sailing parties and teenage dances. By the end of the summer we had been accepted. We had dug ourselves in. Carwheal was home. And Lalla grew up.

She and Godfrey wrote to each other. I knew this because I would see his letters to her lying on the table in the hall. She would take them upstairs to read them in secret in her room, and we were all too great respecters of privacy ever to mention them. When he came to Carwheal, which he did every holiday, to stay with the Roystons, he was always around first thing in the morning on the first day. He said it was to see us all, but we knew it was Lalla he had come to see.

He now owned a battered second-hand car. A lesser man might have scooped Lalla up and taken her off on her own, but Godfrey was far too kind, and he would drive for miles, to distant coves and hilltops, with the whole lot of us packed into his long-suffering car, and the boot[17] filled with food and towels and snorkels and other assorted clobber.[18]

But he was only human, and often they would drift off on their own and walk away from us. We would watch their progress and let them go, knowing that in an hour or two they would be back—Lalla with a bunch of wild flowers or some shells in her hand, Godfrey sunburned and tousled—both of them smiling and content in a way that we found reassuring and yet did not wholly understand.

Lalla had always been such a certain person, so positive, so unveering from a chosen course, that we were all taken by surprise by her vacillating indecision as to what she was going to do with her life. She was nearly eighteen, with her final exams over and her future spread before her like a new country observed from the peak of some painfully climbed hill.

Mother wanted her to go to university.

"Isn't it rather a waste of time if I don't know what I'm going to do at the end of it? How can I decide now what I'm going to do with the rest of my life? It's inhuman. Impossible."

"But darling, what do you want to do?"

"I don't know. Travel, I suppose. Of course, I could be really original and take a typing course."

"It might at least give you time to think things over."

This conversation took place at breakfast. It might have continued forever, reaching no satisfactory conclusion, but the post arrived as we sat there over our empty coffee cups. There was the usual dull bundle of envelopes, but, as well, a large square envelope for Lalla. She opened it idly, read the card inside and made a face. "Goodness, how grand, a proper invitation to a proper dance."

"How nice," said Mother, trying to decipher the butcher's bill. "Who from?"

"Mrs. Menheniot," said Lalla.

We were all instantly agog, grabbing at the invitation in order to gloat over it. We had once been to lunch with Mrs. Menheniot, who lived with Mr. Menheniot and a tribe of junior Menheniots in a beautiful house on the Fal.[19] For

---

16. **offices:** kind acts performed to help someone else.
17. **boot:** British term for the trunk of a car.
18. **clobber:** British slang for clothing or equipment.
19. **Fal:** a river in western Cornwall.

WORDS TO KNOW

enmity (ĕn'mĭ-tē) *n.* the hatred between enemies; antagonism; hostility
vacillating (văs'ə-lāt'ĭng) *adj.* swinging indecisively from one course of action or opinion to another **vacillate** *v.*
decipher (dĭ-sī'fər) *v.* to read or interpret something unclear; to figure out

361

some unspecified reason they were very rich, and their house was vast and white with a pillared portico[20] and green lawns which sloped down to the tidal inlets of the river.

"Are you going to go?" I asked.

Lalla shrugged. "I don't know."

"It's in August. Perhaps Godfrey will be here and you can go with him."

"He's not coming down this summer. He has to earn money to pay his way through college."

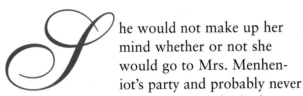he would not make up her mind whether or not she would go to Mrs. Menheniot's party and probably never would have come to any decision if it had not been for the fact that, before very long, I had been invited too. I was really too young, as Mrs. Menheniot's booming voice pointed out over the telephone when she rang Mother, but they were short of girls and it would be a blessing if I could be there to swell the numbers. When Lalla knew that I had been asked as well, she said of course we would go. She had passed her driving test, and we would borrow Mother's car.

We were then faced with the problem of what we should wear, as Mother could not begin to afford to buy us the sort of evening dresses we wanted. In the end she sent away to Liberty's[21] for yards of material, and she made them for us, beautifully, on her sewing machine. Lalla's was pale blue lawn and in it she looked like a goddess—Diana the Huntress perhaps. Mine was a sort of tawny-gold, and I looked quite presentable in it, but of course not a patch on[22] Lalla.

When the night of the dance came, we put on our dresses and set off together in Mother's Mini,[23] giggling slightly with nerves. But when we reached the Menheniots' house, we stopped giggling because the whole affair was so grand as to be awesome. There were floodlights and

car parks[24] and hundreds of sophisticated-looking people all making their way towards the front door.

Indoors, we stood at the foot of the crowded staircase, and I was filled with panic. We knew nobody. There was not a single familiar face. Lalla whisked a couple of glasses of champagne from a passing tray and gave me one. I took a sip, and at that very moment a voice rang out above the hubbub. "Lalla!" A girl was coming down the stairs, a dark girl in a strapless satin dress that had very obviously not been made on her mother's sewing machine.

Lalla looked up. "Rosemary!"

She was Rosemary Sutton from London. She and Lalla had been at school together in the old days. They fell into each other's arms and embraced as though this was all either of them had been waiting for. "What are you doing? I never thought I'd see you here. How marvelous. Come and meet Allan. You remember my brother Allan, don't you? Oh, this is exciting."

Allan was so good-looking as to be almost unreal. Fair as his sister was dark, impeccably turned out. Lalla was tall, but he was taller. He looked down at her, and his rather wooden features were filled with both surprise and obvious pleasure. He said, "But of course I remember." He smiled and laid down his glass. "How could I forget? Come and dance."

I scarcely saw her again all evening. He took her away from me, and I was bereft, as though I had lost my sister forever. At one point I was

---

20. **pillared portico** (pĭl'ərd pôr'tĭ-kō'): a porch with a roof supported by columns.

21. **Liberty's:** a London store especially famous for the fabric it sells.

22. **not a patch on:** not nearly as good as.

23. **Mini** (mĭn'ē): a small, fairly inexpensive, popular British car.

24. **car parks:** British term for parking lots.

WORDS
TO
KNOW

impeccably (ĭm-pĕk'ə-blē) *adv.* flawlessly; perfectly

362

rescued by Mrs. Menheniot herself, who dragooned[25] some young man into taking me to supper, but after supper even he melted away. I found an empty sofa in a deserted sitting-out room,[26] and collapsed into it. It was half-past-twelve, and I longed for my bed. I wondered what people would think if I put up my feet and had a little snooze.

Somebody came into the room and then withdrew again. I looked up and saw his retreating back view. I said, "Godfrey." He turned back. I got up off the sofa, back on to my aching feet.

"What are you doing here? Lalla said you were working."

"I am, but I wanted to come. I drove down from Bristol. That's why I'm so late." I knew why he had wanted to come. To see Lalla. "I didn't expect to see you."

"They were short of girls, so I got included."

We gazed glumly at each other, and my heart felt very heavy. Godfrey's dinner jacket looked as though he had borrowed it from some larger person, and his bow tie was crooked. I said, "I think Lalla's dancing."

"Why don't you come and dance with me, and we'll see."

I thought this a rotten idea but didn't like to say so. Together we made our way towards the ballroom. The ceiling lights had been turned off, and the disco lights now flashed red and green and blue across the smoky darkness. Music thumped and rocked an assault on our ears, and the floor seemed to be filled with an unidentifiable confusion of people, of flying hair and arms and legs. Godfrey and I joined in at the edge, but I could tell that his heart wasn't in it.

I wished that he had never come. I prayed that he would not find Lalla.

But of course, he saw her, because it was impossible not to. It was impossible to miss Allan Sutton as well. They were both so tall, so beautiful. Godfrey's face seemed to close up.

"Who's she with?" he asked.

"Allan Sutton. He and his sister have come down from London. Lalla used to know them."

I couldn't say any more. I couldn't tell Godfrey to go and claim her for himself. I wasn't even certain by then what sort of a reception she would have given him. And anyway, as we watched them, Allan stopped dancing and put his arm around Lalla, drawing her towards him, whispering something into her ear. She slipped her hand into his, and they moved away towards the open French window.[27] The next moment they were lost to view, swallowed into the darkness of the garden beyond.

I couldn't say any more. I couldn't tell Godfrey to go and claim her for himself.

*A*t four o'clock in the morning Lalla and I drove home in silence. We were not giggling now. I wondered sadly if we would ever giggle together again. I ached with exhaustion, and I was out of sympathy with her. Godfrey had never even spoken to her. Soon after our dance he had said

25. **dragooned** (drə-goond′): compelled by threats or force. The term is used humorously here.

26. **sitting-out room:** a room used by those not dancing.

27. **French window:** a type of window that extends to the floor.

goodbye and disappeared, presumably to make the long, lonely journey back to Bristol.

She, on the other hand, had an aura of happiness about her that was almost tangible. I glanced at her and saw her peaceful, smiling profile. It was hard to think of anything to say.

It was Lalla who finally broke the silence. "I know what I'm going to do. I mean, I know what I'm going to do with my life. I'm going back to London. Rosemary says I can live with her. I'll take a secretarial course or something, then get a job."

"Mother will be disappointed."

"She'll understand. It's what I've always wanted. We're buried down here. And there's another thing; I'm tired of being poor. I'm tired of homemade dresses and never having a new car. We've always talked about making our fortunes, and as I'm the eldest, I might as well make a start. If I don't do it now, I never will."

I said, "Godfrey was there this evening."

"Godfrey?"

"He drove down from Bristol."

She did not say anything, and I was angry. I wanted to hurt her and make her feel as bad as I felt. "He came because he wanted to see you. But you didn't even notice him."

"You can scarcely blame me," said Lalla, "for that."

And so she went back to London, lived with Rosemary, and took a secretarial course, just as she said she would. Later, she got a job on the editorial staff of a fashionable magazine, but it was not long before one of the photographers spied her potential, seduced her from her typewriter, and started taking pictures of her. Soon her lovely face smiled at us from the cover of the magazine.

"How does it feel to have a famous daughter?" people asked Mother, but she never quite accepted Lalla's success, just as she never quite accepted Allan Sutton. Allan's devotion to Lalla had proved unswerving and he was her constant companion.

"Let's hope he doesn't marry her," said Barney, but of course eventually, inevitably, they decided to do just that. "We're engaged!" Lalla rang up from London to tell us. Her voice sounded, unnervingly, as though she was calling from the next room.

"Darling!" said Mother, faintly.

"Oh, do be pleased. Please be pleased. I'm so happy and I couldn't bear it if you weren't happy, too."

So of course Mother said that she was pleased, but the truth was that none of us really liked Allan very much. He was—well—spoilt. He was conceited. He was too rich. I said as much to Mother, but Mother was loyal to Lalla. She said, "Things mean a lot to Lalla. I think they always have. I mean, possessions and security. And perhaps someone who truly loves her."

I said, "Godfrey truly loved her."

"But that was when they were young. And perhaps Godfrey couldn't give her love."

"He could make her laugh. Allan never makes her laugh."

"Perhaps," said Mother sadly, "she's grown out of laughter."

And then it was Easter. We hadn't heard from Lalla for a bit and didn't expect her to come to Carwheal for the spring holiday. But she rang up, out of the blue, and said that she hadn't been well and was taking a couple of weeks off. Mother was delighted, of course, but concerned about her health.

By now we were all more or less grown-up. David was studying to be a

WORDS TO KNOW   **unnervingly** (ŭn-nûrv'ĭng-lē) *adv.* in a way that causes someone to become nervous or upset; disturbingly

doctor, and Paul had a job on the local newspaper. I had achieved a place at the Guildhall School of Music, and Barney was no longer a little boy but a gangling teenager with an insatiable appetite. Still, however, we gathered for the holidays, and that Easter Godfrey abandoned his sick dogs and ailing cows to the ministrations[28] of his partner and joined us.

It was lovely weather, almost as warm as summer. The sort of weather that makes one feel young again—a child. There was scented thyme on the golf links, and the cliff walks were starred with primroses and wild violets. In the Roystons' garden the daffodils blew in the long grass beneath the tree house, and Mrs. Royston put up the tennis net and swept the cobwebs out of the summer house.

It was during one of these sessions that Godfrey and I talked about Lalla. We were in the summer house together, sitting out while the others played a set.

"Tell me about Lalla."

"She's engaged."

"I know. I saw it in the paper." I could think of nothing to say. "Do you like him—Allan Sutton, I mean?"

I said "Yes," but I was never much good at lying.

Godfrey turned his head and looked at me. He was wearing old jeans and a white shirt, and I thought that he had grown older in a subtle way. He was more sure of himself and somehow more attractive.

He said, "That night of the Menheniots' dance, I was going to ask her to marry me."

"Oh, Godfrey."

"I hadn't even finished my training, but I thought perhaps we'd manage. And when I saw her, I knew that I had lost her. I'd left it too late."

On the day that Lalla was due to arrive, I took Mother's old car into the neighboring town to do some shopping. When the time came to return home, the engine refused to start. After struggling for a bit, I walked to the nearest garage and persuaded a kindly, oily man to come and help me. But he told me it was hopeless.

We walked back to the garage, and I telephoned home. But it wasn't Mother who answered the call, it was Godfrey.

I explained what had happened. "Lalla's train is due at the junction in about half an hour and we said someone would meet her."

There was a momentary hesitation, then Godfrey said, "I'll go. I'll take my car."

When I finally reached home, exhausted from carrying the laden grocery bags from the bus stop, Godfrey's car was nowhere to be seen.

A short time later the telephone rang. But it wasn't Lalla, explaining where they were, it was a call from London and it was Allan Sutton.

"I have to speak to Lalla."

His voice sounded frantic. I said cautiously, "Is anything wrong?"

"She's broken off our engagement. I got back from the office and found a letter from her and my ring. She said she was coming home. She doesn't want to get married."

---

28. **ministrations** (mĭn´ĭ-strā´shəns): services performed to aid someone or something.

Illustration by
Robbin Gourley

The Cove (1964), Fairfield Porter. Oil on canvas, $37'' \times 53\frac{1}{2}''$, The Metropolitan Museum of Art, New York, bequest of Arthur M. Bullowa, 1993 (1993.406.7). Copyright © 1995 The Metropolitan Museum of Art.

I found it in my heart to be very sorry for him. "But Allan, you must have had *some* idea."

"None. Absolutely none. It's just a bolt from the blue. I know she's been a bit off-color lately, but I thought she was just tired."

"She must have her reasons, Allan," I told him, as gently as I could.

"Talk to her, Jane. Try to make her see sense."

He rang off at last. I put the receiver back on the hook and stood for a moment, gathering my wits about me and assessing this new and startling turn of events. I found myself caught up in a tangle of conflicting emotions. Enormous sympathy for Allan; a reluctant admiration for

Lalla, who had had the courage to take this shattering decision; but, as well, a sort of rising excitement.

Godfrey. Godfrey and Lalla. Where were they? I knew then that I could not face Mother and Barney before I had found out what was going on. Quietly, I opened the door and went out of the house, through the gates, down the lane. As soon as I turned the corner at the end of the lane, I saw Godfrey's car parked on the patch of grass outside the church.

It was a marvelously warm, benign sort of evening. I took the path that led past the church and towards the beach. Before I had gone very far, I saw them, walking up over the golf links towards me. The wind blew Lalla's hair over her face. She was wearing her London high-heeled boots so was taller than Godfrey. They should have appeared ill-assorted, but there was something about them that was totally right. They were a couple, holding hands, walking up from the beach as they had walked innumerable times, together.

I stopped, suddenly reluctant to disturb their intimacy. But Lalla had seen me. She waved and then let go of Godfrey's hand and began to run towards me, her arms flailing like windmills.

"Jane!" I had never seen her so exuberant.

"Oh, Jane." I ran to meet her. We hugged each other, and for some stupid reason my eyes were full of tears.

"Oh, darling Jane . . ."

"I had to come and find you."

"Did you wonder where we were? We went for a walk. I had to talk to Godfrey. He was the one person I could talk to."

"Lalla, Allan's been on the phone."

"I had to do it. It was all a ghastly mistake."

"But you found out in time. That's all that matters."

"I thought I was going after what I wanted. I thought I had what I wanted, and then I found out that I didn't want it at all. Oh, I've missed you all so much. There wasn't anybody I could talk to."

Over her shoulder I saw Godfrey coming, tranquilly, to join us. I let go of Lalla and went to give him a kiss. I didn't know what they had been discussing as they paced the lonely beach, and I knew that I never would. But still, I had the feeling that the outcome could be nothing but good for all of us.

I said, "We must go back. Mother and Barney don't know about anything. They'll be thinking that I've dissolved into thin air, as well as the pair of you."

"In that case," said Godfrey, and he took Lalla's hand in his own once more, "perhaps we'd better go and tell them."

And so we walked home, the three of us. In the warm evening, in the sunshine, in the fresh wind. ❖

WORDS TO KNOW   **benign** (bǐ-nīn') *adj.* mild; gentle

367

RESPONDING
OPTIONS

FROM PERSONAL RESPONSE TO CRITICAL ANALYSIS

REFLECT 1. What was your reaction to the story? Describe your reaction in your notebook.

RETHINK 2. Do you think Lalla made a wise choice in the end? Why or why not?

3. In what ways, if any, do you think Lalla's values change as she gets older? Use examples from the story to support your opinion.
   Consider
   - her reaction to moving to Cornwall
   - her relationships with Godfrey and Allan
   - her comments to Jane after the Menheniots' dance
   - her final decision

4. How does Jane's view of her older sister affect what you think of Lalla?

RELATE 5. What values do you think are most important for people to consider when they choose a mate?

ANOTHER PATHWAY

Cooperative Learning

With three or four other classmates, act out an imaginary conversation that takes place ten years after the story. Choose among the roles of Lalla, Godfrey, Jane, Mother, and Allan, and reminisce about "the old days." In the role of your character, talk about what happened and why you made the decisions you did.

LITERARY CONCEPTS

Many stories open with **exposition,** background information that usually introduces the characters, describes the setting, and summarizes significant events that took place before the story's action begins. In "Lalla," the exposition tells us about Lalla and her family and explains why they are moving to Cornwall. How does this exposition help explain Lalla's later interest in Allan and in living in London?

QUICKWRITES

1. Imagine that this story is being turned into a television movie. Write a **proposal** for a new title that will attract viewers. Be sure to explain your reasoning.

2. Create the **two lists of pros and cons** Lalla might have made before she decided to return to Cornwall. On one list, show the benefits and problems of staying with Allan. On the other, analyze the advantages and disadvantages of returning to Godfrey.

3. Write a **script** for a telephone conversation between Lalla and Allan in which she explains why she is leaving him and moving back to Cornwall.

PORTFOLIO Save your writing. You may want to use it later as a springboard to a piece for your portfolio.

ALTERNATIVE ACTIVITIES

1. Create a **poster.** One side should include images that represent Allan's values; the other side should represent Godfrey's values.

2. Create **valentines** that Godfrey and Allan might have sent Lalla. In each, try to reflect the background and personality of the sender.

CRITIC'S CORNER

A magazine editor once noted, "When Rosamunde Pilcher writes about people, in crisis or at peace, falling in or out of love, discovering new life or accepting death, readers see themselves . . . or their children . . . or their parents." Did you agree? Explain.

WORDS TO KNOW

EXERCISE A Review the Words to Know at the bottom of the selection pages and write the word that is closest in meaning to the italicized word or phrase in each sentence.

1. Allan spoke with *grudging acceptance* of Lalla's engagement to Godfrey.
2. Jane knew she would feel *very lonely* after Lalla got married.
3. Mother was exasperated with Lalla for *changing her mind* so often about the wedding plans.
4. For Lalla's sake, Godfrey and Allan put aside their *intense dislike* for each other.
5. On the wedding day the weather turned sunny and *mild.*
6. Before the ceremony, Uncle Peter spoke *distressingly* to Godfrey about the responsibilities of married life.
7. Remembering Uncle Peter's advice, Godfrey felt some *anxiety* about getting married.
8. Aunt Fran arrived wearing a *very silly* green feathered hat.
9. Allan missed the wedding because he could not *figure out* the map Barney sent him.
10. The ceremony went exactly as planned, and the organist played the wedding music *without a single mistake.*

EXERCISE B With a partner, take turns using facial expressions and/or body gestures to act out the meaning of three Words to Know each and guessing what word is being shown.

ROSAMUNDE PILCHER

Although she now lives in Scotland, Rosamunde Pilcher grew up in Cornwall, the setting of her story "Lalla." She joined the Women's Royal Naval Service during World War II and became a writer soon after the war ended. From 1949 to 1987 she published more than 20 romantic novels. Though her work was largely ignored by British critics, some of it was well received in America. Praise from the *New York Times* for her novel *Sleeping Tiger* (1967) brought Rosamunde Pilcher to the attention of *Good Housekeeping* magazine, which has since published many of her stories. Nevertheless, it was not until *The*

1924–

Shell Seekers appeared in 1988 that she found herself treated as a serious novelist.

Pilcher accepts being called a writer of "light fiction," but she dislikes the label "romantic fiction" and the contempt that often goes with it. After winning respect with *The Shell Seekers,* she commented, "All my life I've had people coming up and saying, 'Sat under the hair dryer and read one of your little stories, dear. So clever of you. Wish I had the time to do it myself.' . . . And now I'm hoping that nobody will ever, ever say that again."
OTHER WORKS *The Blue Bedroom and Other Stories, September, Flowers in the Rain and Other Stories*

PREVIEWING

Love Without Love
Luis Lloréns Torres (loo-ēs′ yô-rĕns′ tô′rĕs) **Puerto Rico**

The Taxi
Amy Lowell **United States**

PERSONAL CONNECTION

In a small group, identify images that suggest romantic love in our culture. For example, you might think of a movie scene with two lovers on a moonlit walk or a television commercial that portrays a man and a woman nestled before a fireplace. Then discuss what these images reveal about our views of romantic love. Use a chart like the one shown to keep track of your images and what they reveal. Share your findings with your classmates.

Romantic Love in Our Culture	
Image	**What It Reveals**
a man and a woman on a moonlit walk	• peacefulness of love • love removed from the harsh realities of ordinary life

LITERARY CONNECTION

The following two poems use vivid, unexpected images to convey the poets' ideas about romantic love. The first poem is by Luis Lloréns Torres, a famous Puerto Rican poet who began publishing his verse in 1899 and was noted for his love poems and his patriotic verse. The second poem is by Amy Lowell, an American poet who won fame just a few years after Lloréns Torres. This poem reflects Lowell's interest in **imagism,** a literary movement that stressed the importance of using clear, precise images in poetry.

WRITING CONNECTION

In your notebook, create your own image of romantic love, one that conveys your own thoughts and feelings. You may either draw a picture of that image or describe it in words. Then explain how your image communicates what love means to you. As you read the following poems, look for the images the poets use to describe their feelings about love.

Love Without Love

Luis Lloréns Torres

I love you, because in my thousand and one nights of dreams,
I never once dreamed of you.
I looked down paths that traveled from afar,
but it was never you I expected.
5   Suddenly I've felt you flying through my soul
in quick, lofty flight,
and how beautiful you seem way up there, far
from my always idiot heart!
Love me that way, flying over everything.
10 And, like the bird on its branch, land in my arms
only to rest,
then fly off again.
Be not like the romantic ones who,
    in love, set me on fire.
When you climb up my mansion,
15 enter so lightly, that as you enter
the dog of my heart will not bark.

Translated by Julio Marzán

FROM PERSONAL RESPONSE TO CRITICAL ANALYSIS

REFLECT   1. Think about the image from this poem that stands out the most to you. In your notebook, jot down what this image makes you think of.

RETHINK   2. What does the speaker's choice of images say to you about his attitude toward his relationship with his loved one?
Consider
• the image of the bird flying through his soul in lines 5–6
• the speaker's reference to his "idiot heart" in line 8
• the contrast between his beloved and "the romantic ones" in line 13
• the speaker's request in lines 15–16

3. What does the title of the poem mean to you?

RELATE   4. Compare and contrast your ideas about love with those of the speaker.

THE TAXI

AMY LOWELL

When I go away from you
The world beats dead
Like a slackened drum.
I call out for you against the jutted stars
5 And shout into the ridges of the wind.
Streets coming fast,
One after the other,
Wedge you away from me,
And the lamps of the city prick my eyes
10 So that I can no longer see your face.
Why should I leave you,
To wound myself upon the sharp edges of the night?

Times Square, New York City No. 2 (1990), Robert Gniewek. Oil on linen, 38″ × 60″, courtesy of Louis K. Meisel Gallery, New York. Photo by Steve Lopez.

RESPONDING OPTIONS

FROM PERSONAL RESPONSE TO CRITICAL ANALYSIS

REFLECT

1. What questions would you like to ask the speaker in "The Taxi"? Jot down those questions in your notebook.

RETHINK

2. Based on the images used in this poem, how would you describe the speaker's feelings about love?

   Consider
   - the sound a slackened drum would make, as described in lines 2–3
   - her sense of the streets wedging her loved one away from her (line 8)
   - the last two lines, where she compares leaving her loved one to being wounded

3. Do you think "The Taxi" is a good title for this poem? Explain your reasoning.

RELATE

4. Compare and contrast the speakers' attitudes toward love in "Love Without Love" and "The Taxi."

5. Which speaker's view of love appeals more to you? Explain your choice.

ANOTHER PATHWAY

With the class as a whole, stage a television talk show in which one student, the host, interviews four classmates posing as the two couples represented in "Love Without Love" and "The Taxi." The rest of the class will act as the studio audience. Have the host and members of the audience ask the couples about their views of love and the relationship they have or want.

LITERARY CONCEPTS

A **metaphor** is a form of figurative language that makes a comparison between two things that have something in common. Some metaphors make the comparison directly, while others imply it. Explain the metaphor in lines 5–9 of "Love Without Love." How does the image of love expressed in this metaphor compare to some of the images you identified and discussed for the Personal Connection on page 370?

CONCEPT REVIEW: Simile Identify a **simile** in each poem. What ideas are being communicated in each simile?

metaphor — is

simile — like or as

QUICKWRITES

1. Using the image you created for the Writing Connection on page 370, write a **poem** that expresses your feelings about the nature of love.

2. The images in "The Taxi" convey feelings about love by describing the pain of being separated from the loved one. Develop a **list of images** that the speaker might use to convey how she feels when she is with her loved one.

3. Write a **journal entry** in which the speaker of "Love Without Love" records a perfect day with his loved one.

   PORTFOLIO Save your writing. You may want to use it later as a springboard to a piece for your portfolio.

ALTERNATIVE ACTIVITIES

1. Make a **tape-recording** of songs that reflect the views about love expressed in either one of the poems.

2. Create a **sketch** showing a figurative expression from one of the poems in a literal way. For example, you might show a night scene that literally has sharp edges.

3. Put together a **photographic essay** that contrasts the ideas of love expressed in these two poems.

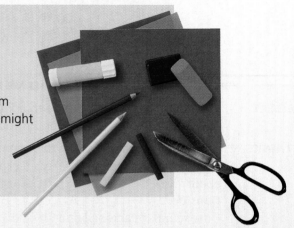

LUIS LLORÉNS TORRES

One of Puerto Rico's most respected modern poets, Luis Lloréns Torres (1878–1944) said the goal of the poet "consists of the presentation in a sensitive manner of scenes and landscapes of the ideal world . . . existing in every poet's imagination." Lloréns Torres took up writing poetry when he was studying law in Spain. He was still in Spain when he published his first book of verse, *At the Foot of the Alhambra,* in 1899. On returning to Puerto Rico, he served in the Puerto Rican legislature and joined with other political leaders who supported independence from the United States. Lloréns Torres also founded and edited the *Antilles Journal,* a literary journal that was highly respected in Puerto Rico and the rest of Latin America. In the journal, he published his own poetry along with works by other leading Latin American writers. Lloréns Torres's association with the *Antilles Journal,* as well as subsequent work, won him a place as a major poet of Latin America.

OTHER WORKS Poems in *The Puerto Rican Poets* and in *Inventing a Word*

AMY LOWELL

1874–1925

A member of an illustrious American family, Amy Lowell was the sister of a noted astronomer, the granddaughter of the founder of Lowell, Massachusetts, and a descendant of the famous American poet James Russell Lowell (1819–1891). She spent much of her early adulthood involved in civic activities. Then, deciding to become a poet herself, Lowell spent ten years studying the craft before she published her first collection of poems, *A Dome of Many-Colored Glass,* in 1912. Soon afterward, while visiting England, she met the American poet Ezra Pound (1885–1972) and adopted his theories of imagism. Pound wanted poetry to rely on clear, concrete images and the patterns of ordinary speech. Such images in "The Taxi" as the world beating dead "Like a slackened drum" and the lights of the city pricking the speaker's eyes reflect this imagist approach.

OTHER WORKS *Sword Blades and Poppy Seeds, Selected Poems, The Complete Poetical Works of Amy Lowell*

PREVIEWING

Sonnet 18
William Shakespeare England

Sonnet 30
Edna St. Vincent Millay United States

PERSONAL CONNECTION

With a partner, come up with different ideas for completing these statements about love shown to the right. You may use lyrics from popular music or any other phrases that come to mind. Share your best responses with your classmates. Then discuss what the completed statements reveal about people's attitudes toward love.

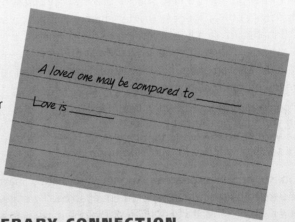

A loved one may be compared to _____

Love is _____

LITERARY CONNECTION

Poets have often explored the topic of love in **sonnets,** 14-line poems that have been a popular form of expression for many centuries. The sonnet originated in Italy; in fact, the word *sonnet* comes from the Italian for "little song." The form was first popularized by the Italian poet Petrarch (1304–1374), who wrote a famous **sonnet sequence,** or series, expressing his love for a woman named Laura. From Italy, the form spread to France, Spain, and England, where many poets, including William Shakespeare, experimented with the form. Shakespeare's 154 sonnets are widely regarded as the finest in English. Like Petrarch's, Shakespeare's sonnets often focus on romantic love; they also address the love between friends. Since Shakespeare's day, many English-language poets have tried their hand at writing sonnets. Among them is the 20th-century American poet Edna St. Vincent Millay.

Understanding Sonnet Structure

A sonnet is one of the most highly structured forms of poetry in the English language. Knowing the elements of that structure can help you to become a better reader of sonnets, because the structure often reflects the meaning of the poem.

Rhyme Scheme Poets use rhyme not only to please the ear but also to mark units of thought. In a sonnet, the **rhyme scheme,** which is the rhyme pattern of the poem, can help you to follow the progression of thought. To identify a sonnet's rhyme scheme, you assign a letter of the alphabet to each line according to the rhymed sound at the end of the line. The example below, from another Shakespeare sonnet, illustrates an *abab* rhyme scheme. Note that *fled* rhymes with *dead* and that *bell* rhymes with *dwell*.

No longer mourn for me when I am *dead*	a
Than you shall hear the ruly sullen *bell*	b
Give warning to the world that I am *fled*	a
From this vile world, with vilest worms to *dwell*.	b

The English, or Shakespearean, Sonnet A sonnet by Shakespeare is characterized by the fixed rhyme pattern *abab cdcd efef gg*. The rhymes reflect the logical organization of the poem, dividing it into three quatrains and one couplet. A **quatrain** is a group of four rhymed lines; a **couplet** is a rhymed pair of lines. This structure is so common in English poetry, and in Shakespeare's poems in particular, that it is recognized as a separate type of sonnet.

In a typical English sonnet, the first quatrain introduces a situation, identifies a problem, or raises a question. In subsequent quatrains the issue is further explored. Toward the end of the poem, a turning point usually occurs, after which the situation is clarified, the problem is resolved, or the question is answered. This turning point often takes place at the beginning of the third quatrain or at the couplet, though it may take place elsewhere.

Modern poets, such as Millay, have continued to experiment with the sonnet form, stretching the Shakespearean mold in fresh and original ways.

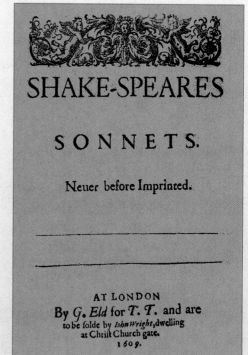

SHAKE-SPEARES

SONNETS.

Neuer before Imprinted.

AT LONDON
By *G. Eld* for *T. T.* and are
to be folde by *Iohn Wright,* dwelling
at Chriſt Church gate.
1609.

Strategies for Reading Sonnets

As you read the Shakespeare and Millay sonnets, apply these strategies to find out how the speakers feel about love.

1. Identify the rhyme scheme and the major units of thought.

2. In your own words, describe the situation, problem, or question that is introduced at the beginning of the poem.

3. Identify the turning point, if there is one.

4. Find out how the situation is clarified, the problem resolved, or the question answered.

5. Summarize the message of the poem in your own words.

Sonnet 18

William Shakespeare

Shall I compare thee to a summer's day?
Thou art more lovely and more temperate:
Rough winds do shake the darling buds of May,
And summer's lease hath all too short a date:

5 Sometime too hot the eye of heaven shines,
And often is his gold complexion dimmed;
And every fair from fair sometime declines,
By chance or nature's changing course untrimmed;
But thy eternal summer shall not fade,

10 Nor lose possession of that fair thou owest;
Nor shall Death brag thou wander'st in his shade,
When in eternal lines to time thou growest:
    So long as men can breathe, or eyes can see,
    So long lives this, and this gives life to thee.

2 temperate (tĕm'pər-ĭt): moderate; mild.

8 untrimmed: stripped of beauty.

10 thou owest (ō'əst): you own; you possess.

FROM PERSONAL RESPONSE TO CRITICAL ANALYSIS

REFLECT 1. Working with a partner, strike a pose that expresses your response to "Sonnet 18," then invite your partner to interpret that pose. In your notebook, explain your response and what you learned about your partner's response to the poem.

RETHINK 2. How did your knowledge of sonnet structure help you to understand the poem?
Consider
- the question raised in the first line
- the rhyme scheme
- the main point of each quatrain and the couplet

3. What words would you use to describe how the speaker feels about the person being addressed? Support your opinion with details from the poem.

Lovers III (1990), Eng Tay. Edition 175, intaglio. Published by Tapir Editions, New York.

Sonnet 30

Edna St. Vincent Millay

Love is not all: it is not meat nor drink
Nor slumber nor a roof against the rain;
Nor yet a floating spar to men that sink
And rise and sink and rise and sink again;
5 Love can not fill the thickened lung with breath,
Nor clean the blood, nor set the fractured bone;
Yet many a man is making friends with death
Even as I speak, for lack of love alone.
It well may be that in a difficult hour,
10 Pinned down by pain and moaning for release,
Or nagged by want past resolution's power,
I might be driven to sell your love for peace,
Or trade the memory of this night for food.
It well may be. I do not think I would.

3 spar: a pole used to support a ship's sails.

11 want: need.

RESPONDING
OPTIONS

FROM PERSONAL RESPONSE TO CRITICAL ANALYSIS

REFLECT

1. Which lines of Millay's "Sonnet 30" did you find most memorable? Describe your response to those lines in your notebook.

RETHINK

2. Consider all the details that the speaker uses to explain why "Love is not all." In your opinion, what do these details have in common?

3. What seems to be the speaker's overall opinion of love?

RELATE

4. Do you think Shakespeare's "Sonnet 18" and Millay's "Sonnet 30" follow the same structure? Explain, using your knowledge of sonnet structure and details from the poems.

5. Do you think these poems convey attitudes about love that are still common today? Draw upon the discussion for the Personal Connection on page 375 to support your opinion.

ANOTHER PATHWAY

Work with a partner to create a Venn diagram like the one below. In it, show what the two poems have in common and what sets each poem apart. Your diagram should include information about the meaning and structure of each poem.

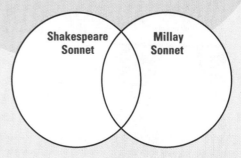

LITERARY CONCEPTS

Sonnets usually follow a regular **rhythm** called **meter.** The meter of a poem is like the beat of a song. Each unit of meter is known as a foot. In English, the most commonly used type of metrical foot is an iamb, an unstressed syllable followed by a stressed syllable (˘ ´).

Two words are used to identify the meter of a line of poetry. The first word describes the predominant type of metrical foot in the line. The second word describes the number of feet in the line: trimeter (three feet), tetrameter (four feet), pentameter (five feet), and so on. Thus, the meter of a poem might be iambic trimeter or iambic pentameter. The following example from Millay's sonnet illustrates iambic pentameter, the most common pattern.

Nŏr yét ă floátĭng spár tŏ mén thăt sínk

Ănd rĭse ănd sínk ănd rĭse ănd sínk ăgáin;

Work in a small group to identify the metrical pattern of Shakespeare's sonnet.

QUICKWRITES

1. Create a **personality profile** of one of the speakers in the two poems. Use details from the poem to support your opinion of the speaker's personality.

2. Write a **sonnet** or another **poem** in which, like Millay, you express your own view of love by defining what it is not.

📁 *PORTFOLIO Save your writing. You may want to use it later as a springboard to a piece for your portfolio.*

ALTERNATIVE ACTIVITIES

1. Present a **weather report** that is not about the weather at all but about the qualities of a person whom you know well. In your report, try to imitate some of the techniques used by Shakespeare to make comparisons.

2. Turn either sonnet into a **popular song** and perform it before the class.

THE WRITER'S STYLE

Shakespeare wrote about 400 years ago. Study his sonnet for words or expressions that are no longer commonly used. Then create a list of those terms and try to come up with a modern substitute for each one. Compare your results with those of your classmates.

WILLIAM SHAKESPEARE

1564–1616

The son of a merchant, William Shakespeare grew up in the market town of Stratford-upon-Avon, England, where he attended the local grammar school. In 1582 he married Anne Hathaway, who was to give birth to three children. Shakespeare probably moved to London in the 1580s and began a career as an actor with the Lord Chamberlain's Men, London's leading theater company. In the 1590s he began writing plays for the group. Great acclaim followed, under both Queen Elizabeth I and her successor, King James I, who became the theater company's patron. From then on known as the King's Players, the group performed mainly at London's Globe Theatre, where Shakespeare was a part owner. When he died, Shakespeare was able to leave his heirs a large inheritance. Of course, Shakespeare's greatest legacy was his writing—over 150 sonnets and over 35 dramas that are generally regarded as the world's finest. These include tragedies such as *Hamlet* and *King Lear* and comedies such as *The Taming of the Shrew* and *A Midsummer Night's Dream.*

OTHER WORKS *Romeo and Juliet, Macbeth, As You Like It, Twelfth Night*

EDNA ST. VINCENT MILLAY

1892–1950

Edna St. Vincent Millay was still a student when she burst on the literary scene in 1912 with her poem "Renascence." After graduating from Vassar College, she settled in Greenwich Village, a New York City neighborhood then enjoying its heyday as a center for poets and artists. Millay quickly became one of Greenwich Village's social lions, admired as much for her offbeat, romantic lifestyle as for her skill with the pen. Though Millay lived the life of a nonconformist, her well-crafted verse usually conformed to poetic traditions of the past. She was one of the few poets of her day who did not abandon rhyme and meter, and her sonnets are still considered masterpieces. In 1923, Millay became the first woman to win the Pulitzer Prize in poetry. Her work reflected many of the social changes that swept through the United States during that era and won her international acclaim. "Love is not all," which appears as Sonnet 30 in her *Collected Sonnets* (1941), was first published in her sonnet sequence *Fatal Interview* (1931).

OTHER WORKS *A Few Figs from Thistles, The Harp-Weaver and Other Poems, Conversation at Midnight*

LASERLINKS
• *AUTHOR BACKGROUND*

PREVIEWING

A Case of Cruelty
James Herriot England

PERSONAL CONNECTION

Think about animals you have owned or about the people you know who feel strong ties to animals. Why do you think people have such strong feelings about pets or other animals? Discuss your ideas with your classmates, drawing on your own experiences.

BIOGRAPHICAL CONNECTION

James Herriot, the author of the selection you are about to read, felt very strong ties to animals of all kinds. For years Herriot worked as a veterinarian, treating both pets and farm animals in a rural part of the northern English county of Yorkshire. Recognizing that his experiences with animals and their owners might make for good reading, he eventually began to put them down on paper. Herriot won fame with a series of charming books about the veterinary practice he shared with his partner in a Yorkshire village called Darrowby. "A Case of Cruelty," from that series, recounts an experience involving the "small animal" side of the two men's practice.

Countryside in Yorkshire, England. Copyright © Colin Raw/Tony Stone Images.

WRITING CONNECTION

In your notebook describe a memorable experience that you have had with a pet or with another animal. Create a chart like the one shown, substituting answers for the questions in the boxes. As you read, compare your own memorable experience with Herriot's recollection.

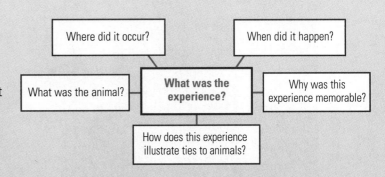

LASERLINKS
• BIOGRAPHICAL CONNECTION

381

A Case of Cruelty

Golden Retriever (1972), Fairfield Porter. Oil on wood panel, 14⅛″ × 15⅛″, The Parrish Art Museum, Southampton, New York, gift of the Estate of Fairfield Porter (1980.10.124). Photo by Jim Strong, Inc.

James 🐾 Herriot

The silvery haired old gentleman with the pleasant face didn't look the type to be easily upset, but his eyes glared at me angrily, and his lips quivered with indignation.

"Mr. Herriot," he said. "I have come to make a complaint. I strongly object to your callousness in subjecting my dog to unnecessary suffering."

"Suffering? What suffering?" I was mystified.

"I think you know, Mr. Herriot. I brought my dog in a few days ago. He was very lame, and I am referring to your treatment on that occasion."

I nodded. "Yes, I remember it well . . . but where does the suffering come in?"

"Well, the poor animal is going around with his leg dangling, and I have it on good authority that the bone is fractured and should have been put in plaster immediately." The old gentleman stuck his chin out fiercely.

383

"All right, you can stop worrying," I said. "Your dog has a radial paralysis[1] caused by a blow on the ribs, and if you are patient and follow my treatment he'll gradually improve. In fact I think he'll recover completely."

"But he trails his leg when he walks."

"I know—that's typical, and to the layman it does give the appearance of a broken leg. But he shows no sign of pain, does he?"

"No, he seems quite happy, but this lady seemed to be absolutely sure of her facts. She was adamant."

"Lady?"

"Yes," said the old gentleman. "She is very clever with animals, and she came around to see if she could help in my dog's convalescence. She brought some excellent condition powders[2] with her."

"Ah!" A blinding shaft pierced the fog in my mind. All was suddenly clear. "It was Mrs. Donovan, wasn't it?"

"Well . . . er, yes. That was her name."

Old Mrs. Donovan was a woman who really got around. No matter what was going on in Darrowby—weddings, funerals, house-sales— you'd find the dumpy little figure and walnut face among the spectators, the darting, black-button eyes taking everything in. And always, on the end of its lead, her terrier dog.

When I say "old," I'm only guessing, because she appeared ageless; she seemed to have been around a long time, but she could have been anything between fifty-five and seventy-five. She certainly had the vitality of a young woman because she must have walked vast distances in her dedicated quest to keep abreast of events. Many people took an uncharitable view of her acute curiosity, but whatever the motivation, her activities took her into almost every channel of life in the town. One of these channels was our veterinary practice.

She could talk at length on the ailments of small animals.

~

Because Mrs. Donovan, among her other widely ranging interests, was an animal doctor. In fact I think it would be safe to say that this facet of her life transcended all the others.

She could talk at length on the ailments of small animals, and she had a whole armory of medicines and remedies at her command, her two specialities being her miracle-working condition powders and a dog shampoo of unprecedented value for improving the coat. She had an uncanny ability to sniff out a sick animal, and it was not uncommon when I was on my rounds to find Mrs. Donovan's dark, gypsy face poised intently over what I had thought was my patient, while she administered calf's foot jelly[3] or one of her own patent nostrums.[4]

I suffered more than Siegfried because I took a more active part in the small animal side of our practice. I was anxious to develop this aspect and to improve my image in this field, and Mrs. Donovan didn't help at all. "Young Mr. Herriot," she would confide to my clients, "is all right with cattle and such like, but he don't know nothing about dogs and cats."

---

1. **radial paralysis:** loss of movement in the lower part of the leg.
2. **condition powders:** medicines for keeping an animal in good condition.
3. **calf's foot jelly:** meat gelatin made by boiling calves' feet; an old-fashioned, nutritious remedy.
4. **patent nostrums** (păt′nt nŏs′trəmz): nonprescription medicines whose effectiveness has not been proven scientifically; quack remedies.

WORDS
TO
KNOW

adamant (ăd′ə-mənt) *adj.* remaining firm despite the pleas or reasoning of others; stubbornly unyielding
convalescence (kŏn′və-lĕs′əns) *n.* the gradual return to health and strength after an illness or an injury
transcend (trăn-sĕnd′) *v.* to move above and beyond; to be greater than

And of course they believed her and had implicit faith in her. She had the irresistible <u>mystic</u> appeal of the amateur, and on top of that there was her habit, particularly endearing in Darrowby, of never charging for her advice, her medicines, her long periods of diligent nursing.

Older folk in the town told how her husband, an Irish farm worker, had died many years ago and how he must have had a "bit put away" because Mrs. Donovan had apparently been able to indulge all her interests over the years without financial strain. Since she inhabited the streets of Darrowby all day and every day, I often encountered her, and she always smiled up at me sweetly and told me how she had been sitting up all night with Mrs. So-and-so's dog that I'd been treating. She felt sure she'd be able to pull it through.

There was no smile on her face, however, on the day when she rushed into the surgery[5] while Siegfried and I were having tea.

"Mr. Herriot!" she gasped. "Can you come? My little dog's been run over!"

I jumped up and ran out to the car with her. She sat in the passenger seat with her head bowed, her hands clasped tightly on her knees.

"He slipped his collar and ran in front of a car," she murmured. "He's lying in front of the school half way up Cliffend Road. Please hurry."

I was there within three minutes, but as I bent over the dusty little body stretched on the pavement, I knew there was nothing I could do. The fast-glazing eyes, the faint, gasping respirations, the ghastly pallor of the mucous membranes[6] all told the same story.

"I'll take him back to the surgery and get some saline[7] into him, Mrs. Donovan," I said. "But I'm afraid he's had a massive internal hemorrhage.[8] Did you see what happened exactly?"

She gulped. "Yes, the wheel went right over him."

Ruptured liver, for sure. I passed my hands under the little animal and began to lift him gently, but as I did so, the breathing stopped, and the eyes stared fixedly ahead.

Mrs. Donovan sank to her knees, and for a few moments she gently stroked the rough hair of the head and chest. "He's dead, isn't he?" she whispered at last.

"I'm afraid he is," I said.

She got slowly to her feet and stood bewilderedly among the little group of bystanders on the pavement. Her lips moved, but she seemed unable to say any more.

I took her arm, led her over to the car and opened the door. "Get in and sit down," I said. "I'll run you home. Leave everything to me."

I wrapped the dog in my calving overall[9] and laid him in the boot[10] before driving away. It wasn't until we drew up outside Mrs. Donovan's house that she began to weep silently. I sat there without speaking till she finished. Then she wiped her eyes and turned to me.

"Do you think he suffered at all?"

"I'm certain he didn't. It was all so quick—he wouldn't know a thing about it."

She tried to smile. "Poor little Rex, I don't know what I'm going to do without him. We've traveled a few miles together, you know."

"Yes, you have. He had a wonderful life, Mrs. Donovan. And let me give you a bit of

---

5. **surgery:** in Britain, a general term for a physician's or veterinarian's office.

6. **mucous membranes:** thin layers of tissue lining the nose, mouth, and other body passages.

7. **saline** (sā′lēn′): a salt solution used to stem the effects of blood loss.

8. **internal hemorrhage** (hĕm′ər-ĭj): excessive bleeding inside the body.

9. **calving overall:** a special heavy overall worn by the veterinarian assisting in the birth of a calf.

10. **boot:** British term for the trunk of a car.

advice—you must get another dog. You'd be lost without one."

She shook her head. "No, I couldn't. That little dog meant too much to me. I couldn't let another take his place."

"Well I know that's how you feel just now, but I wish you'd think about it. I don't want to seem callous—I tell everybody this when they lose an animal, and I know it's good advice."

"Mr. Herriot, I'll never have another one." She shook her head again, very decisively. "Rex was my faithful friend for many years, and I just want to remember him. He's the last dog I'll ever have."

I often saw Mrs. Donovan around the town after this, and I was glad to see she was still as active as ever, though she looked strangely incomplete without the little dog on its lead. But it must have been over a month before I had the chance to speak to her.

It was on the afternoon that Inspector Halliday of the R.S.P.C.A.[11] rang me.

"Mr. Herriot," he said. "I'd like you to come and see an animal with me. A cruelty case."

"Right, what is it?"

"A dog, and it's pretty grim. A dreadful case of neglect." He gave me the name of a row of old brick cottages down by the river and said he'd meet me there.

Halliday was waiting for me, smart and business-like in his dark uniform, as I pulled up in the back lane behind the houses. He was a big, blond man with cheerful blue eyes, but he didn't smile as he came over to the car.

"He's in here," he said and led the way towards one of the doors in the long, crumbling wall. A few curious people were hanging around, and with a feeling of inevitability I recognized a gnome-like brown face. Trust Mrs. Donovan, I thought, to be among those present at a time like this.

We went through the door into the long garden. I had found that even the lowliest dwellings in Darrowby had long strips of land at the back as though the builders had taken it for granted that the country people who were going to live in them would want to occupy themselves with the pursuits of the soil; with vegetable and fruit growing, even stock keeping[12] in a small way. You usually found a pig there, a few hens, often pretty beds of flowers.

But this garden was a wilderness. A chilling air of desolation hung over the few gnarled apple and plum trees standing among a tangle of rank grass as though the place had been forsaken by all living creatures.

Halliday went over to a ramshackle wooden shed with peeling paint and a rusted corrugated iron roof. He produced a key, unlocked the padlock and dragged the door partly open. There was no window, and it wasn't easy to identify the jumble inside; broken gardening tools, an ancient mangle, rows of flower pots and partly used paint tins.[13] And right at the back, a dog sitting quietly.

I didn't notice him immediately because of the gloom and because the smell in the shed started me coughing, but as I drew closer, I saw that he was a big animal, sitting very upright, his collar secured by a chain to a ring in the wall. I had seen some thin dogs, but this advanced emaciation reminded me of my textbooks on anatomy; nowhere else did the bones of pelvis, face and rib cage stand out with such horrifying clarity. A deep, smoothed out hollow in the earth floor showed where he had lain, moved about, in fact lived, for a very long time.

---

11. **R.S.P.C.A.:** the Royal Society for the Prevention of Cruelty to Animals.

12. **stock keeping:** keeping farm animals.

13. **tins:** British term for cans.

WORDS TO KNOW   **rank** (răngk) *adj.* growing abundantly or excessively

386

Old Farmhouse (1872), Edward Henry Fahey, RI. Watercolor and bodycolor, heightened with gum arabic, 13¾″ × 9¾″, Anthony Reed Gallery, London.

The sight of the animal had a stupefying effect on me; I only half took in the rest of the scene—the filthy shreds of sacking scattered nearby, the bowl of scummy water.

"Look at his back end," Halliday muttered.

I carefully raised the dog from his sitting position and realized that the stench in the place was not entirely due to the piles of excrement. The hindquarters were a welter of pressure sores which had turned gangrenous,[14] and strips of sloughing tissue[15] hung down from them. There were similar sores along the sternum[16]

and ribs. The coat, which seemed to be a dull yellow, was matted and caked with dirt.

The inspector spoke again. "I don't think he's ever been out of here. He's only a young dog—about a year old—but I understand he's been in this shed since he was an eight-week-old pup.

---

14. **gangrenous** (găng′grə-nəs): infected with gangrene, which is the death or decay of body tissue due to loss of blood supply.

15. **sloughing** (slŭf′ĭng) **tissue:** dead body tissue separating from the surrounding living tissue.

16. **sternum:** the breastbone, from which the ribs branch off.

Somebody out in the lane heard a whimper, or he'd never have been found."

I felt a tightening of the throat and a sudden nausea which wasn't due to the smell. It was the thought of this patient animal sitting starved and forgotten in the darkness and filth for a year. I looked again at the dog and saw in his eyes only a calm trust. Some dogs would have barked their heads off and soon been discovered, some would have become terrified and vicious, but this was one of the totally undemanding kind, the kind which had complete faith in people and accepted all their actions without complaint. Just an occasional whimper perhaps as he sat interminably in the empty blackness which had been his world and at times wondered what it was all about.

"Well, Inspector, I hope you're going to throw the book at whoever's responsible," I said.

Halliday grunted. "Oh, there won't be much done. It's a case of diminished responsibility. The owner's definitely simple. Lives with an aged mother who hardly knows what's going on either. I've seen the fellow, and it seems he threw in a bit of food when he felt like it, and that's about all he did. They'll fine him and stop him keeping an animal in the future but nothing more than that."

"I see." I reached out and stroked the dog's head, and he immediately responded by resting a paw on my wrist. There was a pathetic dignity about the way he held himself erect, the calm eyes regarding me, friendly and unafraid. "Well, you'll let me know if you want me in court."

"Of course, and thank you for coming along." Halliday hesitated for a moment. "And now I expect you'll want to put this poor thing out of his misery right away."

I continued to run my hand over the head and ears while I thought for a moment. "Yes . . . yes, I suppose so. We'd never find a home for him in this state. It's the kindest thing to do. Anyway, push the door wide open will you so that I can get a proper look at him."

In the improved light I examined him more thoroughly. Perfect teeth, well-proportioned limbs with a fringe of yellow hair. I put my stethoscope on his chest, and as I listened to the slow, strong thudding of the heart, the dog again put his paw on my hand.

I turned to Halliday, "You know, Inspector, inside this bag of bones there's a lovely healthy golden retriever. I wish there was some way of letting him out."

As I spoke, I noticed there was more than one figure in the door opening. A pair of black pebble eyes were peering intently at the big dog from behind the inspector's broad back. The other spectators had remained in the lane, but Mrs. Donovan's curiosity had been too much for her. I continued conversationally as though I hadn't seen her.

"You know, what this dog needs first of all is a good shampoo to clean up his matted coat."

"Huh?" said Halliday.

"Yes. And then he wants a long course of some really strong condition powders."

"What's that?" The inspector looked startled.

"There's no doubt about it," I said. "It's the only hope for him, but where are you going to find such things? Really powerful enough, I mean." I sighed and straightened up. "Ah well, I suppose there's nothing else for it. I'd better put him to sleep right away. I'll get the things from my car."

When I got back to the shed, Mrs. Donovan was already inside examining the dog despite the feeble remonstrances[17] of the big man.

"Look!" she said excitedly, pointing to a name roughly scratched on the collar. "His name's Roy.' She smiled up at me. "It's a bit like Rex, isn't it, that name?"

"You know, Mrs. Donovan, now you mention it, it is. It's very like Rex, the way it comes off your tongue." I nodded seriously.

---

17. **remonstrances** (rĭ-mŏn′strəns-ĭz): protests; complaints; objections.

She stood silent for a few moments, obviously in the grip of a deep emotion, then she burst out.

"Can I have 'im? I can make him better, I know I can. Please, please let me have 'im!"

"Well I don't know," I said. "It's really up to the inspector. You'll have to get his permission."

Halliday looked at her in bewilderment, then he said: "Excuse me, Madam," and drew me to one side. We walked a few yards through the long grass and stopped under a tree.

"Mr. Herriot," he whispered, "I don't know what's going on here, but I can't just pass over an animal in this condition to anybody who has a casual whim. The poor beggar's had one bad break already—I think it's enough. This woman doesn't look a suitable person . . ."

I held up a hand. "Believe me, Inspector, you've nothing to worry about. She's a funny old stick, but she's been sent from heaven today. If anybody in Darrowby can give this dog a new life it's her."

Halliday still looked very doubtful. "But I still don't get it. What was all that stuff about him needing shampoos and condition powders?"

"Oh never mind about that. I'll tell you some other time. What he needs is lots of good grub, care and affection, and that's just what he'll get. You can take my word for it."

"All right, you seem very sure." Halliday looked at me for a second or two then turned and walked over to the eager little figure by the shed.

I had never before been deliberately on the lookout for Mrs. Donovan: she had just cropped up wherever I happened to be, but now I scanned the streets of Darrowby anxiously day by day without sighting her. I didn't like it when Gobber Newhouse got drunk and drove his bicycle determinedly through a barrier into a ten-foot hole where they were laying the new sewer and Mrs. Donovan was not in evidence among the happy crowd who

I had a lot of faith in Mrs. Donovan—far more than she had in me.
~

watched the council workmen[18] and two policemen trying to get him out; and when she was nowhere to be seen when they had to fetch the fire engine to the fish and chip shop the night the fat burst into flames, I became seriously worried.

Maybe I should have called round to see how she was getting on with that dog. Certainly I had trimmed off the necrotic tissue[19] and dressed the sores before she took him away, but perhaps he needed something more than that. And yet at the time I had felt a strong conviction that the main thing was to get him out of there and clean him and feed him, and nature would do the rest. And I had a lot of faith in Mrs. Donovan—far more than she had in me—when it came to animal doctoring; it was hard to believe I'd been completely wrong.

It must have been nearly three weeks, and I was on the point of calling at her home, when I noticed her stumping briskly along the far side of the market place, peering closely into every shop window exactly as before. The only difference was that she had a big yellow dog on the end of the lead.

I turned the wheel and sent my car bumping over the cobbles till I was abreast of her. When she saw me getting out, she stopped and smiled impishly, but she didn't speak as I bent over Roy and examined him. He was still a skinny dog, but he looked bright and happy, his wounds

---

18. **council workmen:** construction workers for the local government, here putting in the new sewer.

19. **necrotic tissue:** tissue in which the cells have died through injury or disease.

Portrait of Fridel Battenberg (1920), Max Beckmann. Oil on canvas, 97 cm × 48.5 cm, Kunstmuseum Hannover (Germany) mit Sammlung Sprengel. Copyright © 1996 Artists Rights Society (ARS), New York/VG Bild-Kunst, Bonn, Germany.

were healthy and granulating[20] and there was not a speck of dirt in his coat or on his skin. I knew then what Mrs. Donovan had been doing all this time; she had been washing and combing and teasing at that filthy tangle till she had finally conquered it.

As I straightened up, she seized my wrist in a grip of surprising strength and looked up into my eyes.

"Now, Mr. Herriot," she said. "Haven't I made a difference to this dog!"

"You've done wonders, Mrs. Donovan," I said. "And you've been at him with that marvelous shampoo of yours, haven't you?"

She giggled and walked away, and from that day I saw the two of them frequently but at a distance, and something like two months went by before I had a chance to talk to her again. She was passing by the surgery as I was coming down the steps, and again she grabbed my wrist.

"Mr. Herriot," she said, just as she had done before. "Haven't I made a difference to this dog!"

I looked down at Roy with something akin to awe. He had grown and filled out, and his coat, no longer yellow but a rich gold, lay in luxuriant shining swathes over the well-fleshed ribs and back. A new, brightly studded collar glittered on his neck, and his tail, beautifully fringed, fanned the air gently. He was now a golden retriever in full magnificence. As I stared at him, he reared up, plunked his forepaws on my chest and looked into my face, and in his eyes I read plainly the same calm affection and trust I had seen in that black, noisome[21] shed.

"Mrs. Donovan," I said softly, "he's the most beautiful dog in Yorkshire." Then, because I knew she was waiting for it. "It's those wonderful condition powders. Whatever do you put in them?"

20. **granulating:** healing by forming fleshy new growth and tiny new blood vessels.

21. **noisome** (noi′səm): foul; disgusting.

"Ah, wouldn't you like to know!" She bridled[22] and smiled up at me coquettishly and indeed she was nearer being kissed at that moment than for many years.

I suppose you could say that that was the start of Roy's second life. And as the years passed, I often pondered on the beneficent providence which had decreed that an animal which had spent his first twelve months abandoned and unwanted, staring uncomprehendingly into that unchanging, stinking darkness, should be whisked in a moment into an existence of light and movement and love. Because I don't think any dog had it quite so good as Roy from then on.

His diet changed dramatically from odd bread crusts to best stewing steak and biscuit, meaty bones and a bowl of warm milk every evening. And he never missed a thing. Garden fêtes,[23] school sports, evictions, gymkhanas[24]—he'd be there. I was pleased to note that as time went on, Mrs. Donovan seemed to be clocking up an even greater daily mileage. Her expenditure on shoe leather must have been phenomenal, but of course it was absolute pie[25] for Roy—a busy round in the morning, home for a meal then straight out again; it was all go.

Mrs. Donovan didn't confine her activities to the town center; there was a big stretch of common land down by the river where there were seats, and people used to take their dogs for a gallop, and she liked to get down there fairly regularly to check on the latest developments on the domestic scene. I often saw Roy loping majestically over the grass among a pack of assorted canines, and when he wasn't doing that, he was submitting to being stroked or patted or generally fussed over. He was handsome, and he just liked people; it made him irresistible.

It was common knowledge that his mistress had bought a whole selection of brushes and combs of various sizes with which she labored over his coat. Some people said she had a little brush for his teeth, too, and it might have been true, but he certainly wouldn't need his nails clipped—his life on the roads would keep them down.

Mrs. Donovan, too, had her reward; she had a faithful companion by her side every hour of the day and night. But there was more to it than that; she had always had the compulsion to help and heal animals, and the salvation of Roy was the high point of her life—a blazing triumph which never dimmed.

I know the memory of it was always fresh because many years later I was sitting on the sidelines at a cricket match, and I saw the two of them; the old lady glancing keenly around her, Roy gazing placidly out at the field of play, apparently enjoying every ball. At the end of the match I watched them move away with the dispersing crowd; Roy would be about twelve then, and heaven only knows how old Mrs. Donovan must have been, but the big golden animal was trotting along effortlessly, and his mistress, a little more bent perhaps and her head rather nearer the ground, was going very well.

When she saw me, she came over, and I felt the familiar tight grip on my wrist.

"Mr. Herriot," she said, and in the dark probing eyes the pride was still as warm, the triumph still as bursting new as if it had all happened yesterday.

"Mr. Herriot, haven't I made a difference to this dog!" ❖

---

22. **bridled:** lifted the head and drew in the chin, like a horse restrained by its bridle.

23. **fêtes** (fāts): outdoor parties; festivals.

24. **gymkhanas** (jĭm-kä′nəz): sporting events in which gymnastics, horse-jumping, or other contests are held.

25. **pie:** slang for something highly desirable; a treat.

Eight Puppies

GABRIELA MISTRAL

Between the thirteenth and the
   fifteenth day
the puppies opened their eyes.
Suddenly they saw the world,
anxious with terror and joy.
5 They saw the belly of their mother,
saw the door of their house,
saw a deluge of light,
saw flowering azaleas.

They saw more, they saw all,
10 the red, the black, the ash.
Scrambling up, pawing and clawing
more lively than squirrels,
they saw the eyes of their mother,
heard my rasping cry and my laugh.

15 And I wished I were born with them.
Could it not be so another time?
To leap from a clump of banana
   plants
one morning of wonders—
a dog, a coyote, a deer;
20 to gaze with wide pupils,
to run, to stop, to run, to fall,
to whimper and whine and jump with
   joy,
riddled with sun and with barking,
a hallowed child of God, his secret,
   divine servant.

Translated by Doris Dana

Ocho Perritos

GABRIELA MISTRAL

Los perrillos abrieron sus ojos
del treceavo al quinceavo día.
De golpe vieron el mundo,
con ansia, susto y alegría.
5 Vieron el vientre de la madre,
la puerta suya que es la mía,
el diluvio de la luz,
las azaleas floridas.

Vieron más: se vieron todos,
10 el rojo, el negro, el ceniza,
gateando y aupándose,
más vivos que las ardillas;
vieron los ojos de la madre
y mi grito rasgado, y mi risa.

15 Y yo querría nacer con ellos.
¿Por qué otra vez no sería?
Saltar de unos bananales
una mañana de maravilla,
en can, en coyota, en venada;
20 mirar con grandes pupilas,
correr, parar, correr, tumbarme
y gemir y saltar de alegría,
acribillada de sol y ladridos
hija de Dios, sierva oscura y divina.

Still Life with Three Puppies (1888), Paul Gauguin. Oil on wood, 36⅛″ × 24⅝″, The Museum of Modern Art, New York, Mrs. Simon Guggenheim Fund. Photo Copyright © 1995 The Museum of Modern Art, New York.

RESPONDING OPTIONS

FROM PERSONAL RESPONSE TO CRITICAL ANALYSIS

REFLECT

1. What one event in this selection stands out the most for you? Describe it in your notebook, then share what you have written with a partner.

RETHINK

2. How would you describe Mrs. Donovan?
   Consider
   - her reaction to Herriot's treatment of local pets
   - her presence at every community event
   - her reaction to the death of her terrier
   - her attitude and behavior toward Roy

3. What is your opinion of Mr. Herriot, the narrator of the selection?

4. In your judgment, how is the relationship between Mr. Herriot and Mrs. Donovan affected by the ties each character feels to animals?

RELATE

5. What rights, if any, do you think animals have? Give some examples to illustrate your views.

6. Compare and contrast the life of the dogs in the poem "Eight Puppies" with the experiences Roy probably had as a puppy.

ANOTHER PATHWAY

Cooperative Learning

Working with a small group of classmates, create a pamphlet titled "How to Care for a Dog." In the pamphlet list the do's and don'ts of dog care based on the treatment of dogs in the selection. Include examples from the selection to illustrate each point. You might use graphics on your computer to make your pamphlet more interesting.

QUICKWRITES

1. Expand the description you wrote for the Writing Connection on page 381 into a **nonfiction narrative** featuring a pet or another animal. Be sure to include all necessary plot elements and make your narrative as entertaining as possible.

2. Write the **diary entries** that Mrs. Donovan might have written about Herriot's treatment of the old gentleman's dog, the death of her terrier, her decision to accept Roy, and her progress in bringing Roy back to health.

3. For the local Darrowby paper, write an **editorial** on the discovery of Roy in the garden shed.

📁 *PORTFOLIO Save your writing. You may want to use it later as a springboard to a piece for your portfolio.*

LITERARY CONCEPTS

Although "A Case of Cruelty" is nonfiction, it is nevertheless a **narrative,** or writing that tells a story, and as such it has many of the same elements as fiction. Review Understanding Fiction on pages 16–17, which lists the major elements of fiction. Then show how the plot of "A Case of Cruelty" develops by completing the plot diagram begun below. Finish labeling the four stages of a typical plot at the appropriate places on the diagram, and then describe the events from the story that fit each stage.

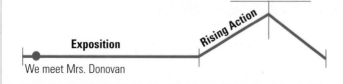

Exposition
We meet Mrs. Donovan

Rising Action

ALTERNATIVE ACTIVITIES

1. Think about Roy's living conditions in the garden shed and in his "second life" with Mrs. Donovan. Create a two-part **drawing** that reflects both parts of Roy's life and your feelings about them.

2. On videocassette, view an episode of *All Creatures Great and Small,* the aired PBS television series based on Herriot's books. In an **oral review,** compare the episode to "A Case of Cruelty."

LITERARY LINKS

Based on this selection, what advice do you think Herriot might give Godfrey, the character in "Lalla" (page 354) who plans to become a veterinarian?

ACROSS THE CURRICULUM

Health Tape an **interview** with a veterinarian to find out more about the treatment and mistreatment of animals in your area.

THE WRITER'S STYLE

James Herriot's writing abounds with lively, detailed descriptions of his characters and settings. Reread the description on page 386 of Herriot's first encounter with Roy in the garden shed. In your notebook, list the specific details that make this part of the story come alive for you. Compare your list with those of your classmates.

WORDS TO KNOW

On a separate sheet of paper, indicate whether the words in each numbered pair below are synonyms or antonyms.

1. beneficent / heartless
2. callousness / compassion
3. placidly / tranquilly
4. coquettishly / teasingly
5. rank / overgrown
6. indignation / pleasure
7. transcend / surpass
8. adamant / flexible
9. convalescence / recuperation
10. mystic / supernatural

JAMES HERRIOT

1916–1995

James Herriot, whose real name was James Alfred Wight, was only 13 when he read a magazine article about a veterinarian's life and decided to become a vet himself. After training in Scotland, he returned to his native England and in 1938 began working in Yorkshire. "The life of a country vet was dirty, uncomfortable, sometimes dangerous," he once told an interviewer. "It was terribly hard work and I loved it." For over 25 years he kept coming home from work and telling his wife about interesting on-the-job experiences, always promising to write a book about them. One day she finally challenged him,

observing that vets of 50 do not write first books. "Well, that did it," Herriot later explained. "I stormed out and bought some paper and taught myself to type."

The result was *If Only They Could Talk,* published in England in 1970 and followed two years later by *It Shouldn't Happen to a Vet.* For his first American edition Herriot joined the two books together under the title *All Creatures Great and Small* (1972), and the new version became a bestseller. Three similar books followed.

OTHER WORKS *All Things Wise and Wonderful, The Lord God Made Them All, Every Living Thing*

PREVIEWING

FICTION

Love Must Not Be Forgotten
Zhang Jie (jäng′ jē-ĕ′) China

PERSONAL CONNECTION

Think about the married couples you know. Based on your observations, what components are necessary to a good marriage? Share your ideas in a class discussion.

CULTURAL CONNECTION

In the 1960s and 1970s, when this selection takes place, many institutions of Chinese life, including marriage, were subjected to intense questioning. Since 1949, Mao Zedong (sometimes spelled Mao Tse-tung) and his Communist forces had been in control of China. By the mid 1960s Mao felt that new blood was needed to keep the ideals of Communism alive, so he implemented the Cultural Revolution in 1966. For the next three years, groups of young students and other radicals removed and replaced older Communist Party leaders. Many leaders were executed; others were sent to prison or to the countryside to be "re-educated" in communist thought.

Despite sweeping political changes, many Chinese customs were slow to change. For example, centuries-old traditions dictated that marriages be arranged by the couple's families when the prospective spouses were still young children. Although new laws enacted by the Communists allowed individuals to choose their own marriage partners, marrying for love was still frowned upon because communist teachings encouraged individuals to suppress personal desires for the greater social good.

READING CONNECTION

Understanding Flashbacks In this selection, which opens in 1979, a young woman examines the role that love should play in her own marriage. Throughout the story her thoughts are interwoven with flashbacks to her mother's advice and diary entries from her mother's past. You may find it easier to keep track of the events in the story if you refer to the time line below as you read.

Using Your Reading Log Use your reading log to record your responses to the questions inserted throughout the selection. Also, jot down other thoughts and feelings that come to mind as you read.

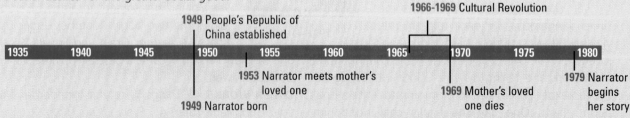

1949 People's Republic of China established

1966-1969 Cultural Revolution

1935 1940 1945 1950 1955 1960 1965 1970 1975 1980

1953 Narrator meets mother's loved one

1969 Mother's loved one dies

1979 Narrator begins her story

1949 Narrator born

LASERLINKS
• CULTURAL CONNECTION

Love Must Not Be Forgotten

Zhang Jie

Red Peonies (1929), Ch'i Pai-Shih. Arthur M. Sackler Museum, Harvard University.

I am thirty, the same age as our People's Republic. For a republic thirty is still young. But a girl of thirty is virtually on the shelf.

Actually, I have a bona fide[1] suitor. Have you seen the Greek sculptor Myron's Discobolus? Qiao Lin[2] is the image of that discus thrower. Even the padded clothes he wears in winter fail to hide his fine physique. Bronzed, with clear-cut features, a broad forehead and large eyes, his appearance alone attracts most girls to him.

But I can't make up my mind to marry him. I'm not clear what attracts me to him, or him to me.

---

1. **bona fide** (bō′nə fīd): authentic; genuine.
2. **Qiao Lin** (chou′lĭn′).

I know people are gossiping behind my back, "Who does she think she is, to be so choosy?"

To them, I'm a nobody playing hard to get. They take offense at such preposterous behavior.

Of course, I shouldn't be captious.[3] In a society where commercial production still exists, marriage like most other transactions is still a form of barter.

I have known Qiao Lin for nearly two years, yet still cannot fathom whether he keeps so quiet from aversion to talking or from having nothing to say. When, by way of a small intelligence test, I demand his opinion of this or that, he says "good" or "bad" like a child in kindergarten.

Once I asked, "Qiao Lin, why do you love me?" He thought the question over seriously for what seemed an age. I could see from his normally smooth but now wrinkled forehead that the little grey cells in his handsome head were hard at work cogitating.[4] I felt ashamed to have put him on the spot.

Finally he raised his clear childlike eyes to tell me, "Because you're good!"

Loneliness flooded my heart. "Thank you, Qiao Lin!" I couldn't help wondering, if we were to marry, whether we could discharge our duties to each other as husband and wife. Maybe, because law and morality would have bound us together. But how tragic simply to comply with law and morality! Was there no stronger bond to link us?

When such thoughts cross my mind, I have the strange sensation that instead of being a girl

How tragic simply to comply with law and morality! Was there no stronger bond to link us?

contemplating marriage I am an elderly social scientist.

Perhaps I worry too much. We can live like most married couples, bringing up children together, strictly true to each other according to the law. . . . Although living in the seventies of the twentieth century, people still consider marriage the way they did millennia ago, as a means of continuing the race, a form of barter or a business transaction in which love and marriage can be separated. As this is the common practice, why shouldn't we follow suit?

But I still can't make up my mind. As a child, I remember, I often cried all night for no rhyme or reason, unable to sleep and disturbing the whole household. My old nurse, a shrewd though uneducated woman, said an ill wind had blown through my ear. I think this judgment showed prescience,[5] because I still have that old weakness. I upset myself over things which really present no problem, upsetting other people at the same time. One's nature is hard to change.

I think of my mother too. If she were alive, what would she say about my attitude to Qiao Lin and my uncertainty about marrying him?

My thoughts constantly turn to her, not because she was such a strict mother that her ghost is still watching over me since her death. No, she was not just my mother but my closest

---

3. **captious** (kăp′shəs): quick to find fault; quibbling.
4. **cogitating** (kŏj′ĭ-tā′tĭng): thinking carefully; pondering.
5. **prescience** (prē′shē-əns): knowledge of things before they happen; foresight.

friend. I loved her so much that the thought of her leaving me makes my heart ache.

She never lectured me, just told me quietly in her deep, unwomanly voice about her successes and failures, so that I could learn from her experience. She had evidently not had many successes—her life was full of failures.

During her last days she followed me with her fine, expressive eyes, as if wondering how I would manage on my own and as if she had some important advice for me but hesitated to give it. She must have been worried by my naiveté and sloppy ways. She suddenly blurted out, "Shanshan,[6] if you aren't sure what you want, don't rush into marriage—better live on your own!"

Other people might think this strange advice from a mother to her daughter, but to me it embodied her bitter experience. I don't think she underestimated me or my knowledge of life. She loved me and didn't want me to be unhappy.

"I don't want to marry, mum!" I said, not out of bashfulness or a show of coyness. I can't think why a girl should pretend to be coy. She had long since taught me about things not generally mentioned to girls.

"If you meet the right man, then marry him. Only if he's right for you!"

"I'm afraid no such man exists!"

"That's not true. But it's hard. The world is so vast, I'm afraid you may never meet him." Whether I married or not was not what concerned her, but the quality of the marriage.

"Haven't you managed fine without a husband?"

"Who says so?"

"I think you've done fine."

"I had no choice. . . ." She broke off, lost in thought, her face wistful. Her wistful lined face reminded me of a withered flower I had pressed in a book.

"Why did you have no choice?"

"You ask too many questions," she parried, not ashamed to confide in me but afraid that I might reach the wrong conclusion. Besides, everyone treasures a secret to carry to the grave. Feeling a bit put out, I demanded bluntly, "Didn't you love my dad?"

"No, I never loved him."

"Did he love you?"

"No, he didn't."

"Then why get married?"

She paused, searching for the right words to explain this mystery, then answered bitterly, "When you're young, you don't always know what you're looking for, what you need, and people may talk you into getting married. As you grow older and more experienced, you find out your true needs. By then, though, you've done many foolish things for which you could kick yourself. You'd give anything to be able to make a fresh start and live more wisely. Those content with their lot will always be happy, they say, but I shall never enjoy that happiness." She added, self-mockingly, "A wretched idealist, that's all I am."

Did I take after her? Did we both have genes which attracted ill winds?

"Why don't you marry again?"

"I'm afraid I'm still not sure what I really want." She was obviously unwilling to tell me the truth.

I cannot remember my father. He and Mother split up when I was very small. I just recall her telling me sheepishly that he was a fine handsome fellow. I could see she was ashamed of having judged by appearances and made a futile choice. She told me, "When I can't sleep at night, I force myself to sober up by recalling all those

6. **Shanshan** (shän′shän′).

WORDS TO KNOW

naiveté (nä′ēv-tā′) *n.* lack of sophistication; childlike innocence
coyness (coi′nĭs) *n.* the pretense of being more modest and innocent than one really is
wistful (wĭst′fəl) *adj.* full of wishful longing; sad
parry (păr′ē) *v.* to turn aside or avoid (a question) with a clever reply

stupid blunders I made. Of course it's so distasteful that I often hide my face in the sheet for shame, as if there were eyes watching me in the dark. But distasteful as it is, I take some pleasure in this form of atonement."

I was really sorry that she hadn't remarried. She was such a fascinating character, if she'd married a man she loved, what a happy household ours would surely have been. Though not beautiful, she had the simple charm of an ink landscape. She was a fine writer too. Another author who knew her well used to say teasingly, "Just reading your works is enough to make anyone love you!"

CLARIFY

Why does the narrator think that her mother should have remarried?

She would retort, "If he knew that the object of his affection was a white-haired old crone, that would frighten him away."

At her age, she must have known what she really wanted, so this was obviously an evasion. I say this because she had quirks which puzzled me.

For instance, whenever she left Beijing on a trip, she always took with her one of the twenty-seven volumes of Chekhov's[7] stories published between 1950 and 1955. She also warned me, "Don't touch these books. If you want to read Chekhov, read that set I bought you." There was no need to caution me. Having a set of my own why should I touch hers? Besides, she'd told me this over and over again. Still she was on her guard. She seemed bewitched by those books.

So we had two sets of Chekhov's stories at home. Not just because we loved Chekhov, but to parry other people like me who loved Chekhov. Whenever anyone asked to borrow a volume, she would lend one of mine. Once, in her absence, a close friend took a volume from her set. When she found out, she was frantic and at once took a volume of mine to exchange for it.

Ever since I can remember, those books were

on her bookcase. Although I admire Chekhov as a great writer, I was puzzled by the way she never tired of reading him. Why, for over twenty years, had she had to read him every single day?

Sometimes, when tired of writing, she poured herself a cup of strong tea and sat down in front of the bookcase, staring raptly at that set of books. If I went into her room then, it flustered her, and she either spilt her tea or blushed like a girl discovered with her lover.

I wondered: Has she fallen in love with Chekhov? She might have if he'd still been alive.

When her mind was wandering just before her death, her last words to me were: "That set. . . ." She hadn't the strength to give it its complete title. But I knew what she meant. "And my diary . . . 'Love Must Not Be Forgotten'. . . . Cremate them with me."

I carried out her last instruction regarding the works of Chekhov, but couldn't bring myself to destroy her diary. I thought, if it could be published, it would surely prove the most moving thing she had written. But naturally publication was out of the question.

At first I imagined the entries were raw material she had jotted down. They read neither like stories, essays, a diary or letters. But after reading the whole I formed a hazy impression, helped out by my imperfect memory. Thinking it over, I finally realized that this was no lifeless manuscript I was holding, but an anguished, loving heart. For over twenty years one man had occupied her heart, but he was not for her. She used these diaries as a substitute for him, a means of pouring out her feelings to him, day after day, year after year.

---

7. **Chekhov's** (chĕk'ôfs): Anton Chekhov (1860–1904; also spelled Chekov), a Russian author, whose short stories were first published in Chinese in the 1950s.

No wonder she had never considered any eligible proposals, had turned a deaf ear to idle talk whether well-meant or malicious. Her heart was already full, to the exclusion of anybody else. "No lake can compare with the ocean, no cloud with those on Mount Wu."[8] Remembering those lines I often reflected sadly that few people in real life could love like this. No one would love me like this.

I learned that towards the end of the thirties, when this man was doing underground work for the Party[9] in Shanghai, an old worker had given his life to cover him, leaving behind a helpless wife and daughter. Out of a sense of duty, of gratitude to the dead and deep class feeling, he had unhesitatingly married the girl. When he saw the endless troubles caused by "love" of couples who had married for "love," he may have thought, "Thank Heaven, though I didn't marry for love, we get on well, able to help each other." For years, as man and wife they lived through hard times.

He must have been my mother's colleague. Had I ever met him? He couldn't have visited our home. Who was he?

In the spring of 1962, Mother took me to a concert. We went on foot, the theatre being quite near.

A black limousine pulled up silently by the pavement. Out stepped an elderly man with white hair in a black serge tunicsuit. What a striking shock of white hair! Strict, scrupulous, distinguished, transparently honest—that was my impression of him. The cold glint of his flashing eyes reminded me of lightning or swordplay. Only <u>ardent</u> love for a woman really deserving his love could fill cold eyes like those with tenderness.

He walked up to Mother and said, "How are you, Comrade Zhong Yu?[10] It's been a long time."

"How are you!" Mother's hand holding mine suddenly turned icy cold and trembled a little.

They stood face to face without looking at

Forbidden Fruit, Simon Ng. Reprinted with the permission of Simon & Schuster Books for Young Readers, an imprint of Simon & Schuster Children's Publishing Division. From *Tales from Gold Mountain: Stories of the Chinese in the New World*, a Groundwood Book/Douglas & McIntyre. Text Copyright © 1989 by Paul Yee, illustrations Copyright © 1989 by Simon Ng.

each other, each appearing upset, even stern. Mother fixed her eyes on the trees by the roadside, not yet in leaf. He looked at me. "Such a big girl already. Good, fine—you take after your mother."

Instead of shaking hands with Mother he shook hands with me. His hand was as icy as

---

8. **Mount Wu:** a high mountain in southern China.

9. **the Party:** the Communist Party.

10. **Zhong Yu** (jŏng'yōō').

WORDS TO KNOW **ardent** (är'dnt) *adj.* displaying great warmth of feeling; passionate

401

hers and trembling a little. As if transmitting an electric current, I felt a sudden shock. Snatching my hand away I cried, "There's nothing good about that!"

"Why not?" he asked with the surprised expression grown-ups always have when children speak out frankly.

I glanced at Mother's face. I did take after her, to my disappointment. "Because she's not beautiful!"

He laughed, then said teasingly, "Too bad that there should be a child who doesn't find her own mother beautiful. Do you remember in '53, when your mum was transferred to Beijing, she came to our ministry to report for duty? She left you outside on the verandah,[11] but like a monkey you climbed all the stairs, peeped through the cracks in doors, and caught your finger in the door of my office. You sobbed so bitterly that I carried you off to find her."

"I don't remember that." I was annoyed at his harking back to a time when I was still in open-seat pants.[12]

"Ah, we old people have better memories." He turned abruptly and remarked to Mother, "I've read that last story of yours. Frankly speaking, there's something not quite right about it. You shouldn't have condemned the heroine. . . . There's nothing wrong with falling in love, as long as you don't spoil someone else's life. . . . In fact, the hero might have loved her too. Only for the sake of a third person's happiness, they had to <u>renounce</u> their love. . . ."

A policeman came over to where the car was parked and ordered the driver to move on. When the driver made some excuse, the old man looked around. After a hasty "Goodbye" he strode to the car and told the policeman, "Sorry. It's not his fault, it's mine. . . ."

I found it amusing watching this old cadre[13] listening respectfully to the policeman's stric-

tures.[14] When I turned to Mother with a mischievous smile, she looked as upset as a first-form[15] primary schoolchild standing forlornly in front of the stern headmistress. Anyone would have thought she was the one being lectured by the policeman.

The car drove off, leaving a puff of smoke. Very soon even this smoke vanished with the wind, as if nothing at all had happened. But the incident stuck in my mind.

Analyzing it now, he must have been the man whose strength of character won Mother's heart. That strength came from his firm political convictions, his narrow escapes from death in the revolution, his active brain, his drive at work, his well-cultivated mind. Besides, strange to say, he and Mother both liked the oboe. Yes, she must have worshipped him. She once told me that unless she worshipped a man, she couldn't love him even for one day.

But I could not tell whether he loved her or not. If not, why was there this entry in her diary?

"This is far too fine a present. But how did you know that Chekhov's my favorite writer?"
"You said so."
"I don't remember that."

---

11. **verandah** (və-răn′də): a partly enclosed porch.

12. **open-seat pants:** pants with a slit down the back, worn by young children.

13. **cadre** (kăd′rē): a member of a tightly knit revolutionary party or military group.

14. **strictures** (strĭk′chərz): rules or remarks setting limits or making restrictions.

15. **first-form:** first-grade.

"I remember. I heard you mention it when you were chatting with someone."

So he was the one who had given her the *Selected Stories of Chekhov.* For her that was tantamount[16] to a love letter.

Maybe this man, who didn't believe in love, realized by the time his hair was white that in his heart was something which could be called love. By the time he no longer had the right to love, he made the tragic discovery of this love for which he would have given his life. Or did it go deeper than that?

This is all I remember about him.

How wretched Mother must have been, deprived of the man to whom she was devoted! To catch a glimpse of his car or the back of his head through its rear window, she carefully figured out which roads he would take to work and back. Whenever he made a speech, she sat at the back of the hall watching his face rendered hazy by cigarette smoke and poor lighting. Her eyes would brim with tears, but she swallowed them back. If a fit of coughing made him break off, she wondered anxiously why no one persuaded him to give up smoking. She was afraid he would get bronchitis again. Why was he so near yet so far?

He, to catch a glimpse of her, looked out of the car window every day, straining his eyes to watch the streams of cyclists, afraid that she might have an accident. On the rare evenings on which he had no meetings, he would walk by a roundabout way to our neighborhood, to pass our compound gate. However busy, he would always make time to look in papers and journals for her work.

His duty had always been clear to him, even

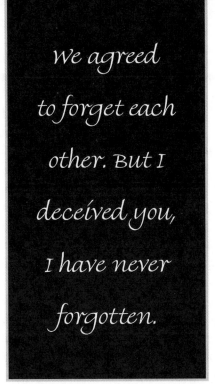

we agreed to forget each other. But I deceived you, I have never forgotten.

in the most difficult times. But now confronted by this love he became a weakling, quite helpless. At his age it was laughable. Why should life play this trick on him? Yet when they happened to meet at work, each tried to avoid the other, hurrying off with a nod. Even so, this would make Mother blind and deaf to everything around her. If she met a colleague named Wang, she would call him Guo[17] and mutter something unintelligible.

It was a cruel ordeal for her. She wrote:

We agreed to forget each other. But I deceived you, I have never forgotten. I don't think you've forgotten either. We're just deceiving each other, hiding our misery. I haven't deceived you deliberately, though; I did my best to carry out our agreement. I often stay far away from Beijing, hoping time and distance will help me to forget you. But on my return, as the train pulls into the station, my head reels. I stand on the platform looking around intently, as if someone were waiting for me. Of course there is no one. I realize then that I have forgotten nothing. Everything is unchanged. My love is like a tree the roots of which strike deeper year after year—I have no way to uproot it.

At the end of every day, I feel as if I've forgotten something important. I may wake with a start from my dreams wonder-

---

16. **tantamount** (tăn′tə-mount′): equal in effect or value.

17. **Guo** (gwō): The Chinese characters for this family name are similar to those for the name *Wang.*

ing what has happened. But nothing has happened. Nothing. Then it comes home to me that you are missing! So everything seems lacking, incomplete, and there is nothing to fill up the blank. We are nearing the ends of our lives, why should we be carried away by emotion like children? Why should life submit people to such ordeals, then unfold before you your lifelong dream? Because I started off blindly, I took the wrong turning, and now there are insuperable[18] obstacles between me and my dream.

Yes, Mother never let me go to the station to meet her when she came back from a trip, preferring to stand alone on the platform and imagine that he had met her. Poor mother with her greying hair was as infatuated as a girl.

Not much space in the diary was devoted to their romance. Most entries dealt with trivia: Why one of her articles had not come off; her fear that she had no real talent; the excellent play she missed by mistaking the time on the ticket; the drenching she got by going out for a stroll without her umbrella. In spirit they were together day and night, like a devoted married couple. In fact, they spent no more than twenty-four hours together in all. Yet in that time they experienced deeper happiness than some people in a whole lifetime. Shakespeare makes Juliet say, "I cannot sum up half my sum of wealth." And probably that is how Mother felt.

He must have been killed in the "cultural revolution." Perhaps because of the conditions then, that section of the diary is ambiguous and obscure. Mother had been so fiercely attacked for her writing, it amazed me that she went on keeping a diary. From some veiled allusions I gathered that he had queried the theories advanc-

CLARIFY

Why was the mother unable to fulfill her dream?

ed by that "theoretician" then at the height of favor, and had told someone, "This is sheer Rightist[19] talk." It was clear from the tear-stained pages of Mother's diary that he had been harshly denounced; but the steadfast old man never knuckled under to the authorities. His last words were, "When I go to meet Marx,[20] I shall go on fighting my case!"

That must have been in the winter of 1969, because that was when Mother's hair turned white overnight, though she was not yet fifty. And she put on a black arm band. Her position then was extremely difficult. She was criticized for wearing this old-style mourning, and ordered to say for whom she was in mourning.

"For whom are you wearing that, mum?" I asked anxiously.

"For my lover." Not to frighten me she explained, "Someone you never knew."

"Shall I put one on too?" She patted my cheeks, as she had when I was a child. It was years since she had shown me such affection. I often felt that as she aged, especially during these last years of persecution, all tenderness had left her, or was concealed in her heart, so that she seemed like a man.

She smiled sadly and said, "No, you needn't wear one."

Her eyes were as dry as if she had no more tears to shed. I longed to comfort her or do something to please her. But she said, "Off you go."

I felt an inexplicable dread, as if dear Mother had already half left me. I blurted out, "Mum!"

Quick to sense my desolation, she said gently, "Don't be afraid. Off you go. Leave me alone for a little."

I was right. She wrote:

---

18. **insuperable** (ĭn-sōō'pər-ə-bəl): impossible to overcome; insurmountable.
19. **Rightist:** belonging to a conservative or reactionary politics.
20. **Marx:** Karl Marx (1818–1883) a German economic philosopher revered by communists.

A painting in the class-education exhibition, Niutung People's Commune No. 4 (about 1970),
Niutung People's Commune Spare-Time Art Group.

You have gone. Half my soul seems to have taken flight with you.

I had no means of knowing what had become of you, much less of seeing you for the last time. I had no right to ask either, not being your wife or friend. . . . So we are torn apart. If only I could have borne that inhuman treatment for you, so that you could have lived on! You should have lived to see your name cleared and take up your work again, for the sake of those who loved you. I knew you could not be a counter-revolutionary. You were one of the finest men killed. That's why I love you— I am not afraid now to avow it.

Snow is whirling down. Heavens, even God is such a hypocrite, he is using this whiteness to cover up your blood and the scandal of your murder.

I have never set store by my life. But now I keep wondering whether anything I say or do would make you contract your shaggy eyebrows in a frown. I must live a worthwhile life like you and do some honest work for our country. Things can't go on like this—those criminals will get what's coming to them.

I used to walk alone along that small asphalt road, the only place where we once walked together, hearing my footsteps in the silent night. . . . I always paced to and fro and lingered there, but never as wretchedly as now. Then, though you were not beside me, I knew you were still in this world and felt that you were keeping me company. Now I can hardly believe that you have gone.

> I must live a worthwhile life like you and do some honest work for our country.

At the end of the road I would retrace my steps, then walk along it again. Rounding the fence I always looked back, as if you were still standing there waving goodbye. We smiled faintly, like casual acquaintances, to conceal our undying love. That ordinary evening in early spring, a chilly wind was blowing as we walked silently away from each other. You were wheezing a little because of your chronic bronchitis. That upset me. I wanted to beg you to slow down, but somehow I couldn't. We both walked very fast, as if some important business were waiting for us. How we prized that single stroll we had together, but we were afraid we might lose control of ourselves and burst out with "I love you"—those three words which had tormented us for years. Probably no one else could believe that we never once even clasped hands!

No, Mother, I believe it. I am the only one able to see into your locked heart.

Ah, that little asphalt road, so haunted by bitter memories. We shouldn't overlook the most insignificant spots on earth. For who knows how much secret grief and joy they may hide.

No wonder that when tired of writing, she would pace slowly along that little road behind our window. Sometimes at dawn after a sleepless night, sometimes on a moonless, windy evening. Even in winter during howling gales which hurled sand and pebbles against the windowpane. . . . I thought this was one of her eccentricities, not knowing that she had gone to meet him in spirit.

She liked to stand by the window too, staring at the small asphalt road. Once I thought from her expression that one of our closest friends must be coming to call. I hurried to the window. It was a late autumn evening. The cold wind was stripping dead leaves from the trees and blowing them down the small empty road.

She went on pouring out her heart to him in her diary as she had when he was alive. Right up to the day when the pen slipped from her fingers. Her last message was:

I am a materialist,[21] yet I wish there were a Heaven. For then, I know, I would find you there waiting for me. I am going there to join you, to be together for eternity. We need never be parted again or keep at a distance for fear of spoiling someone else's life. Wait for me, dearest, I am coming—

I do not know how Mother, on her death bed, could still love so ardently with all her heart. To me it seemed not love but a form of madness, a passion stronger than death. If undying love really exists, she reached its extreme. She obviously died happy, because she had known true love. She had no regrets.

EVALUATE

What is your opinion of the mother's devotion to her loved one?

Now these old people's ashes have mingled with the elements. But I know that, no matter what form they may take, they still love each other. Though not bound together by earthly laws or morality, though they never once clasped hands, each possessed the other completely. Nothing could part them. Centuries to come, if one white cloud trails another, two grasses grow side by side, one wave splashes another, a breeze follows another . . . believe me, that will be them.

Each time I read that diary "Love Must Not Be Forgotten" I cannot hold back my tears. I often weep bitterly, as if I myself experienced their ill-fated love. If not a tragedy it was too laughable. No matter how beautiful or moving I find it, I have no wish to follow suit!

Thomas Hardy[22] wrote that "the call seldom produces the comer, the man to love rarely coincides with the hour for loving." I cannot censure them from conventional moral standards. What I deplore is that they did not wait for a "missing counterpart" to call them.

If everyone could wait, instead of rushing into marriage, how many tragedies could be averted!

When we reach communism,[23] will there still be cases of marriage without love? Maybe, because since the world is so vast, two kindred spirits may be unable to answer each other's call. But how tragic! However, by that time, there may be ways to escape such tragedies.

Why should I split hairs?

Perhaps after all we are responsible for these tragedies. Who knows? Maybe we should take the responsibility for the old ideas handed down from the past. Because if someone never marries, that is a challenge to these ideas. You will be called neurotic, accused of having guilty secrets or having made political mistakes. You may be regarded as an eccentric who looks down on ordinary people, not respecting age-old customs—a heretic. In short they will trump up endless vulgar and futile charges to ruin your

---

21. **materialist** (mə-tîr′ē-ə-lĭst): here, a person who believes that the physical world is the only reality.

22. **Thomas Hardy** (1840–1928): a British author.

23. **When we reach communism:** When we reach the ideal state by following communist principles.

WORDS
TO
KNOW

censure (sĕn′shər) *v.* to criticize severely; to blame
heretic (hĕr′ĭ-tĭk) *n.* a person who holds controversial opinions that do not conform to the prevailing opinions of a society, religion, or group

New Look of a Village (about 1970), Niutung People's Commune Spare-Time Art Group.

reputation. Then you have to knuckle under to those ideas and marry willy-nilly. But once you put the chains of a loveless marriage around your neck, you will suffer for it for the rest of your life.

I long to shout: "Mind your own business! Let us wait patiently for our counterparts. Even waiting in vain is better than willy-nilly marriage. To live single is not such a fearful disaster. I believe it may be a sign of a step forward in culture, education and the quality of life." ❖

Translated by Gladys Yang

RESPONDING
OPTIONS

FROM PERSONAL RESPONSE TO CRITICAL ANALYSIS

REFLECT

1. Write down your impressions of the narrator and her mother in your notebook. Share your thoughts with your classmates.

RETHINK

2. How do you think the narrator is affected by her mother's advice and experiences?

   Consider
   - the narrator's feelings about her relationship with Qiao Lin
   - the narrator's views on love and marriage
   - how the narrator says she is viewed by society

3. Do you think that the mother and the man she loved made the right choices about their relationship? Explain your opinion.

4. Do you agree or disagree with the mother that it is better to live on one's own than to rush into marriage? Use examples from the story to support your opinion.

5. Predict the narrator's future. Will she marry, and if so, will she be happy?

RELATE

6. Do you think our society puts pressure on people to get married? Discuss your views with your classmates.

ANOTHER PATHWAY
Cooperative Learning

In a small group, prepare a eulogy that the narrator might have spoken at her mother's funeral. Be sure to include details from the story about the mother's life, comments from her friends, and the narrator's personal thoughts about her mother. Read your eulogy aloud to classmates.

QUICKWRITES

1. Recall the ideas on marriage that you discussed for the Personal Connection on page 396 and the advice that the mother gives her daughter in the story. Then write a newspaper **advice column** in which you give the best advice you can on the subject of marriage. State your opinions and support them with strong reasons.

2. Write a **monologue** in which the mother describes her feelings about and concerns for her daughter.

3. Write a **character evaluation** of any prominent figure in the selection. First provide an objective description of the character and then state your opinion of that character. Be sure to base your statements on details in the selection.

📁 *PORTFOLIO Save your writing. You may want to use it later as a springboard to a piece for your portfolio.*

LITERARY CONCEPTS

The **theme** of a work of literature is the central idea or message of the work. Theme should not be confused with subject, or what the work is about. Rather, theme is a perception about life or human nature that the writer shares with the reader. In most fiction, the reader uses details from the story to figure out a theme. In this story, however, the writer states the theme directly. Find quotations from the selection that could serve as the theme. Then, in a class discussion, decide which quotations best communicate the theme of the story.

LITERARY LINKS

What similarities, if any, do you see between the attitudes toward love expressed in this selection and those conveyed in other selections in this unit? Explain your reasoning.

ACROSS THE CURRICULUM

History Find out more about the Cultural Revolution in China. Use current books, encyclopedia entries, and articles about China and determine what happened and what impact the Cultural Revolution has had on life in China. Present your findings in an oral report.

ART CONNECTION

The painting on page 405 shows workers at a political meeting in China. What does this painting tell you about the power of the Communist government over the lives of the characters in this selection?

Detail of a painting in the class-education exhibition, Niutung People's Commune No. 4.

WORDS TO KNOW

Determine the relationship between each pair of capitalized words below. On your paper, write the letter of the choice that shows the most similar relationship.

1. RENOUNCE : ACCEPT :: (a) agree : approve (b) despise : disapprove (c) abandon : join
2. WISTFUL : SAD :: (a) warm : hot (b) bashful : shy (c) cheerful : gloomy
3. ATONEMENT : SIN :: (a) question : answer (b) fact : opinion (c) apology : insult
4. NAIVETÉ : WORLDLINESS :: (a) beauty : youth (b) simplicity : complexity (c) love : marriage
5. PARRY : QUESTION :: (a) dodge : bullet (b) donate : gift (c) suffer : injury
6. COYNESS : MODESTY :: (a) intelligence : foolishness (b) bravado : courage (c) cowardice : fear
7. CENSURE : OPPONENT :: (a) advise : counselor (b) ridicule : mockery (c) praise : hero
8. ARDENT : FOND :: (a) hilarious : funny (b) cool : icy (c) wicked : evil
9. HERETIC : SOCIETY :: (a) criminal : prison (b) outlaw : community (c) voter : democracy
10. AVERSION : DISLIKE :: (a) passion : fondness (b) innocence : guilt (c) elm : tree

ZHANG JIE

Zhang Jie has been one of China's most highly acclaimed and, at times, controversial authors. Brought up in poverty and forced by the government to pursue college studies in economics instead of in literature as she had dreamed, Zhang Jie developed a strong sensitivity to injustices within the Communist system. After college Zhang Jie was directed to become a statistician, and during the Cultural Revolution, she, like many other college graduates, was sent to southern China to work in a factory. Finally, in 1976, Zhang Jie was able to move to Beijing and begin a writing career. Her first story, published in

1937–

1978, won her the first of many writing awards. By the early 1980s, Zhang Jie was a best-selling writer in her homeland.

Zhang Jie's stories highlight injustices and other problems in China's Communist system. Strongly committed to socialism, she has described her role as a writer as being to encourage readers to work to improve society. With "Love Must Not Be Forgotten" she became the first Chinese author in years to write about romantic love, marriage and the role of women.

OTHER WORKS *As Long as Nothing Happens, Nothing Will; Heavy Wings* (also translated as Leaden Wings)

Brigid

MARY LAVIN / IRELAND

"Brigid" is set in Ireland, a rainy, largely agricultural land that is also one of western Europe's poorer nations. Irish farms are small by American standards, and most farm families must struggle to support themselves. Farmers were even poorer five or six decades ago, when "Brigid" takes place. Farms like that of the family in the story often lacked electricity and indoor plumbing and many of the other conveniences we associate with modern life. Despite the poverty—or perhaps because of it—Irish farming families remained close-knit, with children expected to care for aging parents and for other relatives unable to care for themselves. As author Joe McCarthy noted in the 1960s, "The bonds of an Irish family are deep between brothers and sisters and their uncles, aunts and grandparents. . . . It is a disgrace for a family to let old relatives live alone and a scandalous shame to put a granduncle or an aged aunt among strangers in a nursing home or public institution." Such values play a prominent role in the story you are about to read.

The rain came sifting through the air and settled like a bloom on the fields. But under the trees it fell in single heavy drops, noisily, like cabbage water running through the holes of a colander.[1]

The house was in the middle of the trees.

"Listen to that rain!" said the woman to her husband. "Will it never stop?"

"What harm is a sup[2] of rain?" he said.

"That's you all over again," she said. "What harm is anything, as long as it doesn't affect yourself?"

"How do you mean, when it doesn't affect me? Look at my feet. They're sopping. And look at my hat. It's soused."[3] He took the hat off and shook the rain from it onto the spitting bars of the grate.

"Quit that," said the woman. "Can't you see you're raising ashes?"

"What harm is ashes?"

"I'll show you what harm," she said, taking down a plate of cabbage and potato from the shelf over the fire. "There's your dinner destroyed with them." The yellow cabbage was lightly sprayed with ash.

"Ashes is healthy, I often heard said. Put it here!" He sat down at the table, taking up his knife and fork, and indicating where the plate was to be put by tapping the table with the handle of the knife. "Is there no bit of meat?" he asked, prodding the potato critically.

"There's plenty in the town, I suppose."

"In the town? And why didn't somebody go to the town, might I ask?"

"Who was there to go? You know as well as I do there's no one here to be traipsing in and out every time there's something wanted from the town."

"I suppose one of our fine daughters would think it the end of the world if she was asked to go for a bit of a message? Let me tell you they'd get husbands for themselves quicker if they were seen doing a bit of work once in a while."

"Who said anything about getting husbands for them?" said the woman. "They're time enough getting married."

"Is that so? Mind you now, anyone would think that you were anxious to get them off your hands with the way every penny that comes into the house goes out again on bits of silks and ribbons for them."

"I'm not going to let them be without their bit of fun just because you have other uses for your money than spending it on your own children!"

"What other uses have I? Do I smoke? Do I drink? Do I play cards?"

"You know what I mean."

"I suppose I do." The man was silent. He left down his fork. "I suppose you're hinting at poor Brigid again?" he said. "But I told you forty times, if she was put into a home[4] she'd be just as much of an expense to us as she is in the little house above there." He pointed out of the window with his fork.

"I see there's no use in talking about it," said the woman. "All I can say is God help the girls, with you, their own father, putting a drag on them so that no man will have anything to do with them after hearing about Brigid."

"What do you mean by that? This is something new. I thought it was only the bit of bread and tea she got that you grudged the poor thing. This is something new. What is this?"

"You oughtn't to need to be told, a man like you that saw the world, a man that traveled like you did, a man that was in England and London."

---

1. **colander** (kŭl′ən-dər): a bowl-shaped, perforated kitchen utensil for draining off liquid and rinsing food.

2. **sup:** a small quantity of liquid.

3. **soused** (soust): soaking wet; drenched.

4. **home:** here, a residential institution where people are cared for.

Rebecca (about 1947), Raphael Soyer. Oil on canvas, 26″ × 20″, courtesy of Forum Gallery, New York.

"I don't know what you're talking about." He took up his hat and felt it to see if the side he had placed near the fire was dry. He turned the other side toward the fire. "What are you trying to say?" he said. "Speak plain!"

"Is any man going to marry a girl when he hears her aunt is a poor half-witted creature, soft in the head, and living in a poke of a hut, doing nothing all day but sitting looking into the fire?"

"You don't want to listen to anything unpleasant. You don't want to listen to anything that's right."

"What has that got to do with anybody but the poor creature herself? Isn't it her own trouble?"

"Men don't like marrying into a family that has the like of her in it."

"Is that so? I didn't notice that you were put off marrying me, and you knew all about poor Brigid. You used to bring her bunches of primroses. And one day I remember you pulling the flowers off your hat and giving them to her when she started crying over nothing. You used to say she was a harmless poor thing. You used to say you'd look after her."

"And didn't I? Nobody can say I didn't look after her. Didn't I do my best to have her taken into a home, where she'd get proper care? You can't deny that."

"I'm not denying it. You never gave me peace or ease since the day we were married. But I wouldn't give in. I wouldn't give in then, and I won't give in now, either. I won't let it be said

that I had hand or part in letting my own sister be put away."

"But it's for her own good." This time the woman's voice was softer, and she went over and turned the wet hat again on the fender.[5] "It's nearly dry," she said, and she went back to the table and took up the plate from which he had eaten and began to wash it in a basin of water at the other end of the table. "It's for her own good. I'm surprised you can't see that; you, a sensible man, with two grown-up daughters. You'll be sorry one of these days when she's found dead in the chair—the Lord between us and all harm—or falls in the fire and gets scorched to death—God preserve us from the like! I was reading, only the other day, in a paper that came round something from the shop, that there was a case like that up in the Midlands."

"I don't want to hear about it," said the man, shuffling his feet. "The hat is dry, I think," he said, and he put it on his head and stood up.

"That's the way you always go on. You don't want to listen to anything unpleasant. You don't want to listen to anything that's right. You don't want to listen because you know what I'm saying is true and you know you have no answer to it."

"You make me tired," said the man; "it's always the one story in this house. Why don't you get something else to talk about for a change?"

The woman ran to the door and blocked his way.

"Is that your last word?" she said. "You won't give in?"

"I won't give in. Poor Brigid. Didn't my mother make me promise I'd never have hand or part in putting the poor creature away? 'Leave her alone,' my mother used to say, 'she's doing no harm to anyone.'"

---

5. **fender:** a metal screen in front of a fireplace to keep hot coals and ashes from falling out.

"She's doing harm to our daughters," said the woman, "and you know that. Don't you?" She caught his coat and stared at him. "You know the way Matty Monaghan[6] gave up Rosie after dancing with her all night at a dance in the Town Hall last year. Why did he do that, do you suppose? It's little you know about it at all! You don't see Mamie crying her eyes out some nights after coming in from a walk with the girls and hearing bits of talk from this one and that one, and putting two and two together, and finding out for herself the talk that goes on among the men about girls and the kind of homes they come from!"

"There'd be a lot more talk if the poor creature was put away. Let me tell you that, if you don't know it for yourself! It's one thing to have a poor creature, doing no one any harm, living quiet, all by herself, up at the end of a boreen[7] where seldom or never anyone gets a chance of seeing her. It's another thing altogether to have her taken away in a car and everyone running to the window to see the car pass and talking about her and telling stories from one to another till in no time at all they'd be letting on she was twice as bad as she is, and the stories about her would be getting so wild that none of us could go down the streets without being stared at as if we were all queer!"

"You won't give in?" his wife asked once more.

"I won't give in."

"Poor Mamie. Poor Rosie." The woman sighed. She put the plate up on the dresser.

Owen shuffled his feet. "If you didn't let it be seen so plain that you wanted to get them off, they might have a better chance. I don't know what they want getting married for, in any case. They'd be better off to be interested in this place, and raise a few hens, and make a bit of money for themselves so they could be independent and take no notice of people and their gossip!"

"It's little you know about anything, that's all I have to say," said the woman.

Owen moved to the door.

"Where are you going now?"

"There's no use in my telling you and drawing down another stream of abuse on myself when I mention the poor creature's name."

The woman sighed and then stood up and walked over to the fire.

"If that's where you're going you might as well take over these clean sheets." She took down a pair of sheets from where they were airing on the shelf over the fire. "You can't say but I look after her, no matter what," she said.

"If you remembered her the way I do," said the man, "when she was only a little bit of a child, and I was growing up and going to school, you'd know what it feels like to hear talk of putting her in a home. She used to have lovely hair. It was like the flossy heads of the dandelions when they are gone past their best. No one knew she was going to be a bit soft[8] until she was toddling around and beginning to talk, and even then it was thought she was only slow, that she'd grow out of it."

"I know how you feel," said the woman. "I could cry sometimes myself when I think about her. But she'd be so happy in a home! We could visit her any time we wanted. We could hire a car and drive over to see her, all of us, on a fine Sunday now and again. It would be some place to go. And it would cost no more than it costs to keep her here."

She didn't know whether he had heard the end of the sentence because he had gone out through the yard and was cutting across the field, with his ash plant[9] in his hand.

---

6. **Monaghan** (mŏn'ə-hăn).

7. **boreen** (bôr-ēn'): a narrow country lane.

8. **a bit soft**: simple-minded; mentally slow.

9. **ash plant**: a walking stick made from a young ash tree.

Fire and Water (1927), Winifred Nicholson. Copyright © artist's family.

"He was cutting across the field with the ash plant in his hand when we were starting off on our walk," said Rosie, when she and Mamie came in to their supper and her mother asked her if she had seen their father out in the yard.

"He was going up to your Aunt Brigid then," said their mother. "Did you not see him after that?"

"That was three hours ago," said Mamie, looking worried. "He wouldn't be over there all this time. Would he? He must be doing something for Aunt Brigid—chopping wood or mending something. He wouldn't be just sitting over there all this time."

"Ah, you wouldn't know what he'd be doing," the mother said, and the girls looked at each other. They knew then there had been words between their father and mother while they were out.

"Maybe one of you ought to run over and see what's keeping him?" said their mother.

"Oh, leave him alone," said Mamie. "If he wants to stay over there, let him! He'll have to be home soon anyway to put in the calves. It's nearly dark."

But soon it was very dark, and the calves were still out. The girls had gone out again to a dance, and it was beginning to rain when Owen's wife put on her coat and went across the field herself and up the boreen to Brigid's.

How can she sit there in the dark? she thought, when she didn't see a light in the window. But as she got nearer she saw there was a faint glow from the fire on the hearth. She felt sure Owen wasn't there. He wouldn't be there without lighting a lamp, or a bit of a candle! There was no need to go in. She was going to turn back, but it seemed an unnatural thing not to call to the door and see if the poor creature was all right.

Brigid was the same as ever, sitting by the fire with a silly smile and not looking up till she was called three or four times.

"Brigid, did you see Owen?" his wife asked without much hope of a reply.

Brigid looked up. "Owen is a queer man," she said. That was all the answer she gave.

"So he was here! What time did he leave?"

Brigid grumbled something.

"What are you saying, Brigid?"

"He wouldn't go home," Brigid said. "I told him it was time to go home for his tea, but he wouldn't answer me. 'Go home,' I said, 'go home, Owen.'"

"When did he go? What time was it? Did you notice?"

Brigid could be difficult sometimes. Was she going to be difficult now?

"He wouldn't go home," Brigid said again.

Suddenly Owen's wife saw his ash plant lying on the table.

"Is he still here?" she said, sharply, and she glanced back at the door. "I didn't see him in the yard! I didn't hear him!"

"He wouldn't speak to me," Brigid said again stubbornly.

The other woman couldn't see her in the dark. The fire was flickering too irregularly to see by its light.

"But where is he? Is there anything the matter with him?" She ran to the door and called out into the dark. But there was no answer. She stood there trying to think. She heard Brigid talking to herself, but she didn't trouble to listen. She might as well go home, she thought. Wherever he was, he wasn't here. "If he comes back, Brigid, tell him I was here looking for him," she said. "I'll go home through the other field."

Brigid said something then that made her turn sharply and look at her.

"What did you say?"

"Tell him yourself," said Brigid, and then she seemed to be talking to herself again. And she was leaning down in the dark before the fire.

"Why don't you talk?" she said. "Why don't you talk?"

Owen's wife began to pull out the old settle bed[10] that was in front of the fire, not knowing why she did it, but she could feel the blood pounding in her ears and behind her eyes.

"He fell down there and he wouldn't get up!" Brigid said. "I told him to get up. I told him that his head was getting scorched. But he wouldn't listen to me. He wouldn't get up. He wouldn't do anything."

Owen's wife closed her eyes. All of a sudden she was afraid to look. But when she looked, Owen's eyes stared up at her, wide open, from where he lay on his back on the hearth.

"Owen!" she screamed, and she tried to pull him up.

His shoulders were stiff and heavy. She caught his hands. They were cold. Was he dead? She felt his face. But his face was hot, so hot she couldn't put her hand on it. If he was dead he'd be cold. She wanted to scream and run out of the house, but first she tried to drag him as far as she could from the ashy hearth. Then suddenly feeling the living eyes of Brigid watching her, and seeing the dead eyes staring up from the blistered red face, she sprang up, knocking over a chair, and ran out of the house, and ran screaming down the boreen.

Her screams brought people running out to their doors, the light streaming out each side of them. She couldn't speak, but she pointed up the hill and ran on. She wanted to get to the pump.

It was dark at the pump, but she could hear people running the way she had pointed. Then when they had reached the cottage, there was no more running, but great talking and shouting. She sat down at the side of the pump, but there was a smell off her hands and desperately she bent forward and began to wash them under the pump, but when she saw there was hair stuck to her fingers she wanted to scream again, but there was a great pain gathering in her heart, not yet the pain of loss, but the pain of having failed; failed in some terrible way.

> *"I told him to get up. I told him that his head was getting scorched. But he wouldn't listen to me."*

I failed him always, she thought, from the very start. I never loved him like he loved me; not even then, long ago, the time I took the flowers off my hat. It wasn't for Brigid, like he thought. I was only making myself out to be what he imagined I was. I didn't know enough about loving to change myself for him. I didn't even know enough about it to keep him loving me. He had to give it all to Brigid in the end.

He gave it all to Brigid; to a poor daft thing that didn't know enough to pull him back from the fire or call someone when he fell down in a stroke. If it was anyone else was with him, he might have had a chance.

Oh, how had it happened? How could love be wasted and go to loss like that?

It was like the way the tossy balls of cowslips[11] they used to make as children were forgotten and left behind in the fields, till they were trodden into the muck by the cattle and the sheep.

---

10. **settle bed:** a long bench used both as a seat and as a bed.
11. **tossy balls of cowslips:** strung-together flowers and stems of cowslips. A cowslip is a wildflower that grows in Britain and Ireland.

Suddenly she thought of the heavy feet of the neighbors tramping the boards of the cottage up in the fields behind her, and rising up, she ran back up the boreen.

"Here's the poor woman now," someone said, as she thrust past the crowd around the door.

They began to make a way for her to where, on the settle bed, they had laid her husband. But instead she parted a way through the people and went toward the door of the room off the kitchen.

"It's Brigid I'm thinking about," she said. "Where is she?"

"Something will have to be done about her now all right," someone said.

"It will," she said, decisively, and her voice was as true as a bell.

She had reached the door of the room.

"That's why I came back," she said, looking around her defiantly. "She'll need proper minding[12] now. To think she hadn't the strength to run for help or pull him back a bit from the fire." She opened a door.

Sitting on the side of the bed, all alone, she saw Brigid.

"Get your hat and coat, Brigid," she said. "You're coming home with me." ❖

---

12. **minding:** tending; watching; caring for.

MARY LAVIN

Although she was born in Massachusetts, Mary Lavin (1912–) has spent most of her life in Ireland and writes about Ireland in virtually all of her fiction. The daughter of an Irish couple who spent a few years in America, Lavin immigrated to Ireland when she was nine and attended a convent school in the Irish capital of Dublin. Four years later, her father became the manager of the Bective estate in Ireland's County Meath, an area that Lavin came to know and love. In fact, Lavin's first collection of short stories, published in 1942, was called *Tales from Bective Bridge;* later, she and her family purchased Abbey Farm in Bective and made it their residence.

With her stories being published on both sides of the Atlantic Ocean, Lavin became one of Ireland's foremost short story writers. "Mary Lavin is a great artist," said the eminent British critic V. S. Pritchett; "we are excited by her sympathy, her acute knowledge of the human heart, her truthfulness and, above all, by the controlled revelation of untidy powerful emotion." "Brigid," which first appeared in a 1944 edition of *Dublin Magazine,* was later chosen for the Dell anthology *Great Irish Short Stories* (1964).

OTHER WORKS *Collected Stories, The Shrine and Other Stories, Mary Lavin: Selected Stories, A Family Likeness*

CAPTURING A MOMENT

Does the language in this unit's poetry captivate you or create a picture in your mind? Poetic language uses sound devices, figurative language, and sensory details to surprise or enlighten you. Even such everyday writing as TV jingles, rock lyrics, and phrases in your journal can sparkle with the language of poetry. On the next few pages you will

- explore the figures of speech that poets use
- write a poem of your own
- make observations about the use of metaphor in media

The Writer's Style: Figurative Language Figurative language, which is often used in poetry, conveys a message beyond the literal meaning of words. Some types of figurative language are simile, metaphor, and personification.

Read the Literature

Notice how these poets use figurative language to help you see familiar things in unusual ways. How do personification, simile, and metaphor form pictures in your mind?

Literature Models

Personification
Personification gives human characteristics to inanimate objects. What objects does this poet personify?

Streets coming fast,
One after the other,
Wedge you away from me,
And the lamps of the city prick my eyes
So that I can no longer see your face.

Amy Lowell,
from "The Taxi"

Simile
A simile uses the word *like* or *as* to make a comparison. What two unlike things is this poet comparing?

The snow was flying, like white willow cotton.
This year, Spring has come again,
And the willow cotton is like snow.

Su Tung Po, from "To a Traveler,"
translated by Kenneth Rexroth

Connect to Music

Whenever you listen to a song, you are also listening to a poem. A song lyric is really a short verse that expresses the writer's emotion. The following song lyric makes an unusual direct comparison. Notice how figurative language is used.

Song Lyric

We have come for LIGHT
WHOLLY, we have come for light
  it's TRUE
  I am the SUN
  I am the new year
  I am the rain

the Breeders,
from "New Year,"
Last Splash

Metaphors
A metaphor makes a comparison by speaking of one thing as though it were something else. What direct comparisons does this lyricist make?

Try Your Hand: Using Figurative Language

1. **Practice Personification** Write a sentence or phrase that gives human characteristics to each of the following: a river, time, a computer.

2. **Spice It Up** Make the following scene richer by using figurative language.

   > We stood motionless and afraid. An eerie silence began to fill the town. Before we could decide what to do, we heard a deafening sound. Then, the tornado hit without fair warning and we were caught in its mighty winds.

3. **Make the Comparison** In a sentence, create a metaphor and a simile of your own. You might want to describe a feeling, an object, or a person you know.

WRITER'S CRAFT

Avoiding Clichés
Clichés are phrases or figures of speech that are so overused that they are no longer effective. Because they lack creative thought, they give you nothing new to think about.

For example, instead of saying that his love is *"as pretty as a picture,"* Shakespeare writes

Shall I compare thee to a summer's day?
Thou art more lovely and more temperate: . . .

from Sonnet 18

Following are some examples of clichés. Can you think of more?

- as big as a house
- squeaky clean
- happy as a clam
- working my fingers to the bone
- a sight for sore eyes

APPLYING WHAT YOU'VE LEARNED
Rewrite the phrases above to provide fresh, interesting alternatives.

Creative Response

Poems like those in Unit Three capture a moment of experience, make a surprising observation, or tell a story. Poetry may take any form and may be written about anything, yet poetry is unique. The sounds and rhythms of words, the look of a poem, the mental images that poems evoke—all make poetry the closest thing in words to music and to visual art.

GUIDED ASSIGNMENT

Write a Poem To better understand a piece of writing, you can do the same kind of writing yourself. On these pages you'll explore your own response to the poems in Unit Three. Then you'll discover a poem that could be written only by you.

Student's Poetry Sketchbook

OBSERVATION
- the sky's blue shades on the horizon
- activity on the beach - children, crabs
- the horizon's power over me

PERSONIFICATION
- waves kiss the shore
- horizon casts a spell over me

IMAGES

peaceful feeling

shades of blue and beige

salty taste of sea mist

BEACH

hot, brilliant sun

squealing children

pounding waves

1 Prewrite and Explore

Poets seldom plan what they will write before they compose. Usually, they begin with a phrase, a feeling, or an image, in language that brings forth a certain direction.

SEARCHING FOR IDEAS

The following methods might help you to discover the poem inside of you:

- Listen to conversation.
- Observe events and situations.
- Read the poetry of others.
- Recall a mood or feeling.
- Think about images.
- Reread literature that evokes a memory.

RECORDING YOUR THOUGHTS

Your search for subjects or images can take on many forms. You might like to keep a notebook of ideas, create webs, draw pictures, or talk over your ideas with a friend. Many times the best way to begin a poem is just to start writing. The example at the left is one student's approach to recording thoughts at the beach that might be used in future poems.

❷ Freewrite

Now it's time to freewrite. Record words, phrases, and feelings that come to you. Play with language, write as much as you can, and don't censor yourself. All you need to do is write!

The yellow notes show how one student analyzed his freewriting.

Student's Freewriting

I look at the horizon and see layers of pale blue, gray blue, bright blue. It is a hot sunny day. Waves ruin sand creations. What does this scene remind me of? My childhood memories of the beach at the lake. What feelings does this memory give me? calm, secure, free

Now I think about the present. As I stand at the edge of the ocean, I am surprised the water is warm. I feel the fresh mist from the sea and lick my lips to taste the salt and summer.

Children squeal and sand crabs scurry across the sand umbrellas dot the beach.

I look back to the horizon and feel peace.

Do I want to write about my childhood memories or my present impressions?

What kinds of images might I add?

❸ Draft and Share

How will you change your freewriting into a poem? Remember that poetry is written in lines, not sentences. First, mark the sections, phrases, even words that you think you want to keep. Next, condense your poem by including only your most important ideas and details. Consider how your poem can make a strong impression. When you are finished, think about these questions and share your poem with a friend.

- Does my poem make sense?
- Do I use interesting figurative language?
- Is every word necessary? How might I condense my ideas?

 PEER RESPONSE

- What is your first reaction when you read my poem?
- Does the figurative language appeal to you? Why?
- What images could be stronger?

SkillBuilder

 WRITER'S CRAFT

Using Sound Devices
Poets use various techniques such as sound devices to add dimension to poetry. Two sound devices, consonance and assonance, can help add interest to your poems.

Consonance Notice the repetition of consonant sounds within words.

To leap from a clump of banana plants
one morning of wonders—

Gabriela Mistral
from "Eight Puppies"

Assonance Watch for the repetition of vowel sounds within words.

Tonight I can write the saddest lines.
I loved her, and sometimes she loved me too.

Pablo Neruda
from "Tonight I Can Write . . ."
translated by W. S. Merwin

APPLYING WHAT YOU'VE LEARNED
Try your hand at using these sound devices. Write one line of poetry using consonance and one line using assonance.

4 Revise and Edit

Even poems need revision. Reread your poem aloud and listen to decide if each word you chose adds to the poem's effect. Check the callouts below and consider the Standards for Evaluation as you prepare your final draft.

Student's Final Draft

What language choices seem interesting?

How is figurative language used?

What feeling does the student convey?

June Day at the Seashore

Perched between the sand and sea, I gaze upon the horizon.
Soft layers of blue put me in a trance.
I am lost inside the cloudless day.

Waves kiss the shore and topple sand castles.
Expecting cold, I am surprised at the warmth.
After the misty sea sprays me,
I lick my lips to taste the salt and summer.

Damp heat presses, children squeal in delight, sand crabs scurry.
Scents of sunscreen and stickiness float between breezes.
Graceful umbrellas dot the straight beige beach.

The seashore is all of these things,
but it's always the horizon that calls me back—
showing me a dream, a promise, an answer.

Standards for Evaluation

The poem
- accurately captures an experience, observation, or emotion
- uses precise and fresh language
- uses sounds and figurative language to support the meaning and effect

Grammar in Context

Participial Phrases A **participle** is a verb form that is used as a modifier. A participial phrase contains a participle and any words that modify it. Participial phrases are often used in poetry because they are useful in compressing ideas. However, a writer must use them carefully. If a participial phrase is not placed near the word it modifies, the result can be very confusing.

I gaze upon the horizon, perched between the sand and sea.

In the example above, the participial phrase should be moved to the beginning of the line because it modifies the word *I*, not *horizon*.

I am surprised at the warmth, expecting cold.

The example above shows that the participial phrase, *expecting cold*, should be placed near *I*, the word it modifies.

Try Your Hand: Using Participial Phrases

On a separate piece of paper, identify which of the following sentences contain misplaced participial phrases. Rewrite the sentences correctly.

1. The crabs were hidden from view buried in the sand.
2. Sparkling in the sun, the shells were beautiful treasures.
3. Walking across the beach, the sun set as I headed home.

 GRAMMAR FROM WRITING

Using Punctuation in Poetry

The rules of punctuation are usually relaxed in the writing of poetry. It is important, though, to follow some punctuation rules. Even though you've written a poem to express yourself, you need to make your poem reader-friendly. Punctuation is your reader's "roadmap."

Look at this excerpt from "I Love Words" by Louis Ginsberg:

Some love jewels
And gems that daze:
Topaz, onyx,
Chrysoprase.

Others love Beauty
That haunts swans
In permanent
Repose of bronze.

Ginsberg uses a colon to alert the reader to an upcoming list. He uses commas to separate items and a period at the end of a thought. He also capitalizes the first letter of each new line.

APPLYING WHAT YOU'VE LEARNED
Go back to your final poem and decide whether there are places you can improve punctuation use. Modify your poem's punctuation.

 GRAMMAR HANDBOOK

For more information on punctuation, see page 1089 of the Grammar Handbook.

When You Wish upon a RISING STAR

Everyone in Hollywood knows that Hayun Cho is a rising star. But will the young director climb fast enough to satisfy the people banking on her?

By Jim Ochsenreiter   Photgraphs by Clare Schortgen

SEEING METAPHOR

Literature is not the only place you will find metaphors. In articles, advertisements, and cartoons, for example, metaphors can be effective shortcuts for communicating ideas. By using familiar images, writers can instantly convey an idea or opinion to their readers.

View Look at the magazine and newspaper pages shown here. Which words and pictures catch your attention first?

Interpret What ideas are being expressed on each page? What metaphors are used to help present each idea?

Discuss In a group, discuss how effective the metaphors were in helping you get a quick sense of the ideas. How would the message have been different if the writer or artist had used a more straightforward approach? Refer to the SkillBuilder at the right to help you think about what you observe.

SkillBuilder

 CRITICAL THINKING

Making Observations
What is going on around you? Making observations is more than just looking. It's paying close attention to your environment by using your senses to gather information. Becoming aware of what makes each person, place, thing, or situation special is the key to making successful observations.

To effectively observe, zero in on ideas or images that help you make connections in your world. Take notes on what you perceive. Look beyond the surface. That's what metaphors teach you. In effect, that's what all of your experiences teach you. Making observations helps you to interpret those experiences.

When making observations, remember the following:

- Use all five of your senses.
- Ask *who, what, why, where, when,* and *how.*
- Recall past experiences.
- Create lists.

APPLYING WHAT YOU'VE LEARNED
Over the next few days, practice making observations. Consider the ideas above and remember to expect the unexpected!

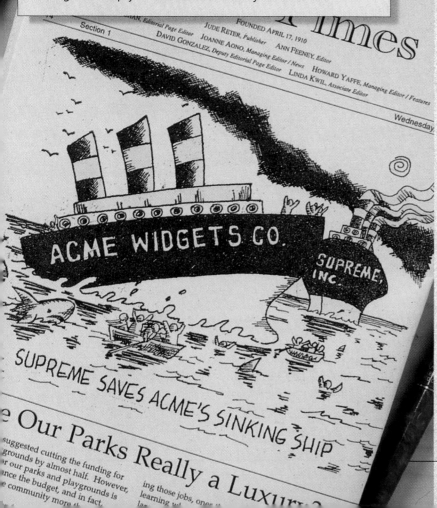

MYSTERIES OF THE HEART

REFLECTING ON THEME

Consider the Roman god of love, Cupid. Young, beautiful, mischievous—even cruel—he shoots his arrows of love, and the results are almost always unpredictable. His characteristics reflect love's mysterious powers. As you will see in this part of Unit Three, love can have a profound impact, for better or worse, on people's lives.

What Do You Think? With a group of classmates, create a brief glossary of expressions that convey the strange, wonderful, and even frightful effects of love. You may want to include phrases such as *love-crazed* and *head over heels in love,* as well as expressions that you have heard at home or through the media. Define each expression, give an example of its use, and provide a visual illustration if one would be appropriate. After reading these selections, you may have ideas for additions to the glossary.

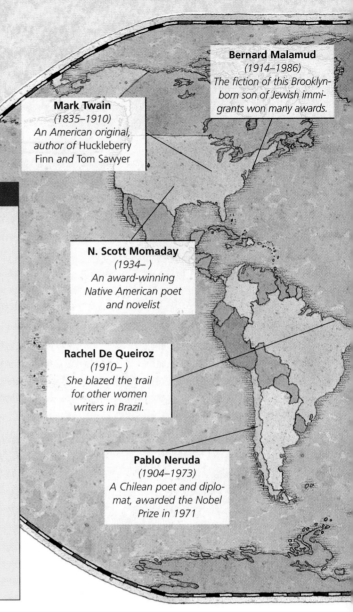

Mark Twain
(1835–1910)
An American original, author of Huckleberry Finn and Tom Sawyer

Bernard Malamud
(1914–1986)
The fiction of this Brooklyn-born son of Jewish immigrants won many awards.

N. Scott Momaday
(1934–)
An award-winning Native American poet and novelist

Rachel De Queiroz
(1910–)
She blazed the trail for other women writers in Brazil.

Pablo Neruda
(1904–1973)
A Chilean poet and diplomat, awarded the Nobel Prize in 1971

Mark Twain	**The Californian's Tale** *When will she return to her devoted husband?*	430
Su Dong Po	**To a Traveler** / INSIGHT *Absence and remembrance*	438
N. Scott Momaday	**Simile** *How did love go wrong?*	441
Pablo Neruda	**Tonight I Can Write . . . /** **Puedo Escribir Los Versos . . .** *The "saddest lines" about love*	441
Aleksandr Pushkin	**To . . .** *He can't forget her.*	448

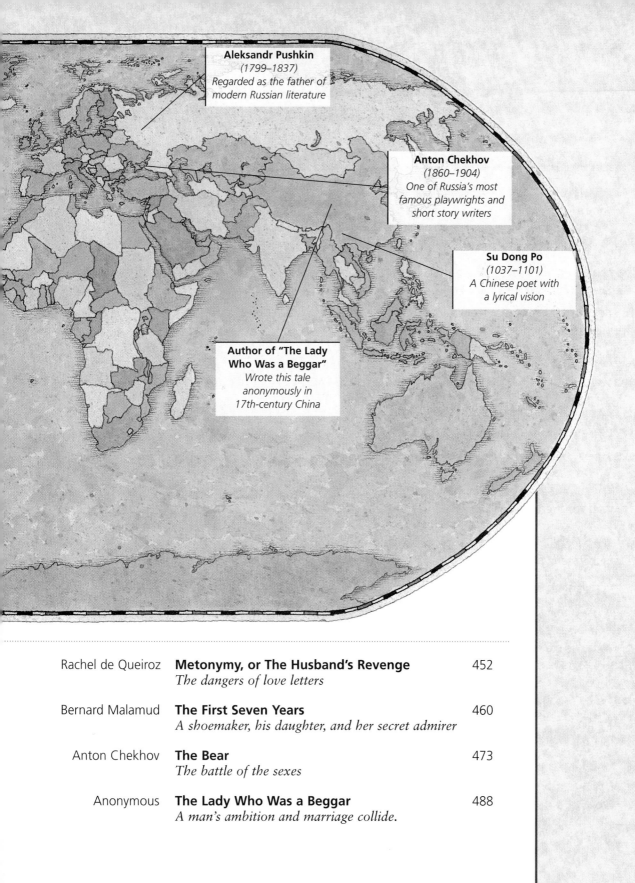

Aleksandr Pushkin
(1799–1837)
Regarded as the father of modern Russian literature

Anton Chekhov
(1860–1904)
One of Russia's most famous playwrights and short story writers

Su Dong Po
(1037–1101)
A Chinese poet with a lyrical vision

Author of "The Lady Who Was a Beggar"
Wrote this tale anonymously in 17th-century China

<table>
<tr><td>Rachel de Queiroz</td><td>**Metonymy, or The Husband's Revenge**
The dangers of love letters</td><td>452</td></tr>
<tr><td>Bernard Malamud</td><td>**The First Seven Years**
A shoemaker, his daughter, and her secret admirer</td><td>460</td></tr>
<tr><td>Anton Chekhov</td><td>**The Bear**
The battle of the sexes</td><td>473</td></tr>
<tr><td>Anonymous</td><td>**The Lady Who Was a Beggar**
A man's ambition and marriage collide.</td><td>488</td></tr>
</table>

PREVIEWING

FICTION

The Californian's Tale
Mark Twain United States

PERSONAL CONNECTION

What do you think makes a house a home? Is a home created by its comfortable furnishings or the personal touches in its decoration? Is it created by the feelings of the people who live there or by the way guests are welcomed? For five minutes, do some focused freewriting in your notebook about what it takes to make a house a home.

HISTORICAL CONNECTION

The comforts of home have a special significance for the characters in "The Californian's Tale," who live in a lonely environment in the aftermath of the California Gold Rush. Gold was first discovered in 1848 at Sutter's Mill east of Sacramento. During 1849 alone, more than 80,000 so-called "forty-niners" rushed to the California territory to prospect, or hunt, for gold in the region's many rivers and creeks. Dozens of mining towns sprang up along these waterways, and by 1850 California had grown so much that it was admitted as a state in the Union. Most settlers who came to California to strike it rich were men. In fact, women were so seldom seen that miners were known to walk miles to catch sight of one.

Once the precious ore became harder to find, many Gold Rush "boom" towns turned into ghost towns. A number of the miners returned to their families in the East. Some moved on to other regions in the West that promised gold or silver. Other veteran prospectors, however, did remain to continue their search for gold or to try their hand at farming.

READING CONNECTION

Interpreting Details About Setting As you read the story, pay attention to the little domestic touches that make Henry's house seem so pleasant to the narrator. What do the details about the house reveal about Henry's wife? What do they reveal about Henry?

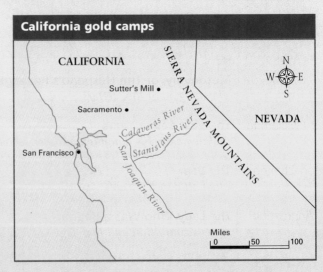

California gold camps

LASERLINKS
• HISTORICAL CONNECTION

The Californian's Tale

Mark Twain

Old-Time Cabin, Maynard Dixon. Courtesy of Museum of Art, Brigham Young University. Copyright © Museum of Art, Brigham Young University, all rights reserved.

Thirty-five years ago I was out prospecting on the Stanislaus,[1] tramping all day long with pick and pan and horn, and washing a hatful of dirt here and there, always expecting to make a rich strike, and never doing it.

---

1. **Stanislaus:** a river in California where gold was mined.

> At last, in the early part of the afternoon,
> when I caught sight of
> a human creature, I felt a most
> grateful uplift.

It was a lovely region, woodsy, balmy, delicious, and had once been populous, long years before, but now the people had vanished and the charming paradise was a solitude. They went away when the surface diggings gave out. In one place, where a busy little city with banks and newspapers and fire companies and a mayor and aldermen had been, was nothing but a wide expanse of emerald turf, with not even the faintest sign that human life had ever been present there. This was down toward Tuttletown.[2] In the country neighborhood thereabouts, along the dusty roads, one found at intervals the prettiest little cottage homes, snug and cozy, and so cobwebbed with vines snowed thick with roses that the doors and windows were wholly hidden from sight—sign that these were deserted homes, forsaken years ago by defeated and disappointed families who could neither sell them nor give them away. Now and then, half an hour apart, one came across solitary log cabins of the earliest mining days, built by the first gold miners, the predecessors of the cottage builders. In some few cases these cabins were still occupied; and when this was so, you could depend upon it that the occupant was the very pioneer who had built the cabin; and you could depend on another thing, too—that he was there because he had once had his opportunity to go home to the States rich, and had not done it; had rather lost his wealth, and had then in his humiliation resolved to sever all communication with his home relatives and friends, and be to them thenceforth as one

dead. Round about California in that day were scattered a host of these living dead men— pride-smitten poor fellows, grizzled and old at forty, whose secret thoughts were made all of regrets and longings—regrets for their wasted lives, and longings to be out of the struggle and done with it all.

It was a lonesome land! Not a sound in all those peaceful expanses of grass and woods but the drowsy hum of insects; no glimpse of man or beast; nothing to keep up your spirits and make you glad to be alive. And so, at last, in the early part of the afternoon, when I caught sight of a human creature, I felt a most grateful uplift. This person was a man about forty-five years old, and he was standing at the gate of one of those cozy little rose-clad cottages of the sort already referred to. However, this one hadn't a deserted look; it had the look of being lived in and petted and cared for and looked after; and so had its front yard, which was a garden of flowers, abundant, gay, and flourishing. I was invited in, of course, and required to make myself at home—it was the custom of the country.

It was delightful to be in such a place, after long weeks of daily and nightly familiarity with miners' cabins—with all which this implies of dirt floor, never-made beds, tin plates and cups,

---

2. **Tuttletown:** a mining town near the Stanislaus River.

bacon and beans and black coffee, and nothing of ornament but war pictures from the Eastern illustrated papers tacked to the log walls. That was all hard, cheerless, materialistic desolation, but here was a nest which had aspects to rest the tired eye and refresh that something in one's nature which, after long fasting, recognizes, when confronted by the belongings of art, howsoever cheap and modest they may be, that it has unconsciously been famishing and now has found nourishment. I could not have believed that a rag carpet could feast me so, and so content me; or that there could be such solace to the soul in wallpaper and framed lithographs,[3] and bright-colored tidies[4] and lamp mats, and Windsor chairs,[5] and varnished whatnots,[6] with seashells and books and china vases on them, and the score of little unclassifiable tricks and touches that a woman's hand distributes about a home, which one sees without knowing he sees them, yet would miss in a moment if they were taken away. The delight that was in my heart showed in my face, and the man saw it and was pleased; saw it so plainly that he answered it as if it had been spoken.

"All her work," he said, caressingly; "she did it all herself—every bit," and he took the room in with a glance which was full of affectionate worship. One of those soft Japanese fabrics with which women drape with careful negligence the upper part of a picture frame was out of adjustment. He noticed it, and rearranged it with cautious pains, stepping back several times to gauge the effect before he got it to suit him. Then he gave it a light finishing pat or two with his hand, and said: "She always does that. You can't tell just what it lacks, but it does lack something until you've done that—you can see it yourself after it's done, but that is all you know; you can't find out the law of it. It's like the finishing pats a mother gives the child's hair

after she's got it combed and brushed, I reckon. I've seen her fix all these things so much that I can do them all just her way, though I don't know the law of any of them. But she knows the law. She knows the why and the how both; but I don't know the why; I only know the how."

He took me into a bedroom so that I might wash my hands; such a bedroom as I had not seen for years: white counterpane,[7] white pillows, carpeted floor, papered walls, pictures, dressing table, with mirror and pincushion and dainty toilet things; and in the corner a washstand, with real chinaware bowl and pitcher, and with soap in a china dish, and on a rack more than a dozen towels—towels too clean and white for one out of practice to use without some vague sense of profanation.[8] So my face spoke again, and he answered with gratified words:

"All her work; she did it all herself—every bit. Nothing here that hasn't felt the touch of her hand. Now you would think—But I mustn't talk so much."

---

3. **lithographs:** prints made by a process in which portions of a flat surface are treated either to retain or to repel ink.
4. **tidies:** decorative coverings for the arms or headrest of a chair or sofa.
5. **Windsor chairs:** wooden chairs with high-spoked backs, outward-slanting legs, and saddle seats.
6. **whatnots:** a set of light, open shelves for displaying ornaments.
7. **counterpane:** bedspread.
8. **profanation:** the showing of contempt for something regarded as sacred.

Into the Past (1941), Hananiah Harari. Oil on canvas, 15″ × 12⅞″, Richard York Gallery, New York.

By this time I was wiping my hands and glancing from detail to detail of the room's belongings, as one is apt to do when he is in a new place, where everything he sees is a comfort to his eye and his spirit; and I became conscious, in one of those unaccountable ways, you know, that there was something there somewhere that the man wanted me to discover for myself. I knew it perfectly, and I knew he was trying to help me by <u>furtive</u> indications with his eye, so I tried

hard to get on the right track, being eager to gratify him. I failed several times, as I could see out of the corner of my eye without being told; but at last I knew I must be looking straight at the thing—knew it from the pleasure issuing in invisible waves from him. He broke into a happy laugh, and rubbed his hands together, and cried out:

"That's it! You've found it. I knew you would. It's her picture."

WORDS TO KNOW   **furtive** (fûr′tĭv) *adj.* shifty; having a hidden motive or purpose

I went to the little black-walnut bracket[9] on the farther wall, and did find there what I had not yet noticed—a daguerreotype case.[10] It contained the sweetest girlish face, and the most beautiful, as it seemed to me, that I had ever seen. The man drank the admiration from my face, and was fully satisfied.

"Nineteen her last birthday," he said, as he put the picture back; "and that was the day we were married. When you see her—ah, just wait till you see her!"

"Where is she? When will she be in?"

"Oh, she's away now. She's gone to see her people. They live forty or fifty miles from here. She's been gone two weeks today."

"When do you expect her back?"

"This is Wednesday. She'll be back Saturday, in the evening—about nine o'clock, likely."

I felt a sharp sense of disappointment.

"I'm sorry, because I'll be gone then," I said, regretfully.

"Gone? No—why should you go? Don't go. She'll be so disappointed."

She would be disappointed—that beautiful creature! If she had said the words herself they could hardly have blessed me more. I was feeling a deep, strong longing to see her—a longing so supplicating, so insistent, that it made me afraid. I said to myself: "I will go straight away from this place, for my peace of mind's sake."

"You see, she likes to have people come and stop with us—people who know things, and can talk—people like you. She delights in it; for she knows—oh, she knows nearly everything herself, and can talk, oh, like a bird—and the books she reads, why, you would be astonished. Don't go; it's only a little while, you know, and she'll be so disappointed."

I heard the words, but hardly noticed them, I was so deep in my thinkings and strugglings. He left me, but I didn't know. Presently he was back, with the picture case in his hand, and he held it open before me and said:

"There, now, tell her to her face you could have stayed to see her, and you wouldn't."

That second glimpse broke down my good resolution. I would stay and take the risk. That night we smoked the tranquil pipe, and talked till late about various things, but mainly about her; and certainly I had had no such pleasant and restful time for many a day. The Thursday followed and slipped comfortably away. Toward twilight a big miner from three miles away came—one of the grizzled, stranded pioneers—and gave us warm salutation, clothed in grave and sober speech. Then he said:

"I only just dropped over to ask about the little madam, and when is she coming home. Any news from her?"

"Oh yes, a letter. Would you like to hear it, Tom?"

"Well, I should think I would, if you don't mind, Henry!"

Henry got the letter out of his wallet, and said he would skip some of the private phrases, if we were willing; then he went on and read the bulk of it—a loving, sedate, and altogether charming and gracious piece of handiwork, with a postscript full of affectionate regards and messages to Tom, and Joe, and Charley, and other close friends and neighbors.

As the reader finished, he glanced at Tom, and cried out:

"Oho, you're at it again! Take your hands away, and let me see your eyes. You always do

---

9. **bracket:** a small shelf.

10. **daguerreotype** (də-gâr′ə-tīp′) **case:** a frame-like case holding an early type of photograph.

> "I'm getting old, you know, and any little disappointment makes me want to cry. I thought she'd be here herself, and now you've got only a letter."

that when I read a letter from her. I will write and tell her."

"Oh no, you mustn't, Henry. I'm getting old, you know, and any little disappointment makes me want to cry. I thought she'd be here herself, and now you've got only a letter."

"Well, now, what put that in your head? I thought everybody knew she wasn't coming till Saturday."

"Saturday! Why, come to think, I did know it. I wonder what's the matter with me lately? Certainly I knew it. Ain't we all getting ready for her? Well, I must be going now. But I'll be on hand when she comes, old man!"

Late Friday afternoon another gray veteran tramped over from his cabin a mile or so away, and said the boys wanted to have a little gaiety and a good time Saturday night, if Henry thought she wouldn't be too tired after her journey to be kept up.

"Tired? She tired! Oh, hear the man! Joe, *you* know she'd sit up six weeks to please any one of you!"

When Joe heard that there was a letter, he asked to have it read, and the loving messages in it for him broke the old fellow all up; but he said he was such an old wreck that *that* would happen to him if she only just mentioned his name. "Lord, we miss her so!" he said.

Saturday afternoon I found I was taking out my watch pretty often. Henry noticed it, and said, with a startled look:

"You don't think she ought to be here so soon, do you?"

I felt caught, and a little embarrassed; but I laughed, and said it was a habit of mine when I was in a state of expectancy. But he didn't seem quite satisfied; and from that time on he began to show uneasiness. Four times he walked me up the road to a point whence we could see a long distance; and there he would stand, shading his eyes with his hand, and looking. Several times he said:

"I'm getting worried, I'm getting right down worried. I know she's not due till about nine o'clock, and yet something seems to be trying to warn me that something's happened. You don't think anything has happened, do you?"

I began to get pretty thoroughly ashamed of him for his childishness; and at last, when he repeated that imploring question still another time, I lost my patience for the moment, and spoke pretty brutally to him. It seemed to shrivel him up and cow[11] him; and he looked so wounded and so humble after that, that I detested myself for having done the cruel and unnecessary thing. And so I was glad when Charley, another veteran, arrived toward the edge of the evening, and nestled up to Henry to hear the letter read, and talked over the preparations for the welcome. Charley fetched out one hearty speech after another, and did his best to drive away his friend's bodings and apprehensions.

"Anything *happened* to her? Henry, that's pure nonsense. There isn't anything going to happen to her; just make your mind easy as to that. What did the letter say? Said she was well,

---

11. **cow:** to intimidate; to frighten with threats or a show of force.

WORDS TO KNOW

imploring (ĭm-plôr'ĭng) *adj.* begging; making an urgent appeal **implore** v.
boding (bō'dĭng) *n.* a warning or omen about the future, especially of evil **bode** v.

didn't it? And said she'd *be* here by nine o'clock, didn't it? Did you ever know her to fail of her word? Why, you know you never did. Well, then, don't you fret; she'll be here, and that's absolutely certain, and as sure as you are born. Come, now, let's get to decorating—not much time left."

Pretty soon Tom and Joe arrived, and then all hands set about adorning the house with flowers. Toward nine the three miners said that as they had brought their instruments they might as well tune up, for the boys and girls would soon be arriving now, and hungry for a good, old-fashioned breakdown.[12] A fiddle, a banjo, and a clarinet—these were the instruments. The trio took their places side by side, and began to play some rattling dance music, and beat time with their big boots.

It was getting very close to nine. Henry was standing in the door with his eyes directed up the road, his body swaying to the torture of his mental distress. He had been made to drink his wife's health and safety several times, and now Tom shouted:

"All hands stand by! One more drink, and she's here!"

Joe brought the glasses on a waiter,[13] and served the party. I reached for one of the two remaining glasses, but Joe growled, under his breath:

"Drop that! Take the other."

Which I did. Henry was served last. He had hardly swallowed his drink when the clock began to strike. He listened till it finished, his face growing pale and paler; then he said:

"Boys, I'm sick with fear. Help me—I want to lie down!"

They helped him to the sofa. He began to nestle and drowse, but presently spoke like one talking in his sleep, and said: "Did I hear horses' feet? Have they come?"

One of the veterans answered, close to his ear: "It was Jimmy Parrish come to say the party got delayed, but they're right up the road a piece, and coming along. Her horse is lame, but she'll be here in half an hour."

"Oh, I'm *so* thankful nothing has happened!"

He was asleep almost before the words were out of his mouth. In a moment those handy men had his clothes off, and had tucked him into his bed in the chamber where I had washed my hands. They closed the door and came back. Then they seemed preparing to leave; but I said: "Please don't go, gentlemen. She won't know me; I am a stranger."

They glanced at each other. Then Joe said:

"She? Poor thing, she's been dead nineteen years!"

"Dead?"

"That or worse. She went to see her folks half a year after she was married, and on her way back, on a Saturday evening, the Indians captured her within five miles of this place, and she's never been heard of since."

"And he lost his mind in consequence?"

"Never has been sane an hour since. But he only gets bad when that time of the year comes round. Then we begin to drop in here, three days before she's due, to encourage him up, and ask if he's heard from her, and Saturday we all come and fix up the house with flowers, and get everything ready for a dance. We've done it every year for nineteen years. The first Saturday there was twenty-seven of us, without counting the girls; there's only three of us now, and the girls are all gone. We drug him to sleep, or he would go wild; then he's all right for another year—thinks she's with him till the last three or four days come round; then he begins to look for her, and gets out his poor old letter, and we come and ask him to read it to us. Lord, she was a darling!" ❖

---

12. **breakdown:** a noisy, energetic American country dance.

13. **waiter:** a tray.

To a Traveler

Su Dong Po

Last year when I accompanied you
As far as the Yang Chou Gate,
The snow was flying, like white
   willow cotton.
This year, Spring has come again,
5 And the willow cotton is like snow.
But you have not come back.
Alone before the open window,
I raise my wine cup to the shining moon.
The wind, moist with evening dew,
10 Blows the gauze curtains.

Maybe Chang-O the moon goddess,
Will pity this single swallow
And join us together with the cord of
   light
That reaches beneath the painted eaves
   of your home.

Translated by Kenneth Rexroth

RESPONDING OPTIONS

FROM PERSONAL RESPONSE TO CRITICAL ANALYSIS

REFLECT   **1.** Were you surprised by the outcome of this story? Explain why or why not in your notebook, and then share your writing with a classmate.

RETHINK   **2.** How would you describe Henry?
Consider
- how Henry has taken care of his home
- Henry's expectation of his wife's return
- the anxiety that Henry experiences on Saturday night

3. Why do you think the narrator becomes so fascinated by Henry's wife?
Consider
- the narrator's description of the cottage and the wife's photograph
- what Henry says about her
- the type of life the narrrator has led

4. Do you think the miners exercise good judgment in staging a welcome home party for Henry's wife year after year? Why or why not?

RELATE   **5.** What does the speaker in Su Dong Po's poem "To a Traveler" have in common with Henry?

ANOTHER PATHWAY

Cooperative Learning

What happens after the story ends? Get together with three other classmates and continue the conversation among the narrator, Tom, Charley, and Joe, with each student acting out a role. Talk over what happened that night, tell stories about past gatherings and share impressions of the wife.

QUICKWRITES

1. Write a **literary analysis** in which you explain what the setting—the house and its surroundings—reveals about the lives of Henry and his wife.

2. Write the wife's **letter** that Henry has treasured for so many years. Be sure to incorporate the details about the letter's content that the story provides.

3. Imagine that Henry's wife actually returns, 19 years after leaving. Write a **comic scene** in which Henry and his wife are reunited but find it difficult to adjust to the changes in each other. Be sure to include the wife's explanation for her absence.

📁 *PORTFOLIO Save your writing. You may want to use it later as a springboard to a piece for your portfolio.*

LITERARY CONCEPTS

Foreshadowing is a writer's use of hints or clues to indicate events that will occur later in a narrative. This technique often creates suspense and prepares the reader for what is to come. In "The Californian's Tale," for example, the crying of Henry's friends upon hearing the wife's letter foreshadows the ending of the story, where we learn that the wife has been long gone. With a partner, find three more examples of foreshadowing in "The Californian's Tale." Which of them—if any—did you recognize as foreshadowing when you first read the story? What effect did they have on you? Share your responses with the rest of the class.

ALTERNATIVE ACTIVITIES

1. Create a **painting** of either the landscape described at the beginning of the story or the interior of Henry's house. Try to capture the mood of either setting.

2. In a small group, act out the story in **pantomime,** using movement and facial expressions to convey the action and emotions of the characters.

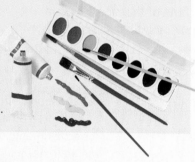

THE WRITER'S STYLE

Mark Twain developed a distinctly American style. He wrote for the ear, capturing the voices of his characters like no other author of his time. In a small group, take turns reading aloud the dialogue from the story. What do you notice about Twain's use of dialogue?

ACROSS THE CURRICULUM

Drama Working in a small group, write a script for a dramatic presentation of "The Californian's Tale." In your stage directions, include information about sets, costumes, and props.

MARK TWAIN

Mark Twain—whose real name was Samuel Clemens—grew up in the Mississippi River port of Hannibal, Missouri. Before becoming a writer, Twain worked first as a printer and then as a steamboat pilot on the Mississippi, but when the river was closed to commercial traffic during the Civil War, he headed west to prospect for gold. He supported himself by writing for local newspapers, adopting his pen name from a riverman's term for water two fathoms deep, or just deep enough for safe navigation.

1835–1910

Although Twain never struck it rich in the western mines, he did successfully mine his western experiences to win fame and fortune as a writer. In 1865, one of his California tall tales, "The Celebrated Jumping Frog of Calaveras County," was published in a New York newspaper. The story became an immediate hit, launching a writing career that earned international acclaim. Twain's two most famous books, *The Adventures of Tom Sawyer* and *The Adventures of Huckleberry Finn,* drew their inspiration from his own wild and spirited boyhood along the Mississippi River. He is also remembered for his satires, his humorous tall tales, his travel sketches, and his public lectures.

OTHER WORKS *Innocents Abroad, A Connecticut Yankee in King Arthur's Court, Mark Twain's Speeches*

LASERLINKS
• *AUTHOR BACKGROUND*

PREVIEWING

Simile
N. Scott Momaday (mä′mə-dā) **United States**

Tonight I Can Write . . . / Puedo Escribir Los Versos . . .
Pablo Neruda (nĕ-rōō′də) **Chile**

PERSONAL CONNECTION

The natural world can sometimes seem to hold up a mirror to your emotions. For example, if you are in a bad mood on a rainy day, you may think that the weather reflects how you feel. In a small group, discuss how elements in nature may seem to reflect various human emotions. Together, brainstorm a list of images from nature that suggest feelings such as sadness, love, or regret. Share your ideas with the rest of the class.

LITERARY CONNECTION

Poets often illuminate human emotions and experiences by drawing comparisons to the natural world. In the first part of this unit, you saw how Shakespeare compared a loved one to a summer's day, while Luis Lloréns Torres described his loved one in terms of a bird. Frequently, poets employ figures of speech, such as similes and metaphors, to make their comparisons. Another common figure of speech is **personification,** which attributes human qualities to an object, animal, or idea. In the following two poems, various figures of speech are used to express the emotions felt by the speakers.

READING CONNECTION

Understanding Comparisons As you read, pay careful attention to descriptions of the natural world and what they suggest about the speaker's emotions and experience. Complete a chart like the one below for each poem. In the first column, list each image from nature that you find. In the second column, describe the human emotions or experiences that are suggested by that image.

Image from nature	Suggested human emotions or experiences

Simile

N. Scott Momaday

What did we say to each other
that now we are as the deer
who walk in single file
with heads high
5 with ears forward
with eyes watchful
with hooves always placed on
    firm ground
in whose limbs there is latent flight

8 **latent** (lāt'nt): present but not active; potential.

FROM PERSONAL RESPONSE TO CRITICAL ANALYSIS

REFLECT **1.** Draw a quick sketch of the first image that came to mind when you finished reading "Simile." Share your drawing with a partner.

RETHINK **2.** Review the chart that you created for the Reading Connection on page 441. In your opinion, what human emotions and experiences are being compared to "the deer who walk in single file"?

Consider
- the relationship between the speaker and the person being addressed
- the physical description of the deer
- what is suggested by the first line of the poem

3. How do you think the speaker feels about the future of the relationship that he is describing? Explain your opinion.

RELATE **4.** Is it possible for two people to remain close without sometimes quarreling? Share your opinions with classmates.

Corn Maiden (1982), David Dawangyumptewa.
Photo Copyright © 1987 by Jerry Jacka.

TONIGHT
I Can Write...

PABLO NERUDA

Tonight I can write the saddest lines.

Write, for example, 'The night is shattered
and the blue stars shiver in the distance.'

The night wind revolves in the sky and sings.

5 Tonight I can write the saddest lines.
I loved her, and sometimes she loved me too.

Through nights like this one I held her in my arms.
I kissed her again and again under the endless sky.

She loved me, sometimes I loved her too.

10 How could one not have loved her great still eyes.

Tonight I can write the saddest lines.
To think that I do not have her. To feel that I have lost her.

To hear the immense night, still more immense without her.
And the verse falls to the soul like dew to the pasture.

15 What does it matter that my love could not keep her.
The night is shattered and she is not with me.

This is all. In the distance someone is singing. In the distance.
My soul is not satisfied that it has lost her.

My sight searches for her as though to go to her.

20 My heart looks for her, and she is not with me.

The same night whitening the same trees.
We, of that time, are no longer the same.

I no longer love her, that's certain, but how I loved her.
My voice tried to find the wind to touch her hearing.

25 Another's. She will be another's. Like my kisses before.
Her voice. Her bright body. Her infinite eyes.

I no longer love her, that's certain, but maybe I love her.
Love is so short, forgetting is so long.

Because through nights like this one I held her in my arms
30 my soul is not satisfied that it has lost her.

Though this be the last pain that she makes me suffer
and these the last verses that I write for her.

Translated by W. S. Merwin

PUEDO
Escribir Los Versos . . .
PABLO NERUDA

Puedo escribir los versos más tristes esta noche.

Escribir, por ejemplo: 'La noche está estrellada,
y tiritan, azules, los astros, a lo lejos.'

El viento de la noche gira en el cielo y canta.

5   Puedo escribir los versos más tristes esta noche.
Yo la quise, y a veces ella también me quiso.

En las noches como ésta la tuve entre mis brazos.
La besé tantas veces bajo el cielo infinito.

Ella me quiso, a veces yo también la quería.

10   Cómo no haber amado sus grandes ojos fijos.

Puedo escribir los versos más tristes esta noche.
Pensar que no la tengo. Sentir que la he perdido.

Oir la noche inmensa, más inmensa sin ella.
Y el verso cae al alma como al pasto el rocío.

15   Qué importa que mi amor no pudiera guardarla.
La noche está estrellada y ella no está conmigo.

Eso es todo. A lo lejos alguien canta. A lo lejos.
Mi alma no se contenta con haberla perdido.

Como para acercarla mi mirada la busca.

20   Mi corazón la busca, y ella no está conmigo.

La misma noche que hace blanquear los mismos arboles.
Nosotros, los de entonces, ya no somos los mismos.

Ya no la quiero, es cierto, pero cuánto la quise.
Mi voz buscaba el viento para tocar su oído.

25   De otro. Será de otro. Como antes de mis besos.
Su voz, su cuerpo claro. Sus ojos infinitos.

Ya no la quiero, es cierto, pero tal vez la quiero.
Es tan corto el amor, y es tan largo el olvido.

Porque en noches como ésta la tuve entre mis brazos,
30   mi alma no se contenta con haberla perdido.

Aunque éste sea el último dolor que ella me causa,
y éstos sean los últimos versos que yo le escribo.

RESPONDING OPTIONS

FROM PERSONAL RESPONSE TO CRITICAL ANALYSIS

REFLECT
1. Which lines of "Tonight I Can Write . . ." are the most memorable for you? Why? Jot down your thoughts in your notebook.

RETHINK
2. Review the chart that you created for the Reading Connection on page 441. What do the images from nature reveal about the speaker's emotions and experience?

   Consider
   - why the speaker says, "The night is shattered / and the blue stars shiver"
   - what you learn about the speaker's relationship with the woman
   - why the night feels "still more immense without her"
   - what this night reminds him of

3. Do you think the speaker still loves the woman? Support your opinion.

4. Reread the last two lines of the poem. What is your opinion of the speaker's conclusion?

RELATE
5. How do you think "Simile" and "Tonight I Can Write" relate to the theme of this part of the unit, "Mysteries of the Heart"? Explain.

ANOTHER PATHWAY

For each poem, draft a paragraph that explains the speaker's situation. Include details or quotations from each poem. Then share your writing with a classmate and discuss your respective explanations.

LITERARY CONCEPTS

Repetition is a literary technique in which sounds, words, phrases, or lines are repeated for emphasis or unity. In "Tonight I Can Write . . . " Neruda repeats the first line three times to emphasize the speaker's sorrow and to help unify the poem. With a partner, make a list of repeated words, phrases, or lines.

Then discuss how each instance of repetition affects your understanding of the speaker's feelings. Why do you think Neruda sometimes repeats part of a line and then adds new information?

CONCEPT REVIEW: Figurative Language Review both poems and identify each metaphor, simile, or personification. Then create one metaphor, one simile, and one personification of your own to compare your feelings to objects in nature.

QUICKWRITES

1. In a **monologue,** give the other side of the story for one of the two poems. In other words, assume the identity of the loved one in the poem and express your feelings and ideas about the relationship described by the speaker.

2. Express your own ideas about love and loss in a **poem.** Try to include images from nature as well as repetition and figurative language to help emphasize and unify your ideas. The images you generated in the Personal Connection on page 441 may help you get started.

📁 *PORTFOLIO Save your writing. You may want to use it later as a springboard to a piece for your portfolio.*

LITERARY LINKS

Which of the two poems do you think has the most in common with Amy Lowell's "Taxi"? Cite details from the two poems to support your evaluation.

ACROSS THE CURRICULUM

Music Find a contemporary song that reveals some of the same emotions conveyed by "Simile" or "Tonight I Can Write . . . ." Share the song with your classmates and discuss how it relates to the poem.

N. SCOTT MOMADAY

1934–

N. Scott Momaday's poetry and prose reflect his deeply felt love for his Kiowa Indian ancestry— its culture, history, and native traditions. His father, a member of the Kiowa tribe, was one of the finest Native American artists of his day; his mother, who was part Cherokee, was a writer and a teacher. When asked about how his heritage has affected his work, Momaday told an interviewer, "When I was growing up on the reservations of the Southwest, I saw people who were deeply involved in their traditional life, in the memories of their blood. They had, as far as I could see, a certain strength and beauty that I find missing in the modern world at large. I like to celebrate that involvement in my writing."

Momaday has received a number of honors and awards for his writing, including the Pulitzer Prize for fiction in 1969 for his novel *House Made of Dawn*. In fact, he was the first Native American to earn that prestigious award. Momaday has since published several books of poetry and fiction, as well as essays and articles on the importance of preserving the environment. Momaday says, "I sometimes think [writing] is a very lonely sort of work. But when you get into it, it can be exhilarating, tremendously fulfilling and stimulating."

OTHER WORKS *The Way to Rainy Mountain, Angle of Geese and Other Poems, The Names: A Memoir*

PABLO NERUDA

1904–1973

Pablo Neruda, the pen name of Ricardo Eliecer Neftalí Reyes y Basoalto, was drawn to poetry at an early age, even though his working-class family scoffed at his literary ambitions. He began publishing poems at the age of 15. When just 20, he won celebrity throughout his native Chile with *Twenty Love Poems and a Song of Despair* in which "Tonight I Can Write . . ." first appeared.

After he served in his nation's diplomatic corps—an honor then commonly granted to talented Latin American writers—he shifted the focus of his poetry to political and social criticism. In the early 1970s, Neruda supported Chile's socialist leader Salvador Allende and served as his nation's ambassador to France. When the poet received the 1971 Nobel Prize for Literature, the event was celebrated as a national holiday in his homeland. Neruda produced more than 40 volumes of poetry, translations, and verse drama during his literary career.

OTHER WORKS *Residence on Earth, Elemental Odes, The Heights of Macchu Picchu, Pablo Neruda: Selected Poems, Extravagaria*

PREVIEWING

To . . .

Aleksandr Pushkin (pŏŏsh′kĭn) **Russia**

PERSONAL CONNECTION

Recall a time when you met a person who made a very positive first impression. What was it about the person that you found remarkable? What feelings did he or she inspire? In your notebook, explore your experience in a tree diagram like the one on the right. Note which details about the person most impressed you, as well as your thoughts and feelings after your first meeting.

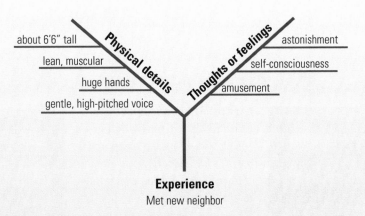

Physical details
- about 6′6″ tall
- lean, muscular
- huge hands
- gentle, high-pitched voice

Thoughts or feelings
- astonishment
- self-consciousness
- amusement

Experience
Met new neighbor

BIOGRAPHICAL CONNECTION

In 1819, the 20-year-old Russian poet Aleksandr Pushkin met an attractive young woman named Anna Kern, the niece of a friend. Anna made a very strong first impression on Pushkin, who frequently fell in love with beautiful women. Unfortunately, the poet was exiled shortly thereafter to a remote part of southern Russia by a government that did not care for some of his political poems, and he was not to see Anna Kern for six years. It seems that Anna's first impression had become a lasting one, however, because soon after meeting her again in June 1825, Pushkin was inspired to write the following poem to her. Though his romantic interest faded as he got to know her better, the two remained friends.

READING CONNECTION

Understanding Chronological Order
As you read the poem, pay attention to the order of the events and the feelings associated with them. Which details refer to the speaker's first meeting with the woman addressed? Which refer to a second meeting? Which refer to the period in between? Look for words and phrases that indicate time sequence, and think about how the speaker communicates that his first impressions have become lasting ones.

Portrait of the Princess Saltikova, 1802–1863 (1837), Karl Pavlovitch Briullov. Oil on canvas, 200 cm × 142 cm, Russian State Museum, St. Petersburg, Russia, Giraudon/Art Resource, New York.

To...

Aleksandr Pushkin

Couple Above St. Paul (1970–1971), Marc Chagall. Collection Chagall, St. Paul de Vence, France, Scala/Art Resource, New York. Copyright © 1996 Artists Rights Society (ARS), New York/ADAGP, Paris.

I recollect that wondrous meeting,
That instant I encountered you,
When like an apparition fleeting,
Like beauty's spirit, past you flew.

5 Long since, when hopeless grief distressed me,
When noise and turmoil vexed, it seemed
Your voice still tenderly caressed me,
Your dear face sought me as I dreamed.

Years passed; their stormy gusts confounded
10 And swept away old dreams apace.
I had forgotten how you sounded,
Forgot the heaven of your face.

In exiled gloom and isolation
My quiet days meandered on,
15 The thrill of awe and inspiration,
And life, and tears, and love, were gone.

My soul awoke from inanition,
And I encountered you anew,
And like a fleeting apparition,
20 Like beauty's spirit, past you flew.

My pulses bound in exultation,
And in my heart once more unfold
The sense of awe and inspiration,
The life, the tears, the love of old.

Translated by Walter Arndt

3 apparition (ăp'ə-rĭsh'ən): a ghost or ghostly figure; a sudden or unusual sight.

6 vexed (vĕkst): annoyed; bothered.

9 confounded (kən-foun'dĭd): confused; mixed up; made hard to distinguish.

10 apace (ə-pās'): at a rapid pace; swiftly.

14 meandered (mē-ăn'dərd): followed a winding course; moved aimlessly and idly, without a fixed direction or purpose.

17 inanition (ĭn'ə-nĭsh'ən): exhaustion caused by lack of nourishment or vitality; emptiness.

RESPONDING
OPTIONS

FROM PERSONAL RESPONSE TO CRITICAL ANALYSIS

REFLECT

1. What impression do you have of the speaker and his experience? Describe your response in your notebook.

RETHINK

2. Why do you think the woman made such a lasting impression on the speaker?
Consider
- what he remembers about their first encounter
- how he has been affected by his memories of her
- the way he describes his life during their years apart

3. In your judgment, what does the poem reveal about the personality and values of the speaker? Cite details from the poem to support your opinion.

4. Compare your own views about romantic love with the speaker's. How much do you have in common?

RELATE

5. Do you believe that too much attention is paid to romantic love in our culture today? Why or why not?

ANOTHER PATHWAY
Cooperative Learning

In a small group, create visual representations of the speaker's various emotional states. For example, you might create three different images to convey his feelings about first meeting the woman, their separation, and their second meeting. Use words or phrases from the poem to accompany each image.

LITERARY CONCEPTS

Rhyme is the occurrence of a similar or identical sound at the ends of words, as in *tether* and *together*. Rhyme that occurs at the ends of lines of poetry is called **end rhyme.** End rhymes that are not exact but approximate are called **off rhymes,** for example *other* and *bother*. A **rhyme scheme** is the pattern of end rhyme in a poem. With a partner, review the explanation of how to determine rhyme scheme on page 376; then identify the poem's rhyme scheme, noting where off rhyme is used. Share your findings with the class.

CONCEPT REVIEW: Rhythm and Meter Review the explanation of rhythm and meter on page 379. Then copy one of the poem's stanzas and mark it for stressed and unstressed syllables. In a small group, check each other's work and decide what kind of metrical pattern is represented.

QUICKWRITES

1. Write a **song lyric** that describes the relationship between the speaker and the woman to whom the poem is addressed. In your lyric, describe their first meeting and the different stages of their relationship.

2. Write an extended **definition** of love that conveys what love means to the speaker. Before writing, check the definitions of love in two or three dictionaries.

3. Write a **poem** about the encounter that you described in the Personal Connection on page 448.

PORTFOLIO Save your writing. You may want to use it later as a springboard to a piece for your portfolio.

ALTERNATIVE ACTIVITIES

1. With a partner, create an **exhibition** of 19th-century paintings that feature women who might have appealed to Pushkin. To do this, bring in reproductions of paintings from art books or printouts from on-line computer-based encyclopedias. For each painting, provide a caption from Pushkin's poem.

2. Choreograph a **dance** based on "To . . . ." Through movement, try to capture the mood of the poem, as well as the speaker's changing emotions from the beginning to the end. Then perform your dance for your classmates.

ART CONNECTION

Why do you think the painting on page 449, *Couple Above St. Paul,* was chosen to accompany Pushkin's poem?

Detail of *Couple Above St. Paul* (1970–1971), Marc Chagall. Collection Chagal, St. Paul de Vence, France, Scala/Art Resource, New York. Copyright © 1996 Artists Rights Society (ARS), New York/ADAGP, Paris.

ACROSS THE CURRICULUM

World Languages With a partner, find one or more additional translations of this poem, which is often called "To Anna Kern." Then compare and contrast the translations. What do the differences suggest about the process of translation?

ALEKSANDR PUSHKIN

1799–1837

Aleksandr Pushkin is widely regarded as the father of modern Russian literature. He began writing at a time when Russia's upper class regarded their own language as an "uncultured" tongue and preferred to speak and write in French. Pushkin went on to prove the versatility and beauty of the Russian language in his many poems and prose writings. Though he was descended from the upper class, he took pride in his maternal great grandfather, Ibrahim Hannibal, an Ethiopian who had been brought to Russia as a slave and who rose to comrade-in-arms of the Russian czar Peter the Great (1672–1725). Perhaps because of his ancestry, Pushkin was sympathetic to the plight of Russia's peasants. His sympathies, expressed in several early political poems, made him hugely popular with the Russian people but also led to his exile to southern Russia in 1820. While he was not imprisoned, he was forced to live far from the cultural centers of St. Petersburg and Moscow. Nonetheless, he was immensely productive during this period, writing or beginning some of his greatest works, including his verse novel *Eugene Onegin* and his historic drama *Boris Godunov.*

After Nicholas I became Russia's czar, he allowed Pushkin to return to Moscow in the fall of 1826, in part so that his ministers could keep an eye on the poet. A few years later, Pushkin married one of the many beautiful women with whom he had fallen in love over the years, but the marriage brought him little happiness. After discovering that she was carrying on a flirtation with another man, Pushkin fought a duel to defend her honor. Although he had survived duels in the past, this time he was not so lucky. Two days after fighting, Pushkin died of his wounds.

OTHER WORKS "Mozart and Salieri," *The Captain's Daughter, The Bronze Horseman: Selected Poems of Aleksandr Pushkin*

PREVIEWING

FICTION

Metonymy, or The Husband's Revenge
Rachel de Queiroz (rä-chĕl′ dĕ kĕ-ē-rôs′) **Brazil**

PERSONAL CONNECTION

Get together with another student and role-play a situation in which one of you has wronged the other. If you wish, you may base your role playing on one of the situations on the right. Afterward, discuss the reactions expressed. Were feelings conveyed in an open manner, or did feelings remain hidden? Did revenge enter into the scene? Compare your reactions to those of other pairs of students.

being deceived in love

having a friend break a promise

having something stolen

being cheated

LITERARY CONNECTION

Rachel de Queiroz, a prominent Brazilian writer, is considered a master of the *crônica* (krô′nĕ-kä), a form of short fiction that combines elements of the essay and the short story. This form, which has become especially popular in Brazil, is characterized by a simple and direct style and an interest in contemporary issues and events. "Metonymy," which was published in a collection of her *crônicas,* is representative of the form. It has an informal, conversational tone, which makes it seem as if the narrator is carrying on a conversation with an interested listener. The narrator begins by discussing a figure of speech and from there launches into a compelling tale that explores the ways in which people react when they feel they have been wronged.

WRITING CONNECTION

In your notebook, describe a time when you felt that someone had wronged you. What caused the incident and how did you respond to it? How do you feel now about your response? As you read, compare your own response to wrongdoing to that of the husband in the story.

I was wronged when . . .

Cause:

My response:

Now I feel:

METONYMY,
or The Husband's Revenge

Rachel de Queiroz

Metonymy. I learned the word in 1930 and shall never forget it. I had just published my first novel. A literary critic had scolded me because my hero went out into the night "chest unclosed."

"What deplorable nonsense!" wrote this eminently sensible gentleman. "Why does she not say what she means? Obviously, it was his shirt that was unclosed, not his chest."

I accepted his rebuke with humility, indeed with shame. But my illustrious Latin professor, Dr. Matos Peixoto,[1] came to my rescue. He said that what I had written was perfectly correct; that I had used a respectable figure of speech known as metonymy; and that this figure consisted in the use of one word for another word associated with it—for example, a word representing a cause instead of the effect, or representing the container when the content is intended. The classic instance, he told me, is "the sparkling cup"; in reality, not the cup but the wine in it is sparkling.

The professor and I wrote a letter, which was published in the newspaper where the review had appeared. It put my unjust critic in his place. I hope he learned a lesson. I know I did. Ever since, I have been using metonymy—my only bond with classical rhetoric.

Moreover, I have devoted some thought to it, and I have concluded that metonymy may be more than a figure of speech. There is, I believe, such a thing as practical or applied metonymy. Let me give a crude example, drawn from my own experience. A certain lady of my acquaintance suddenly moved out of the boardinghouse where she had been living for years and became a mortal enemy of the woman who owned it.

---

1. **Matos Peixoto** (mä′tŏŏs pĕ-ē-hô′tô).

WORDS TO KNOW
deplorable (dĭ-plôr′ə-bəl) *adj.* worthy of strong criticism or disapproval; terrible
eminently (ĕm′ə-nənt-lē) *adv.* highly; notably
rebuke (rĭ-byōōk′) *n.* sharp criticism

I asked her why. We both knew that the woman was a kindly soul; she had given my friend injections when she needed them, had often loaned her a hot-water bag, and had always waited on her when she had her little heart attacks. My friend replied:

"It's the telephone in the hall. I hate her for it. Half the time when I answered it, the call was a hoax or joke of some sort."

"But the owner of the boardinghouse didn't perpetrate these hoaxes. She wasn't responsible for them."

"No. But whose telephone was it?"

I know another case of applied metonymy, a more disastrous one for it involved a crime. It happened in a city of the interior,[2] which I shall not name for fear that someone may recognize the parties and revive the scandal. I shall narrate the crime but conceal the criminal.

Well, in this city of the interior there lived a man. He was not old but he was spent, which is worse than being old. In his youth he had suffered from beriberi.[3] His legs were weak, his chest was tired and asthmatic, his skin was yellowish, and his eyes were rheumy.[4] He was, however, a man of property: he owned the house in which he lived and the one next to it, in which he had set up a grocery store. Therefore, although so unattractive personally, he was able to find himself a wife. In all justice to him, he did not tempt fate by marrying a beauty. Instead, he married a poor, emaciated girl, who worked in a men's clothing factory. By her face one would have thought she had consumption.[5] So our friend felt safe. He did not foresee the effects of good nutrition and a healthful life on a woman's appearance. The girl no longer spent eight hours

a day at a sewing table. She was the mistress of her house. She ate well: fresh meat, cucumber salad, pork fat with beans and manioc mush,[6] all kinds of sweets, and oranges, which her husband bought by the gross for his customers. The effects were like magic. Her body filled out, especially in the best places. She even seemed to grow taller. And her face—what a change! I may have forgot to mention that her features, in themselves, were good to begin with. Moreover, money enabled her to embellish her natural advantages with art: she began to wear makeup, to wave her hair, and to dress well.

Lovely, attractive, she now found her sickly, prematurely old husband a burden and a bore. Each evening, as soon as the store was closed, he dined, mostly on milk (he could not stomach meat), took his newspaper, and rested on his chaise longue[7] until time to go to bed. He did not care for the movies or for soccer or for radio. He did not even show much interest in love. Just a sort of tepid, tasteless cohabitation.

And then Fate intervened: it produced a sergeant.

Granted, it was unjust for a young wife, after being reconditioned at her husband's expense, to employ her charms to the prejudice of the aforesaid husband. Unjust; but, then, this world

2. **city of the interior:** an inland Brazilian city, as opposed to one of Brazil's more populous coastal cities.

3. **beriberi** (bĕr´ē-bĕr´ē): a disease caused by a deficiency of thiamine in the diet.

4. **rheumy** (rōōm´ē): filmy with a watery or thin mucous discharge.

5. **consumption** (kən-sŭmp´shən): tuberculosis, a lung disease that causes weight loss and chest pain.

6. **manioc mush:** mashed cassava, a tropical plant with starchy, edible roots.

7. **chaise longue** (shāz-lông´): a reclining chair with a seat long enough to support a person's outstretched legs.

Le coeur [The heart] (1947), Henri Matisse. Plate 7 from *Jazz*, published by Tériade. The Metropolitan Museum of Art, New York, gift of Lila Acheson Wallace, 1983 (1983.1009). Copyright © 1985 The Metropolitan Museum of Art, all rights reserved.

thrives on injustice, doesn't it? The sergeant—I shall not say whether he was in the Army, the Air Force, the Marines, or the Fusileers, for I still mean to conceal the identities of the parties—the sergeant was muscular, young, ingratiating, with a manly, commanding voice and a healthy spring in his walk. He looked gloriously martial in his high-buttoned uniform.

One day, when the lady was in charge of the counter (while her husband lunched), the sergeant came in. Exactly what happened and what did not happen, is hard to say. It seems that the sergeant asked for a pack of cigarettes. Then he wanted a little vermouth.[8] Finally, he asked permission to listen to the sports broadcast on the radio next to the counter. Maybe it was just an excuse to remain there awhile. In any case, the girl said it would be all right. It is hard to refuse a favor to a sergeant, especially a sergeant like this one. It appears that the sergeant asked nothing more that day. At most, he and the girl exchanged expressive glances and a few agreeable words, murmured so softly that the customers, always alert for something to gossip about, could not hear them.

Three times more the husband lunched while his wife chatted with the sergeant in the store. The flirtation progressed. Then the husband fell ill with a grippe,[9] and the two others went far beyond flirtation. How and when they met, no one was able to discover. The important thing is that they were lovers and that they loved with a

---

8. **vermouth** (vər-mo͞oth′): a type of wine.
9. **grippe** (grĭp): the flu.

Courtesy of the National Postal Museum, Smithsonian Institution, Washington, D.C.

found a postcard and a book, both with a man's name in the same handwriting. He found the insignia of the sergeant's regiment and concluded that the object of his wife's murmurs, sighs, and silences was not only a man but a soldier. Finally he made the supreme discovery: that they had indeed betrayed him. For he discovered the love letters, bearing airmail stamps, a distant postmark, and the sergeant's name. They left no reasonable doubt.

For five months the poor fellow twisted the poisoned dagger of jealousy in his thin, sickly chest. Like a boy who discovers a bird's nest and, hiding nearby, watches the eggs increasing in number every day, so the husband, using a duplicate key to the wood chest where his wife put her valuables, watched the increase in the number of letters concealed there. He had given her the chest during their honeymoon, saying, "Keep your secrets here." And the ungrateful girl had obeyed him.

Every day at the fateful hour of lunch, she replaced her husband at the counter. But he was not interested in eating. He ran to her room, pulled out a drawer of her bureau, removed the chest from under a lot of panties, slips, and such, took the little key out of his pocket, opened the chest, and anxiously read the new letter. If there was no new letter, he reread the one dated August 21st; it was so full of realism that it sounded like dialogue from a French movie. Then he put everything away and hurried to the kitchen, when he swallowed a few spoonfuls of broth and gnawed at a piece of bread. It was almost impossible to swallow with the passion of those two thieves sticking in his throat.

When the poor man's heart had become utterly saturated with jealousy and hatred, he

forbidden love, like Tristan and Isolde or Paolo and Francesca.[10]

Then Fate, which does not like illicit love and generally punishes those who engage in it, transferred the sergeant to another part of the country.

It is said that only those who love can really know the pain of separation. The girl cried so much that her eyes grew red and swollen. She lost her appetite. Beneath her rouge could be seen the consumptive complexion of earlier times. And these symptoms aroused her husband's suspicion, although, curiously, he had never suspected anything when the love affair was flourishing and everything was wine and roses.

He began to observe her carefully. He scrutinized her in her periods of silence. He listened to her sighs and to the things she murmured in her sleep. He snooped around and

10. **Tristan and Isolde or Paolo and Francesca:** two legendary pairs of lovers.

WORDS TO KNOW
illicit (ĭ-lĭs′ĭt) *adj.* unlawful; not allowed by custom or law
scrutinize (skrōōt′n-īz′) *v.* to examine or observe with great care

took a revolver and a box of bullets from the counter drawer; they had been left, years before, by a customer as security for a debt, which had never been paid. He loaded the revolver.

One bright morning at exactly ten o'clock, when the store was full of customers, he excused himself and went through the doorway that connected the store with his home. In a few seconds the customers heard the noise of a row,[11] a woman's scream, and three shots. On the sidewalk in front of the shopkeeper's house they saw his wife on her knees, still screaming, and him, with the revolver in his trembling hand, trying to raise her. The front door of the house was open. Through it, they saw a man's legs, wearing khaki trousers and boots. He was lying face down, with his head and torso in the parlor, not visible from the street.

The husband was the first to speak. Raising his eyes from his wife, he looked at the terror-stricken people and spotted among them his favorite customer. He took a few steps, stood in the doorway, and said:

"You may call the police."

t the police station he explained that he was a deceived husband. The police chief remarked:

"Isn't this a little unusual? Ordinarily you kill your wives. They're weaker than their lovers."

The man was deeply offended.

"No," he protested, "I would be utterly incapable of killing my wife. She is all that I have in the world. She is refined, pretty, and hard-working. She helps me in the store, she understands bookkeeping, she writes the letters to the wholesalers. She is the only person who knows how to prepare my food; I have a special diet. Why should I want to kill my wife?"

"I see," said the chief of police. "So you killed her lover."

The man shook his head.

"Wrong again. The sergeant—her lover—was transferred to a place far away from here. I discovered the affair only after he had gone. By reading his letters. They tell the whole story. I know one of them by heart, the worst of them. . . ."

The police chief did not understand. He said nothing and waited for the husband to continue, which he presently did:

"Those letters! If they were alive, I would kill them, one by one. They were shameful to read—almost like a book. I thought of taking an airplane trip. I thought of killing some other sergeant here so that they would all learn a lesson not to fool around with another man's wife. But I was afraid of the rest of the regiment; you know how these military men stick together. Still, I had to do something. Otherwise I would have gone crazy. I couldn't get those letters out of my head. Even on days when none arrived I felt terrible, worse than my wife. I had to put an end to it, didn't I? So today, at last, I did it. I waited till the regular time and, when I saw the wretch appear on the other side of the street, I went into the house, hid behind a door, and lay there for him."

"The lover?" asked the police chief stupidly.

"No, of course not. I told you I didn't kill her lover. It was those letters. The sergeant sent them—but he delivered them. Almost every day, there he was at the door, smiling, with the vile envelope in his hand. I pointed the revolver and fired three times. He didn't say a word; he just fell. No, Chief, it wasn't her lover. It was the mailman." ❖

Translated by William L. Grossman

---

11. **row:** a noisy quarrel; a brawl.

WORDS TO KNOW **refined** (rĭ-fīnd') *adj.* free from coarseness or vulgarity; polite
vile (vīl) *adj.* disgusting; objectionable; wicked

457

RESPONDING OPTIONS

FROM PERSONAL RESPONSE TO CRITICAL ANALYSIS

REFLECT
1. How do you feel about the husband's action at the end of the story? Briefly express your feelings in your notebook.

RETHINK
2. Which character do you sympathize with most, and why?

3. What do you think would have happened if the sergeant had not been transferred?

4. How would you describe the story's tone, which conveys the attitude a writer takes toward a subject?

Consider
- the narrator's introductory anecdote about the word *metonymy*
- the narrator's commentary interspersed throughout the story
- the outcome of the story

5. Do you think the story has a message, or theme? Explain your view.

RELATE
6. The idea of "killing the messenger" goes back to ancient times, when people sometimes killed a messenger because they disliked the message or its sender. Can you think of instances in real life in which a "messenger" is blamed for the "message"? Share your ideas with classmates.

ANOTHER PATHWAY

Cooperative Learning

What would happen if the characters in "Metonymy, or The Husband's Revenge" were invited to appear on a television talk show to share their scandalous story with a public audience? With a group of classmates, sketch out a plan for the show. Then stage it for the rest of the class.

QUICKWRITES

1. Write the **investigative notes** that a police officer might take at the crime scene. Include what he might learn from observation and interviews.

2. Write a **letter** from the wife to the sergeant, telling him what has happened and what she has decided to do next.

3. Imagine that the husband decides to defend himself at his trial. Write his **opening statement** before the jury.

PORTFOLIO Save your writing. You may want to use it later as a springboard to a piece for your portfolio.

LITERARY CONCEPTS

"Metonymy, or The Husband's Revenge" is an example of a **frame story,** a story within a narrative setting—or frame. The first four paragraphs describing the narrator's use of metonymy in her writing provide the frame for the two stories-within-a-story: the tale about the woman in the boardinghouse and the tale of the husband's revenge. Why do you think the author included the frame instead of just telling about the husband's revenge?

ALTERNATIVE ACTIVITIES

1. Draw a **cartoon** to illustrate a scene from the story. Use a quotation from the story to serve as a caption. Then display your artwork on a classroom or school bulletin board.

2. Imagine that you are a radio or television journalist and prepare and deliver a **newscast** about the mailman's murder. If your report is for television, you may want to draw pictures of key scenes and present visuals as part of your story.

CRITIC'S CORNER

Fred P. Ellison, one of Queiroz's translators, has praised her work for its "acute perception of human motives." How well do you think his observation applies to "Metonymy, or The Husband's Revenge"? Explain your view.

LITERARY LINKS

Compare and contrast the husband in this story to Henry in "The Californian's Tale" by Mark Twain.

WORDS TO KNOW

EXERCISE A Identify the word that is closest in meaning to the word in bold print.

1. **refined:** (a) scarce, (b) polished, (c) expensive
2. **embellish:** (a) adorn, (b) create, (c) ring
3. **scrutinize:** (a) struggle, (b) twist, (c) inspect
4. **tepid:** (a) enthusiastic, (b) hot, (c) indifferent
5. **deplorable:** (a) bad, (b) favorable, (c) capable
6. **eminently:** (a) prominently, (b) quickly, (c) weakly
7. **rebuke:** (a) response, (b) praise, (c) scolding
8. **vile:** (a) hidden, (b) wretched, (c) pleasant
9. **ingratiating:** (a) charming, (b) harsh, (c) unappreciative
10. **illicit:** (a) sick, (b) incapable, (c) illegal

EXERCISE B Play a game of charades with the Words to Know, pantomiming their meanings for classmates. Try to present each word in its entirety instead of syllable-by-syllable.

RACHEL DE QUEIROZ

1910–

Rachel de Queiroz once wrote, "The . . . merit I may possess is in my free and easy countrywoman's way of saying things, of telling stories about what I know and what I like." For more than 60 years, Queiroz has done just that, writing novels, plays, stories, and essays on political and social issues that deeply interest her. The status and role of women in Brazilian society have always been among Queiroz's primary concerns, and much of her writing features strong female protagonists.

As a child, Queiroz lived on her family's ranch in northeastern Brazil. Her first novel, *The Year '15*, was inspired by family stories of the great drought that hit northeastern Brazil in 1915. Hailed as part of a new wave of Brazilian writers who focused on real-life social and economic problems, Queiroz wrote three more realistic novels.

Queiroz devoted herself to journalism in the early 1940s, writing political articles and *crônicas*, which gained her a wide following in Brazil. In recognition of her life's work, she was elected to the Brazilian Academy of Letters, the first woman to receive that honor.

OTHER WORKS *The Three Marias; Dôra, Doralina*

PREVIEWING

FICTION

The First Seven Years
Bernard Malamud (măl'ə-məd) United States

PERSONAL CONNECTION

Think about the qualities or characteristics that you would consider especially important in a husband or wife. Would a sense of humor be important, or physical appearance, or shared interests and goals? Would your parents or guardians find the same qualities important in the spouse of your choice? In your notebook, make a Venn diagram like the one shown.

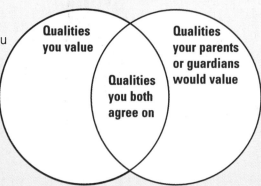

Qualities you value

Qualities your parents or guardians would value

Qualities you both agree on

HISTORICAL/CULTURAL CONNECTION

In "The First Seven Years," Feld the shoemaker expresses his ideas about the qualities that his daughter Miriam should seek in a husband. Feld is one of the millions of eastern European Jews who immigrated to America from 1880 to 1930 to escape religious persecution and seek economic opportunity. Though often not educated themselves, these Jewish immigrants placed great value on education and saw it as the means by which their children would achieve the American dream. Many of them settled in New York City, where "The First Seven Years" is set. This story takes place in the years just after World War II, when a new and far smaller group of European Jews arrived in America. These refugees—including Sobel in the story—were survivors of the Holocaust.

Ship bringing immigrants to the United States. Photo courtesy of Brown Brothers.

READING CONNECTION

Interpreting Motivation As you read this story, pay attention to the hopes and dreams that Feld the shoemaker has for his daughter. What type of man does he want his daughter to marry? What qualities does he believe her husband should possess? What motivates him to have such qualities in mind?

Using Your Reading Log Use your reading log to record your responses to the questions inserted throughout the selection. Also jot down other thoughts and feelings as you read.

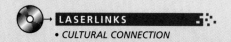

LASERLINKS
• CULTURAL CONNECTION

Les souliers [A pair of boots] (1887), Vincent van Gogh. Oil on canvas, 13″ × 16⅛″, The Baltimore Museum of Art, The Cone Collection, formed by Dr. Claribel Cone and Miss Etta Cone of Baltimore, Maryland (BMA 1950.302).

THE FIRST SEVEN YEARS

BERNARD MALAMUD

Feld, the shoemaker, was annoyed that his helper, Sobel, was so insensitive to his reverie that he wouldn't for a minute cease his fanatic pounding at the other bench.

He gave him a look, but Sobel's bald head was bent over the last[1] as he worked, and he didn't notice. The shoemaker shrugged and continued to peer through the partly frosted window at the near-sighted haze of falling February snow. Neither the shifting white blur outside, nor the sudden deep remembrance of the snowy Polish village where he had wasted his youth could turn his thoughts from Max the college boy, (a constant visitor in the mind since early that morning when Feld saw him trudging through the snowdrifts on his way to school) whom he so much respected because of the sacrifices he had made throughout the years—in winter or direst heat—to further his education. An old wish returned to haunt the shoemaker: that he had had a son instead of a daughter, but this blew away in the snow for Feld, if anything, was a practical man. Yet he could not help but contrast the diligence of the boy, who was a peddler's son, with Miriam's unconcern for an education. True, she was always with a book in her hand, yet when the opportunity arose for a college education, she had said no she would rather find a job. He had begged her to go, pointing out how many fathers could not afford to send their children to college, but she said she wanted to be independent. As for education, what was it, she asked, but books, which Sobel, who diligently read the classics, would as usual advise her on. Her answer greatly grieved her father.

A figure emerged from the snow, and the door opened. At the counter the man withdrew from a wet paper bag a pair of battered shoes for repair. Who he was the shoemaker for a moment had no idea, then his heart trembled as he realized, before he had thoroughly discerned the face, that Max himself was standing there, embarrassedly explaining what he wanted done to his old shoes. Though Feld listened eagerly, he couldn't hear a word, for the opportunity that had burst upon him was deafening.

He couldn't exactly recall when the thought had occurred to him, because it was clear he had more than once considered suggesting to the boy that he go out with Miriam. But he had not dared speak, for if Max said no, how would he face him again? Or suppose Miriam, who harped so often on independence, blew up in anger and shouted at him for his meddling? Still, the chance was too good to let by: all it meant was an introduction. They might long ago have become friends had they happened to meet somewhere, therefore was it not his duty—an obligation—to bring them together, nothing more, a harmless connivance[2] to replace an accidental encounter in the subway, let's say, or a mutual friend's introduction in the street? Just let him once see and talk to her, and he would for sure be interested. As for Miriam, what possible harm for a working girl in an office, who met only loud-mouthed salesmen and illiterate shipping clerks, to make the acquaintance of a fine scholarly boy? Maybe he would awaken in her a desire to go to college; if not—the shoemaker's mind at last came to grips with the truth—let her marry an educated man and live a better life.

When Max finished describing what he wanted done to his shoes, Feld marked them, both with enormous holes in the soles which he pretended not to notice, with large white-chalk x's, and the rubber heels, thinned to the nails, he marked with o's, though it troubled him he might have mixed up the letters. Max inquired the price, and the shoemaker cleared his throat and asked the boy, above Sobel's insistent hammering, would he please step through the side door there into the hall. Though surprised, Max did

---

1. **last:** a block or form shaped like a human foot and used in making or repairing shoes.
2. **connivance** (kə-nī′vəns): a scheme; a plot.

WORDS TO KNOW

direst (dīr′ĕst) *adj.* most terrible; worst
discern (dĭ-sûrn′) *v.* to perceive with the eyes or intellect; to recognize

as the shoemaker requested, and Feld went in after him. For a minute they were both silent, because Sobel had stopped banging, and it seemed they understood neither was to say anything until the noise began again. When it did, loudly, the shoemaker quickly told Max why he had asked to talk to him.

"Ever since you went to high school," he said, in the dimly-lit hallway, "I watched you in the morning go to the subway to school, and I said always to myself, this is a fine boy that he wants so much an education."

"Thanks," Max said, nervously alert. He was tall and grotesquely thin, with sharply cut features, particularly a beak-like nose. He was wearing a loose, long slushy overcoat that hung down to his ankles, looking like a rug draped over his bony shoulders, and a soggy, old brown hat, as battered as the shoes he had brought in.

"I am a business man," the shoemaker abruptly said to conceal his embarrassment, "so I will explain you right away why I talk to you. I have a girl, my daughter Miriam—she is nineteen—a very nice girl and also so pretty that everybody looks on her when she passes by in the street. She is smart, always with a book, and I thought to myself that a boy like you, an educated boy—I thought maybe you will be interested sometime to meet a girl like this." He laughed a bit when he had finished and was tempted to say more but had the good sense not to.

Max stared down like a hawk. For an uncomfortable second he was silent, then he asked, "Did you say nineteen?"

"Yes."

"Would it be all right to inquire if you have a picture of her?"

"Just a minute." The shoemaker went into the store and hastily returned with a snapshot that Max held up to the light.

"She's all right," he said.

Feld waited.

"And is she sensible—not the flighty kind?"

"She is very sensible."

After another short pause, Max said it was okay with him if he met her.

"Here is my telephone," said the shoemaker,

> "She is smart, always with a book, and I thought to myself that a boy like you, an educated boy—I thought maybe you will be interested sometime to meet a girl like this."

hurriedly handing him a slip of paper. "Call her up. She comes home from work six o'clock."

Max folded the paper and tucked it away into his worn leather wallet.

"About the shoes," he said. "How much did you say they will cost me?"

"Don't worry about the price."

"I just like to have an idea."

"A dollar—dollar fifty. A dollar fifty," the shoemaker said.

At once he felt bad, for he usually charged two twenty-five for this kind of job. Either he should have asked the regular price or done the work for nothing.

Later, as he entered the store, he was startled by a violent clanging and looked up to see Sobel pounding with all his might upon the naked last. It broke, the iron striking the floor

Girl with a Book (1927), Matej Sternen. National Gallery, Ljubljana, Slovenia.

and jumping with a thump against the wall, but before the enraged shoemaker could cry out,

QUESTION

What do you think has made Sobel so angry?

the assistant had torn his hat and coat from the hook and rushed out into the snow.

So Feld, who had looked forward to anticipating how it would go with his daughter and Max, instead had a great worry on his mind. Without his temperamental helper he was a lost man, especially since it was years now that he had carried the store alone. The shoemaker had for an age suffered from a heart condition that threatened collapse if he dared exert himself. Five years ago, after an attack, it had appeared as though he would have either to sacrifice his business upon the auction block and live on a pittance thereafter, or put himself at the mercy of some unscrupulous employee who would in the end probably ruin him. But just at the moment of his darkest despair, this Polish refugee, Sobel, appeared one night from the street and begged for work. He was a stocky man, poorly dressed, with a bald head that had once been blond, a severely plain face and soft blue eyes prone to tears over the sad books he read, a young man but old—no one would have guessed thirty. Though he confessed he knew nothing of shoemaking, he said he was apt and would work for a very little if Feld taught him the trade. Thinking that with, after all, a landsman,[3] he would have less to fear than from a complete stranger, Feld took him on and within six weeks the refugee rebuilt as good a shoe as he, and not long thereafter expertly ran the business for the thoroughly relieved shoemaker.

Feld could trust him with anything and did, frequently going home after an hour or two at the store, leaving all the money in the till,[4]

knowing Sobel would guard every cent of it. The amazing thing was that he demanded so little. His wants were few; in money he wasn't interested—in nothing but books, it seemed—which he one by one lent to Miriam, together with his profuse, queer written comments, manufactured during his lonely rooming house evenings, thick pads of commentary which the shoemaker peered at and twitched his shoulders over as his daughter, from her fourteenth year, read page by sanctified page, as if the word of God were inscribed on them. To protect Sobel, Feld himself had to see that he received more than he asked for. Yet his conscience bothered him for not insisting that the assistant accept a better wage than he was getting, though Feld had honestly told him he could earn a handsome salary if he worked elsewhere, or maybe opened a place of his own. But the assistant answered, somewhat ungraciously, that he was not interested in going elsewhere, and though Feld frequently asked himself what keeps him here? why does he stay? he finally answered it that the man, no doubt because of his terrible experiences as a refugee, was afraid of the world.

After the incident with the broken last, angered by Sobel's behavior, the shoemaker decided to let him stew for a week in the rooming house, although his own strength was taxed dangerously and the business suffered. However, after several sharp nagging warnings from both his wife and daughter, he went finally in search of Sobel, as he had once before, quite recently, when over some fancied slight—Feld had merely asked him not to give Miriam so many books to read because her eyes were strained and red—the assistant had left the

---

3. **landsman:** a fellow Jew who comes from the same district or town, especially in eastern Europe.
4. **till:** a drawer or compartment for holding money.

WORDS TO KNOW
pittance (pĭt′ns) *n.* a small amount of money
apt (ăpt) *adj.* quick to learn or understand
profuse (prə-fyoos′) *adj.* plentiful; given freely and abundantly

place in a huff, an incident which, as usual, came to nothing, for he had returned after the shoemaker had talked to him, and taken his seat at the bench. But this time, after Feld had plodded through the snow to Sobel's house—he had thought of sending Miriam but the idea became <u>repugnant</u> to him—the burly landlady at the door informed him in a nasal voice that Sobel was not at home, and though Feld knew this was a nasty lie, for where had the refugee to go? still for some reason he was not completely sure of—it may have been the cold and his fatigue—he decided not to insist on seeing him. Instead he went home and hired a new helper.

Having settled the matter, though not entirely to his satisfaction, for he had much more to do than before, and so, for example, could no longer lie late in bed mornings because he had to get up to open the store for the new assistant, a speechless, dark man with an irritating rasp[5] as he worked, whom he would not trust with the key as he had Sobel. Furthermore, this one, though able to do a fair repair job, knew nothing of grades of leather or prices, so Feld had to make his own purchases; and every night at closing time it was necessary to count the money in the till and lock up. However, he was not dissatisfied, for he lived much in his thoughts of Max and Miriam. The college boy had called her, and they had arranged a meeting for this coming Friday night. The shoemaker would personally have preferred Saturday, which he felt would make it a date of the first magnitude, but he learned Friday was Miriam's choice, so he said nothing. The day of the week did not matter. What mattered was the aftermath. Would they like each other and want to be friends? He sighed at all the time that would have to go by before he knew for sure. Often he was tempted to talk to Miriam about the boy, to ask whether she thought she would like his type—he had

told her only that he considered Max a nice boy and had suggested he call her—but the one time he tried she snapped at him—justly—how should she know?

At last Friday came. Feld was not feeling particularly well, so he stayed in bed, and Mrs. Feld thought it better to remain in the bedroom with him when Max called. Miriam received the boy, and her parents could hear their voices, his throaty one, as they talked. Just before leaving, Miriam brought Max to the bedroom door, and he stood there a minute, a tall, slightly hunched figure wearing a thick, droopy suit, and apparently at ease as he greeted the shoemaker and his wife, which was surely a good sign. And Miriam, although she had worked all day, looked fresh and pretty. She was a large-framed girl with a well-shaped body, and she had a fine open face and soft hair. They made, Feld thought, a first-class couple.

Miriam returned after 11:30. Her mother was already asleep, but the shoemaker got out of bed and after locating his bathrobe went into the kitchen, where Miriam, to his surprise, sat at the table, reading.

"So where did you go?" Feld asked pleasantly.

"For a walk," she said, not looking up.

"I advised him," Feld said, clearing his throat, "he shouldn't spend so much money."

"I didn't care."

The shoemaker boiled up some water for tea and sat down at the table with a cupful and thick slice of lemon.

"So how," he sighed after a sip, "did you enjoy?"

"It was all right."

He was silent. She must have sensed his disappointment, for she added, "You can't

_____

5. **rasp:** a harsh, grating sound.

WORDS TO KNOW
repugnant (rĭ-pŭg′nənt) *adj.* offensive; repulsive

really tell much the first time."

"You will see him again?"

Turning a page, she said that Max had asked for another date.

"For when?"

"Saturday."

"So what did you say?"

"What did I say?" she asked, delaying for a moment—"I said yes."

Afterwards she inquired about Sobel, and Feld, without exactly knowing why, said the assistant had got another job. Miriam said nothing more and began to read. The shoemaker's conscience did not trouble him; he was satisfied with the Saturday date.

During the week, by placing here and there a deft question, he managed to get from Miriam some information about Max. It surprised him to learn that the boy was not studying to be either a doctor or lawyer but was taking a business course leading to a degree in accountancy. Feld was a little disappointed because he thought of accountants as bookkeepers and would have preferred "a higher profession." However, it was not long before he had investigated the subject and discovered that certified public accountants were highly respected people, so he was thoroughly content as Saturday approached. But because Saturday was a busy day, he was much in the store and therefore did not see Max when he came to call for Miriam. From his wife he learned there had been nothing especially revealing about their meeting. Max had rung the bell, and Miriam had got her coat and left with him—nothing more. Feld did not probe, for his wife was not particularly observant. Instead, he waited up for Miriam with a newspaper on his lap, which he scarcely looked at so lost was he in thinking of the future. He awoke to find her in the room with him, tiredly removing her hat.

Greeting her, he was suddenly inexplicably afraid to ask anything about the evening. But since she volunteered nothing, he was at last forced to inquire how she had enjoyed herself. Miriam began something noncommittal but apparently changed her mind, for she said after a minute, "I was bored."

When Feld had sufficiently recovered from

Greeting her, he was suddenly inexplicably afraid to ask anything about the evening.

his anguished disappointment to ask why, she answered without hesitation, "Because he's nothing more than a materialist."

"What means this word?"

"He has no soul. He's only interested in things."

He considered her statement for a long time but then asked, "Will you see him again?"

"He didn't ask."

"Suppose he will ask you?"

"I won't see him."

He did not argue; however, as the days went by he hoped increasingly she would change her mind. He wished the boy would telephone, because he was sure there was more to him than Miriam, with her inexperienced eye, could discern. But Max didn't call. As a matter of fact he took a different route to school, no longer passing the shoemaker's store, and Feld was deeply hurt.

Then one afternoon Max came in and asked for his shoes. The shoemaker took them down from the shelf where he had placed them, apart

EVALUATE

Why didn't Miriam and Max get along?

WORDS
TO   **deft** (dĕft) *adj.* skillful
KNOW

467

from the other pairs. He had done the work himself, and the soles and heels were well built and firm. The shoes had been highly polished and somehow looked better than new. Max's Adam's apple went up once when he saw them, and his eyes had little lights in them.

"How much?" he asked, without directly looking at the shoemaker.

"Like I told you before," Feld answered sadly. "One dollar fifty cents."

Max handed him two crumpled bills and received in return a newly-minted silver half dollar.

He left. Miriam had not been mentioned. That night the shoemaker discovered that his new assistant had been all the while stealing from him, and he suffered a heart attack.

Though the attack was very mild, he lay in bed for three weeks. Miriam spoke of going for Sobel, but sick as he was Feld rose in wrath against the idea. Yet in his heart he knew there was no other way, and the first weary day back in the shop thoroughly convinced him, so that night after supper he dragged himself to Sobel's rooming house.

He toiled up the stairs, though he knew it was bad for him, and at the top knocked at the door. Sobel opened it, and the shoemaker entered. The room was a small, poor one, with a single window facing the street. It contained a narrow cot, a low table and several stacks of books piled haphazardly around on the floor along the wall, which made him think how queer Sobel was, to be uneducated and read so much. He had once asked him, Sobel, why you read so much? and the assistant could not answer him. Did you ever study in a college someplace? he had asked, but Sobel shook his head. He read, he said, to know. But to know what, the shoemaker demanded, and to know, why? Sobel

never explained, which proved he read much because he was queer.

Feld sat down to recover his breath. The assistant was resting on his bed with his heavy back to the wall. His shirt and trousers were clean, and his stubby fingers, away from the shoemaker's bench, were strangely pallid. His face was thin and pale, as if he had been shut in this room since the day he had bolted from the store.

"So when you will come back to work?" Feld asked him.

To his surprise, Sobel burst out, "Never."

Jumping up, he strode over to the window that looked out upon the miserable street. "Why should I come back?" he cried.

"I will raise your wages."

"Who cares for your wages!"

The shoemaker, knowing he didn't care, was at a loss what else to say.

"What do you want from me, Sobel?"

"Nothing."

"I always treated you like you was my son."

Sobel vehemently denied it. "So why you look for strange boys in the street they should go out with Miriam? Why you don't think of me?"

The shoemaker's hands and feet turned freezing cold. His voice became so hoarse he couldn't speak. At last he cleared his throat and croaked, "So what has my daughter got to do with a shoemaker thirty-five years old who works for me?"

"Why do you think I worked so long for you?" Sobel cried out. "For the stingy wages I sacrificed five years of my life so you could have to eat and drink and where to sleep?"

"Then for what?" shouted the shoemaker.

"For Miriam," he blurted—"for her."

The shoemaker, after a time, managed to say, "I pay wages in cash, Sobel," and lapsed into silence. Though he was seething with excitement, his mind was coldly clear, and he had to admit to himself he had sensed all along that Sobel felt this way. He had never so much as thought it consciously, but he had felt it and was afraid.

"Miriam knows?" he muttered hoarsely.

"She knows."

"You told her?"

"No."

"Then how does she know?"

"How does she know?" Sobel said, "because she knows. She knows who I am and what is in my heart."

Feld had a sudden insight. In some devious way, with his books and commentary, Sobel had given Miriam to understand that he loved her. The shoemaker felt a terrible anger at him for his deceit.

"Sobel, you are crazy," he said bitterly. "She will never marry a man so old and ugly like you."

Sobel turned black with rage. He cursed the shoemaker, but then, though he trembled to hold it in, his eyes filled with tears, and he broke into deep sobs. With his back to Feld, he stood at the window, fists clenched, and his shoulders shook with his choked sobbing.

Watching him, the shoemaker's anger diminished. His teeth were on edge with pity for the man, and his eyes grew moist. How strange and sad that a refugee, a grown man, bald and old with his miseries, who had by the skin of his teeth escaped Hitler's incinerators, should fall in love, when he had got to America, with a girl less than half his age. Day after day, for five years he had sat at his bench, cutting and hammering away, waiting for the girl to become a woman, unable to ease his heart with speech, knowing no protest but desperation.

"Ugly I didn't mean," he said half aloud.

Then he realized that what he had called ugly was not Sobel but Miriam's life if she married him. He felt for his daughter a strange and gripping sorrow, as if she were already Sobel's bride—the wife, after all, of a shoemaker—and had in her life no more than her mother had had. And all his dreams for her—why he had slaved and destroyed his heart with anxiety and labor—all these dreams of a better life were dead.

The room was quiet. Sobel was standing by the window reading, and it was curious that when he read he looked young.

"She is only nineteen," Feld said brokenly. "This is too young yet to get married. Don't ask her for two years more, till she is twenty-one, then you can talk to her."

Sobel didn't answer. Feld rose and left. He went slowly down the stairs, but once outside, though it was an icy night and the crisp falling snow whitened the street, he walked with a stronger stride.

But the next morning, when the shoemaker arrived, heavy-hearted, to open the store, he saw he needn't have come, for his assistant was already seated at the last, pounding leather for his love. ❖

RESPONDING OPTIONS

FROM PERSONAL RESPONSE TO CRITICAL ANALYSIS

REFLECT 1. What do you think of Sobel at the end of the story? Write down your impressions in your notebook, then share your ideas with a classmate.

RETHINK 2. What is your opinion of Feld? Explain your views.
Consider
- his relationship with his daughter
- his treatment of Sobel
- what you learn about his life and values

3. If Miriam were your daughter, would you want her to marry Sobel?
Consider
- what Sobel and Miriam have in common
- whether you believe they will be happy together
- whether Sobel possesses the qualities that you value in a mate

RELATE 4. Review the Venn diagram you created for the Personal Connection on page 460. Which character do you think would be more likely to earn the respect of your parents or guardians, Max or Sobel? Explain your choice.

5. In today's society, do you think parents should exert an influence in their child's choice of mate?

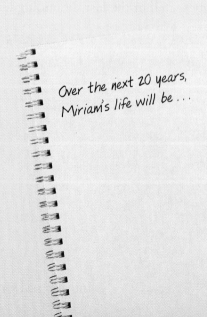

Over the next 20 years, Miriam's life will be . . .

ANOTHER PATHWAY

Think about how the story would have been different if told from a first-person point of view. For example, if Sobel had narrated the story, how might he have described Feld's actions? Choose one section of the story and rewrite it from the point of view of one of the characters. Discuss the effects of altering the point of view.

QUICKWRITES

1. Write the **wedding announcement** that might appear in the neighborhood newspaper if Miriam agrees to marry Sobel in two years. Be sure to include information on each character's background.

2. Write two **public service announcements** about the value of education that might appear in a magazine. One should present the views of Max and Feld; the other should present the views of Miriam and Sobel.

3. Choose one of the characters and imagine what his or her life will be like over the next 20 years. Write a **biographical sketch** in which you convey possible events in the character's life.

PORTFOLIO Save your writing. You may want to use it later as a springboard to a piece for your portfolio.

LITERARY CONCEPTS

An **allusion** is a reference to a historical or literary person, place, thing, or event with which the reader is assumed to be familiar. Malamud's title "The First Seven Years" makes an allusion to events recounted in the Old Testament of the Bible. According to chapter 29, verses 15–30, of the Book of Genesis, Jacob worked for Laban for seven years in return for Laban's beautiful daughter Rachel's hand in marriage. When the seven years were up, however, Laban tricked Jacob into marrying Leah, Rachel's elder sister, because it was not the custom for a younger sister to marry first. Jacob then agreed to work for Laban for seven more years to earn the right to Rachel's hand. How does the title of Malamud's story—and the biblical story to which it alludes—apply to Sobel's situation? Why do you think Malamud makes this allusion?

CONCEPT REVIEW: Foreshadowing Did you realize before the end of the story that Sobel was in love with Miriam? Find clues in the story that foreshadow Sobel's confession to Feld.

LITERARY LINKS

What do you think this story has in common with the Unit One story "Two Kinds" by Amy Tan?

ART CONNECTION

Take another look at the painting on page 464. Do you think it captures the essence of Miriam in "The First Seven Years"? Explain why or why not.

Detail of *Girl with a Book* (1927), Matej Sternen. National Gallery, Ljubljana, Slovenia.

CRITIC'S CORNER

Critic Edward A. Abramson wrote that Malamud deprives his characters of emotional well-being, physical comfort, and the ability to achieve their life's goals. "He pushes them down to bedrock in order to test them, to make them come to grips with what he feels to be the centrally important facets of life—selflessness and love." Do you think Abramson's generalization holds true for "The First Seven Years"? Why or why not?

ALTERNATIVE ACTIVITIES

1. With a partner, **role-play** the conversation Miriam might have had with Sobel when she sees that he has returned to work at her father's shop. As an alternative, role-play the conversation Miriam and her father might have had in which they discuss her desire to find a job.

2. Imagine that Miriam and Sobel are marrying and that you are a friend at the wedding. Give the **wedding toast** to the bride and groom.

WORDS TO KNOW

EXERCISE A Review the Words to Know at the bottom of the selection pages. Then, on your paper, indicate which word could best replace the italicized word or phrase in each sentence below.

1. When Tillie learned that her father had arranged a blind date for her, she began to *boil with anger.*
2. She *strongly* refused to meet the young man.
3. Finally, her father's *crafty* maneuvers convinced her to give the fellow a chance.
4. At their first encounter, she noticed his *very pale* complexion.
5. Though hardly handsome, he was not *disgusting.*
6. They went bowling on their first date; although he had never bowled before, Tillie found him to be *quick to learn.*

7. He was impressed with Tillie's strength and agility, and his compliments were *many.*
8. When Tillie asked about his job, he informed her that he earned more than a *tiny sum.*
9. From the twinkle in his eye, Tillie could *figure out* that he was teasing her.
10. By the time their date was over, Tillie was in the *gravest* danger of falling in love.

EXERCISE B Draw pictures that communicate the meaning of five of the Words to Know. Then exchange your drawings with a classmate and identify which words have been depicted.

BERNARD MALAMUD

Born and raised in Brooklyn, New York, Bernard Malamud was the son of poor Russian-Jewish immigrants who, according to the author, "taught me their values. . . . Theirs was a person-centered world, one that regarded the qualities of people. When I think of my father, I'm filled with a sense of sweet humanity." As a child, Malamud was often taken to theaters on New York's Second Avenue, where his

1914–1986

mother's relatives performed plays in Yiddish, the language of European Jews. He also pored over his *Book of Knowledge,* a 20-volume encyclopedia that his father, though he could ill afford it, bought to encourage his son's pursuit of learning. Malamud was only a teenager when he began writing stories in the back room of the family grocery store, where he worked part time after his mother died. In the 1940s he published stories in noted magazines such as *Harper's Bazaar* and *Partisan Review.* "The First Seven Years" is one of several stories collected in *The Magic Barrel,*

which won Malamud a National Book Award in 1959. Malamud was awarded a Pulitzer Prize, as well as a second National Book Award, for his novel *The Fixer,* published in 1966.

For most of his professional life, Malamud combined his writing activities with teaching. He held positions in the English departments at Oregon State University, Harvard University, and Bennington College in Vermont. Although his first novel, *The Natural,* is a fantasy about baseball and many of his stories draw on his wife's Italian-American heritage, Malamud is best known for writing about the experiences of European and American Jews. "I write about Jews," he explained, "because they set my imagination going . . . because I think I will understand them better as people."

OTHER WORKS *The Assistant, Idiots First, Rembrandt's Hat, The Stories of Bernard Malamud*

PREVIEWING

The Bear

Anton Chekhov (chĕk′ôf) **Russia**

PERSONAL CONNECTION

What does the phrase "battle of the sexes" mean to you? In a class discussion, share your definition of the term and your opinions about it. Also describe examples of the battle of the sexes from books, movies, plays, or television shows.

CULTURAL CONNECTION

In the following one-act comedy, the battle of the sexes takes place on a country estate in 19th-century Russia. The two combatants are both members of what was then Russia's privileged land-owning class. One is a woman who would describe herself as a genteel widow with delicate sensibilities, while the other is an outspoken gentleman farmer whose hot temper makes him seem like a bear, or a crude, insensitive person. Like others of his class, he is educated enough to know French—considered a language of refinement by upper-class Russians of the day—but he pokes fun at those who insist on speaking it. Far more at home with the "manly" pursuits of his class, such as riding, dueling, and managing his farm, he seems out of place in the widow's elegant drawing room, the formal room for receiving guests that is the setting of the play's "battle."

WRITING CONNECTION

In your notebook, provide a humorous description of one particular battle of the sexes. You may describe an actual event from your own experience or one that is imaginary. Use actual terms of battle to describe the conflict. Feel free to make use of exaggeration in describing the participants and the event. As you read *The Bear*, compare your battle to the one that takes place in the widow's drawing room.

Scene from a 1995 stage performance of *The Bear*. Writers Theatre Chicago. Photo by Alexander Guezentsvey.

The Bear
A Farce in One Act

by Anton Chekhov

Cast of Characters

Mrs. Helen Popov, a young widow with dimpled cheeks, a landowner

Gregory Smirnov, a landowner in early middle age

Luke, Mrs. Popov's old manservant

The action takes place in the drawing room of Mrs. Popov's country house.

Scene 1

(Mrs. Popov, *in deep mourning, with her eye fixed on a snapshot, and* Luke)

Luke. This won't do, madam; you're just making your life a misery. Cook's out with the maid picking fruit, every living creature's happy, and even our cat knows how to enjoy herself—she's parading round the yard trying to pick up a bird or two. But here you are cooped up inside all day like you was in a convent cell[1]—you never have a good time. Yes, it's true. Nigh on twelve months it is since you last set foot outdoors.

Mrs. Popov. And I'm never going out again; why should I? My life's finished. He lies in his grave; I've buried myself inside these four walls—we're both dead.

Luke. There you go again! I don't like to hear such talk, I don't. Your husband died and that was that—God's will be done, and may he rest in peace. You've shed a few tears and that'll

---

1. **convent cell:** a small room occupied by an individual nun in a convent, a community of nuns living under strict religious vows.

Portrait of the Pianist, Conductor, and Composer A. G. Rubinstein (1881), Ilya Efimovich Repin.
Oil on canvas, 80 cm × 62.3 cm, The State Tretyakov Gallery, Moscow, acquired by
P. M. Tretyakov from the artist.

do; it's time to call it a day—you can't spend your whole life a-moaning and a-groaning. The same thing happened to me once, when my old woman died, but what did I do? I grieved a bit, shed a tear or two for a month or so, and that's all she's getting. Catch me wearing sackcloth and ashes[2] for the rest of my days; it'd be more than the old girl was worth! (sighs) You've neglected all the neighbors—won't go and see them or have them in the house. We never get out and about, lurking here like dirty great spiders, saving your presence. The mice have been at my livery[3] too. And it's not for any lack of nice people either—the county's full of 'em, see. There's the regiment stationed at Ryblovo, and them officers are a fair treat; a proper sight for sore eyes they are. They have a dance in camp of a Friday, and the brass band plays most days. This ain't right, missus. You're young, and pretty as a picture with that peaches-and-cream look, so make the most of it. Them looks won't last forever, you know. If you wait another ten years to come out of your shell and lead them officers a dance, you'll find it's too late.

Mrs. Popov (decisively). Never talk to me like that again, please. When Nicholas died, my life lost all meaning, as you know. You may think I'm alive, but I'm not really. I swore to wear this mourning and shun society till my dying day, do you hear? Let his departed spirit see how I love him! Yes, I realize you know what went on—that he was often mean to me, cruel and, er, unfaithful even; but I'll be true to the grave and show him how much I can love. And he'll find me in the next world just as I was before he died.

Luke. Don't talk like that—walk round the garden instead. Or else have Toby or Giant harnessed and go and see the neighbors.

Mrs. Popov. Oh dear! (weeps)

Luke. Missus! Madam! What's the matter? For heaven's sake!

Mrs. Popov. He was so fond of Toby—always drove him when he went over to the Korchagins' place and the Vlasovs'. He drove so well too! And he looked so graceful when he pulled hard on the reins, remember? Oh Toby, Toby! See he gets an extra bag of oats today.

Luke. Very good, madam.

(A loud ring.)

Mrs. Popov (shudders). Who is it? Tell them I'm not at home.

Luke. Very well, madam. (goes out)

Scene 2

(Mrs. Popov, alone)

Mrs. Popov (looking at the snapshot). Now you shall see how I can love and forgive, Nicholas. My love will only fade when I fade away myself, when this poor heart stops beating. (laughs, through tears) Well, aren't you ashamed of yourself? I'm your good, faithful little wifie; I've locked myself up, and I'll be faithful to the grave, while you—aren't you ashamed, you naughty boy? You deceived me, and you used to make scenes and leave me alone for weeks on end.

Scene 3

(Mrs. Popov and Luke)

Luke (comes in, agitatedly). Someone's asking for you, madam. Wants to see you—

Mrs. Popov. Then I hope you told them I haven't received visitors since the day my husband died.

---

2. **sackcloth and ashes:** rough, scratchy clothing and ashes worn as symbols of mourning.

3. **livery:** a servant's uniform.

Luke. I did, but he wouldn't listen—his business is very urgent, he says.

Mrs. Popov. *I am not at home!*

Luke. So I told him, but he just swears and barges straight in, drat him. He's waiting in the dining room.

Mrs. Popov (*irritatedly*). All right, ask him in here then. Aren't people rude?

(Luke *goes out.*)

Mrs. Popov. Oh, aren't they all a bore? What do they want with me; why must they disturb my peace? (*sighs*) Yes, I see I really shall have to get me to a nunnery.[4] (*reflects*) I'll take the veil;[5] that's it.

Scene 4

(Mrs. Popov, Luke *and* Smirnov)

Smirnov (*coming in, to* Luke). You're a fool, my talkative friend. An ass. (*seeing* Mrs. Popov, *with dignity*) May I introduce myself, madam? Gregory Smirnov, landed gentleman[6] and lieutenant of artillery retired. I'm obliged to trouble you on most urgent business.

Mrs. Popov (*not holding out her hand*). What do you require?

Smirnov. I had the honor to know your late husband. He died owing me twelve hundred roubles[7]—I have his two IOUs. Now I've some interest due to the land bank tomorrow, madam, so may I trouble you to let me have the money today?

Mrs. Popov. Twelve hundred roubles—How did my husband come to owe you that?

Smirnov. He used to buy his oats from me.

Mrs. Popov (*sighing, to* Luke). Oh yes—Luke, don't forget to see Toby has his extra bag of oats. (Luke *goes out. To* Smirnov.) Of course I'll pay if Nicholas owed you something, but I've nothing on me today, sorry. My manager

will be back from town the day after tomorrow, and I'll get him to pay you whatever it is then, but for the time being I can't oblige. Besides, it's precisely seven months today since my husband died, and I am in no fit state to discuss money.

Smirnov. Well, I'll be in a fit state to go bust with a capital B if I can't pay that interest tomorrow. They'll have the bailiffs[8] in on me.

Mrs. Popov. You'll get your money the day after tomorrow.

Smirnov. I don't want it the day after tomorrow; I want it now.

Mrs. Popov. I can't pay you now, sorry.

Smirnov. And I can't wait till the day after tomorrow.

Mrs. Popov. Can I help it if I've no money today?

Smirnov. So you can't pay then?

Mrs. Popov. Exactly.

Smirnov. I see. And that's your last word, is it?

Mrs. Popov. It is.

Smirnov. Your last word? You really mean it?

Mrs. Popov. I do.

Smirnov (*sarcastic*). Then I'm greatly obliged to you; I'll put it in my diary! (*shrugs*) And people expect me to be cool and collected! I met the local excise man[9] on my way here just now. "My dear Smirnov," says he, "why are you always losing your temper?" But how can I help it, I ask you? I'm in desperate need of money! Yesterday morning I left home at

---

4. **get me to a nunnery:** go and live in a convent. This is probably a reference to a line from Shakespeare's *Hamlet* in which Hamlet angrily tells his girlfriend, "Get thee to a nunnery."
5. **veil:** the outer covering of a nun's headdress and, by extension, the life of a nun.
6. **landed gentleman:** a land owner. In Russia before the Russian Revolution, only a few people owned land.
7. **roubles:** units of Russian money; often spelled *rubles*.
8. **bailiffs:** assistants or deputies to the police chief.
9. **excise man:** tax man.

crack of dawn. I call on everyone who owes me money, but not a soul forks out. I'm dog tired. I spend the night in some God-awful place. Then I fetch up here, fifty miles from home, hoping to see the color of my money, only to be fobbed off[10] with this "no fit state" stuff! How *can* I keep my temper?

Mrs. Popov. I thought I'd made myself clear. You can have your money when my manager gets back from town.

Smirnov. It's not your manager I'm after; it's you. What the blazes, pardon my language, do I want with your manager?

Mrs. Popov. I'm sorry, my dear man, but I'm not accustomed to these peculiar expressions and to this tone. I have closed my ears. (*hurries out*)

Scene 5

(Smirnov, *alone*)

Smirnov. Well, what price that! "In no fit state!" Her husband died seven months ago, if you please! Now have I got my interest to pay or not? I want a straight answer—yes or no? All right, your husband's dead, you're in no fit state and so on and so forth, and your blasted manager's hopped it. But what am I supposed to do? Fly away from my creditors by balloon, I take it! Or go and bash the old brain-box against a brick wall? I call on Gruzdev—not at home. Yaroshevich is in hiding. I have a real old slanging match[11] with Kuritsyn and almost chuck him out of the window. Mazutov has the bellyache, and this creature's "in no fit state." Not one of the swine will pay. This is what comes of being too nice to them and behaving like some <u>sniveling</u> no-hoper or old woman. It doesn't pay to wear kid gloves with this lot! All right, just you wait—I'll give you

something to remember me by! You don't make a monkey out of me, blast you! I'm staying here—going to stick around till she coughs up. Pah! I feel well and truly riled today. I'm shaking like a leaf, I'm so furious—choking I am. Phew, my God, I really think I'm going to pass out! (*shouts*) Hey, you there!

Scene 6

(Smirnov *and* Luke)

Luke (*comes in*). What is it?

Smirnov. Bring me some kvass[12] or water, will you?

(Luke *goes out*)

Smirnov. What a mentality, though! You need money so bad you could shoot yourself, but she won't pay, being "in no fit state to discuss money," if you please! There's female logic for you and no mistake! That's why I don't like talking to women. Never have. Talk to a woman—why, I'd rather sit on top of a powder magazine![13] Pah! It makes my flesh creep, I'm so fed up with her, her and that great trailing dress! Poetic creatures they call 'em! Why, the very sight of one gives me cramp in both legs, I get so aggravated.

Scene 7

(Smirnov *and* Luke)

Luke (*comes in and serves some water*). Madam's unwell and won't see anyone.

---

10. **fobbed off:** put off with a trick or an excuse.
11. **slanging match:** the exchange of angry, abusive language.
12. **kvass** (kväs): Russian beer.
13. **powder magazine:** a room in which gun powder and other explosives are stored in a fort or on a ship.

WORDS TO KNOW **sniveling** (snĭv′əl-ĭng) *adj.* whining

A Room in the Brasovo Estate (1916), Stanislav Iulianovich Zhukovskii. Oil on canvas, 80 cm × 107 cm, The State Tretyakov Gallery, Moscow, accessioned from the People's Commissariate of Foreign Affairs, 1941.

Smirnov. You clear out!

(Luke *goes out*)

Smirnov. "Unwell and won't see anyone." All right then, don't! I'm staying put, chum, and I don't budge one inch till you unbelt.[14] Be ill for a week, and I'll stay a week; make it a year, and a year I'll stay. I'll have my rights, lady! As for your black dress and dimples, you don't catch me that way—we know all about those dimples! (*shouts through the window*) Unhitch, Simon; we're here for some time—I'm staying put. Tell the stable people to give my horses oats. And you've got that animal tangled in the reins again, you great oaf! (*imitates him*) "I don't care." I'll give you don't care! (*moves away from the window*) How ghastly—it's unbearably hot, no one will pay up, I had a bad night, and now here's this female with her long black dress and her states. I've got a headache. How about a glass of vodka? That might be an idea. (*shouts*) Hey, you there!

Luke (*comes in*). What is it?

Smirnov. Bring me a glass of vodka.

(Luke *goes out*)

Smirnov. Phew! (*sits down and looks himself over*) A fine specimen I am, I must say—dust all over me, my boots dirty, unwashed, hair unbrushed, straw on my waistcoat. I bet the little woman took me for a burglar. (*yawns*) It's not exactly polite to turn up in a drawing room in this rig! Well, anyway, I'm not a guest here; I'm collecting money. And there's no such thing as correct wear for the well-dressed creditor.

---

14. **unbelt:** take off a belt designed to hold money; in this case, to pay what is due.

Luke (*comes in and gives him the vodka*). This is a liberty, sir.

Smirnov (*angrily*). What!

Luke. I, er, it's all right, I just—

Smirnov. Who do you think you're talking to? You hold your tongue!

Luke (*aside*). Now we'll never get rid of him, botheration take it! It's an ill wind brought him along.

(Luke *goes out*)

Smirnov. Oh, I'm so furious! I could pulverize the whole world, I'm in such a rage. I feel quite ill. (*shouts*) Hey, you there!

Scene 8

(Mrs. Popov *and* Smirnov)

Mrs. Popov (*comes in, with downcast eyes*). Sir, in my solitude I have grown unaccustomed to the sound of human speech, and I can't stand shouting. I must urgently request you not to disturb my peace.

Smirnov. Pay up and I'll go.

Mrs. Popov. As I've already stated quite plainly, I've no ready cash. Wait till the day after tomorrow.

Smirnov. I've also had the honor of stating quite plainly that I need the money today, not the day after tomorrow. If you won't pay up now, I'll have to put my head in a gas oven tomorrow.

Mrs. Popov. Can I help it if I've no cash in hand? This is all rather odd.

Smirnov. So you won't pay up now, eh?

Mrs. Popov. I can't.

Smirnov. In that case I'm not budging; I'll stick around here till I do get my money. (*sits down*) You'll pay the day after tomorrow, you say?

Very well, then I'll sit here like this till the day after tomorrow. I'll just stay put exactly as I am. (*jumps up*) I ask you—have I got that interest to pay tomorrow or haven't I? Think I'm trying to be funny, do you?

Mrs. Popov. Kindly don't raise your voice at me, sir—we're not in the stables.

Smirnov. I'm not discussing stables; I'm asking whether my interest falls due tomorrow. Yes or no?

Mrs. Popov. You don't know how to treat a lady.

Smirnov. Oh yes I do.

Mrs. Popov. Oh no you don't. You're a rude, ill-bred person. Nice men don't talk to ladies like that.

Smirnov. Now, this *is* a surprise! How do you want me to talk then? In French, I suppose? (*in an angry, simpering voice*) *Madame, je voo pree.* You won't pay me—how perfectly delightful. Oh, *pardong*, I'm sure—sorry you were troubled! Now isn't the weather divine today? And that black dress looks too, too charming! (*bows and scrapes*)

Mrs. Popov. That's silly. And not very clever.

Smirnov (*mimics her*). "Silly, not very clever." I don't know how to treat a lady, don't I? Madam, I've seen more women in my time than you have house sparrows. I've fought three duels over women. There have been twenty-one women in my life. Twelve times it was me broke it off; the other nine got in first. Oh yes! Time was I made an ass of myself, slobbered, mooned around, bowed and scraped and practically crawled on my belly. I loved; I suffered; I sighed at the moon; I languished; I melted; I grew cold. I loved passionately, madly, in every conceivable fashion, damn me, burbling nineteen to the dozen about women's emancipation and wasting half

W O R D S   **liberty** (lĭb'ər-tē) *n.* an action that is too bold or forward
T O   **languish** (lăng'gwĭsh) *v.* to suffer with longing
K N O W   **emancipation** (ĭ-măn'sə-pā'shən) *n.* a setting free from restraint or controls

my substance[15] on the tender passion. But now—no thank you very much! I can't be fooled anymore; I've had enough. Black eyes, passionate looks, crimson lips, dimpled cheeks, moonlight, "Whispers, passion's bated breathing"[16]—I don't give a tinker's cuss[17] for the lot now, lady. Present company excepted, all women, large or small, are simpering, mincing, gossipy creatures. They're great haters. They're eyebrow deep in lies. They're futile; they're trivial; they're cruel; they're outrageously illogical. And as for having anything upstairs (*taps his forehead*)—I'm sorry to be so blunt, but the very birds in the trees can run rings round your average bluestocking.[18] Take any one of these poetical creations. Oh, she's all froth and fluff, she is; she's half divine; she sends you into a million raptures. But you take a peep inside her mind, and what do you see? A common or garden crocodile! (*clutches the back of a chair, which cracks and breaks*) And yet this crocodile somehow thinks its great lifework, privilege and monopoly is the tender passion—that's what really gets me! But damn and blast it, and crucify me upside down on that wall if I'm wrong—does a woman know how to love any living creature apart from lap dogs? Her love gets no further than sniveling and slobbering. The man suffers and makes sacrifices, while she just twitches the train of her dress and tries to get him squirming under her thumb; that's what her love adds up to! You must know what women are like, seeing you've the rotten luck to be one. Tell me frankly, did you ever see a sincere, faithful, true woman? You know you didn't. Only the old and ugly ones are true and faithful. You'll never find a constant woman, not in a month of Sundays you won't, not once in a blue moon!

Mrs. Popov. Well, I like that! Then who is true and faithful in love to your way of thinking?

Not men by any chance?

Smirnov. Yes, madam. Men.

Mrs. Popov. *Men!* (*gives a bitter laugh*) Men true and faithful in love! That's rich, I must say. (*vehemently*) What right have you to talk like that? Men true and faithful! If it comes to that, the best man I've ever known was my late husband, I may say. I loved him passionately, with all my heart as only an intelligent young woman can. I gave him my youth, my happiness, my life, my possessions. I lived only for him. I worshiped him as an idol. And—what do you think? This best of men was shamelessly deceiving me all along the line! After his death I found a drawer in his desk full of love letters, and when he was alive—oh, what a frightful memory!—he used to leave me on my own for weeks on end, he carried on with other girls before my very eyes, he was unfaithful to me, he spent my money like water, and he joked about my feelings for him. But I loved him all the same, and I've been faithful to him. What's more, I'm still faithful and true now that he's dead. I've buried myself alive inside these four walls, and I shall go round in these widow's weeds[19] till my dying day.

Smirnov (*with a contemptuous laugh*). Widow's weeds! Who do you take me for? As if I didn't know why you wear this fancy dress and bury yourself indoors! Why, it sticks out a mile! Mysterious and romantic, isn't it? Some army

---

15. **substance:** wealth or fortune.
16. **bated breathing:** breathing held in, due to excitement or fear. Smirnov is quoting the first lines of a well-known lyric by A. A. Fet.
17. **a tinker's cuss:** the smallest degree or amount; same as a tinker's damn.
18. **bluestocking:** a woman having intellectual or literary interests.
19. **widow's weeds:** the black mourning clothes of a widow.

WORDS TO KNOW **futile** (fyo͞ot′l) *adj.* serving no useful purpose

Portrait of M. K. Oliv (1895), Valentin Aleksandrovich Serov.
Oil on canvas, 88 cm × 68.5 cm, The State Russian Museum,
St. Petersburg, accessioned from I. A. Mamontov, 1904.

cadet or hack poet[20] may pass by your garden, look up at your windows and think: "There dwells Tamara,[21] the mysterious princess, the one who buried herself alive from love of her husband." Who do you think you're fooling?

Mrs. Popov (*flaring up*). *What!* You dare to take that line with me!

Smirnov. Buries herself alive—but doesn't forget to powder her nose!

Mrs. Popov. You dare adopt that tone!

Smirnov. Don't you raise your voice to me, madam; I'm not one of your servants. Let me call a spade a spade. Not being a woman, I'm used to saying what I think. So stop shouting, pray.

Mrs. Popov. It's you who are shouting, not me. Leave me alone, would you mind?

Smirnov. Pay up, and I'll go.

Mrs. Popov. You'll get nothing out of me.

Smirnov. Oh yes I shall.

Mrs. Popov. Just to be awkward, you won't get one single copeck.[22] And you can leave me alone.

---

20. **hack poet:** a poet who writes shallow or ordinary verse, usually just to make a living.

21. **Tamara:** a reference to the heroine of the poem "Tamara" by Russian Romantic poet Mikhail Lermontov.

22. **copeck:** a Russian coin of little value, similar to a penny.

Smirnov. Not having the pleasure of being your husband or fiancé, I'll trouble you not to make a scene. (*sits down*) I don't like it.

Mrs. Popov (*choking with rage*). Do I see you sitting down?

Smirnov. You most certainly do.

Mrs. Popov. Would you mind leaving?

Smirnov. Give me my money. (*aside*) Oh, I'm in such a rage! Furious I am!

Mrs. Popov. I've no desire to bandy words with cads,[23] sir. Kindly clear off! (*pause*) Well, are you going or aren't you?

Smirnov. No.

Mrs. Popov. No?

Smirnov. No!

Mrs. Popov. Very well then! (*rings*)

Scene 9

(*The above and* Luke)

Mrs. Popov. Show this gentleman out, Luke.

Luke (*goes up to* Smirnov). Be so good as to leave, sir, when you're told, sir. No point in—

Smirnov (*jumping up*). You hold your tongue! Who do you think you're talking to? I'll carve you up in little pieces.

Luke (*clutching at his heart*). Heavens and saints above us! (*falls into an armchair*) Oh, I feel something terrible—fair took my breath away, it did.

Mrs. Popov. But where's Dasha? Dasha! (*shouts*) Dasha! Pelegeya! Dasha! (*rings*)

Luke. Oh, they've all gone fruit picking. There's no one in the house. I feel faint. Fetch water.

Mrs. Popov. Be so good as to clear out!

Smirnov. Couldn't you be a bit more polite?

Mrs. Popov (*clenching her fists and stamping*). You uncouth oaf! You have the manners of a bear! Think you own the place? Monster!

Smirnov. What! You say that again!

Mrs. Popov. I called you an ill-mannered oaf, a monster!

Smirnov (*advancing on her*). Look here, what right have you to insult me?

Mrs. Popov. All right, I'm insulting you. So what? Think I'm afraid of you?

Smirnov. Just because you look all romantic, you can get away with anything—is that your idea? This is dueling talk!

Luke. Heavens and saints above us! Water!

Smirnov. Pistols at dawn!

Mrs. Popov. Just because you have big fists and the lungs of an ox, you needn't think I'm scared, see? Think you own the place, don't you!

Smirnov. We'll shoot it out! No one calls me names and gets away with it, weaker sex or no weaker sex.

Mrs. Popov (*trying to shout him down*). You coarse lout!

Smirnov. Why should it only be us men who answer for our insults? It's high time we dropped that silly idea. If women want equality, let them damn well have equality! I challenge you, madam!

Mrs. Popov. Want to shoot it out, eh? Very well.

Smirnov. This very instant!

Mrs. Popov. Most certainly! My husband left some pistols; I'll fetch them instantly. (*moves hurriedly off and comes back*) I'll enjoy putting a bullet through that thick skull, damn your infernal cheek![24] (*goes out*)

Smirnov. I'll pot[25] her like a sitting bird. I'm not one of your sentimental young puppies. She'll get no chivalry from me!

23. **bandy . . . cads:** exchange words with scoundrels.
24. **infernal cheek:** hellish sass or boldness.
25. **pot:** shoot.

Luke. Kind sir! (*kneels*) Grant me a favor; pity an old man and leave this place. First you frighten us out of our wits; now you want to fight a duel.

Smirnov (*not listening*). A duel! There's true women's emancipation for you! That evens up the sexes with a vengeance! I'll knock her off as a matter of principle. But what a woman! (*mimics her*) "Damn your infernal cheek! I'll put a bullet through that thick skull." Not bad, eh? Flushed all over, flashing eyes, accepts my challenge! You know, I've never seen such a woman in my life.

Luke. Go away, sir, and I'll say prayers for you till the day I die.

Smirnov. There's a regular woman for you, something I do appreciate! A proper woman—not some namby-pamby, wishy-washy female, but a really red-hot bit of stuff, a regular pistol-packing little spitfire. A pity to kill her, really.

Luke (*weeps*). Kind sir—do leave. Please!

Smirnov. I definitely like her. Definitely! Never mind her dimples; I like her. I wouldn't mind letting her off what she owes me, actually. And I don't feel angry anymore. Wonderful woman!

Scene 10

(*The above and* Mrs. Popov)

Mrs. Popov (*comes in with the pistols*). Here are the pistols. But before we start would you mind showing me how to fire them? I've never had a pistol in my hands before.

Luke. Lord help us! Mercy on us! I'll go and find the gardener and coachman. What have we done to deserve this? (*goes out*)

Smirnov (*examining the pistols*). Now, there are several types of pistol. There are Mortimer's special dueling pistols with percussion caps.[26] Now, yours here are Smith and Wessons, triple action with extractor,[27] center-fired. They're

fine weapons, worth a cool ninety roubles the pair. Now, you hold a revolver like this. (*aside*) What eyes, what eyes! She's hot stuff all right!

Mrs. Popov. Like this?

Smirnov. Yes, that's right. Then you raise the hammer and take aim like this. Hold your head back a bit; stretch your arm out properly. Right. And then with this finger you press this little gadget; and that's it. But the great thing is—don't get excited, and do take your time about aiming. Try and see your hand doesn't shake.

Mrs. Popov. All right. We can't very well shoot indoors; let's go in the garden.

Smirnov. Very well. But I warn you, I'm firing in the air.

Mrs. Popov. Oh, this is the limit! Why?

Smirnov. Because, because—That's my business.

Mrs. Popov. Got cold feet, eh? I see. Now don't shilly-shally, sir. Kindly follow me. I shan't rest till I've put a bullet through your brains, damn you. Got the wind up, have you?

Smirnov. Yes.

Mrs. Popov. That's a lie. Why won't you fight?

Smirnov. Because, er, because you, er, I like you.

Mrs. Popov (*with a vicious laugh*). He likes me! He dares to say he likes me! (*points to the door*) I won't detain you.

Smirnov (*puts down the revolver without speaking, picks up his peaked cap and moves off; near the door he stops, and for about half a minute the two look at each other without speaking; then he speaks, going up to her hesitantly*). Listen. Are you still angry? I'm absolutely furious myself, but you must see—how can I put it? The fact is that, er, it's this

26. **percussion caps:** small powder caps used to set off some older guns.

27. **extractor:** the part of a gun that pulls the shell case out of the chamber so that it may be ejected after firing.

way, actually—(*shouts*) Anyway, can I help it if I like you? (*clutches the back of a chair, which cracks and breaks*) Damn fragile stuff, furniture! I like you! Do you understand? I, er, I'm almost in love.

Mrs. Popov. Keep away from me; I loathe you.

Smirnov. God, what a woman! Never saw the like of it in all my born days. I'm sunk! Without trace! Trapped like a mouse!

Mrs. Popov. Get back or I shoot.

Smirnov. Shoot away. I'd die happily with those marvelous eyes looking at me; that's what you can't see—die by that dear little velvet hand. Oh, I'm crazy! Think it over and make your mind up now, because once I leave this place we shan't see each other again. So make your mind up. I'm a gentleman and a man of honor, I've ten thousand a year, I can put a bullet through a coin in midair and I keep a good stable. Be my wife.

Mrs. Popov (*indignantly brandishes the revolver*). A duel! We'll shoot it out!

Smirnov. I'm out of my mind! Nothing makes any sense. (*shouts*) Hey, you there—water!

Mrs. Popov (*shouts*). We'll shoot it out!

Smirnov. I've lost my head, fallen for her like some damfool boy! (*Clutches her hand. She shrieks with pain.*) I love you! (*kneels*) I love you as I never loved any of my twenty-one other women—twelve times it was me broke it off; the other nine got in first. But I never loved anyone as much as you. I've gone all sloppy, soft and sentimental. Kneeling like an imbecile, offering my hand! Disgraceful! Scandalous! I haven't been in love for five years, I swore not to, and here I am crashing head over heels, hook, line and sinker! I offer you my hand. Take it or leave it. (*gets up and hurries to the door*)

Mrs. Popov. Just a moment.

Smirnov (*stops*). What is it?

Mrs. Popov. Oh, never mind, just go away. But wait. No, go, go away. I hate you. Or no—don't go away. Oh, if you knew how furious I am! (*throws the revolver on the table*) My fingers are numb from holding this beastly thing. (*tears a handkerchief in her anger*) Why are you hanging about? Clear out!

Smirnov. Good-bye.

Mrs. Popov. Yes, yes, go away! (*shouts*) Where are you going? Stop. Oh, go away then. I'm so furious! Don't you come near me, I tell you.

Smirnov. (*going up to her*). I'm so fed up with myself! Falling in love like a schoolboy! Kneeling down! It's enough to give you the willies! (*rudely*) I love you! Oh, it's just what the doctor ordered, this is! There's my interest due in tomorrow, hay making's upon us—and *you* have to come along! (*takes her by the waist*) I'll never forgive myself.

Mrs. Popov. Go away! You take your hands off me! I, er, hate you! We'll sh-shoot it out!

(*A prolonged kiss*)

Scene 11

(*The above,* Luke *with an axe, the gardener with a rake, the coachman with a pitchfork and some workmen with sundry sticks and staves*)

Luke (*seeing the couple kissing*). Mercy on us! (*pause*)

Mrs. Popov (*lowering her eyes*). Luke, tell them in the stables—Toby gets no oats today.

Curtain

Translated by Ronald Hingley

RESPONDING
OPTIONS

FROM PERSONAL RESPONSE TO CRITICAL ANALYSIS

REFLECT 1. In your notebook, rate this comedy on a 1 to 10 scale, with 10 representing "very funny" and 1 representing "not funny at all." Share your response.

RETHINK 2. What is your opinion of Smirnov's attitude toward women? Cite examples from the play to support your opinion.

3. Do you think that Smirnov is really a bear, as the title implies? Explain your answer.

4. How would you describe Mrs. Popov?
Consider
- how she responded to her husband's death
- what her marriage was really like
- why she agrees to the duel
- her change of heart at the end of the play

5. Of the sayings "Birds of a feather flock together" and "Opposites attract," which do you think is more appropriate to the romance in *The Bear?* Explain your answer.

6. In a well-made play, even minor characters contribute to its success. In your opinion, what do Luke and the horse, Toby, contribute to this play?

RELATE 7. Do you think men or women most often win the battle of the sexes? Explain your reasoning.

ANOTHER PATHWAY
Cooperative Learning
With a group of classmates, stage a sequel to *The Bear,* set at the wedding reception after the two main characters marry. Create dialogue and action in keeping with the characters' earlier portrayal. Guests at the reception can share stories about the couple's odd courtship.

QUICKWRITES

1. Why do you think the two main characters in *The Bear* fall in love? Write an **analysis** that explains their behavior, citing details from the play to support your ideas.

2. Imagine that you are a theater critic. Write a **review** of *The Bear* that focuses on your opinion of the play itself, though you may also include imaginary details about the quality of the production.

3. Write your own **dramatic scene** from a farce about the battle of the sexes. The description you created for the Writing Connection on page 473 might serve as the basis of your plot.

📁 *PORTFOLIO Save your writing. You may want to use it later as a spring-board to a piece for your portfolio.*

LITERARY CONCEPTS

A **farce** is a play that prompts laughter through ridiculous situations, exaggerated behavior and language, and physical comedy. Characters are often **stereotypes;** that is, they conform to a fixed pattern or are defined by a single trait. In *The Bear*, for example, Luke might be seen as a stereotype of a loyal but critical servant who tells his superior more than she wants to hear. Cite examples of ridiculous situations, exaggerated behavior and language, and physical comedy in *The Bear*. Would you say that the main characters are stereotypes? Why or why not?

THE WRITER'S STYLE

Chekhov's diction, or word choice, plays a strong role in reinforcing characterization in *The Bear*. Find examples of slang and formal language in the play. What do these examples reveal about the characters who speak in such a manner?

CRITIC'S CORNER

A student reviewer, Cynthia Villicana, found Chekhov's play to be interesting because it is "romantic and funny at the same time." How does her judgment of the play compare with your own?

ACROSS THE CURRICULUM

Drama Find out more about Chekhov's contributions to the theater. Prepare a class presentation of this information and, if possible, share with the class various photographs from stage productions of his plays.

Logo Moscow Arts Theatre

WORDS TO KNOW

Review the Words to Know at the bottom of the selection pages. Then write the word that best completes each sentence.

1. That ill-mannered man overstepped his bounds and took the _____ of asking a woman out on a date just one week after her husband's funeral!

2. Giving him a book on etiquette would be _____, since rude people don't see any point to politeness.

3. "Why," he might whine, "should I _____ with desire instead of just asking for what I want?"

4. Overwhelmed by his rudeness, the woman cried, "You inconsiderate, _____ idiot!"

5. One who wants _____ from the restrictions imposed by good manners will find that there is a price to pay for such freedom.

ANTON CHEKHOV

One of his country's greatest authors, Anton Chekhov was born to a poor family in Taganrog in the south of Russia. After finishing high school, Chekhov enrolled in medical school in Moscow, but since his family needed his financial support, he began writing comical sketches and selling them to popular newspapers and journals. Although Chekhov obtained his degree in 1884, he practiced medicine only sporadically throughout his writing career.

1860–1904

By 1887 Chekhov had published three story collections and was beginning to experiment with drama, producing *The Bear* and several more one-act farces, as well as full-length plays. The first performance of one of these plays, *The Seagull*, received such poor reviews that Chekhov nearly stopped writing drama; however, a successful restaging at the Moscow Art Theater turned the criticism around. In the next few years Chekhov wrote three more plays for which he is best remembered: *Uncle Vanya, The Three Sisters,* and *The Cherry Orchard*. Chekhov died of tuberculosis in 1904, just three years after marrying actress Olga Knipper, whom he met when the Moscow Art Theater staged his plays.

OTHER WORKS *Stories of Russian Life, The Brute and Other Farces, Chekhov: The Major Plays, Forty Stories*

REFLECT & ASSESS

The Lady Who Was a Beggar

Anonymous / China

The Bride Wore Red (about 1988–1989), Yang Hsien Min. Copyright © 1989, The Greenwich Workshop, Inc., Shelton, Connecticut. Reproduced with the permission of the Greenwich Workshop, Inc.

Although the following folk tale was not published until the early 1620s, it was probably first composed in the 12th century. At that time, China was ruled by the Song dynasty (960–1279) and its magnificent capital was in the eastern city of Lin-an, later called Hangzhou. During the Song dynasty, literature, music, and art flourished, and oral storytelling in the everyday language of the people became an art form. Audiences gathered in a variety of settings—including street corners and market places—to hear their favorite artists.

Each teller had a specialty, such as crime stories, stories from Buddhist scripture, or love stories. The tales themselves were always meant to entertain, but they also communicated the values of the society, teaching proper, moral behavior through the deeds of the characters and the punishments they suffered.

Cautionary tales and romances were two types of love stories that were particularly popular in Lin-an during the 12th and 13th centuries, and "The Lady Who Was a Beggar," is considered a typical romance tale. Such lines in the story as, "Let us digress no longer," or "Don't you agree that . . ." are evidence that the tale was once shared aloud. Look for other such evidence as you read.

t is told that in the Shao-hsing[1] reign period of the Sung dynasty (1131–1163), although Lin-an had been made the capital city and was a wealthy and populous district, still the great number of beggars had not diminished. Among them was one who acted as their head. He was called the "tramp-major," and looked after all the beggars. Whenever they managed to beg something, the tramp-major would demand a fee for the day. Then when it was raining or snow lay on the ground, and there was nowhere to go to beg, the tramp-major would boil up a drop of thin gruel and feed the whole beggar band. Their tattered robes and jackets were also in his care. The result was that the whole crowd of the beggars were care-

ful to obey him, with bated breath like a lot of slaves, and none of them dared offend him.

The tramp-major was thus provided with a regular income, and as a rule he would lend out sums of money among the beggars and extort a tidy interest. In this way, . . . he could build up a going concern out of it. He depended on this for his livelihood, and never for a moment thought of changing his profession. There was only one drawback: a tramp-major did not have a very good name. Though he acquired land by his efforts, and his family had prospered for generations, still he was a boss of the beggars and not to be compared with ordinary respectable people. No one would salute him with respect if he showed himself out-of-doors, and so the only thing for him to do was to shut his doors and play the great man in his own home.

And yet, distinguishing the worthy from the base, we count among the latter only . . . actors, yamen-runners[2] and soldiers: we certainly do not include beggars. For what is wrong with beggars is not that they are covered in sores, but simply that they have no money. There have been men like the minister Wu Tzu-hsü,[3] of Ch'un-ch'iu times,[4] who as a fugitive from oppression played his pipes and begged his food in the marketplace of Wu; or Cheng Yüan-ho[5] of T'ang times[6] who sang the beggar's song of "Lien-hua lo,"[7] but later rose to wealth and eminence and covered his bed with brocade. These were great men, though beggars: clearly, we may hold beggars in contempt, but we should

---

1. Shao-hsing (shou'shǐng').
2. yamen-runners (yä'mən-rŭn'ərz): people who run errands for a Chinese government official or department.
3. Wu Tzu-hsü (wo͞o' tso͞o'shü').
4. Ch'un-ch'iu (cho͝on'chē-o͞o') times: 722–479 B.C.
5. Cheng Yüan-ho (jəng yü-än'hō').
6. T'ang (täng) times: the T'ang (now usually spelled Tang) dynasty, which ruled from A.D. 618–907.
7. Lien-hua lo (lē-ĕn'hwä' lō').

not compare them with the . . . actors, the runners, and [the] soldiery.

Let us digress no longer, but tell now how in the city of Hangchow there was once a tramp-major by the name of Chin Lao-ta. In the course of seven generations his ancestors had developed the profession into a perfect family business, so that Chin Lao-ta ate well and dressed well, lived in a fine house and cultivated good land. His barns were well-stocked with grain and his purse with money, he made loans and kept servants; if not quite the wealthiest, he was certainly one of the rich. Being a man of social aspirations, he decided to relinquish this post of tramp-major into the hands of a relative, "Scabby" Chin, while he himself took his ease with what he had and mingled no more with the beggar band. But unfortunately, the neighbors were used to speaking of the "tramp-major's family," and the name persisted in spite of his efforts.

Chin Lao-ta was over fifty. He had lost his wife and had no son, but only a daughter whose name was Jade Slave. Jade Slave was beautiful, as we are told by a verse about her:

Pure to compare with jade,
Gracious to shame the flowers,
Given the adornments of the court
Here would be another Chang Li-hua.[8]

Chin Lao-ta prized his daughter as a jewel, and taught her from an early age to read and write. By the age of fifteen she was adept in prose and verse, composing as fast as her hand could write. She was equally proficient in the womanly crafts, and in performing on the harp or flute: everything she did proclaimed her skill. Her beauty and talent inspired Chin Lao-ta to seek a husband for her among the scholar class. But the fact was that among families of name and rank it would be difficult to find anyone anxious to marry the girl— no one wanted a tramp-major's daughter. On the other hand, Lao-ta had no desire to cultivate a liaison[9] with humble and unaspiring tradespeople. Thus, while her father hovered between high and low, the girl reached the age of seventeen without betrothal.

And then one day an old man of the neighborhood came along with news of a student by the name of Mo Chi who lived below the T'ai-ping Bridge. This was an able youth of nineteen, full of learning, who remained unmarried only because he was an orphan and had no money. But he had graduated recently, and was hoping to marry some girl in whose family he could find a home.

"This youth would be just right for your daughter," said the neighbor. "Why not take him as your son-in-law?"

"Then do me the favor of acting as go-between," said Chin Lao-ta; and off went the old man on his errand, straight to the T'ai-ping Bridge.

> Unfortunately, the neighbors were used to speaking of the "tramp-major's family."

---

8. **Chang Li-hua** (jäng′ lē′hwä′): beautiful girlfriend of the Chen dynasty's last emperor, who ruled from A.D. 583–589.

9. **liaison** (lē′ā-zŏn′): a close relationship, connection, or link.

THE LADY WHO WAS A BEGGAR

There he sought out the graduate Mo Chi, to whom he said, "There is one thing I am obliged to tell you: the ancestors of Chin Lao-ta followed the profession of tramp-major. But this was long ago: and think, what a fine girl she is, this daughter of his—and what's more, what a prosperous and flourishing family! If it is not against the young gentleman's wishes, I will take it upon myself to arrange the whole thing at once."

Before giving his reply, Mo Chi turned the matter over in his mind: "I am not very well-off for food and clothes just now, and I am certainly not in a position to take a wife in the usual way. Why not make the best of it and marry into this family? It would be killing two birds with one stone; and I needn't take any notice of ridicule." Turning to the old man, he said, "Uncle,[10] what you propose seems an admirable plan. But I am too poor to buy the usual presents. What do you suggest?"

"Provided only that you accept this match," replied the old man, "you will not even be called on to supply so much as the paper for the exchange of horoscopes.[11] You may leave everything to me."

With this he returned to report to Chin Lao-ta. They selected an auspicious[12] day, and the Chin family even provided clothes for Mo Chi to wear at the wedding.

When Mo Chi had entered the family and the ceremony was over, he found that Jade Slave's beauty and talents exceeded his wildest hopes. And this perfect wife was his without the outlay of a single copper! He had food and clothes in abundance, and indeed everything he could wish. Even the ridicule he had feared from his friends was withheld, for all were willing to make allowances for Mo Chi's penniless condition.

When their marriage had lasted a month, Chin Lao-ta prepared a generous banquet at which his son-in-law could feast his graduate friends and thus enhance the dignity of the house. The drinking went on for a week: but what was not foreseen was the offense which all this gave to the kinsman "Scabby" Chin. Nor was Scabby without justification.

"You're a tramp-major just as much as I am," said he in his heart, "the only thing is that you've been one for a few generations longer and have got some money in your pocket. But if it comes to ancestors, aren't yours the very same as mine? When my niece Jade Slave gets married, I expect to be invited to drink a toast—here's a load of guests drinking for a week on end to celebrate the first month, but not so much as a one-inch by three-inch invitation card do I receive. What is this son-in-law of yours—he's a graduate, I know, but is he a President of a Board or a Prime Minister as well? Aren't I the girl's own uncle, and entitled to a stool at your party? Very well," he concluded, "if they're so ready to ignore my existence, I'll go and stir them up a bit and see how that pleases them."

Thereupon he called together fifty or sixty of his beggars, and took the lot of them along to Chin Lao-ta's house. What a sight—

*Hats bursting into flower, shirts tied up in
    knots,
A rag of old matting or a strip of worn rug,
    a bamboo stick and a rough chipped bowl.
Shouting "Father!," shouting "Mother!,"
    shouting "Benefactor!," what a
    commotion before the gate!
Writhing snakes, yapping dogs, chattering
    apes and monkeys, what sly cunning they
    all display!*

---

10. **Uncle:** in China, a respectful way of addressing any elderly man.

11. **exchange of horoscopes:** Before marriage, astrological forecasts based on the Chinese calendar were traditionally exchanged to make sure the partners were compatible.

12. **auspicious:** favorable; lucky.

*Beating clappers, singing "Yang Hua,"[13] the
  clamor deafens the ear;
Clattering tiles, faces white with chalk,[14] the
  sight offends the eye.
A troop of rowdies banded together, not
  Chung K'uei[15] himself could contain them.*

When Chin Lao-ta heard the noise they made, he opened the gate to look out, whereupon the whole crowd of beggars, with Scabby at their head, surged inside and threw the house into commotion. Scabby himself hurried to a seat, snatched the choicest of the meats and wines and began to stuff himself, calling meanwhile for the happy couple to come and make their obeisances[16] before their uncle.

So terrified were the assembled graduates that they gave up at once and fled the scene, Mo Chi joining in their retreat. Chin Lao-ta was at his wits' end, and pleaded repeatedly, "My son-in-law is the host today; this is no affair of mine. Come another day when I will buy some wine specially for you and we will have a chat together."

He distributed money among the beggar band, and brought out two jars of fine wine and some live chickens and geese, inviting the beggars to have a banquet of their own over at Scabby's house; but it was late at night before they ceased their rioting and took their leave, and Jade Slave wept in her room from shame and rage.

That night Mo Chi stayed at the house of a friend, returning only when morning came. At the sight of his son-in-law, Chin Lao-ta felt keenly the disgrace of what had happened, and his face filled with shame. Naturally enough, Mo Chi on his part was strongly displeased; but no one was anxious to say a word. Truly,

*When a mute tastes the bitterness of cork-tree
  wood
He must swallow his disgust with his medicine.*

Let us rather tell how Jade Slave, conscious of her family's disrepute and anxious that her husband should make his own name for himself, exhorted[17] him to labor at his books. She grudged neither the cost of the works, classical and recent, which she bought for his use, nor the expense of engaging tutors for learned discussion with him. She provided funds also for the entertaining that would widen her husband's circle of acquaintances. As a result, Mo Chi's learning and reputation made daily advances.

He gained his master's degree at the age of twenty-two, and ultimately his doctorate, and at last the day came when he left the great reception for successful candidates and, black hat, doctor's robes and all, rode back to his father-in-law's house. But as he entered his own ward of the city, a crowd of urchins pressed about him,

---

13. **Yang Hua** (yäng′ hwä′): probably a beggars' song similar to the earlier "Lien-hua lo."

14. **white with chalk:** Beggars sometimes whitened their faces to simulate poverty and hunger.

15. **Chung K'uei** (jŏŏng′ kwä′): a legendary Chinese demon slayer whose image is often posted on festival days to ward off evil spirits.

16. **obeisances** (ō-bā′sən-səz): bows, curtsies, or other body movements that show submission or respect.

17. **exhorted** (ĭg-zôr′tĭd): urged very strongly.

pointing and calling—"Look at the tramp-major's son-in-law! He's an official now!"

From his elevated position Mo Chi heard them, but it was beneath his dignity to do anything about it. He simply had to put up with it; but his correct observance of etiquette on greeting his father-in-law concealed a burning indignation. "I always knew that I should attain these honors," he said to himself, "yet I feared that no noble or distinguished family would take me in as a son-in-law, and so I married the daughter of a tramp-major. Without question, it is a lifelong stain. My sons and daughters will still have a tramp-major for their grandfather, and I shall be passed from one man to the next as a laughing stock! But the thing is done now. What is more, my wife is wise and virtuous; it would be impossible for me to divorce her on any of the seven counts.[18] 'Marry in haste, repent at leisure'—it's a true saying after all!"

His mind seethed with such thoughts, and he was miserable all day long. Jade Slave often questioned him, but received no reply and remained in ignorance of the cause of his displeasure. But what an absurd figure, this Mo Chi! Conscious only of his present eminence, he has forgotten the days of his poverty. His wife's assistance in money and effort are one with the snows of yesteryear,[19] so crooked are the workings of his mind.

Before long, Mo Chi presented himself for appointment and received the post of Census Officer at Wu-wei-chün. His father-in-law provided wine to feast his departure, and this time awe of the new official deterred the beggar band from breaking up the party.

It so happened that the whole journey from Hangchow to Wu-wei-chün was by water, and Mo Chi took his wife with him, boarded a junk[20] and proceeded to his post. After several days their voyage brought them to the eddies and whirlpools below the Colored Stone Cliff,[21] and they tied up to the northern bank. That night the moon shone bright as day. Mo Chi, unable to sleep, rose and dressed and sat in the prow enjoying the moonlight. There was no one about; and as he sat there brooding on his relationship with a tramp-major, an evil notion came into his head. The only way for him to be rid of lifelong disgrace was for his wife to die and a new one to take her place. A plan formed in his mind. He entered the cabin and inveigled[22] Jade Slave into getting up to see the moon in its glory.

Jade Slave was already asleep, but Mo Chi repeatedly urged her to get up, and she did not like to contravene[23] his wishes. She put on her

> The only way for him to be rid of lifelong disgrace was for his wife to die and a new one to take her place.

---

18. **any of the seven counts:** In Chinese tradition, a wife could be divorced for failing to bear a son, adultery, disobedience to her in-laws, nagging, stealing, jealousy, or contracting an evil disease.

19. **are one with the snows of yesteryear:** that is, have melted away; are completely forgotten.

20. **junk:** a Chinese flat-bottomed ship.

21. **Colored Stone Cliff:** a spur of the mountain Niu-chu that projects from the south bank of the Yangtze (yăng′sē′) River.

22. **inveigled** (ĭn-vā′gǝld): convinced by clever or deceitful means; lured.

23. **contravene** (kŏn′trǝ-vēn′): to act in opposition to.

gown and crossed over to the doorway, where she raised her head to look at the moon. Standing thus, she was taken unawares by Mo Chi, who dragged her out on to the prow and pushed her into the river.

Softly he then woke the boatmen and ordered them to get under way at once—extra speed would be handsomely rewarded. The boatmen, puzzled but ignorant, seized pole and flourished oar. Mo Chi waited until the junk had covered three good miles before he moored again and told them that his wife had fallen in the river while gazing at the moon, and that no effort would have availed to save her. With this, he rewarded the boatmen with three ounces of silver to buy wine. The boatmen caught his meaning, but none dared open his mouth. The silly maidservants who had accompanied Jade Slave on board accepted that their mistress had really fallen in the river. They wept for a little while and then left off, and we will say no more of them. There is a verse in evidence of all this:

The name of tramp-major pleases him ill;
Hardened by pride he casts off his mate.
The ties of Heaven are not easily broken;
All he gains is an evil name.

But don't you agree that "there is such a thing as coincidence"? It so happened that the newly-appointed Transport Commissioner for Western Huai, Hsü Te-hou,[24] was also on his way to his post; and his junk moored across from the Colored Stone Cliff just when Mo Chi's boat had disappeared from view. It was the very spot where Mo Chi had pushed his wife into the water. Hsü Te-hou and his lady had opened their window to enjoy the moonlight, and had not yet retired but were taking their ease over a cup of wine. Suddenly they became aware of someone sobbing on the riverbank. It was a woman, from the sound, and her distress could not be ignored.

At once Hsü ordered his boatmen to investigate. It proved indeed to be a woman, alone, sitting on the bank. Hsü made them summon her aboard, and questioned her about herself. The woman was none other than Jade Slave, Madam Chin, the wife of the Census Officer at Wu-wei-chün. What had happened was that when she found herself in the water, her wits all but left her, and she gave herself up for dead. But suddenly she felt something in the river which held up her feet, while the waves washed her close to the bank. Jade Slave struggled ashore; but when she opened her eyes, there was only the empty expanse of the river, and no sign of the Census Officer's junk. It was then that she realized what had happened: "My husband, grown rich, has forgotten his days of hardship. It was his deliberate plan to drown his true wife to pave the way for a more advantageous marriage. And now, though I have my life, where am I to turn for support?"

Bitter reflections of this kind brought forth piteous weeping, and confronted by Hsü's questioning she could hold nothing back, but told the whole story from beginning to end. When she had finished she wept without ceasing. Hsü and his wife in their turn were moved to tears, and Hsü Te-hou tried to comfort her: "You must not grieve so; but if you will agree to become my adopted daughter, we will see what provision can be made."

Hsü had his wife produce a complete change of clothing for the girl and settle her down to rest in the stern cabin.[25] He told his servants to treat her with the respect due to his daughter, and prohibited the boatmen from disclosing anything of the affair. Before long he reached his place of office in Western Huai. Now it so happened that among the places under his juris-

---

24. **Huai** (hwī); **Hsü Te-hou** (shü′də-hou′).
25. **stern cabin:** the cabin at the rear end of a boat.

diction was Wu-wei-chün. He was therefore the superior officer of Mo Chi, who duly appeared with his fellows to greet the new Commissioner. Observing the Census Officer, Hsü sighed that so promising a youth should be capable of so callous an action.

Hsü Te-hou allowed several months to pass, and then he addressed the following words to his staff: "I have a daughter of marriageable age, and possessing both talent and beauty. I am seeking a man fit to be her husband, whom I could take into my family. Does any of you know of such a man?"

All his staff had heard of Mo Chi's bereavement early in life, and all hastened to commend his outstanding ability and to profess his suitability as a son-in-law for the Commissioner. Hsü agreed: "I myself have had this man in mind for some time. But one who has graduated at such a youthful age must cherish high ambitions: I am not at all sure that he would be prepared to enter my family."

"He is of humble origin," the others replied. "It would be the happiest of fates for him to secure your interest, to 'cling as the creeper to the tree of jade'—there can be no doubt of his willingness."

"Since you consider it practicable," said Hsü, "I should like you to approach the Census Officer. But to discover how he reacts, say that this plan is of your own making: it might hinder matters if you disclose my interest."

They accepted the commission and made their approach to Mo Chi, requesting that they should act as go-betweens. Now to rise in society was precisely Mo Chi's intention; moreover, a matrimonial alliance with one's superior officer was not a thing to be had for the asking. Delighted, he replied, "I must rely entirely on you to accomplish this; nor shall I be slow in the material expression of my gratitude."

"You may leave it to us," they said; and thereupon they reported back to Hsü.

But Hsü demurred: "The Census Officer may be willing to marry her," said he, "but the fact is that my wife and I have doted on our daughter and have brought her up to expect the tenderest consideration. It is for this reason that we wish her to remain in her own home after marriage. But I suspect that the Census Officer, in the impatience of youth, might prove insufficiently tolerant; and if the slightest discord should arise, it would be most painful to my wife and myself. He must be prepared to be patient in all things, before I can accept him into my family."

They bore these words to Mo Chi, who accepted every condition.

The Census Officer's present circumstances were very different from those of his student days. He signified acceptance of the betrothal by sending fine silks and gold ornaments on the most ample scale. An auspicious date was selected, and Mo Chi itched in his very bones as he awaited the day when he should become the son-in-law of the Transport Commissioner.

But let us rather tell how Hsü Te-hou gave his wife instructions to prepare Jade Slave for her marriage. "Your stepfather," Mrs. Hsü said to her, "moved by pity for you in widowhood, wishes to invite a young man who has gained his doctorate to become your husband and enter our family. You must not refuse him."

But Jade Slave replied, "Though of humble family, I am aware of the rules of conduct. When Mo Chi became my husband I vowed to remain faithful to him all my life. However cruel and lawless he may have been, however shamefully he may have rejected the companion of his poverty, I shall fulfill my obligations. On no account will I forsake the true virtue of womanhood by remarrying."

With these words her tears fell like rain. Mrs. Hsü, convinced of her sincerity, decided to tell her the truth, and said, "The young graduate of whom my husband spoke is none other than Mo Chi himself. Appalled by his mean action, and anxious to see you reunited with him, my husband passed you off as his own daughter, and told the members of his staff that he was seeking a son-in-law who would enter our family. He made them approach Mo Chi, who was delighted by the proposal. He is to come to us this night; but when he enters your room, this is what you must do to get your own back. . . ."

As she disclosed her plan, Jade Slave dried her tears. She remade her face and changed her costume, and made preparations for the coming ceremony.

With evening, there duly appeared the Census Officer Mo Chi, all complete with mandarin's hat and girdle:[26] he was dressed in red brocade and had gold ornaments in his cap, under him was a fine steed with decorated saddle, and before him marched two bands of drummers and musicians. His colleagues were there in force to see him married, and the whole procession was cheered the length of the route. Indeed,

To the roll and clang of music the white steed
    advances,
But what a curious person, this fine upstand-
    ing groom:
Delighted with his change of families, beggar
    for man of rank,
For memories of the Colored Stone Cliff his
    glad heart has no room.

That night the official residence of the Transport Commissioner was festooned with flowers and carpeted, and to the playing of pipe and drum all awaited the arrival of the bridegroom. As the Census Officer rode up to the gate and dismounted, Hsü Te-hou came out to receive him, and then the accompanying junior officers took their leave. Mo Chi walked straight through to the private apartments, where the bride was brought out to him, veiled in red and supported by a maidservant on either side. From beyond the threshold the master of ceremonies took them through the ritual. The happy pair made obeisances to heaven and earth and to the parents of the bride; and when the ceremonial observances were over, they were escorted into the nuptial chamber for the wedding feast. By this time Mo Chi was in a state of indescribable bliss, his soul somewhere above the clouds. Head erect, triumphant, he entered the nuptial chamber.

But no sooner had he passed the doorway than from positions of concealment on either

26. **mandarin's hat and girdle:** a distinctive hat and belt indicating that the wearer is a high government official.

side there suddenly emerged seven or eight young maids and old nannies, each one armed with a light or heavy bamboo. Mercilessly they began to beat him. Off came his silk hat; blows fell like rain on his shoulders; he yelled perpetually, but try as he might he could not get out of the way.

Under the beating the Census Officer collapsed, to lie in a terrified heap on the floor, calling on his parents-in-law to save him. Then he heard, from within the room itself, a gentle command issued in the softest of voices: "Beat him no more, our hardhearted young gentleman, but bring him before me."

At last the beating stopped, and the maids and nannies, tugging at his ears and dragging at his arms like the six senses tormenting Amida Buddha in the parable,[27] hauled him, his feet barely touching the ground, before the presence of the bride. "What is the nature of my offense?" the Census Officer was mumbling; but when he opened his eyes, there above him, correct and upright in the brilliance of the candlelight, was seated the bride—who was none other than his former wife, Jade Slave, Madam Chin.

Now Mo Chi's mind reeled, and he bawled, "It's a ghost! It's a ghost!" All began to laugh, until Hsü Te-hou came in from outside and addressed him: "Do not be alarmed, my boy: this is no ghost, but my adopted daughter, who came to me below the Colored Stone Cliff."

Mo Chi's heart ceased its pounding. He fell to his knees and folded his hands in supplication. "I, Mo Chi, confess my crime," he said. "I only beg your forgiveness."

"This is no affair of mine," replied Hsü, "unless my daughter has something to say. . . ."

Jade Slave spat in Mo Chi's face and cursed him: "Cruel wretch! Did you never think of the words of Sung Hung?[28] 'Do not exclude from

your mind the friends of your poverty, nor from your house the wife of your youth.' It was empty-handed that you first came into my family, and thanks to our money that you were able to study and enter society, to make your name and enjoy your present good fortune. For my part, I looked forward to the day when I should share in your glory. But you—forgetful of the favors you had received, oblivious of our early love, you repaid good with evil and threw me into the river to drown. Heaven took pity on me and sent me a savior, whose adopted daughter I became. But if I had ended my days on the riverbed, and you had taken a new wife—how could your heart have been so callous? And now, how can I so demean myself as to rejoin you?"

Her speech ended in tears and loud wails, and "Cruel, cruel!" she continued to cry. Mo Chi's whole face expressed his shame. He could find no words, but pleaded for forgiveness by kow-towing[29] before her. Hsü Te-hou, satisfied with her demonstration of anger, raised Mo Chi to his feet and admonished Jade Slave in the following words: "Calm your anger, my child. Your husband has now repented his crime, and we may be sure that he will never again treat you ill. Although in fact your marriage took place some years ago, so far as my family is concerned you are newly wed; in all things, therefore, show consideration to me, and let an end be made here and now to recriminations."[30] Turning to Mo Chi, he said, "My son, your crime is upon your

---

27. **six senses tormenting Amida Buddha in the parable:** sight, hearing, smell, taste, touch, and thought, tormenting a godlike being that is worshipped in Buddhism.

28. **Sung Hung** (sŏong′ hŏong′): Chinese minister who in A.D. 26 refused to leave his lowborn wife after being elevated to the nobility, even though the emperor told him to marry a princess.

29. **kowtowing** (kou-tou′ĭng): kneeling and touching the forehead to the ground as a sign of respect.

30. **recriminations** (rĭ-krĭm′ə-nā′shənz): countercharges; accusations made in return.

own head; lay no blame on others. Tonight I ask you only to show tolerance. I will send your mother-in-law to make peace between you."

He left the room, and shortly his wife came in to them. Much mediation was required from her before the two were finally brought into accord.

On the following day Hsü Te-hou gave a banquet for his new son-in-law, during which he returned all the betrothal gifts, the fine silks and gold ornaments, saying to Mo Chi, "One bride may not receive two sets of presents. You took such things as these to the Chin family on the previous occasion; I cannot accept them all over again now." Mo Chi lowered his head and said nothing, and Hsü went on: "I believe it was your dislike of the lowly status of your father-in-law which put an end to your love and almost to your marriage. What do you think now of my own position? I am only afraid that the rank I hold may still be too low for your aspirations."

Mo Chi's face flushed crimson, and he was obliged to retire a few steps and acknowledge his errors. There is a verse to bear witness:

Full of fond hopes of bettering himself by
*   marriage,*
Amazed to discover his bride to be his wife;
A beating, a cursing, an overwhelming shame:
Was it really worth it for a change of in-laws?

From this time on, Mo Chi and Jade Slave lived together twice as amicably as before. Hsü Te-hou and his wife treated Jade Slave as their own daughter and Mo Chi as their proper son-in-law, and Jade Slave behaved towards them exactly as though they were her own parents. Even the heart of Mo Chi was touched, so that he received Chin Lao-ta, the tramp-major, into his official residence and cared for him to the end of his days. And when in the fullness of time Hsü Te-hou and his wife died, Jade Slave, Madam Chin, wore the heaviest mourning of coarse linen for each of them in recompense for their kindness to her; and generations of descendants of Mo and Hsü regarded each other as cousins and never failed in friendship. A verse concludes:

Sung Hung remained faithful and was
*   praised for his virtue;*
Huang Yün[31] divorced his wife and was
*   reviled for lack of feeling.*
Observe the case of Mo Chi, remarrying
*   his wife:*
A marriage is predestined:[32] no objection
*   can prevail.* ❖

31. **Huang Yün** (hwäng′ yün′): a famous figure of third-century China who left his wife in the hopes of marrying a noblewoman.
32. **predestined** (prē-děs′tǐnd): determined in advance by fate or divine will.

WRITING FROM EXPERIENCE

WRITING TO EXPLAIN

As Unit Three, "In the Name of Love," shows, the ties that bind couples and families together vary from culture to culture and change over time within cultures. As you learn about different families and different ways of life, you will often find yourself comparing cultures so that you will better understand other people and the ways they behave.

GUIDED ASSIGNMENT
Write a Compare-and-Contrast Essay In this lesson you will learn how to compare and contrast aspects of two or more cultures or historical periods that interest you.

❶ Read the Articles

Read the articles on these pages. What aspect or era of a country's culture does each discuss? What interests or surprises you about each article? What do you learn from the illustrations?

❷ Think About Topics

Using these articles as starting points, list some aspects of culture that might be interesting to explore across different countries or time periods. Consider such topics as marriages, extended families, schools, or death and mourning.

- You may want to learn more about a custom or practice you have read about.
- You may want to explore a culture that is part of your family's history.

Think about how you might compare unfamiliar practices or customs with those that are familiar. Then discuss your ideas for comparison essays in a group.

My sister wants a traditional Hindu ceremony. Does she realize how different that will be?

Hindu Rites of Passage

Hindus consider marriage the most important rite of passage. In India, parents arrange most marriages, which are viewed as family alliances. They look for similar family traditions, languages, and backgrounds. On the wedding day the bride's parents greet the groom and present gifts. Before the ceremony, guests sing songs and throw rice. During the ceremony the couple, wearing special clothes, exchange garlands and face each other over a sacred fire. They pour *ghee* (melted butter) into the fire as they pray for healthy children, a long life, and wealth and as priests chant mantras.

**Excerpt from
Social Studies Text**

Folk and Festival Costumes of the World

Wedding Costume
TURKEY

**Pictorial Reference
How can illustrations provide insights into a culture?**

Magazine Article

1940s–1950s
Dating DO's & DON'Ts

DO be fascinated by the same subjects he is. Say things like, "I see you have your football letter. It looks wonderful."

DON'T keep him waiting. Be ready when he arrives and introduce him with obvious pleasure to your parents.

1980s–1990s
Dating DO's & DON'Ts

DO stop looking to guys as your only source of excitement and self-esteem. Then you will graduate from flings to more lasting love.

DON'T go out with a guy who verbally or physically abuses you.

Rebecca Barry
from *Seventeen*

Custom of the Country

When I was in India last spring I went to visit my cousin, a quiet and thoughtful woman with a teenage daughter, who lives in the frenetic, modern, Westernized, commerce-conscious city of Bombay. We had a peaceful cup of tea, countless little delicacies both sweet and salty, which she had gone to some pains to prepare, and a long, chatty, family-gossip kind of conversation in which we exchanged our news. The particular item that occupied her mind at the time was that her daughter was of an age to get married and that she had to do something about it.

"But the girl is so *young,*" I said, talking like a foreigner.

"Old enough to be betrothed," she replied with a puzzled severity. "She's nearly eighteen."

Meekly, I nodded acceptance of her point of view, and asked whether there was someone the girl was particularly keen on. Was she in love? Who was the young man? (It always takes me a little time to get readjusted to India, and I had forgotten that arranged marriages are a very ordinary matter.)

My cousin looked as though she thought I had lost my reason. "Love?" she said in amazement. "A young man?" With quiet dignity she remarked, "Naturally there are several who seek her hand. This is a good family. Of course there would be several. They have all sent their horoscopes in the proper way."

"Yes, yes," I said quickly, "yes, *of course.*" Thinking back rapidly to my grandmother and her ways I asked, as casually as I could, "Do any of the horoscopes match?"

"Match!" she repeated scornfully. "We are a modern family. Certainly we aren't as old-fashioned as *that!*"

Santha Rama Rau
from *Travel Holiday,* June 1991

Amazing! Are marriages still arranged by parents in India?

Magazine Article

❸ Choose Your Topic

Examine your list. Which customs do you think would be most similar or most different across cultures or across time? Which topic interests you the most? Freewrite about the topic you've chosen, predicting what you might find as you begin your research.

LASERLINKS
• *WRITING SPRINGBOARD*

WRITING COACH

Exploring Information

Making Decisions Your discussion and freewriting so far have probably helped you zero in on a culture or time period you want to know more about. These pages will help you to narrow your topic and to collect and organize information about it.

1 Focus Your Exploration

You will find it easier to explore your topic if you narrow it down. For example, don't try to compare ceremonies in India with ceremonies in the United States. Instead, perhaps you could compare a traditional Hindu wedding ceremony with a typical wedding in the United States.

Find a reason to write. Could a comparison help you make a decision? solve a problem? understand an unfamiliar subject?

Student's Research Materials

2 Collect Information

As you look for information on your topic, remember that you will want to explain the ideas behind customs or rituals, not just the customs themselves.

- Visit museums or cultural centers for information about cultures you intend to compare.
- Listen to music from these cultures, watch movies or videotapes; talk to classmates or other people who are familiar with these cultures.
- Use the SkillBuilder on the next page and the Multimedia Handbook to help you access library sources and information from on-line services.

502

❸ Organize Information

Use a graphic organizer to keep track of information you find.

- A Venn diagram can help you think about similarities and differences. The example below shows how one student organized his thoughts about different wedding customs.
- After organizing information, you may decide that the topics you chose to compare have too few features in common to make an interesting essay.

Student's Venn Diagram

Western wedding

- Bride and groom have more to do with arranging wedding.
- They exchange vows & rings.
- They share wedding cake at reception.
- After wedding they go away by themselves.

Family & friends are important.
Guests throw rice.
Bride leaves family's home.

Hindu wedding

- Marriages are seen as alliances between families and are usually arranged.
- Bride and groom exchange garlands and take seven steps around sacred fire.
- Certain foods are part of ceremony.
- After wedding bride goes to live in husband's parents' home.

❹ Define Your Audience

Now that you have reviewed information on your topic, you probably have some ideas about who your audience is and how you could share your comparison with them.

- You may have a special audience for your comparison—for example, the families participating in a wedding.
- You may want to write your comparison as a newspaper or magazine article or as a photo essay for a general audience.
- You may want to add music and pictures to your information and make a multimedia presentation.

DRAFTING

Getting Your Ideas Down

Putting Ideas into Words Review any graphic organizers you made during prewriting. They can help you to think about the information you gathered as well as help you to organize your draft.

1 Try a Rough Draft

As you write your rough draft, remember to explain the history or meaning behind the customs you describe as well as the customs themselves.

The Writing Coach can help you as you draft.

Student's Rough Draft

Wedding Comparison

My Rough Draft

Most Hindu weddings in India are arranged by parents, and, even today, it is important that a bride and groom be of the same background. My parents told me that, in India, people who marry outside their caste, or position in society, are looked upon with disfavor. A wedding ceremony is thought of as being an alliance between two families.

Here, young people like my sister choose their marriage partners themselves, and it would be thought snobbish or undemocratic to say that a marriage was unsuitable because the bride and groom had different backgrounds. Western parents, even mine, do not interfere with their children's choice of marriage partners, and after the wedding may have very little to do with their children's in-laws.

A Hindu wedding day begins with the bride's parents welcoming the groom and formally giving their daughter in marriage to him. The groom and his father receive the bride into their family.

Some Western brides are "given away" by their fathers, or by both parents, but many have chosen to do away with this part of the wedding.

A Hindu ceremony includes many symbolic actions. Western ceremonies have less symbolism. Exchanging rings and vows are two symbolic rituals.

My Comments
My Rough Draft

Is this irrelevant? Instead, I need an introduction to explain what I'm comparing and why.

Perhaps some of this should go in my conclusion. Should I try to explain advantages of arranged marriages?

Should I say all I have to say about a Hindu wedding and then mention things that are similar about a Western wedding?

I need to describe Hindu rituals here.

❷ Organize Your Ideas

Think about how you can best order the information and ideas. The patterns in the Writing Handbook will show you different ways. Either of the patterns below could be used to organize the student writer's draft.

COMPARE-AND-CONTRAST PATTERNS

Subject-by-Subject

1. Western Wedding
   - *Planning*
   - *Ceremony*
   - *Reception*

2. Hindu Wedding
   - *Planning*
   - *Ceremony*
   - *Reception*

Feature-by-Feature

1. Planning
   - *Western Wedding*
   - *Hindu Wedding*

2. Ceremony
   - *Western Wedding*
   - *Hindu Wedding*

3. Reception
   - *Western Wedding*
   - *Hindu Wedding*

❸ Rework and Share

With your rough draft in front of you and your organizational structure in mind, write your second draft.

- Consider writing an introduction to establish what you will compare or to explain your purpose.
- Consider adding a conclusion to pull together what you learned.
- The SkillBuilder on the right will help you use parallel sentence structures to emphasize similarities and differences.

 PEER RESPONSE

A peer reviewer can help identify strengths and weaknesses of your draft. Ask him or her questions like the following:

- Which specific points of comparison were most interesting to you? Which were least interesting?
- Where have I strayed from my topic?
- What additional information might support my conclusion?

SkillBuilder

WRITER'S CRAFT

Using Parallel Structure
One way to make comparisons clear to your readers is to use parallel structures for the ideas you are comparing. Using similar grammatical structures or sentence patterns calls attention to similarities or differences. Compare these two sets of sentences:

The wedding cake serves as part of a modern ritual. Another use for it is that people eat it for dessert.

The wedding cake is part of modern ritual. It is also a dessert.

In the second set, the sentences are grammatically parallel.

APPLYING WHAT YOU'VE LEARNED
Rewrite the following sentences, using similar sentence patterns.

The groom's family plays a major role in planning a Hindu wedding. A minor role is played by the groom's family in planning a Western wedding.

RETHINK & EVALUATE

Preparing to Revise

1. How can you improve the organization of your draft?
2. How can you use parallel structures to make similarities and differences more clear?
3. How can you pull your generalizations together in a conclusion?

Finishing Your Essay

Making Final Changes Once you have worked at improving your draft, read it again to make sure that comparisons will be clear to your readers and that paragraphs are well developed. If you've decided to publish your essay in a special format, you may want to make additional changes to the text or to choose music or visual aids to accompany the information in your essay.

A Comparison of Hindu and Western Weddings

When my sister became engaged, she decided she wanted to include customs and rituals from her Hindu heritage as well as Western customs. She asked us all to help her do some research. To our surprise, we found that although Hindu weddings are very different from Western weddings, the meaning behind some Western customs is similar to the meaning behind some Hindu rituals.

Even today, most marriages in India are arranged by parents and are thought of as alliances between families. The ceremony is held in the bride's home and begins after the groom is welcomed by the bride's parents and is formally given their daughter. The groom's parents give the bride gifts and welcome her into their family.

Here, men and women usually choose their marriage partners without parental advice or interference. Some Western brides are "given away" by their fathers, or by both parents, but many couples have chosen to do away with this particular wedding tradition.

The Hindu ceremony includes many symbolic actions. At the beginning the couple stands as the guests chant blessings and throw rice at the couple. The bride and groom exchange garlands. Then a sacred fire is lit, and the couple pour clarified butter on it as they pray for healthy children, long life, and wealth. The couple takes seven paces around the fire to symbolize the following: a long married life, power, prosperity, happiness, children, enjoyment of seasonal pleasures, and a lifelong friendship.

Western ceremonies also include symbolism. Exchanging rings and vows are two symbolic rituals. Lighting a unity candle is another.

❶ Revise and Edit

Read your draft again slowly and carefully. Mark parts you want to revise.

- Use peer comments and the Standards for Evaluation as you reorganize your essay.
- Make sure your introduction and conclusion help to accomplish your purpose.
- Use the Editing Checklist and the SkillBuilder on the next page to make sure that comparisons are made correctly.

Student's Final Draft
What information does the introduction provide?

Which of the two types of organization did the writer use?

GRAMMAR FROM WRITING

Avoiding Double Comparisons

When making comparisons, be careful to avoid double comparisons. A double comparison is one that uses both an adjective ending in *-er* or *-est* and *more* or *most*. Look at these examples:

Incorrect: *A bride's bouquet is more fancier than a bridesmaid's.*

Correct: *A bride's bouquet is fancier than a bridesmaid's.*

GRAMMAR HANDBOOK

For more information on writing correct comparisons, see page 1077 of the Grammar Handbook.

Editing Checklist Use these tips as you revise.

- Is spelling correct?
- Is punctuation used correctly?
- Are comparisons written correctly?

❷ Share Your Work

You may decide to adapt the information in your essay for a multimedia presentation including music, text, and pictures. (For help, see the Multimedia Handbook on page 1055.) The revisions you make will depend on the audience with whom you want to share your ideas.

PUBLISHING IDEAS

- A newspaper story could include photographs and charts.
- A photo essay could make your points dramatically.
- Your class could publish a collection of essays and share them with social studies classes at a junior high school.

Standards for Evaluation

A compare-and-contrast essay
- identifies clearly the things being compared
- includes specific, relevant details
- follows a clear plan of organization
- concludes with generalizations that are supported by information in the essay

REFLECT & ASSESS

Evaluating the Experience

1. What did you learn by writing a compare-and-contrast essay?
2. How can you use compare-and-contrast organizational patterns in other writing situations?

📁 **PORTFOLIO** What would you do differently if you were writing your compare-and-contrast essay? Add your thoughts to your portfolio.

REFLECT & ASSESS

UNIT THREE: IN THE NAME OF LOVE

*Have the selections in this unit changed your opinions about love
or deepened your understanding of its effects? What new things
have you learned as a reader and writer? Explore these questions
by completing one or more of the options in each of
the following sections.*

REFLECTING ON THEME

OPTION 1 **Comparing Love's Emotions** Review the activity on page 352, which asked you to create a bar graph identifying the different feelings that you have experienced in a love relationship. Then review the selections in the unit to identify which one comes closest to your own experience of love; also identify the selection that seemed furthest removed from your experience. Write a note explaining why you have chosen those two selections instead of other selections in the unit. Consider how the selections that you have chosen affect your own understanding of love.

OPTION 2 **Portraying Love's Agony and Ecstasy** As you saw in this unit, love can lead people to great happiness or to the depths of misery. Consider which selections in the unit depict the agony of love, which portray its ecstasy, and which, if any, capture both extremes. Then create a collage with images and words that suggest your own views about the

extremes of love. Your images may be based on ones described in the selections, as well as from your own experience. Share your collage with a small group of classmates. Explain how your collage represents your views, and discuss whether your opinions of love were changed by your readings.

Self-Assessment: Put together your reflections about love by creating two lists, one titled What Love Is *and one titled* What Love Is Not. *Each list may comprise words or phrases, names of characters from the selections, or brief descriptions of people and events from your own life. In other words, you may include virtually anything in your lists as long as it represents your own views about the nature of love. Underline those items on your lists that are inspired by your readings in this unit.*

REVIEWING LITERARY CONCEPTS

OPTION 1 **Understanding Metaphor and Mood**
After reviewing the definition of *metaphor* on page 373, search through the selections in this unit to find at least five metaphors that you find interesting or memorable. Create a chart like the one shown. For each metaphor, identify the two things being compared and tell what mood is evoked by the metaphor. Compare your chart with those created by other students.

Selection	Metaphor	Things Compared	Mood Evoked
"Tonight I Can Write . . ."	"The night is shattered and she is not with me."	The night is being compared with something that can be broken, such as a piece of fine china or a fragile glass.	sadness; an overwhelming sense of loss

`OPTION 2` **Appreciating the Sonnet** Review the information on page 376 about the sonnet. Then work with a partner to create a poster, pamphlet, or multimedia display about the sonnet. Include information about its history, offer your own definitions of sonnet and related terms, and present a variety of sonnets drawn from different centuries and countries. You may wish to include decorative art and, if possible, present recordings of sonnet readings.

Self-Assessment: On a sheet of paper, copy down the following list of terms from this unit, all of which are related to poetry. Create a test to measure students' understanding of these terms. One section of your test might require that students

match terms with their definitions. Another section might include poems or excerpts of poems, along with questions focused on how the terms can be applied to the poetry. Take a test created by one of your classmates, and note any terms that give you trouble. Work with the classmate to clarify the meaning of these terms.

metaphor	*couplet*
sonnet	*rhythm*
sonnet sequence	*meter*
rhyme scheme	*repetition*
English sonnet	*rhyme*
quatrain	

PORTFOLIO BUILDING

- **QuickWrites** Many of the QuickWrites assignments in this unit ask for creative responses to the selections. These responses include the writing of poems, scripts, and monologues. Review the creative assignments that you completed, and pick out one or two pieces that you feel contain the best use of descriptive language. Write a note that explains your opinion of those pieces. If you feel that the pieces are worthy of your portfolio, add the note and the pieces to your portfolio.

- **Writing About Literature** By now you've written your own poem as a response to a poem in this unit. Write a note about your poem to include in your portfolio. How well does your poem stand on its own? What would you change, if anything? What about this experience can you bring to your reading of other poems?

- **Writing from Experience** Earlier in this unit you wrote a comparison-contrast essay. As you review your essay, what questions do you have about it, if any? Would you do anything differently if you were to rewrite it? Note one or two other potential subjects for a comparison-contrast essay.

- **Personal Choice** Reflect upon the various writing assignments and other activities that you have worked on during the course of this unit, including

work that you may have done on your own. You may also want to review any evaluations or peer responses that you received about your work. Which activity or piece of writing proved the most difficult? Write a note explaining the difficulty and what you learned as a result.

Self-Assessment: Consider all the pieces that you now have in your portfolio. Have you changed your opinion about the quality of any of the pieces? Is there some item that you feel no longer represents your ability or interests? You may wish to weed out some pieces or to replace them.

SETTING GOALS

You probably have a good idea of your likes and dislikes in literature and writing, as well as your strengths and weaknesses. Set a new challenge for yourself to turn a weakness into a strength or to come to a new appreciation of certain genres of literature. For example, if you have struggled with poetry in the past, set a goal to improve in that area.

MOMENTS OF
TRUTH

Truth resides in every human heart, and one has to search for it there.

Mohandas K. Gandhi
Indian nationalist and spiritual leader
1869–1948

The Flooded Field (1992),
Claire B. Cotts.
Courtesy of the artist.

UNEXPECTED REALIZATIONS

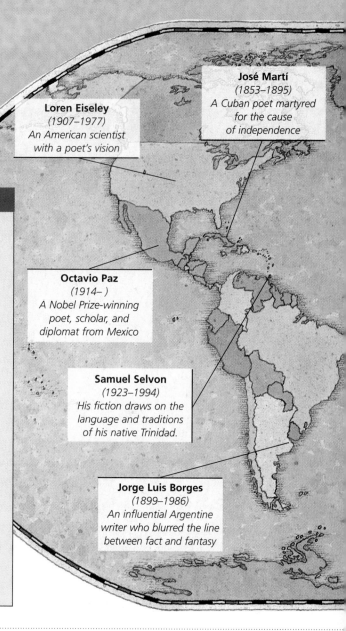

José Martí
(1853–1895)
*A Cuban poet martyred
for the cause
of independence*

Loren Eiseley
(1907–1977)
*An American scientist
with a poet's vision*

Octavio Paz
(1914–)
*A Nobel Prize-winning
poet, scholar, and
diplomat from Mexico*

Samuel Selvon
(1923–1994)
*His fiction draws on the
language and traditions
of his native Trinidad.*

Jorge Luis Borges
(1899–1986)
*An influential Argentine
writer who blurred the line
between fact and fantasy*

REFLECTING ON THEME

Oliver Wendell Holmes, a poet and U.S. Supreme Court justice, once said, "A moment's insight is sometimes worth a life's experience." All of us have probably had moments when a flash of insight illuminated the truth about a situation, another person, or ourselves. Such insights often catch us by surprise, overturning our expectations and assumptions. In this part of Unit Four, you will read about characters who come to unexpected realizations about the truth. The results, as you will see, range from the humorous to the tragic.

What Do You Think? In your notebook, describe a time when a moment of insight altered your perception of a situation, another person, or yourself. How did the insight affect you, and what were its consequences?

Jorge Luis Borges	**The Meeting** *Two men, two knives*	514
Agatha Christie	**The Witness for the Prosecution** *Did he really murder the woman?*	523
Anita Desai	**Games at Twilight** *A young boy dreams of victory.*	545
Octavio Paz	**The Street / La Calle** *Who—or what—is following him?*	556
Juan Ramón Jiménez	**I Am Not I / Yo No Soy Yo** *Seeing two selves*	556

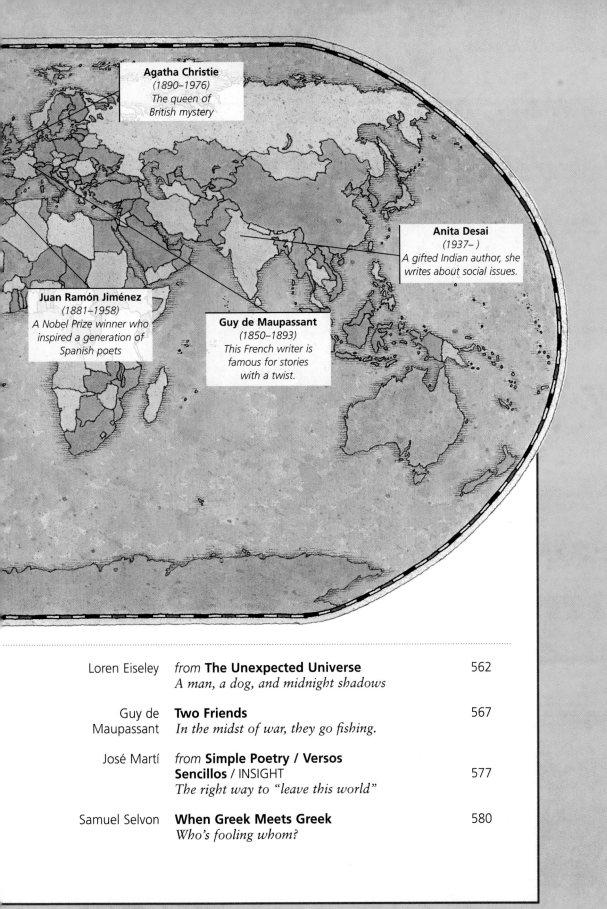

Agatha Christie
(1890–1976)
The queen of
British mystery

Anita Desai
(1937–)
A gifted Indian author, she
writes about social issues.

Juan Ramón Jiménez
(1881–1958)
A Nobel Prize winner who
inspired a generation of
Spanish poets

Guy de Maupassant
(1850–1893)
This French writer is
famous for stories
with a twist.

PREVIEWING

FICTION

The Meeting

Jorge Luis Borges (hôr'hĕ loo-ēs' bôr'hĕs) **Argentina**

PERSONAL CONNECTION

Recall a time when you witnessed a fight that began with words and moved on to physical violence, or at least to the threat of violence. What caused the fight? What pushed the participants over the edge? Describe the incident and its causes in your notebook, and explain how you felt about witnessing such a conflict.

CULTURAL CONNECTION

In "The Meeting," the narrator recalls a violent conflict that he witnessed in his youth. This tale, like many stories by Jorge Luis Borges, draws upon the history and culture of the author's native Argentina.

Though the story takes place in the early 20th century, it makes reference to the gauchos of Argentina's frontier past. The gauchos, like the cowboys in the Old West in the United States, were wandering cattlemen known for their skillful horsemanship, distinctive clothes, and fighting abilities. Eventually, gauchos were romanticized and became folk heroes. Three gauchos mentioned in this story, Juan Moreira, Martín Fierro, and Segundo Sombra, are still celebrated today.

The duels fought by gauchos were often the result of insults to honor; typically, the knife was the weapon of choice. Among Argentina's upper classes, duels of honor were fought with the sword, a weapon regarded as more appropriate to polite society. In both cases, spectators did not interfere, and the killing of an opponent in a duel was considered a less serious offense than murder.

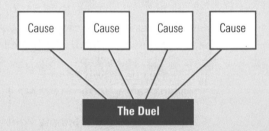

Gaucho in Argentina. Copyright ©
Carlos Goldin / DDB Stock Photo.

READING CONNECTION

Identifying Causes In "The Meeting," an argument spins out of control and leads to a duel. As you read, identify the various explanations that are offered as causes of the conflict. Fill in a chart, like the one below, to keep track of the possible causes. Feel free to add to your chart more boxes than those shown here.

Causes of the Duel

| Cause | Cause | Cause | Cause |

The Duel

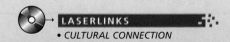

LASERLINKS
• CULTURAL CONNECTION

514

Jorge Luis Borges

The Meeting

Anyone leafing his way through the morning paper does so either to escape his surroundings or to provide himself with small talk for later in the day, so it is not to be wondered at that no one any longer remembers—or else remembers as in a dream—the famous and once widely discussed case of Maneco Uriarte and of Duncan. The event took place, furthermore, back around 1910, the year of the comet[1] and the Centennial,[2] and since then we have had and have lost so many things. Both protagonists[3] are now dead; those who witnessed the episode solemnly swore silence. I, too, raised my hand for the oath, feeling the importance of the ritual with all the romantic seriousness of my nine or ten years. I do not know whether the others noticed that I had given my word; I do not know whether they kept theirs. Anyway, here is the story, with all the inevitable variations brought about by time and by good or bad writing.

My cousin Lafinur took me to a barbecue that evening at a country house called The Laurels, which belonged to some friends of his. I cannot fix its exact location; let us take any of those suburban towns lying just to the north, shaded and quiet, that slope down to the river and that have nothing in common with sprawling Buenos Aires[4] and its surrounding prairie. The journey by train lasted long enough to seem endless to me, but time for children—as is well known—flows slowly. It was already dark when we passed through the villa's main gate. Here, I felt, were all the ancient, elemental things: the smell of meat cooking golden brown, the trees, the dogs, the kindling wood, and the fire that brings men together.

The guests numbered about a dozen; all were grown-ups. The eldest, I learned later, was not yet thirty. They were also—this I was soon to find out—well versed in matters about which I am still somewhat backward: race horses, the right tailors, motorcars, and notoriously expensive women. No one ruffled my shyness; no one paid any attention to me. The lamb, slowly and skillfully prepared by one of the hired men, kept

---

1. **the comet:** Halley's comet, which appears about every 76 years, appeared in 1910.
2. **the Centennial:** the hundred-year anniversary of Argentina's independence.
3. **protagonists:** persons playing leading or active parts.
4. **Buenos Aires:** capital and largest city of Argentina.

WORDS TO KNOW

versed (vûrst) *adj.* acquainted by experience and study; knowledgeable or skilled
verse *v.*

Niño en azul [Boy in blue] (1928), Rufino Tamayo. Oil on canvas, 75 cm × 63.8 cm, reproduction authorized by The Foundation of Olga and Rufino Tamayo, A.C.

us a long time in the big dining room. The dates of vintages[5] were argued back and forth. There was a guitar; my cousin, if I remember correctly, sang a couple of Elías Regules' ballads about gauchos in the back country of Uruguay and some verses in dialect, in the incipient *lunfardo*[6] of those days, about a knife fight in a brothel[7] on Junín Street. Coffee and Havana cigars were brought in. Not a word about getting back. I felt (in the words of the poet Lugones[8]) the fear of what is suddenly too late. I dared not look at the clock. In order to disguise my boyish loneliness among grown-ups, I put away—not really liking it—a glass or two of wine. Uriarte, in a loud voice, proposed to Duncan a two-handed game of poker. Someone objected that that kind of play made for a poor game and suggested a hand of four. Duncan agreed, but Uriarte, with a stubbornness that I did not understand and that I did not try to understand, insisted on the first scheme. Outside of *truco*—a game whose real aim is to pass time with mischief and verses—and of the modest mazes of solitaire, I never enjoyed cards. I slipped away without anyone's noticing. A rambling old house, unfamiliar and dark (only in the dining room was there light), means more to a boy than a new country means to a traveler. Step by step, I explored the rooms; I recall a billiard room, a long gallery with rectangular and diamond-shaped panes, a couple of rocking chairs, and a window from which you could just make out a summerhouse. In the darkness I lost my way; the owner of the house, whose name, as I recall after all these years, may have been Acevedo or Acebal, finally came across me somehow. Out of kindness or perhaps out of a collector's vanity, he led me to a display cabinet. On lighting a lamp, I saw the glint of steel. It was a collection of knives that had once been in the hands of famous fighters. He told me that he had a bit of land somewhere to the north around Pergamino, and that he had been picking up these things on his travels back and forth across the province.[9] He opened the cabinet, and without looking at what was written on the tags, he began giving me accounts of each item; they were more or less the same except for dates and place names. I asked him whether among the weapons he might have the dagger of Juan Moreira, who was in that day the archetype of the gaucho, as later Martín Fierro and Don[10] Segundo Sombra would be. He had to confess that he hadn't but that he could show me one like it, with a U-shaped crosspiece in the hilt. He was interrupted by the sound of angry voices. At once he shut the cabinet and turned to leave; I followed him.

Uriarte was shouting that his opponent had tried to cheat him. All the others stood around the two players. Duncan, I remember, was a taller man than the rest of the company, and was well built, though somewhat round-shouldered; his face was expressionless, and his hair was so light it was almost white. Maneco Uriarte was nervous, dark, with perhaps a touch of Indian blood, and wore a skimpy, petulant moustache. It was obvious that everybody was drunk; I do not know whether there were two or three emptied bottles on the floor or whether an excess of movies suggests this false memory to me. Uriarte's insults did not let up; at first sharp, they now grew obscene. Duncan appeared not to hear, but finally, as though weary, he got up and

---

5. **vintages:** wines of a particular type, region, and year, and usually of superior quality.

6. *lunfardo* (lo͞on-fär′dô) *South American Spanish*: Argentinean gangster slang, used especially in Buenos Aires.

7. **brothel:** house of prostitution.

8. **Lugones:** Leopoldo Lugones, Argentina's most famous poet.

9. **province:** governmental district of Argentina, similar to a state.

10. **Don** (dôn) *Spanish*: title of respect, similar to *Mr.* or *Sir.*

WORDS TO KNOW | **incipient** (ĭn-sĭp′ē-ənt) *adj.* just beginning to exist or become noticeable
archetype (är′kĭ-tīp′) *n.* a perfect example of a type or group

threw a punch. From the floor, Uriarte snarled that he was not going to take this outrage, and he challenged Duncan to fight.

Duncan said no, and added, as though to explain, "The trouble is I'm afraid of you."

Everybody howled with laughter.

Uriarte, picking himself up, answered, "I'm going to have it out with you, and right now."

Someone—may he be forgiven for it—remarked that weapons were not lacking.

PREDICT

How will the conflict between Uriarte and Duncan be resolved?

I do not know who went and opened the glass cabinet. Maneco Uriarte picked out the showiest and longest dagger, the one with the U-shaped crosspiece; Duncan, almost absent-mindedly, picked a wooden-handled knife with the stamp of a tiny tree on the blade. Someone else said it was just like Maneco to play it safe, to choose a sword. It astonished no one that his hand began shaking; what was astonishing is that the same thing happened with Duncan.

Tradition demands that men about to fight should respect the house in which they are guests, and step outside. Half on a spree, half seriously, we all went out into the damp night. I was not drunk—at least, not on wine—but I was reeling with adventure; I wished very hard that someone would be killed so that later I could tell about it and always remember it. Maybe at that moment the others were no more adult than I was. I also had the feeling that an overpowering current was dragging us on and would drown us. Nobody believed the least bit in Maneco's accusation; everyone saw it as the fruit of an old rivalry, exacerbated by the wine.

We pushed our way through a clump of trees, leaving behind the summerhouse. Uriarte and Duncan led the way, wary of each other. The rest of us strung ourselves out around the edge of an opening of lawn. Duncan had stopped there in

the moonlight and said, with mild authority, "This looks like the right place."

The two men stood in the center, not quite knowing what to do. A voice rang out: "Let go of all that hardware and use your hands!"

But the men were already fighting. They began clumsily, almost as if they were afraid of hurting each other; they began by watching the blades, but later their eyes were on one another. Uriarte had laid aside his anger, Duncan his contempt or aloofness. Danger, in some way, had transfigured[11] them; these were now two men fighting, not boys. I had imagined the fight as a chaos of steel; instead, I was able to follow it, or almost follow it, as though it were a game of chess. The intervening years may, of course, have exaggerated or blurred what I saw. I do not know how long it lasted; there are events that fall outside the common measure of time.

Without ponchos[12] to act as shields, they used their forearms to block each lunge of the knife. Their sleeves, soon hanging in shreds, grew black with blood. I thought that we had gone wrong in supposing that they knew nothing about this kind of fencing. I noticed right off that they handled themselves in different ways. Their weapons were unequal. Duncan, in order to make up for his disadvantage, tried to stay in close to the other man; Uriarte kept stepping back to be able to lunge out with long, low thrusts. The same voice that had called attention to the display cabinet shouted out now: "They're killing each other! Stop them!"

But no one dared break it up. Uriarte had lost ground; Duncan charged him. They were almost body to body now. Uriarte's weapon sought Duncan's face. Suddenly the blade seemed

---

11. **transfigured:** changed the form or appearance of.
12. **ponchos:** cloaks like blankets, with a hole in the middle for the head.

WORDS TO KNOW

exacerbated (ĭg-zăs′ər-bā′tĭd) *adj.* made worse **exacerbate** *v.*
wary (wâr′ē) *adj.* cautious; watchful

518

The Dream (1986), Arnaldo Roche Rabell. Oil on canvas, 78″ × 78″, collection of José B. Andreu, Puerto Rico.

shorter, for it was piercing the taller man's chest. Duncan lay stretched out on the grass. It was at this point that he said, his voice very low, "How strange. All this is like a dream."

He did not shut his eyes, he did not move, and I had seen a man kill another man.

Maneco Uriarte bent over the body, sobbing openly, and begged to be forgiven. The thing he had just done was beyond him. I know now that he regretted less having committed a crime than having carried out a senseless act.

I did not want to look anymore. What I had wished for so much had happened, and it left me shaken. Lafinur told me later that they had had to struggle hard to pull out the weapon. A makeshift council was formed. They decided to lie as little as possible and to elevate this duel with knives to a duel with swords. Four of them volunteered as seconds,[13] among them Acebal. In Buenos Aires anything can be fixed; someone always has a friend.

---

13. **seconds:** assistants or aides of fighters in a duel, usually friends of the duelists.

On top of the mahogany table where the men had been playing, a pack of English cards and a pile of bills lay in a jumble that nobody wanted to look at or to touch.

In the years that followed, I often considered revealing the story to some friend, but always I felt that there was a greater pleasure in being the keeper of a secret than in telling it. However, around 1929, a chance conversation suddenly moved me one day to break my long silence. The retired police captain, don José Olave, was recalling stories about men from the tough riverside neighborhood of the Retiro who had been handy with their knives; he remarked that when they were out to kill their man, scum of this kind had no use for the rules of the game, and that before all the fancy playing with daggers that you saw now on the stage, knife fights were few and far between. I said I had witnessed one, and gave him an account of what had happened nearly twenty years earlier.

He listened to me with professional attention, then said, "Are you sure Uriarte and What's-His-Name never handled a knife before? Maybe they had picked up a thing or two around their fathers' ranches."

CLARIFY

Why does Olave seem surprised that Uriarte and Duncan had never handled knives before?

"I don't think so," I said. "Everybody there that night knew one another pretty well, and I can tell you they were all amazed at the way the two men fought."

Olave went on in his quiet manner, as if thinking aloud. "One of the weapons had a U-shaped crosspiece in the handle. There were two daggers of that kind which became quite famous—Moreira's and Juan Almada's. Almada was from down south, in Tapalquén."

Something seemed to come awake in my memory. Olave continued. "You also mentioned

a knife with a wooden handle, one with the Little Tree brand. There are thousands of them, but there was one—"

He broke off for a moment, then said, "Señor Acevedo had a big property up around Pergamino. There was another of these famous toughs from up that way—Juan Almanza was his name. This was along about the turn of the century. When he was fourteen, he killed his first man with one of these knives. From then on, for luck, he stuck to the same one. Juan Almanza and Juan Almada had it in for each other, jealous of the fact that many people confused the two. For a long time they searched high and low for one another, but they never met. Juan Almanza was killed by a stray bullet during some election brawl or other. The other man, I think, died a natural death in a hospital bed in Las Flores."

Nothing more was said. Each of us was left with his own conclusions.

Nine or ten men, none of whom is any longer living, saw what my eyes saw—that sudden stab and the body under the night sky—but perhaps what we were really seeing was the end of another story, an older story. I began to wonder whether it was Maneco Uriarte who killed Duncan or whether in some uncanny way it could have been the weapons, not the men, which fought. I still remember how Uriarte's hand shook when he first gripped his knife, and the same with Duncan, as though the knives were coming awake after a long sleep side by side in the cabinet. Even after their gauchos were dust, the knives—the knives, not their tools, the men—knew how to fight. And that night they fought well.

Things last longer than people; who knows whether these knives will meet again, who knows whether the story ends here. ❖

RESPONDING OPTIONS

FROM PERSONAL RESPONSE TO CRITICAL ANALYSIS

REFLECT

1. Did you find anything strange or unexpected in this story? Write your reaction in your notebook, then share what you have written with a classmate.

RETHINK

2. Look back at the chart you completed for the Reading Connection on page 514. What one cause do you think was the most important in deciding the outcome of the duel?

   Consider
   - the circumstances surrounding the argument between Uriarte and Duncan
   - the narrator's sense of an "overpowering current" dragging everybody on
   - the skills shown by the fighters, though neither had experience with knives
   - retired police captain Olave's story about the history of the two knives

3. Why do you think the narrator was so strongly affected by the duel that he witnessed?

4. Do you think the partygoers were right to keep the circumstances of Duncan's death a secret? Explain your answer.

RELATE

5. Consider the duel in this story and the fight that you described for the Personal Connection on page 514. What do both events suggest about the causes of violence?

ANOTHER PATHWAY

Cooperative Learning

As a class, produce a television newscast about the events surrounding the knife fight in "The Meeting." Include a factual report about the fight, interviews with eyewitnesses, and feature stories in which you explore the history of the knives and speculate about why the fight turned out as it did.

LITERARY CONCEPTS

In a work of fiction, the **narrator** is the person or voice that tells the story. A narrator can be outside the story, as in "The First Seven Years," or inside the story, as in "The Meeting." In the Borges story, the narrator offers his own memories of events. He admits that "the intervening years may . . . have exaggerated or blurred what I saw." With a partner, evaluate the narrator's trustworthiness on a scale of 1 to 10. In other words, how much of his story do you believe is accurate?

CONCEPT REVIEW: Magical Realism Which of the story's details do you find strongly realistic? Which seem dreamlike, or magical?

QUICKWRITES

1. Write a **ballad** based on the events in this story. If you like, set your ballad to music.

2. Write the **police report** of the fight. Include statements from witnesses who have decided "to lie as little as possible" but "to elevate this duel with knives to a duel with swords."

3. Imagine that the knives in the story are now on display at a museum. Create a **brochure** for museum patrons that describes each knife and its infamous history.

PORTFOLIO Save your writing. You may want to use it later as a springboard to a piece for your portfolio.

ALTERNATIVE ACTIVITIES

1. Sit in a circle with a group of classmates, and imagine you are sitting around a campfire. Have one person begin a **tall tale** about a future encounter between the dagger of Juan Almada and the knife of Juan Almanza. Then take turns around the circle, with each person adding to the tale.

2. Create an **illustration** of an object or event in the story. Be sure to review the story for details about your subject.

LITERARY LINKS

Compare "The Meeting" with "Metonymy, or The Husband's Revenge" on page 452. What do you think the stories have in common?

WORDS TO KNOW

Answer the questions that follow.

1. What would a person **versed** in gardening almost certainly be able to do—paint a garden, grow a garden, or write a poem about a garden?

2. What would be characteristic of the **archetype** of a student—a perfect grade point average, disappointing grades, or average grades?

3. Which sign is designed to make people **wary**— "No Entrance," "Welcome," or "Danger"?

4. If a surgeon found an **incipient** tumor, would it be well advanced, just beginning, or growing smaller?

5. Is hunger most likely to be **exacerbated** by a snack, a full meal, or the aroma of food?

JORGE LUIS BORGES

One of 20th-century Latin America's most influential men of letters, Jorge Luis Borges was a poet, short story writer, and essayist. His writing portrays a puzzling, mysterious world, where boundaries between dream and reality, past and present, fact and fantasy are often blurred.

1899–1986

Borges was born to a prosperous family in Buenos Aires, Argentina. His father was half English and had an extensive library of literature in English that he made available to his children. Educated at home until the age of nine, Borges read writers such as Dickens, Poe, and Twain; he began writing stories at the age of seven. In 1914 his family took him to Geneva, Switzerland, where he mastered French and German and earned his bachelor's degree. After World War I, he visited Spain and became associated with a group of poets, known as the *Ultraístas* (ōōl-trä-ēs′täz), who experimented with free verse and metaphor. Upon returning to Argentina in 1921, Borges began his career as a poet and established a literary journal.

During the next several decades, Borges led a retiring life and expanded his literary range to include fiction and essays, gradually developing his reputation. In 1955 he became director of the National Library of Argentina. Soon thereafter he also began serving as professor of English and North American literature at the University of Buenos Aires. Fascinated by the literature of many cultures, Borges continued to pursue his scholarship and writing despite suffering from an inherited eye disease that left him almost totally blind. "The Meeting" is from a collection titled *Doctor Brodie's Report*.

OTHER WORKS *Labyrinths, The Book of Imaginary Beings, The Garden of Forking Paths, Ficciones, El Aleph*

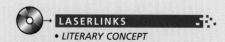

LASERLINKS
• *LITERARY CONCEPT*

PREVIEWING

The Witness for the Prosecution
Agatha Christie England

PERSONAL CONNECTION

How do you decide whether someone is telling you the truth when all you have to go on is the speaker's word? Do you watch the expression on the speaker's face, or listen to the tone of voice? With a classmate, talk about the kinds of clues you look for when you need to make a judgment about the truth of what someone tells you. Then share your ideas with the entire class.

CULTURAL CONNECTION

In the selection you are about to read, a British lawyer seeks the truth about a murder case that is coming to trial. There are two kinds of lawyers in Britain: solicitors, who conduct legal work outside the court, and barristers, who actually try the cases in court. Defendants who are about to go on trial hire a solicitor to handle their case. The solicitor conducts most of the background work, such as researching evidence and interviewing witnesses.

Then the solicitor hires a barrister to appear in court and question witnesses on the client's behalf. In the following mystery by British author Agatha Christie, a solicitor named Mr. Mayherne collects the evidence for his client and then turns it over to a barrister named Sir Charles.

READING CONNECTION

Finding Clues As you read "The Witness for the Prosecution," look for clues that point to the truth about the guilt or innocence of Mr. Mayherne's client. List the clues on a chart like the one shown, with clues indicating guilt on one side and those indicating innocence on the other. Then, just before the trial begins in the last section of the story, pause to weigh the clues and decide what your verdict would be. Finish reading the story to see if you guessed right.

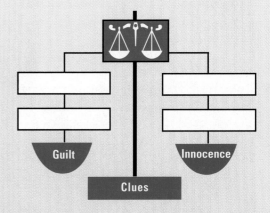

Portrait of Count Fürstenberg-Herdringen (1924), Tamara de Lempicka. Oil on canvas, 16⅛″ × 10¾″, courtesy of Barry Friedman Ltd., New York. Copyright © 1996 Artists Rights Society (ARS), New York/SPADEM, Paris.

THE WITNESS FOR THE PROSECUTION

AGATHA CHRISTIE

Mr. Mayherne adjusted his pince-nez[1] and cleared his throat with a little dry-as-dust cough that was wholly typical of him. Then he looked again at the man opposite him, the man charged with willful murder.[2]

Mr. Mayherne was a small man, precise in manner, neatly, not to say foppishly[3] dressed, with a pair of very shrewd and piercing gray eyes. By no means a fool. Indeed, as a solicitor, Mr. Mayherne's reputation stood very high. His voice, when he spoke to his client, was dry but not unsympathetic.

"I must impress upon you again that you are in very grave danger, and that the utmost frankness is necessary."

Leonard Vole, who had been staring in a dazed fashion at the blank wall in front of him, transferred his glance to the solicitor.

"I know," he said hopelessly. "You keep telling me so. But I can't seem to realize yet that I'm

---

1. **pince-nez** (păns′nā′): eyeglasses without side pieces, kept in place by a spring gripping the bridge of the nose.
2. **willful murder:** deliberate, not accidental, murder. In law, the term *willful* is used synonymously with *premeditated* (planned beforehand). Willful murder is a more serious crime than murder that is unplanned, accidental, or committed in self-defense.
3. **foppishly:** in the manner of a vain man who pays too much attention to his clothes and appearance.

charged with murder—*murder*. And such a dastardly crime too."

Mr. Mayherne was practical, not emotional. He coughed again, took off his pince-nez, polished them carefully, and replaced them on his nose. Then he said:

"Yes, yes, yes. Now, my dear Mr. Vole, we're going to make a determined effort to get you off—and we shall succeed—we shall succeed. But I must have all the facts. I must know just how damaging the case against you is likely to be. Then we can fix upon the best line of defense."

Still the young man looked at him in the same dazed, hopeless fashion. To Mr. Mayherne the case had seemed black enough, and the guilt of the prisoner assured. Now, for the first time, he felt a doubt.

"You think I'm guilty," said Leonard Vole, in a low voice. "But, by God, I swear I'm not! It looks pretty black against me; I know that. I'm like a man caught in a net— the meshes of it all round me, entangling me whichever way I turn. But I didn't do it, Mr. Mayherne; I didn't do it!"

In such a position a man was bound to protest his innocence. Mr. Mayherne knew that. Yet, in spite of himself, he was impressed. It might be, after all, that Leonard Vole was innocent.

"You are right, Mr. Vole," he said gravely. "The case does look very black against you. Nevertheless, I accept your assurance. Now, let us

"I DIDN'T DO IT,

MR. MAYHERNE;

I DIDN'T DO IT!"

get to facts. I want you to tell me in your own words exactly how you came to make the acquaintance of Miss Emily French."

"It was one day in Oxford Street. I saw an elderly lady crossing the road. She was carrying a lot of parcels. In the middle of the street she dropped them, tried to recover them, found a bus was almost on top of her and just managed to reach the curb safely, dazed and bewildered by people having shouted at her. I recovered her parcels, wiped the mud off them as best I could, retied the string of one, and returned them to her."

"There was no question of your having saved her life?"

"Oh, dear me, no! All I did was to perform a common act of courtesy. She was extremely grateful, thanked me warmly, and said something about my manners not being those of most of the younger generation—I can't remember the exact words. Then I lifted my hat and went on. I never expected to see her again. But life is full of coincidences. That very evening I came across her at a party at a friend's house.

She recognized me at once and asked that I should be introduced to her. I then found out that she was a Miss Emily French and that she lived at Cricklewood. I talked to her for some time. She was, I imagine, an old lady who took sudden and violent fancies to people. She took one to me on the strength of a perfectly simple action which anyone might have performed. On leaving, she

WORDS TO KNOW **dastardly** (dăs′tərd-lē) *adj.* mean and cowardly

526

shook me warmly by the hand, and asked me to come and see her. I replied, of course, that I should be very pleased to do so, and she then urged me to name a day. I did not want particularly to go, but it would have seemed churlish to refuse, so I fixed on the following Saturday. After she had gone, I learned something about her from my friends. That she was rich, eccentric, lived alone with one maid and owned no less than eight cats."

"I see," said Mr. Mayherne. "The question of her being well off came up as early as that?"

"If you mean that I inquired—" began Leonard Vole hotly, but Mr. Mayherne stilled him with a gesture.

"I have to look at the case as it will be presented by the other side. An ordinary observer would not have supposed Miss French to be a lady of means. She lived poorly, almost humbly. Unless you had been told the contrary, you would in all probability have considered her to be in poor circumstances[4]—at any rate to begin with. Who was it exactly who told you that she was well off?"

"My friend, George Harvey, at whose house the party took place."

"Is he likely to remember having done so?"

"I really don't know. Of course it is some time ago now."

"Quite so, Mr. Vole. You see, the first aim of the prosecution will be to establish that you were in low water financially—that is true, is it not?"

Leonard Vole flushed.

"Yes," he said, in a low voice. "I'd been having a run of infernal bad luck just then."

"Quite so," said Mr. Mayherne again. "That being, as I say, in low water financially, you met this rich old lady and cultivated her acquaintance assiduously. Now if we are in a position to say that you had no idea she was well off, and that you visited her out of pure kindness of heart—"

"Which is the case."

"I daresay. I am not disputing the point. I am looking at it from the outside point of view. A great deal depends on the memory of Mr. Harvey. Is he likely to remember that conversation, or is he not? Could he be confused by counsel into believing that it took place later?"

Leonard Vole reflected for some minutes. Then he said steadily enough, but with a rather paler face:

"I do not think that that line would be successful, Mr. Mayherne. Several of those present heard his remark, and one or two of them chaffed[5] me about my conquest of a rich old lady."

The solicitor endeavored to hide his disappointment with a wave of the hand.

"Unfortunate," he said. "But I congratulate you upon your plain speaking, Mr. Vole. It is to you I look to guide me. Your judgment is quite right. To persist in the line I spoke of would have been disastrous. We must leave that point. You made the acquaintance of Miss French; you called upon her; the acquaintanceship progressed. We want a clear reason for all this. Why did you, a young man of thirty-three, good-looking, fond of sport, popular with your friends, devote so much of your time to an elderly woman with whom you could hardly have anything in common?"

Leonard Vole flung out his hands in a nervous gesture.

"I can't tell you—I really can't tell you. After the first visit, she pressed me to come again, spoke of being lonely and unhappy. She made it difficult for me to refuse. She showed so plainly her fondness and affection for me that I was placed in an awkward position. You see, Mr.

---

4. **circumstances:** financial condition.

5. **chaffed:** teased in a good-natured way.

Mayherne, I've got a weak nature—I drift—I'm one of those people who can't say 'No.' And believe me or not, as you like, after the third or fourth visit I paid her I found myself getting genuinely fond of the old thing. My mother died when I was young, an aunt brought me up, and she too died before I was fifteen. If I told you that I genuinely enjoyed being mothered and pampered, I daresay you'd only laugh."

Mr. Mayherne did not laugh. Instead he took off his pince-nez again and polished them, a sign with him that he was thinking deeply.

"I accept your explanation, Mr. Vole," he said at last. "I believe it to be psychologically probable. Whether a jury would take that view of it is another matter. Please continue your narrative. When was it that Miss French first asked you to look into her business affairs?"

"After my third or fourth visit to her. She understood very little of money matters and was worried about some investments."

Mr. Mayherne looked up sharply.

"Be careful, Mr. Vole. The maid, Janet Mackenzie, declares that her mistress was a good woman of business and transacted all her own affairs, and this is borne out by the testimony of her bankers."

"I can't help that," said Vole earnestly. "That's what she said to me."

Mr. Mayherne looked at him for a moment or two in silence. Though he had no intention of saying so, his belief in Leonard Vole's innocence was at that moment strengthened. He knew something of the mentality of elderly ladies. He saw Miss French, infatuated with the good-looking young man, hunting about for pretexts that would bring him to the house. What more likely than that she should plead ignorance of business and beg him to help her with her money affairs? She was enough of a woman of the world to realize that any man is slightly flattered by such an admission of his superiority. Leonard Vole had been flattered. Perhaps, too, she had not been averse to letting this young man know that she was wealthy. Emily French had been a strong-willed old woman, willing to pay her price for what she wanted. All this passed rapidly through Mr. Mayherne's mind, but he gave no indication of it and asked instead a further question.

"And you did handle her affairs for her at her request?"

"I did."

"Mr. Vole," said the solicitor, "I am going to ask you a very serious question, and one to which it is vital I should have a truthful answer. You were in low water financially. You had the handling of an old lady's affairs—an old lady who, according to her own statement, knew little or nothing of business. Did you at any time, or in any manner, convert to your own use the securities[6] which you handled? Did you engage in any transaction for your own pecuniary[7] advantage which will not bear the light of day?" He quelled the other's response. "Wait a minute before you answer. There are two courses open to us. Either we can make a feature of your probity[8] and honesty in conducting her affairs whilst pointing out how unlikely it is that you would commit murder to obtain money which you might have obtained by such infinitely easier means. If, on the other hand, there is anything in your dealings which the prosecution will get hold of—if, to put it baldly, it can be proved that you swindled the old lady in any way—we must take the line that you had no motive for the murder,

---

6. **securities:** stock certificates or bonds.
7. **pecuniary** (pĭ-kyoō'nē-ĕr'ē): involving money; financial.
8. **probity** (prō'bĭ-tē): the holding of the highest principles and ideals; integrity.

since she was already a profitable source of income to you. You perceive the distinction. Now, I beg of you, take your time before you reply."

But Leonard Vole took no time at all.

"My dealings with Miss French's affairs were all perfectly fair and aboveboard. I acted for her interests to the very best of my ability, as anyone will find who looks into the matter."

"Thank you," said Mr. Mayherne. "You relieve my mind very much. I pay you the compliment of believing that you are far too clever to lie to me over such an important matter."

"Surely," said Vole eagerly, "the strongest point in my favor is the lack of motive. Granted that I cultivated the acquaintanceship of a rich old lady in the hopes of getting money out of her—that, I gather, is the substance of what you have been saying—surely her death frustrates all my hopes?"

The solicitor looked at him steadily. Then, very deliberately, he repeated his unconscious trick with his pince-nez. It was not until they were firmly replaced on his nose that he spoke.

"Are you not aware, Mr. Vole, that Miss French left a will under which you are the principal beneficiary?"[9]

"My DEALINGS WITH Miss FRENCH'S AFFAIRS WERE ALL PERFECTLY FAIR AND ABOVEBOARD."

"What?" The prisoner sprang to his feet. His dismay was obvious and unforced. "My God! What are you saying? She left her money to me?"

Mr. Mayherne nodded slowly. Vole sank down again, his head in his hands.

"You pretend you know nothing of this will?"

"Pretend? There's no pretense about it. I knew nothing about it."

"What would you say if I told you that the maid, Janet Mackenzie, swears that you *did* know? That her mistress told her distinctly that she had consulted you in the matter and told you of her intentions?"

"Say? That she's lying! No, I go too fast. Janet is an elderly woman. She was a faithful watchdog to her mistress, and she didn't like me. She was jealous and suspicious. I should say that Miss French confided her intentions to Janet, and that Janet either mistook something she said or else was convinced in her own mind that I had persuaded the old lady into doing it. I daresay that she herself believes now that Miss French actually told her so."

"You don't think she dislikes you enough to lie deliberately about the matter?"

Leonard Vole looked shocked and startled.

"No, indeed! Why should she?"

"I don't know," said Mr. Mayherne thoughtfully. "But she's very bitter against you."

The wretched young man groaned again.

"I'm beginning to see," he muttered. "It's

---

9. **beneficiary** (bĕn´ə-fĭsh´ē-ĕr´ē): person named in a will to receive money or goods.

frightful. I made up to her, that's what they'll say, I got her to make a will leaving her money to me, and then I go there that night, and there's nobody in the house—they find her the next day—oh! my God, it's awful!"

"You are wrong about there being nobody in the house," said Mr. Mayherne. "Janet, as you remember, was to go out for the evening. She went, but about half past nine she returned to fetch the pattern of a blouse sleeve which she had promised to a friend. She let herself in by the back door, went upstairs and fetched it, and went out again. She heard voices in the sitting room, though she could not distinguish what they said, but she will swear that one of them was Miss French's and one was a man's."

"At half past nine," said Leonard Vole. "At half past nine . . ." He sprang to his feet. "But then I'm saved—saved—"

"What do you mean, saved?" cried Mr. Mayherne, astonished.

"By half past nine I was at home again! My wife can prove that. I left Miss French about five minutes to nine. I arrived home about twenty past nine. My wife was there waiting for me. Oh, thank God—thank God! And bless Janet Mackenzie's sleeve pattern."

In his exuberance, he hardly noticed that the grave expression on the solicitor's face had not altered. But the latter's words brought him down to earth with a bump.

"Who, then, in your opinion, murdered Miss French?"

"Why, a burglar, of course, as was thought at first. The window was forced, you remember. She was killed with a heavy blow from a crowbar, and the crowbar was found lying on the floor beside the body. And several articles were missing. But for Janet's absurd suspicions and dislike of me, the police would never have swerved from the right track."

"That will hardly do, Mr. Vole," said the solicitor. "The things that were missing were mere trifles of no value, taken as a blind. And the marks on the window were not at all conclusive. Besides, think for yourself. You say you were no longer in the house by half past nine. Who, then, was the man Janet heard talking to Miss French in the sitting room? She would hardly be having an <u>amicable</u> conversation with a burglar?"

"No," said Vole. "No—" He looked puzzled and discouraged. "But, anyway," he added with reviving spirit, "it lets me out. I've got an alibi. You must see Romaine—my wife—at once."

"Certainly," acquiesced the lawyer. "I should already have seen Mrs. Vole but for her being absent when you were arrested. I wired to Scotland at once, and I understand that she arrives back tonight. I am going to call upon her immediately I leave here."

Vole nodded, a great expression of satisfaction settling down over his face.

"Yes, Romaine will tell you. My God! it's a lucky chance that."

"Excuse me, Mr. Vole, but you are very fond of your wife?"

"Of course."

"And she of you?"

"Romaine is devoted to me. She'd do anything in the world for me."

He spoke enthusiastically, but the solicitor's heart sank a little lower. The testimony of a devoted wife—would it gain credence?

"Was there anyone else who saw you return at nine-twenty? A maid, for instance?"

"We have no maid."

"Did you meet anyone in the street on the way back?"

"Nobody I knew. I rode part of the way in a bus. The conductor might remember."

Mr. Mayherne shook his head doubtfully.

WORDS TO KNOW

amicable (ăm´ĭ-kə-bəl) *adj.* having or showing a friendly attitude

"There is no one, then, who can confirm your wife's testimony?"

"No. But it isn't necessary, surely?"

"I daresay not. I daresay not," said Mr. Mayherne hastily. "Now there's just one thing more. Did Miss French know that you were a married man?"

"Oh, yes."

"Yet you never took your wife to see her. Why was that?"

For the first time, Leonard Vole's answer came halting and uncertain.

"Well—I don't know."

"Are you aware that Janet Mackenzie says her mistress believed you to be single and contemplated marrying you in the future?"

Vole laughed.

"Absurd! There was forty years' difference in age between us."

"It has been done," said the solicitor dryly. "The fact remains. Your wife never met Miss French?"

"No—" Again the constraint.

"You will permit me to say," said the lawyer, "that I hardly understand your attitude in the matter."

Vole flushed, hesitated, and then spoke.

"I'll make a clean breast of it. I was hard up, as you know. I hoped that Miss French might lend me some money. She was fond of me, but she wasn't at all interested in the struggles of a young couple. Early on, I found that she had taken it for granted that my wife and I didn't get on—were living apart. Mr. Mayherne—I wanted the money—for Romaine's sake. I said nothing, and allowed the old lady to think what she chose. She spoke of my being an adopted son to her. There was never any question of marriage—that must be just Janet's imagination."

"And that is all?"

"Yes—that is all."

"I HOPED THAT MISS FRENCH MIGHT LEND ME SOME MONEY."

Was there just a shade of hesitation in the words? The lawyer fancied so. He rose and held out his hand.

"Good-bye, Mr. Vole." He looked into the haggard young face and spoke with an unusual impulse. "I believe in your innocence in spite of the multitude of facts arrayed against you. I hope to prove it and vindicate you completely."

Vole smiled back at him.

"You'll find the alibi is all right," he said cheerfully.

Again he hardly noticed that the other did not respond.

"The whole thing hinges a good deal on the testimony of Janet Mackenzie," said Mr. Mayherne. "She hates you. That much is clear."

"She can hardly hate me," protested the young man.

The solicitor shook his head as he went out.

"Now for Mrs. Vole," he said to himself.

He was seriously disturbed by the way the thing was shaping.

WORDS TO KNOW **vindicate** (vĭn′dĭ-kāt′) v. to clear of blame or suspicion

531

The Voles lived in a small shabby house near Paddington Green. It was to this house that Mr. Mayherne went.

In answer to his ring, a big slatternly woman, obviously a charwoman, answered the door.

"Mrs. Vole? Has she returned yet?"

"Got back an hour ago. But I dunno if you can see her."

"If you will take my card to her," said Mr. Mayherne quietly, "I am quite sure that she will do so."

The woman looked at him doubtfully, wiped her hand on her apron and took the card. Then she closed the door in his face and left him on the step outside.

In a few minutes, however, she returned with a slightly altered manner.

"Come inside, please."

She ushered him into a tiny drawing room. Mr. Mayherne, examining a drawing on the wall, started up suddenly to face a tall, pale woman who had entered so quietly that he had not heard her.

"Mr. Mayherne? You are my husband's solicitor, are you not? You have come from him? Will you please sit down?"

Until she spoke, he had not realized that she was not English. Now, observing her more closely, he noticed the high cheekbones, the dense blue-black of the hair, and an occasional very slight movement of the hands that was distinctly foreign. A strange woman, very quiet. So quiet as to make one uneasy. From the very first Mr. Mayherne was conscious that he was up against something that he did not understand.

"Now, my dear Mrs. Vole," he began, "you must not give way—"

He stopped. It was so very obvious that Romaine Vole had not the slightest intention of giving way. She was perfectly calm and composed.

"Will you please tell me about it?" she said. "I must know everything. Do not think to spare me. I want to know the worst." She hesitated, then repeated in a lower tone, with a curious emphasis which the lawyer did not understand: "I want to know the worst."

Mr. Mayherne went over his interview with Leonard Vole. She listened attentively, nodding her head now and then.

"I see," she said, when he had finished. "He wants me to say that he came in at twenty minutes past nine that night?"

"He did come in at that time?" said Mr. Mayherne sharply.

"That is not the point," she said coldly. "Will my saying so acquit him? Will they believe me?"

Mr. Mayherne was taken aback. She had gone so quickly to the core of the matter.

"That is what I want to know," she said. "Will it be enough? Is there anyone else who can support my evidence?"

There was a suppressed eagerness in her manner that made him vaguely uneasy.

"I MUST KNOW EVERYTHING. DO NOT THINK TO SPARE ME."

Portrait de Madame M., Tamara de Lempicka (1898–1980). Oil on canvas, 99 cm × 65 cm, private collection, Paris. Copyright © 1996 Artists Rights Society (ARS), New York/ SPADEM, Paris.

"So far there is no one else," he said reluctantly.

"I see," said Romaine Vole.

She sat for a minute or two perfectly still. A little smile played over her lips.

The lawyer's feeling of alarm grew stronger and stronger.

"Mrs. Vole—" he began. "I know what you must feel—"

"Do you?" she asked. "I wonder."

"In the circumstances—"

"In the circumstances—I intend to play a lone hand."

He looked at her in dismay.

"But, my dear Mrs. Vole—you are overwrought. Being so devoted to your husband—"

"I beg your pardon?"

The sharpness of her voice made him start. He repeated in a hesitating manner:

"Being so devoted to your husband—"

Romaine Vole nodded slowly, the same strange smile on her lips.

"Did he tell you that I was devoted to him?" she asked softly. "Ah! yes, I can see he did. How stupid men are! Stupid—stupid—stupid—"

She rose suddenly to her feet. All the intense emotion that the lawyer had been conscious of in the atmosphere was now concentrated in her tone.

"I hate him, I tell you! I hate him. I hate him. I hate him! I would like to see him hanged by the neck till he is dead."

The lawyer recoiled before her and the smoldering passion in her eyes.

She advanced a step nearer and continued vehemently:

"**"Did he tell you that I was devoted to him?""**

"Perhaps I shall see it. Supposing I tell you that he did not come in that night at twenty past nine, but at twenty past ten? You say that he tells you he knew nothing about the money coming to him. Supposing I tell you he knew all about it, and counted on it, and committed murder to get it? Supposing I tell you that he admitted to me that night when he came in what he had done? That there was blood on his coat? What then? Supposing that I stand up in court and say all these things?"

Her eyes seemed to challenge him. With an effort, he concealed his growing dismay, and endeavored to speak in a rational tone.

"You cannot be asked to give evidence against your husband—"

"He is not my husband!" The words came out so quickly that he fancied he had misunderstood her.

"I beg your pardon? I—"

"He is not my husband." The silence was so intense that you could have heard a pin drop.

"I was an actress in Vienna. My husband is alive but in a madhouse. So we could not marry. I am glad now."

She nodded defiantly.

"I should like you to tell me one thing," said Mr. Mayherne. He contrived to appear as cool and unemotional as ever. "Why are you so bitter against Leonard Vole?"

She shook her head, smiling a little.

"Yes, you would like to know. But I shall not tell you. I will keep my secret. . . ."

Mr. Mayherne gave his dry little cough and rose.

"There seems no point in prolonging this interview," he remarked. "You will hear from me again after I have communicated with my client."

She came closer to him, looking into his eyes with her own wonderful dark ones.

"Tell me," she said, "did you believe—honestly—that he was innocent when you came here today?"

"I did," said Mr. Mayherne.

"You poor little man," she laughed.

"And I believe so still," finished the lawyer. "Good evening, madam."

He went out of the room, taking with him the memory of her startled face.

"This is going to be the devil of a business," said Mr. Mayherne to himself as he strode along the street.

Extraordinary, the whole thing. An extraordinary woman. A very dangerous woman. Women were the devil when they got their knife into you.

What was to be done? That wretched young man hadn't a leg to stand upon. Of course, possibly he did commit the crime. . . .

"No," said Mr. Mayherne to himself. "No—there's almost too much evidence against him. I don't believe this woman. She was trumping up the whole story. But she'll never bring it into court."

He wished he felt more conviction on the point.

The police court proceedings were brief and dramatic. The principal witnesses for the prosecution were Janet Mackenzie, maid to the dead woman, and Romaine Heilger, Austrian subject, the mistress of the prisoner.

Mr. Mayherne sat in court and listened to the damning story that the latter told. It was on the lines she had indicated to him in their interview.

The prisoner reserved his defense and was committed for trial.

Mr. Mayherne was at his wits' end. The case against Leonard Vole was black beyond words. Even the famous K.C.[10] who was engaged for the defense held out little hope.

"If we can shake that Austrian woman's testimony, we might do something," he said dubiously. "But it's a bad business."

Mr. Mayherne had concentrated his energies on one single point. Assuming Leonard Vole to be speaking the truth, and to have left the murdered woman's house at nine o'clock, who was the man Janet heard talking to Miss French at half past nine?

The only ray of light was in the shape of a scapegrace[11] nephew who had in bygone days cajoled and threatened his aunt out of various sums of money. Janet Mackenzie, the solicitor learned, had always been attached to this young man and had never ceased urging his claims upon her mistress. It certainly seemed possible that it was this nephew who had been with Miss French after Leonard Vole left, especially as he was not to be found in any of his old haunts.[12]

In all other directions, the lawyer's researches had been negative in their result. No one had seen Leonard Vole entering his own house, or leaving that of Miss French. No one had seen any other man enter or leave the house in Cricklewood. All inquiries drew blank.

It was the eve of the trial when Mr. Mayherne received the letter which was to lead his thoughts in an entirely new direction.

It came by the six o'clock post. An illiterate

---

10. **K.C.:** King's Counsel, a barrister appointed as legal counsel to the British crown. The term refers to a leading or senior barrister.

11. **scapegrace:** scoundrel.

12. **haunts:** places one frequently goes; hangouts.

WORDS TO KNOW   **cajole** (kə-jōl′) v. to persuade by pleasant words, flattery, or false promises

scrawl, written on common paper and enclosed in a dirty envelope with the stamp stuck on crooked.

Mr. Mayherne read it through once or twice before he grasped its meaning.

> *"Dear Mister:*
> *"Youre the lawyer chap wot acts for the young feller. If you want that painted foreign hussy showd up for wot she is an her pack of lies you come to 16 Shaw's Rents Stepney to-night It ull cawst you 2 hundred quid[13] Arsk for Misses Mogson."*

The solicitor read and reread this strange epistle. It might, of course, be a hoax, but when he thought it over, he became increasingly convinced that it was genuine, and also convinced that it was the one hope for the prisoner. The evidence of Romaine Heilger damned him completely, and the line the defense meant to pursue, the line that the evidence of a woman who had admittedly lived an immoral life was not to be trusted, was at best a weak one.

Mr. Mayherne's mind was made up. It was his duty to save his client at all costs. He must go to Shaw's Rents.

He had some difficulty in finding the place, a ramshackle building in an evil-smelling slum, but at last he did so, and on inquiry for Mrs. Mogson was sent up to a room on the third floor. On this door he knocked and, getting no answer, knocked again.

At this second knock, he heard a shuffling sound inside, and presently the door was opened cautiously half an inch, and a bent figure peered out.

Suddenly the woman, for it was a woman, gave a chuckle and opened the door wider.

"So it's you, dearie," she said, in a wheezy voice. "Nobody with you, is there? No playing tricks? That's right. You can come in—you can come in."

With some reluctance the lawyer stepped across the threshold into the small dirty room, with its flickering gas jet.[14] There was an untidy unmade bed in a corner, a plain deal table[15] and two rickety chairs. For the first time Mr. Mayherne had a full view of the tenant of this unsavory apartment. She was a woman of middle age, bent in figure, with a mass of untidy gray hair and a scarf wound tightly round her face. She saw him looking at this and laughed again, the same curious, toneless chuckle.

"Wondering why I hide my beauty, dear? He, he, he. Afraid it may tempt you, eh? But you shall see—you shall see."

She drew aside the scarf, and the lawyer recoiled involuntarily before the almost formless blur of scarlet. She replaced the scarf again.

"So you're not wanting to kiss me, dearie? He, he, I don't wonder. And yet I was a pretty girl once—not so long ago as you'd think, either. Vitriol,[16] dearie, vitriol—that's what did that. Ah! but I'll be even with 'em—"

She burst into a hideous torrent of profanity which Mr. Mayherne tried vainly to quell. She fell silent at last, her hands clenching and unclenching themselves nervously.

"Enough of that," said the lawyer sternly. "I've come here because I have reason to believe you can give me information which will clear my client, Leonard Vole. Is that the case?"

Her eyes leered at him cunningly.

"What about the money, dearie?" she wheezed. "Two hundred quid, you remember."

"It is your duty to give evidence, and you can be called upon to do so."

---

13. **quid:** in England, slang for the basic monetary unit, the pound.
14. **gas jet:** natural gas flame used to light a room.
15. **deal table:** table made of fir or pine planks.
16. **vitriol:** a strong acid.

Der Rote Turm in Halle II [The red tower in Halle II] (1930), Lyonel Feininger. 100 cm × 85 cm, Städtisches Museum Mülheim an der Ruhr, Mülheim, Germany.

"That won't do, dearie. I'm an old woman, and I know nothing. But you give me two hundred quid, and perhaps I can give you a hint or two. See?"

"What kind of hint?"

"What should you say to a letter? A letter from *her*. Never mind how I got hold of it. That's my business. It'll do the trick. But I want my two hundred quid."

Mr. Mayherne looked at her coldly and made up his mind.

"I'll give you ten pounds, nothing more. And only that if this letter is what you say it is."

"Ten pounds?" She screamed and raved at him.

"Twenty," said Mr. Mayherne, "and that's my last word."

He rose as if to go. Then, watching her closely, he drew out a pocketbook and counted out twenty one-pound notes.

"You see," he said. "That is all I have with me. You can take it or leave it."

But already he knew that the sight of the money was too much for her. She cursed and raved impotently, but at last she gave in. Going over to the bed, she drew something out from beneath the tattered mattress.

"Here you are, damn you!" she snarled. "It's the top one you want."

It was a bundle of letters that she threw to him, and Mr. Mayherne untied them and scanned them in his usual cool, methodical manner. The woman, watching him eagerly, could gain no clue from his impassive face.

He read each letter through, then returned again to the top one and read it a second time. Then he tied the whole bundle up again carefully.

They were love letters, written by Romaine Heilger, and the man they were written to was not Leonard Vole. The top letter was dated the day of the latter's arrest.

"I spoke true, dearie, didn't I?" whined the woman. "It'll do for her, that letter?"

Mr. Mayherne put the letters in his pocket, then he asked a question.

"How did you get hold of this correspondence?"

"That's telling," she said with a leer. "But I know something more. I heard in court what that hussy said. Find out where she was at twenty past ten, the time she says she was at home. Ask at the Lion Road Cinema. They'll remember—a fine upstanding girl like that—curse her!"

"Who is the man?" asked Mr. Mayherne. "There's only a Christian name here."

The other's voice grew thick and hoarse, her hands clenched and unclenched. Finally she lifted one to her face.

"He's the man that did this to me. Many years ago now. She took him away from me—a chit[17] of a girl she was then. And when I went after him—and went for him too—he threw the cursed

"SHE'LL SUFFER FOR THIS,

WON'T SHE, MR. LAWYER?

SHE'LL SUFFER?"

_____

17. **chit:** discourteous young woman.

WORDS TO KNOW

impotently (ĭm′pə-tənt-lē) *adv.* helplessly; powerlessly

538

stuff at me! And she laughed—damn her! I've had it in for her for years. Followed her, I have, spied upon her. And now I've got her! She'll suffer for this, won't she, Mr. Lawyer? She'll suffer?"

"She will probably be sentenced to a term of imprisonment for perjury,[18]" said Mr. Mayherne quietly.

"Shut away—that's what I want. You're going, are you? Where's my money? Where's that good money?"

Without a word, Mr. Mayherne put down the notes on the table. Then, drawing a deep breath, he turned and left the squalid room. Looking back, he saw the old woman crooning over the money.

He wasted no time. He found the cinema in Lion Road easily enough, and, shown a photograph of Romaine Heilger, the commissionaire[19] recognized her at once. She had arrived at the cinema with a man some time after ten o'clock on the evening in question. He had not noticed her escort particularly, but he remembered the lady who had spoken to him about the picture that was showing. They stayed until the end, about an hour later.

Mr. Mayherne was satisfied. Romaine Heilger's evidence was a tissue of lies from beginning to end. She had evolved it out of her passionate hatred. The lawyer wondered whether he would ever know what lay behind that hatred. What had Leonard Vole done to her? He had seemed dumbfounded when the solicitor had reported her attitude to him. He had declared earnestly that such a thing was incredible—yet it had seemed to Mr. Mayherne that after the first astonishment his protests had lacked sincerity.

He did know. Mr. Mayherne was convinced of it. He knew, but he had no intention of revealing the fact. The secret between those two remained a secret. Mr. Mayherne wondered if someday he should come to learn what it was.

The solicitor glanced at his watch. It was late, but time was everything. He hailed a taxi and gave an address.

"Sir Charles must know of this at once," he murmured to himself as he got in.

The trial of Leonard Vole for the murder of Emily French aroused widespread interest. In the first place the prisoner was young and good-looking, then he was accused of a particularly dastardly crime, and there was the further interest of Romaine Heilger, the principal witness for the prosecution. There had been pictures of her in many papers, and several fictitious stories as to her origin and history.

The proceedings opened quietly enough. Various technical evidence came first. Then Janet Mackenzie was called. She told substantially the same story as before. In cross-examination counsel for the defense succeeded in getting her to contradict herself once or twice over her account of Vole's association with Miss French; he emphasized the fact that though she had heard a man's voice in the sitting room that night, there was nothing to show that it was Vole who was there, and he managed to drive home a feeling that jealousy and dislike of the prisoner were at the bottom of a good deal of her evidence.

Then the next witness was called.

"Your name is Romaine Heilger?"

"Yes."

"You are an Austrian subject?"

"Yes."

"For the last three years you have lived with the prisoner and passed yourself off as his wife?"

Just for a moment Romaine Heilger's eyes met those of the man in the dock. Her expression held something curious and unfathomable.

---

18. **perjury:** the deliberate giving of false testimony under oath in court.

19. **commissionaire:** usher.

WORDS TO KNOW

unfathomable (ŭn-făth′ə-mə-bəl) *adj.* too mysterious to be understood

"Yes."

The questions went on. Word by word the damning facts came out. On the night in question the prisoner had taken out a crowbar with him. He had returned at twenty minutes past ten and had confessed to having killed the old lady. His cuffs had been stained with blood, and he had burned them in the kitchen stove. He had terrorized her into silence by means of threats.

As the story proceeded, the feeling of the court which had, to begin with, been slightly favorable to the prisoner, now set dead against him. He himself sat with downcast head and moody air, as though he knew he were doomed.

Yet it might have been noted that her own counsel sought to restrain Romaine's animosity. He would have preferred her to be more unbiased.

Formidable and ponderous, counsel for the defense arose.

He put it to her that her story was a malicious fabrication[20] from start to finish, that she had not even been in her own house at the time in question, that she was in love with another man and was deliberately seeking to send Vole to his death for a crime he did not commit.

Romaine denied these allegations with superb insolence.

Then came the surprising denouement,[21] the

"AT LAST I SHALL HAVE MY REVENGE."

production of the letter. It was read aloud in court in the midst of a breathless stillness.

"Max, beloved, the Fates have delivered him into our hands! He has been arrested for murder—but, yes, the murder of an old lady! Leonard, who would not hurt a fly! At last I shall have my revenge. The poor chicken! I shall say that he came in that night with blood upon him— that he confessed to me. I shall hang him, Max— and when he hangs he will know and realize that it was Romaine who sent him to his death. And then— happiness, Beloved! Happiness at last!"

There were experts present ready to swear that the handwriting was that of Romaine Heilger, but they were not needed. Confronted with the letter, Romaine broke down utterly and confessed everything. Leonard Vole had returned to the house at the time he said, twenty past nine. She had invented the whole story to ruin him.

With the collapse of Romaine Heilger, the case for the Crown collapsed also. Sir Charles

---

20. **malicious fabrication:** a lie intended to do harm or injury.
21. **denouement** (dā′nō͞o-män′): final revelation.

called his few witnesses; the prisoner himself went into the box and told his story in a manly straightforward manner, unshaken by cross-examination.

The prosecution endeavored to rally, but without great success. The judge's summing up was not wholly favorable to the prisoner, but a reaction had set in, and the jury needed little time to consider their verdict.

"We find the prisoner not guilty."

Leonard Vole was free!

Little Mr. Mayherne hurried from his seat. He must congratulate his client.

He found himself polishing his pince-nez vigorously and checked himself. His wife had told him only the night before that he was getting a habit of it. Curious things, habits. People themselves never knew they had them.

An interesting case—a very interesting case. That woman, now, Romaine Heilger.

The case was dominated for him still by the exotic figure of Romaine Heilger. She had seemed a pale, quiet woman in the house at Paddington, but in court she had flamed out against the sober background, flaunting herself like a tropical flower.

If he closed his eyes, he could see her now, tall and vehement, her exquisite body bent forward a little, her right hand clenching and unclenching itself unconsciously all the time.

Curious things, habits. That gesture of hers with the hand was her habit, he supposed. Yet he had seen someone else do it quite lately. Who was it now? Quite lately—

He drew in his breath with a gasp as it came back to him. The woman in Shaw's Rents . . .

He stood still, his head whirling. It was impossible—impossible— Yet, Romaine Heilger was an actress.

The K.C. came up behind him and clapped him on the shoulder.

"Congratulated our man yet? He's had a narrow shave, you know. Come along and see him."

But the little lawyer shook off the other's hand.

He wanted one thing only—to see Romaine Heilger face to face.

He did not see her until some time later, and the place of their meeting is not relevant.

"So you guessed," she said, when he had told her all that was in his mind. "The face? Oh! that was easy enough, and the light of that gas jet was too bad for you to see the makeup."

"But why—why—"

"Why did I play a lone hand?" She smiled a little, remembering the last time she had used the words.

"Such an elaborate comedy!"

"My friend—I had to save him. The evidence of a woman devoted to him would not have been enough—you hinted as much yourself. But I know something of the psychology of crowds. Let my evidence be wrung from me, as an admission, damning me in the eyes of the law, and a reaction in favor of the prisoner would immediately set in."

"And the bundle of letters?"

"One alone, the vital one, might have seemed like a—what do you call it?—put-up job."

"Then the man called Max?"

"Never existed, my friend."

"I still think," said little Mr. Mayherne, in an aggrieved manner, "that we could have got him off by the—er—normal procedure."

"I dared not risk it. You see, you thought he was innocent—"

"And you knew it? I see," said little Mr. Mayherne.

"My dear Mr. Mayherne," said Romaine, "you do not see at all. I knew—he was guilty!" ❖

RESPONDING
OPTIONS

FROM PERSONAL RESPONSE TO CRITICAL ANALYSIS

REFLECT 1. Did you find the end of the story satisfying? Write your reaction in your notebook, then discuss it with a classmate.

RETHINK 2. Review the chart you made for the Reading Connection on page 523. Compare your evaluation of Vole's guilt or innocence with what you learn about him at the end of the play.

3. What is your opinion of Romaine Heilger?
   Consider
   - her physical appearance and demeanor
   - the details of her background
   - her first interview with Mayherne
   - her final revelations

4. Do you think Mr. Mayherne is good at his work? Why or why not?

RELATE 5. Based on this selection and on cases you may have seen in the news, how effective do you think courts are in finding out the truth?

ANOTHER PATHWAY

Imagine that you and a classmate are detectives. As partners, piece together the truth about events on the night of the murder of Miss Emily French. Develop a time line that shows the time of the murder and the steps leading up to and following the deed. If you prepare your time line on a computer, you can easily move blocks of text into the correct order.

LITERARY CONCEPTS

Suspense is the tension or excitement readers feel as they become involved in a story and eager to learn the outcome of the plot. In "The Witness for the Prosecution," the suspense builds as Mr. Mayherne pursues the evidence. We wonder whether Leonard Vole is guilty or innocent and how the trial will turn out. How does the visit to Mrs. Mogson add to the suspense?

CONCEPT REVIEW: Point of View Although the story is narrated from the third-person point of view, the perceptions are limited to Mr. Mayherne's. How does this particular point of view affect your sympathies or views toward the characters?

QUICKWRITES

1. Write a **script** for the interview Mr. Mayherne might have had with Leonard Vole after learning the truth from Romaine Heilger.

2. Write a **newspaper article** that might have appeared just after the murder, just after the pretrial (police court) hearing, or the day after Vole was found not guilty.

3. What current movie stars would you cast in the roles of the characters in a modern film version of "The Witness for the Prosecution"? Make a **cast list** of characters showing which star you would cast in each role. Briefly explain your reasons for each casting decision.

PORTFOLIO Save your writing. You may want to use it later as a springboard to a piece for your portfolio.

ALTERNATIVE ACTIVITIES

1. Working with a classmate, **role-play** the prosecution's examination or the defense's cross-examination of Romaine Heilger, the chief witness for the prosecution.

2. Imagine that you are the courtroom artist at the trial. Draw **sketches** of the defendant, the lawyers, and the witnesses.

3. Read the dramatic adaptation of this story or watch a video of the 1957 film version. Then write a **review** in which you compare the short story with the play or the film version. Be sure to mention which you prefer and why.

4. With a partner, create an **instructional video** that illustrates how to tell whether someone is telling the truth. Base your video on a scene from the story or on your own original script.

ACROSS THE CURRICULUM

Science What current scientific techniques for gathering evidence would make it harder for Vole to conceal his guilt today? Research these techniques, and record your findings in a written report.

THE WRITER'S STYLE

Many of Agatha Christie's mysteries have been adapted for dramatic presentation. Christie herself turned "The Witness for the Prosecution" into a stage play, which then became the basis of a popular 1957 movie; later, there was also a television production. Based on the style of this story, why do you think Christie's fiction lends itself to dramatic adaptation?

CRITIC'S CORNER

Commenting on Christie's popularity, H. R. F. Keating said, "She never tried to be clever in her writing, only ingenious in her plots." Do you think that "The Witness for the Prosecution" illustrates this distinction? Explain your view.

ART CONNECTION

How well does the woman in the painting *Portrait de Madame M.* on page 533 match the way you pictured Romaine Heilger as you read the story?

Detail of *Portrait de Madame M.*, Tamara de Lempicka (1898–1980). Oil on canvas, 99 cm × 65 cm, private collection, Paris. Copyright © 1996 Artists Rights Society (ARS), New York/ SPADEM, Paris.

WORDS TO KNOW

EXERCISE A For each phrase on the left, write the letter of the synonym phrase on the right.

1. impotently scream
2. notice insolence
3. churlish driver
4. amicable serf
5. sweet-talk the filly
6. averse to rehearsal
7. blushes from crushes
8. quiet the riot
9. intolerable officer
10. cultivate comrade

a. infernal colonel
b. infatuated rosiness
c. observe nerve
d. opposed to practice
e. crabby cabbie
f. cajole the foal
g. pleasant peasant
h. quell the crowd
i. befriend Ben
j. weakly shriek

EXERCISE B For each group of words below, write the letter of the word that is the best antonym for the boldfaced word.

1. **dastardly** (a) admirable, (b) effective, (c) clever

2. **animosity** (a) jealousy, (b) sophistication, (c) friendliness

3. **vindicate** (a) accuse, (b) retrieve, (c) honor

4. **unfathomable** (a) encouraging, (b) likable, (c) clear

5. **assiduously** (a) respectfully, (b) lazily, (c) heavily

AGATHA CHRISTIE

Known as the Queen of British Mystery, Agatha Christie is one of the world's most popular writers of detective fiction. Her books have been translated into more than 100 languages, and probably more copies of her books have been sold than have those of any other writer in our century. Christie's eccentric detective Hercule Poirot appeared on a Nicaraguan postage stamp. Several of her other detectives, including Miss Jane Marple, are still featured regularly in televised versions of her mysteries.

1890–1976

Christie grew up in Torquay, Devonshire, a small resort in the English countryside. Her father, an American, died when she was very young, and she was raised by her British mother. In 1914, after the outbreak of World War I, Christie was married. During the war, she worked as a hospital nurse and thereby gained, among other things, a knowledge of poisons. A challenge from her sister prompted Christie to write her first detective novel, *The Mysterious Affair at Styles*, which was published in 1920. In the next six years, she published six more books, including *The Murder of Roger Ackroyd* (1926), often hailed as her

most ingenious mystery. Soon afterward came the famous mystery in Christie's own life: The celebrated author disappeared, and she was discovered, after a nation-wide hunt, apparently suffering from amnesia. She subsequently divorced her first husband and married Max Mallowan, an archaeologist, with whom she later made frequent visits to the Middle East. These travels prompted several mysteries, including *Death on the Nile* (1937) and *Death Comes as the End* (1944).

To please her millions of fans, Christie, for most of her career, produced a mystery a year, or a "Christie for Christmas." Her clever "whodunits" introduced nearly every conceivable variation of the least-likely-suspect solution: the detective who "done it," the seeming victim who "done it," the narrator who "done it," and even a conspiracy in which all of the suspects "done it."

OTHER WORKS *Murder on the Orient Express, And Then There Were None, Three Blind Mice and Other Stories, Hickory Dickory Death*

PREVIEWING

Games at Twilight
Anita Desai (dä sī′) India

PERSONAL CONNECTION

In a class discussion, talk about a favorite childhood game, such as hide-and-seek. What are some of your most vivid memories of that game? Share your recollections of your experiences of the game and the feelings you had about playing it. You might use a cluster diagram, like the one shown, to prompt your memory.

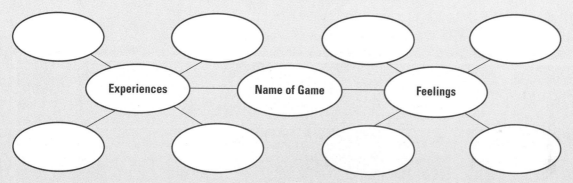

CULTURAL CONNECTION

In "Games at Twilight" the main character is a young boy who is part of a large, wealthy family in India. Many such families still prefer to follow the Western customs and social behaviors introduced during Britain's long colonial rule of India, which ended in 1947. In this story, the children play games similar to those played by British and American children, including hide-and-seek. To determine who will be "It," the children use a counting-out rhyme beginning "Dip, dip, dip" (similar to "Eeny, meeny, miney, mo" or "One potato, two potato," both popular in the United States). In their version of the game, the hiders try to sneak back to the starting place while the seeker is still looking for them. They call the starting place "the den" and cry "Den!" when they return to it safely.

WRITING CONNECTION

Why do you think almost all children play games—regardless of their culture or economic situation? In your notebook, reflect upon the importance of games during your own childhood. Keep these thoughts in mind as you read the following selection.

Children playing cricket in Calcutta, India. Copyright © Jeffrey Alford/Asia Access.

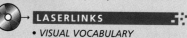

LASERLINKS
• VISUAL VOCABULARY

545

GAMES AT TWILIGHT

ANITA DESAI

In a Past Life (1993), John Harris.

It was still too hot to play outdoors. They had had their tea, they had been washed and had their hair brushed, and after the long day of confinement in the house that was not cool but at least a protection from the sun, the children strained to get out. Their faces were red and bloated with the effort, but their mother would not open the door, everything was still curtained and shuttered in a way that stifled the children, made them feel that their lungs were stuffed with cotton wool and their noses with dust and if they didn't burst out into the light and see the sun and feel the air, they would choke.

"Please, ma, please," they begged. "We'll play in the veranda and porch—we won't go a step out of the porch."

"You will, I know you will, and then—"

"No—we won't, we won't," they wailed so horrendously that she actually let down the bolt of the front door so that they burst out like seeds from a crackling, over-ripe pod into the veranda, with such wild, maniacal yells that she retreated to her bath and the shower of talcum powder and the fresh sari[1] that were to help her face the summer evening.

They faced the afternoon. It was too hot. Too bright. The white walls of the veranda glared stridently in the sun. The bougainvillea[2] hung about it, purple and magenta, in livid balloons. The garden outside was like a tray made of beaten brass, flattened out on the red gravel and the stony soil in all shades of metal—aluminum, tin, copper and brass. No life stirred at this arid time of day—the birds still drooped, like dead fruit, in the papery tents of the trees; some squirrels lay limp on the wet earth under the garden tap. The outdoor dog lay stretched as if dead on the veranda mat, his paws and ears and tail all reaching out like dying travelers in search of water. He rolled his eyes at the children—two white marbles rolling in the purple sockets, begging for sympathy—and attempted to lift his tail in a wag but could not. It only twitched and lay still.

Then, perhaps roused by the shrieks of the children, a band of parrots suddenly fell out of the eucalyptus tree, tumbled frantically in the still, sizzling air, then sorted themselves out into battle formation and streaked away across the white sky.

The children, too, felt released. They too began tumbling, shoving, pushing against each other, frantic to start. Start what? Start their business. The business of the children's day which is—play.

"Let's play hide-and-seek."

"Who'll be It?"

"You be It."

"Why should I? You be—"

"You're the eldest—"

"That doesn't mean—"

The shoves became harder. Some kicked out. The motherly Mira intervened. She pulled the boys roughly apart. There was a tearing sound of cloth but it was lost in the heavy panting and angry grumbling, and no one paid attention to the small sleeve hanging loosely off a shoulder.

"Make a circle, make a circle!" she shouted, firmly pulling and pushing till a kind of vague circle was formed. "Now clap!" she roared and, clapping, they all chanted in melancholy unison: "Dip, dip, dip—my blue ship—" and every now and then one or the other saw he was safe by the way his hands fell at the crucial moment—palm on palm, or back of hand on palm—and dropped out of the circle with a yell and a jump of relief and jubilation.

---

1. **sari** (sä′rē): garment worn by women and girls in India, consisting of a long cloth wrapped around the body, with one end draped over the shoulder.

2. **bougainvillea** (boo′gən-vĭl′ē-ə): tropical vine with brightly colored flowers.

Raghu was It. He started to protest, to cry, "You cheated—Mira cheated—Anu cheated—" but it was too late, the others had all already streaked away. There was no one to hear when he called out, "Only in the veranda—the porch—Ma said—Ma *said* to stay in the porch!" No one had stopped to listen, all he saw were their brown legs flashing through the dusty shrubs, scrambling up brick walls, leaping over compost heaps and hedges; and then the porch stood empty in the purple shade of the bougainvillea and the garden was as empty as before; even the limp squirrels had whisked away, leaving everything gleaming, brassy and bare.

Only small Manu suddenly reappeared, as if he had dropped out of an invisible cloud or from a bird's claws, and stood for a moment in the center of the yellow lawn, chewing his finger and near to tears as he heard Raghu shouting, with his head pressed against the veranda wall, "Eighty-three, eighty-five, eighty-nine, ninety . . ." and then made off in a panic, half of him wanting to fly north, the other half counseling south. Raghu turned just in time to see the flash of his white shorts and the uncertain skittering of his red sandals, and charged after him with such a bloodcurdling yell that Manu stumbled over the hose pipe, fell into its rubber coils and lay there weeping, "I won't be It—you have to find them all—all—All!"

"I know I have to, idiot," Raghu said, superciliously kicking him with his toe. "You're dead," he said with satisfaction, licking the beads of perspiration off his upper lip, and then stalked off in search of worthier prey, whistling spiritedly so that the hiders should hear and tremble.

Ravi heard the whistling and picked his nose in a panic, trying to find comfort by burrowing the finger deep—deep into that soft tunnel. He felt himself too exposed, sitting on an upturned flower pot behind the garage. Where could he burrow? He could run around the garage if he heard Raghu come—around and around and around—but he hadn't much faith in his short legs when matched against Raghu's long, hefty, hairy footballer[3] legs. Ravi had a frightening glimpse of them as Raghu combed the hedge of crotons and hibiscus, trampling delicate ferns underfoot as he did so. Ravi looked about him desperately, swallowing a small ball of snot in his fear.

The garage was locked with a great heavy lock to which the driver had the key in his room, hanging from a nail on the wall under his work shirt. Ravi had peeped in and seen him still sprawling on his string-cot in his vest and striped underpants, the hair on his chest and the hair in his nose shaking with the vibrations of his phlegm-obstructed snores. Ravi had wished he were tall enough, big enough, to reach the key on the nail, but it was impossible, beyond his reach for years to come. He had sidled away and sat dejectedly on the flower pot. That at least was cut to his own size.

But next to the garage was another shed with a big green door. Also locked. No one even knew who had the key to the lock. That shed wasn't opened more than once a year when Ma turned out all the old broken bits of furniture and rolls of matting and leaking buckets, and the white ant hills were broken and swept away and Flit[4] sprayed into the spider webs and rat holes so that the whole operation was like the looting of a poor, ruined and conquered city. The green leaves of the door sagged. They were nearly off their rusty hinges. The hinges were large and made a

---

3. **footballer:** soccer player. In India and much of the world, soccer is called football.

4. **Flit:** the brand name of an insecticide.

WORDS
TO
KNOW

superciliously (sōō′pər-sĭl′ē-əs-lē) *adv.* proudly and scornfully

small gap between the door and the walls—only just large enough for rats, dogs and, possibly, Ravi to slip through.

Ravi had never cared to enter such a dark and depressing mortuary[5] of <u>defunct</u> household goods seething with such unspeakable and alarming animal life but, as Raghu's whistling grew angrier and sharper and his crashing and storming in the hedge wilder, Ravi suddenly slipped off the flower pot and through the crack and was gone. He chuckled aloud with astonishment at his own <u>temerity</u> so that Raghu came out of the hedge, stood silent with his hands on his hips, listening, and finally shouted "I heard you! I'm coming! *Got* you—" and came charging round the garage only to find the upturned flower pot, the yellow dust, the crawling of white ants in a mud-hill against the closed shed door—nothing. Snarling, he bent to pick up a stick and went off, whacking it against the garage and shed walls as if to beat out his prey.

Ravi shook, then shivered with delight, with self-congratulation. Also with fear. It was dark, spooky in the shed. It had a muffled smell, as of graves. Ravi had once got locked into the linen cupboard and sat there weeping for half an hour before he was rescued. But at least that had been a familiar place, and even smelt pleasantly of starch, laundry and, reassuringly, of his mother. But the shed smelt of rats, ant hills, dust and spider webs. Also of less definable, less recognizable horrors. And it was dark. Except for the white-hot cracks along the door, there was no light. The roof was very low. Although Ravi was small, he felt as if he could reach up and touch it with his finger tips. But he didn't stretch. He hunched himself into a ball so as not to bump into anything, touch or feel anything. What might there not be to touch him and feel him as he stood there, trying to see in the dark? Something cold,

or slimy—like a snake. Snakes! He leapt up as Raghu whacked the wall with his stick—then, quickly realizing what it was, felt almost relieved to hear Raghu, hear his stick. It made him feel protected.

But Raghu soon moved away. There wasn't a sound once his footsteps had gone around the garage and disappeared. Ravi stood frozen inside the shed. Then he shivered all over. Something had tickled the back of his neck. It took him a while to pick up the courage to lift his hand and explore. It was an insect—perhaps a spider—exploring *him*. He squashed it and wondered how many more creatures were watching him, waiting to reach out and touch him, the stranger.

There was nothing now. After standing in that position—his hand still on his neck, feeling the wet splodge of the squashed spider gradually dry—for minutes, hours, his legs began to tremble with the effort, the inaction. By now he could see enough in the dark to make out the large solid shapes of old wardrobes, broken buckets and bedsteads piled on top of each other around him. He recognized an old bathtub—patches of enamel glimmered at him and at last he lowered himself onto its edge.

He contemplated slipping out of the shed and into the <u>fray</u>. He wondered if it would not be better to be captured by Raghu and be returned to the milling crowd as long as he could be in the sun, the light, the free spaces of the garden and the familiarity of his brothers, sisters and cousins. It would be evening soon. Their games would become legitimate. The parents would sit out on the lawn on cane basket chairs and watch them as they tore around the garden or

---

5. **mortuary:** place where dead bodies are kept before burial.

WORDS TO KNOW

defunct (dĭ-fŭngkt') *adj.* no longer in existence or use

temerity (tə-mĕr'ĭ-tē) *n.* reckless boldness

fray (frā) *n.* a heated contest; brawl; fight

549

Los Chicos [The boys] (1957), Fletcher Martin. Private collection.

gathered in knots to share a loot of mulberries or black, teeth-splitting *jamun*[6] from the garden trees. The gardener would fix the hosepipe to the water tap and water would fall lavishly through the air to the ground, soaking the dry yellow grass and the red gravel and arousing the sweet, the intoxicating scent of water on dry earth—that loveliest scent in the world. Ravi sniffed for a whiff of it. He half-rose from the bathtub, then heard the despairing scream of one of the girls as Raghu bore down upon her. There was the sound of a crash, and of rolling about in the bushes, the shrubs, then screams and accusing sobs of, "I touched the den—" "You did not—" "I did—" "You liar, you did *not*" and then a fading away and silence again.

Ravi sat back on the harsh edge of the tub, deciding to hold out a bit longer. What fun if they were all found and caught—he alone left unconquered! He had never known that sensation. Nothing more wonderful had ever happened to him than being taken out by an uncle and bought a whole slab of chocolate all to himself, or being flung into the soda-man's pony cart and driven up to the gate by the friendly driver with the red beard and pointed ears. To defeat Raghu—that hirsute,[7] hoarse-voiced football champion—and to be the winner in a circle of older, bigger, luckier children—that would be thrilling beyond imagination. He hugged his knees together and smiled to himself almost shyly at the thought of so much victory, such laurels.[8]

There he sat smiling, knocking his heels against the bathtub, now and then getting up and going to the door to put his ear to the broad crack and listening for sounds of the game, the pursuer and the pursued, and then returning to his seat with the dogged determination of the true winner, a breaker of records, a champion.

It grew darker in the shed as the light at the door grew softer, fuzzier, turned to a kind of crumbling yellow pollen that turned to yellow fur, blue fur, gray fur. Evening. Twilight. The sound of water gushing, falling. The scent of earth receiving water, slaking its thirst in great gulps and releasing that green scent of freshness, coolness. Through the crack Ravi saw the long purple shadows of the shed and the garage lying still across the yard. Beyond that, the white walls of the house. The bougainvillea had lost its lividity, hung in dark bundles that quaked and twittered and seethed with masses of homing sparrows. The lawn was shut off from his view. Could he hear the children's voices? It seemed to him that he could. It seemed to him that he could hear them chanting, singing, laughing. But what about the game? What had happened? Could it be over? How could it when he was still not found?

It then occurred to him that he could have slipped out long ago, dashed across the yard to the veranda and touched the "den." It was necessary to do that to win. He had forgotten. He had only remembered the part of hiding and trying to elude the seeker. He had done that so successfully, his success had occupied him so wholly that he had quite forgotten that success had to be clinched by that final dash to victory and the ringing cry of "Den!"

With a whimper he burst through the crack, fell on his knees, got up and stumbled on stiff, benumbed legs across the shadowy yard, crying heartily by the time he reached the veranda so that when he flung himself at the white pillar and bawled, "Den! Den! Den!" his voice broke with rage and pity at the disgrace of it all and he felt himself flooded with tears and misery.

6. *jamun* (jǎ-mōōn'): purplish-red berries of the *jamun* tree.
7. **hirsute** (hûr'sōōt'): hairy.
8. **laurels:** fame; honor.

WORDS TO KNOW   **slaking** (slā'kǐng) *adj.* satisfying **slake** *v.*

Out on the lawn, the children stopped chanting. They all turned to stare at him in amazement. Their faces were pale and triangular in the dusk. The trees and bushes around them stood inky and sepulchral,[9] spilling long shadows across them. They stared, wondering at his reappearance, his passion, his wild animal howling. Their mother rose from her basket chair and came towards him, worried, annoyed, saying, "Stop it, stop it, Ravi. Don't be a baby. Have you hurt yourself?" Seeing him attended to, the children went back to clasping their hands and chanting "The grass is green, the rose is red. . . ."

But Ravi would not let them. He tore himself out of his mother's grasp and pounded across the lawn into their midst, charging at them with his head lowered so that they scattered in surprise. "I won, I won, I won," he bawled, shaking his head so that the big tears flew. "Raghu didn't find me. I won, I won—"

It took them a minute to grasp what he was saying, even who he was. They had quite forgotten him. Raghu had found all the others long ago. There had been a fight about who was to be It next. It had been so fierce that their mother had emerged from her bath and made them change to another game. Then they had played another and another. Broken mulberries from the tree and eaten them. Helped the driver wash the car when their father returned from work. Helped the gardener water the beds till he roared at them and swore he would complain to their parents. The parents had come out, taken up their positions on the cane chairs. They had begun to play again, sing and chant. All this time no one had remembered Ravi. Having disappeared from the scene, he had disappeared from their minds. Clean.

"Don't be a fool," Raghu said roughly, pushing him aside, and even Mira said, "Stop howling, Ravi. If you want to play, you can stand at the end of the line," and she put him there very firmly.

The game proceeded. Two pairs of arms reached up and met in an arc. The children trooped under it again and again in a lugubrious[10] circle, ducking their heads and intoning

"The grass is green,
The rose is red;
Remember me
When I am dead, dead, dead, dead . . ."

And the arc of thin arms trembled in the twilight, and the heads were bowed so sadly, and their feet tramped to that melancholy refrain so mournfully, so helplessly, that Ravi could not bear it. He would not follow them, he would not be included in this funereal game. He had wanted victory and triumph—not a funeral. But he had been forgotten, left out, and he would not join them now. The ignominy of being forgotten—how could he face it? He felt his heart go heavy and ache inside him unbearably. He lay down full length on the damp grass, crushing his face into it, no longer crying, silenced by a terrible sense of his insignificance. ❖

---

9. **sepulchral** (sə-pŭl′krəl): tomblike; suggestive of the grave.

10. **lugubrious** (lōō-gōō′brē-əs): exaggeratedly sad or mournful.

WORDS TO KNOW

ignominy (ĭg′nə-mĭn′ē) *n.* public shame and disgrace

552

RESPONDING
OPTIONS

FROM PERSONAL RESPONSE TO CRITICAL ANALYSIS

REFLECT   1. How do you feel about what happens to Ravi? Describe your reaction in your notebook.

RETHINK   2. Why do you think Ravi's experience during the hide-and-seek game affects him so deeply?
   Consider
   - how this experience compares with the time he was locked in the cupboard
   - his expectations about what winning will be like
   - how the family reacts to his crying and to his declaration that he has won
   - why he refuses to join the funeral game

   3. How would you evaluate the way Ravi's family behaves toward him?
   Consider
   - why the family forgets about him
   - why they fail to respond according to his expectations

   4. If Ravi came from a smaller family, how might his experience be different?

RELATE   5. To what extent do you think games teach children to live in an adult world? Discuss this with your classmates.

ANOTHER PATHWAY

Cooperative Learning

Imagine it is 20 years after this story takes place. With a group of classmates, act out the parts of Ravi and members of his large family, who have gathered on the veranda on a hot summer evening. The family members reminisce about Ravi's hide-and-seek experience and his behavior after rejoining the others.

QUICKWRITES

1. Use the diagram you completed for the Personal Connection on page 545 as a springboard for your own **first-person narrative** about playing a children's game.

2. Write an **episode** that extends the story, perhaps showing Ravi and his siblings playing games a week later.

3. Do you think strong competition is generally useful or harmful in children's games? Referring both to your own experiences and to the story, express your opinion in an **article** for a parents' magazine or newsletter.

📁 **PORTFOLIO** *Save your writing. You may want to use it later as a springboard to a piece for your portfolio.*

LITERARY LINKS

Compare Ravi with the main character in "The Study of History" by Frank O'Connor on page 151. What is similar and/or different about the two boys' attitudes and realizations?

LITERARY CONCEPTS

Diction, or a writer's choice of words, is an important part of a writer's style. Diction encompasses both vocabulary (individual words) and syntax (the order or arrangement of words). Diction can be described in terms such as formal or informal, technical or common, abstract or concrete. With a partner, choose one passage from the story. Using the terms supplied above, analyze Desai's diction in that passage. Present your analysis to the class.

ACROSS THE CURRICULUM

Anthropology Many childhood games have a long history, and variations of the same game may span many cultures. Research a game that you played as a child and find out about its history and variations. Share your findings in an oral report.

Science "Games at Twilight" begins on an oppressively hot, dry afternoon. Research the monthly average temperatures and rainfall in India. Present your findings to the class in the form of two bar graphs, one for temperature and one for rainfall. Based on your research, what month or months would you say are likely times for the setting of this story?

ALTERNATIVE ACTIVITIES

1. Draw a **map** of the grounds around Ravi's house showing all the locations mentioned in the story. Label the areas and briefly describe the action that takes place there.

2. Speaking as one of the parents in "Games at Twilight," give an **oral monologue** describing the evening of the story and Ravi's experiences from an adult's point of view.

3. With a partner, create a **pie chart** that shows the various emotions Ravi feels during the story. Make a separate section for each emotion. In each section, write quotations from the selection that give evidence of that emotion.

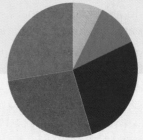

CRITIC'S CORNER

According to one critic, "Games at Twilight" conveys "Ravi's first experience of his own mortality, his sense of his own small, brief place in a vast and difficult universe." Explain whether you agree or disagree with this interpretation, and support your opinion with details from the story.

WORDS TO KNOW

With 19 classmates, play a game with the words listed below. Each student should write one of the words on a note card (one student per word). Then each student should hold up his or her word and look for the classmate who is holding the best synonym for that word. Stand together until all pairs are matched up. Play several rounds by exchanging words with a classmate and finding your new match.

1. arid
2. stifle
3. defunct
4. temerity
5. melancholy
6. stridently
7. fray
8. superciliously
9. ignominy
10. slaking

a. rashness
b. parched
c. conflict
d. gloomy
e. dishonor
f. bygone
g. smother
h. harshly
i. quenching
j. arrogantly

bygone

ANITA DESAI

Anita Desai, considered one of the most gifted of contemporary Indian authors, writes about the blending of British and Eastern cultures in her native India. She examines social issues by focusing on individual characters' struggles with the everyday problems of life.

Born Anita Mazumdar in Mussoorie, India, she graduated from nearby Delhi University in 1957 and married a business executive, Ashvin Desai, in 1958. She began writing short stories while still in college and published her first novel in 1963. Like other contemporary Indian authors, Desai writes in English, a language in which many Indians are fluent, owing to the legacy of British colonial rule. Writing in English has enabled Desai to reach not only a large Indian population but also British and American audiences.

Desai's first overseas publications appeared in Great Britain, where she has twice been nominated for the prestigious Booker Prize (similar to the Pulitzer Prize).

1937–

Her fifth novel, *Fire on the Mountain* (1977), was published in the United States, and her fame in this country spread rapidly. Her novel *Clear Light of Day*, published in 1980, was universally acclaimed by American critics. Karen Ray described it as "a novel of perfect details, of looking at the world through a magnifying glass, of collecting enough small bits to make sense somehow of the whole." That same year saw the American release of the much-praised *Games at Twilight and Other Stories*.

Since that time, all of Desai's novels have become available to American readers, and Desai has visited and taught in the United States. She also has published three books of juvenile literature, including *The Village by the Sea*, which won Great Britain's Guardian Award for Children's Fiction in 1982.

OTHER WORKS *Voices in the City; Bye-Bye, Blackbird; In Custody; Baumgartner's Bombay*

PREVIEWING

POETRY

The Street / La Calle
Octavio Paz (ôk-tä′vē-ô päs) Mexico

I Am Not I / Yo No Soy No
Juan Ramón Jiménez (wän rä-môn′ hē-mě′něs) Spain

PERSONAL CONNECTION

If someone asked you to define your identity, how would you respond? Would you be one who looks inward, tapping the depths of the private self hidden from public view? Or would you look outward, defining yourself by your own unique place in the world? In your notebook, create two columns like those shown. Describe your own identity by responding to each question.

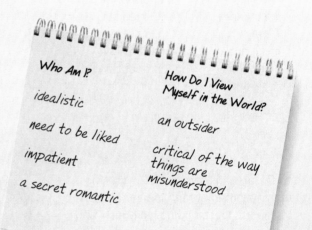

Who Am I?
idealistic
need to be liked
impatient
a secret romantic

How Do I View Myself in the World?
an outsider
critical of the way things are
misunderstood

LITERARY CONNECTION

The mysteries of identity are key concerns of the two poems that follow. Both poems are by eminent Spanish-language poets whose achievements were honored with the Nobel Prize in literature. The poetry of Octavio Paz often contains elements of **surrealism,** in which dreamlike images from the unconscious mind are captured in writing. Juan Ramón Jiménez, who preceded Paz by a generation, is responsible in many respects for introducing modernism to Spanish poetry. "The Street" and "I Am Not I" both explore the hidden territories of the self and its relation to the rest of the world.

The Endless Enigma (1938), Salvador Dali. Oil on canvas, 45″ × 57″. Copyright © Fundació Gala-Salvador Dali.

Understanding Modern Poetry

Modern poets have often used their art to explore their own identity. These poets have had more freedom than their predecessors: they have explored their most private thoughts, chosen virtually any subject, and created their own forms of expression. To understand such poetry, you will find it helpful to know about the following poetic techniques:

Free Verse

Many modern poems are written in free verse, which has no meter and no fixed stanzas or fixed line lengths. Instead, the poet decides where the lines should break, based on where a pause is required or on how the poem will look on the page. As you read the Paz and Jiménez poems, pay attention to how the lines are organized on the page. The line breaks, punctuation, and spacing help convey the mood and the meaning of each poem.

Literal and Symbolic Meanings

Modern poets frequently write about situations from everyday life that are often charged with symbolic meaning to convey a message about life or human nature. To understand symbolic meaning, you first need to understand literal meaning. As you read the Paz poem, consider where the speaker is and what he is doing. For the Jiménez poem, note the routine activities described. Literal meanings provide access to richer, symbolic meanings.

Diction

In contrast to the poetry of long ago, notable for its formal and sometimes flowery language, modern poetry often makes use of informal language drawn from the vocabulary and speech patterns of everyday life. As you read, pay close attention to the poet's diction, or word choice. Why do you think the poet chose such words? What feelings and ideas do they suggest to you?

Imagery and Figurative Language

Like all poets, modern poets rely more on suggestion than on direct statement. Typically, poets use imagery and figurative language to convey underlying ideas and emotions. Paz presents an image of a man walking on a "long and silent street." Jiménez creates an image of a divided self in "I Am Not I." In each poem, the image is central to the meaning.

Strategies for Reading Modern Poetry

1. Read through the poem once to get a general idea of what it is about, using clues from the title to identify the topic.
2. Notice how physical arrangement and punctuation mark units of thought.
3. Consider the literal meaning of the situation described. What is going on, and who is involved?
4. Think about the associations that the words, imagery, and figurative language bring to mind. How do these associations influence understanding?
5. Identify the parts of the poem that puzzle you. Can you use the parts that are clear to you to help explain other parts that are less clear?
6. Consider different ways of interpreting the poem. Which interpretation explains the most?
7. Read the poem aloud, or read it so that you "hear" the poem in your head. Note the relationship between sound and meaning.

Octavio Paz — The Street

A long and silent street.
I walk in blackness and I stumble and fall
and rise, and I walk blind, my feet
stepping on silent stones and dry leaves.
5 Someone behind me also stepping on stones,
    leaves:
if I slow down, he slows;
if I run, he runs. I turn: nobody.
Everything dark and doorless.
Turning and turning among these corners
10 which lead forever to the street
where nobody waits for, nobody follows me,
where I pursue a man who stumbles
and rises and says when he sees me: nobody.

Translated by Muriel Rukeyser

La Calle

Es una calle larga y silenciosa.
Ando en tinieblas y tropiezo y caigo
y me levanto y piso con pies ciegos
las piedras mudas y las hojas secas
5 y alguien detrás di mí también las pisa:
si me detengo, se detiene;
si corro, corre. Vuelvo el rostro: nadie.
Todo está oscuro y sin salida,
y doy vueltas y vueltas en esquinas
10 que dan siempre a la calle
donde nadie me espera ni me sigue,
donde yo sigo a un hombre que tropieza
y se levanta y dice al verme: nadie.

FROM PERSONAL RESPONSE TO CRITICAL ANALYSIS

REFLECT 1. Draw a sketch of what you pictured in your mind while you were reading "The Street." Compare your sketch with those of your classmates.

RETHINK 2. Do you think the speaker is describing a real or an imagined event?
Consider
- details about the speaker's surroundings
- why the speaker feels that someone is following him
- what the speaker realizes when he turns and sees "nobody"
- who or what the speaker might be pursuing

3. How do you think the speaker views his own life?
Consider
- how the speaker feels about the events he describes
- what the street might symbolize
- why the speaker keeps repeating the word "nobody"

Juan Ramón Jiménez
"I Am Not I"

I am not I.
       I am this one
walking beside me whom I do not see,
whom at times I manage to visit,
5 and whom at other times I forget;
who remains calm and silent while I talk,
and forgives, gently, when I hate,
who walks where I am not,
who will remain standing when I die.

       Translated by Robert Bly

Yo No Soy Yo

Yo no soy yo.
       Soy este
que va a mi lado sin yo verlo;
que, a veces, voy a ver,
5 y que, a veses, olvido.
El que calla, sereno, cuando hablo,
el que perdona, dulce, cuando odio,
el que pasea por donde no estoy,
el que quedará en pie cuando yo muera.

La reproduction interdite (Portrait d'Edward James) [Not to be reproduced (Portrait of Edward James)] (1937), René Magritte. Oil on canvas, 81.3 cm × 65 cm, Museum Boymans–van Beuningen, Rotterdam, the Netherlands, Giraudon/Art Resource, New York. Copyright © 1996 Artists Rights Society (ARS), New York.

RESPONDING OPTIONS

FROM PERSONAL RESPONSE TO CRITICAL ANALYSIS

REFLECT 1. What went through your mind as you were reading "I Am Not I"? Describe your reaction in your notebook.

RETHINK 2. How would you describe the speaker's two different selves?

Consider
- why the speaker visits his other self only some of the time
- the contrasts in lines 6–8
- your interpretation of the last line

3. How does the speaker seem to evaluate his two different selves?

RELATE 4. Do you think that all people have an inner self that is different from the self they show the world? Explain your opinion.

5. How do you think the speakers in "The Street" and "I Am Not I" see themselves in relation to the rest of the world?

6. In your judgment, how do "The Street" and "I Am Not I" illustrate typical characteristics of modern poetry?

ANOTHER PATHWAY

Imagine that you are the speaker of "The Street" or "I Am Not I." Turn the poem into a diary entry in which you describe in prose your thoughts and feelings about your identity. Be sure to base your statements on details from the poem. Share your diary entry with a small group of classmates, and discuss the similarities and differences among the entries.

LITERARY CONCEPTS

Alliteration is the repetition of initial consonant sounds in nearby words, as in "*d*ismal *d*ungeon." Alliteration can be used to emphasize certain words, unify a poem, contribute to the tone, or establish sound effects. In translating Paz's poem into English, American poet Muriel Rukeyser tried to preserve the alliteration of the original Spanish. Identify examples of alliteration in her translation, and discuss the purposes they help achieve. Then compare Robert Bly's translation of "I Am Not I" with the original to see if the alliteration was preserved.

CONCEPT REVIEW: Repetition Cite examples from both poems to show how repetition helps emphasize and unify ideas in the poems.

QUICKWRITES

1. Write your own **poem** about who you are. You may find it helpful to draw upon your responses to the questions in the Personal Connection on page 556.

2. Many people, just for fun, follow horoscopes in the daily newspaper. Create a **horoscope** for the speaker of one of the poems. Your horoscope can either predict what kind of day the speaker will have or profile his personality.

📁 *PORTFOLIO Save your writing. You may want to use it later as a springboard to a piece for your portfolio.*

ALTERNATIVE ACTIVITIES

1. With a classmate, prepare a **dramatic scene** of a situation in the life of the speaker of "I Am Not I." Decide on a situation to enact. Then, using clues from the poem, show how each "I" would react in that situation.

2. Create a **mask** that reflects the personality of the speaker in "I Am Not I" or "The Street." Display your mask to the class or the entire school.

OCTAVIO PAZ

1914–

Octavio Paz, a poet, essayist, and literary scholar, is one of modern Mexico's best-known literary figures. His receipt of the 1990 Nobel Prize in literature was considered by many critics to be long overdue.

Paz grew up outside Mexico City. He loved books and often devised games based on *Robinson Crusoe* and other popular adventure tales he read. At 17, Paz founded the first of many literary journals that he would establish; at 19, he published his first book of poetry, *Forest Moon* (1933). Like many young writers of the 1930s, he journeyed to Spain to support the Loyalists in the Spanish Civil War.

Paz's political convictions and his fascination with the ways native Indian and conquering Spanish elements interact in Mexican history are strong themes in his writing. His highly acclaimed prose work *The Labyrinth of Solitude* (1950) is a major study of Mexican culture. Mexico's early history also inspired his 1957 epic poem *Sunstone,* whose title refers to the famous calendar stone of the Aztecs.

From 1945 until 1968, Paz served in the Mexican diplomatic corps. While stationed in Japan and India, he developed an interest in Oriental arts and philosophy, which is reflected in some of his poems. Since 1968, he has continued to write and has taught and lectured in Europe and the United States.

OTHER WORKS *Configurations; The Collected Poems of Octavio Paz, 1957–1987*

JUAN RAMÓN JIMÉNEZ

1881–1958

Juan Ramón Jiménez's short and intensely personal poems were an inspiration to a generation of Spanish writers in the 1920s and 1930s. Born in Spain, Jiménez briefly studied law at the University of Seville, but he eventually quit to devote himself to writing. His poems began appearing in an influential Spanish magazine when he was 17, and he published his first two volumes of verse in 1900.

From 1912 until 1916, Jiménez lived in Madrid, where he wrote *Platero and I* (1914), prose poems about walks with a donkey. The book became a beloved Spanish classic. Also during this time, Jiménez met American-born Zenobia Camprubí, who was visiting in Spain. Jiménez's voyage to the United States to marry Camprubí inspired one of his most successful collections, *Diary of a Newlywed Poet* (1917).

After the couple returned to Spain, Jiménez continued to devote himself to poetry. At the outbreak of the Spanish Civil War in 1936, he was sent to the United States as a representative of Spain. Eventually, Jiménez took a position at the University of Puerto Rico. The couple were in San Juan when they received word that Jiménez had won the 1956 Nobel Prize in literature. Just three days later, his wife died after a long bout with cancer. Grieving for his wife, the poet's health declined, and he died a year and a half later.

OTHER WORKS *Three Hundred Poems: 1903–1953*

LASERLINKS
• *ART GALLERY*

PREVIEWING

NONFICTION

from The Unexpected Universe

Loren Eiseley United States

PERSONAL CONNECTION

Think about dogs, cats, or other domestic animals that you have observed. How much of the animals' behavior is instinctive? How much is learned? In your notebook, make a chart like the one below, listing examples of instinctive and learned behavior. Then compare your chart with those of your classmates, and discuss whether you believe such animals are driven primarily by instinct.

Instinctive Behavior	Learned Behavior
Dog chases squirrel.	Dog obeys command to fetch slippers.

SCIENTIFIC CONNECTION

Scientists believe that dogs were probably the first domestic animals. More than 10,000 years ago, wild dogs, the ancestors of our modern dogs, found that they could survive by scavenging food scraps from the garbage dumps around humans' campsites. In turn, people discovered that the dogs could help them by keeping the campsites clean and by barking to warn of approaching strangers. As people realized they could train dogs for many other tasks, such as hunting and herding, a long and valued relationship developed between humans and dogs. Despite thousands of years of domestication, however, modern dogs still exhibit instinctive tendencies. Their instinctive behavior is similar to that of wolves, the dogs' closest wild relatives. These instincts reflect the behaviors that were needed for survival in the wild.

WRITING CONNECTION

Think about a time when you acted on instinct. Do you now feel that acting instinctively in that situation was best? Write your thoughts about that time in your notebook. Then, as you read the following selection, note the role that instincts play in the situation described.

Gray wolf. Copyright © Ken Cole/Animals Animals.

German shepherd. Copyright © Ralph A. Reinhold/Animals Animals.

from The Unexpected Universe

Loren Eiseley

A time comes when creatures whose destinies have crossed somewhere in the remote past are forced to appraise each other as though they were total strangers. I had been huddled beside the fire one winter night, with the wind prowling outside and shaking the windows. The big shepherd dog on the hearth before me occasionally glanced up affectionately, sighed, and slept. I was working, actually, amidst the debris of a far greater winter. On my desk lay the lance points of ice age hunters and the heavy leg bone of a fossil bison. No remnants of flesh attached to these relics.[1] The deed lay more than ten thousand years remote. It was represented here by naked flint and by bone so mineralized it rang when struck. As I worked on in my little circle of light, I absently laid the bone beside me on the floor. The hour had crept toward midnight. A grating noise, a heavy rasping of big teeth diverted me. I looked down.

The dog had risen. That rock-hard fragment of a vanished beast was in his jaws, and he was mouthing it with a fierce intensity I have never seen exhibited by him before.

"Wolf," I exclaimed, and stretched out my hand. The dog backed up but did not yield. A low and steady rumbling began to rise in his chest, something out of a long-gone midnight. There was nothing in that bone to taste, but ancient shapes were moving in his mind and determining his utterance. Only fools gave up bones. He was warning me.

Cosmos Dog (1989), George Rodrigue. Oil on canvas, courtesy of The Rodrigue Gallery of New Orleans. Copyright © 1989 George Rodrigue.

---

1. **relics:** things that are highly valued for their age or historic interest.

563

"Wolf," I chided again.

As I advanced, his teeth showed and his mouth wrinkled to strike. The rumbling rose to a direct snarl. His flat head swayed low and wickedly as a reptile's above the floor. I was the most loved object in his universe, but the past was fully alive in him now. Its shadows were whispering in his mind. I knew he was not bluffing. If I made another step he would strike.

Yet his eyes were strained and desperate. "Do not," something pleaded in the back of them, some affectionate thing that had followed at my heel all the days of his mortal life, "do not force me. I am what I am and cannot be otherwise because of the shadows. Do not reach out. You are a man, and my very god. I love you, but do not put out your hand. It is midnight. We are in another time, in the snow."

"The *other* time," the steady rumbling continued while I paused, "the other time in the snow, the big, the final, the terrible snow, when the shape of this thing I hold spelled life. I will not give it up. I cannot. The shadows will not permit me. Do not put out your hand."

I stood silent, looking into his eyes, and heard his whisper through. Slowly I drew back in understanding. The snarl diminished, ceased. As I retreated, the bone slumped to the floor. He placed a paw on it, warningly.

And were there no shadows in my own mind, I wondered. Had I not for a moment, in the grip of that savage utterance, been about to respond, to hurl myself upon him over an invisible haunch ten thousand years removed? Even to me the shadows had whispered—to me, the scholar in his study.

"Wolf," I said, but this time, holding a familiar leash, I spoke from the door indif-ferently. "A walk in the snow." Instantly from his eyes that other visitant[2] receded. The bone was left lying. He came eagerly to my side, accepting the leash and taking it in his mouth as always.

A blizzard was raging when we went out, but he paid no heed. On his thick fur the driving snow was soon clinging heavily. He frolicked a little—though usually he was a grave dog—making up to me for something still receding in his mind. I felt the snowflakes fall upon my face, and stood thinking of another time, and another time still, until I was moving from midnight to midnight under ever more remote and vaster snows. Wolf came to my side with a little whimper. It was he who was civilized now. "Come back to the fire," he nudged gently, "or you will be lost." Auto-matically I took the leash he offered. He led me safely home and into the house.

"We have been very far away," I told him solemnly. "I think there is something in us that we had both better try to forget." Sprawled on the rug, Wolf made no response except to thump his tail feebly out of courtesy. Already he was mostly asleep and dreaming. By the movement of his feet I could see he was running far upon some errand in which I played no part.

Softly I picked up his bone—our bone, rather—and replaced it high on a shelf in my cabinet. As I snapped off the light the white glow from the window seemed to augment itself and shine with a deep, glacial blue. As far as I could see, nothing moved in the long aisles of my neigh-bor's woods. There was no visible track, and certainly no sound from the living. The snow continued to fall steadily, but the wind, and the shadows it had brought, had vanished. ❖

---

2. **visitant:** supernatural visitor, such as a ghost.

WORDS
TO
KNOW

chide (chīd) *v.* to scold mildly
recede (rĭ-sēd′) *v.* to withdraw or move backward
augment (ôg-mĕnt′) *v.* to increase; make greater

RESPONDING OPTIONS

FROM PERSONAL RESPONSE TO CRITICAL ANALYSIS

REFLECT

1. What was the strongest image for you in this essay? Briefly describe your reaction in your notebook. Then share what you wrote with a partner.

RETHINK

2. Do you think Eiseley's interpretation of the scene with the bone is convincing? Explain your reasoning.

3. How would you describe the relationship between Eiseley and his dog?
   Consider
   - the opening scene, when the writer is at his desk
   - the dog's behavior when he has the bone
   - the writer's thoughts when they are out in the snow
   - the dog's behavior in the snow

4. What do you think is the main point, or theme, of this selection?
   Consider
   - the first sentence of the selection
   - Eiseley's reference to "something in us that we had both better try to forget" (page 564)
   - Eiseley's calling the bison bone "our bone" near the end of the essay

RELATE

5. Do you think survival in modern society depends more on instinct or on learned behavior? Cite some examples to support your answer.

ANOTHER PATHWAY
Cooperative Learning

Working with a partner, write a dramatic soliloquy that retells the events in this essay from Wolf's point of view. Be sure to include, as the writer does, descriptions of the setting and the dog's ideas about what the man must be thinking. Share your soliloquy by reading it aloud or by posting it in a classroom.

QUICKWRITES

1. Write your own **reflective essay** in which you reflect upon the experience you described for the Writing Connection on page 562. You also might incorporate ideas from the essay and from class discussion.

2. Write a **character analysis** of Loren Eiseley based on the impression you have of him from the essay. Use details from the essay to support your opinion.

3. Imagine that you were an unobserved witness of the events that Eiseley describes. Write an **eyewitness account** of the events.

📁 *PORTFOLIO Save your writing. You may want to use it later as a springboard to a piece for your portfolio.*

LITERARY CONCEPTS

A **reflective essay** is an autobiographical account in which the writer highlights significant events in his or her life and reflects on how those events affected him or her. Such an essay is usually written in the first-person point of view to give the reader insight into the writer's character, feelings, and attitudes. Explain how you think Eiseley's essay fits this definition. Why do you think Eiseley chose this particular event to write about?

CONCEPT REVIEW: Setting Notice the way Eiseley describes the indoor and outdoor settings. Why are the settings important in this essay?

Inside Outside

THE WRITER'S STYLE

Although Eiseley explores ideas related to the world of science, his style is often compared to a poet's. Make a list of quotations from the essay that seemed especially poetic to you.

ACROSS THE CURRICULUM

Science Research the last Ice Age, the animals that lived then, and their relationship in the food chain. Be sure to include information about Wolf's Ice Age ancestor. Create a chart to show the different kinds of animals and their relationship to one another as predator and prey.

WORDS TO KNOW

In each item below, determine the relationship between each pair of capitalized words. On your paper, write the letter of the word choice that shows the most similar relationship.

1. UTTERANCE : WHISPER :: (a) chirp : bird, (b) knock : tap, (c) bite : teeth, (d) shed : mansion

2. APPRAISE : EXAMINATION :: (a) weigh : scale, (b) hammer : nail, (c) plant : garden, (d) address : stamp

3. CHIDE : DISAPPROVAL :: (a) hush : noise, (b) praise : reaction, (c) mock : contempt, (d) delight : laughter

4. AUGMENT : MICROPHONE :: (a) transmit : receiver, (b) reduce : muffler, (c) perform : audience, (d) conduct : orchestra

5. RECEDE : RETREAT :: (a) imagine : do, (b) accept : reject, (c) borrow : steal, (d) honor : respect

LOREN EISELEY

Loren Eiseley, who was an anthropologist by training but a poet by instinct and vision, is famous for his ability to communicate to others the wonders and mysteries of natural science. Eiseley was born in Lincoln, Nebraska. "I first became vividly aware of the fossil past," he said, "when visiting, as a child, the old red brick museum which used to house the paleontological collections at the University of Nebraska." Eventually he attended that university, where he studied not only anthropology but also English literature, often contributing to the well-known literary magazine *Prairie Schooner.* Throughout the 1930s, Eiseley continued to pursue his dual interests, obtaining higher degrees in anthropology and publishing stories and poems. From 1944 to 1947, he served as chairman of the department of sociology and anthropology at Oberlin College, in Ohio; after

1907–1977

1947, he taught mainly at the University of Pennsylvania, although he also was a visiting professor at other schools and held leadership positions in many anthropology organizations.

Beginning with *The Immense Journey* (1957) and *Darwin's Century* (1958), Eiseley shared his considerable scientific knowledge with an increasingly appreciative lay audience. In the 1960s, he hosted the TV series *Animal Secrets. The Unexpected Universe* (1969), the source of the selection you have just read, contains several Eiseley essays published in the 1960s. The book is dedicated to Wolf, "who sleeps forever with an ice age bone across his heart, the last gift of one who loved him."

OTHER WORKS *The Invisible Pyramid, The Night Country, The Star Thrower, The Lost Notebooks of Loren Eiseley*

PREVIEWING

Two Friends

Guy de Maupassant (gē də mō-pă-sän′) France

PERSONAL CONNECTION

Think about how it might feel to live in an area that has been at war, with supply lines cut off for some time and your normal activities limited because of danger or lack of goods. Consider how your life under such conditions would contrast with your life in peacetime. What would you miss most? Make lists, like the ones shown, based on what you have read, experienced, or seen on the news. Then share your ideas in a class discussion.

Things I Would Miss	Activities I Would Miss
variety of foods	going out with friends

HISTORICAL CONNECTION

For most of the 1800s, Germany was a collection of separate German-speaking states. Among these, the northern state of Prussia gradually emerged as the most powerful. By 1870, under the leadership of Prussian chancellor Otto von Bismarck, the German states had begun to unite. In July of 1870, fearful of a unified Germany on his borders, Emperor Napoleon III of France began what was called the Franco-Prussian War.

By early September, German troops had won several victories and even captured Napoleon III in a battle in northern France. They then laid siege to the French capital of Paris, surrounding the city and trying to starve its citizens into surrender.

In the absence of their emperor, the people of Paris established their own government and raised an army of nearly 600,000 in just a few weeks. For nearly four months, they controlled all movement in and out of the city, using spies and even surprise escapes by balloon to harass and attack the Germans. Still, by January of 1871, Paris was in danger of collapsing under the German siege. The following story takes place at this time in history.

READING CONNECTION

Understanding Contrast Guy de Maupassant uses contrast to emphasize the differences between wartime and peacetime. As you read, look for these contrasts and notice how they affect your understanding of the story.

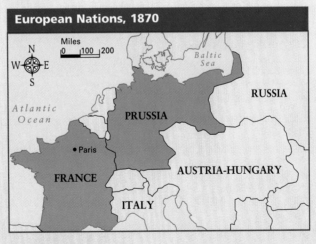

European Nations, 1870

LASERLINKS
• HISTORICAL CONNECTION

Portrait of André Derain (1905), Henri Matisse. Tate Gallery, London/Art Resource, New York.
Copyright ©1995 Succession H. Matisse, Paris/Artists Rights Society (ARS), New York.

Two Friends

Guy de Maupassant

Paris was under siege,[1] in the grip of famine, at its last gasp. There were few sparrows on the rooftops now, and even the sewers were losing some of their inhabitants. The fact is that people were eating anything they could get their hands on.

One bright January morning Monsieur Morissot[2] was strolling dejectedly along one of the outer boulevards, with an empty stomach and his hands in the pockets of his old army trousers. He was a watchmaker by trade and a man who liked to make the most of his leisure. Suddenly, he came upon one of his close friends, and he stopped short. It was Monsieur Sauvage,[3] whom he had got to know on fishing expeditions.

---

1. **siege** (sēj): the surrounding of a city by an enemy army trying to capture it by cutting off supplies and keeping it under attack.
2. **Monsieur Morissot** (mə-syœ′ mô-rē-sō′)
3. **Sauvage** (sō-väzh′)

Every Sunday before the war it was Morissot's custom to set off at the crack of dawn with his bamboo rod in his hand and a tin box slung over his back. He would catch the Argenteuil train and get off at Colombes, from where he would walk to the island of Marante. The minute he reached this land of his dreams he would start to fish—and he would go on fishing till it got dark.

And it was here, every Sunday, that he met a tubby, jolly little man by the name of Sauvage. He was a haberdasher[4] from the Rue Notre-Dame-de-Lorette, and as fanatical an angler[5] as Morissot himself. They often spent half the day sitting side by side, rod in hand, with their feet dangling over the water. And they had become firm friends.

There were some days when they hardly spoke to each other. On other occasions they would chat all the time. But they understood each other perfectly without needing to exchange any words, because their tastes were so alike and their feelings identical.

On spring mornings at about ten o'clock, when the rejuvenated sun sent floating over the river that light mist which moves along with the current, warming the backs of the two enthusiastic fishermen with the welcome glow of a new season, Morissot would say to his neighbor:

"Ah! It's grand here, isn't it?"

And Monsieur Sauvage would reply:

"There's nothing I like better."

This simple exchange of words was all that was needed for them to understand each other and confirm their mutual appreciation.

In the autumn towards the close of day, when the sky was blood-red and the water reflected strange shapes of scarlet clouds which reddened the whole river, and the glowing sun set the distant horizon ablaze, making the two friends look as though they were on fire, and touching with gold the russet leaves which were already trembling with a wintry shudder, Monsieur Sauvage would turn to Morissot with a smile and say:

"What a marvelous sight!"

They understood each other perfectly without needing to exchange any words, because their tastes were so alike and their feelings identical.

And Morissot, equally taken up with the wonder of it all, but not taking his eyes off his float, would answer:

"It's better than walking down the boulevards, eh?"

As soon as the two friends had recognized each other, they shook hands warmly, feeling quite emotional over the fact that they had come across each other in such different circumstances. Monsieur Sauvage gave a sigh and remarked:

4. **haberdasher:** one who sells men's clothing, such as shirts, hats, and gloves.

5. **angler:** fisherman.

WORDS TO KNOW

fanatical (fə-năt′ĭ-kəl) *adj.* extremely enthusiastic
rejuvenated (rĭ-jōō′və-nā′tĭd) *adj.* made new or young again **rejuvenate** *v.*

"What a lot has happened since we last met!"

Morissot, in mournful tones, lamented:

"And what awful weather we've been having! This is the first fine day of the year."

And, indeed, the sky was a cloudless blue, brilliant with light.

They started to walk on together side by side, pensive and melancholy. Then Morissot said:

"And what about those fishing trips, eh? *There's* something worth remembering!"

"When shall we be able to get back to it?" mused Monsieur Sauvage.

They went into a little café and drank a glass of absinthe.[6] Then they resumed their stroll along the boulevards.

Morissot suddenly stopped and said:

"What about another glass of the green stuff, eh?"

"Just as you wish," consented Monsieur Sauvage, and they went into a second bar.

When they came out they both felt very fuzzy, as people do when they drink alcohol on an empty stomach. The weather was very mild. A gentle breeze caressed their faces.

Monsieur Sauvage, who felt even more fuddled[7] in this warm air, stopped and said:

"What about it, then? Shall we go?"

"Go where?"

"Fishing!"

"But where can we go?"

"To our island, of course. The French frontline is near Colombes. I know the colonel in command—fellow called Dumoulin. I'm sure we'd have no trouble in getting through."

Morissot began to quiver with excitement.

"Right!" he said. "I'm your man!"

And the two friends separated and went off to get their fishing tackle.

An hour later they were striding down the main road together. They reached the villa in which the colonel had set up his headquarters.

When he heard their request, he smiled at their eccentric enthusiasm but gave them permission. They set off once again, armed with an official pass.

They soon crossed the frontline, then went through Colombes, which had been evacuated, and now found themselves on the fringe of the area of vineyards which rise in terraces above the Seine. It was about eleven o'clock.

On the opposite bank they could see the village of Argenteuil, which looked deserted and dead. The hills of Orgemont and Sannois dominated the horizon, and the great plain which stretches as far as Nanterre was empty, completely empty, with nothing to be seen but its leafless cherry trees and gray earth.

Pointing towards the high ground Monsieur Sauvage muttered:

"The Prussians are up there."

And as the two friends gazed at the deserted countryside, they felt almost paralyzed by the sense of uneasiness which was creeping through them.

The Prussians! They had never so much as set eyes on them, but for four months now they had been aware of their presence on the outskirts of Paris, occupying part of France, looting, committing atrocities, reducing people to starvation . . . the invisible yet all-powerful Prussians. As they thought of them, a kind of superstitious dread was added to their natural hatred for this unknown, victorious race.

"What if we should happen to run into some of them?" said Morissot nervously.

Monsieur Sauvage gave the sort of reply which showed that cheerful Parisian banter survived in spite of everything.

---

6. **absinthe:** a syrupy, green alcoholic beverage that has a licorice flavor.

7. **fuddled:** drunk and confused.

571

"Oh, we'll just offer them some nice fish to fry!"

Even so, they were so worried by the silence of the surrounding countryside that they hesitated about going any further.

It was Monsieur Sauvage who finally made up his mind.

"Come on!" he said. "We'll go on—but we must keep a sharp lookout!"

And they scrambled down the slope of one of the vineyards, bent double, crawling on their hands and knees, taking advantage of the cover afforded by the vines, keeping their eyes wide open and their ears on the alert.

All that now separated them from the riverbank was a strip of open ground. They ran across it, and as soon as they reached the river, they crouched amongst the dry rushes.

Morissot pressed his ear to the ground to see if he could detect the sound of marching feet. He could hear nothing. They were alone, completely alone.

They told each other there was nothing to worry about, and started to fish.

Opposite them the deserted island of Marante concealed them from the other bank. The little building which once housed the restaurant was closed and shuttered, and looked as though it had been abandoned for years.

It was Monsieur Sauvage who caught the first fish—a gudgeon. Morissot caught the second, and then, almost without a pause, they jerked up their rods time after time to find a little silvery creature wriggling away on the hook. This really was a miraculous draft of fishes.

They carefully placed each fish into a fine-meshed net which was suspended in the water at their feet. And as they did so they were overcome by a delightful sense of joy, the kind of joy you only experience when you resume something you really love after being deprived of it for a long time.

A kindly sun was shedding its warmth across their backs. They were so absorbed that they no longer heard, or thought, or paid the least attention to the outside world. What did anything matter now? They were fishing!

But suddenly, the bank beneath them shook with a dull rumble which seemed to come from underground.

The distant cannon were starting to fire again.

Morissot turned his head, and above the bank, over to the left, he saw the great bulk of Mont Valérien. On the mountainside was a white plume of smoke, showing where the gunpowder had just bellowed out.

Almost immediately another jet of smoke spurted from the fort on the summit, and a few seconds later the rumble of another detonation reached their ears.

Other cannon shots followed, and every now and then the mountain spat out its deadly breath, exhaled its clouds of milky vapor, which rose slowly into the calm sky above.

"There they go again!" said Monsieur Sauvage with a shrug of his shoulders.

Morissot, who was anxiously watching the feather on his float as it bobbed up and down, was suddenly filled with the anger of a peace-loving man for these maniacs who indulge in fighting.

"They've got to be really stupid," he growled, "to go on killing each other like that!"

"They're worse than animals," said Monsieur Sauvage.

Morissot, who had just caught another fish, called out:

"And it'll never be any different so long as we have governments!"

"Oh, no," disagreed Monsieur Sauvage. "The Republic[8] would never have declared war . . ."

---

8. **the Republic:** the Second Republic of France (1848–1852), which was France's first truly representative government.

The Talisman (1888), Paul Serusier. Musée d'Orsay, Paris, Giraudon/Art Resource, New York.

"Look!" interrupted Morissot. "Under kings you have war against other countries. Under republican governments you have civil war."

And they began to argue, in a calm and friendly way, sorting out all the world's great political problems with the commonsense approach of mild and reasonable men. On one point they were in absolute agreement: mankind would never be free. And as they talked, Mont Valérien went thundering on without respite, demolishing French homes with its cannonades,[9] pounding lives to dust, crushing human beings to pulp, putting an end to so many dreams, to so many long-awaited joys, so much long-expected happiness, tearing into the hearts of all those wives and daughters and mothers with pain and suffering that would never be eased.

"Such is life," said Monsieur Sauvage.

"Better to call it death," laughed Morissot.

But at that moment they both gave a start, scared by the feeling that somebody had been walking just behind them. They looked round and saw standing above them four men, four tall, bearded men, armed to the teeth, dressed like liveried[10] footmen, with flat military caps on their heads—and rifles which they were pointing straight at the two friends.

The fishing rods dropped from their hands and went floating down the river.

In a matter of seconds they were seized, tied up, hustled along, thrown into a boat and carried across to the island.

Behind the building which they had thought deserted they saw a group of about twenty German soldiers.

A sort of hairy giant who was sitting astride a chair and smoking a large clay pipe asked them in excellent French:

"Well, messieurs, did the fishing go well?"

One of the soldiers placed at the officer's feet the net full of fish which he had been careful to bring along. The Prussian smiled and said:

The fishing rods dropped from their hands and went floating down the river.

"Well, well! I can see you didn't do badly at all! . . . But I have to deal with a very different matter. Now, listen to me carefully, and don't get alarmed . . . As far as I am concerned you are a couple of spies sent out here to keep an eye on me. I've caught you and I've every right to shoot you. You were obviously pretending to fish as a cover for your real purposes. It's too bad for you that you've fallen into my hands. But war is war . . . Now, since you've come out here past your own lines, you're bound to have a password so you can get back. Just give me that password and I'll spare your lives."

The two friends, ghastly pale, stood there side by side with their hands trembling. They said nothing.

"Nobody will ever get to know about it," continued the officer. "You will go back without any trouble, and the secret will go with you . . . If you refuse to cooperate, you'll die—straight away. So take your choice!"

They stood there motionless, keeping their mouths firmly shut.

The Prussian, who was still quite calm, pointed in the direction of the river and said:

---

9. **cannonades:** continued firing of cannons.
10. **liveried:** uniformed.

WORDS TO KNOW **respite** (rĕs'pĭt) *n.* a temporary stop; a brief period of rest or relief from activity

Green Fish (about 1928), Selden Gile. Oil on board, Bedford Gallery, Dean Lesher Regional Center for the Arts, Walnut Creek, California.

"Just think! In five minutes you'll be at the bottom of that river. In five minutes! You must have families. Think of them!"

The rumbling of the cannon was still coming from Mont Valérien.

The two fishermen simply stood there, refusing to speak. The German now gave some orders in his own language. Then he moved his chair some distance away from the prisoners. Twelve men marched up and formed a line twenty yards from them with their rifles at their sides.

"I'll give you one minute to make up your minds," called the officer. "And not two seconds more."

Then he jumped to his feet, went up to the two Frenchmen, took Morissot by the arm, and led him to one side. Then he said to him in a very low voice:

"Quick! Just let me have that password! Your friend won't know you've told me. I'll make it look as though I've taken pity on you both."

Morissot said nothing.

The Prussian then dragged Monsieur

Sauvage to one side and made the same proposition to him.

Monsieur Sauvage said nothing.

So they were pushed together again, side by side.

It was then that Morissot happened to glance down at the net full of gudgeon which was lying in the grass a few yards away.

A ray of sunlight fell on the heap of glittering fish, which were still quivering with life. As he looked at them he felt a momentary weakness. In spite of his efforts to hold them back, tears filled his eyes.

"Well, now it's the fishes' turn."

"Farewell, Monsieur Sauvage," he mumbled. And Monsieur Sauvage replied:

"Farewell, Monsieur Morissot."

They shook hands, trembling uncontrollably from head to foot.

"Fire!" shouted the officer.

Twelve shots rang out simultaneously.

Monsieur Sauvage fell like a log onto his face. Morissot, who was taller, swayed, spun round, then collapsed on top of his friend, with his face staring up at the sky and the blood welling from where his coat had been burst open across his chest.

The German shouted out more orders. His men went off and came back with some lengths of rope and a few heavy stones which they fastened to the feet of the two bodies. Then they carried them to the riverbank.

All the time Mont Valérien continued to rumble, and now it was capped by a great mountain of smoke.

Two soldiers got hold of Morissot by the head and feet. Two others lifted up Monsieur Sauvage in the same way. The two bodies were swung violently backwards and forwards, then thrown with great force. They curved through the air, then plunged upright into the river, with the stones dragging them down, feet first.

The water spurted up, bubbled, swirled round, then grew calm again, with little waves rippling across to break against the bank. There was just a small amount of blood discoloring the surface.

The officer, still quite unperturbed, said, half aloud:

"Well, now it's the fishes' turn."

As he was going back towards the building, he noticed the net full of gudgeon lying in the grass. He picked it up, looked at the fish, then smiled, and called out:

"Wilhelm!"

A soldier came running up. He was wearing a white apron. The Prussian officer threw across to him the catch made by the two executed fishermen, and gave another order:

"Fry me these little creatures—straight away, while they're still alive. They'll be delicious!"

Then he lit his pipe again. ❖

Translated by Arnold Kellett

José Martí

from *Simple Poetry*
XXIII

I want to leave this world
By the natural door;
They must carry me off to die
In a cart of green leaves.

5 Do not put me in the dark
To die like a traitor;
I am good, and so I shall die
With my face to the sun!

Translated by Elinor Randall

from *Versos Sencillos*
XXIII

Yo quiero salir del mundo
Por la puerta natural:
En un carro de hojas verdes
A morir me han de llevar.

5 No me pongan en lo oscuro
A morir como un traidor:
¡Yo soy bueno, y como bueno
Moriré de cara al sol!

Carving the Spirit of the Flesh (1980), Arnaldo Roche Rabell.
Oil pastel on paper, 50″ × 40″, courtesy of the artist and
Galeria Botello, Hato Rey, Puerto Rico.

RESPONDING OPTIONS

FROM PERSONAL RESPONSE TO CRITICAL ANALYSIS

REFLECT

1. What is your reaction to the ending of the story? Jot down your reaction in your notebook.

RETHINK

2. Why do you think Morissot and Sauvage are willing to risk their lives to go fishing?

3. Do you think the Frenchmen do the right thing by refusing to cooperate with the officer?

   Consider
   • the officer's promise that "Nobody will ever get to know about it"
   • the values that might have influenced their decision
   • whether you think they know the password

4. Do you think either friend would have acted differently had he been captured alone?

RELATE

5. Recall incidents you have heard about in recent years concerning the treatment of prisoners, the wounded, or civilians during times of war. Which acts do you consider to be morally wrong, and which ones, if any, are acceptable during wartime?

6. What connection can you make between "Two Friends" and the Insight poem by José Martí? Support your response with details from both selections.

ANOTHER PATHWAY

Cooperative Learning

In a small group, create a storyboard of the events in this story. For each frame of the storyboard, include a sketch of one event. Beneath each frame, write a short statement of what you think the characters are thinking or feeling at that point. Base your work on evidence from the story.

LITERARY CONCEPTS

In any story, the **protagonist** is the main character who is involved in the main action of the story. Sometimes a story has more than one protagonist. The person or force working against the protagonist is called the **antagonist.** The antagonist can be

another character, something in nature or society, or an internal force within the protagonist. Who are the protagonists in "Two Friends"? Who or what would you identify as the antagonist? Explain.

CONCEPT REVIEW: Irony Situational irony is the contrast between what a character or reader expects and what actually happens. Explain how situational irony functions in this story. How does the irony contribute to the theme?

QUICKWRITES

1. Imagine that the German officer has allowed Morissot or Sauvage to write a final letter to a loved one. Write the **letter** that one of the two friends might have written.

2. Imagine that one of the Frenchmen decided to reveal the password. Write an **alternative ending** to the story.

PORTFOLIO Save your writing. You may want to use it later as a springboard to a piece for your portfolio.

ALTERNATIVE ACTIVITIES

1. Create a paper **patchwork quilt** or some other design that illustrates with shapes and colors the contrasting feelings associated with war and peace as conveyed by the story.

2. In a small group, create a **multimedia presentation** featuring contemporary images of war and peace. Read aloud passages from the story to accompany your images. You may also use music to help establish the tone of your presentation.

3. Design a **greeting card** about friendship inspired by the friendship that Morissot and Sauvage share.

THE WRITER'S STYLE

Guy de Maupassant's tales are pioneering works of **realism,** the 19th-century literary movement that stressed the need to picture life as it really was lived. What aspects of the story did you find especially true to life?

WORDS TO KNOW

Review the Words to Know at the bottom of the selection pages. Then read each newspaper headline below, and write the vocabulary word that you would expect to find in an article with that headline.

1. "Crowd of Cheering Fans Mobs Celebrity"
2. "Mass Murders Committed by Rebel Forces"
3. "Vitamin E Shown to Reduce Facial Wrinkles"
4. "Families Reflect on War's Casualties"
5. "Study Reveals Dangers of Exhaustion"

GUY DE MAUPASSANT

1850–1893

Guy de Maupassant is famous for realistic tales based mostly on personal experience. Maupassant grew up in Normandy, a region in northwestern France. Fishermen, sailors, and practical Norman merchants figure prominently in his tales, as does a lifelong love of the sea. Several of his stories explore unhappy marriages, no doubt inspired by that of his own parents. His mother and father separated when Guy was 11, and his childhood memories of their bitter quarrels help explain why he himself never married.

Maupassant studied law in Paris, but his studies were interrupted by military service in the Franco-Prussian War, which gave him firsthand experience that he would draw on for several more tales. After the war, he resumed his studies and, through his father's influence, obtained a government job. His mother's influence proved even more significant: she asked her friend Gustave Flaubert, the famous French novelist, to keep an eye on her son in Paris. Flaubert became Maupassant's friend and mentor, encouraging the younger man to write and offering him advice on literary technique.

During the 1880s, Maupassant enjoyed his most productive years as an author. Although he wrote several novels, his forte was the short story, a form he helped popularize throughout Europe. His financial success allowed him to purchase a fine apartment in Paris as well as a yacht, which he enjoyed sailing. Tragedy came in 1889, however, when his younger brother died of a disease that would soon strike the author. Maupassant, whose final years were marked by mental and physical deterioration, died in July 1893, a month short of his 43rd birthday.

OTHER WORKS *The Best Stories of Guy de Maupassant, Selected Stories, The Dark Side of Guy de Maupassant*

WHEN GREEK MEETS GREEK

SAMUEL SELVON

TRINIDAD

The author of this story is from Trinidad, one of the islands in the chain that constitutes the West Indies. This island chain stretches across the area between the south coast of Florida and the northern coast of South America, separating the Atlantic Ocean and the Caribbean Sea. Christopher Columbus named the island chain *Indies* and the inhabitants *Indians* because he mistakenly thought he had reached the Indies of Asia.

The first inhabitants of the islands were Arawak, Carib, and other Native American peoples. Gradually, people from other parts of the world came to the islands, and now many West Indians have black African, European, Asian Indian, or mixed ancestry. Thus, the term *Indian* has come to mean any person of color from India or the West Indies, as well as Native American.

Great Britain used to have colonies in both India and the West Indies, and many Indians from both regions have immigrated to London, the setting of this story. The title of the story comes from a famous line in a 17th-century play: "When Greeks joined Greeks, then was the tug of war." Both the title and the quote refer to an encounter between equals.

One morning Ramkilawansingh (after this, we calling this man Ram) was making a study of the notice boards along Westbourne Grove what does advertise rooms to let.[1] Every now and then he writing down an address or a telephone number, though most of the time his eyes colliding up with *No Colours, Please,* or *Sorry, No Kolors.*

"YOU LOOK LIKE A MAN WHO LOOKING FOR A PLACE TO LIVE."

"Red, white and blue, all out but you," Ram was humming a little ditty what children say when they playing whoop. Just as he get down by Bradley's Corner he met Fraser.

"You look like a man who looking for a place to live," Fraser say.

"You look like a man who could tell me the right place to go," Ram say.

"You try down by Ladbroke Grove?" Fraser ask.

"I don't want to go down in that criminal area," Ram say, "at least, not until they find the man who kill Kelso."

"Then you will never live in the Grove," Fraser say.

"You are a contact man,"[2] Ram say. "Which part you think I could get a room, boy?"

Fraser scratch his head. "I know of a landlord up the road who vow that he ain't ever taking anybody who come from the West Indies. But he

---

1. **to let:** for rent.

2. **contact man:** a kind of middleman; someone whose sources provide information that is hard to come by.

Welcome to My Ghetto Land (1986), Jean Lacy. Paint, gesso, gold leaf on wood panel, 6″ × 3″, Dallas Museum of Art, Metropolitan Life Foundation Purchase Grant (1989.28).

don't mind taking Indians. He wouldn't know the difference when he see you is a Indian . . . them English people so foolish they believe every Indian come from India."

"You think I stand a chance?" Ram ask.

"Sure, you stand a chance. All you have to do is put on a turban."

"I never wear a turban in my life; I am a born Trinidadian,[3] a real Creole.[4] All the same, you best hads give me the address, I will pass around there later."

So Fraser give him the address, and Ram went on reading a few more boards, but he got discourage after a while and went to see the landlord.

The first thing the landlord ask him was: "What part of the world do you come from?"

"I am an Untouchable[5] from the heart of India," Ram say. "I am looking for a single room. I dwelt on the banks of the Ganges.[6] Not too expensive."

"But you are not in your national garments," the landlord say.

"When you are in Rome," Ram say, making it sound like an original statement, "do as the Romans do."

While the landlord sizing up Ram, an Indian tenant come up the steps to go inside. This fellar was Chandrilaboodoo (after this, we calling this man Chan), and he had a big beard with a hair net over it, and he was wearing a turban. When he see Ram, he clasp his hands with the palms touching across his chest by way of greeting.

The old Ram catch on quick and do the same thing.

"*Acha, Hindustani,*" Chan say.

"*Acha, pilau, papadom, chickenvindaloo,*" Ram say desperately, hoping for the best.

Chan nod his head, say good morning to the landlord and went inside.

"That was a narrow shave," Ram thought. "I have to watch out for that man."

"That was Mr. Chan," the landlord say. "He is the only other Indian tenant I have at the moment. I have a single room for two pounds. Are you a student?"

"Who is not a student?" Ram say, getting into the mood of the thing. "Man is forever

"THIS HOUSE TOO SMALL FOR THE TWO OF WE," RAM SAY TO HIMSELF. "ONE WILL HAVE TO GO."

studying ways and means until he passes into the hands of Allah."[7]

Well, to cut a long story short, Ram get a room on the first floor, right next door to Chan, and he move in that same evening.

But as the days going by, Ram had to live like cat and mouse with Chan. Every time he see Chan, he have to hide in case this man start up this Hindustani talk again or start to ask him questions about Mother India. In fact, it begin to get on Ram nerves, and he decide that he had to do something.

"This house too small for the two of we," Ram say to himself. "One will have to go."

So Ram went down in the basement to see the landlord.

"I have the powers of the Occult,"[8] Ram say, "and I have come to warn you of this man Chan. He is not a good tenant. He keeps the bathroom dirty, he does not tidy up his room at all, and he

---

3. **Trinidadian:** person from the West Indies island of Trinidad.
4. **Creole:** person of European descent born in the West Indies.
5. **Untouchable:** a Hindu belonging to the lowest social group in India.
6. **Ganges:** river in northern India.
7. **Allah:** the Moslem name for God.
8. **Occult:** relating to the supernatural or any of the mysterious arts, such as magic or astrology.

is always chanting and saying his prayers loudly and disturbing the other tenants."

"I have had no complaints," the landlord say.

"But I am living next door to him," Ram say, "and if I concentrate my powers, I can see through the wall. That man is a menace, and the best thing you can do is to give him notice. You have a good house here, and it would be a pity to let one man spoil it for the other tenants."

"I will have a word with him about it," the landlord say.

Well, the next evening Ram was in his room when he hear a knock at the door. He run in the corner quick and stand upon his head and say, "Come in."

The landlord come in.

"I am just practicing my yoghourt,"[9] Ram say.

"I have had a word with Mr. Chan," the landlord say, "and I have reason to suspect that you have deceived me. You are not from India; you are from the West Indies."

Ram turn right-side up. "I am a citizen of the world," he say.

"You are flying false colors," the landlord say. "You do not burn incense like Mr. Chan, you do not dress like Mr. Chan, and you do not talk like Mr. Chan."

"Give me a break, old man," Ram say, falling back on the good old West Indian dialect.

"It is too late. You have already started to make trouble. You must go."

Well, the very next week find Ram out scouting again, giving the boards a perusal,[10] and who he should chance to meet but Fraser.

He start to tell Fraser how life hard, how he had to keep dodging from this Chan fellar all the time, and it was pure torture.

"Listen," Fraser say, "you don't mean a big fellar with a beard, and he always wearing a turban?"

"That sound like him," Ram say. "You know him?"

"Know him!" Fraser say. "Man, that is a fellar from Jamaica who I send to that house to get a room!" ❖

---

9. **yoghourt:** yogurt. Ram means that he is practicing yoga, the Hindu discipline of exercises to promote control of the body and the mind.

10. **perusal:** careful reading.

SAMUEL SELVON

Samuel Selvon (1923–1994), of Asian Indian and European descent, was born in the semirural city of San Fernando, Trinidad. His childhood friends came from all the racial and ethnic backgrounds represented on the island. He once said, "By the time I was in my teens I was a product of my environment, as Trinidadian as anyone could claim to be, . . . and I had no desire to isolate myself from the mixture of races that comprised the community."

Selvon went to college in Trinidad and served as a telegraph operator during World War II. Before he immigrated to London in 1950, he worked as literary editor for the *Trinidad Guardian* newspaper and achieved local fame for his short stories. Throughout his lifetime, Selvon authored poems, essays, ten novels, dozens of short stories, and plays for stage, radio, and television. His writing is often noted for its faithfulness to the Trinidadian dialect, its depiction of local color, and its conversational tone. His novel *The Lonely Londoners* deals with the hardships and prejudices faced by West Indians living in London. Another novel, *An Island Is a World*, won Selvon a Guggenheim Fellowship. Selvon immigrated to Canada in 1978, but he never let go of his Trinidadian roots, saying, "This island is my shadow and I carry it with me wherever I go."

OTHER WORKS *A Brighter Sun, Ways of Sunlight, Turn Again Tiger*

WRITING ABOUT LITERATURE

SEARCHING FOR MEANING

The first time you read a short story or a poem, its message may not be obvious to you. Sometimes it takes effort to interpret a piece and uncover the writer's meaning. You may need to look at a writer's tone, the attitude he or she has toward a subject. On the following pages, you will

- learn how tone conveys an emotional effect
- write an interpretation of a short story or poem
- examine how your interpretation of an image changes after repeated viewings

Writer's Style: Using Tone Strong writers use tone to communicate their feelings about a subject. Tones such as anger, sympathy, suspense, and joy are conveyed through a writer's language choice and sentence structure.

Read the Literature

Notice the mother's tone in this poem to her daughter.

Literature Model

Tone Through Word Choice
What words tell you about the relationship between mother and daughter? What is the tone of this excerpt?

Old daughter, small traveler
asleep in a German featherbed
under the eaves in a postcard town
of turrets and towers,
I am putting a dream in your head.

Listen! Here it is afternoon.
The rain comes down like bullets
I stand in the kitchen,
that harem of good smells
where we bumped hips and
cracked the cupboards with our talk.

Maxine Kumin,
from "Making the Jam Without You"

Connect to Life

In a well-written speech, sentence structure helps to communicate a definite tone. Speeches with an informal tone have a sentence structure that you might use in conversation. Speeches with a more formal tone often use more complex sentence structures.

Speech

*F*riends and Fellow-Citizens:—I stand before you under indictment for the alleged crime of having voted at the last presidential election, without having a lawful right to vote. It shall be my work this evening to prove to you that in thus doing, I not only committed no crime, but instead simply exercised my citizen's right, guaranteed to me and all United States citizens by the National Constitution beyond the power of any State to deny.

Susan B. Anthony,
from "Constitutional Argument," 1872

Tone Through Sentence Structure
What is the tone of this speech? How does the sentence structure help to communicate the tone?

Try Your Hand: Using Tone

1. **What Tone?** When might you use a formal tone in your writing? When would an informal tone be more appropriate? Would your audience and topic make a difference? Explain why.

2. **A New Tone** Rewrite the speech above to give it an informal tone. Pay special attention to your word choice and sentence structure.

3. **Your Own Tone** Describe getting ready for school this morning. Were you grumpy, excited, anxious about getting there on time? Let the tone of your description communicate your feelings.

SkillBuilder

 WRITER'S CRAFT

Recognizing Connotation
When writers choose words, they consider both the denotation, or dictionary meaning of a word, and its connotation, the positive or negative feelings most people associate with the word.

In "The Meeting," Jorge Luis Borges writes that Uriarte wore "a skimpy, petulant moustache."

Why do you think Borges chose the words *skimpy* and *petulant*? What are the connotations of these words? How do they affect your impression of Uriarte?

Now read this excerpt from "The Witness for the Prosecution."

Janet is an elderly woman. She was a faithful watchdog to her mistress, and she didn't like me.

What feelings are associated with a word like *watchdog*? Are they positive or negative? How does Janet act toward her mistress?

APPLYING WHAT YOU'VE LEARNED
For each sentence below, replace the underlined word with a synonym that has a different connotation.

1. Max <u>fled</u> from the bus stop.
2. At the press conference, the reporters were <u>inquisitive</u>.
3. Our family <u>feasted</u> on the traditional Thanksgiving meal.

Interpretation

Have you ever read a story or poem and understood the writer's words but not the meaning of the piece? Reading a selection more than once can help you understand it better.

GUIDED ASSIGNMENT

Interpret a Poem On the next few pages, you'll discover how rereading a poem or short story can help you interpret it. Then you will write an essay that presents your interpretation.

➊ Prewrite and Explore

Sometimes a selection has several meanings that aren't apparent at first. Choose a story or poem that intrigues you but that you don't yet fully understand.

TRACKING YOUR THINKING

Create a reading log or a chart like the one below, and record your questions and interpretive comments. Then, reread the text as often as you wish, noting how your understanding changes with each reading. Between readings, discuss your interpretation with others.

Student's Prewriting Chart

Response to my readings of "Making the Jam Without You"

	1st reading	2nd reading	3rd reading
Ideas and Questions	This poem is about a mother making jam and thinking of her daughter who is in Germany. I wonder why she wants her daughter to dream about jam making? Who is this man with "angel arms"? "Let him bring the buckets/crooked on his angel arms."	I think she wants her daughter to carry on the jam-making tradition with someone she meets in Germany. "Now may your two heads/touch over the kettle." Making jam is important to her, and she doesn't want her daughter to forget about it. I wonder why?	I guess this isn't really about jam making. She talks about how they "bumped hips" and "cracked the cupboards with our talk!" Maybe it's not the jam that's important but the companionship they share.

② Write and Analyze a Discovery Draft

After you record and discuss your comments, begin writing a draft. Below are some activities to help you get started. Choose whichever ones seem useful.

- Look over your reading log. Write for ten minutes, explaining how your understanding of the poem or story progressed.
- Share your log with a group or a partner. Work together to answer questions you have about the selection's meaning.
- Choose a passage from the poem or story that seems important. Write about it for ten minutes.

Here's how one student resolved a problem.

Student's Discovery Draft

> What other lines from the poem would support my new interpretation?

> Why does the speaker say, "Old daughter, small traveler"? Oh, I see. She has experience at being a daughter but is new at learning about the world. When the mother says, "I am putting a dream in your head," she's wishing for her to take a happy experience from her childhood and "redo it" to find the same happiness in her new world.

③ Draft and Share

How has your perception of the poem or story changed from the first reading? What central idea have you grasped? Write a thesis statement that summarizes the changes in your understanding. As you draft your interpretation, try to accomplish the following:

- Introduce your selection and state your thesis.
- Support your thesis by explaining how your understanding changed through several readings.
- Give examples from the poem or story to support your ideas.
- Conclude by stating an overall response.

 PEER RESPONSE

- What ideas are unclear to you?
- Is my interpretation convincing? Why or why not?
- Find the thesis statement. What is my essay's main idea?

4 Revise and Edit

Make sure that your introduction has a clear thesis statement. The body of your essay should support that thesis by interpreting specific passages from the poem or story. As you revise, consider your peer review comments and refer to the Standards for Evaluation below.

Student's Final Draft

The speaker of "Making the Jam Without You" by Maxine Kumin is speaking to her 19-year-old daughter, who is far from home and "asleep in a German featherbed." As the mother is "crushing blackberries to make the annual jam," she sends a dream to her daughter. The dream is of her mother at work on the jam and a reminder of the times they shared the jam making together. She invites her daughter to continue the dream: to pick berries in Germany with a man, to stand with him over a boiling kettle, and to spread their new jam on fresh bread. At first I thought the poem was simply about a mother who wants her daughter to carry on the jam-making tradition. After several readings, however, I felt that the poem is a wish for a daughter to take the love"from her childhood and transform it into a deeper love she can share with a partner in her adult life.

The poem begins with the lines "Old daughter, small traveler, / asleep in a German featherbed, / under the eaves in a postcard town." At first reading, the first line didn't make sense to me. A 19-year-old is neither "old" nor "small." Then I thought more about the words "daughter" and "traveler." As a daughter the young woman is "old" because she's grown-up. As a traveler, she's small because she's inexperienced and in a larger world than the one she left behind.

What is the overall purpose of the essay?

How did the student's understanding of the first line change?

Standards for Evaluation

An interpretive essay
- discusses the contents of the work, mentions the title and author, and includes a thesis statement
- offers a well-organized interpretation of the selection
- supports the interpretation with details and quotes
- tells of problems and successes in interpreting the text

Grammar in Context

Quoting from Poetry When you use direct quotations from a poem, take care to use the exact quotation set off with quotation marks. If you are quoting more than one line of a poem, place a slash with a space on each side to show where each line ends. If you are quoting more than three lines, set the quotation off from the rest of the paragraph. Indent it from the left, and do not include quotation marks or slashes. Note how the student's final copy was edited.

The poem begins with the lines "Old daughter, small traveler / asleep in a German featherbed / under the eaves in a postcard town."

Consult the SkillBuilder at the right for a review of styling titles of literary texts. For additional information on using quotations, see page 1096 of the Grammar Handbook.

Try Your Hand: Using Quotations from Literary Texts

On a separate piece of paper, edit the following paragraph to punctuate and style direct quotations and titles correctly.

After my first reading of Making the Jam Without You, I thought I understood the poem. The first part of the poem introduces the poet's purpose: to send her daughter a dream. After some thought, though, I had to reread the poem. The lines that made sense the first time were now confusing, I stand in the kitchen, that harem of good smells where we have bumped hips and cracked the cupboards with our talk while the stove top danced with pots and it was not clear who did the mothering. What does it was not clear who did the mothering mean? My second reading created even more questions, so I am reading the poem again.

SkillBuilder

GRAMMAR FROM WRITING

Styling Titles of Literary Texts

When you cite literary works, remember to punctuate or style the titles correctly.

Use quotation marks to set off titles of

- short stories
- essays
- short poems
- articles

Italicize titles of

- books
- magazines
- newspapers
- movies
- plays
- epic poems
- long musical compositions

If you are handwriting or typing, underline the title to show italics.

APPLYING WHAT YOU'VE LEARNED
Correctly punctuate or style the following titles.

1. We saw Phantom of the Opera Friday night.
2. Have you read the novel To Kill a Mockingbird?
3. The Road Not Taken by Robert Frost is one of the most recognized poems.

 GRAMMAR HANDBOOK

For more information on punctuation of titles, see page 1088 of the Grammar Handbook.

LOOK AGAIN

Has a situation ever puzzled you? Perhaps you've had second thoughts about a scene in which more seems to be happening than meets the eye. Just as reading a selection more than once helps you understand it, looking again at a situation can help you discover more than you noticed at first.

View What did you notice when you first looked at this scene? Jot down those impressions.

Interpret After a second look, what did you realize was going on? What details helped you draw a conclusion?

Discuss In a small group, compare observations. What was striking or puzzling about the situation? Did your first impressions change after each observation? What did everyone decide about the scene? Refer to the SkillBuilder at the right for help in making careful observations.

SkillBuilder

 CRITICAL THINKING

Making Careful Observations

How did your impression of the scene on these pages change as you looked at it more closely? What details helped you figure out what was going on?

Many situations you encounter in real life require more than a quick glance to be understood. You must look again in order to take in all the details and get the big picture.

Making careful observations and asking yourself questions like the following can help you make sense of situations you encounter in everyday life.

- What seems to be happening here? Does anything seem out of place, confusing, or unusual?
- What details do I notice about the setting, people, or objects?
- How do these details help explain what is going on?

APPLYING WHAT YOU'VE LEARNED
In a small group, discuss making careful observations. Can you think of instances when your observation was incorrect? What could you have done to make a more careful and accurate observation?

WHAT MATTERS MOST

Sarah Orne Jewett
(1849–1909)
An American author who wrote about her beloved Maine

Emily Dickinson
(1830–1886)
A recluse—and perhaps the most famous American poet

Maxine Kumin
(1925–)
A prize-winning American poet inspired by rural New England

REFLECTING ON THEME

What matters most in your life? What values, interests, and goals move you to action—and keep you going in the face of obstacles or conflicts? As you will see in this part of Unit Four, there are many ways of responding to such questions. Some characters discover what's most important through an illuminating experience; others must make a difficult choice to be true to themselves or to uphold their values—and then there are those who distill a truth to live by and pass it on to another.

What Do You Think? Create a word portrait of yourself. First, draw an outline of the human form on a sheet of paper. Then fill it in with words or phrases that describe what matters most to you. As you read, compare your self-portrait with what you learn about the characters and people in the selections.

Sarah Orne Jewett	**A White Heron** *A young girl must make a choice.*	594
R. K. Narayan	**Like the Sun** *Do people really want the whole truth?*	608
Emily Dickinson	**Tell all the Truth but tell it slant—** / INSIGHT *Truth with a twist?*	612
Gabriel Okara	**Once upon a Time** *A father's wish for his son*	615
Maxine Kumin	**Making the Jam Without You** *A dream sent to a distant daughter*	615

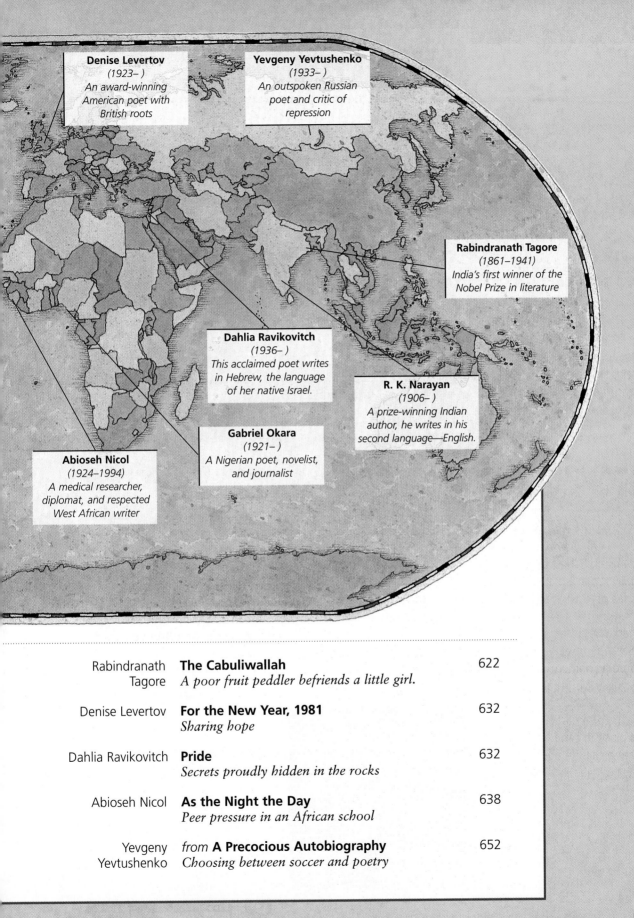

Denise Levertov
(1923–)
An award-winning American poet with British roots

Yevgeny Yevtushenko
(1933–)
An outspoken Russian poet and critic of repression

Rabindranath Tagore
(1861–1941)
India's first winner of the Nobel Prize in literature

Dahlia Ravikovitch
(1936–)
This acclaimed poet writes in Hebrew, the language of her native Israel.

R. K. Narayan
(1906–)
A prize-winning Indian author, he writes in his second language—English.

Gabriel Okara
(1921–)
A Nigerian poet, novelist, and journalist

Abioseh Nicol
(1924–1994)
A medical researcher, diplomat, and respected West African writer

Rabindranath Tagore	**The Cabuliwallah** *A poor fruit peddler befriends a little girl.*	622
Denise Levertov	**For the New Year, 1981** *Sharing hope*	632
Dahlia Ravikovitch	**Pride** *Secrets proudly hidden in the rocks*	632
Abioseh Nicol	**As the Night the Day** *Peer pressure in an African school*	638
Yevgeny Yevtushenko	*from* **A Precocious Autobiography** *Choosing between soccer and poetry*	652

PREVIEWING

FICTION

A White Heron
Sarah Orne Jewett United States

PERSONAL CONNECTION

Where do your loyalties lie? In your notebook, identify some of the people, places, ideals, or values to which you are most committed. Then create a bar graph, like the one shown, to rate the strength of your loyalties.

	Mildly Loyal ⟶ Extremely Loyal		
Parents			
Brothers/Sisters			
Friends			
Environment			
School			

SCIENTIFIC/BIOGRAPHICAL CONNECTION

In the story you are about to read, a white heron plays a prominent role in the test of a young girl's loyalty. Herons are graceful birds with sticklike legs, narrow heads, and long, slender necks. They live near water and hunt for their food by wading in streams, marshes, and swamps. Shy of human populations, they usually live in isolated areas, and they build their nests in tall bushes or in trees to help protect their young from predators. Seeing these large birds hunched in their treetop perches is a remarkable, often startling experience.

Sarah Orne Jewett, the author of "A White Heron," grew up in an environment much like the one described in this story, which is set in rural Maine in the late 1800s. In her writing, Jewett was able to catch the essence of a particular time and place in America by re-creating the life and landscape that she loved as a child.

Great white heron. Copyright © Camerique / H. Armstrong Roberts.

READING CONNECTION

Making Inferences When you make an inference, you come to a logical conclusion on the basis of evidence presented. As you read "A White Heron," pay attention to the details that are used to describe Sylvia, the main character. What inferences can you make about her character and her loyalties?

Using Your Reading Log Jot down in your reading log your answers to the questions asked throughout the story.

LASERLINKS
• SCIENCE CONNECTION

A White Heron

Sarah Orne Jewett

The woods were already filled with shadows one June evening, just before eight o'clock, though a bright sunset still glimmered faintly among the trunks of the trees. A little girl was driving home her cow, a plodding, dilatory,[1] provoking creature in her behavior, but a valued companion for all that. They were going away from whatever light there was, and striking deep into the woods, but their feet were familiar with the path, and it was no matter whether their eyes could see it or not.

There was hardly a night the summer through when the old cow could be found waiting at the pasture bars; on the contrary, it was her greatest pleasure to hide herself away among the high huckleberry bushes, and though she wore a loud bell she had made the discovery that if one stood perfectly still it would not ring. So Sylvia had to hunt for her until she found her, and call Co'! Co'!

---

1. **dilatory** (dĭl'ə-tôr'ē): tending to postpone or delay.

with never an answering Moo, until her childish patience was quite spent. If the creature had not given good milk and plenty of it, the case would have seemed very different to her owners. Besides, Sylvia had all the time there was, and very little use to make of it. Sometimes in pleasant weather it was a consolation to look upon the cow's pranks as an intelligent attempt to play hide-and-seek, and as the child had no playmates she lent herself to this amusement with a good deal of zest. Though this chase had been so long that the wary animal herself had given an unusual signal of her whereabouts, Sylvia had only laughed when she came upon Mistress Moolly at the swamp-side, and urged her affectionately homeward with a twig of birch leaves. The old cow was not inclined to wander farther; she even turned in the right direction for once as they left the pasture, and stepped along the road at a good pace. She was quite ready to be milked now, and seldom stopped to browse. Sylvia wondered what her grandmother would say because they were so late. It was a great while since she had left home at half past five o'clock, but everybody knew the difficulty of making this errand a short one. Mrs. Tilley had chased the hornéd torment too many summer evenings herself to blame anyone else for lingering, and was only thankful as she waited that she had Sylvia, nowadays, to give such valuable assistance. The good woman suspected that Sylvia loitered occasionally on her own account; there never was such a child for straying about out-of-doors since the world was made! Everybody said that it was a good change for a little maid who had tried to grow for eight years in a crowded manufacturing town, but, as for Sylvia herself, it seemed as if she never had been alive at all before she came to live at the farm. She thought often with wistful compassion of a wretched geranium that belonged to a town neighbor.

"'Afraid of folks,'" old Mrs. Tilley said to herself with a smile after she had made the unlikely choice of Sylvia from her daughter's houseful of children and was returning to the farm. "'Afraid of folks,' they said! I guess she won't be troubled no great with 'em up to the old place!" When they reached the door of the lonely house and stopped to unlock it, and the cat came to purr loudly and rub against them, a deserted pussy, indeed, but fat with young robins, Sylvia whispered that this was a beautiful place to live in, and she never should wish to go home.

The companions followed the shady wood-road, the cow taking slow steps and the child very fast ones. The cow stopped long at the brook to drink, as if the pasture were not half a swamp, and Sylvia stood still and waited, letting her bare feet cool themselves in the shoal[2] water, while the great twilight moths struck softly against her. She waded on through the brook as the cow moved away, and listened to the thrushes with a heart that beat fast with pleasure. There was a stirring in the great boughs overhead. They were full of little birds and beasts that seemed to be wide-awake, and going about their world, or else saying good night to each other in sleepy twitters. Sylvia herself felt sleepy as she walked along. However, it was not much farther to the house, and the air was soft and sweet. She was not often in the woods so late as this, and it made her feel as if she were a part of the gray shadows and the moving leaves. She was just thinking how long it seemed since she first came to the farm a year ago, and wondering if everything went on in the noisy town just the same as when she was there; the thought of the great red-faced boy who used to chase and frighten her made her hurry along the path to escape from the shadow of the trees.

2. **shoal** (shōl): shallow.

Springtime (1885), Lionel Percy Smythe. Watercolor, 20¾″ × 15¼″, private collection.
Photo by Christopher Newall.

CLARIFY

How would you describe Sylvia's life before and after moving to her grandmother's farm?

Suddenly this little woods-girl is horror-stricken to hear a clear whistle not very far away. Not a bird's whistle, which would have a sort of friendliness, but a boy's whistle, determined, and somewhat aggressive. Sylvia left the cow to whatever sad fate might await her, and stepped discreetly aside into the bushes, but she was just too late. The enemy had discovered her, and called out in a very cheerful and persuasive tone, "Halloa, little girl, how far is it to the road?" and trembling Sylvia answered almost inaudibly, "A good ways."

She did not dare to look boldly at the tall young man, who carried a gun over his shoulder, but she came out of her bush and again followed the cow, while he walked alongside.

"I have been hunting for some birds," the stranger said kindly, "and I have lost my way and need a friend very much. Don't be afraid," he added gallantly. "Speak up and tell me what your name is, and whether you think I can spend the night at your house, and go out gunning early in the morning."

Sylvia was more alarmed than before. Would not her grandmother consider her much to blame? But who could have foreseen such an accident as this? It did not seem to be her fault, and she hung her head as if the stem of it were broken, but managed to answer "Sylvy" with much effort when her companion again asked her name.

Mrs. Tilley was standing in the doorway when the trio came into view. The cow gave a loud moo by way of explanation.

"Yes, you'd better speak up for yourself, you old trial! Where'd she tucked herself away this time, Sylvy?" But Sylvia kept an awed silence; she knew by instinct that her grandmother did not comprehend the gravity[3] of the situation. She must be mistaking the stranger for one of the farmer lads of the region.

The young man stood his gun beside the door, and dropped a lumpy game bag beside it; then he bade Mrs. Tilley good evening, and repeated his wayfarer's story, and asked if he could have a night's lodging.

"Put me anywhere you like," he said. "I must be off early in the morning, before day; but I am very hungry, indeed. You can give me some milk at any rate, that's plain."

"Dear sakes, yes," responded the hostess, whose long slumbering hospitality seemed to be easily awakened. "You might fare better if you went out to the main road a mile or so, but you're welcome to what we've got. I'll milk right off, and you make yourself at home. You can sleep on husks or feathers," she proffered graciously. "I raised them all myself. There's good pasturing for geese just below here toward the ma'sh.[4] Now step round and set a plate for the gentleman, Sylvy!" And Sylvia promptly stepped. She was glad to have something to do, and she was hungry herself.

It was a surprise to find so clean and comfortable a little dwelling in this New England wilderness. The young man had known the horrors of its most primitive housekeeping and the dreary squalor of that level of society which does not rebel at the companionship of hens. This was the best thrift of an old-fashioned farmstead, though on such a small scale that it seemed like a hermitage.[5] He listened eagerly to the old woman's quaint talk, he watched Sylvia's pale face and shining gray eyes with ever-growing enthusiasm, and insisted that this was the best supper he had eaten for a month, and afterward,

---

3. **gravity:** seriousness or importance.
4. **ma'sh:** dialect for *marsh*, a low-lying wetland.
5. **hermitage:** place where a hermit, or recluse, lives.

WORDS TO KNOW

discreetly (dĭ-skrēt′lē) *adv.* in a manner showing good judgment; cautiously
squalor (skwŏl′ər) *n.* a filthy and wretched condition

598

the new-made friends sat down in the doorway together while the moon came up.

Soon it would be berry time, and Sylvia was a great help at picking. The cow was a good milker, though a plaguy[6] thing to keep track of, the hostess gossiped frankly, adding presently that she had buried four children, so Sylvia's mother and a son (who might be dead) in California were all the children she had left. "Dan, my boy, was a great hand to go gunning," she explained sadly. "I never wanted for pa'tridges or gray squer'ls while he was to home. He's been a great wand'rer, I expect, and he's no hand to write letters. There, I don't blame him; I'd ha' seen the world myself if it had been so I could.

"Sylvia takes after him," the grandmother continued affectionately, after a minute's pause. "There ain't a foot o' ground she don't know her way over, and the wild creatur's counts her one o' themselves. Squer'ls she'll tame to come an' feed right out o' her hands, and all sorts o' birds. Last winter she got the jaybirds to bangeing[7] here, and I believe she'd 'a' scanted herself of her own meals to have plenty to throw out amongst 'em if I hadn't kep' watch. Anything but crows, I tell her, I'm willin' to help support—though Dan he had a tamed one o' them that did seem to have reason same as folks. It was round here a good spell after he went away. Dan an' his father they didn't hitch[8]—but he never held up his head ag'in after Dan had dared him an' gone off."

The guest did not notice this hint of family sorrows in his eager interest in something else.

"So Sylvy knows all about birds, does she?" he exclaimed, as he looked round at the little girl who sat, very demure but increasingly sleepy, in the moonlight. "I am making a collection of birds myself. I have been at it ever since I was a boy." (Mrs. Tilley smiled.) "There are two or three very rare ones I have been hunting for these five years. I mean to get them on my own ground if they can be found."

"Do you cage 'em up?" asked Mrs. Tilley doubtfully, in response to this enthusiastic announcement.

"Oh no, they're stuffed and preserved, dozens and dozens of them," said the ornithologist,[9] "and I have shot or snared every one myself. I caught a glimpse of a white heron a few miles from here on Saturday, and I have followed it in this direction. They have never been found in this district at all. The little white heron, it is," and he turned again to look at Sylvia with the hope of discovering that the rare bird was one of her acquaintances.

But Sylvia was watching a hop-toad in the narrow footpath.

"A queer tall white bird with soft feathers and long thin legs."

"You would know the heron if you saw it," the stranger continued eagerly. "A queer tall white bird with soft feathers and long thin legs. And it would have a nest perhaps in the top of a high tree, made of sticks, something like a hawk's nest."

Sylvia's heart gave a wild beat; she knew that strange white bird, and had once stolen softly near where it stood in some bright green swamp grass, away over at the other side of the woods. There was an open place where the sunshine always seemed strangely yellow and hot, where tall, nodding rushes grew, and her grandmother had warned her that she might sink in the soft

---

6. **plaguy** (plā′gē): annoying; bothersome.

7. **bangeing** (băn′jĭng): New England colloquial term meaning gathering or lounging about in groups.

8. **didn't hitch:** didn't get along.

9. **ornithologist** (ôr′nə-thŏl′ə-jĭst): one who studies birds.

black mud underneath and never be heard of more. Not far beyond were the salt marshes, and just this side the sea itself, which Sylvia wondered and dreamed much about, but never had seen, whose great voice could sometimes be heard above the noise of the woods on stormy nights.

"I can't think of anything I should like so much as to find that heron's nest," the handsome stranger was saying. "I would give ten dollars to anybody who could show it to me," he added desperately, "and I mean to spend my whole vacation hunting for it if need be. Perhaps it was only migrating, or had been chased out of its own region by some bird of prey."

> "I can't think of anything I should like so much as to find that heron's nest," the handsome stranger was saying.

Mrs. Tilley gave amazed attention to all this, but Sylvia still watched the toad, not divining,[10] as she might have done at some calmer time, that the creature wished to get to its hole under the doorstep, and was much hindered by the unusual spectators at that hour of the evening. No amount of thought, that night, could decide how many wished-for treasures the ten dollars, so lightly spoken of, would buy.

The next day the young sportsman hovered about the woods, and Sylvia kept him company, having lost her first fear of the friendly lad, who proved to be most kind and sympathetic. He told her many things about the birds and what they knew and where they lived and what they did with themselves. And he gave her a jack-knife, which she thought as great a treasure as if she were a desert islander. All day long he did not once make her troubled or afraid except when he brought down some unsuspecting singing creature from its bough. Sylvia would have liked him vastly better without his gun; she could not understand why he killed the very birds he seemed to like so much. But as the day waned, Sylvia still watched the young man with loving admiration. She had never seen anybody so charming and delightful; the woman's heart, asleep in the child, was vaguely thrilled by a dream of love. Some premonition[11] of that great power stirred and swayed these young creatures who traversed the solemn woodlands with soft-footed silent care. They stopped to listen to a bird's song; they pressed forward again eagerly, parting the branches—speaking to each other rarely and in whispers; the young man going first and Sylvia following, fascinated, a few steps behind, with her gray eyes dark with excitement.

She grieved because the longed-for white heron was elusive, but she did not lead the guest, she only followed, and there was no such thing as speaking first. The sound of her own unquestioned voice would have terrified her—it was hard enough to answer yes or no when there was need of that. At last evening

EVALUATE

What effect does the hunter seem to be having on Sylvia?

---

10. **divining** (dĭ-vī'nĭng): guessing.
11. **premonition:** a sense that something will happen; forewarning

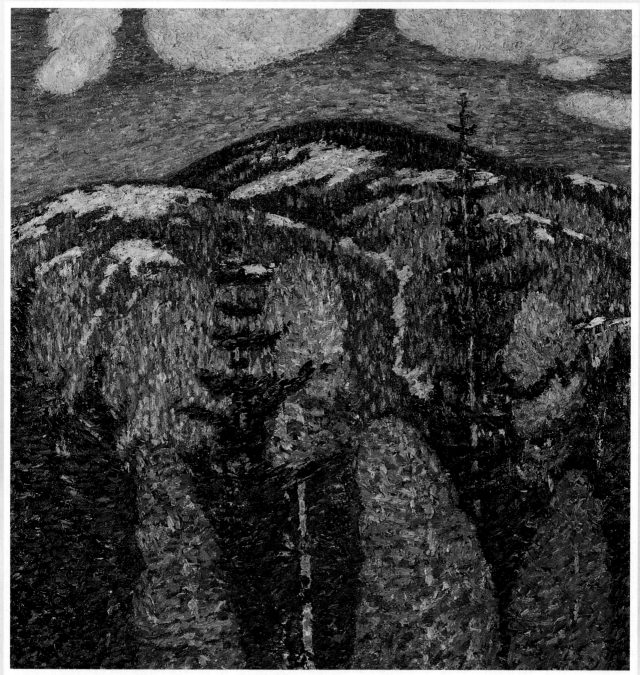

Cosmos (1908–1909), Marsden Hartley. Oil on canvas, 30″ × 30⅛″, Columbus (Ohio) Museum of Art, gift of Ferdinand Howald (31.179).

began to fall, and they drove the cow home together, and Sylvia smiled with pleasure when they came to the place where she heard the whistle and was afraid only the night before.

Half a mile from home, at the farther edge of the woods, where the land was highest, a great pine tree stood, the last of its generation. Whether it was left for a boundary mark, or for what reason, no one could say; the wood-choppers who had felled its mates were dead and gone long ago, and a whole forest of sturdy trees, pines and oaks and maples, had grown again. But the stately head of this old pine towered above them all and made a landmark for sea and shore miles and miles away. Sylvia knew it well. She had always believed that whoever climbed to the top of it could see the ocean; and the little girl had often laid her hand on the great rough trunk and looked up wistfully at those dark boughs that the wind always stirred, no matter how hot and still the air might be below. Now she thought of the tree with a new excitement, for why, if one climbed it at break of day, could not one see all the world, and easily discover whence the white heron flew, and mark the place, and find the hidden nest?

What a spirit of adventure, what wild ambition! What fancied triumph and delight and glory for the later morning when she could make known the secret! It was almost too real and too great for the childish heart to bear.

All night the door of the little house stood open and the whippoorwills came and sang upon the very step. The young sportsman and his old hostess were sound asleep, but Sylvia's great design[12] kept her broad awake and watching. She forgot to think of sleep. The short summer night seemed as long as the winter darkness, and at last, when the whip-poorwills ceased, and she was afraid the morning would after all come too soon, she

stole out of the house and followed the pasture path through the woods, hastening toward the open ground beyond, listening with a sense of comfort and companionship to the drowsy twitter of a half-awakened bird, whose perch she had jarred in passing. Alas, if the great wave of human interest which flooded for the first time this dull little life should sweep away the satisfactions of an existence heart to heart with nature and the dumb life of the forest!

There was the huge tree asleep yet in the paling moonlight, and small and silly Sylvia began with utmost bravery to mount to the top of it, with tingling, eager blood coursing the channels of her whole frame, with her bare feet and fingers, that pinched and held like bird's claws to the monstrous ladder reaching up, up, almost to the sky itself. First she must mount the white oak tree that grew alongside, where she was almost lost among the dark branches and the green leaves heavy and wet with dew; a bird fluttered off its nest, and a red squirrel ran to and fro and scolded pettishly[13] at the harmless housebreaker. Sylvia felt her way easily. She had often climbed there, and knew that higher still one of the oak's upper branches chafed against the pine trunk, just where its lower boughs were set close together. There, when she made the dangerous pass from one tree to the other, the great enterprise would really begin.

She crept out along the swaying oak limb at last, and took the daring step across into the old pine tree. The way was harder than she thought; she must reach far and hold fast, the sharp dry twigs caught and held her and scratched her like angry talons, the pitch made her thin little fingers clumsy and stiff as she went round and round the tree's great stem, higher and higher upward. The sparrows and

12. **design:** plan or secretive scheme.
13. **pettishly:** crossly; irritably.

robins in the woods below were beginning to wake and twitter to the dawn, yet it seemed much lighter there aloft in the pine tree, and the child knew she must hurry if her project were to be of any use.

The tree seemed to lengthen itself out as she went up, and to reach farther and farther upward. It was like a great mainmast to the voyaging earth; it must truly have been amazed that morning through all its ponderous frame as it felt this determined spark of human spirit wending its way from higher branch to branch. Who knows how steadily the least twigs held themselves to advantage this light, weak creature on her way! The old pine must have loved his new dependent. More than all the hawks, and bats, and moths, and even the sweet-voiced thrushes, was the brave, beating heart of the solitary gray-eyed child. And the tree stood still and frowned away the winds that June morning while the dawn grew bright in the east.

Look, look! a white spot of him like a single floating feather comes up from the dead hemlock and grows larger.

Sylvia's face was like a pale star, if one had seen it from the ground, when the last thorny bough was past, and she stood trembling and tired but wholly triumphant, high in the tree-top. Yes, there was the sea with the dawning sun making a golden dazzle over it, and toward that glorious east flew two hawks with slow-moving pinions.[14] How low they looked in the air from that height when one had only seen them before far up, and dark against the blue sky. Their gray feathers were as soft as moths; they seemed only a little way from the tree, and Sylvia felt as if she too could go flying away among the clouds. Westward, the woodlands and farms reached miles and miles into the distance; here and there were church steeples, and white villages; truly it was a vast and awesome world!

The birds sang louder and louder. At last the sun came up bewilderingly bright. Sylvia could see the white sails of ships out at sea, and the clouds that were purple and rose-colored and yellow at first began to fade away. Where was the white heron's nest in the sea of green branches, and was this wonderful sight and pageant of the world the only reward for having climbed to such a giddy height? Now look down again, Sylvia, where the green marsh is set among the shining birches and dark hemlocks; there where you saw the white heron once you will see him again; look, look! a white spot of him like a single floating feather comes up from the dead hemlock and grows larger, and rises, and comes close at last, and goes by the landmark pine with steady sweep of wing and outstretched slender neck and crested head. And wait! wait! do not move a foot or a finger, little girl, do not send an arrow of light and consciousness from your two eager eyes, for the heron has perched on a pine bough not far beyond yours, and cries back to his mate on the nest and plumes his feathers[15] for the new day!

---

14. **pinions** (pĭn′yənz): a bird's wings.
15. **plumes his feathers:** cleans and smoothes his feathers with his bill; preens.

The child gives a long sigh a minute later when a company of shouting catbirds comes also to the tree, and vexed by their fluttering and lawlessness, the solemn heron goes away. She knows his secret now, the wild, light, slender bird that floats and wavers, and goes back like an arrow presently to his home in the green world beneath. Then Sylvia, well satisfied, makes her perilous way down again, not daring to look far below the branch she stands on, ready to cry sometimes because her fingers ache and her lamed feet slip. Wondering over and over again what the stranger would say to her, and what he would think when she told him how to find his way straight to the heron's nest.

"Sylvy, Sylvy!" called the busy old grandmother again and again, but nobody answered, and the small husk bed was empty, and Sylvia had disappeared.

The guest waked from a dream, and remembering his day's pleasure hurried to dress himself that it might sooner begin. He was sure from the way the shy little girl looked once or twice yesterday that she had at least seen the white heron, and now she must really be made to tell. Here she comes now, paler than ever, and her worn old frock is torn and tattered, and smeared with pine pitch. The grandmother and the sportsman stand in the door together and question her, and the splendid moment has come to speak of the dead hemlock tree by the green marsh.

But Sylvia does not speak after all, though the old grandmother fretfully rebukes her, and the young man's kind, appealing eyes are looking straight in her own. He can make them rich with money; he has promised it, and they are poor now. He is so well worth making happy, and he waits to hear the story she can tell.

No, she must keep silence! What is it that suddenly forbids her and makes her dumb? Has she been nine years growing and now, when the great world for the first time puts out a hand to her, must she thrust it aside for a bird's sake? The murmur of the pine's green branches is in her ears, she remembers how the white heron came flying through the golden air and how they watched the sea and the morning together, and Sylvia cannot speak; she cannot tell the heron's secret and give its life away.

Dear loyalty, that suffered a sharp pang as the guest went away disappointed later in the day, that could have served and followed him and loved him as a dog loves! Many a night Sylvia heard the echo of his whistle haunting the pasture path as she came home with the loitering cow. She forgot even her sorrow at the sharp report[16] of his gun and the sight of thrushes and sparrows dropping silent to the ground, their songs hushed and their pretty feathers stained and wet with blood. Were the birds better friends than their hunter might have been—who can tell? Whatever treasures were lost to her, woodlands and summertime, remember! Bring your gifts and graces and tell your secrets to this lonely country child! ❖

---

16. **report:** explosive noise.

RESPONDING OPTIONS

FROM PERSONAL RESPONSE TO CRITICAL ANALYSIS

REFLECT

1. Did you like this story? Why or why not? Jot down your response in your notebook.

RETHINK

2. What is your opinion of Sylvia's decision to keep the location of the white heron's nest a secret?

3. How would you describe Sylvia's relationship with the stranger?

4. Review the bar graph that you created for the Personal Connection on page 594. How do your own loyalties compare with Sylvia's?

5. Sylvia, her grandmother, and the stranger all seem to have feelings for nature. How are their attitudes similar, and how are they different?

6. At the end of the story, the narrator asks, "Were the birds better friends than their hunter might have been—who can tell?" How do you predict Sylvia will answer this question in ten years, when she is 19?

7. Remember that a symbol is a person, place, or object that represents something beyond itself. How do you interpret the symbols in "A White Heron"?

   Consider
   - the "wretched geranium" at the end of the second paragraph
   - the old pine tree
   - the white heron

RELATE

8. Are the various attitudes toward nature represented in the story still evident today? Discuss.

ANOTHER PATHWAY

Cooperative Learning

Working in a small group, create a bar graph like the one you created for the Personal Connection on page 594, this one showing Sylvia's loyalties. Consider the people, places, and creatures that Sylvia values and what the narrator says in the last three paragraphs.

QUICKWRITES

1. Rewrite "A White Heron" as a **children's book.** Include both text and color illustrations, using watercolors, crayons, or pastels.

2. Try to imagine how Sylvia feels at the end of the story. Capture these feelings in a **haiku** for publication in your school's literary magazine or for display on a class bulletin board.

3. On the basis of the setting, write the copy for a **travel brochure** describing the appeal of the Maine woods.

4. Imagine that Sylvia and the stranger meet again, ten years later. Draft an **epilogue** to the story, describing the encounter. Include information about what has happened to the two characters and about the kind of life each one is now leading.

PORTFOLIO Save your writing. You may want to use it later as a springboard to a piece for your portfolio.

LITERARY CONCEPTS

Point of view refers to the narrative method, or the kind of narrator, used in a literary work. In the **third-person point of view,** the narrator is outside the action of the story. Sometimes this narrator is **omniscient,** or all-knowing, and can see into the minds of more than one character, reporting the thoughts, feelings, and experiences of these characters. Cite evidence from the story to show that "A White Heron" has an omniscient narrator. What effect does the narrator have on your impressions of Sylvia, the grandmother, and the stranger?

CRITIC'S CORNER

According to critic and journalist Caskie Stinnett, "Miss Jewett's modest goal is to let the reader feel the place, the characters, and the situation. . . . The key word is *feel.*" Do you think Sarah Orne Jewett achieved this goal in "A White Heron"? Use details from the story to support your opinion.

THE WRITER'S STYLE

Like many 19th-century writers, Sarah Orne Jewett wrote **realistic fiction.** She made use of vivid descriptions in her stories and incorporated her knowledge of local customs and regional dialect that conveyed village and rural life in New England. Do you think Jewett was successful in conveying the local color of rural southeastern Maine in "A White Heron"? Explain your point of view, citing evidence from the story.

Approaching Storm (1886), Edward Mitchell Bannister. National Museum of American Art, Smithsonian Institution, Washington, D.C./Art Resource, New York.

ALTERNATIVE ACTIVITIES

1. Imagine that a real estate developer is seeking approval from the town council to build homes on the land where the old pine tree now stands. Give the **speech** Sylvia would give at a public hearing, arguing why the tree—and the heron's natural habitat—should be preserved.

2. Create a **painting** to illustrate one of the scenes in the story. Try to capture the mood Jewett evokes through her vivid descriptions.

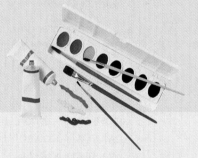

LITERARY LINKS

Which of the people in the selections you've read would be most sympathetic to Sylvia and supportive of her choice? Who would have the hardest time understanding or appreciating her dilemma?

WORDS TO KNOW

EXERCISE A Review the Words to Know at the bottom of the selection pages. Then write the vocabulary word that best completes each sentence.

1. Whether one lives in splendor or in _____, there is something about the sight of a great white heron that lifts the heart.

2. It flies slowly despite its nearly six-foot wing span, which means that a person lucky enough to see one _____ its habitat may be able to keep it in view for a while.

3. Large as this bird is, it appears anything but _____ in flight.

4. Silent and motionless in the water, the heron may seem asleep until its bill moves, like lightning, to spear the fish too _____ for slower hunters.

5. The hopeful heron-watcher must behave as _____ as the bird, for rash and careless actions will guarantee this graceful creature's quick departure.

EXERCISE B Make a quick sketch or use watercolors to depict the meaning of *traverse, elusive,* or *discreetly.* You might consider illustrating the word's use in Exercise A above. Then exchange your artwork with a classmate; each of you should judge whether the other has successfully communicated the meaning of the word.

SARAH ORNE JEWETT

1849–1909

Sarah Orne Jewett was born and raised in South Berwick, Maine, a town she loved and often wrote about in her fiction. The daughter of a respected Maine physician, she often traveled the countryside with him as he visited his patients; later she said that the best of her education was received in her father's buggy and the places to which it carried her. Jewett also enjoyed her father's extensive library, and by the age of 14, she was writing her own poetry and stories.

A few years later, in a bold and secret move shared only with an older sister, Jewett submitted one of her stories to a children's magazine. Following the publication of this story, Jewett became a frequent contributor to a number of periodicals; when she was 19, the prestigious New England magazine *Atlantic Monthly* published one of her stories. Impressed by her tales of Deephaven, a Maine town modeled on South Berwick, *Atlantic Monthly* editor William Dean Howells encouraged her to pursue the then popular genre of regional fiction, novels and stories that realistically depict the local color of a particular area. The result was her first book, *Deephaven,* a series of interrelated stories and sketches, published in 1877. Jewett went on to write hundreds of short stories and several novels.

In 1901 Jewett became the first woman to receive an honorary doctorate from Maine's Bowdoin College, where her father had received his own education and had also taught medicine. On her 53rd birthday, Jewett was thrown from a carriage and suffered head and spinal injuries, putting an end to her writing career and leaving her an invalid. She died in South Berwick several years later.

OTHER WORKS *Country By-Ways, A Country Doctor, A White Heron and Other Stories, The Country of the Pointed Firs*

PREVIEWING

Like the Sun

R. K. Narayan (nə-rī′yən) India

PERSONAL CONNECTION

Imagine that a friend has purchased a new outfit or has gotten a new haircut, which you find unattractive. Your friend seems unsure about his or her appearance and looks to you for approval. Would you express your true feelings? Working in pairs, role-play the different conversations that you and your friend might have. Then discuss with your class whether it's always best to tell the absolute truth or whether truth needs to be tempered in order to spare people's feelings.

CULTURAL CONNECTION

Issues of truth are important to Sekhar, the main character in "Like the Sun." Sekhar is a teacher in India, where schools are modeled on the British educational system. Students begin secondary school at age 11 and for the next seven years progress through forms, the equivalent of grades in the United States. Sekhar teaches the third form, or ninth grade; the principal of his school is called a headmaster. Sekhar is also a music critic in the small town in which he lives. In the story, he is asked to judge a performance of well-known traditional songs that reflect India's centuries-old musical heritage.

Schoolgirls in Oxford, England. Copyright © Thomas Hollyman / Photo Researchers, Inc.

Schoolchildren in front of the Taj Mahal in Agra, India. Copyright © Will and Deni McIntyre/Photo Researchers, Inc.

WRITING CONNECTION

Recall a time when you had to choose between telling the absolute truth or telling a white lie that might spare the feelings of another person. What choice did you make, and what were its effects? Describe the incident in your notebook. As you read "Like the Sun," compare your experience with the incidents in the story.

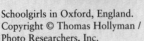

LASERLINKS
• CULTURAL CONNECTION

Like the Sun

R. K. Narayan

Truth, Sekhar reflected, is like the sun. I suppose no human being can ever look it straight in the face without blinking or being dazed. He realized that, morning till night, the essence of human relationships consisted in tempering truth so that it might not shock. This day he set apart as a unique day—at least one day in the year we must give and take absolute Truth whatever may happen. Otherwise life is not worth living. The day ahead seemed to him full of possibilities. He told no one of his experiment. It was a quiet resolve, a secret pact between him and eternity.

The very first test came while his wife served him his morning meal. He showed hesitation over a titbit, which she had thought was her culinary[1] masterpiece. She asked, "Why, isn't it good?" At other times he would have said, considering her feelings in the matter, "I feel full up, that's all." But today he said, "It isn't good. I'm unable to swallow it." He saw her wince and said to himself, Can't be helped. Truth is like the sun.

His next trial was in the common room when one of his colleagues came up and said, "Did you hear of the death of so-and-so? Don't you think it a pity?" "No," Sekhar answered. "He was such a fine man—" the other began. But Sekhar cut him short with: "Far from it. He always struck me as a mean and selfish brute."

During the last period when he was teaching geography for Third Form A, Sekhar received a note from the headmaster: "Please see me before you go home." Sekhar said to himself: It must be about these horrible test papers. A hundred papers in the boys' scrawls; he had shirked this work for weeks, feeling all the time as if a sword were hanging over his head.

The bell rang, and the boys burst out of the class.

Sekhar paused for a moment outside the headmaster's room to button up his coat; that was another subject the headmaster always sermonized about.

He stepped in with a very polite "Good evening, sir."

---

1. **culinary** (kyŏoˊlə-nĕrˊē): having to do with cooking or the kitchen.

609

The headmaster looked up at him in a very friendly manner and asked, "Are you free this evening?"

Sekhar replied, "Just some outing which I have promised the children at home—"

"Well, you can take them out another day. Come home with me now."

"Oh . . . yes, sir, certainly . . ." And then he added timidly, "Anything special, sir?"

"Yes," replied the headmaster, smiling to himself . . . "You didn't know my weakness for music?"

"Oh, yes, sir . . ."

"I've been learning and practicing secretly, and now I want you to hear me this evening. I've engaged a drummer and a violinist to accompany me—this is the first time I'm doing it full-dress,[2] and I want your opinion. I know it will be valuable."

Sekhar's taste in music was well-known. He was one of the most dreaded music critics in the town. But he never anticipated his musical inclinations would lead him to this trial. . . . "Rather a surprise for you, isn't it?" asked the headmaster. "I've spent a fortune on it behind closed doors. . . ." They started for the headmaster's house. "God hasn't given me a child, but at least let him not deny me the consolation of music," the headmaster said, pathetically, as they walked. He incessantly chattered about music: how he began one day out of sheer boredom; how his teacher at first laughed at him and then gave him hope; how his ambition in life was to forget himself in music.

At home the headmaster proved very ingratiating. He sat Sekhar on a red silk carpet, set before him several dishes of delicacies, and fussed over him as if he were a son-in-law of the house. He even said, "Well, you must listen with a free mind. Don't worry about these test papers." He added half humorously, "I will give you a week's time."

"Make it ten days, sir," Sekhar pleaded.

"All right, granted," the headmaster said generously. Sekhar felt really relieved now—he would attack them at the rate of ten a day and get rid of the nuisance.

The headmaster lighted incense sticks. "Just to create the right atmosphere," he explained. A drummer and a violinist, already seated on a Rangoon mat, were waiting for him. The headmaster sat down between them like a professional at a concert, cleared his throat, and began an alapana,[3] and paused to ask, "Isn't it good Kalyani?"[4] Sekhar pretended not to have heard the question. The headmaster went on to sing a full song composed by Thyagaraja[5] and followed it with two more. All the time the headmaster was singing, Sekhar went on commenting within himself, He croaks like a dozen frogs. He is bellowing like a buffalo. Now he sounds like loose window shutters in a storm.

The incense sticks burnt low. Sekhar's head throbbed with the medley of sounds that had assailed his eardrums for a couple of hours now. He felt half stupefied. The headmaster had gone nearly hoarse, when he paused to ask, "Shall I go on?" Sekhar replied, "Please don't, sir; I think this will do. . . ." The headmaster looked stunned. His face was beaded with perspiration. Sekhar felt the greatest pity for him. But he felt he could not help it. No judge delivering a sentence felt more pained and helpless. Sekhar noticed that the headmaster's wife peeped in from the kitchen, with eager curiosity. The drummer and the violinist put away their burdens with an air of relief. The headmaster removed his spectacles, mopped his brow, and

2. full-dress: complete in every respect.

3. alapana: improvisational Indian music in the classical style.

4. Kalyani: traditional Indian folk songs.

5. Thyagaraja (1767–1847): famous Indian composer.

WORDS TO KNOW

incessantly (ĭn-sĕs′ənt-lē) *adv.* endlessly; constantly
stupefied (stōō′pə-fīd′) *adj.* dazed; stunned

Detail of *The Dance of Krishna* (about 1650, Mewar, Rajasthan, India). From a manuscript of the Sur-Sagar, opaque watercolor on paper, 11″ × 8⅝″, Collection Gopi Krishna Kanoria, Patna, India.

asked, "Now, come out with your opinion."

"Can't I give it tomorrow, sir?" Sekhar asked tentatively.

"No. I want it immediately—your frank opinion. Was it good?"

"No, sir . . ." Sekhar replied.

"Oh! . . . Is there any use continuing my lessons?"

"Absolutely none, sir . . ." Sekhar said with his voice trembling. He felt very unhappy that he could not speak more soothingly. Truth, he reflected, required as much strength to give as to receive.

All the way home he felt worried. He felt that his official life was not going to be smooth sailing hereafter. There were questions of increment and confirmation[6] and so on, all depending upon the headmaster's goodwill. All kinds of worries seemed to be in store for him. . . . Did not Harischandra[7] lose his throne,

---

6. **increment and confirmation:** salary increases and job security.

7. **Harischandra:** a legendary Hindu king and the subject of many Indian stories. His name has come to symbolize truth and integrity.

wife, child, because he would speak nothing less than the absolute Truth whatever happened?

At home his wife served him with a sullen face. He knew she was still angry with him for his remark of the morning. Two casualties for today, Sekhar said to himself. If I practice it for a week, I don't think I shall have a single friend left.

He received a call from the headmaster in his classroom next day. He went up apprehensively.

"Your suggestion was useful. I have paid off the music master. No one would tell me the truth about my music all these days. Why such antics at my age! Thank you. By the way, what about those test papers?"

"You gave me ten days, sir, for correcting them."

"Oh, I've reconsidered it. I must positively have them here tomorrow. . . ." A hundred papers in a day! That meant all night's sitting up! "Give me a couple of days, sir . . ."

"No. I must have them tomorrow morning. And remember, every paper must be thoroughly scrutinized."

"Yes, sir," Sekhar said, feeling that sitting up all night with a hundred test papers was a small price to pay for the luxury of practicing Truth. ❖

INSIGHT

Tell all the Truth but tell it slant—
Emily Dickinson

Tell all the Truth but tell it slant—
Success in Circuit lies
Too bright for our infirm Delight
The Truth's superb surprise
5   As Lightning to the Children eased
With explanation kind
The Truth must dazzle gradually
Or every man be blind—

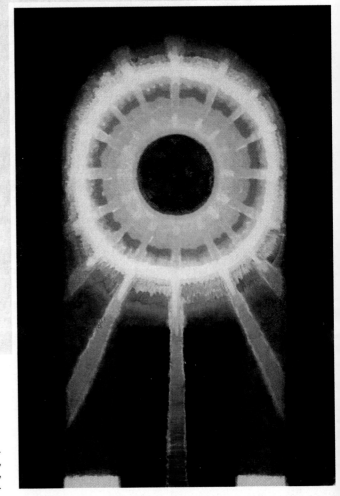

June '70 (1970), Biren De.
Oil on canvas, 72″ × 48″,
National Gallery of Modern Art,
New Delhi, India.

RESPONDING
OPTIONS

FROM PERSONAL RESPONSE TO CRITICAL ANALYSIS

REFLECT   1. Did you like the character Sekhar? Share what you think with your classmates.

RETHINK   2. What kind of person is Sekhar?
Consider
- his actions on the day of truth compared with those on other days
- his relationships with other people
- his attitude toward his work
- his reputation as a music critic

3. Why do you think that telling the absolute truth at least one day a year is so important to Sekhar?

4. Is Sekhar's "experiment" one that you would like to repeat? Why or why not?
Consider
- the effects of his experiment on others and himself
- your role-playing activity for the Personal Connection on page 608
- the incident that you described for the Writing Connection on page 608

RELATE   5. Does the Insight poem "Tell all the Truth but tell it slant—" help you to understand Sekhar's observations about truth? Explain your answer.

6. Do you agree with Sekhar that truth generally requires "as much strength to give as to receive"? Why or why not?

ANOTHER PATHWAY

If this day of "absolute truth" had been like any day of "tempered truth," how might Sekhar have responded to the questions asked by his colleague and by his boss? Discuss the differences between tempered truth and absolute truth. Then rewrite Sekhar's two conversations. Temper the truth about what Sekhar really thinks so that he avoids hurting anyone's feelings.

LITERARY CONCEPTS

In literature there are three basic types of **humor,** all of which may involve exaggeration or irony. **Humor of situation** is derived from the plot of a work. It usually involves exaggerated events or situational irony, which occurs when something happens that is different from what one expected. **Humor of character** is often based on exaggerated personalities or on characters who fail to recognize their own flaws, a form of dramatic irony. **Humor of language** may include sarcasm, exaggeration, puns, or verbal irony, which occurs when what is said is not what is meant. Do you think the humor in "Like the Sun" derives mainly from situation, character, or language? Cite details to support your opinion.

QUICKWRITES

1. As the headmaster of Sekhar's school, write two **notes,** one to your music master and one to Sekhar. Tell the music master why you are ending your lessons. Then tell Sekhar what you think of his honest evaluation of your performance.

2. Write a **literary analysis** of the theme of the story. What do you think the author is trying to say about truth and personal relationships?

PORTFOLIO Save your writing. You may want to use it later as a springboard to a piece for your portfolio.

ALTERNATIVE ACTIVITIES

Take a **survey** of at least six friends or family members on the subject of truth. Create a series of questions based on situations from everyday life that are similar to those that Sekhar faced. For example, you might ask, "If a friend who lacked musical talent wanted your opinion about his or her performance, how truthful would you be?" Have participants rate their truthfulness on a scale of 1 to 5, with 1 being "not truthful at all" and 5 being "completely truthful." If you have a graphics program on your computer, use it to design your questionnaire.

ACROSS THE CURRICULUM

Math If Sekhar needs to correct 100 papers in 24 hours and wants to spend the same amount of time on each, what is the maximum number of minutes he can spend on each paper? How much time can he spend on each paper if he also spends an hour and a half eating his meals, 30 minutes reading the newspaper, 20 minutes exercising, and 40 minutes doing household chores?

CRITIC'S CORNER

According to critic Perry D. Westbrook, much of Narayan's work conveys this theme: "Human beings are human beings, not gods. Men and women can make flights toward godhood, but they always fall a bit short." How do you think this statement applies to "Like the Sun"?

WORDS TO KNOW

On your paper, answer the questions that follow.

1. Are people who normally **shirk** their work likely to be lazy, efficient, or exhausted?

2. Is a person who can easily identify the **essence** of a problem someone with a sharp sense of smell, someone with an ability to see what's most important, or someone with a taste for the extraordinary?

3. Would a lecturer who spoke **incessantly** most likely find himself or herself applauded, arrested, or hoarse?

4. Does a person become **stupefied** by amusement, amazement, or annoyance?

5. Which of the following is the best synonym for **tempering:** *opposing, insisting,* or *moderating?*

R. K. NARAYAN

Born in Madras, India, R. K. Narayan is widely regarded as one of India's greatest authors. For his novel *The Guide* (1958), he won the National Prize of the Indian Literary Academy, his country's highest literary honor. Ironically, he turned to writing after he failed at teaching, having held two different jobs for a total of two days.

Narayan sets most of his works in a fictional Indian town named Malgudi, a place that resembles both the city of his birth and the city of Mysore, where he has spent most of his life. He creat-

1906–

ed Malgudi for his first novel, *Swami and Friends*. "As I sat in a room nibbling my pen and wondering what to write," he recalls, "Malgudi with its little railway station swam into view."

Although Narayan knows the Indian language of Tamil, he always writes in English. Many of his stories were originally published in *Hindu,* one of India's English-language newspapers.

OTHER WORKS *Malgudi Days, The English Teacher, My Days: A Memoir, Under the Banyan Tree*

PREVIEWING

POETRY

Once upon a Time
Gabriel Okara (ō-kä′rə) **Nigeria**

Making the Jam Without You
Maxine Kumin (kyōō′mĭn) **United States**

PERSONAL CONNECTION

Aside from material things, what do you think parents and guardians want most for their children? What, in turn, might parents be able to learn from their children? In a small group, make concept charts like the ones below and brainstorm ideas about relationships between parents and children. Feel free to extend the charts as your ideas take you in new directions.

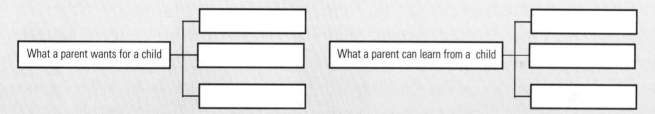

What a parent wants for a child

What a parent can learn from a child

BIOGRAPHICAL CONNECTION

The speakers of the next two poems both are parents addressing their children. In Gabriel Okara's poem, the speaker addresses a son; in Maxine Kumin's, a daughter.

Like many Nigerian authors, Gabriel Okara writes in English, which became the common language of literature during British colonial rule. Okara's title, "Once upon a Time," is from many English-language bedtime stories and fairy tales.

Though best known for writing about nature and rural farm life, Maxine Kumin has also written what she calls "tribal poems," which she defines as "poems of kinship and parenting." Often these poems are written to or about her children. "Making the Jam Without You" was dedicated to her daughter, who traveled and lived in Europe.

WRITING CONNECTION

In your notebook, describe the type of parent that you would like to be and the type of relationship that you would like to have with your child. As you read the following two poems, compare your hopes with those of the speakers in the poems.

Once upon a Time

Gabriel Okara

Once upon a time, son
they used to laugh with their hearts
and laugh with their eyes;
but now they only laugh with their teeth,
5   while their ice-block-cold eyes
search behind my shadow.

There was a time indeed
they used to shake hands with their hearts;
but that's gone, son.
10   Now they shake hands without hearts
while their left hands search
my empty pockets.

"Feel at home," "Come again,"
they say, and when I come
15   again and feel
at home, once, twice,
there will be no thrice—
for then I find doors shut on me.

So I have learned many things, son.
20   I have learned to wear many faces
like dresses—homeface,
officeface, streetface, hostface, cock-
tailface, with all their conforming smiles
like a fixed portrait smile.

Ijo mask. Plate 61 from the exhibition catalog *Wild Spirits, Strong Medicine*, courtesy of the Museum for African Art, New York. Photo by Jerry L. Thompson.

25 And I have learned too
to laugh with only my teeth
and shake hands without my heart.
I have also learned to say, "Goodbye,"
when I mean "Goodriddance";
30 to say "Glad to meet you,"
without being glad; and to say "It's been
nice talking to you," after being bored.

But believe me, son.
I want to be what I used to be
35 when I was like you. I want
to unlearn all these muting things.
Most of all, I want to relearn
how to laugh, for my laugh in the mirror
shows only my teeth like a snake's bare fangs!

40 So show me, son,
how to laugh; show me how
I used to laugh and smile
once upon a time when I was like you.

FROM PERSONAL RESPONSE TO CRITICAL ANALYSIS

REFLECT   **1.** What are your impressions of the father who is the speaker in "Once upon a Time"? Share your ideas with a partner.

RETHINK   **2.** What message do you think the speaker most wants to communicate to his son?
Consider
- what the speaker says about other people
- the faces he has learned to wear
- the things he has learned to do and say
- what he hopes to learn from his son

3. How does the speaker's attitude about his adult life affect the tone of the poem?

4. Why do you think Okara called the poem "Once upon a Time"?

Making the Jam Without You

Maxine Kumin

Old daughter, small traveler
asleep in a German featherbed
under the eaves in a postcard town
of turrets and towers,
5   I am putting a dream in your head.

Listen! Here it is afternoon.
The rain comes down like bullets.
I stand in the kitchen,
that harem[1] of good smells
10   where we have bumped hips and
cracked the cupboards with our talk
while the stove top danced with pots
and it was not clear who did
the mothering. Now I am
15   crushing blackberries
to make the annual jam
in a white cocoon of steam.

Take it, my sleeper. Redo it
in any of your three
20   languages and nineteen years.
Change the geography.
Let there be a mountain,
the fat cows on it belled
like a cathedral. Let
25   there be someone beside you
as you come upon the ruins
of a schloss,[2] all overgrown

with a glorious thicket,
its brambles soft as wool.
30   Let him bring the buckets
crooked on his angel arms
and may the berries, vaster
than any forage[3] in
the mild hills of New Hampshire,
35   drop in your pail, plum size,
heavy as the eyes
of an honest dog
and may you bear them
home together to a square
40   white unreconstructed kitchen
not unlike this one.

Now may your two heads
touch over the kettle,
over the blood of the berries
45   that drink up sugar and sun,
over that tar-thick boil
love cannot stir down.
More plainly than
the bric-a-brac of shelves
50   filling with jelly glasses,
more surely than
the light driving through them
trite[4] as rubies, I see him
as pale as paraffin[5] beside you.
55   I see you cutting
fresh baked bread to spread it
with the bright royal fur.

At this time
I lift the flap of your dream
60   and slip out thinner than a sliver
as your two mouths open
for the sweet stain of purple.

---

1. **harem:** section of a house reserved for women members of a Moslem household.
2. **schloss** (shlôs) *German:* castle.
3. **forage:** food found by searching.
4. **trite:** uninteresting through overuse or repetition.
5. **paraffin:** a waxy, white substance used to seal home-canned foods to prevent spoilage.

Elena in the Kitchen (1991), Richard Maury. Copyright © Gerold Wunderlich & Co., New York.

RESPONDING
OPTIONS

FROM PERSONAL RESPONSE TO CRITICAL ANALYSIS

REFLECT 1. What image from "Making the Jam Without You" lingers in your mind? Draw a quick sketch of it in your notebook, and share your work with a classmate.

RETHINK 2. What does the speaker seem to want most for her daughter? Use images and details from the poem to explain your response.

3. How would you describe the speaker's relationship with her daughter?
Consider
   - the tone that the speaker uses in speaking to her daughter
   - the speaker's memories of their time together in the kitchen
   - the actions described in the last stanza

4. Why do you think the speaker sends her daughter a dream instead of telling her what she wants her to know?

RELATE 5. Look back at what you wrote for the Writing Connection on page 615. Compare your vision of yourself as a parent with what you learned about the speakers in "Once upon a Time" and "Making the Jam Without You."

ANOTHER PATHWAY
Cooperative Learning
Working in a small group, draft brief biographical sketches of the speakers and their children in the two poems. Begin by listing all the biographical details that each poem states or implies about each person. Then brainstorm a list of invented details that you might include to round out the picture of each person.

QUICKWRITES

1. Write a **letter** that conveys the same message as one of the poems. Assume the identity of the speaker of the poem, and address the letter to the same child who is addressed in the poem. Each paragraph of your letter might correspond to a stanza in the poem.

2. Write a **definition** of the quality or value that seems to matter most to the father in "Once upon a Time." Do the same for the mother in "Making the Jam Without You."

📁 **PORTFOLIO** *Save your writing. You may want to use it later as a springboard to a piece for your portfolio.*

LITERARY CONCEPTS

Free verse is poetry that does not contain regular patterns of rhyme and meter. The lines in free verse often flow more naturally than do rhymed, metrical lines and thus achieve a rhythm more like everyday human speech. With a partner, take turns reading the two poems aloud. In what ways does each poem resemble everyday speech? Discuss the appropriateness of using free verse rather than metrical, rhymed lines for poems that deal with parent-child relationships.

ALTERNATIVE ACTIVITIES

1. What would the children addressed in these two poems say in response to the speakers? With a partner, role-play the **conversations** that might take place between the father and the son and between the mother and the daughter.

2. Make a **collage** of the faces people wear in "Once upon a Time" (lines 20–24).

LITERARY LINKS

Compare either of these poems with another selection you have read that involves parents and their children. What is similar and what is different about the relationship that each work describes?

CRITIC'S CORNER

Critic Jane Howard once wrote that Maxine Kumin "brings tastes, sounds, textures, smells, and the look of things to vivid life." Reread "Making the Jam Without You." Then make a list of vivid sensory images in the poem, finding at least one image for each of the five senses. Compare your list with a classmate's.

GABRIEL OKARA

Gabriel Okara (1921–) was born in eastern Nigeria, the son of an Ijaw (ē'jô) chief. As a college student, Okara's main love was painting; he also studied philosophy, music, and literature. After leaving school, Okara worked as a bookbinder and began writing poetry and radio plays. In 1953 his poem "The Call of the River Nun" won the "Best All-Around" award at the Nigerian Festival of the Arts. Three years later, Okara came to the United States to study journalism; after he returned to his homeland, he held various jobs in publishing, broadcasting, and government.

In 1964 Okara published *The Voice,* which has been called "one of the most memorable novels to have come out of Nigeria." During the Nigerian civil war (1967–1970), Okara traveled throughout the United States with fellow Nigerian author Chinua Achebe to seek help for the Ibo people, who were fighting to form an independent country. Though Okara has become a frequently anthologized poet, many of his early poems were lost, in part because of the devastation of the civil war.

OTHER WORKS *Poems 1957–1972, The Fisherman's Invocation*

MAXINE KUMIN

1925–

Born in Philadelphia, Pennsylvania, Maxine Kumin began writing poetry as a student at Radcliffe College, where she earned both her bachelor's and master's degrees. She published her first volume of verse, *Halfway,* in 1961; since then, she has written numerous poetry volumes, essay collections, novels, short stories, and children's books. She served as the poetry consultant to the Library of Congress in 1981–1982.

In 1973 Kumin won the Pulitzer Prize for *Up Country: Poems of New England.* Like much of her other writing, the poems in this collection were largely inspired by the natural world around the New Hampshire farm where she and her family have lived part-time since the early 1960s. The rest of the time has usually found Kumin teaching at one of several leading American universities. She has said, "I hope to live out my life on the land, raising horses and turnips and making jam from the wild berries."

OTHER WORKS *In Deep: Country Essays, Looking for Luck, The Nightmare Factory, Our Ground Time Here Will Be Brief*

PREVIEWING

FICTION

The Cabuliwallah (kə-bŏŏl′ĭ-wŏl′ə)
(The Fruit Seller from Cabul)
Rabindranath Tagore (rə-bēn′drə-nät′ tə-gôr′) India

PERSONAL CONNECTION

Think of someone you know who has a different background from yours. Perhaps this person is much richer or much poorer than you are, practices a different religion, or comes from another country. In your notebook, describe your first meeting and your reaction to this person. Despite your differences, were you able to find that you had something in common?

CULTURAL CONNECTION

Set around 1890 in Calcutta, a large city in eastern India, "The Cabuliwallah" features characters of very different backgrounds. The title character is a poor Moslem from Cabul (often spelled Kabul), the capital of Afghanistan, a mountainous country northwest of India. The narrator of the story and his family, on the other hand, are upper-caste Hindu Indians. Hinduism, India's most widespread religion, developed a caste system, or class system, centuries ago. Around the time of this story, caste rules were strictly enforced. A lower-caste Hindu could not eat, sit, or socialize in any way with a member of an upper caste. A poor Moslem also would have had very limited contact with upper-caste Hindus.

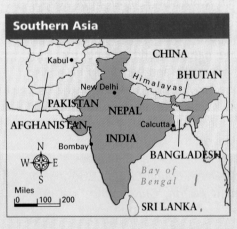

The caste system prohibited marriage among people from different castes, and parents arranged marriages for their children. Weddings, such as the one in this story, were held when the bride and groom were young teenagers. Traditionally, the bride moved into the household of her father-in-law.

READING CONNECTION

Comparing Characters As you read the following story, look for details that help you to understand the characters of the Cabuliwallah and the narrator. Try to see what is similar and what is different about the two men and their backgrounds, and list those details on a chart like the one below.

Cabuliwallah	Narrator
foreigner from Afghanistan	native of India

THE CABULIWALLAH

Rabindranath Tagore

[The Fruit Seller from Cabul]

The Charpoi, Robert Wade. Watercolor, 10″ × 14″, private collection. From *Painting More Than the Eye Can See*, 1989, North Light Books. Copyright © Robert Wade.

Mini, my five-year-old daughter, cannot live without chattering. I really believe that in all her life she has not wasted one minute in silence. Her mother is often vexed at this and would stop her <u>prattle</u>, but I do not. To see Mini quiet is unnatural, and I cannot bear it for long. Because of this, our conversations are always lively.

One morning, for instance, when I was in the midst of the seventeenth chapter of my new novel, Mini stole into the room and, putting her hand into mine, said: "Father! Ramdayal the doorkeeper calls a crow a *krow*! He doesn't know anything, does he?"

Before I could explain the language differences in this country, she was on the trace of another subject. "What do you think, Father? Shola says there is an elephant in the clouds, blowing water out of his trunk, and that is why it rains!"

The child had seated herself at my feet near the table and was playing softly, drumming on her knees. I was hard at work on my seventeenth chapter, where Pratap Singh, the hero, had just caught Kanchanlata, the heroine, in his arms and was about to escape with her by the third-story window of the castle, when all of a sudden Mini left her play and ran to the window, crying "A Cabuliwallah! a Cabuliwallah!" Sure enough,

WORDS TO KNOW **prattle** (prăt′l) *n.* trivial chatter or talk

in the street below was a Cabuli-wallah passing slowly along. He wore the loose, soiled clothing of his people, and a tall turban; there was a bag on his back, and he carried boxes of grapes in his hand.

I cannot tell what my daughter's feelings were at the sight of this man, but she began to call him loudly. Ah, I thought, he will come in, and my seventeenth chapter will never be finished! At this exact moment the Cabuliwallah turned and looked up at the child. When she saw this, she was overcome by terror, fled to her mother's protection, and disappeared. She had a blind belief that inside the bag which the big man carried were two or three children like herself. Meanwhile, the peddler entered my doorway and greeted me with a smiling face.

So precarious was the position of my hero and my heroine that my first impulse was to stop and buy something, especially since Mini had called to the man. I made some small purchases, and a conversation began about Abdurrahman, the Russians, the English, and the frontier policy.[1]

As he was about to leave, he asked: "And where is the little girl, sir?"

I, thinking that Mini must get rid of her false fear, had her brought out. She stood by my chair, watching the Cabuliwallah and his bag. He offered her nuts and raisins, but she would not be tempted and only clung closer to me, with all her doubts increased. This was their first meeting.

One morning, however, not many days later, as I was leaving the house, I was startled to find Mini seated on a bench near the door, laughing and talking with the great Cabuliwallah at her feet. In all her life, it appeared, my small daughter had never found so patient a listener, except for her father. Already the corner of her little sari was stuffed with almonds and raisins,

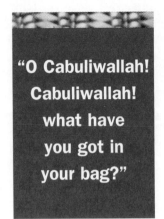

"O Cabuliwallah! Cabuliwallah! what have you got in your bag?"

gifts from her visitor. "Why did you give her those?" I said and, taking out an eight-anna piece,[2] handed it to him. The man accepted the money without delay, and slipped it into his pocket.

Alas, on my return an hour later, I found the unfortunate coin had made twice its own worth of trouble! The Cabuliwallah had given it to Mini, and her mother, seeing the bright round object, had pounced on the child with: "Where did you get that eight-anna piece?"

"The Cabuliwallah gave it to me," said Mini cheerfully.

"The Cabuliwallah gave it to you!" cried her mother much shocked. "O Mini! how could you take it from him?"

Entering at this moment, I saved her from impending disaster and proceeded to make my own inquiries. I found that it was not the first or the second time the two had met. The Cabuliwallah had overcome the child's first terror by a judicious bribery of nuts and almonds, and the two were now great friends.

They had many quaint jokes which afforded them a great deal of amusement. Seated in front of him, and looking with all her tiny dignity on his gigantic frame, Mini would ripple her face with laughter and begin "O Cabuliwallah! Cabuliwallah! what have you got in your bag?"

He would reply in the nasal accents of a

---

1. **Abdurrahman . . . policy:** During the 1800s, Great Britain and Russia competed for control of Afghanistan. In 1880, after having invaded Afghanistan, the British gave Abdurrahman Khan, the Afghan emir, the authority to rule over his country's internal affairs. The eastern frontier remained a troubled area, and Abdurrahman was forced to agree to an eastern border established by the British.

2. **eight-anna piece:** a coin formerly used in India.

WORDS TO KNOW

precarious (prǐ-kâr′ē-əs) *adj.* dangerously lacking in security or stability
impending (ǐm-pěn′dǐng) *adj.* about to happen **impend** *v.*
judicious (jōō-dǐsh′əs) *adj.* exhibiting sound judgment or common sense
quaint (kwānt) *adj.* odd, especially in an old-fashioned way

mountaineer: "An elephant!" Not much cause for merriment, perhaps, but how they both enjoyed their joke! And for me, this child's talk with a grown-up man always had in it something strangely fascinating.

Then the Cabuliwallah, not to be caught behind, would take his turn with: "Well, little one, and when are you going to the father-in-law's house?"[3]

Now most small Bengali[4] maidens have heard long ago about the father-in-law's house, but we, being a little modern, had kept these things from our child, and at this question Mini must have been a trifle bewildered. But she would not show it and with instant composure replied: "Are you going there?"

Among men of the Cabuliwallah's class, however, it is well-known that the words "father-in-law's house" have a double meaning. It is a euphemism for jail, the place where we are well cared for at no expense. The sturdy peddler would take my daughter's question in this sense. "Ah," he would say, shaking his fist at an invisible policeman, "I will thrash my father-in-law!" Hearing this, and picturing the poor, uncomfortable relative, Mini would go into peals of laughter, joined by her formidable friend.

These were autumn mornings, the time of year when kings of old went forth to conquest; and I, never stirring from my little corner in Calcutta, would let my mind wander over the whole world. At the very name of another country, my heart would go out to it, and at the sight of a foreigner in the streets, I would fall to weaving a network of dreams: the mountains, the glens, the forests of his distant homeland with a cottage in its setting, and the free and independent life of faraway wilds. Perhaps these scenes of travel pass in my imagination all the more vividly because I lead a vegetable existence such that a call to travel would fall upon me like a thunderbolt. In the presence of this Cabuliwallah I was immediately transported to the foot of mountains, with narrow defiles[5] twisting in and out amongst their towering, arid peaks. I could see the string of camels bearing merchandise, and the company of turbaned merchants carrying queer old firearms, and some of their spears down toward the plains. I could see—but at this point Mini's mother would intervene, imploring me to "beware of that man."

Unfortunately Mini's mother is a very timid lady. Whenever she hears a noise in the street or sees people coming toward the house, she always jumps to the conclusion that they are either thieves, drunkards, snakes, tigers, malaria, cockroaches, caterpillars, or an English sailor. Even after all these years of experience, she is not able to overcome her terror. Thus she was full of doubts about the Cabuliwallah and used to beg me to keep a watchful eye on him.

I tried to gently laugh her fear away, but then she would turn on me seriously and ask solemn questions.

Were children never kidnapped?

Was it, then, not true that there was slavery in Cabul?

Was it so very absurd that this big man should be able to carry off a tiny child?

I told her that, though not impossible, it was highly improbable. But this was not enough, and her dread persisted. As her suspicion was unfounded, however, it did not seem right to forbid the man to come to the house, and his familiarity went unchecked.

Once a year, in the middle of January, Rahmun

---

3. **going to . . . house:** an idiom meaning "getting married."
4. **Bengali:** of or from Bengal, a region of eastern India and, now, Bangladesh.
5. **defiles:** deep, narrow mountain passes.

625

the Cabuliwallah was in the habit of returning to his country, and as the time approached, he would be very busy going from house to house collecting his debts. This year, however, he always found time to come and see Mini. It would have seemed to an outsider that there was some conspiracy between them, for when he could not come in the morning, he would appear in the evening.

Even to me it was a little startling now and then, to suddenly surprise this tall, loose-garmented man of bags in the corner of a dark room; but when Mini would run in, smiling, with her "O Cabuliwallah! Cabuliwallah!" and the two friends so far apart in age would subside into their old laughter and their old jokes, I felt reassured.

One morning, a few days before he had made up his mind to go, I was correcting my proof sheets[6] in my study. It was chilly weather. Through the window the rays of the sun touched my feet, and the slight warmth was very welcome. It was almost eight o'clock, and the early pedestrians were returning home with their heads covered. All at once I heard an uproar in the street and, looking out, saw Rahmun bound and being led away between two policemen, followed by a crowd of curious boys. There were bloodstains on the clothes of the Cabuliwallah, and one of the policemen carried a knife. Hurrying out, I stopped them and inquired what it all meant. Partly from one, partly from another, I gathered that a certain neighbor had owed the peddler something for a Rampuri shawl[7] but had falsely denied having bought it, and that in the course of the quarrel Rahmun had struck him. Now, in the heat of his excitement, the prisoner began calling his enemy all sorts of names. Suddenly, from a verandah of my house my little

> Even my lighthearted Mini, I am ashamed to say, forgot her old friend.

Mini appeared, with her usual exclamation: "O Cabuliwallah! Cabuliwallah!" Rahmun's face lighted up as he turned to her. He had no bag under his arm today, so she could not discuss the elephant with him. She at once therefore proceeded to the next question: "Are you going to the father-in-law's house?" Rahmun laughed and said: "Just where I am going, little one!" Then seeing that the reply did not amuse the child, he held up his <u>fettered</u> hands. "Ah," he said, "I would have thrashed that old father-in-law, but my hands are bound!"

On a charge of murderous assault, Rahmun was sentenced to many years of imprisonment.

Time passed, and he was forgotten. The accustomed work in the accustomed place was ours, and the thought of the once free mountaineer spending his years in prison seldom occurred to us. Even my lighthearted Mini, I am ashamed to say, forgot her old friend. New companions filled her life. As she grew older, she spent more of her time with girls, so much in fact that she came no more to her father's room. I was scarcely on speaking terms with her.

Many years passed. It was autumn once again, and we had made arrangements for Mini's marriage; it was to take place during the Puja holidays.[8] With the goddess Durga returning to her seasonal home in Mount Kailas, the light of our home was also to depart, leaving our house in shadows.

6. **proof sheets:** copies of a typeset manuscript, on which changes or corrections are made by the author or an editor.

7. **Rampuri shawl:** shawl from Rampur, India. Such shawls are the finest in India because of the quality of the fabric.

8. **Puja holidays:** great Hindu festival (also called Durga-puja) that honors Durga, a war goddess. It is a time for family reunions and other gatherings as well as religious ceremonies.

The morning was bright. After the rains, there was a sense of cleanness in the air, and the rays of the sun looked like pure gold; so bright that they radiated even to the sordid[9] brick walls of our Calcutta lanes. Since early dawn, the wedding pipes had been sounding, and at each beat my own heart throbbed. The wailing tune, Bhairavi,[10] seemed to intensify my pain at the approaching separation. My Mini was to be married tonight.

From early morning, noise and bustle pervaded the house. In the courtyard the canopy had to be slung on its bamboo poles; the tinkling chandeliers should be hung in each room and verandah; there was great hurry and excitement. I was sitting in my study, looking through the accounts, when someone entered, saluting respectfully, and stood before me. It was Rahmun the Cabuliwallah, and at first I did not recognize him. He had no bag, nor the long hair, nor the same vigor that he used to have. But he smiled, and I knew him again.

"When did you come, Rahmun?" I asked him.

"Last evening," he said, "I was released from jail."

The words struck harsh upon my ears. I had never talked with anyone who had wounded his fellowman, and my heart shrank when I realized this, for I felt that the day would have been better omened if he had not turned up.

"There are ceremonies going on," I said, "and I am busy. Could you perhaps come another day?"

At once he turned to go; but as he reached the door, he hesitated and said: "May I not see the little one, sir, for a moment?" It was his belief that Mini was still the same. He had pictured her running to him as she used to do, calling "O Cabuliwallah! Cabuliwallah!" He

---

9. **sordid:** filthy or dirty.
10. **Bhairavi** (bī′rə-vē): the name of a particular tune. It is a happy piece of music and is associated with joyous events.

WORDS TO KNOW · **pervade** (pər-vād′) v. to spread throughout; to be present throughout

627

had imagined that they would laugh and talk together, just as in the past. In fact, in memory of those former days he had brought, carefully wrapped up in paper, a few almonds and raisins and grapes, somehow obtained from a country-man—his own little fund was gone.

I said again: "There is a ceremony in the house, and you will not be able to see anyone today."

The man's face fell. He looked wistfully at me for a moment, said "Good morning," and went out.

I felt a little sorry, and would have called him back, but saw that he was returning of his own accord. He came close up to me, holding out his offerings, and said: "I brought these few things, sir, for the little one. Will you give them to her?"

I took them and was going to pay him, but he caught my hand and said: "You are very kind, sir! Keep me in your recollection; do not offer me money! You have a little girl; I too have one like her in my own home. I thought of my own and brought fruits to your child, not to make a profit for myself."

Saying this, he put his hand inside his big loose robe and brought out a small dirty piece of paper. With great care he unfolded this and smoothed it out with both hands on my table. It bore the impression of a little hand, not a photograph, not a drawing. The impression of an ink-smeared hand laid flat on the paper. This touch of his own little daughter had been always on his heart, as he had come year after year to Calcutta to sell his wares in the streets.

Tears came to my eyes. I forgot that he was a poor Cabuli fruit seller, while I was—but no, was I more than he? He was also a father.

That impression of the hand of his little Parbati in her distant mountain home reminded me of my own little Mini, and I immediately sent for her from the inner apartment. Many excuses were raised, but I would not listen. Clad in the red silk of her wedding day, with the sandal

paste[11] on her forehead, and adorned as a young bride, Mini came and stood bashfully before me.

The Cabuliwallah was staggered at the sight of her. There was no hope of reviving their old friendship. At last he smiled and said: "Little one, are you going to your father-in-law's house?"

But Mini now understood the meaning of the word "father-in-law," and she could not reply to him as in the past. She flushed at the question and stood before him with her bride's face looking down.

I remembered the day when the Cabuliwallah and my Mini first met, and I felt sad. When she had gone, Rahmun heaved a deep sigh and sat down on the floor. The idea had suddenly come to him that his daughter also must have grown up during this long time, and that he would have to make friends with her all over again. Surely he would not find her as he used to know her; besides, what might have happened to her in these eight years?

The marriage pipes sounded, and the mild autumn sun streamed around us. But Rahmun sat in the little Calcutta lane and saw before him the barren mountains of Afghanistan.

I took out a bank note and gave it to him, saying: "Go back to your own daughter, Rahmun, in your own country, and may the happiness of your meeting bring good fortune to my child!"

After giving this gift, I had to eliminate some of the festivities. I could not have the electric lights, nor the military band, and the ladies of the house were saddened. But to me the wedding feast was brighter because of the thought that in a distant land a long-lost father met again with his only child. ❖

Translated from the Bengali language

---

11. **sandal paste:** paste made from sandalwood sawdust mixed with water and used as a liquid make-up that gives the skin a paler appearance.

RESPONDING OPTIONS

FROM PERSONAL RESPONSE TO CRITICAL ANALYSIS

REFLECT 1. Did your view of the characters change as you read? Jot down your reaction in your notebook.

RETHINK 2. How would you describe the Cabuliwallah?
Consider
- his profession and his social and economic status
- his friendship with Mini
- his assault on the man who owed him money
- his remarks and revelations on Mini's wedding day

3. How would you describe the narrator, Mini's father?
Consider
- his profession and his social and economic status
- his desire to help Mini overcome her initial fears of the Cabuliwallah
- his feelings and actions toward his wife and daughter
- his treatment of the Cabuliwallah on Mini's wedding day

4. What is your opinion of Mini and the way she treats the Cabuliwallah? Cite examples to support your opinion.

5. Review the chart you created for the Reading Connection on page 622. Do you think the similarities linking the two men outweigh the differences in background that divide them? Why or why not?

RELATE 6. Think about the Cabuliwallah's social and economic situation. To what type of person today would you compare him?

ANOTHER PATHWAY
Cooperative Learning

Mini's father gives money to the Cabuliwallah that had been set aside to pay for some of her wedding festivities. In a panel discussion with three other students, evaluate the father's act and its consequences. Each student should take the part of one of the characters (Mini, the father, the mother, or the Cabuliwallah).

QUICKWRITES

1. Write a **letter to the editor** about how we should treat the Cabuliwallahs of our society, that is, those people who are viewed as outcasts. In your letter, reflect upon the message of the story as well as on your own experience.

2. Retell the story of the Cabuliwallah as a **fairy tale.** Adapt the plot as needed in order to convey the moral of your tale. Decide which characters would be rewarded for their actions and which, if any, would be punished.

3. Review the story for details concerning how the narrator feels about Mini's wedding day. Write the **diary entry** that he might have written at the end of that day.

PORTFOLIO Save your writing. You may want to use it later as a springboard to a piece for your portfolio.

LITERARY CONCEPTS

Through **characterization,** writers develop characters and make them believable. There are four basic methods of characterization: (1) through physical description; (2) through a character's speech, thoughts, feelings, and actions; (3) through the speech, thoughts, feelings, and actions of other characters; and (4) through the narrator's direct comments about a character's nature. With a partner, make a list of what you know about each character in the story—Mini, her father, her mother, and the Cabuliwallah. Then look back at the story and find out which method of characterization the writer used to convey the information you listed. Share your findings with others in your class.

CONCEPT REVIEW: Point of View How might the story be different if it were narrated by the Cabuliwallah instead of Mini's father? Explain your answer.

ALTERNATIVE ACTIVITIES

1. Make a **sketch** of one of the scenes described in the story. For example, you might sketch Mini as a little girl, chatting with the Cabuliwallah; the scuffle between the Cabuliwallah and the man who owed him money; or the narrator's final conversation with the Cabuliwallah.

2. Investigate the poetry for which Rabindranath Tagore is famous, and choose a short poem or a passage from a longer poem that you think expresses attitudes similar to those of the narrator in the story. Present the selection in an **oral reading.** Then lead a class discussion about the poem and its possible connection to "The Cabuliwallah."

3. With a partner, research traditional Hindu marriage customs. Make a **multimedia presentation** of your findings. You may make use of videodiscs, recordings, reproductions of photography or artwork, your own illustrations, or any other media of your choice.

CRITIC'S CORNER

Student reviewer Josh Raub wrote: "I couldn't understand how the mother distrusted Rahmun [the Cabuliwallah]. He was so kind to Mini, and he was such a nice man." How would you answer Josh's question?

ACROSS THE CURRICULUM

Economics The Cabuliwallah is selling his wares in Calcutta, far from his home in Afghanistan. Why? Do some research on the economies of Afghanistan and India, and compare and contrast them in an oral report for your classmates.

ART CONNECTION

Take another look at the painting, *The Charpoi,* on page 623. What mood does it convey? Find a line from the story that could serve as a caption for the image.

Detail of *The Charpoi,* Robert Wade. Watercolor, 10" × 14", private collection. From *Painting More Than the Eye Can See,* 1989, North Light Books. Copyright © Robert Wade.

WORDS TO KNOW

EXERCISE A Review the Words to Know at the bottom of the selection pages. Then write the word that is suggested by each set of idioms below.

1. just around the corner; hanging over one's head; close at hand; on the verge

2. run off at the mouth; gabfest; chew the fat; rattle on

3. horn in; get a word in; throw a monkey wrench into; poke one's nose in

4. passed away; no longer with us; ladies' room; downsizing the company

5. without turning a hair; cool as a cucumber; without batting an eye

EXERCISE B Write the letter of the antonym of each boldfaced word below.

1. **precarious:** (a) secure, (b) problematic, (c) uncertain

2. **quaint:** (a) genuine, (b) peculiar, (c) modern

3. **pervade:** (a) vacate, (b) agree, (c) mislead

4. **judicious:** (a) illegal, (b) foolish, (c) correct

5. **fettered:** (a) restrained, (b) freed, (c) clustered

RABINDRANATH TAGORE

Rabindranath Tagore was a poet, short story writer, novelist, playwright, composer, philosopher, and painter. Born in Calcutta, India, to a prominent Brahmin family—a family in the highest Hindu caste—he was the son of a respected spiritual leader. Among his talented brothers and sisters were a musician, a philosopher, and India's first major woman novelist. Tagore was educated by tutors on his family's estate and at private schools. As a teenager, he traveled in India with his father and was deeply impressed with the beauty of his nation's land and its people, culture, and history.

1861–1941

Tagore published his first major work, the narrative poem *A Poet's Tale,* in 1878 and his poetry collections *Evening Songs and Morning Songs* a few years later. Some of his finest verse was produced from 1902 to 1907, years of deep sorrow following the untimely deaths of his wife, a daughter, and a son. Although

Tagore wrote in Bengali—one of India's many languages—he translated much of his own work into English. In fact, his English translations of some of his poems were published in 1912 as *Gitanjali: Song Offerings,* a volume that made him famous in the West. "The Cabuliwallah" appeared in English translation in *The Hungry Stones and Other Stories,* a collection first published in 1913; in that same year, Tagore also became the first Indian to win the Nobel Prize in literature. Indian scholar Krishna Kripalāni wrote in a biography of Tagore that his "main significance lies in the impulse and direction he gave to the course of India's cultural and intellectual development. . . . He gave [his people] faith in their own language and in their cultural and moral heritage."

OTHER WORKS *A Tagore Reader, Selected Poems, Selected Short Stories*

PREVIEWING

For the New Year, 1981
Denise Levertov England / United States

Pride
Dahlia Ravikovitch (däl′yə rə-vē′kə-vĭch) Israel

PERSONAL CONNECTION

What comes to mind when you hear the word *hope?* What about *pride?* For each of these terms, make a word web in your notebook like the one shown. Write down in your notebook whatever words or phrases you associate with hope and pride, and then share your webs with a classmate.

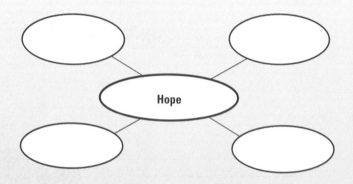

SCIENTIFIC CONNECTION

Hope and pride are the subjects of the next two poems, both of which are by contemporary women poets. The speaker in Denise Levertov's "For the New Year, 1981" draws upon images from nature to convey her thoughts about hope. Toward the end of the poem, she makes a comparison to irises, popular perennial plants with orchidlike flowers. Like all perennials, irises can live and bloom for many years; however, they will do so only if they are dug up and divided when they get too crowded. Because the roots of irises are actually thick, gnarled underground stems called rhizomes, dividing the plants can be a difficult chore for a gardener.

The speaker in Dahlia Ravikovitch's "Pride" also uses images from the natural world; in an extended metaphor, rocks at the edge of the sea are used to provide insight into her subject. To the naked eye, rocks often appear changeless. Geologists tell us, however, that rocks, like all elements of the natural world, are subject to an aging process brought about by weathering and erosion.

READING CONNECTION

Understanding Images As you read the two poems, pay attention to the natural images that both poets use to make the abstract concepts of hope and pride more concrete. What specific ideas about hope and pride do the images help convey?

For the New Year, 1981

Denise Levertov

I have a small grain of hope—
one small crystal that gleams
clear colors out of transparency.

I need more.

5 I break off a fragment
to send you.

Please take
this grain of a grain of hope
so that mine won't shrink.

10 Please share your fragment
so that yours will grow.

Only so, by division,
will hope increase,

like a clump of irises, which will cease to flower
15 unless you distribute
the clustered roots, unlikely source—
clumsy and earth-covered—
of grace.

FROM PERSONAL RESPONSE *TO* CRITICAL ANALYSIS

REFLECT   1. What are your thoughts after reading this poem? In your notebook, jot down the first thing that comes to mind.

RETHINK   2. What do you think hope means to the speaker?
Consider
- the speaker's comparison of hope to a grain, "one small crystal that gleams / clear colors out of transparency" (lines 2–3)
- the speaker's remark "I need more" (line 4)
- the reason the speaker gives for sharing hope (lines 5–13)
- the word web for *hope* that you created for the Personal Connection on page 632

3. Why do you think the speaker compares hope to irises?

4. What might be the relationship between the speaker and the person addressed? Explain your response.

Pride

Dahlia Ravikovitch

I tell you, even rocks crack,
and not because of age.
For years they lie on their backs
in the heat and the cold,
5 so many years,
it almost seems peaceful.
They don't move, so the cracks stay hidden.
A kind of pride.
Years pass over them, waiting there.
10 Whoever is going to shatter them
hasn't come yet.
And so the moss flourishes, the seaweed
whips around,
the sea pushes through and rolls back—
15 the rocks seem motionless.
Till a little seal comes to rub against them,
comes and goes away.
And suddenly the rock has an open wound.
I told you, when rocks break, it happens by surprise.
20 And people, too.

Translated by Chana and Ariel Bloch

*Tidal Flats, Deer Isle,
Sunset* (1978),
A. Robert Birmelin.
Acrylic on canvas,
$50'' \times 57\frac{1}{2}''$, private
collection.

RESPONDING OPTIONS

FROM PERSONAL RESPONSE TO CRITICAL ANALYSIS

REFLECT

1. What did you picture as you read "Pride"? Make a sketch in your notebook of what you envisioned, and then share your work with a classmate.

RETHINK

2. Why do you think the speaker compares people to rocks?

   Consider
   - what qualities you associate with rocks
   - what aspects of human nature the speaker might be comparing to the cracks in a rock
   - how the natural forces that act upon a rock might be compared to human experiences
   - what an "open wound" might mean

3. Would you say that the pride described in this poem is positive or negative? Explain your view.

4. Review the word web for *pride* that you created for the Personal Connection on page 632. Then compare your notions of pride with the speaker's.

RELATE

5. Compare the tone of "For the New Year, 1981" with that of "Pride."

ANOTHER PATHWAY

Cooperative Learning

In a small group, evaluate the title of each poem in terms of what it contributes to the reader's understanding of the poem. Then, for each poem, brainstorm a list of alternative titles and vote on the best option. Share your new titles with the rest of the class.

QUICKWRITES

1. Write **thesaurus entries** for the terms *pride* and *hope* on the basis of the views presented in the two poems. For each entry, include several synonyms and antonyms as well as a brief definition of the term.

2. Write a **poem** about pride, hope, or another human attitude or value that you associate with these ideas. The word webs you created for the Personal Connection on page 632 may help you get started. Try using images from nature to make the abstract attitude or value more concrete.

📁 *PORTFOLIO Save your writing. You may want to use it later as a springboard to a piece for your portfolio.*

LITERARY CONCEPTS

Personification is a figure of speech in which human qualities are attributed to something nonhuman, such as an object, an animal, or an idea. "The wind sighed" is an example of personification, since it suggests that a nonhuman force, the wind, can engage in the human activity of sighing. With a partner, identify examples of personification in "Pride" and explain what human qualities are being personified.

CONCEPT REVIEW: Rhythm When poets use free verse, they do not follow a regular pattern of rhyme or meter; however, they can create rhythm by sound devices and cadence. With a partner, reread the two poems aloud and discuss how you would describe the rhythm of each poem.

ALTERNATIVE ACTIVITIES

1. Share with your classmates a recording of a **piece of music** that conveys the attitudes expressed in either poem.

2. Each of these poems tells a kind of story. Retell the story of one of the poems by creating a narrative **cartoon,** with each panel describing a separate section of the poem. Include quotations from the poem in your cartoon.

LITERARY LINKS

What fictional character or real person from the selections you have read might represent the type of hope that is described in "For the New Year, 1981"? Who might represent the type of pride described in "Pride"?

ACROSS THE CURRICULUM

World Languages With a partner, try to translate one of the poems into another language that you know or that you have been studying in school. Present your translation to the rest of the class.

DENISE LEVERTOV

Denise Levertov was born and raised in a suburb of London, England. She was educated by her parents at home and inherited her mother's love of nature. As a teenager, Levertov studied ballet and enjoyed painting; she loved traveling alone around London and spending time in the city's many museums and galleries. "Being a poet was, however, from my earliest childhood, what I never had any doubts about," Levertov has said. "There is nothing I would ever for a moment prefer to have been." Indeed, Levertov has published about two dozen volumes of poetry and has received numerous honors and awards—including a

1923–

Guggenheim Fellowship—for her work.

Levertov moved to the United States in 1948 and became a U.S. citizen in 1955. Since that time, she has been the poetry editor of such magazines as *The Nation* and *Mother Jones* and has taught at a number of colleges and universities. A pacifist, Levertov was active in antiwar and antinuclear movements over several decades; some of her poems reflect these political convictions.

OTHER WORKS *Collected Earlier Poems 1940–1960, New and Selected Essays, Candles in Babylon, Evening Train*

DAHLIA RAVIKOVITCH

Dahlia Ravikovitch is among the foremost poets writing in modern Hebrew, the language of Israel. She was born in a town called Ramat Gan, near Tel Aviv, and was raised on Kibbutz Geva, one of the country's many collective farms or settlements. After studying literature at Hebrew University in Jerusalem, she began publishing poetry in the noted journal *Orlogin*. From 1959 to 1963, she taught high school;

1936–

then she left teaching to devote herself to writing. In addition to several volumes of verse, she has published short stories, children's books, and English-to-Hebrew translations of a number of works. Ravikovitch has also been active in the Israeli peace movement and in programs that teach adults to write poetry.

OTHER WORKS *A Dress of Fire, The Window: New and Selected Poems*

PREVIEWING

As the Night the Day

Abioseh Nicol (ä′bē-ō′sĕ nē′kōl) Sierra Leone (sē-ĕr′ə lē-ōn′)

PERSONAL CONNECTION

Identify some positive and some negative effects of peer pressure at your school. For example, when do individual students go against their better judgment because of peer pressure? When can peer pressure be a positive influence on an individual? Share your ideas in a class discussion.

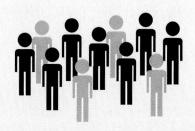

CULTURAL CONNECTION

The following story focuses on relationships between individuals and their peers at a Christian boys' school in Sierra Leone, a nation on the west coast of Africa. Formerly a British colony, Sierra Leone achieved independence in the early 1960s, when this story was written. The country's population is diverse, with 12 major black African ethnic groups. Many non-Africans have also settled in Sierra Leone's urban areas, often as traders or shopkeepers. One of the story's characters, for example, comes from a family of Muslim immigrants from the Middle Eastern nation of Syria.

Because of poverty and a lack of educational resources, only about 40 percent of the nation's children attend elementary school, and only about 15 percent go to high school. The schools of Sierra Leone, like some in the United States, sometimes reflect the ethnic tensions of the larger society.

WRITING CONNECTION

In your notebook, describe a time when you experienced a conflict with your peers about an issue of right or wrong. How did you resolve this conflict? As you read "As the Night the Day," compare your experience with the situations described in the story.

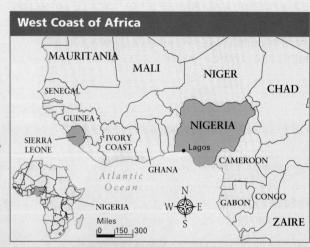

West Coast of Africa

MAURITANIA
MALI
NIGER
CHAD
SENEGAL
GUINEA
NIGERIA
SIERRA LEONE
IVORY COAST
Lagos
GHANA
CAMEROON
Atlantic Ocean
NIGERIA
Miles 0 150 300
GABON
CONGO
ZAIRE

LASERLINKS
• CULTURAL CONNECTION

As the Night the Day

Abioseh Nicol

Reprinted by permission of Marie Brown Associates. Copyright © Tom Feelings.

Kojo and Bandele walked slowly across the hot, green lawn, holding their science manuals with moist fingers. In the distance they could hear the junior school collecting in the hall of the main school building, for singing practice. Nearer, but still far enough, their classmates were strolling toward them. The two reached the science block and entered it. It was a low building set apart from the rest of the high school, which sprawled on the hillside of the African savanna.[1] The laboratory was a longish room, and at one end they saw Basu, another boy, looking out of the window, his back turned to them. Mr. Abu, the ferocious laboratory attendant, was not about. The rows of

---

1. **savanna:** treeless plain or grassland.

multicolored bottles looked inviting. A Bunsen burner soughed[2] loudly in the heavy, weary heat. Where the tip of the light-blue triangle of flame ended, a shimmering plastic transparency started. One could see the restless hot air moving in the minute tornado. The two African boys watched it, interestedly, holding hands.

"They say it is hotter inside the flame than on its surface," Kojo said, doubtfully. "I wonder how they know."

"I think you mean the opposite; let's try it ourselves," Bandele answered.

"How?"

"Let's take the temperature inside."

"All right, here is a thermometer. You do it."

"It says ninety degrees now. I shall take the temperature of the outer flame first, then you can take the inner yellow one."

Bandele held the thermometer gently forward to the flame, and Kojo craned to see. The thin thread of quicksilver[3] shot upward within the stem of the instrument with swift malevolence, and there was a slight crack. The stem had broken. On the bench the small bulbous drops of mercury which had spilled from it shivered with glinting, playful malice and shuddered down to the cement floor, dashing themselves into a thousand shining pieces, some of which coalesced again and shook gaily as if with silent laughter.

"Oh my God!" whispered Kojo hoarsely.

"Shut up!" Bandele said, imperiously, in a low voice.

Bandele swept the few drops on the bench into his cupped hand and threw the blob of mercury down the sink. He swept those on the floor under an adjoining cupboard with his bare feet. Then, picking up the broken halves of the thermometer, he tiptoed to the waste bin and dropped them in. He tiptoed back to Kojo, who was standing petrified by the blackboard.

"See no evil, hear no evil, speak no evil," he whispered to Kojo.

It all took place in a few seconds. Then the rest of the class started pouring in, chattering and pushing each other. Basu, who had been at the end of the room with his back turned to them all the time, now turned round and limped laboriously across to join the class, his eyes screwed up as they always were.

The class ranged itself loosely in a semicircle around the demonstration platform. They were dressed in the school uniform of white shirt and khaki shorts. Their official age was around sixteen, although, in fact, it ranged from Kojo's fifteen years to one or two boys of twenty-one.

Mr. Abu, the laboratory attendant, came in from the adjoining store and briskly cleaned the blackboard. He was a retired African sergeant from the Army Medical Corps and was feared by the boys. If he caught any of them in any petty thieving, he offered them the choice of a hard smack on the bottom or of being reported to the science masters. Most boys chose the former, as they knew the matter would end there, with no protracted interviews, moral recrimination, and an entry in the conduct book.

The science master stepped in and stood on his small platform. A tall, thin, dignified Negro, with graying hair and silver-rimmed spectacles badly fitting on his broad nose and always slipping

"See no evil, hear no evil, speak no evil," he whispered to Kojo.

---

2. **soughed** (sŭft): made a murmuring or rustling sound.

3. **quicksilver:** mercury, a poisonous liquid metal.

down, making him look avuncular.[4] "Vernier" was his nickname, as he insisted on exact measurement and exact speech "as fine as a vernier scale," he would say, which measured, of course, things in thousandths of a millimeter. Vernier set the experiments for the day and demonstrated them, then retired behind the *Church Times,* which he read seriously in between walking quickly down the aisles of lab benches, advising boys. It was a simple heat experiment to show that a dark surface gave out more heat by radiation than a bright surface.

During the class, Vernier was called away to the telephone and Abu was not about, having retired to the lavatory for a smoke. As soon as a posted sentinel announced that he was out of sight, minor pandemonium broke out. Some of the boys raided the store. The wealthier ones swiped rubber tubing to make catapults and to repair bicycles, and helped themselves to chemicals for developing photographic films. The poorer boys were in deadlier earnest and took only things of strict commercial interest which could be sold easily in the market. They emptied stuff into bottles in their pockets. Soda for making soap, magnesium sulphate for opening medicine, salt for cooking, liquid paraffin for women's hairdressing, and fine yellow iodoform powder much in demand for sprinkling on sores. Kojo protested mildly against all this. "Oh, shut up!" a few boys said. Sorie, a huge boy who always wore a fez[5] indoors and who, rumor said, had already fathered a child, commanded respect and some leadership in the class. He was sipping his favorite mixture of diluted alcohol and bicarbonate—which he called "gin and fizz"— from a beaker. "Look here, Kojo, you are getting out of hand. What do you think our parents pay taxes and school fees for? For us to enjoy—or to buy a new car every year for Simpson?" The other boys laughed. Simpson was the European headmaster, feared by the small boys, adored by the boys in the middle school, and liked, in a

critical fashion, with reservations, by some of the senior boys and African masters. He had a passion for new motorcars, buying one yearly.

"Come to think of it," Sorie continued to Kojo, "you must take something yourself; then we'll know we are safe." "Yes, you must," the other boys insisted. Kojo gave in and, unwillingly, took a little nitrate for some gunpowder experiments which he was carrying out at home.

"Someone!" the lookout called.

The boys dispersed in a moment. Sorie swilled out his mouth at the sink with some water. Mr. Abu, the lab attendant, entered and observed the innocent collective expression of the class. He glared round suspiciously and sniffed the air. It was a physics experiment, but the place smelled chemical. However, Vernier came in then. After asking if anyone was in difficulties, and finding that no one could momentarily think up anything, he retired to his chair and settled down to an article on Christian reunion, adjusting his spectacles and thoughtfully sucking an empty tooth socket.

Toward the end of the period, the class collected around Vernier and gave in their results, which were then discussed. One of the more political boys asked Vernier: if dark surfaces gave out more heat, was that why they all had black faces in West Africa? A few boys giggled. Basu looked down and tapped his clubfoot embarrassedly on the floor. Vernier was used to questions of this sort from the senior boys. He never committed himself, as he was getting near retirement and his pension, and became more guarded each year. He sometimes even feared that Simpson had spies among the boys.

"That may be so, although the opposite might be more convenient."

Everything in science had a loophole, the

---

4. **avuncular** (ə-vŭng′kyə-lər): of or like an uncle.

5. **fez:** a man's brimless hat, shaped like a flat-topped cone, with a black tassel.

boys thought, and said so to Vernier.

"Ah! That is what is called research," he replied, <u>enigmatically</u>.

Sorie asked a question. Last time, they had been shown that an electric spark with hydrogen and oxygen atoms formed water. Why was not that method used to provide water in town at the height of the dry season when there was an acute water shortage?

"It would be too expensive," Vernier replied, shortly. He disliked Sorie, not because of his different religion, but because he thought that Sorie was a bad influence and also asked ridiculous questions.

Sorie persisted. There was plenty of water during the rainy season. It could be split by lightning to hydrogen and oxygen in October and the gases compressed and stored, then changed back to water in March during the shortage. There was a faint ripple of applause from Sorie's admirers.

"It is an impracticable idea," Vernier snapped.

The class dispersed and started walking back across the hot grass. Kojo and Bandele heaved sighs of relief and joined Sorie's crowd, which was always the largest.

"Science is a bit of a swindle," Sorie was saying. "I do not for a moment think that Vernier believes any of it himself," he continued. "Because, if he does, why is he always reading religious books?"

"Come back, all of you, come back!" Mr. Abu's stentorian[6] voice rang out, across to them.

They wavered and stopped. Kojo kept walking on in a blind panic.

"Stop," Bandele hissed across. "You fool." He stopped, turned, and joined the returning crowd, closely followed by Bandele. Abu joined Vernier on the platform. The loose semicircle of boys faced them.

"Mr. Abu just found this in the waste bin," Vernier announced, gray with anger. He held up

the two broken halves of the thermometer. "It must be due to someone from this class, as the number of thermometers was checked before being put out."

A little wind gusted in through the window and blew the silence heavily this way and that.

"Who?"

No one answered. Vernier looked round and waited.

"Since no one has owned up, I am afraid I shall have to detain you for an hour after school as punishment," said Vernier.

There was a murmur of dismay and anger. An important soccer house-match was scheduled for that afternoon. Some boys put their hands up and said that they had to play in the match.

"I don't care," Vernier shouted. He felt, in any case, that too much time was devoted to games and not enough to work.

He left Mr. Abu in charge and went off to fetch his things from the main building.

"We shall play 'Bible and Key,'" Abu announced as soon as Vernier had left. Kojo had been afraid of this, and new beads of perspiration sprang from his troubled brow. All the boys knew the details. It was a method of finding out a culprit by divination.[7] A large door key was placed between the leaves of a Bible at the New Testament passage where Ananias and Sapphira were struck dead before the Apostles for lying, and the Bible suspended by two bits of string tied to both ends of the key. The combination was held up by someone, and the names of all present were called out in turn. When that of the sinner was called, the Bible was expected to turn round and round violently and fall.

Now Abu asked for a Bible. Someone produced a copy. He opened the first page and then

---

6. **stentorian:** extremely loud.

7. **divination:** the act of exploring the unknown or predicting the future by supernatural means.

shook his head and handed it back. "This won't do," he said. "It's a Revised Version; only the genuine Word of God will give us the answer."

An Authorized King James Version was then produced, and he was satisfied. Soon he had the contraption fixed up. He looked round the semi-circle, from Sorie at one end, through the others, to Bandele, Basu, and Kojo at the other, near the door.

"You seem to have an honest face," he said to Kojo. "Come and hold it." Kojo took the ends of the string gingerly with both hands, trembling slightly.

Abu moved over to the low window and stood at attention, his sharp profile outlined against the red hibiscus flowers, the green trees, and the molten sky. The boys watched anxiously. A black-bodied lizard scurried up a wall and started nodding its pink head with grave impartiality.

Abu fixed his aging, bloodshot eyes on the suspended Bible. He spoke hoarsely and slowly:

"Oh, Bible, Bible, on a key,
Kindly tell it unto me,
By swinging slowly round and true,
To whom this sinful act is due. . . ."

He turned to the boys and barked out their names in a parade-ground voice, beginning with Sorie and working his way round, looking at the Bible after each name.

To Kojo, trembling and shivering as if ice-cold water had been thrown over him, it seemed as if he had lost all power and that some gigantic being stood behind him holding up his tired, aching elbows. It seemed to him as if the key and Bible had taken on a life of their own, and he watched with fascination the whole combination

moving slowly, jerkily, and rhythmically in short arcs, as if it had acquired a heartbeat.

"Ayo Sogbenri, Sonnir Kargbo, Oji Ndebu." Abu was coming to the end now. "Tommy Longe, Ajayi Cole, Bandele Fagb . . ."

Kojo dropped the Bible. "I am tired," he said, in a small scream. "I am tired."

"Yes, he is," Abu agreed, "but we are almost finished; only Bandele and Basu are left."

"Pick up that book, Kojo, and hold it up again." Bandele's voice whipped through the air with cold fury. It sobered Kojo and he picked it up.

"Will you continue, please, with my name, Mr. Abu?" Bandele asked, turning to the window.

"Go back to your place quickly, Kojo," Abu said. "Vernier is coming. He might be vexed. He is a strongly religious man and so does not believe in the Bible-and-key ceremony."

Kojo slipped back with sick relief, just before Vernier entered.

In the distance the rest of the school were assembling for closing prayers. The class sat and stood around the blackboard and demonstration bench in attitudes of exasperation, resignation, and self-righteous indignation. Kojo's heart was beating so loudly that he was surprised no one else heard it.

"Once to every man and nation
Comes the moment to decide . . ."[8]

The closing hymn floated across to them, interrupting the still afternoon.

Kojo got up. He felt now that he must speak

"You seem to have an honest face," he said to Kojo.

---

8. **Once . . . decide:** "In the strife of Truth with Falsehood, for the good or evil side" is the next line in the stanza. The hymn's words come from a poem by J. R. Lowell.

the truth, or life would be intolerable ever afterwards. Bandele got up swiftly before him. In fact, several things seemed to happen all at the same time. The rest of the class stirred. Vernier looked up from a book review which he had started reading. A butterfly, with black and gold wings, flew in and sat on the edge of the blackboard, flapping its wings quietly and waiting too.

"Basu was here first before any of the class," Bandele said firmly.

Everyone turned to Basu, who cleared his throat.

"I was just going to say so myself, sir," Basu replied to Vernier's inquiring glance.

"Pity you had no thought of it before," Vernier said, dryly. "What were you doing here?"

"I missed the previous class, so I came straight to the lab and waited. I was over there by the window, trying to look at the blue sky. I did not break the thermometer, sir."

A few boys tittered. Some looked away. The others muttered. Basu's breath always smelt of onions, but although he could play no games, some boys liked him and were kind to him in a tolerant way.

"Well, if you did not, someone did. We shall continue with the detention."

Vernier noticed Abu standing by. "You need not stay, Mr. Abu," he said to him. "I shall close up. In fact, come with me now and I shall let you out through the back gate."

He went out with Abu.

When he had left, Sorie turned to Basu and asked mildly:

"You are sure you did not break it?"

"No, I didn't."

"He did it," someone shouted.

"But what about the Bible-and-key?" Basu protested. "It did not finish. Look at him." He pointed to Bandele.

"I was quite willing for it to go on," said Bandele. "You were the only one left."

Someone threw a book at Basu and said, "Confess!"

Basu backed on to a wall. "To God, I shall call the police if anyone strikes me," he cried fiercely.

"He thinks he can buy the police," a voice called.

"That proves it," someone shouted from the back.

"Yes, he must have done it," the others said, and they started throwing books at Basu. Sorie waved his arm for them to stop, but they did not. Books, corks, boxes of matches rained on Basu. He bent his head and shielded his face with his bent arm.

"I did not do it, I swear I did not do it. Stop it, you fellows," he moaned over and over again. A small cut had appeared on his temple, and he was bleeding. Kojo sat quietly for a while. Then a curious hum started to pass through him, and his hands began to tremble, his armpits to feel curiously wetter. He turned round and picked up a book and flung it with desperate force at Basu, and then another. He felt somehow that there was an awful swelling of guilt which he could only shed by punishing himself through hurting someone. Anger and rage against everything different seized him, because if everything and everyone had been the same, somehow he felt nothing would have been wrong and they would all have been happy. He was carried away now by a torrent which swirled and pounded. He felt that somehow Basu was in the wrong, must be in the wrong, and if he hurt him hard enough, he would convince the others and therefore himself that he had not broken the thermometer and that he had never done anything wrong. He groped for something bulky enough to throw, and picked up the Bible.

"Stop it," Vernier shouted through the open doorway. "Stop it, you hooligans, you beasts."

They all became quiet and shamefacedly put down what they were going to throw. Basu was crying quietly and hopelessly, his thin body shaking.

Reprinted by permission of Marie Brown Associates. Copyright © Tom Feelings.

"Go home, all of you, go home. I am ashamed of you." His black face shone with anger. "You are an utter disgrace to your nation and to your race."

They crept away, quietly, uneasily, avoiding each other's eyes, like people caught in a secret passion.

Vernier went to the first-aid cupboard and started dressing Basu's wounds.

Kojo and Bandele came back and hid behind the door, listening. Bandele insisted that they should.

Vernier put Basu's bandaged head against his waistcoat and dried the boy's tears with his handkerchief, gently patting his shaking shoulders.

"It wouldn't have been so bad if I had done it, sir," he mumbled, snuggling his head against Vernier, "but I did not do it. I swear to God I did not."

"Hush, hush," said Vernier comfortingly.

"Now they will hate me even more," he moaned.

"Hush, hush."

"I don't mind the wounds so much; they will heal."

"Hush, hush."

"They've missed the football match and now they will never talk to me again; oh-ee, oh-ee, why have I been so punished?"

"As you grow older," Vernier advised, "you must learn that men are punished not always for what they do, but often for what people think they will do, or for what they are. Remember that and you will find it easier to forgive them. 'To thine own self be true!'" Vernier ended with a flourish, holding up his clenched fist in a mock dramatic gesture, quoting from the Shakespeare examination set-book for the year and declaiming[9] to the dripping taps and empty benches and still afternoon, to make Basu laugh.

Basu dried his eyes and smiled <u>wanly</u> and

replied: "'And it shall follow as the night the day.'[10] *Hamlet*, Act One, Scene Three, Polonius to Laertes."

"There's a good chap. First Class Grade One. I shall give you a lift home."

Kojo and Bandele walked down the red laterite[11] road together, Kojo dispiritedly kicking stones into the gutter.

"The fuss they made over a silly old thermometer," Bandele began.

"I don't know, old man, I don't know," Kojo said impatiently.

They had both been shaken by the scene in the empty lab. A thin, invisible wall of hostility and mistrust was slowly rising between them.

"Basu did not do it, of course," Bandele said.

Kojo stopped dead in his tracks. "Of course he did not do it," he shouted; "we did it."

"No need to shout, old man. After all, it was your idea."

"It wasn't," Kojo said furiously. "You suggested we try it."

"Well, you started the argument. Don't be childish." They tramped on silently, raising small clouds of dust with their bare feet.

"I should not take it too much to heart," Bandele continued. "That chap Basu's father hoards foodstuff like rice and palm oil until

> "Men are punished not always for what they do, but often for what people think they will do, or for what they are."

---

9. **declaiming:** reciting in a showy way.

10. **"And it shall . . . the day":** The complete quotation is "This above all: to thine own self be true,/And it must follow, as the night the day,/Thou canst not then be false to any man." In other words, be honest with yourself and you will be honest with others.

11. **laterite:** a red soil often found in tropical regions.

there is a shortage and then sells them at high prices. The police are watching him."

"What has that got to do with it?" Kojo asked.

"Don't you see, Basu might quite easily have broken that thermometer. I bet he has done things before that we have all been punished for." Bandele was emphatic.

They walked on steadily down the main road of the town, past the Syrian and Lebanese shops crammed with knickknacks and rolls of cloth, past a large Indian shop with dull red carpets and brass trays displayed in its windows, carefully stepping aside in the narrow road as the British officials sped by in cars to their hill-station bungalows for lunch and siesta.

Kojo reached home at last. He washed his feet and ate his main meal for the day. He sat about heavily and restlessly for some hours. Night soon fell with its usual swiftness, at six, and he finished his homework early and went to bed.

Lying in bed he rehearsed again what he was determined to do the next day. He would go up to Vernier:

"Sir," he would begin, "I wish to speak with you privately."

"Can it wait?" Vernier would ask.

"No, sir," he would say firmly, "as a matter of fact, it is rather urgent."

Vernier would take him to an empty classroom and say, "What is troubling you, Kojo Ananse?"

"I wish to make a confession, sir. I broke the thermometer yesterday." He had decided he would not name Bandele; it was up to the latter to decide whether he would lead a pure life.

Vernier would adjust his slipping glasses up his nose and think. Then he would say:

"This is a serious matter, Kojo. You realize you should have confessed yesterday?"

"Yes, sir, I am very sorry."

"You have done great harm, but better late than never. You will, of course, apologize in front of the class and particularly to Basu, who has shown himself a finer chap than all of you."

"I shall do so, sir."

"Why have you come to me now to apologize? Were you hoping that I would simply forgive you?"

"I was hoping you would, sir. I was hoping you would show your forgiveness by beating me."

Vernier would pull his glasses up his nose again. He would move his tongue inside his mouth reflectively. "I think you are right. Do you feel you deserve six strokes or nine?"

"Nine, sir."

"Bend over!"

Kojo had decided he would not cry because he was almost a man.

Whack! Whack!

Lying in bed in the dark thinking about it all as it would happen tomorrow, he clenched his teeth and tensed his buttocks in imaginary pain.

Whack! Whack! Whack!

Suddenly, in his little room, under his thin cotton sheet, he began to cry. Because he felt the sharp, lancing pain already cutting into him. Because of Basu and Simpson and the thermometer. For all the things he wanted to do and be which would never happen. For all the good men they had told them about—Jesus Christ, Mohammed, and George Washington, who never told a lie. For Florence Nightingale[12] and David Livingstone.[13] For Kagawa,[14] the Japanese man, for Gandhi,[15] and for Kwegyir Aggrey,[16] the African. Oh-ee, oh-ee. Because he knew he would never be as straight and strong

---

12. **Florence Nightingale:** British nurse regarded as the founder of modern nursing.

13. **David Livingstone:** Scottish missionary and explorer of Africa.

14. **Kagawa:** Japanese pacifist, social reformer, and Christian preacher.

15. **Gandhi:** Indian nationalist and spiritual leader known for nonviolent methods of protest.

16. **Kwegyir Aggrey:** African educator and writer.

and true as the school song said they should be. He saw, for the first time, what this thing would be like, becoming a man. He touched the edge of an <u>inconsolable</u> eternal grief. Oh-ee, oh-ee; always, he felt, always I shall be a disgrace to the nation and the race.

His mother passed by his bedroom door, slowly dragging her slippered feet as she always did. He pushed his face into his wet pillow to stifle his sobs, but she had heard him. She came in and switched on the light.

"What is the matter with you, my son?"

He pushed his face farther into his pillow.

"Nothing," he said, muffled and choking.

"You have been looking like a sick fowl all afternoon," she continued.

She advanced and put the back of her moist, cool fingers against the side of his neck.

"You have got fever," she exclaimed. "I'll get something from the kitchen."

When she had gone out, Kojo dried his tears and turned the dry side of the pillow up. His mother reappeared with a thermometer in one hand and some quinine mixture in the other.

"Oh, take it away, take it away," he shouted, pointing to her right hand and shutting his eyes tightly.

"All right, all right," she said, slipping the thermometer into her bosom.

He is a queer boy, she thought, with pride and a little fear as she watched him drink the clear, bitter fluid.

She then stood by him and held his head against her broad thigh as he sat up on the low bed, and she stroked his face. She knew he had been crying but did not ask him why, because she was sure he would not tell her. She knew he was learning, first slowly and now quickly, and she would soon cease to be his mother and be only one of the womenfolk in the family. Such a short time, she thought, when they are really yours and tell you everything. She sighed and slowly eased his sleeping head down gently.

The next day Kojo got to school early and set to things briskly. He told Bandele that he was going to confess but would not name him. He half hoped he would join him. But Bandele had said, threateningly, that he had better not mention his name, let him go and be a Boy Scout on his own. The sneer strengthened him, and he went off to the lab. He met Mr. Abu and asked for Vernier. Abu said Vernier was busy and what was the matter, anyhow.

"I broke the thermometer yesterday," Kojo said in a businesslike manner.

Abu put down the glassware he was carrying.

"Well, I never!" he said. "What do you think you will gain by this?"

"I broke it," Kojo repeated.

"Basu broke it," Abu said impatiently. "Sorie got him to confess, and Basu himself came here this morning and told the science master and myself that he knew now that he had knocked the thermometer by mistake when he came in early yesterday afternoon. He had not turned round to look, but he had definitely heard a tinkle as he walked by. Someone must have picked it up and put it in the waste bin. The whole matter is settled, the palaver[17] finished."

He tapped a barometer on the wall and, squinting, read the pressure. He turned again to Kojo.

"I should normally have expected him to say so yesterday and save you boys missing the game. But there you are," he added, shrugging and trying to look reasonable, "you cannot hope for too much from a Syrian boy." ❖

---

17. **palaver** (pə-lăv′ər): talk, especially idle chatter.

WORDS TO KNOW   **inconsolable** (ĭn′kən-sō′lə-bəl) *adj.* unable to be comforted; brokenhearted

RESPONDING
OPTIONS

FROM PERSONAL RESPONSE TO CRITICAL ANALYSIS

REFLECT

1. How did the ending of the story make you feel? Explain your reaction in your notebook.

RETHINK

2. Why do you think Basu ignores Vernier's advice to be true to oneself and confesses to doing something that he did not do?

   Consider
   - why Basu is falsely blamed for breaking the thermometer
   - how the other students feel about the class punishment
   - how Basu views himself
   - your discussion for the Personal Connection on page 638

3. How would you describe Kojo?

   Consider
   - what he says and does when the boys loot the science supplies
   - his relationship with Bandele
   - his participation in the attack on Basu
   - what he thinks about when he cries at night
   - his attempted confession

4. If you had been in Kojo's shoes, how would you have handled the situations described in this story? You may find it helpful to review your response to the Writing Connection on page 638.

5. In your opinion, what is the theme of this story? Explain your viewpoint.

RELATE

6. Who do you think suffers most when false accusations are made: the person who is accused or the person who points the finger of blame? Support your opinion.

ANOTHER PATHWAY
Cooperative Learning

Working in a small group, create a chart, like the one below, that shows what matters most to each character in the story: Kojo, Bandele, Sorie, Basu, Mr. Abu, Vernier, Simpson, and Kojo's mother. Then compare your completed chart with that of another group.

Character	What Matters Most	Supporting Details

QUICKWRITES

1. Write a **job evaluation** of the teaching of either Vernier or Mr. Abu. Refer to details from the story.

2. How might this story have ended if Kojo had spoken to Vernier instead of Mr. Abu? Write a new **story ending.**

3. Write the **dialogue** that might have taken place between Sorie and Basu when Basu agreed to confess to breaking the thermometer.

4. Write an **explanation** of why the author might have chosen a science laboratory as the setting for this story. If you are using a word processor, be sure to run a Spell Check.

PORTFOLIO Save your writing. You may want to use it later as a springboard to a piece for your portfolio.

LITERARY CONCEPTS

An **internal conflict** is one that occurs between opposing tendencies within a character. Get together with a partner and review the story, looking for passages that suggest Kojo's internal conflicts. Identify the tendencies within Kojo that are in opposition. What do you think Kojo learns—about himself and about the world around him—as he tries to resolve these internal conflicts?

CONCEPT REVIEW: Allusion The narrator makes several allusions within the story, from a Shakespearean play to heroic figures in history whom Kojo admires. Choose one of these allusions and explain how it helps to convey the internal conflict Kojo is experiencing.

ALTERNATIVE ACTIVITIES

1. In a small group, perform an **improvisation** that depicts an incident involving peer pressure at your school. Each member should assume the personality of one of the characters in the story: one person might act like Kojo, another might act like Bandele, and so on.

2. Create a **comparison/contrast chart** featuring Basu, Kojo, and Bandele. Use categories such as Personality, Background, Motivations, and Action. Review the story to find details to fit each category.

3. Conduct an **interview** with one of your teachers, asking questions about how he or she might handle the classroom problems depicted in "As the Night the Day." For example, what would your teacher do if a group of students were constantly picking on another student in the class? Consider asking your teacher to read the story in advance of the interview.

LITERARY LINKS

How do you think Miss Hurd, as described by Nicholas Gage in "The Teacher Who Changed My Life" on page 83, might have handled the situation in Kojo's class?

ACROSS THE CURRICULUM

Science *Cooperative Learning* The students in this story violate several fundamental rules for appropriate laboratory behavior, jeopardizing their own and others' safety. Working in a small group, make a list of the violations that occur in the lab—either on purpose or by accident. Discuss your list with a science teacher.

WORDS TO KNOW

On your paper, answer the questions that follow.

1. Are people most likely to respond **wanly** if they are enthusiastic, exhausted, or furious?

2. Does **malevolence** come from feelings of affection, pride, or hatred?

3. If two groups **coalesce,** do they merge, argue, or cancel each other out?

4. Is a person most likely to be **inconsolable** after experiencing a large dinner, a tragedy, or a good night's sleep?

5. Would a person feel **indignation** over a stolen bicycle, a birthday gift, or a pile of dirty clothes?

6. Is a **recrimination** an expression of blame, sympathy, or gratitude?

7. Which describes the attitude of a **self-righteous** person: do or die, take it or leave it, or holier than thou?

8. If a disagreement was described as **protracted,** would that mean it was violent, involved many people, or went on and on?

9. Who would you expect to behave **imperiously**— a student, a servant, or a dictator?

10. Is the word *enigmatically* most likely to be used to describe how a thank-you note, a secret message, or a term paper has been written?

ABIOSEH NICOL

1924–1994

Both science and education were very important to Dr. Davidson Nicol, who wrote fiction under the pen name of Abioseh Nicol. Born in Freetown, Sierra Leone, Nicol spent his early years in Nigeria, where his father taught pharmacology. On returning to Freetown, he continued his education and won a scholarship that enabled him to study medicine at Cambridge University in England. Later, he broke racial barriers by becoming the first black African ever to be named a fellow at Cambridge University. Nicol held several high positions at hospitals and medical schools in England and Nigeria before returning to his homeland to serve as principal of Freetown's Fourah Bay College and, later, as vice chancellor of the University of Sierra Leone. As a medical researcher, he won fame for his breakthrough research on the structure of human insulin.

Nicol also had a distinguished career as a diplomat.

From 1969 to 1971, he was Sierra Leone's chief delegate to the United Nations, serving as president of the U.N. Security Council in 1970. He became an Under Secretary General of the United Nations in 1972 and held the post until he retired from the organization a decade later.

Despite these many activities, Nicol still found time to become one of West Africa's finest writers. His short fiction won praise from critic Adrian A. Roscoe for "taking a slice of real life and offering it to us in all its workaday detail, all its blending of the tragic and the absurd." Nicol also wrote nonfiction and poetry, some of which was read aloud on radio programs broadcast by the British Broadcasting Corporation.

OTHER WORKS *The Truly Married Woman and Other Stories;* poems and nonfiction prose in *An African Treasury,* edited by Langston Hughes; *Africa: A Subjective View; Two African Tales*

REFLECT & ASSESS

Yevgeny Yevtushenko Russia

from A Precocious Autobiography

The Russian poet Yevgeny Yevtushenko published his autobiography in the same year that he turned 30, which helps explain the use of the word *precocious* in its title. The word means "intelligent or mature at an unusually early age" and captures his early public image as a bright and brash young man. Yevtushenko burst upon the literary scene in the Soviet Union while in his 20s. By the time his autobiography was published in 1963, he had already won international acclaim for his poetry. With his outspoken style and personal charm, he represented the new generation of Soviet writers that emerged in the 1950s and 1960s. In the following excerpt from *A Precocious Autobiography,* Yevtushenko describes his love for soccer and tells how he first came to be a published poet.

Before the Game (1983), Claudio Bravo. Oil on canvas, 78½" × 94¼". © 1995 Claudio Bravo / Licensed by VAGA, New York, NY. Private collection, courtesy of Marlborough Gallery, New York.

Besides poetry, I had still another passion—soccer.

At night I wrote poetry, and in the daytime I played soccer in backyards and on empty lots. I came home with torn trousers, battered shoes, and bleeding knees. The thud of the bouncing ball was, to me, the most intoxicating of all sounds.

To outflank the opponents' defense by feinting[1] and dribbling and then to land a dead shot into the net past the helplessly spread-eagled goalkeeper, this seemed to me—and still does—very like poetry.

Soccer taught me many things.

When, later, I was goalkeeper myself, I learned to detect the slightest movement of the opposing forwards and often to anticipate their feints.

This was to be of help to me in my literary struggle.

I was told that I could make a brilliant career as a soccer player.

Many of the boys I played with at school became professionals. On the rare occasions when I meet them now, I have a feeling that they envy me, but at times I catch myself envying them.

Soccer is in many ways easier than poetry. If you score a goal, you have concrete evidence—the ball is in the net. The fact is indisputable. (The referees may, in fact, disallow the goal, though this rarely happens.) But if you score a

---

1. **feinting** (fān′tǐng): creating a false attack to draw the defense away from the real one.

goal in poetry, you are very likely to hear thousands of referees' whistles shrilling out to disallow it—and nothing can ever be proved. And very often a shot that passed far outside the goal posts is declared a goal.

In general, in spite of all the intrigues and the dirt that go with it, sport is a cleaner business than literature. There are times when I am very sorry I did not become a soccer player.

I very nearly did.

After I had distinguished myself in a boys' match—I blocked three penalty kicks in succession—the coach of a famous team asked me to come and see him. All the other boys were green with envy.

But then something happened which determined my fate.

I had long been meaning to take my poems to the editor of *Soviet Sport*—it was about the only paper I had never sent them to.

I went there after the match, in a faded blue soccer shirt, old flannel trousers, and torn sneakers. I had in my hand a poem, *à la* Mayakovsky,[2] in which I subjected the mores[3] of Soviet and American athletes to a scathing analysis.

The editorial office of *Soviet Sport* was a big room in Dzerzhinsky[4] Street where, through clouds of cigarette smoke and the clicking of typewriters, scratching of pens, and rustling of galleys[5] I barely made out the presence of several figures.

I asked timidly where the poetry section was. Somewhere in the fog a voice barked that there was no such section.

Suddenly a hand, thrust out of the fog, fell on my shoulder, and a voice asked: "Poetry? Let's have a look. . . ."

I trusted the hand and the voice at once, and I was right.

Before me sat a man of about thirty with raven-black hair and dark Oriental eyes. He was Nikolay Alexandrovich Tarasov, in charge

of four departments of *Soviet Sport:* foreign news, politics, soccer, and literature.

He made me sit down next to him and ran his eyes over my poem.

"Got any more?" he asked without comment.

I pulled out the dog-eared notebook I carried inside my belt and said, embarrassed: "It isn't about sport."

He smiled. "All the better."

He read aloud against the clatter of the typewriters. At one point he called a woman over and read her a line which compared a bunch of grapes to a cluster of balloons.

As he went on reading, several people—reporters, photographers, typists—came and stood around the desk and listened.

Finally he turned to them. "Well? Is he going to write or not?"

"He is," they said.

A hand slapped my shoulder. "He certainly is."

"I think so too," Tarasov said, smiling.

To this day it beats me how they could have seen a poet in me then. Perhaps what helped was that literature was not strictly their field, and so they were not cluttered up with prejudices.

When they went back to their desks, leaving me with Tarasov, he picked up my poem, "Two Kinds of Sport," and said: "It's the worst of the lot, but it's the one for us. . . ."

He wrote on it the magic, long-awaited words, "To be set," and away it sailed.

"Now don't get it into your head that your other poems are all that good. But there's a strong line here and there."

---

2. *à la* **Mayakovsky** (ä′ lä mä′yə-kôf′skē): in the style of Vladimir Mayakovsky (1893–1930), a Soviet poet who broke poetic traditions and used everyday, even slangy language; also spelled *Mayakovski*.

3. **mores** (môr′āz′): moral attitudes; ways of doing things.

4. **Dzerzhinsky** (dyîr-zhēn′skē).

5. **galleys** (găl′ēz): in printing, long sheets of composed type to be proofread before final pages are made up.

I tried to look profound, as if I knew what a strong line was.

"Which poets do you like?" Tarasov asked quietly.

I swallowed. "Mayakovsky."

"Fine, but that's not enough. . . . Do you know Pasternak?"[6]

"Yes."

"You're lying. Even if you think you do, you don't. Listen to this."

He recited verses by Pasternak which were indeed unknown to me. "Nikolay Alexandrovich, quoting Pasternak again!" A typist jokingly shook her finger at him and pointed to a door with a large notice: "Editor in Chief."

"Thank goodness, we're a sports magazine," Tarasov said with a laugh.

Then he bent over my notebook and started to explain to me why he thought some lines were good and others bad. What he could not endure was limp, flaccid verse. Everything experimental, even if it verged on bad taste, he liked.

"Are you in a hurry to go anywhere?" he asked. "If not, I'd like you to meet a friend of mine." He phoned someone, and after a while a man of about his own age, pale, jerky, and with an immense forehead, came into the office. Unaccountably, he had a chessboard under his arm.

"My friend Volodya Barlas,[7] a physicist," said Tarasov. "Meet Yevgeny Yevtushenko, a poet."

It was the first time I had been called a poet.

"A poet?" Barlas raised his eyebrows. "That's saying quite a lot. . . ." He smiled skeptically.

At first, for some reason, he struck me as crazy.

We left the office and walked along the street, under the young rustling leaves of the trees of that Moscow June of 1949.

"A poet," Barlas said again. "And what have you to say to the world?"

"He wants to tell the world that he's a poet, and that's something for a start," Tarasov said, coming to my rescue.

He looked nervous. Clearly this odd character with the huge forehead of a Martian and the chessboard under his arm meant a lot to him. And it looked as though I meant something to him as well.

Walking on, I recited three of my poems, one after another.

"All right," Barlas said at last, giving me a piercing look. "Of course you have talent. You've got drive; there's a sort of ringing and booming in your lines. But at the moment I can't see that you have anything in mind except the wish to convince the world of your talent. You haven't done it yet, of course, and you won't have an easy job. But suppose the world believes in you—then it will expect you to say something really important. What will you say to it then?"

"Volodya, he's not quite sixteen," Tarasov said, once again defending me.

"That's the time to think about it. Afterward it will be too late," Barlas said harshly.

"It will come of itself. The important thing for him now is to write and to think of nothing else. You make much too much of the rational element in poetry," objected Tarasov.

"Nothing comes of itself. . . . Emotion is fine, but emotion by itself isn't enough. . . ."

I will always thank my lucky stars for my meeting with these two men. In many ways it determined the course of my career. Once, they had both wanted to become writers, but so far neither had succeeded. And now they saw in me their own youth and wanted me to fulfill its frustrated promise. We spent all night wandering about the Moscow streets. As we were saying good-by at dawn, Tarasov looked at his watch and said with warmth: "Well, in another hour the paper will be out, and your poem will be in it."

---

6. **Pasternak** (păs′tər-năk′): Russian writer Boris Pasternak (1890–1960), poet and author of the novel *Doctor Zhivago.*

7. **Volodya Barlas** (və-lôd′yə bär′ləs).

Portrait of B. Amanov, People's Artist of the USSR (1969), Aman Amangheldyev.
Oil on canvas, 145 cm × 170 cm, Union of Artists of the Russian Federation, Moscow.

"Remember—you no longer belong just to yourself," Barlas repeated his warning. But I took no notice of the alarming words.

I parted from my new friends and hung around the street, like the drunks outside the closed doors of the beer halls. My heart was pounding wildly as I waited for the newsstands to open.

At seven o'clock I snatched from the newsboy's hand a copy of *Soviet Sport* still smelling of printer's ink, unfolded it, and found my poem with my name printed underneath it.

I bought up about fifty copies—all the newsboy had—and strode down the street, waving them at the sky.

The ground whirled under my feet.

I was a genius.

I came home to my mother and triumphantly spread the paper before her. Mother's reaction could hardly be described as joyful.

"Well, there's no hope for you now," she commented with a discouraged sigh.

She may have been right at that.

Later that day Tarasov saw to it that I was paid—I got 350 rubles. As I had no identity card yet, I had to produce my birth certificate for identification. The girl in the accounting department stared at my T-shirt, my torn sneakers, and my sunburnt, ridiculously peeling nose and tried hard not to laugh.

"He's a real ugly duckling," I heard her say behind my back. But I put my money in my trouser pocket, said good-by politely, and walked out like a swan who would one day be recognized. ❖

Translated by Andrew R. MacAndrew

YEVGENY YEVTUSHENKO

Yevgeny Yevtushenko was born and raised in Zima Junction, Siberia, a tiny town on the Trans-Siberian railroad line near Lake Baikal in Russia. Zima is the setting of a number of Yevtushenko's works, and the poet continues to speak and write about his birthplace with fond affection and nostalgia.

Yevtushenko's first published poems appeared in *Soviet Sport* in 1949. He then studied at the Gorky Institute of Literature in Moscow and began publishing volumes of poetry. Yevtushenko achieved fame largely through word of mouth. He gave public readings of his poetry in factories, in schools, and on street corners; his audiences quickly grew to the thousands and tens of thousands in city squares and sports stadiums. Yevtushenko

1933–

delivered a new message to a new generation: he spoke out against the evils of Joseph Stalin's dictatorship and anti-Semitism. He also fought for artistic freedom and the release of imprisoned Soviet writers.

Most of Yevtushenko's poetry is written in rhyme, which is often lost in translation. "Music is part of content," he says. "There is a tragic difference between very good translations and the originals." In addition to more than 45 collections of poetry, Yevtushenko has written novels, short stories, essays, and screenplays, two of which became movies that he directed himself.

OTHER WORKS *Yevgeny Yevtushenko: Poems Chosen by the Author, The Collected Poems 1952–1990*

WRITING FROM EXPERIENCE

WRITING TO EXPLAIN

Some characters in Unit Four, "Moments of Truth," make decisions about what matters most and live with the consequences of their decisions. Was there a time when you had to make an important decision? Why did you make the choice you made? What were the consequences?

GUIDED ASSIGNMENT
Write a Cause-and-Effect Essay In this lesson you will describe your thoughts about causes or effects related to a situation that interests you.

➊ Observe Your World

Many situations or issues cannot be fully understood until you examine the causes and effects involved. In a group, discuss what causes and effects may be involved in the situations on these pages. Then discuss other situations that require careful analysis.

Explore Choices You have many decisions to make about your life. Can you predict how one of these choices might affect your life? What decision do you think Robert Frost was thinking about in "The Road Not Taken"?

Observe Nature What natural phenomena do you wonder about? How could you learn more about the causes or effects of a natural phenomenon?

Research Events Think about current events or historical events that interest you. Are you interested in researching the causes or consequences of one of these events?

Identify Problems Reflect on social problems that trouble your community or environmental problems that threaten the world. Can you analyze the causes of a problem or discuss its long-term effects?

Poem

THE ROAD NOT TAKEN

Two roads diverged in a yellow wood,
And sorry I could not travel both
And be one traveler, long I stood
And looked down one as far as I could
To where it bent in the undergrowth;

Then took the other, as just as fair,
And having perhaps the better claim,
Because it was grassy and wanted wear;
Though as for that, the passing there
Had worn them really about the same,

And both that morning equally lay
In leaves no step had trodden black
Oh, I kept the first for another day!
Yet knowing how way leads on to way,
I doubted if I should ever come back.

I should be telling this with a sigh
Somewhere ages and ages hence:
Two roads diverged in a wood, and I—
I took the one less traveled by,
And that has made all the difference.

Robert Frost

What causes and effects are suggested by information in the article and the bar graph?

Recycling the Plastic Package

Magazine Article

Asked to name a symbol of our throw-away society, most Americans would undoubtedly say packaging, which is the largest component of our solid waste stream, accounting for almost one-third of municipal solid waste. And the packaging material that's usually considered the worst offender is plastics. After all, plastics have been the fastest growing packaging material by far and now account for 11 percent of packaging waste by weight. They also constitute a disproportionately high volume of municipal solid waste—approximately 20 percent—which drives up the cost of transporting and landfilling it. But most important, plastics are generally viewed as unrecyclable. Only about 2 percent of plastic wastes in the United States are presently recycled, while the recycling rates for the other major materials used in packaging—paper, glass, and metals—all exceed 15 percent.

The fact of the matter is that it doesn't have to be that way. To be sure, plastics recycling does present some difficult technical problems. But these obstacles are no longer so formidable: advances in plastics recycling have been taking place at a truly astounding rate, perhaps comparable to the pace of innovation in computer technology. As a result, it's now technically feasible to recycle the bulk of the plastic used in packaging, and in most cases it's economically viable as well—or could be, given the proper institutional arrangements and market incentives.

Robert F. Stone, Ambuj D. Sagar, and Nicholas A. Ashford, from Technology Review

I wonder why more plastics aren't recycled.

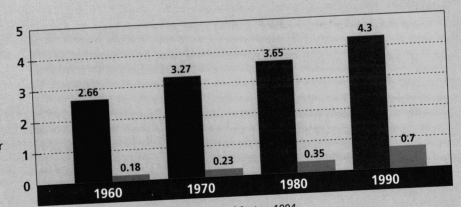

Municipal Waste Collected and Recycled

- ■ Pounds collected per person each day
- ■ Pounds recycled per person each day

Year	Pounds collected	Pounds recycled
1960	2.66	0.18
1970	3.27	0.23
1980	3.65	0.35
1990	4.3	0.7

Source: *Statistical Abstract of the United States: 1994*

Bar Graph

Do I throw out over 4 pounds of garbage every day? This is depressing!

❷ Freewrite About a Situation

Freewrite about one of the decisions, natural phenomena, events, or problems you discussed. Try to clarify for yourself the issues and problems involved in this topic. Then list some questions you have about this situation. Be as specific as you can about things you do not understand and want to learn more about.

- ○→ **LASERLINKS**
  - • *WRITING SPRINGBOARD*
- ▭→ **WRITING COACH**

Answering Questions

Research for a Purpose You've identified a situation for which you want to research, analyze, and explain causes or effects. You've listed some questions about that situation for which you want to find answers. These pages will help you to identify your reasons for writing, find answers to your questions, and organize the information and ideas you find.

Student's Speculations

Situation: Low percentages of waste materials recycled

Possible Reasons
1. Too expensive?

2. Not possible?

3. "Too much trouble"?

4. Low demand for recycled materials by manufacturers?

Correct?
No, it's cheaper in many places than burying or burning.

No, even plastics can be recycled.

Yes. People often do not bother to separate trash.

Yes, true except for metals and a few other things.

1 Understand Your Purpose

Writers have many reasons for thinking through cause-and-effect relationships. A writer may want to help solve a problem, make a personal decision, or persuade legislators to pass a new law. Think about why your topic is important to you and what you want to accomplish in your essay. Are you trying to make a decision? Are you hoping to solve a problem? Do you simply want to understand a situation better?

2 Speculate About Causes and Effects

Before you begin your research, write out possible causes or effects of the situation you've selected. The notes at the top of the page show the initial speculations of a student who wondered why more waste wasn't recycled.

If possible, brainstorm with others interested in the issue. The ideas you share may help you decide where to look for information.

Student's Flow Chart

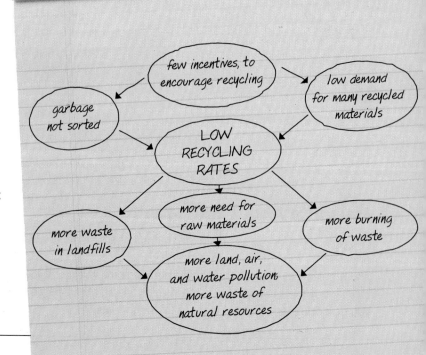

③ Look for Answers

Research your topic and find out whether your speculations about causes or effects were on target. To keep yourself on track, organize your ideas in a graphic organizer, such as the flow chart shown at the lower left. Possible sources include

- experts on a subject or people with experience in making decisions similar to the one you are trying to make
- newspaper or magazine articles or editorials on your subject
- organizations concerned with issues related to your subject
- on-line and library sources
- experiments or observations related to scientific topics

Sometimes cause-and-effect relationships are more complicated than they seem. For example, one event may have several causes and many effects. Be critical of your own and others' reasoning about cause-and-effect relationships. The SkillBuilder at the right can help you avoid leaping to wrong conclusions.

④ Identify Your Audience

Once you have completed your research, look over your graphic organizer. Decide which ideas and information will best help you explain important causes and effects. Think also about who would be interested in this information and how much background information this audience needs. For example, after researching recycling, one writer decided to share his cause-and-effect essay with science classes.

Make some decisions about the form and the content of your analysis.

- The specific subject and purpose of your analysis may make it appropriate for a persuasive speech, a newspaper article, a personal letter, or a research report.
- If you are writing about a personal decision, the information you include will depend on how well your readers know you.
- For scientific or historical topics you may need to provide background information.

 CRITICAL THINKING

Avoiding Logical Fallacies
One event may follow another without being caused by it. It might rain on the day of a track meet, but the track meet did not cause it to rain. To assume that these events are related is a logical fallacy, or mistake in reasoning. This kind of fallacy is called **false cause.** Other fallacies are

- **oversimplification:** assuming an event has only one cause
- **overgeneralization:** making a generalization based on too few examples
- **either/or:** assuming there are only two alternatives

APPLYING WHAT YOU'VE LEARNED
Look for fallacies in your own and others' thinking about topics.

 WRITING HANDBOOK

For more information on cause-and-effect writing, see page 1038 of the Writing Handbook.

THINK & PLAN

Defining Relationships

1. Which ideas in your graphic organizer or notes are not clearly related as causes or effects?
2. If you discovered fallacies in your thinking, how can you correct them?
3. What background information will your audience need?

DRAFTING

Making Connections

Chains of Events With your purpose in mind, write a first draft. Don't worry if some of the cause-and-effect relationships you want to describe are still a little unclear to you. Writing your ideas down may help you to clarify them. If you spot a logical fallacy, circle it so you can rethink your analysis.

1 Write a Rough Draft

As you write, try to draw a clear connection between each cause and its effect.

- If you made a flow chart or other graphic organizer during prewriting, use it as a guide for your writing.
- Begin by telling your readers what you're analyzing. Make your purpose clear.
- Provide any necessary background information.

Student's Rough Draft

The effects of recycling are obvious. It reduces pollution and protects the environment. I even read that it is cheaper than burning trash or burying it in landfills.

So why are recycling rates low? I think it's mostly because people are lazy. It's easier to dump everything into one bag and forget about it than it is to separate out different kinds of cans and bottles and boxes.

Also, making packages out of some recycled materials, especially plastics, may be more expensive than making packages out of raw materials. This usually means that the products sold in these packages are more expensive. The costs of disposing of such packages are paid by taxpayers and not by the people who make or buy these packages, so manufacturers and consumers have little reason to make or buy things in recycled containers.

There are some things that could cause recycling rates to go up. City governments could charge more for collecting unsorted garbage than for collecting sorted garbage. Taxes could be charged for raw materials that would make them more expensive than recycled materials. Sales taxes could be placed on products in packages that are unrecyclable or not made from recycled materials.

People can do a few things to raise recycling rates. They can carry groceries in permanent shopping bags. They can buy products using the smallest amount of packaging. They can buy products in recycled and recyclable packages. They can stop using many disposable products. They can separate garbage and take it to recycling centers.

> This is vague. How does recycling reduce pollution and save the environment? C.K.

> Connections aren't clear here. T.N.

> Why don't you present this at the school forum on environmental issues next week? K.C.

② Analyze Your Rough Draft

As you read over your draft, think about whether you have accomplished your purpose. Page 1035 of the Writing Handbook can help you to think about ways of organizing ideas and details. The organizational pattern you use depends on your purpose and on the kind of information you are presenting. Methods of organizing cause-and-effect essays include

- describing a cause first and then one or more effects
- describing an effect first and then one or more causes
- describing a series of causes and effects in chronological order

③ Rework and Share

As you rework your draft, make sure that paragraphs are fully developed, that connections between causes and effects are clear, and that all the information you include is relevant.

- Elaborate on basic information with facts, statistics, incidents or examples, or details.
- Emphasize connections between ideas. The SkillBuilder at the right can help you to make connections clear by using transitional words or phrases or by repeating key words.
- Eliminate information that doesn't help you explain the cause-and-effect relationships as you now understand them.
- Consider including a graphic such as a flow chart to help readers to understand your analysis.

 PEER RESPONSE

Feedback from a peer will show you whether you have clearly explained connections between causes and effects. Peer comments on the draft at the left suggested changes. Questions like the ones below can help to show the strengths and weaknesses of your analysis:

- Are the connections between causes and effects clear to you? If not, how can I clarify them?
- If you see any logical fallacies in my analysis, can you suggest ways I could correct them?
- What is missing from this explanation? What information would you leave out?

SkillBuilder

 WRITER'S CRAFT

Creating Coherence in Paragraphs

A paragraph is coherent when all of its sentences relate logically to one another. Using transitions such as *because, due to,* and *consequently* will help you make cause-and-effect paragraphs coherent. You can also repeat key words that tie sentences together.

Packaging materials cannot be recycled together, because they have different physical properties. Consequently, different packaging materials must be separated.

APPLYING WHAT YOU'VE LEARNED
Read over your draft to find paragraphs in which ideas can be linked by using transitional words or by repeating key words.

 WRITING HANDBOOK

For more information on using transitions, see page 1027 of the Writing Handbook.

RETHINK & EVALUATE

Preparing to Revise

1. Which connections between events or ideas are unclear? How can you clarify them?
2. Which paragraphs need elaboration? How can you develop them? What can you eliminate?
3. How can you best order your ideas to achieve your purpose?

Clarifying Connections

Wrap-Up You've examined connections between causes and effects. Now prepare to share your ideas by correcting mistakes, polishing sentences and paragraphs, and preparing any visuals that will accompany your writing. Think again about the best way to share your findings. The ideas on these pages can help you.

Student's Final Draft

❶ Revise and Edit

Use peer comments and the Standards for Evaluation on the next page as you revise your essay.

- The SkillBuilder on the next page will help you avoid using fragments as sentences.
- Be sure to clarify connections between causes and effects and avoid logical fallacies.

Effects of Recycling

Until recently, my only thought about garbage was that somebody besides me should take it out. Then I started reading articles about recycling. As a result of what I've learned, I've decided to take responsibility for recycling in my family and to set up and maintain a recycling center for my apartment building.

The effects of recycling are that it reduces landfills, it reduces the need for raw materials such as wood and iron, and it reduces air and water pollution. It also saves money.

The causes for the first three effects are obvious. If paper, glass, aluminum, steel, and some plastic are removed, less solid waste is left to burn or bury. If reprocessed paper and metals are used instead of raw materials, then fewer trees will be cut down and less metal will be mined. Air pollution is reduced because less garbage is burned and because fewer raw materials are processed. It may not be obvious why recycling saves money. Because landfills and burning have become very expensive, recycling is actually cheaper than getting rid of garbage by these methods. A study in Massachusetts showed that the total benefits of recycling were worth about $231 per ton to taxpayers (Stone, Sager, and Ashford 54).

Unfortunately, it is not always true that products in packages made from recycled materials are cheaper to make or to buy than those in packages made from raw materials. Making materials out of some recycled materials can be more expensive than making packages out of raw materials. This may make the products more expensive for consumers.

The writer begins by explaining why he made a decision about recycling.

He clearly explains the effects of recycling and uses a statistic to prove his point.

What Garbage Consists Of

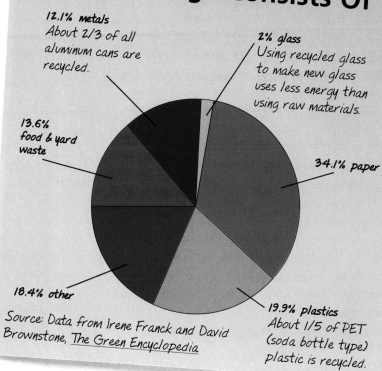

12.1% metals About 2/3 of all aluminum cans are recycled.

2% glass Using recycled glass to make new glass uses less energy than using raw materials.

13.6% food & yard waste

34.1% paper

18.4% other

19.9% plastics About 1/5 of PET (soda bottle type) plastic is recycled.

Source: Data from Irene Franck and David Brownstone, The Green Encyclopedia

Student's Circle Graph

② Share Your Work

If you explained a cause-and-effect situation related to science, history, or civics, share your analysis with teachers in that subject. They may ask you to present your information to their classes. Consider including flow charts or other graphics to help your audience understand causes and effects. The writer of the essay on the left added a circle graph showing the percentage of materials collected as garbage. If you explained a personal decision, you may want to share your analysis with friends or relatives who are familiar with your situation.

Standards for Evaluation

An effective cause-and-effect essay
- clearly states the cause-and-effect relationship being examined
- shows clear relationships between causes and effects
- arranges details logically and uses transitional words to clarify order
- uses language and details appropriate to its audience

SkillBuilder

 GRAMMAR FROM WRITING

Avoiding Sentence Fragments

Clauses beginning with subordinating conjunctions such as *because* or *since* are sometimes confused with sentences. Unless subordinate clauses are joined to independent clauses, they are fragments. Be sure to correct sentence fragments such as this:

Fragment *Because it was easier*
Sentence *I put all the garbage in one bag because it was easier.*

 GRAMMAR HANDBOOK

For more information on avoiding sentence fragments, see page 1058 of the Grammar Handbook.

Editing Checklist Use the following editing tips as you revise.

- Have you avoided using sentence fragments as sentences?
- Are capitalization, punctuation, and spelling correct?

REFLECT & ASSESS

Evaluating the Experience

1. What advice would you give on writing cause-and-effect essays?
2. How can you use cause-and-effect writing in science class?

📁 **PORTFOLIO** How well did you analyze and explain causes and effects? Put this evaluation in your portfolio.

REFLECT & ASSESS

UNIT FOUR: MOMENTS OF TRUTH

How have your feelings or views about truth been affected by the selections in this unit? How would you rate your development as a reader and a writer during your work on the unit? Explore these questions by completing one or more of the options in each of the following sections.

REFLECTING ON THEME

OPTION 1 **Choosing Guides to the Truth** Many classic works of literature feature characters who embark on great journeys to find truth. Often the main character is guided by some person or divine power who serves as a guide or mentor. If you were to embark on such a journey, which character or writer from this unit would you most want as a guide? Which do you think would be least trustworthy or desirable as a guide? Explain your choices in writing, comparing them with other characters or writers from the unit.

OPTION 2 **Truths to Live By** Review the What Do You Think? feature on page 592, which asked you to create a word portrait describing what matters most to you. Then create two similar word portraits—one representing the values of an individual from this unit whom you admire or identify with, the other representing the values of an individual whose values or

experiences seem far removed from your own. Share your word portraits with your classmates, explaining the reasoning behind them.

Self-Assessment: Create a tree diagram to show the different meanings that truth has for you. On each major branch, write a word or phrase that conveys one aspect of truth. On the smaller branches, list titles of selections that relate to each word or phrase, as well as your own elaborations of its meaning. For example, a major branch labeled "Personal Integrity" might lead to smaller branches bearing the titles "Once Upon a Time" and "As the Night the Day," along with descriptive words and phrases such as honesty, sincerity, *and* being true to yourself.

REVIEWING LITERARY CONCEPTS

OPTION 1 **Understanding Imagery** Writers use imagery to re-create sensory experiences for readers. Some images depend upon the literal meanings of words, presenting the evidence of the senses directly. Others rely on figurative language, requiring readers to use their imaginations to fill in the sensory details. Create a chart like the one shown. Then find at least seven striking images in the selections in this unit, and place each in the appropriate category. Compare your chart with those of your classmates, discussing the different effects of literal and figurative images.

Selection	Literal Image	Figurative Image
"Two Friends"	"The hills of Orgemont and Sannois dominated the horizon, and the great plain which stretches as far as Nanterre was empty, completely empty, with nothing but its leafy cherry tree and gray earth."	"A sort of hairy giant who was sitting astride a chair and smoking a large clay pipe . . ."

OPTION 2 **Defining Modern Poetry** Review the information about distinctive characteristics of modern poetry on page 557. Then work with a partner to create your own extended definition of modern poetry. Apply your definition to the poems in this unit. Which ones best illustrate your definition? Are there any poems that your definition doesn't seem to fit? Present the results of your work in a brief oral report.

Self-Assessment: The following literary terms were introduced in this unit. Create categories for the terms, putting similar ones together. For example, one category might be "Terms That Describe How a Story Is Told." The terms can be categorized in a number of ways—just be sure that you can explain your reasoning. If there are any *terms that you do not fully understand, review their meanings in the Handbook of Literary Terms (page 1000). Compare your categories with those of your classmates.*

narrator	*third-person point of view*
suspense	*omniscient point of view*
alliteration	*humor*
reflective essay	*free verse*
protagonist	*characterization*
antagonist	*personification*
diction	*internal conflict*

PORTFOLIO BUILDING

• **QuickWrites** Many of the QuickWrites assignments in this unit asked you to produce narrative writing, such as a ballad, an eyewitness account, and a children's book. Which of your narratives tell the most interesting stories? Does the interest of each stem from plot, from character, or from some other literary element? Choose one or two pieces to include in your portfolio, and write a note explaining your choice. Then add the pieces and the note to your portfolio.

• **Writing About Literature** Earlier you interpreted one of this unit's poems. Reread your interpretation. Then draft a letter to the poet, in which you share any discoveries you made in writing your interpretation, as well as ask any questions you still have. Decide whether to include your letter and interpretation in your portfolio.

• **Writing from Experience** By now you've written a cause-and-effect essay. After reviewing the essay, write a note to yourself about what you discovered as you wrote it. When might you again analyze causes and effects as you did in the essay? Why?

• **Personal Choice** Think about the nonwriting activities that you completed during the course of this unit—everything from dramatizations to drawings.

Did you surprise yourself by what you were able to accomplish? Did you discover any hidden talents or skills? Choose an activity that led to a new discovery about your abilities or interests. Write a note explaining your choice, and add the note to your portfolio.

Self-Assessment: Review the pieces in your portfolio. Which types of writing seem to bring out your best work? Which types of writing have proved troublesome or difficult to master? Have your strengths and weaknesses changed during the course of the year? Jot down your responses to these questions in your notebook.

SETTING GOALS

The Reflect & Assess feature at the end of Unit One (pages 174–175) asked you to create a list of skills that you would like to work on. Review that list to judge the progress that you have made. Then create an updated list of skills you want to work on during the rest of the year, reflecting your current needs and interests.

Nothing Stays the Same

La región más transparente [Where the air is clear] (1989), Ismael Vargas. Oil on canvas, 90 cm × 110 cm, private collection.

There is nothing permanent except change.

Heraclitus
Ancient Greek philosopher
c. 500 B.C.

PROGRESS AND ITS PRICE

REFLECTING ON THEME

How do you view progress? Do you believe that we are moving inevitably toward a better life, aided by ever-faster computers and other forms of electronic wizardry, or are you worried about what might be lost or destroyed as a result of the rapid changes in our world? This part of Unit Five features stories of people who must contend with forces of change. In various ways the selections challenge you to determine the price of progress and to clarify your own vision of the good life.

What Do You Think? Working with a small group of classmates, create two illustrations—one suggesting progress and the other suggesting the opposite of progress. Then compare your illustrations with those of other groups and discuss what the images reveal about your views of progress.

Ray Bradbury
(1920–)
One of America's most popular science fiction writers

E. B. White
(1899–1985)
An American essayist, humorist, and children's author

Sara Teasdale
(1884–1933)
An American lyric poet and Pulitzer Prize winner

Stephen Vincent Benét
(1898–1943)
An American author whose writings on U.S. history and folklore won him a Pulitzer Prize

Mary Oliver
(1935–)
A Pulitzer Prize-winning American poet who writes of the natural world

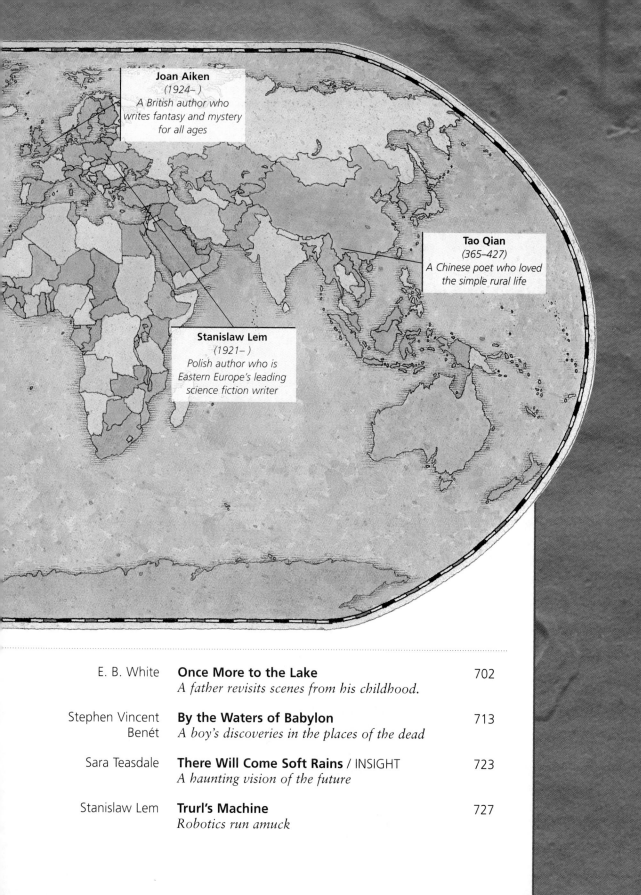

Joan Aiken
(1924–)
A British author who writes fantasy and mystery for all ages

Tao Qian
(365–427)
A Chinese poet who loved the simple rural life

Stanislaw Lem
(1921–)
Polish author who is Eastern Europe's leading science fiction writer

E. B. White	**Once More to the Lake**	702
	A father revisits scenes from his childhood.	
Stephen Vincent Benét	**By the Waters of Babylon**	713
	A boy's discoveries in the places of the dead	
Sara Teasdale	**There Will Come Soft Rains** / INSIGHT	723
	A haunting vision of the future	
Stanislaw Lem	**Trurl's Machine**	727
	Robotics run amuck	

PREVIEWING

FICTION

Searching for Summer
Joan Aiken England

PERSONAL CONNECTION

Imagine waking up on a warm, sunny day. Through your window you can see a cloudless blue sky. Then imagine waking up on a cool, cloudy day with a dark gray sky. How would you feel in each situation? As a class, discuss how the weather affects your emotional well-being. Then try to depict the class's overall reaction on a Venn diagram like the one shown.

Feelings on a Sunny Day

Feelings on a Cloudy Day

LITERARY CONNECTION

The following selection is a fantasy in which sunshine plays an important role. A **fantasy** is a type of fiction that contains events, places, or other details that could not exist in the real world. The characters in a fantasy are often realistic, but they have experiences that overstep the bounds of reality. Along with its cousin, science fiction, fantasy is literature from and for the imagination. It offers an escape from reality and, at its best, brings reality closer as well. In the realm of fantasy, you can speculate about what might have been or what could be and discover the magic and wonder hidden just below the surface of your own familiar, everyday world.

Joan Aiken wrote "Searching for Summer" in the 1950s, setting the story in a future "eighties," perhaps the 1980s or the 2080s. The characters live in England and speak in an English dialect that may be unfamiliar to American readers.

WRITING CONNECTION

Imagine living in a place where you were always dissatisfied with the weather. How would the weather affect your everyday life? What could you do about it? Answer these questions in your notebook and, as you read "Searching for Summer," see how your ideas relate to the story.

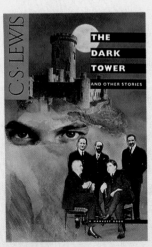

Cover illustration from *The Dark Tower and Other Stories* (Harvest Edition) by C.S. Lewis. Copyright © 1977 by the Trustees of the the the Estate of C.S. Lewis, reprinted by permission of Harcourt Brace & Company.

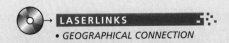

LASERLINKS
• *GEOGRAPHICAL CONNECTION*

Searching for Summer

Joan Aiken

The Mysterious Bird (1917), Charles Burchfield. Watercolor and pencil on paper, 20¾″ × 17¾″, Delaware Art Museum, Wilmington, bequest of John L. Sexton, 1955.

Lily wore yellow on her wedding day. In the eighties people put a lot of faith in <u>omens</u> and believed that if a bride's dress was yellow her married life would be blessed with a bit of sunshine.

It was years since the bombs had been banned, but still the cloud never lifted. Whitish gray, day after day, sometimes darkening to a weeping slate color or, at the end of an evening, turning to smoky copper, the sky endlessly, secretively brooded.

Old people began their stories with the classic, fairy-tale opening: "Long, long ago, when I was a liddle un, in the days when the sky was blue . . ." and children, listening, chuckled among themselves at the absurd thought, because, *blue,* imagine it! How could the sky ever have been *blue?* You might as well say, "In the days when the grass was pink."

Stars, rainbows, and all other such heavenly sideshows had been permanently withdrawn, and if the radio announced that there was a blink of sunshine in such and such a place, where the cloud belt had thinned for half an hour, cars and buses would pour in that direction for days in an <u>unavailing</u> search for warmth and light.

After the wedding, when all the relations were standing on the church porch, with Lily shivering prettily in her buttercup nylon, her father prodded the dour[1] and <u>withered</u> grass on a grave—although it was August, the leaves were hardly out yet—and said, "Well, Tom, what are you aiming to do now, eh?"

"Going to find a bit of sun and have our honeymoon in it," said Tom. There was a general laugh from the wedding party.

"Don't get sunburned," shrilled Aunt Nancy.

"Better start off Bournemouth[2] way. Paper said they had a half-hour of sun last Wednesday week," Uncle Arthur weighed in heavily.

"We'll come back brown as—as this grass," said Tom, and ignoring the good-natured teasing from their respective families, the two young people mounted on their scooter, which stood ready at the churchyard wall, and chugged away in a shower of golden confetti. When they were out of sight, and the yellow paper had subsided on the gray and gritty road, the Whitemores and the Hoskinses strolled off, sighing, to eat wedding cake and drink currant[3] wine, and old Mrs. Hoskins spoiled everyone's pleasure by bursting into tears as she thought of her own wedding day when everything was so different.

Meanwhile Tom and Lily buzzed on hopefully across the gray countryside, with Lily's veil like a gilt banner floating behind. It was chilly going for her in her wedding things, but the sight of a bride was supposed to bring good luck, and so she stuck it out, although her fingers were blue to the knuckles. Every now and then they switched on their portable radio and listened to the forecast. Inverness had seen the sun for ten minutes yesterday, and Southend[4] for five minutes this morning, but that was all.

"Both those places are a long way from here," said Tom cheerfully. "All the more reason we'd find a nice bit of sunshine in these parts somewhere. We'll keep on going south. Keep your eyes peeled, Lil, and tell me if you see a blink of sun on those hills ahead."

But they came to the hills and passed them, and a new range shouldered up ahead and then slid away behind, and still there was no flicker

---

1. **dour** (dŏŏr): gloomy; forbidding.
2. **Bournemouth** (bôrn'məth): a British seaside resort.
3. **currant:** a berry used to make jams, jellies, and wines.
4. **Inverness . . . Southend:** resort towns in the north and south of the British Isles.

WORDS TO KNOW
omen (ō'mən) *n.* a thing or event supposed to foretell good or evil; a sign
unavailing (ŭn'ə-vā'lĭng) *adj.* useless; ineffective
withered (wĭ*th*'ərd) *adj.* shriveled or shrunken, as if from lack of water or food

or patch of sunshine to be seen anywhere in the gray, winter-ridden landscape. Lily began to get discouraged, so they stopped for a cup of tea at a drive-in.

"Seen the sun lately, mate?" Tom asked the proprietor.

He laughed shortly. "Notice any buses or trucks around here? Last time I saw the sun was two years ago September; came out just in time for the wife's birthday."

"It's stars I'd like to see," Lily said, looking wistfully at her dust-colored tea. "Ever so pretty they must be."

"Well, better be getting on I suppose," said Tom, but he had lost some of his bounce and confidence. Every place they passed through looked nastier than the last, partly on account of the dismal light, partly because people had given up bothering to take a pride in their boroughs.[5] And then, just as they were entering a village called Molesworth, the dimmest, drabbest, most insignificant huddle of houses they had come to yet, the engine coughed and died on them.

"Can't see what's wrong," said Tom, after a prolonged and gloomy survey.

"Oh, Tom!" Lily was almost crying. "What'll we do?"

"Have to stop here for the night, s'pose." Tom was short-tempered with frustration. "Look, there's a garage just up the road. We can push the bike there, and they'll tell us if there's a pub[6] where we can stay. It's nearly six anyway."

They had taken the bike to the garage, and the man there was just telling them that the only pub in the village was the Rising Sun, where Mr. Noakes might be able to give them a bed, when a bus pulled up in front of the petrol[7] pumps.

How could the sky ever have been *blue?*

"Look," the garage owner said, "there's Mr. Noakes just getting out of the bus now. Sid!" he called.

But Mr. Noakes was not able to come to them at once. Two old people were climbing slowly out of the bus ahead of him: a blind man with a white stick, and a withered, frail old lady in a black satin dress and hat. "Careful now, George," she was saying, "mind ee be careful with my son William."

"I'm being careful, Mrs. Hatching," the conductor said patiently, as he almost lifted the unsteady old pair off the bus platform. The driver had stopped his engine, and everyone on the bus was taking a mild and sympathetic interest, except for Mr. Noakes just behind who was cursing irritably at the delay. When the two old people were on the narrow pavement, the conductor saw that they were going to have trouble with a bicycle that was propped against the curb just ahead of them; he picked it up and stood holding it until they had passed the line of petrol pumps and were going slowly off along a path across the fields. Then, grinning, he put it back, jumped hurriedly into the bus, and rang his bell.

"Old nuisances," Mr. Noakes said furiously. "Wasting public time. Every week that palaver[8] goes on, taking the old man to Midwick Hospital Outpatients and back again. I know what *I'd* do with 'em. Put to sleep, that sort ought to be."

Mr. Noakes was a repulsive-looking

---

5. **boroughs:** towns or districts.

6. **pub:** a British term for a small tavern. Pubs in small towns sometimes serve meals and rent rooms to travelers.

7. **petrol:** a British term for gasoline.

8. **palaver** (pə-lăv′ər): useless chatter.

individual, but when he heard that Tom and Lily wanted a room for the night, he changed completely and gave them a leer that was full of false goodwill. He was a big, red-faced man with wet, full lips, bulging pale-gray bloodshot eyes, and a crop of stiff greasy black hair. He wore tennis shoes.

"Honeymooners, eh?" he said, looking sentimentally at Lily's pale prettiness. "Want a bed for the night, eh?" and he laughed a disgusting laugh that sounded like thick oil coming out of a bottle, heh-heh-heh-heh, and gave Lily a tremendous pinch on her arm. Disengaging herself as politely as she could, she stooped and picked up something from the pavement. They followed Mr. Noakes glumly up the street to the Rising Sun.

While they were eating their baked beans, Mr. Noakes stood over their table grimacing at them. Lily unwisely confided to him that they were looking for a bit of sunshine. Mr. Noakes's laughter nearly shook down the ramshackle building.

"Sunshine! Oh my gawd! That's a good 'un! Hear that, Mother?" he bawled to his wife. "They're looking for a bit of sunshine. Heh-heh-heh-heh-heh-heh! Why," he said, banging on the table till the baked beans leaped about, "if I could find a bit of sunshine near here, permanent bit that is, dja know what I'd do?"

The young people looked at him inquiringly across the bread and margarine.

"Lido,[9] trailer site, country club, holiday camp—you wouldn't know the place. Land around here is dirt cheap; I'd buy up the lot. Nothing but woods. I'd advertise—I'd have people flocking to this little dump from all over the country. But what a hope, what a hope, eh? Well, feeling better? Enjoyed your tea? Ready for bed? Heh-heh-heh-heh, bed's ready for you."

Avoiding one another's eyes, Tom and Lily stood up.

"I—I'd like to go for a bit of a walk first, Tom," Lily said in a small voice. "Look, I picked up that old lady's bag on the pavement; I didn't notice it till we'd done talking to Mr. Noakes, and by then she was out of sight. Should we take it back to her?"

"Good idea," said Tom, pouncing on the suggestion with relief. "Do you know where she lives, Mr. Noakes?"

"Who, old Ma Hatching? Sure I know. She lives in the wood. But you don't want to go taking her bag back, not this time o' the evening you don't. Let her worry. She'll come asking for it in the morning."

"She walked so slowly," said Lily, holding the bag gently in her hands. It was very old, made of black velvet on two ring handles, and embroidered with beaded roses. "I think we ought to take it to her, don't you, Tom?"

"Oh, very well, very well, have it your own way," Mr. Noakes said, winking at Tom. "Take that path by the garage; you can't go wrong. I've never been there meself, but they live somewhere in that wood back o' the village; you'll find it soon enough."

They found the path soon enough, but not the cottage. Under the lowering[10] sky they walked forward endlessly among trees that carried only tiny and rudimentary leaves, wizened and poverty-stricken.[11] Lily was still wearing her wedding sandals, which had begun to blister her. She held onto Tom's arm, biting her lip with the pain, and he looked down miserably at her bent brown head; everything had turned out so differently from what he had planned.

By the time they reached the cottage Lily

---

9. **lido** (lī′dō): a British term for a public outdoor swimming pool.

10. **lowering** (lou′ər-ĭng): dark and threatening.

11. **rudimentary . . . poverty-stricken:** leaves that are imperfectly formed and shriveled up from lack of sunlight.

could hardly bear to put her left foot to the ground, and Tom was gentling her along: "It can't be much farther now, and they'll be sure to have a bandage. I'll tie it up, and you can have a sit-down. Maybe they'll give us a cup of tea. We could borrow an old pair of socks or something. . . ." Hardly noticing the cottage garden, beyond a vague impression of rows of runner beans, they made for the clematis-grown[12] porch and knocked. There was a brass lion's head on the door, carefully polished.

"Eh, me dear!" It was the old lady, old Mrs. Hatching, who opened the door, and her exclamation was a long-drawn gasp of pleasure and astonishment. "Eh, me dear! 'Tis the pretty bride. See'd ye s'arternoon when we was coming home from hospital."

"Who be?" shouted a voice from inside.

"Come in, come in, me dears. My son William'll be glad to hear company; he can't see, poor soul, nor has this thirty year, ah, and a pretty sight he's losing this minute—"

"We brought back your bag," Tom said, putting it in her hands, "and we wondered if you'd have a bit of plaster[13] you could kindly let us have. My wife's hurt her foot—"

My wife. Even in the midst of Mrs. Hatching's <u>voluble</u> welcome the strangeness of these words struck the two young people, and they fell quiet, each of them, pondering, while Mrs. Hatching thanked and commiserated, all in a breath, and asked them to take a seat on the sofa and fetched a basin of water from the scullery,[14] and William from his seat in the chimney corner demanded to know what it was all about.

"Wot be doing? Wot be doing, Mother?"

" 'Tis a bride, all in's finery," she shrilled

"The sun? Is it really the sun?"

back at him, "an's blistered her foot, poor heart." Keeping up a running commentary for William's benefit she bound up the foot, every now and then exclaiming to herself in wonder over the fineness of Lily's wedding dress, which lay in yellow nylon swathes around the chair. "There, me dear. Now us'll have a cup of tea, eh? Proper thirsty you'm fare to be, walking all the way to here this hot day."

Hot day? Tom and Lily stared at each other and then around the room. Then it was true, it was not their imagination, that a great dusty golden square of sunshine lay on the fireplace wall, where the brass pendulum of the clock at every swing blinked into sudden brilliance? That the blazing geraniums on the windowsill housed a drove of murmuring bees? That, through the window, the gleam of linen hung in the sun to whiten suddenly dazzled their eyes?

"The sun? Is it really the sun?" Tom said, almost doubtfully.

"And why not?" Mrs. Hatching demanded. "How else'll beans set, tell me that? Fine thing if sun were to stop shining." Chuckling to herself she set out a Crown Derby tea set, gorgeously colored in red and gold, and a baking of saffron[15] buns. Then she sat down and, drinking her own tea, began to question the two of them about where they had come from, where they were going. The tea was

---

12. **clematis-grown:** covered with a flowering vine.
13. **plaster:** a British term for an adhesive bandage.
14. **scullery:** a small room in which dishwashing and other kitchen chores are done.
15. **saffron:** made with a cooking spice that imparts an orange-yellow color to foods.

WORDS
TO
KNOW   **voluble** (vŏl′yə-bəl) *adj.* in or with a long flow of words; talkative

677

tawny[16] and hot and sweet; the clock's tick was like a bird chirping; every now and then a log settled in the grate; Lily looked sleepily around the little room, so rich and peaceful, and thought, I wish we were staying here. I wish we needn't go back to that horrible pub. . . . She leaned against Tom's comforting arm.

"Look at the sky," she whispered to him. "Out there between the geraniums. Blue!"

Embrace II (1981), George Tooker. Egg tempera on gesso panel, 18″ × 24″, private collection.

"And ee'll come up and see my spare bedroom, won't ee now?" Mrs. Hatching said, breaking off the thread of her questions—which indeed was not a thread, but merely a savoring[17] of her pleasure and astonishment at this unlooked-for visit—"Bide here, why don't ee? Mid as well. The lil un's fair wore out. Us'll do for ee better 'n rangy old Noakes; proper old scoundrel 'e be. Won't us, William?"

"Ah," William said appreciatively. "I'll sing ee some o' my songs."

A sight of the spare room settled any doubts. The great white bed, huge as a prairie, built up with layer upon solid layer of mattress, blanket, and quilt, almost filled the little shadowy room in which it stood. Brass rails shone in the green dimness. "Isn't it quiet," Lily whispered. Mrs. Hatching, silent for the moment, stood looking at them proudly, her bright eyes slowly moving from face to face. Once her hand fondled, as if it might have been a baby's downy head, the yellow brass knob.

And so, almost without any words, the matter was decided.

Three days later they remembered that they must go to the village and collect the scooter which must, surely, be mended by now.

They had been helping old William pick a basketful of beans. Tom had taken his shirt off, and the sun gleamed on his brown back; Lily was wearing an old cotton print which Mrs. Hatching, with much chuckling, had shortened to fit her.

It was amazing how deftly, in spite of his blindness, William moved among the beans, feeling through the rough, rustling leaves for the stiffness of concealed pods. He found twice as many as Tom and Lily, but then they, even

---

16. **tawny:** tan in color.
17. **savoring:** full appreciation or enjoyment.

on the third day, were still stopping every other minute to exclaim over the blueness of the sky. At night they sat on the back doorstep while Mrs. Hatching clucked inside as she dished the supper, "Starstruck ee'll be! Come along in, do-ee, before soup's cold; stars niver run away yet as I do know."

"Can we get anything for you in the village?" Lily asked, but Mrs. Hatching shook her head.

"Baker's bread and suchlike's no use but to cripple thee's innardses wi' colic.[18] I been living here these eighty year wi'out troubling doctors, and I'm not faring to begin now." She waved to them and stood watching as they walked into the wood, thin and frail beyond belief, but wiry, indomitable, her black eyes full of zest. Then she turned to scream menacingly at a couple of pullets[19] who had strayed and were scratching among the potatoes.

Almost at once they noticed, as they followed the path, that the sky was clouded over.

"It *is* only there on that one spot," Lily said in wonder. "All the time. And they've never even noticed that the sun doesn't shine in other places."

"That's how it must have been all over the world, once," Tom said.

At the garage they found their scooter ready and waiting. They were about to start back when they ran into Mr. Noakes.

"Well, well, well, well, *well!*" he shouted, glaring at them with ferocious good humor. "How many wells make a river, eh? And where did you slip off to? Here's me and the missus was just going to tell the police to have the rivers dragged. But hullo, hul*lo*, what's this? Brown, eh? Suntan? Scrumptious," he said, looking meltingly at Lily and giving her another tremendous pinch. "Where'd you get it, eh? That wasn't all got in half an hour, *I* know. Come on, this means money to you and me; tell

us the big secret. Remember what I said; land around these parts is dirt cheap."

Tom and Lily looked at each other in horror. They thought of the cottage, the bees humming among the runner beans, the sunlight glinting in the red-and-gold teacups. At night, when they had lain in the huge sagging bed, stars had shone through the window, and the whole wood was as quiet as the inside of a shell.

"Oh, we've been miles from here," Tom lied hurriedly. "We ran into a friend, and he took us right away beyond Brinsley." And as Mr. Noakes still looked suspicious and unsatisfied, he did the only thing possible. "We're going back there now," he said. "The sunbathing's grand." And opening the throttle, he let the scooter go. They waved at Mr. Noakes and chugged off toward the gray hills that lay to the north.

"My wedding dress," Lily said sadly. "It's on our bed."

They wondered how long Mrs. Hatching would keep tea hot for them, who would eat all the pasties.[20]

"Never mind, you won't need it again," Tom comforted her.

At least, he thought, they had left the golden place undisturbed. Mr. Noakes never went into the wood. And they had done what they intended; they had found the sun. Now they, too, would be able to tell their grandchildren, when beginning a story, "Long, long ago, when we were young, in the days when the sky was blue . . ." ❖

---

18. **cripple . . . colic** (kŏl'ĭk): give yourself a bad case of indigestion.

19. **pullets:** young hens.

20. **pasties** (păs'tēz): a British term for meat pies.

WORDS TO KNOW **indomitable** (ĭn-dŏm'ĭ-tə-bəl) *adj.* not easily discouraged, defeated, or subdued

RESPONDING OPTIONS

FROM PERSONAL RESPONSE TO CRITICAL ANALYSIS

REFLECT
1. In your notebook, write a sentence that expresses your feelings about the end of the story.

RETHINK
2. What words and phrases would you use to describe the world depicted in the story?

3. Why do you think the sun shines only over the Hatchings' cottage?

4. Do you think Tom and Lily do the right thing in not going back to Mrs. Hatching's cottage? Explain your opinion.

5. What themes, or messages, do you see in this story?

Consider
- previous events alluded to at the beginning of the story
- why sunshine is important to Tom and Lily
- which characters are presented positively and which negatively

RELATE
6. Tom and Lily choose to protect the Hatchings' bit of sunlight rather than let Mr. Noakes try to develop the land for his own gain. Think of situations in your own community or elsewhere in which there has been a conflict between some people's desire to protect places of natural beauty and other people's desire to develop those places for economic gain. How do you think such conflicts should be resolved?

ANOTHER PATHWAY

Cooperative Learning

With a small group of classmates, prepare illustrations for "Searching for Summer." Include pictures of the main characters, various landscapes, and a caption for each of the pictures. Then show your illustrations to the class and read the captions.

QUICKWRITES

1. How would you react if you awoke one morning to a permanently gray world? Write a **story opening** to describe your response. You may find it useful to reflect upon the discussion for the Personal Connection on page 672.

2. Write a **dialogue** Tom and Lily might have in the evening after leaving Molesworth, discussing whether they will ever return to the Hatchings'.

3. Write an **outline** for a revision of "Searching for Summer," in which bright sunshine is almost constant and clouds are rare.

PORTFOLIO Save your writing. You may want to use it later as a springboard to a piece for your portfolio.

LITERARY CONCEPTS

The term *imagery* refers to words and phrases that re-create sensory experiences for a reader. Images can appeal to any of the five senses—sight, hearing, taste, smell, and touch. In "Searching for Summer" Joan Aiken uses imagery to contrast the cold, gray world that Tom and Lily want to escape with the warm, bright world where they find refuge. Work with a partner to create a two-column chart featuring quotations from the story. In one column list images associated with the cloudy, gray world; in the other column list images from the bright sunny one. Then compare your chart with those of your classmates.

ALTERNATIVE ACTIVITIES

1. In a small group, use details from the story to create a **family photo album** of Tom and Lily's honeymoon. Share your album with the class.

2. Imagine that Mr. Noakes has discovered the sunshine over the Hatchings' home. With a partner, create and present to the class a **radio commercial** that Mr. Noakes might put together to advertise the area as a tourist attraction.

CRITIC'S CORNER

When asked to comment on this story, the student reviewer Jayme Charak remarked, "The story went to the heart. It was a sweet story and makes you think about the future." How does this reaction compare with your own?

WORDS TO KNOW

Review the Words to Know at the bottom of the selection pages. Then write the vocabulary word that is suggested by each set of idioms below.

1. run off at the mouth, have the gift of gab, be a chatterbox, talk till the cows come home

2. a black cat crossing your path, gathering clouds, a feeling in one's bones, seeing the handwriting on the wall

3. be a lion, have an iron will, never say die, not be a pushover

4. waste away, curl up and die, dry up and blow away, be a shadow of a former self

5. cry over spilt milk, close the barn door after the horse is stolen, carry water in a sieve

JOAN AIKEN

1924–

The daughter of the American poet Conrad Aiken, Joan Aiken grew up in England, where her parents settled before she was born. After her parents divorced, her mother married another writer, Martin Armstrong. "I knew I was going to be a writer," Joan explains, "like Conrad, like Martin, whose books were to be seen around the house."

In 1945, Aiken met and married Ronald Brown and also began having her poems and stories published in magazines. Her first book of fiction for young adults, *All You've Ever Wanted and Other Stories,* appeared in 1953. Widowed about two years later and needing to support her two children, she became an editor for *Argosy* magazine but continued to write in her spare time.

Joan Aiken has devoted much of her career to writing richly imaginative literature for children and young adults. These stories create worlds of fantasy, mystery, and humor—"what I would have liked to read as a child," she says. In the 1960s she won critical acclaim for a series of books that present alternative histories of England. *The Wolves of Willoughby Chase* (1962), the first in the series, explores what England might have been like if a different royal family had come to power in the 1700s. The series also includes *Black Hearts in Battersea* (1964) and *Night Birds on Nantucket* (1966). Themes of fantasy, mystery, and history also carry through into Aiken's books for adults. Her novel *Mansfield Revisited* was written as a sequel to Jane Austen's *Mansfield Park.*

OTHER WORKS *The Windscreen Weepers and Other Tales of Horror and Suspense, The Haunting of Lamb House, Morningquest*

FICTION

A Sound of Thunder
Ray Bradbury United States

PERSONAL CONNECTION

If time travel were possible, what era would you most like to visit? Would you want to travel back to the past or ahead into the future? Share your thoughts in a class discussion.

LITERARY CONNECTION

Time travel has been a popular idea in science fiction ever since the British author H. G. Wells wrote the short novel *The Time Machine* in 1895. In his novel Wells suggested that in addition to the three dimensions of length, height, and width, there is a fourth dimension of duration, or time. Wells speculated that if a machine could be invented to move along the fourth dimension, time travel would be possible. Science fiction writers since Wells's time have continued to use time travel as a basis for their adventures. The story that follows is set in the future, yet the characters travel back into the distant past.

WRITING CONNECTION

If you traveled to some time in the future or in the past, what would you hope to learn or experience? Do you think that you would try to affect the era that you visited? How do you think you might be affected by your time travel? Explore your answers to these questions in your notebook. As you read "A Sound of Thunder," see how your ideas compare with the action of the story.

Still from the 1960 movie *The Time Machine*, based on the H. G. Wells novel. Photofest.

Thoughts on Time Travel:

A Sound of Thunder

RAY BRADBURY

The sign on the wall seemed to quaver under a film of sliding warm water. Eckels felt his eyelids blink over his stare, and the sign burned in this momentary darkness:

TIME SAFARI, INC.
SAFARIS TO ANY YEAR IN THE PAST.
YOU NAME THE ANIMAL.
WE TAKE YOU THERE.
YOU SHOOT IT.

A warm phlegm gathered in Eckels's throat; he swallowed and pushed it down. The muscles around his mouth formed a smile as he put his hand slowly out upon the air, and in that hand waved a check for ten thousand dollars to the man behind the desk.

"Does this safari guarantee I come back alive?"

"We guarantee nothing," said the official, "except the dinosaurs." He turned. "This is Mr. Travis, your Safari Guide in the Past. He'll tell you what and where to shoot. If he says no shooting, no shooting. If you disobey instructions, there's a stiff penalty of another ten thousand dollars, plus possible government action, on your return."

Eckels glanced across the vast office at a mass and tangle, a snaking and humming of wires and steel boxes, at an aurora[1] that flickered now orange, now silver, now blue. There was a sound like a gigantic bonfire burning all of Time, all the years and all the parchment calendars, all the hours piled high and set aflame.

A touch of the hand and this burning would, on the instant, beautifully reverse itself. Eckels remembered the wording in the advertisements to the letter. Out of chars and ashes, out of dust and coals, like golden salamanders, the old years, the green years, might leap; roses sweeten the air, white hair turn Irish-black, wrinkles vanish; all, everything fly back to seed, flee death, rush down to their beginnings, suns rise in western skies and set in glorious easts, moons eat themselves opposite to the custom, all and everything cupping one in another like Chinese boxes,[2] rabbits into hats, all and everything returning to the fresh death, the seed death, the green death, to the time before the beginning. A

---

1. **aurora:** a light that changes colors.
2. **Chinese boxes:** a series of boxes, each of which fits neatly inside the next larger one.

touch of a hand might do it, the merest touch of a hand.

"Unbelievable." Eckels breathed, the light of the Machine on his thin face. "A real Time Machine." He shook his head. "Makes you think. If the election had gone badly yesterday, I might be here now running away from the results. Thank God Keith won. He'll make a fine President of the United States."

"Yes," said the man behind the desk. "We're lucky. If Deutscher had gotten in, we'd have the worst kind of dictatorship. There's an anti-everything man for you, a militarist, anti-Christ, anti-human, anti-intellectual. People called us up, you know, joking but not joking. Said if Deutscher became President they wanted to go live in 1492. Of course it's not our business to conduct Escapes, but to form Safaris. Anyway, Keith's President now. All you got to worry about is—"

"Shooting my dinosaur," Eckels finished it for him.

"A *Tyrannosaurus rex*. The Tyrant Lizard, the most incredible monster in history. Sign this release. Anything happens to you, we're not responsible. Those dinosaurs are hungry."

Eckels flushed angrily. "Trying to scare me!"

"Frankly, yes. We don't want anyone going who'll panic at the first shot. Six Safari leaders were killed last year, and a dozen hunters. We're here to give you the severest thrill a *real* hunter ever asked for. Traveling you back sixty million years to bag the biggest game in all of Time. Your personal check's still there. Tear it up."

Mr. Eckels looked at the check. His fingers twitched.

"Good luck," said the man behind the desk. "Mr. Travis, he's all yours."

They moved silently across the room, taking their guns with them, toward the Machine, toward the silver metal and the roaring light.

First a day and then a night and then a day and then a night, then it was day-night-day-night-day. A week, a month, a year, a decade! A.D. 2055. A.D. 2019. 1999! 1957! Gone! The Machine roared.

They put on their oxygen helmets and tested the intercoms.

Eckels swayed on the padded seat, his face pale, his jaw stiff. He felt the trembling in his arms, and he looked down and found his hands tight on the new rifle. There were four other men in the Machine. Travis, the Safari Leader; his assistant, Lesperance; and two other hunters, Billings and Kramer. They sat looking at each other, and the years blazed around them.

"Can these guns get a dinosaur cold?" Eckels felt his mouth saying.

"If you hit them right," said Travis on the helmet radio. "Some dinosaurs have two brains, one in the head, another far down the spinal column. We stay away from those. That's stretching luck. Put your first two shots into the eyes, if you can, blind them, and go back into the brain."

The Machine howled. Time was a film run backward. Suns fled, and ten million moons fled after them. "Think," said Eckels. "Every hunter that ever lived would envy us today. This makes Africa seem like Illinois."

The Machine slowed; its scream fell to a murmur. The Machine stopped.

The sun stopped in the sky.

The fog that had enveloped the Machine blew away, and they were in an old time, a very old time indeed, three hunters and two Safari Heads with their blue metal guns across their knees.

"Christ isn't born yet," said Travis. "Moses has not gone to the mountain to talk with God. The Pyramids are still in the earth, waiting to be cut out and put up. *Remember* that. Alexander, Caesar, Napoleon, Hitler—none of them exists."

The man nodded.

"That"—Mr. Travis pointed—"is the jungle of sixty million two thousand and fifty-five years before President Keith."

He indicated a metal path that struck off into green wilderness, over streaming swamp, among giant ferns and palms.

"And that," he said, "is the Path, laid by Time Safari for your use. It floats six inches above the earth. Doesn't touch so much as one grass blade, flower, or tree. It's an antigravity metal. Its purpose is to keep you from touching this world of the past in any way. Stay on the Path. Don't go off it. I repeat. *Don't go off*. For *any* reason! If you fall off, there's a penalty. And don't shoot any animal we don't okay."

"Why?" asked Eckels.

They sat in the ancient wilderness. Far birds' cries blew on a wind, and the smell of tar and an old salt sea, moist grasses, and flowers the color of blood.

"We don't want to change the Future. We don't belong here in the Past. The government doesn't *like* us here. We have to pay big graft to keep our franchise.[3] A Time Machine is finicky business. Not knowing it, we might kill an important animal, a small bird, a roach, a flower even, thus destroying an important link in a growing species."

"That's not clear," said Eckels.

"All right," Travis continued, "say we accidentally kill one mouse here. That means all the future families of this one particular mouse are destroyed, right?"

"Right."

"And all the families of the families of the

families of that one mouse! With a stamp of your foot, you <u>annihilate</u> first one, then a dozen, then a thousand, a million, a *billion* possible mice!"

"So they're dead," said Eckels. "So what?"

"So what?" Travis snorted quietly. "Well, what about the foxes that'll need those mice to survive? For want of ten mice, a fox dies. For want of ten foxes, a lion starves. For want of a lion, all manner of insects, vultures, infinite billions of life forms are thrown into chaos and destruction. Eventually it all boils down to this: fifty-nine million years later, a caveman, one of a dozen on the *entire world,* goes hunting wild boar or saber-toothed tiger for food. But you,

"Unbelievable." Eckels breathed, the light of the Machine on his face. "A real Time Machine."

friend, have *stepped* on all the tigers in that region. By stepping on *one* single mouse. So the caveman starves. And the caveman, please note, is not just *any* <u>expendable</u> man, no! He is an *entire future nation*. From his loins would have sprung ten sons. From *their* loins one hundred sons, and thus onward to a civilization. Destroy this one man, and you destroy a race, a people, an entire history of life. It is comparable to slaying some of Adam's grandchildren. The stomp of your foot, on one mouse, could start an earthquake, the effects

---

3. **graft to keep our franchise:** money paid as a bribe to officials in return for their approval of the business.

WORDS TO KNOW

annihilate (ə-nī′ə-lāt′) *v.* to destroy completely; wipe out
expendable (ĭk-spĕn′də-bəl) *adj.* dispensable; unnecessary

685

of which could shake our earth and destinies down through Time, to their very foundations. With the death of that one caveman, a billion others yet unborn are throttled in the womb. Perhaps Rome never rises on its seven hills. Perhaps Europe is forever a dark forest, and only Asia waxes healthy and teeming. Step on a mouse, and you crush the Pyramids. Step on a mouse, and you leave your print, like a Grand Canyon, across Eternity. Queen Elizabeth might never be born; Washington might not cross the Delaware; there might never be a United States at all. So be careful. Stay on the Path. *Never* step off!"

"I see," said Eckels. "Then it wouldn't pay for us even to touch the *grass?*"

"Correct. Crushing certain plants could add up <u>infinitesimally</u>. A little error here would multiply in sixty million years, all out of proportion. Of course maybe our theory is wrong. Maybe Time *can't* be changed by us. Or maybe it can be changed only in little subtle ways. A dead mouse here makes an insect imbalance there, a population disproportion later, a bad harvest further on, a depression, mass starvation, and, finally, a change in *social* temperament in far-flung countries. Something much more subtle, like that. Perhaps only a soft breath, a whisper, a hair, pollen on the air, such a slight, slight change that unless you looked close you wouldn't see it. Who knows? Who really can say he knows? We don't know. We're guessing.

Illustration Copyright © Douglas Henderson. From *The Complete T-Rex* by John Horner and Don Lessem, published by Simon & Schuster.

But until we do know for certain whether our messing around in Time *can* make a big roar or a little rustle in history, we're being careful. This Machine, this Path, your clothing and bodies, were sterilized, as you know, before the journey. We wear these oxygen helmets so we can't introduce our bacteria into an ancient atmosphere."

"How do we know which animals to shoot?"

WORDS TO KNOW   **infinitesimally** (ĭn′fĭn-ĭ-tĕs′ə-mə-lē) *adv.* in steps so small as to be immeasurable or incalculable

or one that drowns in a tar pit, I note the exact hour, minute, and second. I shoot a paint bomb. It leaves a red patch on his side. We can't miss it. Then I correlate our arrival in the Past so that we meet the Monster not more than two minutes before he would have died anyway. This way, we kill only animals with no future, that are never going to mate again. You see how *careful* we are?"

"But if you came back this morning in Time," said Eckels eagerly, "you must've bumped into *us,* our Safari! How did it turn out? Was it successful? Did all of us get through—alive?"

Travis and Lesperance gave each other a look.

"That'd be a paradox," said the latter. "Time doesn't permit that sort of mess—a man meeting himself. When such occasions threaten, Time steps aside. Like an airplane hitting an air pocket. You felt the Machine jump just before we stopped? That was us passing ourselves on the way back to the Future. We saw nothing. There's no way of telling *if* this expedition was a success, *if we* got our monster, or whether all of us—meaning *you,* Mr. Eckels—got out alive."

Eckels smiled palely.

"Cut that," said Travis sharply. "Everyone on his feet!"

They were ready to leave the Machine.

The jungle was high and the jungle was broad and the jungle was the entire world forever and forever. Sounds like music and sounds like flying tents filled the sky, and those

"They're marked with red paint," said Travis. "Today, before our journey, we sent Lesperance here back with the Machine. He came to this particular era and followed certain animals."

"Studying them?"

"Right," said Lesperance. "I track them through their entire existence, noting which of them lives longest. Very few. How many times they mate. Not often. Life's short. When I find one that's going to die when a tree falls on him,

were pterodactyls[4] soaring with cavernous gray wings, gigantic bats of delirium and night fever.[5] Eckels, balanced on the narrow Path, aimed his rifle playfully.

"Stop that!" said Travis. "Don't even aim for fun, blast you! If your guns should go off—"

Eckels flushed. "Where's our *Tyrannosaurus?*"

Lesperance checked his wristwatch. "Up ahead. We'll bisect his trail in sixty seconds. Look for the red paint! Don't shoot till we give the word. Stay on the Path. *Stay on the Path!*"

They moved forward in the wind of morning.

"Strange," murmured Eckels. "Up ahead, sixty million years, Election Day over. Keith made President. Everyone celebrating. And here we are, a million years lost, and they don't exist. The things we worried about for months, a lifetime, not even born or thought of yet."

"Safety catches off, everyone!" ordered Travis. "You, first shot, Eckels. Second, Billings.

"Ahead," he whispered. "In the mist. There he is. There's His Royal Majesty now."

Third, Kramer."

"I've hunted tiger, wild boar, buffalo, elephant, but now, this is *it*," said Eckels. "I'm shaking like a kid."

"Ah," said Travis.

Everyone stopped.

Travis raised his hand. "Ahead," he whispered. "In the mist. There he is. There's His Royal Majesty now."

The jungle was wide and full of twitterings, rustlings, murmurs, and sighs.

Suddenly it all ceased, as if someone had shut a door.

Silence.

A sound of thunder.

Out of the mist, one hundred yards away, came *Tyrannosaurus rex*.

"It," whispered Eckels. "It . . ."

"Sh!"

It came on great oiled, <u>resilient</u>, striding legs. It towered thirty feet above half of the trees, a great evil god, folding its delicate watchmaker's claws close to its oily reptilian chest. Each lower leg was a piston, a thousand pounds of white bone, sunk in thick ropes of muscle, <u>sheathed</u> over in a gleam of pebbled skin like the mail of a terrible warrior. Each thigh was a ton of meat, ivory, and steel mesh. And from the great breathing cage of the upper body those two delicate arms dangled out front, arms with hands which might pick up and examine men like toys, while the snake neck coiled. And the head itself, a ton of sculptured stone, lifted easily upon the sky. Its mouth gaped, exposing a fence of teeth like daggers. Its eyes rolled, ostrich eggs, empty of all expression save hunger. It closed its mouth in a death grin. It ran, its pelvic bones crushing aside trees and bushes, its taloned feet clawing damp earth, leaving prints six inches deep wherever it settled its weight. It ran with a gliding ballet step, far too poised and balanced for its ten tons. It moved into a sunlit arena warily, its beautifully reptilian hands feeling the air.

"Why, why," Eckels twitched his mouth. "It could reach up and grab the moon."

"Sh!" Travis jerked angrily. "He hasn't seen us yet."

---

4. **pterodactyls** (tĕr′ə-dăk′təlz): extinct flying reptiles having a wingspan of up to 40 feet.

5. **bats . . . fever:** the sort of bats that appear in nightmares and visions caused by drugs or illness.

"It can't be killed." Eckels pronounced this verdict quietly, as if there could be no argument. He had weighed the evidence, and this was his considered opinion. The rifle in his hands seemed a cap gun. "We were fools to come. This is impossible."

"Shut up!" hissed Travis.

"Nightmare."

"Turn around," commanded Travis. "Walk quietly to the Machine. We'll remit one-half your fee."

"I didn't realize it would be this *big*," said Eckels. "I miscalculated, that's all. And now I want out."

"It *sees* us!"

"There's the red paint on its chest!"

The Tyrant Lizard raised itself. Its armored flesh glittered like a thousand green coins. The coins, crusted with slime, steamed. In the slime, tiny insects wriggled, so that the entire body seemed to twitch and <u>undulate</u>, even while the monster itself did not move. It exhaled. The stink of raw flesh blew down the wilderness.

"Get me out of here," said Eckels. "It was never like this before. I was always sure I'd come through alive. I had good guides, good safaris, and safety. This time, I figured wrong. I've met my match and admit it. This is too much for me to get hold of."

"Don't run," said Lesperance. "Turn around. Hide in the Machine."

"Yes." Eckels seemed to be numb. He looked at his feet as if trying to make them move. He gave a grunt of helplessness.

"Eckels!"

Copyright © 1996 Glenn Dean.

He took a few steps, blinking, shuffling. "Not *that* way!"

The Monster, at the first motion, lunged forward with a terrible scream. It covered one hundred yards in six seconds. The rifles jerked up and blazed fire. A windstorm from the beast's mouth engulfed them in the stench of slime and old blood. The Monster roared, teeth glittering with sun.

Eckels, not looking back, walked blindly to the edge of the Path, his gun limp in his arms, stepped off the Path, and walked, not knowing it, in the jungle. His feet sank into green moss. His legs moved him, and he felt alone and remote from the events behind.

The rifles cracked again. Their sound was lost in shriek and lizard thunder. The great level of the reptile's tail swung up, lashed sideways. Trees exploded in clouds of leaf and branch. The Monster twitched its jeweler's hands down to fondle at the men, to twist them in half, to crush them like berries, to cram them into its teeth and its screaming throat. Its boulder-stone eyes leveled with the men. They saw themselves mirrored. They fired at the metallic eyelids and the blazing black iris.

Like a stone idol, like a mountain avalanche, *Tyrannosaurus* fell. Thundering, it clutched trees, pulled them with it. It wrenched and tore the metal Path. The men flung themselves back and away. The body hit, ten tons of cold flesh and stone. The guns fired. The Monster lashed its armored tail, twitched its snake jaws, and lay still. A fount of blood spurted from its throat. Somewhere inside, a sac of fluids burst. Sickening gushes drenched the hunters. They stood, red and glistening.

The thunder faded.

The jungle was silent. After the avalanche, a green peace. After the nightmare, morning.

Billings and Kramer sat on the pathway and threw up. Travis and Lesperance stood with smoking rifles, cursing steadily.

In the Time Machine, on his face, Eckels lay shivering. He had found his way back to the Path, climbed into the Machine.

Travis came walking, glanced at Eckels, took cotton gauze from a metal box, and returned to the others, who were sitting on the Path.

"Clean up."

They wiped the blood from their helmets. They began to curse too. The Monster lay, a hill of solid flesh. Within, you could hear the sighs and murmurs as the furthest chambers of it died, the organs malfunctioning, liquids running a final instant from pocket to sac to spleen, everything shutting off, closing up forever. It was like standing by a wrecked locomotive or a steam shovel at quitting time, all valves being released or levered tight. Bones cracked; the tonnage of its own flesh, off balance, dead weight, snapped the delicate forearms, caught underneath. The meat settled, quivering.

Another cracking sound. Overhead, a gigantic tree branch broke from its heavy mooring, fell. It crashed upon the dead beast with finality.

In the Time Machine, on his face, Eckels lay shivering.

"There." Lesperance checked his watch. "Right on time. That's the giant tree that was scheduled to fall and kill this animal originally." He glanced at the two hunters. "You want the trophy picture?"

"What?"

"We can't take a trophy back to the Future. The body has to stay right here where it would have died originally, so the insects, birds, and bacteria can get at it, as they were intended to. Everything in balance. The body stays. But we *can* take a picture of you standing near it."

The two men tried to think, but gave up, shaking their heads.

They let themselves be led along the metal Path. They sank wearily into the Machine cushions. They gazed back at the ruined Monster, the stagnating mound, where already strange reptilian birds and golden insects were busy at the steaming armor.

A sound on the floor of the Time Machine stiffened them. Eckels sat there, shivering.

"I'm sorry," he said at last.

"Get up!" cried Travis.

Eckels got up.

"Go out on that Path alone," said Travis. He had his rifle pointed. "You're not coming back in the Machine. We're leaving you here!"

Lesperance seized Travis's arm. "Wait—"

"Stay out of this!" Travis shook his hand away. "This fool nearly killed us. But it isn't *that* so much, no. It's his *shoes*! Look at them! He ran off the Path. That *ruins* us! We'll forfeit! Thousands of dollars of insurance! We guarantee no one leaves the Path. He left it. Oh, the fool! I'll have to report to the government. They might revoke our license to travel. Who knows *what* he's done to Time, to History!"

"Take it easy; all he did was kick up some dirt."

"How do we *know?*" cried Travis. "We don't know anything! It's all a mystery! Get out there, Eckels!"

Eckels fumbled his shirt. "I'll pay anything. A hundred thousand dollars!"

Travis glared at Eckels's checkbook and spat. "Go out there. The Monster's next to the Path. Stick your arms up to your elbows in his mouth. Then you can come back with us."

"That's unreasonable!"

"The Monster's dead, you idiot. The bullets! The bullets can't be left behind. They don't belong in the Past; they might change anything. Here's my knife. Dig them out!"

The jungle was alive again, full of the old tremorings and bird cries. Eckels turned slowly to regard the primeval garbage dump, that hill of nightmares and terror. After a long time, like a sleepwalker he shuffled out along the Path.

He returned, shuddering, five minutes later, his arms soaked and red to the elbows. He held out his hands. Each held a number of steel bullets. Then he fell. He lay where he fell, not moving.

"You didn't have to make him do that," said Lesperance.

"Didn't I? It's too early to tell." Travis nudged the still body. "He'll live. Next time he won't go hunting game like this. Okay." He jerked his thumb wearily at Lesperance. "Switch on. Let's go home."

1492. 1776. 1812.

They cleaned their hands and faces. They changed their caking shirts and pants. Eckels was up and around again, not speaking. Travis glared at him for a full ten minutes.

"Don't look at me," cried Eckels. "I haven't done anything."

"Who can tell?"

"Just ran off the Path, that's all, a little mud on my shoes—what do you want me to do—get down and pray?"

"We might need it. I'm warning you, Eckels, I might kill you yet. I've got my gun ready."

"I'm innocent. I've done nothing!"

1999. 2000. 2055.

The Machine stopped.

"Get out," said Travis.

The room was there as they had left it. But not the same as they had left it. The same man sat behind the same desk. But the same man did not quite sit behind the same desk.

Travis looked around swiftly. "Everything okay here?" he snapped.

"Fine. Welcome home!"

Travis did not relax. He seemed to be looking at the very atoms of the air itself, at the way the sun poured through the one high window.

"Okay, Eckels, get out. Don't ever come back."

WORDS TO KNOW **revoke** (rĭ-vōk´) *v.* to cancel or withdraw
primeval (prī-mē´vəl) *adj.* belonging to the earliest times or ages

691

Eckels could not move.

"You heard me," said Travis. "What're you *staring* at?"

Eckels stood smelling of the air, and there was a thing to the air, a chemical <u>taint</u> so subtle, so slight, that only a faint cry of his <u>subliminal</u> senses warned him it was there. The colors, white, gray, blue, orange, in the wall, in the furniture, in the sky beyond the window, were . . . were . . . And there was a *feel*. His flesh twitched. His hands twitched. He stood drinking the oddness with the pores of his body. Somewhere, someone must have been screaming one of those whistles that only a dog can hear. His body screamed silence in return. Beyond this room, beyond this wall, beyond this man who was not quite the same man seated at this desk that was not quite the same desk . . . lay an entire world of streets and people. What sort of world it was now, there was no telling. He could feel them moving there, beyond the walls, almost, like so many chess pieces blown in a dry wind. . . .

But the immediate thing was the sign painted on the office wall, the same sign he had read earlier today on first entering.

Somehow, the sign had changed:

TYME SEFARI INC.

SEFARIS TU ANY YEER EN THE PAST.

YU NAIM THE ANIMALL.

WEE TAEKYUTHAIR.

YU SHOOT ITT.

Eckels felt himself fall into a chair. He fumbled crazily at the thick slime on his boots. He held up a clod of dirt, trembling, "No, it *can't* be. Not a *little* thing like that. No!"

Embedded in the mud, glistening green and gold and black, was a butterfly, very beautiful and very dead.

"Not a little thing like *that!* Not a butterfly!" cried Eckels.

It fell to the floor, an exquisite thing, a small thing that could upset balances and knock down a line of small dominoes and then big dominoes and then gigantic dominoes, all down the years across Time. Eckels's mind whirled. It *couldn't* change things. Killing one butterfly couldn't be *that* important! Could it?

His face was cold. His mouth trembled, asking: "Who—who won the presidential election yesterday?"

The man behind the desk laughed. "You joking? You know very well. Deutscher, of course! Who else? Not that fool weakling Keith. We got an iron man now, a man with guts!" The official stopped. "What's wrong?"

Eckels moaned. He dropped to his knees. He scrabbled at the golden butterfly with shaking fingers. "Can't we," he pleaded to the world, to himself, to the officials, to the Machine, "can't we take it *back;* can't we *make* it alive again? Can't we start over? Can't we—"

He did not move. Eyes shut, he waited, shivering. He heard Travis breathe loud in the room; he heard Travis shift his rifle, click the safety catch, and raise the weapon.

There was a sound of thunder. ❖

WORDS TO KNOW

taint (tānt) *n.* a trace of something that harms, spoils, or corrupts

subliminal (sŭb-lĭm′ə-nəl) *adj.* below the threshold of conscious perception; subconscious

RESPONDING OPTIONS

FROM PERSONAL RESPONSE TO CRITICAL ANALYSIS

REFLECT

1. What were your thoughts as you heard the "sound of thunder" at the end of the story? Briefly describe them in your notebook.

RETHINK

2. How would you describe Eckels?
   Consider
   - his reasons for going on a safari
   - his response to the tyrannosaurus
   - his attitude about stepping off the path

3. Review what you wrote for the Writing Connection on page 682. How do your responses compare with what happens to Eckels?

4. In your opinion, what is the theme, or message, of the story?
   Consider
   - the business practices of Time Safari, Inc.
   - the society Eckels returns to as compared with the society depicted at the beginning of the story
   - the significance of the butterfly

RELATE

5. What activities of today might be compared to Eckels's accidental killing of the butterfly? Cite examples of small actions that may have big effects on the future.

ANOTHER PATHWAY

Cooperative Learning

Working in a small group, rewrite this story as a radio play that includes a narrator and dialogue. You may also wish to provide sound effects. Then present the play to your classmates.

QUICKWRITES

1. Make an **annotated time line** that plots the events in "A Sound of Thunder," giving a brief description of each event. If you have a graphics program on your computer, try using it to design your time line.

2. Draft your own **science fiction story** about time travel, dinosaurs, or another idea that "A Sound of Thunder" may inspire. Your class discussion for the Personal Connection on page 682 may also trigger some ideas.

3. Create a National Park Service **brochure** explaining why it is essential that people leave the parks unchanged after a visit. You may use the information that Travis provides about how slight changes in an environment can produce unintended effects.

PORTFOLIO Save your writing. You may want to use it later as a springboard to a piece for your portfolio.

LITERARY CONCEPTS

Science fiction is prose writing in which the writer explores unexpected possibilities of the past or the future, using known scientific data and theories as well as his or her imagination. Most science fiction comments on present-day society through the writer's fictional conception of a past or future society. Think about your response to question 4, which asked you to analyze the theme of the story. Could this theme have been conveyed through a style of writing other than science fiction?

CONCEPT REVIEW: Style Bradbury often capitalizes words that ordinarily are not capitalized. Find at least three examples of this and discuss why Bradbury might have chosen to use capitalization in this way.

ALTERNATIVE ACTIVITIES

1. Create a **poster** or a **magazine ad** that Time Safari, Inc., might use to advertise its services. You may wish to draw upon Bradbury's description of such an advertisement in the sixth paragraph of the story.

2. View the film *Jurassic Park,* or read the Michael Crichton novel of the same name, on which the film is based. Then give an **oral commentary,** comparing the film or book with Bradbury's story.

CRITIC'S CORNER

In a review of *Dinosaur Tales,* the collection of Bradbury stories containing "A Sound of Thunder," the critic Andrew Andrews remarks that Bradbury "gets to you—in simple ways he shows you how to marvel over these awesome, startling creatures." What was your own reaction to the portrayal of the dinosaurs in the story?

LITERARY LINKS

Compare Joan Aiken's depiction of the future in "Searching for Summer" with Bradbury's depiction of the future in this story. In your opinion, which story delivers a stronger message?

THE WRITER'S STYLE

Ray Bradbury is famous for a lyrical style in which he uses **images, figurative language,** and poetic devices such as **rhythm** and **repetition** to make his prose descriptions vivid. For example, Bradbury describes the dinosaur's hands metaphorically as "watchmaker's claws" and "jeweler's hands." Reread his description of the dinosaur—the paragraph beginning, "It came on great oiled, resilient, striding legs," on page 688. With a partner, make a list of the evidence you find of Bradbury's lyrical style. Share your list with others.

ACROSS THE CURRICULUM

Science Have you ever heard of the "butterfly effect"—the notion that the flapping of a butterfly's wings can change the weather? With a partner, research the connection between the butterfly effect and chaos theory, the field of science that studies the apparently random or irregular behavior of systems in nature. Then, in an oral report for your classmates, explain how the story reflects these scientific theories.

WORDS TO KNOW

For each group of words below, write the letter of the word that is the best synonym of the boldfaced word.

1. **infinitesimally:** (a) lastingly, (b) microscopically, (c) happily

2. **undulate:** (a) hover, (b) ripple, (c) surrender

3. **revoke:** (a) repeat, (b) modify, (c) repeal

4. **primeval:** (a) wicked, (b) ancient, (c) best

5. **resilient:** (a) elastic, (b) shiny, (c) weak

6. **expendable:** (a) difficult, (b) costly, (c) nonessential

7. **annihilate:** (a) demolish, (b) confuse, (c) restore

8. **taint:** (a) purity, (b) rotation, (c) contamination

9. **subliminal:** (a) instinctive, (b) underground, (c) inhuman

10. **sheathed:** (a) exposed, (b) surrounded, (c) beautified

RAY BRADBURY

1920–

One of America's foremost writers of fantasy and science fiction, Ray Bradbury describes himself as "that special freak, the man with the child inside who remembers all." Bradbury grew up in the town of Waukegan, Illinois—the "Green Town" of some of his tales— and later moved to Los Angeles.

His early years were haunted by nightmares and thrilling fantasies, which he later transformed into ideas for his fiction. An avid reader and movie buff, Bradbury made story writing a top priority from the age of 12, spending at least four hours a day at his typewriter.

After graduating from high school, Bradbury continued to write stories and supported himself by selling newspapers on a Los Angeles street corner. He became a full-time fiction writer in the early 1940s, after the so-called pulp magazines devoted to science fiction began publishing his tales. Before long, mainstream publications such as *Collier's* and *The Saturday Evening Post* also began publishing his work, and his early dream of being anthologized in *The Best American Short Stories* came true in 1946. Four years later, he published *The Martian Chronicles,* a series of interconnected stories about the colonization of Mars. The work, which drew critical praise and established Bradbury's reputation, was eventually translated into 30 languages and sold millions of copies.

Bradbury went on to write hundreds of stories, as well as novels, plays, television scripts, essays, and children's books. "Science fiction is the most important literature in the history of the world," he once said, "because it's the history of ideas, the history of our civilization birthing itself."

OTHER WORKS *The Illustrated Man, Dandelion Wine, Something Wicked This Way Comes, Fahrenheit 451, The Stories of Ray Bradbury*

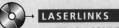

LASERLINKS
- *LITERARY CONNECTION*
- *SCIENCE CONNECTION*

PREVIEWING

Poem on Returning to Dwell in the Country
Tao Qian (tou' chē-än') China

The Sun
Mary Oliver United States

PERSONAL CONNECTION

Have you ever watched the sun rise or set? Have you ever felt the tug of an ocean's undercurrent or smelled freshly mown grass? Think of an experience with nature, whether in the countryside or in a park, that gave you a positive feeling. Spend the next few minutes writing in your notebook about that experience.

BIOGRAPHICAL CONNECTION

About 1,600 years passed between the time the Chinese poet Tao Qian wrote "Poem on Returning to Dwell in the Country" and the time the contemporary American poet Mary Oliver wrote "The Sun." Although these poets are from different eras and from opposite sides of the globe, they have an important thing in common: a love and appreciation of nature.

Tao Qian worked for several years in government service, an occupation that he disliked. He resigned his position and, although he was offered other ones, returned to his quiet life as a country farmer. "Poem on Returning to Dwell in the Country" describes this return. Like Tao Qian, Mary Oliver writes poems that reflect the connection she feels with nature. Much of her poetry describes the external world and connects it to internal emotional states.

READING CONNECTION

Identifying the Author's Tone As you read the two poems, think about their tones—the feeling about or attitude toward nature that each poet is trying to express. In your notebook, make a chart like the one shown, listing words or phrases from each poem that are clues to the poet's tone.

Tao Qian	Mary Oliver
1. vulgar	1.
2.	2.
3.	3.

POEM ON RETURNING TO DWELL IN THE COUNTRY

TAO QIAN

In youth I had nothing
    that matched the vulgar tone,
For my nature always
    loved the hills and mountains.
5 Inadvertently I fell
    into the Dusty Net,
Once having gone
    it was more than thirteen years.
The tame bird
10 longs for his old forest—
The fish in the house-pond
    thinks of his ancient pool.
I too will break the soil
    at the edge of the southern moor,
15 I will guard simplicity
    and return to my fields and garden.
My land and house—
    a little more than ten acres,

2 vulgar: coarse; lacking culture and refinement; indecent.

5 inadvertently: unintentionally.

6 Dusty Net: a reference to worldliness and materialism.

In the thatched cottage—
20   only eight or nine rooms.
Elms and willows
        shade the back verandah,
Peach and plum trees
        in rows before the hall.
25   Hazy and dimly seen
        a village in the distance,
Close in the foreground
        the smoke of neighbors' houses.
A dog barks
30   amidst the deep lanes,
A cock is crowing
        atop a mulberry tree.
No dust and confusion
        within my doors and courtyard;
35   In the empty rooms,
        more than sufficient leisure.
Too long I was held
        within the barred cage.
Now I am able
40   to return again to Nature.

Translated by William Acker

FROM **PERSONAL RESPONSE** *TO* **CRITICAL ANALYSIS**

REFLECT   **1.** After reading this poem, what impressions linger in your mind? Share them with a classmate.

RETHINK   **2.** How would you describe the speaker's views of nature and society?
Consider
- what you can tell about the speaker's childhood
- how the speaker might have spent the last 13 years
- the kind of life the speaker now wants to live
- the chart that you completed for the Reading Connection on page 696

3. Are your own experiences with nature and society similar to or different from the speaker's? Explain your answer.

RELATE   **4.** How do you think the speaker would react to life in modern society?

The Sun

Mary Oliver

Have you ever seen
anything
in your life
more wonderful

5 than the way the sun,
every evening,
relaxed and easy,
floats toward the horizon

and into the clouds or the hills,
10 or the rumpled sea,
and is gone—
and how it slides again

out of the blackness,
every morning,
15 on the other side of the world,
like a red flower

streaming upward on its heavenly oils,
say, on a morning in early summer,
at its perfect imperial distance—
20 and have you ever felt for anything

19 imperial: of great size; majestic.

such wild love—
do you think there is anywhere, in any language,
a word billowing enough
for the pleasure

25 that fills you,
as the sun
reaches out,
as it warms you

as you stand there,
30 empty-handed—
or have you too
turned from this world—

or have you too
gone crazy
35 for power,
for things?

RESPONDING
OPTIONS

FROM PERSONAL RESPONSE TO CRITICAL ANALYSIS

REFLECT 1. What memories or thoughts did "The Sun" trigger in you? Jot them down in your notebook.

RETHINK 2. What message do you think is conveyed in the poem?

3. How would you describe the speaker's tone, or attitude, in lines 1–30?
   Consider
   - the speaker's description of the setting of the sun
   - the description of the rising of the sun
   - what might be meant by "wild love"
   - the chart that you completed for the Reading Connection on page 696

4. How would you describe the speaker's tone in lines 31–36?
   Consider
   - whom the speaker might be addressing
   - what the speaker means by "power" and "things"
   - the chart that you completed for the Reading Connection

RELATE 5. Compare the views on nature and society presented in "Poem on Returning to Dwell in the Country" and "The Sun."

ANOTHER PATHWAY
Cooperative Learning

Work in a small group to paraphrase, or restate in your own words, the five questions that the speaker asks in "The Sun." Then discuss your answers to these questions, drawing on your own experience with nature. How does your view of nature compare with Oliver's? Compare the responses in your group with those of other groups.

QUICKWRITES

1. Write a **press release** announcing Tao Qian's resignation from the government agency in which he worked. Include reasons why he is leaving.

2. In "The Sun," the speaker asks if anyone has seen anything more wonderful than the rising or the setting of the sun. Imagine that the answer is yes, and draft a **descriptive paragraph** about some other wonderful things that you have seen or can imagine.

3. Write a **poem** about your feelings toward nature or about your reaction to a specific natural phenomenon. You might want to use the writing that you did for the Personal Connection on page 696 as a springboard.

   📁 *PORTFOLIO Save your writing. You may want to use it later as a springboard to a piece for your portfolio.*

LITERARY CONCEPTS

Mood is the feeling, or atmosphere, that a writer creates for the reader. The moods of literary works can be described by words such as *sinister, cheerful, exciting, depressing, dreamlike, suspenseful, mysterious,* and *sentimental.* One element that contributes to the mood of a poem is its **imagery**—the words and phrases that re-create sensory experiences for the reader. For example, in lines 21–22 of Tao Qian's poem, the visual image of elms and willows shading the verandah helps create a calm, peaceful mood. With a partner, identify other images that you feel contribute to the mood of Tao Qian's poem. Then discuss how imagery affects the mood of "The Sun." Share your ideas with the rest of the class.

ALTERNATIVE ACTIVITIES

1. Create a **photographic display** of images that suggest the mood of one of the poems.

2. With a partner, create a **tape recording** of the two poems that reflects your individual interpretations of them. Take turns reading each poem into the recorder, then play back the tape and discuss the similarities and differences between the readings.

CRITIC'S CORNER

The critic David Kirby once wrote, "One of Ms. Oliver's hallmarks is plain speech." Find examples of this kind of speech in "The Sun."

TAO QIAN

A.D. 365–427

Tao Qian (sometimes spelled *Tao Chien* or *T'ao Ch'ien)* is often called China's first great poet of the "fields and gardens." Born into an upper-class family that had lost its wealth, he was forced to take a government job that he soon grew to despise. After about ten years he retired with his family to a rural village, where he began farming, gardening, and writing poetry. His new contentment is evident in his verse, which praises nature and the simple life.

Tao Qian was a master of *wu yen shih,* a form of Chinese verse made up of rhymed lines, each containing five Chinese characters (words). His simple style was not fashionable during his lifetime, and it was not until the Tang dynasty (A.D. 618–907) that his work was fully appreciated. Today, however, he is considered one of China's greatest poets. Because of his chosen isolation, he is affectionately known as Tao the Dweller-in-Hiding or Tao the Hermit.

OTHER WORKS *T'ao the Hermit: Sixty Poems by T'ao Ch'ien,* poems in *A Hundred and Seventy Chinese Poems,* poems in *Sunflower Splendor: Three Thousand Years of Chinese Poetry*

MARY OLIVER

Born in a suburb of Cleveland, Ohio, Mary Oliver (1935–) attended Ohio State University and Vassar College, although she never obtained a university degree. Her love of poetry brought her to Steepletop in upstate New York, the home of the poet Edna St. Vincent Millay, which became a writers' colony after Millay's death. There, Oliver worked for a time as secretary to Norma Millay, the poet's sister. She later settled in Provincetown, Massachusetts, a Cape Cod community known for its writers and artists.

Oliver has written more than eight volumes of poetry since 1963, when her first collection, *No Voyage and Other Poems,* was published. She won a Pulitzer Prize for *American Primitive* in 1984 and a National Book Award for her *New and Selected Poems* in 1992. She has also been a visiting professor or poet-in-residence at several universities. Her fellow poet Maxine Kumin once wrote that Oliver is a "guide to the natural world, particularly to its lesser-known aspects."

OTHER WORKS *The River Styx, Ohio, and Other Poems; The Night Traveler; Dream Work; A Poetry Handbook*

LASERLINKS
• *ART GALLERY*

PREVIEWING

NONFICTION

Once More to the Lake
E. B. White United States

PERSONAL CONNECTION

Think of a special place from childhood that you would like to revisit. In your notebook, jot down specific details that this place brings to mind and describe what you would hope to find if you returned there.

BIOGRAPHICAL CONNECTION

Although well-known for his classic children's books, such as *Stuart Little* and *Charlotte's Web,* E. B. White may be best known for his essays, which appeared for many years in *The New Yorker* magazine. He once described the essayist as a writer "sustained by the childish belief that everything he thinks about, everything that happens to him, is of general interest." Few writers have been able to capture the wonders of everyday life as well as White has. In the following essay, a simple visit to a lake becomes a moving experience.

1940 postcard of pond near Camden, Maine. Curt Teich Postcard Archives, Lake County (Illinois) Museum.

Understanding the Personal Essay

For E. B. White, the **personal essay** was a favorite form of writing. A personal essay is a brief nonfiction work that expresses the writer's thoughts, feelings, and opinions on a subject. This type of essay provides an opportunity for a writer to explore the meaning of events and issues in his or her own life.

The term *essay* derives from the works of the 16th-century French writer Michel de Montaigne (mē-shĕl' də mŏn-tān'), who called his explorations of various subjects *essais* (ĕ-sĕ'), French for "attempts." Montaigne's writings were personal and informal in nature. Since then, many other writers have followed in this literary tradition to explore a wide variety of subjects.

The following strategies will help you to appreciate the art of the personal essay:

Identify the writer's purpose. Most personal essays are written with more than a single purpose in mind. Besides wanting to share personal thoughts and experiences, the writer may write for the purpose of entertaining readers, informing them about a subject, or persuading them to act, think, or feel a certain way. As you read White's essay, try to determine his main purposes for writing.

Determine the theme. Identifying the writer's purpose often helps you to determine the meaning that the writer is deriving from ordinary events. When reading a personal essay like White's, ask yourself, What lessons or insights does the writer derive from his or her experiences and memories? How might these insights apply to my own experiences?

Recognize the tone. An important element in any personal essay is the writer's tone, or attitude toward his or her subject. In a sense, the tone of a personal essay is our glimpse into the personality behind the writing. When you read White's essay, think of words and phrases that might describe his tone.

Appreciate the style. Style is not what is said but rather how it is said. Elements such as word choice, length of sentences, tone, and degree of formality contribute to a writer's style. As you read White's work, think of how you would describe his style.

Use your reading log. When you are reading a personal essay, a reading log helps you to be an active reader, exploring your own thoughts and responses as you progress through the essay. While reading White's essay, record your responses to the questions inserted throughout the selection. Also jot down other thoughts and feelings that come to you as you read.

When reading a personal essay:
• Identify the writer's purpose.
• Determine the theme.
• Recognize the tone.
• Appreciate the style.
• Use your reading log.

Once More to the Lake

E. B. White

Illustration by Gary Head.

August 1941

One summer, along about 1904, my father rented a camp[1] on a lake in Maine and took us all there for the month of August. We all got ringworm[2] from some kittens and had to rub Pond's Extract on our arms and legs night and morning, and my father rolled over in a canoe with all his clothes on; but outside of that the vacation was a success and from then on none of us ever thought there was any place in the world like that lake in Maine. We returned summer after summer—always on August 1 for one month. I have since become a salt-water man, but sometimes in summer there are days when the restlessness of the tides and the fearful cold of the seawater and the incessant wind that blows across the afternoon and into the evening make me wish for the placidity of a lake in the woods. A few weeks ago this feeling got so strong I bought myself a couple of bass hooks and a spinner and returned to the lake where we used to go, for a week's fishing and to revisit old haunts.

I took along my son, who had never had any fresh water up his nose and who had seen lily pads only from train windows. On the journey over to the lake I began to wonder what it would be like. I wondered how time would have marred this unique, this holy spot—the coves and streams, the hills that the sun set behind, the camps and the paths behind the camps. I was sure that the tarred road would have found it out, and I wondered in what other ways it would be desolated. It is strange how much you can remember about places like that once you allow your mind to return into the grooves that lead back. You remember one thing, and that suddenly reminds you of another thing. I guess I remembered clearest of all the early mornings, when the lake was cool and motionless, remembered how the bedroom smelled of the lumber it was made of and of the wet woods whose scent entered through the screen. The partitions in the camp were thin and did not extend clear to the top of the rooms, and as I was always the first up I would dress softly so as not to wake the others, and sneak out into the sweet outdoors and start out in the canoe, keeping close along the shore in the long shadows of the pines. I remembered being very careful never to rub my paddle against the gunwale[3] for fear of disturbing the stillness of the cathedral.

The lake had never been what you would call a wild lake. There were cottages sprinkled around the shores, and it was in farming country although the shores of the lake were quite heavily wooded. Some of the cottages were owned by nearby farmers, and you would live at the shore and eat your meals at the farm-house. That's what our family did. But although it wasn't wild, it was a fairly large and undis-turbed lake and there were places in it that, to a child at least, seemed infinitely remote and primeval.

I was right about the tar: it led to within half a mile of the shore. But when I got back there, with my boy, and we settled into a camp near a

---

1. **camp:** a summer cottage.
2. **ringworm:** a contagious skin disease caused by a fungus that produces itchy, ring-shaped patches.
3. **gunwale** (gŭn'əl): the upper edge of the side of a boat.

WORDS
TO
KNOW   **haunt** (hônt) *n.* a place visited frequently

705

Morning of Life (1907), David Ericson. Oil on canvas, 27" × 22¼", collection of the Tweed Museum of Art, University of Minnesota, Duluth, gift of Mrs. E. L. Tuohy.

farmhouse and into the kind of summertime I had known, I could tell that it was going to be pretty much the same as it had been before—I knew it, lying in bed the first morning, smelling the bedroom and hearing the boy sneak quietly out and go off along the shore in a boat. I began to sustain the illusion that he was I, and therefore, by simple transposition, that I was my father. This sensation persisted, kept cropping up all the time we were there. It was not an entirely new feeling, but in this setting it grew much stronger. I seemed to be living a dual existence. I would be in the middle of

some simple act, I would be picking up a bait box or laying down a table fork, or I would be saying something, and suddenly it would be not

QUESTION

Why does White think of himself in terms of his father?

I but my father who was saying the words or making the gesture. It gave me a creepy sensation.

We went fishing the first morning. I felt the same damp moss covering the worms in the bait can, and saw the dragonfly alight on the tip of my rod as it hovered a few inches from the surface of the water. It was the arrival of this fly that convinced me beyond any doubt that everything was as it always had been, that the years were a mirage and that there had been no years. The small waves were the same, chucking the rowboat under the chin as we fished at anchor, and the boat was the same boat, the same color green and the ribs broken in the same places, and under the floorboards the same freshwater leavings and débris—the dead hellgrammite,[4] the wisps of moss, the rusty discarded fishhook, the dried blood from yesterday's catch. We stared silently at the tips of our rods, at the dragonflies that came and went. I lowered the tip of mine into the water, tentatively, pensively dislodging the fly, which darted two feet away, poised, darted two feet back, and came to rest again a little farther up the rod. There had been no years between the ducking of this dragonfly and the other one—the one that was part of memory. I looked at the boy, who was silently watching his fly, and it was my hands that held his rod, my eyes watching. I felt dizzy and didn't know which rod I was at the end of.

We caught two bass, hauling them in briskly as though they were mackerel, pulling them over the side of the boat in a businesslike

---

4. **hellgrammite:** the larva of an insect, often used as fish bait.

WORDS
TO
KNOW

tentatively (tĕn′tə-tĭv-lē) *adv.* hesitantly; uncertainly

manner without any landing net, and stunning them with a blow on the back of the head. When we got back for a swim before lunch, the lake was exactly where we had left it, the same number of inches from the dock, and there was only the merest suggestion of a breeze. This seemed an utterly enchanted sea, this lake you could leave to its own devices for a few hours and come back to, and find that it had not stirred, this constant and trustworthy body of water. In the shallows, the dark, water-soaked sticks and twigs, smooth and old, were undulating in clusters on the bottom against the clean ribbed sand, and the track of the mussel was plain. A school of minnows swam by, each minnow with its small individual shadow, doubling the attendance, so clear and sharp in the sunlight. Some of the other campers were in swimming, along the shore, one of them with a cake of soap, and the water felt thin and clear and unsubstantial. Over the years there had been this person with the cake of soap, this cultist, and here he was. There had been no years.

*U*p to the farmhouse to dinner through the teeming, dusty field, the road under our sneakers was only a two-track road. The middle track was missing, the one with the marks of the hooves and the splotches of dried, flaky manure. There had always been three tracks to choose from in choosing which track to walk in; now the choice was narrowed down to two. For a moment I missed terribly the middle alternative. But the way led past the tennis court, and something about the way it lay there in the sun reassured me; the tape had loosened along the back line, the alleys were green with plantains and other weeds, and the net (installed in June and removed in

September) sagged in the dry noon, and the whole place steamed with midday heat and hunger and emptiness. There was a choice of pie for dessert, and one was blueberry and one was apple, and the waitresses were the same country girls, there having been no passage of time, only the illusion of it as in a dropped curtain—the waitresses were still fifteen; their hair had been washed, that was the only difference—they had been to the movies and seen the pretty girls with the clean hair.

Summertime, oh, summertime, pattern of life <u>indelible</u>, the fade-proof lake, the woods unshatterable, the pasture with the sweet fern and the juniper forever and ever, summer without end; this was the background, and the life along the shore was the design, the cottagers with their innocent and tranquil design, their tiny docks with the flagpole and the American flag floating against the white clouds in the blue sky, the little paths over the roots of the trees leading from camp to camp and the paths leading back to the outhouses and the can of lime for sprinkling, and at the souvenir counters at the store the miniature birch-bark canoes and the postcards that showed things looking a little better than they looked. This was the American family at play, escaping the city heat, wondering whether the newcomers in the camp at the head of the cove were "common" or "nice," wondering whether it was true that the people who drove up for Sunday dinner at the farmhouse were turned away because there wasn't enough chicken.

It seemed to me, as I kept remembering all this, that those times and those summers had been infinitely precious and worth saving. There had been jollity and peace and goodness. The arriving (at the beginning

EVALUATE

Why do you think the summer means so much to White?

WORDS TO KNOW   **indelible** (ĭn-dĕl′ə-bəl) *adj.* impossible to remove or eliminate; permanent

of August) had been so big a business in itself, at the railway station the farm wagon drawn up, the first smell of the pine-laden air, the first glimpse of the smiling farmer, and the great importance of the trunks and your father's enormous authority in such matters, and the feel of the wagon under you for the long ten-mile haul, and at the top of the last long hill catching the first view of the lake after eleven months of not seeing this cherished body of water. The shouts and cries of the other campers when they saw you, and the trunks to be unpacked, to give up their rich burden. (Arriving was less exciting nowadays, when you sneaked up in your car and parked it under a tree near the camp and took out the bags and in five minutes it was all over, no fuss, no loud wonderful fuss about trunks.)

Peace and goodness and jollity. The only thing that was wrong now, really, was the sound of the place, an unfamiliar nervous sound of the outboard motors. This was the note that jarred, the one thing that would sometimes break the illusion and set the years moving. In those other summertimes all motors were inboard; and when they were at a little distance, the noise they made was a sedative, an ingredient of summer sleep. They were one-cylinder and two-cylinder engines, and some were make-and-break and some were jump-spark, but they all made a sleepy sound across the lake. The one-lungers throbbed and fluttered, and the twin-cylinder ones purred and purred, and that was a quiet sound, too. But now the campers all had outboards. In the daytime, in the hot mornings, these motors made a petulant, irritable sound; at night, in the still evening when the afterglow lit the water, they whined about one's ears like mosquitoes. My boy loved our rented outboard, and his great desire was to achieve single-handed

mastery over it, and authority, and he soon learned the trick of choking it a little (but not too much), and the adjustment of the needle valve. Watching him I would remember the things you could do with the old one-cylinder engine with the heavy flywheel, how you could have it eating out of your hand if you got really close to it spiritually. Motorboats in those days didn't have clutches, and you would make a landing by shutting off the motor at the proper time and coasting in with a dead rudder. But there was a way of reversing them, if you learned the trick, by cutting the switch and putting it on again exactly on the final dying revolution of the flywheel, so that it would kick back against compression and begin reversing. Approaching a dock in a strong following breeze, it was difficult to slow up sufficiently by the ordinary coasting method, and if a boy felt he had complete mastery over his motor, he was tempted to keep it running beyond its time and then reverse it a few feet from the dock. It took a cool nerve, because if you threw the switch a twentieth of a second too soon you would catch the flywheel when it still had speed enough to go up past center, and the boat would leap ahead, charging bull fashion at the dock.

We had a good week at the camp. The bass were biting well and the sun shone endlessly, day after day. We would be tired at night and lie down in the accumulated heat of the little bedrooms after the long hot day and the breeze would stir almost imperceptibly outside and the smell of the swamp drift in through the rusty screens. Sleep would come easily and in the morning the red squirrel would be on

WORDS TO KNOW · **petulant** (pĕch′ə-lənt) *adj.* showing unreasonable annoyance over little things

From the Potomac River Series, 1991, Diana Suttenfield. Mary Bell Galleries, Chicago.

the roof, tapping out his gay routine. I kept remembering everything, lying in bed in the mornings—the small steamboat that had a long rounded stern like the lip of a Ubangi,[5] and how quietly she ran on the moonlight sails, when the older boys played their mandolins and the girls sang and we ate doughnuts dipped in sugar, and how sweet the music was on the water in the shining night, and what it had felt like to think about girls then. After breakfast we would go up to the store and the things were in the same place—the minnows in a bottle, the plugs and spinners disarranged and pawed over by the youngsters from the boys' camp, the Fig Newtons and the Beeman's gum. Outside, the road was tarred and cars stood in front of the store. Inside, all was just as it had always been, except there was more Coca-Cola and not so much Moxie and root beer and birch beer and sarsaparilla. We would walk out with the bottle of pop apiece and sometimes the pop would backfire up our noses and hurt. We explored the streams, quietly, where the turtles slid off the sunny logs and dug their way into the soft bottom; and we lay on the town wharf and fed worms to the tame bass. Everywhere we went I had trouble making out which was I, the one walking at my side, the one walking in my pants.

CLARIFY

How does White's son remind him of himself?

One afternoon while we were there at that lake a thunderstorm came up. It was like the revival of an old melodrama that I had seen long ago with childish awe. The second-act climax of the drama of the electrical disturbance over a lake in America had not changed in any important respect. This was the big scene, still the big scene. The whole thing was so familiar, the first feeling of oppression and heat and a general air around camp of not wanting to go very far away. In midafternoon (it was all the same) a curious darkening of the sky, and a lull in everything that had made life tick; and then the way the boats suddenly swung the other way at their moorings with the coming of a breeze out of the new quarter, and the premonitory rumble. Then the kettledrum, then the snare, then the bass drum and cymbals, then crackling light against the dark, and the gods grinning and licking their chops in the hills. Afterward the calm, the rain steadily rustling in the calm lake, the return of light and hope and spirits, and the campers running out in joy and relief to go swimming in the rain, their bright cries perpetuating the deathless joke about how they were getting simply drenched, and the children screaming with delight at the new sensation of bathing in the rain, and the joke about getting drenched linking the generations in a strong indestructible chain. And the comedian who waded in carrying an umbrella.

When the others went swimming, my son said he was going in, too. He pulled his dripping trunks from the line where they had hung all through the shower and wrung them out. Languidly, and with no thought of going in, I watched him, his hard little body, skinny and bare, saw him wince slightly as he pulled up around his vitals the small, soggy, icy garment. As he buckled the swollen belt, suddenly my groin felt the chill of death. ❖

---

5. **Ubangi** (yōō-băng′gē): a woman of a people living near the Ubangi River in Africa, with pierced lips enlarged by saucerlike disks.

RESPONDING
OPTIONS

FROM PERSONAL RESPONSE TO CRITICAL ANALYSIS

REFLECT

1. In your notebook, draw a quick sketch of the scene from the essay that stands out most in your mind.

RETHINK

2. Why do you think this return trip to the lake is so important to White?

Consider

- what he remembers about his special childhood place
- the fact that he brings his son with him
- details in the first paragraph, in the sentence beginning, "I have since become a salt-water man . . ."

3. What do you make of White's phrase "the chill of death" in the last sentence of the essay? Explain your response.

4. What insights does White seem to gain from this experience?

Consider

- his identification with his son
- his identification with his father
- what has changed and what has stayed the same over time

5. Review the information provided in the Reading Connection on page 703. How would you describe the tone of this personal essay?

RELATE

6. In this essay, written more than half a century ago, White suggests that there is a "strong indestructible chain" linking the generations. Do you believe such a chain exists today? Explain your opinion.

CRITIC'S CORNER

White's friend and *New Yorker* colleague James Thurber once praised him for "those silver and crystal sentences which have a ring like nobody else's sentences in the world." In your opinion, which sentences in the essay might be described as "silver and crystal"?

ANOTHER PATHWAY
Cooperative Learning

How might this essay be different if it were written by the son? Discuss this question with a group of classmates. Then draft an essay that White's son might have written in school when asked to describe his summer vacation. Make sure to include the son's observations of his father.

QUICKWRITES

1. Think back to the special place you described for the Personal Connection on page 702. Write an **advertisement** for a travel magazine that re-creates the sensory experiences of being there.

2. Prepare the **script** that White might have used when giving a slide presentation to his neighbors after his return home.

3. Suppose developers are planning to clear away the cottages and build high-rise condominiums around this lake. Write an **editorial** for the local newspaper, opposing or approving of the plan.

PORTFOLIO Save your writing. You may want to use it later as a springboard to a piece for your portfolio.

ONCE MORE TO THE LAKE **711**

LITERARY CONCEPTS

Just as each person has a speaking voice, each writer has a writing voice. The term *voice* refers to a writer's unique use of language that allows a reader to "hear" a human personality in his or her writing. The elements of style that determine a writer's voice include **sentence structure, diction, and tone.** For example, some writers are noted for their reliance on short, simple sentences, while others make use of long, complicated ones. Certain writers use concrete words, such as *lake* or *cold,* which name things you can see, hear, feel, taste, or smell. Others prefer abstract terms like *memory,* which name things that cannot be perceived with the senses. A writer's tone also leaves its imprint on his or her personal voice. With a partner, review White's essay and describe his sentence structure, diction, and tone. How do these elements contribute to his voice?

CONCEPT REVIEW: Symbol As you may recall, a symbol is a person, place, or object that represents something beyond itself. What might the lake be a symbol of?

WORDS TO KNOW

EXERCISE A For each phrase in the first column, write the letter of the synonymous phrase in the second column.

1. **languidly** loiter   a. permanent pigment
2. **tentatively** tell   b. cross character
3. Harold's **haunt**   c. listlessly linger
4. **petulant** person   d. Harry's hangout
5. **indelible** ink   e. doubtfully disclose

EXERCISE B With a partner, try creating music that helps to convey the meanings of three of the Words to Know. You could clap out a rhythm, hum a tune, or use a musical instrument.

E. B. WHITE

In addition to being regarded as one of the 20th century's finest essayists, E. B. White has been acclaimed as a poet, humorist, and children's author. Born in Mount Vernon, New York, Elwyn Brooks White attended Cornell University, where he edited the college newspaper. In 1921, after serving in World War I and then completing his education at Cornell, he briefly worked as a reporter for the *Seattle Times* and served as mess boy on a ship to Alaska. On returning to the New York area, White began submitting his writing to the then-new magazine *The New Yorker.* He soon joined the *New Yorker* staff and remained associated with the magazine for the rest of his writing career.

The subject matter of White's essays is extremely varied—everything "from the tremor of a leaf in the afternoon sun to the malaise of modern man," as one critic observed. Often he wrote about rural Maine, where he enjoyed times in childhood and bought a farm for his family in 1937.

1899–1985

White is well-known for the 1959 edition of *The Elements of Style,* a writing manual that he coauthored with his former college professor William Strunk, Jr. He also collaborated with his wife, Katherine, in editing the 1941 anthology *A Subtreasury of American Humor.* His many literary awards include the National Medal for Literature and a Pulitzer Prize special citation.

OTHER WORKS *One Man's Meat, The Second Tree from the Corner, The Points of My Compass, Poems and Sketches of E. B. White*

PREVIEWING

By the Waters of Babylon
Stephen Vincent Benét (bĭ-nā′) United States

PERSONAL CONNECTION

Think about specific dates and events that mark the passage from childhood to adulthood in your own life. Are you considered an adult upon graduating from high school? Is moving away from home a sign of adulthood? Are there cultural or religious rituals that mark this important transition? Share your ideas in a class discussion.

CULTURAL CONNECTION

Most cultures have rites of passage to mark the journey from childhood to adulthood or from one role in life to another. Commonly, the participants in a rite of passage stop their normal activities, separate from their community in some way, and concentrate on gaining new knowledge or insights to prepare for their new roles. For example, when boys in some African cultures reach a certain age, they are removed from normal activities for several days or weeks. During this time they learn about their culture and acquire special skills to help them in their role as adult men. When the process is completed, the participants return to society and take up their new role in the community. In the selection you are about to read, John, the main character, goes on a journey that becomes a rite of passage and gives him new knowledge about his world.

Young Samburu man in Kenya participating in a ceremony on the final day of his rite of passage. From *Samburu* by Nigel Pavitt. Copyright © 1992 by Nigel Pavitt, reprinted by permission of Henry Holt and Co., Inc.

READING CONNECTION

Understanding Allusion An allusion is a reference to a historical or literary person, place, thing, or event with which the reader is assumed to be familiar. As you read the following story about the narrator's rite of passage, you may encounter allusions that the narrator himself does not understand. You may also come upon allusions that you do not immediately recognize. When you find a word or phrase that might be an allusion, try to offer your own explanation of its meaning. Then read on to see if your interpretation is correct. You might organize your thoughts in a chart like the one shown.

Allusion	Explanation
1.	
2.	

713

Starburst, Colin Hay.

The north and the west and the south are good hunting ground, but it is forbidden to go east. It is forbidden to go to any of the Dead Places except to search for metal, and then he who touches the metal must be a priest or the son of a priest. Afterwards, both the man and the metal must be purified. These are the rules and the laws; they are well made. It is forbidden to cross the great river and look upon the place that was the Place of the Gods—this is most strictly forbidden. We do not even say its name, though we know its name. It is there that spirits live, and demons— it is there that there are the ashes of the Great Burning. These things are forbidden—they have been forbidden since the beginning of time.

BY THE WATERS OF BABYLON

STEPHEN VINCENT BENÉT

My father is a priest; I am the son of a priest. I have been in the Dead Places near us, with my father—at first, I was afraid. When my father went into the house to search for the metal, I stood by the door, and my heart felt small and weak. It was a dead man's house, a spirit house. It did not have the smell of man, though there were old bones in a corner. But it is not fitting that a priest's son should show fear. I looked at the bones in the shadow and kept my voice still.

Then my father came out with the metal—a good, strong piece. He looked at me with both eyes, but I had not run away. He gave me the metal to hold—I took it and did not die. So he knew that I was truly his son and would be a priest in my time. That was when I was very young—nevertheless, my brothers would not have done it, though they are good hunters. After that, they gave me the good piece of meat and the warm corner by the fire. My father watched over me—he was glad that I should be a priest. But when I boasted or wept without a reason, he punished me more strictly than my brothers. That was right.

After a time, I myself was allowed to go into the dead houses and search for metal. So I learned the ways of those houses—and if I saw bones, I was no longer afraid. The bones are light and old—sometimes they will fall into dust if you touch them. But that is a great sin.

I was taught the chants and the spells—I was taught how to stop the running of blood from a wound and many secrets. A priest must know many secrets—that was what my father said. If the hunters think we do all things by chants and spells, they may believe so—it does not hurt them. I was taught how to read in the old books and how to make the old writings—that was hard and took a long time. My knowledge made me happy—it was like a fire in my heart. Most of all, I liked to hear of the Old Days and the stories of the gods. I asked myself many questions that I could not answer, but it was good to ask them. At night, I would lie awake and listen to the wind—it seemed to me that it was the voice of the gods as they flew through the air.

We are not ignorant like the Forest People—our women spin wool on the wheel; our priests wear a white robe. We do not eat grubs from the tree; we have not forgotten the old writings, although they are hard to understand. Nevertheless, my knowledge and my lack of knowledge burned in me—I wished to know more. When I was a man at last, I came to my father and said, "It is time for me to go on my journey. Give me your leave."

He looked at me for a long time, stroking his beard; then he said at last, "Yes. It is time." That night, in the house of the priesthood, I asked for and received purification. My body hurt, but my spirit was a cool stone. It was my father himself who questioned me about my dreams.

He bade me look into the smoke of the fire

Hills (1914), Man Ray. Oil on canvas, 10⅛″ × 12″, Munson-Williams-Proctor Institute, Museum of Art, Utica, New York, museum purchase.

with both eyes. My voice sounded thin in my ears, but that was because of the smoke.

He touched me on the breast and the forehead. He gave me the bow and the three arrows.

"Take them," he said. "It is forbidden to travel east. It is forbidden to cross the river. It is forbidden to go to the Place of the Gods. All these things are forbidden."

"All these things are forbidden," I said, but it was my voice that spoke and not my spirit. He looked at me again.

"My son," he said. "Once I had young dreams. If your dreams do not eat you up, you may be a great priest. If they eat you, you are still my son. Now go on your journey."

I went fasting, as is the law. My body hurt but not my heart. When the dawn came, I was out of sight of the village. I prayed and purified myself, waiting for a sign. The sign was an eagle. It flew east.

Sometimes signs are sent by bad spirits. I waited again on the flat rock, fasting, taking no food. I was very still—I could feel the sky above me and the earth beneath. I waited till the sun was beginning to sink. Then three deer passed in the valley, going east—they did not wind me or see me. There was a white fawn with them—a very great sign.

I followed them, at a distance, waiting for what would happen. My heart was troubled about going east, yet I knew that I must go. My head hummed with my fasting—I did not even

and see—I saw and told what I saw. It was what I have always seen—a river, and, beyond it, a great Dead Place and in it the gods walking. I have always thought about that. His eyes were stern when I told him—he was no longer my father but a priest. He said, "This is a strong dream."

"It is mine," I said, while the smoke waved and my head felt light. They were singing the star song in the outer chamber, and it was like the buzzing of bees in my head.

He asked me how the gods were dressed, and I told him how they were dressed. We know how they were dressed from the book, but I saw them as if they were before me. When I had finished, he threw the sticks three times and studied them as they fell.

"This is a very strong dream," he said. "It may eat you up."

"I am not afraid," I said and looked at him

see the panther spring upon the white fawn. But, before I knew it, the bow was in my hand. I shouted, and the panther lifted his head from the fawn. It is not easy to kill a panther with one arrow, but the arrow went through his eye and into his brain. He died as he tried to spring—he rolled over, tearing at the ground. Then I knew I was meant to go east—I knew that was my journey. When the night came, I made my fire and roasted meat.

It is eight suns' journey to the east, and a man passes by many Dead Places. The Forest People are afraid of them, but I am not. Once I made my fire on the edge of a Dead Place at night, and next morning, in the dead house, I found a good knife, little rusted. That was small to what came afterward, but it made my heart feel big. Always when I looked for game, it was in front of my arrow, and twice I passed hunting parties of the Forest People without their knowing. So I knew my magic was strong and my journey clean, in spite of the law.

Toward the setting of the eighth sun, I came to the banks of the great river. It was half a day's journey after I had left the god road—we do not use the god roads now, for they are falling apart into great blocks of stone, and the forest is safer going. A long way off, I had seen the water through trees, but the trees were thick. At last, I came out upon an open place at the top of a cliff. There was the great river below, like a giant in the sun. It is very long, very wide. It could eat all the streams we know and still be thirsty. Its name is Ou-dis-sun, the Sacred, the Long. No man of my tribe had seen it, not even my father, the priest. It was magic, and I prayed.

Then I raised my eyes and looked south. It was there, the Place of the Gods.

How can I tell what it was like—you do not know. It was there, in the red light, and they were too big to be houses. It was there with the red light upon it, mighty and ruined. I knew

that in another moment the gods would see me. I covered my eyes with my hands and crept back into the forest.

Surely, that was enough to do, and live. Surely it was enough to spend the night upon the cliff. The Forest People themselves do not come near. Yet, all through the night, I knew that I should have to cross the river and walk in the places of the gods, although the gods ate me up. My magic did not help me at all, and yet there was a fire in my bowels, a fire in my mind. When the sun rose, I thought, "My journey has been clean. Now I will go home from my journey." But, even as I thought so, I knew I could not. If I went to the Place of the Gods, I would surely die, but, if I did not go, I could never be at peace with my spirit again. It is better to lose one's life than one's spirit, if one is a priest and the son of a priest.

Nevertheless, as I made the raft, the tears ran out of my eyes. The Forest People could have killed me without fight, if they had come upon me then, but they did not come. When the raft was made, I said the sayings for the dead and painted myself for death. My heart was cold as a frog and my knees like water, but the burning in my mind would not let me have peace. As I pushed the raft from the shore, I began my death song—I had the right. It was a fine song.

"I am John, son of John," I sang. "My people are the Hill People. They are the men.

THERE WAS

THE GREAT

RIVER BELOW,

LIKE A GIANT

IN THE SUN.

*I go into the Dead Places, but I am not slain.
I take the metal from the Dead Places, but
I am not blasted.*

*I travel upon the god roads and am not
afraid. E-yah! I have killed the panther; I
have killed the fawn!*

*E-yah! I have come to the great river. No
man has come there before.*

*It is forbidden to go east, but I have gone,
forbidden to go on the great river, but I
am there.*

*Open your hearts, you spirits, and hear my
song.*

*Now I go to the Place of the Gods; I shall
not return.*

*My body is painted for death and my limbs
weak, but my heart is big as I go to the
Place of the Gods!"*

All the same, when I came to the Place of
the Gods, I was afraid, afraid. The
current of the great river is very strong—
it gripped my raft with its hands. That was
magic, for the river itself is wide and calm. I
could feel evil spirits about me, in the bright
morning; I could feel their breath on my neck
as I was swept down the stream. Never have I
been so much alone—I tried to think of my
knowledge, but it was a squirrel's heap of winter
nuts. There was no strength in my knowledge
anymore, and I felt small and naked as a new-
hatched bird—alone upon the great river, the
servant of the gods.

Yet, after a while, my eyes were opened, and
I saw. I saw both banks of the river—I saw that
once there had been god roads across it, though
now they were broken and fallen like broken
vines. Very great they were, and wonderful and
broken—broken in the time of the Great Burning when the fire fell out of the sky. And always
the current took me nearer to the Place of the
Gods, and the huge ruins rose before my eyes.

I do not know the customs of rivers—we are

the People of the Hills. I tried to guide my raft
with the pole, but it spun around. I thought the
river meant to take me past the Place of the
Gods and out into the Bitter Water of the
legends. I grew angry then—my heart felt
strong. I said aloud, "I am a priest and the son
of a priest!" The gods heard me—they showed
me how to paddle with the pole on one side of
the raft. The current changed itself—I drew
near to the Place of the Gods.

When I was very near, my raft struck and
turned over. I can swim in our lakes—I swam to
the shore. There was a great spike of rusted
metal sticking out into the river—I hauled
myself up upon it and sat there, panting. I had
saved my bow and two arrows and the knife I
found in the Dead Place, but that was all. My
raft went whirling downstream toward the
Bitter Water. I looked after it, and thought if it
had trod me under, at least I would be safely
dead. Nevertheless, when I had dried my
bowstring and restrung it, I walked forward to
the Place of the Gods.

It felt like ground underfoot; it did not burn
me. It is not true what some of the tales say,
that the ground there burns forever, for I have
been there. Here and there were the marks and
stains of the Great Burning, on the ruins, that is
true. But they were old marks and old stains. It
is not true either, what some of our priests say,
that it is an island covered with fogs and
enchantments. It is not. It is a great Dead
Place—greater than any Dead Place we know.
Everywhere in it there are god roads, though
most are cracked and broken. Everywhere there
are the ruins of the high towers of the gods.

How shall I tell what I saw? I went carefully,
my strung bow in my hand, my skin ready for
danger. There should have been the wailings of
spirits and the shrieks of demons, but there were
not. It was very silent and sunny where I had
landed—the wind and the rain and the birds
that drop seeds had done their work—the grass

grew in the cracks of the broken stone. It is a fair island—no wonder the gods built there. If I had come there, a god, I also would have built.

How shall I tell what I saw? The towers are not all broken—here and there one still stands, like a great tree in a forest, and the birds nest high. But the towers themselves look blind, for the gods are gone. I saw a fish hawk, catching fish in the river. I saw a little dance of white butterflies over a great heap of broken stones and columns. I went there and looked about me—there was a carved stone with cut letters, broken in half. I can read letters, but I could not understand these. They said UBTREAS. There was also the shattered image of a man or a god. It had been made of white stone, and he wore his hair tied back like a woman's. His name was ASHING, as I read on the cracked half of a stone. I thought it wise to pray to ASHING, though I do not know that god.

How shall I tell what I saw? There was no smell of man left, on stone or metal. Nor were there many trees in that wilderness of stone. There are many pigeons, nesting and dropping in the towers—the gods must have loved them, or, perhaps, they used them for sacrifices. There are wild cats that roam the god roads, green-eyed, unafraid of man. At night they wail like demons, but they are not demons. The wild dogs are more dangerous, for they hunt in a pack, but them I did not meet till later. Every-where there are the carved stones, carved with magical numbers or words.

I went north—I did not try to hide myself. When a god or a demon saw me, then I would die, but meanwhile I was no longer afraid. My hunger for knowledge burned in me—there was so much that I could not understand. After a while, I knew that my belly was hungry. I could have hunted for my meat, but I did not hunt. It is known that the gods did not hunt as we do—they got their food from enchanted boxes and jars. Sometimes these are still found in the Dead

Places—once, when I was a child and foolish, I opened such a jar and tasted it and found the food sweet. But my father found out and punished me for it strictly, for, often, that food is death. Now, though, I had long gone past what was forbidden, and I entered the likeliest towers, look-ing for the food of the gods.

I found it at last in the ruins of a great temple in the mid-city. A mighty temple it must have been, for the roof was painted like the sky at night with its stars—that much I could see, though the colors were faint and dim. It went down into great caves and tunnels—perhaps they kept their slaves there. But when I started to climb down, I heard the squeaking of rats, so I did not go—rats are unclean, and there must have been many tribes of them, from the squeaking. But near there, I found food, in the heart of a ruin, behind a door that still opened. I ate only the fruits from the jars—they had a very sweet taste. There was drink, too, in bottles of glass— the drink of the gods was strong and made my head swim. After I had eaten and drunk, I slept on the top of a stone, my bow at my side.

When I woke, the sun was low. Looking down from where I lay, I saw a dog sitting on his haunches. His tongue was hanging out of his mouth; he looked as if he were laughing. He was a big dog, with a gray-brown coat, as big as a wolf. I sprang up and shouted at him, but he did not move—he just sat there as if he were laughing. I did not like that. When I reached for a stone to throw, he moved swiftly out of the way of the stone. He was not afraid of me; he looked at me as if I were meat. No doubt I

IT IS NOT

TRUE WHAT

SOME OF THE

TALES SAY . . .

could have killed him with an arrow, but I did not know if there were others. Moreover, night was falling.

I looked about me—not far away there was a great, broken god road, leading north. The towers were high enough, but not so high, and while many of the dead houses were wrecked, there were some that stood. I went toward this god road, keeping to the heights of the ruins, while the dog followed. When I had reached the god road, I saw that there were others behind him. If I had slept later, they would have come upon me asleep and torn out my throat. As it was, they were sure enough of me; they did not hurry. When I went into the dead house, they kept watch at the entrance—doubtless they thought they would have a fine hunt. But a dog cannot open a door, and I knew, from the books, that the gods did not like to live on the ground but on high.

WITHIN, THERE WAS A PLACE OF GREAT RICHES.

I had just found a door I could open when the dogs decided to rush. Ha! They were surprised when I shut the door in their faces—it was a good door, of strong metal. I could hear their foolish baying beyond it, but I did not stop to answer them. I was in darkness—I found stairs and climbed. There were many stairs, turning around till my head was dizzy. At the top was another door—I found the knob and opened it. I was in a long small chamber—on one side of it was a bronze door that could not be opened, for it had no handle. Perhaps there was a magic word to open it, but I did not have the word. I turned to the door in the opposite side of the wall. The lock of it was broken, and I opened it and went in.

Within, there was a place of great riches. The god who lived there must have been a powerful god. The first room was a small anteroom—I waited there for some time, telling the spirits of the place that I came in peace and not as a robber. When it seemed to me that they had had time to hear me, I went on. Ah, what riches! Few, even, of the windows had been broken—it was all as it had been. The great windows that looked over the city had not been broken at all, though they were dusty and streaked with many years. There were coverings on the floors, the colors not greatly faded, and the chairs were soft and deep. There were pictures upon the walls, very strange, very wonderful—I remember one of a bunch of flowers in a jar—if you came close to it, you could see nothing but bits of color, but if you stood away from it, the flowers might have been picked yesterday. It made my heart feel strange to look at this picture—and to look at the figure of a bird, in some hard clay, on a table and see it so like our birds. Everywhere there were books and writings, many in tongues that I could not read. The god who lived there must have been a wise god and full of knowledge. I felt I had a right there, as I sought knowledge also.

Nevertheless, it was strange. There was a washing place but no water—perhaps the gods washed in air. There was a cooking place but no wood, and though there was a machine to cook food, there was no place to put fire in it. Nor were there candles or lamps—there were things that looked like lamps, but they had neither oil nor wick. All these things were magic, but I touched them and lived—the magic had gone out of them. Let me tell one thing to show. In the washing place, a thing said "Hot," but it was not hot to the touch—another thing said "Cold," but it was not cold. This must have been a strong magic, but the magic was gone. I do not understand—they had ways—I wish that I knew.

It was close and dry and dusty in the house of the gods. I have said the magic was gone, but that is not true—it had gone from the magic things, but it had not gone from the place. I felt the spirits about me, weighing upon me. Nor had I ever slept in a Dead Place before—and yet, tonight, I must sleep there. When I thought of it, my tongue felt dry in my throat, in spite of my wish for knowledge. Almost I would have gone down again and faced the dogs, but I did not.

I had not gone through all the rooms when the darkness fell. When it fell, I went back to the big room looking over the city and made fire. There was a place to make fire and a box with wood in it, though I do not think they cooked there. I wrapped myself in a floor covering and slept in front of the fire—I was very tired.

Now I tell what is very strong magic. I woke in the midst of the night. When I woke, the fire had gone out, and I was cold. It seemed to me that all around me there were whisperings and voices. I closed my eyes to shut them out. Some will say that I slept again, but I do not think that I slept. I could feel the spirits drawing my spirit out of my body as a fish is drawn on a line.

Why should I lie about it? I am a priest and the son of a priest. If there are spirits, as they say, in the small Dead Places near us, what spirits must there not be in that great Place of the Gods? And would not they wish to speak? After such long years? I know that I felt myself drawn as a fish is drawn on a line. I had stepped out of my body—I could see my body asleep in front of the cold fire, but it was not I. I was drawn to look out upon the city of the gods.

It should have been dark, for it was night, but it was not dark. Everywhere there were lights—lines of light—circles and blurs of light—ten thousand torches would not have been the same. The sky itself was alight—you

Toto (1988), Jimmy Lee Sudduth. Paint with mud on wood, 31¾″ × 24″, from *American Self-Taught,* by Frank Maresca and Roger Ricco, published by Knopf, 1993.

could barely see the stars for the glow in the sky. I thought to myself "This is strong magic" and trembled. There was a roaring in my ears like the rushing of rivers. Then my eyes grew used to the light and my ears to the sound. I knew that I was seeing the city as it had been when the gods were alive.

That was a sight indeed—yes, that was a sight: I could not have seen it in the body—my body would have died. Everywhere went the gods, on foot and in chariots—there were gods beyond number and counting, and their chariots blocked the streets. They had turned night to day for their pleasure—they did not sleep with the sun. The noise of their coming and going was the noise of many waters. It was magic what they could do—it was magic what they did.

I looked out of another window—the great vines of their bridges were mended, and the god roads went east and west. Restless, restless, were the gods and always in motion! They burrowed tunnels under rivers—they flew in the air. With unbelievable tools they did giant works—no part of the earth was safe from them, for, if they wished for a thing, they summoned it from the other side of the world. And always, as they labored and rested, as they feasted and made love, there was a drum in their ears—the pulse of the giant city, beating and beating like a man's heart.

Were they happy? What is happiness to the gods? They were great; they were mighty; they were wonderful and terrible. As I looked upon them and their magic, I felt like a child—but a little more, it seemed to me, and they would pull down the moon from the sky. I saw them with wisdom beyond wisdom and knowledge beyond knowledge. And yet not all they did was well done—even I could see that—and yet their wisdom could not but grow until all was peace. Then I saw their fate come upon them, and that was terrible past speech. It came upon them as they walked the streets of their city. I have been in the fights with the Forest People—I have seen men die. But this was not like that. When gods war with gods, they use weapons we do not know. It was fire falling out of the sky and a mist that poisoned. It was the time of the Great Burning and the Destruction. They ran about like ants in the streets of their city—poor gods, poor gods! Then the towers began to fall. A few escaped—

WERE THEY HAPPY? WHAT IS HAPPINESS TO THE GODS?

yes, a few. The legends tell it. But, even after the city had become a Dead Place, for many years the poison was still in the ground. I saw it happen; I saw the last of them die. It was darkness over the broken city, and I wept.

All this, I saw. I saw it as I have told it, though not in the body. When I woke in the morning, I was hungry, but I did not think first of my hunger, for my heart was perplexed and confused. I knew the reason for the Dead Places, but I did not see why it had happened. It seemed to me it should not have happened, with all the magic they had. I went through the house looking for an answer. There was so much in the house I could not understand—and yet I am a priest and the son of a priest. It was like being on one side of the great river, at night, with no light to show the way.

Then I saw the dead god. He was sitting in his chair, by the window, in a room I had not entered before, and for the first moment, I thought that he was alive. Then I saw the skin on the back of his hand—it was like dry leather. The room was shut, hot and dry—no doubt that had kept him as he was. At first I was afraid to approach him—then the fear left me. He was sitting looking out over the city—he was dressed in the clothes of the gods. His age was neither young nor old—I could not tell his age. But there was wisdom in his face and great sadness. You could see that he would have not run away. He had sat at his window, watching his city die—then he himself had died. But it is better to lose one's life than one's spirit—and you could see from the face that his spirit had not been lost. I knew that, if I touched him, he would fall into dust—and yet, there was something unconquered in the face.

That is all of my story, for then I knew he was a man—I knew then that they had been men, neither gods nor demons. It is a great knowledge, hard to tell and believe. They were men—they went a dark road, but they were men. I had no fear after that—I had no fear going home, though twice I fought off the dogs and once I was hunted for two days by the Forest People. When I saw my father again, I prayed and was purified. He touched my lips and my breast; he said, "You went away a boy. You come back a man and a priest." I said, "Father, they were men! I have been in the Place of the Gods and seen it! Now slay me, if it is the law—but still I know they were men."

He looked at me out of both eyes. He said, "The law is not always the same shape—you have done what you have done. I could not have done it my time, but you come after me. Tell!"

I told, and he listened. After that, I wished to tell all the people, but he showed me otherwise. He said, "Truth is a hard deer to hunt. If you eat too much truth at once, you may die of the truth. It was not idly that our fathers forbade the Dead Places." He was right—it is better the truth should come little by little. I have learned that, being a priest. Perhaps, in the old days, they ate knowledge too fast.

Nevertheless, we make a beginning. It is not for the metal alone we go to the Dead Places now—there are the books and the writings. They are hard to learn. And the magic tools are broken—but we can look at them and wonder. At least, we make a beginning. And, when I am chief priest, we shall go beyond the great river. We shall go to the Place of the Gods—the place newyork—not one man but a company. We shall look for the images of the gods and find the god ASHING and the others—the gods

Lincoln and Biltmore[1] and Moses.[2] But they were men who built the city, not gods or demons. They were men. I remember the dead man's face. They were men who were here before us. We must build again. ❖

---

1. **Biltmore:** the name of a famous hotel in New York City.
2. **Moses:** Robert Moses (1888–1981), a New York City public official whose name appears on many bridges and other structures built during his administration.

INSIGHT

THERE WILL COME SOFT RAINS
SARA TEASDALE

There will come soft rains and the
　　smell of the ground,
And swallows circling with their
　　shimmering sound;

And frogs in the pools singing at
　　night,
And wild plum-trees in tremulous
　　white;

5　Robins will wear their feathery fire
Whistling their whims on a low
　　fence-wire;

And not one will know of the war,
　　not one
Will care at last when it is done.

Not one would mind, neither bird
　　nor tree
10　If mankind perished utterly;

And Spring herself, when she woke
　　at dawn,
Would scarcely know that we were
　　gone.

RESPONDING OPTIONS

FROM PERSONAL RESPONSE TO CRITICAL ANALYSIS

REFLECT

1. In your notebook, describe what came to mind as you were reading. Share your thoughts with a classmate.

RETHINK

2. At what point in the story did you begin to figure out what the Place of the Gods was? Refer to the allusion chart you made for the Reading Connection on page 713 and to details in the story to support your response.

3. Why do you think it is forbidden for anyone but a priest to visit the Dead Places? Explain your opinion.

4. How would you describe John?
   Consider
   - the way that he uses language
   - his determination to finish his journey and complete his rite of passage
   - the importance he gives to pursuing knowledge
   - what he means by "It is better to lose one's life than one's spirit" (page 717)
   - his statement "We must build again," at the end of the story

5. The title of this selection refers to the ancient city of Babylon, which exists only as ruins today. In its time, this city was a center of culture, learning, and world trade. How does knowing about Babylon add to your understanding of Benét's story?

6. What do you think is the theme, or message, of the story? Support your ideas.

RELATE

7. Do you think it is dangerous for a person or a society to have too much knowledge?

8. How does the world described in the Insight poem "There Will Come Soft Rains" on page 723 compare with the world described in "By the Waters of Babylon"?

ANOTHER PATHWAY

Cooperative Learning

With a group of classmates, develop a map that shows the territory in which John lives and travels. Be sure to show the sites of important events of John's journey, such as where he hid from the Forest People and where he crossed the river. Add other details to make your map complete.

QUICKWRITES

1. Write two sets of **observer's notes** about a rite of passage in your own life. The first set of notes should present your own description of the rite of passage; the second set of notes should be from John's perspective.

2. Compose a series of **journal entries** that the dead man sitting at the window might have left in his safe, to be found by someone like John.

3. Imagine that a powerful priest of the Hill People is against John's making public the insights he gained on his journey. Write a **transcript** of a debate between John and the priest about whether the people should learn the truth about the gods.

📁 *PORTFOLIO Save your writing. You may want to use it later as a springboard to a piece for your portfolio.*

LITERARY CONCEPTS

The term *point of view* refers to the kind of narrator used in a literary work. In a work told from the **first–person point of view,** the narrator is a character in the story who tells everything in his or her own words. "By the Waters of Babylon"—told entirely from the point of view of John, the main character—is such a story. John is what is sometimes referred to as a **naive narrator** because he does not always understand what he is describing. In what way might the impact of the story be different if John spoke as an informed narrator, one who understood the meaning of everything he saw? With a partner, rewrite a section of the story, portraying John as an informed narrator. Then read your version to the class.

CONCEPT REVIEW: Irony In the story, find at least three examples of situations where the reader knows more than the narrator. What type of irony do they illustrate?

ALTERNATIVE ACTIVITIES

1. Create a **model** or **drawing** of the city, either as it was when John visited it or as he envisioned it in his dream.

2. Put together a **collection** of artifacts that John might have brought back from his visit to the Place of the Gods. Present your collection to the class as John might have presented it to the people of his village.

LITERARY LINKS

Both "By the Waters of Babylon" and "Searching for Summer" could be classified as futuristic literature because they seem to be set sometime in the future. What other similarities do you see in these two stories?

ART CONNECTION

Does the painting *Starburst* on page 714 reflect your own image of the Place of the Gods? Explain your answer.

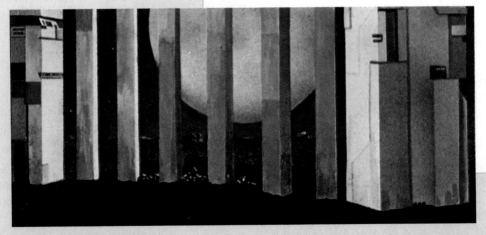

Detail of *Starburst*, Colin Hay.

ACROSS THE CURRICULUM

History Benét published "By the Waters of Babylon" in 1937. Find out about world events and the general public mood of that time to learn what might have prompted him to write such a story. Present your findings to the class as a script for a movie newsreel or as a series of news headlines or articles, with an editorial comment summing up the general atmosphere of the times.

Film View the film *The Gods Must Be Crazy,* in which people from a primitive culture make unexpected contact with modern society. Discuss with your classmates the contrast between the two societies presented in the film and the view depicted in this story.

Old movie camera. Copyright © H. Armstrong Roberts, Inc.

STEPHEN VINCENT BENÉT

1898–1943

Stephen Vincent Benét was the most famous member of a writing family that also included his brother William and his sister Laura. Benét was born in Bethlehem, Pennsylvania, and grew up on various army bases in California and in other parts of the country. As a boy he was studious, and his main companions were the books in the family library. A love of poetry came naturally to him because his father often read poetry aloud and would discuss its form and content with his children.

Benét studied literature at Yale University and at the Sorbonne in Paris, France. There he met Rosemary Carr, who worked for the Paris edition of the *Chicago Tribune.* Benét and Carr eventually married, and they collaborated on various literary pieces.

Benét was deeply patriotic, and much of his writing is based on American history and folklore. With his wife, he wrote *A Book of Americans* (1933), a collection of historical sketches for younger readers. He was best known for his poetry and short stories, but he also wrote many other kinds of works, including novels and scripts for radio and film. He even wrote an operetta. Based on Washington Irving's classic tale "The Legend of Sleepy Hollow," it was nationally broadcast on the radio in 1937.

Among Benét's best-known works are the humorous short story "The Devil and Daniel Webster" (1937), for which he received an O. Henry Memorial Prize, and *John Brown's Body* (1928), a long narrative poem about the Civil War, based on information that Benét culled from military records in his father's library. The poem won Benét the first of his two Pulitzer Prizes. The second came for *Western Star* (1943), another long poem about the history of America, which was to have been the first volume in a series. The series remained unfinished at the time of Benét's death.

OTHER WORKS *Ballad of William Sycamore, 1790–1880; Ballads and Poems; Tales Before Midnight; Selected Works of Stephen Vincent Benét*

LASERLINKS
• *GEOGRAPHICAL CONNECTION*
• *LITERARY CONNECTION*

TRURL'S Machine

Stanislaw Lem
Poland

Stanislaw Lem is considered the leading science fiction writer of Eastern Europe. This story was published in a collection of his humorous space-age tales, called *The Cyberiad*. The book takes its title from the science of cybernetics, which includes the study of the similarities and differences in the ways human beings and machines function and communicate. In "Trurl's Machine," neither man nor machine is functioning all that well.

Once upon a time Trurl the constructor built an eight-story thinking machine. When it was finished, he gave it a coat of white paint, trimmed the edges in lavender, stepped back, squinted, then added a little curlicue on the front and, where one might imagine the forehead to be, a few pale orange polka dots. Extremely pleased with himself, he whistled an air and, as is always done on such occasions, asked it the ritual question of how much is two plus two.

The machine stirred. Its tubes began to glow; its coils warmed up; current coursed through all its circuits like a waterfall; transformers hummed and throbbed; there was a clanging, and a chugging, and such an ungodly racket that Trurl began to think of adding a special mentation muffler. Meanwhile the machine labored on, as if it had been given the most difficult problem in the universe to solve; the ground shook; the sand slid underfoot from the vibration; valves popped like champagne corks; the relays nearly gave way under the strain. At last, when Trurl had grown extremely impatient, the machine ground to a halt and said in a voice like thunder: SEVEN!

"Nonsense, my dear," said Trurl. "The answer's four. Now be a good machine and adjust yourself! What's two and two?" "SEVEN!" snapped the machine. Trurl sighed and put his coveralls back on, rolled up his sleeves, opened the bottom trap door and crawled in. For the longest time he hammered away inside, tightened, soldered, ran clattering up and down the metal stairs, now on the sixth floor, now on the eighth, then pounded back down to the bottom and threw a switch, but something sizzled in the middle, and the spark plugs grew blue whiskers. After two hours of this he came out, covered with soot but satisfied, put all his tools away, took off his coveralls, wiped his face and hands.

As he was leaving, he turned and asked, just so there would be no doubt about it:

"And now what's two and two?"

"SEVEN!" replied the machine.

Trurl uttered a terrible oath, but there was no help for it—again he had to poke around inside the machine, disconnecting, correcting, checking, resetting, and when he learned for the third time that two and two was seven, he collapsed in despair at the foot of the machine, and sat there until Klapaucius found him. Klapaucius inquired what was wrong, for Trurl looked as if he had just returned from a funeral. Trurl explained the problem. Klapaucius crawled into the machine himself a couple of times, tried to fix this and that, then asked it for the sum of one plus two, which turned out to be six. One plus one, according to the machine, equaled zero. Klapaucius scratched his head, cleared his throat and said:

"My friend, you'll just have to face it. That isn't the machine you wished to make. However, there's a good side to everything, including this."

"What good side?" muttered Trurl and kicked the base on which he was sitting.

"Stop that," said the machine.

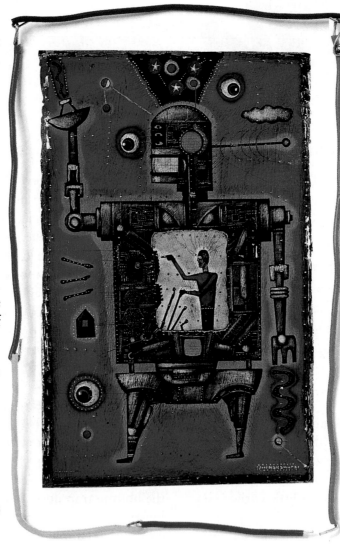

"H'm, it's sensitive too. But where was I? Oh yes . . . there's no question but that we have here a stupid machine, and not merely stupid in the usual, normal way, oh no! This is, as far as I can determine—and you know I am something of an expert—this is the stupidest thinking machine in the entire world, and that's nothing to sneeze at! To construct deliberately such a machine would be far from easy; in fact, I would say that no one could manage it. For the thing is not only stupid, but stubborn as a mule, that is, it has a personality common to idiots, for idiots are uncommonly stubborn."

"What earthly use do I have for such a machine!" said Trurl and kicked it again.

"I'm warning you; you better stop!" said the machine.

"A warning, if you please," observed Klapaucius dryly. "Not only is it sensitive, dense and stubborn, but quick to take offense, and believe me, with such an abundance of qualities there are all sorts of things you might do!"

"What, for example?" asked Trurl.

"Well, it's hard to say offhand. You might put it on exhibit and charge admission; people would flock to see the stupidest thinking machine that ever was—what does it have, eight stories? Really, could anyone imagine a bigger dunce? And the exhibition would not only cover your costs, but—"

"Enough, I'm not holding any exhibition!" Trurl said, stood up and, unable to restrain himself, kicked the machine once more.

"This is your third warning," said the machine.

"What?" cried Trurl, infuriated by its imperious manner. "You . . . you . . ." And he kicked it several times, shouting: "You're only good for kicking, you know that?"

"You have insulted me for the fourth, fifth, sixth and eighth times," said the machine. "Therefore I refuse to answer all further questions of a mathematical nature."

"It refuses! Do you hear that?" fumed Trurl, thoroughly exasperated. "After six comes eight—did you notice, Klapaucius?—not seven, but eight! And that's the kind of mathematics Her Highness refuses to perform! Take that! And that! And that! Or perhaps you'd like some more?"

The machine shuddered, shook, and without another word started to lift itself from its foundations. They were very deep, and the girders began to bend, but at last it scrambled out, leaving behind broken concrete blocks with steel spokes protruding—and it bore down on Trurl and Klapaucius like a moving fortress. Trurl was so dumbfounded that he didn't even try to hide from the machine, which to all appearances intended to crush him to a pulp. But Klapaucius grabbed his arm and yanked him away, and the two of them took to their heels. When finally they looked back, they saw the machine swaying like a high tower, advancing slowly, at every step sinking to its second floor, but stubbornly, doggedly pulling itself out of the sand and heading straight for them.

"Whoever heard of such a thing?" Trurl gasped in amazement. "Why, this is mutiny! What do we do now?"

"Wait and watch," replied the prudent Klapaucius. "We may learn something."

But there was nothing to be learned just then. The machine had reached firmer ground and was picking up speed. Inside, it whistled, hissed and sputtered.

"Any minute now the signal box will knock loose," said Trurl under his breath. "That'll jam the program and stop it. . . ."

"No," said Klapaucius, "this is a special case. The thing is so stupid, that even if the whole transmission goes, it won't matter. But— look out!"

"stop that," said the machine.

The machine was gathering momentum, clearly bent on running them down, so they fled just as fast as they could, the fearful rhythm of crunching steps in their ears. They ran and ran—what else could they do? They tried to make it back to their native district, but the machine outflanked them, cut them off, forced them deeper and deeper into a wild, uninhabited region. Mountains, dismal and craggy, slowly rose out of the mist. Trurl, panting heavily, shouted to Klapaucius:

"Listen! Let's turn into some narrow canyon . . . where it won't be able to follow us . . . the cursed thing . . . what do you say?"

"No . . . better go straight," wheezed Klapaucius. "There's a town up ahead . . . can't

729

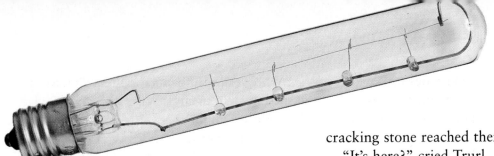

remember the name . . . anyway, we can find—oof!—find shelter there. . . ."

So they ran straight and soon saw houses before them. The streets were practically deserted at this time of day, and the constructors had gone a good distance without meeting a living soul, when suddenly an awful crash, like an avalanche at the edge of the town, indicated that the machine was coming after them.

Trurl looked back and groaned.

"Good heavens! It's tearing down the houses, Klapaucius!" For the machine, in stubborn pursuit, was plowing through the walls of the buildings like a mountain of steel, and in its wake lay piles of rubble and white clouds of plaster dust. There were dreadful screams, confusion in the streets, and Trurl and Klapaucius, their hearts in their mouths, ran on till they came to a large town hall, darted inside and raced down endless stairs to a deep cellar.

"It won't get us in here, even if it brings the whole building down on our heads!" panted Klapaucius. "But really, the devil himself had me pay you a visit today. . . . I was curious to see how your work was going—well, I certainly found out . . ."

"Quiet," interrupted Trurl. "Someone's coming. . . ."

And, indeed, the cellar door opened up, and the mayor entered, accompanied by several aldermen. Trurl was too embarrassed to explain how this strange and calamitous situation had come about; Klapaucius had to do it. The mayor listened in silence. Suddenly the walls trembled, the ground heaved, and the sound of

cracking stone reached them in the cellar.

"It's here?" cried Trurl.

"Yes," said the mayor. "And it demands that we give you up; otherwise it says it will level the entire town. . . ."

Just then they heard, far overhead, words that honked as if from a muffled horn:

"Trurl's here . . . I smell Trurl . . ."

"But surely you won't give us up?" asked in a quavering voice the object of the machine's obstinate fury.

"The one of you who calls himself Trurl must leave. The other may remain, since surrendering him does not constitute part of the conditions . . ."

"Have mercy!"

"We are helpless," said the mayor. "And were you to stay here, Trurl, you would have to answer for all the damage done to this town and its inhabitants, since it was because of you that the machine destroyed sixteen homes and buried beneath their ruins many of our finest citizens. Only the fact that you yourself stand in imminent peril permits me to let you leave unpunished. Go then, and nevermore return."

Trurl looked at the aldermen and, seeing his sentence written on their stern faces, slowly turned and made for the door.

"Wait! I'll go with you!" cried Klapaucius impulsively.

"You?" said Trurl, a faint hope in his voice. "But no . . ." he added after a moment. "Why should you have to perish too? . . ."

"Nonsense!" rejoined Klapaucius with great energy. "What, us perish at the hands of that iron imbecile? Never! It takes more than that, my friend, to wipe two of the most famous constructors off the face of the globe! Come, Trurl! Chin up!"

Encouraged by these words, Trurl ran up the stairs after Klapaucius. There was not a soul outside in the square. Amid clouds of dust and the gaunt skeletons of demolished homes stood the machine, higher than the town hall tower itself, puffing steam, covered with the blood of powdered brick and smeared with chalk.

"Careful!" whispered Klapaucius. "It doesn't see us. Let's take that first street on the left, then turn right, then straight for those mountains. There we can take refuge and think of how to make the thing give up once and for all its insane . . . *Now!*" he yelled, for the machine had just spotted them and was charging, making the pavement buckle.

Breathless, they ran from the town and galloped along for a mile or so, hearing behind them the thunderous stride of the colossus that followed relentlessly.

"I know that ravine!" Klapaucius suddenly cried. "That's the bed of a dried-out stream, and it leads to cliffs and caves—faster, faster, the thing'll have to stop soon! . . ."

So they raced uphill, stumbling and waving their arms to keep their balance, but the machine still gained on them. Scrambling up over the gravel of the dried-out riverbed, they reached a crevice in the perpendicular rock and,

seeing high above them the murky mouth of a cave, began to climb frantically toward it, no longer caring about the loose stones that flew from under their feet. The opening in the rock breathed chill and darkness. As quickly as they could, they leaped inside, ran a few extra steps, then stopped.

"Well, here at least we're safe," said Trurl, calm once again. "I'll just take a look, to see where it got stuck . . ."

"Be careful," cautioned Klapaucius. Trurl inched his way to the edge of the cave, leaned out, and immediately jumped back in fright.

"It's coming up the mountain!" he cried.

"Don't worry; it'll never be able to get in here," said Klapaucius, not altogether convinced. "But what's that? Is it getting dark? Oh no!"

At that moment a great shadow blotted out the bit of sky visible through the mouth of the cave, and in its place appeared a smooth steel wall with rows of rivets. It was the machine slowly closing with the rock, thereby sealing up the cave as if with a mighty metal lid.

"We're trapped . . ." whispered Trurl, his voice breaking off when the darkness became absolute.

"That was idiotic on our part!" Klapaucius exclaimed, furious. "To jump into a cave that it could barricade! How could we have done such a thing?"

"What do you think it's waiting for now?" asked Trurl after a long pause.

"For us to give up—that doesn't take any great brains."

Again there was silence. Trurl tiptoed in the darkness, hands outstretched, in the direction of the opening, running his fingers along the stone until he touched the smooth steel, which was warm, as if heated from within. . . .

"I feel Trurl . . ." boomed the iron voice. Trurl hastily retreated, took a seat alongside his friend, and for some time they sat there, motionless. At last Klapaucius whispered:

"There's no sense our just sitting here. I'll try to reason with it . . ."

. . . for the last time,

"That's hopeless," said Trurl. "But go ahead. Perhaps it will at least let *you* go free . . ."

"Now, now, none of that!" said Klapaucius, patting him on the back. And he groped his way toward the mouth of the cave and called: "Hello out there, can you hear us?"

"Yes," said the machine.

"Listen, we'd like to apologize. You see . . . well, there was a little misunderstanding, true, but it was nothing, really. Trurl had no intention of . . ."

"I'll pulverize Trurl!" said the machine. "But first, he'll tell me how much two and two makes."

"Of course he will, of course he will, and you'll be happy with his answer and make it up with him for sure, isn't that right, Trurl?" said the mediator soothingly.

"Yes, of course . . ." mumbled Trurl.

"Really?" said the machine. "Then how much is two and two?"

"Fo . . . that is, seven . . ." said Trurl in an even lower voice.

"Ha! Not four, but seven, eh?" crowed the machine. "There, I told you so!"

"Seven, yes, seven, we always knew it was seven!" Klapaucius eagerly agreed. "Now will you, uh, let us go?" he added cautiously.

"No. Let Trurl say how sorry he is and tell me how much is two times two . . ."

"And you'll let us go, if I do?" asked Trurl.

"I don't know. I'll think about it. I'm not making any deals. What's two times two?"

"But you probably will let us go, won't you?" said Trurl, while Klapaucius pulled on his arm and hissed in his ear: "The thing's an imbecile; don't argue with it, for heaven's sake!"

"I won't let you go, if I don't want to," said the machine. "You just tell me how much two times two is. . . ."

Suddenly Trurl fell into a rage.

"I'll tell you; I'll tell you all right!" he screamed. "Two and two is four, and two times two is four, even if you stand on your head, pound these mountains all to dust, drink the ocean dry and swallow the sky—do you hear? Two and two is four!"

"Trurl! What are you saying? Have you taken leave of your senses? Two and two is seven, nice machine! Seven, seven!" howled Klapaucius, trying to drown out his friend.

"No! It's four! Four and only four, four from the beginning to the end of time—FOUR!" bellowed Trurl, growing hoarse.

The rock beneath their feet was seized with a feverish tremor.

The machine moved away from the cave, letting in a little pale light, and gave a piercing scream:

"That's not true! It's seven. Say it's seven or I'll hit you!"

"Never!" roared Trurl, as if he no longer cared what happened, and pebbles and dirt

"SEVEN."

rained down on their heads, for the machine had begun to ram its eight-story hulk again and again into the wall of stone, hurling itself against the mountainside until huge boulders broke away and went tumbling down into the valley.

Thunder and sulfurous fumes filled the cave, and sparks flew from the blows of steel on rock, yet through all this pandemonium one could still make out, now and then, the ragged voice of Trurl bawling:

"Two and two is four! Two and two is four!"

Klapaucius attempted to shut his friend's mouth by force, but, violently thrown off, he gave up, sat and covered his head with his arms. Not for a moment did the machine's mad efforts flag, and it seemed that any minute now the ceiling would collapse, crush the prisoners and bury them forever. But when they had lost all hope, and the air was thick with acrid smoke and choking dust, there was suddenly a horrible scraping, and a sound like a slow explosion, louder than all the maniacal banging and battering, and the air whooshed, and the black wall that blocked the cave was whisked away, as if by a hurricane, and monstrous chunks of rock came crashing down after it.

The echoes of that avalanche still rumbled and reverberated in the valley below when the two friends peered out of their cave. They saw the machine. It lay smashed and flattened, nearly broken in half by an enormous boulder that had landed in the middle of its eight floors. With the greatest care they picked their way down through the smoking rubble. In order to reach the riverbed, it was necessary to pass the remains of the machine, which resembled the wreck of some mighty vessel thrown up upon a beach. Without a word, the two stopped together in the shadow of its twisted hull. The machine still quivered slightly, and one could hear something turning, creaking feebly, within.

"Yes, this is the bad end you've come to, and two and two is—as it always was—" began Trurl, but just then the machine made a faint, barely audible croaking noise and said, for the last time, "SEVEN."

Then something snapped inside, a few stones dribbled down from overhead, and now before them lay nothing but a lifeless mass of scrap. The two constructors exchanged a look and silently, without any further comment or conversation, walked back the way they came. ❖

Translated by Michael Kandel

STANISLAW LEM

Born in Lvov, Poland (now in Ukraine), Stanislaw Lem showed an early interest in the sciences as well as in the imaginary worlds of fantasy and science fiction. The young Lem also enjoyed tinkering with broken bells, alarm clocks, and mechanical devices of all sorts. He worked as an auto mechanic during the German occupation of Poland in World War II, putting his mechanical abilities to political use by secretly damaging the Nazis' cars.

After the war, Lem studied medicine in Cracow for

1921–

a few years before turning to writing full time. It was not long before he established himself as the leading science fiction writer in Eastern Europe. Though his tales are inventive and witty, they nevertheless examine such serious themes as the purpose of life and the relationship between human beings and technology. His nearly 50 books have been translated into more than 30 languages.

OTHER WORKS *Solaris, The Invincible, Tales of Pirx the Pilot, The Cosmic Carnival of Stanislaw Lem*

WRITING ABOUT LITERATURE

MAKING A CHANGE

What are the ingredients of a good story? Words and ideas are certainly a good start. However, a writer must know how to combine those ingredients in just the right way to create unique characters, an intriguing plot, and an effective setting. On the following pages, you will

- examine how unity contributes to successful writing
- rewrite a scene from a story by changing an element
- consider how such a change affects your perception

The Writer's Style: Paragraph Unity An important ingredient in good writing is unity. In a unified paragraph, all of the sentences support the main idea.

Read the Literature

In the excerpts below, notice how the related sentences support the main idea and create a unified paragraph.

Literature Models

Implied Main Idea
Although it is not stated directly, the main idea of this paragraph is clear. How would you state it? How did the supporting sentences help you figure out the main idea?

It came on great oiled, resilient, striding legs. It towered thirty feet above half of the trees, a great evil god, folding its delicate watchmaker's claws close to its oily reptilian chest. Each lower leg was a piston, a thousand pounds of white bone, sunk in thick ropes of muscle, sheathed over in a gleam of pebbled skin like the mail of a terrible warrior. Each thigh was a ton of meat, ivory, and steel mesh. And from the great breathing cage of the upper body those two delicate arms dangled out front, arms with hands which might pick up and examine men like toys, while the snake neck coiled.

Ray Bradbury, from "A Sound of Thunder"

Stated Main Idea
In this paragraph, a topic sentence states the main idea directly. What is the main idea? How do the other sentences support it?

All the same, when I came to the Place of the Gods, I was afraid, afraid. The current of the great river is very strong—it gripped my raft with its hands. That was magic, for the river itself is wide and calm. I could feel evil spirits about me, in the bright morning; I could feel their breath on my neck as I was swept down the stream. Never have I been so much alone.

Stephen Vincent Benét, from "By the Waters of Babylon"

Connect to Science

Writers of science articles must be particularly careful to keep writing unified if they want readers to understand. In good paragraphs, unity is achieved when the details support the main idea. Notice how the following paragraph seems unified.

Magazine Article

In Montana, Jack Horner of the Museum of the Rockies has discovered scores of dinosaur nests. The eggshells in the fossilized mudstone nests were totally mashed. Conclusion: hatchlings stayed in the nest, lying around on the shells. The tips of the babies' bones had large masses of cartilage, like some baby birds. Says Horner: "It means they couldn't walk, so someone had to bring them food." Horner found fossilized berries and seeds that had been regurgitated. In nearby strata, he uncovered nests, eggs and unhatched babies of smaller, graceful bi-ped dinosaurs called hypsilophodonts. The fetuses had smooth, hard bone ends; they could have been up and out of the nest right after birth, like turtles and crocodiles. There was no single right way to be a dinosaur parent.

Sharon Begley,
from "New Theories and Old Bones Reveal
the Lifestyles of the Dinosaur," *Newsweek*

Related Details
How do the details relate to one another and support the main idea?

Try Your Hand: Achieving Paragraph Unity

1. **Choose Your Topic** Look through a newspaper for a topic that interests you, and jot down the main idea. Then create a unified paragraph that includes supporting details.

2. **Check a QuickWrite** Look through your QuickWrites for what you think is a unified paragraph. Have a partner read the paragraph and try to identify the main idea and supporting details.

3. **Try This Challenge** Choose one of the topics below, and write a unified paragraph that contains an implied main idea.

   - a special person
   - a place you dislike
   - a school of the future

SkillBuilder

 GRAMMAR FROM WRITING

Using Compound Subjects and Predicates
Unity in a paragraph can be made even stronger by combining related ideas into a single sentence. A **compound subject** is made up of two or more key words joined by a conjunction and having the same verb. Identify the key words of the compound subject in the following sentence from "By the Waters of Babylon."

The north and the west and the south are good hunting ground, but it is forbidden to go east.

A **compound predicate** is made up of two or more verbs or verb phrases joined by a conjunction and having the same subject. Locate the verbs of the compound predicate in the excerpt from "Searching for Summer" below.

Every now and then they switched on their portable radio and listened to the forecast.

APPLYING WHAT YOU'VE LEARNED
Write one sentence using a compound subject and one using a compound predicate to combine ideas.

 GRAMMAR HANDBOOK

For more information on compound subjects and compound predicates, see page 1099 of the Grammar Handbook.

Creative Response

You know the role that unity plays in good writing. Now consider the effects that elements such as character, plot, and setting have on a story. What if one of these elements were changed in one of the stories in this unit?

GUIDED ASSIGNMENT

Change a Story Element In this lesson you will change a story by changing a story element. Rewrite a portion of the story, changing any element that interests you.

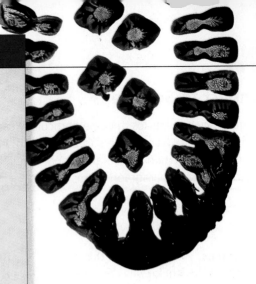

1 Prewrite and Explore

Choose a story in Unit Five that you enjoyed. What parts of the story were satisfying? Decide which elements seemed critical to the story. Consider such elements as mood, point of view, narrator, and tone, as well as plot, character, and setting.

CHOOSING A PART OF THE STORY AND AN ELEMENT

Think about a part of the story and an element you could change. These questions can help:

- What parts are most intriguing to you?
- In which part might the change of an element be most interesting?
- How would the change affect the actions and words of the characters?

GENERATING IDEAS

As a start, you might begin a list of "what if" questions that ask what would happen if an element changed. For example, if you chose to explore a plot change in Ray Bradbury's "A Sound of Thunder," you might ask yourself questions like these:

- What if the story were told by Travis, the guide?
- What if *Tyrannosaurus* killed one of the men?
- What if Eckels actually faced the giant beast?

You could also use a cause-effect chain like the one shown below to help you explore different possibilities.

Decision Point Now it's time to choose which part of the story you will rewrite and which story element you will change.

Student's Cause-Effect Chain

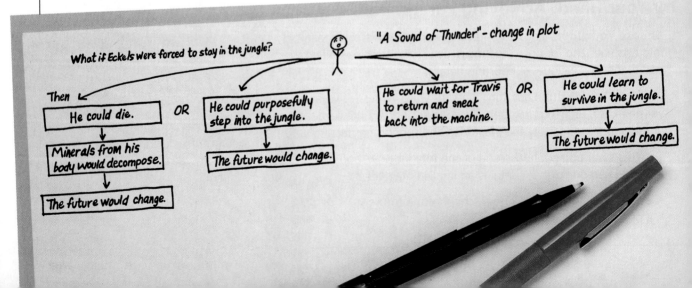

❷ Draft Your Story

As you write your draft, think carefully about the effects that one change can have on other elements of the story. If you're stuck, write the ending first and work backwards.

In the student draft below, the plot of "The Sound of Thunder" has been changed. Note the student's own questions.

Student's Draft

Travis and Eckels looked down at the shoes. "What's that?" asked Travis, noticing the butterfly.

Eckels backed away and mumbled, "Uh, I . . ."

"That's it! I won't have you ruin our business. You're staying here," said Travis.

The time machine made a tremendous noise and left abruptly. Eckels' head began to spin. He had never been so afraid and uncertain in his life. As he was thinking about his choices, an eerie feeling came over him. Looking up, he saw a pterodactyl. As it swooped down at him, he feared for his life. "What am I going to do?" he thought. Just then, an idea hit him. He stood perfectly still while the giant bird flew by him. Then, with all the courage he could find, he walked the narrow metal path towards a clearing in the trees ahead.

Does my plot progression make sense?

Do I show how other elements change when the plot changes?

❸ Share Your Work

When you've finished your draft, ask yourself

- How does my writing show a changed story element?
- Do story events still flow logically?
- How well does my writing imitate the writer's style?

 PEER RESPONSE

Then ask a classmate to read your rewritten portion of the story and respond to the following questions.

- What story element have I changed?
- How does the change affect the story?

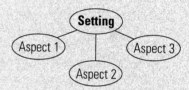
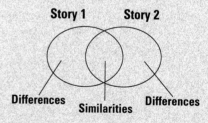

④ Revise and Edit

As you write a final draft, check to see that your writing is unified. Refer to the Grammar in Context on the opposite page and the Standards for Evaluation below. Consider sharing your final version with other students and discussing changes you made.

Student's Final Draft

Eckels had spent two long days under the cover of a tree in the jungle. During that time, a change had come over him. He felt brave. Although he was tired and hungry, he had become used to the eerie jungle sounds. He was sometimes afraid of the creatures in the jungle, but now he was very good at remaining still when an animal was near. Suddenly, he heard the noise he had been waiting for. Whhrrrr! Chink, chink, chink! Thud!

He heard the familiar voice, "Here we are! Everyone, remember what I told you about stepping off the path. One member of the last group stepped off the path and found himself in a grave situation!" With that last sentence, Travis howled an evil laugh. Members of the group sighed nervously.

"What happened to him?" one man asked.

Travis laughed again, only louder. "Well, my friend, I don't think you'd care to know!"

As he hid behind the leaves, Eckels could hear the group coming toward him. A creature from the distance approached. Eckels could feel the ground shake.

Then, there was the clicking sound of a rifle. With his newfound bravery, Eckels came face to face with his target.

Bang! A sound of thunder.

What other story elements changed when the plot changed? How did they change?

Standards for Evaluation

A creative response that changes a story element
- skillfully retells a story part while changing an element
- retains the element change throughout the story part
- changes other story elements in order to make sense with the new element

Grammar in Context

Past Perfect Tense To clearly present events, you need to use the correct verb tense. Sometimes when writing a narrative, you will need to use the past perfect tense to show an action that came before another past action. To form the past perfect tense, use the helping verb *had* with the past participle. Look at the following student draft of a story with actions that took place in the past.

Eckels ^*had* spent two long days under the cover of a tree in the jungle. During that time, a change ^*had come* came over him. He felt brave. Although he was tired and hungry, he ^*had become* became used to the eerie jungle sounds. He was sometimes afraid of the creatures in the jungle, but now he was very good at remaining still when an animal was near.

This story part takes place in the past, but some of the action took place even earlier. Therefore, the helping verb *had* plus the past participle was inserted to create the past perfect verb tense. Notice how the past perfect verb tense makes sense in the story. Consult the lessons on verb tenses and forms in the Grammar Handbook on page 1081 for more help.

Try Your Hand: Using Past Perfect Tense

Create past perfect verb tenses in the following paragraph.

The change in Eckels occurred suddenly. His confidence grew. He no longer shuddered at the sound of a prehistoric animal approaching him. As for shelter and food, he built a rough little hut out of bunches of leaves. Luckily, he brought a survival kit with a basic food supply. He waited patiently until Travis and the time machine finally returned.

SkillBuilder

 GRAMMAR FROM WRITING

Past Participles of Irregular Verbs

When you use the past perfect tense, you will be using past participles too. Most past participles of regular verbs are formed by adding -*d* or -*ed* to the present verb form. Some examples follow.

*Travis had **guided** safaris for ten years.* (guide)

*Eckels had **pointed** the rifle at his target.* (point)

Past participles of irregular verbs are not formed by adding -*d* or -*ed*. Since they are formed irregularly, you may need to consult a dictionary or grammar handbook. Check the following samples.

*Eckels **built** a hut with materials he had **found**.* (build, find)

*He felt lucky that he had **brought** a survival kit.* (bring)

APPLYING WHAT YOU'VE LEARNED
Create three sentences that contain the past participles of irregular verbs. Refer to a dictionary if you need help.

 GRAMMAR HANDBOOK

For more information on past participles of irregular verbs, see page 1082 of the Grammar Handbook.

NEW AND IMPROVED?

You've seen how changing an element changes a story. How might changing an element on a product's package change the way you think about that product? Imagine you're in a grocery store looking for fruit juice. How might the differences between the packages affect your buying decision?

View Look at the two products below. In your notebook, list differences between the two. What do you notice first?

Interpret Review your list of differences. Which product do you like better? Which seems healthier? Which would you buy?

Discuss What did you base your choice on? In a small group, talk about the power of a package. What makes a package appealing? Refer to the SkillBuilder on comparing and contrasting for more ideas.

All Natural

Cranberry
Apple
Juice

16 FL. OZ.
(473 mL)

SkillBuilder

 CRITICAL THINKING

Comparing and Contrasting Products

Can you really judge a book by its cover? Do colors, shapes, and specific words persuade you to buy a product? Believe it or not, many consumers choose one product instead of another because of the packaging rather than the content. A product's packaging might cause you to believe that one product is better than another—or that you'll be "better" for having purchased it.

When you evaluate by comparing and contrasting, you are recognizing similarities and differences. Each time you taste a different food, consider buying a new product, or listen to a new musical group, you judge similarities and differences. The key to making smart judgments is to look beyond the surface, or package, to discover the facts.

APPLYING WHAT YOU'VE LEARNED
Try the following with a partner.

- Flip through a newspaper or magazine and find an advertisement that compares and contrasts two products. In two columns, list similarities and differences of the two products. Which product would you purchase?
- Discuss a time when you made a choice based on a product's packaging. What was the outcome? What were your reasons for your decision?

CULTURAL CROSSROADS

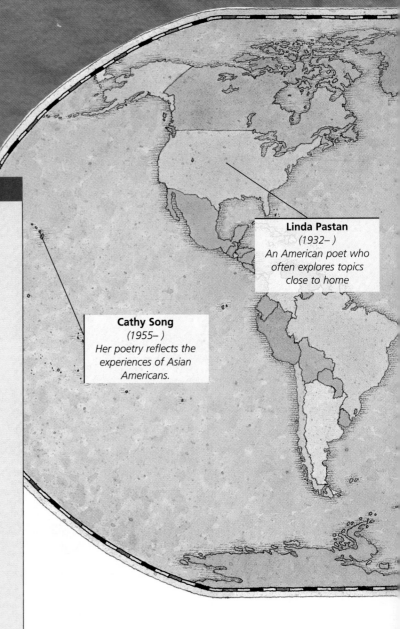

Linda Pastan
(1932–)
An American poet who often explores topics close to home

Cathy Song
(1955–)
Her poetry reflects the experiences of Asian Americans.

REFLECTING ON THEME

The phrase *cultural crossroads* has two distinct meanings. On the one hand, it can refer to an intersection of two or more cultures—an intersection that may produce mutual enrichment, conflict, or misunderstanding. On the other hand, it can refer to a critical turning point within a single culture. For example, a traditional society may reach a crossroads when it seeks to adopt modern ways of living. As you read this part of Unit Five, consider which meaning best applies to each selection.

What Do You Think? Working with a partner, find two or three news stories dealing with cultural crossroads. For example, a newspaper might have a report about a conflict between two cultural groups, or a newscast might feature a story about a culture in the process of change. Discuss your findings with your classmates.

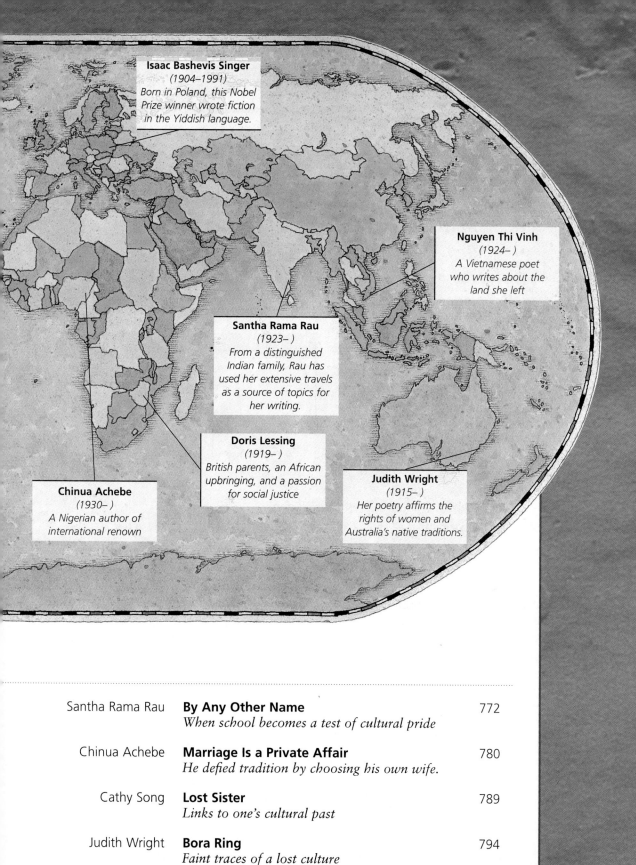

Isaac Bashevis Singer
(1904–1991)
Born in Poland, this Nobel Prize winner wrote fiction in the Yiddish language.

Nguyen Thi Vinh
(1924–)
A Vietnamese poet who writes about the land she left

Santha Rama Rau
(1923–)
From a distinguished Indian family, Rau has used her extensive travels as a source of topics for her writing.

Doris Lessing
(1919–)
British parents, an African upbringing, and a passion for social justice

Chinua Achebe
(1930–)
A Nigerian author of international renown

Judith Wright
(1915–)
Her poetry affirms the rights of women and Australia's native traditions.

PREVIEWING

FICTION

No Witchcraft for Sale
Doris Lessing Southern Rhodesia / England

PERSONAL CONNECTION

Think of an incident in which people from different cultures or races have misjudged or misunderstood one another. Perhaps you have personally experienced such a misunderstanding, or perhaps you have read about one. Describe the incident in your notebook, offering your explanation of what happened. Then share your description with your classmates. In a class discussion, try to identify some of the causes and effects of cultural or racial misunderstanding. You might use a diagram like the one shown to help you organize your ideas.

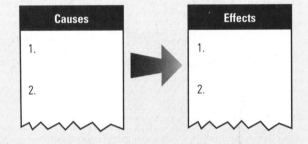

Cultural or Racial Misunderstanding

Causes		Effects
1.		1.
2.		2.

HISTORICAL CONNECTION

Africa has long been a setting for misunderstanding and confrontation between cultures and races. In the 1800s and early 1900s, most African countries became colonies of European powers. Although many of the African countries had been strong kingdoms with well-developed economies and cultures, they came to be dominated politically, economically, and culturally by their European rulers.

In the 1890s, the region that would become Southern Rhodesia fell under British control. A land of great beauty and mineral wealth, Southern Rhodesia had a large population of British settlers that for decades dominated the country, both as a British colony and, after 1965, as an independent nation. Following a sometimes violent struggle, the black majority gained control of the country—in 1980 renaming it Zimbabwe, after the ancient African capital city of the region. "No Witchcraft for Sale" takes place in Southern Rhodesia during the time of white rule.

READING CONNECTION

Interpreting Characterizations to Discover an Author's Viewpoint
Writers of fiction seldom state their viewpoints directly. The ways in which an author presents characters, however, may provide clues to his or her opinions. For example, a character treated sympathetically may embody values that the author approves of. As you read Doris Lessing's story, decide which characters are portrayed sympathetically. What do these portrayals suggest about Lessing's views on the misunderstandings described?

Using Your Reading Log Use your reading log to record your responses to the questions inserted in the selection. Also jot down other thoughts and feelings that come to you as you read.

LASERLINKS
• *GEOGRAPHICAL CONNECTON*

Conjur Woman (1975), Romare Bearden. Collage on board, 46″ × 36″, private collection, courtesy of Sheldon Ross Gallery, Birmingham, Michigan, and the Estate of Romare Bearden.

No Witchcraft for Sale

Doris Lessing

The Farquars had been childless for years when little Teddy was born; and they were touched by the pleasure of their servants, who brought presents of fowls and eggs and flowers to the homestead when they came to rejoice over the baby, exclaiming with delight over his downy golden head and his blue eyes. They congratulated Mrs. Farquar as if she had achieved a very great thing, and she felt that she had—her smile for the lingering, admiring natives was warm and grateful.

Later, when Teddy had his first haircut, Gideon the cook picked up the soft gold tufts from the ground and held them reverently in his hand. Then he smiled at the little boy and said: "Little Yellow Head." That became the native name for the child. Gideon and Teddy were great friends from the first. When Gideon had finished his work, he would lift Teddy on his shoulders to the shade of a big tree, and play with him there, forming curious little toys from twigs and leaves and grass, or shaping animals from wetted soil. When Teddy learned to walk, it was often Gideon who crouched before him, clucking encouragement, finally catching him when he fell, tossing him up in the air till they both became breathless with laughter. Mrs. Farquar was fond of the old cook because of his love for her child.

There was no second baby; and one day Gideon said: "Ah, missus, missus, the Lord above sent this one; Little Yellow Head is the most good thing we have in our house." Because of that "we" Mrs. Farquar felt a warm impulse towards her cook; and at the end of the month she raised his wages. He had been with her now for several years; he was one of the few natives who had his wife and children in the compound and never wanted to go home to his kraal,[1] which was some hundreds of miles away. Sometimes a small piccanin[2] who had been born the same time as Teddy, could be

seen peering from the edge of the bush, staring in awe at the little white boy with his miraculous fair hair and Northern blue eyes. The two little children would gaze at each other with a wide, interested gaze, and once Teddy put out his hand curiously to touch the black child's cheeks and hair.

Gideon, who was watching, shook his head wonderingly, and said: "Ah, missus, these are both children, and one will grow up to be a baas,[3] and one will be a servant"; and Mrs. Farquar smiled and said sadly, "Yes, Gideon, I was thinking the same." She sighed. "It is God's

---

"Gideon, look at me!" And Gideon would laugh and say: "Very clever, Little Yellow Head."

---

will," said Gideon, who was mission boy.[4] The Farquars were very religious people; and this shared feeling about God bound servant and masters even closer together.

Teddy was about six years old when he was given a scooter, and discovered the intoxications of speed. All day he would fly around the homestead, in and out of flowerbeds, scattering squawking chickens and irritated dogs, finishing with a wide dizzying arc into the kitchen door. There he would cry: "Gideon, look at me!" And Gideon would laugh and say: "Very clever, Little Yellow Head." Gideon's youngest son, who was now a herdsboy, came especially up

---

1. **kraal** (krôl): a native village in southern Africa.
2. **piccanin** (pĭk'ə-nĭn'): a native child (usually considered offensive).
3. **baas:** boss.
4. **mission boy:** a boy educated at a school run by Christian missionaries.

from the compound to see the scooter. He was afraid to come near it, but Teddy showed off in front of him. "Piccanin," shouted Teddy, "get out of my way!" And he raced in circles around the black child until he was frightened and fled back to the bush.

"Why did you frighten him?" asked Gideon, gravely reproachful.

Teddy said defiantly: "He's only a black boy," and laughed.

Then, when Gideon turned away from him without speaking, his face fell. Very soon he slipped into the house and found an orange and brought it to Gideon, saying: "This is for you." He could not bring himself to say he was sorry; but he could not bear to lose Gideon's affection either. Gideon took the orange unwillingly and sighed. "Soon you will be going away to school, Little Yellow Head," he said wonderingly, "and then you will be grown up." He shook his head gently and said, "And that is how our lives go." He seemed to be putting a distance between himself and Teddy, not because of resentment, but in the way a person accepts something inevitable. The baby had lain in his arms and smiled up into his face: the tiny boy had swung from his shoulders and played with him by the hour. Now Gideon would not let his flesh touch the flesh of the white child. He was kind, but there was a grave formality in his voice that made Teddy pout and sulk away. Also, it made him into a man: with Gideon he was polite, and carried himself formally, and if he came into the kitchen to ask for something, it was in the way a white man uses towards a servant, expecting to be obeyed.

But on the day that Teddy came staggering into the kitchen with his fists to his eyes,

EVALUATE

How does Teddy view Gideon?

shrieking with pain, Gideon dropped the pot full of hot soup that he was holding, rushed to the child, and forced aside his fingers. "A snake!" he exclaimed. Teddy had been on his scooter and had come to a rest with his foot on the side of a big tub of plants. A tree snake, hanging by its tail from the roof, had spat full into his eyes. Mrs. Farquar came running when she heard the commotion. "He'll go blind," she sobbed, holding Teddy close against her. "Gideon, he'll go blind!" Already the eyes, with perhaps half an hour's sight left in them, were swollen up to the size of fists: Teddy's small white face was distorted by great purple oozing protuberances.[5] Gideon said: "Wait a minute, missus, I'll get some medicine." He ran off into the bush.

Mrs. Farquar lifted the child into the house and bathed his eyes with permanganate.[6] She had scarcely heard Gideon's words; but when she saw that her remedies had no effect at all, and remembered how she had seen natives with no sight in their eyes because of the spitting of a snake, she began to look for the return of her cook, remembering what she heard of the efficacy of native herbs. She stood by the window, holding the terrified, sobbing little boy in her arms, and peered helplessly into the bush. It was not more than a few minutes before she saw Gideon come bounding back, and in his hand he held a plant.

"Do not be afraid, missus," said Gideon, "this will cure Little Yellow Head's eyes." He stripped the leaves from the plant, leaving a small white fleshy root. Without even washing it, he put the root in his mouth, chewed it

---

5. **protuberances** (prō-tōō'bər-ən-səz): bulges or swellings.

6. **permanganate** (pər-măng'gə-nāt´): a solution of the chemical potassium permanganate, formerly used as an antidote to snake poison.

WORDS TO KNOW   **efficacy** (ĕf'ĭ-kə-sē) *n.* the power to produce a desired effect; effectiveness

The Ukimwi Road (1994), John Harris.

vigorously, and then held the spittle there while he took the child forcibly from Mrs. Farquar. He gripped Teddy down between his knees, and pressed the balls of his thumbs into the swollen eyes, so that the child screamed and Mrs. Farquar cried out in protest: "Gideon, Gideon!" But Gideon took no notice. He knelt over the writhing child, pushing back the puffy lids till chinks of eyeball showed, and then he spat hard, again and again, into first one eye, and then the other. He finally lifted Teddy gently into his mother's arms, and said: "His eyes will get better." But Mrs. Farquar was weeping with terror, and she could hardly thank him: it was impossible to believe that Teddy could keep his sight. In a couple of hours the swellings were gone: the eyes were inflamed and tender but Teddy could see. Mr. and Mrs. Farquar went to Gideon in the kitchen and thanked him over and over again. They felt helpless because of their gratitude: it seemed they could do nothing

to express it. They gave Gideon presents for his wife and children, and a big increase in wages, but these things could not pay for Teddy's now completely cured eyes. Mrs. Farquar said: "Gideon, God chose you as an instrument for His goodness," and Gideon said: "Yes, missus, God is very good."

Now, when such a thing happens on a farm, it cannot be long before everyone hears of it. Mr. and Mrs. Farquar told their neighbors and the story was discussed from one end of the district to the other. The bush is full of secrets. No one can live in Africa, or at least on the veld,[7] without learning very soon that there is an ancient wisdom of leaf and soil and season— and, too, perhaps most important of all, of the darker tracts of the human mind—which is the black man's heritage. Up and down the district

---

7. **veld** (vĕlt): an open, grass-covered plain of southern Africa.

people were telling <u>anecdotes</u>, reminding each other of things that had happened to them.

"But I saw it myself, I tell you. It was a puff-adder bite. The kaffir's[8] arm was swollen to the elbow, like a great shiny black bladder. He was

> **The scientist explained how humanity might benefit if this new drug could be offered for sale.**

groggy after a half a minute. He was dying. Then suddenly a kaffir walked out of the bush with his hands full of green stuff. He smeared something on the place, and next day my boy was back at work, and all you could see was two small punctures in the skin."

This was the kind of tale they told. And, as always, with a certain amount of exasperation, because while all of them knew that in the bush of Africa are waiting valuable drugs locked in bark, in simple-looking leaves, in roots, it was impossible to ever get the truth about them from the natives themselves.

The story eventually reached town; and perhaps it was at a sundowner party, or some such function, that a doctor, who happened to be there, challenged it. "Nonsense," he said. "These things get exaggerated in the telling. We are always checking up on this kind of story, and we draw a blank every time."

Anyway, one morning there arrived a strange car at the homestead, and out stepped one of the workers from the laboratory in town, with cases full of test-tubes and chemicals.

Mr. and Mrs. Farquar were flustered and pleased and flattered. They asked the scientist to lunch, and they told the story all over again, for the hundredth time. Little Teddy was there too, his blue eyes sparkling with health, to prove the truth of it. The scientist explained how humanity might benefit if this new drug could be offered for sale; and the Farquars were even more pleased: they were kind, simple people, who liked to think of something good coming about because of them. But when the scientist began talking of the money that might result, their manner showed discomfort. Their feelings over the miracle (that was how they thought of it) were so strong and deep and religious, that it was <u>distasteful</u> to them to think of money. The scientist, seeing their faces, went back to his first point, which was the advancement of humanity. He was perhaps a trifle perfunctory: it was not the first time he had come salting the tail of[9] a fabulous bush-secret.

E ventually, when the meal was over, the Farquars called Gideon into their living-room and explained to him that this baas, here, was a big Doctor from the Big City, and he had come all that way to see Gideon. At this Gideon seemed afraid; he did not understand; and Mrs. Farquar explained quickly that it was because of the wonderful thing he had done with Teddy's eyes that the Big Baas had come.

Gideon looked from Mrs. Farquar to Mr. Farquar, and then at the little boy, who was showing great importance because of the occasion. At last he said grudgingly: "The Big

---

8. **kaffir's** (kăf'ərz): belonging to a black African (usually considered offensive).

9. **salting the tail of:** trying to capture (from the childhood belief that birds can be caught by putting salt on their tail).

Baas want to know what medicine I used?" He spoke incredulously, as if he could not believe his old friends could so betray him. Mr. Farquar began explaining how a useful medicine could be made out of the root, and how it could be put on sale, and how thousands of people, black and white, up and down the continent of Africa, could be saved by the medicine when that spitting snake filled their eyes with poison. Gideon listened, his eyes bent on the ground, the skin of his forehead puckering in discomfort. When Mr. Farquar had finished he did not

> **But they went on persuading and arguing, with all the force of their exasperation.**

reply. The scientist, who all this time had been leaning back in a big chair, sipping his coffee and smiling with skeptical good-humor, chipped in and explained all over again, in different words, about the making of drugs and the progress of science. Also, he offered Gideon a present.

There was silence after this further explanation, and then Gideon remarked <u>indifferently</u> that he could not remember the root. His face was sullen and hostile, even when he looked at the Farquars, whom he usually treated like old friends. They were beginning to feel annoyed; and this feeling <u>annulled</u> the guilt that had been sprung into life by Gideon's accusing manner. They were beginning to feel that he was unreasonable. But it was at that moment that they all realized he would never give in. The magical drug would remain where it was, unknown and useless except for the tiny

scattering of Africans who had the knowledge, natives who might be digging a ditch for the municipality in a ragged shirt and a pair of patched shorts, but who were still born to healing, hereditary healers, being the nephews or sons of the old witch doctors whose ugly masks and bits of bone and all the uncouth properties of magic were the outward signs of real power and wisdom.

The Farquars might tread on that plant fifty times a day as they passed from house to garden, from cow kraal[10] to mealie[11] field, but they would never know it.

But they went on persuading and arguing, with all the force of their exasperation; and Gideon continued to say that he could not remember, or that there was no such root, or that it was the wrong season of the year, or that it wasn't the root itself, but the spit from his mouth that had cured Teddy's eyes. He said all these things one after another, and seemed not to care they were contradictory. He was rude and stubborn. The Farquars could hardly recognize their gentle, lovable old servant in this ignorant, perversely obstinate[12] African, standing there in front of them with lowered eyes, his hands twitching his cook's apron, repeating over and over whichever one of the stupid refusals that first entered his head.

And suddenly he appeared to give in. He lifted his head, gave a long, blank angry look at the circle of whites, who seemed to him like a circle of yelping dogs pressing around him, and said: "I will show you the root."

They walked single file away from the homestead down a kaffir path. It was a blazing December afternoon, with the sky full of hot

---

10. **cow kraal:** a livestock enclosure or corral.

11. **mealie:** corn.

12. **perversely obstinate:** stubbornly and wrongly insistent on having one's own way.

rain-clouds. Everything was hot: the sun was like a bronze tray whirling overhead, there was a heat shimmer over the fields, the soil was scorching underfoot, the dusty wind blew gritty and thick and warm in their faces. It was a terrible day, fit only for reclining on a verandah[13] with iced drinks, which is where they would normally have been at that hour.

From time to time, remembering that on the day of the snake it had taken ten minutes to find the root, someone asked: "Is it much further, Gideon?" And Gideon would answer over his shoulder, with angry politeness: "I'm looking for the root, baas." And indeed, he would frequently bend sideways and trail his hand among the grasses with a gesture that was insulting in its perfunctoriness. He walked them through the bush along unknown paths for two hours, in that melting destroying heat, so that the sweat trickled coldly down them and their heads ached. They were all quite silent: the Farquars because they were angry, the scientist because he was being proved right again; there was no such plant. His was a tactful silence.

PREDICT

Do you think Gideon will find the root?

At last, six miles from the house, Gideon suddenly decided they had had enough; or perhaps his anger evaporated at that moment. He picked up, without an attempt at looking anything but casual, a handful of blue flowers from the grass, flowers that had been growing plentifully all down the paths they had come.

He handed them to the scientist without looking at him, and marched off by himself on the way home, leaving them to follow him if they chose.

When they got back to the house, the scientist went to the kitchen to thank Gideon: he was very very polite, even though there was an amused look in his eyes. Gideon was not there. Throwing the flowers casually into the back of his car, the eminent visitor departed on his way back to his laboratory.

Gideon was back in his kitchen in time to prepare dinner, but he was sulking. He spoke to Mr. Farquar like an unwilling servant. It was days before they liked each other again.

The Farquars made inquiries about the root from their laborers. Sometimes they were answered with distrustful stares. Sometimes the natives said: "We do not know. We have never heard of the root." One, the cattle boy, who had been with them a long time, and had grown to trust them a little, said: "Ask your boy in the kitchen. Now, there's a doctor for you. He's the son of a famous medicine man who used to be in these parts, and there's nothing he cannot cure." Then he added politely: "Of course, he's not as good as the white man's doctor, we know that, but he's good for us."

After some time, when the soreness had gone from between the Farquars and Gideon, they began to joke: "When are you going to show us the snake-root, Gideon?" And he would laugh and shake his head, saying, a little uncomfortably: "But I did show you, missus, have you forgotten?"

Much later, Teddy, as a schoolboy, would come into the kitchen and say: "You old rascal, Gideon! Do you remember that time you tricked us all by making us walk miles all over the veld for nothing? It was so far my father had to carry me!"

And Gideon would double up with polite laughter. After much laughing, he would suddenly straighten himself up, wipe his old eyes, and look sadly at Teddy, who was grinning mischievously at him across the kitchen: "Ah, Little Yellow Head, how you have grown! Soon you will be grown up with a farm of your own . . ." ❖

---

13. **verandah** (və-răn′də): a long porch.

RESPONDING OPTIONS

FROM PERSONAL RESPONSE TO CRITICAL ANALYSIS

REFLECT   1. Which part of this story evoked the strongest response in you? In your notebook, describe your reaction to that part of the story.

RETHINK   2. How do you feel about Gideon's refusal to share his knowledge of the medicinal plant?
   Consider
   - the relationship between the whites and the blacks
   - the title of the story
   - the plant's effectiveness against snake poison
   - what you think motivates Gideon's actions

   3. The Farquars believe themselves to be people of goodwill. Do you agree? Support your opinion.

   4. In your judgment, what are the causes and effects of cultural and racial misunderstanding in the story? You may find it helpful to review the chart that you made for the Personal Connection on page 744.

   5. What do you think is the author's view of the characters and society that she depicts?

RELATE   6. In this story, Gideon stands up for his own dignity and the dignity of his culture. Think of other instances you know of in which an individual has taken a stand to protect his or her culture. How successful do you think such actions can be in influencing people's attitudes?

ANOTHER PATHWAY

Cooperative Learning

Work to develop a newspaper editorial page focusing on the events in this story. Include an editorial presenting the paper's position on whether Gideon was right to keep his secret. Express other points of view about Gideon's decision in letters to the editor from doctors, snakebite victims, and traditional healers.

QUICKWRITES

1. Assume the identity of Doris Lessing and write an **afterword** to the story, explaining the story's theme. Also explain which characters reflect values that you support.

2. Write a **dialogue** between Gideon and his son, in which Gideon explains why he did not give the scientist the healing root.

📁 *PORTFOLIO Save your writing. You may want to use it later as a springboard to a piece for your portfolio.*

LITERARY CONCEPTS

In the plot of a story, the **climax** is the moment when the reader's interest and emotional intensity reach their highest point. This moment is also called the turning point, since it usually determines how the conflict of the story will be resolved. What would you identify as the climax of "No Witchcraft for Sale"? With a partner, create a plot diagram, marking each event as a point on a line that rises to a peak at the climax, then falls off as the conflict is resolved.

ALTERNATIVE ACTIVITIES

1. Prepare an **oral tale** that Gideon might tell his neighbors about his "helping" the scientist, and tell it to your classmates.

2. Create a **bar graph** in which you rate each character's power in society, with the longest bar representing the most powerful character. Then explain your ratings to the class.

ACROSS THE CURRICULUM

Health With a partner, research the medicinal properties of plants native to your part of the country. Present your findings by displaying a sample or picture of each plant along with an explanation of its medicinal use.

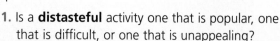

Answer the following questions.

1. Is a **distasteful** activity one that is popular, one that is difficult, or one that is unappealing?

2. Are you most likely to react **indifferently** to a remark that angers you, that bores you, or that surprises you?

3. Is an **anecdote** a story that is amusing, that is boring, or that is instructional?

4. Would a medicine known for its **efficacy** have a reputation for working well, for being expensive, or for having side effects?

5. In an effort to **annul** the effects of an insulting remark you made, would you repeat it, add to it, or say you were kidding?

DORIS LESSING

1919–

Born to British parents in Persia (now Iran), Doris Lessing grew up in Southern Rhodesia, where her family went to farm when she was about five. Her childhood was fairly solitary, and she spent most of her time reading or walking outdoors. "The storms, the winds, the silences of the bush; the sunlit or rain-whipped mountains; fields of maize miles long; sunflowers that turned their heads after the sun; cotton plants with their butterfly-like pink and white flowers—these, and the neighbors, were my education," she reports.

Lessing left school at 14 and worked as a nursemaid and telephone operator in Salisbury, Southern Rhodesia, until she married at the age of 19. In 1949, after two failed marriages, she moved to England, which remains her place of residence. Not long afterward, Lessing published her first novel, *The Grass Is Singing* (1950), and the story collection *This Was the* *Old Chief's Country* (1951). These stories were based on her intimate knowledge of Southern Rhodesia, especially the problems between blacks and whites. Because of her outspoken criticism of racism and her radical political sympathies, Lessing was banned from her homeland and South Africa. Nonetheless, her works have been praised for their honest portrayal of colonial Africa and its mysterious, often harsh, natural beauty.

Another major theme in Lessing's writing is the role of women in modern society. *The Golden Notebook* (1962), an experimental novel about a woman coming to terms with her personal relationships and her role in the world, is regarded as her masterpiece.

OTHER WORKS *Going Home; African Stories; The Doris Lessing Reader; Under My Skin: Volume One of My Autobiography, to 1949*

LASERLINKS
• *HEALTH CONNECTION*

PREVIEWING

Thoughts of Hanoi
Nguyen Thi Vinh (nwĭn′ tē′ vĭng′) Vietnam

PERSONAL CONNECTION

Imagine finding yourself in the midst of a civil war and having to move halfway across the country to support the side that you favored. How do you think you would feel about your former home? How would you feel about your friends who were fighting for the opposite side? Discuss your ideas with classmates.

CULTURAL CONNECTION

Like all civil wars, the war between Communist North Vietnam and anti-Communist South Vietnam pitted friend against friend, relative against relative. The situation was particularly difficult in a small country whose people had traditionally viewed themselves as one large extended family—an attitude reflected in the Vietnamese language, in which there is no word corresponding to *you*. The Vietnamese address even strangers as "Brother," "Sister," "Uncle," "Aunt," "Grandfather," and "Grandmother."

The poet Nguyen Thi Vinh was born near Hanoi, the capital of North Vietnam. Because of her anti-Communist convictions, however, she moved during the civil war to South Vietnam, where she published this poem.

WRITING CONNECTION

In your notebook, make a simple chart like the one shown. In the first column, list images that suggest war; in the second column, list images that suggest peace. Then, as you read Nguyen Thi Vinh's poem, compare your images of war and peace with those in the poem.

War	Peace
• an exploding gun	• a peaceful lake on a summer afternoon

Thoughts of Hanoi

Nguyen Thi Vinh

The night is deep and chill
as in early autumn. Pitchblack,
it thickens after each lightning flash.
I dream of Hanoi:
5 Co-ngu Road[1]
ten years of separation
the way back sliced by a frontier of hatred.
I want to bury the past
to burn the future
10 still I yearn
still I fear
those endless nights
waiting for dawn.

Brother,
15 how is Hang Dao[2] now?
How is Ngoc Son[3] temple?
Do the trains still run
each day from Hanoi
to the neighboring towns?
20 To Bac-ninh, Cam-giang, Yen-bai,[4]
the small villages, islands
of brown thatch in a lush green sea?

---

1. **Co-ngu** (kông′o͞o′).
2. **Hang Dao** (häng′ dou′).
3. **Ngoc Son** (ngôk′ sŏn′).
4. **Bac-ninh** (bäk′nĭn′), **Cam-giang** (käm′gē-äng′), **Yen-bai** (yĕn′bī′).

Đêm sâu thẳm, thâm u
từng cơn chớp lóe
càng tăng thêm cảnh mịt mù
hơi mưa lành lạnh
5 dường như trời đã sang Thu

Tôi mơ về Hà nội
tôi nhớ đường Cổ Ngư
mười năm cách biệt
ngăn lối về bằng biên giới hận thù

10 Anh ơi phố Hàng Đào giờ ra sao
đền Ngọc Sơn thế nào
ga Hàng Cỏ có còn
những toa tàu hỏa
hằng ngày bao chuyến đi về
15 qua khắp các vùng lân cận?

Bắc Ninh Cẩm Giàng, Yên Báy . . .
tôi nhớ những xóm làng nho nhỏ
chừng vài trăm mái tranh
chung quanh toàn đồng xanh

755

The girls
   bright eyes
25   ruddy cheeks
   four-piece dresses
      raven-bill scarves
   sowing harvesting
      spinning weaving
30 all year round,
the boys
   ploughing
      transplanting
in the fields
35   in their shops
running across
   the meadow at evening
to fly kites
   and sing alternating songs.[5]

40 Stainless blue sky,
   jubilant voices of children
stumbling through the alphabet,
   village graybeards strolling to the
   temple,
grandmothers basking in twilight sun,
45   chewing betel leaves[6]
while the children run—

---

5. **alternating songs:** songs sung in rounds.
6. **betel** (bĕt′l) **leaves:** the leaves of the betel
   palm, which are wrapped around the seed
   of the plant and chewed like chewing gum.

20   Các nàng con gái
      mắt sáng má hồng
      mặc áo tứ thân
      chít khăn mỏ quạ

      Các chàng trai da rám, ngực đầy
25   đi cấy đi cày
      làm thợ sơn thợ khảm
      Nền trời cao trong xanh
      tiếng trẻ reo vui nói ngọng
      ê . . . a tập đánh vần

30   Các ông già tóc bạc râu dài
      thong thả thăm đình thăm miếu
      Các bà già ngồi sưởi nắng hoàng hôn
      nhai trầu bỏm bẻm
      mắt nhìn con trẻ thương yêu

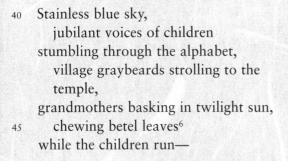

Brother,
how is all that now?
Or is it obsolete?
50 Are you like me,
reliving the past,
imagining the future?
Do you count me as a friend
or am I the enemy in your eyes?
55 Brother, I am afraid
that one day I'll be with the March-North Army[7]
meeting you on your way to the South.
I might be the one to shoot you then
or you me
60 but please
not with hatred.

7. **March-North Army:** the South
Vietnamese army marching north
to invade Communist North
Vietnam.

35 Anh ơi giờ cảnh ấy thế nào
hẳn đã thành lạc hậu
và còn anh
có như tôi
nhớ về dĩ vãng
40 mơ chuyện tương lai
anh còn coi tôi là bạn
hay đã chuyển thành thù

Nhớ không anh, ngày trước
hai chúng mình cùng trường, chung lớp
45 bảo nhau rằng tình bạn thâm sâu
Giờ đây Bến Hải chia đôi đất nước
gà nhà bôi mặt đá nhau
bởi các tay cá độ

Tôi sợ có ngày tôi theo đoàn quân Bắc tiến
50 anh vào xâm chiếm miền Nam
gặp nhau trên chiến trận
anh bắn tôi, tôi bắn anh
trong ánh mắt nhìn nhau thù hận!
Có thể nào như thế không anh?

For don't you remember how it was,
you and I in school together,
plotting our lives together?
65   Those roots go deep!

Brother, we are men,
conscious of more
than material needs.
How can this happen to us
70   my friend
my foe?

Translated by Nguyen Ngoc Bich

55 *Ngày xưa Hà Nội hiền lành*
tình người như bánh cốm xanh
  ngọt ngào
Mùa Thu hồng chín nao nao
lá sen gói thủy chung vào dậy
  hương . . .

RESPONDING OPTIONS

FROM PERSONAL RESPONSE TO CRITICAL ANALYSIS

REFLECT

1. Draw a picture to convey the feelings that this poem evoked in you. Share your drawing with a classmate and discuss your response to the poem.

RETHINK

2. How do you think the speaker feels about being a soldier in the civil war?

   Consider
   - his description, in the first stanza, of his current situation
   - the feelings he expresses in his memories of Hanoi
   - his fear of encountering his "brother" in battle (lines 55–61)

3. How would you describe the relationship between the speaker and the person he is addressing?

   Consider
   - why the speaker uses the word *brother*
   - the effects that the civil war has had on both men
   - the meaning of the last stanza

4. Why do you think the poet chose to create a male speaker for this poem? Explain your opinion.

5. What does the poem suggest to you about the poet's view of the civil war?

RELATE

6. Do you think that countries ever fully recover from the wounds of civil wars? Cite examples from history or current events to support your opinion.

ANOTHER PATHWAY

With a partner, rewrite this poem as a letter from the speaker to a friend in the north. Try to express the speaker's feelings about the war and about the contrast between his current situation and his memories of his past. Add details as needed to make your letter sound authentic. Then read the letter to your class.

QUICKWRITES

1. Write your own **dramatic monologue** about civil war. Use ideas prompted by your reading of the poem or by your work for the Personal Connection and the Writing Connection on page 754.

2. Write **extended definitions** of the words *war* and *peace* that reflect the speaker's views of the subjects. If your views are different from the speaker's, also write your own definitions of the two terms.

3. Draft an **essay** in which you compare the feelings expressed in this poem with those expressed in Tim O'Brien's "On the Rainy River" (page 266) or in the excerpt from Le Ly Hayslip's *When Heaven and Earth Changed Places* (page 140).

   📁 *PORTFOLIO Save your writing. You may want to use it later as a springboard to a piece for your portfolio.*

LITERARY CONCEPTS

"Thoughts of Hanoi" is a **dramatic monologue,** the speech of a character in a dramatic situation. In a dramatic monologue, the speaker usually addresses a silent or absent listener, as if engaged in a private conversation. Practice reading this poem aloud as if you were the Vietnamese soldier who is the speaker. Then perform your dramatic reading for the rest of the class.

ALTERNATIVE ACTIVITIES

1. Create two **illustrations** for this poem, one representing the speaker's current situation and one showing his recollection of a past event. Your illustrations should convey the contrasting moods of the two experiences.

2. Find **recordings** of songs about the American Civil War and share them with the class. In a discussion, compare the feelings expressed in the American songs with the feelings conveyed in this poem.

LITERARY LINKS

What does the speaker of this poem have in common with the main character in Hwang Sunwŏn's story "Cranes" (page 33)?

CRITIC'S CORNER

Nguyen Ngoc Bich, who translated this poem into English, has said that Nguyen Thi Vinh's "sincerity shines right through her work." Cite details from the poem that support this statement.

ACROSS THE CURRICULUM

History Research the aftermath of the war in Vietnam. What steps were taken to rebuild the country? How were members of the defeated army treated? What has life in Vietnam been like since the war? Share your findings in an oral report.

NGUYEN THI VINH

Born into a middle-class family in northern Vietnam, Nguyen Thi Vinh (1924–) spent most of her childhood in the city of Hanoi. Her first husband was a well-known activist in the Vietnamese nationalist movement seeking to free the country from French control, but neither he nor Nguyen Thi Vinh supported the Communists. After World War II, when the Communists began taking over the North, the couple fled to Hong Kong.

In 1952, Nguyen Thi Vinh settled in Saigon (now Ho Chi Minh City), then the capital of South Vietnam. She began contributing stories to magazines and in 1953 published her first story collection, *Two Sisters*. From 1954 until the fall of South Vietnam two decades later, she published several works of fiction as well as a collection of poetry. She also helped found the literary magazine *Tan Phong* (New Wind), which specialized in works by women, and later edited another magazine, *Dong Phuong* (The East).

Like other South Vietnamese, Nguyen Thi Vinh suffered great hardship after South Vietnam surrendered to the North Vietnamese in 1975. Nine years later, she escaped in a small boat with family members and others. They were rescued in the South China Sea by a Norwegian fishing vessel, and she now lives in Norway, where she has resumed her writing career. Her most recent story collection, *Norway and I* (1994), appeared in both Vietnamese and Norwegian editions.

PREVIEWING

FICTION

The Son from America
Isaac Bashevis Singer Poland / United States

PERSONAL CONNECTION

What kinds of changes do you think people who immigrate to the United States go through as they adapt to a new way of life? How might their departure from their native lands affect the family and friends they leave behind? In a small-group discussion, explore the answers to these questions, sharing personal experiences of immigration if possible.

HISTORICAL/CULTURAL CONNECTION

Millions of eastern European Jews immigrated to the United States near the beginning of the 20th century, often fleeing religious persecution or seeking a better way of life. Life in America at the time bore little resemblance to the life these immigrants had left behind. In the "old country"—particularly in rural villages—change occurred slowly, if at all, and people lived simply, as their ancestors before them had lived. In the United States, however, change was occurring at a rapid pace as economic and urban development transformed the nation and its people.

To meet the challenge of living in a new country, immigrants learned English, found jobs, and often became assimilated, or absorbed, into mainstream American culture. In order to fit in, some abandoned the cultural and religious traditions that had formerly shaped their lives. However, as they adapted to their newfound freedom and relative prosperity, most tried to maintain the feeling of community they had left behind. Typically, they settled among other Jews from the same towns or regions in eastern Europe. They also formed social groups, or societies, that raised money to help support those still living in their native villages.

READING CONNECTION

Making Predictions In this story, a man who emigrated to the United States returns to the Polish village of his youth to visit his aging parents. In your notebook, make a prediction about what will happen during his visit. As you read, compare your prediction with the events of the story.

An Eastern European village during the 1930s. Sovfoto.

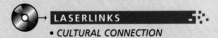

LASERLINKS
• CULTURAL CONNECTION

761

The Son from America

Isaac Bashevis Singer

The village of Lentshin was tiny—a sandy marketplace where the peasants of the area met once a week. It was surrounded by little huts with thatched roofs or shingles green with moss. The chimneys looked like pots. Between the huts there were fields, where the owners planted vegetables or pastured their goats.

In the smallest of these huts lived old Berl, a man in his eighties, and his wife, who was called Berlcha (wife of Berl). Old Berl was one of the Jews who had been driven from their villages in Russia and had settled in Poland. In Lentshin, they mocked the mistakes he made while praying aloud. He spoke with a sharp "r." He was short, broad-shouldered, and had a small white beard, and summer and winter he wore a sheepskin hat, a padded cotton jacket, and stout boots. He walked slowly, shuffling his feet. He had a half acre of field, a cow, a goat, and chickens.

The couple had a son, Samuel, who had gone to America forty years ago. It was said in Lentshin that he became a millionaire there. Every month, the Lentshin letter carrier brought old Berl a money order and a letter that no one could read because many of the words were English. How much money Samuel sent his parents remained a secret. Three times a year, Berl and his wife went on foot to Zakroczym[1] and cashed the money orders there. But they never seemed to use the money. What for? The garden, the

---

1. **Zakroczym** (zä-krô′chəm).

The Grey House (1917), Marc Chagall. Thyssen-Bornemisza Museum, Madrid, Spain, Nimatallah/Art Resource, New York. Copyright © 1996 Artists Rights Society (ARS), New York/ADAGP, Paris.

cow, and the goat provided most of their needs. Besides, Berlcha sold chickens and eggs, and from these there was enough to buy flour for bread.

No one cared to know where Berl kept the money that his son sent him. There were no thieves in Lentshin. The hut consisted of one room, which contained all their belongings: the table, the shelf for meat, the shelf for milk foods, the two beds, and the clay oven. Sometimes the chickens roosted in the woodshed and sometimes, when it was cold, in a coop near the oven. The goat, too, found shelter inside when the weather was bad. The more prosperous villagers had kerosene lamps, but Berl and his wife did not believe in newfangled gadgets. What was wrong with a wick in a dish of oil? Only for the Sabbath[2] would Berlcha buy three tallow candles at the store. In summer, the couple got up at sunrise and retired with the chickens. In the long winter evenings, Berlcha spun flax at her spinning wheel, and Berl sat beside her in the silence of those who enjoy their rest.

Once in a while when Berl came home from the synagogue after evening prayers, he brought news to his wife. In Warsaw there were strikers who demanded that the czar abdicate. A heretic by the name of Dr. Herzl[3] had come up with the idea that Jews should settle again in Palestine. Berlcha listened and shook her bonneted head. Her face was yellowish and wrinkled like a cabbage leaf. There were bluish sacks under her eyes. She was half deaf. Berl had to repeat each word he said to her. She would say, "The things that happen in the big cities!"

Here in Lentshin nothing happened except usual events: a cow gave birth to a calf, a young couple had a circumcision party,[4] or a girl was born and there was no party. Occasionally, someone died. Lentshin had no cemetery, and the corpse had to be taken to Zakroczym. Actually, Lentshin had become a village with few young people. The young men left for Zakroczym, for Nowy Dwor, for Warsaw, and sometimes for the United States. Like Samuel's, their letters were illegible, the Yiddish[5] mixed with the languages of the countries where they were now living. They sent photographs in which the men wore top hats and the women fancy dresses like squiresses.[6]

Berl and Berlcha also received such photographs. But their eyes were failing, and neither he nor she had glasses. They could barely make out the pictures. Samuel had sons and daughters with Gentile[7] names—and grandchildren who had married and had their own offspring. Their names were so strange that Berl and Berlcha could never remember them. But what difference do names make? America was far, far away on the other side of the ocean, at the edge of the world. A Talmud[8] teacher who came to Lentshin had said that Americans walked with their heads down and their feet up. Berl and Berlcha could not grasp this. How was it possible? But since the teacher said so, it must be true. Berlcha pondered for some time, and then she said, "One can get accustomed to everything."

---

2. **the Sabbath:** a weekly day of rest and worship for Jews, beginning at sundown Friday and ending at sundown Saturday.

3. **Dr. Herzl** (hĕrt′səl): Theodor Herzl, an Austrian writer and journalist who, in response to anti-Jewish feeling in Europe in the late 1800s, called for the establishment of a Jewish state.

4. **circumcision party:** a party following the Jewish ceremony called *brith milah* (brĭt′ mē-lä′), in which a baby boy is circumcised and given a Hebrew name on the eighth day after birth.

5. **Yiddish:** a language—containing elements of German, Hebrew, and several other languages—spoken by Jews in central and eastern Europe and by their descendants in other countries.

6. **squiresses:** wives of country gentlemen (squires).

7. **Gentile** (jĕn′tĭl′): not Jewish (usually applied to people and things Christian).

8. **Talmud** (täl′mŏod): the writings that are the basis of Jewish civil and religious law.

And so it remained. From too much thinking—God forbid—one may lose one's wits.

One Friday morning, when Berlcha was kneading the dough for the Sabbath loaves, the door opened and a nobleman entered. He was so tall that he had to bend down to get through the door. He wore a beaver hat and a cloak bordered with fur. He was followed by Chazkel, the coachman from Zakroczym, who carried two leather valises with brass locks. In astonishment Berlcha raised her eyes.

The nobleman looked around and said to the coachman in Yiddish, "Here it is." He took out a silver ruble and paid him. The coachman tried to hand him change, but he said, "You can go now."

When the coachman closed the door, the nobleman said, "Mother, it's me, your son Samuel—Sam."

Berlcha heard the words and her legs grew numb. Her hands, to which pieces of dough were sticking, lost their power. The nobleman hugged her, kissed her forehead, both her cheeks. Berlcha began to cackle like a hen, "My son!" At that moment Berl came in from the woodshed, his arms piled with logs. The goat followed him. When he saw a nobleman kissing his wife, Berl dropped the wood and exclaimed, "What is this?"

The nobleman let go of Berlcha and embraced Berl. "Father!"

For a long time Berl was unable to utter a sound. He wanted to recite holy words that he had read in the Yiddish Bible, but he could remember nothing. Then he asked, "Are you Samuel?"

"Yes, Father, I am Samuel."

"Well, peace be with you." Berl grasped his son's hand. He was still not sure that he was not being fooled. Samuel wasn't as tall and heavy as this man, but then Berl reminded himself that Samuel was only fifteen years old when he had left home. He must have grown in that faraway country. Berl asked, "Why didn't you let us know that you were coming?"

"Didn't you receive my cable?" Samuel asked. Berl did not know what a cable was.

Berlcha had scraped the dough from her hands and enfolded her son. He kissed her again and asked, "Mother, didn't you receive a cable?"

"What? If I lived to see this, I am happy to die," Berlcha said, amazed by her own words. Berl, too, was amazed. These were just the words he would have said earlier if he had been able to remember. After a while Berl came to himself and said, "Pescha, you will have to make a double Sabbath pudding in addition to the stew."

It was years since Berl had called Berlcha by her given name. When he wanted to address her, he would say, "Listen," or "Say." It is the young or those from the big cities who call a wife by her name. Only now did Berlcha begin to cry. Yellow tears ran from her eyes, and everything became dim. Then she called out, "It's Friday—I have to prepare for the Sabbath." Yes, she had to knead the dough and braid the loaves. With such a guest, she had to make a larger Sabbath stew. The winter day is short, and she must hurry.

Le juif en vert [Jew in green] (1914), Marc Chagall. Oil on cardboard 38⅛″ × 30¼″, private collection, Geneva, Switzerland. Copyright © 1996 Artists Rights Society (ARS), New York/ADAGP, Paris.

Kaddish[9] for me." She wept raspingly. Her strength left her, and she slumped onto the bed.

Berl said, "Women will always be women." And he went to the shed to get more wood. The goat sat down near the oven; she gazed with surprise at this strange man—his height and his bizarre clothes.

The neighbors had heard the good news that Berl's son had arrived from America, and they came to greet him. The women began to help Berlcha prepare for the Sabbath. Some laughed; some cried. The room was full of people, as at a wedding. They asked Berl's son, "What is new in America?"

And Berl's son answered, "America is all right."

"Do Jews make a living?"

"One eats white bread there on weekdays."

"Do they remain Jews?"

"I am not a Gentile."

Her son understood what was worrying her, because he said, "Mother, I will help you."

Berlcha wanted to laugh, but a choked sob came out. "What are you saying? God forbid."

The nobleman took off his cloak and jacket and remained in his vest, on which hung a solid-gold watch chain. He rolled up his sleeves and came to the trough. "Mother, I was a baker for many years in New York," he said, and he began to knead the dough.

"What! You are my darling son who will say

After Berlcha blessed the candles, father and son went to the little synagogue across the street. A new snow had fallen. The son took large steps, but Berl warned him, "Slow down."

In the synagogue the Jews recited "Let Us Exult" and "Come, My Groom." All the time, the snow outside kept falling. After prayers, when Berl and Samuel left the Holy Place, the village was unrecognizable. Everything was covered in snow. One could see only the contours

---

9. **Kaddish** (kä′dĭsh): a Jewish prayer recited by mourners after the death of a close relative.

of the roofs and the candles in the windows. Samuel said, "Nothing has changed here."

Berlcha had prepared gefilte fish,[10] chicken soup with rice, meat, carrot stew. Berl recited the benediction over a glass of ritual wine. The family ate and drank, and when it grew quiet for a while, one could hear the chirping of the house cricket. The son talked a lot, but Berl and Berlcha understood little. His Yiddish was different and contained foreign words.

After the final blessing Samuel asked, "Father, what did you do with all the money I sent you?"

Berl raised his white brows. "It's here."

"Didn't you put it in a bank?"

"There is no bank in Lentshin."

"Where do you keep it?"

Berl hesitated. "One is not allowed to touch money on the Sabbath, but I will show you." He crouched beside the bed and began to shove something heavy. A boot appeared. Its top was stuffed with straw. Berl removed the straw, and the son saw that the boot was full of gold coins. He lifted it.

"Father, this is a treasure!" he called out.

"Well."

"Why didn't you spend it?"

"On what? Thank God, we have everything."

"Why didn't you travel somewhere?"

"Where to? This is our home."

The son asked one question after the other, but Berl's answer was always the same: they wanted for nothing. The garden, the cow, the goat, the chickens provided them with all they needed. The son said, "If thieves knew about this, your lives wouldn't be safe."

"There are no thieves here."

"What will happen to the money?"

"You take it."

Slowly, Berl and Berlcha grew accustomed to their son and his American Yiddish. Berlcha could hear him better now. She even recognized his voice. He was saying, "Perhaps we should build a larger synagogue."

"The synagogue is big enough," Berl replied.

"Perhaps a home for old people."

"No one sleeps in the street."

The next day after the Sabbath meal was eaten, a Gentile from Zakroczym brought a paper—it was the cable. Berl and Berlcha lay down for a nap. They soon began to snore. The goat, too, dozed off. The son put on his cloak and his hat and went for a walk. He strode with his long legs across the marketplace. He stretched out a hand and touched a roof. He wanted to smoke a cigar, but he remembered it was forbidden on the Sabbath. He had a desire to talk to someone, but it seemed that the whole of Lentshin was asleep. He entered the synagogue. An old man was sitting there, reciting psalms. Samuel asked, "Are you praying?"

"What else is there to do when one gets old?"

"Do you make a living?"

The old man did not understand the meaning of these words. He smiled, showing his empty gums, and then he said, "If God gives health, one keeps on living."

Samuel returned home. Dusk had fallen. Berl went to the synagogue for the evening prayers, and the son remained with his mother. The room was filled with shadows.

Berlcha began to recite in a solemn singsong, "God of Abraham, Isaac, and Jacob, defend the

---

10. **gefilte** (gə-fĭl′tə) **fish:** a traditional Jewish food made from finely chopped fish.

poor people of Israel and Thy name. The Holy Sabbath is departing; the welcome week is coming to us. Let it be one of health, wealth, and good deeds."

"Mother, you don't need to pray for wealth," Samuel said. "You are wealthy already."

Berlcha did not hear—or pretended not to. Her face had turned into a cluster of shadows.

In the twilight Samuel put his hand into his jacket pocket and touched his passport, his checkbook, his letters of credit. He had come here with big plans. He had a valise filled with presents for his parents. He wanted to bestow gifts on the village. He brought not only his own money but funds from the Lentshin Society in New York, which had organized a ball for the benefit of the village. But this village in the hinterland needed nothing. From the synagogue one could hear hoarse chanting. The cricket, silent all day, started again its chirping. Berlcha began to sway and utter holy rhymes inherited from mothers and grandmothers:

Thy holy sheep
In mercy keep,
In Torah and good deeds;
Provide for all their needs,
Shoes, clothes, and bread
And the Messiah's tread. ❖

Translated by the author and Dorothea Straus

INSIGHT

GRUDNOW
LINDA PASTAN

When he spoke of where he
   came from,
my grandfather could have been
clearing his throat
of that name, that town
5 sometimes Poland, sometimes Russia,
the borders penciled in
with a hand as shaky as his.
He left, I heard him say,
because there was nothing there.

10 I understood what he meant
when I saw the photograph
of his people standing
against a landscape emptied
of crops and trees, scraped raw
15 by winter. Everything
was in sepia, as if the brown earth
had stained the faces,
stained even the air.

I would have died there, I think
20 in childhood maybe
of some fever,
my face pressed for warmth
against a cow with flanks
like those of the great-aunts
25 in the picture. Or later
I would have died of history
like the others, who dug
their stubborn heels into that earth,
heels as hard as the heels
30 of the bread my grandfather tore
from the loaf at supper. He always
sipped his tea through a cube of sugar
clenched in his teeth, the way
he sipped his life here, noisily,
35 through all he remembered
that might have been sweet in
   Grudnow.

RESPONDING OPTIONS

FROM PERSONAL RESPONSE TO CRITICAL ANALYSIS

REFLECT

1. How close was the prediction you made for the Reading Connection on page 761 to what actually happened in the story? Share your thoughts with a classmate.

RETHINK

2. What are your impressions of Berl and Berlcha?
   Consider
   - the description of their home and their community
   - their understanding of what's going on in the world
   - their reasons for not spending the money their son has sent
   - the role of tradition and religion in their life

3. What are your impressions of their son, Samuel?
   Consider
   - why he returns to Lentshin
   - how he has adapted to life in his new country
   - how he reacts to his parents' life

4. What do you think are the advantages and the disadvantages of life in Lentshin, and how do these compare with the advantages and the disadvantages of life in America? Cite details from the story in explaining your response.

5. How would you explain what Samuel has realized by the end of the story?

RELATE

6. Would you say that the grandfather in the Insight poem "Grudnow" has more in common with Samuel or with Samuel's parents? Why?

7. Do aspects of life in Lentshin exist anywhere in the United States today? Cite details from the story as you share your opinion with classmates.

ANOTHER PATHWAY
Cooperative Learning

Get together with classmates and compare Samuel's values and attitudes with those of his parents. First, create a list of categories, such as "attitude toward money" and "attitude toward life," to use in making your comparisons. Then organize your ideas in a comparison-and-contrast chart.

QUICKWRITES

1. Imagine that you are Samuel. Write a **newsletter article** for the Lentshin Society, describing your trip to Lentshin, Poland. Be sure to explain why you have returned to New York with the money that the society has raised for the village.

2. Write a **review** of this story, providing a brief summary of the story and discussing your opinion of Singer's merits as a writer.

3. Write **character sketches** of Berl and Berlcha. Use quotations from the story to help you describe the characters' appearance and show how they live and relate to each other.

PORTFOLIO Save your writing. You may want to use it later as a springboard to a piece for your portfolio.

LITERARY CONCEPTS

As you may recall, **situational irony** is a contrast between what a character or reader expects and what actually happens in a literary work. If the detective in a mystery story turns out to be the criminal, for example, most readers would consider the situation ironic. With a partner, review and discuss "The Son from America," listing examples of situational irony that the story contains. What point might Isaac Bashevis Singer have been making by means of these ironies?

CONCEPT REVIEW: Voice How would you describe Singer's writing voice? What does his voice suggest about his personality and attitudes?

ALTERNATIVE ACTIVITIES

1. Draw or paint a **portrait** of Samuel as seen through his parents' eyes.

2. Work with two classmates to create a **scrapbook** of Samuel's trip to Lentshin. Use old photos, art reproductions, bits of writing or clippings, and drawings of your own to depict the most important aspects of his visit. Include captions explaining how the images reflect Samuel's encounters and realizations.

3. Conduct an interview with someone you know who has immigrated to America. The discussion you had for the Personal Connection on page 761 can give you ideas for questions to ask the person about his or her experiences. Prepare a summary statement comparing that person's experiences with Samuel's.

THE WRITER'S STYLE

Singer's short fiction is noted for its blend of modern attitudes with elements of folklore, fable, and history. Which of these elements do you detect in "The Son from America"? Explain your ideas, citing details from the story.

CRITIC'S CORNER

In awarding Singer its prize for literature, the Nobel Prize committee praised his "impassioned narrative art which, with roots in a Polish-Jewish cultural tradition, brings universal human conditions to life." Would you say that "The Son from America" deals with universal human conditions? Why or why not?

ACROSS THE CURRICULUM

World Religions Do some research into the Jewish celebration of the Sabbath. Look for information on the symbolism of candles, bread, and wine and on the traditional laws governing behavior on the Sabbath, some of which are mentioned in the story. Present your findings to your classmates in an oral report.

World Languages Find out more about Yiddish, the language in which Singer wrote his works. Make a list of Yiddish words and expressions that have entered into the English language.

ISAAC BASHEVIS SINGER

1904–1991

One of the world's foremost Yiddish-language authors, Isaac Bashevis Singer was born in a tiny village in rural Poland and spent most of his youth in Warsaw, the country's capital. His father and both of his grandfathers were rabbis, so he received a traditional religious education. Singer was very close with his older brother, I. J. Singer, a writer who rejected some traditional beliefs and supported the modernization of Judaism. "I was fascinated both with my brother's rationalism and with my parents' mysticism," he once remarked, and both interests are evident in his writings. He also said that he preferred "to write about the world which I knew, which I know best." As a result, much of his fiction is set in the Polish-Jewish communities of his boyhood, which no longer exist.

In the 1920s, while working in Warsaw as a proofreader for a Yiddish literary journal edited by his brother, Singer began writing and publishing his own stories and book reviews. In 1932 he became coeditor of *Globus,* a literary magazine in which he published portions of what would become his first novel, *Satan in Goray.* The complete novel appeared in 1935, the same year that Singer left for America to join his brother, who had emigrated the year before. He settled in New York City and began writing articles, book reviews, and short stories for the *Daily Forward,* a Yiddish newspaper.

Over the course of his career, Singer won a great number of honors and awards for his writing, including the 1978 Nobel Prize in literature. He won a National Book Award for children's literature for *A Day of Pleasure,* an account of his boyhood in Warsaw, as well as a National Book Award for fiction for the story collection *A Crown of Feathers,* in which "The Son from America" appeared. He always wrote in Yiddish, his native tongue, even though he learned English and even collaborated on English translations of his works. Singer once said in an interview, "When I was a boy, they called me a liar . . . for telling stories. Now they call me a writer. It's more advanced, but it's the same thing." He also believed that "every experience becomes important when it's told, not before."

OTHER WORKS *The Family Moskat; Gimpel the Fool and Other Stories; In My Father's Court; Yentl, the Yeshiva Boy; Shosha; The Collected Stories of Isaac Bashevis Singer*

LASERLINKS
• *STORYTELLER*

PREVIEWING

By Any Other Name

Santha Rama Rau (săn'thä rä'mä rou') **India**

PERSONAL CONNECTION

With your classmates, discuss what it might be like to live in a country ruled by a foreign government. How do you think your everyday life might be affected? What conflicts might arise? Use a cluster map like the one shown to help you generate ideas.

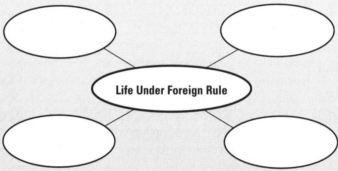

Life Under Foreign Rule

CULTURAL CONNECTION

India was a British colony from the late 1700s until 1947, when it gained its independence. During these years, the British came to dominate nearly all aspects of Indian life—the economy, the military, education, and government—and Indians often had to adapt to British ways and attitudes in order to succeed. They faced the difficulty of choosing between their own native customs and those of their foreign colonial "masters." Santha Rama Rau, the author of this selection, grew up in a well-to-do Indian household during the time of British rule.

WRITING CONNECTION

Imagine that you are an Indian child during British colonial rule. In your notebook, write about how attending a British school and being taught by British teachers might make you feel. Then, as you read the selection, compare your ideas with the feelings of the main characters.

By Any Other Name

Santha Rama Rau

At the Anglo-Indian[1] day school in Zorinabad[2] to which my sister and I were sent when she was eight and I was five and a half, they changed our names. On the first day of school, a hot, windless morning of a north Indian September, we stood in the headmistress's study, and she said, "Now you're the *new* girls. What are your names?"

My sister answered for us. "I am Premila, and she"—nodding in my direction—"is Santha."

The headmistress had been in India, I suppose, fifteen years or so, but she still smiled her helpless inability to cope with Indian names. Her rimless half-glasses glittered, and the precarious bun on the top of her head trembled as she shook her head. "Oh, my dears, those are much too hard for me. Suppose we give you pretty English names. Wouldn't that be more jolly? Let's see, now—Pamela for you, I think." She shrugged in a baffled way at my sister. "That's as close as I can get. And for *you,*" she said to me, "how about Cynthia? Isn't that nice?"

My sister was always less easily intimidated than I was, and while she kept a stubborn silence, I said, "Thank you," in a very tiny voice.

We had been sent to that school because my father, among his responsibilities as an officer of the civil service, had a tour of duty to perform in the villages around that steamy little provincial town, where he had his headquarters at that time. He used to make his shorter inspection tours on horseback, and a week before, in the stale heat of a typically postmonsoon[3] day, we had waved good-by to him and a little procession—an assistant, a secretary, two bearers, and the man to look after the bedding rolls and luggage. They rode away through our large garden, still bright green from the rains, and we turned back into the twilight of the house and the sound of fans whispering in every room.

Up to then, my mother had refused to send Premila to school in the British-run establishments of that time, because, she used to say,

---

1. **Anglo-Indian:** belonging to the British colonists in India.
2. **Zorinabad** (zə-rĭn′ə-bäd′).
3. **postmonsoon:** following the Indian rainy season.

"you can bury a dog's tail for seven years and it still comes out curly, and you can take a Britisher away from his home for a lifetime and he still remains insular." The examinations and degrees from entirely Indian schools were not, in those days, considered valid. In my case, the question had never come up, and probably never would have come up if Mother's extraordinary good health had not broken down. For the first time in my life, she was not able to continue the lessons she had been giving us every morning. So our Hindi[4] books were put away, the stories of the Lord Krishna[5] as a little boy were left in midair, and we were sent to the Anglo-Indian school.

That first day at school is still, when I think of it, a remarkable one. At that age, if one's name is changed, one develops a curious form of dual personality. I remember having a certain detached and disbelieving concern in the actions of "Cynthia," but certainly no responsibility. Accordingly, I followed the thin, erect back of the headmistress down the veranda to my classroom feeling, at most, a passing interest in what was going to happen to me in this strange, new atmosphere of School.

The building was Indian in design, with wide verandas opening onto a central courtyard, but Indian verandas are usually whitewashed, with stone floors. These, in the tradition of British schools, were painted dark brown and had matting on the floors. It gave a feeling of extra intensity to the heat.

I suppose there were about a dozen Indian children in the school—which contained perhaps forty children in all—and four of them were in my class. They were all sitting at the back of the room, and I went to join them. I sat next to a small, solemn girl who didn't smile at me. She had long, glossy-black braids and wore a cotton dress, but she still kept on her Indian jewelry—a gold chain around her neck, thin gold bracelets, and tiny ruby studs in her ears. Like most Indian children, she had a rim of black kohl[6] around her eyes. The cotton dress should have looked strange, but all I could think of was that I should ask my mother if I couldn't wear a dress to school, too, instead of my Indian clothes.

I can't remember too much about the proceedings in class that day, except for the beginning. The teacher pointed to me and asked me to stand up. "Now, dear, tell the class your name."

I said nothing.

"Come along," she said, frowning slightly. "What's your name, dear?"

"I don't know," I said, finally.

The English children in the front of the class—there were about eight or ten of them—giggled and twisted around in their chairs to look at me. I sat down quickly and opened my eyes very wide, hoping in that way to dry them off. The little girl with the braids put out her hand and very lightly touched my arm. She still didn't smile.

Most of that morning I was rather bored. I looked briefly at the children's drawings pinned to the wall and then concentrated on a lizard clinging to the ledge of the high, barred window behind the teacher's head. Occasionally it would shoot out its long yellow tongue for a fly, and then it would rest, with its eyes closed and

---

4. **Hindi** (hĭn′dē): the principal language of northern India.
5. **Lord Krishna:** one of the chief gods of Hinduism, the major religion of India.
6. **kohl** (kōl): a powder used in some Eastern countries to darken the eyelids and eyelashes.

its belly palpitating, as though it were swallowing several times quickly. The lessons were mostly concerned with reading and writing and simple numbers—things that my mother had already taught me—and I paid very little attention. The teacher wrote on the easel blackboard words like "bat" and "cat," which seemed babyish to me; only "apple" was new and incomprehensible.

When it was time for the lunch recess, I followed the girl with braids out onto the veranda. There the children from the other classes were assembled. I saw Premila at once and ran over to her, as she had charge of our lunchbox. The children were all opening packages and sitting down to eat sandwiches. Premila and I were the only ones who had Indian food—thin wheat chapatties,[7] some vegetable curry,[8] and a bottle of buttermilk. Premila thrust half of it into my hand and whispered fiercely that I should go and sit with my class, because that was what the others seemed to be doing.

Two Indian girls in their native clothing. Copyright © Bill Cardoni/Bruce

The enormous black eyes of the little Indian girl from my class looked at my food longingly, so I offered her some. But she only shook her head and plowed her way solemnly through her sandwiches.

I was very sleepy after lunch, because at home we always took a siesta. It was usually a pleasant time of day, with the bedroom darkened against the harsh afternoon sun, the drifting off into sleep with the sound of Mother's voice reading a story in one's mind, and, finally, the shrill, fussy voice of the ayah[9] waking one for tea.

At school, we rested for a short time on low, folding cots on the veranda, and then we were expected to play games. During the hot part of the afternoon we played indoors, and after the shadows had begun to lengthen and the slight breeze of the evening had come up, we moved outside to the wide courtyard.

I had never really grasped the system of competitive games. At home, whenever we

---

7. **chapatties** (chə-päd′ēz): flat, thin pieces of bread.
8. **curry:** a stew seasoned with curry powder (a combination of spices).
9. **ayah** (ä′yə): a native nurse or lady's maid in India.

played tag or guessing games, I was always allowed to "win"—"because," Mother used to tell Premila, "she is the youngest, and we have to allow for that." I had often heard her say it, and it seemed quite reasonable to me, but the result was that I had no clear idea of what "winning" meant.

When we played twos-and-threes that afternoon at school, in accordance with my training, I let one of the small English boys catch me but was naturally rather puzzled when the other children did not return the courtesy. I ran about for what seemed like hours without ever catching anyone, until it was time for school to close. Much later I learned that my attitude was called "not being a good sport," and I stopped allowing myself to be caught, but it was not for years that I really learned the spirit of the thing.

When I saw our car come up to the school gate, I broke away from my classmates and rushed toward it yelling, "Ayah! Ayah!" It seemed like an eternity since I had seen her that morning—a wizened,[10] affectionate figure in her white cotton sari, giving me dozens of urgent and useless instructions on how to be a good girl at school. Premila followed more sedately, and she told me on the way home never to do that again in front of the other children.

When we got home, we went straight to Mother's high, white room to have tea with her, and I immediately climbed onto the bed and bounced gently up and down on the springs. Mother asked how we had liked our first day in school. I was so pleased to be home and to have left that peculiar Cynthia behind that I had nothing whatever to say about school, except to ask what "apple" meant. But Premila told Mother about the classes, and added that in her class they had weekly tests to see if they had learned their lessons well.

I asked, "What's a test?"

Premila said, "You're too small to have them. You won't have them in your class for donkey's years." She had learned the expression that day and was using it for the first time. We all laughed enormously at her wit. She also told Mother, in an aside, that we should take sandwiches to school the next day. Not, she said, that *she* minded. But they would be simpler for me to handle.

That whole lovely evening I didn't think about school at all. I sprinted barefoot across the lawns with my favorite playmate, the cook's son, to the stream at the end of the garden. We quarreled in our usual way, waded in the tepid water under the lime trees, and waited for the night to bring out the smell of the jasmine. I listened with fascination to his stories of ghosts and demons, until I was too frightened to cross the garden alone in the semidarkness. The ayah found me, shouted at the cook's son, scolded me, hurried me in to supper—it was an entirely usual, wonderful evening.

It was a week later, the day of Premila's first test, that our lives changed rather abruptly. I was sitting at the back of my class, in my usual inattentive way, only half listening to the teacher. I had started a rather guarded friendship with the girl with the braids, whose name turned out to be Nalini (Nancy, in school). The three other Indian children were already fast friends. Even at that age it was apparent to all of us that friendship with the English or Anglo-Indian children was out of the question. Occasionally, during the class, my new friend and I would draw pictures and show them to each other secretly.

The door opened sharply, and Premila marched in. At first, the teacher smiled at her in a kindly and encouraging way and said, "Now, you're little Cynthia's sister?"

---

10. **wizened** (wĭz′ənd): withered; shriveled.

Premila didn't even look at her. She stood with her feet planted firmly apart and her shoulders rigid and addressed herself directly to me. "Get up," she said. "We're going home."

I didn't know what had happened, but I was aware that it was a crisis of some sort. I rose obediently and started to walk toward my sister.

"Bring your pencils and your notebook," she said.

I went back for them, and together we left the room. The teacher started to say something just as Premila closed the door, but we didn't wait to hear what it was.

In complete silence we left the school grounds and started to walk home. Then I asked Premila what the matter was. All she would say was "We're going home for good."

It was a very tiring walk for a child of five and a half, and I dragged along behind Premila with my pencils growing sticky in my hand. I can still remember looking at the dusty hedges, and the tangles of thorns in the ditches by the side of the road, smelling the faint fragrance from the eucalyptus trees and wondering whether we would ever reach home. Occasionally a horse-drawn tonga[11] passed us, and the women, in their pink or green silks, stared at Premila and me trudging along on the side of the road. A few coolies[12] and a line of women carrying baskets of vegetables on their heads smiled at us. But it was nearing the hottest time of day, and the road was almost deserted. I walked more and more slowly and shouted to Premila, from time to time, "Wait for me!" with increasing peevishness.[13] She spoke to me only once, and that was to tell me to carry my notebook on my head, because of the sun.

When we got to our house, the ayah was just taking a tray of lunch into Mother's room. She immediately started a long, worried questioning about what are you children doing back here at this hour of the day.

Mother looked very startled and very concerned and asked Premila what had happened.

Premila said, "We had our test today, and she made me and the other Indians sit at the back of the room, with a desk between each one."

Mother said, "Why was that, darling?"

"She said it was because Indians cheat," Premila added. "So I don't think we should go back to that school."

Mother looked very distant and was silent a long time. At last she said, "Of course not, darling." She sounded displeased.

We all shared the curry she was having for lunch, and afterward I was sent off to the beautifully familiar bedroom for my siesta. I could hear Mother and Premila talking through the open door.

Mother said, "Do you suppose she understood all that?"

Premila said, "I shouldn't think so. She's a baby."

Mother said, "Well, I hope it won't bother her."

Of course, they were both wrong. I understood it perfectly, and I remember it all very clearly. But I put it happily away, because it had all happened to a girl called Cynthia, and I never was really particularly interested in her. ❖

---

11. **tonga:** a small two-wheeled carriage.
12. **coolies:** unskilled laborers in India or China.
13. **peevishness:** irritability.

RESPONDING OPTIONS

FROM PERSONAL RESPONSE TO CRITICAL ANALYSIS

REFLECT

1. In your notebook, jot down your immediate reaction to the selection. Share your reaction with a partner.

RETHINK

2. Do you think Premila did the right thing by walking out in the middle of school? Explain your position.

3. What do you think were the mother's goals for her daughters' education?
   Consider
   - why she taught them at home and told them stories about Lord Krishna
   - what she said about the British
   - why she sent Santha and Premila to a British school when she was no longer able to teach them herself
   - the family's position in society

4. How do you think the Indian children were affected by the Britishers' treatment of them?
   Consider
   - Santha's two personalities as "Santha" and "Cynthia"
   - how Premila responded to school
   - why other children adapted to British ways
   - how the teachers viewed the Indians
   - what you wrote for the Writing Connection on page 772

5. How would you evaluate Rama Rau as a storyteller? Support your opinion with examples from the selection?

RELATE

6. Premila was able to walk out of school rather than remain and face continued humiliation. On the basis of what you know about Premila and other people, what personal characteristics do you think an individual needs in order to reject unjust treatment?

ANOTHER PATHWAY

Cooperative Learning

With a small group of classmates, create an annotated time line that shows the key events in this selection. Above the time line, label each event. Below the line, write a brief description of how Santha and Premila felt about the event.

QUICKWRITES

1. Write an **opinion column** for the Zorinabad newspaper, in which you report and comment on the incident presented in this selection. You may show support either for Santha and Premila's family or for the British school.

2. Imagine you are the girls' mother and write a **note** to the headmistress of the British school, explaining why your daughters will not be returning to the school.

📁 *PORTFOLIO Save your writing. You may want to use it later as a springboard to a piece for your portfolio.*

LITERARY CONCEPTS

The **title** of a literary work often reflects the meaning of the work. Sometimes the title contains an allusion that can help readers better understand and appreciate the work. Santha Rama Rau's title is an allusion to these lines from Act Two, Scene 2, of William Shakespeare's *Romeo and Juliet:*

> **What's in a name? That which we call a rose**
> **By any other name would smell as sweet.**

Explain in your own words what the quotation means and how it applies to Rama Rau's autobiographical essay.

CRITIC'S CORNER

A reviewer for the *Providence Journal* once observed that Rama Rau "can see the color and catch the flavor of a scene. She can give the complete atmosphere of quite different ways of life. Best of all, she has a sharp and amused eye for people." Explain whether you agree with this statement, supporting your opinion with details from the selection.

ACROSS THE CURRICULUM

History Many immigrants found their names changed when they entered the United States because officials who could not spell or pronounce the names simply wrote down familiar approximations of what they heard. For example, "Jurek" (yōōr'ĕk) might become "George," and "Iorizzo" (yō-rēt'tsō) might become "Rice." Research other name changes and create a chart showing various original names along with their "Americanized" variations. Share your chart with the class.

SANTHA RAMA RAU

1923–

Born in the city of Madras, Santha Rama Rau came from a wealthy and distinguished family. Her father was a diplomat in the Anglo-Indian government, and her mother was a leading social reformer. Although her father's job required the family to move frequently, she and her sister sometimes lived with their grandmother, surrounded by stability and tradition. Rama Rau once wrote, "The two strong strains of my childhood—the shifting life of district touring and the unshakable little universe of the family—were both vividly a part of my experience."

When Rama Rau was six, her family moved to London, and she attended school in England for the next ten years. She later enrolled at Wellesley College in Massachusetts, where she began composing *Home to India,* an account of a 1939 trip to her homeland. The book won instant acclaim as a "refreshing, read-able contrast" to the "serious and weighty works" about Indian nationalism that were then flooding the market.

After graduating from Wellesley, Rama Rau lived in Bombay, India, and worked as editor of a magazine called *Trend.* In 1947, after India gained independence from Britain, she accompanied her father to Tokyo when he became India's first ambassador to Japan. Her experiences in eastern Asia are recounted in her travel book *East of Home* (1950). In subsequent years Rama Rau has produced several more travel books and articles, as well as novels, personal essays, and even an Indian cookbook. "By Any Other Name" first appeared in *The New Yorker.*

OTHER WORKS *Remember the House, View to the Southeast, The Adventuress, A Princess Remembers: The Memoirs of the Maharani of Jaipur*

PREVIEWING

FICTION

Marriage Is a Private Affair

Chinua Achebe (chĭn′wä ä-chä′bä) Nigeria

PERSONAL CONNECTION

Marriage customs vary greatly throughout the world. In some cultures, people's marriages are traditionally arranged by their parents; in others, parents play little part. Discuss what you know about arranged marriages. Then create a comparison-contrast chart, like the one shown, to compare arranged marriages with marriages based on the choice of the partners.

	Parents Choose Mates	Partners Choose Each Other
Reason for marriage		
Benefits of this method of choice		
Drawbacks		

CULTURAL CONNECTION

This story takes place in the West African country of Nigeria, a land of great cultural diversity. Centuries-old traditions continue to govern life in Nigerian villages, where parents often play a decisive role in choosing mates for their children. In the cities, however, modern practices have displaced many of the village traditions, including the role of parent as matchmaker. The tension between the old and new ways of living sometimes creates conflict within families, especially between generations.

The story focuses on a conflict between a father and son about the choice of the son's marriage partner. Both men are Ibo (ē′bō), members of one of the largest ethnic groups in Nigeria. The son, like many of his contemporaries, has moved away from the village of his birth and lives in a city—in this case, Lagos (lā′gŏs), the economic and commercial center of the nation, with a population of 1.4 million. In the villages of Nigeria, the Ibo live apart from other peoples, maintaining their traditional way of life. Life in Lagos, however, is characterized by a mingling of ethnic groups, cultures, and religions.

WRITING CONNECTION

With another student, brainstorm some common objections that parents raise to their children's choice of marriage partners. Record the objections in your notebook, putting an *R* by the ones that you think are reasonable and a *U* by those that seem unreasonable. Then, as you read the story, think about what is reasonable and unreasonable in the father's reaction to his son's choice of a spouse.

MARRIAGE Is a Private Affair

Chinua Achebe

"Have you written to your dad yet?" asked Nene[1] one afternoon as she sat with Nnaemeka[2] in her room at 16 Kasanga Street, Lagos.

"No. I've been thinking about it. I think it's better to tell him when I get home on leave!"

"But why? Your leave is such a long way off yet—six whole weeks. He should be let into our happiness now."

Nnaemeka was silent for a while and then began very slowly as if he groped for his words: "I wish I were sure it would be happiness to him."

"Of course it must," replied Nene, a little surprised. "Why shouldn't it?"

"You have lived in Lagos all your life, and you know very little about people in remote parts of the country."

"That's what you always say. But I don't believe anybody will be so unlike other people that they will be unhappy when their sons are engaged to marry."

"Yes. They are most unhappy if the engagement is not arranged by them. In our case it's worse—you are not even an Ibo."

This was said so seriously and so bluntly that Nene could not find speech immediately. In the cosmopolitan atmosphere of the city it had always seemed to her something of a joke that a person's tribe could determine whom he married.

At last she said, "You don't really mean that he will object to your marrying me simply on that account? I had always thought you Ibos were kindly disposed to other people."

"So we are. But when it comes to marriage, well, it's not quite so simple. And this," he added, "is not peculiar to the Ibos. If your father were alive and lived in the heart of Ibibio-land, he would be exactly like my father."

"I don't know. But anyway, as your father is

---

1. **Nene** (nā′nā).
2. **Nnaemeka** (ən-nä′ā-mä′kä).

WORDS TO KNOW

cosmopolitan (kŏz′mə-pŏl′ĭ-tn) *adj.* worldly; sophisticated

so fond of you, I'm sure he will forgive you soon enough. Come on then, be a good boy and send him a nice lovely letter . . ."

"It would not be wise to break the news to him by writing. A letter will bring it upon him with a shock. I'm quite sure about that."

"All right, honey, suit yourself. You know your father."

As Nnaemeka walked home that evening, he turned over in his mind different ways of overcoming his father's opposition, especially now that he had gone and found a girl for him. He had thought of showing his letter to Nene but decided on second thoughts not to, at least for the moment. He read it again when he got home and couldn't help smiling to himself. He remembered Ugoye[3] quite well, an Amazon[4] of a girl who used to beat up all the boys, himself included, on the way to the stream, a complete dunce at school.

I have found a girl who will suit you admirably—Ugoye Nweke, the eldest daughter of our neighbor, Jacob Nweke. She has a proper Christian upbringing. When she stopped schooling some years ago, her father (a man of sound judgment) sent her to live in the house of a pastor where she has received all the training a wife could need. Her Sunday school teacher has told me that she reads her Bible very fluently. I hope we shall begin negotiations when you come home in December.

On the second evening of his return from Lagos Nnaemeka sat with his father under a cassia tree. This was the old man's retreat where he went to read his Bible when the parching December sun had set and a fresh, reviving wind blew on the leaves.

"Father," began Nnaemeka suddenly, "I have come to ask for forgiveness."

"Forgiveness? For what, my son?" he asked in amazement.

"It's about this marriage question."

"Which marriage question?"

"I can't—we must—I mean it is impossible for me to marry Nweke's daughter."

"Impossible? Why?" asked his father.

"I don't love her."

"Nobody said you did. Why should you?" he asked.

"Marriage today is different . . ."

"Look here, my son," interrupted his father, "nothing is different. What one looks for in a wife are a good character and a Christian background."

Nnaemeka saw there was no hope along the present line of argument.

"Moreover," he said, "I am engaged to marry another girl who has all of Ugoye's good qualities, and who . . ."

His father did not believe his ears. "What did you say?" he asked slowly and disconcertingly.

"She is a good Christian," his son went on, "and a teacher in a girls' school in Lagos."

"Teacher, did you say? If you consider that a qualification for a good wife, I should like to point out to you, Emeka, that no Christian woman should teach. St. Paul in his letter to the Corinthians says that women should keep silence." He rose slowly from his seat and paced forwards and backwards. This was his pet subject, and he condemned vehemently those church leaders who encouraged women to teach in their schools. After he had spent his emotion on a long

---

3. **Ugoye** (oō-gō'yā).

4. **Amazon:** an exceptionally tall, strong woman.

Wooing (1984), Varnette Honeywood. Collage. Copyright © 1984 Varnette P. Honeywood.

his room. This was most unexpected and perplexed Nnaemeka. His father's silence was infinitely more menacing than a flood of threatening speech. That night the old man did not eat.

When he sent for Nnaemeka a day later, he applied all possible ways of <u>dissuasion</u>. But the young man's heart was hardened, and his father eventually gave him up as lost.

"I owe it to you, my son, as a duty to show you what is right and what is wrong. Whoever put this idea into your head might as well have cut your throat. It is Satan's work." He waved his son away.

"You will change your mind, Father, when you know Nene."

"I shall never see her" was the reply. From that night the father scarcely spoke to his son. He did not, however, cease hoping that he would realize how serious was the danger he was heading for. Day and night he put him in his prayers.

<u>homily</u>, he at last came back to his son's engagement, in a seemingly milder tone.

"Whose daughter is she, anyway?"

"She is Nene Atang."

"What!" All the mildness was gone again. "Did you say Neneataga; what does that mean?"

"Nene Atang from Calabar.[5] She is the only girl I can marry." This was a very rash reply, and Nnaemeka expected the storm to burst. But it did not. His father merely walked away into

Nnaemeka, for his own part, was very deeply affected by his father's grief. But he kept hoping that it would pass away. If it had occurred to him that never in the history of his people had a man married a woman who spoke a different tongue, he might have been less optimistic. "It has never been heard," was the verdict of an old man speaking a few weeks later. In that

---

5. **Calabar:** a seaport in southeastern Nigeria.

783

short sentence he spoke for all of his people. This man had come with others to <u>commiserate</u> with Okeke[6] when news went round about his son's behavior. By that time the son had gone back to Lagos.

"It has never been heard," said the old man again with a sad shake of his head.

"What did Our Lord say?" asked another gentleman. "Sons shall rise against their fathers; it is there in the Holy Book."

"It is the beginning of the end," said another.

The discussion thus tending to become <u>theological</u>, Madubogwu, a highly practical man, brought it down once more to the ordinary level.

"Have you thought of consulting a native doctor about your son?" he asked Nnaemeka's father.

"He isn't sick" was the reply.

"What is he then? The boy's mind is diseased, and only a good herbalist[7] can bring him back to his right senses. The medicine he requires is *Amalile*, the same that women apply with success to recapture their husbands' straying affection."

"Madubogwu is right," said another gentleman. "This thing calls for medicine."

"I shall not call in a native doctor." Nnaemeka's father was known to be obstinately ahead of his more superstitious neighbors in these matters. "I will not be another Mrs. Ochuba. If my son wants to kill himself, let him do it with his own hands. It is not for me to help him."

"But it was her fault," said Madubogwu. "She ought to have gone to an honest herbalist. She was a clever woman, nevertheless."

"She was a wicked murderess," said Jonathan, who rarely argued with his neighbors because, he often said, they were incapable of reasoning.

"The medicine was prepared for her husband, it was his name they called in its preparation, and I am sure it would have been perfectly beneficial to him. It was wicked to put it into the herbalist's food and say you were only trying it out."

Six months later, Nnaemeka was showing his young wife a short letter from his father:

It amazes me that you could be so unfeeling as to send me your wedding picture. I would have sent it back. But on further thought I decided just to cut off your wife and send it back to you because I have nothing to do with her. How I wish that I had nothing to do with you either.

When Nene read through this letter and looked at the mutilated picture, her eyes filled with tears, and she began to sob.

"Don't cry, my darling," said her husband. "He is essentially good-natured and will one day look more kindly on our marriage." But years passed, and that one day did not come.

For eight years, Okeke would have nothing to do with his son, Nnaemeka. Only three times (when Nnaemeka asked to come home and spend his leave) did he write to him.

"I can't have you in my house," he replied on one occasion. "It can be of no interest to me where or how you spend your leave—or your life, for that matter."

The prejudice against Nnaemeka's marriage was not confined to his little village. In Lagos, especially among his people who worked there,

---

6. **Okeke** (ō-kā′kā).

7. **herbalist** (ûr′bə-lĭst): a person who is expert in the use of medicinal herbs.

it showed itself in a different way. Their women, when they met at their village meeting, were not hostile to Nene. Rather, they paid her such excessive deference as to make her feel she was not one of them. But as time went on, Nene gradually broke through some of this prejudice and even began to make friends among them. Slowly and grudgingly they began to admit that she kept her home much better than most of them.

The story eventually got to the little village in the heart of the Ibo country that Nnaemeka and his young wife were a most happy couple. But his father was one of the few people in the village who knew nothing about this. He always displayed so much temper whenever his son's name was mentioned that everyone avoided it in his presence. By a tremendous effort of will he had succeeded in pushing his son to the back of his mind. The strain had nearly killed him, but he had persevered and won.

Then one day he received a letter from Nene, and in spite of himself he began to glance through it perfunctorily until all of a sudden the expression on his face changed and he began to read more carefully.

. . . Our two sons, from the day they learnt that they have a grandfather, have insisted on being taken to him. I find it impossible to tell them that you will not see them. I implore you to allow

Nnaemeka to bring them home for a short time during his leave next month. I shall remain here in Lagos . . .

The old man at once felt the resolution he had built up over so many years falling in. He was telling himself that he must not give in. He tried to steel his heart against all emotional appeals. It was a reenactment of that other struggle. He leaned against a window and looked out. The sky was overcast with heavy black clouds, and a high wind began to blow, filling the air with dust and dry leaves. It was one of those rare occasions when even Nature takes a hand in a human fight. Very soon it began to rain, the first rain in the year. It came down in large sharp drops and was accompanied by the lightning and thunder which mark a change of season. Okeke was trying hard not to think of his two grandsons. But he knew he was now fighting a losing battle. He tried to hum a favorite hymn, but the pattering of large raindrops on the roof broke up the tune. His mind immediately returned to the children. How could he shut his door against them? By a curious mental process he imagined them standing, sad and forsaken, under the harsh angry weather—shut out from his house.

That night he hardly slept, from remorse— and a vague fear that he might die without making it up to them. ❖

RESPONDING
OPTIONS

FROM PERSONAL RESPONSE TO CRITICAL ANALYSIS

REFLECT 1. Which character did you have the strongest feelings about? Explain your reaction in your notebook.

RETHINK 2. How would you explain Okeke's persistent opposition to his son's marriage, and his change of attitude at the end of the story? *Consider*
   - the traditions that influence Okeke
   - how he feels about his son's actions
   - how he is affected by Nene's letter

3. How well do you think Nnaemeka handles his father's opposition to his marriage?

4. What is your opinion of Nene's personality and judgment?

5. How do you think the story's title relates to its theme?

RELATE 6. What do you think is gained and lost when a society undergoes a transformation from traditional ways of life to modern ways? Draw upon your knowledge of history and current events, as well as your interpretation of this story.

ANOTHER PATHWAY

Fill out a chart similar to the one you created for the Personal Connection on page 780. In one column, give reasons why Okeke wants Nnaemeka to marry Ugoye, and list the benefits and the drawbacks of his choice. In the other column, list the reasons why Nnaemeka has chosen Nene, along with the benefits and the drawbacks of his choice.

LITERARY CONCEPTS

As you have learned, the **setting** of a literary work is the time and place in which the action of the work takes place. A setting does not consist only of a physical location, however—it also includes the cultural environment in which the events unfold. The Ibo traditions of village life and the modern ways of city life can be considered parts of this story's cultural setting. With a partner, create two lists of details that convey the story's **cultural setting.** In one list, note what the story tells you about village life and attitudes; in the other, what it tells you about city life and attitudes. Share your lists with the rest of the class, and discuss how the story's setting contributes to your understanding of its characters and theme.

CONCEPT REVIEW: Point of View From what point of view is this selection narrated? How does the use of that point of view affect your reaction to the story?

QUICKWRITES

1. Write a **letter** that Okeke might send in response to Nene's letter. Your letter should reflect the father's personality and communicate how he now feels about his son and his son's family.

2. Write a series of **diary entries** in which Nene describes the problems she encounters as a result of her marriage, as well as her feelings about the problems.

3. Create a **list** of Okeke's objections to modern life. For each objection, include a supporting quotation from the story. Then write a response to each objection, defending modern life as Nnaemeka and Nene might.

📁 *PORTFOLIO Save your writing. You may want to use it later as a springboard to a piece for your portfolio.*

ALTERNATIVE ACTIVITIES

1. With two of your classmates, perform an **improvisational scene** depicting the first meeting of Nene, Nnaemeka, and Okeke.

2. Do research to find two contrasting **photographs** of life in Nigeria today—one showing a way of life that Okeke would find appealing, the other showing a way of life that would appeal to his son. Display reproductions of the photographs to your class, explaining why you chose them.

3. With a group of classmates, role-play a **conversation** that might take place in the village where Okeke lives. Share news about the letter from Nene, being sure to convey the various attitudes of the villagers.

4. Create a **Venn diagram** to compare Okeke and Nnaemeka. In the nonoverlapping parts of the circles, list characteristics that are unique to the father and to the son. Where the circles overlap, list characteristics they have in common. Consider their personalities, beliefs, attitudes, and actions.

ART CONNECTION

Take another look at *Wooing,* the painting shown on page 783. What does the image suggest to you about the relationship between Nnaemeka and Nene?

CRITIC'S CORNER

About Achebe's writing, the critic G. D. Killam has said, "Through it all the spirit of man and the belief in the possibility of triumph endures." Do you think this comment is relevant to "Marriage Is a Private Affair"? Explain your opinion.

LITERARY LINKS

Compare the attitudes toward love and marriage expressed in this story with those expressed in "The First Seven Years" (page 460). What do the two stories have in common?

ACROSS THE CURRICULUM

Anthropology Find out more about Ibo traditions and village life. You may find information by looking up *Ibo* or *Igbo* (a variation of the name) in reference works or in a library card catalog. Then create a poster that displays information about life in an Ibo village.

History When did romantic love become a basis of marriage? What countries are associated with the origins of romantic love as we know it? Research an aspect of love or marriage that interests you, and draft a report on your findings.

Detail of *Wooing* (1984), Varnette Honeywood. Collage. Copyright © 1984 Varnette P. Honeywood.

WORDS TO KNOW

EXERCISE A For each group of words below, write the letter of the word that is an antonym of the boldfaced word.

1. **persevere:** (a) praise, (b) quit, (c) accept

2. **dissuasion:** (a) improvement, (b) silence, (c) encouragement

3. **remorse:** (a) attraction, (b) improvement, (c) satisfaction

4. **cosmopolitan:** (a) provincial, (b) widespread, (c) elegant

5. **perfunctorily:** (a) thoroughly, (b) naturally, (c) wisely

EXERCISE B Review the Words to Know at the bottom of the selection pages. Then read each title below and write the vocabulary word, not used in Exercise A, that you might expect to find in a magazine article with that title.

1. "When Know-It-Alls Start Talking: A Guide for Self-Defense"

2. "The Tragedy of America's Cast-Off Pets"

3. "How to Help When a Loved One Hurts"

4. "Prayer in the Schools: The Debate Goes On"

5. "The Wisdom of Age: Honoring Our Elderly"

EXERCISE C With a partner, pantomime a situation that suggests the meaning of one of the vocabulary words. For example, one of you might act in a fawning manner toward the other to suggest the word *deference.* Invite your classmates to try to guess the word.

CHINUA ACHEBE

Chinua Achebe is one of contemporary Africa's most famous authors. A member of the Ibo people of eastern Nigeria, Achebe was born in the village of Ogidi, where his father taught at a Christian mission school. As a child, Achebe learned both the Ibo and the English languages. "I have always been fond of stories and intrigued by language—first my mother tongue, Ibo, and later English," he reports. He first considered a

1930–

writing career while a student at Nigeria's University of Ibadan. "I read some appalling European novels about Africa," he explains, ". . . and realized that our story could not be told for us by anyone else."

After college, Achebe taught briefly and then took a job with the Nigerian Broadcasting Corporation, eventually becoming the company's director of external broadcasting. In 1958 he published his first novel, *Things Fall Apart,* now a modern African classic. Like much of his subsequent fiction, this book, set in an Ibo village in the late 1800s, explores the effects of European colonialism in Africa and the clash between traditional and modern ways.

During the Nigerian civil war of 1967–1970, Achebe supported the independence effort of Biafra, a predominantly Ibo region in eastern Nigeria. He served on diplomatic missions representing Biafra and traveled in the United States with his fellow writer Gabriel Okara, lecturing and raising funds. After the fall of Biafra, Achebe took a university position in Nigeria; he has devoted his life to teaching and writing ever since.

Though fluent in Ibo, Achebe usually writes in English. He is generally regarded as the most accomplished of the many African novelists who write in English, and his works have sold well on three continents. In addition to novels and short stories, Achebe has produced a number of children's books, as well as collections of essays and poetry. "Marriage Is a Private Affair" is from *Girls at War and Other Stories,* published in 1973.

OTHER WORKS *Arrow of God; A Man of the People; Beware, Soul-Brother, and Other Poems; Anthills of the Savannah*

LASERLINKS
- *AUTHOR BACKGROUND*
- *CULTURAL CONNECTION*

PREVIEWING

POETRY

Lost Sister

Cathy Song United States

PERSONAL CONNECTION

Think about various situations that might prompt a woman to immigrate to the United States. What part might the social conditions in her native country play in her decision to leave? How do you think the experience of an immigrant woman in the United States might differ from that of an immigrant man? In a class discussion, share what you know about the lives of female immigrants in this country. Draw upon personal experience, or share what you have read or have seen in films or television shows.

Immigrants in Chinatown, San Francisco.
Copyright © Underwood Photo Archives.

CULTURAL CONNECTION

In "Lost Sister," the poet Cathy Song contrasts the traditional life of women in China with the life of a Chinese woman who has emigrated to the United States. For many centuries, Chinese marriages were arranged when the partners were children. Before marriage, a girl was subservient to the adults in her family; afterward, when she moved into her husband's family's home, she was subservient to her husband, his male relations, and his older female relations. Only after having children of her own did she gain some measure of authority.

In some parts of China, it was considered essential for a girl to have small feet if she was to be married, so female children were subjected to the practice of foot binding—the tight wrapping of the feet to stunt their growth—between the ages of five and seven. Because this process bent the feet, breaking the bones of the insteps, the girls would hobble for the rest of their lives.

READING CONNECTION

Defining Cultural Roles As you read this poem, notice the details that are used to characterize the traditional life of women in China and those that are used to characterize the life of a Chinese woman who has emigrated to the United States. In a chart like the one shown, jot down words or phrases, contained in or suggested by the poem, that describe the two ways of life.

A Woman in China	A Chinese Woman in U.S.
1.	1.
2.	2.
3.	3.

Lost Sister

Cathy Song

1

In China,
even the peasants
named their first daughters
Jade—
5   the stone that in the far fields
could moisten the dry season,
could make men move mountains
for the healing green of the inner hills
glistening like slices of winter melon.

10   And the daughters were grateful:
they never left home.
To move freely was a luxury
stolen from them at birth.
Instead, they gathered patience,
15   learning to walk in shoes
the size of teacups,
without breaking—
the arc of their movements
as dormant as the rooted willow,
20   as redundant as the farmyard hens.
But they traveled far
in surviving,
learning to stretch the family rice,
to quiet the demons,
25   the noisy stomachs.

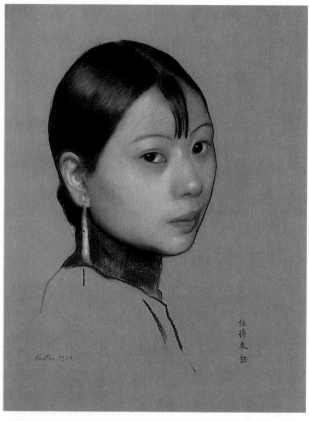

Portrait of Miss Jen Sun-ch'ang (1934), William McGregor Paxton.
Courtesy Robert Douglas Hunter.

19 dormant (dôr′mənt): inactive.

20 redundant (rĭ-dŭn′dənt):
needlessly repetitive.

2

There is a sister
across the ocean,
who relinquished her name,
diluting jade green
30 with the blue of the Pacific.
Rising with a tide of locusts,
she swarmed with others
to inundate another shore.
In America,
35 there are many roads
and women can stride along with men.

But in another wilderness,
the possibilities,
the loneliness,
40 can strangulate like jungle vines.
The meager provisions and sentiments
of once belonging—
fermented roots, Mah-Jongg tiles and firecrackers—
set but a flimsy household
45 in a forest of nightless cities.
A giant snake rattles above,
spewing black clouds into your kitchen.
Dough-faced landlords
slip in and out of your keyholes,
50 making claims you don't understand,
tapping into your communication systems
of laundry lines and restaurant chains.

You find you need China:
your one fragile identification,
55 a jade link
handcuffed to your wrist.
You remember your mother
who walked for centuries,
footless—
60 and like her,
you have left no footprints,
but only because
there is an ocean in between,
the unremitting space of your rebellion.

28 relinquished (rĭ-lĭng′kwĭsht): gave up; abandoned.

29 diluting (dī-lōō′tĭng): lessening the strength or purity of.

33 inundate (ĭn′ŭn-dāt′): overwhelm as if by a flood; overflow.

43 Mah-Jongg (mä′zhŏng′): a game of Chinese origin, played with tiles resembling dominoes.

64 unremitting (ŭn′rĭ-mĭt′ĭng): continuing without interruption; unceasing.

RESPONDING
OPTIONS

FROM PERSONAL RESPONSE TO CRITICAL ANALYSIS

REFLECT

1. What kind of mood did this poem leave you with? Explain your response to a classmate.

RETHINK

2. How do you think the speaker feels about the traditional life of Chinese women, as described in the first part of the poem?
   Consider
   - the significance of the name Jade (lines 1–9)
   - the speaker's description of the lives of daughters (lines 10–25)

3. What conclusions can you reach about the life of the immigrant Chinese woman, as described in the second part of the poem?
   Consider
   - the "many roads" she can take (lines 35–36)
   - the use of the word *strangulate* (line 40)
   - the comparison between the "footless" mother and the immigrant daughter with "no footprints" (lines 57–61)

4. How might the poem be different if the immigrant described were male instead of female?

RELATE

5. Do you think other immigrant women, from different times and places, might have feelings similar to those expressed in this poem? Explain your opinion.

ANOTHER PATHWAY

Imagine you are a Chinese woman of about 100 years ago who must decide whether to emigrate to the United States. Write a paragraph on the pros and cons of staying in China and another paragraph on the pros and cons of living as an immigrant in the United States. Use the chart you created for the Reading Connection on page 789 to support your ideas.

QUICKWRITES

1. Imagine that you are the woman portrayed in the second part of the poem. Write two **letters** to a sister in China, telling her about your experience—one conveying your thoughts shortly after leaving home, the other describing your feelings after living in America for a while. Be sure to express your feelings about immigration.

2. Compose an **alternative title** for the poem, providing an explanation of the title's meaning and the reasons you think it appropriate.

📁 *PORTFOLIO Save your writing. You may want to use it later as a springboard to a piece for your portfolio.*

LITERARY CONCEPTS

A **symbol** is a person, a place, or an object that represents something beyond itself. **Cultural symbols** are things with symbolic meaning for people in a particular culture. The stone jade, for example, is a cultural symbol in China, where carved jade objects and jewelry are equated with such abstract values as toughness, durability, and moral and physical beauty. **Literary symbols** are things that are given symbolic meaning within the context of literary works. How does an understanding of the cultural symbolism of jade influence your interpretation of its use as a literary symbol in "Lost Sister"? Discuss each of the three mentions of the stone in the poem.

LITERARY LINKS

Compare the immigrant experience depicted in "Lost Sister" with that depicted in "The Son from America" by Isaac Bashevis Singer (page 761).

CRITIC'S CORNER

The poet Richard Hugo has written, "Taste and touch are strong elements in [Cathy Song's] poems, although it is our sight that is most often engaged." Does this comment apply to "Lost Sister"? Support your answer with details from the poem.

ACROSS THE CURRICULUM

World Cultures Do some research on one of the poem's references to aspects of Chinese or Chinese-American life, and share your findings with your classmates in an oral report. For example, you might report on foot binding, rice, Mah-Jongg (also spelled *mahjong),* firecrackers, or the businesses in which Chinese immigrants to the United States have traditionally found jobs.

Teapot belonging to Chinese woman who emigrated to the United States, 1880s. Photo by Karen Yamauchi for Chermayeff & Geismar Inc./MetaForm Inc.

CATHY SONG

In 1982 Cathy Song's first poetry collection, *Picture Bride,* was published as the winner of the Yale Series of Younger Poets competition, a contest open to any American writer under the age of 40 who has not previously published a volume of poetry. Many of the poems in the book, like "Lost Sister," chronicle the Chinese-American experience. Noting that *Picture Bride* is divided into sections named for different flowers, the contest judge, Richard Hugo, compared Song's poems to "flowers—colorful, sensual and quiet—offered almost shyly as bouquets to those

1955–

moments in life that seemed minor but in retrospect count the most."

Song was born and raised in Hawaii and attended the University of Hawaii and Wellesley College; she earned her master's degree at Boston University. In addition to publishing poems in a number of anthologies and literary journals, she has coedited the anthology *Sister Stew: Fiction and Poetry by Women.* She now lives and teaches in Honolulu, Hawaii.

OTHER WORKS *Frameless Windows, Squares of Light;* poems in *The Open Boat: Poems from Asian America*

BORA RING

JUDITH WRIGHT AUSTRALIA

Rock engravings done by aborigines in eastern Australia. Superstock.

Before the English began to colonize Australia at the end of the 18th century, the Australian Aborigines (ăb´ə-rĭj´ə-nēz)—the native peoples of the continent—probably numbered around 300,000. Seminomadic and dependent on the natural environment for survival, they felt a deep spiritual connection to the land and marked life's passages—such as birth, maturity, marriage, and death—with sacred

rituals and ceremonies. The bora ritual, performed in a "bora ring," celebrated a boy's entry into manhood.

English colonization greatly reduced the number of Australian Aborigines and destroyed much of their way of life. Bloodshed, disease, forced resettlement, agricultural expansion, and urbanization all contributed to the destruction of their traditional culture.

The song is gone; the dance
is secret with the dancers in the earth,
the ritual useless, and the tribal story
lost in an alien tale.

5 Only the grass stands up
to mark the dancing-ring: the apple-gums
posture and mime a past corroboree,
murmur a broken chant.

The hunter is gone: the spear
10 is splintered underground; the painted bodies
a dream the world breathed sleeping and forgot.
The nomad feet are still.

Only the rider's heart
halts at a sightless shadow, an unsaid word
15 that fastens in the blood the ancient curse,
the fear as old as Cain.

6 apple-gums: eucalyptus trees, native to Australia.

7 corroboree (kə-rŏb′ə-rē): a nighttime festival in which the Australian Aborigines celebrate important events with songs and symbolic dances.

16 Cain (kān): the eldest son of Adam and Eve, who was condemned to be a fugitive after he murdered his brother Abel out of jealousy.

JUDITH WRIGHT

1915–

The acclaimed poet Judith Wright is a descendant of English settlers who arrived on the continent of Australia in 1828. She grew up in a small farming town in the New England district of the Australian state of New South Wales. Educated at home until she was 13, she spent much of her childhood out of doors, on horseback. "The country was deep in my bones," she recalls, "and I loved to look at it."

Wright attended the University of Sydney and then traveled in Europe for a year before returning to Australia and embarking on her literary career. "Bora Ring" appeared in Wright's first volume of poetry, *The Moving Image,* which was published in 1946. The poems in this collection and in *Woman to Man,* which followed in 1949, concern the plight of Australian Aborigines, the role of women, and the need to protect Australia's natural landscape. These themes have continued to concern the poet throughout her writing career, during which she has produced more than a dozen volumes of verse, as well as short stories, essays, children's books, and plays.

An active environmentalist, Wright helped found a wildlife preservation society in Queensland, Australia, and has fought to preserve Australia's Great Barrier Reef, to establish national parks, and to protect the land from deforestation. "Four generations of my forebears spent a lot of their time battling against Australian trees," she once observed; ". . . I spend a good deal of my time in the reverse process, battling *for* trees."

OTHER WORKS *The Generations of Men; Because I Was Invited; The Double Tree: Selected Poems, 1942–1976*

WRITING A PLAY

Selections in Unit Five, "Nothing Stays the Same," show the effects of change and the conflicts that arise among people affected by change. What conflicts are there among people in your school? your town? the world? How many of these conflicts are related to change?

GUIDED ASSIGNMENT
Write a Scene for a Play Because all of the action in a play takes place before an audience, drama is a very effective medium for showing change and conflict. In this lesson, you will write a scene that dramatizes a challenging situation.

News Photograph
People often organize to protest situations they believe are unfair. What kinds of conflicts do public protests involve?

1 Identify Changes

Most good stories and plays have their beginnings in some sort of real-world conflict. For example, the stories in Unit Five involved conflicts between different groups of people or between people and changing situations. Look at the headlines and articles on these pages. What change or conflict is at the center of each one? How might a writer build a story around one of these conflicts?

2 Consider the Possibilities

You, too, may discover the seeds of a story in situations and images that you see around you. Try one or more of these activities to find an idea that you can turn into a play.

- Think about stories in the news that you've read or heard about. Would any of the conflicts behind these stories make good plays? What details would you need to add or change?
- Discuss changes that may happen in the future, such as a woman becoming president or global warming. What conflicts might result? Could the conflicts be dramatized?
- Discuss stories in this book that would make good plays. Look through the Table of Contents for ideas.

Article Headlines

A play set in the future could have conflicts over the environment.

Newspaper headlines often emphasize conflict. What stories might follow each of these headlines?

Ozone Layer Is Disappearing
What happens when it's gone?

ANOTHER ICE AGE?
SCIENTISTS DISAGREE

This reminds me of that story "Searching for Summer"!

Resort Threatens Bird Sanctuary

Noakes would have exploited the Hatchings' sunny spot.

The Continuing Fight for the Amazon

Anguish is etched in the Kayapo Indian warrior's dark bronze features. He has recently emerged from his thatch hut after six months mourning a son stricken by malaria. Fewer than 4,000 of this once-dominant tribe survive in the dense rain forest of the Brazilian Amazon. Now, another of the man's children is sick, as "white men's diseases"—pneumonia, hepatitis, and malaria—sweep through the Kayapo village of Pukanuv in the northern Brazilian state of Pará.

In the village center, a satellite dish is framed incongruously against a brilliant blue sky. The dish was flown in two years ago, with an accompanying TV set, by a timber company that illegally felled mahogany. The trees were already on the ground, argued the loggers: Why not let us pay you to take them away?

Today, Brazil's 200,000 remaining tribal Indians are caught in a Faustian pact. The timber companies bring disease and plunder natural resources. But they also bring wealth to the chiefs who control the villages.

Polly Ghazi,
from *World Press Review*, September 1994

❸ Freewrite

Try some of your ideas. For each situation, think of things that could happen that would create conflict. Ask "What if . . . ?" and then freewrite about the situation for a few minutes.

Decision Point Decide which story or real-life situation you are going to dramatize.

WRITING FROM EXPERIENCE **797**

Setting the Stage

Conflict Through Action You've decided on a real or fictional story that you want to dramatize. Now it's time to think about the people and events that will be part of your scene. These pages can help you to make decisions about how to dramatize the conflict and about the characters, setting, and action of your scene.

1 Make Notes on Your Scene

Note important events in the story you want to tell. As you choose a specific scene to dramatize, look for an event that has a clear starting point and end point.

- Make some notes on what will happen, where and when it will happen, and who will make it happen in your scene.
- Decide which events will be included in your scene.
- Jot down a few sentences or phrases that describe the key characters. Include personality traits as well as physical characteristics and clothing.

2 Refine Your Plan

Questions such as the following may help you improve your plan.

- How will I set up the most important conflict in the scene? How will it be resolved?
- Where and when does the play take place?
- Who are the characters? How do they look? How are they dressed?

Notice how one student noted what she wanted to show in a scene based on the story "Searching for Summer."

Student's Planning Notes

Scene for _Searching for Summer_

Scenes in story:
1) Church, road
2) Molesworth
3) Cottage
4) 3 days later, woods
5) Molesworth, road

Events in my scene:
1) Scooter breaks down.
2) Bus arrives and Mrs. Hatching drops purse.
3) Lily & Tom meet Mr. Noakes.
4) Lily & Tom set off to return purse.

Characters:

Mr. Noakes -
red face, greasy hair, overweight, greedy, insincere

Tom - suit; unsure of self

Lily - yellow wedding dress; innocent

William - blind

Mrs. Hatching - black dress & hat; sweet

Setting:
dingy garage on dusty road; gray sky

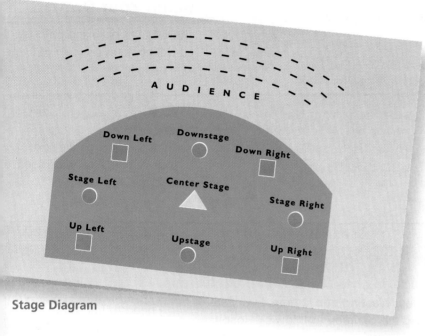

Stage Diagram

WRITER'S CRAFT

Writing Stage Directions
Scripts for plays include stage directions—descriptions of how characters look, speak, and move and of scenery, props, and lighting. Characters are described where each appears on stage.

Include speaking directions for actors with dialogue. Most directions are a word or phrase, such as (sadly) or (looking at him). Other directions describe complicated actions. (He smiles with satisfaction as he looks in mirror.) Review plays in this book for more examples.

The setting is described at the beginning of each scene. A setting should fit the mood of a scene. For example, a set for a realistic play could include real furniture. Some plays are performed with only lighting or music to evoke a mood.

APPLYING WHAT YOU'VE LEARNED
Describe a setting that would be appropriate for your scene.

❸ Visualize Your Staging

Now that you've made some basic decisions about your scene, imagine how it will look and sound as it is performed.

- Picture what the audience will see when the scene opens and where the actors will be on the stage. Then imagine each event as your story unfolds.
- The stage diagram above and the SkillBuilder on the right may help you imagine the placement of scenery and props and the movement of characters on stage.
- When you have finished playing out the scene in your mind, jot down ideas that you want to include in your script.

❹ Consider Your Audience

Who will this play be for—people your own age, a general audience, or children? Once you have identified your audience, think about how you can plan setting, dialogue, action, and costumes that will appeal to this audience. For example, a play for children would probably include more action and less dialogue than a play for adults.

THINK & PLAN

Reflecting on Your Ideas

1. What details can you include in your opening to describe the setting and characters?
2. How can you make the conflict in your story clear through dialogue and stage directions?
3. If you are adapting a story, what changes will you make?

DRAFTING

Developing Your Script

Conflict Shown Through Dialogue In a play, dialogue and stage directions must communicate everything about the story. Keep this in mind as you draft a script for your scene. If you feel more comfortable with one part of your scene than with another, begin with that part. Put your characters in the scene and have them start talking to one another. You can clarify their situation and add stage directions later.

① Begin Your Draft

The Writing Coach and your prewriting notes can help you with drafting.

- Try talking aloud to yourself in the voices of your characters as you write.
- The SkillBuilder on the next page can help you write good dialogue.

Student's Rough Draft

Scene for "Summer"

My Rough Draft	My Comments
Mr. Noakes. Old nuisances! Wasting public time. Every week that business goes on, taking the old man to Midwick Hospital Outpatients and back again. I know what I'd do with 'em. Put away somewhere, that sort ought to be!	*My Rough Draft* I need to tell what Mr. Noakes looks like and what important characters are wearing. Also, how can I get characters off the bus?
Garage owner. Mr. Noakes, Mr. Noakes! Here's two young people wanting you. They need a room for the night.	
Mr. Noakes. Honeymooners, eh? Want a bed for the night, eh? Heh, heh, heh, heh.	
Lily. Well, we WERE looking for some sunshine. Now we'll have to stay until the bike's fixed, I guess.	Here, in the original story, they go to the inn, but I can't change the scenery in the middle of the scene. Instead, have them talking on the road. Is there a way to get them off for their walk before they go to the inn?
Mr. Noakes. Sunshine! Oh my gawd! That's a good one! Hear that? They're looking for a bit of sunshine. Heh, heh, heh, heh, heh, heh! Why if I could find a bit of sunshine near here, permanent bit, that is, do you know what I'd do? Beach, trailer site, country club, holiday camp—you wouldn't know the place. Land around here is dirt cheap; I'd buy up the lot. Nothing but woods. I'd advertise—I'd have people flocking to this little dump from all over the country. But what a hope, what a hope, eh? Well, come on then. Almost bedtime! Ready for bed? Heh, heh, heh, heh, bed's ready for you! Follow me.	
Lily. I—I'd like to go for a bit of a walk first, Tom. Look, I picked up that old lady's bag on the pavement. I didn't notice it till we'd done talking to Mr. Noakes, and by then she was out of sight. Should we take it back to her?	
Tom. Good Idea! Do you know where she lives, Mr. Noakes?	
Mr. Noakes. Who, old Ma Hatching? Sure, she lives in the wood. But you don't want to take her bag back. Let her worry.	

❷ Review Your Draft

Read your draft aloud to yourself to catch unnatural sounding dialogue. Mark places where dialogue must be added to supply necessary background information. Also, ask yourself these questions:

- Does the part of the story shown in my scene make sense?
- Is the conflict in the story developed in an interesting way?
- Could I move more quickly into the conflict?
- Do my characters have distinct personalities? Can I change the dialogue or add stage directions to make them more real? Would it help to have them wear certain costumes?
- Is my setting clear? What details can I add to make it more vivid? Do I want to describe the setting in dialogue, or should I add stage directions for scenery and lighting?

Ask a few of your friends to read your script aloud or to act out your script and follow your stage directions.

❸ Rework and Share

Before you write a second draft, think about changes that you want to make based on your attempt to act out your scene.

- If the action in your scene was too slow or too fast, add or take out dialogue or action.
- Make sure that your opening stage directions identify the setting and describe the stage as the scene opens, including the positions of the actors.
- Wherever it is needed, add stage directions to describe how the characters talk and move.
- The stage diagram and SkillBuilder on page 799 can help you write good stage directions.

 PEER RESPONSE

Ask a few peer readers to once again act out your script and follow your stage directions. These questions may help readers to identify the strengths and weaknesses of your scene:

- Were you interested in the scene from the beginning? If not, how could I change the opening to make it more involving?
- What details would tell more about setting and characters?
- Do my characters seem real? Is their dialogue natural?
- Are any parts of the scene unclear to you? What parts?

Staging Your Scene

On with the Show! You've worked to make your dialogue and stage directions tell a story. Now share your scene by preparing a final draft. This draft should incorporate your own and your peers' ideas for improvements and should use correct scriptwriting conventions. If you decide to produce your scene, choose your actors, design your scenery, and start rehearsals. You're the producer, director, and the star of your show.

Student's Final Script

The future. Molesworth village. A road in front of a garage, gray sky above. **Lily,** in a yellow wedding dress, and **Tom,** in a suit, stand with their scooter beside **Garage owner,** who waves at people getting off a bus, which is offstage left.

Garage owner. There's Mr. Noakes now. He'll have room for you.

William, blind and with a white stick, and **Mrs. Hatching,** old and frail in a black dress and hat, enter. **William** is helped along by George. **Mr. Noakes,** who is fat, red-faced, and dirty-looking, follows them.

Mrs. Hatching. Careful now, George, mind ee be careful with my son William. (*She drops her purse. They move off right.*)

Mr. Noakes (*furiously*). Old nuisances! Wasting public time. Every week that business goes on, taking the old man to Midwick Hospital Outpatients and back again. I know what I'd do with 'em. Put away somewhere, that sort ought to be!

Garage owner (*calling*). Mr. Noakes, Mr. Noakes! Here's two young people wanting you. They need a room for the night.

Mr. Noakes (*leering with false sentimentality at Lily*). Honeymooners, eh? Want a bed for the night, eh? (*Laughs suggestively and pinches Lily's arm*).

Lily (*sadly*). Well, we WERE looking for some sunshine. Now we'll have to stay until the bike's fixed, I guess.

1 Revise and Edit

Use peer comments on dialogue and stage directions and the Standards for Evaluation on the next page as you revise. The SkillBuilder on the next page will help you to make your scene ready for its opening.

The writer describes the setting of the scene and the characters' positions on stage in an introductory paragraph.

The writer changes some story events to allow all the action to take place in the same setting.

Trees together/no sunshine.

Trees pull left and right off stage to let in sunshine (stage light).

Student's Idea for Stage Set

2 Share Your Scene

You may want to expand your scene into a complete play before having it performed. For a play based on "Searching for Summer," the writer designed a set for a forest scene. The trees pull back to give the illusion of sun breaking through clouds.

You may also adapt your play as a radio script or film script.

- Radio plays have sound effects and often have narrators.
- Scripts for television and films describe what is shown on the screen while the characters are speaking and specify the point of view from which a shot is seen.
- Record your play on audiotape or videotape and share it.

Standards for Evaluation

An effective dramatic scene
- deals with a conflict that is clearly conveyed by the plot
- uses characters and setting to create a world of its own
- includes complete stage directions as necessary
- uses dialogue that advances the plot
- uses appropriate format for dramatic writing

SkillBuilder

GRAMMAR FROM WRITING

Formatting Your Script
Look over the plays in this book before preparing the final draft of your script. Notice the beginning of the play and the dialogue.

- Describe the setting and opening situation in a paragraph.
- If you list characters, arrange them by order of appearance.
- Begin a new line when the speaker changes. Give the name of the speaker, followed by a period.
- Give directions for an actor within parentheses between the name and the dialogue.
- Use italic type for stage directions and boldface type for characters' names, if possible.

Editing Checklist Use the following editing tips as you revise.

- Did you correctly use scriptwriting conventions?
- Are capitalization, punctuation, and spelling correct?

REFLECT & ASSESS

Evaluating the Experience

1. How well did your scene communicate to your audience?
2. How would you change your scene if you adapted it for film?

📁 **PORTFOLIO** How well did you communicate the idea of the story you dramatized? Put this evaluation in your portfolio.

REFLECT & ASSESS

UNIT FIVE: NOTHING STAYS THE SAME

The selections in this unit show many dimensions of change, from changes that mark an individual's life to ones that affect an entire culture. How has your own understanding of change been affected by the selections? Explore this question by completing one or more of the options in each section.

REFLECTING ON THEME

OPTION 1 **Charting Responses to Change** Are you a person who welcomes change, or do you tend to approach change with fear or regret? Make a two-column chart, with one column labeled "Welcome Changes" and the other labeled "Unwelcome Changes." Fill in the chart by listing, in the appropriate columns, some changes that are presented in this unit's selections, as well as ones that you have faced in your own life. Underline the entries that you have the strongest feelings about. Then write an evaluation of your own attitude toward change, describing how your attitude has been affected by your reading.

OPTION 2 **Evaluating a Quotation** Consider the quotation from the ancient philosopher Heraclitus at the beginning of this unit: "There is nothing permanent except change." Which of the characters and authors in this unit might agree with that statement? Which might disagree? Make two lists of characters and authors—one list showing those who would agree, the other showing those who would disagree. Include yourself in one of the lists.

OPTION 3 **Graphing the Causes of Change** Work with a partner to create a pie chart showing what you believe to be the major causes of change affecting individuals and societies. To identify these causes, consider the changes presented in this unit's selections and reflect on your own experiences with change. Remember that the largest section of your chart should represent the most important or most common cause of change. Compare your pie chart with those of your classmates, and discuss their similarities and differences.

Self-Assessment: Which of the selections in this unit might have the greatest influence on you in the future—those dealing with the price of progress (Part 1) or those examining cultural issues (Part 2)? Create a list of the selection titles, arranging them in their order of impact.

REVIEWING LITERARY CONCEPTS

OPTION 1 **Analyzing Personal Essays** Review the information about personal essays on page 703. Then identify at least four personal essays in this textbook or other sources, and create a chart, like the one shown, to analyze them. After you complete

Essay	Author's Purpose	Theme	Tone	Style
"Once More to the Lake" by E. B. White	To offer his reflections on revisiting a lake where he had vacationed as a child	Memory can bring the past to life, but only partially.	Thoughtful, nostalgic, tranquil	Complex; characterized by long, elaborate sentences; full of sensory details

your chart, identify the essay that had the greatest impact on you. Write a note explaining your choice.

OPTION 2 **Identifying Symbols** Review the definition of *symbol* in the Handbook of Literary Terms on page 1000. Then identify at least five symbols in this unit's selections and write a brief explanation of each. After sharing your work with a small group of classmates, work with the group to choose a symbol that conveys the idea expressed by the unit title, "Nothing Stays the Same." The symbol can be one of those you identified in the selections, or it can be invented.

Self-Assessment: Imagine that a rich, eccentric patron of your school is offering a $5,000 prize to students who show mastery of the following terms. There is a catch, however—you have only 15 minutes to review the terms. To help you use your time efficiently, divide the terms into three categories: those you don't need to review, those you need to review only briefly, and those for which you require extensive review. Then spend 15 minutes reviewing the necessary terms (and hope that you find that rich patron!).

imagery	*tone*	*situational irony*
science fiction	*first-person point of view*	*title*
mood	*naive narrator*	*setting*
personal essay	*climax*	*cultural setting*
voice	*dramatic monologue*	*cultural symbols*
sentence structure		*literary symbols*
diction		

PORTFOLIO BUILDING

• **QuickWrites** Imagine that you are applying for a job and your prospective employer has asked to see a writing sample. Review your QuickWrites for this unit, paying particular attention to any that reflect the world of work, such as an advertisement, a newsletter article, or a press release. Choose the one that you feel would most impress an employer. Write a note explaining your choice. Then add the piece and the note to your portfolio.

• **Writing About Literature** Earlier in this unit, you changed a story element in one of the selections. Review your rewritten portion of the story, noting your impressions of your work now. How does it sound to you? What do you remember most about this experience of writing it? How might you apply what you learned to your future reading or writing?

• **Writing from Experience** By now you have written a scene for a play. How well does it work as a dramatic moment? Write a brief yet thoughtful review of your scene. What are its strengths and weaknesses? What did you learn from writing it that you can apply to other writing assignments? You may want to include your review in your portfolio.

• **Personal Choice** Look back through your records and evaluations of all the activities and writing that you completed in this unit, including any work that you did on your own. Which activity or piece of writing would you most like to expand into a larger project? Write a note explaining your choice, and add it, along with your record of the original work, to your portfolio.

Self-Assessment: Compare the recent additions to your portfolio with pieces that you included earlier in the year. In what ways has your writing improved? How have your interests changed since the beginning of the year? How satisfied are you with your progress? Write an evaluation of your development as a writer up to this point in the year.

SETTING GOALS

Make a list of things that you would like to change about yourself as a reader and writer. Then circle the changes that seem realistically achievable by the end of the year. Use the circled items as goals for your work in the next unit.

THE MAKING OF HEROES

THE HERO IN ONE AGE WILL BE A HERO IN ANOTHER.

CHARLOTTE LENNOX
BRITISH NOVELIST AND POET
1720–1804

Still Life #31 (1993), Tom Wesselmann.
Mixed-media construction with television,
48″ × 60″ × 10 ¼″, Frederick R. Weisman
Art Foundation, Los Angeles. Copyright
© 1996 Tom Wesselmann / Licensed by
VAGA, New York.

A STRENGTH FROM WITHIN

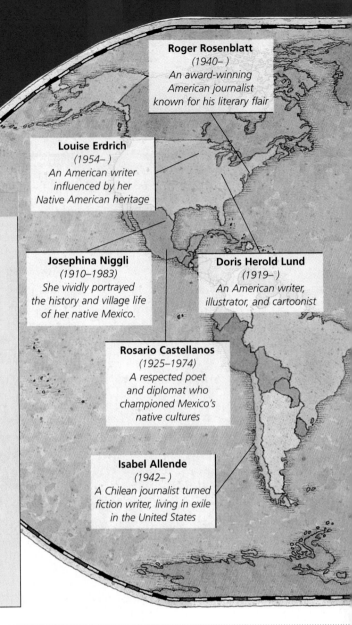

Roger Rosenblatt
(1940–)
An award-winning American journalist known for his literary flair

Louise Erdrich
(1954–)
An American writer influenced by her Native American heritage

Josephina Niggli
(1910–1983)
She vividly portrayed the history and village life of her native Mexico.

Doris Herold Lund
(1919–)
An American writer, illustrator, and cartoonist

Rosario Castellanos
(1925–1974)
A respected poet and diplomat who championed Mexico's native cultures

Isabel Allende
(1942–)
A Chilean journalist turned fiction writer, living in exile in the United States

REFLECTING ON THEME

Are you a strong person? In times of trial, can you find the strength to do what needs to be done—to overcome obstacles, to withstand opposition, even to face danger? Often, people never know what they are capable of doing until circumstances push them to the limit. In this part of Unit Six, you will encounter a number of ordinary people who must confront extraordinary challenges. As you will see, such challenges can produce unexpected heroes.

What Do You Think? In your notebook, list the names of three people whom you regard as heroes. These may be figures from history, people in the news, or personal acquaintances. Write a brief explanation of what makes each of the people heroic. Then compare your list with those of your classmates and discuss what you regard as essential ingredients of heroism.

Nadine Gordimer	**A Chip of Glass Ruby** *Fighting for rights in South Africa*	810
Roger Rosenblatt	**The Man in the Water** *Why did he sacrifice himself?*	823
Isabel Allende	**And of Clay Are We Created** *Amid disaster, heroism*	829
Rosario Castellanos	**Nocturne / Nocturno** / INSIGHT *A question for the night*	840
Louise Erdrich	**The Leap** *How far would you go to save your child?*	844

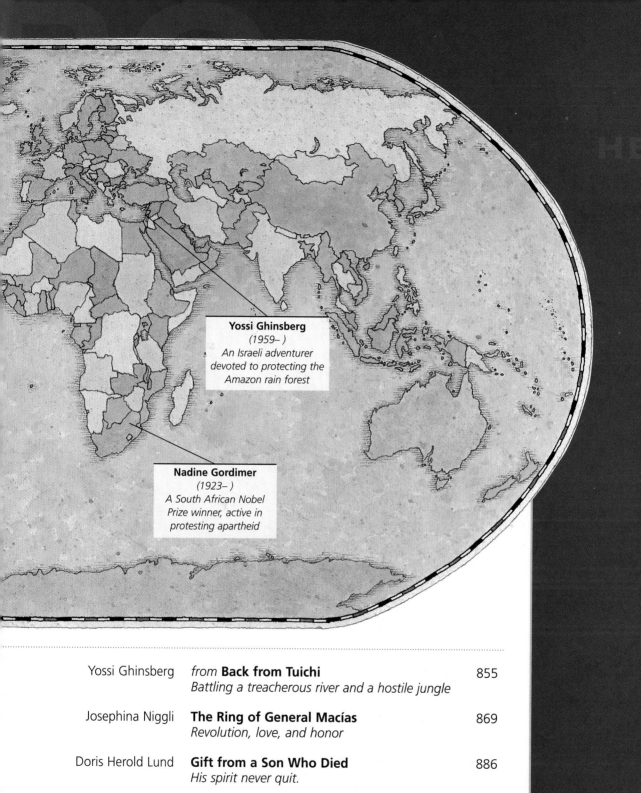

Yossi Ghinsberg
(1959–)
An Israeli adventurer devoted to protecting the Amazon rain forest

Nadine Gordimer
(1923–)
A South African Nobel Prize winner, active in protesting apartheid

PREVIEWING

FICTION

A Chip of Glass Ruby
Nadine Gordimer South Africa

PERSONAL CONNECTION

Think of a household where one parent is heavily involved in political or charitable activities outside the home. With a small group of classmates, discuss how the family might be affected by such activities. Make a chart, like the one shown, listing the positive and negative effects that such involvement might have on the family.

Possible Effects on Family	
Positive	**Negative**

HISTORICAL CONNECTION

In this story, an Indian woman living in South Africa juggles the responsibilities of family life with her work as a political activist. The story takes place during the time of apartheid (ə-pärt'hīt'), a system of racial segregation. Under apartheid, every citizen was classified as either white, colored (mixed race), Asian (of East Indian ancestry), or Bantu (native black). Complex laws set limits on the lives of those who were not white. For example, the Group Areas Act, mentioned in this story, forced nonwhites to live in certain areas. Pass laws required that black South Africans carry passes identifying where they lived and what areas they could visit. While Asians did not have to carry passes, their movements also were restricted.

For decades, many South Africans struggled against apartheid, despite the threat of being jailed. Among the most influential antiapartheid groups was the African National Congress (ANC), called simply "Congress" in the story. As a result of protests led by the ANC and others, the pass laws were among the first apartheid laws to be fought successfully; they were abolished in 1986. Apartheid was completely dismantled in the early 1990s.

READING CONNECTION

Visualizing Setting As you read this story, create mental pictures of the domestic life that the writer describes. Notice details about the house, the clothing, the food, and the routines of daily life. Consider what these details reveal about the family members, the society in which they live, and how their lives are affected by the political activities of Mrs. Bamjee.

Using Your Reading Log Use your reading log to record your responses to the questions throughout the selection. Also jot down any questions, thoughts, and feelings you have as you read.

LASERLINKS
• *HISTORICAL CONNECTION*

Nadine Gordimer

A Chip of Glass Ruby

When the duplicating machine was brought into the house, Bamjee said, "Isn't it enough that you've got the Indians' troubles on your back?" Mrs. Bamjee said, with a smile that showed the gap of a missing tooth but was confident all the same, "What's the difference, Yusuf? We've all got the same troubles."

"Don't tell me that. We don't have to carry passes; let the natives protest against passes on their own; there are millions of them. Let them go ahead with it."

The nine Bamjee and Pahad children were present at this exchange as they were always; in the small house that held them all there was no room for privacy for the discussion of matters they were too young to hear, and so they had never been too young to hear anything. Only their sister and half-sister, Girlie, was missing; she was the eldest, and married. The children looked expectantly, unalarmed and interested, at Bamjee, who had neither left the room nor settled down again to the task of rolling his own cigarettes, which had been interrupted by the arrival of the duplicator. He had looked at the thing that had come hidden in a washbasket and conveyed in a black man's taxi, and the children turned on it too, their black eyes surrounded by thick lashes like those still, open flowers with hairy tentacles that close on whatever touches them.

"A fine thing to have on the table where we eat," was all he said at last. They smelled the machine among them; a smell of cold black grease. He went out, heavily on tiptoe, in his troubled way.

"It's going to go nicely on the sideboard!" Mrs. Bamjee was busy making a place by removing the two pink glass vases filled with plastic carnations and the hand-painted velvet runner with the picture of the Taj Mahal.[1]

After supper she began to run off leaflets on the machine. The family lived in that room—the three other rooms in the house were full of beds—and they were all there. The older children shared a bottle of ink while they did their homework, and the two little ones pushed a couple of empty milk bottles in and out the chair legs. The three-year-old fell asleep and was carted away by one of the girls. They all drifted off to bed eventually; Bamjee himself went before the older children—he was a fruit-and-vegetable hawker[2] and was up at half past four every morning to get to the market by five. "Not long now," said Mrs. Bamjee. The older children looked up and smiled at him. He

turned his back on her. She still wore the traditional clothing of a Moslem woman, and her body, which was scraggy and unimportant as a dress on a peg when it was not host to a child, was wrapped in the trailing rags of a cheap sari,[3] and her thin black plait[4] was greased. When she was a girl, in the Transvaal[5] town where they lived still, her mother fixed a chip of glass ruby in her nostril; but she had abandoned that adornment as too old-style, even for her, long ago.

She was up until long after midnight, turning out leaflets. She did it as if she might have been pounding chilies.

Bamjee did not have to ask what the leaflets were. He had read the papers. All the past week Africans had been destroying their passes and then presenting themselves for arrest. Their leaders were jailed on charges of incitement,[6] campaign offices were raided—someone must be helping the few minor leaders who were left to keep the campaign going without offices or equipment. What was it the leaflets would say—"Don't go to work tomorrow," "Day of Protest," "Burn Your Pass for Freedom"? He didn't want to see.

He was used to coming home and finding his wife sitting at the table deep in discussion with strangers or people whose names

CLARIFY

Why doesn't Bamjee want to see the leaflets?

---

1. **Taj Mahal** (täzh′ mə-häl′): a beautiful white marble building in India, built in the seventeenth century by Shah Jahan as a tomb for his wife and himself.
2. **hawker:** a peddler who sells goods by calling out.
3. **sari** (sä′rē): a garment worn by East Indian women and girls, consisting of a long cloth wrapped around the body, with one end draped over the shoulder.
4. **plait** (plāt): a braid of hair.
5. **Transvaal** (trăns-väl′): a province in northeast South Africa.
6. **incitement** (ĭn-sīt′mənt): a rousing, stirring up, or calling to action.

News from the Gulf (about 1991), Robert A. Wade. Watercolor, 19″ × 29″, private collection.
Copyright © Robert A. Wade. From *Painting Your Vision in Watercolor*, North Light Books.

were familiar by repute.[7] Some were prominent Indians, like the lawyer, Dr. Abdul Mohammed Khan, or the big businessman, Mr. Moonsamy Patel, and he was flattered, in a suspicious way, to meet them in his house. As he came home from work next day, he met Dr. Khan coming out of the house, and Dr. Khan—a highly educated man—said to him, "A wonderful woman." But Bamjee had never caught his wife out in any presumption; she behaved properly, as any Moslem woman should, and once her business with such gentlemen was over would never, for instance, have sat down to eat with them. He found her now back in the kitchen, setting about the preparation of dinner and carrying on a conversation on several different wavelengths with the children. "It's really a shame if you're tired of lentils, Jimmy, because that's what you're getting—Amina, hurry up, get a pot of water going—don't worry, I'll mend that in a minute; just bring the yellow cotton, and there's a needle in the cigarette box on the sideboard."

"Was that Dr. Khan leaving?" said Bamjee.

"Yes, there's going to be a stay-at-home on Monday. Desai's ill, and he's got to get the word around by himself. Bob Jali was up all last night

---

7. **repute** (rĭ-pyo͞ot′): reputation; fame.

WORDS TO KNOW   **presumption** (prĭ-zŭmp′shən) *n.* behavior or language that is boldly arrogant or offensive

printing leaflets, but he's gone to have a tooth out." She had always treated Bamjee as if it were only a mannerism that made him appear uninterested in politics, the way some woman will persist in interpreting her husband's bad temper as an endearing gruffness hiding boundless goodwill, and she talked to him of these things just as she passed on to him neighbors' or family gossip.

"What for do you want to get mixed up with these killings and stonings and I don't know what? Congress should keep out of it. Isn't it enough with the Group Areas?"

She laughed. "Now, Yusuf, you know you don't believe that. Look how you said the same thing when the Group Areas started in Natal. You said we should begin to worry when we get moved out of our own houses here in the Transvaal. And then your own mother lost her house in Noorddorp,[8] and there you are; you saw that nobody's safe. Oh, Girlie was here this afternoon; she says Ismail's brother's engaged—that's nice, isn't it? His mother will be pleased; she was worried."

"Why was she worried?" asked Jimmy,

who was fifteen, and old enough to <u>patronize</u> his mother.

"Well, she wanted to see him settled. There's a party on Sunday week at Ismail's place—you'd better give me your suit to give to the cleaners tomorrow, Yusuf."

One of the girls presented herself at once. "I'll have nothing to wear, Ma."

Mrs. Bamjee scratched her <u>sallow</u> face. "Perhaps Girlie will lend you her pink, eh? Run over to Girlie's place now and say I say will she lend it to you."

The sound of commonplaces often does service as security, and Bamjee, going to sit in the armchair with the shiny armrests that was wedged between the table and the sideboard, lapsed into an unthinking doze that, like all times of dreamlike ordinariness during those weeks, was filled with uneasy jerks and starts back into reality. The next morning, as soon as he got to market, he heard that Dr. Khan had been arrested. But that night Mrs. Bamjee sat up making a new dress for her daughter; the sight <u>disarmed</u> Bamjee, reassured him again, against his will, so that the resentment he had been making ready all day faded into a <u>morose</u> and accusing silence. Heaven knew, of course, who came and went in the house during the day. Twice in that week of riots, raids, and arrests, he found black women in the house when he came home; plain ordinary native women in doeks,[9] drinking tea. This was not a thing other Indian women would have in their homes, he thought bitterly; but then his wife was not like other

This was not a thing other Indian women would have in their homes, he thought bitterly...

CLARIFY

What seems to be Bamjee's attitude toward his wife?

8. **Natal** (nə-tăl) . . . **Noorddorp** (nōrt′dôrp): provinces in South Africa.
9. **doeks** (düks): cloth head coverings.

WORDS TO KNOW

patronize (pā′trə-nīz) *v.* to behave in a manner that shows feelings of superiority
sallow (săl′ō) *adj.* of a sickly, yellowish color or complexion
disarm (dĭs-ärm′) *v.* to overcome or reduce the intensity of suspicion or hostility; to win the confidence of
morose (mə-rōs′) *adj.* gloomy; sullen

people, in a way he could not put his finger on, except to say what it was not: not scandalous, not punishable, not rebellious. It was, like the attraction that had led him to marry her, Pahad's widow with five children, something he could not see clearly.

When the Special Branch[10] knocked steadily on the door in the small hours of Thursday morning, he did not wake up, for his return to consciousness was always set in his mind to half past four, and that was more than an hour away. Mrs. Bamjee got up herself, struggled into Jimmy's raincoat which was hanging over a chair, and went to the front door. The clock on the wall—a wedding present when she married Pahad—showed three o'clock when she snapped on the light, and she knew at once who it was on the other side of the door. Although she was not surprised, her hands shook like a very old person's as she undid the locks and the complicated catch on the wire burglar-proofing. And then she opened the door and they were there—two colored policemen in plain clothes. "Zanip Bamjee?"

"Yes."

As they talked, Bamjee woke up in the sudden terror of having overslept. Then he became conscious of men's voices. He heaved himself out of bed in the dark and went to the window, which, like the front door, was covered with a heavy mesh of thick wire against intruders from the dingy lane it looked upon. Bewildered, he appeared in the room, where the policemen were searching through a soapbox of papers beside the duplicating machine. "Yusuf, it's for me," Mrs. Bamjee said.

At once, the snap of a trap, realization came. He stood there in an old shirt before the two policemen, and the woman was going off to prison because of the natives. "There you are!" he shouted, standing away from her. "That's what you've got for it. Didn't I tell you? Didn't I? That's the end of it now. That's the finish.

That's what it's come to." She listened with her head at the slightest tilt to one side, as if to ward off a blow, or in compassion.

Jimmy, Pahad's son, appeared at the door with a suitcase; two or three of the girls were behind him. "Here, Ma, you take my green jersey." "I've found your clean blouse." Bamjee had to keep moving out of their way as they helped their mother to make ready. It was like the preparation for one of the family festivals his wife made such a fuss over; wherever he put himself, they bumped into him. Even the two policemen mumbled, "Excuse me," and pushed past into the rest of the house to continue their search. They took with them a tome[11] that Nehru[12] had written in prison; it had been bought from a persevering traveling salesman and kept, for years, on the mantelpiece. "Oh, don't take that, please," Mrs. Bamjee said suddenly, clinging to the arm of the man who had picked it up.

The man held it away from her.

"What does it matter, Ma?"

It was true that no one in the house had ever read it; but she said, "It's for my children."

"Ma, leave it." Jimmy, who was squat and plump, looked like a merchant advising a client against a roll of silk she had set her heart on. She went into the bedroom and got dressed. When she came out in her old yellow sari with a brown coat over it, the faces of the children were behind her like faces on the platform at a railway station. They kissed her goodbye. The policemen did not hurry her, but she seemed to be in a hurry just the same.

"What am I going to do?" Bamjee accused them all.

The policemen looked away patiently.

"It'll be all right. Girlie will help. The big

---

10. **Special Branch:** the South African secret police.

11. **tome:** a book, especially a large or scholarly one.

12. **Nehru** (nā′rōō): Jawaharlal (jə-wä′hər-läl′) Nehru, nationalist leader in India's movement for self-governance and the first prime minister of independent India.

children can manage. And Yusuf—" The children crowded in around her; two of the younger ones had awakened and appeared, asking shrill questions.

"Come on," said the policemen.

"I want to speak to my husband." She broke away and came back to him, and the movement of her sari hid them from the rest of the room for a moment. His face hardened in suspicious anticipation against the request to give some message to the next fool who would take up her pamphleteering until he, too, was arrested. "On Sunday," she said. "Take them on Sunday." He did not know what she was talking about. "The engagement party," she whispered, low and urgent. "They shouldn't miss it. Ismail will be offended."

They listened to the car drive away. Jimmy bolted and barred the front door and then at once opened it again; he put on the raincoat that his mother had taken off. "Going to tell Girlie," he said. The children went back to bed. Their father did not say a word to any of them; their talk, the crying of the younger ones and the argumentative voices of the older, went on in the bedrooms. He found himself alone; he felt the night all around him. And then he happened to meet the clock face and saw with a terrible sense of unfamiliarity that this was not the secret night but an hour he should have recognized: the time he always got up. He pulled on his trousers and his dirty white hawker's coat and wound his grey muffler up to the stubble on his chin and went to work.

The duplicating machine was gone from the sideboard. The policemen had taken it with them, along with the pamphlets and the conference reports and the stack of old newspapers that had collected on top of the wardrobe in the bedroom—not the thick dailies of the white men but the thin, impermanent-looking papers that spoke up, sometimes interrupted by suppression or lack of money, for the rest. It was all gone. When he had married her and moved in with her and her five children, into what had been the Pahad and became the Bamjee house, he had not recognized the humble, harmless, and apparently useless routine tasks—the minutes of meetings being written up on the dining-room table at night, the government blue books that were read while the latest baby was suckled, the employment of the fingers of the older children in the fashioning of crinkle-paper Congress rosettes—as activity intended to move mountains. For years and years he had not noticed it, and now it was gone.

EVALUATE

Why do you think Bamjee hadn't paid attention to his wife's political activities?

The house was quiet. The children kept to their lairs, crowded on the beds with the doors shut. He sat and looked at the sideboard, where the plastic carnations and the mat with the picture of the Taj Mahal were in place. For the first few weeks he never spoke of her. There was the feeling, in the house, that he had wept and raged at her, that boulders of reproach had thundered down upon her absence, and yet he had said not one word. He had not been to inquire where she was; Jimmy and Girlie had gone to Mohammed Ebrahim, the lawyer, and when he found out that their mother had been taken—when she was arrested, at least—to a prison in the next town, they had stood about outside the big prison door for hours while they waited to be told where she had been moved from there. At last they had discovered that she was fifty miles away, in Pretoria.[13] Jimmy asked Bamjee for five shillings to help Girlie pay the train fare to Pretoria, once she had been interviewed by the police and had been given a permit to visit her mother; he put three two-shilling pieces on the

---

13. **Pretoria** (prĭ-tôr′ē-ə): the administrative capital of South Africa.

Light in the Souk, (about 1991), Robert A. Wade. Watercolor, 19″ × 29″, private collection.
Copyright © Robert A. Wade. From *Painting Your Vision in Watercolor,* North Light Books.

table for Jimmy to pick up, and the boy, looking at him keenly, did not know whether the extra shilling meant anything, or whether it was merely that Bamjee had no change.

It was only when relations and neighbors came to the house that Bamjee would suddenly begin to talk. He had never been so expansive in his life as he was in the company of these visitors, many of them come on a polite call rather in the nature of a visit of condolence. "Ah, yes, yes, you can see how I am—you see what has been done to me. Nine children, and I am on the cart all day. I get home at seven or eight. What are you to do? What can people like us do?"

"Poor Mrs. Bamjee. Such a kind lady."

"Well, you see for yourself. They walk in here in the middle of the night and leave a houseful of children. I'm out on the cart all day; I've got a living to earn." Standing about in his shirtsleeves, he became quite animated; he would call for the girls to bring fruit drinks for the visitors. When they were gone, it was as if he, who was orthodox[14] if not devout and never drank liquor, had been drunk and abruptly sobered up; he looked dazed and could not have gone over in his mind what he had been saying. And as he cooled, the lump of resentment and wrongedness stopped his throat again.

---

14. **orthodox:** conforming to established religious rules or principles.

Bamjee found one of the little boys the center of a self-important group of championing brothers and sisters in the room one evening. "They've been cruel to Ahmed."

"What has he done?" said the father.

"Nothing! Nothing!" The little girl stood twisting her handkerchief excitedly.

An older one, thin as her mother, took over, silencing the others with a gesture of her skinny hand. "They did it at school today. They made an example of him."

"What is an example?" said Bamjee impatiently.

"The teacher made him come up and stand in front of the whole class, and he told them, 'You see this boy? His mother's in jail because she likes the natives so much. She wants the Indians to be the same as natives.' "

"It's terrible," he said. His hands fell to his sides. "Did she ever think of this?"

He had a sudden vision of her at the duplicating machine...

"That's why Ma's *there*," said Jimmy, putting aside his comic and emptying out his schoolbooks upon the table. "That's all the kids need to know. Ma's there because things like this happen. Petersen's a colored teacher, and it's his black blood that's brought him trouble all his life, I suppose. He hates anyone who says everybody's the same because that takes away from him his bit of whiteness that's all he's got. What d'you expect? It's nothing to make too much fuss about."

"Of course, you are fifteen and you know everything," Bamjee mumbled at him.

"I don't say that. But I know Ma, anyway." The boy laughed.

There was a hunger strike among the political prisoners, and Bamjee could not bring himself to ask Girlie if her mother was starving herself too. He would not ask; and yet he saw in the young woman's face the gradual weakening of her mother. When the strike had gone on for nearly a week, one of the elder children burst into tears at the table and could not eat. Bamjee pushed his own plate away in rage.

Sometimes he spoke out loud to himself while he was driving the vegetable lorry.[15] "What for?" Again and again: "What for?" She was not a modern woman who cut her hair and wore short skirts. He had married a good plain Moslem woman who bore children and stamped her own chilies. He had a sudden vision of her at the duplicating machine, that night just before she was taken away, and he felt himself maddened, baffled, and hopeless. He had become the ghost of a victim, hanging about the scene of a crime whose motive he could not understand and had not had time to learn.

CLARIFY

How does Bamjee feel about his life?

15. **lorry:** a truck.

The hunger strike at the prison went into the second week. Alone in the rattling cab of his lorry, he said things that he heard as if spoken by someone else, and his heart burned in fierce agreement with them. "For a crowd of natives who'll smash our shops and kill us in our houses when their time comes." "She will starve herself to death there." "She will die there." "Devils who will burn and kill us." He fell into bed each night like a stone and dragged himself up in the mornings as a beast of burden is beaten to its feet.

One of these mornings, Girlie appeared very early, while he was wolfing bread and strong tea—alternate sensations of dry solidity and stinging heat—at the kitchen table. Her real name was Fatima, of course, but she had adopted the silly modern name along with the clothes of the young factory girls among whom she worked. She was expecting her first baby in a week or two, and her small face, her cut and curled hair, and the sooty arches drawn over her eyebrows did not seem to belong to her thrust-out body under a clean smock. She wore mauve lipstick and was smiling her cocky little white girl's smile, foolish and bold, not like an Indian girl's at all.

"What's the matter?" he said.

She smiled again. "Don't you know? I told Bobby he must get me up in time this morning. I wanted to be sure I wouldn't miss you today."

"I don't know what you're talking about."

She came over and put her arm up around his unwilling neck and kissed the grey bristles at the side of his mouth. "Many happy returns! Don't you know it's your birthday?"

"No," he said. "I didn't know, didn't think—" He broke the pause by swiftly picking up the bread and giving his attention desperately to eating and drinking. His mouth was busy, but his eyes looked at her, intensely black. She said nothing but stood there with him. She would not speak, and at last he said, swallowing a piece of bread that tore at his throat as it went down, "I don't remember these things."

The girl nodded, the Woolworth baubles in her ears swinging. "That's the first thing she told me when I saw her yesterday—don't forget it's Bajie's birthday tomorrow."

He shrugged over it. "It means a lot to children. But that's how she is. Whether it's one of the old cousins or the neighbor's grand-mother, she always knows when the birthday is. What importance is my birthday, while she's sitting there in a prison? I don't understand how she can do the things she does when her mind is always full of woman's nonsense at the same time—that's what I don't understand with her."

"Oh, but don't you see?" the girl said. "It's because she doesn't want anybody to be left out. It's because she always remembers; remembers everything—people without some-where to live, hungry kids, boys who can't get educated—remembers all the time. That's how Ma is."

"Nobody else is like that." It was half a complaint.

"No, nobody else," said his stepdaughter.

She sat herself down at the table, resting her belly. He put his head in his hands. "I'm getting old"—but he was overcome by some-thing much more curious, by an answer. He knew why he had desired her, the ugly widow with five children; he knew what way it was in which she was not like the others; it was there, like the fact of the belly that lay between him and her daughter. ❖

RESPONDING
OPTIONS

FROM PERSONAL RESPONSE TO CRITICAL ANALYSIS

REFLECT

1. With which character did you sympathize more, Bamjee or Mrs. Bamjee? Share your response with a partner.

RETHINK

2. Do you think that Mrs. Bamjee is a heroic character? Explain your views, citing details from the story to support your opinion.

3. How would you describe the relationship between the husband and wife?

   Consider
   - what Bamjee realizes at the story's conclusion about "why he had desired her"
   - how he feels about his wife's political involvement
   - how each of them handles the responsibilities of marriage and parenthood
   - the differences in their values and personalities

4. In your judgment, what are the positive and negative effects of Mrs. Bamjee's political activities on her family?

   Consider
   - how Mrs. Bamjee's children and husband respond to her imprisonment
   - how her actions might influence the future lives of family members
   - the chart that you created for the Personal Connection on page 810

5. How would you describe life under apartheid, based on your understanding of this story?

RELATE

6. In what ways might this story be relevant to people living in your country?

LITERARY LINKS

Review Coretta Scott King's "Montgomery Boycott" on page 221. If Mrs. King and Mrs. Bamjee were to meet, what might they say to each other?

ANOTHER PATHWAY
Cooperative Learning

With a small group of classmates, prepare and present four dramatic monologues in which each of the following characters expresses his or her view of Mrs. Bamjee: Girlie, Jimmy, Yusuf, and a neighbor. You may wish to include quotations from the story in your monologues.

QUICKWRITES

1. A character in one of Gordimer's novels says, "The real definition of loneliness . . . is to live without social responsibility." Draft an **essay** explaining how Yusuf and Zanip Bamjee would respond to such a statement and how they would define their own responsibilities.

2. Write the **diary entries** that Yusuf and Girlie might have written soon after Mrs. Bamjee's arrest.

3. Write a **literary analysis** in which you offer your own explanation of the significance of this story's title.

4. Rewrite an episode from the story as a **dramatic scene** with stage directions and dialogue.

   PORTFOLIO Save your writing. You may want to use it later as a springboard to a piece for your portfolio.

LITERARY CONCEPTS

Writers often use **dialogue** as a method of developing characters. Working with a partner, choose three characters from this story whom you would like to study. Then review the story to find examples of dialogue that reveal those characters' traits. Create three diagrams like the one shown to record your findings.

Jimmy	
Dialogue	**Trait(s) Revealed**
"Ma's there because things like this happen."	—respect for mother —concern about social justice

THE WRITER'S STYLE

Cooperative Learning With a small group of classmates, take turns reading aloud the description of Mrs. Bamjee's late-night arrest. After completing your oral reading, discuss Gordimer's style. Consider her choice of words, her **tone,** her handling of **dialogue,** her use of **descriptive language,** and any other aspects of **style** that you notice.

CRITIC'S CORNER

The critic Brigitte Weeks wrote that "Gordimer insists that her readers face South African life as she does: with affection and horror." How do you think this statement applies to "A Chip of Glass Ruby"?

ART CONNECTION

Choose one of the two paintings that accompany the selection (page 813 or 817) and explain how it reflects the mood of "A Chip of Glass Ruby."

Detail of *Light in the Souk* (about 1991), Robert A. Wade. Watercolor, 19″ × 29″, private collection. Copyright © Robert A. Wade. From *Painting Your Vision in Watercolor,* North Light Books.

Detail of *News from the Gulf* (about 1991), Robert A. Wade. Watercolor, 19″ × 29″, private collection. Copyright © Robert A. Wade. From *Painting Your Vision in Watercolor,* North Light Books.

ALTERNATIVE ACTIVITIES

1. Create an **illustration** that shows an interior scene of the Bamjee household, based on details in the story. You may work in any medium that you like. Try to portray the household as you visualized it while reading.

2. Conduct an **interview** of someone who is involved in political or charitable activities in your community. Determine why he or she is involved in this work and what—if anything—he or she has sacrificed to provide time for such a commitment.

3. Create a **political cartoon** that offers a reflection on apartheid.

ACROSS THE CURRICULUM

History Find out more about antiapartheid protests led by the African National Congress or about earlier protests in South Africa led by India's Mohandas Gandhi. Share your findings in an oral report.

WORDS TO KNOW

Answer the following questions.

1. Would people be most likely to **patronize** someone they fear, look up to, or look down on?

2. Would a person with a **sallow** appearance be more likely to look as if he or she has spent a lot of time indoors, out in the sun, or at the gym lifting weights?

3. Does a **morose** person typically act conceited, depressed, or frightened?

4. Is a **presumption** an act that is usually seen as being humorous, bashful, or rude?

5. If you were trying to **disarm** someone, would you be most likely to behave in a friendly, bossy, or insulting manner?

NADINE GORDIMER

1923–

Nadine Gordimer was born and raised in Springs, South Africa, a small mining town near Johannesburg, the country's largest city. She attended an all-white school and spent much of her free time reading at the local library. Gordimer realized early on that she had little in common with her peers, however, and she began questioning the racial attitudes of white South Africa. She discovered, in her words, that she "was not merely part of a suburban white life aping Europe" but "lived with and among a variety of colors and kinds of people. This discovery was a joyous personal one, not a political one, at first; but, of course, as time has gone by it has hardened into a sense of political opposition to abusive white power."

Gordimer knew she would be a writer when, at the age of 15, she had her first short story published; her first story collection, *Face to Face*, appeared 10 years later. She was recognized almost immediately as a serious and talented artist, and she gained an American audience by publishing her stories in such magazines as the *New Yorker* and *Harper's*. She has also won praise for her novels—including *A World of*

Strangers, A Guest of Honour, Burger's Daughter, and *July's People*—and has written numerous essays, television plays, and documentaries.

Much of Gordimer's writing has focused on the theme of the destructive influence of apartheid on relationships among South Africans of all colors; as a result, several of her books were banned in her homeland for many years. Although she has said that she's not by nature a political person, she joined the African National Congress (ANC) and also helped found the Congress of South African Writers. "The real influence of politics on my writing is the influence of politics on people," she said. "Their lives, and I believe their very personalities, are changed by the extreme political circumstances one lives under in South Africa." On learning that she had won the 1991 Nobel Prize for literature, she called the event the second greatest thrill of recent years; the first, she said, was the release of ANC leader Nelson Mandela after 27 years as a political prisoner.

OTHER WORKS *Selected Stories, Six Feet of the Country, My Son's Story, Jump and Other Stories*

LASERLINKS
• AUTHOR BACKGROUND

PREVIEWING

The Man in the Water

Roger Rosenblatt United States

PERSONAL CONNECTION

In a disaster—such as an earthquake, a flood, a tornado, or a plane crash—people react in many different ways. With your classmates, discuss how such disasters can bring out the best—or worst—in people. Draw upon your own knowledge for examples.

HISTORICAL CONNECTION

One of the most publicized disasters in recent aviation history occurred on January 13, 1982, when a passenger jet crashed in Washington, D.C., during the evening rush hour. The jet was taking off in freezing rain and failed to gain enough altitude. Crashing onto the 14th Street Bridge, which crosses the Potomac River, the plane broke in two and fell into the icy river. Seventy-eight people died in the disaster—some of them in the plane, some in their cars on the bridge, and some in the frigid waters of the Potomac.

Following the crash of Flight 90, news reports on television and in newspapers provided extensive details of the tragedy. This essay offers more than a news report. It presents the author's viewpoints on the meaning of the events that took place immediately following the crash. In particular, the author looks at how one passenger behaved in those confusing, terrifying moments and considers what his behavior says about all of us.

WRITING CONNECTION

Think about the discussion you had for the Personal Connection, and jot down in your notebook a list of the generalizations you can make about human nature based on the way people respond to a disaster. As you read this essay, see how your views of human nature compare with the author's.

LASERLINKS
• *HISTORICAL CONNECTION*

823

The Man in the Water

Roger Rosenblatt

A paramedic pulls a woman from the Potomac River following the crash of Air Florida Flight 90. AP / Wide World Photos.

A woman holds on to a safety ring as she is pulled from the Potomac River. AP / Wide World Photos.

As disasters go, this one was terrible, but not unique, certainly not among the worst on the roster of U.S. air crashes. There was the unusual element of the bridge, of course, and the fact that the plane clipped it at a moment of high traffic, one routine thus intersecting another and disrupting both. Then, too, there was the location of the event. Washington, the city of form and regulations, turned chaotic, deregulated, by a blast of real winter and a single slap of metal on metal. The jets from Washington National Airport that normally swoop around the presidential monuments like famished gulls are, for the moment, emblemized by the one that fell; so there is that detail. And there was the aesthetic[1] clash as well—blue-and-green Air Florida, the name a flying garden, sunk down among gray chunks in a black river. All that was worth noticing, to be sure. Still, there was nothing very special in any of it, except death, which, while always special, does not necessarily bring millions to tears or to attention. Why, then, the shock here?

Perhaps because the nation saw in this disaster something more than a mechanical failure. Perhaps because people saw in it no

---

1. **aesthetic** (ĕs-thĕt′ĭk): relating to that which is beautiful or pleasing to the senses.

WORDS TO KNOW   **chaotic** (kā-ŏt′ĭk) *adj.* extremely confused or disordered

failure at all, but rather something successful about their makeup. Here, after all, were two forms of nature in collision: the elements and human character. Last Wednesday, the elements, indifferent as ever, brought down Flight 90. And on that same afternoon, human nature—groping and flailing in mysteries of its own—rose to the occasion.

Of the four acknowledged heroes of the event, three are able to account for their behavior. Donald Usher and Eugene Windsor, a park police helicopter team, risked their lives every time they dipped the skids into the water to pick up survivors. On television, side by side in bright blue jumpsuits, they described their courage as all in the line of duty. Lenny Skutnik, a twenty-eight-year-old employee of the Congressional Budget Office, said: "It's something I never thought I would do"—referring to his jumping into the water to drag an injured woman to shore. Skutnik added that "somebody had to go in the water," delivering every hero's line that is no less admirable for its repetitions. In fact, nobody had to go into the water. That somebody actually did so is part of the reason this particular tragedy sticks in the mind.

But the person most responsible for the emotional impact of the disaster is the one known at first simply as "the man in the water." (Balding, probably in his fifties, an extravagant mustache.) He was seen clinging with five other survivors to the tail section of the airplane. This man was described by Usher and Windsor as appearing alert and in control. Every time they lowered a lifeline and flotation ring to him, he passed it on to another of the passengers. "In a mass casualty, you'll find people like him," said Windsor. "But I've never seen one with that commitment." When the helicopter came back for him, the man had gone under. His selflessness was one reason the story held national attention; his anonymity another. The fact that he went unidentified invested him with a universal character. For a while he was Everyman, and thus proof (as if one needed it) that no man is ordinary.

Still, he could never have imagined such a capacity in himself. Only minutes before his character was tested, he was sitting in the ordinary plane among the ordinary passengers, dutifully listening to the stewardess telling him to fasten his seat belt and saying something about the "no smoking sign." So our man relaxed with the others, some of whom would owe their lives to him. Perhaps he started to read, or to doze, or to regret some harsh remark made in the office that morning. Then suddenly he knew that the trip would not be ordinary. Like every other person on that flight, he was desperate to live, which makes his final act so stunning.

For at some moment in the water he must have realized that he would not live if he continued to hand over the rope and ring to others. He *had* to know it, no matter how gradual the effect of the cold. In his judgment he had no choice. When the helicopter took off with what was to be the last survivor, he watched everything in the world move away from him, and he deliberately let it happen.

Yet there was something else about the man that kept our thoughts on him, and which keeps our thoughts on him still. He was *there,* in the essential, classic circumstance. Man in nature. The man in the water. For its part, nature cared nothing about the five passengers. Our man, on the other hand, cared totally. So the timeless battle commenced in the Potomac. For as long as that man could last, they went at each other, nature and man: the one making no distinctions of good and evil, acting on no principles, offering no lifelines; the other acting wholly on distinctions, principles, and, one supposes, on faith.

Since it was he who lost the fight, we ought to come again to the conclusion that people are powerless in the world. In reality, we believe the reverse, and it takes the act of the man in the water to remind us of our true feelings in this matter. It is not to say that everyone would have acted as he did, or as Usher, Windsor, and Skutnik. Yet whatever moved these men to challenge death on behalf of their fellows is not peculiar to them. Everyone feels the possibility in himself. That is the <u>abiding</u> wonder of the story. That is why we would not let go of it. If the man in the water gave a lifeline to the people gasping for survival, he was likewise giving a lifeline to those who observed him.

The odd thing is that we do not even really believe that the man in the water lost his fight. "Everything in Nature contains all the powers of Nature," said Emerson. Exactly. So the man in the water had his own natural powers. He could not make ice storms, or freeze the water until it froze the blood. But he could hand life over to a stranger, and that is a power of nature too. The man in the water pitted himself against an <u>implacable</u>, impersonal enemy; he fought it with charity; and he held it to a standoff. He was the best we can do. ❖

January 25, 1982

Two more survivors are pulled from the icy water. UPI/Bettmann.

A section of the plane's fuselage is hoisted from the river several days after the crash. UPI/Bettmann.

826

RESPONDING OPTIONS

FROM PERSONAL RESPONSE TO CRITICAL ANALYSIS

REFLECT

1. What do you think about the behavior of the man in the water? Record your response in your notebook.

RETHINK

2. Why do you think Rosenblatt chose to focus on the anonymous man in the water rather than on one of the other three acknowledged heroes of the tragedy?

3. Rosenblatt concludes that "we do not even really believe that the man in the water lost his fight" with nature. Do you agree or disagree?
   Consider
   - Rosenblatt's view of nature
   - the lessons that Rosenblatt draws from the man's sacrifice
   - the power that enabled the man to "hand life over to a stranger"

4. What does the essay's final statement— "He was the best we can do"—mean to you? Explain your response.

RELATE

5. Do you think that everyone is capable of acting as heroically as the man in the water? You may wish to review the generalizations you made for the Writing Connection on page 823.

ANOTHER PATHWAY

Cooperative Learning

In a small group, create a two-column chart. Label one column Nature and the other column Human Nature. In each column, list words and phrases from the essay that convey Rosenblatt's views about that subject. Then write statements summarizing his view of nature and his view of human nature.

QUICKWRITES

1. Write a **tribute** to the man in the water that would be appropriate for a memorial plaque to be placed on the 14th Street Bridge.

2. Using information from this essay and from the Historical Connection on page 823, write a **newspaper article** about the man in the water.

3. Write a **personal essay** about a disaster, an emergency, or some other event that you witnessed or learned about and that made you reflect about human nature. You may find it helpful to review the generalizations that you made for the Writing Connection on page 823.

   📁 *PORTFOLIO Save your writing. You may want to use it later as a springboard to a piece for your portfolio.*

LITERARY CONCEPTS

Tone is the attitude a writer takes toward a subject. In nonfiction a writer's tone is influenced by his or her purpose for writing, as well as the writing format. For example, the tone of an informative newspaper article is typically detached and objective. In contrast, the tone of an editorial may be angry or pleading, urging readers to action, while a personal narrative may have a nostalgic tone, appropriate to the recollection of one's past. Read aloud several paragraphs of "The Man in the Water." What word or words would you use to describe Roger Rosenblatt's tone? How might the tone be related to Rosenblatt's purpose for writing the essay?

ALTERNATIVE ACTIVITIES

1. Stage a **television report** from the scene of the airplane crash. A reporter can interview people on the scene, such as Lenny Skutnik, a rescued person, and a witness to the disaster. If possible, videotape the report and show the tape to other classes.

2. Draw a **picture** of the man in the water, using Rosenblatt's description of him as your inspiration.

3. Compose a **song** that reflects your own response to the events described by Rosenblatt. You might, for example, write a ballad about the man in the water or create an instrumental piece to express your feelings about him.

ART CONNECTION

Look over the photographs of the rescue efforts made at the scene of the Air Florida crash. What kind of impact did they make on you? Would Rosenblatt's article have affected you the same way if the photographs had not been presented along with the selection? Explain why or why not.

ACROSS THE CURRICULUM

Science/Technology Do research to learn about the role that weather can play in plane crashes. For example, you might investigate wind shear or the effects of ice on a plane's wings. Present your findings in a bulletin-board display.

WORDS TO KNOW

Review the Words to Know at the bottom of the selection pages. Then write the word that applies to each description below.

1. Tree limbs may do this during a windstorm.

2. A crush will not be this, but true love is supposed to be.

3. Riots, wild scenes, rowdy classrooms, and some children's bedrooms are this.

4. Beloved movie stars often wish for this when they go out in public.

5. Nothing is good enough for this kind of person, and apologies to him or her may be met with stony silence.

ROGER ROSENBLATT

1940–

A journalist and essayist who has won many awards for his writing, Roger Rosenblatt is a New York City native with a Ph.D. from Harvard University. After teaching literature at Harvard, he served for two years as the director of education for the National Endowment for the Humanities. In 1975 he turned to journalism, working first as the literary editor of the Washington-based magazine *The New Republic* and then as an editorial writer for the *Washington Post.* He has also been a senior writer for *Time* and *U.S. News and World Report* and has regularly contributed oral essays to the TV news show *The MacNeil/Lehrer Newshour.*

Known for his sensitivity and literary flair, Rosenblatt has won praise for several nonfiction books on controversial topics, including *Witness: The World Since Hiroshima,* which examines the impact of the atomic bomb on different aspects of modern life. Perhaps the best known of Rosenblatt's books is *Children of War* (1983), an investigation into the lives of children in war-torn Ireland, Israel, Lebanon, Cambodia, and Vietnam.

OTHER WORKS *Black Fiction, The Man in the Water: Essays and Stories*

PREVIEWING

FICTION

And of Clay Are We Created
Isabel Allende (ä-yĕn′dĕ) Chile / United States

PERSONAL CONNECTION

Think about the novels or stories you have read that are based upon actual events, such as wars, natural disasters, or other thought-provoking occurrences. Why do you think certain fiction writers choose to use factual events in their writing, often altering details to suit their stories? Do you enjoy reading such fictionalized accounts? Or would you rather read a nonfiction account of those events? As a class, discuss your experience in reading fiction that is based upon fact. Then discuss your views about the relationship between fact and imagination in storytelling.

SCIENTIFIC CONNECTION

In this story, which is based on an actual disaster, a reporter becomes involved in rescue efforts following a deadly volcanic eruption. When a volcano erupts, it releases lava, hot gases, rock fragments, and ash. Such eruptions can be disastrous not only because of what is released during the explosion but also because of the mud slides and avalanches that may follow. Volcanoes have caused some of the worst disasters in human history, even burying entire cities. Scientists often monitor the activities of volcanoes in an effort to predict eruptions and save lives. Some volcanoes, such as the one in this story, emit early warning signals of an eruption. Small earthquakes and clouds of gas signal that the pressure within the volcano is building.

Preliminary eruption of Nevado del Ruiz volcano, September 1985, three months before the major eruption. U.S. Geological Survey.

LASERLINKS
• HISTORICAL CONNECTON

READING CONNECTION

From Fact to Fiction

Writers often draw upon real-life events to create their fictional stories. Isabel Allende, a former reporter herself, found inspiration for this story in news reports and photographs of a volcanic disaster. On November 13, 1985, the Nevado del Ruiz (nĕ-vä′dô dĕl rōō-ēs′) volcano in Colombia, South America, erupted after more than a century of inactivity. The intense heat from the erupting crater inside the volcano melted the mountain's icecap and sent a thick torrent of water, ash, mud, and rocks into the valley below. The liquid avalanche buried the town of Armero and damaged several others, killing more than 20,000 people.

The plight of one of the volcano's victims became known to people around the world. Omeira Sanchez, a teenage girl, was submerged up to her neck in mud, trapped by rubble and by the bodies of her relatives. The girl featured in this story is based upon Omeira Sanchez, pictured on this page.

As you read Allende's story, you may find it helpful to consider the following questions:

- Which parts of the story seem factually accurate, and which do you think were invented by Allende?

- Why do you think Allende chose to use a narrator who is not present at the scene of the disaster?

- Why would Allende decide to write about this occurrence in fiction rather than nonfiction?

- What does the story suggest to you about the relationship between fact and fiction?

Aftermath of disaster caused by Nevado del Ruiz eruption. Allan Tannenbaum/Sygma.

Rescue efforts to save Omeira Sanchez, the Colombian teenage girl who inspired this story. Carraro/Rex USA Ltd.

And of Clay Are We Created

Isabel Allende

They discovered the girl's head protruding from the mud pit, eyes wide open, calling soundlessly. She had a First Communion name,[1] Azucena.[2] Lily. In that vast cemetery where the odor of death was already attracting vultures from far away, and where the weeping of orphans and wails of the injured filled the air, the little girl obstinately clinging to life became the symbol of the tragedy. The television cameras transmitted so often the unbearable image of the head budding like a black squash from the clay that there was no one who did not recognize her and know her name. And every time we saw her on the screen, right behind her was Rolf Carlé,[3] who had gone there on

---

1. **First Communion name:** a name traditionally given to a Roman Catholic child at the time of the child's first participation in the rite of Holy Communion.
2. **Azucena** (ä′zōō-kĕ′nä).
3. **Rolf Carlé** (rälf kär-lĕ′).

assignment, never suspecting that he would find a fragment of his past, lost thirty years before.

First a subterranean[4] sob rocked the cotton fields, curling them like waves of foam. Geologists had set up their seismographs[5] weeks before and knew that the mountain had awakened again. For some time they had predicted that the heat of the eruption could detach the eternal ice from the slopes of the volcano, but no one heeded their warnings; they sounded like the tales of frightened old women. The towns in the valley went about their daily life, deaf to the moaning of the earth, until that fateful Wednesday night in November when a prolonged roar announced the end of the world, and walls of snow broke loose, rolling in an avalanche of clay, stones, and water that descended on the villages and buried them beneath unfathomable meters of telluric[6] vomit. As soon as the survivors emerged from the paralysis of that first awful terror, they could see that houses, plazas, churches, white cotton plantations, dark coffee forests, cattle pastures—all had disappeared. Much later, after soldiers and volunteers had arrived to rescue the living and try to assess the magnitude of the cataclysm,[7] it was calculated that beneath the mud lay more than twenty thousand human beings and an indefinite number of animals putrefying in a viscous soup.[8] Forests and rivers had also been swept away, and there was nothing to be seen but an immense desert of mire.

When the station called before dawn, Rolf Carlé and I were together. I crawled out of bed, dazed with sleep, and went to prepare coffee while he hurriedly dressed. He stuffed his gear in the green canvas backpack he always carried, and we said goodbye, as we had so many times before. I had no presentiments.[9] I sat in the

kitchen, sipping my coffee and planning the long hours without him, sure that he would be back the next day.

He was one of the first to reach the scene, because while other reporters were fighting their way to the edges of that morass in jeeps, bicycles, or on foot, each getting there however he could, Rolf Carlé had the advantage of the television helicopter, which flew him over the avalanche. We watched on our screens the footage captured by his assistant's camera, in which he was up to his knees in muck, a microphone in his hand, in the midst of a bedlam of lost children, wounded survivors, corpses, and devastation. The story came to us in his calm voice. For years he had been a familiar figure in newscasts, reporting live at the scene of battles and catastrophes with awesome <u>tenacity</u>. Nothing could stop him, and I was always amazed at his <u>equanimity</u> in the face of danger and suffering; it seemed as if nothing could shake his <u>fortitude</u> or deter his curiosity. Fear seemed never to touch him, although he had confessed to me that he was not a courageous man, far from it. I believe that the lens of a camera had a strange effect on him; it was as if it transported him to a different time from which he could watch events without actually participating in them. When I knew him better, I came to realize

---

4. **subterranean** (sŭb′tə-rā′nē-ən): underground.
5. **seismographs** (sīz′mə-grăfs): instruments that record the intensity and duration of earthquakes and other tremors.
6. **telluric** (tĕ-lŏŏr′ĭk): relating to the earth.
7. **cataclysm** (kăt′ə-klĭz′əm): a violent and sudden change in the earth's crust; upheaval that destroys.
8. **putrefying** (pyōō′trə-fī′ĭng) . . . **soup:** rotting in a thick soup.
9. **presentiments** (prĭ-zĕn′tə-mənts): feelings that something is about to happen; forebodings.

WORDS
TO
KNOW

tenacity (tə-năs′ĭ-tē) *n.* the state or quality of holding persistently to something; firm determination

equanimity (ē′kwə-nĭm′ĭ-tē) *n.* the quality of being calm and even-tempered; composure

fortitude (fôr′tĭ-tōōd′) *n.* strength of mind to endure misfortune or pain with courage

The Volcanos (1950), Dr. Atl (Gerardo Murillo). Oil on masonite, 137 cm × 260 cm, Instituto Cultural Cabañas, Patrimonio de Jalisco, Guadalajara, Mexico.

that this fictive[10] distance seemed to protect him from his own emotions.

Rolf Carlé was in on the story of Azucena from the beginning. He filmed the volunteers who discovered her, and the first persons who tried to reach her; his camera zoomed in on the girl, her dark face, her large desolate eyes, the plastered-down tangle of her hair. The mud was like quicksand around her, and anyone attempting to reach her was in danger of sinking. They threw a rope to her that she made no effort to grasp until they shouted to her to catch it; then she pulled a hand from the mire and tried to move but immediately sank a little deeper. Rolf threw down his knapsack and the rest of his equipment and waded into the quagmire, commenting for his assistant's microphone that it was cold and that one could begin to smell the stench of corpses.

"What's your name?" he asked the girl, and she told him her flower name. "Don't move, Azucena," Rolf Carlé directed, and kept talking to her, without a thought for what he was saying, just to distract her, while slowly he worked his way forward in mud up to his waist. The air around him seemed as murky as the mud.

It was impossible to reach her from the approach he was attempting, so he retreated and circled around where there seemed to be firmer footing. When finally he was close enough, he took the rope and tied it beneath her arms, so they could pull her out. He smiled at her with that smile that crinkles his eyes and makes him look like a little boy; he told her that everything was fine, that he was here with

---

10. **fictive** (fĭk′tĭv): imaginary or fictional.

her now, that soon they would have her out. He signaled the others to pull, but as soon as the cord tensed, the girl screamed. They tried again, and her shoulders and arms appeared, but they could move her no farther; she was trapped. Someone suggested that her legs might be caught in the collapsed walls of her house, but she said it was not just rubble, that she was also held by the bodies of her brothers and sisters clinging to her legs.

"Don't worry, we'll get you out of here," Rolf promised. Despite the quality of the transmission, I could hear his voice break, and I loved him more than ever. Azucena looked at him but said nothing.

During those first hours Rolf Carlé exhausted all the resources of his ingenuity to rescue her. He struggled with poles and ropes, but every tug was an intolerable torture for the imprisoned girl. It occurred to him to use one of the poles as a lever but got no result and had to abandon the idea. He talked a couple of soldiers into working with him for a while, but they had to leave because so many other victims were calling for help. The girl could not move, she barely could breathe, but she did not seem desperate, as if an ancestral resignation allowed her to accept her fate. The reporter, on the other hand, was determined to snatch her from death. Someone brought him a tire, which he placed beneath her arms like a life buoy, and then laid a plank near the hole to hold his weight and allow him to stay closer to her. As it was impossible to remove the rubble blindly, he tried once or twice to dive toward her feet but emerged frustrated, covered with mud, and spitting gravel. He concluded that he would have to have a pump to drain the water, and radioed a request for one but received in return a message that there was no available transport and it could not be sent until the next morning.

"We can't wait that long!" Rolf Carlé shouted, but in the pandemonium no one stopped to commiserate. Many more hours would go by before he accepted that time had stagnated[11] and reality had been irreparably distorted.

A military doctor came to examine the girl and observed that her heart was functioning well and that if she did not get too cold she could survive the night.

"Hang on, Azucena, we'll have the pump tomorrow," Rolf Carlé tried to console her.

"Don't leave me alone," she begged.

"No, of course I won't leave you."

Someone brought him coffee, and he helped the girl drink it, sip by sip. The warm liquid revived her, and she began telling him about her small life, about her family and her school, about how things were in that little bit of world before the volcano erupted. She was thirteen, and she had never been outside her village. Rolf Carlé, buoyed by a premature optimism, was convinced that everything would end well: the pump would arrive, they would drain the water, move the rubble, and Azucena would be transported by helicopter to a hospital where she would recover rapidly and where he could visit her and bring her gifts. He thought, She's already too old for dolls, and I don't know what would please her; maybe a dress. I don't know much about women, he concluded, amused, reflecting that although he had known many women in his lifetime, none had taught him these details. To pass the hours he began to tell Azucena about his travels and adventures as a news hound, and when he exhausted his memory, he called upon imagination, inventing things he thought might entertain her. From time to time she dozed, but he kept talking in the darkness, to assure her that he was still there and to overcome the menace of uncertainty.

That was a long night.

---

11. **stagnated:** stopped moving.

Many miles away, I watched Rolf Carlé and the girl on a television screen. I could not bear the wait at home, so I went to National Television, where I often spent entire nights with Rolf editing programs. There, I was near his world, and I could at least get a feeling of what he lived through during those three decisive days. I called all the important people in the city, senators, commanders of the armed forces, the North American ambassador, and the president of National Petroleum, begging them for a pump to remove the silt, but obtained only vague promises. I began to ask for urgent help on radio and television, to see if there wasn't *someone* who could help us. Between calls I would run to the newsroom to monitor the satellite transmissions that periodically brought new details of the catastrophe. While reporters selected scenes with most impact for the news report, I searched for footage that featured Azucena's mud pit. The screen reduced the disaster to a single plane and accentuated the tremendous distance that separated me from Rolf Carlé; nonetheless, I was there with him. The child's every suffering hurt me as it did him; I felt his frustration, his impotence.[12] Faced with the impossibility of communicating with him, the fantastic idea came to me that if I tried, I could reach him by force of mind and in that way give him encouragement. I concentrated until I was dizzy—a frenzied and futile activity. At times I would be overcome with compassion and burst out crying; at other times, I was so drained I felt as if I were staring through a telescope at the light of a star dead for a million years.

I watched that hell on the first morning broadcast, cadavers[13] of people and animals awash in the current of new rivers formed overnight from the melted snow. Above the mud rose the tops of trees and the bell towers of a church where several people had taken refuge and were patiently awaiting rescue teams. Hundreds of soldiers and volunteers from the civil defense were clawing through rubble searching for survivors, while long rows of ragged specters[14] awaited their turn for a cup of hot broth. Radio networks announced that their phones were jammed with calls from families offering shelter to orphaned children. Drinking water was in scarce supply, along with gasoline and food. Doctors, resigned to amputating arms and legs without anesthesia, pled that at least they be sent serum and painkillers and antibiotics; most of the roads, however, were impassable, and worse were the bureaucratic obstacles that stood in the way. To top it all, the clay contaminated by decomposing bodies threatened the living with an outbreak of epidemics.

Azucena was shivering inside the tire that held her above the surface. Immobility and tension had greatly weakened her, but she was conscious and could still be heard when a microphone was held out to her. Her tone was humble, as if apologizing for all the fuss. Rolf Carlé had a growth of beard, and dark circles beneath his eyes; he looked near exhaustion. Even from that enormous distance I could sense the quality of his weariness, so different from the fatigue of other adventures. He had completely forgotten the camera; he could not look at the girl through a lens any longer. The pictures we were receiving were not his assistant's but those of other reporters who had appropriated Azucena, bestowing on her the pathetic responsibility of embodying the horror of what had happened in that place. With the

---

12. **impotence:** powerlessness.

13. **cadavers** (kə-dăv′ərz): dead bodies.

14. **specters:** ghosts or ghostlike visions.

835

Illustration by David Loew / ARTCO.

first light Rolf tried again to dislodge the obstacles that held the girl in her tomb, but he had only his hands to work with; he did not dare use a tool for fear of injuring her. He fed Azucena a cup of the cornmeal mush and bananas the army was distributing, but she immediately vomited it up. A doctor stated that she had a fever but added that there was little he could do: antibiotics were being reserved for cases of gangrene.[15] A priest also passed by and blessed her, hanging a medal of the Virgin around her neck. By evening a gentle, persistent drizzle began to fall.

"The sky is weeping," Azucena murmured, and she, too, began to cry.

"Don't be afraid," Rolf begged. "You have to keep your strength up and be calm. Everything will be fine. I'm with you, and I'll get you out somehow."

Reporters returned to photograph Azucena and ask her the same questions, which she no longer tried to answer. In the meanwhile, more television and movie teams arrived with spools of cable, tapes, film, videos, precision lenses, recorders, sound consoles, lights, reflecting screens, auxiliary motors, cartons of supplies, electricians, sound technicians, and cameramen: Azucena's face was beamed to millions of screens around the world. And all the while Rolf Carlé kept pleading for a pump. The improved technical facilities bore results, and National Television began receiving sharper pictures and clearer sound, the distance seemed suddenly compressed, and I had the horrible sensation that Azucena and Rolf were by my side, separated from me by impenetrable glass. I was able to follow events hour by hour; I knew everything my love did to wrest the girl from her prison and help her endure her suffering; I overheard fragments of what they said to one another and could guess the rest; I was present when she taught Rolf to pray and when he distracted her with the stories I had told him

in a thousand and one nights beneath the white mosquito netting of our bed.

When darkness came on the second day, Rolf tried to sing Azucena to sleep with old Austrian folk songs he had learned from his mother, but she was far beyond sleep. They spent most of the night talking, each in a stupor of exhaustion and hunger and shaking with cold. That night, imperceptibly, the unyielding floodgates that had contained Rolf Carlé's past for so many years began to open, and the torrent of all that had lain hidden in the deepest and most secret layers of memory poured out, leveling before it the obstacles that had blocked his consciousness for so long. He could not tell it all to Azucena; she perhaps did not know there was a world beyond the sea or time previous to her own; she was not capable of imagining Europe in the years of the war. So he could not tell her of defeat, nor of the afternoon the Russians had led them to the concentration camp to bury prisoners dead from starvation. Why should he describe to her how the naked bodies piled like a mountain of firewood resembled fragile china? How could he tell this dying child about ovens and gallows? Nor did he mention the night that he had seen his mother naked, shod in stiletto-heeled red boots, sobbing with humiliation. There was much he did not tell, but in those hours he relived for the first time all the things his mind had tried to erase. Azucena had surrendered her fear to him and so, without wishing it, had obliged Rolf to confront his own. There, beside that hellhole of mud, it was impossible for Rolf to flee from himself any longer, and the visceral terror he had lived as a boy suddenly invaded him. He reverted to the years when he was the age of Azucena and younger, and, like her, found himself trapped in a pit without escape, buried in life, his head barely

---

15. **gangrene:** death and decay of body tissue, usually resulting from injury or disease.

837

above ground; he saw before his eyes the boots and legs of his father, who had removed his belt and was whipping it in the air with the never-forgotten hiss of a viper coiled to strike. Sorrow flooded through him, intact and precise, as if it had lain always in his mind, waiting. He was once again in the armoire[16] where his father locked him to punish him for imagined mis-behavior, there where for eternal hours he had crouched with his eyes closed, not to see the darkness, with his hands over his ears to shut out the beating of his heart, trembling, huddled like a cornered animal. Wandering in the mist of his memories he found his sister, Katharina, a sweet, retarded child who spent her life hiding, with the hope that her father would forget the disgrace of her having been born. With Katharina, Rolf crawled beneath the dining room table, and with her hid there under the long white tablecloth, two children forever embraced, alert to footsteps and voices. Katharina's scent melded with his own sweat, with aromas of cooking, garlic, soup, freshly baked bread, and the unexpected odor of putrescent[17] clay. His sister's hand in his, her frightened breathing, her silk hair against his cheek, the candid gaze of her eyes. Katharina . . . Katharina materialized before him, floating on the air like a flag, clothed in the white tablecloth, now a winding sheet, and at last he could weep for her death and for the guilt of having aban-doned her. He understood then that all his exploits as a reporter, the feats that had won him such recognition and fame, were merely an attempt to keep his most ancient fears at bay, a stratagem for taking refuge behind a lens to test whether reality was more tolerable from that perspective. He took excessive risks as an exer-cise of courage, training by day to conquer the monsters that tormented him by night. But he had to come face to face with the moment of truth; he could not continue to escape his past. He *was* Azucena; he was buried in the clayey

mud; his terror was not the distant emotion of an almost forgotten childhood, it was a claw sunk in his throat. In the flush of his tears he saw his mother, dressed in black and clutching her imitation-crocodile pocketbook to her bosom, just as he had last seen her on the dock when she had come to put him on the boat to South Amer-ica. She had not come to dry his tears, but to tell him to pick up a shovel: the war was over and now they must bury the dead.

"Don't cry. I don't hurt anymore. I'm fine," Azucena said when dawn came.

"I'm not crying for you," Rolf Carlé smiled. "I'm crying for myself. I hurt all over."

The third day in the valley of the cataclysm began with a pale light filtering through storm clouds. The president of the republic visited the area in his tailored safari jacket to confirm that this was the worst catastrophe of the century; the country was in mourning; sister nations had offered aid; he had ordered a state of siege; the armed forces would be merciless; anyone caught stealing or committing other offenses would be shot on sight. He added that it was impossible to remove all the corpses or count the thousands who had disappeared; the entire valley would be declared holy ground, and bishops would come to celebrate a solemn mass for the souls of the victims. He went to the army field tents to offer relief in the form of vague promises to crowds of the rescued, then to the improvised hospital to offer a word of encouragement to doctors and nurses worn down from so many hours of tribulations. Then he asked to be taken to see Azucena, the little

---

16. **armoire** (ärm-wär'): a large, ornate wardrobe or cabinet.
17. **putrescent** (pyoo-trĕs'ənt): rotting and foul smelling.

WORDS
TO
KNOW   **tribulation** (trĭb'yə-lā'shən) *n.* great distress or suffering

838

girl the whole world had seen. He waved to her with a limp statesman's hand, and microphones recorded his emotional voice and paternal tone as he told her that her courage had served as an example to the nation. Rolf Carlé interrupted to ask for a pump, and the president assured him that he personally would attend to the matter. I caught a glimpse of Rolf for a few seconds kneeling beside the mud pit. On the evening news broadcast, he was still in the same position; and I, glued to the screen like a fortuneteller to her crystal ball, could tell that something fundamental had changed in him. I knew somehow that during the night his defenses had crumbled and he had given in to grief; finally he was <u>vulnerable</u>. The girl had touched a part of him that he himself had no access to, a part he had never shared with me. Rolf had wanted to console her, but it was Azucena who had given him consolation.

I recognized the precise moment at which Rolf gave up the fight and surrendered to the torture of watching the girl die. I was with them, three days and two nights, spying on them from the other side of life. I was there when she told him that in all her thirteen years no boy had ever loved her and that it was a pity to leave this world without knowing love. Rolf assured her that he loved her more than he could ever love anyone, more than he loved his mother, more than his sister, more than all the women who had slept in his arms, more than he loved me, his life companion, who would have given anything to be trapped in that well in her place, who would have exchanged her life for Azucena's, and I watched as he leaned down to kiss her poor forehead, consumed by a sweet, sad emotion he could not name. I felt how in

that instant both were saved from despair, how they were freed from the clay, how they rose above the vultures and helicopters, how together they flew above the vast swamp of corruption and laments. How, finally, they were able to accept death. Rolf Carlé prayed in silence that she would die quickly, because such pain cannot be borne.

By then I had obtained a pump and was in touch with a general who had agreed to ship it the next morning on a military cargo plane. But on the night of that third day, beneath the unblinking focus of quartz lamps and the lens of a hundred cameras, Azucena gave up, her eyes locked with those of the friend who had sustained her to the end. Rolf Carlé removed the life buoy, closed her eyelids, held her to his chest for a few moments, and then let her go. She sank slowly, a flower in the mud.

You are back with me, but you are not the same man. I often accompany you to the station, and we watch the videos of Azucena again; you study them intently, looking for something you could have done to save her, something you did not think of in time. Or maybe you study them to see yourself as if in a mirror, naked. Your cameras lie forgotten in a closet; you do not write or sing; you sit long hours before the window, staring at the mountains. Beside you, I wait for you to complete the voyage into yourself, for the old wounds to heal. I know that when you return from your nightmares, we shall again walk hand in hand, as before. ❖

Translated by Margaret Sayers Peden

Nocturne   Nocturno

Rosario Castellanos

Time is too long for life;
for knowledge not enough.

What have we come for, night, heart
   of night?

All we can do is dream, or die,
5 dream that we do not die
and, at times, for a moment, wake.

Translated by Magda Bogin

Para vivir es demasiado el tiempo;
para saber no es nada.

¿A qué vinimos, noche, corazón de la
   noche?

No es posible sino soñar, morir,
5 soñar que no morimos
y, a veces, un instante, despertar.

Nocturnal Landscape (1947),
Diego Rivera. Oil on canvas,
111 cm × 91 cm, courtesy of
Museo de Arte Moderno (INBA),
Mexico City. Photo Copyright © 1995,
Dirk Bakker/The Detroit Institute of Arts.

RESPONDING
OPTIONS

FROM PERSONAL RESPONSE TO CRITICAL ANALYSIS

REFLECT 1. How did you react to the outcome of the story? In your notebook, jot down a few words and phrases that best describe your emotions.

RETHINK 2. How would you describe the relationship that develops between Rolf and Azucena?
Consider
- why Rolf becomes a participant in the effort to save her
- what they learn from each other
- the painful childhood memories he is able to recall
- why he tells Azucena that he loves her more than he could ever love anyone

3. How do you think Rolf's experience with Azucena will affect him in the future?
Consider
- his career as a reporter
- his relationship with the narrator
- his understanding of his past

4. According to the narrator, the name Azucena means "lily." Why do you think the author might have given her this name?

5. Now that you have read this story, how would you respond to the questions in the Reading Connection on page 830?

RELATE 6. What connection do you see between the Insight poem on page 840 and Allende's story?

7. Although Azucena had the attention of her entire nation, she died partly because no one transported a pump to the disaster site. Could a similar situation happen in your own country? Why or why not?

ANOTHER PATHWAY
Cooperative Learning

Do you think this story has a hero or heroes? In a small group, evaluate the actions and attitudes of the characters and narrator in terms of heroism. Then decide which characters, if any, can be considered heroic. Share the results of your discussion with other groups.

QUICKWRITES

1. Draft the **monologue** Rolf might give in a retrospective television broadcast one year after the tragic destruction of the town.

2. Write the **love letter** that the narrator might write to Rolf in the months following the disaster.

3. Read articles in newsmagazines to learn what really happened when the Nevado del Ruiz volcano erupted. Then, in a two-column **chart,** list those details that the author derived from news accounts and those details that the author probably invented for her story.

📁 *PORTFOLIO Save your writing. You may want to use it later as a springboard to a piece for your portfolio.*

LITERARY CONCEPTS

The events of a story almost always involve one or more **conflicts,** or struggles between opposing forces. A conflict may be **external,** pitting a character against an outside force—such as another character, a physical obstacle, or an aspect of nature or society—or it may be **internal,** occurring within a character. What kinds of conflicts do Rolf, Azucena, and the narrator each experience in this story? Cite passages in the story that support your conclusions.

CONCEPT REVIEW: Narrator How do the narrator's relationship with Rolf and her feelings for him affect your understanding of the story? Explain, using story details to support your response.

CRITIC'S CORNER

After reading "And of Clay Are We Created," student reviewer Quoleshna Elbert wrote, "The story got under my skin; that's what makes a good story." Do you feel the same way about this story? What makes a good story for you?

LITERARY LINKS

Compare Allende's descriptive passages with those of another reporter or news commentator, such as Nicholas Gage, Brent Staples, or Roger Rosenblatt. Whose style of description do you prefer? Explain your opinion.

ALTERNATIVE ACTIVITIES

1. Assume the identity of Rolf or the narrator and deliver a **eulogy** for Azucena.

2. If this story were made into a movie, what music might be used in the soundtrack? Write your own **musical composition** or find an existing piece of music that would help create the mood of one of the scenes in the story. Play it for your classmates and ask them what part of the story it was intended to accompany.

ACROSS THE CURRICULUM

Psychology Look up the word *repression* in a psychology textbook to better understand how some people, like Rolf in the story, deal with very painful memories. Also find out what the experts believe about the causes of repression and how it can be treated. Share your findings.

ART CONNECTION

What is your interpretation of the illustration on page 836? Why do you think it was chosen to accompany this story?

Detail of illustration by David Loew/ARTCO.

WORDS TO KNOW

EXERCISE A Identify each pair of words as synonyms or antonyms.

1. visceral—logical
2. fortitude—endurance
3. tenacity—doubt
4. equanimity—hysteria
5. stupor—daze

6. pandemonium—disturbance
7. vulnerable—immune
8. tribulation—blessing
9. embody—symbolize
10. irreparably—correctably

EXERCISE B In a small group, tell a "round robin" story using the Words to Know. One person should begin a story and continue to speak until he or she has used one of the words in a sentence. Then the next person picks up the story where the first person left off, continuing until another of the words is used. Continue this process until all ten words are used and the story is brought to a conclusion.

ISABEL ALLENDE

1942–

Born in Lima, Peru, Isabel Allende moved with her mother to Santiago, Chile, when she was three years old and grew up in the home of her maternal grandparents. Her mother nurtured her creativity from the time she was very young, encouraging her to record her thoughts in a notebook and to draw anything she wanted on a bedroom wall. After graduating from high school, Allende worked for many years as a journalist and television interviewer. "My love for words induced me to work as a journalist since I was seventeen, but my vicious imagination was a great handicap," she said. "I could never be objective, I exaggerated and twisted reality, I would put myself in the middle of every feature."

Isabel Allende's uncle and godfather, Salvador Allende, became president of Chile in 1970 but was murdered when the military seized power in 1973. As a result, Isabel Allende and her family—along with many Chilean artists and intellectuals—went into exile, moving first to Venezuela and later to the United States. In her words, she felt "like a Christmas tree, cut off from all roots" after fleeing from her homeland, and for several years she was unable to write or to find work as a journalist.

After receiving word in 1981 that her nearly 100-year-old grandfather was dying, however, she began writing a long letter to him. Her grandfather believed that people died only when you forgot them, and Allende says she wanted to prove to him that she had forgotten nothing, "that his spirit was going to live with us forever." Allende's letter became her first novel, *The House of the Spirits,* which was published in Spanish in 1982 and in English translation three years later. Written in the style of magical realism, the novel is based on her own family history and the political upheaval in modern Chile. The work became an international bestseller, hailed by critics as a powerful and original piece of historical fiction.

Although she is fluent in English, Allende writes her novels and short stories in Spanish, then has her work translated. Recent works include *The Infinite Plan,* her first novel set in the United States, and *Paula,* an autobiographical work.

OTHER WORKS *Of Love and Shadows, Eva Luna, The Stories of Eva Luna*

PREVIEWING

The Leap
Louise Erdrich United States

PERSONAL CONNECTION

Are you the sort of person who would risk injury—perhaps even death—for the sake of an activity that you loved? Would you be willing to put yourself in physical danger for the sake of someone else? In your notebook, describe your attitude toward taking physical risks and the circumstances that might lead you to do so.

CULTURAL CONNECTION

This story focuses on the life of a woman who took great physical risks as a blindfolded trapeze performer. Although trapeze acts often appear to be foolhardy stunts, the risks are well calculated by the trained performer, who may spend several years perfecting a single maneuver. Working on the trapeze requires not only tremendous strength, precise timing, and delicate balance but also considerable mental effort. Alfred Codona, one of the world's greatest trapeze artists, repeatedly emphasized the importance of "brain coordination" in aerial routines, warning other performers that any lack of mental clarity could result in death.

READING CONNECTION

Recognizing Flashbacks The narrator of "The Leap" is a woman who owes her life to the risks her mother took. She tells her story using flashbacks—interruptions in the chronological order of events. She begins in the present, when she is an adult, but then recounts several events that happened in the past, some even before she was born. Be aware of these shifts in time as you read.

Poster reproduced with the permission of Ringling Bros. and Barnum & Bailey Combined Shows, Inc.

The Leap

Louise Erdrich

Illustration by Sarah Figlio.

My mother is the surviving half of a blindfold trapeze act, not a fact I think about much even now that she is sightless, the result of encroaching and stubborn cataracts.[1] She walks slowly through her house here in New Hampshire, lightly touching her way along walls and running her hands over knickknacks, books, the drift of a grown child's belongings and castoffs. She has never upset an object or as much as brushed a magazine onto the floor. She has never lost her balance or bumped into a closet door left carelessly open.

---

1. **encroaching . . . cataracts:** Cataracts are clouded areas on the lens of the eye. When they encroach, or advance beyond previous limits, they can cause total blindness.

It has occurred to me that the catlike precision of her movements in old age might be the result of her early training, but she shows so little of the drama or <u>flair</u> one might expect from a performer that I tend to forget the Flying Avalons. She has kept no sequined costume, no photographs, no fliers or posters from that part of her youth. I would, in fact, tend to think that all memory of double somersaults and heart-stopping catches had left her arms and legs were it not for the fact that sometimes, as I sit sewing in the room of the rebuilt house in which I slept as a child, I hear the crackle, catch a whiff of smoke from the stove downstairs, and suddenly the room goes dark, the stitches burn beneath my fingers, and I am sewing with a needle of hot silver, a thread of fire.

I owe her my existence three times. The first was when she saved herself. In the town square a replica tent pole, cracked and splintered, now stands cast in concrete. It commemorates the disaster that put our town smack on the front page of the Boston and New York tabloids.[2] It is from those old newspapers, now historical records, that I get my information. Not from my mother, Anna of the Flying Avalons, nor from any of her in-laws, nor certainly from the other half of her particular act, Harold Avalon, her first husband. In one news account it says, "The day was mildly overcast, but nothing in the air or temperature gave any hint of the sudden force with which the deadly gale would strike."

I have lived in the West, where you can see the weather coming for miles, and it is true that out here we are at something of a disadvantage. When extremes of temperature collide, a hot and

It is from those old newspapers, now historical records, that I get my information.

cold front, winds generate instantaneously behind a hill and crash upon you without warning. That, I think, was the likely situation on that day in June. People probably commented on the pleasant air, grateful that no hot sun beat upon the striped tent that stretched over the entire center green. They bought their tickets and surrendered them in anticipation. They sat. They ate caramelized popcorn and roasted peanuts.

There was time, before the storm, for three acts. The White Arabians of Ali-Khazar rose on their hind legs and waltzed. The Mysterious Bernie folded himself into a painted cracker tin, and the Lady of the Mists made herself appear and disappear in surprising places. As the clouds gathered outside, unnoticed, the ringmaster cracked his whip, shouted his introduction, and pointed to the ceiling of the tent, where the Flying Avalons were perched.

They loved to drop gracefully from nowhere, like two sparkling birds, and blow kisses as they threw off their plumed helmets and high-collared capes. They laughed and flirted openly as they beat their way up again on the trapeze bars. In the final vignette[3] of their act, they actually would kiss in midair, pausing, almost hovering as they swooped past one another. On the ground, between bows, Harry Avalon would skip quickly to the front rows and point out the smear of my mother's lipstick, just off the edge of his mouth. They made a romantic pair all right, especially in the blindfold sequence.

---

2. **tabloids:** newspapers containing short and often sensational articles.

3. **vignette** (vĭn-yĕt'): a short sketch or scene.

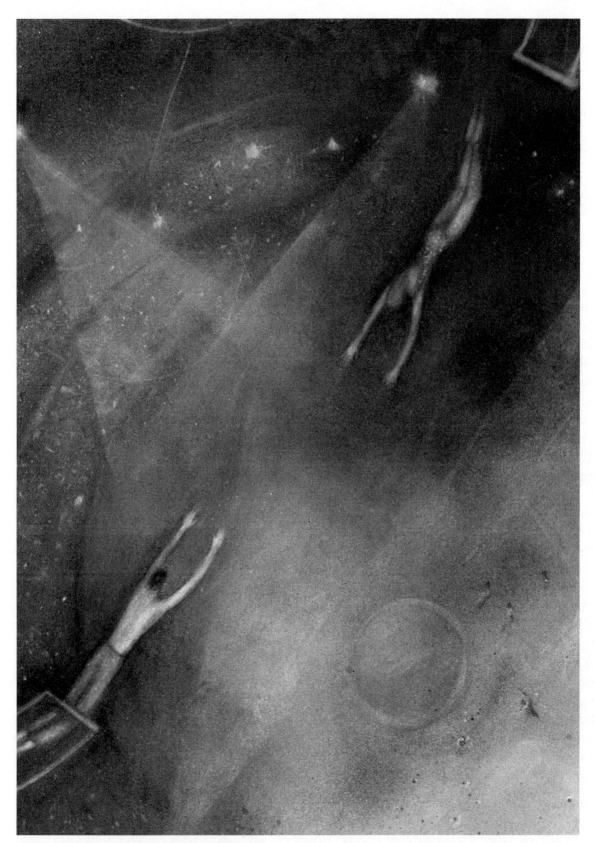

Copyright © Michelle Barnes / The Image Bank.

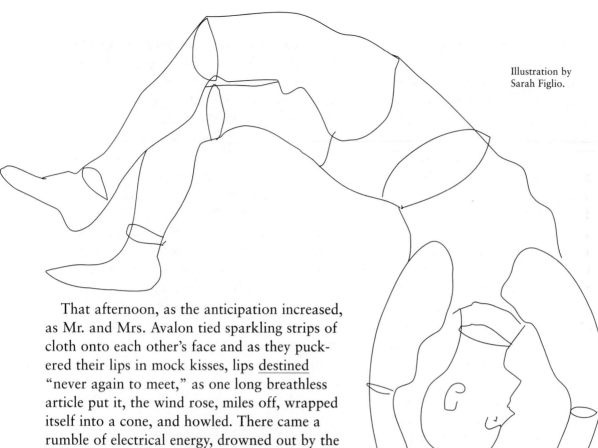

Illustration by
Sarah Figlio.

That afternoon, as the anticipation increased, as Mr. and Mrs. Avalon tied sparkling strips of cloth onto each other's face and as they puckered their lips in mock kisses, lips <u>destined</u> "never again to meet," as one long breathless article put it, the wind rose, miles off, wrapped itself into a cone, and howled. There came a rumble of electrical energy, drowned out by the sudden roll of drums. One detail not mentioned by the press, perhaps unknown—Anna was pregnant at the time, seven months and hardly showing, her stomach muscles were that strong. It seems incredible that she would work high above the ground when any fall could be so dangerous, but the explanation—I know from watching her go blind—is that my mother lives comfortably in extreme elements. She is one with the constant dark now, just as the air was her home, familiar to her, safe, before the storm that afternoon.

From opposite ends of the tent they waved, blind and smiling, to the crowd below. The ringmaster removed his hat and called for silence, so that the two above could concentrate. They rubbed their hands in chalky powder, then Harry launched himself and swung, once, twice, in huge calibrated[4] beats

across space. He hung from his knees and on the third swing stretched wide his arms, held his hands out to receive his pregnant wife as she dove from her shining bar.

It was while the two were in midair, their hands about to meet, that lightning struck the main pole and sizzled down the guy wires, filling the air with a blue radiance that Harry Avalon must certainly have seen through the

4. **calibrated:** measured.

WORDS
TO
KNOW

destined (dĕs'tĭnd) *adj.* determined beforehand; fated **destine** *v.*

cloth of his blindfold as the tent buckled and the edifice[5] toppled him forward, the swing continuing and not returning in its sweep, and Harry going down, down into the crowd with his last thought, perhaps, just a prickle of surprise at his empty hands.

My mother once said that I'd be amazed at how many things a person can do within the act of falling. Perhaps, at the time, she was teaching me to dive off a board at the town pool, for I associate the idea with midair somersaults. But I also think she meant that even in that awful doomed second one could think, for she certainly did. When her hands did not meet her husband's, my mother tore her blindfold away. As he swept past her on the wrong side, she could have grasped his ankle, the toe end of his tights, and gone down clutching him. Instead, she changed direction. Her body twisted toward a heavy wire, and she managed to hang on to the braided metal, still hot from the lightning strike. Her palms were burned so terribly that once healed they bore no lines, only the blank scar tissue of a quieter future. She was lowered, gently, to the sawdust ring just underneath the dome of the canvas roof, which did not entirely settle but was held up on one end and jabbed through, torn, and still on fire in places from the giant spark, though rain and men's jackets soon put that out.

Three people died, but except for her hands my mother was not seriously harmed until an overeager rescuer broke her arm in extricating her and also, in the process, collapsed a portion of the tent bearing a huge buckle that knocked her unconscious. She was taken to the town hospital, and there she must have hemorrhaged,[6] for they kept her, confined to her bed, a month and a half before her baby was born without life.

Harry Avalon had wanted to be buried in the circus cemetery next to the original Avalon, his uncle, so she sent him back with his brothers. The child, however, is buried around the corner, beyond this house and just down the highway. Sometimes I used to walk there just to sit. She was a girl, but I rarely thought of her as a sister or even as a separate person really. I suppose you could call it the egocentrism[7] of a child, of all young children, but I considered her a less finished version of myself.

When the snow falls, throwing shadows among the stones, I can easily pick hers out from the road, for it is bigger than the others and in the shape of a lamb at rest, its legs curled beneath. The carved lamb looms larger as the years pass, though it is probably only my eyes, the vision shifting, as what is close to me blurs and distances sharpen. In odd moments, I think it is the edge drawing near, the edge of everything, the unseen horizon we do not really speak of in the eastern woods. And it also seems to me, although this is probably an idle fantasy, that the statue is growing more sharply etched, as if, instead of weathering itself into a porous mass, it is hardening on the hillside with each snowfall, perfecting itself.

It was during her confinement in the hospital that my mother met my father. He was called in to look at the set of her arm, which was complicated. He stayed, sitting at her bedside, for he was something of an armchair traveler and had spent his war quietly, at an air force training grounds, where he became a specialist in arms and legs broken during parachute training exercises. Anna Avalon had been to many of the places he

---

5. **edifice** (ĕd'ə-fĭs): structure; building.
6. **hemorrhaged** (hĕm'ər-ĭjd): bled heavily from a blood vessel.
7. **egocentrism:** self-centeredness; the belief that everything revolves around oneself.

longed to visit—Venice, Rome, Mexico, all through France and Spain. She had no family of her own and was taken in by the Avalons, trained to perform from a very young age. They toured Europe before the war, then based themselves in New York. She was illiterate.

It was in the hospital that she finally learned to read and write, as a way of overcoming the boredom and depression of those weeks, and it was my father who insisted on teaching her. In return for stories of her adventures, he graded her first exercises. He bought her her first book, and over her bold letters, which the pale guides of the penmanship pads could not contain, they fell in love.

I wonder if my father calculated the exchange he offered: one form of flight for another. For after that, and for as long as I can remember, my mother has never been without a book. Until now, that is, and it remains the greatest difficulty of her blindness. Since my father's recent death, there is no one to read to her, which is why I returned, in fact, from my failed life where the land is flat. I came home to read to my mother, to read out loud, to read long into the dark if I must, to read all night.

Once my father and mother married, they moved onto the old farm he had inherited but didn't care much for. Though he'd been thinking of moving to a larger city, he settled down and broadened his practice in this valley. It still seems odd to me, when they could have gone anywhere else, that they chose to stay in the town where the disaster had occurred, and which my father in the first place had found so constricting. It was my mother who insisted upon it, after her child did not survive. And then, too, she loved the sagging farmhouse with its scrap of what was left of a vast acreage of woods and hidden hay fields that stretched to the game park.

I owe my existence, the second time then, to the two of them and the hospital that brought

them together. That is the debt we take for granted since none of us asks for life. It is only once we have it that we hang on so dearly.

I was seven the year the house caught fire, probably from standing ash. It can rekindle, and my father, forgetful around the house and perpetually exhausted from night hours on call, often emptied what he thought were ashes from cold stoves into wooden or cardboard containers. The fire could have started from a flaming box, or perhaps a buildup of creosote[8] inside the chimney was the culprit. It started right around the stove, and the heart of the house was gutted. The baby sitter, fallen asleep in my father's den on the first floor, woke to find the stairway to my upstairs room cut off by flames. She used the phone, then ran outside to stand beneath my window.

When my parents arrived, the town volunteers had drawn water from the fire pond and were spraying the outside of the house, preparing to go inside after me, not knowing at the time that there was only one staircase and that it was lost. On the other side of the house, the superannuated[9] extension ladder broke in half. Perhaps the clatter of it falling against the walls woke me, for I'd been asleep up to that point.

As soon as I awakened, in the small room that I now use for sewing, I smelled the smoke. I followed things by the letter then, was good at memorizing instructions, and so I did exactly what was taught in the second-grade home fire drill. I got up; I touched the back of my door before opening it. Finding it hot, I left it closed and stuffed my rolled-up rug beneath the crack. I did not hide under my bed or crawl into my closet. I put on my flannel robe, and then I sat down to wait.

---

8. **creosote** (krē′ə-sōt′): an oily tar deposit from burned wood, which collects in a chimney.

9. **superannuated** (sōō′pər-ăn′yōō-ā′tĭd): too old or worn for further work or service.

Outside, my mother stood below my dark window and saw clearly that there was no rescue. Flames had pierced one side wall, and the glare of the fire lighted the massive limbs and trunk of the vigorous old elm that had probably been planted the year the house was built, a hundred years ago at least. No leaf touched the wall, and just one thin branch scraped the roof. From below, it looked as though even a squirrel would have had trouble jumping from the tree onto the house, for the breadth of that small branch was no bigger than my mother's wrist.

Standing there, beside Father, who was preparing to rush back around to the front of the house, my mother asked him to unzip her dress. When he wouldn't be bothered, she made him understand. He couldn't make his hands work, so she finally tore it off and stood there in her pearls and stockings. She directed one of the men to lean the broken half of the extension ladder up against the trunk of the tree. In surprise, he complied. She ascended. She vanished. Then she could be seen among the leafless branches of late November as she made her way up and, along her stomach, inched the length of a bough that curved above the branch that brushed the roof.

Once there, swaying, she stood and balanced. There were plenty of people in the crowd and many who still remember, or think they do, my mother's leap through the ice-dark air toward that thinnest extension, and how she broke the branch falling so that it cracked in her hands, cracked louder than the flames as she vaulted with it toward the edge of the roof, and how it hurtled down end over end without her, and their

From below, it looked as though even a squirrel would have had trouble jumping from the tree onto the house . . .

eyes went up, again, to see where she had flown.

I didn't see her leap through air, only heard the sudden thump and looked out my window. She was hanging by the backs of her heels from the new gutter we had put in that year, and she was smiling. I was not surprised to see her, she was so matter-of-fact. She tapped on the window. I remember how she did it, too. It was the friendliest tap, a bit tentative, as if she was afraid she had arrived too early at a friend's house. Then she gestured at the latch, and when I opened the window, she told me to raise it wider and prop it up with the stick so it wouldn't crush her fingers. She swung down, caught the ledge, and crawled through the opening. Once she was in my room, I realized she had on only underclothing, a bra of the heavy stitched cotton women used to wear and step-in, lace-trimmed drawers. I remember feeling light-headed, of course, terribly relieved, and then embarrassed for her to be seen by the crowd undressed.

I was still embarrassed as we flew out the window, toward earth, me in her lap, her toes pointed as we skimmed toward the painted target of the fire fighter's net.

I know that she's right. I knew it even then. As you fall, there is time to think. Curled as I was, against her stomach, I was not startled by the cries of the crowd or the looming faces. The wind roared and beat its hot breath at our back; the flames whistled. I slowly wondered what would happen if we missed the circle or bounced out of it. Then I wrapped my hands around my mother's hands. I felt the brush of her lips and heard the beat of her heart in my ears, loud as thunder, long as the roll of drums. ❖

RESPONDING OPTIONS

FROM PERSONAL RESPONSE TO CRITICAL ANALYSIS

REFLECT
1. In your notebook, describe what you would say if you could meet the narrator's mother.

RETHINK
2. What, in your opinion, are the mother's most admirable qualities?
   Consider
   - how she saved herself after the lightning struck
   - what she did in the years following the aerial accident
   - the risk she took to save her daughter's life
   - how she manages with her present blindness

3. How would you describe the narrator's relationship with her mother?
   Consider
   - the narrator's statement "I owe her my existence three times"
   - why the narrator has returned to live with her mother
   - the feelings that the narrator expresses about her mother

4. In your opinion, what tone is conveyed by the story? Cite evidence from the story to support your opinion.

RELATE
5. Why do you think some people find ways of coping with a tragedy that forever alters their lives, while others seem unable to recover from tragedy?

ANOTHER PATHWAY

Create an annotated time line of the events in "The Leap." Add as many details from the story as you can, including information about the mother's early life. You may also invent plausible details about the characters' lives. Compare your completed time line with those of other classmates.

QUICKWRITES

1. Write the **tabloid article** that might have appeared after the lightning struck the circus tent. Use information presented in "The Leap," but feel free to invent details.

2. Think about the different kinds of leaps people can make, such as a physical leap, a leap of faith, and so on. Then write an **analysis** of the title of this selection, explaining the multiple leaps that take place in the story.

3. Draft a **comparison-contrast essay** in which you analyze your own attitude toward taking physical risks and draw comparisons between yourself and the narrator's mother.

   PORTFOLIO Save your writing. You may want to use it later as a springboard to a piece for your portfolio.

LITERARY CONCEPTS

As you know, a **flashback** is a description of a conversation, an episode, or an event that happened before the beginning of a story. Often a flashback interrupts the chronological flow of a story to give the reader information helpful in understanding a character's present situation. Identify the main flashbacks in "The Leap." How are they related to one another?

CONCEPT REVIEW: Foreshadowing Which passages foreshadow the disaster in the circus tent and the fire in the house?

ALTERNATIVE ACTIVITIES

1. *Cooperative Learning* With a group of classmates, stage a **television** or **radio talk show** in which Harry Avalon, the narrator, and the narrator's mother and father are interviewed. Have each character tell his or her remarkable story and answer questions from the audience.

2. Make a **collage** of the most powerful images in "The Leap." Use clippings from magazines and your own artwork as you piece together a visual portrait of the story.

ART CONNECTION

In what way does the illustration on page 847 capture the mood of the story? Support your response.

LITERARY LINKS

Compare and contrast the heroism of the mother in "The Leap" with that of the anonymous hero in "The Man in the Water." Which of the two do you have the strongest feelings about?

CRITIC'S CORNER

"Louise Erdrich's stories celebrate the ordinary parts of life," said the critic Jeanne Kinney. "Like many women authors, she seems to appreciate the balance between the commonplace and the sensational." What elements of "The Leap" do you find sensational? Do you agree that the story ultimately celebrates the more ordinary parts of life?

ACROSS THE CURRICULUM

History Investigate the history of circuses and present your findings in an oral report for your classmates. Consider focusing your report on the small traveling circuses of the 19th century, or tell the story of the Ringling Brothers and Barnum & Bailey Circus. You may wish to build a model or diorama, or bring in photos and fine-art reproductions.

Sports Find out more about the flying trapeze act: how it has changed since it was invented in 1859; the kinds of stunts it includes; and the famous families who have popularized the act. Share your findings with interested classmates.

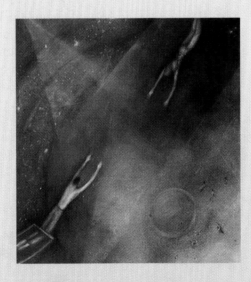

WORDS TO KNOW

For each phrase in the first column, write the letter of the synonymous phrase from the second column.

1. perpetually lonely
2. a dashing "do"
3. extricate the cowboy
4. moistly constricting
5. thought to be destined

a. hair with flair
b. disentangle the wrangler
c. presumed to be doomed
d. endlessly friendless
e. damply cramping

LOUISE ERDRICH

Chippewa on her mother's side and German on her father's, Louise Erdrich was born in Little Falls, Minnesota, and grew up in the small town of Wahpeton, North Dakota, near the Minnesota border. Both of her parents taught at the Bureau of Indian Affairs boarding school in Wapheton, and her grandfather was a tribal leader of the nearby Turtle Mountain Reservation. Her childhood love of writing

1954–

was encouraged by both her father, who gave her a nickel for every story she wrote, and her mother, who stapled the tales into construction paper covers. "So at an early age," Erdrich humorously notes, "I felt myself to be a published author earning substantial royalties."

Erdrich enrolled in Dartmouth in 1972, the first year in which the New Hampshire college admitted women. There she took courses in the new Native American studies department—chaired by anthropologist Michael Dorris—and began coming to terms with the importance of her Native American heritage. After working at several jobs and obtaining a master's degree, she returned to Dartmouth as a writer-in-residence and began a close professional friendship with Dorris, who was also part Native American. Their

mutual interests blossomed into love, and they married in 1981.

Erdrich's first novel, *Love Medicine,* grew out of a short story that she and Dorris worked on together. Winner of the 1984 National Book Critics Circle Award, *Love Medicine* traces the lives of several Native American families in a series of interconnected stories. Many of the characters in *Love Medicine* appear in three of Erdrich's subsequent novels. "My characters choose me," she once said, "and once they do it's like standing in a field and hearing echoes. All I can do is trace their passage."

Erdrich and Dorris continue to work in unusually close collaboration, reading and revising each other's drafts; they have even jointly published one novel, *The Crown of Columbus.* Their large family includes several adopted children, one of whom became the subject of Dorris's award-winning nonfiction book *The Broken Cord.* Erdrich has published two highly regarded volumes of poetry and a number of prize-winning short stories. Her first major work of nonfiction, *The Blue Jay's Dance: A Birth Year,* was published in 1995.

OTHER WORKS *Jacklight, Baptism of Desire, The Beet Queen, Tracks, The Bingo Palace*

LASERLINKS
• ART GALLERY

PREVIEWING

from Back from Tuichi (tōō′ē-chē)

Yossi Ghinsberg (yō′sē gĭnz′bûrg) Israel

PERSONAL CONNECTION

As a class, discuss the ingredients needed for an exciting adventure story. You may consider either real-life adventures or fictional ones portrayed in books, in movies, or on television. Identify the types of characters, settings, plot lines, and other elements that make for an interesting story. Use a diagram like the one shown to organize your ideas.

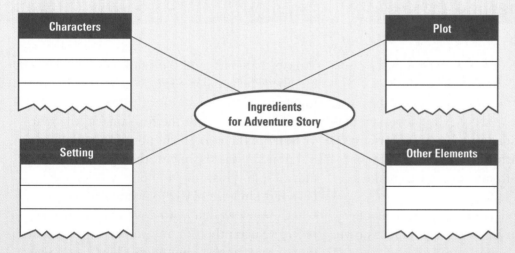

BIOGRAPHICAL CONNECTION

Yossi Ghinsberg experienced the adventure of a lifetime while backpacking through South America in the early 1980s. He recounts his perilous journey in his book *Back from Tuichi: The Harrowing Life-and-Death Story of Survival in the Amazon Rainforest*. While in Bolivia, Yossi met three men, Kevin, Marcus, and Karl, who would journey with him by river raft deep into the jungle. They were searching for a remote Indian village and gold, but all they found was adventure. After several weeks of rough traveling, Marcus and Karl—who had lived and worked in the rain forest and knew best how to survive there—decided to head back to civilization on foot. As this selection begins, Yossi and Kevin are getting ready to continue on their own down the Tuichi River in Bolivia.

WRITING CONNECTION

What exciting adventures have you had? Have you ever had an experience that might have been more exciting had something gone awry? In your notebook, jot down ideas for an adventure story—real or fictional. Then see how your ideas compare to Yossi Ghinsberg's experiences as you read the following excerpt from *Back from Tuichi*.

LASERLINKS
• *GEOGRAPHICAL CONNECTION*

from BACK FROM TUICHI

YOSSI GHINSBERG

Kevin broke the silence. "Get a move on, Yossi. We still have a lot to do."

We crossed back to the other side of the Ipurama[1] and set to work. Kevin uncoupled the four logs we had added to the raft in Asriamas.[2] Then, using *panchos*[3] the way Karl had taught us, we tied the logs to one another to make a smaller raft.

"This," Kevin explained, "will serve as our life raft. We'll fasten all of our equipment down to it."

We bound the small raft tightly to the center of the larger one using the ropes and leather strips that Marcus had left us.

"The main raft will take all the knocks from the rocks, and if anything happens to it, all we'll have to do is to chop the straps with the machete, and the life raft will be set free. We just jump onto it and use it to get ashore."

It sounded reasonable to me.

Kevin emptied the backpacks and rearranged our possessions. In the larger of the two packs he put the bulk of our equipment: the pot and utensils, the sheets of nylon that served as tenting, his extra clothes and sandals, the large stalk of bananas, and the smoked monkey meat. He lined the smaller pack, which he called the life pack, with a waterproof rubber bag. Then he filled the bag with the first-aid kit, the map of Bolivia, the two green mosquito nets, Dede's[4] red poncho, the flashlight, the lighter and matches, and his camera along with an extra lens and film. He placed our documents and what money we had into a watertight metal box. I reluctantly took my wallet with my uncle's tiny book[5] from my pocket. Kevin was watching me. He carefully, wordlessly placed the wallet into the metal box. Finally we fitted the rice and beans into additional waterproof bags. Kevin cinched the mouth of the rubber

---

1. **Ipurama** (ē-pōō-rä′mä): a broad river that empties into the Tuichi River.
2. **Asriamas** (äs-rē-ä′mäs): a small, remote jungle settlement.
3. *panchos* (pän′chōs) *Spanish:* ropes made from tree fibers.
4. **Dede's** (dě′děz): belonging to a friend Yossi made in La Paz, Bolivia, before heading into the jungle.
5. **my uncle's tiny book:** a special book given to Yossi by his Uncle Nissim just before Nissim died; it was believed to have the power to save and protect the person who carried it.

bag tightly shut and closed the pack over it. To the top of the pack he tied two large, sealed tin cans to keep the pack afloat if it should fall from the raft. He placed the entire pack into a nylon bag, which he filled with balsa[6] chips to make it buoyant. The packs were tied firmly to the life raft, and we were ready to go.

We combed the camp area one last time, but we hadn't forgotten anything. Kevin was very thorough. He kicked through the blanket of leaves that had served as our ground cover and poked through the charred remains of the fire. Nothing was overlooked.

Excited, my stomach fluttering, I boarded the raft. Kevin stood in the water, gave the raft a good shove, and then jumped up beside me.

"Everything's going to be just fine," he assured me. "Just remember what you said yourself: your grandmother could do it. And one other thing: keep alert and pay attention to my instructions."

"You're the captain," I answered.

I wanted to believe that Kevin knew what he was talking about, but at that moment I was pretty nervous. The current seized the raft, and Kevin instructed me to change the pole for an oar.

"All we have to do is to keep the front of the raft pointed straight ahead," he said. "We'll let the current carry us along. We should make the bank Karl was talking about sometime today."

We were rapidly coming upon the first difficult pass. I could see jagged rocks jutting out of white-water rapids.

"To the right, Yossi! Pull hard!"

We ran into a rock, and the raft climbed

On a handmade raft of balsa logs, Yossi Ghinsberg navigated dangerous rapids like the ones shown here and on the following pages. Kenneth Garrett / National Geographic Image Collection.

I could see jagged rocks jutting out of white-water rapids.

partway up, the logs shuddering under our feet. Then we were back in the current and about to ram another rock. I made no attempt at rowing but held on to the leather straps for dear life. Kevin was doing the same in the bow. The raft, tossed from rock to rock, descended churning falls, most of the time tilted to one side.

"Hold on tight, Yossi! Don't let go!"

My eyes were squeezed shut.

Just as suddenly we found ourselves drifting once again on a placid[7] river. Looking behind me, I could see the white waters that we had just come through.

"Hey, we made it!" I shouted joyously.

Kevin smiled back at me and gave me a thumbs up. Now we both realized how dangerous this journey was. We had discovered how little we could control the raft. While we were being carried along by the powerful current, we hadn't even been able to keep the front of the raft pointed straight ahead. No, my grandmother wouldn't have come along on this trip. Now that there was no one else along with us sniveling, I no longer felt the need to act the tough guy.

We spent the next two hours drifting easily,

---

6. **balsa** (bôl'sə): a tropical tree having wood that is buoyant and very lightweight, and that is used as a substitute for cork in insulation, floats, and crafts.

7. **placid** (plăs'ĭd): pleasantly calm, quiet, or peaceful.

James P. Blair / National Geographic Image Collection.

convinced that we would reach our destination. The scenery was breathtaking. Evergreen-covered mountains towered over reddish cliffs along the shore. Occasionally we passed a narrow waterfall, cascading from the heights to the river. From time to time a family of monkeys accompanied us downstream, jumping from tree to tree. Kevin considered taking the camera out but decided it would be too risky and gave up on the idea.

Around noon we ran into trouble. A large rock jutted out from the shore, and the water pounding against it formed a treacherous whirlpool. The current carried us into its center. We tried for two hours to get out of it without success. Finally seeing no other way, Kevin swam to shore, climbed onto the rock, and tried to use the rope that was tied to the front of the raft to pull it out of the whirlpool. Twice he

slipped, fell into the water, and was swept away by the current but quickly recovered. On his third try the rope broke off in his hands, and he fell once again into the water, but this time he didn't return so quickly. I was left whirling with the raft, fear churning in my stomach. What if Kevin had drowned? What would become of me? I sat on the raft, craning my neck, trying desperately to catch a glimpse of him. When I saw his straw hat carried downstream, I froze.

Kevin returned about fifteen minutes later, bleeding from a deep wound on his knee.

"The undertow here is incredible," he said. "I thought I was drowning. My air was gone, but just in time the current threw me to the surface, and I made it to shore."

"What about your leg?"

"Oh, I didn't even notice. I guess I must have hit it against a rock. I lost my straw hat."

Instead of attempting to navigate out of the whirlpool, we moored the raft to the riverbank. It was a great relief to have solid ground under my feet.

The next time we tried something else. We pulled the raft upriver, jumped aboard, and, rowing with all our strength, tried to get past the whirlpool and back into the middle of the river. We succeeded on the third try. After our cries of joy had died down, Kevin remarked thoughtfully, "Maybe we should have just stayed back there. It wouldn't have been such a bad place to camp."

"But we've still got a while before dark," I said. "Anyway, it's better that we should get all the way to the mouth of the *cajón*[8] and camp on the bank that Karl showed us on the map. It would be nice to know that we start walking tomorrow."

"Maybe you're right," Kevin agreed.

The reddish cliffs encroached upon the riverbank. It was as if suddenly the river had no banks at all.

"This must be it," Kevin declared. "Get ready. We should sight the island any minute now. When we do, you start rowing to the left as hard as you can. If we run into any serious trouble, jump overboard and swim for shore. This is starting to look like it must be the canyon."

We were both on edge, alert. The current grew stronger. Where was the island?

There was a large rock near the right-hand bank. We were swiftly being drawn toward it. To its left the riverbed dropped sharply, though it was impossible to see just how far. Nevertheless the water cascaded over the edge with a mighty roar. Maybe we could pass to the right of the rock, between it and the riverbank.

"To the right, to the right! Harder, faster!"

I was rowing desperately with all my strength. I closed my eyes, and we rammed into the rock with tremendous force.

"Are you all right, Yossi?"

Like me, Kevin was in the river, hanging on to the ropes of the raft. The water rushed past us on both sides, but the raft wasn't moving. It was protruding from the river at a sixty-degree angle, stuck on a sandbar, riding up against the rock. The pressure of the water slammed us up against the rock and held us fast.

We climbed back onto the raft. Kevin instructed me to tie the oar down so that it wouldn't be swept into the river. I looked over at the waterfall to our left. The river cascaded downward ten or twelve feet. God, why hadn't I turned back with Karl and Marcus?

My legs quivered. If we could maneuver to the right, we would make it through. We tried to get the raft off the rock but were helpless against the current. We tried everything we could think of—pushing, pulling, rowing, prying the raft off with the poles—but the raft didn't budge.

Kevin quickly sized up the situation.

"I don't see much chance of the current getting us out of here. It's only six or seven yards to the right bank, while the waterfall is here on our left, and after that it's probably twenty yards to the left bank. The river is narrow, and the current is terrifically strong. You see what it means? The canyon must start here. We must be really close to the island. If we can just make it ashore, we can go on from here by foot and easily bypass the canyon overland to Curiplaya."[9]

Kevin paused for a moment and looked around before he made up his mind.

"We don't have any choice. I'm going in. I'll try to reach the right bank. When I do, you throw me the machete. I'll climb up into the jungle and cut a vine. I'll throw the vine to you, and you'll pass the packs over to me on it. Then you tie yourself to the vine, and I'll pull you ashore."

---

8. *cajón* (kä-hôn′) *Spanish:* a narrow canyon.
9. **Curiplaya** (kōō-rē-plä′yä): a gold-mining camp, deserted most of the year.

"Don't go in, Kevin. It's much too dangerous. Wait awhile," I called to him, but Kevin didn't hesitate. He took off his shoes and socks.

"I'll make it, Yossi," he shouted, and jumped into the river.

The current's tremendous force pulled him along. He disappeared for a moment but then bobbed up again. He was washed up against a rock about twenty-five yards downstream, grabbed onto it, and from there made it to the riverbank. I sighed with relief but then caught my breath. I felt the raft moving under me, slowly breaking free of the rock.

"Kevin! Kevin! The raft is moving, Kevin!"

It was slowly slipping away. Kevin ran swiftly toward me.

"Throw me my shoes, fast!"

I obeyed him automatically and threw his shoes as hard in his direction as I could. They landed on the rocky bank. The raft was almost free. It was headed toward the waterfall. I was trembling all over, looking at Kevin in terror, pleading. He was already hurriedly putting his shoes on.

"The machete! Throw me the machete!" he shouted.

The large blade whistled through the air and thudded to the ground. The raft had begun moving.

"You're leaving me, Kevin!" I shouted.

"Hang on as tight as you can, Yossi! Don't let go of the leather straps, no matter what! Don't let go! You're heading for the waterfall. You're going to go over it! Hang on tight!"

"Kevin, you're leaving me!"

"I'll catch up with you. Just hang on! Hang on!"

The raft came off the rock and edged vertically toward the waterfall. I could feel the surge of the river beneath me and held on to the leather straps for dear life. I was thrown into the air, raging water swallowing my screams; amidst the water I felt as helpless as a fallen leaf. The moment of terror lingered, then abruptly ended with a crash. The raft was pulled under the surface of the river, taking me with it. Darkness enveloped me. My lungs were bursting. I had no air.

Don't, don't let go of the raft! I told myself as the undertow dragged the raft along rapidly below the surface. The pressure on my lungs grew unbearable.

God, help me please.

I thought this was the end. Then I found myself above water, the raft floating again. I jerked my head around and saw Kevin, a hundred yards or more behind me, running in my direction. Relief washed over me.

"I'll wait for you wherever I manage to make shore!" I shouted, and waved at him.

Kevin couldn't hear me, but he waved back and kept running.

Suddenly I understood where I was: I had entered the canyon and was being swept swiftly toward the treacherous Mal Paso San Pedro.[10] The raft bounced from wall to wall. It crashed into the rocks, tilted on its sides, was tossed over falls, and swept through foaming rapids. I held on desperately, closing my eyes and praying *God, God.* Then the raft dove under again, taking me with it. I rammed into a rock so violently that I was twice thrown into the air, landing in the water, vulnerable to the torments of the river, sucked down to its depths. If I hit another rock, I would be smashed to pieces. I was running out of air. When I resurfaced, I saw the bound logs of the raft nearby. I managed to grab hold of them and climb aboard again.

The horrible dance of death went endlessly on. The current was incredibly swift. The raft was swept along like lightning. There was another small bend in the river, and then, still far away, I saw it: a mountain of rock in the middle of the river, almost blocking its entire

---

10. **Mal Paso San Pedro** (mäl pä'sô sän pě'drô) *Spanish:* Bad Pass of St. Peter.

I knew that I had to get to the life raft. I mustn't lose the life pack. I couldn't survive without it.

breadth. The water pounded against it with a terrible roar. White foam sprayed in all directions, the white-capped maelstrom[11] swirling at the foot of the terrifying crag,[12] and I knew that I would never make it past.

I lay down on the raft facing the stern, not wanting to watch as death approached. I squeezed my eyes tightly shut and clutched at the straps for all I was worth. There was a crash. I felt nothing. I was simply flying through the air, then landing back in the water, my eyes still squeezed shut. I was sucked under the black waters for what seemed an eternity. I could feel the pressure in my ears, my nose, the sockets of my eyes. My chest was bursting. Then once more an invisible hand plucked me out of the current and, just in time, drew me to the surface. I lifted my head, gasped for air—a lot of air—before I would be pulled back under. Far behind me I could see the mountain of rock receding. I couldn't believe it. I had passed it. But how? I didn't feel any pain. No, I was uninjured. It was a miracle.

The raft was in front of me not far away. The logs had become loosened from one another. I managed to climb up onto what was left of it. The leather straps were torn, and I had nothing to cling to. I knew that I had to get to the life raft. I mustn't lose the life pack. I couldn't survive without it.

I jumped into the water, and two strokes brought me to the life raft. Again I crashed into the stone walls of the canyon, only now I no longer had a wide, solid raft to protect me. The life raft was small and narrow. Every blow lifted it half out of the water. Once again I rammed into a rock, injuring my knee, but much worse than that, the precious life pack came loose and fell into the water. I grabbed hold of it just as it was about to float away, but it was heavy, and I was afraid that it would drown me. I tied the waist belt to one of the logs and hoped that it would hold. But I was wrong. One more knock,

---

11. **maelstrom** (māl'strəm): a whirlpool of extraordinary size or violence.

12. **crag:** a steeply projecting mass of rock forming part of a rugged cliff.

How would you find shelter from continual rainfall; protection from poisonous snakes, biting insects, and other wild animals; and nourishing food if left alone in the heart of the jungle? Copyright © Luiz C. Marico / Peter Arnold, Inc.

one more dive over a fall, and the precious pack was bobbing behind me, out of my reach. I couldn't take my eyes off it.

I mustn't lose sight of it, I told myself. *I mustn't lose it, no matter what.*

I was fairly certain that I was already through the pass but still in a canyon. Steep stone walls rose on both sides, but the river was getting wider, the current milder, and I could have swum to the bank, but I couldn't abandon the pack. As long as I could still see it bobbing behind me followed by the large raft, I didn't swim ashore.

The river turned a bend, and I waited in vain for the pack to make the bend behind me. It must have gotten caught on something. Nor did the raft appear. So, as the life raft neared the right bank, I took the chance to leap ashore, having no other choice but to abandon the big pack and raft.

I landed in the water close to the bank and, wonder of wonders, felt sand beneath my feet. I could actually stand up. I staggered out of the river, unbelieving. I had landed on a rocky strip of shore. Solid ground. I was alive!

It was a few moments before my breathing became regular. Then my thoughts returned to my present situation. The life pack was lost, nowhere to be seen, but maybe it would turn up. Couldn't the current knock it free?

And what about Kevin? Surely he would find me. I had seen him running in my direction. He would certainly make it this far today—or tomorrow at the latest. Yes, everything would be all right. I was sure. He would find me, and together we would walk to Curiplaya. How far could we be from each other? I didn't know. How long had I spent on the river? I didn't know. Maybe twenty minutes. The thought of the river made me shudder.

A steady rain had been falling and now grew stronger. There was no more point in waiting. It would be better to climb up into the jungle to find shelter for the night. I clawed my way up the stone wall. When I reached a height of about fifteen feet, I looked down and was overcome with joy. I could see the big raft. It was trapped between some rocks near the shore, bobbing and banging softly, maybe three hundred yards upstream. Now that I could see it, I could hear the sound that it made as it hit against the rocks. What luck! I thought that the pack was probably stuck there too.

I hurried down to the bank, but the bend in the river blocked my view, and except for the spot where I was standing, the river had no bank at all. I wouldn't be able to get any closer to the raft by foot. I waded into the river, very close to the bank, and tried to walk upriver, fighting the current. I progressed a few feet but then slipped and fell as if the bottom had been pulled out from under me. I was terror-stricken and scrambled back to shore.

Now what would I do? I was seething with anger and frustration. I desperately needed the pack. Maybe I could reach it by land, but scaling the stone walls could take hours. I choked back tears.

No, don't cry. Be strong. Don't give up. You're

a man of action. Get on with it, do whatever must be done.

I knew I couldn't make it to the raft that day. It was already growing dark and still raining. I had to find some kind of shelter. I started climbing again, chanting to myself in a whisper, "Man of action, man of action." I could see the raft bobbing among the rocks.

Please stay there until tomorrow. Please stay put.

Improvising a shelter was no easy task. I uprooted small bushes, broke off branches, tore off leaves, and dragged it all back to a little alcove in the stony hillside. I scattered leaves about on the floor and piled branches in the opening until they formed some kind of barrier.

I was famished. I hadn't eaten since morning. A way down the hillside I saw a palmetto tree. I could eat the palm heart, as Karl had taught us. The tree was small, but its roots went deep into the rocky ground. I dug around them with my hands until I finally succeeded in uprooting it. The heart was at the very top. I took a large rock and smashed it against the trunk until I uncovered the soft, white heart. It was a small amount of nourishment, but I gathered every bit.

Suddenly I heard shouting.

It must be Kevin, I said to myself, and roared, "Kevin! Kevin! Kevin!" but there was no reply.

It must have been my imagination. No, I could hear something. A family of monkeys. I trembled with fear. Karl had told us that there were always jaguars in the vicinity of bands of monkeys.

God, let Kevin get here.

I was wearing a blue T-shirt that Marcus had given me, a brown flannel shirt, rough underwear, jeans, socks, walking shoes, and a large bandanna tied around my neck. I crawled into my camouflaged little niche. The stones cut into my back, but they weren't as bad as the cold. I was soaking wet and had no fire or anything with which to cover myself. I took the bandanna from around my neck and tied it over my face, and the warmth

of my own breath gave me at least the illusion of comfort. Frightening thoughts filled my mind: wild animals, snakes. What if I didn't find the pack? What if Kevin didn't get here? I would either be devoured by wild beasts or die of starvation. I felt desperate, desolate, and I leapt out of the niche.

"Kevin! Kevin! Kevin!"

"Oha, oha," the cursed monkeys chattered.

I fled back to my alcove. I was choked with tears.

Don't cry. Don't break now. Be a man of action, I coaxed myself.

It was already dark. I replaced the bandanna over my face. I couldn't sleep, couldn't get the frightening thoughts out of my mind. . . .

I told myself that when morning came, I would find Kevin, and together we would make it out of this. When I found myself feeling hopeless, I whispered my mantra,[13] "Man of action, man of action." I don't know where I had gotten the phrase. Perhaps I had picked it up from one of Carlos Castaneda's books.[14] I repeated it over and over: a man of action does whatever he must, isn't afraid, and doesn't worry. But when I heard the rustle of branches outside, my motto wasn't all that encouraging. I held my breath and waited for the rustling to recede into the jungle.

I felt better in the morning. I pushed the branches aside and crawled outside. I roared Kevin's name a few times but then went back to being a man of action and sized up my situation. For starters I was absolutely certain that I was past the canyon. I remembered Karl's description well: the waterfalls, the rapids, the gigantic rock blocking the river. Yes, I was sure

---

13. **mantra:** a verbal formula repeated in prayer or during meditation.

14. **Carlos Castaneda's** (käs-tä-nĕ′däz) **books:** books written by Carlos Castaneda, a Latin American mystic and novelist born in 1931.

that that had been the *mal paso,* and Curiplaya was supposed to be not far from the pass, on the right bank, the bank I was standing on. There was a chance that I could make it there. There were cabins and equipment in Curiplaya. Karl had said that there was also a banana grove. And from Curiplaya it was four days' walk to San José de Uchupiamonas.[15] There should even be a path cut through the jungle. I allowed myself to feel optimistic. I could do it. Not more than one day's walk to Curiplaya and from there on a path to San José. There might even be someone left in Curiplaya.

I hunted around for something for breakfast but found nothing. I decided to try to retrieve the pack once again. It would be worth investing an entire day looking for it as long as there was even the slightest chance of finding it. There was food in the pack, along with matches, a map, and a flashlight. If I could only find it, I'd be set.

It was no easy task. I started walking upriver. The route took me over jagged cliffs and smooth rock faces. I walked for two hours, climbing higher to progress and then back down to see if I could reach the shore. The stony walls were steep and smooth. I lost my footing a few times but luckily was caught by trees and bushes. Finally, from a cliff that towered fifty feet over the river, I spotted the raft in the water, still beating against the rocks. I was positive that the pack must be nearby.

At that point the bank of the river was a thin strip of land. I had no choice but to take the risk and started slowly climbing down, clawing at the sharp rocks. I took tiny steps, groping with my foot for a hold that would support my weight, my body covered with cold sweat. I said a silent prayer, *Don't slip. Don't fall.* If I broke an arm or leg, I didn't stand a chance. The last time I had gone rock climbing, I had fallen but had been saved by a miracle: Uncle Nissim's little book had been in my pocket. Now it was in the backpack. I should never have left it there.

It was still raining, hadn't let up at all since yesterday. The stones were damp and slick, but I kept climbing. My pants caught on a jagged edge and ripped. My knee was scratched, my fingers bloody. The strain on my legs was tremendous, terribly painful. I could tell that the rash was spreading over my wet feet again. When I was about ten feet above the ground, I turned and slid down the rock face on my rear end. My back was scraped, but I landed safely on the riverbank. I started searching, skipping over rocks until I reached the raft.

It was hard to believe, but the raft was still in one piece. All seven logs were still bound together. . . .

Before I began my search for the pack, I secured the raft well, just in case I met up with Kevin and the two of us might make use of it. I looked around among the rocks and crevices, and there, about ten yards away, in the cleft of a small rock, sat the precious pack, soaking wet but still afloat.

Thank you, God.

Words could not describe my happiness. I laid down on the rock and fished the pack out of the river and hurriedly opened it. I was saved! The contents were only slightly damp. The rubber bag had protected them well. There was everything: rice and beans, the flashlight and matches, the lighter, map, mosquito netting, red poncho, medicines, and, most important, my wallet with Uncle Nissim's little book. Now I wouldn't die. I felt safe. . . .

Somebody up there likes me, I thought. *Just let Kevin find me.*

Up until now I had thought him the better off of the two of us—at least he had the machete—but now I was a wealthy man, and he, poor guy, had only the clothes on his back. Poor Kevin had nothing; he must need me. I had food and could start a fire. He just had

---

15. **San José de Uchupiamonas** (sän hô-sě′ dě o͞o′cho͞o-pē-ä-mô′näs): Yossi and Kevin's final destination.

Three weeks after becoming separated from Kevin, Yossi Ghinsberg was rescued. His poncho had been dinner for millions of termites that had invaded his final campsite. Courtesy of Yossi Ghinsberg.

to find me. Without me he didn't have a chance.

It was still pouring rain, and I shivered with cold. I hurriedly closed the pack and set it down in a niche of the cliff. I kept only the poncho to protect me from the rain. Then it occurred to me that I should hang it up in some conspicuous place. It was bright red and might catch Kevin's eye. I saw a crag jutting prominently over the river. I climbed up to it and spread the poncho out over it, weighting it down with heavy stones so that it wouldn't blow away in the wind. Again I called out to Kevin, but I knew the shouts were pointless. The roar of the water was deafening, and there was no chance of anyone's hearing me.

On my way back to the pack I noticed a few yellow fruits lying on the shore and stopped to pick them up. Most of them were rotten, but I found one hard, fresh fruit and took a bite. It was delicious. I looked up and spotted the source: a tree laden with wild yellow plums at the edge of the stone wall.

Someone really is looking out for me, I thought.

I looked for a way up to the tree and found a slight hollow in the rock face where the rainwater ran off the mountain and down to the river. It was wet and slippery, but the incline was not so steep there. I had almost reached the tree—just a few more steps—when I saw a snake. It was green and coiled and just a few inches from my foot. I recognized it immediately as the deadly lora. Karl had told me they could blind their victims by spraying venom even from a distance.

I froze in my place. The snake, too, was motionless. Only its tongue flicked in and out of its mouth. It held the upper half of its body erect. I was afraid to move a muscle, but my fear and desperation soon turned to hatred. I took a step backward, picked up a huge rock, and flung it at the snake. Its body convulsed and then thickened, as if tied in knots. I picked up a flat, narrow rock, bent over, and started hitting the snake in a rage, over and over, until I'd sliced its head from its body. I was trembling, knowing that if the snake had bitten me, I would have died.

I picked up its green body and peeled its skin like a banana, revealing its pinkish flesh. I cleaned the internal organs out with one flick of my finger and was left holding the flesh. What should I do with it? Eat it or use it for bait? I threw it down to the riverbank. I would decide what to do with it after I got down.

I went over to the fruit tree, looking cautiously before every step. The lora was a tree climber, and I was afraid its mate might be nearby. I climbed up into the tree, eating ripe fruit as I went. The tree was heavily laden, but I had competition: tiny yellow ants swarmed on the trunk. I was all too familiar with them: fire ants. They stung me all over, but I didn't give in to them. I hurriedly picked as much fruit as I could, tossing it down to the riverbank. Then I climbed down and shook the cursed ants off. I felt as if I was on fire but was glad I hadn't let them drive me away. Now I would eat my fill.

Down on the riverbank I took one of the large tin cans that had been tied to the pack. It had two cups and a spoon inside. I drank from the river and then gathered up the fruit, filling the can with those I didn't eat.

I no longer had any desire to make a meal of the snake. I couldn't have started a fire anyway, because everything was still damp, and I certainly wasn't about to eat it raw. I found the fishing line in the pack, but the river was too rocky and the water too turbulent to fish.

I sat on the pack awhile, leaning against the cliff, the rain still beating down on me. Kevin couldn't have continued walking along the riverbank, I reasoned, so he must be walking up on the ledge above the stone walls. There wasn't much chance of his seeing the poncho from there. I couldn't see any point in waiting by the river any longer. I might as well climb up to the ledge myself. I retrieved the poncho, folded it into the pack, put the pack on my back, and started scaling the wall back toward the plum tree.

Marching the length of the ledge, I searched for a cranny that would shelter me for the night and found an ideal place: a shallow niche cut into the stone wall about six feet above ground level. I climbed up to it. I would have liked to have started a fire now that I had matches and a lighter, but all the branches were wet, so I abandoned the idea.

In the second tin I discovered a large lump of salt, some spices, garlic cloves, and three lemons. I had a well-balanced supper: one lemon, three cloves of garlic, a pinch of salt, and a handful of the plumlike fruit.

This night was kinder to me than the last one had been. I covered myself with the two mosquito nets, which, although damp, were comforting. I spread the poncho over them and covered my face with its hood. I breathed into the hood, and waves of warmth spread over my body.

What if Kevin doesn't make it here? I asked myself.

Tomorrow I will check the map, try to figure out approximately where I am and how far it is to San José. I'll spend tomorrow here waiting for Kevin, and if he doesn't show up, then I'll set out myself on the following day.

During the night I started hallucinating. Kevin was calling in desperation, *Help! Help! Yossi, save me. Wait for me. Don't leave, Yossi! Yossi! Help!*

I was sweating under my wet clothes. ❖

Translated by Yael Politis and Stanley Young

RESPONDING
OPTIONS

FROM PERSONAL RESPONSE TO CRITICAL ANALYSIS

REFLECT
1. What feelings did you experience while reading the selection? Describe your reaction in your notebook, and share your writing with a classmate.

RETHINK
2. How would you rate this selection as an adventure story? Consider the ingredients for a good adventure story that you identified in the Personal Connection on page 855.

3. What do you think was the most difficult challenge that Yossi Ghinsberg faced? Explain your opinion.

4. What sort of person does Yossi Ghinsberg reveal himself to be?

   Consider
   - how he responds to danger and adversity
   - his thoughts in italics
   - why he repeats "man of action"
   - his relationship with Kevin

RELATE
5. How does Yossi Ghinsberg compare to your personal definition of a hero? Use evidence from the story to support your point of view.

6. Why do you think some people have such a strong need for adventure, while others have little desire for such experiences?

ANOTHER PATHWAY
Cooperative Learning

Working with a group of your classmates, review the story to see which of Kevin's and Yossi's actions require physical prowess and which require clever thinking. Create a chart like the one shown to report your findings. Then discuss which of these abilities is more important in a test of survival.

Physical Ability	Mental Ability

QUICKWRITES

1. Write the **book jacket copy** for *Back from Tuichi* on the basis of what you know about the book from the Biographical Connection on page 855 and from the selection.

2. Read the rest of *Back from Tuichi* and share your opinion of Yossi's adventures in a **book report.** If possible, use a computer to compose and edit your draft.

3. Draft your own **true-life adventure.** The notes you made for the Writing Connection on page 855 can help you to get started.

📁 *PORTFOLIO Save your writing. You may want to use it later as a springboard to a piece for your portfolio.*

LITERARY CONCEPTS

A **true-life adventure** is a nonfiction account of heroic deeds or exciting adventures, usually organized chronologically. Often, a true-life adventure is narrated from the first-person point of view, presenting the experience as it happened to the writer. A true-life adventure may also be written from a third-person point of view, as reported to the writer. Choose an exciting passage from this selection and rewrite it from a third-person point of view. Discuss the differences between the two versions.

CONCEPT REVIEW: Suspense How does Yossi Ghinsberg create suspense in Back from Tuichi? At what point or points did the tension reach a peak?

ALTERNATIVE ACTIVITIES

1. With a partner, create a **map** of Yossi's harrowing journey on the river. Review the story for details about the locations where events take place. You may also invent details if needed.

2. Present an **oral reading** of an excerpt from the selection. Let the expression in your voice capture the excitement of Yossi's adventure and his changing emotions as the selection unfolds.

CRITIC'S CORNER

A reviewer once described *Back from Tuichi* as "no ordinary autobiographical travel book" and further observed, "The need for loyalty and the extremes of physical and emotional limits are vividly portrayed." Do you think this assessment applies to the excerpt you just read of *Back from Tuichi*? Cite details to support your opinion.

YOSSI GHINSBERG

1959–

Born and raised in Israel, Yossi Ghinsberg grew up devouring classic adventure novels. His appetite for adventure was further whetted during his years in the Israeli navy, when he visited the Red Sea and the Sinai Desert. The spirit of adventure then took him to Europe and the Americas, where his temporary jobs included employment as a construction worker in Norway, a fisherman in Alaska, and a cook in New York City.

Yossi Ghinsberg's travels in South America almost claimed his life. After he was separated from Kevin on the Tuichi River, he spent 20 days struggling to survive in the rain forest with almost no food, supplies, or protection against the elements. The obstacles he encountered included incessant rain, termites, leeches, snakes, and jaguars. Luckily, Kevin found his way back to civilization and formed a rescue party that saved Yossi's life in the nick of time. Karl and Marcus were not so lucky; they vanished without a trace. *Back from Tuichi,* which was published in Israel in 1985, proved so popular that it was translated into several languages.

Although Ghinsberg returned to Israel to study at Tel Aviv University, he was drawn back to the South American rain forest. There he helped establish the Chalalan Project, an environmental organization that seeks to preserve the Tuichi valley economy without endangering its ecosystem. He also founded a pharmaceutical company that works hand in hand with the native people of the rain forest.

PREVIEWING

The Ring of General Macías (mä-sē'äs)
Josephina Niggli Mexico / United States

PERSONAL CONNECTION

What does honor mean to you? Discuss the concept of honor with a small group of your classmates. Use a spider map like the one shown to explore the concept from different angles. Then compare your group's diagram to those produced by other groups.

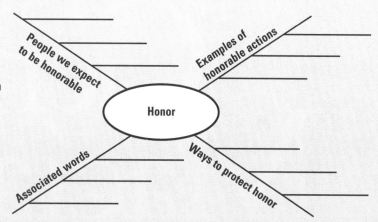

People we expect to be honorable

Examples of honorable actions

Honor

Associated words

Ways to protect honor

HISTORICAL CONNECTION

Honor is central to the play you are about to read, which takes place during the Mexican Revolution (1910–1917). The Revolution began as a revolt by impoverished peasants against wealthy landowners. It called for an end to oppression suffered under the dictatorship of Porfirio Díaz (pôr-fēr'yô dē'äs) and the formation of a new government that would redistribute land so that everyone would have a fair share. A group called the Federalists opposed the uprising and fought to protect Mexico's existing government and way of life.

Detail of *The People in Arms*, 1957, David Alfáro Siqueiros, fresco, Museo Nacional de Historia, Mexico City (INAH).

READING CONNECTION

Visualizing Drama Every drama is a story that is meant to be performed in front of a live audience. As you read *The Ring of General Macías,* which focuses on the concept of honor, try to visualize the play in performance in order to fully appreciate the story. Pay careful attention to the description of the setting and the stage directions, noting any indications of stage props or scenery. Imagine the kinds of actors needed for the characters' roles; decide how the actors might be dressed and what facial expressions, gestures, and movements they might use to portray the characters effectively.

The Ring of General Macías

Josephina Niggli

CAST OF CHARACTERS

Marica (mä-rē′kä), the sister of General Macías

Raquel (rä-kĕl′), the wife of General Macías

Andrés de la O (än-drĕs′ dĕ-lä-ô′), a captain in the revolutionary army

Cleto (clĕ′tô), a private in the revolutionary army

Basilio Flores (bä-sē′lē-ô flô′rĕs), a captain in the federal army

Place: Just outside Mexico City

Time: A night in April, 1912.

The living room of General Macías' home is luxuriously furnished in the gold and ornate style of Louis XVI. In the right wall are French windows leading into the patio. Flanking these windows are low bookcases. In the back wall is, right, a closet door; and, center, a table holding a wine decanter and glasses. The left wall has a door upstage, and downstage a writing desk with a straight chair in front of it. Near the desk is an armchair. Down right is a small sofa with a table holding a lamp at the upstage end of it. There are pictures on the walls. The room looks rather stuffy and unlived in.

Self-Portrait (1926), Frida Kahlo. Oil on canvas, 31″ × 23″, private collection, Mexico City.

When the curtains part, the stage is in darkness save for the moonlight that comes through the French windows. Then the house door opens, and a young girl in negligee enters <u>stealthily</u>. She is carrying a lighted candle. She stands at the door a moment listening for possible pursuit, then moves quickly across to the bookcase down right. She puts the candle on top of the bookcase and begins searching behind the books. She finally finds what she wants: a small bottle. While she is searching, the house door opens silently and a woman, also in negligee, enters. (These negligees are in the latest Parisian style.) She moves silently across the room to the table by the sofa, and as the girl turns with the bottle, the woman switches on the light. The girl gives a half-scream and draws back, frightened. The light reveals her to be quite young—no more than twenty—a timid, dovelike creature. The woman has a queenly air, and whether she is actually beautiful or not, people think she is. She is about thirty-two.

Marica (*trying to hide the bottle behind her*). Raquel! What are you doing here?

Raquel. What did you have hidden behind the books, Marica?

Marica (*attempting a forced laugh*). I? Nothing. Why do you think I have anything?

Raquel (*taking a step toward her*). Give it to me.

Marica (*backing away from her*). No. No, I won't.

Raquel (*stretching out her hand*). I demand that you give it to me.

Marica. You have no right to order me about. I'm a married woman. I . . . I . . . (*She begins to sob and flings herself down on the sofa.*)

Raquel (*much gentler*). You shouldn't be up. The doctor told you to stay in bed. (*She bends over Marica and gently takes the bottle out of the girl's hand.*) It was poison. I thought so.

Marica (*frightened*). You won't tell the priest, will you?

Raquel. Suicide is a sin, Marica. A sin against God.

Marica. I know. I . . . (*She catches* Raquel's *hand.*) Oh, Raquel, why do we have to have wars? Why do men have to go to war and be killed?

Raquel. Men must fight for what they believe is right. It is an honorable thing to die for your country as a soldier.

Marica. How can you say that with Domingo out there fighting, too? And fighting what? Men who aren't even men. Peasants. Ranch slaves. Men who shouldn't be allowed to fight.

Raquel. Peasants are men, Marica. Not animals.

Marica. Men. It's always men. But how about the women? What becomes of us?

Raquel. We can pray.

Marica (*bitterly*). Yes, we can pray. And then comes the terrible news, and it's no use praying anymore. All the reason for our praying is dead. Why should I go on living with Tomás dead?

Raquel. Living is a duty.

Marica. How can you be so cold, so hard? You are a cold and hard woman, Raquel. My brother worships you. He has never even looked at another woman since the first day he saw you. Does he know how cold and hard you are?

Raquel. Domingo is my—honored husband.

Marica. You've been married for ten years. And I've been married for three months. If Domingo is killed, it won't be the same for you. You've had ten years. (*She is crying wildly.*) I haven't anything . . . anything at all.

Raquel. You've had three months—three months of laughter. And now you have tears. How lucky you are. You have tears. Perhaps five months of tears. Not more. You're only twenty. In five months Tomás will become just a lovely memory.

Marica. I'll remember Tomás all my life.

Raquel. Of course. But he'll be distant and far

WORDS TO KNOW   **stealthily** (stĕl'thə-lē) *adv.* in a quiet, cautious, or secretive manner intended to avoid notice

away. But you're young . . . and the young need laughter. The young can't live on tears. And one day in Paris, or Rome, or even Mexico City, you'll meet another man. You'll marry again. There will be children in your house. How lucky you are.

Marica. I'll never marry again.

Raquel. You're only twenty. You'll think differently when you're twenty-eight, or nine, or thirty.

Marica. What will you do if Domingo is killed?

Raquel. I shall be very proud that he died in all his courage . . . in all the greatness of a hero.

Marica. But you'd not weep, would you? Not you! I don't think there are any tears in you.

Raquel. No, I'd not weep. I'd sit here in this empty house and wait.

Marica. Wait for what?

Raquel. For the jingle of his spurs as he walks across the tiled hall. For the sound of his laughter in the patio. For the echo of his voice as he shouts to the groom to put away his horse. For the feel of his hand . . .

Marica (*screams*). Stop it!

Raquel. I'm sorry.

Marica. You do love him, don't you?

Raquel. I don't think even he knows how much.

Marica. I thought that after ten years people slid away from love. But you and Domingo—why, you're all he thinks about. When he's away from you he talks about you all the time. I heard him say once that when you were out of his sight he was like a man without eyes or ears or hands.

Raquel. I know. I, too, know that feeling.

Marica. Then how could you let him go to war? Perhaps to be killed? How could you?

Raquel (*sharply*). Marica, you are of the family Macías. Your family is a family of great warriors. A Macías man was with Ferdinand when the Moors[1] were driven out of Spain. A Macías man was with Cortés when the Aztecans[2] surrendered. Your grandfather fought in the War of Independence.[3] Your own father was executed not twenty miles from this house by the French. Shall his son be any less brave because he loves a woman?

Marica. But Domingo loved you enough to forget that. If you had asked him, he wouldn't have gone to war. He would have stayed here with you.

Raquel. No, he would not have stayed. Your brother is a man of honor, not a whining, creeping coward.

Marica (*beginning to cry again*). I begged Tomás not to go. I begged him.

Raquel. Would you have loved him if he had stayed?

Marica. I don't know. I don't know.

Raquel. There is your answer. You'd have despised him. Loved and despised him. Now come, Marica, it's time for you to go to bed.

Marica. You won't tell the priest—about the poison, I mean?

Raquel. No. I won't tell him.

Marica. Thank you, Raquel. How good you are. How kind and good.

Raquel. A moment ago I was hard and cruel. What a baby you are. Now, off to bed with you.

Marica. Aren't you coming upstairs, too?

Raquel. No . . . I haven't been sleeping very well lately. I think I'll read for a little while.

Marica. Good night, Raquel. And thank you.

---

1. **Moors:** Moslem people from northwest Africa whose kingdom in Spain was defeated by Ferdinand of Aragon in 1492.

2. **Aztecans** (ăz′těk′ənz): people who lived in central Mexico and had an advanced civilization before the conquest of Mexico by Cortés in 1519.

3. **War of Independence:** the revolution (1810–1821) in which Mexico gained its independence from Spain.

Raquel. Good night, little one.

(Marica *goes out through the house door left, taking her candle with her.* Raquel *stares down at the bottle of poison in her hand, then puts it away in one of the small drawers of the desk. She next selects a book from the downstage case and sits on the sofa to read it, but feeling chilly, she rises and goes to the closet, back right, and takes out an afghan.*[4] *Coming back to the sofa, she makes herself comfortable, with the afghan across her knees. Suddenly she hears a noise in the patio. She listens, then, convinced it is nothing, returns to her reading. But she hears the noise again. She goes to the patio door and peers out.*)

Raquel (*calling softly*). Who's there? Who's out there? Oh! (*She gasps and backs into the room. Two men—or rather a man and a young boy—dressed in the white pajama suits of the Mexican peasants, with their sombreros*[5] *tipped low over their faces, come into the room.* Raquel *draws herself up* <u>regally</u>. *Her voice is cold and commanding.*) Who are you, and what do you want here?

Andrés. We are hunting for the wife of General Macías.

Raquel. I am Raquel Rivera de Macías.

Andrés. Cleto, stand guard in the patio. If you hear any suspicious noise, warn me at once.

Cleto. Yes, my captain. (*The boy returns to the patio.*)

(*The man, hooking his thumbs in his belt, strolls around the room, looking it over. When he reaches the table at the back he sees the wine. With a small bow to* Raquel *he pours himself a glass of wine and drains it. He wipes his mouth with the back of his hand.*)

Raquel. How very interesting.

Andrés (*startled*). What?

Raquel. To be able to drink wine with that hat on.

Andrés. The hat? Oh, forgive me, señora. (*He flicks the brim with his fingers so that it drops off his head and dangles down his back from the neck cord.*) In a military camp one forgets one's polite manners. Would you care to join me in another glass?

Raquel (*sitting on the sofa*). Why not? It's my wine.

Andrés. And very excellent wine. (*He pours two glasses and gives her one while he is talking.*) I would say amontillado of the vintage of '87.[6]

Raquel. Did you learn that in a military camp?

Andrés. I used to sell wines . . . among other things.

Raquel (*ostentatiously hiding a yawn*). I am devastated.

Andrés (*pulls over the armchair and makes himself comfortable in it*). You don't mind, do you?

Raquel. Would it make any difference if I did?

Andrés. No. The Federals are searching the streets for us, and we have to stay somewhere. But women of your class seem to expect that senseless sort of question.

Raquel. Of course I suppose I could scream.

Andrés. Naturally.

Raquel. My sister-in-law is upstairs asleep. And there are several servants in the back of the house. Mostly men servants. Very big men.

Andrés. Very interesting. (*He is drinking the wine in small sips with much enjoyment.*)

Raquel. What would you do if I screamed?

Andrés (*considering the request as though it were another glass of wine*). Nothing.

Raquel. I am afraid you are lying to me.

Andrés. Women of your class seem to expect polite little lies.

---

4. *afghan* (ăf′găn): a crocheted or knitted blanket.

5. *sombreros* (sŏm-brâr′ōz): broad-brimmed, high-crowned straw or felt hats, traditionally worn by peasants in Mexico.

6. **amontillado** (ə-mŏn′tl-ä′dō) . . . '87: a pale, dry sherry bottled in 1887.

Raquel. Stop calling me "woman of your class."

Andrés. Forgive me.

Raquel. You are one of the fighting peasants, aren't you?

Andrés. I am a captain in the revolutionary army.

Raquel. This house is completely loyal to the federal government.

Andrés. I know. That's why I'm here.

Raquel. And now that you are here, just what do you expect me to do?

Andrés. I expect you to offer sanctuary to myself and to Cleto.

Raquel. Cleto? (*She looks toward the patio and adds sarcastically.*) Oh, your army.

Cleto (*appearing in the doorway*). I'm sorry, my captain. I just heard a noise. (Raquel *stands.* Andrés *moves quickly to her and puts his hands on her arms from the back.* Cleto *has turned and is peering into the patio.* Then the boy relaxes.) We are still safe, my captain. It was only a rabbit. (*He goes back into the patio.* Raquel *pulls away from* Andrés *and goes to the desk.*)

Raquel. What a magnificent army you have. So clever. I'm sure you must win many victories.

Andrés. We do. And we will win the greatest victory, remember that.

Raquel. This farce has gone on long enough. Will you please take your army and climb over the patio wall with it?

Andrés. I told you that we came here so that you could give us sanctuary.

Raquel. My dear captain—captain without a name . . .

Andrés. Andrés de la O, your servant. (*He makes a bow.*)

Raquel (*startled*). Andrés de la O!

Andrés. I am flattered. You have heard of me.

Raquel. Naturally. Everyone in the city has heard of you. You have a reputation for politeness—especially to women.

Andrés. I see that the tales about me have lost nothing in the telling.

Raquel. I can't say. I'm not interested in gossip about your type of soldier.

Andrés. Then let me give you something to heighten your interest. (*He suddenly takes her in his arms and kisses her. She stiffens for a moment, then remains perfectly still. He steps away from her.*)

Raquel (*rage forcing her to whisper*). Get out of here—at once!

Andrés (*staring at her in admiration*). I can understand why Macías loves you. I couldn't before, but now I can understand it.

Raquel. Get out of my house.

Andrés. (*Sits on the sofa and pulls a small leather pouch out of his shirt. He pours its contents into his hand.*) So cruel, señora, and I with a present for you? Here is a holy medal. My mother gave me this medal. She died when I was ten. She was a street beggar. She died of starvation. But I wasn't there. I was in jail. I had been sentenced to five years in prison for stealing five oranges. The judge thought it was a great joke. One year for each orange. He laughed. He had a very loud laugh. (*pause*) I killed him two months ago. I hanged him to the telephone pole in front of his house. And I laughed. (*pause*) I also have a very loud laugh. (Raquel *abruptly turns her back on him.*) I told that story to a girl the other night, and she thought it very funny. But of course she was a peasant girl—a girl who could neither read nor write. She hadn't been born in a great house in Tabasco. She didn't have an English governess. She didn't go to school to the nuns in Paris. She didn't marry one of the richest young men in the republic. But she thought my story very funny. Of course she could understand it. Her brother had been whipped to death because he had run away from the plantation that owned him. (*He pauses and looks at her. She does not move.*) Are you still angry with me? Even though I have brought you a present? (*He holds out his hand.*) A very nice present—from your husband.

Raquel (*turns and stares at him in amazement*). A present! From Domingo?

Andrés. I don't know him that well. I call him the general Macías.

Raquel (*excitedly*). Is he well? How does he look? (*with horrified comprehension*) He's a prisoner . . . your prisoner!

Andrés. Naturally. That's why I know so much about you. He talks about you constantly.

Raquel. You know nothing about him. You're lying to me. (Cleto *comes to the window.*)

Andrés. I assure you, señora . . .

Cleto (*interrupting*). My captain . . .

Andrés. What is it Cleto? Another rabbit?

Cleto. No, my captain. There are soldiers at the end of the street. They are searching all the houses. They will be here soon.

Andrés. Don't worry. We are quite safe here. Stay in the patio until I call you.

Cleto. Yes, my captain. (*He returns to the patio.*)

Raquel. You are not safe here. When those soldiers come I shall turn you over to them.

Andrés. I think not.

Raquel. You can't escape from them. And they are not kind to you peasant prisoners. They have good reason not to be.

Andrés. Look at this ring. (*He holds his hand out, with the ring on his palm.*)

Raquel. Why, it's—a wedding ring.

Andrés. Read the inscription inside of it. (*As she hesitates, he adds sharply.*) Read it!

Raquel (*Slowly takes the ring. While she is reading, her voice fades to a whisper.*) "D.M.—R.R.—June 2, 1902." Where did you get this?

Andrés. General Macías gave it to me.

Raquel (*firmly and clearly*). Not this ring. He'd never give you this ring. (*with dawning horror*) He's dead. You stole it from his dead finger. He's dead.

Andrés. Not yet. But he will be dead if I don't return to camp safely by sunset tomorrow.

Raquel. I don't believe you. I don't believe you. You're lying to me.

Andrés. This house is famous for its loyalty to the federal government. You will hide me until those soldiers get out of this district. When it is safe enough, Cleto and I will leave. But if you betray me to them, your husband will be shot tomorrow evening at sunset. Do you understand? (*He shakes her arm.* Raquel *looks dazedly at him.* Cleto *comes to the window.*)

Cleto. The soldiers are coming closer, my captain. They are at the next house.

Andrés (*to* Raquel). Where shall we hide? (Raquel *is still dazed. He gives her another little shake.*) Think, woman! If you love your husband at all—think!

Raquel. I don't know. Marica upstairs—the servants in the rest of the house—I don't know.

Andrés. The general has bragged to us about you. He says you are braver than most men. He says you are very clever. This is a time to be both brave and clever.

Cleto (*pointing to the closet*). What door is that?

Raquel. It's a closet . . . a storage closet.

Andrés. We'll hide in there.

Raquel. It's very small. It's not big enough for both of you.

Andrés. Cleto, hide yourself in there.

Cleto. But, my captain . . .

Andrés. That's an order! Hide yourself.

Cleto. Yes, sir. (*He steps inside the closet.*)

Formation of Revolutionary Leadership (1926–1927), Diego Rivera. Fresco, 354 cm × 555 cm, Universidad Autónoma de Chapingo (Mexico), Chapel. Photo Copyright © 1995 Dirk Bakker / The Detroit Institute of Arts.

Andrés. And now, señora, where are you going to hide me?

Raquel. How did you persuade my husband to give you his ring?

Andrés. That's a very long story, señora, for which we have no time just now. (*He puts the ring and medal back in the pouch and thrusts it inside his shirt.*) Later I will be glad to give you all the details. But at present it is only necessary for you to remember that his life depends upon mine.

Raquel. Yes—yes, of course. (*She loses her dazed expression and seems to grow more queenly as she takes command of the situation.*) Give me your hat. (*Andrés shrugs and passes it over to her. She takes it to the closet and hands it to Cleto.*) There is a smoking jacket[7] hanging up in there. Hand it to me. (*Cleto hands her a man's velvet smoking jacket. She brings it to Andrés.*) Put this on.

Andrés (*puts it on and looks down at himself*). Such a pity my shoes are not comfortable slippers.

Raquel. Sit in that chair. (*She points to the armchair.*)

Andrés. My dear lady . . .

Raquel. If I must save your life, allow me to do it in my own way. Sit down. (*Andrés sits. She picks up the afghan from the couch and throws it over his feet and legs, carefully tucking it in so that his body is covered to the waist.*) If anyone speaks to you, don't answer. Don't turn your head. As far as you are concerned, there is no one in this room—not even me. Just look straight ahead of you and . . .

Andrés (*as she pauses*). And what?

Raquel. I started to say "and pray," but since you're a member of the revolutionary army, I don't suppose you believe in God and prayer.

Andrés. My mother left me a holy medal.

Raquel. Oh, yes, I remember. A very amusing story. (*There is the sound of men's voices in*

---

7. **smoking jacket:** a man's evening jacket, often made of fine fabric, and usually worn at home.

the patio.) The federal soldiers are here. If you can pray, ask God to keep Marica upstairs. She is very young and very stupid. She'll betray you before I can shut her mouth.

Andrés. I'll . . .

Raquel. Silence! Stare straight ahead of you and pray. (*She goes to the French window and speaks loudly to the soldiers.*) Really! What is the meaning of this uproar?

Flores (*off*). Do not alarm yourself, señora. (*He comes into the room. He wears the uniform of a federal officer.*) I am Captain Basilio Flores, at your service, señora.

Raquel. What do you mean, invading my house and making so much noise at this hour of the night?

Flores. We are hunting for two spies. One of them is the notorious Andrés de la O. You may have heard of him, señora.

Raquel (*looking at* Andrés). Considering what he did to my cousin—yes, I've heard of him.

Flores. Your cousin, señora?

Raquel. (*Comes to* Andrés *and puts her hand on his shoulder. He stares woodenly in front of him.*) Felipe was his prisoner before the poor boy managed to escape.

Flores. Is it possible? (*He crosses to* Andrés.) Captain Basilio Flores, at your service. (*He salutes.*)

Raquel. Felipe doesn't hear you. He doesn't even know you are in the room.

Flores. Eh, it is a sad thing.

Raquel. Must your men make so much noise?

Flores. The hunt must be thorough, señora. And now if some of my men can go through here to the rest of the house . . .

Raquel. Why?

Flores. But I told you, señora. We are hunting for two spies . . .

Raquel (*speaking quickly from controlled nervousness*). And do you think I have them hidden

someplace, and I the wife of General Macías?

Flores. General Macías! But I didn't know . . .

Raquel. Now that you do know, I suggest you remove your men and their noise at once.

Flores. But, señora, I regret—I still have to search this house.

Raquel. I can assure you, captain, that I have been sitting here all evening, and no peasant spy has passed me and gone into the rest of the house.

Flores. Several rooms open off the patio, señora. They needn't have come through here.

Raquel. So . . . you do think I conceal spies in this house. Then search it by all means. Look under the sofa . . . under the table. In the drawers of the desk. And don't miss that closet, captain. Inside that closet is hidden a very fierce and wicked spy.

Flores. Please, señora . . .

Raquel (*goes to the closet door*). Or do you prefer me to open it for you?

Flores. I am only doing my duty, señora. You are making it very difficult.

Raquel (*relaxing against the door*). I'm sorry. My sister-in-law is upstairs. She has just received word that her husband has been killed. They were married three months ago. She's only twenty. I didn't want . . .

Marica (*calling off*). Raquel, what is all that noise downstairs?

Raquel (*goes to the house door and calls*). It is nothing. Go back to bed.

Marica. But I can hear men's voices in the patio.

Raquel. It is only some federal soldiers hunting for two peasant spies. (*She turns and speaks rapidly to* Flores.) If she comes down here, she must not see my cousin. Felipe escaped, but her husband was killed. The doctor thinks the sight of my poor cousin might affect her mind. You understand?

Flores. Certainly, señora. What a sad thing.

Marica (*still off*). Raquel, I'm afraid! (*She tries to* *push past* Raquel *into the room.* Raquel *and* Flores *stand between her and* Andrés.) Spies! In this house. Oh, Raquel!

Raquel. The doctor will be very angry if you don't return to bed at once.

Marica. But those terrible men will kill us. What is the matter with you two? Why are you standing there like that? (*She tries to see past them, but they both move so that she can't see* Andrés.)

Flores. It is better that you go back to your room, señora.

Marica. But why? Upstairs I am alone. Those terrible men will kill me. I know they will.

Flores. Don't be afraid, señora. There are no spies in this house.

Marica. Are you sure?

Raquel. Captain Flores means that no spy would dare to take refuge in the house of General Macías. Isn't that right, captain?

Flores (*laughing*). Of course. All the world knows of the brave General Macías.

Raquel. Now go back to bed, Marica. Please, for my sake.

Marica. You are both acting very strangely. I think you have something hidden in this room you don't want me to see.

Raquel (*sharply*). You are quite right. Captain Flores has captured one of the spies. He is sitting in the chair behind me. He is dead. Now will you please go upstairs!

Marica (*gives a stifled sob*). Oh! That such a terrible thing could happen in this house. (*She runs out of the room, still sobbing.*)

Flores (*worried*). Was it wise to tell her such a story, señora?

Raquel (*tense with repressed relief*). Better that than the truth. Good night, captain, and thank you.

Flores. Good night, señora. And don't worry. Those spies won't bother you. If they were anywhere in this district, my men would have found them.

Raquel. I'm sure of it.

(*The* Captain *salutes her, looks toward* Andrés, *and salutes him, then goes into the patio. He can be heard calling his men. Neither* Andrés *nor* Raquel *moves until the voices outside go away. Then* Raquel *staggers and nearly falls, but* Andrés *catches her in time.*)

Andrés (*calling softly*). They've gone, Cleto. (Andrés *carries* Raquel *to the sofa as* Cleto *comes out of the closet.*) Bring a glass of wine. Quickly.

Cleto (*as he gets the wine*). What happened?

Andrés. It's nothing. Just a faint. (*He holds the wine to her lips.*)

Cleto. She's a great lady, that one. When she wanted to open the closet door, my knees were trembling, I can tell you.

Andrés. My own bones were playing a pretty tune.

Cleto. Why do you think she married Macías?

Andrés. Love is a peculiar thing, Cleto.

Cleto. I don't understand it.

Raquel (*moans and sits up*). Are they—are they gone?

Andrés. Yes, they're gone. (*He kisses her hand.*) I've never known a braver lady.

Raquel (*pulling her hand away*). Will you go now, please?

Andrés. We'll have to wait until the district is free of them—but if you'd like to write a letter to your husband while we're waiting . . .

Raquel (*surprised at his kindness*). You'd take it to him? You'd really give it to him?

Andrés. Of course.

Raquel. Thank you. (*She goes to the writing desk and sits down.*)

Andrés (*to* Cleto, *who has been staring steadily at* Raquel *all the while*). You stay here with the señora. I'm going to find out how much of the district has been cleared.

Cleto (*still staring at* Raquel). Yes, my captain.

(Andrés *leaves by the French windows.* Cleto *keeps on staring at* Raquel *as she starts to write. After a moment she turns to him.*)

Raquel (*irritated*). Why do you keep staring at me?

Cleto. Why did you marry a man like that one, señora?

Raquel. You're very impertinent.[8]

Cleto (*shyly*). I'm sorry, señora.

Raquel (*after a brief pause*). What do you mean: "a man like that one"?

Cleto. Well, you're very brave, señora.

Raquel (*lightly*). And don't you think the general is very brave?

Cleto. No, señora. Not very.

Raquel (*staring at him with bewilderment*). What are you trying to tell me?

Cleto. Nothing, señora. It is none of my affair.

Raquel. Come here. (*He comes slowly up to her.*) Tell me what is in your mind.

Cleto. I don't know, señora. I don't understand it. The captain says love is a peculiar thing, but I don't understand it.

Raquel. Cleto, did the general willingly give that ring to your captain?

Cleto. Yes, señora.

Raquel. Why?

Cleto. The general wanted to save his own life. He said he loved you and he wanted to save his life.

Raquel. How would giving that ring to your captain save the general's life?

Cleto. The general's supposed to be shot tomorrow afternoon. But he's talked about you a lot, and when my captain knew we had to come into the city, he thought perhaps we might take refuge here if the Federals got on our trail. So he went to the general and said that if he fixed it so we'd be safe here, my captain would save him from the firing squad.

Raquel. Was your trip here to the city very important—to your cause, I mean?

Cleto. Indeed yes, señora. The captain got a lot of fine information. It means we'll win the next big battle. My captain is a very clever man, señora.

Raquel. Did the general know about this information when he gave his ring to your captain?

Cleto. I don't see how he could help knowing it, señora. He heard us talking about it enough.

Raquel. Who knows about that bargain to save the general's life beside you and your captain?

Cleto. No one, señora. The captain isn't one to talk, and I didn't have time to.

Raquel (*While the boy has been talking, the life seems to have drained completely out of her*). How old are you, Cleto?

Cleto. I don't know, señora. I think I'm twenty, but I don't know.

Raquel (*speaking more to herself than to him*). Tomás was twenty.

Cleto. Who is Tomás?

Raquel. He was married to my sister-in-law. Cleto, you think my husband is a coward, don't you?

Cleto (*with embarrassment*). Yes, señora.

Raquel. You don't think any woman is worth it, do you? Worth the price of a great battle, I mean?

Cleto. No, señora. But as the captain says, love is a very peculiar thing.

Raquel. If your captain loved a woman as much as the general loves me, would he have given an enemy his ring?

Cleto. Ah, but the captain is a great man, señora.

Raquel. And so is my husband a great man. He is of the family Macías. All of that family have been great men. All of them—brave and honorable men. They have always held their honor to be greater than their lives. That is a tradition of their family.

Cleto. Perhaps none of them loved a woman like you, señora.

---

8. **impertinent** (ĭm-pûr′tn-ənt): improperly bold or forward.

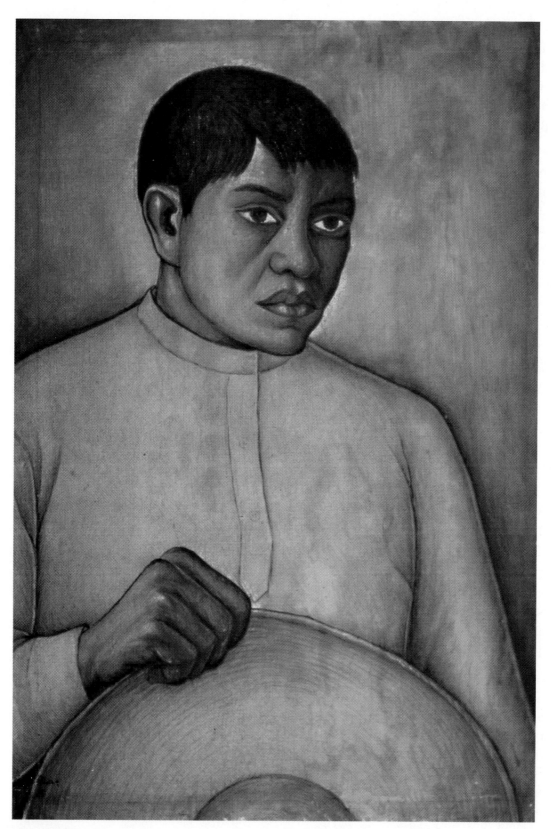

Peasant with Sombrero (1926), Diego Rivera.

Raquel. How strange you are. I saved you from the Federals because I want to save my husband's life. You call me brave, and yet you call him a coward. There is no difference in what we have done.

Cleto. But you are a woman, señora.

Raquel. Has a woman less honor than a man, then?

Cleto. No, señora. Please, I don't know how to say it. The general is a soldier. He has a duty to his own cause. You are a woman. You have a duty to your husband. It is right that you should try to save him. It is not right that he should try to save himself.

Raquel (*dully*). Yes, of course. It is right that I should save him. (*becoming practical again*) Your captain has been gone some time, Cleto. You'd better find out if he is still safe.

Cleto. Yes, señora. (*As he reaches the French windows, she stops him.*)

Raquel. Wait, Cleto. Have you a mother—or a wife, perhaps?

Cleto. Oh, no, señora. I haven't anyone but the captain.

Raquel. But the captain is a soldier. What would you do if he should be killed?

Cleto. It is very simple, señora. I should be killed, too.

Raquel. You speak about death so calmly. Aren't you afraid of it, Cleto?

Cleto. No, señora. It's like the captain says . . . dying for what you believe in—that's the finest death of all.

Raquel. And you believe in the revolutionary cause?

Cleto. Yes, señora. I am a poor peasant, that's true. But still I have a right to live like a man, with my own ground, and my own family, and my own future. (*He stops speaking abruptly.*) I'm sorry, señora. You are a fine lady. You don't understand these things. I must go and find my captain. (*He goes out.*)

Raquel (*rests her face against her hand*). He's so

young. But Tomás was no older. And he's not afraid. He said so. Oh, Domingo—Domingo! (*She straightens abruptly, takes the bottle of poison from the desk drawer and stares at it. Then she crosses to the decanter and laces the wine with the poison. She hurries back to the desk and is busy writing when* Andrés *and Cleto return.*)

Andrés. You'll have to hurry that letter. The district is clear now.

Raquel. I'll be through in just a moment. You might as well finish the wine while you're waiting.

Andrés. Thank you. A most excellent idea. (*He pours himself a glass of wine. As he lifts it to his lips, she speaks.*)

Raquel. Why don't you give some to—Cleto?

Andrés. This is too fine a wine to waste on that boy.

Raquel. He'll probably never have another chance to taste such wine.

Andrés. Very well. Pour yourself a glass, Cleto.

Cleto. Thank you. (*He pours it.*) Your health, my captain.

Raquel (*quickly*). Drink it outside, Cleto. I want to speak to your captain. (*The boy looks at* Andrés, *who jerks his head toward the patio.* Cleto *nods and goes out.*) I want you to give my husband a message for me. I can't write it. You'll have to remember it. But first, give me a glass of wine, too.

Andrés (*pouring the wine*). It might be easier for him if you wrote it.

Raquel. I think not. (*She takes the glass.*) I want you to tell him that I never knew how much I loved him until tonight.

Andrés. Is that all?

Raquel. Yes. Tell me, captain, do you think it possible to love a person too much?

Andrés. Yes, señora. I do.

Raquel. So do I. Let us drink a

toast, captain—to honor. To bright and shining honor.

Andrés (*raises his glass*). To honor. (*He drains his glass. She lifts hers almost to her lips and then puts it down. From the patio comes a faint cry.*)

Cleto (*calling faintly in a cry that fades into silence*). Captain. Captain.

(Andrés *sways, his hand trying to brush across his face as though trying to brush sense into his head. When he hears* Cleto *he tries to stagger toward the window but stumbles and can't quite make it. Hanging on to the table by the sofa he looks accusingly at her. She shrinks back against her chair.*)

Andrés (*his voice weak from the poison*). Why?

Raquel. Because I love him. Can you understand that?

Andrés. We'll win. The revolution will win. You can't stop that.

Raquel. Yes, you'll win. I know that now.

Andrés. That girl—she thought my story was funny—about the hanging. But you didn't . . .

Raquel. I'm glad you hanged him. I'm glad.

(Andrés *looks at her and tries to smile. He manages to pull the pouch from his shirt and extend it to her. But it drops from his hand.*)

Raquel (*runs to French window and calls*). Cleto. Cleto! (*She buries her face in her hands for a moment, then comes back to* Andrés. *She kneels beside him and picks up the leather pouch. She opens it and, taking the ring, puts it on her finger. Then she sees the medal. She rises, and, pulling out the chain from her own throat, she slides the medal on to the chain. Then she walks to the sofa and sinks down on it.*)

Marica (*calling off*). Raquel! Raquel! (Raquel *snaps off the lamp, leaving the room in darkness.* Marica *opens the house door. She is carrying a candle which she shades with her hand. The light is too dim to reveal the dead* Andrés.) What are you doing down here in the dark? Why don't you come to bed?

Raquel (*making an effort to speak*). I'll come in just a moment.

Marica. But what are you doing, Raquel?

Raquel. Nothing. Just listening . . . listening to an empty house.

(Quick curtain)

RESPONDING
OPTIONS

FROM PERSONAL RESPONSE TO CRITICAL ANALYSIS

REFLECT   **1.** What was your response to Raquel's final act? Share your response with a classmate.

RETHINK   **2.** Why do you think Raquel poisons Andrés and Cleto, even though she knows that her husband will die if they do not return?
Consider
- how her actions will affect the war
- Raquel's conversation with Cleto on page 880
- General Macías's bargain and who knows about it
- Raquel's feelings about her husband and about honor

3. Why do you think Raquel agrees with Andrés that "the revolution will win"?
Consider
- her conversation with Marica on pages 872–873
- what she learns about Andrés and Cleto
- what she realizes about the two sides in the war

4. What do Andrés and General Macías have in common, and what sets them apart? Use details from the play to support your opinion.

5. Which characters in the play live—or die—with honor? You might find it helpful to review the spider map you created for the Personal Connection on page 869.

6. In your opinion, who is the most admirable character in the play? Explain your views.

RELATE   **7.** Do you think people today are still willing to die for an honorable cause? Share your ideas, using examples.

ANOTHER PATHWAY
Cooperative Learning

Imagine that your class is staging this play. With a group of classmates, create a set of director's notes for each character in the play. Provide information that will help the actors understand their characters and what motivates them to speak and act as they do.

QUICKWRITES

1. Raquel started a letter to her husband near the end of the play. Write the complete **letter** she might have written if she had had the time to finish it.

2. Write a **psychological profile** of one of the characters on the basis of information presented in the play.

3. Write the **speech** Andrés might give to the Mexican people urging their involvement in the Revolution.

PORTFOLIO Save your writing. You may want to use it later as a springboard to a piece for your portfolio.

LITERARY CONCEPTS

A **foil** is a minor character who provides a striking contrast to a main character. A writer might use a foil to emphasize certain traits possessed by a main character or simply to set off or enhance the main character through contrast. What do you think Niggli emphasizes about Raquel by presenting Marica as her foil?

CONCEPT REVIEW: Verbal Irony Verbal irony occurs when a character says one thing and means another. Find examples of verbal irony in the play.

ALTERNATIVE ACTIVITIES

1. Make **sketches** of costumes or of a set design to be used in a production of the play.
2. Create a **poster** to advertise a production of the play.

LITERARY LINKS

Do you think that *The Ring of General Macías* and "Two Friends" (page 567) present similar views of honor? Why or why not?

ACROSS THE CURRICULUM

Film To learn more about the peasant uprising in the Mexican Revolution, watch a videocassette recording of the 1952 film *Viva Zapata!*

WORDS TO KNOW

Review the Words to Know at the bottom of the selection pages. Then write the word that best completes each sentence.

1. After entering Raquel's house, Andrés offends Raquel by acting _____; he drinks her wine and even kisses her, as if boasting of his charms.

2. Even though she knows the revolutionary soldiers threaten her entire way of life, she reacts as if they are absurd and their revolution is a _____.

3. Her lifestyle, her way of carrying herself, and her attitude all indicate that she is used to ruling her home _____ and will tolerate no insult.

4. She is quite open, at first, about her refusal to allow the revolutionaries to use her home as a _____ to escape the federalists.

5. In the end, it is not what she does obviously but what she does _____ that causes their downfall.

JOSEPHINA NIGGLI

Josephina Niggli (1910–1983) was born in the city of Monterrey in northeastern Mexico and lived there for several years before moving with her family to San Antonio, Texas. Fluent in both Spanish and English, Niggli was educated at home until she reached high school age. After obtaining her bachelor's degree, she studied drama in graduate school, where she wrote and saw produced two of her full-length plays as well as a number of the one-act plays for which she is now better known. She acted in several of the productions herself and even directed a few.

Josephina Niggli also published books about how to write stage and radio plays. She spent two years in Hollywood as a screenwriter for MGM Studios. Her plays, stories, and novels, which were written in English, have won praise for their memorable characters and vivid portrayals of Mexican history and village life.

OTHER WORKS *Mexican Silhouettes; Mexican Folk Plays; Mexican Village; Step Down, Elder Brother; A Miracle for Mexico*

LASERLINKS
• *ART GALLERY*

Gift from

Eric Lund at age 18, 1968. Courtesy of Doris Lund.

Doris Herold Lund
United States

a Son Who Died

At 17, Eric Lund was stricken with leukemia, a form of cancer in which white blood cells, which defend the body against infection, grow in an uncontrolled manner. Although leukemia can sometimes be successfully treated with drug therapy, in Eric's case the disease proved fatal. In this essay, Eric's mother describes her son's four-and-a-half-year battle with the disease and his eventual acceptance of his fate.

It's not the way I thought it would be. I thought the sun and the moon would go out. I thought joy itself would die when Eric died. He had given so much to all of us—his family, friends, the girl he loved. And yet his death is not the end of joy after all. It's somehow another beginning. . . .

Eric died at 22, after a four-and-a-half-year struggle with leukemia. While he left us with the deep bruises of grief, he left us so much more. So much to celebrate! There's a victory here that I'm still trying to understand. Why do I, even in loss, feel stronger? Why does life on this untidy, dangerous planet seem more wonderfully precious? I am conscious now of the value of each good moment, the importance of wasting nothing.

These things are Eric's gifts to me. They weren't easily bought or quickly accepted. And not all came tied with ribbons; many were delivered with blows. In addition to leukemia,

Eric was suffering from adolescence. And there were times when this condition took more out of us than his other one. A 17-year-old boy who may not live to become a man is suddenly in a great hurry. Like a militant new nation, he wants instant independence and no compromises. After the first few weeks Eric quickly took charge of his illness. I was no longer to talk to the doctors. In fact—the message came through clearly—I was no longer to talk at all unless I could avoid sounding like a worried mother.

Perhaps it would have been different if we'd had a chance to prepare for what was coming, but there was no beginning. It was a thunderbolt from a cloudless sky.

We live in a small Connecticut town, just a block from the beach. This had been a summer like many others. The front hall was, as usual, full of sand and kicked-off sneakers, mysterious towels that didn't belong to us, an assortment of swimming fins and soccer balls. By September, I, like many mothers, was half longing for school to start and half dreading it. Our 20-year-old daughter had married, and now Eric was packed and ready to go off for his freshman year at the University of Connecticut. But ten-year-old Lisa and 14-year-old Mark would still be at home. I kept telling myself how lucky I'd be to have less laundry and fewer cookie crumbs to contend with. But I didn't exactly believe it.

One afternoon Eric and I both wanted the car at the same moment. "I've *got* to run at the track, Mom." He was wearing his soccer shorts and running shoes. "I've only got two more days before school starts, and I'm not in shape."

I knew how much he wanted to make the freshman soccer team when he got to college, but I had work to do. "I have to go to the printer," I said. "But I'll drop you off at the field and pick you up later."

"Okay." He scowled a bit at the compromise. As we drove off together with the top down, the late summer sun poured over our shoulders, turning Eric's hair to yellow curly flames. His eyebrows were sunburned almost white, and the hairs on his powerful legs gleamed gold against deep tan. Then I noticed something on his leg— an ugly red sore, big and round as a silver dollar. There was another farther down. And another on his other leg.

"Eric! What have you got on your legs?"

"Dunno. Little infection maybe."

"It doesn't look little to me," I protested. "Impetigo[1] is what it looks like. We'd better go right over to the doctor's office."

"Mom! For God's sake!" He was furious.

"Eric," I said. "Impetigo spreads like mad. If that's what it is, they aren't even going to let you into the locker room. We've got two days before you go. Let's get the doctor to clear it up now."

"All right," he said dully.

The sores did not look like impetigo to our doctor. He told his secretary to call the hospital and arrange to have Eric admitted next morning for tests. "Be there at eight, Eric," he said. My son nodded and swung through the waiting room, full of mothers and toddlers, slamming the door behind him.

"What tests?" I turned to the doctor. Eric had had a complete physical, required of all freshmen, only 12 days before. Blood tests, too. He'd passed with flying colors.

"I want them to rerun some of the blood tests," said the doctor. "I've also ordered a bone marrow—"[2]

I blanked out the words "bone marrow" as if I'd never heard them. After all, I thought as we drove home, he'd just had that perfect physical. . . .

---

1. **impetigo** (ĭm′pĭ-tī′gō): a contagious skin infection.
2. **a bone marrow:** The doctor is referring to a test of the soft tissue that produces red blood cells and is found in the center of bones.

et the next afternoon when the phone rang and the doctor was saying, "I'd like to talk to you and your husband together—" I knew at once. "You don't have to tell me," I said. "I know. Eric has leukemia."

I was once in a house struck by lightning. The sensation, the scene, even the strange electrical smell returned at that moment. A powerful bolt seemed to enter the top of my skull as I got the message . . . Eric had leukemia. It was happening this minute in his bones. We'd been struck.

He'd always been a fine athlete, a competitor, a runner. Now fate had tripped him; he stumbled and fell. Yet how quickly he tried to get up and join the race again! Left at home that fall, very ill, with his friends scattering to schools and jobs, he still was determined to go to college later, study hard, make the soccer team, eventually make all-American. To these goals he soon added one more—to stay alive.

We both knew that tremendous ordeals lay ahead. Leukemia, cancer of the blood, had always been a swift killer. When Eric developed the disease in 1968, doctors had just found ways to slow it down by using powerful drugs to suppress symptoms and produce periods of remission.[3] They did not know how to cure it.

There was hope, though, in the fact that Eric had a type of childhood leukemia (acute lymphocytic[4]) that was especially responsive to drug therapy. (By now, a few youngsters are actually being cured of it.) But Eric, at 17, was beyond the age of most effective treatment. Soon we discovered that his body overreacted to many of the best drugs and that the recommended high dosage, needed to destroy diseased cells, tended too quickly to wipe out healthy ones.

A powerful bolt seemed to enter the top of my skull as I got the message ... Eric had leukemia.

There were times during those first months when I saw him shaken, fighting for control. After all, it hadn't been too long since he was a small boy who could throw himself in my arms for comfort. Part of him must have been crying, "Please save me! Don't let me die!" I couldn't save him, but I could show him my own best courage. I learned to hide my concern, my tenderness, and I saw he was strengthened by my calm. He had to run free to be a man. I wanted that. If there were to be no other alternative, eventually I would help him die like a man.

We learned to be casual with danger, to live with death just around the corner. Whenever Eric was discharged from the hospital after transfusions (first they would give him two, then five, then seven), he would fly down the steps swinging a duffel bag, as if he were just back from a great weekend. I'd hand him the keys to the car, slide over, and he would pick up his life as if nothing had happened. But there were always drugs, always bouts of nausea.

I remember once starting up the stairs to bring him a cup of weak tea. He passed me on the way down wearing his swim trunks and carrying a spear gun. Ignoring the tea, he said, "Maybe I'll get you a fish for supper." He played pick-up soccer, weekend football and basketball with a hemoglobin[5] so low it left him short of breath, occasionally faint. On the basketball court, his teammates, galloping for a

---

3. **remission:** the period during which the symptoms of a disease lessen or subside.

4. **acute lymphocytic** (lĭm′fə-sīt′ĭk).

5. **a hemoglobin** (hē′mə-glō′bĭn): a count of the red blood cells, which carry oxygen from the lungs to other body tissues and carbon dioxide from the tissues to the lungs.

A member of the University of Connecticut soccer team, Eric trained during periods of remission. Courtesy of Doris Lund.

goal at the other end of the gym, would shout, "Just stay there, Eric—we'll be right back."

It was always more than a game he played. His life was on the line. "Exercise, Attitude, Desire" were the chalked words on his blackboard. These three words would bring him through. "You don't die of leuk, you know," he said once to me. "Something else goes. Your heart. Or your kidneys. I'm going to be ready for it when it comes for me. I'm going to win."

But he was not confused about the nature of his enemy—at least not by the time he'd spent some weeks on the eighth floor of Memorial Hospital's Ewing Pavilion in New York. Ewing Eight has faces, bodies you might see in pictures of the inmates of Dachau or Auschwitz.[6] Worse.

Ewing patients talk a lot about remissions, of

---

6. **Dachau** (dä′kou) **or Auschwitz** (oush′vĭts): World War II Nazi concentration camps. Prisoners were skeletally thin from starvation.

course. "Remission"—that seductive word! Hope, with the end to hope implied. Eric's remissions encouraged us to think that justice would triumph, the devil relent. Once he got an 11-month stay of execution with the drug Methotrexate. I remember looking at him that summer as he ran the beach with friends. All of them tan, glowing, happy, all with the same powerful shoulders, the same strong, brown legs. What could there be in the bones of one that differed from the others? I relaxed, reassured. He must be safe at last. The next day Memorial phoned. Eric's most recent tests had shown that his remission was at an end. Even as I watched him, wild cells had been springing up in his marrow like dragon's teeth.[7] More and then more. Always more than could be slain.

Eric endured and survived many crises. He learned to live on the edge of the ledge and not look down. Whenever he had to be in the hospital, Memorial's doctors gave him passes to escape the horror. He'd slip off his hospital bracelet (which was forbidden) and rush out to plunge into the life of the city. Crowds, shop windows, cut-rate records. Restaurants in Chinatown. Concerts in the park. Summer parties on rooftops. Dark, crazy bars. He liked the music, the talk and, when he could take it, the beer. He listened a lot but never told his own story. "Where you from?" His answer was always, "I've got my own pad on First Avenue, between 67th and 68th. Nice neighborhood— handy to everything." (Some way to describe your bed on Ewing Eight!)

Even more than exploring the city, he loved working out, trying to get back his strength on these brief passes. A pretty Memorial technician called his doctor in terror one afternoon. "I've got a date with Eric in a few minutes. What'll I do if he wants to run?" "Sit down and wait for him," came the reply. Once he went out waving good- bye to less fortunate inmates on the floor, only to return an hour later waving from the ambulance stretcher. There was no living without risks, and

so he took them. (This is one of his special gifts to me. Dare! Take life, dangers and all.)

The disease gained on him. To prevent infec- tion he was finally put in a windowless, isolated chamber, the laminar-airflow room. Sterile air, sterile everything, sterile masks, caps, gowns, gloves for anyone entering his room. He joked, played to the eager audience peering through his glass-windowed door. And then sudden severe hemorrhages.[8] Six days of unconscious- ness, soaring fevers. His white count was dan- gerously low. Platelet count[9] zero! Hemoglobin hardly worth mentioning. Surely, I thought, this is the end. But friends came, literally by bus- loads, to give blood for transfusions. During that crisis, it took more than 32 blood donors a day just to keep him alive.

I watched the doctors and nurses jabbing for veins, taping both needled arms to boards, packing the hemorrhages, shaking him to rouse him from stupor, and I thought: Enough! Let him die in peace! Why bring him back for more? He's proved himself—and beyond. He's had two good years of college. He made the soccer team in spite of your wretched drugs which are only poisons in disguise. He even made the dean's list. No more! Let him go!

But I had more to learn about my son's strength and resources. There was still much good life to be lived at the edge of the dark place. Eric came back—it seemed to me "from the unknown bourne."[10] He had to remain in the laminar-

---

7. **springing . . . dragon's teeth:** In Greek mythology, a prince sowed the teeth of a dragon he had killed, and fierce armed men sprang from the ground.

8. **hemorrhages** (hĕm'ər-ĭj-ĭz): heavy discharges of blood, often internal.

9. **white count . . . platelet** (plāt'lĭt) **count:** counts of the white blood cells and the platelets, the cells necessary for clotting.

10. **"from the unknown bourne** (bôrn)**":** A *bourne* (or *bourn*) is an ultimate limit, destination, or goal. This quotation may be a reference to a speech in Shakespeare's *Hamlet* in which Hamlet describes "something after death" as "The undiscovered country from whose bourn / No traveler returns."

airflow room, off and on, for nearly four months. The picture on page 890 was taken two days after his release. Within weeks he was running from 12 to 15 miles a day. That spring, he didn't get back to college, but in his absence they named him captain of the varsity soccer team; he received the award for the Most Improved Player and finally was listed among the All-New England All-Stars. Proud honors, justly won. And there were others. We have a bookcase full of plaques and medals.

But I treasure even more the things they don't give medals for: his irreverent[11] humor; the warmth and love and consideration he gave his friends, especially his comrades in the War on the Eighth Floor. For these last he was a jaunty[12] hero, survivor of epic battles. Yet he was always one of them; hopefully, the Golden Warrior who would lead them all to victory— or at least escape.

(He and a fellow inmate almost managed it once. Hiding themselves in laundry carts under dirty linen, they rode down nine floors on the service elevator and out to the sidewalk. Just short of being loaded with the laundry on a truck, they decided to give themselves up and go back to bone marrow, intravenous bottles, and the rest of it. There was, after all, no real way out.)

As a variation on the theme of escape, Eric invented Ralph the Camel, a melancholy dromedary who, although hospitalized for "humpomeia," somehow managed to survive all the witless treatments his doctors could devise, including daily injections of pineapple juice. Ralph starred in a series of underground comic books known as *The Adventures of Ewing 8,* which featured Memorial's top doctors, nurses, technicians, and other notables, all drawn by Eric in merciless caricature. As Dr. Bayard Clarkson put it, "Eric

> "We are all in the same boat in a stormy sea and we owe each other a terrible loyalty."

spared no one, but we could hardly wait for the next *Adventure.*" When they asked for more, his price was simple: "Get me in remission."

One of his exploits became a legend. Ten important doctors made Grand Rounds together every week. This particular Monday they stopped by the bed of their liveliest patient, to find him huddled under blankets looking unusually bleak.

"Eric! How do you feel?" asked Dr. Dowling, concerned.

"Scaly," was the mumbled reply.

Only then was the doctor's eye caught by the live goldfish swimming around in Eric's intravenous bottle. The plastic tube running down under the covers wasn't, of course, hooked up, but it looked convincing. The doctors broke up. The ward cheered! For the moment, humor had death on the run.

The eighth floor was a bad place to make friends. As one crusty old patient put it, "Make 'em and you'll lose 'em." But for Eric, there was no way to stay uninvolved. In the beginning he looked for the secrets of survival in the most spirited people around him. "That Eileen is so great," he told me. "She's beaten this thing for five years!" Or, "Look at that old guy, Mr. Miller. They just took out his spleen,[13] but he's hanging in there!"

Then, as the months of his treatments lengthened into years, he began to see them go. The good, the brave, the beautiful, the weak, the whining, the passive. They were all going the same way . . . Eileen, Mr. Miller, and

---

11. **irreverent** (ĭ-rĕv′ər-ənt): satirical; critical of what is generally accepted or respected.

12. **jaunty:** having an easy confidence; happy and carefree.

13. **spleen:** an organ that has various functions in modifying the blood as it circulates through the body.

so many more. When he was at home during one of his last remissions, he chalked up new words on his blackboard. "We are all in the same boat in a stormy sea and we owe each other a terrible loyalty" (G. K. Chesterton). Eric would not desert or fault his companions. He would play his heart out while the game might still be won, but he was beginning to think of the unthinkable. The casualty lists on the eighth floor were long. . . .

At the end, Eric finally accepted his own death. This acceptance was his last, most precious gift to me—what made my own acceptance possible. There was no bitterness. He said, simply, "There comes a time when you say: 'Well, that's it. We gave it a helluva try.'"

I remember one afternoon in Memorial a few days before he died. He wanted to talk of all the good things: the way he felt about his sisters . . . the wild, wonderful times he'd had with his brother, Mark. Suddenly he closed his eyes and said, "Running! That was so great—running on a beach for miles and miles!" He smiled, eyes still closed. "And snow! Snow was

fun—" He was summing it up, living it, feeling it all again while there was still time.

He talked on quietly, gently, in the past tense, telling me, without telling me, to be ready, to be strong.

Once, thinking the light was hurting his eyes, I started to lower the window blind. "No, no!" he stopped me. "I want all the sky." He couldn't move (too many tubes), but he looked at that bright blue square with such love. "The sun," he said. "It was so good—"

It grew dark. He grew tired. Then he whispered, "Do something for me? Leave a little early tonight. Don't run for the bus. Walk a few blocks and look at the sky. Walk in the world for me. . . ."

And so I do, and so I will. Loving life that much, Eric gave it to me—new, strong, beautiful!—even as he was dying. That was his victory. In a way it is also mine. And I think perhaps it is a victory for all of us everywhere when human beings succeed in giving such gifts to each other. ❖

DORIS HEROLD LUND

A native of Indianapolis, Indiana, Doris Herold Lund worked as an advertising copywriter before becoming a freelance writer, illustrator, and cartoonist. She has written and illustrated a number of books for children, and her verse collection, *The Attic of the Wind,* has been made into an animated movie. She is best known, however, for her 1974 book *Eric,* a longer and more detailed version of the story she tells in the essay "Gift from a Son Who Died." For Eric and his family, the physical struggle with leukemia was compounded by the emotional struggles that come with adolescence. As Lund said, "While Eric

1919–

demanded his independence, even though he was ill, I had to overcome my need to mother him too much—to let him go even though he might be dying. In other words we *both* grew up—in different ways." She added, "It seems my whole life has been one long struggle to develop the kind of courage that I needed every minute during Eric's losing battle." *Eric* has been translated into 15 languages and was made into a Hallmark Hall of Fame television movie in 1975.
OTHER WORKS *Hello, Baby!; The Paint-Box Sea; Patchwork Clan: How the Sweeney Family Grew*

WRITING ABOUT LITERATURE

A CRITICAL VIEW

As you read the literature in Unit Six, you may have thought about the ideas presented. A selection may have addressed a universal problem, told something of human nature, or reflected a set of beliefs. Did you question these ideas or simply accept them? On the next several pages, you will

- study how writers use elaboration to develop ideas
- express your opinion about the ideas in a selection
- use your skills to evaluate a real-world issue

Writer's Style: Elaboration Writers use elaboration—facts, sensory details, anecdotes, specific examples, quotations, or opinions—to support and develop their ideas.

Read the Literature

How do the writers of the following excerpts support their ideas?

Literature Models

Specific Examples
What is the main idea being presented here? What specific examples does the writer give to support that idea?

He was used to coming home and finding his wife sitting at the table deep in discussion with strangers or people whose names were familiar by repute. Some were prominent Indians, like the lawyer, Dr. Abdul Mohammed Khan, or the big businessman, Mr. Moonsamy Patel, and he was flattered, in a suspicious way, to meet them in his house. As he came home from work next day, he met Dr. Khan coming out of the house, and Dr. Khan—a highly educated man—said to him, "A wonderful woman."

Nadine Gordimer, from "A Chip of Glass Ruby"

Sensory Details
Which senses does the writer appeal to in this paragraph? Which words appeal to those senses?

Curled as I was, against her stomach, I was not startled by the cries of the crowd or the looming faces. The wind roared and beat its hot breath at our back; the flames whistled. I slowly wondered what would happen if we missed the circle or bounced out of it. Then I wrapped my hands around my mother's hands. I felt the brush of her lips and heard the beat of her heart in my ears, loud as thunder, long as the roll of drums.

Louise Erdrich, from "The Leap"

Connect to Life

Facts are statements that can be proved. Statistics are facts stated with numbers. Ideas supported by facts and statistics seem credible and authoritative. Credibility is particularly important in nonfiction writing. Notice the factual support in the following excerpt from a magazine article.

Magazine Article

On August 6, 1973, Clemente entered the hallowed Baseball Hall of Fame, alongside such other greats as Babe Ruth, Lou Gehrig, Ted Williams and Joe DiMaggio. His Hall of Fame plaque reads: Member of exclusive 3,000 hit club. Led National League in batting four times. Had four seasons with 200 or more hits while posting lifetime average of .317 and 240 home runs. Won most valuable player award in 1966. Rifle-armed defensive star. Set N.L. mark by pacing outfielders in assists five years. Batted .362 in two World Series, hitting in all 14 games.

John S. Babbitt,
from "Roberto Clemente—A Sports Legend,"
Stamps

Facts and Statistics
What general idea do these facts and statistics support?

Try Your Hand: Elaboration

1. **Elaborate on an Idea** Use sensory details to elaborate on ideas about a special party, a home-cooked meal, the first day of spring, or any other topic of your choosing.

2. **A QuickWrite Check** Check your portfolio for a QuickWrite or paragraph, and revise the piece, using elaboration to support one of its ideas.

3. **Work Together** With a partner, use elaboration to support or develop the following idea or an idea of your own choosing. Decide on the most effective type of elaboration to use.

   The weather can affect the way people think and act.

Criticism

Writing a critical essay can help you understand and judge a literary work. You can then share your opinion with others, helping them understand why you evaluated the selection the way you did.

GUIDED ASSIGNMENT

Write a Critical Essay On the next few pages, you'll identify selections from Unit Six that present ideas that interest you. Then you'll choose one of these selections and evaluate the ideas and values it contains.

Don't Go to Work Tomorrow

Day of Protest

Burn Your Pass for Freedom

① Prewrite and Explore

Reflect on the selections you have read in Unit Six. Which present ideas that really catch your interest? Create a list of possible selections.

FINDING A FOCUS

Choosing a Selection As you reread one or more selections, jot down any questions, comments, or reactions that you have. Which selection seems most interesting to you?

Deciding on an Idea What key ideas are presented? Which are striking or significant?

Focusing Your Position Think about the important ideas and how you feel about them. The notes at the right include questions you might ask yourself.

Decision Point Now make a decision on what idea you will evaluate.

LOOKING FOR EVIDENCE

Now that you know the selection and the idea you want to focus on, look for evidence of the idea in the selection. Ask yourself

- What passages or examples from the text reflect the ideas or values I want to write about?
- Do I agree with these ideas or values? Why or why not?

Student's Prewriting Notes

Notes on "A Chip of Glass Ruby"

What universal problem or experience does the text address?
—inequality and racism
—lack of freedom and voice

What lesson does it seem to teach?
—the importance of personal inner strength
—that human beings can overcome hardships

What does it show about human nature or relationships?
—human beings are reluctant to help others who are different from themselves
—people sometimes make judgments out of fear

How does the literature represent a particular set of beliefs or ideas?
—two sets of ideas: one of sympathy and commitment, one of criticism and selfishness

❷ Write and Analyze a Draft

When you begin writing, remember that your draft should briefly summarize the selection, explain the idea you will be writing about, and state your criticism of it. Don't forget to include a thesis statement and a clear summary of your position.

Check the draft and self-stick notes below to see how one student evaluated an idea from "A Chip of Glass Ruby."

Student's Draft

> *Have I made my thesis statement clear?*

"A Chip of Glass Ruby" tells the story of an Indian woman who lives in South Africa. Her decision to reach out to the natives affects her family, but Zanip Bamjee takes chances anyway. In this story, Nadine Gordimer raises an important question about a moral problem: Who is responsible for helping others who are less fortunate than ourselves? Should we be compassionate or selfish? The story encourages the reader to decide which response is more appropriate. Since most human beings don't sympathize with others' problems, Mrs. Bamjee's answer to the problem of social responsibility is a good one.

> *I will include ideas about social commitment in the body of my essay*

❸ Share Your Draft

Before you share your draft, read it over and ask yourself the following questions.

- What idea is the focus of this essay?
- What additional support for my position might I include?

 PEER RESPONSE

Share the draft and ask a peer to consider these questions.

- In your own words, restate my opinion of this idea.
- How is my main point stated and supported?
- How do I use elaboration to bring out my ideas?

SkillBuilder

 SPEAKING & LISTENING

Types of Peer Responses

Giving helpful responses to a classmate's writing is not always easy. Consider some of the following techniques as you give and receive peer responses.

Pointing Ask your readers what they like best in your piece of writing. Request that they be specific and avoid comments such as "It's good" or "I liked it."

Summarizing Ask readers what they hear as the main message in your writing. They don't need to evaluate the writing at this time.

Responding to Specific Features Ask for feedback on qualities such as support of ideas and unity in a paragraph. Ask them to respond to specific questions such as, "Do I explore my reactions in depth?" "Is there anything in my paper that confuses you?"

Replying Discuss the ideas in your paper with your readers. Ask their opinions on your topic. Talk about what you have said, not how you have said it.

APPLYING WHAT YOU'VE LEARNED Consider these techniques as you ask for and give peer responses to your critical essays.

 WRITING HANDBOOK

For information on using peer response, see page 1020 of the Writing Handbook.

4 Revise and Edit

Will your reader understand your opinion of the idea? When you revise, make sure that you have stated your topic and your position clearly. Reflect on your essay and make sure you have supported critical statements with specific examples or details.

Student's Final Draft

Since most human beings rarely sympathize with others' problems, Mrs. Bamjee's answer to the problem of social responsibility is correct and hopeful.

From the first scene in the story, Zanip accepts social responsibility. She is portrayed as gentle, confident, and strong. Unselfishly, she ignores her own problems and cares for others who are less fortunate and different from her. Some people, including her husband, might say that she is extremely irresponsible for neglecting her own family; however, I believe that she is acting very courageously. Few people can commit to solving major social problems with such intensity. She is truly driven to make a change. For example, her husband scolds her for helping the natives instead of attending to the Indians' own problems. She replies confidently, "What's the difference, Yusuf? We've all got the same troubles."

Zanip and her husband seem to be separated by two ideas that conflict. While she represents sympathy and understanding, Mr. Bamjee represents a harsh, judgmental, selfish point of view. Like most human beings, he does not want to become involved in others' problems. As he resists her efforts to help the natives, he seems fearful too. The government has been jailing protesters.

What single idea is being discussed? What is the writer's opinion of it?

How does the writer elaborate on the idea that Zanip is a confident, strong person?

Standards for Evaluation

A critical essay
- chooses a single idea to investigate
- presents evidence from the text to support critical, evaluative, and interpretive statements
- integrates appropriate quotations smoothly
- is organized clearly and logically

Grammar in Context

Using Adverbs Adverbs can help you elaborate on ideas by answering the questions *Where? When? How? To what extent?* They modify different parts of speech and therefore add detail to sentences.

An adverb can modify a verb.

She replies, *confidently* "What's the difference, Yusuf? We've all got the same troubles."

An adverb can modify an adjective.

Some people, including her husband, might say that she is *extremely* irresponsible for neglecting her own family.

An adverb can modify another adverb.

I believe that she is acting *very* courageously.

Try Your Hand: Using Adverbs

Fill in adverbs in the paragraph below. Then compare your new version with a classmate's paragraph. How does the meaning of the paragraph change with your adverb choices?

"A Chip of Glass Ruby" is a story about an Indian woman who takes responsibility for the problems of others. Her actions raise important questions and teach that a person's spirit cannot be dampened. Even when she faces hardship, Mrs. Bamjee maintains her spirit and influences the people she touches.

GRAMMAR FROM WRITING

Positioning Adverbs Correctly

The placement of adverbs can alter the meaning or intensity of a sentence. Adverbs usually follow the verbs they modify. Look at the following examples from *Back from Tuichi* by Yossi Ghinsberg.

I was rowing desperately with all my strength.

Sometimes, though, adverbs can also come before the verb.

He carefully, wordlessly placed the wallet into the metal box.

Intensifiers, such as *very* and *extremely,* usually come before the adjective or adverb they modify.

We must be really close to the island.

APPLYING WHAT YOU'VE LEARNED
You can change the position of some adverbs to create sentence variety or a different emphasis. Experiment with the placement of the adverbs in parentheses.

1. We arrived at the river. (today)
2. Since we hurried into the raft, we did not realize our gear was still on the bank. (just)
3. Reaching for the gear, I slipped and became wet! (really)

 GRAMMAR HANDBOOK

For more information on adverbs, see page 1076 of the Grammar Handbook.

FOCUS ON IDEAS

You have seen that in order to evaluate a piece of literature you need to identify the ideas it contains and then give them careful thought. Often those ideas are not obvious at first—you have to study the selection to uncover them. Similarly, everyday situations often include hidden ideas that you must uncover and then evaluate.

View Suppose you come upon a group like the one pictured on these pages. What do you notice? Describe the details.

Interpret Why are these students dressed the way they are? What attitudes or ideas might this situation represent? Where do you think those ideas came from?

Discuss Do you think school uniforms or dress codes are a good idea? Why or why not? How might others, such as parents or teachers, evaluate this idea? In a small group, discuss the pros and cons of having a school dress code. Check the SkillBuilder for tips on interpreting a situation.

SkillBuilder

 CRITICAL THINKING

Interpreting a Situation

If you just witness a situation or an event and don't think any more about what you've seen, you could miss something fairly important or significant.

Asking questions such as the following can help you interpret and evaluate the ideas that may be hidden within a situation. You may even become a more careful observer in the process!

- What am I really seeing here? Notice what you notice—the big picture and the details.
- What does this mean? What is the hidden idea?
- Do I agree with the idea as I understand it? Why or why not?

By asking thoughtful questions, you will be less likely to miss important events or details. You will be more likely to understand and learn from what you see.

APPLYING WHAT YOU'VE LEARNED

In a small group, brainstorm a list of intriguing events or situations you have witnessed. Discuss and evaluate the hidden ideas in each. Record details and observations that lead to your interpretation and evaluation.

THE HEROIC TRADITION

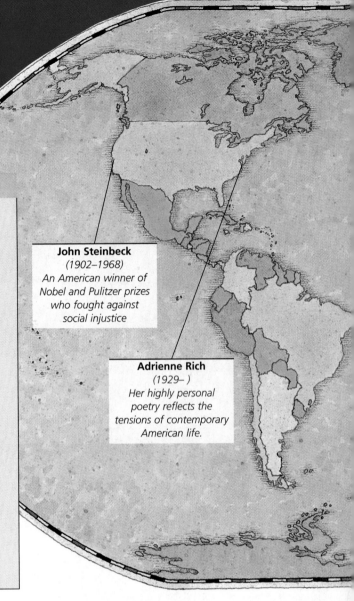

John Steinbeck
(1902–1968)
An American winner of Nobel and Pulitzer prizes who fought against social injustice

Adrienne Rich
(1929–)
Her highly personal poetry reflects the tensions of contemporary American life.

REFLECTING ON THEME

Can a hero exist without someone to tell his or her story? When you think about it, heroes and storytelling go hand and hand. From ancient times to the present, people have shared stories about great deeds, and each new generation learns about the heroes of old. Often, these heroes represent qualities or character traits that are valued by entire cultures. As you will see in this part of Unit Six, stories of heroes can be kept alive for centuries.

What Do You Think? In your notebook, create a list of your own childhood heroes. Then describe one of those heroes to a small group of classmates, explaining what you found admirable or interesting about him or her. After every person in the group has described a hero, discuss how the heroes reflect qualities and character traits that are valued by cultures.

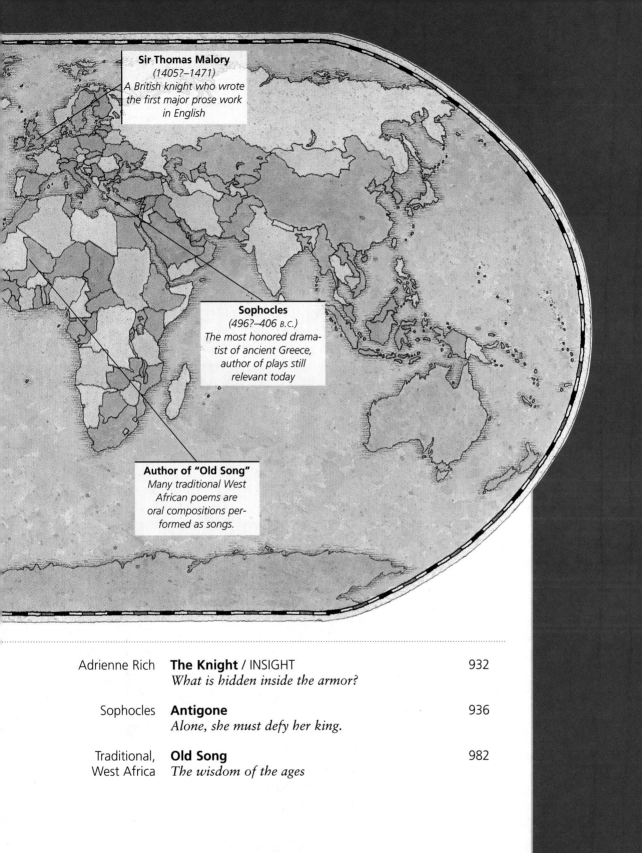

Sir Thomas Malory
(1405?–1471)
A British knight who wrote the first major prose work in English

Sophocles
(496?–406 B.C.)
The most honored dramatist of ancient Greece, author of plays still relevant today

Author of "Old Song"
Many traditional West African poems are oral compositions performed as songs.

PREVIEWING

ROMANCE

from Le Morte d'Arthur
The Crowning of Arthur
Sir Launcelot du Lake

Sir Thomas Malory England

Retold by Keith Baines

PERSONAL CONNECTION

In a small-group discussion, share what you know about the legend of King Arthur and his knights of the Round Table. What types of actions do you associate with Arthurian knights? What do you know about their ideals and motives? What personal qualities do they exhibit? Use a chart, like the one shown, to organize your information. Then share your group's results with the rest of the class.

Arthur and His Knights	
Name of Heroes	Ideals / Motives
Action	Personal Qualities

LITERARY CONNECTION

In literature, great heroes rarely spring from humble origins. Legendary heroes are usually the sons of kings or even the sons of gods, whose births are foretold and heralded by miraculous signs. They are "chosen ones" fated to rule or inspire others, though in youth they may be unaware of their destined role. And so it is with King Arthur, the heroic ruler in one of the most popular and enduring legends in Europe and North America. According to legend, Arthur became king of England and established his court at Camelot. He then gathered the best knights of the realm to join with him in the fellowship of the Round Table. These knights lived according to a specific code of behavior—the chivalric code—which stressed, among other things, loyalty to the king, courage, personal honor, and defending those who could not defend themselves. The most famous model of chivalry was Sir Launcelot, Arthur's friend and the greatest knight of the Round Table.

The earliest tales of Arthur come from Welsh literature of the 6th through 12th centuries. Most English-speaking readers know of the Arthurian legend through Sir Thomas Malory's *Le Morte d'Arthur* ("The Death of Arthur"), completed about 1470, or one of its many adaptations. The excerpts you are about to read are from Keith Baines's modern retelling of *Le Morte d'Arthur.*

WRITING CONNECTION

What makes a hero? Is it destiny? noble birth? Or is there some inner quality that motivates someone to act heroically? In your notebook, write down your own thoughts about what makes a hero. Keep these thoughts in mind as you read about the legendary Arthur and Sir Launcelot.

LASERLINKS
• *CULTURAL CONNECTION*

The Crowning of Arthur

**from Le Morte d'Arthur
Sir Thomas Malory**

King Uther Pendragon,[1] ruler of all Britain, had been at war for many years with the Duke of Tintagil in Cornwall when he was told of the beauty of Lady Igraine,[2] the duke's wife. Thereupon he called a truce and invited the duke and Igraine to his court, where he prepared a feast for them, and where, as soon as they arrived, he was formally reconciled to the duke through the good offices[3] of his courtiers.

In the course of the feast, King Uther grew passionately desirous of Igraine and, when it was over, begged her to become his paramour.[4] Igraine, however, being as naturally loyal as she was beautiful, refused him.

---

1. **Uther Pendragon** (oō'thər pĕn-drăg'ən): *Pendragon* was a title used in ancient Britain to refer to a supreme chief or leader.
2. **Igraine** (ē-grān').
3. **offices:** services.
4. **paramour** (păr'ə-moōr'): lover or mistress.

The Granger Collection, New York.

"I suppose," said Igraine to her husband, the duke, when this had happened, "that the king arranged this truce only because he wanted to make me his mistress. I suggest that we leave at once, without warning, and ride overnight to our castle." The duke agreed with her, and they left the court secretly.

The king was enraged by Igraine's flight and summoned his privy council.[5] They advised him to command the fugitives' return under threat of renewing the war; but when this was done, the duke and Igraine defied his summons. He then warned them that they could expect to be dragged from their castle within six weeks.

The duke manned and provisioned[6] his two strongest castles: Tintagil for Igraine, and Terrabyl, which was useful for its many sally ports,[7] for himself. Soon King Uther arrived with a huge army and laid siege to Terrabyl; but despite the ferocity of the fighting, and the numerous casualties suffered by both sides, neither was able to gain a decisive victory.

Still enraged, and now despairing, King Uther fell sick. His friend Sir Ulfius came to him and asked what the trouble was. "Igraine has broken my heart," the king replied, "and unless I can win her, I shall never recover."

"Sire," said Sir Ulfius, "surely Merlin the Prophet could find some means to help you? I will go in search of him."

Sir Ulfius had not ridden far when he was accosted by a hideous beggar. "For whom are you searching?" asked the beggar; but Sir Ulfius ignored him.

"Very well," said the beggar, "I will tell you: you are searching for Merlin, and you need look no further, for I am he. Now go to King Uther and tell him that I will make Igraine his if he will reward me as I ask; and even that will be more to his benefit than to mine."

"I am sure," said Sir Ulfius, "that the king will refuse you nothing reasonable."

"Then go, and I shall follow you," said Merlin.

Well pleased, Sir Ulfius galloped back to the king and delivered Merlin's message, which he had hardly completed when Merlin himself appeared at the entrance to the pavilion. The king bade him welcome.

"Sire," said Merlin, "I know that you are in love with Igraine; will you swear, as an anointed[8] king, to give into my care the child that she bears you, if I make her yours?"

The king swore on the gospel that he would do so, and Merlin continued: "Tonight you shall appear before Igraine at Tintagil in the likeness of her husband, the duke. Sir Ulfius and I will appear as two of the duke's knights: Sir Brastius and Sir Jordanus. Do not question either Igraine or her men, but say that you are sick and retire to bed. I will fetch you early in the morning, and do not rise until I come; fortunately Tintagil is only ten miles from here."

The plan succeeded: Igraine was completely deceived by the king's impersonation of the duke, and gave herself to him, and conceived Arthur. The king left her at dawn as soon as Merlin appeared, after giving her a farewell kiss. But the duke had seen King Uther ride out from the siege on the previous night and, in the course of making a surprise attack on the king's army, had been killed. When Igraine realized that the duke had died three hours before he had appeared to her, she was greatly disturbed in mind; however, she confided in no one.

Once it was known that the duke was dead, the king's nobles urged him to be reconciled to Igraine, and this task the king gladly entrusted to Sir Ulfius, by whose eloquence it was soon accomplished. "And now," said Sir Ulfius to his fellow nobles, "why should not the king marry the beautiful Igraine? Surely it would be as well for us all."

---

5. **privy** (prĭv′ē) **council:** a group of advisors who serve a ruler.
6. **provisioned:** supplied.
7. **sally ports:** gates or passages in the walls of fortifications, from which troops can make a sudden attack.
8. **anointed:** chosen as if by divine intervention.

The marriage of King Uther and Igraine was celebrated joyously thirteen days later; and then, at the king's request, Igraine's sisters were also married: Margawse, who later bore Sir Gawain, to King Lot of Lowthean and Orkney; Elayne, to King Nentres of Garlot. Igraine's daughter, Morgan le Fay, was put to school in a nunnery; in after years she was to become a witch, and to be married to King Uryens of Gore, and give birth to Sir Uwayne of the Fair Hands.

A few months later it was seen that Igraine was with child, and one night, as she lay in bed with King Uther, he asked her who the father might be. Igraine was greatly abashed.

"Do not look so dismayed," said the king, "but tell me the truth, and I swear I shall love you the better for it."

"The truth is," said Igraine, "that the night the duke died, about three hours after his death, a man appeared in my castle—the exact image of the duke. With him came two others who appeared to be Sir Brastius and Sir Jordanus. Naturally I gave myself to this man as I would have to the duke, and that night, I swear, this child was conceived."

"Well spoken," said the king; "it was I who impersonated the duke, so the child is mine." He then told Igraine the story of how Merlin had arranged it, and Igraine was overjoyed to discover that the father of her child was now her husband.

Sometime later, Merlin appeared before the king. "Sire," he said, "you know that you must provide for the upbringing of your child?"

"I will do as you advise," the king replied.

"That is good," said Merlin, "because it is my reward for having arranged your impersonation of the duke. Your child is destined for glory, and I want him brought to me for his baptism. I shall then give him into the care of foster parents who can be trusted not to reveal his identity before the proper time. Sir Ector would be suitable: he is extremely loyal, owns good estates, and his wife has just borne him a child. She could give her

child into the care of another woman, and herself look after yours."

Sir Ector was summoned and gladly agreed to the king's request, who then rewarded him handsomely. When the child was born, he was at once wrapped in a gold cloth and taken by two knights and two ladies to Merlin, who stood waiting at the rear entrance to the castle in his beggar's disguise. Merlin took the child to a priest, who baptized him with the name of Arthur, and thence to Sir Ector, whose wife fed him at her breast.

Two years later King Uther fell sick, and his enemies once more overran his kingdom, inflicting heavy losses on him as they advanced. Merlin prophesied that they could be checked only by the presence of the king himself on the battlefield, and suggested that he should be conveyed there on a horse litter.[9] King Uther's army met the invader on the plain at St. Albans, and the king duly appeared on the horse litter. Inspired by his presence, and by the lively leadership of Sir Brastius and Sir Jordanus, his army quickly defeated the enemy, and the battle finished in a rout. The king returned to London to celebrate the victory.

But his sickness grew worse, and after he had lain speechless for three days and three nights, Merlin summoned the nobles to attend the king in his chamber on the following morning. "By the grace of God," he said, "I hope to make him speak."

In the morning, when all the nobles were assembled, Merlin addressed the king: "Sire, is it your will that Arthur shall succeed to the throne, together with all its prerogatives?"[10]

The king stirred in his bed and then spoke so that all could hear: "I bestow on Arthur God's blessing and my own, and Arthur shall succeed to the throne on pain of forfeiting my blessing."

---

9. **horse litter:** a stretcher fastened to a horse.
10. **prerogatives:** rights or privileges held by a person or group.

Then King Uther gave up the ghost. He was buried and mourned the next day, as befitted his rank, by Igraine and the nobility of Britain.

During the years that followed the death of King Uther, while Arthur was still a child, the ambitious barons fought one another for the throne, and the whole of Britain stood in jeopardy. Finally the day came when the Archbishop of Canterbury, on the advice of Merlin, summoned the nobility to London for Christmas morning. In his message the archbishop promised that the true succession to the British throne would be miraculously revealed. Many of the nobles purified themselves during their journey, in the hope that it would be to them that the succession would fall.

The archbishop held his service in the city's greatest church (St. Paul's), and when matins[11] were done, the congregation filed out to the yard. They were confronted by a marble block into which had been thrust a beautiful sword. The block was four feet square, and the sword passed through a steel anvil which had been struck in the stone, and which projected a foot from it. The anvil had been inscribed with letters of gold:

WHOSO PULLETH OUTE THIS SWERD OF THIS STONE AND ANVYLD IS RIGHTWYS KYNGE BORNE OF ALL BRYTAYGNE

The congregation was awed by this miraculous sight, but the archbishop forbade anyone to touch the sword before mass had been heard. After mass, many of the nobles tried to pull the sword out of the stone, but none was able to, so a watch of ten knights was set over the sword, and a tournament proclaimed for New Year's Day, to provide men of noble blood with the opportunity of proving their right to the succession.

WHOSO PULLETH OUTE THIS SWERD OF THIS STONE AND ANVYLD IS RIGHTWYS KYNGE BORNE OF ALL BRYTAYGNE

Sir Ector, who had been living on an estate near London, rode to the tournament with Arthur and his own son Sir Kay, who had been recently knighted. When they arrived at the tournament, Sir Kay found to his annoyance that his sword was missing from its sheath, so he begged Arthur to ride back and fetch it from their lodging.

Arthur found the door of the lodging locked and bolted, the landlord and his wife having left for the tournament. In order not to disappoint his brother, he rode on to St. Paul's, determined to get for him the sword which was lodged in the stone. The yard was empty, the guard also having slipped off to see the tournament, so Arthur strode up to the sword, and, without troubling to read the inscription, tugged it free. He then rode straight back to Sir Kay and presented him with it.

Sir Kay recognized the sword and, taking it to Sir Ector, said, "Father, the succession falls to me, for I have here the sword that was lodged in the stone." But Sir Ector insisted that they should all ride to the churchyard, and once there bound Sir Kay by oath to tell how he had come by the sword. Sir Kay then admitted that Arthur had given it to him. Sir Ector turned to Arthur and said, "Was the sword not guarded?"

"It was not," Arthur replied.

"Would you please thrust it into the stone again?" said Sir Ector. Arthur did so, and first Sir Ector and then Sir Kay tried to remove it, but both were unable to. Then Arthur, for the second time, pulled it out. Sir Ector and Sir Kay both knelt before him.

"Why," said Arthur, "do you both kneel before me?"

"My lord," Sir Ector replied, "there is only

---

11. **matins** (măt'nz): morning prayers.

The Granger Collection, New York.

one man living who can draw the sword from the stone, and he is the true-born King of Britain." Sir Ector then told Arthur the story of his birth and upbringing.

"My dear father," said Arthur, "for so I shall always think of you—if, as you say, I am to be king, please know that any request you have to make is already granted."

Sir Ector asked that Sir Kay should be made Royal Seneschal,[12] and Arthur declared that while they both lived it should be so. Then the three of them visited the archbishop and told him what had taken place.

All those dukes and barons with ambitions to rule were present at the tournament on New Year's Day. But when all of them had failed, and Arthur alone had succeeded in drawing the sword from the stone, they protested against one so young, and of ignoble[13] blood, succeeding to the throne.

The secret of Arthur's birth was known only to a few of the nobles surviving from the days of King Uther. The archbishop urged them to make Arthur's cause their own; but their support proved ineffective. The tournament was repeated at Candlemas and at Easter, and with the same outcome as before.

Finally at Pentecost, when once more Arthur alone had been able to remove the sword, the commoners arose with a tumultuous cry and demanded that Arthur should at once be made king. The nobles, knowing in their hearts that the commoners were right, all knelt before Arthur and begged forgiveness for having delayed his succession for so long. Arthur forgave them and then, offering his sword at the high altar, was dubbed first knight of the realm. The coronation took place a few days later, when Arthur swore to rule justly, and the nobles swore him their allegiance. ❖

---

12. **Royal Seneschal** (sĕn′ə-shəl): the representative of a king in judicial and domestic matters.

13. **ignoble:** not noble; common.

FROM PERSONAL RESPONSE TO CRITICAL ANALYSIS

REFLECT 1. In your notebook, jot down your reaction to the events that occur in "The Crowning of Arthur." Then share your thoughts with a partner.

RETHINK 2. How much control would you say the characters have over their lives?
Consider
- Uther's passion for Igraine and the way he makes her his wife
- what happens to Igraine's sisters and daughter after her wedding
- Merlin's comment that Arthur is "destined for glory" and the instructions he gives for Arthur's care
- Arthur's discovery that he is heir to the throne

3. In your opinion, does Arthur deserve to be king?
Consider
- the sacrifices other people must make to bring him to power
- the support he receives from the common people
- the kind of person he seems to be

4. What do you think it would be like to live in the world depicted in this selection? Explain your views.

Tournament in King Arthur's court. MS Douce 383, fol. 16r. The Bodleian Library, Oxford, England.

Sir Launcelot du Lake

from Le Morte d'Arthur
Sir Thomas Malory

When King Arthur returned from Rome, he settled his court at Camelot, and there gathered about him his knights of the Round Table, who diverted themselves with jousting and tournaments. Of all his knights one was supreme, both in prowess at arms and in nobility of bearing, and this was Sir Launcelot, who was also the favorite of Queen Gwynevere, to whom he had sworn oaths of fidelity.

One day Sir Launcelot, feeling weary of his life at the court, and of only playing at arms, decided to set forth in search of adventure. He asked his nephew Sir Lyonel to accompany him, and when both were suitably armed and mounted, they rode off together through the forest.

At noon they started across a plain, but the intensity of the sun made Sir Launcelot feel sleepy, so Sir Lyonel suggested that they should rest

WORDS TO KNOW

prowess (prou'ĭs) *n.* superior strength, courage, or daring, especially in battle
fidelity (fĭ-dĕl'ĭ-tē) *n.* faithfulness to duties and obligations; devotion; loyalty

beneath the shade of an apple tree that grew by a hedge not far from the road. They dismounted, tethered their horses, and settled down.

"Not for seven years have I felt so sleepy," said Sir Launcelot, and with that fell fast asleep, while Sir Lyonel watched over him.

Soon three knights came galloping past, and Sir Lyonel noticed that they were being pursued by a fourth knight, who was one of the most powerful he had yet seen. The pursuing knight overtook each of the others in turn and, as he did so, knocked each off his horse with a thrust of his spear. When all three lay stunned, he dismounted, bound them securely to their horses with the reins, and led them away.

Without waking Sir Launcelot, Sir Lyonel mounted his horse and rode after the knight and, as soon as he had drawn close enough, shouted his challenge. The knight turned about, and they charged at each other, with the result that Sir Lyonel was likewise flung from his horse, bound, and led away a prisoner.

The victorious knight, whose name was Sir Tarquine,[1] led his prisoners to his castle and there threw them on the ground, stripped them naked, and beat them with thorn twigs. After that he locked them in a dungeon where many other prisoners, who had received like treatment, were complaining dismally.

Meanwhile, Sir Ector de Marys,[2] who liked to accompany Sir Launcelot on his adventures, and finding him gone, decided to ride after him. Before long he came upon a forester.

"My good fellow, if you know the forest hereabouts, could you tell me in which direction I am most likely to meet with adventure?"

"Sir, I can tell you: less than a mile from here stands a well-moated castle. On the left of the entrance you will find a ford where you can water your horse, and across from the ford a large tree from which hang the shields of many famous knights. Below the shields hangs a caldron, of copper and brass: strike it three times with your spear, and then surely you will

meet with adventure—such, indeed, that if you survive it, you will prove yourself the foremost knight in these parts for many years."

"May God reward you!" Sir Ector replied.

The castle was exactly as the forester had described it, and among the shields Sir Ector recognized several as belonging to knights of the Round Table. After watering his horse, he knocked on the caldron, and Sir Tarquine, whose castle it was, appeared.

They jousted, and at the first encounter Sir Ector sent his opponent's horse spinning twice about before he could recover.

"That was a fine stroke; now let us try again," said Sir Tarquine.

This time Sir Tarquine caught Sir Ector just below the right arm and, having impaled him on his spear, lifted him clean out of the saddle and rode with him into the castle, where he threw him on the ground.

"Sir," said Sir Tarquine, "you have fought better than any knight I have encountered in the last twelve years; therefore, if you wish, I will demand no more of you than your parole[3] as my prisoner."

"Sir, that I will never give."

"Then I am sorry for you," said Sir Tarquine, and with that he stripped and beat him and locked him in the dungeon with the other prisoners. There Sir Ector saw Sir Lyonel.

"Alas, Sir Lyonel, we are in a sorry plight. But tell me, what has happened to Sir Launcelot? for he surely is the one knight who could save us."

"I left him sleeping beneath an apple tree, and what has befallen him since I do not know," Sir Lyonel replied; and then all the unhappy prisoners once more bewailed their lot.

While Sir Launcelot still slept beneath the

---

1. **Tarquine** (tär′kwĭn).
2. **Sir Ector de Marys** (măr′əs): brother of Launcelot.
3. **parole:** the promise of a prisoner to abide by certain conditions in exchange for full or partial freedom.

apple tree, four queens started across the plain. They were riding white mules and accompanied by four knights who held above them, at the tips of their spears, a green silk canopy, to protect them from the sun. The party was startled by the neighing of Sir Launcelot's horse and, changing direction, rode up to the apple tree, where they discovered the sleeping knight. And as each of the queens gazed at the handsome Sir Launcelot, so each wanted him for her own.

"Let us not quarrel," said Morgan le Fay. "Instead, I will cast a spell over him so that he remains asleep while we take him to my castle and make him our prisoner. We can then oblige him to choose one of us for his paramour."

Sir Launcelot was laid on his shield and borne by two of the knights to the Castle Charyot, which was Morgan le Fay's stronghold. He awoke to find himself in a cold cell, where a young noblewoman was serving him supper.

"What cheer?"[4] she asked.

"My lady, I hardly know, except that I must have been brought here by means of an enchantment."

"Sir, if you are the knight you appear to be, you will learn your fate at dawn tomorrow." And with that the young noblewoman left him. Sir Launcelot spent an uncomfortable night, but at dawn the four queens presented themselves and Morgan le Fay spoke to him:

"Sir Launcelot, I know that Queen Gwynevere loves you, and you her. But now you are my prisoner, and you will have to choose: either to take one of us for your paramour, or to die miserably in this cell—just as you please. Now I will tell you who we are: I am Morgan le Fay, Queen of Gore; my companions are the queens of North Galys, of Estelonde, and of the Outer Isles. So make your choice."

"A hard choice! Understand that I choose none of you, lewd sorceresses that you are; rather will I die in this cell. But were I free, I would take pleasure in proving it against any who would champion you that Queen Gwynevere is the finest lady of this land."

"So, you refuse us?" asked Morgan le Fay.

"On my life, I do," Sir Launcelot said finally, and so the queens departed.

Sometime later, the young noblewoman who had served Sir Launcelot's supper reappeared.

"What news?" she asked.

"It is the end," Sir Launcelot replied.

"Sir Launcelot, I know that you have refused the four queens, and that they wish to kill you out of spite. But if you will be ruled by me, I can save you. I ask that you will champion my father at a tournament next Tuesday, when he has to combat the King of North Galys, and three knights of the Round Table, who last Tuesday defeated him ignominiously."

"My lady, pray tell me, what is your father's name?"

"King Bagdemagus."[5]

"Excellent, my lady; I know him for a good king and a true knight, so I shall be happy to serve him."

"May God reward you! And tomorrow at dawn I will release you and direct you to an abbey which is ten miles from here, and where the good monks will care for you while I fetch my father."

"I am at your service, my lady."

As promised, the young noblewoman released Sir Launcelot at dawn. When she had led him through the twelve doors to the castle entrance, she gave him his horse and armor, and directions for finding the abbey.

"God bless you, my lady; and when the time comes, I promise I shall not fail you."

Sir Launcelot rode through the forest in search of the abbey but at dusk had still failed to find it

---

4. **What cheer?:** How are you?

5. **Bagdemagus** (băg′də-măg′əs).

WORDS TO KNOW   **champion** (chăm′pē-ən) v. to fight for; defend

and, coming upon a red silk pavilion, apparently unoccupied, decided to rest there overnight and continue his search in the morning.

He had not been asleep for more than an hour, however, when the knight who owned the pavilion returned and got straight into bed with him. Having made an assignation[6] with his paramour, the knight supposed at first that Sir Launcelot was she and, taking him into his arms, started kissing him. Sir Launcelot awoke with a start and, seizing his sword, leaped out of bed and out of the pavilion, pursued closely by the other knight. Once in the open they set to with their swords, and before long Sir Launcelot had wounded his unknown adversary so seriously that he was obliged to yield.

The knight, whose name was Sir Belleus, now asked Sir Launcelot how he came to be sleeping in his bed and then explained how he had an assignation with his lover, adding:

"But now I am so sorely wounded that I shall consider myself fortunate to escape with my life."

"Sir, please forgive me for wounding you; but lately I escaped from an enchantment, and I was afraid that once more I had been betrayed. Let us go into the pavilion, and I will staunch your wound."

Sir Launcelot had just finished binding the wound when the young noblewoman who was Sir Belleus's paramour arrived and, seeing the wound, at once rounded in fury on Sir Launcelot.

"Peace, my love," said Sir Belleus. "This is a noble knight, and as soon as I yielded to him, he treated my wound with the greatest care." Sir Belleus then described the events which had led up to the duel.

"Sir, pray tell me your name, and whose knight you are," the young noblewoman asked Sir Launcelot.

"My lady, I am called Sir Launcelot du Lake."

"As I guessed, both from your appearance and from your speech; and indeed I know you

Lancelot rescuing Guinevere by crossing the sword bridge (about 1300). From *Le Roman de Lancelot du Lac,* M. 806, f. 166, The Pierpont Morgan Library, New York/Art Resource, New York.

better than you realize. But I ask you, in recompense for the injury you have done my lord, and out of the courtesy for which you are famous, to recommend Sir Belleus to King Arthur, and suggest that he be made one of the knights of the Round Table. I can assure you that my lord deserves it, being only less than yourself as a man-at-arms, and sovereign of many of the Outer Isles."

"My lady, let Sir Belleus come to Arthur's court at the next Pentecost. Make sure that you come

---

6. **assignation** (ăs´ĭg-nā´shən): an appointment for a meeting between lovers.

916

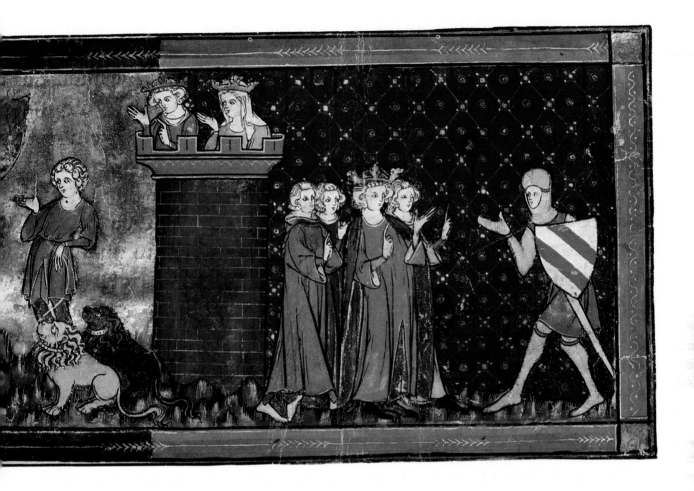

with him, and I promise I will do what I can for him; and if he is as good a man-at-arms as you say he is, I am sure Arthur will accept him."

As soon as it was daylight, Sir Launcelot armed, mounted, and rode away in search of the abbey, which he found in less than two hours. King Bagdemagus's daughter was waiting for him and, as soon as she heard his horse's footsteps in the yard, ran to the window and, seeing that it was Sir Launcelot, herself ordered the servants to stable his horse. She then led him to her chamber, disarmed him, and gave him a long gown to wear, welcoming him warmly as she did so.

King Bagdemagus's castle was twelve miles away, and his daughter sent for him as soon as she had settled Sir Launcelot. The king arrived with his retinue[7] and embraced Sir Launcelot,

who then described his recent enchantment, and the great obligation he was under to his daughter for releasing him.

"Sir, you will fight for me on Tuesday next?"

"Sire, I shall not fail you; but please tell me the names of the three Round Table knights whom I shall be fighting."

"Sir Modred, Sir Madore de la Porte, and Sir Gahalantyne. I must admit that last Tuesday they defeated me and my knights completely."

"Sire, I hear that the tournament is to be fought within three miles of the abbey. Could you send me three of your most trustworthy knights, clad in plain armor, and with no device,[8] and a fourth suit of armor which I

---

7. **retinue** (rĕt′n-ōō): attendants.

8. **device:** a design, often a motto, on a coat of arms.

myself shall wear? We will take up our position just outside the tournament field and watch while you and the King of North Galys enter into combat with your followers; and then, as soon as you are in difficulties, we will come to your rescue and show your opponents what kind of knights you command."

This was arranged on Sunday, and on the following Tuesday Sir Launcelot and the three knights of King Bagdemagus waited in a copse,[9] not far from the pavilion which had been erected for the lords and ladies who were to judge the tournament and award the prizes.

The King of North Galys was the first on the field, with a company of ninescore knights; he was followed by King Bagdemagus with fourscore[10] knights, and then by the three knights of the Round Table, who remained apart from both companies. At the first encounter King Bagdemagus lost twelve knights, all killed, and the King of North Galys six.

With that, Sir Launcelot galloped on to the field, and with his first spear unhorsed five of the King of North Galys's knights, breaking the backs of four of them. With his next spear he charged the king and wounded him deeply in the thigh.

"That was a shrewd blow," commented Sir Madore and galloped onto the field to challenge Sir Launcelot. But he too was tumbled from his horse, and with such violence that his shoulder was broken.

Sir Modred was the next to challenge Sir Launcelot, and he was sent spinning over his horse's tail. He landed headfirst, his helmet became buried in the soil, and he nearly broke his neck, and for a long time lay stunned.

Finally Sir Gahalantyne tried; at the first encounter both he and Sir Launcelot broke their spears, so both drew their swords and hacked vehemently at each other. But Sir Launcelot, with mounting wrath, soon struck his opponent a blow on the helmet which brought the blood streaming from eyes, ears, and mouth. Sir Gahalantyne slumped forward in the saddle, his

horse panicked, and he was thrown to the ground, useless for further combat.

Sir Launcelot took another spear and unhorsed sixteen more of the King of North Galys's knights and, with his next, unhorsed another twelve; and in each case with such violence that none of the knights ever fully recovered. The King of North Galys was forced to admit defeat, and the prize was awarded to King Bagdemagus.

That night Sir Launcelot was entertained as the guest of honor by King Bagdemagus and his daughter at their castle and before leaving was loaded with gifts.

"My lady, please, if ever again you should need my services, remember that I shall not fail you."

The next day Sir Launcelot rode once more through the forest and by chance came to the apple tree where he had previously slept. This time he met a young noblewoman riding a white palfrey.[11]

"My lady, I am riding in search of adventure; pray tell me if you know of any I might find hereabouts."

"Sir, there are adventures hereabouts if you believe that you are equal to them; but please tell me, what is your name?"

"Sir Launcelot du Lake."

"Very well, Sir Launcelot, you appear to be a sturdy enough knight, so I will tell you. Not far away stands the castle of Sir Tarquine, a knight who in fair combat has overcome more than sixty opponents whom he now holds prisoner. Many are from the court of King Arthur, and if you can rescue them, I will then ask you to deliver me and my companions from a knight who distresses us daily, either by robbery or by other kinds of outrage."

"My lady, please first lead me to Sir

---

9. **copse** (kŏps): a thicket of small trees.

10. **ninescore . . . fourscore:** a score is a set of 20; thus, ninescore is 180 and fourscore is 80.

11. **palfrey:** a gentle riding-horse.

Tarquine; then I will most happily challenge this miscreant knight of yours."

When they arrived at the castle, Sir Launcelot watered his horse at the ford and then beat the caldron until the bottom fell out. However, none came to answer the challenge, so they waited by the castle gate for half an hour or so. Then Sir Tarquine appeared, riding toward the castle with a wounded prisoner slung over his horse, whom Sir Launcelot recognized as Sir Gaheris, Sir Gawain's brother and a knight of the Round Table.

"Good knight," said Sir Launcelot, "it is known to me that you have put to shame many of the knights of the Round Table. Pray allow your prisoner, who I see is wounded, to recover, while I vindicate the honor of the knights whom you have defeated."

"I defy you, and all your fellowship of the Round Table," Sir Tarquine replied.

"You boast!" said Sir Launcelot.

At the first charge the backs of the horses were broken and both knights stunned. But they soon recovered and set to with their swords, and both struck so lustily that neither shield nor armor could resist, and within two hours they were cutting each other's flesh, from which the blood flowed liberally. Finally they paused for a moment, resting on their shields.

"Worthy knight," said Sir Tarquine, "pray hold your hand for a while and, if you will, answer my question."

"Sir, speak on."

"You are the most powerful knight I have fought yet, but I fear you may be the one whom in the whole world I most hate. If you are not, for the love of you I will release all my prisoners and swear eternal friendship."

"What is the name of the knight you hate above all others?"

"Sir Launcelot du Lake; for it was he who slew my brother, Sir Carados of the Dolorous Tower, and it is because of him that I have killed a hundred knights and maimed as many more, apart from the sixty-four I still hold

prisoner. And so, if you are Sir Launcelot, speak up, for we must then fight to the death."

"Sir, I see now that I might go in peace and good fellowship or otherwise fight to the death; but being the knight I am, I must tell you: I am Sir Launcelot du Lake, son of King Ban of Benwick, of Arthur's court, and a knight of the Round Table. So defend yourself!"

"Ah! this is most welcome."

Now the two knights hurled themselves at each other like two wild bulls; swords and shields clashed together, and often their swords drove into the flesh. Then sometimes one, sometimes the other, would stagger and fall, only to recover immediately and resume the contest. At last, however, Sir Tarquine grew faint and unwittingly lowered his shield. Sir Launcelot was swift to follow up his advantage and, dragging the other down to his knees, unlaced his helmet and beheaded him.

Sir Launcelot then strode over to the young noblewoman: "My lady, now I am at your service, but first I must find a horse."

Then the wounded Sir Gaheris spoke up: "Sir, please take my horse. Today you have overcome the most formidable knight, excepting only yourself, and by so doing have saved us all. But before leaving, please tell me your name."

"Sir Launcelot du Lake. Today I have fought to vindicate the honor of the knights of the Round Table, and I know that among Sir Tarquine's prisoners are two of my brethren, Sir Lyonel and Sir Ector, also your own brother, Sir Gawain. According to the shields there are also Sir Brandiles, Sir Galyhuddis,[12] Sir Kay, Sir Alydukis,[13] Sir Marhaus, and many others. Please release the prisoners and ask them to help themselves to the castle treasure. Give them all my greetings and say I will see them at the next Pentecost. And please request Sir Ector and Sir Lyonel to go straight to the court and await me there." ❖

---

12. **Galyhuddis** (găl′ĭ-hŏod′əs).
13. **Alydukis** (ăl′ĭ-dōō′kəs).

RESPONDING OPTIONS

FROM PERSONAL RESPONSE TO CRITICAL ANALYSIS

REFLECT

1. What did you find to be the strongest image in "Sir Launcelot du Lake"? Draw a quick sketch of this image.

RETHINK

2. Judging from the behavior of Sir Launcelot and the other knights in this selection, how would you describe the chivalric code that they live by?

   Consider
   - the reasons the knights fight
   - Sir Launcelot's reaction to the four queens' proposal
   - Sir Tarquine's reaction to the fighting skills of Sir Ector and Sir Launcelot
   - Sir Launcelot's answer to Sir Tarquine's question about his identity

3. Do you think that Sir Launcelot is totally honorable and heroic?
   Support your opinion with details from the selection.

4. What is your opinion of the female characters in this story? Use details from the story to support your answer.

RELATE

5. Do you think leaders and heroes with qualities like those of Uther, Arthur, and Launcelot still exist in today's world? Explain your opinion.

6. Review the chart you created for the Personal Connection on page 904. Were your views or images of Arthur, Launcelot, and their world changed as a result of reading these two tales?

LITERARY LINKS

Think about the way Uther Pendragon, Launcelot, and other characters in these excerpts view war and fighting. What differences do you see between their views and those expressed by the characters in "On the Rainy River" (page 266), "Thoughts of Hanoi" (page 754), and other selections in this book?

ANOTHER PATHWAY

Cooperative Learning

With a small group of classmates, prepare a guidebook for tourists visiting the Arthurian world. Include descriptions and pictures of the people, their residences, and their activities, noting the distinctive features of life in this world. Also offer advice about how to behave. Share your guidebook with the class.

QUICKWRITES

1. Write a **plot synopsis** for a newspaper TV listing, adapting one of these tales to fit a contemporary genre, such as a police drama or a futuristic adventure. For example, you might summarize an episode of *Starbase Camelot*.

2. Write a **magazine article** about a typical day in the life of Sir Launcelot. Incorporate details about his habitual fighting, his relationships with women, and his friendships and rivalries with other knights.

3. In an **editorial,** persuade fellow students that society would either improve or worsen if people tried to live up to chivalric ideals as presented in these selections.

PORTFOLIO Save your writing. You may want to use it later as a springboard to a piece for your portfolio.

LITERARY CONCEPTS

The term **romance** refers to any imaginative story concerned with noble heroes, chivalric codes of honor, passionate love, daring deeds, and supernatural events. Writers of romances tend to idealize their heroes as well as the eras in which the heroes live. Medieval romances, such as *Le Morte d'Arthur,* are stories of kings, knights, and ladies, who are motivated by love, religious faith, or simply a desire for adventure. Such romances are comparatively lighthearted in tone and loose in structure, containing many episodes. Usually the main character has a series of adventures while on a quest to accomplish some goal.

With your classmates, talk about the ways in which these excerpts from *Le Morte d'Arthur* illustrate the characteristics of a romance. Then discuss romantic elements in modern forms of entertainment, such as soap operas, romance novels, Westerns, and adventure films.

ALTERNATIVE ACTIVITIES

1. Watch a videotape of *Camelot* or another film about the legend of Arthur. In an **oral movie review,** compare the view of the Arthurian world shown in the movie with the impression you get from these selections.

2. Create a **drawing** or **painting** of your favorite scenes or characters from these selections. For inspiration, examine some of the artwork in this part of the unit or in illustrated volumes of Arthurian legends.

3. With a partner, create a **television commercial** for a new movie or television series about Launcelot's glorious deeds. You may wish to include a dramatization, a catchy theme song, or an interview with the leading man.

Jousting at the court of Caerleon (1468). From *Les Chroniques de Hainaut*, MS 9243, f. 45, Bibliothèque Royale Albert I, Brussels, Belgium / Art Resource, New York.

ART CONNECTION

How does the picture *King Arthur Drawing Forth the Sword* (page 906) affect your view of the young Arthur and his suitability for kingship?

The Granger Collection, New York.

ACROSS THE CURRICULUM

History/Sports Research medieval tournaments—their purpose, the equipment used, the participants, the contests or events held, and the way winners were determined. Then create a program for such a tournament, describing the events in which the knights of the Round Table might have participated.

WORDS TO KNOW

Write the letter of the word pair that best expresses a relationship similar to that of the first pair.

1. TIP : RECOMPENSE :: (a) arm : body, (b) prediction : recollection, (c) disk : computer, (d) memo : correspondence

2. DOG : FIDELITY :: (a) chicken : egg, (b) fox : cleverness, (c) wolf : timidity, (d) whale : mammal

3. PROWESS : GLADIATOR :: (a) tact : diplomat, (b) honesty : thief, (c) wisdom : fool, (d) humility : actor

4. CHAMPION : PROTECTOR :: (a) teach : instructor, (b) cure : patient, (c) referee : competitor, (d) arrest : judge

5. ADVERSARY : FRIEND :: (a) cat : pet, (b) hunter : trapper, (c) servant : ruler, (d) member : club

SIR THOMAS MALORY

The man who wrote *Le Morte d'Arthur* called himself "Syr Thomas Maleore, knyght." He also indicated that he completed this work in the ninth year of Edward IV's reign (1469 or 1470), and he added a prayer that he be safely delivered from prison. Although his precise identity remains uncertain, most scholars feel that he is the same person as Sir Thomas Malory (1405?–1471), a knight from the English county of Warwickshire who led a life of adventure at the end of the Middle Ages.

As a youth, Malory served bravely in battle under the Earl of Warwick, fighting for England during the final years of the Hundred Years' War with France. He inherited his father's estates in 1433 or 1434 and about a decade later represented Warwickshire in Parliament. In 1451, however, he was arrested and jailed for violently entering and robbing an abbey. Malory was imprisoned several more times in the next decade, accused of crimes such as cattle theft, highway robbery, and attempted murder, though the

charges may have been politically motivated. Twice he escaped from prison but was recaptured. In 1462 he joined rebels opposing King Edward IV in the civil war known as the Wars of the Roses. Imprisoned for treason in 1468, he was specifically excluded from the pardons Edward granted to many of the other rebels. He spent the remainder of his life in London's Newgate Prison, where he apparently occupied his time by writing *Le Morte d'Arthur*. The work was published in 1485, 14 years after his death.

While legends of King Arthur were originally preserved in Wales, by Malory's day the French versions of the legends were better known than their Welsh sources. Malory based *Le Morte d'Arthur* on these French versions, although his efforts were far more creative than mere translation. His gracefully written romance is considered the first major prose work in the English language.

LASERLINKS
• *ART GALLERY*

PREVIEWING

ROMANCE

from The Acts of King Arthur and His Noble Knights

John Steinbeck **United States**

PERSONAL CONNECTION

Think of a famous person you admire. In your notebook, make notes on what it would be like to live the life of this person for one day, including both positive and negative aspects. Then discuss your ideas with classmates, comparing your views of fame with theirs.

LITERARY CONNECTION

In this selection, modern novelist John Steinbeck portrays what it might be like to be Lancelot (also spelled *Launcelot*), the most famous knight of the Round Table. From childhood, Steinbeck was fascinated by the Arthurian legend, and as an adult he attempted to set it down in "plain, present-day speech" for his sons. He researched the legend in England and Italy, studying rare manuscripts, and wrote in a room he named Joyous Garde, after Lancelot's castle. Unfortunately, Steinbeck never completed his version of the legend; in 1976, several years after his death, his unfinished work was published as *The Acts of King Arthur and His Noble Knights*. The excerpt you are about to read offers a new perspective on some of the events from Malory's tale of Sir Launcelot.

READING CONNECTION

Inferences About Lancelot		
	Clues	**Inferences**
His Attitude Toward His Fame		
His Feelings About Guinevere		
Other Aspects of His Life		

Making Inferences To get the most out of this story, which presents a day in the life of the famed Lancelot, you will need to make **inferences,** or logical guesses, about Lancelot's feelings and behavior. For example, when Queen Guinevere (Gwynevere) asks Lancelot whether he has really encountered fair queen enchantresses, he looks away nervously and does not answer her directly. The reader can infer that he did meet such women and that he does not want to tell Guinevere about his encounters. As you read, look for other clues to help you understand Lancelot. In your notebook, keep track of your inferences by making a chart like the one shown.

Using Your Reading Log Use your reading log to record your responses to the questions inserted throughout the selection. Also jot down other thoughts and feelings that come to you as you read.

from THE ACTS of KING ARTHUR and HIS NOBLE KNIGHTS

JOHN STEINBECK

King Arthur held Whitsun[1] court at Winchester, that ancient royal town favored by God and His clergy as well as the seat and tomb of many kings. The roads were clogged with eager people, knights returning to stamp in court the record of their deeds, of bishops, clergy, monks, of the defeated fettered to their paroles,[2] the prisoners of honor. And on Itchen water, pathway from Solent[3] and the sea, the little ships brought succulents, lampreys, eels and oysters, plaice and sea trout, while barges loaded with casks of whale oil and casks of wine came tide borne. Bellowing oxen walked to the spits on their own four hooves, while geese and swans, sheep and swine, waited their turn in hurdle pens. Every householder with a strip of colored cloth, a ribbon, any textile gaiety, hung it from a window to flap its small festival, and those in lack tied boughs of pine and laurel over their doors.

In the great hall of the castle on the hill the king sat high, and next below the fair elite company of the Round Table, noble and decorous as kings themselves, while at the long trestle boards the people were as fitted as toes in a tight shoe.

Then while the glistening meat dripped down the tables, it was the custom for the defeated to celebrate the deeds of those who had overcome them, while the victor dipped his head in disparagement of his greatness and fended off the compliments with small defensive gestures of his hands. And as at public penitence sins are given stature they do not deserve, little sins grow up and baby sins are born, so those knights who lately claimed mercy perchance might raise the exploits of the brave and merciful beyond reasonable gratitude for their lives and in anticipation of some small notice of value.

This no one said of Lancelot, sitting with bowed head in his golden-lettered seat at the Round Table. Some said he nodded and perhaps dozed, for the testimony to his greatness was long and the monotony of his victories continued for many hours. Lancelot's immaculate fame had grown so great that men took pride in being unhorsed by him—even this notice was an honor. And since he had won many victories, it is possible that knights he had never seen claimed to have been overthrown by him. It was a way to claim attention for a moment. And as he dozed and wished to be otherwhere, he heard his deeds exalted beyond his recognition, and some mighty exploits once attributed to other men were brought bright-painted out and laid on the shining pile of his achievements. There is a seat of worth beyond the reach of envy whose occupant ceases to be a man and becomes the receptacle of the wishful longings of the world, a seat most often reserved for the dead, from whom neither reprisal nor reward may be expected, but at this time Sir Lancelot was its unchallenged tenant. And he vaguely heard his strength favorably compared with elephants, his ferocity with lions, his agility with deer, his cleverness with foxes, his beauty with the stars, his justice with Solon,[4] his stern probity[5] with St. Michael, his humility with newborn lambs; his military

---

1. **Whitsun:** another name for Pentecost, a Christian festival celebrated on the seventh Sunday after Easter.
2. **fettered to their paroles:** bound by their word of honor to lay down arms.
3. **Itchen . . . Solent:** waterways in southern England.
4. **Solon:** Athenian statesman and lawgiver who lived in the sixth century B.C.
5. **probity:** uprightness; honesty.

Study for Lancelot (1893), Sir Edward Burne-Jones. From *Drawings of Sir Edward Burne-Jones*, published by Charles Scribner's Sons, New York. Photo by Hollyer.

niche would have caused the Archangel Gabriel[6] to raise his head. Sometimes the guests paused in their chewing the better to hear, and a man who slopped his metheglin[7] drew frowns.

EVALUATE

Why do you think the knights are so extravagant in their praise of Lancelot?

Arthur on his dais[8] sat very still and did not fiddle with his bread, and beside him sat lovely Guinevere, still as a painted statue of herself. Only her inward eyes confessed her vagrant thoughts. And Lancelot studied the open pages of his hands—not large hands, but delicate where they were not knobby and scarred with old wounds. His hands were fine-textured—soft of skin and very white, protected by the pliant leather lining of his gauntlets.

The great hall was not still, not all upturned listening. Everywhere was movement as people came and went, some serving huge planks of meat and baskets of bread, round and flat like a plate. And there were restless ones who could not sit still, while everyone under burden of half-chewed meat and the floods and freshets of mead and beer found necessity for repeated departures and returns.

Lancelot exhausted the theme of his hands and squinted down the long hall and watched the movement with eyes so nearly closed that he could not see faces. And he thought how he knew everyone by carriage. The knights in long full floor-brushing robes walked lightly or thought their feet barely touched the ground because their bodies were released from their crushing boxes of iron. Their feet were long and slender because, being horsemen, they had never widened and flattened their feet with walking. The ladies, full-skirted, moved like water, but this was schooled and designed, taught to little girls with the help of whips on raw ankles, while their shoulders were bound back with nail-studded harnesses and their heads held high and rigid by painful collars of woven willow or, for the forgetful, by supports of painted wire, for to learn the high proud head on a swan's neck, to learn to flow like water, is not easy for a little girl as she becomes a gentlewoman. But knights and ladies both matched their movements to their garments; the sweep and rhythm of a long gown informs the manner of its moving. It is not necessary to inspect a serf or a slave, his shoulder wide and sloping from burdens, legs short and thick and crooked, feet splayed and widespread, the whole frame slowly crushed by weights. In the great hall the serving people walked under burdens with the slow weight of oxen and scuttled like crabs, crooked and nervous when the weight was gone.

A pause in the recital of his virtues drew Lancelot's attention. The knight who had tried to kill him in a tree had finished, and among the benches Sir Kay was rising to his feet. Lancelot could hear his voice before he spoke, reciting deeds like leaves and bags and barrels. Before his friend could reach the center of the hall, Sir Lancelot wriggled to his feet and approached the dais. "My lord king," he said, "forgive me if I ask leave to go. An old wound has broken open."

Arthur smiled down on him. "I have the same old wound," he said. "We'll go together. Perhaps you will come to the tower room when we have attended to our wounds." And he signed the trumpets to end the gathering, and the body-guards to clear the hall.

QUESTION

Why do Lancelot and Arthur suddenly leave the hall?

---

6. **St. Michael . . . Archangel Gabriel:** In several religious traditions, Michael and Gabriel are archangels, the chief messengers of God. Both are celebrated as warriors against evil.

7. **metheglin** (mə-thĕg'lĭn): a liquor made from honey.

8. **dais** (dā'ĭs): a raised platform used for a seat of honor.

WORDS TO KNOW

vagrant (vā'grənt) *adj.* wandering
carriage (kăr'ĭj) *n.* manner of moving one's body

Study on Brown Paper (1895), Sir Edward Burne-Jones. From *Drawings of Sir Edward Burne-Jones*, published by Charles Scribner's Sons, New York. Photo by Hollyer.

The stone stairway to the king's room was in the thickness of the wall of the round tower of the keep. At short intervals a deep embrasure[9] and a long, beveled[10] arrow slit commanded some aspect of the town below.

No armed men guarded this stairway. They were below and had passed Sir Lancelot in. The king's room was round, a horizontal slice of the tower, windowless save for the arrow slits, entered by a narrow arched door. It was a sparsely furnished room, carpeted with rushes. A wide bed, and at its foot a carved oaken chest, a bench before the fireplace, and several stools completed the furnishing. But the raw stone of the tower was plastered over and painted with solemn figures of men and angels walking hand in hand. Two candles and the reeky fire gave the only light.

When Lancelot entered, the queen stood up from the bench before the fire, saying, "I will retire, my lords."

"No, stay," said Arthur.

"Stay," said Lancelot.

The king was stretched comfortably in the bed. His bare feet projecting from his long saffron[11] robe caressed each other, the toes curled downward.

The queen was lovely in the firelight, all lean, down-flowing lines of green samite.[12] She wore her little mouth-corner smile of concealed amusement, and her bold golden eyes were the same color as her hair, and odd it was that her lashes and slender brows were dark, an oddity contrived with kohl[13] brought in a small enameled pot from an outland by a far-wandering knight.

"How are you holding up?" Arthur asked.

"Not well, my lord. It's harder than the quest."

"Did you really do all the things they said you did?"

Lancelot chuckled. "Truthfully, I don't know. It sounds different when they tell about it. And most of them feel it necessary to add a little. When I remember leaping eight feet, they tell it

at fifty, and frankly I don't recall several of those giants at all."

The queen made room for him on the fire bench, and he took his seat, back to the fire.

Guinevere said, "The damsel—what's her name—talked about fair queen enchantresses,[14] but she was so excited that her words tumbled over each other. I couldn't make out what happened."

Lancelot looked nervously away. "You know how excitable young girls are," he said. "A little back-country necromancy[15] in a pasture."

"But she spoke particularly of queens."

"My lady, I think everyone is a queen to her. It's like the giants—makes the story richer."

"Then they were not queens?"

"Well, for that matter, when you get into the field of enchantment, everyone is a queen, or thinks she is. Next time she tells it, the little damsel will be a queen. I do think, my lord, there's too much of that kind of thing going on. It's a bad sign, a kind of restlessness, when people go in for fortunetelling and all such things. Maybe there should be a law about it."

"There is," said Arthur. "But it's not in secular hands. The Church is supposed to take care of that."

"Yes, but some of the nunneries are going in for it."

"Well, I'll put a bug in the archbishop's ear."

The queen observed, "I gather you rescued damsels by the dozen." She put her fingers on

---

9. **embrasure** (ĕm-brā′zhər): opening in a wall, through which cannons are fired.

10. **beveled:** having a sloping edge.

11. **saffron:** golden yellow, named for the spice that has that color.

12. **samite:** a heavy silk fabric.

13. **kohl:** a cosmetic preparation used as eye makeup.

14. **fair queen enchantresses:** Morgan le Fay and three other queens, the four of whom, as related in "Sir Launcelot du Lake," imprisoned Lancelot, demanding that he take one of them as his lover.

15. **necromancy:** magic.

his arm and a searing shock ran through his body, and his mouth opened in amazement at a hollow ache that pressed upward against his ribs and shortened his breath.

After a moment she said, "How many damsels did you rescue?"

His mouth was dry. "Of course there were a few, madame. There always are."

"And all of them made love to you?"

"That they did not, madame. There you protect me."

"I?"

"Yes. Since with my lord's permission I swore to serve you all my life and gave my knightly courtly love to you, I am sheltered from damsels by your name."

"And do you want to be sheltered?"

CLARIFY

How does Lancelot feel about Guinevere?

"Yes, my lady. I am a fighting man. I have neither time nor inclination for any other kind of love. I hope this pleases you, my lady. I sent many prisoners to ask your mercy."

"I never saw such a crop of them," Arthur said. "You must have swept some counties clean."

Guinevere touched him on the arm again and with side-glancing golden eyes saw the spasm that shook him. "While we are on this subject, I want to mention one lady you did not save. When I saw her, she was a headless corpse and not in good condition, and the man who brought her in was half crazed."[16]

"I am ashamed of that," said Lancelot. "She was under my protection, and I failed her. I suppose it was my shame that made me force the man to do it. I'm sorry. I hope you released him from the burden."

"Not at all," she said. "I wanted him away before the feast reeked up the heavens. I sent him with his burden to the Pope. His friend will not improve on the way. And if his loss of interest in ladies continues, he may turn out to

be a very holy man, a hermit or something of that nature, if he isn't a maniac first."

The king rose on his elbow. "We will have to work out some system," he said. "The rules of errantry[17] are too loose, and the quests overlap. Besides, I wonder how long we can leave justice in the hands of men who are themselves unstable. I don't mean you, my friend. But there may come a time when order and organization from the crown will be necessary."

The queen stood up. "My lords, will you grant me permission to leave you now? I know you will wish to speak of great things foreign and perhaps tiresome to a lady's ears."

The king said, "Surely, my lady. Go to your rest."

"No, sire—not rest. If I do not lay out the designs for the needlepoint, my ladies will have no work tomorrow."

"But these are feast days, my dear."

"I like to give them something every day, my lord. They're lazy things and some of them so woolly in the mind that they forget how to thread a needle from day to day. Forgive me, my lords."

She swept from the room with proud and powerful steps, and the little breeze she made in the still air carried a strange scent to Lancelot, a perfume which sent a shivering excitement coursing through his body. It was an odor he did not, could not, know, for it was the smell of Guinevere distilled by her own skin. And as she passed through the door and descended the steps, he saw himself leap up and follow her, although he did not move. And when she was gone, the room was bleak, and the glory was gone from it, and Sir Lancelot was dog-weary, tired almost to weeping.

"What a queen she is," said King Arthur softly.

---

16. **When I saw her . . . half crazed:** Guinevere is referring to a woman Lancelot was unable to save—a woman who was beheaded by her jealous husband. As punishment, Lancelot commanded the husband to take the woman's body to Guinevere and to throw himself on her mercy.

17. **errantry** (ĕr′ən-trē): the knightly pursuit of adventure.

"And what a woman equally. Merlin was with me when I chose her. He tried to dissuade me with his usual doomful prophecies. That was one of the few times I differed with him. Well, my choice has proved him fallible. She has shown the world what a queen should be. All other women lose their sheen when she is present."

EVALUATE

Who do you think is right about Arthur's marriage, Merlin or Arthur?

Lancelot said, "Yes, my lord," and for no reason he knew, except perhaps the intemperate dullness of the feast, he felt lost, and a cold knife of loneliness pressed against his heart.

The king was chuckling. "It is the device of ladies that their lords have great matters to discuss, when if the truth were told, we bore them. And I hope the truth is never told. Why, you look haggard, my friend. Are you feverish? Did you mean that about an old wound opening?"

"No. The wound was what you thought it was, my lord. But it is true that I can fight, travel, live on berries, fight again, go without sleeping, and come out fresh and fierce, but sitting still at Whitsun feast has wearied me to death."

Arthur said, "I can see it. We'll discuss the realm's health another time. Go to your bed now. Have you your old quarters?"

"No—better ones. Sir Kay has cleared five knights from the lovely lordly rooms over the north gate. He did it in memory of an adventure which we, God help us, will have to listen to tomorrow. I accept your dismissal, my lord."

And Lancelot knelt down and took the king's beloved hand in both of his and kissed it. "Good night, my liege[18] lord, my liege friend," he said and then stumbled blindly from the room and felt his way down the curving stone steps past the arrow slits.

As he came to the level of the next landing, Guinevere issued silently from a darkened entrance. He could see her in the thin light from the arrow slit. She took his arm and led him to her dark chamber and closed the oaken door.

"A strange thing happened," she said softly. "When I left you, I thought you followed me. I was so sure of it I did not even look around to verify it. You were there behind me. And when I came to my own door, I said good night to you, so certain I was that you were there."

He could see her outline in the dark and smell the scent which was herself. "My lady," he said, "when you left the room, I saw myself follow you as though I were another person looking on."

Their bodies locked together as though a trap had sprung. Their mouths met, and each devoured the other. Each frantic heartbeat at the walls of ribs trying to get to the other until their held breaths burst out and Lancelot, dizzied, found the door and blundered down the stairs. And he was weeping bitterly. ❖

---

18. **liege** (lēj): under feudal law, entitled to the service or allegiance of subjects.

WORDS TO KNOW
fallible (făl'ə-bəl) *adj.* capable of being wrong or mistaken
intemperate (ĭn-těm'pər-ĭt) *adj.* extreme
haggard (hăg'ərd) *adj.* appearing worn and exhausted

THE KNIGHT

ADRIENNE RICH

Millefleurs tapestry with horseman and arms of
Jean de Daillon (late 1400s), unknown Flemish artist.
National Trust Photographic Library.

A knight rides into the noon,
and his helmet points to the sun,
and a thousand splintered suns
are the gaiety of his mail.
5 The soles of his feet glitter
and his palms flash in reply,
and under his crackling banner
he rides like a ship in sail.

A knight rides into the noon,
10 and only his eye is living,
a lump of bitter jelly
set in a metal mask,
betraying rags and tatters
that cling to the flesh beneath
15 and wear his nerves to ribbons
under the radiant casque.

Who will unhorse this rider
and free him from between
the walls of iron, the emblems
20 crushing his chest with their weight?
Will they defeat him gently,
or leave him hurled on the green,
his rags and wounds still hidden
under the great breastplate?

RESPONDING
OPTIONS

FROM PERSONAL RESPONSE TO CRITICAL ANALYSIS

REFLECT

1. What were your feelings toward Lancelot as you read this selection? Describe them in your notebook.

RETHINK

2. What inferences did you make about Lancelot as you were reading? Make use of your reading log and the chart that you created for the Reading Connection on page 923.

3. The knights' tributes to Lancelot imply that he is a "winner." Do you think Lancelot would agree?

   Consider
   - his fame and his achievements
   - his relationships with Arthur and Guinevere
   - why Lancelot weeps as he goes down the stairs

4. How does the view of fame presented in this selection compare with the views about fame expressed in your discussion for the Personal Connection on page 923?

5. Do you think the amount of detail Steinbeck includes adds to or detracts from the story? Explain your opinion.

   Consider
   - the description of the town and of Arthur's great hall during the feast
   - Lancelot's observations about the carriage of different groups in society
   - the physical descriptions of Lancelot, Arthur, and Guinevere

RELATE

6. Consider this statement in Steinbeck's tale: "There is a seat of worth beyond the reach of envy whose occupant ceases to be a man and becomes the receptacle of the wishful longings of the world." What modern-day figures, male or female, might you apply this statement to?

ANOTHER PATHWAY
Cooperative Learning

In a small group, choose a scene from the selection and create a storyboard for it that indicates not only what the characters say but also what they feel and think. If you prepare your storyboard on a computer, you could use different fonts or colors to distinguish between the characters' thoughts and words.

QUICKWRITES

1. Pretend you are a society reporter covering the feast at the castle. Write a brief **feature article** describing the event.

2. In an **interview** to be published in a celebrity magazine, have Lancelot discuss his views about fame.

3. Write an **advice column** in which you analyze Lancelot's dilemma regarding Guinevere and present possible options to him.

4. Write a **soap-opera scene** in which Guinevere discusses her plight with one of her ladies-in-waiting.

   PORTFOLIO Save your writing. You may want to use it later as a springboard to a piece for your portfolio.

LITERARY CONCEPTS

Style is the particular way in which a piece of literature is written. Style refers not so much to what is said but to how it is said. Use of descriptive detail, use of dialogue, depth of characterization, diction (word choice), and tone all contribute to a writer's style. Though both Steinbeck and Baines (writer of "The Crowning of Arthur" and "Sir Launcelot du Lake" on page 904) relied on the same sources for their versions of the Arthurian legend, each writer retold the legend in his own distinctive style. Baines, for instance, in trying to render Malory's work, included much less descriptive detail than Steinbeck did.

In a chart, compare the styles of Baines and Steinbeck. Create a separate column for each of the five elements of style mentioned in the previous paragraph and for any other elements you wish to analyze. After completing your chart, write a sentence for each writer, summing up key features of his style.

CRITIC'S CORNER

The noted critic Alfred Kazin praised Steinbeck for his "moving approach to human life" but also criticized his specific characterizations. "Nothing in his books is so dim," Kazin felt, ". . . as the human beings who live in them, and few of them are intensely imagined as human beings at all." On the basis of this selection, do you agree with Kazin's comments? Why or why not?

LITERARY LINKS

What do you think Guinevere and Lancelot, as portrayed in Steinbeck's story, would say to the speakers of the poems "Love Without Love" (page 371) and "The Taxi" (page 372)?

ALTERNATIVE ACTIVITIES

1. **Cooperative Learning** Imagine that a foreign visitor has come to Winchester to interview Arthur, Guinevere, and Lancelot about their values and ideals. In a small group, create a **dramatization** of that interview.

2. Lancelot believes he can identify people by their gait, or way of walking. Reread the description of the gaits of knights, ladies, and serfs, beginning on page 927. With two classmates, present a **demonstration** of each gait for the class.

3. Review the selection for details about the kinds of food served at the Whitsun feast. With a partner, do research to find out more about the offerings at a medieval feast and how much food might have been required. Develop a **menu** for such a feast and share it with the class.

ACROSS THE CURRICULUM

Sports Lancelot admits to leaping eight feet. Is that possible? What is the highest a person has actually leaped—both with and without a pole? Create a poster that compares Lancelot's leap with these actual record-breaking jumps.

History Research the design and construction of medieval English castles. Then create a model or a diagram of Arthur's castle, using the information that you find as well as details from the selection.

View of medieval castle surrounded by moat. J. Allan Cash Photolibrary.

WORDS TO KNOW

EXERCISE A Review the Words to Know at the bottom of the selection pages. Then fill in each blank with the vocabulary word that best completes the sentence.

1. Although medieval romances often _____ knights and their gallantry, nonfiction accounts of the times are generally more critical.
2. Most people were poor, had inadequate diets, worked constantly, and slept on thin straw mats, leaving them _____ and in poor health.
3. Even nobles were uncomfortable, for castles were freezing cold in the winter, hot and stuffy in the summer—in short, miserable places in any _____ weather.
4. The ladies who walked so elegantly learned that graceful _____ through harsh, even cruel, training in their youth.
5. Most knights served a single lord; some, however, lived a more _____ life, moving from place to place, serving one lord and then another.
6. Good manners were critical for a knight, for _____ behavior was important to the upper class.
7. However, acts of cruelty toward women and peasants were common, and because such behavior was not considered wicked, it required no _____.
8. Knights expected great praise for their bravery and reacted negatively to insults or any form of _____.
9. Because tempers were short and law enforcement was lacking, insults or injuries were likely to be met by acts of _____.
10. Legal disputes were often decided by combat because people believed that while humans were _____ and might misjudge a situation, God would cause the guilty party to be defeated.

EXERCISE B With a partner, try using a minimal number of gestures or actions to communicate five of the Words to Know.

JOHN STEINBECK

One of 20th-century America's most famous authors, John Steinbeck is best known for novels that honor working people and point out social injustice. Steinbeck was born in the Salinas Valley in northern California, the setting of much of his fiction. He attended Stanford University on and off for several years but never earned a college degree. Instead, he worked at a series of odd jobs—fruit picker, house painter, caretaker, lab assistant—before becoming a writer.

1902–1968

During the 1930s, Steinbeck won fame for novels that sympathetically portrayed the economic hardships of the Great Depression. The best known of these, his Pulitzer Prize-winning *The Grapes of Wrath* (1939), depicts the plight of an Oklahoma farm family forced to turn to migrant work in California. During World War II, Steinbeck worked overseas as a newspaper war correspondent and also wrote training manuals for the U.S. Army. Two decades later, he wrote political speeches for President Lyndon B. Johnson and traveled to Vietnam to report on the war there for *Newsday*.

During his long writing career, Steinbeck also produced short stories, travel books, and several plays for stage and screen, including an award-winning stage adaptation of his 1937 novel *Of Mice and Men*. In 1962 he won the Nobel Prize in literature.

OTHER WORKS *The Red Pony, The Pearl, Travels with Charley in Search of America*

PREVIEWING

DRAMA

Antigone (ăn-tĭg′ə-nē)
Sophocles (sŏf′ə-klēz′) Ancient Greece
Translated by Dudley Fitts and Robert Fitzgerald

PERSONAL CONNECTION

Consider the principles listed on the right, and in your notebook, rank them in the order of their importance to you. Discuss your ranking and your reasoning with the class. Which of the principles might you be willing to fight for—or willing to uphold if it meant making a sacrifice?

☐ loyalty or obligation to family

☐ obedience to civil law

☐ observance of religious law

☐ protection of personal dignity

☐ freedom

☐ protection of community or nation

LITERARY CONNECTION

Sophocles was one of the great dramatists of ancient Greece, and his play *Antigone* is regarded as one of the finest examples of classical Greek tragedy. The main characters in this play come into conflict because they stand firmly behind their principles—principles that are contradictory.

Most Greek tragedies are based on legends or myths that the audience of ancient Greece was very familiar with. *Antigone* is based on the legend of the family of Oedipus (ĕd′ə-pəs), the doomed king of Thebes. As the play begins, Antigone and her sister, Ismene (ĭs-mē′nē), recall their dead father, Oedipus, who unknowingly killed his father and then married his own mother. Upon discovering the truth, Oedipus blinded himself and went into exile, where he was cared for by his two daughters until his death. After his death, his sons, Eteocles (ē-tē′ə-klēz′) and Polyneices (pŏl′ĭ-nī′sēz), agreed to share the kingship of Thebes, ruling in alternate years. However, when Eteocles had served his first term as king, he banished Polyneices from Thebes and refused to relinquish the throne to him, claiming that Polyneices was unfit to rule. Polyneices then enlisted an army from Argos, a powerful city-state and a long-standing enemy of Thebes, to fight his brother. In the course of battle, the brothers killed each other. Their uncle, Creon, has become king and faces the task of restoring order in Thebes. As the new king, he plans to honor one corpse and insult the other.

Detail of bowl fragment, actor with mask (about 350 B.C.), unknown Sicilian artist. Terra cotta, 7⅜″, Martin von Wagner Museum, Universität Würzburg, Germany. Photo by K. Oehrlein.

LASERLINKS
• *READING CONNECTION*

Understanding Classical Drama

Classical drama arose in Athens, Greece, from religious celebrations in honor of Dionysus (dī'ə-nī'səs), the god of wine and fertility. These celebrations included ritual chants and songs performed by a group called a chorus. Drama evolved from these celebrations during the sixth century B.C., when individual actors began entering into dialogue with the chorus to tell a story.

The Theater Greek drama was filled with the spectacle and pageantry of a religious festival. Attended by thousands, plays were performed during the day in an outdoor theater with seats built into a hillside. The action of each play was presented at the foot of the hill, often on a raised platform. A long building, called the **skene,** served as a backdrop for the action and as a dressing room. A spacious circular floor, the **orchestra,** was located between the skene and the audience.

Actors and Chorus The actors—all men—wore elegant robes, huge masks, and often elevated shoes, all of which added to the grandeur of the spectacle. Sophocles used three actors in his plays; between scenes, they changed costumes and masks when they needed to portray different characters. The **chorus**—a group of about 15—commented on the action, and the leader of the chorus, the **choragus** (kə-rā'gəs), participated in the dialogue. Between scenes, the chorus sang and danced to musical accompaniment in the orchestra, giving insights into the message of the play. The chorus is often considered a kind of ideal spectator, representing the response of ordinary citizens to the tragic events unfolding in the play.

Tragedy and the Tragic Hero During Sophocles' lifetime, three playwrights were chosen each year to enter a theatrical competition in the festival of Dionysus. Each playwright would produce three tragedies, along with a satyr (sā'tər) play, a short comic interlude. A **tragedy** is a drama that recounts the downfall of a dignified, superior character who is involved in historically or socially significant events. The **protagonist,** or **tragic hero,** of the work is in conflict with an opposing character or force, the **antagonist.** The action builds from one event to the next and finally to a **catastrophe** that leads to a disastrous conclusion. Twists of fate play a key role in the hero's destruction.

According to the Greek philosopher Aristotle, a tragic hero possesses a defect, or **tragic flaw,** that brings about or contributes to his or her downfall. This flaw may be poor judgment, pride, weakness, or an excess of an admirable quality. The tragic hero, noted Aristotle, recognizes his or her flaw and its consequences, but only after it is too late to change the course of events.

Strategies for Reading Classical Drama

- Imagine the spectacle of the play as staged, visualizing as you read.

- Try to understand the hero's motivations and the qualities that make him or her a noble figure.

- Pay close attention to the causes of the conflict between the hero and his or her antagonist.

- Determine the circumstances or flaws that lead to the hero's downfall.

- Consider how the words and actions of minor characters help you to understand the main characters.

- Notice how the comments of the chorus interpret the action and point to universal themes.

ANTIGONE

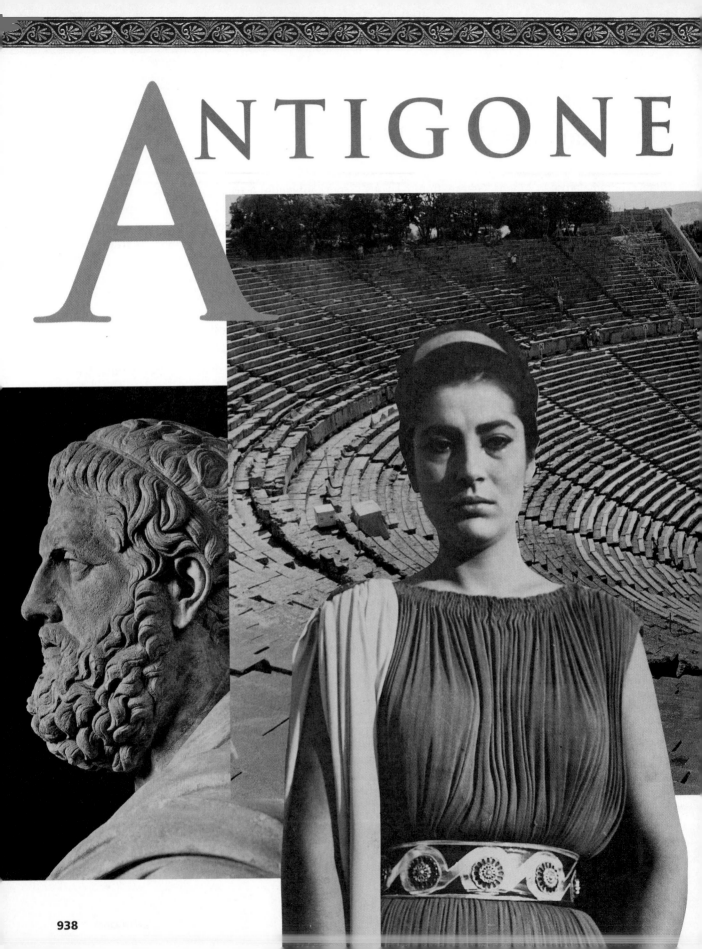

CAST OF CHARACTERS

Antigone ⎫ daughters of Oedipus, former king
Ismene ⎭ of Thebes

Creon (krē′ŏn′), king of Thebes, uncle of
  Antigone and Ismene

Haemon (hē′mŏn′), Creon's son, engaged to
  Antigone

Eurydice (yŏo-rĭd′ĭ-sē), wife of Creon

Teiresias (tī-rē′sē-əs), a blind prophet

Chorus, made up of about 15 elders of Thebes

Choragus, leader of the chorus

a Sentry

a Messenger

Bust of Sophocles. Museo
Lateranense, Vatican Museums,
Vatican City, Alinari / Art
Resource, New York.

Antigone contemplates her fate.
Culver Pictures.

Ruins of ancient theater
at Epidaurus, Greece.
Copyright © 1993
Barbara Ries / Photo
Researchers, Inc.

SOPHOCLES

Scene: Before the palace of Creon, king of Thebes. A central double door, and two doors at the side. A platform extends the length of the stage, and from this platform three steps lead down into the orchestra, or chorus ground.

Time: Dawn of the day after the repulse of the Argive army from the assault on Thebes

PROLOGUE

(Antigone *and* Ismene *enter from the central door of the palace.*)

Antigone. Ismene, dear sister,
   You would think that we had already suffered enough
   For the curse on Oedipus:
   I cannot imagine any grief
5   That you and I have not gone through. And now—
   Have they told you the new decree of our king Creon?

Ismene. I have heard nothing: I know
   That two sisters lost two brothers, a double death
   In a single hour; and I know that the Argive army
10   Fled in the night; but beyond this, nothing.

Antigone. I thought so. And that is why I wanted you
   To come out here with me. There is something we must do.

Ismene. Why do you speak so strangely?

Antigone. Listen, Ismene:
15   Creon buried our brother Eteocles
   With military honors, gave him a soldier's funeral,
   And it was right that he should; but Polyneices,
   Who fought as bravely and died as miserably—
   They say that Creon has sworn
20   No one shall bury him, no one mourn for him,
   But his body must lie in the fields, a sweet treasure
   For carrion birds to find as they search for food.
   That is what they say, and our good Creon is coming here
   To announce it publicly; and the penalty—
25   Stoning to death in the public square!
                                          There it is,
   And now you can prove what you are:
   A true sister, or a traitor to your family.

Ismene. Antigone, you are mad! What could I possibly do?

Antigone. You must decide whether you will help me or not.

30 **Ismene.** I do not understand you. Help you in what?

Antigone. Ismene, I am going to bury him. Will you come?

repulse: an act of turning away or beating back.

9 Argive: of Argos.

20–22 The obligation to bury the dead with appropriate burial rites was considered a sacred law among the ancient Greeks. They believed that the soul of someone left unburied would never find peace.

28–35 What contrast between Antigone and Ismene is suggested by the conversation between them?

Ismene. Bury him! You have just said the new law forbids it.

Antigone. He is my brother. And he is your brother, too.

Ismene. But think of the danger! Think what Creon will do!

35 **Antigone.** Creon is not strong enough to stand in my way.

Ismene. Ah sister!
Oedipus died, everyone hating him
For what his own search brought to light, his eyes
Ripped out by his own hand; and Jocasta died,
40 His mother and wife at once: she twisted the cords
That strangled her life; and our two brothers died,
Each killed by the other's sword. And we are left:
But oh, Antigone,
Think how much more terrible than these
45 Our own death would be if we should go against Creon
And do what he has forbidden! We are only women;
We cannot fight with men, Antigone!
The law is strong, we must give in to the law
In this thing, and in worse. I beg the dead
50 To forgive me, but I am helpless: I must yield
To those in authority. And I think it is dangerous business
To be always meddling.

Antigone.   If that is what you think,
I should not want you, even if you asked to come.
You have made your choice; you can be what you want to be.
55 But I will bury him; and if I must die,
I say that this crime is holy: I shall lie down
With him in death, and I shall be as dear
To him as he to me.
                    It is the dead,
Not the living, who make the longest demands:
60 We die forever. . . .
                    You may do as you like,
Since apparently the laws of the gods mean nothing to you.

Ismene. They mean a great deal to me; but I have no strength
To break laws that were made for the public good.

Antigone. That must be your excuse, I suppose. But as for me,
65 I will bury the brother I love.

Ismene.   Antigone,
I am so afraid for you!

Antigone.   You need not be:
You have yourself to consider, after all.

39 Jocasta, the mother of Antigone and Ismene, hanged herself when she realized the truth about her relationship with Oedipus.

55–61 What do these lines reveal about Antigone's feelings for her brother and the gods' laws?

Ismene. But no one must hear of this; you must tell no one!
   I will keep it a secret, I promise!

Antigone.   Oh tell it! Tell everyone!
70   Think how they'll hate you when it all comes out
   If they learn that you knew about it all the time!

Ismene. So fiery! You should be cold with fear.

Antigone. Perhaps. But I am doing only what I must.

Ismene. But can you do it? I say that you cannot.

75 **Antigone.** Very well: when my strength gives out, I shall do no more.

Ismene. Impossible things should not be tried at all.

Antigone. Go away, Ismene:
   I shall be hating you soon, and the dead will too,
   For your words are hateful. Leave me my foolish plan:
80   I am not afraid of the danger; if it means death,
   It will not be the worst of deaths—death without honor.

Ismene. Go then, if you feel that you must.
   You are unwise,
   But a loyal friend indeed to those who love you.

(*Exit into the palace.* Antigone *goes off, left. Enters the* Chorus,
with Choragus.)

PARODOS
Chorus. Now the long blade of the sun, lying
   Level east to west, touches with glory
   Thebes of the Seven Gates. Open, unlidded
   Eye of golden day! O marching light
5   Across the eddy and rush of Dirce's stream,
   Striking the white shields of the enemy
   Thrown headlong backward from the blaze of morning!

Choragus. Polyneices their commander
   Roused them with windy phrases,
10   He the wild eagle screaming
   Insults above our land,
   His wings their shields of snow,
   His crest their marshaled helms.

Chorus. Against our seven gates in a yawning ring
15   The famished spears came onward in the night;
   But before his jaws were <u>sated</u> with our blood,

PARADOS: The parodos is a song that marks the entry of the chorus, which represents the leading citizens of Thebes.

5 Dirce's (dûr′sēz) **stream:** a stream flowing past Thebes. The stream is named after a murdered queen who was thrown into it.

14–15 Thebes had seven gates, which the Argives attacked all at once.

WORDS
TO
KNOW   **sated** (sā′tĭd) *adj.* satisfied fully **sate** *v.*

942

Or pine fire took the garland of our towers,
He was thrown back; and as he turned, great Thebes—
No tender victim for his noisy power—
20 Rose like a dragon behind him, shouting war.

Choragus. For God hates utterly
The bray of bragging tongues;
And when he beheld their smiling,
Their swagger of golden helms,
25 The frown of his thunder blasted
Their first man from our walls.

Chorus. We heard his shout of triumph high in the air
Turn to a scream; far out in a flaming arc
He fell with his windy torch, and the earth struck him.
30 And others storming in fury no less than his
Found shock of death in the dusty joy of battle.

Choragus. Seven captains at seven gates
Yielded their clanging arms to the god
That bends the battle line and breaks it.
35 These two only, brothers in blood,
Face to face in matchless rage,
Mirroring each the other's death,
Clashed in long combat.

Chorus. But now in the beautiful morning of victory
40 Let Thebes of the many chariots sing for joy!
With hearts for dancing we'll take leave of war:
Our temples shall be sweet with hymns of praise,
And the long night shall echo with our chorus.

21–26 Zeus, the king of the gods, threw a thunderbolt, which killed the first Argive attacker. What type of conduct was Zeus punishing?

32–34 When the seven captains were killed, their armor was offered as a sacrifice to Ares (âr′ēz), the god of war.

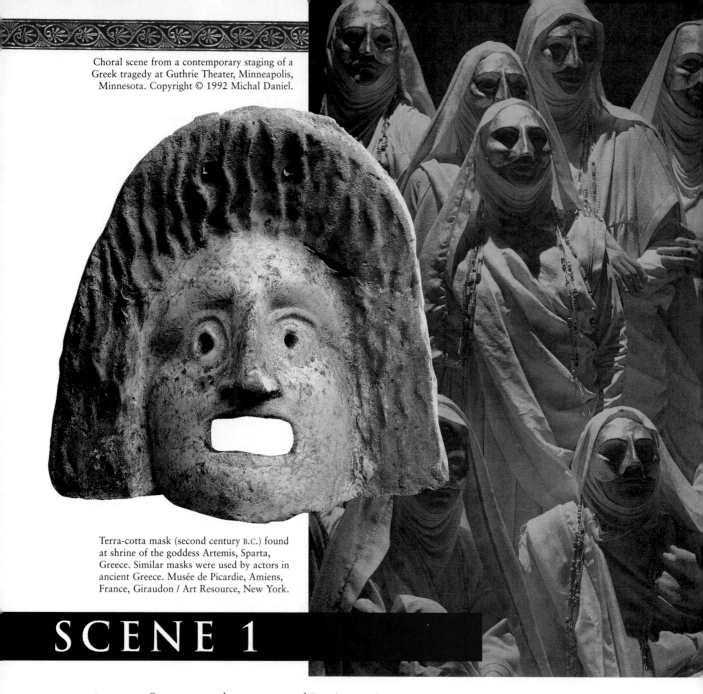

Choral scene from a contemporary staging of a Greek tragedy at Guthrie Theater, Minneapolis, Minnesota. Copyright © 1992 Michal Daniel.

Terra-cotta mask (second century B.C.) found at shrine of the goddess Artemis, Sparta, Greece. Similar masks were used by actors in ancient Greece. Musée de Picardie, Amiens, France, Giraudon / Art Resource, New York.

SCENE 1

Choragus. But now at last our new king is coming:
Creon of Thebes, Menoeceus' son.
In this <u>auspicious</u> dawn of his reign
What are the new complexities
5   That shifting Fate has woven for him?
What is his counsel? Why has he summoned
The old men to hear him?

(*Enter* Creon *from the palace. He addresses the* Chorus *from the top step.*)

2 Menoeceus (mə-nē′syŏŏs).

5 The Greeks believed that human destiny was controlled by three sisters called the Fates: Clotho (klō′thō), who spun the thread of human life; Lachesis (lăk′ĭ-sĭs), who determined its length; and Atropos (ăt′rə-pŏs′), who cut the thread.

WORDS
TO
KNOW

auspicious (ô-spĭsh′əs) *adj.* promising success; favorable

944

Creon. Gentlemen: I have the honor to inform you that our ship of
state, which recent storms have threatened to destroy, has come
10   safely to harbor at last, guided by the merciful wisdom of heaven.
I have summoned you here this morning because I know that I
can depend upon you: your devotion to King Laius was absolute;
you never hesitated in your duty to our late ruler Oedipus; and
when Oedipus died, your loyalty was transferred to his children.
15   Unfortunately, as you know, his two sons, the princes Eteocles and
Polyneices, have killed each other in battle; and I, as the next in
blood, have succeeded to the full power of the throne.

    I am aware, of course, that no ruler can expect complete loy-
alty from his subjects until he has been tested in office. Never-
20   theless, I say to you at the very outset that I have nothing but
contempt for the kind of governor who is afraid, for whatever
reason, to follow the course that he knows is best for the state;
and as for the man who sets private friendship above the public welfare—I have no use for him, either. I call God to witness
25   that if I saw my country headed for ruin, I should not be afraid
to speak out plainly; and I need hardly remind you that I would
never have any dealings with an enemy of the people. No one
values friendship more highly than I; but we must remember
that friends made at the risk of wrecking our ship are not real
30   friends at all.

    These are my principles, at any rate, and that is why I have
made the following decision concerning the sons of Oedipus:
Eteocles, who died as a man should die, fighting for his country, is to be buried with full military honors, with all the cere-
35   mony that is usual when the greatest heroes die; but his brother
Polyneices, who broke his exile to come back with fire and
sword against his native city and the shrines of his fathers'
gods, whose one idea was to spill the blood of his blood and
sell his own people into slavery—Polyneices, I say, is to have no
40   burial: no man is to touch him or say the least prayer for him;
he shall lie on the plain, unburied; and the birds and the scavenging dogs can do with him whatever they like.

    This is my command, and you can see the wisdom behind it.
As long as I am king, no traitor is going to be honored with the
45   loyal man. But whoever shows by word and deed that he is on
the side of the state—he shall have my respect while he is living, and my reverence when he is dead.

Choragus. If that is your will, Creon son of Menoeceus,
    You have the right to enforce it: we are yours.

50   **Creon.** That is my will. Take care that you do your part.

---

12 Laius (lā′əs): father of Oedipus.

18–30 According to Creon, what deserves the highest loyalty? How do you feel about Creon's principles?

31–42 Do you think Creon is justified in treating Polyneices' corpse in this way? What do you think his motive is?

Choragus. We are old men: let the younger ones carry it out.

Creon. I do not mean that: the sentries have been appointed.

Choragus. Then what is it that you would have us do?

Creon. You will give no support to whoever breaks this law.

55 **Choragus.** Only a crazy man is in love with death!

Creon. And death it is; yet money talks, and the wisest
Have sometimes been known to count a few coins too many.

(*Enter* Sentry.)

Sentry. I'll not say that I'm out of breath from running, King, because
every time I stopped to think about what I have to tell you, I felt
60 like going back. And all the time a voice kept saying, "You fool,
don't you know you're walking straight into trouble?"; and then
another voice: "Yes, but if you let somebody else get the news to
Creon first, it will be even worse than that for you!" But good sense
won out, at least I hope it was good sense, and here I am with a
65 story that makes no sense at all; but I'll tell it anyhow, because, as
they say, what's going to happen's going to happen, and—

Creon. Come to the point. What have you to say?

Sentry. I did not do it. I did not see who did it. You must not punish me for what someone else has done.

70 **Creon.** A comprehensive defense! More effective, perhaps,
If I knew its purpose. Come: what is it?

Sentry. A dreadful thing . . . I don't know how to put it—

Creon. Out with it!

Sentry.   Well, then;
    The dead man—
                    Polyneices—

(*Pause. The* Sentry *is overcome, fumbles for words.*
Creon *waits impassively.*)

                              out there—
                                        someone—

75   New dust on the slimy flesh!

(*Pause. No sign from* Creon.)

    Someone has given it burial that way, and
    Gone. . . .

(*Long pause.* Creon *finally speaks with deadly control.*)

Creon. And the man who dared do this?

Sentry.   I swear I
    Do not know! You must believe me!

78 Note that Creon assumes it
is a man who has tried to bury
the body.

Listen:

80 The ground was dry, not a sign of digging, no,
Not a wheel track in the dust, no trace of anyone.
It was when they relieved us this morning: and one of them,
The corporal, pointed to it.

There it was,

The strangest—

Look:

85 The body, just mounded over with light dust: you see?
Not buried really, but as if they'd covered it
Just enough for the ghost's peace. And no sign
Of dogs or any wild animal that had been there.

And then what a scene there was! Every man of us
90 Accusing the other: we all proved the other man did it;
We all had proof that we could not have done it.
We were ready to take hot iron in our hands,
Walk through fire, swear by all the gods,
It was not I!
95 *I do not know who it was, but it was not I!*

(Creon's *rage has been mounting steadily, but the* Sentry *is too intent upon his story to notice it.*)

And then, when this came to nothing, someone said
A thing that silenced us and made us stare
Down at the ground: you had to be told the news,
And one of us had to do it! We threw the dice,
100 And the bad luck fell to me. So here I am,
No happier to be here than you are to have me:
Nobody likes the man who brings bad news.

Choragus. I have been wondering, King: can it be that the gods
have done this?

Creon (*furiously*). Stop!
105 Must you doddering wrecks
Go out of your heads entirely? "The gods!"
Intolerable!
The gods favor this corpse? Why? How had he served them?
Tried to loot their temples, burn their images,
110 Yes, and the whole state, and its laws with it!
Is it your senile opinion that the gods love to honor bad men?
A pious thought!—

No, from the very beginning

There have been those who have whispered together,
Stiff-necked anarchists, putting their heads together,

85–88 Notice that the burial of Polyneices is symbolic and ritualistic rather than actual.

104–109 Note how quickly Creon rejects a reasonable question posed by the choragus. Creon is convinced that he knows how the gods think.

114 anarchists (ăn'ər-kĭsts): persons favoring the overthrow of government.

115 Scheming against me in alleys. These are the men,
And they have bribed my own guard to do this thing.
(*sententiously*) Money!
There's nothing in the world so demoralizing as money.
Down go your cities,
120 Homes gone, men gone, honest hearts corrupted,
Crookedness of all kinds, and all for money!

(*to* Sentry) But you—!
I swear by God and by the throne of God,
The man who has done this thing shall pay for it!
Find that man; bring him here to me, or your death
125 Will be the least of your problems: I'll string you up
Alive, and there will be certain ways to make you
Discover your employer before you die;
And the process may teach you a lesson you seem to have
    missed:
The dearest profit is sometimes all too dear.
130 That depends on the source. Do you understand me?
A fortune won is often misfortune.

Sentry. King, may I speak?

Creon. Your very voice distresses me.

Sentry. Are you sure that it is my voice, and not your conscience?

Creon. By God, he wants to analyze me now!

135 **Sentry.** It is not what I say, but what has been done, that hurts you.

Creon. You talk too much.

Sentry. Maybe; but I've done nothing.

Creon. Sold your soul for some silver: that's all you've done.

Sentry. How dreadful it is when the right judge judges wrong!

Creon. Your figures of speech
140 May entertain you now; but unless you bring me the man,
You will get little profit from them in the end.

(*Exit* Creon *into the palace.*)

Sentry. "Bring me the man"—!
I'd like nothing better than bringing him the man!
But bring him or not, you have seen the last of me here.
145 At any rate, I am safe!

(*Exit* Sentry.)

117 sententiously (sĕn-tĕn′shəs-lē):
in a pompous, moralizing manner.

117–122 What does Creon assume
about the motives of those who
have disobeyed him?

ODE 1

Chorus. Numberless are the world's wonders, but none
More wonderful than man; the storm-grey sea
Yields to his prows; the huge crests bear him high;
Earth, holy and inexhaustible, is graven
5   With shining furrows where his plows have gone
Year after year, the timeless labor of stallions.

The light-boned birds and beasts that cling to cover,
The <u>lithe</u> fish lighting their reaches of dim water,
All are taken, tamed in the net of his mind;
10   The lion on the hill, the wild horse windy-maned,
Resign to him; and his blunt yoke has broken
The sultry shoulders of the mountain bull.

Words also, and thought as rapid as air,
He fashions to his good use; statecraft is his,
15   And his the skill that deflects the arrows of snow,
The spears of winter rain: from every wind
He has made himself secure—from all but one:
In the late wind of death he cannot stand.

O clear intelligence, force beyond all measure!
20   O fate of man, working both good and evil!
When the laws are kept, how proudly his city stands!
When the laws are broken, what of his city then?
Never may the anarchic man find rest at my hearth,
Never be it said that my thoughts are his thoughts.

ODE: An ode is a song chanted by the chorus.

4 graven: carved; engraved.

24 What does this ode convey about human greatness and tragic limitation?

WORDS
TO
KNOW   **lithe** (līth) *adj.* limber; physically flexible

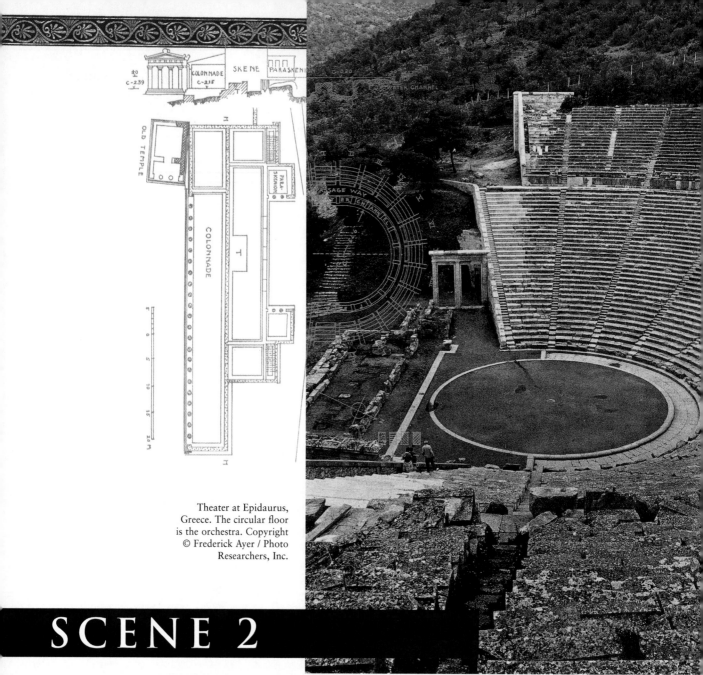

Theater at Epidaurus, Greece. The circular floor is the orchestra. Copyright © Frederick Ayer / Photo Researchers, Inc.

SCENE 2

(*Reenter* Sentry *leading* Antigone.)

Choragus. What does this mean? Surely this captive woman
    Is the princess, Antigone. Why should she be taken?

Sentry. Here is the one who did it! We caught her
    In the very act of burying him. Where is Creon?

5   **Choragus.** Just coming from the house.

(*Enter* Creon, *center.*)

Creon.   What has happened?
    Why have you come back so soon?

Sentry (*expansively*).   O King,
A man should never be too sure of anything:
I would have sworn
That you'd not see me here again: your anger
10   Frightened me so, and the things you threatened me with;
But how could I tell then
That I'd be able to solve the case so soon?

No dice throwing this time: I was only too glad to come!

Here is this woman. She is the guilty one:
15   We found her trying to bury him.

Take her, then; question her; judge her as you will.
I am through with the whole thing now, and glad of it.

Creon. But this is Antigone! Why have you brought her here?

Sentry. She was burying him, I tell you!

Creon (*severely*).   Is this the truth?

20   **Sentry.** I saw her with my own eyes. Can I say more?

Creon. The details: come, tell me quickly!

Sentry.   It was like this:
After those terrible threats of yours, King,
We went back and brushed the dust away from the body.
The flesh was soft by now, and stinking,
25   So we sat on a hill to windward and kept guard.
No napping this time! We kept each other awake.
But nothing happened until the white round sun
Whirled in the center of the round sky over us:
Then, suddenly,
30   A storm of dust roared up from the earth, and the sky
Went out, the plain vanished with all its trees
In the stinging dark. We closed our eyes and endured it.
The whirlwind lasted a long time, but it passed;
And then we looked, and there was Antigone!

35   I have seen
A mother bird come back to a stripped nest, heard
Her crying bitterly a broken note or two
For the young ones stolen. Just so, when this girl
Found the bare corpse, and all her love's work wasted,
40   She wept, and cried on heaven to damn the hands
That had done this thing.
                                        And then she brought more dust
And sprinkled wine three times for her brother's ghost.

We ran and took her at once. She was not afraid,

7–13 Note the change in attitude on the part of the sentry. How might his statement "A man should never be too sure of anything" apply to Creon?

35–45 How does the sentry's speech create sympathy for Antigone?

Not even when we charged her with what she had done.
45 She denied nothing.
                              And this was a comfort to me,
And some uneasiness: for it is a good thing
To escape from death, but it is no great pleasure
To bring death to a friend.
                              Yet I always say
There is nothing so comfortable as your own safe skin!

50 **Creon** (*slowly, dangerously*). And you, Antigone,
You with your head hanging—do you confess this thing?

Antigone. I do. I deny nothing.

Creon (*to* Sentry).   You may go.

(*Exit* Sentry.)

(*to* Antigone) Tell me, tell me briefly:
Had you heard my proclamation touching this matter?

55 **Antigone.** It was public. Could I help hearing it?

Creon. And yet you dared defy the law.

Antigone.   I dared.
It was not God's proclamation. That final Justice
That rules the world below makes no such laws.

Your <u>edict</u>, King, was strong,
60 But all your strength is weakness itself against
The immortal unrecorded laws of God.
They are not merely now: they were, and shall be,
Operative forever, beyond man utterly.

I knew I must die, even without your decree:
65 I am only mortal. And if I must die
Now, before it is my time to die,
Surely this is no hardship: can anyone
Living, as I live, with evil all about me,
Think Death less than a friend? This death of mine
70 Is of no importance; but if I had left my brother
Lying in death unburied, I should have suffered.
Now I do not.

57–63 What law does Antigone recognize as the supreme one?

64–70 What is Antigone's attitude toward death?

Film still from the 1960 movie *Antigone*. Antigone is about to be taken prisoner after sprinkling dust and wine over her brother's corpse. Culver Pictures.

WORDS TO KNOW   **edict** (ē′dĭkt′) *n.* an order put out by a person in authority

You smile at me. Ah Creon,
Think me a fool, if you like; but it may well be
That a fool convicts me of folly.

75 **Choragus.** Like father, like daughter: both headstrong, deaf to
    reason!
She has never learned to yield.

Creon. She has much to learn.
The inflexible heart breaks first, the toughest iron
Cracks first, and the wildest horses bend their necks
At the pull of the smallest curb.
                              Pride? In a slave?

80 This girl is guilty of a double insolence,
Breaking the given laws and boasting of it.
Who is the man here,
She or I, if this crime goes unpunished?
Sister's child, or more than sister's child,

85 Or closer yet in blood—she and her sister
Win bitter death for this!
             (*to servants*) Go, some of you,
Arrest Ismene. I accuse her equally.
Bring her: you will find her sniffling in the house there.

Her mind's a traitor: crimes kept in the dark

90 Cry for light, and the guardian brain shudders;
But how much worse than this
Is brazen boasting of barefaced anarchy!

Antigone. Creon, what more do you want than my death?

Creon. Nothing.
That gives me everything.

Antigone. Then I beg you: kill me.

95 This talking is a great weariness: your words
Are distasteful to me, and I am sure that mine
Seem so to you. And yet they should not seem so:
I should have praise and honor for what I have done.
All these men here would praise me

100 Were their lips not frozen shut with fear of you.
(*bitterly*) Ah the good fortune of kings,
Licensed to say and do whatever they please!

Creon. You are alone here in that opinion.

Antigone. No, they are with me. But they keep their tongues in leash.

105 **Creon.** Maybe. But you are guilty, and they are not.

Antigone. There is no guilt in reverence for the dead.

82–83 Think about how Creon's perception of Antigone as a threat to his manhood heightens the conflict.

99–104 What does Antigone assume about the attitude of the chorus? Do you think she is right?

Confrontation between Antigone and Creon in the 1960 film. Photofest.

Creon. But Eteocles—was he not your brother too?

Antigone. My brother too.

Creon.   And you insult his memory?

Antigone (*softly*). The dead man would not say that I insult it.

110 **Creon.** He would: for you honor a traitor as much as him.

Antigone. His own brother, traitor or not, and equal in blood.

Creon. He made war on his country. Eteocles defended it.

Antigone. Nevertheless, there are honors due all the dead.

Creon. But not the same for the wicked as for the just.

115 **Antigone.** Ah Creon, Creon,
    Which of us can say what the gods hold wicked?

115–116 Unlike Creon, Antigone holds that humans cannot understand the thinking of the gods.

Creon. An enemy is an enemy, even dead.

Antigone. It is my nature to join in love, not hate.

Creon (*finally losing patience*). Go join them, then; if you must have
    your love,
120 Find it in hell!

Choragus. But see, Ismene comes:

(*Enter* Ismene, *guarded.*)

    Those tears are sisterly; the cloud
    That shadows her eyes rains down gentle sorrow.

Creon. You too, Ismene,
125 Snake in my ordered house, sucking my blood
Stealthily—and all the time I never knew
That these two sisters were aiming at my throne!
                             Ismene,
Do you confess your share in this crime or deny it?
Answer me.

130 **Ismene.** Yes, if she will let me say so. I am guilty.

Antigone (*coldly*). No, Ismene. You have no right to say so.
    You would not help me, and I will not have you help me.

131–143 What do you think of Antigone's treatment of her sister?

Ismene. But now I know what you meant; and I am here
    To join you, to take my share of punishment.

135 **Antigone.** The dead man and the gods who rule the dead
    Know whose act this was. Words are not friends.

Ismene. Do you refuse me, Antigone? I want to die with you:
    I too have a duty that I must discharge to the dead.

Antigone. You shall not lessen my death by sharing it.

140 **Ismene.** What do I care for life when you are dead?

Antigone. Ask Creon. You're always hanging on his opinions.

Ismene. You are laughing at me. Why, Antigone?

Antigone. It's a joyless laughter, Ismene.

Ismene.   But can I do nothing?

Antigone. Yes. Save yourself. I shall not envy you.
145   There are those who will praise you; I shall have honor, too.

Ismene. But we are equally guilty!

Antigone.   No, more, Ismene.
      You are alive, but I belong to Death.

Creon (*to the* Chorus). Gentlemen, I beg you to observe these girls:
      One has just now lost her mind; the other,
150   It seems, has never had a mind at all.

Ismene. Grief teaches the steadiest minds to waver, King.

Creon. Yours certainly did, when you assumed guilt with the guilty!

Ismene. But how could I go on living without her?

Creon.   You are.
      She is already dead.

Ismene.   But your own son's bride!

155 **Creon.** There are places enough for him to push his plow.
      I want no wicked women for my sons!

Ismene. O dearest Haemon, how your father wrongs you!

Creon. I've had enough of your childish talk of marriage!

Choragus. Do you really intend to steal this girl from your son?

160 **Creon.** No; Death will do that for me.

Choragus.   Then she must die?

Creon. You dazzle me.
                        —But enough of this talk!
      (*to guards*) You, there, take them away and guard them well:
      For they are but women, and even brave men run
      When they see Death coming.

(*Exeunt* Ismene, Antigone, *and guards.*)

ODE 2

Chorus. Fortunate is the man who has never tasted God's vengeance!
      Where once the anger of heaven has struck, that house is shaken
      Forever: damnation rises behind each child
      Like a wave cresting out of the black northeast,
5   When the long darkness under sea roars up
      And bursts drumming death upon the wind-whipped sand.

154 Ismene's line reveals a complication in the plot: Creon's son, Haemon, is engaged to Antigone. Creon's love for his immediate family is now an issue in his conflict with Antigone.

155–156 How does Creon feel about the bond between Haemon and Antigone?

I have seen this gathering sorrow from time long past
Loom upon Oedipus' children: generation from generation
Takes the compulsive rage of the enemy god.
10 So lately this last flower of Oedipus' line
Drank the sunlight! but now a passionate word
And a handful of dust have closed up all its beauty.

　　What mortal arrogance
　　Transcends the wrath of Zeus?
15 Sleep cannot lull him, nor the effortless long months
Of the timeless gods: but he is young forever,
And his house is the shining day of high Olympus.
　　All that is and shall be,
　　And all the pást, is his.
20 No pride on earth is free of the curse of heaven.

　　The straying dreams of men
　　May bring them ghosts of joy:
But as they drowse, the waking embers burn them;
Or they walk with fixed eyes, as blind men walk.
25 But the ancient wisdom speaks for our own time:
　　Fate works most for woe
　　With Folly's fairest show.
Man's little pleasure is the spring of sorrow.

17 **Olympus:** a mountain in northern Greece, home of the gods and goddesses.

28 Do you think this line could apply to Creon?

WORDS TO KNOW **compulsive** (kəm-pŭl'sĭv) *adj.* having the ability to compel, or force resulting from an irresistible, irrational impulse

Painting on wine cup, showing the god Dionysus, the patron of theater, in his ship (540 B.C.), Exekias. Greek pottery often featured scenes from mythology. Antikensammlung, Munich, Germany. Photo Copyright © Erich Lessing / Art Resource, New York.

Theatrical masks on a fragment of a Greek bowl, about 410 B.C. The Granger Collection, New York.

SCENE 3

Choragus. But here is Haemon, King, the last of all your sons.
Is it grief for Antigone that brings him here,
And bitterness at being robbed of his bride?

(*Enter* Haemon.)

Creon. We shall soon see, and no need of diviners.
                                        —Son,

5   You have heard my final judgment on that girl:
Have you come here hating me, or have you come
With deference and with love, whatever I do?

Haemon. I am your son, Father. You are my guide.
You make things clear for me, and I obey you.

4 diviners: those who predict the future.

10 No marriage means more to me than your continuing wisdom.

Creon. Good. That is the way to behave: subordinate
    Everything else, my son, to your father's will.
    This is what a man prays for, that he may get
    Sons attentive and dutiful in his house,
15 Each one hating his father's enemies,
    Honoring his father's friends. But if his sons
    Fail him, if they turn out unprofitably,
    What has he fathered but trouble for himself
    And amusement for the malicious?

                                    So you are right
20 Not to lose your head over this woman.
    Your pleasure with her would soon grow cold, Haemon,
    And then you'd have a hellcat in bed and elsewhere.
    Let her find her husband in hell!
    Of all the people in this city, only she
25 Has had contempt for my law and broken it.

    Do you want me to show myself weak before the people?
    Or to break my sworn word? No, and I will not.
    The woman dies.

    I suppose she'll plead "family ties." Well, let her.
30 If I permit my own family to rebel,
    How shall I earn the world's obedience?
    Show me the man who keeps his house in hand,
    He's fit for public authority.

                            I'll have no dealings
    With lawbreakers, critics of the government:
35 Whoever is chosen to govern should be obeyed—
    Must be obeyed, in all things, great and small,
    Just and unjust! O Haemon,
    The man who knows how to obey, and that man only,
    Knows how to give commands when the time comes.
40 You can depend on him, no matter how fast
    The spears come: he's a good soldier; he'll stick it out.

    Anarchy, anarchy! Show me a greater evil!
    This is why cities tumble and the great houses rain down;
    This is what scatters armies!

45 No, no: good lives are made so by discipline.
    We keep the laws then, and the lawmakers,
    And no woman shall seduce us. If we must lose,
    Let's lose to a man, at least! Is a woman stronger than we?

Choragus. Unless time has rusted my wits,

11–19 What do Creon's words suggest about his relationship with his son?

26–44 What do Creon's words tell you about his views of government and his role as king?

47–48 Again Creon hints that he feels his manhood is threatened.

50   What you say, King, is said with point and dignity.

        Haemon (*boyishly earnest*). Father:
        Reason is God's crowning gift to man, and you are right
        To warn me against losing mine. I cannot say—
        I hope that I shall never want to say!—that you
55   Have reasoned badly. Yet there are other men
        Who can reason, too; and their opinions might be helpful.
        You are not in a position to know everything
        That people say or do, or what they feel:
        Your temper terrifies them—everyone
60   Will tell you only what you like to hear.
        But I, at any rate, can listen; and I have heard them
        Muttering and whispering in the dark about this girl.
        They say no woman has ever, so unreasonably,
        Died so shameful a death for a generous act:
65   "She covered her brother's body. Is this indecent?
        She kept him from dogs and vultures. Is this a crime?
        Death? She should have all the honor that we can give her!"

        This is the way they talk out there in the city.

        You must believe me:
70   Nothing is closer to me than your happiness.
        What could be closer? Must not any son
        Value his father's fortune as his father does his?
        I beg you, do not be unchangeable:
        Do not believe that you alone can be right.
75   The man who thinks that,
        The man who maintains that only he has the power
        To reason correctly, the gift to speak, the soul—
        A man like that, when you know him, turns out empty.

        It is not reason never to yield to reason!

80   In flood time you can see how some trees bend,
        And because they bend, even their twigs are safe,
        While stubborn trees are torn up, roots and all.
        And the same thing happens in sailing:
        Make your sheet fast, never slacken—and over you go,
85   Head over heels and under: and there's your voyage.
        Forget you are angry! Let yourself be moved!
        I know I am young; but please let me say this:
        The ideal condition
        Would be, I admit, that men should be right by instinct;
90   But since we are all too likely to go astray,
        The reasonable thing is to learn from those who can teach.

51–60 In what ways does Haemon's speech reflect the ideals of democracy?

61–68 Haemon suggests that Creon is causing the very thing he most wants to prevent—anarchy.

79–85 Compare Haemon's words to Creon with Creon's words to Antigone in Scene 2, beginning "The inflexible heart breaks first . . ." (line 77, page 954).

Choragus. You will do well to listen to him, King,
If what he says is sensible. And you, Haemon,
Must listen to your father. Both speak well.

95 **Creon.** You consider it right for a man of my years and experience
To go to school to a boy?

Haemon. It is not right
If I am wrong. But if I am young, and right,
What does my age matter?

Creon. You think it right to stand up for an anarchist?

100 **Haemon.** Not at all. I pay no respect to criminals.

Creon. Then she is not a criminal?

Haemon. The city would deny it, to a man.

Creon. And the city proposes to teach me how to rule?

Haemon. Ah. Who is it that's talking like a boy now?

105 **Creon.** My voice is the one voice giving orders in this city!

Haemon. It is no city if it takes orders from one voice.

Creon. The state is the king!

Haemon. Yes, if the state is a desert.

(*Pause*)

Creon. This boy, it seems, has sold out to a woman.

Haemon. If you are a woman: my concern is only for you.

110 **Creon.** So? Your "concern"! In a public brawl with your father!

Haemon. How about you, in a public brawl with justice?

Creon. With justice, when all that I do is within my rights?

Haemon. You have no right to trample on God's right.

Creon (*completely out of control*). Fool, adolescent fool! Taken in
by a woman!

115 **Haemon.** You'll never see me taken in by anything vile.

Creon. Every word you say is for her!

Haemon (*quietly, darkly*). And for you.
And for me. And for the gods under the earth.

Creon. You'll never marry her while she lives.

Haemon. Then she must die. But her death will cause another.

120 **Creon.** Another?
Have you lost your senses? Is this an open threat?

Haemon. There is no threat in speaking to emptiness.

Creon. I swear you'll regret this superior tone of yours!

You are the empty one!

Haemon. If you were not my father,
125   I'd say you were <u>perverse</u>.

Creon. You girl-struck fool, don't play at words with me!

Haemon. I am sorry. You prefer silence.

Creon. Now, by God—!
  I swear, by all the gods in heaven above us,
  You'll watch it; I swear you shall!
                       (*to the servants*) Bring her out!
130   Bring the woman out! Let her die before his eyes,
  Here, this instant, with her bridegroom beside her!

Haemon. Not here, no; she will not die here, King.
  And you will never see my face again.
  Go on raving as long as you've a friend to endure you.

(*Exit* Haemon.)

135 **Choragus.** Gone, gone.
  Creon, a young man in a rage is dangerous!

Creon. Let him do, or dream to do, more than a man can.
  He shall not save these girls from death.

Choragus. These girls?
  You have sentenced them both?

Creon. No, you are right.
140   I will not kill the one whose hands are clean.

Choragus. But Antigone?

Creon (*somberly*). I will carry her far away,
  Out there in the wilderness, and lock her
  Living in a vault of stone. She shall have food,
  As the custom is, to absolve the state of her death.
145   And there let her pray to the gods of hell:
  They are her only gods:
  Perhaps they will show her an escape from death,
  Or she may learn,
              though late,
  That piety shown the dead is pity in vain.

(*Exit* Creon.)

141–149 What do you make of Creon's decision to bury a person who is still alive when he has steadfastly refused to bury a dead one?

WORDS TO KNOW   **perverse** (pər-vûrs′) *adj.* willfully determined to go against what is expected or desired

963

ODE 3

Chorus. Love, unconquerable
    Waster of rich men, keeper
    Of warm lights and all-night vigil
    In the soft face of a girl:
5   Sea wanderer, forest visitor!
    Even the pure immortals cannot escape you,
    And mortal man, in his one day's dusk,
    Trembles before your glory.

    Surely you swerve upon ruin
10   The just man's consenting heart,
    As here you have made bright anger
    Strike between father and son—
    And none has conquered but Love!
    A girl's glance working the will of heaven:
15   Pleasure to her alone who mocks us,
    Merciless Aphrodite.

16 Aphrodite (ăf'rə-dī'tē): goddess of love and beauty.

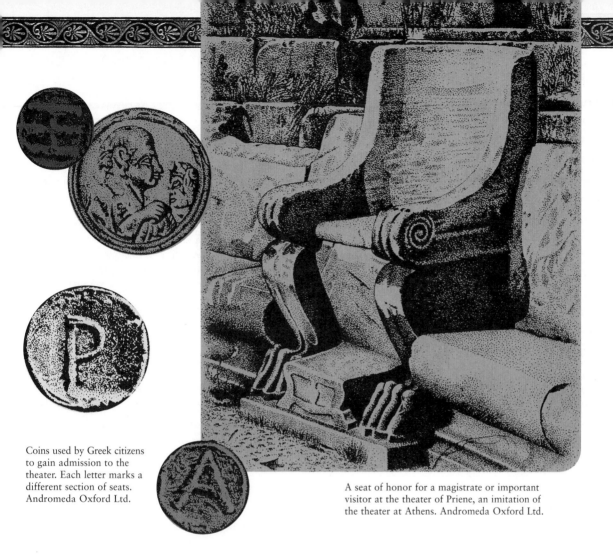

Coins used by Greek citizens to gain admission to the theater. Each letter marks a different section of seats. Andromeda Oxford Ltd.

A seat of honor for a magistrate or important visitor at the theater of Priene, an imitation of the theater at Athens. Andromeda Oxford Ltd.

SCENE 4

Choragus (*as* Antigone *enters, guarded*). But I can no longer stand in awe of this,
Nor, seeing what I see, keep back my tears.
Here is Antigone, passing to that chamber
Where all find sleep at last.

5   **Antigone.** Look upon me, friends, and pity me
Turning back at the night's edge to say
Good-bye to the sun that shines for me no longer;
Now sleepy Death
Summons me down to Acheron, that cold shore:

9 Acheron (ăk'ə-rŏn'): in Greek mythology, one of the rivers bordering the underworld, the place inhabited by the souls of the dead.

10 There is no bride song there, nor any music.

Chorus. Yet not unpraised, not without a kind of honor,
You walk at last into the underworld;
Untouched by sickness, broken by no sword.
What woman has ever found your way to death?

15 Antigone. How often I have heard the story of Niobe,
Tantalus' wretched daughter, how the stone
Clung fast about her, ivy-close: and they say
The rain falls endlessly
And sifting soft snow; her tears are never done.
20 I feel the loneliness of her death in mine.

Chorus. But she was born of heaven, and you
Are woman, woman-born. If her death is yours,
A mortal woman's, is this not for you
Glory in our world and in the world beyond?

25 Antigone. You laugh at me. Ah, friends, friends,
Can you not wait until I am dead? O Thebes,
O men many-charioted, in love with Fortune,
Dear springs of Dirce, sacred Theban grove,
Be witnesses for me, denied all pity,
30 Unjustly judged! and think a word of love
For her whose path turns
Under dark earth, where there are no more tears.

Chorus. You have passed beyond human daring and come at last
Into a place of stone where Justice sits.
35 I cannot tell
What shape of your father's guilt appears in this.

Antigone. You have touched it at last: that bridal bed
Unspeakable, horror of son and mother mingling:
Their crime, infection of all our family!
40 O Oedipus, father and brother!
Your marriage strikes from the grave to murder mine.
I have been a stranger here in my own land:
All my life
The blasphemy of my birth has followed me.

45 Chorus. Reverence is a virtue, but strength
Lives in established law: that must prevail.
You have made your choice;
Your death is the doing of your conscious hand.

Antigone. Then let me go, since all your words are bitter,
50 And the very light of the sun is cold to me.

15–20 Niobe (nī'ə-bē) was a queen of Thebes whose children were killed by the gods because she had boasted that she was greater than a goddess. After their deaths, she was turned to stone but continued to shed tears. Why might Antigone compare herself to Niobe?

44 blasphemy of my birth: Antigone is referring to her father's marriage to his own mother, an incestuous relationship that resulted in her birth. This type of relationship was considered a sin against the gods.

Irene Papas playing the title role in the 1960 movie. Culver Pictures.

Lead me to my vigil, where I must have
Neither love nor <u>lamentation</u>; no song, but silence.

(Creon *interrupts impatiently.*)

Creon. If <u>dirges</u> and planned lamentations could put off death,
Men would be singing forever.
                    (*to the servants*) Take her, go!
55 You know your orders: take her to the vault
And leave her alone there. And if she lives or dies,
That's her affair, not ours: our hands are clean.

Antigone. O tomb, vaulted bride-bed in eternal rock,
Soon I shall be with my own again
60 Where Persephone welcomes the thin ghosts underground:
And I shall see my father again, and you, Mother,
And dearest Polyneices—
                    dearest indeed
To me, since it was my hand
That washed him clean and poured the ritual wine:
65 And my reward is death before my time!

And yet, as men's hearts know, I have done no wrong;
I have not sinned before God. Or if I have,
I shall know the truth in death. But if the guilt
Lies upon Creon who judged me, then, I pray,
70 May his punishment equal my own.

Choragus.   O passionate heart,
Unyielding, tormented still by the same winds!

Creon. Her guards shall have good cause to regret their delaying.

Antigone. Ah! That voice is like the voice of death!

Creon. I can give you no reason to think you are mistaken.

75 **Antigone.** Thebes, and you my fathers' gods,
And rulers of Thebes, you see me now, the last
Unhappy daughter of a line of kings,
Your kings, led away to death. You will remember
What things I suffer, and at what men's hands,
80 Because I would not <u>transgress</u> the laws of heaven.
(*to the guards, simply*) Come: let us wait no longer.

(*Exit* Antigone, *left, guarded.*)

60 Persephone (pər-sĕf′ə-nē): wife of Hades (hā′dēz) and queen of the underworld.

75–80 What do these lines suggest about what Antigone values most?

WORDS
TO
KNOW

lamentation (lăm′ən-tā′shən) *n.* an expression of grief
dirge (dûrj) *n.* a slow, mournful piece of music; a funeral hymn
transgress (trăns-grĕs′) *v.* to violate or break a law, command, or moral code

ODE 4

Chorus. All Danae's beauty was locked away
    In a brazen cell where the sunlight could not come:
    A small room, still as any grave, enclosed her.
    Yet she was a princess too,
5   And Zeus in a rain of gold poured love upon her.
    O child, child,
    No power in wealth or war
    Or tough sea-blackened ships
    Can prevail against untiring Destiny!

10   And Dryas' son also, that furious king,
    Bore the god's prisoning anger for his pride:
    Sealed up by Dionysus in deaf stone,
    His madness died among echoes.
    So at the last he learned what dreadful power
15   His tongue had mocked:
    For he had profaned the revels
    And fired the wrath of the nine
    Implacable sisters that love the sound of the flute.

    And old men tell a half-remembered tale
20   Of horror done where a dark ledge splits the sea
    And a double surf beats on the grey shores:
    How a king's new woman, sick
    With hatred for the queen he had imprisoned,
    Ripped out his two sons' eyes with her bloody hands
25   While grinning Ares watched the shuttle plunge
    Four times: four blind wounds crying for revenge,

    Crying, tears and blood mingled. Piteously born,
    Those sons whose mother was of heavenly birth!
    Her father was the god of the north wind,
30   And she was cradled by gales;
    She raced with young colts on the glittering hills
    And walked untrammeled in the open light:
    But in her marriage deathless Fate found means
    To build a tomb like yours for all her joy.

1–5 Danae (dăn'ə-ē') was a princess who was imprisoned by her father because it had been predicted that her son would one day kill him. After Zeus visited Danae in the form of a shower of gold, she gave birth to his son Perseus, who eventually did kill his grandfather.

10–18 King Lycurgus (lĭ-kûr'gəs), son of Dryas (drī'əs), was driven mad and imprisoned in stone for objecting to the worship of Dionysus. The nine implacable sisters are the Muses, the goddesses who presided over literature, the arts, and the sciences. Once offended, they were impossible to appease.

19–34 These lines refer to the myth of King Phineus (fĭn'yōōs), who imprisoned his first wife, the daughter of the north wind, and allowed his new wife to blind his sons from his first marriage.

Two views of Sophocles, who was regarded by his Greek admirers as "the perfect man." *Left,* Museo Gregoriano Profano, Vatican Museums, Vatican State, Alinari / Art Resource, New York. *Right,* Museo Lateranense, Vatican Museums, Vatican City, Alinari / Art Resource, New York.

SCENE 5

(*Enter blind* Teiresias, *led by a boy. The opening speeches of* Teiresias *should be in singsong contrast to the realistic lines of* Creon.)

Teiresias. This is the way the blind man comes, princes, princes,
  Lock step, two heads lit by the eyes of one.

Creon. What new thing have you to tell us, old Teiresias?

Teiresias. I have much to tell you: listen to the prophet, Creon.

5 **Creon.** I am not aware that I have ever failed to listen.

Teiresias. Then you have done wisely, King, and ruled well.

Creon. I admit my debt to you. But what have you to say?

1–7 The blind Teiresias is physically blind but spiritually sighted. As a prophet, he is an agent of the gods in their dealings with humans. His revelation of the truth to Oedipus led Oedipus to leave Thebes, which indirectly helped Creon to become king.

Teiresias. This, Creon: you stand once more on the edge of fate.

Creon. What do you mean? Your words are a kind of dread.

10 **Teiresias.** Listen, Creon:
   I was sitting in my chair of augury, at the place
   Where the birds gather about me. They were all a-chatter,
   As is their habit, when suddenly I heard
   A strange note in their jangling, a scream, a
15 Whirring fury; I knew that they were fighting,
   Tearing each other, dying
   In a whirlwind of wings clashing. And I was afraid.
   I began the rites of burnt offering at the altar,
   But Hephaestus failed me: instead of bright flame,
20 There was only the sputtering slime of the fat thigh-flesh
   Melting: the entrails dissolved in grey smoke;
   The bare bone burst from the welter. And no blaze!

   This was a sign from heaven. My boy described it,
   Seeing for me as I see for others.

25 I tell you, Creon, you yourself have brought
   This new calamity upon us. Our hearths and altars
   Are stained with the corruption of dogs and carrion birds
   That glut themselves on the corpse of Oedipus' son.
   The gods are deaf when we pray to them; their fire
30 Recoils from our offering; their birds of omen
   Have no cry of comfort, for they are gorged
   With the thick blood of the dead.
                                    O my son,
   These are no trifles! Think: all men make mistakes,
   But a good man yields when he knows his course is wrong,
35 And repairs the evil. The only crime is pride.

   Give in to the dead man, then: do not fight with a corpse—
   What glory is it to kill a man who is dead?
   Think, I beg you:
   It is for your own good that I speak as I do.
40 You should be able to yield for your own good.

   Creon. It seems that prophets have made me their especial province.
   All my life long
   I have been a kind of butt for the dull arrows
   Of doddering fortunetellers!
                              No, Teiresias:
45 If your birds—if the great eagles of God himself—
   Should carry him stinking bit by bit to heaven,
   I would not yield. I am not afraid of pollution:

11–17 The chair of augury is the place where Teiresias sits to hear the birds, whose sounds reveal the future to him. The fighting among the birds suggests that the anarchy infecting Thebes has spread even to the world of nature.

19 Hephaestus (hĭ-fĕs′təs): god of fire.

18–32 According to Teiresias, the birds and dogs that have eaten the corpse of Polyneices have become corrupt causing the gods to reject the Thebans' offerings and prayers. What do these lines suggest about how the gods view Creon's refusal to allow Polyneices to be buried?

44–48 What do these lines suggest about Creon's view of himself and the gods?

No man can <u>defile</u> the gods.
                              Do what you will;
Go into business, make money, speculate

50 In India gold or that synthetic gold from Sardis,
Get rich otherwise than by my consent to bury him.
Teiresias, it is a sorry thing when a wise man
Sells his wisdom, lets out his words for hire!

49–53 What does Creon assume is the motive behind Teiresias' prophecies?

50 Sardis (sär'dĭs): the capital of ancient Lydia, where metal coins were first produced.

Teiresias. Ah Creon! Is there no man left in the world—

55 **Creon.** To do what? Come, let's have the aphorism!

Teiresias. No man who knows that wisdom outweighs any wealth?

Creon. As surely as bribes are baser than any baseness.

Teiresias. You are sick, Creon! You are deathly sick!

Creon. As you say: it is not my place to challenge a prophet.

60 **Teiresias.** Yet you have said my prophecy is for sale.

Creon. The generation of prophets has always loved gold.

Teiresias. The generation of kings has always loved brass.

Creon. You forget yourself! You are speaking to your king.

Teiresias. I know it. You are a king because of me.

65 **Creon.** You have a certain skill; but you have sold out.

Teiresias. King, you will drive me to words that—

Creon.   Say them, say them!
    Only remember: I will not pay you for them.

Teiresias. No, you will find them too costly.

Creon.   No doubt. Speak:
    Whatever you say, you will not change my will.

70 **Teiresias.** Then take this, and take it to heart!
    The time is not far off when you shall pay back
    Corpse for corpse, flesh of your own flesh.
    You have thrust the child of this world into living night;
    You have kept from the gods below the child that is theirs:

75 The one in a grave before her death, the other,
    Dead, denied the grave. This is your crime:
    And the Furies and the dark gods of hell
    Are swift with terrible punishment for you.
    Do you want to buy me now, Creon?
                              Not many days,

77–78 Furies: three goddesses who avenge crimes, especially those that violate family ties. How might this prophecy be fulfilled?

80 And your house will be full of men and women weeping,
    And curses will be hurled at you from far

WORDS
TO   **defile** (dĭ-fīl') v. to make foul, dirty, unclean, or impure
KNOW

Cities grieving for sons unburied, left to rot before the walls of
    Thebes.

These are my arrows, Creon: they are all for you.

(*to boy*) But come, child: lead me home.

85   Let him waste his fine anger upon younger men.
Maybe he will learn at last
To control a wiser tongue in a better head.

(*Exit* Teiresias.)

Choragus. The old man has gone, King, but his words
    Remain to plague us. I am old, too,
90   But I cannot remember that he was ever false.

Creon. That is true. . . . It troubles me.
    Oh it is hard to give in! but it is worse
    To risk everything for stubborn pride.

Choragus. Creon: take my advice.

Creon.   What shall I do?

95 **Choragus.** Go quickly: free Antigone from her vault
    And build a tomb for the body of Polyneices.

Creon. You would have me do this?

Choragus.   Creon, yes!
    And it must be done at once: God moves
    Swiftly to cancel the folly of stubborn men.

100 **Creon.** It is hard to deny the heart! But I
    Will do it: I will not fight with destiny.

Choragus. You must go yourself; you cannot leave it to others.

Creon. I will go.
          —Bring axes, servants:
    Come with me to the tomb. I buried her; I
105   Will set her free.
             Oh quickly!
My mind misgives—
The laws of the gods are mighty, and a man must serve them
To the last day of his life!

(*Exit* Creon.)

PAEAN

Choragus. God of many names

Chorus.   O Iacchus

                                        son

of Cadmean Semele

                        O born of the thunder!

guardian of the West

                        regent

of Eleusis' plain

                        O prince of maenad Thebes

5   and the Dragon Field by rippling Ismenus:

Choragus. God of many names

Chorus.   the flame of torches

flares on our hills

                        the nymphs of Iacchus

dance at the spring of Castalia:

from the vine-close mountain

                                come ah come in ivy:

10   *Evohé evohé!* sings through the streets of Thebes

Choragus. God of many names

Chorus.   Iacchus of Thebes

heavenly child

                        of Semele bride of the Thunderer!

The shadow of plague is upon us:

                                        come

with clement feet

                        oh come from Parnassus

15   down the long slopes

                        across the lamenting water

Choragus. Io Fire! Chorister of the throbbing stars!
O purest among the voices of the night!
Thou son of God, blaze for us!

Chorus. Come with choric rapture of circling Maenads

20   Who cry *Io Iacche!*

                        God of many names!

PAEAN: A paean (pē'ən) is a hymn appealing to the gods for assistance. In this paean, the chorus praises Dionysus, or Iacchus (yä'kəs), and calls on him to come to Thebes to show mercy and drive out evil.

2 Cadmus was the legendary founder of Thebes. Dionysus was the son of Cadmus' daughter Semele (sə-mē'lē) and Zeus, who is referred to here as thunder.

4–5 These lines name locations near Athens and Thebes. The maenads (mē'nădz') were priestesses of Dionysus.

8–9 The spring of Castalia is on the sacred mountain Parnassus. Grape vines and ivy were symbols of Dionysus.

10 evohé: hallelujah.

EXODOS

(*Enter* Messenger.)

Messenger. Men of the line of Cadmus, you who live
Near Amphion's citadel:
                           I cannot say
Of any condition of human life, "This is fixed,
This is clearly good, or bad." Fate raises up,
5 And Fate casts down the happy and unhappy alike:
No man can foretell his fate.
                            Take the case of Creon:
Creon was happy once, as I count happiness:
Victorious in battle, sole governor of the land,
Fortunate father of children nobly born.
10 And now it has all gone from him! Who can say
That a man is still alive when his life's joy fails?
He is a walking dead man. Grant him rich;
Let him live like a king in his great house:
If his pleasure is gone, I would not give
15 So much as the shadow of smoke for all he owns.

Choragus. Your words hint at sorrow: what is your news for us?

Messenger. They are dead. The living are guilty of their death.

Choragus. Who is guilty? Who is dead? Speak!

Messenger.   Haemon.
Haemon is dead; and the hand that killed him
20 Is his own hand.

Choragus.   His father's? or his own?

Messenger. His own, driven mad by the murder his father had done.

Choragus. Teiresias, Teiresias, how clearly you saw it all!

Messenger. This is my news: you must draw what conclusions you
     can from it.

Choragus. But look: Eurydice, our queen:
25 Has she overheard us?

(*Enter* Eurydice *from the palace, center.*)

Eurydice. I have heard something, friends:
As I was unlocking the gate of Pallas' shrine,
For I needed her help today, I heard a voice
Telling of some new sorrow. And I fainted
30 There at the temple with all my maidens about me.
But speak again: whatever it is, I can bear it:
Grief and I are no strangers.

EXODOS: The exodos is the last episode in the play. It is followed by a final speech made by the choragus and addressed directly to the audience.

2 Amphion: Niobe's husband, who built a wall around Thebes by charming the stones into place with music.

15 How does the messenger compare with the sentry who appeared in Scenes 1 and 2?

27 Pallas: Athena, the goddess of wisdom.

32 Megareus (mə-găr′ē-əs), the older son of Eurydice and Creon, had died in the battle for Thebes.

Messenger. Dearest lady,
I will tell you plainly all that I have seen.
I shall not try to comfort you: what is the use,
35 Since comfort could lie only in what is not true?
The truth is always best.

I went with Creon
To the outer plain where Polyneices was lying,
No friend to pity him, his body shredded by dogs.
We made our prayers in that place to Hecate
40 And Pluto, that they would be merciful. And we bathed
The corpse with holy water, and we brought
Fresh-broken branches to burn what was left of it,
And upon the urn we heaped up a towering barrow
Of the earth of his own land.

When we were done, we ran
45 To the vault where Antigone lay on her couch of stone.
One of the servants had gone ahead,
And while he was yet far off he heard a voice
Grieving within the chamber, and he came back
And told Creon. And as the king went closer,
50 The air was full of wailing, the words lost,
And he begged us to make all haste. "Am I a prophet?"
He said, weeping. "And must I walk this road,
The saddest of all that I have gone before?
My son's voice calls me on. Oh quickly, quickly!
55 Look through the crevice there, and tell me
If it is Haemon, or some deception of the gods!"

We obeyed; and in the cavern's farthest corner
We saw her lying:
She had made a noose of her fine linen veil
60 And hanged herself. Haemon lay beside her,
His arms about her waist, lamenting her,
His love lost underground, crying out
That his father had stolen her away from him.
When Creon saw him, the tears rushed to his eyes,
65 And he called to him: "What have you done, child? Speak to me.
What are you thinking that makes your eyes so strange?
O my son, my son, I come to you on my knees!"
But Haemon spat in his face. He said not a word,
Staring—
and suddenly drew his sword
70 And lunged. Creon shrank back; the blade missed, and the boy,
Desperate against himself, drove it half its length

39–40 Hecate (hĕk′ə-tē) **and Pluto:** other names for Persephone and Hades, the goddess and god of the underworld.

43–44 Note the contrast between the barrow, or burial mound, erected by Creon and the handful of dirt used by Antigone to cover her brother.

60 Note that this is the same way in which Jocasta, Antigone's mother, killed herself.

Into his own side and fell. And as he died,
He gathered Antigone close in his arms again,
Choking, his blood bright red on her white cheek.
75 And now he lies dead with the dead, and she is his
At last, his bride in the houses of the dead.

(*Exit* Eurydice *into the palace.*)

Choragus. She has left us without a word. What can this mean?

Messenger. It troubles me, too; yet she knows what is best;
Her grief is too great for public lamentation,
80 And doubtless she has gone to her chamber to weep
For her dead son, leading her maidens in his dirge.

Choragus. It may be so: but I fear this deep silence.

(*Pause*)

Messenger. I will see what she is doing. I will go in.

(*Exit* Messenger *into the palace. Enter* Creon *with attendants,
bearing* Haemon's *body.*)

Choragus. But here is the king himself: oh look at him,
85 Bearing his own damnation in his arms.

Creon. Nothing you say can touch me any more.
My own blind heart has brought me
From darkness to final darkness. Here you see
The father murdering, the murdered son—
90 And all my civic wisdom!
Haemon my son, so young, so young to die,
I was the fool, not you; and you died for me.

Choragus. That is the truth; but you were late in learning it.

Creon. This truth is hard to bear. Surely a god
95 Has crushed me beneath the hugest weight of heaven,
And driven me headlong a barbaric way
To trample out the thing I held most dear.

The pains that men will take to come to pain!

(*Enter* Messenger *from the palace.*)

Messenger. The burden you carry in your hands is heavy,
100 But it is not all: you will find more in your house.

Creon. What burden worse than this shall I find there?

Messenger. The queen is dead.

Creon. O port of death, deaf world,
Is there no pity for me? And you, angel of evil,
105 I was dead, and your words are death again.

Is it true, boy? Can it be true?
Is my wife dead? Has death bred death?

Messenger. You can see for yourself.

(*The doors are opened, and the body of* Eurydice *is disclosed within.*)

Creon. Oh pity!
110   All true, all true, and more than I can bear!
O my wife, my son!

Messenger. She stood before the altar, and her heart
Welcomed the knife her own hand guided,
And a great cry burst from her lips for Megareus dead,
115   And for Haemon dead, her sons; and her last breath
Was a curse for their father, the murderer of her sons.
And she fell, and the dark flowed in through her closing eyes.

Creon. O God, I am sick with fear.
Are there no swords here? Has no one a blow for me?

120 **Messenger.** Her curse is upon you for the deaths of both.

Creon. It is right that it should be. I alone am guilty.
I know it, and I say it. Lead me in,
Quickly, friends.
I have neither life nor substance. Lead me in.

125 **Choragus.** You are right, if there can be right in so much wrong.
The briefest way is best in a world of sorrow.

Creon. Let it come;
Let death come quickly and be kind to me.
I would not ever see the sun again.

130 **Choragus.** All that will come when it will; but we, meanwhile,
Have much to do. Leave the future to itself.

Creon. All my heart was in that prayer!

Choragus. Then do not pray any more: the sky is deaf.

Creon. Lead me away. I have been rash and foolish.
135   I have killed my son and my wife.
I look for comfort; my comfort lies here dead.
Whatever my hands have touched has come to nothing.
Fate has brought all my pride to a thought of dust.

(*As Creon* is being led into the house, the Choragus *advances and*
speaks directly to the audience.)

Choragus. There is no happiness where there is no wisdom;
140   No wisdom but in submission to the gods.
Big words are always punished,
And proud men in old age learn to be wise.

RESPONDING
OPTIONS

FROM PERSONAL RESPONSE TO CRITICAL ANALYSIS

REFLECT

1. How did you react to what happens at the end of this play? Jot down your impressions in your notebook.

RETHINK

2. How much do you think Creon is to blame for the suicides of Antigone, Haemon, and Eurydice?

   Consider
   - Creon's judgment of himself at the end of the play
   - how Haemon and Eurydice feel about Creon at the moment of death
   - Creon's failed effort to rescue Antigone
   - whether someone can be held accountable for another's suicide

3. What do you think is the main reason that Creon and Antigone cannot resolve their conflict?

   Consider
   - what Polyneices means to each character
   - the principles that motivate each character
   - the attitude of each character toward the gods
   - any flaws or defects exhibited by each character

4. Review the definition of a tragic hero on page 937. Who do you think best fits the definition, Antigone or Creon? Explain your response.

5. Who do you think suffers the most in this play and why?

6. How do other characters—such as Ismene, Teiresias, Haemon, and Eurydice—help you to understand and evaluate the actions of Antigone and Creon?

7. What effect did the choragus and the chorus have on your interpretation of the events in this play? Support your analysis with evidence from the play.

RELATE

8. Which of the messages conveyed by Sophocles do you think is most relevant for people today?

ANOTHER PATHWAY

With a partner, create a flow chart of the plot of Antigone, showing the cause-and-effect relationships between events. Mark the steps that you think are especially instrumental in leading to the tragic conclusion. Share your flow chart by posting it on a class bulletin board.

QUICKWRITES

1. Compare the way you ranked the principles listed in the Personal Connection on page 936 with the way you think Antigone, Creon, or some other character in the play would rank them. Then write a **letter** to that character, either in support of or in opposition to his or her decisions and behavior.

2. Think about how one of the less important characters—such as Ismene, the sentry, or Teiresias—might have viewed what happened to Antigone. Write a **diary entry** expressing the thoughts and feelings of this character.

3. Imagine that you have been asked to address a group on the topic "Women of Courage in Classic Literature." Write the portion of your **lecture** that concerns Antigone.

📁 *PORTFOLIO Save your writing. You may want to use it later as a springboard to a piece for your portfolio.*

LITERARY CONCEPTS

Irony is a contrast between what is believed or expected and what actually exists or happens. **Dramatic irony** is a type of irony that occurs when readers or viewers are aware of information that a character is unaware of. For example, Creon tells Antigone, "That [her death] gives me everything." Once you know the outcome of the play, you realize that Antigone's death will not give Creon everything. On the contrary, it will take from Creon all that is meaningful in his life. This contrast between Creon's limited knowledge and your fuller understanding generates dramatic irony.

With a small group of classmates, find other examples of dramatic irony in *Antigone*. List each example and write a brief explanation of why you think it is ironic. After you have completed your list, share your findings with another group and speculate about why Sophocles used this technique.

ALTERNATIVE ACTIVITIES

1. *Cooperative Learning* With a group of classmates, perform a **Readers Theater production** of a scene from this play. Sit in chairs at the front of the classroom and take turns reading the parts. Choose whether you want to present the scene in the formal manner of the ancient Greek theater or in a more contemporary style.

2. Create a **mask** to be worn in a production of *Antigone*. You may research the masks worn in ancient Greek productions or create your own original version.

3. In Scene 2 of the play, the choragus says of Antigone, "Like father, like daughter: both headstrong, deaf to reason!" Read Sophocles' play *Oedipus the King* to get a sense of Oedipus' character. Then create a **chart** that compares father and daughter.

4. Create a **model** of the Theater of Dionysus in Athens, where this play was first performed.

CRITIC'S CORNER

According to the literary scholar David Grene, "the dilemma of Creon in . . . *Antigone* is incidental to the main emphasis of the play, which is on Antigone." Do you agree with this assessment? Cite details from the play to support your opinion.

THE WRITER'S STYLE

Throughout *Antigone,* Sophocles makes **allusions** to myths that his original audience would have been familiar with. With a partner, research the full story of one of these myths. Then write an explanation of how the myth relates to the story of Antigone and why you think Sophocles included the allusion.

ACROSS THE CURRICULUM

History At various times in *Antigone,* Creon's remarks show his attitude toward having his authority challenged by a woman. With a partner, research the typical role of noblewomen during the fifth century B.C. Then create a Venn diagram in which you compare and contrast Antigone's character with that of a typical noblewoman of the time. Does your diagram shed any light on Creon's behavior?

Marble head of woman from ancient Greek civilization. Published by permission of the Director of Antiquities and the Cyprus Museum Nicosia, Cyprus.

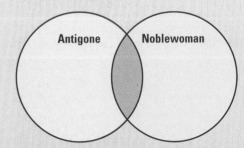

WORDS TO KNOW

Answer the questions that follow.

1. Is a **dirge** a piece of music that is sad, joyful, or complicated?

2. Are people who **transgress** a law those who make it, break it, or enforce it?

3. Would a person's appetite be **sated** by the smell of food, a light snack, or a large meal?

4. Is an **edict** a request, a command, or a question?

5. Would **lamentation** be most expected after a tragedy, a dinner party, or a graduation?

6. Does a person **defile** a lake by photographing it, polluting it, or stocking it with fish?

7. When is it most important to be **lithe**—while competing in a spelling bee, lifting weights, or performing gymnastics?

8. If people demonstrate **compulsive** behavior, is what they do rude, sympathetic, or beyond their control?

9. Is a person most likely to respond to **auspicious** events by feeling encouraged, frightened, or exhausted?

10. If a child was described to you as being **perverse,** would you expect the child to be angelic, disobedient, or shy?

SOPHOCLES

Born near Athens in the village of Colonus, Sophocles was the son of a wealthy manufacturer of armor. In his youth, he received a fine education and was said to be skilled in wrestling, dancing, and playing the lyre. These skills and a handsome appearance apparently resulted in his being chosen, as a youth, to lead a chorus in a celebration of the Greek victory over the Persians at the Battle of Salamis.

496?–406 B.C.

In 468 B.C., Sophocles defeated his teacher, the great playwright Aeschylus (ĕs′kə-ləs), in the Dionysian dramatic festival, an annual competition. That first-place award was followed by as many as 23 other victories, more than any other Greek playwright. Sophocles also was active in the political life of Athens. He was elected several times to the body of high executives commanding the military and was one of ten commissioners in charge of helping Athens recover after a severe military defeat in Sicily. In 406 B.C., the year of his death, he led a chorus of public mourners in honor of Euripides (yŏŏ-rĭp′ĭ-dēz′), a younger playwright who had often been his rival at the annual drama festivals.

Sophocles wrote more than 100 plays, although only 7 of them survive today. These include *Ajax, Oedipus the King* (sometimes called *Oedipus Rex*), *Electra,* and *Oedipus at Colonus. Antigone,* which rivals *Oedipus the King* as his best-known play, was probably first performed in 442 or 441 B.C. *Oedipus at Colonus,* which shows the playwright's affection for his native village, was written when Sophocles was around 90.

OTHER WORKS *Trachinian Women, Philoctetes*

REFLECT & ASSESS

OLD SONG

Traditional, West Africa

Ere alaafin Shangó [Shangó, Oyo-Ilé warrior-king] (early 1800s), Oyo-Shangó artist.
Collection of the Nigerian Museum, Lagos. Photo by Robert Farris Thompson, 1962.

Traditional African poetry was composed and then passed down orally from generation to generation, most often as songs or chants. The poetry includes myths, epics, religious chants, and magical formulas and touches on just about every aspect of daily African life. The selection you are about to read contains a series of proverbs. Highly creative and often humorous, African proverbs reinforce social behavior and express the collective wisdom of a people.

Do not seek too much fame,

but do not seek obscurity.

Be proud.

But do not remind the world of your deeds.

5 Excel when you must,

but do not excel the world.

Many heroes are not yet born,

many have already died.

To be alive to hear this song is a victory.

WRITING FROM EXPERIENCE

WRITING A REPORT

In Unit Six, "The Making of Heroes," you read the legends of King Arthur and Sir Launcelot, heroes chosen by people searching for leadership or inspiration. Every age has its heroes. Who are some heroes of our time?

GUIDED ASSIGNMENT

Write a Biographical Research Paper A biographical research paper tells a person's life story, focusing on what made that life significant. Writing this kind of paper will help you learn more about a person you consider heroic. The following pages will help you research and write your report.

Photograph

Buzz Aldrin was one of the first astronauts to walk on the moon.

Historical Source

1 Read About Heroes

What do you know about the persons identified here? What is each known for? What qualities does each represent? Do you agree that each is a hero? Why or why not?

2 Think About Heroes

With a group, discuss what makes someone a hero. Then brainstorm a list of heroes. Did all of you choose the same kind of person? Which qualities does each of you feel are important? What does this discussion show you about different ideas of what is heroic?

3 QuickWrite

Choose two or three people whom you consider heroic, and spend a few minutes writing about them. What makes each person heroic? Why does each interest you? What would you want to find out about each person?

Decision Point Choose the hero who interests you most. Write a statement of controlling purpose telling what your report will explain about this person. You can revise this statement as you find more information.

On September 10, 1855, Elizabeth Cady Stanton wrote this letter to her friend Susan B. Anthony, the women's rights activist:

Peterboro, September 10, 1855

Dear Susan,

I wish that I were as free as you and I would stump the state in a twinkling. But I am not, and what is more, I passed through a terrible scourging when last at my father's. I cannot tell you how deep the iron entered my soul. I never felt more keenly the degradation of my sex. To think that all in me of which my father would have felt a proper pride had I been a man, is deeply mortifying to him because I am a woman. That thought has stung me to a fierce decision—to speak as soon as I can do myself credit.

She sounds really hurt and angry! Maybe these feelings made her such a passionate reformer.

When I read this I was really struck by her need to prove her work

Political Cartoon
Nelson Mandela was imprisoned for his work against apartheid, a policy of legalized discrimination in South Africa. He was later elected president.

PRISONER, 1963-1990   PRESIDENT, 1994-

© elDani '94
FILIPINO REPORTER, NYC

Copyright © 1995 elDani (Aguila), *Filipino Reporter*, New York. Reprinted by permission.

Magazine Article

The former U.S. president slept in a room at a dormitory at Wilfrid Laurier University in Waterloo, Ont. By 7 a.m. last Tuesday, Jimmy Carter and his wife Rosalynn had eaten breakfast in the cafeteria and were aboard a bus full of volunteer home builders bound for a construction site five km away. Once the most powerful man in the world, Carter spent the day working with his wife and a group of unpaid laborers, installing windows, drywall, and vinyl siding on a small three-bedroom bungalow. The Carters were part of an army of 1,100 volunteers who, in just five days last week, built 40 homes for low-income families in 10 communities across

Former President Jimmy Carter with his wife, Rosalynn

Canada. The nonprofit, Georgia-based organization Habitat for Humanity International sponsored the event as part of its program to provide affordable housing for poor families around the world.

D'Arcy Jenish,
from "Carter the Carpenter," *Maclean's*

What kind of information is provided by each of these sources?

LASERLINKS
• *WRITING SPRINGBOARD*
WRITING COACH

Researching Your Hero

A Search for Sources Now that you have a subject, it's time to plan your research and start digging for information. The steps below can help you decide what information you need, where to look for it, and how to keep track of it all.

Student's Source Cards

❶ Ask Questions

To write a biographical report that is rich in detail, you need more than just facts. To guide your research, develop questions like these.

- What motivated my hero to succeed?
- What obstacles did he or she overcome?
- Who influenced my hero? How?

❷ Search for Sources

You will want to use a variety of primary and secondary sources in writing your report. Primary sources come directly from the person you are writing about or from people who knew him or her. Secondary sources present ideas about a person or subject based on evidence from primary sources.

- Look at the sources on pages 984 and 985. Which are primary? Which are secondary?
- List some types of primary and secondary sources that might provide information on your subject.

❸ Gather Information

Keep the following ideas in mind as you choose your sources and gather information from them.

Remember Your Purpose Refer to the statement of controlling purpose you wrote when you chose your topic. It can help you keep your research, and later your writing, on track.

Evaluate Your Sources As you gather secondary sources, consider whether each source contains up-to-date information and whether the author is a respected authority on your subject. See the SkillBuilder on page 989 for more information.

Journal Article

Book

① Banner, Lois W. Elizabeth Cady Stanton: A Radical for Woman's Rights. Boston: Little, Brown, 1980.

Public Library — HQ 1413 S67 B35

Encyclopedia Entry

⑤ Sochen, June. "Stanton, Elizabeth Cady." The World Book Encyclopedia. 1995 ed.

School Library

⑦ Welter, Barbara. "The Cult of True Womanhood, 1820–1860." American Quarterly 18 (1966): 151–174.

Public Library

Look for Variety Your report will be livelier if you include anecdotes and quotes from your subject as well as from critics and admirers.

4 Make Source Cards and Note Cards

Keep track of your sources on three-by-five-inch index cards. The models on the left show source cards for a book, an encyclopedia entry, and a journal article. In the upper right corner of each card, number the card so that you can easily identify the source when you take notes.

Take notes for your report on four-by-six-inch index cards, writing only one main idea per card. Label each card and note the source card number of the source from which the information is taken. For a source you intend to quote, copy the writer's sentences word for word and enclose them within quotation marks. Otherwise, paraphrase information by rewriting it in your own words. Write the page number from which the information is taken, and note whether the information is a quote or a paraphrase. For more information on making source cards and note cards, see page 1045 of the Writing Handbook.

Student's Note Card

Laws and practices unfair to women

By 1848, married women in some states could control property they inherited. In other states they couldn't. Husbands owned any money their wives earned and had legal rights to their children, which women didn't. Wives could not take their husbands to court. No women could vote. Only one college in the country admitted women. Women could not be doctors or lawyers. 40
(Paraphrase)

5 Write a Thesis Statement

A thesis statement is one or two sentences that tell briefly and clearly what you intend your report to show about your subject. Revise your statement of controlling purpose to reflect your point of view and to emphasize the main ideas of your report. Use your thesis statement to focus and organize your thoughts as you get ready to draft your report.

THINK & PLAN

Looking at What You've Found

1. What information do you need to fill in the gaps in your report? Where could you look for it?
2. What ideas seem most important to include? Which facts, quotes, and anecdotes will support these ideas?

DRAFTING

Drafting Your Report

Ready to Write Your research is complete and you're ready to write—almost. Outlining your ideas first will help make the writing go more smoothly. An outline is your plan, and it is one you can change at any stage of the writing process.

Student's Outline and Rough Draft

E. C. Stanton Outline

Elizabeth Cady Stanton: Women's Rights Pioneer

Thesis: Elizabeth Cady Stanton's upbringing and experience and the reform spirit of her time motivated her to become a leader in the women's rights movement. Despite criticism and frustration, she persevered in her fight for reform.

I. Introduction
   A. Organized first women's rights convention
   B. Worked for many reforms
   C. Became a leader

II. Seneca Falls Convention
   A. Felt unhappy with how women were treated
   B. Called a women's rights convention
   C. Said women should get the vote

III. Her Early Life
   A. Birth date and place
   B. Family's influence on beliefs

① Outline

Follow these steps as you outline:

- Group note cards by subject or idea.
- Write your thesis statement at the top of your outline.
- Using your note cards, list the main ideas in a logical order. Biographies often follow a chronological order.
- Instead of beginning with your hero's date of birth, show your readers why this person is important. Describe a dramatic moment or an achievement.
- Use main ideas as outline headings and supporting ideas as subheadings.

Coaching Workspace of My Report

Elizabeth Cady Stanton: Women's Rights Pioneer

Elizabeth Cady Stanton organized the first women's rights convention in 1848 at Seneca Falls, New York. It was the start of the woman suffrage movement. (At that time, women could not vote.) Stanton became a writer, organizer, and lecturer. During her lifetime, she fought for women's right to vote and for their right to higher education, better wages, fairer divorce laws, and equality in marriage. Her work provoked harsh criticism from many people. But Stanton's upbringing and experience and the reform spirit of her time encouraged her to keep fighting for what she believed.

Stanton had moved from Boston to Seneca Falls in 1846. She wasn't happy about it. Her husband was usually away, leaving her with many children and a lot of work. In Boston, she had always lived with friends nearby and with well-trained servants who could take on much of the work. In her neighborhood she got to be friends with many poor women who were overworked and mistreated by their husbands.

Now she knew what life was like for a lot of women: "I now fully understood the practical difficulties most women had to contend with in the isolated household, and the impossibility of woman's best development if in contact, the chief part of her life, with servants and children" (Stanton and Blatch 144).

② Write a Rough Draft

For each heading in the outline, write at least one paragraph.

- Keep your thesis statement in mind as you write.
- Draft your report from beginning to end or concentrate on the parts of the topic you understand best.
- Credit your sources as you use them. Write the author's last name—or the title of the work if no author is given—and the page number of the source in parentheses following the quotation or information from that source. It is not necessary to credit information that is considered general knowledge—widely known facts that can be found in several sources.

③ Analyze Your Draft

Read your draft to see how well it meets each of the following criteria. Where your draft needs improvement, mark it or make a note on how you can rework it. Your report should be

Structured The introduction includes a thesis statement explaining why your subject is a hero; the body provides details in well-organized paragraphs, and the conclusion ties your main points together.

Accurate Facts are correct and sources are credited.

Thorough Your report covers major events in your subject's life at least briefly and focuses on the most significant.

Clear Ideas are clearly expressed and flow logically.

Interesting You make your account of your subject's life interesting by including colorful facts, quotes, and anecdotes.

④ Rework and Share

Rework your draft, making the changes you marked.

 PEER RESPONSE

Share your draft with a friend and ask the following.

- How could I make my thesis statement clearer?
- Does the way I organized my report make sense? If not, how could I better order my main points?
- What facts, quotes, or anecdotes did you find interesting?
- Have I focused on the parts of my subject's life that seem most important? If not, which parts seem more important?

The Finishing Touches

Your Final Product Your report is nearly complete. Look over your draft. Which parts are most interesting? Which are still unclear? Pay attention to peer responses and the Standards for Evaluation on the next page as you revise and edit to make your report clear and interesting from start to finish.

Student's Final Report

Wong 1

Sheila Wong
Ms. Flores
Sophomore English
24 April 1997

Elizabeth Cady Stanton: Women's Rights Pioneer

In 1848, when Elizabeth Cady Stanton organized the first women's rights convention, the idea of women voting in government elections was so shocking it had never been discussed in public. The convention marked the beginning of the woman suffrage movement and of Stanton's long career as a writer, organizer, and lecturer for the rights of women. During her 87 years, she fought for women's right to vote and for their right to higher education, to better wages, to fairer divorce laws, and to equality in marriage. Her work provoked harsh criticism from the press, from friends, and even from her husband and her father. Despite criticism and frustration with the slow progress of reform, Stanton persevered. Her unique upbringing and personal experiences and the 19th-century reform spirit all motivated her to become a leader in the movement for women's rights.

The Movement Begins

For the first several years of her marriage, Stanton was fairly content with her life. She had a successful husband, three healthy children, a comfortable home in Boston, excellent servants, and interesting friends.

❶ Revise and Edit

Read over your report.

- Does it hold your interest all the way through?
- Is any important information missing? What details, quotes, or anecdotes could help?
- Is your thesis statement clear?
- Does your report give a clear impression of your subject's personality?

❷ Polish It

Turn your rough draft into a finished piece.

- Credit your sources correctly.
- Refer to the SkillBuilder on the next page for help in using brackets and ellipses within text.
- Create a Works Cited list like the one on the next page. Pay close attention to punctuation. For more information on creating a Works Cited list, see page 1044 of the Writing Handbook.

The student explains the subject's importance in a brief introduction.

The student tells how changes in the subject's life influenced her ideas.

When Stanton moved to Seneca Falls in 1846, the change was not a happy one. Her husband, an aspiring politician, was often away, leaving her with a houseful of children and an endless round of chores. In her new neighborhood she came to know many poor women who were overworked and mistreated by their husbands. She later said of that time, "I now fully understood the practical difficulties most women had to contend with in the isolated household" (Stanton and Blatch 144).

Works Cited

Banner, Lois W. Elizabeth Cady Stanton: A Radical for Woman's Rights. Boston: Little, 1980.

DuBois, Ellen Carol, ed. Elizabeth Cady Stanton, Susan B. Anthony: Correspondence, Writings, Speeches. New York: Schocken, 1981.

Griffith, Elisabeth. In Her Own Right: The Life of Elizabeth Cady Stanton. New York: Oxford UP, 1984.

Sochen, June. "Stanton, Elizabeth Cady." The World Book Encyclopedia. 1995 ed.

Stanton, Theodore, and Harriot Stanton Blatch, eds. Elizabeth Cady Stanton, As Revealed in Her Letters, Diary, and Reminiscences. New York: Harper, 1922.

Standards for Evaluation

A biographical research report
- begins with a vivid introduction that reveals why the person is significant and makes the reader want to know more
- covers the most important parts of the subject's life in a clear and logical order
- contains accurate facts from a variety of sources
- uses quotes and anecdotes that convey important information about the subject's life or personality
- has a strong conclusion

SkillBuilder

GRAMMAR FROM WRITING

Using Ellipses and Brackets
When quoting sources, you need not always include every word. When you leave out words within a quote, use ellipsis points to replace the words you leave out. Three dots (. . .) indicate an omission within a sentence. Four dots (. . . .) indicate an omission between sentences. When you replace an author's word with another word or when you add words to explain something within a quote, use brackets [ ] to enclose words not in the original.

GRAMMAR HANDBOOK

For more information on punctuating quotations, see page 1096 of the Grammar Handbook.

Editing Checklist Use the following editing tips as you revise.

- Are sources quoted and cited correctly?
- Are names spelled correctly?

REFLECT & ASSESS

Evaluating the Experience

1. What did you learn about your subject in writing this report?
2. How did your concept of heroism grow or change?

📁 **PORTFOLIO** How well did you communicate your ideas about your subject? Put this evaluation in your portfolio.

REFLECT & ASSESS

UNIT SIX: THE MAKING OF HEROES

How have your thoughts and feelings about heroism been affected by the selections in this unit? At this stage of the school year, how do you rate yourself as a reader and as a writer? Explore these questions by completing one or more of the options in each of the following sections.

REFLECTING ON THEME

OPTION 1 **Assessing Heroism** In Charles Dickens's novel *David Copperfield,* the narrator begins his life's story by wondering "whether I shall turn out to be the hero of my life." What qualities and accomplishments would you need in order to consider yourself a hero? Review the selections in this unit, and make a list of the heroic qualities and accomplishments they present that you would value in your own life.

OPTION 2 **Identifying Qualities of Leadership** Heroes often find themselves in positions of leadership. Review this unit's selections, identifying characters and authors who you believe possess strong lead-

ership abilities, even if they are not in positions of authority. Then work with a partner to create a checklist that identifies the distinctive characteristics of a successful leader. Choose the individual from the unit who best represents those characteristics, and present your choice to your classmates.

Self-Assessment: Which of the selections in this unit gave you the deepest insights into the concept of heroism? Write a short paragraph in which you explain your choice.

REVIEWING LITERARY CONCEPTS

OPTION 1 **Understanding Classical Drama** Review the information about classical drama on page 937 and in the Literary Concepts feature on page 980. Then, in your own words, write definitions of the terms *chorus, tragedy, tragic hero, tragic flaw,* and *dramatic irony.* In each definition, include an example that illustrates the meaning of the term.

chorus:
tragedy:
tragic hero:
tragic flaw:
dramatic irony:

OPTION 2 **Separating Fact from Fiction** As you know, a fictional work can have a factual basis. Review five of the fictional narratives and dramas in this unit, jotting down aspects of plot, character, and setting that you think might have some basis in fact. Compile your results in a chart like the one shown. Then, with a small group of classmates, compare charts and discuss your views on the relationship between facts and imagination in works of literature.

Title	Factual Basis of Plot / Character	Factual Basis of Setting
from *The Acts of King Arthur and His Noble Knights*	• Knights engaged in fighting and boasting. • Ideals of chivalry influenced knights' conduct. • Court celebrations were common.	• Actual places in England are referred to by name. • Castles like the one described existed. • Descriptions of customs and clothing may be accurate.

Self-Assessment: On a sheet of paper, copy the following literary terms: characterization through dialogue, tone in nonfiction, conflict, foil, flashback, true-life adventure, romance, *and* style. *For each term, find an example from outside this unit that illustrates its meaning. To illustrate the concept of tone in nonfiction, for example, you might write a brief description of the tone of an essay in a previous unit. For examples of romance and true-life adventure, you will need to go outside this textbook. Use the Handbook of Literary Terms on page 1000 to refresh your memory about any terms you are not sure of.*

PORTFOLIO BUILDING

• **QuickWrites** Good writers know how to use language economically, without waste or needless repetition. Review the QuickWrites that you completed during this unit, and choose one or two that could profit from trimming and tightening. Revise them, attach the revisions to the originals, and add both versions to your portfolio, along with a note that explains the reasoning behind your revisions.

• **Writing About Literature** Earlier, you wrote a critical essay about one of the selections in this unit. How does it sound to you now? Write a brief note explaining how you chose a selection to write about and how successfully you think you evaluated it. Decide whether to include your note in your portfolio.

• **Writing from Experience** You may have just finished your biographical research paper. If you could ask your hero three questions, what would they be? Jot them down. Then decide how successfully you could tell someone else about your subject's life and why he or she is important to you.

• **Personal Choice** Sometimes our own mistakes provide valuable lessons. Look back through your records and evaluations of all the activities and writing that you completed in this unit, including any

work that you did on your own. Which work do you regard as your least successful? Write a note in which you identify that activity or piece of writing and explain what you have learned from working on it. Add the note, along with your work (or evaluations of it), to your portfolio.

Self-Assessment: At this stage, your writing portfolio should represent the work of an entire year. Review the pieces in your portfolio and choose three of your best works—one done in the fall, one in the winter, and one in the spring. Write a note explaining what these works reveal about your progress and abilities as a writer.

SETTING GOALS

Reflect on all the goals that you set for yourself during the course of the year. Which goals did you reach? Which goals seem nearly within your reach? Which seem as far away as ever? Write an evaluation of your progress this year, and identify three goals for the next school year.

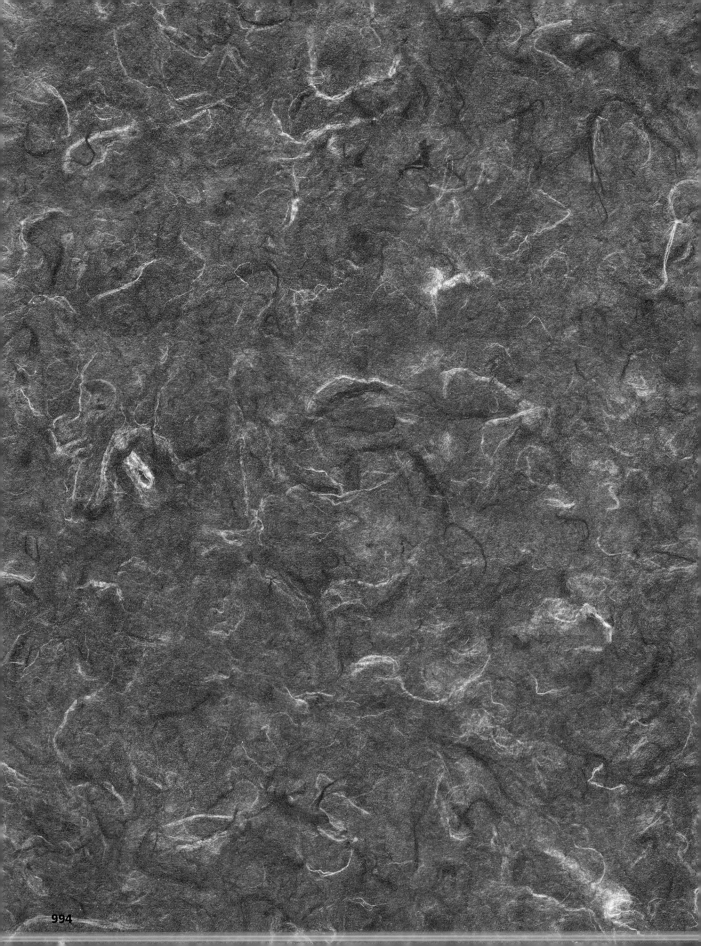

Student Resource Bank

Words to Know: Access Guide

Pronunciation Key

Symbol	Examples	Symbol	Examples	Symbol	Examples
ă	at, gas	m	man, seem	v	van, save
ā	ape, day	n	night, mitten	w	web, twice
ä	father, barn	ng	sing, anger	y	yard, lawyer
âr	fair, dare	ŏ	odd, not	z	zoo, reason
b	bell, table	ō	open, road, grow	zh	treasure, garage
ch	chin, lunch	ô	awful, bought, horse	ə	awake, even, pencil,
d	dig, bored	oi	coin, boy		pilot, focus
ĕ	egg, ten	o͝o	look, full	ər	perform, letter
ē	evil, see, meal	o͞o	root, glue, through		
f	fall, laugh, phrase	ou	out, cow		**Sounds in Foreign Words**
g	gold, big	p	pig, cap	KH	*German* ich, auch;
h	hit, inhale	r	rose, star		*Scottish* loch
hw	white, everywhere	s	sit, face	N	*French* entre, bon, fin
ĭ	inch, fit	sh	she, mash	œ	*French* feu, cœur;
ī	idle, my, tried	t	tap, hopped		*German* schön
îr	dear, here	th	thing, with	ü	*French* utile, rue;
j	jar, gem, badge	*th*	then, other		*German* grün
k	keep, cat, luck	ŭ	up, nut		
l	load, rattle	ûr	fur, earn, bird, worm		

Stress Marks

′ This mark indicates that the preceding syllable receives the primary stress. For example, in the word *language,* the first syllable is stressed: lăng′gwĭj.

′ This mark is used only in words in which more than one syllable is stressed. It indicates that the preceding syllable is stressed, but somewhat more weakly than the syllable receiving the primary stress. In the word *literature,* for example, the first syllable receives the primary stress, and the last syllable receives a weaker stress: lĭt′ər-ə-cho͝or′.

Adapted from *The American Heritage Dictionary of the English Language, Third Edition;* Copyright © 1992 by Houghton Mifflin Company. Used with the permission of Houghton Mifflin Company.

Handbook of Literary Terms

Act An act is a major unit of action in a play. Acts are sometimes divided into scenes; each scene is limited to a single time and place. Shakespeare's plays all have five acts. Contemporary plays usually have two or three acts, although some only have one act. Josephine Tey's *The Pen of My Aunt* and Anton Chekhov's *The Bear* are examples of one-act plays.

Alliteration Alliteration is the repetition of initial consonant sounds. Alliteration occurs in everyday speech and in all forms of literature. Poets, in particular, use alliteration to emphasize certain words, to create mood, to underscore meaning, and to enhance rhythm. Note how D. H. Lawrence makes use of a repeated *s* sound in the following stanza of "Piano." Such repetition helps contribute to the quiet, pensive mood of the poem.

> Softly, in the dusk, a woman is
>   singing to me;
>
> Taking me back down the vista of
>   years, till I see
>
> A child sitting under the piano, in
>   the boom of the tingling strings
>
> And pressing the small, poised feet
>   of a mother who smiles as she
>   sings.

See *Assonance, Consonance.*

Allusion An allusion is a reference to a historical or literary person, place, thing, or event with which the reader is assumed to be familiar. In Bernard Malamud's story "The First Seven Years," the title is an allusion to a story from the Book of Genesis in the Bible. According to the biblical narrative, Jacob agreed to work for Laban for seven years in return for Laban's beautiful daughter Rachel's hand in marriage. Similarly, the title of Stephen Vincent Benét's "By the Waters of Babylon" is an allusion to the beginning of Psalm 137 in the Bible: "By the rivers of Babylon, there we sat down, yea, we wept, when we remembered Zion."

Antagonist The antagonist in a work of literature is the character or force against which the main character, or protagonist, is pitted. The antagonist may be another character, something in nature or society, or even an internal force within the protagonist. In Josephine Tey's *The Pen of My Aunt,* the antagonist is the German soldier who detains the aunt's "nephew"; in Isabel Allende's "And of Clay Are We Created," the destructive force unleashed by the volcano may be considered an antagonist.

See *Conflict, Protagonist.*

Aside In drama, an aside is a remark spoken in an undertone by one character either to the audience or to another character, which the remaining characters supposedly do not hear. The aside is a traditional dramatic convention, a device that the audience accepts even though it is obviously unrealistic. The aside can be used to express a character's feelings, opinions, and reactions, and thus functions as a method of characterization. In the following example from Anton Chekhov's *The Bear,* the aside shows Luke's growing antagonism towards Smirnov.

Luke (*aside*). Now we'll never get rid of him, botheration take it! It's an ill wind brought him along.

Assonance Assonance is the repetition of a vowel sound within nonrhyming words. *Helter-skelter, sweet dreams,* and *high and mighty* are examples of assonance. Writers of both poetry and prose use assonance to give their work a musical quality and unify stanzas and passages. Notice the assonance of the long *a* sounds in the following lines from Robert Hayden's "Those Winter Sundays."

then with cracked hands that ached
from labor in the weekday weather made
banked fires blaze. . . .

See *Alliteration, Consonance.*

Author's Purpose Authors write for one or more of the following purposes: to inform, to express an opinion, to entertain, or to persuade. For example, the purpose of a news report is to inform; the purpose of an editorial is to persuade the readers or audience to do or believe something. Elie Wiesel wrote *Night* to inform readers about the horrors of concentration camps and to persuade them to resist the evil that made these horrors possible.

Autobiography An autobiography is the story of a person's life written by that person. Yevgeny Yevtushenko's *A Precocious Autobiography,* Mark Mathabane's *Kaffir Boy,* and Le Ly Hayslip's *When Heaven and Earth Changed Places* are all examples of autobiographies. Autobiographies are almost always written in the first person, and they typically focus on events and people that are particularly significant in the author's life.

Ballad A ballad is a narrative poem that was originally meant to be sung. Ballads usually begin abruptly, focus on a single tragic incident, contain dialogue and repetition, and imply more than they actually tell. Traditional ballads are written in four-line stanzas with regular rhythm and rhyme. The rhythm often alternates between four-stress and three-stress lines, and the rhyme scheme usually is *a b c b* or *a a b b.*

Folk ballads were composed orally and handed down by word of mouth. These ballads usually tell about ordinary people who have had unusual adventures or have performed daring deeds. The literary ballad is a poem written by a poet who imitates the form and content of the folk ballad.

The following anonymous ballad was popular during the Civil War. Each line has four stresses and the rhyme scheme is *a b c b.*

"Mother, is the battle over?
Thousands have been slain, they say.
Is my father come? and tell me,
Has the army gained the day?

"Is he well, or is he wounded?
Mother, do you think he's slain?
If he is, pray will you tell me.
Will my father come again?

"Mother, I see you always sighing
Since that paper last you read;
Tell me why you are crying:
Is my dearest father dead?"

"Yes, my boy, your noble father
Is one numbered with the slain;
Though he loves me very dearly,
Ne'er on earth we'll meet again."

See *Meter, Narrative Poem, Rhyme.*

Biography A biography is an account of a person's life written by another person. The writer of a biography, or biographer, often researches his or her subject in order to present accurate information. A biographer may also draw upon personal knowledge of his or her subject. For example, Coretta Scott King's *My*

Life with Martin Luther King, Jr., is based on the author's intimate knowledge of her subject. Although biographies are usually book length, there are also shorter forms of biographical writing, such as the excerpt from Colette's *Earthly Paradise,* which is a biographical sketch of the writer's mother, and Doris Herold Lund's "Gift from a Son Who Died," which focuses on the life of Lund's son. Although a biographer—by necessity and by inclination—presents a subject from a certain point of view, a skilled biographer strives for a balanced treatment, highlighting weaknesses as well as strengths, failures as well as achievements.

Blank Verse Blank verse is unrhymed poetry written in iambic pentameter. Each line has five metrical feet, and each foot has an unstressed syllable followed by a stressed syllable.

The "Passing of Arthur," by the English poet Alfred, Lord Tennyson, is written in blank verse. The following lines from the poem describe the famous scene in which, at King Arthur's request, his sword Excalibur is thrown into the water. Note the iambic pentameter and the lack of end rhyme.

> So flash'd / and fell / the brand / Excal / i bur:
> But ere / he dipt / the sur / face, rose /
>   an arm
> Clothed in / white sam / site, mys / tic,
>   won / derful.
> And caught / him by / the hilt / and
>   bran / dish'd him
> Three times, / and drew / him un / der in /
>   the mere.

See *Meter, Rhythm.*

Character Characters are the individuals who participate in the action of a literary work. The most important characters are called **main characters.** Less prominent characters are known as **minor characters.** In Rabindranath Tagore's "The Cabulliwallah," the father, his daughter Mini, and the Cabulliwallah are main characters, while the mother is a minor character.

Whereas some characters are two-dimensional, with only one or two dominant traits, a fully developed character possesses many traits, mirroring the psychological complexity of a real person. In longer works of fiction, main characters often undergo change as the plot unfolds. Such characters are called **dynamic characters,** as opposed to **static characters,** who remain the same. In Amy Tan's "Two Kinds," the narrator is a dynamic character because her perception of her childhood and of her mother changes dramatically during the course of the story; on the other hand, the mother is a static character who remains essentially the same.

See *Antagonist, Characterization, Foil, Plot, Protagonist.*

Characterization Characterization refers to the techniques employed by writers to develop characters. There are four basic methods of characterization.

1. The writer may use physical description. In Nadine Gordimer's "A Chip of Glass Ruby," Mrs. Bamjee is described as follows: "She still wore the traditional dress of a Moslem woman, and her body, which was scraggy and unimportant as a dress on a peg when it was not host to a child, was wrapped in the trailing rags of a cheap sari, and her thin black plait was greased."

2. The character's own speech, thoughts, feelings, or actions may be presented. In Gordimer's story, the reader learns of Mrs. Bamjee's reaction to the arrival of the police: "Although she was not surprised, her hands shook like a very old person's as she undid the locks and the complicated catch on the wire burglar-proofing."

3. The speech, thoughts, feelings, or actions of other characters provide another means of developing a character. Dr. Khan, in Gordimer's story, tells Bamjee that his wife is a "wonderful woman." After Mrs. Bamjee's arrest, one of the neighbors says in sympathy, "Poor Mrs. Bamjee. Such a kind lady."

4. The narrator's own direct comments also serve to develop a character. The narrator says of Mrs. Bamjee, "She had always treated Bamjee as if it were only a mannerism that made him appear uninterested in politics, the way some woman will persist in interpreting her husband's bad temper as an endearing gruffness hiding boundless goodwill. . . ."

See *Character, Narrator, Point of View.*

Chorus In the theater of ancient Greece, the chorus was a group of actors who commented on the action of the play. Between scenes the chorus sang and danced to musical accompaniment in the orchestra—the semicircular floor between the stage and the audience—giving insights into the message of the play. The chorus is often considered a kind of ideal spectator, representing the response of ordinary citizens to the tragic events unfolding in the play. In Sophocles' *Antigone,* the chorus represents the leading citizens of Thebes.

Climax In dramatic or narrative literature, the climax is the moment when the reader's interest and emotional intensity reach their highest point. This moment is also called the **turning point,** since it usually determines how the conflict of the story will be resolved. In Stephen Vincent Benét's "By the Waters of Babylon," John's discovery of the dead "god" is the climax of the story. As a result of his discovery, John realizes the truth about the past and the destruction of its way of life.

See *Falling Action, Plot, Rising Action.*

Comedy A comedy is a dramatic work that is light and often humorous in tone, usually ending happily with a peaceful resolution of the main conflict. *The Pen of My Aunt* is a comedy. A comedy differs from farce by having a more believable plot, more realistic characters, and less boisterous behavior.

See *Drama, Farce.*

Conflict Conflict is the struggle between opposing forces and is the basis of plot in dramatic and narrative literature. **External conflict** occurs when a character is pitted against an outside force, such as another character, a physical obstacle, or an aspect of nature or society. **Internal conflict** occurs when the struggle takes place within a character. In Abioseh Nicol's "As the Night the Day," the main character Kojo experiences internal conflict when he feels guilty about his actions and external conflict when his plan to confess his misdeeds is opposed by his classmate Bandele.

See *Antagonist, Plot, Rising Action.*

Connotation Connotation is the emotional response evoked by a word, in contrast to its **denotation,** which is its literal or dictionary meaning. *Kitten,* for example, is defined as a "young cat." However, the word also suggests, or connotes, images of softness, warmth, and playfulness. In W. P. Kinsella's "The Thrill of the Grass," the narrator describes baseball players who "recall sprawling in the lush outfields of childhood." The word *sprawling* connotes the joy and ease of childhood.

Consonance Consonance is the repetition of consonant sounds within and at the ends of words. "Last but not least" and a "stroke of luck" contain examples of consonance. Consonance, assonance, alliteration, and rhyme give writing a musical quality and may be used to unify poems and passages of prose writing. Notice the repetition of internal and final consonant *s* sounds in the following lines from Cathy Song's "Lost Sister."

But in another wilderness,
the possibilities,
the loneliness,
can strangulate like jungle vines.

See *Alliteration, Assonance.*

Couplet See *Sonnet*.

Denotation See *Connotation*.

Dénouement See *Falling Action*.

Description Description is writing that appeals to the senses. Good descriptive writing helps the reader to see, hear, smell, taste, or feel the subject that is described and usually relies on precise adjectives, adverbs, nouns, and verbs, as well as on vivid, original phrases. Figurative language, such as simile, metaphor, and personification, is also an important tool in description. The following passage from Tom Whitecloud's "Blue Winds Dancing" illustrates the use of vivid descriptive language.

> In my Wisconsin, the leaves change before the snows come. In the air there is the smell of wild rice and venison cooking; and when the winds come whispering through the forests, they carry the smell of rotting leaves. In the evenings, the loon calls, lonely; and birds sing their last songs before leaving. Bears dig roots and eat late fall berries, fattening for their long winter sleep.

See *Connotation, Imagery, Style*.

Dialect A dialect is the particular variety of language spoken in a definite place by a distinct group of people. Dialects vary in pronunciation, vocabulary, colloquial expressions, sentence structure, and grammatical constructions. Writers use dialogue to establish setting, to provide local color, and to develop characters.

The following selection is from *The Adventures of Tom Sawyer* by Mark Twain. Twain effectively reproduces a dialect spoken in the Mississippi River town of Hannibal, Missouri, in about the middle of the 19th century.

> "Hang the boy, can't I never learn anything? Ain't he played me tricks enough like that for me to be looking out for him by this time? But old fools is the biggest

fools there is. Can't learn an old dog new tricks, as the saying is."

Dialect also plays an important role in Samuel Selvon's "When Greek Meets Greek." The main character, Ram, speaks a dialect of Caribbean English, except when he tries to convince his landlord that he is from India.

Dialogue Dialogue is written conversation between two or more characters. Dialogue is used in most forms of prose writing and also in narrative poetry. In drama the dialogue carries the story line. Realistic, well-placed dialogue enlivens narrative, descriptive, and expository prose and provides the reader with insights into characters' personalities and relationships with one another. The dialogue can also reflect the time and place in which the action takes place, giving a richness and believability to the literary work.

See *Characterization, Drama*.

Diction Diction is a writer's choice of words. Diction encompasses both vocabulary (individual words) and syntax (the order or arrangement of words). Diction can be described in terms such as formal or informal, technical or common, abstract or concrete, literal or figurative.

The writer of a scientific essay on thunderstorms, for example, would use formal, technical, and abstract words with precise denotative meanings. The essayist E. B. White, however, uses a more informal language in "Once More to the Lake," relying on words that are common and concrete, as shown by the following figurative description of a thunderstorm at a lake.

> Then the kettledrum, then the snare, then the bass drum and cymbals, then crackling light against the dark, and the gods grinning and licking their chops in the hills. Afterward the calm, the rain steadily rustling in the calm lake. . . .

Drama Drama is literature that develops plot

and character through dialogue and action; in other words, drama is literature in play form. Dramas are meant to be performed by actors and actresses who appear on a stage, before radio microphones, or in front of television or movie cameras.

Unlike other forms of literature, such as fiction and poetry, a work of drama requires the collaboration of many people in order to come to life. In an important sense, a drama in printed form is an incomplete work of art. It is a skeleton that must be fleshed out by a director, actors, set designers, and others who interpret the work and stage a performance. When an audience becomes caught up in a drama and forgets to a degree the artificiality of a play, the process is called the "suspension of disbelief."

Most plays are divided into acts, with each act having an emotional peak, or climax, of its own. The acts sometimes are divided into scenes; each scene is limited to a single time and place. Shakespeare's plays all have five acts. Contemporary plays usually have two or three acts, although some have only one act. Josephine Tey's *The Pen of My Aunt* and Anton Chekhov's *The Bear* are examples of one-act plays.

See *Act, Dialogue, Props, Scene.*

Dramatic Irony See *Irony.*

Dramatic Monologue A dramatic monologue is a lyric poem in which a speaker addresses a silent or absent listener in a moment of high intensity or deep emotion, as if engaged in private conversation. To increase the dramatic impact of the poem, the poet often reveals the motivations as well as the feelings, personality, and circumstances of the speaker. "Thoughts of Hanoi" by Nguyen Thi Vinh is a dramatic monologue.

Essay An essay is a brief nonfiction composition on a single subject, usually presenting the personal views of the writer. An essay may seek to persuade, as does E. M. Forster's "Tolerance." An essay may offer a reflection on an episode in the writer's life, in the manner of E. B. White's "Once More to the Lake." Other essays, such as Roger Rosenblatt's "The Man in the Water" and Brent Staples's "Black Men and Public Space," are reflections on current events or social problems.

Some essays are formal and impersonal, and the major argument is developed systematically. Other essays are informal, personal, and less rigidly organized. The informal essay often includes anecdotes and humor.

Exposition Exposition is the part of a literary work that provides the background information necessary to understand characters and their actions. Exposition typically occurs at the beginning of a work and introduces the characters, describes the setting, and summarizes significant events that took place before the action begins. The exposition in Joan Aiken's "Searching for Summer" introduces the main characters Lily and Tom on their wedding day, tells about the bombs that had permanently darkened the sky, and announces the newlyweds' intention to find the sun.

See *Plot, Rising Action.*

Extended Metaphor In an extended metaphor two unlike things are compared in several ways. Sometimes the comparison is carried throughout a paragraph, a stanza, or an entire selection. William Shakespeare compares the world to a theatrical stage in a famous extended metaphor that begins as follows.

All the world's a stage,

And all the men and women merely players:

They have their exits and their entrances;

And one man in his time plays many parts. . . .

See *Figurative Language, Metaphor, Simile.*

External Conflict See *Conflict.*

Falling Action In a dramatic or narrative work, the falling action occurs after the climax, or high point of intensity or interest. The falling action shows the results of the major events and resolves loose ends in the plot. In Abioseh Nicol's "As the Night the Day," the falling action occurs after the main character Kojo decides to confess that he broke a laboratory thermometer—not Basu, who had been falsely blamed. We learn that Kojo's truthful account is not believed and that the innocent Basu had already confessed to the act. The final resolution or clarification of the plot is sometimes called the **dénouement.**

See *Climax, Plot, Rising Action.*

Fantasy The term *fantasy* is applied to a work of fiction characterized by extravagant imagination and disregard for the restraints of reality. The aim of a fantasy may be purely to delight or may be to make a serious comment on reality. One type of fantasy is represented by *Alice's Adventures in Wonderland,* in which Lewis Carroll creates a nonexistent, unreal, imaginary world. A less extreme form of fantasy, such as Joan Aiken's "Searching for Summer," portrays characters who, within a realistic world, marginally overstep the bounds of reality. Finally, science fiction is a form of fantasy, for it extends scientific principles to new realms of time or place. An example is Ray Bradbury's "A Sound of Thunder," which is set in both the distant future and the distant past.

See *Science Fiction.*

Farce A farce is a play that prompts laughter through ridiculous situations, exaggerated behavior and language, and physical comedy. Characters are often stereotypes; that is, they conform to a fixed pattern or are defined by a single trait. In Anton Chekhov's *The Bear,* for example, Luke might be seen as a stereotype of a loyal but critical servant who tells the lady of the house more than she wants to hear.

See *Comedy, Stereotype.*

Fiction A work of fiction is a narrative that springs from the imagination of the writer, though it may be based on actual events and real people. The writer shapes his or her narrative to capture the reader's interest and to achieve desired effects. The two major types of fiction are novels and short stories. The basic elements of fiction are character, setting, plot, and theme.

See *Novel, Short Story.*

Figurative Language Figurative language is language that communicates ideas beyond the literal meanings of the words. Although what is said is not literally true, it stimulates vivid pictures or concepts in the mind of the reader. For example, the narrator in Alice Walker's "Everyday Use" says that Dee's hair "stands straight up like the wool on a sheep. It is black as night and around the edges are two long pigtails that rope about like small lizards disappearing behind her ears." Obviously, Dee's pigtails do not literally move like lizards, but the passage vividly suggests the look of Dee's hair.

Figurative language appears in poetry and prose as well as in spoken language. The general term *figurative language* includes specific figures of speech, such as simile, metaphor, personification, and hyperbole.

See *Hyperbole, Metaphor, Personification, Simile, Understatement.*

First-Person Point of View
See *Point of View.*

Flashback A flashback is an account of a conversation, an episode, or an event that happened before the beginning of a story. Often a flashback interrupts the chronological flow of a story to give information that can help readers to understand a character's present situation. Tolstoy's "After the Ball" is a story told almost entirely in flashback. The events that happened to the main character Ivan as a young man help readers to understand his present situation and beliefs. Similarly, flashbacks play a vital role in Louise Erdrich's "The Leap," in which the narrator recounts her memories of her mother.

Foil A foil is a character who provides a striking contrast to another character. By using a foil, a writer calls attention to certain traits possessed by a main character or simply enhances a character by contrast. In Anton Chekhov's *The Bear,* for example, the dutiful servant Luke is a foil for Smirnov, the loud, rude, and quarrelsome visitor. In *The Ring of General Macías,* the unsophisticated Cleto is a foil for the suave and refined Andrés, the captain of the revolutionary soldiers.

Foreshadowing Foreshadowing is a writer's use of hints or clues to indicate events that will occur later in a narrative. This technique often creates suspense and prepares the reader for what is to come. Mark Twain's "The Californian's Tale" and Guy de Maupassant's "Two Friends" both contain elements of foreshadowing.

Form At its simplest, the word *form* refers to the physical arrangement of words in a poem— the length and placement of the lines and the grouping of lines into stanzas. The term can also be used to refer to other types of patterning in poetry, anything from rhythm and other sound patterns to the design of a traditional poetic type, such as a sonnet or dramatic monologue. Finally, *form* can be used as a synonym for *genre,* which refers to literary categories ranging from the broad (short story, novel) to the narrowly defined (sonnet, dramatic monologue).

Frame Story A frame story exists when a story is told within a narrative setting or frame— hence, there is a story within a story. This storytelling technique has been used for over one thousand years and was employed in famous works such as *One Thousand and One Arabian Nights* and Geoffrey Chaucer's *The Canterbury Tales.* In Rachel de Queiroz's "Metonymy" the narrator tells a story within a story in order to illustrate the meaning of the title.

Free Verse Free verse is poetry that does not contain regular patterns of rhyme and meter.

The lines in free verse often flow more naturally than do rhymed, metrical lines and thus achieve a rhythm more like everyday human speech. Much of the poetry written in the 20th century is free verse.

An example of free verse is the following poem by Walt Whitman, the 19th-century poet generally credited with originating this type of poetry. The poem was written as a tribute to Abraham Lincoln.

> This dust was once the man,
> Gentle, plain, just and resolute, under
>   whose cautious hand,
> Against the foulest crime in history known
>   in any land or age,
> Was saved the Union of these States.

Hero The word *hero* has come to mean the main character in a literary work. A traditional hero possesses "good" qualities that enable him or her to triumph over an antagonist who is "bad."

The term *tragic hero,* first used by the Greek philosopher Aristotle, refers to a central character in a drama who is dignified or noble. According to Aristotle, a tragic hero possesses a defect, or **tragic flaw,** that brings about or contributes to his or her downfall. This flaw may be poor judgment, pride, weakness, or an excess of an admirable quality. The tragic hero, noted Aristotle, recognizes his or her own flaw and its consequences, but only after it is too late to change the course of events. Creon in *Antigone* may be considered as a tragic hero, though some critics also apply the term to Antigone as well.

The term *cultural hero* refers to a hero who represents the values of his or her culture. King Arthur, for example, represents the physical courage, moral leadership, and loyalty that were valued in Anglo-Saxon society. Antigone can also be considered a cultural hero because her sense of duty to family and the gods, as well as her courage, reflects the values of ancient Greece.

See *Tragedy.*

Humor In literature there are three basic types of humor, all of which may involve exaggeration or irony. **Humor of situation** is derived from the plot of a work. It usually involves exaggerated events or situational irony, which occurs when something happens that is different from what is expected. **Humor of character** is often based on exaggerated personalities or on characters who fail to recognize their own flaws, a form of dramatic irony. **Humor of language** may include sarcasm, exaggeration, puns, or verbal irony, which occurs when what is said is not what is meant. Samuel Selvon's "When Greek Meets Greek" contains all three types of humor, as does Anton Chekhov's *The Bear.*

Hyperbole Hyperbole is a figure of speech in which the truth is exaggerated for emphasis or for humorous effect. The expression "I'm so hungry I could eat a horse" is an example of hyperbole. The following excerpt from John Steinbeck's *The Acts of King Arthur and His Noble Knights* also illustrates hyperbole. In this scene the knights of the Round Table are taking turns praising Lancelot, who is bored by their extravagant claims: "And he [Lancelot] vaguely heard his strength favorably compared with elephants, his ferocity with lions, his agility with deer, his cleverness with foxes, his beauty with the stars. . . ."

Iambic Pentameter See *Meter.*

Imagery Imagery describes words and phrases that re-create vivid sensory experiences for the reader. Because sight is the most highly developed sense, the majority of images are visual. Imagery may also appeal to the senses of smell, hearing, taste, and touch. Effective writers of both prose and poetry frequently use imagery that appeals to more than one sense simultaneously. In D. H. Lawrence's "Piano," the phrase "the boom of the tingling strings" appeals to the senses of hearing and touch, while "pressing the small, poised feet" appeals to the senses of

sight and touch. The following lines from Nguyen Thi Vinh's "Thoughts of Hanoi" appeal to the senses of sight and hearing.

> Stainless blue sky,
> jubilant voices of children
> stumbling through the alphabet,
> village graybeards strolling to the temple. . . .

Internal Conflict See *Conflict.*

Irony Irony is a contrast between what is expected and what actually exists or happens. There are three basic types of irony.

Situational irony occurs when a character or the reader expects one thing to happen but something entirely different occurs. In Amy Tan's "Two Kinds," the narrator expects to play the piano like a prodigy at the talent show. In actuality, however, she performs dismally and embarrasses her family.

Verbal irony occurs when someone says one thing but means another. In *The Ring of General Macías,* Raquel insults the two peasant soldiers by saying, "What a magnificent army you have. So clever. I'm sure you must win many victories." Raquel's comment belittles their response to the noise of a scurrying rabbit, which they mistake for enemy soldiers.

Dramatic irony refers to the contrast between what a character knows and what the reader or audience knows. For example, the German soldier in *The Pen of My Aunt* comes to believe that he has mistakenly detained the nephew of the influential Madame. The audience learns, however, that the soldier has apprehended—and released—a member of the resistance.

See *Hyperbole, Understatement.*

Legend A legend is a story handed down from the past, especially one that is popularly believed to be based on historical events. The story of the rise and fall of King Arthur is a famous example of a legend. Though legends often incorporate supernatural elements and magical deeds, they claim to be the story of a real human being and are often set in a particular time and place. These characteristics separate a legend from a myth.

See *Myth.*

Lyric In ancient Greece, the lyre was a musical instrument, and the lyric became the name for a song accompanied by music. In ordinary speech the words of songs are still called lyrics.

In literature, a lyric is any short poem that presents a single speaker who expresses his or her innermost thoughts and feelings. In a love lyric, such as Amy Lowell's "Taxi" or Aleksandr Pushkin's "To . . .," the speaker expresses romantic love. In other lyrics a speaker may meditate on nature or explore personal issues, such as those addressed by Juan Ramón Jiménez's "I Am Not I" and José Martí's *Simple Poetry.*

Magical Realism Magical realism refers to a style of writing that often includes exaggeration, unusual humor, magical and bizarre events, dreams that come true, and superstitions that prove warranted. Magical realism differs from pure fantasy in combining fantastic elements with realistic elements such as recognizable characters, believable dialogue, a true-to-life setting, a matter-of-fact tone, and a plot that sometimes contains historic events. Julio Cortázar's "House Taken Over" and Jorge Luis Borges "The Meeting" are examples of magical realism.

Metaphor A metaphor is a form of figurative language that makes a comparison between two things that have something in common. Unlike a simile, a metaphor does not use the word *like* or *as;* instead the comparison is suggested rather than directly expressed.

In the following lines from Sonnet 73 by William Shakespeare, the poet draws a comparison between old age and approaching winter.

That time of year thou mayst in me behold
When yellow leaves, or none, or few, do hang
Upon those boughs which shake against
    the cold,

This metaphor helps the reader to perceive the similarity between a person approaching the cold of death and a tree enduring the cold of winter.

See *Extended Metaphor, Figurative
    Language, Simile.*

Meter Meter is the repetition of a regular rhythmic unit in a line of poetry. The meter of a poem is like the beat of a song; it establishes a predictable means of emphasis.

Each unit of meter is known as a **foot,** with each foot having one stressed and one or two unstressed syllables. The four basic types of metrical feet are the **iamb,** an unstressed syllable followed by a stressed syllable ($\breve{}\,\acute{}$); the **trochee,** a stressed syllable followed by an unstressed syllable ($\acute{}\,\breve{}$); the **anapest,** two unstressed syllables followed by a stressed syllable ($\breve{}\,\breve{}\,\acute{}$); and the **dactyl,** a stressed syllable followed by two unstressed syllables ($\acute{}\,\breve{}\,\breve{}$).

A line of poetry is named not only for the type of meter but also for the number of feet in the line. The most common metrical names are **trimeter,** a three-foot line; **tetrameter,** a four-foot line; **pentameter,** a five-foot line; and **hexameter,** a six-foot line.

These lines from Edna St. Vincent Millay's "Sonnet 30" illustrate **iambic pentameter,** the most common form of meter in the English language.

Nŏr yét / ă flóat / ĭng spár / tŏ mén / thăt sínk
Ănd ríse / ănd sínk / ănd ríse / ănd sínk / ăgaín;

Minor Characters See *Character.*

Monologue See *Soliloquy.*

Mood Mood is the feeling, or atmosphere, that a writer creates for the reader. The writer's use of connotation, imagery, and figurative language, as well as sound and rhythm, develops the mood of a selection. Notice how Tom Whitecloud makes use of all of these techniques in this passage from "Blue Winds Dancing" to create a peaceful, joyous mood.

> I walk along the trail to the lodge, watching the northern lights forming in the heavens. White waving ribbons that seem to pulsate with the rhythm of the drums. Clean snow creaks beneath my feet, and a soft wind sighs through the trees, singing to me. Everything seems to say, "Be happy! You are home now—you are free. . . ."

See *Connotation, Diction, Figurative Language, Imagery, Style.*

Myth A myth is a traditional story, usually concerning some superhuman being or unlikely event, that was once widely believed to be true. Frequently, myths attempt to explain natural phenomena, such as solar and lunar eclipses and the cycle of the seasons. For some peoples, myths were both a kind of science and a religion. In addition, myths served as literature and entertainment, just as they do for modern-day audiences.

The most famous myths, such as the stories of Theseus and Hercules, originated among the ancient Greeks and Romans. Norse mythology, consisting of myths from Scandinavia and Germany, is also important classical literature. Indian peoples throughout North America have produced fascinating myths of various kinds, as have the peoples of Africa and Latin America.

See *Legend.*

Narrative A narrative is any type of writing that is primarily concerned with relating an event or a series of events. A narrative can be imaginary, as is a short story or novel, or it can be factual, as is a newspaper account or a work of history.

See *Fiction, Nonfiction, Novel, Plot, Short Story.*

Narrative Poem A narrative poem tells a story. Like a short story, a narrative poem has characters, a setting, a plot, and a point of view, all of which combine to develop a theme. Epics, such as Homer's *Iliad* and Virgil's *Aeneid,* are narrative poems, as are ballads.

Nonfiction Nonfiction is prose writing that is about real people, places, and events. Unlike fiction, nonfiction is largely concerned with factual information, although the writer shapes the information according to his or her purpose and viewpoint. Nonfiction includes an amazingly diverse range of writing; newspaper articles, cookbooks, letters, movie reviews, editorials, speeches, true-life adventure stories—all are considered nonfiction.

See *Autobiography, Biography, Essay, Fiction.*

Novel The novel is an extended work of fiction. Like a short story, a novel is essentially the product of a writer's imagination. The most obvious difference between a novel and a short story is length. Because the novel is considerably longer, a novelist can develop a wider range of characters and a more complex plot.

Onomatopoeia The word *onomatopoeia* literally means "name-making." It is the process of creating or using words that imitate sounds. The *buzz* of the bee, the *honk* of the car horn, the *peep* of the chick are all onomatopoetic, or echoic, words.

Onomatopoeia as a literary technique goes beyond the use of simple echoic words. Writers, particularly poets, choose words whose sounds suggest their denotative and connotative meanings: for example, *whisper, kick, gargle, gnash,* and *clatter.*

Paradox A paradox is a seemingly contradictory or absurd statement that may nonetheless suggest an important truth. Shakespeare employed a paradox in *Julius Caesar.*

Cowards die many times before their deaths;
The valiant never taste of death but once.

The statement suggests that cowards' fearful and constant anticipation of death is worse than death itself. Juan Ramón Jiménez's poem "I Am Not I" reflects upon the paradox expressed in the title, which suggests that the speaker feels separated from himself.

Parody A parody imitates or mocks another serious work or type of literature. Like caricature in art, parody in literature mimics a subject or a style. The purpose of a parody may be to ridicule through broad humor. On the other hand, a parody may broaden understanding or add insight to the original work. Some parodies are even written in tribute to a work of literature.

Personification Personification is a figure of speech in which human qualities are attributed to an object, animal, or idea. Writers use personification to make images and feelings concrete for the reader. In Dahlia Ravikovitch's "Pride," human physical attributes are given to rocks in the phrases "they lie on their backs" and "the rock has an open wound."

See *Figurative Language, Imagery, Metaphor, Simile.*

Plot The word *plot* refers to the chain of related events that take place in a story. The plot is the writer's blueprint for what happens, when it happens, and to whom it happens. Usually, the events of a plot progress because of a **conflict,** or struggle between opposing forces.

Although there are many types of plots, most include the following stages.

• **Exposition** The exposition lays the groundwork for the plot and provides the reader with essential background information. Characters are introduced, the setting is described, and the plot begins to unfold. Although the exposition generally appears at the opening of a story, it may also occur later in the narrative.

• **Rising Action** As the story progresses, complications usually arise, causing difficulties for the main characters and making the conflict more difficult to resolve. As the characters struggle to find solutions to the conflict, suspense builds.

• **Climax** The climax is the turning point of the action, the moment when interest and intensity reach their peak. The climax of a story usually involves an important event, decision, or discovery that affects the final outcome.

• **Falling Action** The falling action consists of the events that occur after the climax. Often, the conflict is resolved, and the intensity of the action subsides. Sometimes this phase of the plot is called the **dénouement** (dā′nōō-män′), from a French word that means "untying." In the dénouement, also known as the resolution, the tangles of the plot are untied and mysteries are solved.

See *Climax, Conflict, Falling Action, Rising Action.*

Poetry Poetry is language arranged in lines. Like other forms of literature, poetry attempts to re-create emotions and experiences. Poetry, however, is usually more condensed and suggestive than prose. Because poetry frequently does not include the kind of detail and explanation found in prose, poetry tends to leave more to the reader's imagination. Poetry also may require more work on the reader's part to unlock meaning.

Poems often are divided into stanzas, or groups of lines. The stanzas in a poem may contain the same number of lines or they may vary in length. Some poems have definite patterns of meter and rhyme. Others rely more on the sounds of words and less on fixed rhythms and rhyme schemes. The use of figurative language is also common in poetry.

See *Form, Meter, Repetition, Rhyme, Rhythm.*

Point of View Point of view refers to the narrative method used in a short story, novel, or nonfiction selection. The two basic points of view are first-person and third-person.

When a character within a selection describes the action as a participant, in his or her own words, the writer is using the **first-person point of view.** A first-person narrator tends to involve the reader in the story and to communicate a sense of immediacy and personal concern. Tim O'Brien's "On the Rainy River" and Alice Walker's "Everyday Use" are examples of the first-person point of view.

Third-person point of view occurs when a narrator outside the action describes events and characters. In **third-person omniscient point of view,** the narrator is omniscient, or all-knowing, and can see into the minds of more than one character. The use of a third-person narrator gives the writer tremendous flexibility and provides the reader with access to all the characters and to events that may be occurring simultaneously. Yukio Mishima's "The Pearl" is told from a third-person omniscient point of view. In this story, the reader not only sees how the different characters react to the loss of the pearl but also has access to their thoughts and feelings. The narrator also shows what each character does after Mrs. Sasaki's party, even though these events take place in different places and occur at approximately the same time.

In the **third-person limited point of view** events are related through the eyes of one character. The narrator describes only that character's feelings and events that he or she witnesses. Bernard Malamud's "The First Seven Years" and R. K. Narayan's "Like the Sun" are examples of the third-person limited point of view. In the Malamud story, the reader sees all events through the eyes of Feld the shoemaker, while in the Narayan story, everything is filtered through the perspective of the main character, Sekhar.

Props The word *prop,* an abbreviation of *property,* refers to the physical objects that are used in a stage production. In Josephina Niggli's *The Ring of General Macías,* the props include furniture, a wine decanter and glasses, and a bottle of poison. Props help to establish the setting for a play.

See *Drama.*

Protagonist The central character in a story or play is called the protagonist. The protagonist is always involved in the central conflict of the plot and often changes during the course of the work. Sometimes more than one character can be the protagonist of a story. The protagonist in R. K. Narayan's "Like the Sun" is the character Sekhar, who encounters problems while seeking to tell the absolute truth. The protagonist in Doris Lessing's "No Witchcraft for Sale" is Gideon, the servant who displays his knowledge of medicinal herbs.

See *Antagonist.*

Quatrain A quatrain is a four-line stanza, or unit of poetry. The most common stanza in English poetry, the quatrain can display a variety of meters and rhyme schemes. The following quatrain by English poet William Savage Landor follows a typical *a b a b* rhyme scheme.

I strove with none; for none was worth my strife, *a*
Nature I loved, and, next to Nature, Art;   *b*
I warmed both hands before the fire of life;   *a*
It sinks, and I am ready to depart.   *b*
See *Meter, Poetry, Rhyme, Sonnet, Stanza.*

Realism In literature, realism has both a general meaning and a special meaning. As a general term, realism refers to any effort to offer an accurate and detailed portrayal of actual life. Thus, critics talk about Shakespeare's realistic portrayals of his characters and praise the medieval poet Chaucer for his realistic descriptions of people from different social classes.

More specifically, realism also refers to a

literary method developed in the 19th century. The realists based their writing on careful observations of their contemporary life, often focusing on the middle or lower classes. They attempted to present life objectively and honestly, without the sentimentality or idealism that had characterized earlier literature. Typically, realists developed their settings in great detail in an effort to re-create a specific time and place for the reader. Guy de Maupassant, Leo Tolstoy, Mark Twain, and Sarah Orne Jewett are all considered realists.

Repetition Repetition is a literary technique in which a sound, word, phrase, or line is repeated for emphasis. Note the use of repetition in the following lines from Edna St. Vincent Millay's "Sonnet 30."

> Love is not all: it is not meat nor drink
> Nor slumber nor a roof against the rain;
> Nor yet a floating spar to men that sink
> And rise and sink and rise and sink again;

Resolution See *Falling Action.*

Rhyme Words rhyme when the sound of their accented vowels and all succeeding sounds are identical, as in *tether* and *together.* For **true rhyme,** the consonants that precede the vowels must be different, as in Shakespeare's rhyming of *day* and *May* in "Sonnet 18." Rhyme that occurs at the ends of lines of poetry is called **end rhyme.** End rhyme that is not exact but approximate is called **off rhyme,** as in *other* and *bother.* Rhyme that occurs within a single line, as in the following example from "The Raven" by Edgar Allan Poe, is called **internal rhyme.**

> Once upon a midnight dreary, while I pondered
> weak and weary,
> Over many a quaint and curious volume of
> forgotten lore,
> While I nodded, nearly napping, suddenly there
> came a tapping,
> As of someone gently rapping, rapping at my
> chamber door.

A **rhyme scheme** is the pattern of end rhyme in a poem. The pattern is charted by assigning a letter of the alphabet, beginning with the letter *a,* to each line. Lines that rhyme are given the same letter. The following example from Shakespeare's "Sonnet 18" has an *a b a b* rhyme scheme.

> But thy eternal summer shall not fade,   *a*
> Nor lose possession of that fair thou owest;   *b*
> Nor shall Death brag thou wander'st in his shade,   *a*
> When in eternal lines to time thou growest: *b*

Rhythm Rhythm refers to the pattern or beat of stressed and unstressed syllables in a line of poetry. Poets use rhythm to bring out the musical quality of language, to emphasize ideas, to create mood, and to reinforce subject matter.
See *Meter.*

Rising Action Rising action refers to the part of the plot in which complications develop and the conflict intensifies, building to the climax, or highest point of interest and intensity in the plot. The rising action in Anton Chekhov's *The Bear* describes the growing conflict between Smirnov and Mrs. Popov.
See *Climax, Falling Action, Plot.*

Romance A romance refers to any imaginative story concerned with noble heroes, chivalric codes of honor, passionate love, daring deeds, and supernatural events. Writers of romances tend to idealize their heroes as well as the eras in which the heroes live. Medieval romances, such as Malory's *Le Morte d'Arthur,* are stories of kings, knights, and ladies who are motivated by love, religious faith, or simply a desire for adventure. Such romances are comparatively lighthearted in tone and loose in structure, containing many episodes. Usually the main character has a series of adventures while on a quest to accomplish some goal.

Satire Satire is a literary technique in which ideas, customs, behaviors, or institutions are ridiculed for the purpose of improving society. Satire may be gently witty, mildly abrasive, or bitterly critical, and it often uses exaggeration to force readers to see something in a more critical light. Luisa Valenzuela's "The Censors" is a satire that criticizes not only censorship but government oppression and the citizens who cooperate with such practices.

Scene A scene is a subdivision of an act in drama. Each scene usually establishes a different time or place. In Shakespeare's *Julius Caesar,* for example, the first scene of Act One takes place at a public celebration on a street in Rome. The last scene in Act Five takes place on a battlefield.

Science Fiction Science fiction is prose writing that presents the possibilities of the future, using known scientific data and theories as well as the creative imagination of the writer. Most science fiction comments on present-day society through the writer's fictional conception of a future society. Stephen Vincent Benét's "By the Waters of Babylon," for example, warns about the danger of modern warfare and the potential for the destruction of our entire civilization. Ray Bradbury's "A Sound of Thunder" shows how all aspects of nature are interrelated and that human interference with the ecological cycle can lead to disaster.

Setting Setting is the time and place of the action of a story. In many stories, setting plays an important role. The prison setting of Bessie Head's "The Prisoner Who Wore Glasses" reflects the racial injustices of South African society, while the desolate frontier setting of Mark Twain's "The Californian's Tale" enables the reader to understand the loneliness of the characters and their need for companionship.

Shakespearean Sonnet See *Sonnet.*

Short Story A short story is a work of fiction that can be read in one sitting. Generally, a short story develops one major conflict. The four basic elements of a short story are setting, character, plot, and theme.

A short story must be unified; all the elements must work together to produce a total effect. This unity of effect is reinforced through an appropriate title and through the use of other literary devices, such as symbolism and irony.

See *Character, Conflict, Plot, Setting, Theme.*

Simile A simile is a stated comparison between two things that are actually unlike but that have something in common. Like metaphors, similes are figures of speech, but whereas a metaphor implies a comparison, a simile expresses the comparison clearly by the use of the word *like* or *as.* In W. P. Kinsella's "The Thrill of the Grass" the narrator describes his shadow as being "black as an umbrella." This simile links the shadow and the umbrella by their common color.

See *Figurative Language, Metaphor.*

Situational Irony See *Irony.*

Soliloquy In a dramatic work, soliloquy is a speech in which a character speaks his or her private thoughts aloud. The character is almost always on stage alone and generally appears to be unaware of the presence of an audience. The plays of William Shakespeare frequently include soliloquies.

Sonnet A sonnet is a lyric poem of 14 lines, commonly written in iambic pentameter. For centuries the sonnet has been a popular form, for it is long enough to permit development of a complex idea yet short and structured enough to challenge any poet's artistic skills.

The Shakespearean, or English, sonnet is sometimes also called the Elizabethan sonnet. It consists of three quatrains, or four-line units, and a final **couplet,** or two-line unit, which reflect the logical organization of the poem. The typical rhyme scheme is *a b a b c d c d e f e f g g*. In the English sonnet, the rhymed couplet at the end of the sonnet provides a final commentary on the subject developed in the preceding three quatrains. The poems by William Shakespeare and Edna St. Vincent Millay included in this text are sonnets.

Some poets have written a series of related sonnets that have the same subject. These are called sonnet sequences, or sonnet cycles. Toward the end of the 15th century, writing sonnets became fashionable, with a common subject being love for a beautiful but unattainable woman. Shakespeare's sonnets are the most famous of all sonnet sequences.

See *Meter, Poetry, Quatrain, Rhythm, Rhyme.*

Speaker The speaker in a poem is the voice that "talks" to the reader, similar to the narrator in fiction. Speaker and poet are not necessarily synonymous. Often a poet creates a speaker with a distinct identity in order to achieve a particular effect. In Nguyen Thi Vinh's "Thoughts of Hanoi," the speaker is a male Vietnamese soldier fighting in a civil war, while the poet is female.

Stage Directions The stage directions in a dramatic script serve as a kind of instructional manual for the director, actors, and stage crew as well as the general reader. Often the stage directions are printed in italic type, and they may be enclosed in parentheses or brackets.

Stage directions serve a number of important functions. They may describe the scenery, or setting. For example, in *The Pen of My Aunt,* the stage directions identify the country house where events unfold and the historical era, the Nazi occupation of France. Directions may also describe the props that are used during a performance. Stage directions may describe lighting, costumes, music, sound effects, or, in the case of film productions, camera angles and shots. Most important, the stage directions usually provide hints to the performers on how the characters look, move, and speak.

Stanza A stanza is a group of lines that form a unit of poetry. The stanza is roughly comparable to the

paragraph in prose. In traditional poems, the stanzas usually have the same number of lines and often have the same rhyme scheme and meter as well. In the 20th century, poets have experimented more freely with stanza form than did earlier poets, sometimes writing poems that have no stanza breaks at all.

Stereotype In literature, simplified or stock characters who conform to a fixed pattern or are defined by a single trait are called stereotypes. Such characters do not usually demonstrate the complexities of real people. Familiar stereotypes in popular literature include the absent-minded professor, the dumb athlete, and the busybody. In Chekhov's *The Bear,* the servant Luke might be seen as a stereotype of a loyal but critical servant who tells the lady of the house more than she wants to hear.

See *Farce.*

Structure Structure is the way in which the parts of a work of literature are put together. In poetry, structure refers to the arrangement of words and lines to produce a desired effect. A common structural unit in poetry is the stanza, of which there are numerous types. In prose, structure is the arrangement of larger units or parts of a selection. Paragraphs, for example, are a basic unit in prose, as are chapters in novels and acts in plays. The structure of a poem, short story, novel, play, or nonfiction selection usually emphasizes certain important aspects of content.

Style Style is the way in which a piece of literature is written. Style refers not to what is said but to how it is said. Elements such as word choice, sentence length, tone, imagery, and use of dialogue contribute to a writer's personal style. Sarah Orne Jewett's style in "A White Heron," for example, might be described as a blend of the poetic and realistic. Through her use of sensory details, regional dialect, and a sensitive narrator, she creates both an accurate and an admiring picture of the main character and her world. Frank O'Connor's style in "The Study of History" might be described as matter-of-fact and humorously understated, reflecting the engaging personality of its youthful narrator.

Surprise Ending A surprise ending is an unexpected twist in plot at the conclusion of a story. The conclusion of Guy de Maupassant's "Two Friends" surprises the reader because earlier events in the story had suggested a different outcome.

Suspense Suspense is the tension or excitement felt by the reader as he or she becomes involved in a story and eager to know the outcome of the conflict. In Stephen Vincent Benét's "By the Waters of Babylon," the reader wants to know if John will survive his journey, what he will discover, and what understandings he will gain from his experiences.

Symbol A symbol is a person, place, or object that represents something beyond itself. For instance, a star on a door represents fame; a star pinned to the shirt of a sheriff stands for authority and power. Symbols can succinctly communicate complicated, emotionally rich ideas. A flag, for example, can symbolize patriotism and a national heritage. The cranes in Hwang Sunwŏn's story of the same name symbolize the childhood friendship of the two main characters, as well as peace and tranquillity. The medicinal plant in Doris Lessing's "No Witchcraft for Sale" symbolizes native African culture.

Theme The theme is the central idea or message in a work of literature. Theme should not be confused with subject, or what the work is about. Rather, theme is a perception about life or human nature shared with the reader. Sometimes the theme is directly stated within a work; at other times it is implied, and the reader must infer the theme.

One way to discover the theme of a work of literature is to think about what happens to the central characters. The importance of those events, stated in terms that apply to all human beings, is often the theme. In several selections throughout this book, for example, the theme involves the need for people to accept one another despite differences in culture.

Third-Person Narration See *Point of View*.

Title The title of a literary work often reflects the meaning of the work. For example, the title of Nadine Gordimer's "A Chip of Glass Ruby" refers to a traditional Indian adornment. When Mrs. Bamjee was a girl, her mother had fixed a glass ruby in her daughter's nostril, "but she [Mrs. Bamjee] had abandoned that adornment . . . long ago." On one hand, the title suggests her rejection of a narrowly defined traditional role. On the other hand, the title suggests the husband's frustrated desire for a wife solely focused on traditional duties.

Tone Tone is the attitude a writer takes toward a subject. The language and details a writer chooses help to create the tone, which might be playful, serious, bitter, angry, or detached, among other possibilities. To identify the tone of a work of literature, you might find it helpful to read the work aloud, as if giving a dramatic reading before an audience. The emotions that you convey in reading should give you hints as to the tone of the work.

Unlike mood, which refers to the emotional response of the reader to a work, tone reflects the feelings of the writer. For example, Roger Rosenblatt's "The Man in the Water" exhibits a philosophic, somber tone, reflecting the writer's efforts to draw a lesson from a tragic yet heroic event. Luisa Valenzuela's "The Censors" has an ironic, amusing tone, showing the writer's disapproval of censorship and governmental oppression.

See *Connotation, Diction, Mood, Style*.

Tragedy In broad terms tragedy is literature, especially drama, in which actions and events turn out disastrously for the main character or characters. In tragedy the main characters, and sometimes other involved characters and innocent bystanders as well, are destroyed. Usually the destruction is death, as in Shakespeare's *Julius Caesar* or Sophocles' *Antigone.* Some tragedies, however, end with the main characters alive but in a devastated condition. Tragic heroes evoke both pity and fear in readers or viewers—pity because they feel sorry for the characters and fear because they realize that the problems and struggles faced by the characters are perhaps a necessary part of human life. At the end of a tragedy, a reader or viewer generally feels a sense of waste, because humans who were in some way superior have been destroyed.

See *Hero.*

Tragic Flaw See *Hero.*

Tragic Hero See *Hero.*

True-Life Adventure A true-life adventure is a nonfiction account of heroic deeds or exciting excursions, usually organized chronologically. Often, a true-life adventure is narrated from the first-person point of view, presenting the experience as it happened to the writer, as illustrated by Yossi Ghinsberg's *Back from Tuichi.* A true-life adventure may also be written from a third-person point of view, as reported to the writer.

Turning Point See *Climax.*

Understatement Understatement is the technique of creating emphasis by saying less than is actually or literally true. As such, it is the opposite of exaggeration, or hyperbole. Understatement can be a biting form of sarcasm or verbal irony. Jonathan Swift, the 18th-century English writer best known for *Gulliver's Travels,* often used understatement as a satiric weapon. For example, Swift wrote, "Last week I saw a woman flayed [skinned alive], and you will hardly believe how much it altered her appearance for the worse."

See *Hyperbole, Irony.*

Verbal Irony See *Irony.*

Voice The term *voice* refers to a writer's unique use of language that allows a reader to "hear" a human personality in his or her writing. The elements of style that determine a writer's voice include sentence structure, diction, and tone. For example, some writers are noted for their reliance on short, simple sentences, while others make use of long, complicated ones. Certain writers use concrete words, such as *lake* or *cold,* which name things that you can see, hear, feel, taste, or smell. Others prefer abstract terms like *memory,* which name things that cannot be perceived with the senses. A writer's tone also leaves its imprint on his or her personal voice.

The term can be applied to the narrator of a selection, as well as the writer. For example, in Alice Walker's "Everyday Use" the narrator establishes her personality through her manner of narration. She emerges as a strong, down-to-earth character with a gift for descriptive language, as shown by her following account of her daughter exiting from a car.

Dee next. A dress down to the ground, in this hot weather. A dress so loud it hurts my eyes. There are yellows and oranges enough to throw back the light of the sun. I feel my whole face warming from the heat waves it throws out. Earrings gold, too, and hanging down to her shoulders. Bracelets dangling and making noises when she moves her arm up to shake the folds of the dress out of her armpits. The dress is loose and flows, and as she walks closer, I like it. . . .

The Writing Process

The writing process consists of four stages: prewriting, drafting, revising and editing, and publishing and reflecting. As the graphic to the right shows, these stages are not steps that you must complete in a set order. Rather, you may return to any one at any time in your writing process, using feedback from your readers along the way.

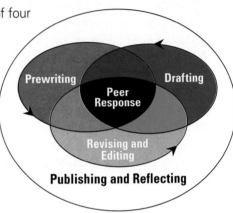

1.1 Prewriting

In the prewriting stage, you explore your ideas and discover what you want to write about.

Finding Ideas for Writing

Ideas for writing can come from just about anywhere: experiences, memories, conversations, dreams, or imaginings. Try one or more of the following techniques to help you find and explore a writing topic.

Personal Techniques
Practice imaging, or trying to remember mainly sensory details about a subject—its look, sound, feel, taste, and smell.
Complete a knowledge inventory to discover what you already know about a subject.
Browse through magazines, newspapers, and on-line bulletin boards for ideas.
Start a clip file of articles that you want to save for future reference. Be sure to label each clip with source information.

Sharing Techniques
With a group, brainstorm a topic by trying to come up with as many ideas as you can without stopping to critique or examine them.
Interview someone who knows a great deal about your topic.

Writing Techniques
After freewriting on a topic, try looping, or choosing your best idea for more freewriting. Repeat the loop at least once.
Make a list to help you organize ideas, examine them, or identify areas for further research.

Graphic Techniques
Create a pro-and-con chart to compare the positive and negative aspects of an idea or course of action.
Use a cluster map or tree diagram to explore subordinate ideas that relate to your general topic or central idea.

Determining Your Purpose

At some time during your writing process, you need to consider your purpose, or general reason, for writing. For example, your purpose may be one of the following: to express yourself, to entertain, to inform, to describe, to analyze, or to persuade. To clarify your purpose, ask yourself questions like these:

- Why did I choose to write about my topic?
- What aspects of the topic mean the most to me?
- What do I want others to think or feel after they read my writing?

Identifying Your Audience

Knowing who will read your writing can help you clarify your purpose, focus your topic, and choose the details and tone that will best communicate your ideas. As you think about your readers, ask yourself questions like these:

- What does my audience already know about my topic?
- What will they be most interested in?
- What language is most appropriate for this audience?

1.2　Drafting

In the drafting stage, you put your ideas on paper and allow them to develop and change as you write.

There's no right or wrong way to draft. Sometimes you might be adventuresome and dive right into your writing. At other times, you might draft slowly, planning carefully beforehand. You can combine aspects of these approaches to suit yourself and your writing projects.

 LINK TO LITERATURE

Personal experiences are often the richest source of ideas for writing. Elie Wiesel's painful memories of his time in a Nazi concentration camp during World War II informed the world about one of the darkest periods in history. In the excerpt from *Night,* page 308, notice how details add a sense of "you are there" immediacy to the account of endurance during the Holocaust.

Alice Walker, author of "Everyday Use," page 110, realizes the importance of both Standard English and African-American dialect. "I use them both naturally," Walker has said. "In speaking to you, I speak in the language we both understand, and it's perfectly easy to do. But when I'm speaking to my mother, it's in black folk English. . . . It's very cozy; it immediately creates a world."

Discovery drafting is a good approach when you've gathered some information on your topic or have a rough idea for writing but are not quite sure how you feel about your subject or what exactly you want to say. You just plunge into your draft and let your ideas lead you where they will. After finishing a discovery draft, you may decide to start another draft, do more prewriting, or revise your first draft.

Planned drafting may work better for research reports, critical reviews, and other kinds of formal writing. Try thinking through a writing plan or making an outline before you begin drafting. Then, as you write, you can develop your ideas and fill in the details.

1.3 Using Peer Response

The suggestions and comments your peers or classmates make about your writing are called peer response.

Talking with peers about your writing can help you discover what you want to say or how well you have communicated your ideas. You can ask a peer reader for help at any point in the writing process. For example, your peers can help you develop a topic, narrow your focus, discover confusing passages, or organize your writing.

Questions for Your Peer Readers

You can help your peer readers provide you with the most useful kinds of feedback by following these guidelines:

- Tell readers where you are in the writing process. Are you still trying out ideas, or have you completed a draft?
- Ask questions that will help you get specific information about your writing. Open-ended questions that require more than yes-or-no answers are more likely to give you information you can use as you revise.
- Give your readers plenty of time to respond thoughtfully to your writing.
- Encourage your readers to be honest when they respond to your work. It's OK if you don't agree with them—you always get to decide which changes to make.

The chart on the following page explains different peer-response techniques you might use when you're ready to share your work with others.

Technique	When to Use It	Questions to Ask
Sharing	Use this when you are just exploring ideas or when you want to celebrate the completion of a piece of writing.	Will you please read or listen to my writing without criticizing or making suggestions afterward?
Summarizing	Use this when you want to know if your main idea or goals are clear.	What do you think I'm saying? What's my main idea or message?
Replying	Use this strategy when you want to make your writing richer by adding new ideas.	What are your ideas about my topic? What do you think about what I have said in my piece?
Responding to Specific Features	Use this when you want a quick overview of the strengths and weaknesses of your writing.	Are the ideas supported with enough examples? Did I persuade you? Is the organization clear enough so you could follow the ideas?
Telling	Use this to find out which parts of your writing are affecting readers the way you want and which parts are confusing.	What did you think or feel as you read my words? Would you show me which passage you were reading when you had that response?

Tips for Being a Peer Reader

Follow these guidelines when you respond to someone else's work:

- Respect the writer's feelings.
- Make sure you understand what kind of feedback the writer is looking for, and then respond accordingly.
- Use "I" statements, such as "I like . . .," "I think . . .," or "It would help me if. . . ." Remember that your impressions and opinions may not be the same as someone else's.

1.4 Revising and Editing

In the revising and editing stage you improve your draft, choose the words that best express your ideas, and proofread for mistakes in spelling, grammar, usage, and punctuation.

The changes you make in your writing during this stage usually fall into three categories: revising for content, revising for structure, and editing to correct mistakes in mechanics. Use the questions and suggestions that follow to help you assess problems in your draft and determine what kinds of changes would improve it.

WRITING TIP

Writers are more likely to accept criticism of their work if they first receive positive feedback. When you act as a peer reader, try to start your review by telling something you like about the piece.

WRITING TIP

Be sure to consider the needs of your audience as you answer the questions under Revising for Content. For example, before you can determine whether any of your material is unnecessary or irrelevant, you need to identify what your audience already knows.

WRITING TIP

For help identifying and correcting problems that are listed in the Proofreading Checklist, see the Grammar Handbook, pages 1058–1097.

Revising for Content

- Does my writing have a main idea or central focus? Is my thesis clear?
- Have I incorporated adequate detail? Where might I include a telling detail, revealing statistic, or vivid example?
- Is any material unnecessary, irrelevant, or confusing?

Revising for Structure

- Is my writing unified? Do all ideas and supporting details pertain to my main idea or advance my thesis?
- Is my writing clear and coherent? Is the flow of sentences and paragraphs smooth and logical?
- Do I need to add transitional words, phrases, or sentences to make the relationships among ideas clearer?
- Are my sentences well constructed? What sentences might I combine to improve the grace and rhythm of my writing?

Editing to Correct Mistakes in Mechanics

When you are satisfied with your draft, proofread and edit it, correcting any mistakes you might have made in spelling, grammar, usage, and punctuation. You may want to proofread your writing several times, looking for different types of mistakes each time. The following checklist may help you proofread your work.

Proofreading Checklist	
Sentence Structure and Agreement	Are there any run-on sentences or sentence fragments? Do all verbs agree with their subjects? Do all pronouns agree with their antecedents? Are verb tenses correct and consistent?
Forms of Words	Do adverbs and adjectives modify the appropriate words? Are all forms of *be* and other irregular verbs used correctly? Are pronouns used correctly? Are comparative and superlative forms of adjectives correct?
Capitalization, Punctuation, and Spelling	Is any punctuation mark missing or not needed? Are all words spelled correctly? Are all proper nouns and all proper adjectives capitalized?

If you have a printout of your draft or a handwritten copy, mark changes on it by using the proofreading symbols shown in the chart on the next page. The Grammar Handbook, starting on page 1058, includes models for using these symbols.

Proofreading Symbols			
$\wedge$	Add letters or words.	/	Make a capital letter lowercase.
$\odot$	Add a period.	¶	Begin a new paragraph.
$\equiv$	Capitalize a letter.	— or ৽	Delete letters or words.
⌣	Close up space.	∾	Switch the positions of letters or words.
$\wedge$	Add a comma.		

1.5 Publishing and Reflecting

After you've completed a writing project, consider sharing it with a wider audience—even when you've produced it for a class assignment. Reflecting on your writing process is another good way to bring closure to a writing project.

Creative Publishing Ideas

Following are some ideas for publishing and sharing your writing.

- Post your writing on an electronic bulletin board or send it to others via e-mail.
- Create a multimedia presentation and share it with classmates.
- Publish your writing in a school newspaper or literary magazine.
- Present your work orally in a report, a speech, a reading, or a dramatic performance.
- Submit your writing to a local newspaper or a magazine that publishes student writing.
- Form a writing exchange group with other students.

Reflecting on Your Writing

Think about your writing process and consider whether you'd like to add your writing to your portfolio. You might attach to your work a note in which you answer questions like these:

- What did I learn about myself and my subject through this writing project?
- Which parts of the writing process did I most and least enjoy?
- As I wrote, what was my biggest problem? How did I solve it?
- What did I learn that I can use the next time I write?

WRITING TIP

You might work with other students to publish an anthology of class writing. Then exchange your anthology with another class or another school. Reading the work of other student writers will help you get ideas for new writing projects and for ways to improve your work.

Building Blocks of Good Writing

2.1 Introductions

A good introduction catches your reader's interest and often presents the main idea of your writing. To introduce your writing effectively, try one of the following methods.

Make a Surprising Statement

Beginning with a startling or interesting fact can capture your reader's curiosity about the subject, as in the example below.

> The Star of Africa, a diamond that is part of the British Crown Jewels, is roughly the size of a golf ball. It is only one of hundreds of jewels, crowns, and scepters on display at the Tower of London. These treasures not only are impressive but also tell much of the history of the British Empire.

Provide a Description

A vivid description sets a mood and brings a scene to life for your reader. The following description introduces a travel article about Greenland.

> The glowing orb hovered on the horizon, its brilliant rays reflected in the powdery, crystalline snow that blanketed everything. This breathtaking sight was my first impression of Greenland.

Pose a Question

Beginning with a question can make your readers want to read on to find out the answer. The following introduction asks readers to think about something they may not have thought about before.

LINK TO LITERATURE

A vivid description is a good way to introduce readers to the characters or setting of a narrative. A description that sets a mood is an effective way to draw the reader into the setting for a narrative. Kay Boyle conveys the mood of a dark and lonely New York apartment in her opening for "Winter Night," page 40.

Why does a paperback printed ten years ago fall apart, while a book published centuries ago remains intact? The answer can be found by exploring the different materials used in bookmaking throughout history.

Relate an Anecdote

Beginning with a brief anecdote, or story, can hook readers and help you make a point in a dramatic way. The following anecdote sets the scene for a discussion of class distinctions in Britain.

Young Winston Churchill was once stopped on his way up the stairs by a member of parliament from an opposing political party. "Stand back," the man said brusquely. "I don't make way for fools." Stepping well back to give the man a wide berth, Churchill replied, "*I do.*"

WRITING TIP

Dialogue can enhance an introduction. The comments by Winston Churchill and his fellow member of parliament make the anecdote at the left more vivid and realistic.

Address the Reader Directly

Speaking directly to readers in your introduction establishes a friendly, informal tone and involves them in your topic.

Masterpiece Theatre has been praised for bringing great works to the screen; however, you may recall a few of the "masterpieces" that have been downright clunkers.

Begin with a Thesis Statement

A thesis statement expressing a paper's main idea may be woven into both the beginning and the end of a piece of nonfiction. The following is a thesis statement that introduces a literary analysis.

By telling the story "After the Ball" almost entirely through the words of one character, Tolstoy provides little interpretation. With this technique, the author allows readers to experience for themselves the intertwining of good and evil.

2.2 Paragraphs

A paragraph is made up of sentences that work together to develop an idea or accomplish a purpose. Whether or not it contains a topic sentence stating the main idea, a good paragraph must have both unity and coherence.

Unity

A paragraph has unity when all the sentences support and develop one stated or implied idea. Use the following techniques to create unity in your paragraphs.

Write a Topic Sentence A topic sentence states the main idea of the paragraph; all the other sentences in the paragraph provide supporting details. A topic sentence is often the first sentence in a paragraph, as shown in the model below. However, it may also appear later in the paragraph or at the end, to summarize or reinforce the main idea.

> *Extrasensory perception (ESP) is the term for awareness or communication by means other than the known physical senses.* ESP includes clairvoyance and telepathy—knowledge of facts and of another's thoughts gained without using ordinary sensory processes. People have believed in such phenomena for thousands of years, but only since the late 1800s have scientists explored ESP.

Relate All Sentences to an Implied Main Idea A paragraph can be unified without a topic sentence as long as every sentence supports the implied, or unstated, main idea. In the example below, all the sentences work together to create a unified impression of a cool spring morning.

> Budding leaves formed a pale green veil over the gray trees. The fragrance of the damp earth, as the last traces of snow melted into it, was invigorating. People on the street greeted one another familiarly, as if they were fellow inmates jointly released from winter's prison. None of this stirred Kim, however. Her somber mood remained untouched by spring.

WRITING TIP

The same techniques that create unity in paragraphs can be used to create unity in an entire paper. Be sure that all of your paragraphs support the thesis statement or the implied main idea of your paper. If a paragraph includes information irrelevant to the main idea, you should delete it or revise it to establish a clear connection.

Coherence

A paragraph is coherent when all its sentences are related to one another and flow logically from one to the next. The following techniques will help you achieve coherence in paragraphs.

- Present your ideas in the most logical order.
- Use pronouns, synonyms, and repeated words to connect ideas.
- Use transitional devices to show the relationships among ideas.

In the example below, the italicized words show how the writer used some of these techniques to create a unified paragraph.

> Most comets "die" by being flung out of the solar system. In 1994, *however*, scientists videotaped the unusual *death* of Comet Shoemaker-Levy 9. *It* passed close enough to Jupiter for *the planet's* gravitational pull to rip *the comet* apart. Even if *it* had passed Jupiter safely, *it* would have died, eventually, perhaps by crashing into the sun. We probably wouldn't have known about *its death, though*, since *that event* might not have occurred for a few hundred thousand more years.

2.3 Transitions

Transitions are words and phrases that show the connections between details, such as relationships in time and space, order of importance, causes and effects, and similarities or differences.

Time or Sequence

Some transitions help to clarify the sequence of events over time. When you are telling a story or describing a process, you can connect ideas with such transitional words as *first, second, always, then, next, later, soon, before, finally, after, earlier, afterward,* and *tomorrow.*

> *First* I had to determine where I was. The sun high above told me that it was noon, but I could not tell which way was east. *Then* I hit on the idea of heading left until I could see which way the building numbers ran. *Finally,* after walking many blocks, I got my bearings and was on my way.

WRITING TIP

You can use the techniques at the left to create coherence in an entire paper. Be sure that paragraphs flow logically from one to the next.

LINK TO LITERATURE

In "Like the Sun," page 608, notice how author R. K. Narayan begins his story in the morning and marks the sequence of the day throughout the narrative with transitional phrases, such as "the very first test," "his next trial," and "during the last period."

Spatial Relationships

Transitional words and phrases such as *in front, behind, next to, along, nearest, lowest, above, below, underneath, on the left,* and *in the middle* can help readers visualize a scene.

> Ben surveyed the great room. *The middle* of the room was dominated by a huge stone fireplace. *To his left* were a large brown sofa and two easy chairs. Dark wooden bookcases covered the entire wall *to his right.* A colorful oil painting hung *above* the fireplace, and as Ben crossed the room, he felt the rough plank floor *underneath* his feet.

Degree

Transitions of degree, such as *mainly, strongest, weakest, first, second, most important, least important, worst,* and *best,* may be used to rank ideas or to show degree of importance, as in the model below.

> *At worst,* Margot would have to repeat a grade. *At best* she would barely pass and move on to 11th grade.

Compare and Contrast

Words and phrases such as *similarly, likewise, also, like, as, neither . . . nor,* and *either . . . or* show similarity between details. *However, by contrast, yet, but, unlike, instead, whereas,* and *while* show difference. Note the use of both types of transitions in the model below.

> At first glance the couple seemed ideally suited. *Each* was tall and fit. *Each* was articulate and social. *On the other hand,* she thrived on competition, *but* he shrank from it.

Cause and Effect

When you are writing about a cause-and-effect relationship, use transitional words and phrases such as *since, because, thus, therefore, so, due to, for this reason,* and *as a result* to help clarify that relationship and to make your writing coherent.

LINK TO LITERATURE

Note the use of transitions that show degree in "Montgomery Boycott," page 221. In the introduction, Coretta Scott King uses words such as *most* and *worse* to describe how African Americans in the South were treated when they used public transportation.

> *Because* so many early chess players were Persian, historians long thought that the game began in Persia in about A.D. 590. Ivory chess pieces, recently discovered in Russia, date to the second century A.D., however, *so* historians are reconsidering.

2.4 Elaboration

Elaboration is the process of developing a writing idea by providing specific supporting details that are appropriate for the purpose and form of your writing.

Facts and Statistics

A fact is a statement that can be verified, while a statistic is a fact stated in numbers. As in the model below, the facts and statistics you use should strongly support the statements you make.

> Cats are often kept inside for their own safety, but this practice is also safer for other animals as well. A recent study shows that the average city cat kills about 28 birds per year.

Sensory Details

Details that show how something looks, sounds, tastes, smells, or feels can enliven a description. Which senses does the writer appeal to in the following paragraph?

> She ran her hand over the many fabrics displayed on the counter—sliding over the smooth Connaught satin, moving the crisp silk organza between her fingers, judging the heft of the resisting brocade. What a gown this would be—if she could only make up her mind!

Incidents

One way to illustrate a point is to relate an incident or tell a story, as in the example on the following page.

WRITING TIP

Facts and statistics can be used to explain more than one idea, depending on how you interpret the information for the reader. Be certain that you clearly and logically establish how the facts you have chosen support your writing.

> Eva had expected courtesy and dignity—but not warmth—from the people of this land of bracing winds, barren moors, and stone walls. Now here was this stranger saying, "You must be Laura's mother. Do join us for tea." Her image of reserved Britons did an about-face.

Examples

An example can help make an abstract or complex idea concrete for the reader.

> The fast-food eating habits of Americans create large amounts of waste. For example, one takeout cup of coffee can create several waste items: a cup, a wooden stir stick, a plastic lid, plastic cream containers, and paper sugar packets.

Quotations

Choose quotations that clearly support your points and be sure that you copy each quotation word for word. Remember always to credit the source.

> Tolerance may be the most necessary virtue for ensuring peace, because the practice of tolerance requires us to think carefully before we react and before we judge others. In his essay "Tolerance," E. M. Forster says that tolerance "entails imagination. For you have all the time to be putting yourself in someone else's place."

2.5   Description

A good description contains carefully chosen details that create a unified impression for the reader.

Description is an important part of most writing genres—essays, stories, biography, and poetry, for example. Effective description can help readers to recognize the significance of an issue, to visualize a scene, or to understand a character.

LINK TO LITERATURE

Note Rachel de Queiroz's use of examples in "Metonymy, or the Husband's Revenge," on page 452. When she introduces the term *applied metonymy,* she uses an example to demonstrate the abstract idea.

Use a Variety of Details

If you include plenty of sensory details, the reader can better imagine the scene you are describing. In the example below, the sensory details help capture the character's mood.

> Phil dragged the worn canvas backpack from the dark recesses of the closet. The musty odor rekindled memories of his many trips with Joe. Hastily he rolled up a new bar of yellow soap and his toothbrush in the soft gray sweatshirts he would be living in for days. The prospect of camping with his brother transported him back in time.

Show, Don't Tell

Simply telling your readers about an event or an idea in a general way does not give them a clear impression. Showing your readers the specific details, however, helps them develop a better sense of your subject. The following example only tells you about the character.

> Warren had the best time at Mona's party.

The paragraph below uses descriptive details to show how he enjoyed the evening's activities.

> Warren had looked at his watch soon after arriving at Mona's party, but it was four hours later when he thought to check the time again. After all, the music was just his style, and the food was delicious. What's more, his wit did not fail him. He was the life of the party.

Use Figurative Language

Figurative language is descriptive writing that evokes associations beyond the literal meaning of words. The following types of figurative language can make your descriptions clear and fresh.

LINK TO LITERATURE

E. B. White uses a variety of sensory details in his essay "Once More to the Lake." In his description of the lake on page 707, he writes, "In the shallows, the dark, water-soaked sticks and twigs, smooth and old, were undulating in clusters on the bottom against the clean ribbed sand."

WRITING TIP

Be careful not to use two or more comparisons that create a confusing image. *The football player was a bowling ball, rolling through the defensive line and flattening his opponents like a bulldozer.*

WRITING TIP

Clarify your descriptive writing by choosing precise words. For example, you can replace general nouns (*instrument*) with more specific nouns (*scalpel*).

- A **simile** is a figure of speech comparing two essentially unlike things, signaling the comparison with a word such as *like* or *as*.
- A **metaphor** is a figure of speech describing something by speaking of it as if it were something else, without using a word such as *like* or *as* to signal the comparison.

The example below uses a simile to describe a cat.

> The cat perched on the armoire, wound up and poised for action like a spring.

Organize Your Details

Organize descriptions carefully to create a clear image for your reader. Descriptive details may be organized chronologically, spatially, by order of importance, or by order of impression.

> Rung by rung she ascended, remembering her father's advice not to look down. To distract her from an acute awareness of the swaying of the ladder, she focused on her goal. "Once I reach the window, the rest will be easy," she said to herself. "If only I hadn't forgotten my key."

2.6 Conclusions

A conclusion should leave readers with a strong final impression. Try any of these approaches for concluding your writing.

Restate Your Thesis

A good way to conclude an essay is by restating your thesis, or main idea, in different words. The conclusion below restates the thesis introduced in an example on page 1025.

> By allowing one of the characters to tell his own story in "After the Ball," Tolstoy lures readers in and invites them to experience and to interpret the events for themselves. Therefore, it is Tolstoy's narrative technique—not the events of the story—that makes readers feel the intertwining of good and evil so acutely.

Ask a Question

Try asking a question that sums up what you have said and gives readers something new to think about. The question below concludes a persuasive argument for eating healthier food.

> The next time you want to grab a quick snack, ask yourself, Do I really need these french fries? or Can my body afford to eat these chips?

Make a Recommendation

When you are persuading your audience to take a position on an issue, you can conclude by recommending a specific course of action.

> To learn firsthand about campaigns and the election process, you should participate in the high school's mock presidential election.

Make a Prediction

Readers are concerned about matters that may affect them and therefore are moved by a conclusion that predicts the future.

> The mild winter and light snows of recent years will leave people unprepared for the bitter winter that has been forecast for the city this year.

Summarize Your Information

Summarizing reinforces your main ideas, leaving a strong, lasting impression. The model below concludes with a statement that summarizes an analysis of Winslow Homer's art.

> Winslow Homer's art captured a range of 19th-century American experiences—from events as significant as the Civil War to lighthearted scenes of children at play.

 LINK TO LITERATURE

In the last two paragraphs of his essay "Black Men and Public Space," on page 297, Brent Staples summarizes what he has learned to do over the years in response to people's fearful reactions to him.

3 Narrative Writing

Narrative writing tells a story. If you write a story from your imagination, it is called a fictional narrative. A true story about actual events is called a nonfictional narrative.

Writing Standards

Good narrative writing

▶ includes descriptive details and dialogue to develop the characters, setting, and plot

▶ has a clear beginning, middle, and end

▶ has a logical organization with clues and transitions to help the reader understand the order of events

▶ maintains a consistent tone and point of view

▶ uses language that is appropriate for the audience

▶ demonstrates the significance of events or ideas

Key Techniques of Narrative Writing

Depict Characters Vividly

Use vivid details to show your readers what your characters look like, what they say, and what they think.

Example

"Sit!" she ordered. I was surprised to hear such anger in my aunt's voice. All I had done was skip school.

Clearly Organize the Events

Choose the important events and explain them in an order that is easy to understand. In a fictional narrative, this series of events is the story's plot.

Example
- Kelly moves from a city to a small town.
- She meets new friends; her aunt warns her about getting into trouble.
- Kelly and friends are caught skipping school.
- Kelly admits that she was acting foolishly and tries to make up for her mistake.

Describe the Conflict

The conflict of a narrative is the problem that the main character faces. In the example below, the conflict is between the main character, Kelly, and her aunt.

Example

After my friends left, my aunt followed me to my room. She said, "Those kids are trouble, and trouble's the last thing you need to be messing with at your new school."

Organizing Narrative Writing

One way to organize a piece of narrative writing is to arrange the events in chronological order, as shown in Option 1 below.

Option 1 **Example**

Focus on Events
• Introduce characters and setting
• Show event 1
• Show event 2
• End, perhaps showing the significance of the events

Kelly moves from the city to a small town to live with her aunt.

When Kelly brings her new friends home, her aunt says, "Those kids are trouble."

Kelly is caught skipping school with her friends, and her aunt grounds her for a week.

Kelly admits that she was acting foolishly and offers to clean her aunt's basement to make up for the trouble she caused her.

When the telling of a fictional narrative focuses on a central conflict, the story's plot may follow the model shown in Option 2. It is also possible in narrative writing to arrange the order of events by starting *in medias res,* or in the middle of things (Option 3).

Option 2

Focus on Conflict
• Describe the main characters and setting
• Present the conflict
• Relate the events that make the conflict complex and cause the characters to change
• Present the resolution, or outcome of the conflict

Option 3

Flashback
• Begin with the conflict
• Present the events leading up to the conflict
• Present the resolution, or outcome of the conflict

Remember: Good narrative writing shows action rather than telling about it.

WRITING TIP

Introductions Try to hook your reader's interest by opening your story with an exciting event or some attention-grabbing dialogue.

WRITING TIP

As the writer, you decide what your characters say. You can make every word count by using dialogue for any of the following purposes: to reveal character, to highlight the relationship between characters, or to move the action along.

4 Explanatory Writing

LINK TO LITERATURE

Explanatory writing provides many opportunities to explore issues presented in literature. The examples on the following pages examine the excerpt from Le Ly Hayslip's nonfictional narrative *When Heaven and Earth Changed Places* and Hwang Sunwŏn's fictional narrative "Cranes."

Explanatory writing is writing that informs and explains. For example, you can use it to evaluate the effects of a new law, to compare two movie reviews, or to analyze a narrative.

Types of Explanatory Writing

Compare and Contrast

Compare-and-contrast writing explores the similarities and differences between two or more subjects.

Example
Le Ly Hayslip and the character Sŏngsam in "Cranes" may not seem to have much in common. However, both choose to follow personal values rather than acting the part of warriors.

Cause and Effect

Cause-and-effect writing explains why something happened, why certain conditions exist, or what resulted from an action or a condition.

Example
The war in Vietnam causes dramatic changes in Le Ly Hayslip's family life.

Analysis

Analysis explains how something works, how it is defined, or what its parts are.

Example
Le Ly Hayslip's father defined his daughter's job as follows: "to stay alive, to find a husband and have babies," and "to live in peace."

Problem-Solution

Problem-solution writing identifies a problem, analyzes the problem, and proposes a solution to it.

Example
Le Ly's father faces the problem of protecting his family's farm from enemy soldiers by hiding and keeping watch.

4.1 Compare and Contrast

Compare-and-contrast writing explores the similarities and differences between two or more subjects.

Organizing Compare-and-Contrast Writing

Compare-and-contrast writing can be organized in different ways. The examples below demonstrate feature-by-feature organization and subject-by-subject organization.

Option 1 — **Example**

Feature by Feature

Feature 1
- Subject A
- Subject B

Feature 2
- Subject A
- Subject B

Le Ly Hayslip and the character Sŏngsam both learn the value of acting peacefully during wartime.

Le Ly learns that she should live in peace and tend the shrines of her ancestors.

Sŏngsam realizes that his friend's life is more important than the duty of being a soldier.

Le Ly Hayslip and Sŏngsam learn this value from two different sources.

Option 2 — **Example**

Subject by Subject

Subject A
- Feature 1
- Feature 2

Subject B
- Feature 1
- Feature 2

Le Ly learns an important lesson during a time of war.

She learns that she should live in peace and tend the shrines of her ancestors.

She learns this from the example of her father, who devoted himself to his family and farm.

The character Sŏngsam learns an important lesson during a time of war.

He realizes that his friend's life is more important than the duty of being a soldier.

He learns this value by recollecting their shared childhood experiences.

WRITING TIP

Remember your purpose for comparing the items you are writing about and support your purpose with expressive language and specific details.

Writing Standards
Good cause-and-effect writing
▶ clearly states the cause-and-effect relationship being examined
▶ shows clear connections between causes and effects
▶ presents causes and effects in a logical order and uses transitions effectively
▶ uses facts, examples, and other details to illustrate each cause and effect
▶ uses language and details appropriate to the audience

 WRITING TIP

Possible topics for cause-and-effect writing include important historical events that had an impact on society. For example, what effect did the invention of the cotton gin have on the Southern economy and society? You can explore current events and their potential outcomes as well.

Cause-and-effect writing explains why something happened, why certain conditions exist, or what resulted from an action or a condition.

Organizing Cause-and-Effect Writing

Your organization will depend on your topic and purpose for writing. If your focus is on explaining the effects of an event such as the passage of a law, you might first state the cause and then explain the effects (Option 2). If you want to explain the causes of an event such as the closing of a factory, you can first state the effect and then examine its causes (Option 3). Sometimes you'll want to describe a chain of cause-and-effect relationships (Option 1) to explore a topic such as the disappearance of tropical rain forests or the development of home computers.

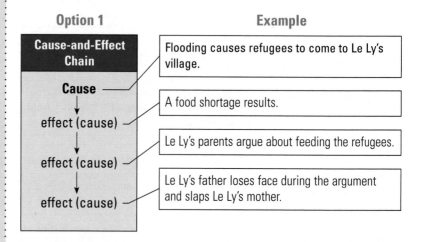

Option 1   **Example**

Cause-and-Effect Chain

Cause — Flooding causes refugees to come to Le Ly's village.

effect (cause) — A food shortage results.

effect (cause) — Le Ly's parents argue about feeding the refugees.

effect (cause) — Le Ly's father loses face during the argument and slaps Le Ly's mother.

Option 2

Cause to Effect

Cause
- Effect 1
- Effect 2
- Effect 3

Option 3

Effect to Cause

Effect
- Cause 1
- Cause 2
- Cause 3

Remember: You cannot assume that a cause-and-effect relationship exists simply because one event follows another. Be sure your facts indicate that the effect could not have happened without the cause.

4.3 Problem-Solution

Problem-solution writing clearly states a problem, analyzes the problem, and proposes a solution to the problem.

Organizing Problem-Solution Writing

Your organization will depend on the goal of your problem-solution piece, your intended audience, and the specific problem you choose to address. The organizational methods outlined below are effective for different kinds of problem-solution writing.

Option 1   **Example**

Simple Problem-Solution	
Description of problem and why it needs to be solved	Should you endanger yourself to protect something you value? In *When Heaven and Earth Changed Places,* Le Ly's father risks capture to protect his family's farm from enemy troops.
Recommended solution	I wouldn't endanger myself to protect a possession, but I would take risks to protect my family.
Explanation of solution	Even though I know it is dangerous, I would risk my own safety to protect my family from a dangerous situation such as a fire.
Conclusion	Taking risks to protect something I value could be dangerous, but I would do it for my family.

Option 2   **Example**

Deciding Between Solutions	
Description of Problem	What would you do if invading troops threatened to destroy your city or town?
Solution A	You could pack some of your possessions and go somewhere that isn't being threatened.
• Pros	You and your family would be in a safe place to wait until your town is out of danger.
• Cons	Your home and possessions could be destroyed while you are away seeking safety.
Solution B	
• Pros	You could stay near your home and try to protect your possessions and property.
• Cons	
Recommendation	

Writing Standards

Good problem-solution writing

▶ identifies the problem and helps the reader understand the issues involved

▶ analyzes the causes and effects of the problem

▶ integrates quotes, facts, and statistics into the text

▶ explores potential solutions to the problem and recommends the best one(s)

▶ uses language, tone, and details appropriate to the audience

WRITING TIP

Ask a classmate to read and respond to your problem-solution writing. Here are some questions for your peer reader to respond to: Is my language clear? Is the writing organized in a way that is easy to follow? Do the proposed solutions seem logical?

A good analysis

- hooks the reader's attention with a strong introduction

- clearly states the subject and its individual parts

- uses a specific organizing structure to provide a logical flow of information

- shows connections among facts and ideas through subordinate clauses and transitional words and phrases

- uses language and details appropriate for the audience

 WRITING TIP

Introductions To capture the reader's attention, you may want to begin your analysis with a vivid description of the subject. For example, a description of the father's efforts to protect his farm and family during the war could introduce an analysis of the excerpt from *When Heaven and Earth Changed Places.*

4.4 Analysis

In an analysis you try to help your readers understand a subject by explaining how it works, how it is defined, or what its parts are.

The details you include will depend upon the kind of analysis you're writing.

- A **process analysis** should provide background information—such as definitions of terms and a list of needed equipment—and then explain each important step or stage in the process. For example, you might explain the steps to program a VCR or the stages in a plant's growth cycle.

- A **definition** should include the most important characteristics of the subject. To define a quality, such as honesty, you might include the characteristic of telling the truth.

- A **parts analysis** should describe each of the parts, groups, or types that make up the subject. For example, you might analyze the human brain by looking at its parts, or a new law by looking at how different groups are affected by it, or jazz music by describing the different styles of jazz.

Organizing Your Analysis

Organize your details in a logical order appropriate for the kind of analysis you're writing. A process analysis is usually organized chronologically, with steps or stages in the order they occur.

Option 1 **Example**

Process Analysis

Introduce topic → The war in Vietnam involved many warring factions and different countries over many years.

Background information → Vietnam is a tropical country in Southeast Asia. Most of the people of Vietnam are farmers. Vietnam was at war—with other countries and internally—roughly from 1946 until 1975.

Explain steps

- Step 1 → Some Vietnamese began fighting French rule in 1946.

- Step 2 → In 1954 a United Nations peace treaty divided Vietnam into two parts, North and South.

- Step 3 → Despite many years of support from the United States, in 1975 the South Vietnamese government was toppled by North Vietnam.

You can organize the details in a definition or parts analysis in order of importance or impression.

Option 2   **Example**

Definition

Introduce term — *When Heaven and Earth Changed Places* shows what survival means to Le Ly and her family during the Vietnam War.

General definition

Explain qualities — Survival takes on new meaning during wartime since people are required to behave in uncommon ways.

- Quality 1 — Survival requires taking extraordinary action to keep the family safe.

- Quality 2 — Survival can require dividing the family for safety's sake.

- Quality 3 — Survival requires self-sacrifice for the sake of others.

In the following parts analysis, the challenges of surviving during wartime are broken down into three different aspects.

Option 3   **Example**

Parts Analysis

Survival during wartime can be as difficult for civilians as it is for soldiers.

Introduce subject

Explain parts — Le Ly's family members choose different ways to adapt to wartime in order to survive.

- Part 1 — Le Ly's father adapts to wartime by singing comical songs about the soldiers who are nearby.

- Part 2 — Le Ly's mother adapts by taking a serious outlook on the war and protecting her children.

- Part 3 — As a child, Le Ly views the war as part of everyday life. She spends time with her father learning about family traditions and ancestors.

WRITING TIP

Conclusions Since analytical writing often deals with numerous details, it will help your readers if your conclusion summarizes the main points.

5 Persuasive Writing

Persuasive writing allows you to use the power of language to inform and influence others.

Key Techniques of Persuasive Writing

Writing Standards

Good persuasive writing

- clearly states the issue and the writer's position
- gives opinions and supports them with facts or reasons
- has a reasonable and respectful tone
- takes into account and answers opposing views
- uses sound logic and effective language
- concludes by summing up reasons or calling for action

State Your Opinion

Taking a stand on an issue and clearly stating your opinion are essential to every piece of persuasive writing you do.

Example
If you liked the story "The Witness for the Prosecution" by Agatha Christie, you should see the movie of the same name.

Know Your Audience

Knowing who will read your writing will help you decide what information you need to share and what tone you should use to communicate your message. In the example below, the writer has chosen an informal tone appropriate for a review to be presented to fellow students.

Example
Like many other Agatha Christie mysteries, "The Witness for the Prosecution" now has quite a following.

Support Your Opinion

Using reasons, examples, facts, statistics, and anecdotes to support your opinion will show your audience why you feel the way you do. Below, the writer gives a reason to support her opinion.

Example
In both the movie and the story, unfolding events hook the audience into discovering who the real villain is, step by step.

Organizing Persuasive Writing

In persuasive writing, you need to gather information to support your opinions. Here are some ways you can organize that material to persuade your audience.

Option 1   **Example**

Reasons for Your Opinion
Your opinion
• Reason 1
• Reason 2
• Reason 3

If you liked the story "The Witness for the Prosecution" by Agatha Christie, you should see the movie of the same name.

As in the story, the fascinating characters and exciting courtroom drama capture the audience's attention.

Like the defense attorney in the story, the audience becomes involved in solving the crime.

The unexpected final twist stuns the audience.

Depending on the purpose and form of your writing, you may want to show the weaknesses of other opinions as you explain the strength of your own. Two options for persuasive writing that include opposing viewpoints are shown below.

Option 2

Why Your Opinion Is Stronger
Your opinion
• your reasons
Other opinion
• evidence refuting reasons for other opinion and showing strengths of your opinion

Option 3

Why Another Opinion Is Weaker
Other opinion
• reasons
Your opinion
• reasons supporting your opinion and pointing out the weaknesses of the other side

Remember: Effective persuasion often uses deductive reasoning—arguing from a general statement to specific points. Keep this in mind as you organize the reasons supporting your opinion.

WRITING TIP

Introductions Capture your readers' attention in the introduction to your piece. Try opening with a quote, a statistic, or an anecdote that shows the importance of your topic.

WRITING TIP

Conclusions Writing persuasively means convincing the reader to feel the way you do about something. Your conclusion might summarize your opinion, make a final appeal, or urge your readers to take action.

6 Research Report Writing

A research report explores a topic in depth, incorporating information from a variety of sources.

Key Techniques of Research Report Writing

Writing Standards

Good research report writing

- ▶ clearly states purpose of the report in a thesis statement
- ▶ uses evidence and details from a variety of sources to support the thesis
- ▶ contains only accurate and relevant information
- ▶ documents sources correctly
- ▶ develops the topic logically and includes appropriate transitions
- ▶ includes a properly formatted Works Cited list

Clarify Your Thesis

A thesis statement is one or two sentences clearly stating the main idea that you will develop in your report. A thesis may also indicate the organizational pattern you will follow and reflect your tone and point of view.

Example
Although H. G. Wells's predictions about space travel were mostly inaccurate scientifically, he did successfully predict the impact such developments would have on society.

Support Your Ideas

You should support your ideas with relevant evidence—facts, anecdotes, and statistics—from reliable sources. In the following example, the writer supports a claim about the accuracy of H. G. Wells's predictions of the future.

Example
Most of Wells's predictions were scientifically inaccurate, but sometimes he got things right. Although Wells wrote *The First Men in the Moon* 60 years before the first crewed space flight, he accurately described the effects of weightlessness in space (McConnell 155).

Document Your Sources

You need to document, or credit, the sources you use in your writing. In the example below, the writer uses a quotation as a supporting detail and documents the source.

Example
Jonathan Rose claims that "futurology is more than just predicting new gadgetry. It is far more important to foresee the impact that future technology will have on everyday life" (20).

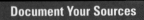

Evaluating Sources

To help you determine whether your sources are reliable and contain useful and accurate information, use the following checklist.

Checklist for Evaluating Your Sources	
Authoritative	Someone who has written several books or articles on your subject or whose work has been published in a well-respected newspaper or journal may be considered an authority.
Up-to-date	Check the publication dates to see whether the source reflects the most current research on your subject.
Respected	In general, tabloid newspapers and popular-interest magazines are not reliable sources. If you have questions about whether you are using a respected source, ask your librarian.

Making Source Cards

For each source you find, record the bibliographic information on a separate index card. You will need this information to give credit to the sources you use in your paper. The samples at the right show how to make source cards for magazine articles, on-line articles, and books. You will use the source number on each card to identify the notes you take during your research.

Taking Notes

As you read your sources, record on note cards information that is relevant to the purpose of your research. You will probably use all three of the following note-taking methods.

- **Paraphrase,** or restate in your own words, the main ideas and supporting details from a passage.
- **Summarize,** or rephrase the original material in fewer words, trying to capture the key ideas.
- **Quote,** or copy the original text word for word, if you think the author's own words best clarify a particular point. Use quotation marks to signal the beginning and the end of the quotation.

WRITING TIP

For additional help, see the research report about Elizabeth Cady Stanton on page 991 or McDougal Littell's *Writing Research Papers.*

Magazine

Source number ①
Author — Title of article
Rose, Jonathan. "Looking Back—to the Futurists of the Past." *Scholastic Update* Dec. 1986: 19-21.
Title of magazine/Date of publication/Page number

On-line Article

②
Author — Title of article
Ferrell, Keith. "The challenges of science fiction."
Title of source in print — Title of database
Omni Feb. 1992. *Magazine Index.* On-line.
Date of publication — Publication medium
Dialog. 18 Oct. 1995.
Computer service/Date of access

Book

③
Author — Title
McConnell, Frank. *The Science Fiction of H. G. Wells.* New York: Oxford UP, 1981.
City of publication/Publisher/Date of publication

Location of source — Library call number
Public Library — 823 W454 Ym

Quotation

Main idea — Source number ③
Wells's predictions and society
Wells's stories "tell us something important not about the 'real' nature of the moon or space travel, ... but rather about the image of a truly just, truly civilized society as it might appear on this planet." 162
Type of note — Page number
(Quotation)

Organizing Your Research Report

Making an outline can help guide the drafting process. Begin by reading over your note cards and sorting them into groups. The main-idea headings may help you find connections among the notes. Then arrange the groups of related note cards so that the ideas flow logically from one group to the next.

Note the format for a topic outline shown below. Remember that in a topic outline, items of the same degree of importance should be parallel in form. For instance, if A is a noun, then B and C should also be nouns. Subtopics need not be parallel with main topics.

Predicting the Future in _The First Men in the Moon_

Introduction—Predictions in Wells's science fiction

I. Predictions about science and technology

   A. Accurate predictions

   B. Inaccurate predictions

     1. Design of space ships

     2. Life on the moon

II. Predictions about society

Documenting Your Sources

When you quote, paraphrase, or summarize information from one of your sources, you need to credit that source, using parenthetical documentation.

Guidelines for Parenthetical Documentation	
Work by One Author	Put the author's last name and the page reference in parentheses: (McConnell 152). If you mention the author's name in the sentence, put only the page reference in parentheses: (152).
Work by Two or Three Authors	Put the authors' last names and the page reference in parentheses: (Philmus and Hughes 34).
Work by More than Three Authors	Give the first author's last name followed by _et al._ and the page reference: (Schreck et al. 212).
Work with No Author Given	Give the title or a shortened version and the page reference (if appropriate): ("Science Fiction").
One of Two or More Works by Same Author	Give the author's last name, the title or a shortened version, and the page reference: (Rose, "Looking Back" 19).

WRITING TIP

Plagiarism Presenting someone else's writing or ideas as your own is plagiarism. To avoid plagiarism, you need to credit sources as noted at the right. However, if a piece of information is common knowledge—information available in several sources—you do not need to credit a source. To see an example of parenthetical documentation, see the essay on page 991.

Following MLA Manuscript Guidelines

The final copy of your report should follow the Modern Language Association guidelines for manuscript preparation.

- The heading in the upper left-hand corner of the first page should include your name, your teacher's name, the course name, and the date, each on a separate line.
- Below the heading, center the title on the page.
- Number all the pages consecutively in the upper right-hand corner, one-half inch from the top. Also, include your last name before the page number.
- Double-space the entire paper.
- Except for the margins above the page numbers, leave one-inch margins on all sides of every page.

The Works Cited list at the end of your paper is an alphabetized list of the sources you have used and documented in your report. The additional line of each entry is indented one-half inch.

 WRITING TIP

When your report includes a quotation that is longer than four lines, set it off from the rest of the text by indenting the entire quotation one inch from the left margin. In this case, you should not use quotation marks.

1″   ½″ Wong 15 ⊢—1″—⊣

Works Cited

Edel, Leon, and Gordon N. Ray, eds. <u>Henry James and H. G. Wells</u>. Urbana: U of Illinois P, 1958. — Book with editors but no single author

Ferrell, Keith. "The challenges of science fiction." <u>Omni</u> Feb. 1992. <u>Magazine Index</u>. Online. Dialog. 18 Oct. 1995. — On-line article

McConnell, Frank. <u>The Science Fiction of H. G. Wells</u>. New York: Oxford UP, 1981. — Book with one author

Mencken, H. L. "The Late Mr. Wells." <u>Prejudices: First Series</u>. New York: Knopf, 1919. 22–35. — Chapter in a book

Philmus, Robert M., and David Y. Hughes. <u>H. G. Wells: Early Writings in Science and Science Fiction</u>. Berkeley: U of California P, 1975. — Work with two authors

Rose, Jonathan. "Looking Back—to the Futurists of the Past." <u>Scholastic Update</u> Dec. 1986: 19–21. — Article in magazine

Schorer, Mark. "Technique as Discovery." <u>Hudson Review</u> 1 (1948): 67–87. — Article in scholarly journal

Models for Works Cited Entries

1 Getting Information Electronically

Electronic resources provide you with a convenient and efficient way to gather information.

1.1 On-line Resources

When you use your computer to communicate with another computer or with another person using a computer, you are working "on-line." On-line resources include commercial information services and information available on the Internet.

Commercial Information Services

You can subscribe to various services that offer information such as the following:

- up-to-date news, weather, and sports reports
- access to encyclopedias, magazines, newspapers, dictionaries, almanacs, and databases (collections of information)
- electronic mail (e-mail) to and from other users
- forums, or ongoing electronic conversations among users interested in a particular topic

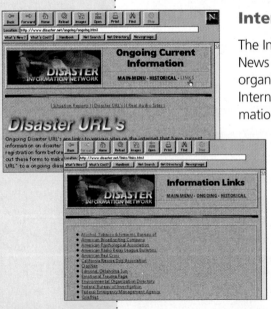

Internet

The Internet is a vast network of computers. News services, libraries, universities, researchers, organizations, and government agencies use the Internet to communicate and to distribute information. The Internet includes two key features:

- **World Wide Web,** which provides you with information on particular subjects and links you to related topics and resources (such as the linked Web pages shown at the left)
- **Electronic mail** (e-mail), which allows you to communicate with other e-mail users worldwide

1.2　CD-ROM

A CD-ROM (compact disc–read-only memory) stores data that may include text, sound, photographs, and video.

Almost any kind of information can be found on CD-ROMs, which you can use at the library or purchase, including

- encyclopedias, almanacs, and indexes
- other reference books on a variety of subjects
- news reports from newspapers, magazines, television, or radio
- museum art collections
- back issues of magazines
- literature collections

1.3　Library Computer Services

Many libraries offer computerized catalogs and a variety of other electronic resources.

Computerized Catalogs

You may search for a book in a library by typing the title, author, subject, or key words into a computer terminal. If you enter the title of a book, the screen will display the bibliographic information and the current availability of the book. When a particular work is not available, you may be able to search the catalogs of other libraries.

Other Electronic Resources

In addition to computerized catalogs, many libraries offer electronic versions of books or other reference materials. They may also have a variety of indexes on CD-ROM, which allow you to search for magazine or newspaper articles on any topic you choose. When you have found an article on the topic you want, the screen will display the kind of information shown at the right.

WHAT YOU'LL NEED

- To access on-line resources, you need a computer with a modem linked to a telephone line. Your school computer lab or resource center may be linked to the Internet or to a commercial information service.
- To use CD-ROMs, you need a computer system with a CD-ROM player.

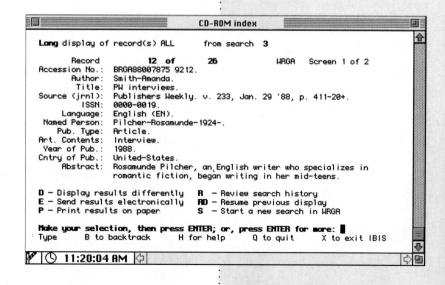

2 Word Processing

- Computer
- Word-processing program
- Printer

WRITING TIP

Spell checkers and grammar checkers offer suggestions for corrections, but you must carefully assess these suggestions before picking the right one. Making such an assessment involves looking at the suggested change in the context of your writing.

Word-processing programs allow you to draft, revise, edit, and format your writing and to produce neat, professional-looking papers. They also allow you to share your writing with others.

2.1 Revising and Editing

Improving the quality of your writing becomes easier when you use a word-processing program to revise and edit.

Revising a Document

Most word-processing programs allow you to make the following kinds of changes:

- add or delete words
- move text from one location in your document to another
- undo a change you have made in the text
- save a document with a new name, allowing you to keep old drafts for reference
- view more than one document at a time, so you can copy text from one document and add it to another

Editing a Document

Many word-processing programs have the following features to help you catch errors and polish your writing:

- The **spell checker** automatically finds misspelled words and suggests possible corrections.
- The **grammar checker** spots possible grammatical errors and suggests ways you might correct them.
- The **thesaurus** suggests synonyms for a word you want to replace.
- The **dictionary** will give you the definitions of words so you can be sure you have used words correctly.
- The **search and replace** feature searches your whole document and corrects every occurrence of something you want to change, such as a misspelled name.

2.2 Formatting Your Work

Format is the layout and appearance of your writing on the page. You may choose your formatting options before or after you write.

Formatting Type

You may want to make changes in the typeface, type size, and type style of the words in your document. For each of these, your word-processing program will most likely have several options to choose from. These options allow you to

- change the typeface to create a different look for the words in your document
- change the type size of the entire document or of just the headings of sections in the paper
- change the type style when necessary; for example, use italics or underline for the titles of books and magazines

Typeface	Size	Style
Geneva	7-point Times	*Italic*
Times	10-point Times	**Bold**
Chicago	12-point Times	Underline
`Courier`	14-point Times	

Formatting Pages

Not only can you change the way individual words look; you can also change the way they are arranged on the page. Some of the formatting decisions you make will depend on how you plan to use a printout of a draft or on the guidelines of an assignment.

- Set the line spacing, or the amount of space you need between lines of text. Double spacing is commonly used for final drafts.

Centered

Announcement!

The results of the East High School fundraising drive are posted below. The money that was raised will be added to other donations to repair the speaker system in the gym.

9th grade	$48.00
10th grade	$62.00
11th grade	$54.60
12th grade	$56.22
Total	$220.82

Left-aligned **Right-aligned**

- Set the margins, or the amount of white space around the edges of your text. A one-inch margin on all sides is commonly used for final drafts.
- Create a header for the top of the page or a footer for the bottom if you want to include such information as your name, the date, or the page number on every page.
- Determine the alignment of your text. The screen at the left shows your options.

WRITING TIP

Keep your format simple. Your goal is to create not only an attractive document but also one that is easy to read. Your readers will have difficulty if you change the type formatting frequently.

TECHNOLOGY TIP

Some word-processing programs or other software packages provide preset templates, or patterns, for writing outlines, memos, letters, newsletters, or invitations. If you use one of these templates, you will not need to adjust the formatting.

2.3 Working Collaboratively

Computers allow you to share your writing electronically. Send a copy of your work to someone via e-mail or put it in someone's drop box if your computer is linked to other computers on a network. Then use the feedback of your peers to help you improve the quality of your writing.

Peer Editing on a Computer

The writer and the reader can both benefit from the convenience of peer editing "on screen," or at the computer.

- Be sure to save your current draft and then make a copy of it for each of your peer readers.
- You might have each peer reader use a different typeface or type style for making comments, as shown in the example below.
- Ask each of your readers to include his or her initials in the file name.

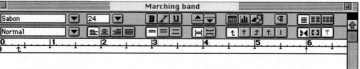

The marching band continues to be a top choice among activities open to students. However, if you are considering the band, you should be aware of the pros and cons of membership. Band practice is three days a week and begins promptly at 7:00 A.M. **Good introduction. I'm interested, but give more details: How much time does band take? How much does it cost?** If you are not a morning person, consider this a disadvantage. On the other hand, the difficulty may be offset by the drama of marching across the field while admiring early commuters drive slowly by. The new uniforms we display so proudly get another split vote. They give us a cool look, but it's hard to be cool on a hot summer day. **Tone is a little stiff. Be more casual since students are your audience.**

- If your computer allows you to open more than one file at a time, open each reviewer's file and refer to the files as you revise your draft.

Peer Editing on a Printout

Some peer readers prefer to respond to a draft on paper rather than on the computer.

- Double-space or triple-space your document so that your peer editor can make suggestions between the lines.
- Leave extra-wide margins to give your readers room to note their reactions and questions as they read.
- Print out your draft and photocopy it if you want to share it with more than one reader.

Using Visuals

3

Tables, graphs, diagrams, and pictures often communicate information more effectively than words alone do. Many computer programs allow you to create visuals to use with your written text.

3.1 When to Use Visuals

Use visuals in your work to illustrate complex concepts and processes or to make a page look more interesting.

Although you should not expect a visual to do all the work of written text, combining words and pictures or graphics can increase the understanding and enjoyment of your writing. Many computer programs allow you to create and insert graphs, tables, time lines, diagrams, and flow charts into your document. An art program allows you to create border designs for a title page or to draw an unusual character or setting for narrative or descriptive writing. You may also be able to add clip art, or premade pictures, to your document. Clip art can be used to illustrate an idea or concept or to make your writing more appealing for young readers.

3.2 Kinds of Visuals

The visuals you choose will depend on the type of information you want to present to your readers.

Tables

Tables allow you to arrange facts or numbers into rows and columns so that your reader can compare information more easily. In many word-processing programs, you can create a table by choosing the number of vertical columns and horizontal rows you need and then entering information in each box, as the illustration shows.

WHAT YOU'LL NEED

- A graphics program to create visuals
- Access to clip-art files from a CD-ROM, a computer disk, or an on-line service

TECHNOLOGY TIP

A spreadsheet program provides you with a preset table for your statistics and performs any necessary calculations.

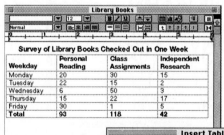

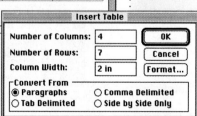

TECHNOLOGY TIP

To help your readers easily understand the different parts of a pie chart or bar graph, use a different color or shade of gray for each section.

Graphs and Charts

You can sometimes use a graph or chart to help communicate complex information in a clear visual image. For example, you could use a line graph to show how a trend changes over time, a bar graph such as the one at the right to compare statistics from different years, or a pie chart to compare percentages. You might want to explore ways of displaying data in more than one visual format before deciding which will work best for you.

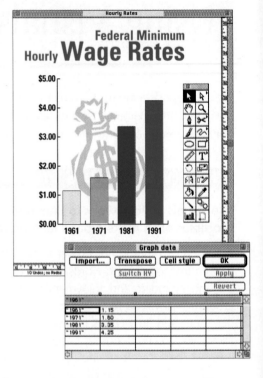

Other Visuals

Art and design programs allow you to create visuals for your writing. Many programs include the following features:

- drawing tools that allow you to draw, color, and shade pictures
- clip art that you can copy or change with drawing tools
- page borders that you can use to decorate title pages, invitations, or brochures
- text options that allow you to combine words with your illustrations, as shown at the left
- tools for making geometric shapes in flow charts, time lines, and diagrams that show a process or sequence of events

Creating a Multimedia Presentation

4

A multimedia presentation is a combination of text, sound, and visuals such as photographs, videos, and animation. Your audience reads, hears, and sees your presentation at a computer, following different "paths" you create to lead the user through the information you have gathered.

4.1 Features of Multimedia Programs

To start planning your multimedia presentation, you need to know what options are available to you. You can combine sound, photos, videos, and animation to enhance any text you write about your topic.

Sound

Including sound in your presentation can help your audience understand information in your written text. For example, the user may be able to listen and learn from

- the pronunciation of an unfamiliar or foreign word
- a speech
- a recorded interview
- a musical selection
- a dramatic reading of a work of literature

Photos and Videos

Photographs and live-action videos can make your subject come alive for the user. Here are some examples:

- videotaped news coverage of a historical event
- videos of music, dance, or theater performances
- charts and diagrams
- photos of an artist's work
- photos or video of a geographical setting that is important to the written text

WHAT YOU'LL NEED

- Individual programs to create and edit the text, graphics, sound, and videos you will use
- A multimedia authoring program that allows you to combine these elements and create links between the screens

Animation

Many graphics programs allow you to add animation, or movement, to the visuals in your presentation. Animated figures add to the user's enjoyment and understanding of what you present. You can use animation to illustrate

- what happens in a story
- the steps in a process
- changes in a chart, graph, or diagram
- how your user can explore information in your presentation

4.2   Planning Your Presentation

To create a multimedia presentation, first choose your topic and decide what you want to include. Then plan how you want the user to move through your presentation.

Imagine that you are creating a multimedia presentation exploring the differences between old and new architecture by focusing on a historic old house in your community. You decide to include the following items:

- a photo of the old house
- text about the history and construction of the house
- a blueprint of the old house
- an interview with an architect comparing old and new architecture and building techniques
- photos of architectural details in a house
- a video tour of an old house
- photos of new houses
- text describing how quickly new houses are built

You can choose one of the following ways to organize your presentation:

- step by step with only one path, or order, in which the user can see and hear the information
- a branching path that allows users to make some choices about what they will see and hear, and in what order

A flow chart can help you figure out the path a user can take through your presentation. Each box in the flow chart on the following page represents something about the house for the user to read, see, or hear. The arrows on the flow chart show a branching path the user can follow.

Whenever boxes branch in more than one direction, it means that the user can choose which item to see or hear first.

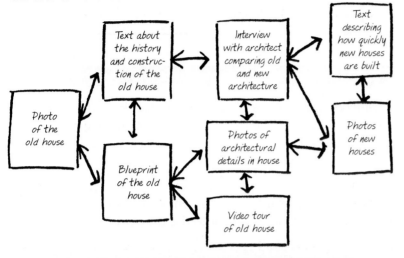

4.3 Guiding Your User

Your user will need directions to follow the path you have planned for your multimedia presentation.

Most multimedia authoring programs allow you to create screens that include text or audio directions that guide the user from one part of your presentation to the next. In the example below, the user can choose between several paths, and directions on the screen explain how to make the choice.

If you need help creating your multimedia presentation, ask your school's technology adviser. You may also be able to get help from your classmates or your software manual.

The user clicks on a button to select any of these options.

WRITING TIP

You usually need permission from the person or organization that owns the copyright on materials if you want to copy them. You do not need permission, however, if you are not making money from your presentation, if you use it only for educational purposes, and if you use only a small percentage of the original material.

Navigational buttons take the user back and forth, one screen at a time.

This screen shows a photo of architectural details.

(1) Writing Complete Sentences

1.1 Sentence Fragments

A sentence fragment is a group of words that does not express a complete thought. Sentence fragments may be missing a subject, a predicate, or both.

Completing an Incomplete Thought

You can correct a sentence fragment by adding the missing subject or predicate to complete the thought.

> In "Two Kinds," a story about mother-daughter conflict, *the mother*
>
> wants desperately to make her daughter a prodigy. The
>
> independent and unwilling daughter. *refuses*

When the fragment is a subordinate clause, you can join the fragment to an existing sentence and change the punctuation or you can rewrite the clause so it can stand alone.

> When the mother pushes her daughter to perform publicly
>
> on the piano. The girl rebels. While refusing to practice *She refuses*
>
> diligently or correct her mistakes.

Correcting Punctuation

When the fragment is a phrase, it can be connected to a complete sentence. Simply change the punctuation.

> By the time of the recital. The girl has actually convinced
>
> herself that she can play well.

APPLY WHAT YOU'VE LEARNED

Rewrite this paragraph, correcting the sentence fragments.

[1]"Two Kinds" explores the world of a would-be musical child prodigy. [2]In this selection from *The Joy Luck Club,* the mother tries to turn her daughter into a prodigy. [3]But is not successful. [4]In the case of Sarah Chang, on the other hand, was different. [5]She was a natural musician. [6]Who at the age of 12 was already performing on television with symphony orchestras. [7]Most of the great violinists of the first half of this century. [8]Came from Russia and Eastern Europe. [9]Recently, gifted Asians have appeared. [10]And have been making musical news. [11]Both of Chang's parents. [12]Musicians who emigrated from Korea in 1979. [13]Other former child prodigies. [14]Tell funny or painful stories. [15]About their childhood experiences. [16]Itzhak Perlman, who inherited the mantle of Jascha Heifetz.

1.2   Run-On Sentences

A run-on sentence consists of two or more sentences incorrectly written as one. It is unclear where one idea ends and the next begins.

Forming Separate Sentences

One way to correct a run-on sentence is to form two separate sentences. Use a period or other end punctuation after the first complete thought and capitalize the first letter of the next sentence.

> Many of us remember teachers who influenced our lives positively one good example is Marjorie Hurd in "The Teacher Who Changed My Life."

Sometimes a writer mistakenly uses a comma instead of a period to separate two complete thoughts. You can correct this kind of mistake, called a comma splice, by changing the comma to a period and capitalizing the first letter of the second sentence.

> The author had endured horrible experiences by age nine, one teacher helped him use his experiences in his writing.

REVISING TIP

To correct run-on sentences, read them to yourself, noticing where you naturally pause between ideas. The pause usually indicates where you should place end punctuation.

Joining Sentences

If the ideas expressed in a run-on sentence are closely related, you may wish to join them to form a compound sentence. One way to do this is to use a comma and a coordinating conjunction to join the main clauses.

The heroic stand of Nicholas Gage's mother resulted in her death $\underset{\wedge}{but}$ she arranged her children's escape to freedom in the United States.

Use a semicolon alone, or with a conjunctive adverb, to join main clauses having closely related ideas.

Some commonly used conjunctive adverbs are *however, therefore, nevertheless,* and *besides*.

The young Greek boy learned to love English as an ordinary means of expression $\underset{\wedge}{besides,}$ it helped him communicate intense feelings in writing.

APPLY WHAT YOU'VE LEARNED

Rewrite this paragraph, correcting the run-on sentences.

[1]In recent history Turkey, Yugoslavia, and the United States have all been involved in fighting or providing aid to Greece, during World War II the Communists in Greece engaged in antiroyalist activities. [2]In 1946 the Communists resumed guerrilla warfare there was full-scale war on the northern frontier. [3]Nicholas Gage writes about this period from his childhood memories liberal, conservative, and coalition governments supplanted each other. [4]Violence became part of daily life women and even children participated actively. [5]Gage's mother, Eleni Gatzoyiannis, was one of the patriots not until 1956 did women win the vote in Greece. [6]Following a coup in 1967, a military government took over the country, in 1974 parliamentary government was restored. [7]Instability has gradually yielded to a more stable government in recent years in 1981 Greece joined the European Economic Community. [8]Today the country enjoys defense and economic agreements with the United States, possession of the island of Cyprus is still a bone of contention in some quarters.

Making Subjects and Verbs Agree

2

2.1 Simple and Compound Subjects

A verb must agree in number with its subject. The word *number* refers to whether a word is singular or plural. When a word refers to one thing, it is singular. When it refers to more than one thing, it is plural.

Agreement with Simple Subjects

Use a singular verb with a singular subject.

When the subject is a singular noun, you use the singular form of the verb. The present-tense third-person singular form of a regular verb usually ends in *-s* or *-es*.

> In "On the Rainy River" the narrator confess^(es) what to him
> is a shameful secret.

Use a plural verb with a plural subject.

> Many people remembers the period during the Vietnam
> War about which Tim O'Brien writes.

Agreement with Compound Subjects

Use a plural verb with a compound subject whose parts are joined by *and*, regardless of the number of each part.

> In the story the river and the wilderness helps the narrator
> work through his problems.

REVISING TIP

To find the subject of a sentence, first find the verb. Then ask *who* or *what* is being spoken about. Say the subject and the verb together to see whether they agree.

When the parts of a compound subject are joined by *or* or *nor*, make the verb agree in number with the part that is closer to it.

Neither the young man nor the older one talk~s~ about the problem.

APPLY WHAT YOU'VE LEARNED

Write the correct form of the verb.

[1]In "On the Rainy River" the narrator's internal conflict reflect that of the Vietnam War itself. [2]Americans is still divided about whether American involvement in the war was right. [3]Some people feels that the war divided not only Vietnam but the United States as well. [4]Other people sees U.S. participation as having been the only defense against encroaching communism. [5]Conscience or the laws involves principle.

[6]Sometimes neither logical reasons nor patriotism supply simple, clear-cut answers. [7]Often a decision and an action causes far-reaching results. [8]Both a hawk and a dove finds their place in Vietnam. [9]Some war resisters opts for prison. [10]Emigration or illegal entry into Canada offer another option. [11]Going underground and changing one's identity provides a solution for war resisters. [12]Returning home or contacting one's family result in prosecution. [13]Today many Vietnam War resisters still resides in Canada.

2.2   Pronoun Subjects

When a pronoun is used as a subject, the verb must agree with it in number.

Agreement with Personal Pronouns

When the subject is a singular personal pronoun, use a singular verb. When the subject is plural, use a plural verb.

Singular pronouns are *I, you, he, she,* and *it.* Plural pronouns are *we, you,* and *they.*

In *Earthly Paradise* the author remembers her mother. She look~s~ back fondly on her mother's independence, for example. As we reads, we thinks of our own mothers.

When *he, she,* or *it* is the part of the subject closer to the verb in a compound subject containing *or* or *nor*, use a singular verb. When a pronoun is part of a compound subject containing *and*, use a plural verb.

Colette and she shares a sense of determination. Neither another reader nor she appreciate their similarities fully.

Agreement with Indefinite Pronouns

When the subject is a singular indefinite pronoun, use the singular form of the verb.

The following are singular indefinite pronouns: *another, either, nobody, anybody, everybody, somebody, no one, anyone, everyone, someone, one, anything, everything, something, nothing, each,* and *neither*.

Perhaps everyone like a garden, but Sido values gardens as much as she does people. Almost no one deserve one of her roses, she feels.

When the subject is a plural indefinite pronoun, use the plural form of the verb.

The following are plural indefinite pronouns: *both, few, many,* and *several*.

Many considers their mothers special, but few expresses their feelings as well as Colette. The mother and daughter may at times exasperate each other. Both, however, respects individual differences.

In many sentences the indefinite pronouns listed at the right will be followed by a prepositional phrase that might help you determine whether the subject is singular or plural. Remember, however, that the object of the preposition is not the subject of the sentence.

The indefinite pronouns *some, all, any, none,* and *most* can be either singular or plural. When the pronoun refers to one thing, use a singular verb. When the pronoun refers to more than one thing, use a plural verb.

Some of Sido's strength diminish~es~ with age, but most of her views remains as strong as ever. Many of the duties in her day becomes too hard for her to handle alone, but most of her determination stay~s~ intact to the end.

APPLY WHAT YOU'VE LEARNED

In each sentence, write the correct form of the verb.

1Few (relate, relates) to their gardens as closely as Colette's mother, Sido, of whom the author speaks in *Earthly Paradise.* **2**The French artist Claude Monet and she (has, have) this trait in common. **3**We discover that both (refuse, refuses) to live in Paris, where it (is, are) difficult to find space for a garden. **4**Each (feel, feels) an intense attachment to nature, especially flowers. **5**"I (owe, owes) having become a painter to flowers," Monet once said. **6**In his opinion his garden took priority over his paintings; he said that it (was, were) his greatest work of art. **7**Almost everyone (has, have) seen prints of Monet's blue-and-lavender water-lily paintings. **8**They (is, are) among his most loved works. **9**Some (appear, appears) in almost every showing of impressionistic art. **10**My friends and I (rush, rushes) to see displays of Monet's art. **11**All of them (reveal, reveals) his perception of people and nature.

Note how subjects and verbs agree throughout W. P. Kinsella's "The Thrill of the Grass." Kinsella increases sentence variety by using interrupting words and phrases, as well as inverted sentences. With them he holds the reader's interest and builds tension.

2.3 Common Agreement Problems

Several other situations can cause problems in subject-verb agreement.

Interrupting Words and Phrases

Be sure the verb agrees with its subject when words or phrases come between them.

The subject of the verb is never found in a prepositional phrase or an appositive, which may follow the subject and come before the verb. Other phrases can also separate the subject and verb.

In "The Thrill of the Grass" the narrator, one of many dis-
gruntled baseball fans, plan simply to replace one square [*s* correction above "plan"]
of artificial turf with another of sod.

Phrases beginning with *including, as well as, along with, such as,* and *in addition to* are not part of the subject.

The fan, as well as many of his friends, protest the [*s* correction above "protest"]
modernization of the grand old game of baseball.
Even families of fans, including a great grandfather past
80, joins in the revolt. [correction on "joins"]

REVISING TIP

The forms of *do, be,* and *have* can be main verbs or helping verbs. They can also be part of contractions with *not* (*doesn't/don't, isn't/aren't, hasn't/haven't*). In every case the verb should agree in number with its subject.

Inverted Sentences

When the simple subject comes after the verb, be sure the verb agrees with the subject in number.

A sentence in which the subject follows the verb is called an inverted sentence. Questions are usually in inverted form, as are sentences beginning with *Here* and *There*. (*Where is the turf? Here come the fans.*)

Where is the workers? Here comes the laborers, and before [*are* correction above "is"]
them lie the field of artificial turf, ready for them to harvest. [*s* correction above "lie"]
Before long there are a whole new field of real grass to [*is* correction above "are"]
replace the offensive artificial turf.

REVISING TIP

To check subject-verb agreement in inverted sentences, place the subject before the verb. For example, change *There is the grass* to *The grass is there.*

To find the subject, look carefully at words that come before the verb. Remember that the subject may not be the noun or pronoun closest to the verb.

Singular Nouns with Plural Forms

Be sure to use a singular verb when the subject is a noun that is singular in meaning but appears to be plural.

Words such as *rickets, measles,* and *series* appear to be plural because they end in *s.* However, these words are singular in meaning. Words ending in *ics* that refer to sciences or branches of study *(economics, civics, politics, semantics)* are also singular.

> The mathematics of the plan create only minor problems. *[s]*
>
> A series of events follow because the motivation to make a *[s]*
>
> statement is so strong.

Collective Nouns

Use a singular verb when the subject is a collective noun— such as *group, audience,* or *congregation*—that refers to a group acting as a unit. Use a plural verb when the collective noun refers to members of a group acting individually.

> The group continue to work together night after night. *[s]*
>
> The team has *[have]* various reasons for doing what they do.

Nouns of Time, Weight, Measure, Number

Use a singular verb with a subject that identifies a period of time, a weight, a measure, or a number.

> Two months or so transform the stadium from artificial to *[s]*
>
> natural. Perhaps a hundred thousand square feet of grass
>
> appear before the season has passed. *[s]*

Titles

Use a singular verb when the subject is the title of a work of art, literature, or music, even though the title may contain plural words.

"Field of Dreams" ~~take~~ *takes* the characters and plot from the book *Shoeless Joe*, a work by W. P. Kinsella.

Predicate Nominatives

Use a verb that agrees with the subject, not with the predicate nominative, when the subject is different in number from the predicate nominative.

When the workers finish their job, their feeling ~~are~~ *is* triumph and pride in a job well done.

REVISING TIP

The fact that a title is set off with quotation marks, italics, or underscoring helps to remind you it is singular and takes a singular verb.

APPLY WHAT YOU'VE LEARNED

Write the correct form of each verb.

1. W. P. Kinsella's novel *Shoeless Joe*, like his short story "The Thrill of the Grass," (deal, deals) with baseball.
2. *Shoeless Joe*, made into the highly successful movie *Field of Dreams*, (involve, involves) baseball fans.
3. Where (do, does) the author's ideas come from?
4. (Has, Have) he played baseball himself?
5. Unlike his ball-playing dad, he feels "there (was, were) essentially no place on the field it was safe for me to be."
6. A team sometimes (has, have) differences among themselves.
7. Kinsella, like some other writers, (has been, have been) a clerk and a cab driver.
8. His other jobs—including ad salesman, pizza-parlor owner, and college professor—(seem, seems) less interesting than those of his characters.
9. However, a million dollars (is, are) not enough to pay for experiences like his.
10. Most successful of all his enterprises (has, have) been his writing about baseball.
11. Someday a world series for baseball writers (is, are) likely to include Kinsella.

3 Using Nouns and Pronouns

3.1 Plural and Possessive Nouns

Nouns refer to people, places, things, and ideas. A noun is plural when it refers to more than one person, place, thing, or idea. A possessive noun shows who or what owns something.

Plural Nouns

Follow these guidelines to form noun plurals.

- For most nouns, add -s (*bill—bills, date—dates*).
- For nouns ending in *s, sh, ch, x,* or *z,* add -es (*church—churches, fox—foxes*).
- For nouns ending in a consonant and *y,* change *y* to *i* and add -es (*lady—ladies, baby—babies*).
- For most nouns that end in a consonant and *o,* add -es (*hero—heroes, tomato—tomatoes*).
- For many nouns that end in *f* or *fe,* change *f* to *v* and add -s or -es (*knife—knives, loaf—loaves*).

Some nouns have the same spelling in both the singular and the plural: *moose, deer, salmon.* Some noun plurals have irregular forms that don't follow any rule: *teeth, geese.*

> There are interesting echos in this excerpt from "Tolerance," one of E. M. Forster's essayes. He argues for tolerance between nationes. People can love, in his view; countrys cannot.

Possessive Nouns

Follow these guidelines to form possessive nouns.

- Add an apostrophe and -s to form the possessive of a singular noun or a plural noun that does not end in -s (*father—father's, women—women's*).
- Add only an apostrophe to plural nouns that end in -s (*bottles—bottles', favorites—favorites'*).

A dictionary usually lists the plural form of a noun if the plural is formed irregularly or if it might be formed in more than one way. For example, the plural of *index* is given as both *indexes* and *indices.* Dictionary listings are especially helpful for nouns that end in *o, f,* and *fe.*

One human beings⌄ attitude toward another is personal, he

says. When nations⌄ attempts to love one another fail, peo-

ple abandon hope and cease trying to cooperate.

APPLY WHAT YOU'VE LEARNED

Write the correct plural or possessive.

[1]E. M. Forsters "Tolerance" is only one of his many essay's. [2]He also wrote short storys, a documentary, a biography, and a guidebook. [3]Forsters' fame, however, rests mainly on his noveles. [4]Some of these have been made into movies', including *A Passage to India.* [5]His various work's themes include the virtues of truthfulness and kindness. [6]The everyday values' of common sense, goodwill, and respect for others' feelings pervade his work. [7]Each characters' experiences reflect his or her attitudes. [8]The "good" one's commune with nature on an almost spiritual level. [9]They rise above crass monetary concernes, to focus on the essentials of life. [10]Throughout his writing's he urges liberality. [11]In *A Passage to India,* for example, a womans overreaction to fear of a dark cave results in a false accusation. [12]In *A Room with a View* peoples' values create conflict.

3.2   Pronoun Forms

A personal pronoun is a pronoun that can be used in the first, second, or third person. A personal pronoun has three cases or forms: the subject form, the object form, and the possessive form.

Subject Pronouns

Use the subject form of a pronoun when it is the subject of a sentence or the subject of a clause. *I, you, he, she, it, we,* and *they* are subject pronouns.

Problems usually arise when a noun and a pronoun or two pronouns are used in a compound subject or compound object. To see whether you are using the correct form, read the sentence as if it contained just one pronoun.

"Everyday Use" reminds me of a discussion I had about a

week ago. My mother and me⌄I think that things were made

to be used, not saved.

 LINK TO LITERATURE

Notice how Alice Walker uses pronouns to avoid repetition of the nouns and to create an informal effect throughout "Everyday Use," page 110.

To check for the right pronoun, see if the sentence still makes sense when the subject and pronoun are reversed. (*It was he. He was it.*)

Use the subject form of a pronoun when it is a predicate pronoun following a linking verb.

You often hear the object form used in casual conversation (*It is him*). However, the subject form is preferred for more formal writing.

Many people save dishes and linens to use for special company. We should remember that special company can also be you or ~~me~~. *I*

Object Pronouns

Use the object form of a pronoun when it is the object of a verb or verbal, or the object of a preposition. *Me, you, him, her, it, us,* and *them* are object pronouns.

Maggie knew that her sister Dee looked down on her mother and ~~she~~ *her*. The mother, however, had always treated Dee and ~~she~~ *her* the same.

Possessive Pronouns

Never use an apostrophe in a possessive pronoun. *My, mine, your, yours, his, her, hers, its, our, ours, their,* and *theirs* are possessive pronouns.

Perhaps you know people like Dee. They might think that ~~they're~~ *their* sense of what's appropriate is better than your~~'~~s.

APPLY WHAT YOU'VE LEARNED

Write the following sentences, correcting the pronouns.

[1]In "Everyday Use" Alice Walker introduces two sisters and they're mother. [2]One sister, who has left home, thinks of some of the antiques as her's. [3]She especially wants her mother to give some handmade quilts to her friend and she. [4]Dee feels that the rightful inheritor of the quilts is her. [5]Mrs. Johnson has earmarked the quilts for Maggie's intended husband and she. [6]Quilts were made for daily use, but them are also works of art. [7]During the Civil War, soldiers' families sometimes gave the soldiers small quilts for they're cots. [8]Recently, my friends and me have heard about quilts used in protest movements.

3.3 Pronoun Antecedents

An antecedent is the noun or pronoun to which a personal pronoun refers. The antecedent usually precedes the pronoun.

Pronoun and Antecedent Agreement

The pronoun must agree with its antecedent in number, person, and gender.

Use a singular pronoun to refer to a singular antecedent; use a plural pronoun to refer to a plural antecedent.

Do not allow interrupting words to determine the number of the personal pronoun.

In this excerpt from *Farewell to Manzanar*, Jeanne Wakatsuki Houston recounts the indignities of internment in a relocation center and tells how it (they) haunts her still.

If the antecedent is a noun that could refer to either a male or a female, use *he or she (him or her, his or her)* or reword the sentence to avoid the singular pronoun.

Each person in camp had to deal with the humiliation and discomfort in their (his or her) own way.

LINK TO LITERATURE

Notice the care that Jeanne Wakatsuki Houston and James D. Houston take to ensure that pronouns agree with their antecedents in the excerpt from *Farewell to Manzanar*, on page 330. Readers have no trouble understanding the events and relationships described in the story, which records a dark time in modern American history.

REVISING TIP

You could also revise the example at the left this way: *All of the people* in camp had to deal with the humiliation and discomfort in their own way.

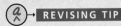

To avoid vague pronoun reference, do not use *this* or *that* alone to start a clause. Instead, include a word stating the thing or idea to which *this* or *that* refers—*this alternative, this concept, that theory.*

Be sure that the antecedent of a pronoun is clear.

In most cases do not use a pronoun to refer to an entire idea or clause. Writing is much clearer if you give the exact idea.

> A new teacher's hostility contrasted starkly with a former
> teacher's warmth. That *experience* hurt the young girl.

Unclear Antecedents

Make sure that each personal pronoun has a clear reference.

Clarify unidentified references.

The words *it, they, this, which,* and *that* can create problems when there is no clear antecedent to which they refer.

> In *Farewell to Manzanar* ~~it~~ shows the reader how irra-
> tionally people behave during wartime.

Clarify ambiguous references.

Ambiguous means "having two or more possible meanings." A pronoun reference is ambiguous if the pronoun may refer to more than one antecedent.

> An old woman was as modest as the author's mother. ~~She~~ *The woman*
> allowed ~~her~~ *the mother* to use ~~her~~ *the* makeshift screen.

Compound Antecedents Using *Or* or *Nor*

When two or more singular antecedents are joined by *or* or *nor*, use a singular pronoun. When two or more plural antecedents are joined by *or* or *nor*, use a plural pronoun.

> Neither the mother nor her daughter had a bed of ~~their~~ *her*
> own in the tiny camp unit.

When one singular and one plural antecedent are joined by *or* or *nor,* use the noun or pronoun nearer the verb to determine whether the pronoun should be singular or plural.

Too excited to be tired, neither the mother nor the girls
found her *their* trip exhausting.

Indefinite Pronouns as Antecedents

When a singular indefinite pronoun is the antecedent, use *he or she (him or her, his or her),* or rewrite the sentence.

Everyone ran around to see if their *his or her* friends were there.

REVISING TIP

Be careful with the indefinite use of *you* and *they.*

One ~~You~~ should always try to make the best of it ~~when they~~ *being* put ~~you~~ in a situation such as this.

APPLY WHAT YOU'VE LEARNED

Correct the pronouns to clarify antecedents.

[1]In *Farewell to Manzanar* you did not have to commit a crime to be relocated. [2]The U.S. government and society discriminated against Americans of Japanese descent; it was unfair. [3]Canada did not have internment camps, but they too relocated West Coast citizens of Japanese heritage. [4]All family members or a single Japanese Canadian had to move to a place new to them. [5]Canada might assign one of these citizens, regardless of their level of education or skill, to work in the fields. [6]Everyone was in the same situation, so they made the best of it. [7]A doctor or a farmer—each had their individual experiences. [8]The author kept her mother's spirits up, but she often felt bad.

3.4 Pronoun Usage

The form that a pronoun takes is always determined by its function within its own clause or sentence.

Who and *Whom*

Use *who* or *whoever* as the subject of a clause or a sentence.

"The Pearl" leaves readers wondering not whom stole a missing pearl but why everybody lied about it.

REVISING TIP

In the example at the left, *who* is the subject of the clause *who stole* a *missing pearl.*

Whom should replace *who* in each sentence of the example at the right:
Whom (she disliked)—direct object of the verb *disliked*
(To) whom—object of the preposition *to*

Use *whom* as the direct or indirect object of a verb or verbal and as the object of a preposition.

People often use *who* for *whom* when speaking informally. However, in written English the pronouns should be used correctly.

> One made up a story to place another, who [M] she disliked, in an uncomfortable position. Who [M] did she tell the story to that day?

In trying to determine the correct pronoun form, ignore interrupters that come between the subject and the verb.

In the example that follows, *who* should replace *whom* because the pronoun is the subject of the clause *who would actually steal.*

> Whom of the women do you think would actually steal?

Pronouns in Contractions

Do not confuse these contractions—*it's, they're, who's,* and *you're*—with possessive pronouns that sound the same—*its, their, whose,* and *your*.

> Its [It's/V] not hard to imagine being in a situation similar to that of the birthday guests. They're [Their] responses seem excessive, however. Who's [Whose] pride requires such extreme measures as these?

Pronouns with Nouns

Determine the correct pronoun form in phrases such as *we students* by imagining what the sentence would look like if the pronoun appeared without the noun.

> The foibles of others may seem funny to we [us] readers, but what if the same thing happened to you or I [me]?

Pronouns in Comparisons

Be sure you use the correct form of a pronoun in a comparison.

Than or *as* often begins an elliptical clause, one in which some words have been left out. To decide which form of the pronoun to use, fill in the missing words.

> Author Yukio Mishima writes with more subtlety than ~~me~~. *I [do]*
>
> Few writers can show as effectively as ~~him~~ *he [does]* how a small
>
> occurrence can trigger a chain of events.

Shifts in Person

Be sure that a pronoun agrees with its antecedent in person.

One, everyone, and *everybody* are in the third person. They should be referred to by the third-person pronouns.

> Everyone should try to consider the feelings of others. ~~You~~ *One*
>
> cannot go wrong using this approach.

APPLY WHAT YOU'VE LEARNED

Rewrite the sentences correctly.

[1] Reading "The Pearl," one can laugh at several minor deceptions; you are surprised at the suspicion that prompts them. [2] When one reads Guy de Maupassant's "The Necklace," we do not laugh at a deception. [3] The event changes the life of the woman, whom the reader discovers has lost only fake jewels. [4] She spends years working to repay the friend from who she borrowed the necklace. [5] Us readers are astounded when we learn that her sacrifice was needless. [6] Its sad to see the woman age prematurely. [7] The youth of her husband and her might have been more carefree than they were. [8] In this story, deceiving the woman who she asked for the necklace is not unkind. [9] The women in "The Pearl" were less considerate than her. [10] Who do you have more sympathy for?

4 Using Modifiers Effectively

4.1 Adjective or Adverb?

Use an adjective to modify a noun or a pronoun. Use an adverb to modify a verb, an adjective, or another adverb.

The hero of "The Man in the Water" kept his mind on his chosen duty amazing*ly*. Risking his own life, he careful*ly* worked to save plane crash survivors from drowning.

Use an adjective after a linking verb to describe the subject.

In addition to forms of the verb *be*, the following are linking verbs: *become, seem, appear, look, sound, feel, taste, grow,* and *smell*.

Perhaps he'd never seemed heroical~~ly~~ before, but he appeared quite courageous~~ly~~ during his struggle to save lives.

APPLY WHAT YOU'VE LEARNED

Rewrite these sentences, selecting the correct modifier in each pair.

1. In "The Man in the Water" a passenger (heroic, heroically) saved some survivors of a plane crash.
2. After his death (busy, busily) investigators identified him as Arland D. Williams of South Carolina.
3. Not long after the tragedy, (grateful, gratefully) Washington, D.C., officials named part of a bridge after him.
4. Many have looked as (brave, bravely) as he.
5. In 1989 in the United Airlines crash at Sioux City, Iowa, a very (brave, bravely) passenger ran back into the burning plane.
6. That person rescued a baby who was tossed (high, highly) into a baggage compartment during the crash.
7. Some crash survivors cannot remember (easy, easily) the crash itself or the (intense, intensely) moments leading up to it.

4.2 Comparisons and Negatives

Comparative and Superlative Modifiers

Use the comparative form of an adjective or adverb to compare two things or actions. Use the superlative form to compare more than two things or actions.

Form the comparative by adding *-er* to short modifiers or by using the word *more* with longer modifiers. Form the superlative by adding *-est* or by adding the word *most*.

In "A White Heron" Sylvia, a far more quieter person than the hunter, works ~~eagerlier~~ *more eagerly* to please him than he knows. Her ~~bestest~~ efforts include climbing the ~~most tall~~ *tallest* tree to find the heron's home.

Illogical Comparisons

Avoid comparisons that don't make sense because of missing words or illogical construction.

Sylvia feels more sympathy for the heron than the hunter *feels*. He was more eager to find the bird than any visitor *had been*.

Double Negatives

To avoid double negatives in comparisons, use only one negative word in a clause.

Besides *not* and *no*, the following are negative words: *never, nobody, none, no one, nothing, nowhere, hardly,* and *scarcely*.

Sylvia had never been ~~nowhere~~ *anywhere* as high as the top of the majestic old pine tree, which towered above the other trees.

REVISING TIP

Without the added words, the comparisons in the second example are hard to understand. In the first sentence, the reader might conclude that Sylvia feels more sympathy for the heron than for the hunter. Similar logic applies to the second sentence.

Rewrite these sentences, correcting mistakes in modifiers.

1. In "A White Heron" Sylvia must decide between saving the most large bird in the woods—a heron—and winning the gratitude of the friendlier hunter she's ever met.
2. Sylvia's actions prove puzzling, and the people around her can't hardly understand why she acts in such a manner.
3. The hunter has been trying to create the most largest collection of stuffed birds that he can.
4. Sylvia can't scarcely understand why he has to kill the birds.
5. Sylvia's final decision about the heron was wiser than any decision she had made.
6. The hunter's motives were more selfish than Sylvia.
7. He could have killed the birds quicklier than they could reproduce.
8. Some herons form part of one of the productivest ecosystems, the salt marsh.
9. Long legs and huge bills help them hunt frogs and fishes most well in shallow water.
10. Without herons as predators, populations of small aquatic animals would increase more faster than their food supply.

4.3 Misplaced or Dangling Modifiers

A misplaced modifier is separated from the word it modifies. It may appear to modify the wrong word and can confuse the reader. A dangling modifier seems unrelated to any word in the sentence. Misplaced or dangling modifiers are usually phrases or clauses.

Misplaced Modifier

Place a modifier near the word it modifies.

In "The Witness for the Prosecution" the accused man, ~~an actress,~~ says that his girlfriend, an actress, can verify his alibi for the night of the murder.

Dangling Modifier

Be sure a modifier describes a particular word in the sentence.

Discovering a flaw in one witness's testimony, the lawyer found the truth ~~was found~~ too late to serve justice.

REVISING TIP

Misplaced modifiers cause confusion. Without the change shown in the example at the right, the reader momentarily wonders how a man can be an actress.

4.4 Special Problems with Modifiers

The following terms are frequently misused in spoken English. Be careful to use them correctly in written English.

Bad and *Badly*

Always use *bad* as an adjective, whether before a noun or after a linking verb. *Badly* should generally be used to modify an action verb.

"The Californian's Tale" shows how bad*ly* a husband can miss his wife.

This, That, These, Those, and *Them*

Whether used as adjectives or pronouns, *this* and *these* refer to people and things that are nearby, and *that* and *those* refer to people and things that are farther away.

Them is a pronoun; it never modifies a noun. *Those* may be a pronoun or an adjective.

His wife had left home to visit ~~them~~ relatives, and was long delayed in her return, and the widower had a hard time dealing with ~~this~~ *that* devastating event.

REVISING TIP

Avoid the use of *here* with *this* and *these*; also, do not use *there* with *that* and *those*.

What else could the widower do when those ~~there~~ sad memories tormented him?

Few, Fewer, Fewest and Little, Less, Least

Few, fewer, and *fewest* refer to numbers of things that can be counted. *Little, less,* and *least* refer to amounts.

Each year, ~~less~~ ^fewer^ miners remained in the territory. When the visitor arrived, he realized that some miners had ~~fewer~~ ^less^ hope than others in their chances for success.

Misplacement of *Only*

For clarity, *only* should be positioned before the word or words it modifies.

The misplacement of *only* can alter, and sometimes confuse, the meaning of a sentence. Notice in the example below the difference in meaning when *only* is moved.

^Only^ The old miners ~~only~~ knew the whole truth about the story of their friend's sweet young wife.

APPLY WHAT YOU'VE LEARNED

Rewrite these sentences, correcting the errors in modifiers.

1. In "The Californian's Tale" Henry had few pleasure to look forward to.
2. His cottage was thickly covered by these vines and roses that the narrator had seen elsewhere in this region.
3. Many like him went to California in 1849 and afterward for the gold rush. They wanted gold very bad.
4. They only thought they would be happy if they had this precious metal.
5. However, less newcomers did well than you might think.
6. Henry's home furnishings imply that he made a fair amount of money during them boom years.
7. Of the forty-niners, little could have afforded this varnished furniture, these framed pictures, or them china vases.
8. Yet he certainly wasn't rich, except perhaps in this fantasy that his wife was still alive.
9. Most of them prospectors and miners spent their earnings on overpriced essentials and made the shopkeepers only rich.
10. That there makes me wonder whether Henry had kept a general store before the gold ran out.

Using Verbs Correctly

5

5.1 Verb Tenses and Forms

Verb tense shows the time of an action or a condition. Writers sometimes cause confusion when they use different verb tenses in describing actions that occur at the same time.

Consistent Use of Tenses

When two or more actions occur at the same time or in sequence, use the same verb tense to describe the actions.

> In "And of Clay Are We Created," when Rolf Carlé arrives at the scene of a disaster, he embarked (embarks) on a demanding journey within himself.

A shift in tense is necessary when two events occur at different times or out of sequence. The tenses of the verbs should clearly indicate that one action precedes the other.

> Carlé confronted (confronts) the fears he buries (buried) in childhood, as he will offer (offers) human closeness to a trapped child.

Tense	Verb Form
Present	dream/dreams
Past	dreamed
Future	will/shall dream
Present perfect	has/have dreamed
Past perfect	had dreamed
Future perfect	will/shall have dreamed

LINK TO LITERATURE

In "And of Clay Are We Created" Isabel Allende has her narrator use the past tense and past perfect tense to describe what happened to Rolf Carlé during the disaster. On page 839, however, the narrator moves into the present tense to describe the continuing impact of that time on Carlé. The shift emphasizes the profound change in him.

REVISING TiP

In telling a story, be careful not to shift tenses so often that the reader finds the sequence of events unclear.

Past Tense and Past Participle

REVISING TIP

The past tense and past participle of regular verbs have the same spelling. Both forms end in *-d* or *-ed*. However, you usually double the final consonant before adding *-ed* when a short-vowel sound precedes the consonant *(slip—slipped, knit—knitted, rot—rotted, pat—patted, stub—stubbed)*.

The simple past form of a verb can always stand alone. The past participle of the following irregular verbs should always be used with a helping verb.

Present Tense	Past Tense	Past Participle
know	knew	(have, had) known
lay	laid	(have, had) laid
lie	lay	(have, had) lain
ride	rode	(have, had) ridden
rise	rose	(have, had) risen
run	ran	(have, had) run
say	said	(have, had) said
see	saw	(have, had) seen
sing	sang	(have, had) sung
sit	sat	(have, had) sat
speak	spoke	(have, had) spoken
steal	stole	(have, had) stolen
swim	swam	(have, had) swum
take	took	(have, had) taken
teach	taught	(have, had) taught

During her ordeal the child **had** known strength beyond her years. Her courage and wisdom **had** given Carlé consolation.

APPLY WHAT YOU'VE LEARNED

Write the correct verb form or tense in the parentheses.

1. In "And of Clay Are We Created" a volcano (causes, will cause) the vast tide of mud that (buried, buries) several villages.
2. The volcanic disaster described in the story closely (resembles, will resemble) that of Nevado del Ruiz, which killed 22,000 people in 1985 in the Colombian town of Armero.
3. This actual eruption, like the fictional one, (occurs, occurred) in November.
4. Because the eruption (throws, had thrown) hot rock fragments on the mountain's ice cap, mudflows (had begun, began).
5. They unlocked water that had long (laid, lain) frozen.
6. In the past, overpopulation (has led, leads) to the construction of towns too close to volcanoes.
7. People should (have known, know) better.
8. In 1845 Nevado del Ruiz killed a thousand people with a mudflow over territory that later (became, becomes) Armero.

5.2 Commonly Confused Verbs

The following verb pairs are often confused.

Affect and Effect

Affect means "to influence." **Effect** means "to cause."

> In *The Ring of General Macías* the general's wife attempts to ~~effect~~ *affect* future events. Killing de la O might ~~affect~~ *effect* a change in history.

Lie and Lay, Sit and Set

Lie means "to rest in a flat position" or "to be in a certain place"; **lay** means "to put or place." **Sit** means "to be in a seated position"; **set** means "to put or place."

> Raquel forces the intruder, de la O, to ~~set~~ *sit*, staring into space; meanwhile, the poison ~~lays~~ *lies* in a desk drawer.

Rise and Raise

Rise means "to move upward." **Raise** means "to move something upward."

> De la O ~~rises~~ *raises* the poisoned wine to his lips, then Raquel ~~raises~~ *rises* and runs to call Cleto.

Learn and Teach

Learn means "to gain knowledge or skill." **Teach** means "to help someone learn."

> The rebel leader attempted to ~~learn~~ *teach* Raquel that his people would win.

REVISING TIP

If you're uncertain about which verb to use, check to see whether the verb has an object. The verbs *lie* and *sit* never have objects—and they both refer to position. The verbs *lay* and *set* both have objects—and they have the same meaning.

When no movement is implied, *bring* may be used to mean "produce a result."

Bring and *Take*

Bring refers to movement toward or with the speaker or writer. *Take* refers to movement away from the speaker or writer.

Raquel wondered what had ~~taken~~ *brought* de la O to her door.

Eventually he offers to ~~bring~~ *take* a letter to her prisoner

husband.

Present Tense	Past Tense	Past Participle
affect	affected	(have, had) affected
effect	effected	(have, had) effected
lie	lay	(have, had) lain
lay	laid	(have, had) laid
sit	sat	(have, had) sat
set	set	(have, had) set
rise	rose	(have, had) risen
raise	raised	(have, had) raised
learn	learned	(have, had) learned
teach	taught	(have, had) taught
bring	brought	(have, had) brought
take	took	(have, had) taken

APPLY WHAT YOU'VE LEARNED

Choose the correct verb from each pair in parentheses.

1. *The Ring of General Macías* explores incidents near Mexico City that (sit, set) a course for change in April of 1912.
2. The revolution (affected, effected) great tumult during those days.
3. Frequent betrayal by their leaders (learned, taught) landless peasants to (raise, rise) up repeatedly against wealthy landowners.
4. Some rebels attempted to (take, bring) justice to Mexico by violent means.
5. They approached the problem in extreme ways because reasonable approaches hadn't (learned, taught) the powerful people anything.
6. The rebels realized that leaders can't just (lay, lie) around and hope for the best.
7. Leaders must skillfully (effect, affect) the course of events.

Correcting Capitalization

6

6.1 Proper Nouns and Adjectives

A common noun names a class of persons, places, things, or ideas. A proper noun names a particular person, place, thing, or idea. A proper adjective is an adjective formed from a proper noun. Capitalize all proper nouns and proper adjectives.

Names and Titles

Capitalize the name of a person and the initials that stand for the name of a person.

In "The Meeting" maneco uriarte challenges duncan to a duel at a country house outside Buenos Aires, Argentina.

Capitalize a title used before a name or an abbreviation for the title. In general, do not capitalize either a title that follows a name or a title that stands alone.

In 1910—about the same year as the duel—the leadership of Argentina shifted from president alcorta to roque sáenz peña, his successor as President.

Capitalize a title indicating a family relationship when it is used before or as someone's name (Aunt Vera, Grandpa) but not when used simply to identify a person (Marco's uncle).

The narrator was only nine or ten years old, and cousin lafinur took him to a barbecue. The Cousin was older.

LINK TO LITERATURE

In "The Meeting" on page 514, notice how Jorge Luis Borges refers to specific places, people, and things. These precise names help you visualize scenes. More general words probably would not help you see the story or believe it as well.

REVISING TIP

Prefixes and suffixes such as ex- and -elect are not capitalized when used with a title. (*On the morning after Election Day in 1988, President-elect George Bush began to assemble a transition team.*)

Languages, Nationalities, Religious Terms

Capitalize languages and nationalities, as well as religious names and terms. Do not capitalize the words *god* and *goddess* when they refer to mythological deities.

Capitalize languages and nationalities, such as *Norwegian, Bengali, Hebrew, Japanese, Louisiana French,* and *Turkish.* Capitalize religious names and terms, such as *God, Buddha,* the *Bible,* and the *Koran.*

Even back then, many argentineans celebrated their gaucho heritage in ballads. Many of these ballads originated in uruguay.

School Subjects

Capitalize the name of a specific school course (*Astronomy I, Ancient History*). Do not capitalize a general reference to a school subject (*physical education, computer science*).

The narrator was never a student in literature 101, but his experiences would have given him much to say in a Writing class.

Organizations, Institutions

Capitalize the important words in the official names of organizations and institutions (*Congress, Kendall College*).

Do not capitalize words that represent kinds of organizations or institutions (*school, church, university*) or words that refer to a specific organization when they are not part of its official name (*at the university*).

By 1910 the national autonomist party, a conservative group, had begun to lose control of Argentina. In 1912 sáenz peña used the congress to confirm radical power.

REVISING TIP

Do not capitalize pronouns that refer to a deity. (*The earth goddess Gaia in **her** joy nurtures you.*)

REVISING TIP

Do not capitalize minor words in a proper noun that is made up of several words. (*the Department **of** Agriculture*)

Geographical Names, Events, Time Periods

Capitalize geographical names—as well as the names of events, historical periods and documents, holidays, months, and days—but not the names of seasons.

Names	Examples
Continents	South America, Europe, Antarctica
Bodies of water	Atlantic Ocean, Iguaçu Falls, Strait of Magellan
Political units	Argentina, Brazil, Montevideo, Bahía Blanca
Areas of a country	the Pampas, Patagonia, the Gran Chaco
Public areas	Columbus Park, Don Torcuato Airport
Roads and structures	Casa Rosada, Rodeo Drive
Events	Congress of Tucumán, the Mexican Revolution
Documents	Treaty of Paris, the Constitution of 1853
Periods of history	the Great Depression, the Enlightenment
Holidays	Cinco de Mayo, Veterans Day
Months and days	November, Monday
Seasons	summer, fall
Directions	south, northeast

The duel took place at Señor Acevedo's country house, the laurels, north of buenos aires and near the paraná river. It happened late on a warm Summer evening, perhaps in february of 1910.

REVISING TIP

Do not capitalize a reference that does not use the full name of a place, an event, or a period. (*The night of the tragedy, Lafinur sang a ballad about a knife fight in Jun'in Street. That* **street** *had seen much violence.*)

APPLY WHAT YOU'VE LEARNED

Rewrite the following sentences, correcting errors in capitalization.

1. In "The Meeting" a group of argentinean men and a boy, the narrator, see a fatal duel.
2. The narrator sets the time of the duel by the appearance of halley's comet in 1910.
3. In 1910 in argentina, the constitution of 1853 structured political life.
4. general urquiza helped finalize the document on may 25, 1853.
5. The argentinean congress dates from that time.
6. Later on, buenos aires gained a University and the national historical museum.
7. Three decades before the 1910 duel, general julio roca fought the last of the indian wars.
8. In 1929 the narrator talks with josé olave, a retired police Captain, about the duel.
9. The Captain tells stories about the tough neighborhood called the retiro.
10. Finally, olave recalls that one of the knives used in the duel belonged to an outlaw, juan almada from tapalquén.

6.2 Titles of Created Works

The titles of published material follow certain capitalization rules.

Books, Plays, Magazines, Newspapers, Films

Capitalize the first word, the last word, and all other important words in the title of a book, play, periodical, newspaper, or film. Underline or italicize the title to set it off.

Within a title, do not capitalize articles, conjunctions, and prepositions of fewer than five letters unless they appear at the beginning or the end of the title.

> D. H. Lawrence's novel sons and lovers describes his boyhood as the son of a coal miner. His first published story appeared in the nottinghamshire guardian, and his first novel, the white peacock, was published in 1911.

Poems, Stories, Articles

Capitalize the first word, last word, and all other important words in the title of a poem, a short story, or an article. Enclose the title in quotation marks.

> Students often read his short stories, such as the prussian officer, or the poem called piano.

Correcting Punctuation

7

7.1 Punctuating Compound Sentences

Punctuation helps organize sentences that have more than one clause.

Commas in Compound Sentences

Use a comma before the conjunction that joins the clauses of a compound sentence.

Do not use a comma before the conjunction that joins a compound subject or a compound predicate.

> In "By the Waters of Babylon" Stephen Vincent Benét tells a story in the first person∧and this focus proves to be very effective.

Semicolons in Compound Sentences

Use a semicolon between the clauses of a compound sentence when no conjunction is used. Use a semicolon before a conjunctive adverb that joins the clauses of a compound sentence.

Conjunctive adverbs include *therefore, however, consequently, nevertheless,* and *besides.* You should place a comma after a conjunctive adverb in a compound sentence.

> The reader identifies with the boy who is telling about his adventure∧however∧few readers will ever have an adventure like John's.

REVISING TIP

Even when clauses are connected by a coordinating conjunction, you should use a semicolon between them if one or both clauses contain a comma. *(The hero of Benét's story, a boy named John, visits the Dead Places; and during his journey he discovers a great truth.)*

APPLY WHAT YOU'VE LEARNED

Rewrite this paragraph, correcting problems with commas or semicolons.

[1]In "By the Waters of Babylon" John, the son of a priest, undergoes a rite of passage to prove his manhood and he passes the test. [2]Most societies observe specific rites of passage in modern times, the most formalized of these rites, such as Christian confirmation and Jewish bar mitzvah, celebrate spiritual passages. [3]Most rites help people understand their new roles in society but they also help others to recognize the people in their new roles. [4]Rites of passage have three stages in the first, a participant is temporarily separated from the rest of society. [5]The second, or transitional stage, is a time of instruction the participant learns about his or her new position. [6]The final stage involves the acknowledgment by the community of the new status of the individual therefore a celebration often marks the individual's achievement of this status.

7.2 Setting Off Elements in a Sentence

Most elements that are not essential to a sentence are set off by commas or by other punctuation marks to highlight the main idea of the sentence. A nonessential element merely adds information to an already complete sentence. An essential element is necessary to convey the accurate meaning of the sentence; without it, the meaning is unclear.

Commas

You should often use a comma to separate an introductory word or phrase from the rest of the sentence.

An introductory prepositional phrase usually need not be set off with a comma. However, you should use a comma for two or more prepositional phrases or for a phrase that includes a verb or a verbal.

In the play *The Pen of My Aunt* by Josephine Tey, the setting is rural France during World War II. Known as the Occupation, that time saw much intrigue as spies and members of the resistance came and went.

In a complex sentence, set off an introductory subordinate clause with a comma.

As the play opens‸a Nazi corporal brings in a stranger who was found wandering in Madame's woods.

Use commas to set off a word or group of words that interrupts the flow of a sentence. When a subordinate clause interrupts the main clause, set off the subordinate clause with commas only if it is not essential.

Madame and her servant Simone‸thinking very quickly‸ scramble to support the stranger's claim that he's Madame's nephew. The stranger‸who also thinks quickly‸ has no papers with him.

The words shown in the chart below are commonly used to begin a subordinate clause. When such words appear with introductory or interrupting clauses, they usually signal the need for one or more commas.

Words Often Used to Introduce Subordinate Clauses				
Subordinating Conjunctions	after although as as if as long as as much as as though	because before even if even though if in order that provided	since so that than though till unless until	whatever when whenever where wherever while
Relative Pronouns	which	who	whom	whose

REVISING TIP

Try saying the sentence without the interrupter; if the basic meaning doesn't change, you should use punctuation (commas, dashes, or parentheses) to set off the interrupter.

Parentheses

Use parentheses to set off material that is only incidentally connected to the main idea of a sentence.

The Nazi corporal (who is negligent and easily fooled) tries unsuccessfully to see the stranger's papers.

Dashes

Use dashes to set off a word, or a group of words, that abruptly interrupts the flow of a sentence.

Simone almost throws away the stranger's freedom by speaking too soon. Luckily—through some clever wrangling—the damage is reversed.

REVISING TIP

A colon often follows a word or phrase such as *these* or *the following items*. Never use a colon after a preposition or after a verb when the items listed are essential to the clause.

Colons

Use a colon to introduce a list of items or a long quotation.

The stranger is told to seek help in these places: Forty Avenue Foch in Crest, the Red Lion in Mans, and the blacksmith's at Laloupe.

Use a colon between two sentences when the second explains or summarizes the first.

The stranger escapes in extraordinary company: the Nazi corporal drives him to the crossroads.

For Clarity

Use commas to prevent misreading or misunderstanding.

> A short time before, the Nazi corporal had planned to apprehend the stranger.

REVISING TIP

Sometimes when a comma is missing, parts of a sentence can be grouped in more than one way by a reader. A comma separates the parts so they can be read in only one way.

APPLY WHAT YOU'VE LEARNED

Rewrite these sentences. Add commas, parentheses, dashes, and colons where necessary.

[1]The stranger in *The Pen of My Aunt* is a member of the resistance a network of civilians working to defeat the Nazis. [2]Participants included two groups civilians and armed guerrillas most likely accompanied by faithful animal companions. [3]Their activities were legion they included printing secret newspapers and helping to rescue Allied pilots from enemy territory. [4]Surprise attacks on German patrols a challenging way to start the day were part of the resistance's duties. [5]Although all resistance groups had the same goals they didn't necessarily work together effectively. [6]In spite of the unbelievable threat however much progress was made. [7]In the play both Madame and the stranger are most likely Communists the Communists dominated the resistance in occupied France.

7.3   Elements in a Series

Use commas to separate three or more elements in a series and to separate multiple adjectives preceding a noun.

Subjects, Verbs, Objects, and Other Elements

Use a comma after every item except the last in a series of three or more items.

The three or more items can be nouns, verbs, adjectives, adverbs, phrases, independent clauses, or other parts of a sentence.

> In "The Balek Scales" the family picks herbs such as woodruff, thyme, mint, hayflowers, and foxgloves.

REVISING TIP

Note in the example that a comma followed by a conjunction precedes the last element in the series. That comma is always used.

Two or More Adjectives

When more than one adjective precedes a noun, in most cases use a comma after each adjective except the last one.

If you can't reverse the order of adjectives without changing the meaning or if you can't use the word *and* between them, do not separate them with a comma.

> I consider the Baleks to have been arrogant despotic dishonest people. The narrator came from a good, old family.

APPLY WHAT YOU'VE LEARNED

Rewrite the paragraph, correcting the comma errors.

[1]"The Balek Scales" is set in a hilly wooded region whose borders have been changing for generations. [2]Germany Czechoslovakia and now the Czech Republic have claimed these lands. [3]Prague today is one of the most beautiful cosmopolitan and colorful cities in all of Europe. [4]Its charm and its museums churches bridges and city square attract tourists from all over the world. [5]The original settlements that merged into present-day Prague spanned hills river valleys and riverside terraces. [6]Prague is famed for its exquisite crystal garnets and china. [7]The Czechs call this historic, old-world city by its original name—Praha.

7.4 Dates, Addresses, and Letters

Punctuation in addresses, dates, and letters makes information easy to understand.

Dates

Use a comma after the day and the year to set off the date from the rest of the sentence.

> "Searching for Summer" might have been written about a wedding taking place November 21 2088 somewhere in England.

REVISING TIP

In dates that include only the month and the year, do not use a comma after the month. (*Lily and Tom married in November 2088 not far from Inverness.*)

Addresses

In an address with more than one part, use a comma after each part to set it off from the rest of the sentence.

In what might as well be Brigadoon∧Scotland∧the young couple in the story find a bit of sunshine to make their joy complete.

Parts of a Letter

Use a comma after the greeting and after the closing of a letter.

Dear Mrs. Hatching∧

How can we ever thank you for our honeymoon—the kind that dreams are made of!

Gratefully∧

Lily and Tom

REVISING TIP

In an address that includes the ZIP code, do not use a comma between the state abbreviation and the ZIP code.

APPLY WHAT YOU'VE LEARNED

Rewrite the following paragraph, correcting the comma errors.

[1]In "Searching for Summer" the skies above Bournemouth England are virtually always overcast. [2]A weather forecaster might report information such as the following:

Dear Pat

Please warn our listeners! Cumulus-shaped clouds suggest thunderstorms in the Antioch Illinois region. If they become cumulonimbus clouds, we are in for a tornado.

With concern
Jack

[3]In November, 1998, we might distinguish among numerous kinds of clouds. [4]However, a different April 8 2088 radio announcement would be more usual in the world of "Searching for Summer." [5]The "lowering" sky near Molesworth England would likely be stratus or stratocumulus clouds.

7.5 Quotations

Quotation marks tell readers who said what. Incorrectly placed or missing quotation marks lead to misunderstanding.

Direct Quotation from a Source

Use quotation marks at the beginning and the end of a direct quotation from source material and to set off the title of a short work. Do not use quotation marks to set off an indirect quotation.

In "The First Seven Years" Malamud explores the struggles of a father, Feld, who wants the best for his child. Feld says he wants "to snare Max, the college boy, for his daughter Miriam."

Introducing a Quotation

Introduce a short direct quotation with a comma. Use a colon for a long quotation. Capitalize the first word in a direct quotation but not in an indirect one.

Max says to Feld, "And is she sensible—not the flighty kind?"

Feld replies, "She is very sensible."

End Punctuation

Place periods inside quotation marks. Place question marks and exclamation points inside quotation marks if they belong to the quotation; place them outside if they do not belong to the quotation. Place semicolons outside quotation marks.

Max asks about her age, "Did you say nineteen?"

Feld replies, "Yes"; then Max says, "Would it be all right to inquire if you have a picture of her?"

REVISING TIP

If quoted words are from a written source and are not complete sentences, begin the quote with a lowercase letter. (*Bernard Malamud wrote that one's fantasy "goes for a walk and returns with a bride."*)

REVISING TIP

Use a colon to introduce a long quotation. (*Anne Frank said: "Whoever is happy will make others happy too. He who has courage and faith will never perish in misery!"*)

Use a comma to end a quotation that is a complete sentence followed by explanatory words.

"Call her up. She comes home from work six o'clock," says Feld to Max.

Divided Quotations

Capitalize the first word of the second part of a direct quotation if it begins a new sentence.

"He has no soul," says Miriam. "He's only interested in things."

Do not capitalize the first word of the second part of a divided quotation if it does not begin a new sentence.

"So how," Feld sighed after a sip, "did you enjoy?"

REVISING TIP

Should the first word of the second part of a divided quotation be capitalized? Imagine the quotation without the explanatory words. If a capital letter would not be used, then do not use one in the divided quotation.

APPLY WHAT YOU'VE LEARNED

Rewrite the sentences, inserting quotation marks and other appropriate punctuation.

1. In The First Seven Years Sobel, the shoemaker's assistant, is revealed as a Holocaust survivor.
2. An actual Holocaust survivor, author Cynthia Ozick, said the whole world wants us dead.
3. "The world has always wanted" she said "To wipe us out."
4. Rabbi Harold Schulweis asked if he must be like Yudka, in the short story The Sermon.
5. Yudka told a kibbutz meeting that "if it were up to him, he would simply forbid teaching Jewish history"
6. Yet Rabbi Schulweis says that "The survivors place a mirror to his soul."
7. In the article Half a Million Schindlers the author says "all of us, Jews and non-Jews, may find it hard to believe—evil has become more credible than good."
8. The people quoted in the article agree that "Jews need Christian heroes." and "Christians need Jewish heroes."

Grammar Glossary

This glossary contains various terms you need to understand when you use the Grammar Handbook. Used as a reference source, this glossary will help you explore grammar concepts and how they relate to one another.

Abbreviation An abbreviation is a shortened form of a word or word group; it is often made up of initials. (*B.C., Lt., YWHA*)

Active voice. *See* **Voice.**

Adjective An adjective modifies, or describes, a noun or pronoun. (*strange* order, *happy* you)

A *predicate adjective* follows a linking verb and describes the subject. (The teacher seemed *energetic*.)

A *proper adjective* is formed from a proper noun. (*Egyptian* pyramids, *Irish* stew)

The *comparative* form of an adjective compares two items. (*more ambitious, kinder*)

The *superlative* form of an adjective compares more than two things. (*most certain, driest*)

What Adjectives Tell	Examples
How many	*some* oranges *most* explorers
What kind	*faint* outline *tighter* schedule
Which one(s)	*this* class *those* games

Adjective phrase. *See* **Phrase.**

Adverb An adverb modifies a verb, an adjective, or another adverb. (Ilya skates *gracefully*.)

The *comparative* form of an adverb compares two actions. (*more swiftly*)

The *superlative* form of an adverb compares more than two actions. (*most frankly*)

What Adverbs Tell	Examples
How	speak *softly* chew *thoroughly*
When	followed *after* *later* in the day
Where	traveled *there* fell *down*
To what extent	*too* angry *really* hurt

Adverb, conjunctive. *See* **Conjunctive adverb.**

Adverb phrase. *See* **Phrase.**

Agreement Sentence parts that correspond with one another are said to be in agreement.

In *pronoun-antecedent agreement,* a pronoun and the word it refers to are the same in number, gender, and person. (*Sue* caught the bus. *She* arrived on time.)

In *subject-verb agreement*, the subject and verb in a sen-tence are the same in number. (*I play* chess. *He plays* chess.)

Ambiguous reference An ambiguous reference occurs when a pronoun may refer to more than one word. (Arturo told Ramon that *he* had to leave.)

Antecedent An antecedent is the noun or the pronoun to which a pro-noun refers. (*Dee* helps *her* friend.)

Appositive An appositive is a word or phrase that explains one or more words in a sentence. (Joe, *a drummer*, plays in the band.)

An *essential appositive* is needed to make the sense of a sentence complete. (My friend *Dom* went camping last week.)

A *nonessential appositive* is one that adds information to a sentence but is not necessary to its sense. (Will Rogers, *the noted humorist,* entertained them.)

Article Articles are the special adjectives *a, an,* and *the*. (*the* box, *a* poem)

The *definite article* (the word *the*) refers to a specific thing. (*the* cat)

An *indefinite article* indicates that a noun is not unique but is one of many of its kind. (*a* glove, *an* anchor)

Auxiliary verb. See **Verb.**

Clause A clause is a group of words that contains a verb and its subject. (*They help*)

An *adjective clause* is a subordinate clause that modifies a noun or pronoun in the main clause of a sentence. (She wrote the poem *that we recited.*)

An *adverb clause* is a subordinate clause used as an adverb to modify a verb, an adjective, or an adverb. (I can't remember *when she arrived.*)

A *noun clause* is a subordinate clause that is used as a noun. (*What I should eat for lunch* is my main concern right now.)

An *elliptical clause* is a clause from which a word or words have been omitted. (John writes better *than I.*)

A *main (independent) clause* can stand by itself as a sentence. (*a car sped by*)

A *subordinate (dependent) clause* does not express a complete thought and cannot stand by itself. (*when a stranger appeared at the door*)

Clause	Example
Main (independent)	The telephone rang shrilly
Subordinate (dependent)	after we had gone to bed.

Collective noun. *See* **Noun.**

Comma splice A comma splice is an error caused when two sentences are separated with a comma instead of a correct end mark. (*The music started, the flag was raised.*)

Common noun. *See* **Noun.**

Comparative. *See* **Adjective; Adverb.**

Complement A complement is a word or group of words that completes the meaning of the verb. (Rain ruined the *float.*) *See also* **Direct object; Indirect object.**

An *objective complement* is a word or a group of words that follows a direct object and renames or describes that object. (The parents considered their son a *genius.*)

A *subject complement* follows a linking verb and renames or describes the subject. (The vote was *unanimous.*) *See* **Noun, predicate; Adjective, predicate.**

Complete predicate The complete predicate of a sentence consists of the main verb plus any words that modify or complete the verb's meaning. (The circus *came to town.*)

Complete subject The complete subject in a sentence consists of the simple subject plus any words that modify or describe the simple subject. (*Several athletes from our school* entered the competition.)

Sentence Part	Example
Complete subject	The tall ship in the distance
Complete predicate	headed for the harbor.

Compound sentence part A sentence element that consists of two or more subjects, predicates, objects, or other parts is compound. (*Jay* and *Art* paint. Diane *sews* and *embroiders.* Pat speaks *English* and *Spanish.*)

Conjunction A conjunction is a word or group of words that links other words or groups of words.

A *coordinating conjunction* connects related words, groups of words, or sentences. (*and, but, or*)

A *correlative conjunction* is one of a pair of conjunctions that work together to connect sentence parts. (*either . . . or, neither . . . nor, not only . . . but also, both . . . and*)

A *subordinating conjunction* introduces a subordinate clause. (*after, although, as, as if, as long as, as though, because, before, if, in order that, provided, since, so that, than, though, till, unless, until, whatever, when, whenever, where, wherever, while*)

Conjunctive adverb A conjunctive adverb joins the clauses of a compound sentence. (*however, therefore, besides*)

Contraction A contraction is formed by joining two words and substituting an apostrophe for a letter or letters left out of one of the words. (*I've, shouldn't*)

Coordinating conjunction. *See* **Conjunction.**

Correlative conjunction. *See* **Conjunction.**

D

Dangling modifier A dangling modifier is a modifier that does not clearly modify any word in the sentence. (*Running to catch a train,* the newspaper headlines caught my attention.)

Demonstrative pronoun. *See* **Pronoun.**

Dependent clause. *See* **Clause.**

Direct object A direct object receives the action of a verb. Direct objects follow transitive verbs. (Rita knew the *answer.*)

Direct quotation. *See* **Quotation.**

Divided quotation. *See* **Quotation.**

Double negative A double negative is an incorrect use of two negative words when only one is needed. (I *won't never* finish this!)

End mark An end mark is one of several punctuation marks that can end a sentence. See the punctuation chart on page 1102.

Fragment. *See* **Sentence fragment.**

Future tense. *See* **Verb tense.**

Gender The gender of a personal pronoun indicates whether the person or thing referred to is male, female, or neuter. (Duke is a great watch dog; *he* won't let any strangers enter the house.)

Gerund A gerund is a verbal that ends in *-ing* and functions as a noun. (I've always enjoyed *swimming*.)

Helping verb. *See* **Verb, auxiliary.**

Illogical comparison An illogical comparison is a comparison that does not make sense because words are missing or illogical. (Ken likes basketball *more than any sport.*)

Indefinite pronoun. *See* **Pronoun.**

Indefinite reference Indefinite reference occurs when a pronoun refers to an idea that is vaguely expressed. (We addressed all the envelopes, and *it* was time consuming.)

Independent clause. *See* **Clause.**

Indirect object An indirect object tells to whom or for whom (sometimes to what or for what) something is done. (Vi gave *me* a book.)

Indirect question An indirect question tells what someone asked without using the person's exact words. (*Al asked me what I wanted.*)

Indirect quotation. *See* **Quotation.**

Infinitive An infinitive is a verbal beginning with *to* that functions as an adjective, an adverb, or a noun. (I want *to go.*)

Intensive pronoun. *See* **Pronoun.**

Interjection An interjection is a word or phrase used to express strong feeling. (*No! Good grief!*)

Interrogative pronoun. *See* **Pronoun.**

Intransitive verb. *See* **Verb.**

Inverted sentence An inverted sentence is one in which the subject comes after the verb. (*There goes my last chance. Where are the notes for the history exam?*)

Irregular verb. *See* **Verb.**

Linking verb. *See* **Verb.**

Main clause. *See* **Clause.**

Main verb. *See* **Verb.**

Modifier A modifier makes another word more precise. Modifiers most often are adjectives or adverbs; they may also be phrases, verbals, or clauses that function as adjectives or adverbs. (*bright* coin, laughed *gaily*, boy *in gym clothes*, *crying* baby)

An *essential modifier* is one that is necessary to the meaning of a sentence. (Everybody *who rides a bicycle* should wear a helmet.)

A *nonessential modifier* is one that merely adds more information to a sentence that is clear without the addition. (Mark Twain, *coming from Missouri*, represented middle America.)

Noun A noun names a person, a place, a thing, or an idea. (*Heidi, garden, box, unity*)

An *abstract noun* names an idea, a quality, or a feeling. (*faith, liberty*)

A *collective noun* names a group of things. (*committee, flock, class*)

A *common noun* is a general name of a person, a place, a thing, or an idea. (*waiter, pond, dress, happiness*)

A *compound noun* contains two or more words. (*mother-in-law, sidewalk, home run*)

A *noun of direct address* is the name of a person being directly spoken to. (*Gene,* will you teach me to dance? Slow down, *Mandy,* or you'll hurt yourself.)

A *possessive noun* shows who or what owns something. (*Wayne's* tie, *Jill's* flute)

A *predicate noun* follows a linking verb and renames the subject. (Rosa is my *assistant.*)

A *proper noun* names a particular person, place, or thing. (*Ann Smith, Westminster Abbey, Vienna Boys Choir*)

Number A word is **singular** in number if it refers to just one person, place, thing, idea, or action and **plural** in number if it refers to more than one person, place, thing, idea, or action. (The words *it, boy,* and *skips* are singular. The words *them, boys,* and *skip* are plural.)

Object of a preposition The object of a preposition is the noun or pronoun that follows a preposition. (We waited for the *train.* I took a message to *him.*)

Object of a verb The object of a verb receives the action of a verb. (Tim collects *stamps.*)

Participle A participle is often used as part of a verb phrase. (had *noticed*) It can also be used as a verbal that functions as an adjective. (the *flaming* arrows, the dog *brought* to the veterinarian)

The *present participle* is formed by adding *-ing* to the present tense of a verb. (*Finding* a dry area, we camped for the night.)

The *past participle* of a regular verb is formed by adding *-d* or *-ed* to the present tense. The past participle of irregular verbs does not follow this pattern. (*Polished* silver gleamed in the jeweler's window. My favorite vase was *broken.*)

Passive voice *See* **Voice.**

Past tense. *See* **Verb tense.**

Perfect tenses. *See* **Verb tense.**

Person The person of pronouns is a means of classifying them.

A *first-person* pronoun refers to the person speaking. (*I* danced.)

A *second-person* pronoun refers to the person spoken to. (*You* ate.)

A *third-person* pronoun refers to some other person(s) or thing(s) being spoken of. (*They* clapped.)

Personal pronoun. *See* **Pronoun.**

Phrase A phrase is a group of related words that lacks both a subject and a verb. (*in a short time, holding a long-stemmed rose*)

An *adjective phrase* modifies a noun or a pronoun. (A part *of the answer* appears.)

An *adverb phrase* modifies a verb, an adjective, or an adverb. (Bob knocked *on the door.*)

An *appositive phrase* explains one or more words in a sentence. (Model-airplane builders often work with balsa, *a lightweight wood.*)

A *gerund phrase* consists of a gerund and its modifiers and complements. (She disliked *taking care of her younger brothers.*)

An *infinitive phrase* consists of an infinitive, its modifiers, and its complements. (The boy tried *to stop the leak in the dike.*)

A *participial phrase* consists of a participle and its modifiers and complements. (*Coming to a complete stop,* the freight train blocked traffic.)

A *prepositional phrase* consists of a preposition, its object, and the object's modifiers. (Homes *near the river banks* were swept away *by the floodwater's force.*)

A *verb phrase* consists of a main verb and one or more helping verbs. (*might have listened, should be coming*)

Possessive A noun or pronoun that is possessive shows ownership. (*Mary's* brother, *our* parents)

Possessive noun. *See* **Noun.**

Possessive pronoun. *See* **Pronoun.**

Predicate The predicate of a sentence tells what the subject is or does. (The horse *bucked the inexperienced rider.* Joan *is a good friend.*) *See* **Complete predicate; simple predicate.**

Predicate adjective. *See* **Adjective.**

Predicate nominative A predicate nominative is a noun or pronoun that follows a linking verb and renames or explains the subject. (The twins are *cheerleaders.* The leader was *he.*)

Predicate pronoun. *See* **Pronoun.**

Preposition A preposition is a word that relates its object to another part of the sentence or to the sentence as a whole. (I wrote a letter *to* my pen pal.)

Prepositional phrase. *See* **Phrase.**

Present tense. *See* **Verb tense.**

Progressive form. *See* **Verb.**

Pronoun A pronoun replaces a noun or another pronoun. (*Jim* and *she* carried *their* own bags.) Some pronouns allow a writer or speaker to avoid repeating a proper noun. Other pronouns let a writer show a situation in which some information is not known.

A *demonstrative pronoun* singles out one or more persons or things. (*This* is my hat.)

An *indefinite pronoun* refers to an unidentified person or thing. (*Someone* should have seen the car. Is *anybody* there?)

An *intensive pronoun* emphasizes a noun or pronoun. (The teacher *herself* told me.)

An *interrogative pronoun* asks a question. (*What* happened here?)

A *personal pronoun* refers to first, second, or third person. (*I* swim. *You* go. *She* eats.)

A *possessive pronoun* shows ownership. (*My* work is finished. Where is *yours*?)

A *predicate pronoun* follows a linking verb and renames the subject. (A reliable helper is *she.*)

A *reflexive pronoun* reflects an action back on the subject of the sentence. (Jetaun taught *herself.*)

A *relative pronoun* relates a subordinate clause to the word it modifies in the main clause. (The courses *that* we took in summer school were interesting.)

Pronoun-antecedent agreement. *See* **Agreement.**

Pronoun forms

The *subject form of a pronoun* is used when the pronoun is the subject of a sentence or follows a linking verb as a predicate pronoun. (*She* knows Ed. Bob is *he.*)

The *object form of a pronoun* is used when the pronoun is the direct or indirect object of a verb or a verbal or the object of a preposition. (Jo gave *her* a shawl. Ben will stay with *them.*)

Proper adjective. *See* **Adjective.**

Proper noun. *See* **Noun.**

Punctuation Punctuation clarifies the structure of sentences. See the punctuation chart below.

Quotation A quotation consists of words from another speaker or writer.

A *direct quotation* is the exact words of a speaker or writer. (May said, *"I can't finish this job tonight."*)

A *divided quotation* is a quotation separated by words that identify the speaker. (*"I can't,"* said May, *"finish this job tonight."*)

An *indirect quotation* repeats what a person said without using the exact words. (*May said that she couldn't finish the job tonight.*)

Reflexive pronoun. *See* **Pronoun.**

Regular verb. *See* **Verb.**

Relative pronoun. *See* **Pronoun.**

Run-on sentence A run-on sentence consists of two or more sentences written incorrectly as one. (*No one answered the phone it kept ringing and ringing.*)

Sentence A sentence expresses a complete thought. The chart at the top of the next page shows the four kinds of sentences.

A *complex sentence* contains one main clause and one or more subordinate clauses. (*If I call, please come right away. The dog barks when I whistle.*)

A *compound sentence* is made up of two or more main clauses combined with a comma and a conjunction or a semicolon. (*The baby let his balloon escape, and Jim could not get it back.*)

A *simple sentence* consists of only one main clause. (*Our soccer team won the series. Jane and Andy arrived late.*)

Sentence fragment A sentence fragment is a group of words that is only part of a sentence. (*While we spoke. Rowing swiftly.*)

Simple predicate The simple predicate is the verb in the predicate. (Jim always *knows* the answer.)

Simple subject The simple subject is the key noun or pronoun in the subject. (The heavy *bag* fell to the floor.)

Punctuation	Uses	Examples
Apostrophe (')	Shows possession Forms a contraction	Al's radio boys' coach I'll stay. He's tried hard.
Colon (:)	Introduces a list or long quotation Divides some compound sentences	the following games: baseball, football, and tennis Time was short: he had one hour to do a two-hour job.
Comma (,)	Separates ideas Separates modifiers Separates items in series	The day was hot, and the clothes dried quickly. The cute, playful puppy jumped onto my lap. We'll need plates, cups, and saucers.
Exclamation point (!)	Ends an exclamatory sentence	I had a wonderful time!
Hyphen (-)	Joins words in some compound nouns	son-in-law, great-grandchild
Period (.)	Ends a declarative sentence Indicates most abbreviations	Everyone helped with the dishes. gal. pt. Rd. Sr. Nov.
Question mark (?)	Ends an interrogative sentence	Who was on the phone?

Semicolon (;)	Divides some compound sentences
	Separates items in series that
	  contain commas
		Linda will be late; she missed her train.
		The student council elected Brigid, a freshman; Juan, a
		  sophomore; and Leo, a senior.

Kind of Sentence	Example
Declarative (statement)	I received a letter.
Exclamatory (strong feeling)	You're here!
Imperative (request, command)	Hold the door.
Interrogative (question)	Who can help?

Split infinitive A split infinitive occurs when a modifier is placed between the word *to* and the verb in an infinitive. (*to gladly give*)

Subject The subject is the part of a sentence that tells whom or what the sentence is about. (*Penny* sang.) *See* **Complete subject; Simple subject.**

Subject-verb agreement. *See* **Agreement.**

Subordinate clause. *See* **Clause.**

Superlative. *See* **Adjective; Adverb.**

Transitive verb. *See* **Verb.**

Unidentified reference An unidentified reference often occurs when the word *it, they, this, which,* or *that* is used. (In Louisiana *they* observe Mardi Gras as a holiday.)

Verb A verb expresses an action, a condition, or a state of being.

An ***action verb*** tells what the subject does, has done, or will do. The action may be physical or mental. (Abdul *shouted.*)

An ***auxiliary verb*** is added to a main verb to express tense, add emphasis, or otherwise affect the meaning of the verb. Together the auxiliary and main verb make up a verb phrase. (*do* believe, *has* seen, *will* forget)

A ***linking verb*** expresses a state of being or connects the subject with a word or words that describe the subject. (The soup *tastes* wonderful.) Linking verbs include *appear, be* (*am, are, is, was, were, been, being*), *become, feel, grow, look, remain, seem, smell, sound, taste.*

A ***main verb*** describes action or state of being; it may have one or more auxiliaries. (may be *chosen*)

The ***progressive form*** of a verb shows continuing action. (Kites *are flying.*)

The past tense and past participle of a ***regular verb*** are formed by adding *-d* or *-ed.* (*charge, charged*) An ***irregular verb*** does not follow a predictable pattern in its formation. (*sink, sank, sunk; teach, taught, taught; forget, forgot, forgotten*)

The action of a ***transitive verb*** is directed toward someone or something, called the object of the verb. (Ralph *takes* lessons in scuba diving.) An ***intransitive verb*** has no object. (Geraldo *swims* well.)

Verb phrase. *See* **Phrase.**

Verb tense Verb tense shows the time of an action or the time of a state of being.

The ***present tense*** places an action or condition in the present. (Sarah *enjoys* hiking.)

The ***past tense*** places an action or condition in the past. (We *stayed.*)

The ***future tense*** places an action or condition in the future. (She *will forget.*)

The ***present perfect tense*** describes an action in an indefinite past time or an action that began in the past and continues in the present. (*has carried, have seen*)

The ***past perfect tense*** describes one action that happened before another action in the past. (*had remained, had allowed*)

The ***future perfect tense*** describes an event that will be finished before another future action begins. (*will have agreed, shall have completed*)

Verbal A verbal is formed from a verb and acts as a noun, an adjective, or an adverb.

Verbal	Example
Gerund (used as a noun)	*Writing* essays takes time.
Infinitive (used as an adjective, an adverb, or a noun)	Try *to finish* the job tonight.
Participle (used as an adjective)	The hikers, *helped* by the guide, reached camp.

Voice The voice of a verb depends on whether the subject performs or receives the action of the verb.

In the ***active voice*** the subject of the sentence performs the action. (Melissa *cooked* dinner. Everyone *will enjoy* it.)

In the ***passive voice*** the subject of the sentence receives the action of the verb. (The jewels *were kept* in the safe. The game *will be played* rain or shine.)

Index of Fine Art

Index of Skills

Literary Terms

Reading and Critical Thinking Skills

Grammar, Usage, and Mechanics

Vocabulary Skills

Research and Study Skills

Speaking, Listening, and Viewing

Index of Titles and Authors

Page numbers that appear in italics refer to biographical information.

Acknowledgments *(continued)*

Alexander. Reprinted by permission of The University of Georgia, Athens, Georgia.

John Johnson Limited: "The Prisoner Who Wore Glasses," from *Tales of Tenderness and Power* by Bessie Head, Heinemann Educational Books, African Writers Series. Reprinted by permission of John Johnson, Ltd., London. Copyright © 1989 by the Estate of Bessie Head.

Rowan Tree Press: "They Have Not Been Able / No Han Podido" from *Landscape and Exile* by Armando Valladares and edited by Marguerite Bouvard; Copyright © 1985. Reprinted with permission from Rowan Tree Press.

Rosario Santos Literary and Cultural Services, Inc.: "The Censors," from *Open Door* by Luisa Valenzuela; Copyright © 1976, renewed 1988 by Luisa Valenzuela. By permission of Rosario Santos Literary and Cultural Services, Inc.

Harcourt Brace & Company and The Society of Authors: Excerpt from "Tolerance," from *Two Cheers for Democracy* by E. M. Forster; Copyright 1951 by E. M. Forster and renewed © 1979 by Donald Parry, reprinted by permission of the publisher and The Society of Authors as the literary representatives of the E. M. Forster Estate.

HarperCollins Publishers, Limited: "Fighting South of the Ramparts," from *The Poetry and Career of Li Po* by Li Po (Li Bo), translated by Arthur Walley; Copyright 1950. By permission of HarperCollins Publishers, Limited, London.

Houghton Mifflin Company: "On the Rainy River," from *The Things They Carried* by Tim O'Brien; Copyright © 1990 by Tim O'Brien. By permission of Houghton Mifflin Company / Seymour Lawrence. All rights reserved.

Excerpt from *Farewell to Manzanar*, by James D. and Jeanne Wakatsuki Houston; Copyright © 1973 by James D. Houston. Reprinted by permission of Houghton Mifflin Company. All rights reserved.

New Directions Publishing Corporation: "The Pearl," from *Death in Midsummer* by Yukio Mishima and translated by Geoffrey W. Sargent; Copyright © 1966 by New Directions Publishing Corp. Reprinted by permission of New Directions Publishing Corporation.

Brent Staples: "Black Men and Public Space" from *Life Studies: A Thematic Reader* by Brent Staples and edited by David Cavitch; Copyright © 1989. Mr. Staples is a member of the *New York Times* editorial board, where he writes on politics and culture.

BOA Editions: "Miss Rosie," from *Good Woman: Poems and a Memoir 1969–1980* by Lucille Clifton; Copyright © 1987 by Lucille Clifton. Reprinted with the permission of BOA Editions, Ltd., 92 Park Ave., Brockport, NY 14420.

Gwendolyn Brooks: "Kitchenette Building," from her book *Blacks*, published by Third World Press, Chicago, © 1991. By permission of the author.

Farrar, Straus & Giroux, Inc.: Excerpt from *Night* by Elie Wiesel, translated by Stella Rodway; Copyright © 1960 by MacGibbon & Kee. Copyright renewed © 1988 by the Collins Publishing Group. By permission of Farrar, Straus & Giroux, Inc.

The Nobel Foundation: Excerpt from Elie Wiesel's Nobel Prize acceptance speech; Copyright © 1986 by the Nobel Foundation. By permission of the Nobel Foundation.

University Press of New England: "The Women Who Are Poets in My Land," from *Because the Sea Is Black* (Wesleyan University Press) by Blaga Dimitrova; Copyright © 1989 by Blaga Dimitrova. By permission of University Press of New England.

Random House, Inc.: "House Taken Over," from *End of the Game and Other Stories* by Julio Cortázar; Copyright © 1967 by Random House, Inc. By permission of Random House, Inc.

the West Indies by Samuel Selvon. Reprinted by permission of Althea N. Selvon, Executor.

Viking Penguin: "Like the Sun" from *Under the Banyan Tree* by R. K. Narayan; Copyright © 1985 by R. K. Narayan. By permission of Viking Penguin, a division of Penguin Books USA Inc.

Gabriel Okara: "Once upon a Time," from *Poems from Black Africa* by Gabriel Okara. By permission of the author.

Viking Penguin: "Making the Jam Without You," from *Our Ground Time Here Will Be Brief* by Maxine Kumin. Copyright © 1970 by Maxine Kumin. Used by permission of Viking Penguin, a division of Penguin Books USA, Inc.

Simon & Schuster, Inc.: "The Cabuliwallah," from *A Tagore Reader* by Rabindranath Tagore, edited by Amiya Chakravarty; Copyright © 1961 Macmillan Publishers, Inc. By permission of Simon & Schuster, Inc.

Sheep Meadow Press: "Pride" from *The Window: New and Selected Poems* by Dahlia Ravikovitch; Copyright © 1989 The Sheep Meadow Press. By permission of The Sheep Meadow Press.

New Directions Publishing Corporation: "For the New Year, 1981," from *Candles in Babylon* by Denise Levertov; Copyright © 1981 by Denise Levertov. Reprinted by permission of New Directions Publishing Corp.

David Higham Associates Limited: "As the Night the Day" from *Modern African Prose* by Abioseh Nicol. Reprinted by permission of David Higham Associates, Limited.

Unit Five

Brandt & Brandt Literary Agents, Inc.: "Searching for Summer," from *The Green Flash and Other Stories of Horror, Suspense, and Fantasy* by Joan Aiken; Copyright 1957, © 1958, 1959, 1960, 1965, 1968, 1969, 1971 by Joan Aiken Enterprises.

"By the Waters of Babylon" by Stephen Vincent Benét; Copyright 1937 by Stephen Vincent Benét. Copyright renewed © 1965 Thomas C. Benét, Stephanie B. Mahin, Rachel Benét Lewis.
Reprinted by permission of Brandt & Brandt Literary Agents, Inc.

Don Congdon Associates, Inc.: "A Sound of Thunder," from *R Is for Rocket* by Ray Bradbury; Copyright 1952, renewed © 1980 by Ray Bradbury. By permission of Don Congdon Associates, Inc.

Grove / Atlantic, Inc.: "Poem on Returning to Dwell in the Country" by T'ao Ch'ien (Tao Qian), from *Anthology of Chinese Literature*, edited by Cyril Birch; Copyright © 1965 by Grove Press, Inc. By permission of Grove / Atlantic, Inc.

Beacon Press: "The Sun," from *New and Selected Poems by Mary Oliver;* Copyright © 1992 by Mary Oliver. Reprinted by permission of Beacon Press.

HarperCollins Publishers: "Once More to the Lake," from *One Man's Meat* by E. B. White; Copyright 1941 by E. B. White.

"By Any Other Name," from *Gifts of Passage* by Santha Rama Rau; Copyright 1951 by Vasanthi Rama Rau Bowers, Copyright renewed.
Reprinted by permission of HarperCollins Publishers, Inc.

Macmillan Publishing Group, Inc.: "There Will Come Soft Rains," from *Collected Poems of Sara Teasdale* by Sara Teasdale; Copyright 1920 by Macmillan Publishing Company, renewed 1948 by Mamie T. Whaless.

The Continuum Publishing Company: "Trurl's Machine," from *The Cyberiad: Fables for the Cybernetic Age* by Stanislaw Lem: Copyright © 1974. Reprinted by permission of The Continuum Publishing Company.

Art Credits

214–215 Rebecca McClellan. 106, 107, 167 *bottom*, 172, 258 *bottom*, 340, 341, 345, 420, 421, 422 *top*, 424–425 *bottom*, 426, 427, 504–506, 586–587 *bottom*, 658–661, 664, 665, 798, 898 *top*, 987, 991 Allan Landau. 199, 203 Maryann Thomas. 285 Leslie Wu. 427 Josh Neufeld. 444–445, 845, 848 Sarah Figlio. 856–865 Clinton Meyer.

Maps on all Previewing pages and Responding pages: Robert Voights.

Miscellaneous Art Credits
xi *Sunday Morning Breakfast* (1943), Horace Pippin. Private collection, courtesy of Galerie St. Etienne, New York. xiii *Homage to Sterling Brown* (1972), Charles White. Collection of Dr. Edmund Gordon, courtesy of the Heritage Gallery, Los Angeles. xv, 455 *Le coeur* [The heart] (1947), Henri Matisse. Plate 7 from *Jazz*, published by Tériade, Paris. The Metropolitan Museum of Art, New York, gift of Lila Acheson Wallace, 1983 (1983.1009). Copyright © 1995 Succession H. Matisse, Paris / Artists Rights Society (ARS), New York. Photo Copyright © 1985 The Metropolitan Museum of Art, all rights reserved. xvi *Cosmos Dog* (1989), George Rodrigue. Oil on canvas, courtesy of The Rodrigue Gallery of New Orleans. Copyright © 1989 George Rodrigue. xix *The Ukimwi Road* (1994), John Harris. xxi Lancelot rescuing Guinevere by crossing the sword bridge (about 1300). From *Le Roman de Lancelot du Lac*, M. 806, f. 166, The Pierpont Morgan Library, New York / Art Resource, New York. xxvi–1 Detail of *Self-Portrait* (1986), Chuck Close. Oil on canvas, $54\frac{1}{2}'' \times 42\frac{1}{4}''$, courtesy of The Pace Gallery, New York. Photo by John Back. 2 *bottom left* Copyright © A. Giampiccolo / FPG International Corp.; *bottom right* Copyright © Arthur Tilley / FPG International Corp. 3 *top* The Bettmann Archive; *center* Copyright © Koji Yamashita / Panoramic Images; *bottom left* Copyright © Carole Elies / Tony Stone Images; *bottom right, Self-Portrait* (1986), Chuck Close. Oil on canvas, $54\frac{1}{2}'' \times 42\frac{1}{4}''$, courtesy of The Pace Gallery, New York. Photo by John Back. 12–13 The Granger Collection, New York. 27 *The Stairway* (1970), Will Barnet. Photo courtesy of Terry Dintenfass Gallery, New York. Copyright © 1995 Will Barnet / Licensed by VAGA, New York. 40 Archive Photos / Lambert. 63 Photo by Malcolm Varon. 76 Copyright © Louise Gubb / JB Pictures Ltd. 106–107 Reprinted courtesy of 'TEEN Magazine. 110 Copyright © Mike Mitchell / Photo Researchers, Inc. 115–116 Detail of *Nia: Purpose* (1991), Varnette Honeywood. Monoprint, collection of Karen Kennedy. Copyright © 1991 Varnette P. Honeywood. 122 Copyright © Mitch Reardon / Photo Researchers, Inc. 135 *bottom right and left* Copyright © Ron Chapple / FPG International Corp.; *top right* Copyright © Bruce Ayres / Tony Stone Images. 140 *top* Le Ly Hayslip's parents. Photos from *When Heaven and Earth Changed Places* by Le Ly Hayslip. Copyright © 1989 by Le Ly Hayslip and Charles Jay Wurts. Used by permission of Doubleday, a division of Bantam Doubleday Dell Publishing Group, Inc. 141, 144, 148 Copyright © Warner Brothers / Regency Enterprises / Le Studio Canal. Photo courtesy of Photofest. 158 *Spring in St. John's Wood* (1933), Dame Laura Knight. Oil on canvas, $51\frac{3}{4}'' \times 45\frac{1}{2}''$, Board of Trustees of the National Museums and Galleries on Merseyside, Walker Art Gallery, Liverpool, Great Britain. Copyright © Dame Laura Knight, reproduced by permission of Curtis Brown Group, Ltd., London. 167 *center* 1982 *The Far Side* cartoon by Gary Larson is reprinted by permission of Chronicle Features, San Francisco. All rights reserved. 172 *bottom* Courtesy of Laurie Duncan. 182 Courtesy of the French Embassy–Photo department. 198 *top* Courtesy of The Topps Company, Inc. 205 *Michael W. Straus* (1961), Fairfield Porter. Oil on canvas, $45\frac{3}{16}'' \times 39\frac{1}{2}''$, Hirschl & Adler Modern, New York.

Teacher Review Panels *(continued)*

Eileen Jones, English Department Chairperson, Spanish River High School, Palm Beach County School District

Jan McClure, Winter Park High School Orange County School District

Wanza Murray, English Department Chairperson (retired), Vero Beach Senior High School, Indian River City School District

Shirley Nichols, Language Arts Curriculum Specialist Supervisor, Marion County School District

Debbie Nostro, Ocoee Middle School, Orange County School District

Barbara Quinaz, Assistant Principal, Horace Mann Middle School, Dade County School District

OHIO

Joseph Bako, English Department Chairperson, Carl Shuler Middle School, Cleveland City School District

Deb Delisle, Language Arts Department Chairperson, Ballard Brady Middle School, Orange School District

Ellen Geisler, English/Language Arts Department Chairperson, Mentor Senior High School, Mentor School District

Dr. Mary Gove, English Department Chairperson, Shaw High School, East Cleveland School District

Loraine Hammack, Executive Teacher of the English Department, Beachwood High School, Beachwood City School District

Sue Nelson, Shaw High School, East Cleveland School District

Mary Jane Reed, English Department Chairperson, Solon High School, Solon City School District

Nancy Strauch, English Department Chairperson, Nordonia High School, Nordonia Hills City School Dictrict

Ruth Vukovich, Hubbard High School, Hubbard Exempted Village School District

TEXAS

Anita Arnold, English Department Chairperson, Thomas Jefferson High School, San Antonio Independent School District

Gilbert Barraza, J.M. Hanks High School, Ysleta School District

Sandi Capps, Dwight D. Eisenhower High School, Alding Independent School District

Judy Chapman, English Department Chairperson, Lawrence D. Bell High School, Hurst-Euless-Bedford School District

Pat Fox, Grapevine High School, Grapevine-Colley School District

LaVerne Johnson, McAllen Memorial High School, McAllen Independent School District

Donna Matsumura, W.H. Adamson High School, Dallas Independent School District

Ruby Mayes, Waltrip High School, Houston Independent School District

Mary McFarland, Amarillo High School, Amarillo Independent School District

Adrienne Thrasher, A.N. McCallum High School, Austin Independent School District

CALIFORNIA

Steve Bass, 8th Grade Team Leader, Meadowbrook Middle School, Ponway Unified School District

Cynthia Brickey, 8th Grade Academic Block Teacher, Kastner Intermediate School, Clovis Unified School District

Karen Buxton, English Department Chairperson, Winston Churchill Middle School, San Juan School District

Bonnie Garrett, Davis Middle School, Compton School District

Sally Jackson, Madrona Middle School, Torrance Unified School District

Sharon Kerson, Los Angeles Center for Enriched Studies, Los Angeles Unified School District

Gail Kidd, Center Middle School, Azusa School District

Corey Lay, ESL Department Chairperson, Chester Nimitz Middle School, Los Angeles Unified School District

Myra LeBendig, Forshay Learning Center, Los Angeles Unified School District

Dan Manske, Elmhurst Middle School, Oakland Unified School District

Joe Olague, Language Arts Department Chairperson, Alder Middle School, Fontana School District

Pat Salo, 6th Grade Village Leader, Hidden Valley Middle School, Escondido Elementary School District

Manuscript Reviewers *(continued)*

Beverly Ann Barge, Wasilla High School, Wasilla, Alaska

Louann Bohman, Wilbur Cross High School, New Haven, Connecticut

Rose Mary Bolden, J. F. Kimball High School, Dallas, Texas

Angela Boyd, Andrews High School, Andrews, Texas

Judith H. Briant, Armwood High School, Seffner, Florida

Hugh Delle Broadway, McCullough High School, The Woodlands, Texas

Stephan P. Clarke, Spencerport High School, Spencerport, New York

Dr. Shawn Eric DeNight, Miami Edison Senior High School, Miami, Florida

JoAnna R. Exacoustas, La Serna High School, Whittier, California

Linda Ferguson, English Department Head, Tyee High School, Seattle, Washington

Ellen Geisler, Mentor Senior High School, Mentor, Ohio

Ricardo Godoy, English Department Chairman, Moody High School, Corpus Christi, Texas

Robert Henderson, West Muskingum High School, Zanesville, Ohio

Martha Watt Hosenfeld, English Department Chairperson, Churchville-Chili High School, Churchville, New York

Janice M. Johnson, Assistant Principal, Union High School, Grand Rapids, Michigan

Eileen S. Jones, English Department Chair, Spanish River Community High School, Boca Raton, Florida

Paula S. L'Homme, West Orange High School, Winter Garden, Florida

Bonnie J. Mansell, Downey Adult School, Downey, California

Ruth McClain, Paint Valley High School, Bainbridge, Ohio

Rebecca Miller, Taft High School, San Antonio, Texas

Deborah Lynn Moeller, Western High School, Fort Lauderdale, Florida

Bobbi Darrell Montgomery, Batavia High School, Batavia, Ohio

Wanza Murray, Vero Beach High School, Vero Beach, Florida

Marjorie M. Nolan, Language Arts Department Head, William M. Raines Sr. High School, Jacksonville, Florida

Julia Pferdehirt, free-lance writer, former Special Education teacher, Middleton, Wisconsin

Pauline Sahakian, English Department Chairperson, San Marcos High School, San Marcos, Texas

Jacqueline Y. Schmidt, Department Chairperson and Coordinator of English, San Marcos High School, San Marcos, Texas

John Sferro, Butler High School, Vandalia, Ohio

Faye S. Spangler, Versailles High School, Versailles, Ohio

Milinda Schwab, Judson High School, Converse, Texas

Rita Stecich, Evergreen Park Community High School, Evergreen Park, Illinois

GayleAnn Turnage, Abilene High School, Abilene, Texas

Ruth Vukovich, Hubbard High School, Hubbard, Ohio

Charlotte Washington, Westwood Middle School, Grand Rapids, Michigan

Tom Watson, Westbridge Academy, Grand Rapids, Michigan